Richelieu's Army

War, Government and Society
France, 1624–1642

The conduct of European war on an unprecedented scale is central to an understanding of the ministry of Richelieu (1624–42), and there has been no previous study of the French army during this period. This book provides a detailed account of the organization of the army, and examines the challenges posed by war to government and society in a period associated with the creation of the 'absolutist state'.

By making extensive use of archival material, the study cuts through myths concerning military and administrative evolution, and confronts typical assumptions about progressive centralization and more effective control of the war-effort by the crown and its agents. Although the European war imposed huge burdens upon the French people, Richelieu's ministry struggled to control the army through traditional administrative and financial mechanisms. Far from strengthening the absolutist authority of government, the waging of war eroded the ministry's control over army officers and troops and incited tensions between soldiers and civilians across French society which in turn contributed to the undermining of existing structures of authority and control.

The book also makes an original and sceptical contribution to the debate about a 'military revolution' in early modern Europe by examining the conduct of war in early seventeenth-century France. In addition, it seeks to contextualize the inadequacy of the war-effort during Richelieu's ministry by providing a view of the military context of French foreign policy after 1625 which challenges many of the orthodoxies about Richelieu's aims and objectives in involving France in the Thirty Years War.

DAVID PARROTT is Fellow and Lecturer in Modern History, New College, Oxford.

CAMBRIDGE STUDIES IN EARLY MODERN HISTORY

Edited by Professor Sir John Elliott, University of Oxford
Professor Olwen Hufton, University of Oxford
Professor H.G. Koenigsberger, University of London
Professor H.M. Scott, University of St Andrews

The idea of an 'early modern' period of European history from the fifteenth to the late eighteenth century is now widely accepted among historians. The purpose of Cambridge Studies in Early Modern History is to publish monographs and studies which illuminate the character of the period as a whole, and in particular focus attention on a dominant theme within it, the interplay of continuity and change as they are presented by the continuity of medieval ideas, political and social organization, and by the impact of new ideas, new methods, and new demands on the traditional structure.

For a list of titles published in the series, please see end of the book

Richelieu's Army

War, Government and Society in
France, 1624–1642

DAVID PARROTT

CAMBRIDGE UNIVERSITY PRESS
Cambridge, New York, Melbourne, Madrid, Cape Town, Singapore, São Paulo

Cambridge University Press
The Edinburgh Building, Cambridge CB2 2RU, UK

Published in the United States of America by Cambridge University Press, New York

www.cambridge.org
Information on this title: www.cambridge.org/9780521792097

© David Parrott 2001

This publication is in copyright. Subject to statutory exception
and to the provisions of relevant collective licensing agreements,
no reproduction of any part may take place without
the written permission of Cambridge University Press.

First published 2001
This digitally printed first paperback version 2006

A catalogue record for this publication is available from the British Library

Library of Congress Cataloguing in Publication data
Parrott, David.
Richelieu's army: war, government and society in France, 1624–1642 / David Parrott.
p.   cm.
Includes bibliographical references and index.
ISBN 0 521 79209 6
1. France – History – Louis XIII, 1610–1643. 2. Richelieu, Armand Jean du Plessis, duc
de, 1585–1642. 3. France. Armée – History – 17th century. 4. France – History,
Military – 1610–1643. I. Title.
DC123.P37 2001
944'.032–dc21   00–065161

ISBN-13 978-0-521-79209-7 hardback
ISBN-10 0-521-79209-6 hardback

ISBN-13 978-0-521-02548-5 paperback
ISBN-10 0-521-02548-6 paperback

To my parents
Fred and Dorothy Parrott

Contents

Acknowledgements		*page* ix
Glossary		xii
List of abbreviations		xvii
Maps		
1	North-east France, 1635–1642	xix
2	Eastern France, 1629–1642	xx
3	Alsace, Lorraine and Franche-Comté	xxi
4	North Italy, 1626–1642	xxii
5	Languedoc, Roussillon and Catalonia, 1637–1642	xxiii
6	Atlantic France and the Pyrenean frontier, 1627–1638	xxiv
	Introduction: war, government and society in France, 1624–1642	1

PART I   THE MILITARY CONTEXT

1	The French art of war during Richelieu's ministry	19
2	France at war, 1624–1642	84
	Aims and methods, 1624–1634	84
	The French war-effort, 1635–1642	110
3	The size of the French army	164

PART II   THE ADMINISTRATIVE CONTEXT

4	Paying for war	225
5	Recruiting and maintaining armies during the Thirty Years War: military enterprise	277
6	The French rejection of entrepreneurship	313
7	The civil administration of the army: the structures	366
	The central structure of the war administration	367
	The administrators with the French army before 1635	373

Contents

PART III RESPONSES AND REACTIONS

8	The management of the war-effort from 1635 to 1642: *commissaires des guerres* and *intendants*	399
9	The ministry and the high command	463
10	The army and the civilian population	505
	Conclusion	547
	Bibliography	557
	Index	579

Acknowledgements

As my colleagues and friends are well aware, this book has been long in gestation. Its origins lie in a more narrowly focused doctoral thesis that was examined back in 1985. Since then further research on Richelieu's army and its wider social and political context has competed with other projects for my time and attention, although these latter have had their own impact on the shape and argument of this work. Some of my scholarly debts therefore extend back to the years of my graduate work. I would especially like to thank Robin Briggs, who both suggested the subject of Richelieu's army as a doctoral study and then provided support, encouragement and advice as my supervisor. From the same period I also owe a great debt to Michael Howard for the time and attention he was prepared to give to my initial thoughts on early modern warfare, and to Cliff Davies and Robert Knecht, doctoral examiners but also unstinting sources of advice and suggestion. All have remained close to the project since then, and I am grateful for their forbearance and willingness to accept my protestations that the book would ultimately appear.

The book would not have been completed at all without an allocation of university research terms, the first two of these granted to me during my years of teaching in the Department of History at the University of York. I remember with deep affection the encouragement, collegiality and stimulation provided by all my colleagues at York, but am particularly grateful to Norman Hampson, Alan Forrest, Dwyryd Jones and Jim Sharpe, with whom I had the opportunity to discuss many of the issues that have shaped my work. Since my return to Oxford I have benefited from further research terms generously granted me by the Warden and Fellows of New College, one of which was prolonged by an award under the British Academy's 'Research Leave Scheme'. Such absences can only be sustained by the willingness of colleagues to absorb extra burdens, and I am most grateful to my fellow historians at New College, Eric Christiansen and Ruth Harris, for facilitating these occasional *exeats*. My intellectual debts to colleagues in Oxford are extensive, though I would especially like to thank John Elliott, Laurence Brockliss, Jeremy Catto, Richard Cooper, Robert Evans, Olwen Hufton, Jonathan Powis, John Robertson, Guy Rowlands, Michael Screech, John Stoye, Helen Watanabe-O'Kelly and Penry Williams for their interest in the project, their innumerable suggestions, ideas and their always profitable conversation.

Acknowledgements

The list of colleagues in the Anglo-Saxon, French and wider European academic worlds to whom I am grateful for advice and guidance, freely given references to their own work and generous and extensive discussion is intimidatingly lengthy. Amongst French colleagues I would particularly like to thank Michel Antoine, Père Jean-Robert Armogathe, Rainer Babel, Françoise Bayard, Lucien Bély, Jean Bérenger, Olivier Chaline, Edward Corp, André Corvisier, Daniel Dessert, Marc Fumaroli, Charles Giry-Deloison, Arlette Jouanna, Bernard Masson, Bruno Neveu, René Pillorget and Jean-Louis Quantin. Outside of the Hexagon, Klaus Bußmann, Arabella Cifani and Franco Monetti, Sven Externbrink, Daniela Ferrari, Bernhard Kroener, Klaus Malettke, Cesare Mozzarelli, Heinz Schilling and Peter Schroeder have all contributed to my research and thinking on war, government and society. I am no less obliged to British and American historians who have offered comments, help and advice, amongst them Simon Adams, Sydney Anglo, Jeremy Black, Richard Bonney, Derek Croxton, Karin Friedrich, Robert Frost, Graham Gibbs, Mark Greengrass, Simon Hodson, James Inglis-Jones, Jonathan Israel, Alan James, Colin Jones, Hellie Koenigsberger, John Lynn, Roger Mettam, Toby Osborne, David Parker, Geoffrey Parker, Simon Pepper, David Potter, Cliff Rogers, John Rogister, Mía Rodriguez-Salgado, Robert Stradling, Christopher Storrs, Geoffrey Symcox and Frank Tallett. By their responsiveness to enquiries, willingness to exchange ideas and openness to debate all have demonstrated that scholarly and collegial values continue to exist in an academic world which at times can seem to have absorbed a depressing ethos of narrow self-promotion. I can only apologize in advance to any others whose names have been inadvertently missed, but whose contribution has been no less considerable. In addition to all those cited above, I would also like to record *in memoriam* three colleagues and close friends – Ragnhild Hatton, Rohan Butler and Jean Jacquart – all of whom made an irreplaceable contribution to my thinking about war and society in the states of the *Ancien Régime*.

The present book rests upon consultation of the holdings of a number of major archives and over the years I have drawn heavily upon the assistance of their archivists. My early work at the Archives de la Guerre was inestimably helped by the kindness, guidance and flexibility of the staff, under the then direction of Marie-Anne Corvisier-de Villèle. I am no less grateful to the staff of the Archives des Affaires Etrangères, and especially to Isabelle Richefort and Monique Constant. The staff of the *salle des manuscrits* of the Bibliothèque Nationale have been consistently helpful and obliging, while the Bibliothèque Mazarine provided a most welcoming and agreeable haven for consulting printed sources.

I am especially aware of a number of particular obligations accumulated in the production of this book. To Joseph Bergin and Hamish Scott I owe not merely their selfless commitment of time and effort to reading and commenting on large sections of this work, but years of encouragement, advice and friendship when the project was in its earlier stages. I am no less grateful to my father, Fred Parrott,

Acknowledgements

whose position outside the world of Richelieu and Claude de Bullion allowed him to read, advise and to go some way to improving the clarity and readability of the text. My sister, Jane Parrott, provided invaluable help with the index and bibliography, while Stéphane Jettot was generous enough to give up some of his time while researching in the Bodleian to correct some of my more egregious errors in transcribing seventeenth-century French. What mistakes remain after all of their efforts are entirely my own responsibility. To the four editors of the Cambridge Studies in Early Modern European History I owe another great debt, as I do for the expert copy-editing of Linda Randall, while the greatest obligation of all is to William Davies, whose professionalism, dynamism, kindness and extraordinary helpfulness in the preparation of the book has been unparalleled.

On a personal note, I would like to thank my sixth-form tutor, Joyce Willcocks, from whose teaching and stimulus I date the beginnings of my interest in Richelieu. I owe an incalculable debt to Roger Clark and above all to Robert Oresko, who have not merely provided me with intellectual and emotional support throughout this period, but have been prepared to put up with a project which has overshadowed a decade of our domestic life. To Robert, as well, I owe a great expansion of my horizons as a historian, and his intellectual influence is a pervasive feature of the entire study. I hope that the work will constitute some sort of tribute, however inadequate, to his encouragement and support over twelve years.

Glossary

armée: (1) The total military establishment maintained by Louis XIII.
(2) Individual army-corps serving in particular campaign theatres – army of the Valtelline, army serving in Franche-Comté, army of Italy, etc.

COMPANY AND REGIMENTAL OFFICERS

I have used the term non-commissioned officer (NCO) to denote those company posts with disciplinary authority below the rank of captain, lieutenant and ensign, though the term is itself an anachronism; 'petty officer' might be more appropriate to a seventeenth-century context, but creates its own confusions for a modern readership.

aide-major: assistant of the regimental (*sergent-*)*major*; liaison between the *major* and the company officers.

anspessade: veteran ranking soldier, allocated the most important positions in a company deployment. The *anspessade* was immediately subordinate to a corporal, but without the formal disciplinary authority of an NCO.

appointé: veteran soldier in a company, though of lower status than an *anspessade*.

archer: ordinary employee and assistant of the *prévôt*.

cornette: (1) Lowest-ranking officer in a company of *cavalerie légère*.
(2) Frequently used to denote the cavalry company itself – 'trois cornettes de cavalerie'.

enseign: lowest-ranking officer in an infantry company, by tradition charged with carrying the company banner. Equivalent in companies of *cavalerie légère* was the *cornette*.

état major: term for all officers and officials in a regiment outside the company hierarchy: *mestre de camp, (sergent-)major, aides-majors, maréchal de logis, commissaire à la conduite*, chaplain, surgeon, the *prévôt* and his lieutenant and *archers*.

guidon: lowest-ranking officer and standard-bearer in company of *gendarmes*.

lieutenant-général: supreme commander of an army-corps – the acting *lieutenant* of the king, commander of all his armies.

Glossary

maréchal: non-hereditary rank granted by the crown to a senior officer, in almost all cases one who had already served as commander of an army-corps. Provided court status equivalent to a *duc sans pairie*. It was not necessary to be a *maréchal* to command an army-corps, but a *maréchal* would enjoy precedence if two commanders were appointed to joint command of an army unless the other commander were a high-ranking *prince du sang* or *prince souverain*, for whom the status of *maréchal* was considered inappropriate.

maréchal de camp: officer of the high command immediately subordinate to the *lieutenant-général* of an army-corps. Overall responsibility for the quartering and encampment of the troops. In theory one or more *maréchaux de camp* was to remain with the army during the winter quarter to maintain discipline.

maréchal des logis: (1) Officer in each infantry regiment, directly under the orders of the *mestre de camp* and the major. Overall responsibility for the lodging of troops, provision of supplies, management of the soldiers at the *étapes*.

(2) Low-ranking NCO in a company of *cavalerie légère*, *dragons* or *gendarmes*, charged with collection and distribution of forage, finding stabling, etc.

maréchal de bataille: officer within the general staff whose original function was to draw up the army for battle according to the plans established by the general.

mestre de camp: commander of a French infantry regiment; commanders of cavalry and foreign mercenary regiments held the title of colonels. (*Mestre [maître] de camp* derived from Spanish *maestro de campo*.)

sergent de bataille: subordinate to the *maréchal de camp* with duties similar to the *maréchal de bataille*, involving the embattling of the army and the general oversight of discipline in quarters. Some confusion of status between the two offices, and by the reign of Louis XIV the office of *maréchal de bataille* had replaced the *sergent*.

sergent-major (*major*): immediate subordinate of the *mestre de camp* in the regimental hierarchy, with authority over all the captains. Had control over the collection and distribution of all munitions to the regiment, and responsibility for drawing up the regiment in order of battle.

WEAPONRY, EQUIPMENT AND PROVISIONING

canon: (1) General term for the artillery pieces present with a French army-corps or in a fortification.

(2) Heavy field or siege piece, weighing around 4,800 lb and firing a shot weighing 30–5 lb.

carabins: ultimately to be superseded by *dragons*, but under Richelieu the standard term for mounted infantry. Those armed with the heavier muskets were sometimes termed *mousquetaires à cheval*.

Glossary

cavalerie légère: the great majority of the French cavalry units. Cavalry armed with a sabre and two pistols, lightly armoured with *cuirasse*, helmet and in some cases arm and leg protection.

corselet: chest and back armour issued to pikemen. Ministers complained frequently that the pikemen declined to wear this cumbersome protection.

culverine: second-heaviest artillery piece, weighing around 3,700 lb, and firing a shot of around 20 lb.

dragons [dragoons]: mounted infantry, armed with muskets or, more usually, lighter firearms, descendants of the sixteenth-century arquebuse. Soldiers would dismount to fight.

flintlock musket (*fusil*): though the matchlock was the standard issue musket for the French (and other European) infantry during the Thirty Years War, numerous examples survive of the more sophisticated flintlock, a musket fired by means of a spark struck from a flint when the trigger was pulled. While the pistols issued to the French cavalry were fired by flint- (wheel-) lock technology, it was considered too expensive and unreliable for adoption by ordinary musketeers. Flintlock muskets remained prestige objects manufactured in relatively small quantities until the later seventeenth century. A small number of mounted infantry – *fusiliers* – were equipped with flintlocks.

gendarme: heavy cavalryman, in most cases still fully armoured. In theory the most prestigious element in the armies, since the companies of *gendarmes* were invariably the personal units of the royal household, major *grands* or the provincial governors. In reality the *gendarmerie* had a reputation for indiscipline and disorder, and played a modest role in campaigning, especially once the *cavalerie légère* had been organized into squadrons or regiments.

matchlock musket: musket fired by means of a 'match' – a length of smouldering fuse applied to the powder in the firing chamber when the musket trigger was pulled. Hence 'match' – quantities of slow-burning fuse issued to infantry with firearms: an extremely large item in the budget of munitions purchase and distribution.

munitionnaire: large-scale supplier prepared to negotiate contracts with the crown for the provision of *pain de munition* to the armies. Frequently linked into networks of other financial speculators.

pain de munition: the basic daily ration of bread provided to the French *infantry* (not cavalry and artillery) by systems of central contracting. The soldiers contributed 1 *sol* per day to this provision, and the crown absorbed the additional costs of providing grain, baking bread and distributing the rations. The bread ration was supposed to weigh 24 ounces.

vivandier: local, small-scale, entrepreneur-merchant who would sell food and

Glossary

drink to the soldiers in camp or garrison to supplement the standard issue of *pain de munition*.

ARMY ORGANIZATION

denier: one twelfth of a *sol*, one 240th of a *livre*.

deniers revenans bons: the financial sums outstanding from the gap between the calculations of the payment of the unit at 'full' strength, and the 'actual' size of the unit as established at the *revue*.

drapeau blanc: the privilege of carrying the king's standard, the *drapeau blanc*, in addition to regimental colours, was accorded to prestige infantry regiments. It was essentially identified with the *vieux* and *petits vieux* regiments, but a sequence of other regiments were accorded this privilege, together with *entretenu* status, during the 1630s.

écu: typically valued at 3 *livres* in 1630s/40s.

étape: prescribed halting-point for units marching down to the campaign theatres, supposedly provided with adequate provisions for the troops collected from the surrounding area or purchased via a local tax.

la colonelle: company in each of the *régiments entretenus* whose officers were nominated by the *colonel général de l'infanterie française*. The captain of this company was titled *lieutenant colonel*, and in theory enjoyed the highest status amongst the captains of the regiment, though this frequently ensured clashes with the captain commanding the company of the regimental *mestre de camp*.

licenciement: the disbandment of a regiment or company, either as a disciplinary penalty or because the numbers of troops in the unit had fallen beneath a minimal effective strength. *Licenciement* usually involved the dismissal of the unit officers and the incorporation of the soldiers and NCOs into other units.

livre tournois: basic unit of currency, though it did not correspond to an actual coin in the French monetary system.

millier: roughly 1,000 lb weight – used largely in connection with quantities of powder, lead, match.

montre: (1) 'Monthly' payment made to both soldiers and officers in the army by the *trésoriers de l'ordinaire et extraordinaire des guerres*. The number of *montres* was reduced by the *bureau des finances* from ten per campaign to eight to six (1634–6), though in practice few troops received more than three or four *montres* per campaign.

(2) Synonymous with *revue* (English 'muster'). French administrative ordinances frequently refer to *montres et revues des gens de guerre*, with no implication that these were different processes.

Glossary

passe-volants: civilians or soldiers from other units, deployed by the unit commander on the day of the *revue* to deceive the *commissaires* and *contrôleurs* about the effective strength of his unit.

petits-vieux régiments: by 1635 this group consisted of seven elite regiments, maintained on a permanent basis and with the right to carry the *drapeau blanc*, but placed in a rank below the *vieux*: Neerestang, Sault, Rambures, Maugiron, Vaubecourt, Bellenaue, Saint-Luc.

pike: one third of the French infantry were armed with pikes, ten to twelve foot staff weapons, headed with an eighteen-inch metal tip. The pikemen were the largest and strongest of the soldiers, who received higher pay and consitituted the core of the infantry unit both in defence and attack.

prêt: basic subsistence payment made to the ordinary soldiers every ten days (in theory) on campaign to permit them to buy food, wine, etc.

réformation: reduction in the number of companies in a unit, usually to concentrate the soldiers and reduce the number of officers. During the winter quarter it was also possible for a full complement of companies to be maintained within a regiment, but at substantially reduced individual strength.

régiment or *compagnie entretenu(e)*: undertaking by the crown and its ministers that a selected regiment or cavalry company would not be disbanded, but would be maintained on a permanent basis regardless of whether France was at war. The unit might undergo a reduction of its effective strength, but the potential to reestablish the unit was always maintained.

revue: assembly of the soldiers in a particular unit or entire army-corps to allow the *commissaires* and *contrôleurs des guerres* to carry out an exact count of the real strength of the force, after which payment would be made – usually into the hands of the unit commander who would then distribute (some of) it to his soldiers.

sol: one twentieth of a livre.

vieux régiments: could include the king's own *régiments des gardes françaises* and *gardes suisses*. Most usually denotes the four oldest 'provincial' regiments of Picardie, Piémont, Champagne and Navarre. To these four were added the Normandie regiment from *c.* 1617 (Père G. Daniel, *Histoire de la milice française*) and Richelieu's *régiment de La Marine* in 1635, though in June 1640 the *Marine* was accorded fifth rank amongst the *vieux* (SHAT $A^1$59, fo. 272).

Abbreviations

AAE MD	Archives des Affaires Etrangères, Mémoires et Documents, France
AAE CP	Archives des Affaires Etrangères, Correspondance Politique
Anselme, *Histoire généalogique*,	Père Anselme de Sainte-Marie, *Histoire généalogique et chronologique de la maison royale de France, des pairs, grands offices de la couronne* . . . (3rd edn), (9 vols.; Paris, 1726–33)
ASMa AG	Archivio di Stato di Mantova, Archivio Gonzaga
ASTo LM	Archivio di Stato di Torino, Lettere Ministri
Aubery, *Richelieu*	A. Aubery, *Mémoires pour servir à l'histoire du cardinal duc de Richelieu* (2 vols.; Paris, 1660)
Avenel	D.L.M. Avenel (ed.), *Lettres, instructions diplomatiques et papiers d'état du cardinal de Richelieu (Collection de documents inédits sur l'histoire de France)* (8 vols.; Paris, 1853–76)
BL	British Library
BN	Bibliothèque Nationale
Code Michau	A.L. Jourdan, J. Decrusy and F.A. Isambert (eds.), *Recueil général des anciennes lois françaises depuis l'an 420 jusqu'à la Révolution de 1789* (28 vols.; Paris, 1821–33), XVI
Grillon	P. Grillon (ed.), *Les papiers de Richelieu. Section politique intérieure: correspondance et papiers d'état* (6 vols. to date; Paris, 1975–)
Hanotaux, *Richelieu*	G. Hanotaux and duc de La Force, *L'histoire du cardinal de Richelieu* (6 vols.; Paris, 1893–1947)
Michaud and Poujoulat	J. Michaud and J. Poujoulat (eds.), *Mémoires pour servir a l'histoire de la France depuis le XIIIe siècle jusqu'à la fin du XVIIIe* – 3e série (10 vols.; Paris, 1838)
Ms.fr.	Manuscrit français
Ms.fr. PO	Manuscrit français, Pièces Originales
n.d.	no date
Petitot and Monmerqué	C. Petitot and L. de Monmerqué (eds.), *Collection des mémoires relatifs à l'histoire de France – 2e série* (52 vols.; Paris, 1824–9)

List of abbreviations

Pinard, *Chronologie*	M. Pinard, *Chronologie historique militaire* (7 vols.; Paris, 1760–4)
Richelieu, *Mémoires*	Richelieu, *Mémoires*, in Petitot and Monmerqué, XXII–XXX (numbered as I–IX in text)
SHAT	Service Historique de l'Armée de Terre (Archives de la Guerre, Vincennes)

MAP 1 North-east France, 1635–1642

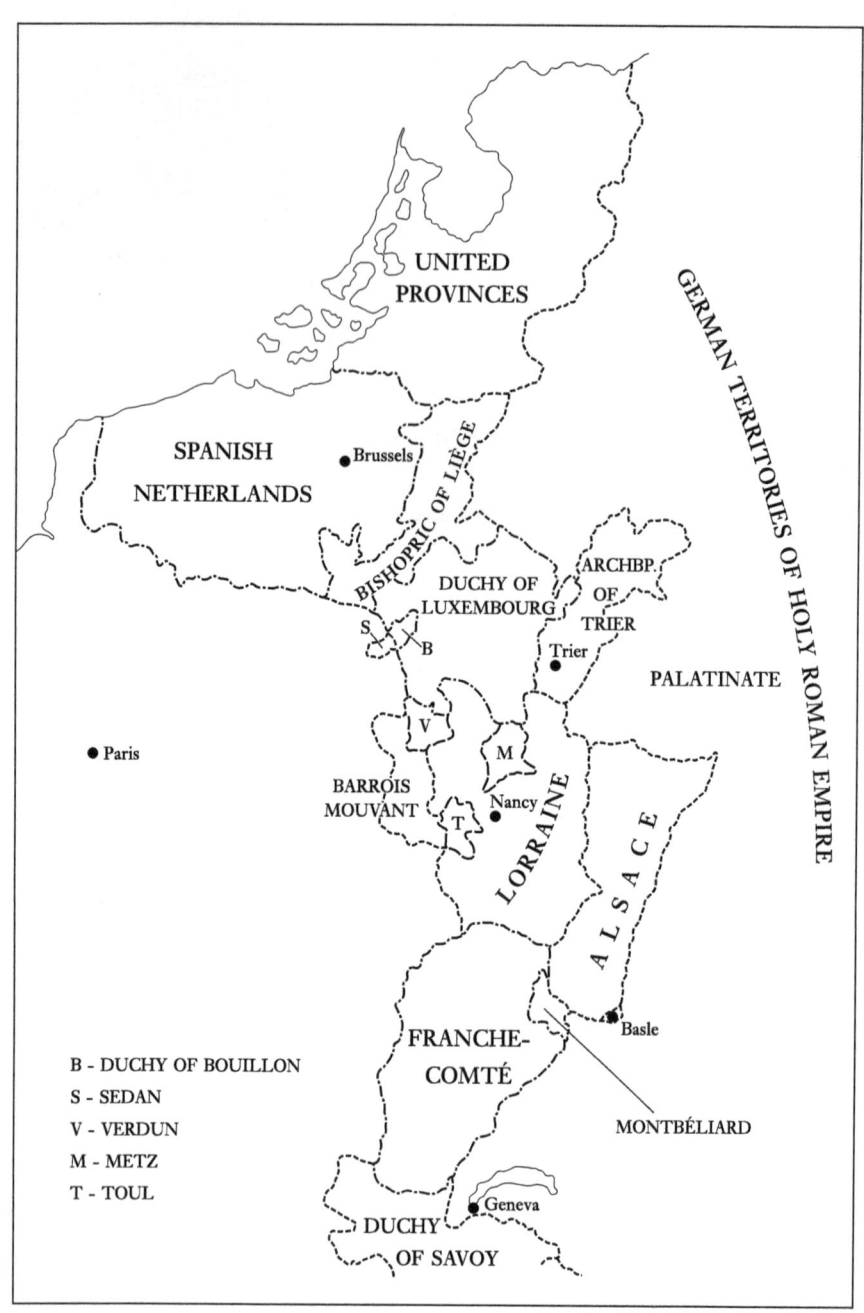

MAP 2 Eastern France, 1629–1642

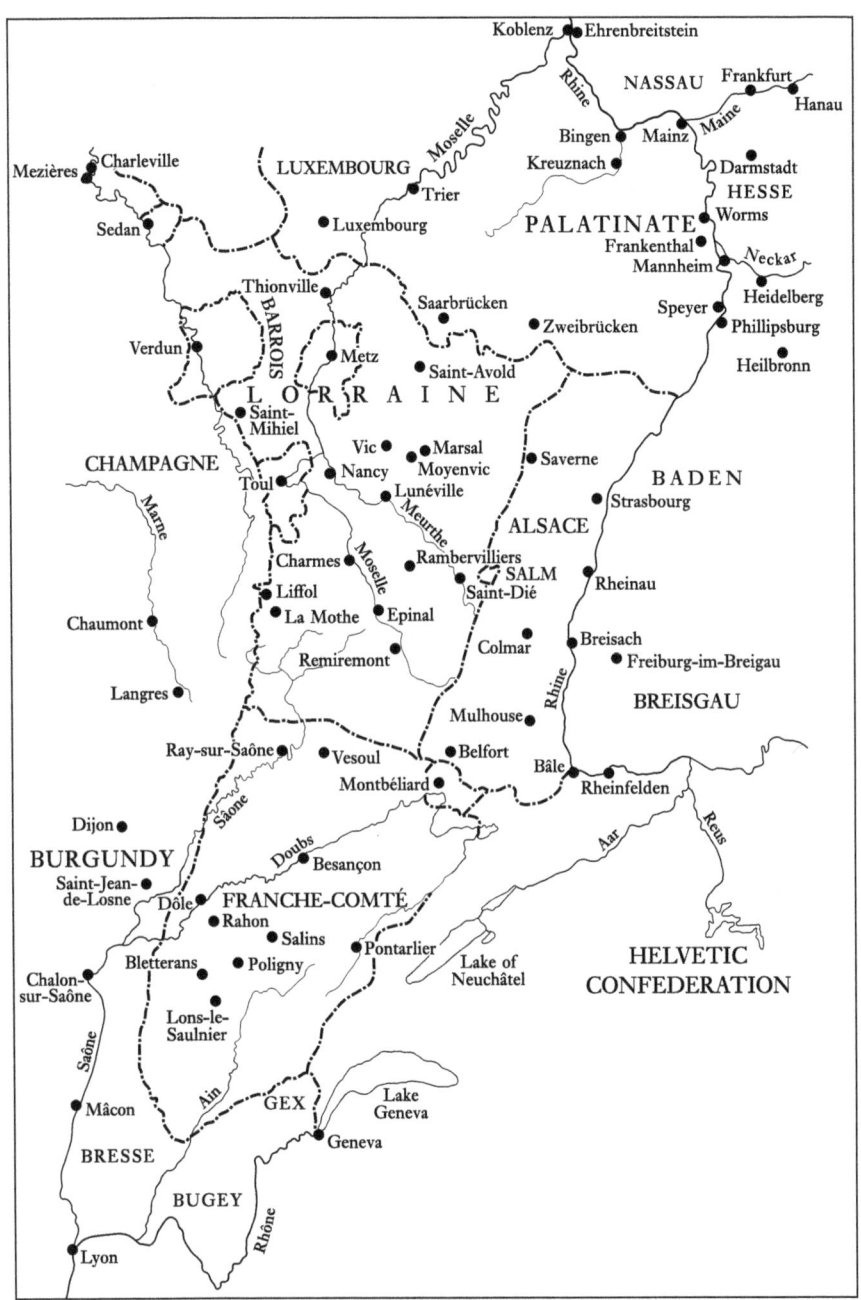

MAP 3 Alsace, Lorraine and Franche-Comté

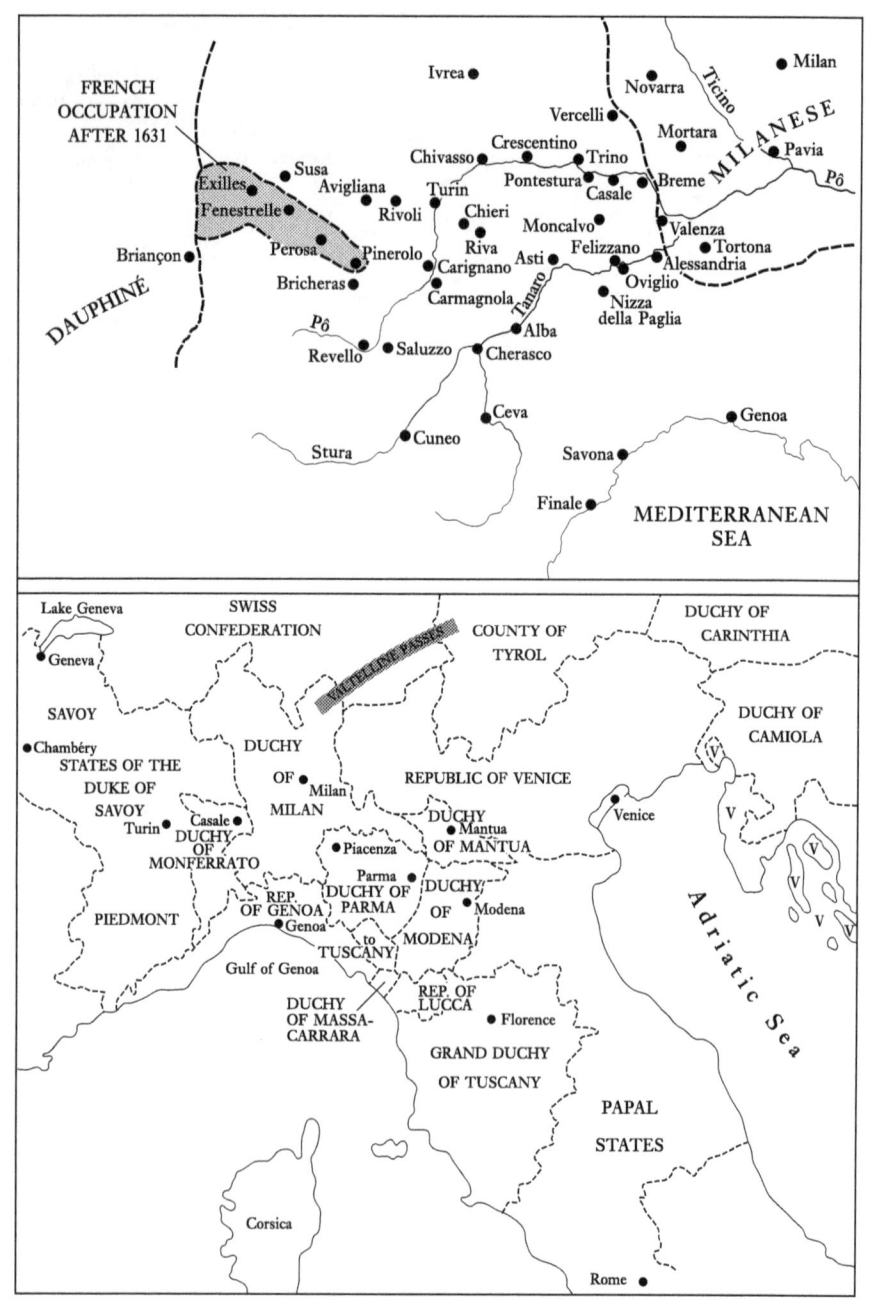

MAP 4 North Italy, 1626–1642

MAP 5 Languedoc, Roussillon and Catalonia, 1637–1642

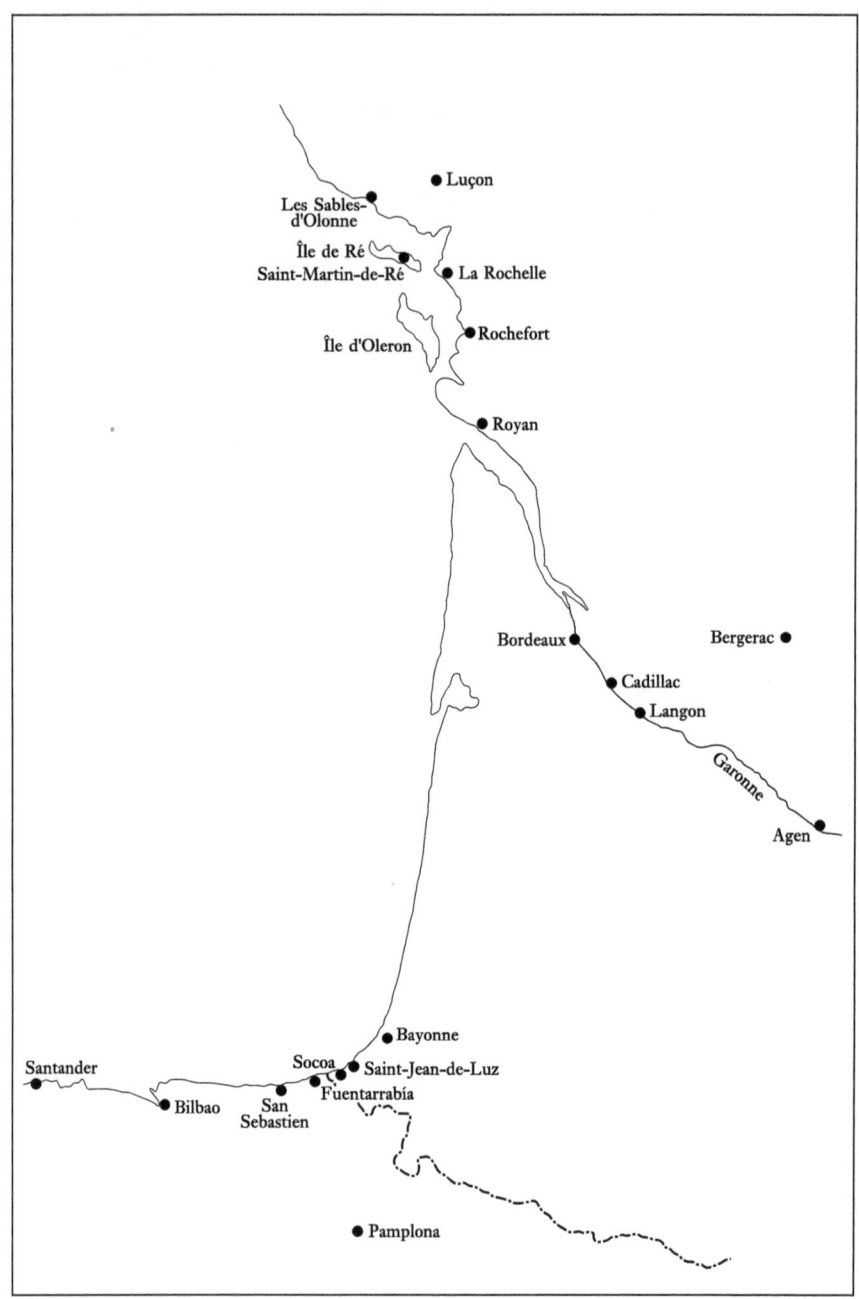

MAP 6 Atlantic France and the Pyrenean frontier, 1627–1638

INTRODUCTION

War, government and society in France, 1624–1642

The present book provides an account of the French army during the ministry of the cardinal de Richelieu. No detailed examination has previously been attempted of the military administration at what is widely considered to be a formative moment in French history; Richelieu's army, in contrast to almost every other aspect of his ministry, has not attracted its historians. Even where the organization and deployment of the army is directly relevant to the conduct of foreign policy, the issues have received little detailed attention since the eighteenth century.[1] The conduct of war and the formulation of strategy, the manner in which French armies fought during the Thirty Years War, the means by which supposedly unprecedented numbers of troops were raised, maintained, funded, supplied and controlled, have all received summary treatment in most historical accounts of the ministry. One reason for this neglect is the presence of pervasive assumptions about the broader relationship between the army, government and society in Richelieu's France, assumptions which have created their own generalized image of military organization and its evolution in this period.

The period of conflict upon which Louis XIII and Richelieu embarked from 1629 with the intervention in north Italy, and above all from 1635 when France was committed to open war with the Habsburg powers of Spain and Austria, was marked by an uninterrupted series of campaigns, fought in multiple theatres, and requiring a larger and more sustained military commitment than any previous war in French history. Waging such a war placed great pressure upon the administrative and fiscal capacities of the French state.

---

[1] The six-volume biography of Richelieu by G. Hanotaux, completed by the duc de La Force, *L'histoire du cardinal de Richelieu* (6 vols.; Paris, 1893–1947), provides a surprisingly perfunctory account of the waging of war and its relationship to foreign policy. For sustained, detailed, narrative with emphasis on the deployment of military resources, it is necessary to return to M. Le Vassor, *Histoire du règne de Louis XIII* (10 vols.; Amsterdam, 1701–11), or H. Griffet, *Histoire du règne de Louis XIII* (3 vols.; Paris, 1758). Detailed, but narrowly focused, accounts of the war-effort are provided in A.M.R.A. vicomte de Noailles, *Épisodes de la Guerre de Trente Ans* (3 vols.: *Bernard de Saxe-Weimar*, *Le cardinal de La Valette* and *Le maréchal de Guébriant*; Paris, 1906–13); another work which provides substantial amounts of detail focused upon particular campaign theatres is G. Fagniez, *Le Père Joseph et Richelieu, 1577–1638* (2 vols.; Paris, 1894). The most comprehensive account of the conduct of war during Richelieu's ministry can probably be obtained from selective reading of the documents collected and published by D.L.M. Avenel (ed.), *Lettres, instructions diplomatiques et papiers d'état du cardinal de Richelieu* (8 vols.; Paris, 1853–76).

Introduction

Traditional interpretations of the ministry have attributed France's capacity to meet the challenge of the struggle with the Habsburgs directly to the will-power and determination of Richelieu. Richelieu's abilities and political vision set him apart from his contemporaries and gave him the relentless energy to pursue an undeviating series of policies for the benefit of France and its monarchy. The war-effort, on which Richelieu recognized the survival and aggrandizement of the Bourbon monarchy would depend, was to be sustained through a strengthening of central government and the crushing of opposition to royal authority – an authority conflated with that of the first minister in these hagiographic interpretations. As with much of the historical picture of Richelieu, the starting point is the cardinal's own writings. The four-fold programme laid out in his *Testament politique* was easily read as a statement both of aims and methods: Richelieu claimed that he had served his king by abasing the power of the Habsburgs and asserting the renown of Louis XIII amongst foreign rulers, by crushing the political and military independence of the Huguenots, by curbing the arrogance and assertiveness of the *grands*, and by reducing all of the king's subjects to due obedience. These achievements contributed, it is implied, to a mutually reinforcing scheme, in which the ability to fight effectively in Europe was a direct consequence of reforms at home which had successfully curbed the spirit of unrest and insubordination that had dogged previous French bids to assert her international status.[2] This model of assertive domestic policies justified as a means to facilitate power abroad was adopted by Richelieu's earliest biographers.[3] By the nineteenth century it had become orthodoxy amongst those historians who accepted Richelieu's preeminence as the shaping force in early seventeenth-century French history. Moreover, those aspects of Richelieu's policies concerned to constrain the self-interest and disruptive potential of a society dominated by corporate, local and individual authority were interpreted in a wider context where Richelieu was considered to have enhanced the power of the central state. For Georges d'Avenel, Richelieu was the revolutionary who had destroyed local and institutional independence, the privileges and liberties vested in an essentially aristocratic society, but had done this as a means to create a centralized, powerful state, able to wage large-scale war and to assert France's interests abroad.[4] These views were echoed in the works of numerous administrative historians, for whom

---

[2] Richelieu, *Testament politique*, ed. F. Hildesheimer, (Paris, 1995), pp. 41–3.

[3] C. Vialart, *Histoire du ministère d'Armand-Jean du Plessis, cardinal duc de Richelieu* (4 vols.; Amsterdam, 1649), I. 2–4 'ces qualitez éminentes qui eslevoient Monsieur le Cardinal au dessus du reste des hommes'; A. Aubery, *Histoire du cardinal duc de Richelieu* (Paris, 1660), pp. 575–618; G. Dugrès, *Life of Richelieu* (London, 1643), p. 45: 'The Cardinal's chiefest end was to make the king of France absolute, glorious and renowned, and his Kingdom to flourish. To obtain it, he removed all the obstacles either at home, or abroad, that could be any hindrance to his proceedings.'

[4] G. d'Avenel, *Richelieu et la monarchie absolue* (4 vols.; Paris, 1884–90), I. 1–165, 'La monarchie traditionelle'; I. 167–247, 'La monarchie absolue': 'La révolution de 1789 était accomplie dans les idées, avant d'être commencée dans les faits; la révolution de 1624 fut exécutée en même temps dans les faits et dans les idées' (I. 186). The psychological ambiguities embedded in Avenel's perceptive

Introduction

the key factor in shaping governmental change and the development of a more powerful administration remained the dynamic and reformist role of *le grand cardinal*.[5] The army is given some attention in these accounts, principally in terms of the challenge which autonomous structures of command and control presented to the ministry and the crown; a number of typical issues are examined, most of which are derived from the classic work of the eighteenth-century Jesuit historian, Père Gabriel Daniel.[6] The conclusions of these works echo the central role allocated to Richelieu in other aspects of government and administration; the concept of *Richelieu's* army, shaped and controlled by the efforts of the cardinal himself, was accepted without serious qualification.[7]

Explanations of political and even social change as the product of an individual's will, though by no means completely rejected, have enjoyed less favour amongst twentieth-century historians. One element contributing to this shift in studies of seventeenth-century France has been a reassessment of the aims and methods of Richelieu. From the omniscient and visionary statesman whose accomplished grasp of France's true interests was weakened only when his policies were misunderstood or misapplied by allies and subordinates, an alternative model has emerged of Richelieu as an essentially expedient and pragmatic politician. The cardinal was seen rather as operating within the same political world as his contemporaries, sharing their motivations and interests, and confronting problems and demands on a day-to-day basis rather than pursuing far-sighted, long-term plans; this picture gave much less support to claims that domestic reform and enhancement of international power were the results of the assertiveness of a strong-willed individual.[8] While Richelieu's political abilities are

---

and intelligent assessment of Richelieu's ministry would be worthy of study in their own right: a revealing indication of political and social tensions in *fin de siècle* France.

[5] A. Dareste de La Chavanne, *Histoire de l'administration en France* (4 vols.; Paris, 1848), I. 49, II. 310–18; A. Chéruel, *Histoire de l'administration monarchique en France depuis l'avènement de Philippe-Auguste jusqu'à la mort de Louis XIV* (2 vols.; Paris, 1855), I. 295–318; J. Caillet, *De l'administration en France sous le ministère du cardinal de Richelieu* (Paris, 1857): 'Richelieu est l'admirable génie qui tire la France de l'anarchie dans laquelle elle s'épuisait' (p. 129); E. Boutaric, *Les institutions militaires de la France avant les armées permanentes* (Paris, 1863), pp. 341–96; Though the eight volumes of the *Lettres de Richelieu* edited by D.L.M. Avenel in fact yields much material which nuances and corrects this interpretation, the editorial commentary and the principle behind making a collection based solely on Richelieu's active correspondence indicate that the project was conceived within this traditional interpretation of the cardinal's centrality to the political process.

[6] G. Daniel, *Histoire de la milice françoise* (2 vols.; Paris, 1721).

[7] A curious exception to this is provided by Xavier Audoin, whose *Histoire de l'administration de la guerre* (4 vols.; Paris, 1811), II. 142–90, identifies Henri IV as the great military reformer and treats Richelieu's responses to the problems of army administration with dismissive contempt. At the other end of the century, Louis André, in his *Michel Le Tellier et l'organisation de l'armée monarchique* (Paris, 1906), pp. 24–33, gives Richelieu brief credit for reforming intentions, but attributes practical success to Le Tellier's post-1643 administration as *secrétaire d'État de la guerre*.

[8] The issue is perceptively discussed in the context of Richelieu's career before 1624 by J. Bergin, *The Rise of Richelieu* (New Haven and London, 1991), pp. 1–11. A series of essays in J.H. Elliott and L. Brockliss (eds.), *The World of the Favourite* (New Haven and London, 1999) – notably by Elliott,

Introduction

not denied in these more recent studies, they do emphasize that his decision to challenge the Habsburg powers drew France into decades of warfare which did not form part of any grand project to revolutionize the power of the monarchy. Far from possessing a long-term and skilfully conceived design to sustain the war-effort by an uncompromising assault upon privilege and local autonomy, Richelieu was inclined to avoid confrontation with established interests, and would have preserved the institutional *status quo* so far as possible.[9] On this interpretation, Richelieu's personal achievement lay less in the conscious implementation of institutional reform, more in the articulation and realignment of political ideas which might be used to justify ministerial policies *post facto*. It was Richelieu and his agents' invigoration of theories of *raison d'état*, both in attempting to justify a foreign policy waged on behalf of protestant allies against the Habsburgs and in equating resistance to ministerial authority with resistance to the crown, which represented the clearest contribution of the cardinal to the reshaping of political life in early seventeenth-century France.[10] As historians of other early modern states have emphasized, the impact of such a shift in the ideological underpinnings of royal power should not be underestimated. Yet these accounts also demonstrate that unless an institutional apparatus already exists or comes into being to exploit this ideological shift, it may well remain a potential rather than an actual factor in political life; what might appear to be new ways of thinking about political authority may remain latent within a traditional framework of practical politics and political assumptions.[11] Aside from the articulation of *raison d'état*, Richelieu's temperamental conservatism and an awareness of the risks of a 'revolutionary' reshaping of government both militated against the kind of 'root and branch' institutional reform attributed to him by earlier generations of historians, who seemed unable to resist the concept of a conscious drive towards monarchical 'absolutism'.

A. Feros and Brockliss – locate Richelieu within this wider context of contemporary politics and the maintenance of favour.

[9] The most extreme example of such an interpretation is offered by J.R. Major, whose *Representative Government in Early Modern France* (New Haven and London, 1980), pp. 487–621, presents an improbable dichotomy between Michel de Marillac as the exponent of royal authoritarianism achieved through institutional reform, and Richelieu as the expedient politician, essentially concerned to maintain the war-effort at whatever long-term price to institutional authority.

[10] See especially the classic study by E. Thuau, *Raison d'Etat et pensée politique à l'époque de Richelieu* (Paris, 1966), esp. pp. 351–409; W. Church, *Richelieu and Reason of State* (Princeton, 1972), pp. 173–282; S. Skalweit, 'Richelieu's Staatsidee', *Geschichte in Wissenschaft und Unterricht*, 2 (1962). Recent works have given priority to this development of political theory in a context of wider political pragmatism: F. Hildesheimer, *Richelieu: une certain idée de l'état* (Paris, 1985), pp. 39–47; J.H. Elliott, *Richelieu and Olivares* (Cambridge, 1984), pp. 113–42; R.J. Knecht, *Richelieu* (London, 1991), pp. 169–89; R. Bonney, 'Absolutism: what's in a name?', *French History*, 1 (1987), 93–117.

[11] Recent works on early Stuart politics have drawn attention to these distinctions between political practice and potentially 'absolutist' ideology, and have argued that the ideological context needs more nuanced examination in the light of the assumptions of the various political actors: see, for example, J. Sommerville, *Politics and Ideology in England, 1603–1640* (London, 1986); G. Burgess, *Absolute Monarchy and the Stuart Constitution* (New Haven and London, 1996).

Introduction

Yet although it may be accepted that Richelieu himself was not the direct instigator of a political process that reshaped French government and society, this does not end debate about the extent and nature of practical political change in this period. While few twentieth-century historians have suggested that Richelieu's ministry was characterized by a conscious attempt to create a royal 'absolutism', they none the less affirm that the effect of a militant foreign policy pursued from the 1630s was to create a more centralized and authoritarian state. In this, they move from specific historical case studies to general theories of state development. Richelieu's ministry is located within a wider debate about the impact of warfare on the changing relationship between central power and the autonomy, privileges and political identity of the governed in early modern Europe. This debate is strongly influenced by the social sciences, and above all by the state-building models of Max Weber and his successors. As Weber proposed in his *Essays on Sociology* of 1906: 'The bureaucratic tendency has chiefly been influenced by needs arising from the creation of standing armies as determined by power politics and by the development of public finance connected with the military establishment.'[12] Thus in its most general form the debate concerns the role of warfare in the process of political modernization, the means by which a 'medieval' Europe characterized by separatist corporations, local autonomy and private administration is transformed into a 'modern' world of bureaucratic central government.[13]

The underlying assumption is that early modern European rulers and their councillors were constrained by a mass of political and social prejudices within a political culture which inclined them to seek compromise and to work within existing structures of privilege and authority.[14] Even *had* they seen the fiscal or political benefits of challenging these structures, they were no less constrained by the lack of agencies capable of bringing about substantial change in a 'normative' political environment. The forces of regional autonomy, privileged interest and influence were too strongly entrenched in the political system to permit the development of powerful centralizing institutions. War is seen as changing this situation in that it forced rulers and their agents to confront obstruction and resistance with coercion – often deployed by the army itself – and to develop bureaucratic systems which could improve administrative efficiency. Though the mental world of the early modern ruler was shaped by dynastic assumptions about

---

[12] M. Weber, 'The presuppositions and causes of bureaucracy', in R.K. Merton (ed.), *A Reader in Bureaucracy* (New York, 1960), pp. 66–7.

[13] The other classic statement of the relationship between war and state building is provided in the 1906 lecture by Otto Hintze, 'Military organization and the organization of the state', introduced and translated by F. Gilbert, *The Historical Essays of Otto Hintze* (New York, 1975), pp. 178–215.

[14] H. Scott (ed.), *The European Nobilities of the Seventeenth and Eighteenth Centuries* (2 vols.; London, 1995), I. 35–52.

Introduction

composite kingdoms, princely sovereignty and aristocratic privilege,[15] warfare when waged for sufficiently high stakes had the capacity to break down this conservative consensus and open the way to change in specific areas of government vital to military success. Precisely because these areas were narrowly defined and related to the needs of military institutions, it is not necessary to seek any radical and self-conscious blueprint for coherent, centralized government. Yet cumulatively these changes contributed to reshaping the entire structure of power in European states in the direction of centralized monarchies underpinned by effective coercive power and operated by professional administrators. In its fullest form, the thesis extends well beyond issues of administrative change. Heavy emphasis is laid upon existing trends towards territorial, linguistic and legal unity, on the assumption that these will facilitate the necessary changes in political and social organization. Such states have an inbuilt advantage in the race to deploy their military forces most effectively – producing the largest and most powerful armies, able to sustain the lengthiest and most costly wars – and can go on to achieve wider goals in a competitive international environment. Hence, it is argued, the growing power and effectiveness of the European 'nation states', and the weakness or extinction of other forms of political organization – composite monarchies or states in which sovereignty is ambiguous, or consciously dissipated, such as those within the Holy Roman Empire. In other, more recent, accounts these deterministic explanations are played down, and the discussion focuses on the motivation and mechanisms for political change in early modern states: why did developments conducive to more authoritarian or centralized administration occur in some states and not in others, and what explains the chronology of their emergence?

Such recent arguments about the primary role of warfare in transforming political and social relations in European states have been developed with considerable sophistication and a strong awareness of the divergences in the political and organizational paths and chronologies pursued by different states. In some cases the links between war and state development form a central element in the argument, usually incorporated into a wider discussion of factors in state formation.[16] In others it forms the background to a discussion of the distinctive

---

[15] R. Oresko, G. Gibbs and H. Scott (eds.), *Royal and Republican Sovereignty in Early Modern Europe* (Cambridge, 1997), pp. 5–12.

[16] S. Finer, 'State and nation-building in Europe: the role of the Military', in C. Tilly (ed.), *The Formation of National States in Western Europe* (Princeton, 1975), pp. 84–163, and C. Tilly, 'Armies, wars and states', in Tilly (ed.), *Formation of National States*, pp. 73–6; R. Bean, 'War and the birth of the nation state', *Journal of Economic History*, 33 (1973), 203–21; W.H. McNeill, *The Pursuit of Power. Technology, Armed Force and Society since A.D. 1000* (Oxford, 1982); B. Downing, *The Military Revolution and Political Change. Origins of Democracy and Autocracy in Early Modern Europe* (Princeton, 1992), is explicitly concerned with this theme of the military-driven reshaping of European political systems, and throughout is explicit about the debt to Weber's theories: 'Having benefited from themes in Weber's works, I believe that military organization has been one of the basic building blocks of all civilizations, quite as important to political development as economic

Introduction

path taken by European states and the wider consequences for the exercise of power at both a national and an international level.[17]

All of these works, whether based on wide-ranging sociological theory or the accumulation of historical comparisons, place military organization at the heart of a debate about political change or modernization in early modern Europe. Unlike other variants of 'modernization theory' which located the primary motor for change in economic/agrarian development, industrialization, social conflict or geopolitical factors, the stress on the centrality of warfare and developing structures of military organization has enjoyed steady and relatively uncontroversial acceptance, and has clearly profited from the revival of interest in the role and definition of 'the state' in political theory.[18] A further contribution to the sharpening of the interpretation was the emergence and subsequent elaboration of the theory of an early modern 'military revolution', initially articulated so coherently by Michael Roberts.[19] By linking concepts of state formation with an array of specific military changes, the 'military revolution' has ensured that the adage that 'war made the state' has become a commonplace in thinking about early modern history.

Though much of this argument for war and administrative change would appear to derive from general theories of state development, its essential characteristics have been imported into historical discussion of individual states. And in this respect France in the first half of the seventeenth century represents a paradigmatic case.[20] Most notable amongst the French historians who have argued that

---

structures' (p. 14); T. Ertman, *The Birth of Leviathan: Building States and Regimes in Medieval and Early Modern Europe* (Cambridge, 1997), pp. 1–34, provides a wide-ranging introductory discussion of state-building theories; W. Reinhard, 'Power elites, state servants, ruling classes and the growth of state power', in W. Reinhard (ed.), *Power Elites and State Building* (Oxford, 1996), pp. 9–14.

[17] P. Kennedy, *The Rise and Fall of the Great Powers. Economic Change and Military Conflict from 1500–2000* (London, 1988), pp. 89–91: 'All remarks about the general rise in government spending, or about new organizations for revenue-collecting, or about the changing relationship between kings and estates in early modern Europe, remain abstract until the central importance of military conflict is recalled' (p. 91); M. Mann, *The Sources of Social Power*, vol. I: *A History of Power from the Beginning to A.D. 1760* (Cambridge, 1986), pp. 453–8, 478–81, 483–90; K. Rasler and W. Thompson, *War and State Making. The Shaping of the Global Powers* (Boston, 1989), pp. 205–19; D. Kaiser, *Politics and War. European Conflict from Philip II to Hitler* (London, 1990), pp. 7–137.

[18] See introductory comments by T. Skocpol in: P. Evans, D. Rueschemeyer and T. Skocpol (eds.), *Bringing the State Back In* (Cambridge, 1985), pp. 3–37.

[19] M. Roberts, 'The military revolution, 1560–1660' (Belfast, 1955), reprinted in M. Roberts, *Essays in Swedish History* (London, 1967), pp. 195–225. The 'military revolution' makes explicit appearances in many of the works cited above – for example, McNeill, *Pursuit of Power*, pp. 127–32, and Kennedy, *Great Powers*, pp. 56–7. See also J. Cornette, 'La révolution militaire et l'état moderne', *Revue d'histoire moderne et contemporaine*, 41 (1994), 698–709.

[20] Many of the general theorists have supported their arguments by deploying the example of political change in the France of Richelieu and Mazarin: Hintze, 'Military organization', pp. 199–201; S. Finer, 'State and nation-building', pp. 124–34; C. Tilly, *Coercion, Capital and European States, AD 990–1992* (Oxford, 1990), pp. 26, 75–91; Downing, *Military Revolution*, pp. 121–7.

Introduction

military demands brought about a transformation of the institutions of French government was Roland Mousnier. Mousnier argued forcefully that the nature of *Ancien Régime* government and society was radically transformed by warfare: 'la guerre a été le plus puissant facteur de transformation de 1598 à 1789'.[21] Above all, the demands of war in the first half of the seventeenth century led to the evolution of an administration based upon agents despatched from the centre holding short-term commissions; these commissions provided the authority to override the established proprietary officials who administered the financial and judicial systems but whose compliance with the crown and its ministers remained conditional. The driving force behind this administrative initiative was the conflict into which France was drawn after 1635, and which necessitated massively increased levels of funding, more effective mobilization of military resources and the suppression of resistance.[22]

This model of political change stimulated by France's involvement in the Thirty Years War has been adopted by numerous French historians working in fields such as popular revolt, provincial and institutional studies.[23] Amongst historians outside of France, the development of commissioned *intendants* during the ministries of Richelieu and Mazarin received a definitive treatment from Richard Bonney, while other Anglo-Saxon historians have examined the impact of the war-effort on particular institutions and relations between central and provincial government.[24]

---

[21] R. Mousnier, *Les institutions de la France sous la monarchie absolue, 1598–1715* (2 vols.; Paris, 1974–80), II. 10.

[22] Mousnier, *Les institutions*, II. 489–96, 574–7; R. Mousnier, 'Etat et commissaire. Recherches sur la création des intendants des provinces (1634–48)', in R. Mousnier, *La plume, la faucille et le marteau. Institutions et société en France du Moyen Age à la Révolution* (Paris, 1970), pp. 179–99; R. Mousnier, 'Les crises intérieures françaises de 1610 à 1659 . . .', in K. Repgen (ed.), *Krieg und Politik 1618–1648* (Munich, 1988), pp. 169–83; R. Mousnier, *L'Homme Rouge ou la vie du cardinal de Richelieu (1585–1642)* (Paris, 1992), pp. 623–33.

[23] G. Pagès, *La monarchie de l'Ancien Régime en France de Henri IV à Louis XIV* (3rd edn, Paris, 1941), pp. 103–10; P. Goubert, *L'Ancien Régime* (2 vols.; Paris, 1973) II. 65–92; E. Esmonin, *Etudes sur la France du XVIIe et XVIIIe siècles* (Paris, 1964), pp. 13–32; Y.-M. Bercé, *Histoire des croquants. Etude des soulèvements populaires au XVIIe siècle dans le sud-ouest de la France* (2 vols.; Geneva, 1974), I. 83–118; P. Deyon, 'The French nobility and absolute monarchy in the first half of the seventeenth century', in P.J. Coveney (ed.), *France in Crisis, 1620–1675* (London, 1977), pp. 231–46; J.F. Pernot, 'Le rôle de la guerre dans le développement de la théorie de la monarchie moderne', *Revue historique des armées*, 3 (1979), 41–70; Cornette, 'La révolution militaire', 709.

[24] R. Bonney, *Political Change in France under Richelieu and Mazarin, 1624–1661* (Oxford, 1978); D.C. Baxter, *Servants of the Sword. French Intendants of the Army, 1630–1670* (Urbana Il., 1976), pp. 60–85; R. Harding, *Anatomy of a Power Elite. The Provincial Governors of Early Modern France* (New Haven and London, 1978), pp. 191–217; A. Lloyd Moote, *The Revolt of the Judges* (Princeton, 1971), pp. 36–63; S. Kettering, *Judicial Politics and Urban Revolt in Seventeenth-Century France: The Parlement of Aix, 1629–1659* (Princeton, 1978), pp. 51–80; J.H. Kitchens, 'Judicial commissions and the Parlement of Paris', *French Historical Studies*, 12 (1982), 323–50; R. Giesey, 'State-building in early modern France: the role of royal officialdom', *Journal of Modern History*, 55 (1983), 191–207; S. Hanley, *The 'Lit de Justice' of the kings of France: Constitutional Ideology in Legend, Ritual and Discourse* (Princeton, 1983), pp. 281–95; D. Hickey, *The Coming of French Absolutism: The Struggle for Tax Reform in the Province of Dauphiné, 1540–1640* (Toronto, 1986), pp. 166–78;

Introduction

A product of these works is a well-established thesis about the development of the army in the context of administration and politics during Richelieu's ministry. The size of the army was increased from its previous maximum strength of perhaps 50,000–75,000 troops in earlier conflicts up to a post-1635 force of 125,000–150,000 soldiers. The scale of this military activity demanded better systems of troop quartering within France, especially during the winter months, and better networks of supply points for troops moving across the provinces to the campaign theatres. Larger forces hugely increased the problems of recruitment, supply and discipline, and these were handled by a great expansion in the authority and competence of the secretary of state for war and his staff in the *bureau de la guerre*. Beneath this central office extended a network of commissioned administrators, the *intendants d'armée*, granted wide-ranging authority within the individual army-corps to handle matters of finance, supply and discipline. Whereas in the past, major campaign armies had been commanded by the king himself in the presence of senior government ministers, war fought in multiple campaigns required the crown to delegate authority to individual generals. Those senior military offices with the most extensive and dangerous powers were abolished (the *connétable*) or had their authority drastically curtailed (the *colonel général de l'infanterie*), while the corps commanders were subject to supervision by the central agents, the *intendants*.

Little of this change could occur independently of a wider political and social context. A huge increase in the size of the army needed to be paid for, and this in turn drove up the burden of taxation to unprecedented levels. Assessing and collecting revenues in these circumstances revealed the grave weaknesses of a fiscal administration based upon venality of office and steeped in local and corporate self-interest. Moreover, the ever-tightening fiscal vice drove peasants and artisans into violent resistance and incited legal and administrative obstruction from the provincial elites. Unable to forgo revenues on which the war-effort depended, the civil counterparts of the commissioned *intendants d'armée*, the provincial *intendants*, were granted ever-increasing powers to assess taxation, to supervise collection and to repress disorders. The billeting of soldiers in the provinces over the winter months, stockpiling of grain magazines and other food supplies, control of civil-military disorders, supervision of recruitment and the passage of troops, were all also placed under the authority of these provincial *intendants*. The central administration was both better informed about the situation in the provinces, thanks to the steady stream of correspondence from its new provincial agents, and more interventionist in all matters which threatened to disrupt the war-effort. The presence of troops in the frontier provinces gave the crown the practical opportunity to impose its authority in the face of local obstruction or non-

---

D. Parker, *Class and State in Ancien Régime France. The Road to Modernity?* (London, 1996), pp. 158–67.

Introduction

cooperation in matters of billeting, payment of taxes or supply. *Raison d'état*, which had hitherto existed as a theoretical concept used by Richelieu's publicists to argue for the legitimacy of war against catholic powers, now provided a justification for an increasingly assertive and authoritarian central regime, based upon the overriding authority of agents acting directly under royal commission.

Such an interpretation of changes in French government and administration brought about by the demands of the war-effort offers a corrective to the improbable view that Richelieu himself could shape policy in accordance with some vision of monarchical absolutism. While not denying that he was more powerful and influential than any other subject of Louis XIII, it is more realistic to recognize that government initiatives – for example, the proliferation of the commissioned *intendants* – owed as much to *ad hoc* decisions and actions by subordinate ministers, or should be seen as pragmatic responses to institutional or provincial pressure. Moreover, challenging the view of Richelieu's political omnicompetence creates awareness that his actions took place in the wider context of a Court in which numerous interests and factions were in play and constantly needed to be taken into account. Richelieu was not a free agent, confident that Louis XIII would identify his policies with the interests of the Bourbon monarchy and the good of France.[25]

Yet this shift in the perception of the ministry's war-effort and its consequences is not wholly satisfactory. At the level of general theory, the assumptions linking the more effective waging of war with bureaucratic rationality and centralization need more scrutiny. There is an obvious danger in adopting a model which was developed to explain the relationship of war to political change in later nineteenth- and early twentieth-century European states, and assuming that it can be applied to earlier periods and societies.[26] It is not axiomatic that central control over the funding and organization of the army and over the level of military activity is the most effective method of waging war. It can certainly be contended that decentralization and the contracting out of military functions into the hands of individual commanders or administrator-entrepreneurs may prove a more efficient means to manage a war-effort in a state lacking existing, wide-ranging structures of revenue extraction, where administrative office is largely the private property of institutional elites, and where the power and influence of a provincial ruling class is too great easily to challenge or sidestep. Far from evading the 'rational' path towards centralization and institutional modernization, rulers and their councillors may be acting more rationally in working within existing

---

[25] A point made by two recent biographies of Louis XIII: P. Chevallier, *Louis XIII, roi cornélien* (Paris, 1979); A. Lloyd Moote, *Louis XIII. The Just* (Berkeley, Calif., 1989).

[26] The extent to which Weber's original linkage between war, military organization and administrative rationalization was extrapolated from historical experience of the Prussian state in the eighteenth and nineteenth centuries has been remarked upon by numbers of commentators – cf. Evans, Rueschmeyer and Skocpol (eds.), *Bringing the State Back In*, pp. 350–1.

Introduction

military/administrative systems, strengthening decentralized and delegated authority and collaborating with established interests. Within a 'long perspective', extending to wars waged by mass conscript armies and requiring the mobilization of a huge proportion of the state's resources, it might appear that there is an inexorable progress towards ever-more centralized and tightly controlled military and civil administration, but there were important periods of history when such a process was not at all evident.[27]

More specific doubts about the character of central and provincial government have been raised by numbers of recent studies of seventeenth-century French institutional structures. Historians have been prepared to question the assumption that the relations between government and French society were transformed under Richelieu, or at least that they were transformed in ways which laid the foundations of a centralized, authoritarian and bureaucratic regime. These studies emphasize continuities with traditional mechanisms of government and administration, and the reliance on mechanisms which tended to consolidate the strength of corporatist and provincial interest. Contrasting with the emphasis on the evolving role of commissioned agents of central authority in civil and military administration is an argument for the dominance of clientelism, a ministerial reliance on elaborate but informal networks of connections within the whole range of existing central and provincial institutions as a means to enforce ministerial policies.[28] The establishment of networks of patronage created a disincentive to weaken the power of existing institutions, since it was through offering rewards to individuals or groups within these structures that the ministers would hope to obtain reciprocal support and assistance. Moreover, underpinning particular clientage relationships was a general awareness of broader networks of established influence extending through society which ought to be respected if government based heavily upon the deployment of personalized relationships was to work to the benefit of the centre.[29] Understanding of the fiscal system in particular has

---

[27] The issue of state control of the military versus contracting receives a particularly important treatment in the study by I.A.A. Thompson, *War and Government in Habsburg Spain, 1560–1620* (London, 1976).

[28] Y. Durand (ed.), *Clientèles et fidélités en Europe à l'époque moderne* (Paris, 1981); K. Dunkley, 'Patronage and power in seventeenth-century France. Richelieu's clients and the Estates of Brittany', *Parliaments, Estates and Representation*, 1 (1981), 1–12; S. Kettering, *Patrons, Brokers and Clients in Seventeenth-Century France* (Oxford, 1986); S. Kettering, 'Patronage in early modern France', *French Historical Studies*, 17 (1992), 839–62; C. Giry-Deloison and R. Mettam (eds.), *Patronages et clientélismes 1550–1750 (France, Angleterre, Espagne, Italie)* (Lille, 1995). Clientelism is not necessarily regarded as incompatible with the development of an administration making greater use of agents acting under commission, as Kettering herself points out: *Patrons*, pp. 232–7. Nor is it the case that historians such as Mousnier and Bonney, who have stressed administrative development through commissions, have ignored the role of clientage in the political context of early seventeenth-century France. Durand's volume is both a *Festschrift* for Mousnier and a response to the latter's call for a systematic study of clienteles, while see, for example, Bonney, *Political Change*, pp. 88–9, 300–1.

[29] The now classic work on established influences in a provincial power structure is that of W. Beik,

Introduction

benefited from the attention given to the interactions between central government and established networks of influence and institutional authority. A group of historians have demonstrated the entrenched position of private financiers at the heart of the ministerial regime, bound to the ministers and the *bureau des finances* as members of clienteles involved in contracting loans which both held the regime together and, paradoxically, represented one of its greatest inflexibilities.[30] At a less developed stage is the detailed study of the persistent power of great noble Houses, for too long seen as the obvious victims of a ministerial drive to centralization. A feature of these studies has been the recognition that, far from seeking to eliminate the power and influence of the great nobles, the aim of the ministers was to incorporate a significant number of these families into political alliances capable both of underpinning the political ambitions of a hard-pressed regime and of underwriting the ministers' own aspirations to high social status.[31] All of this work has focused on the practical impact of the ministry and its policies, particularly at the provincial level, in order to demonstrate that patterns of established interests and traditional channels of authority remained largely in place. Some have also argued that when Richelieu's ministry, under severe fiscal and administrative pressure, did attempt selectively to break with these patterns, the result was often counter-productive, failing to strengthen the control of the central regime.[32]

Absolutism and Society in Seventeenth-Century France. State Power and Provincial Aristocracy in Languedoc (Cambridge, 1985); J.B. Collins, *Classes, Estates and Order in Early Modern Brittany* (Cambridge, 1994), pp. 1–29, 187–228, 271–88; J. Bergin, 'Richelieu and his bishops? Ministerial power and episcopal patronage under Louis XIII', in J. Bergin and L.W.B. Brockliss (eds.), *Richelieu and his Age* (Oxford, 1992), pp. 175–202. A study of a later period but making similar points about respect for institutional structures is provided by A. Hamscher, *The Parlement of Paris after the Fronde, 1653–1673* (Pittsburgh, 1976), pp. 119–202.

[30] A. Guéry, 'Les finances de la monarchie française sous l'Ancien Régime', *Annales ESC*, 33 (1978), 216–39; D. Dessert, 'Le "laquais-financier" au Grand Siècle: mythe ou réalité? *Dix-septième siècle*, 122 (1979), 21–36; R.J. Bonney, *The King's Debts. Finance and Politics in France, 1589–1661* (Oxford, 1981); D. Dessert, *Argent, pouvoir et société au Grand Siècle* (Paris, 1984); F. Bayard, *Le monde des financiers au XVIIe siècle* (Paris, 1988); J. Collins, *The Fiscal Limits of Absolutism. Direct Taxation in Early Seventeenth-Century France* (Berkeley, 1988).

[31] A. Jouanna, *Le devoir de révolte: la noblesse française et la gestion de l'état moderne, 1559–1661* (Paris, 1989), pp. 212–399; R. Mettam, 'The French nobility, 1610–1715', in Scott (ed.), *European Nobilities*, I. 114–41; Parrott, 'Richelieu, the *grands* and the French army', in Bergin and Brockliss (eds.), *Richelieu and his Age*, pp. 135–42; Parker, *Class and State*, pp. 136–57; K. Béguin, *Les princes de Condé. Rebelles, courtisans et mécènes dans la France du Grand Siècle* (Paris, 1999), pp. 26–111; J. Bérenger, *Turenne* (Paris, 1987), pp. 163–90; J. Inglis-Jones, 'The Grand Condé in exile: power politics in France, Spain and the Spanish Netherlands', DPhil thesis, University of Oxford, 1994, pp. 15–44; S. Hodson, 'Sovereigns and subjects: the princes of Sedan and the dukes of Bouillon in early modern France, c. 1450–1652', DPhil thesis, University of Oxford, 2000. For ministerial ambitions, see notably J. Bergin, *Cardinal Richelieu. Power and the Pursuit of Wealth* (New Haven and London, 1985), and R. Oresko, 'The marriage of the nieces of Cardinal Mazarin. Public policy and private strategy in seventeenth-century Europe', in R. Babel (ed.), *Frankreich im europäischen Staatensystem der Frühen Neuzeit* (Sigmaringen, 1995), pp. 109–51.

[32] See notably Beik, *Absolutism and Society*, pp. 98–112.

Introduction

These works have confined themselves to aspects of civil society, albeit aspects that were certainly touched by the impact of warfare. The obvious absence in all of these discussions – whether well-established arguments for change brought about by warfare, or revisionist assertions of institutional and governmental continuity – is an examination of the army itself. Did the French crown in the first half of the seventeenth century respond to the demands of its war-effort by a series of far-reaching administrative reforms touching the organization of the army? Alternatively, did the demands push reluctant and conservative ministers into specific, limited modification and innovation in certain key areas while seeking to leave the surrounding administration untouched? If neither of these was the case, and continuity was everywhere more apparent than change, then just how was this apparently unprecedented military effort sustained, and what were the political and social costs of seeking to maintain the *status quo*?

A primary purpose of the present study is to contribute to these debates about political and administrative change. Although it is a chronologically limited study, the conclusions reach beyond the two decades of French history under examination. It is an approach to the army which draws overwhelmingly upon the evidence of primary, and especially manuscript, source material. Archivally based research provides the essential means to break through a myth-encrusted history of army, state and society; a history built up of successive layers of received opinion shaped partly by nineteenth-century nationalist assumptions, partly by the contribution of detailed but poorly contextualized traditional military history, and partly by reliance on the published self-justifications of contemporaries – most notably of Richelieu himself.

Returning to the archival material, and above all the two dense collections of correspondence in the Archives des Affaires Etrangères, permits the detailed examination of policy-making and action in response to the problems of the army as these appeared to both the embattled ministers and to the commanders and senior administrators in the field. Sequences of letters provide insights into the formulation of strategy, blunt assessments of available resources and priorities, and sharply focused views about the problems of organization, control and maintenance. They also make clear the extent of factional rivalries at Court and amongst the army-corps, the competition for attention and resources amongst the corps commanders and their subordinates, and the pervasive networks of clientage linking ministers, administrators and officers.

The first three chapters of the work are concerned with the military context of the French war-effort. The first examines the way in which the French armies undertook campaigns, their debts to other European styles of warfare, the training and deployment of troops, the strengths and weaknesses of their fighting methods. The second chapter provides an overview of the conduct of foreign policy between 1624 and 1642, draws contrasts between the ways in which Richelieu

Introduction

would have wished to wage war in these decades and the actual circumstances of the French war-effort, and seeks to discuss the consequences of this in terms of available military resources. The third looks at a key issue in the relationship between military aims and resources, the size of the French army during this period of warfare.

The remaining chapters of the book are concerned with the administrative context of the war-effort. This section begins with an examination of the difficulties of financing the army, and the failure of the ministry to provide more than a proportion of the funds necessary to meet the costs of the war-effort. The consequence of this is discussed in the two subsequent chapters: the crown's policies towards the recruitment and maintenance of the individual units in the army is compared with the systems of other European powers; the extent to which the crown sought to transfer the costs of recruiting and maintaining the troops on to the shoulders of the unit officers and the high command is examined in detail. In confronting an officer-corps which felt itself to be exploited by the crown and in consequence took a restricted view of its service obligations, the ministry needed an extensive, well-supported and responsive civil administration with the armies. In practice an almost entirely proprietary military administration was supplemented by agents acting under special commission, but whose authority was ill-defined and who were frequently installed on an *ad hoc* basis. Those administrators who were prepared to act as agents of ministerial authority came up against the continuing power and networks of influence possessed by the high command, considered in chapter 9. The final chapter examines the impact of this military system upon the civilian population of France, focusing upon troop movement across the provinces, the organization of winter quartering and the wider impact of indiscipline and violence between the military and civilians.

It becomes evident from examining these issues that while the war-effort may have been unprecedented, the means by which it was sustained were a combination of traditional mechanisms suited to a smaller military establishment, and a resort to massive decentralization: the high command, ministerial *fidèles* and clients, and unit officers were all expected to bear a substantial element of the financing and maintenance of the army through the war years. The price of this system was an unprecedented level of officer absenteeism, tolerance of soldiers' indiscipline and even desertion, and overt evasion of the obligation to maintain units at acceptable strength. Despite these challenges to military effectiveness, but largely in consequence of its dependence on the contributions of the officer-corps, the ministry compromised with established interests, particularly with the senior officers who were largely drawn from the highest ranks of the *noblesse d'épée*. Richelieu's much-cited rhetoric cannot conceal the evidence that the status and influence of the great nobility in the army was maintained, and in significant respects reinforced, during this period; administrators with the army-corps were

Introduction

well aware that they could expect no support from the ministers – or even the crown – in the event of a clash with senior officers. A civilian administration that was inadequate to the challenges of an expanding war-effort lurched from expedient to contradictory expedient, failing to provide adequate support systems for the army, failing to sustain numbers through effective recruitment, failing to keep the army supplied throughout a campaign, and failing to protect civilian populations from the depredations of a poorly paid, ill-supplied and undisciplined soldiery.

Yet for all this the army was kept in being. A war-effort which consisted for the most part of campaigns waged through grinding, attritional strategies was sustained, and Richelieu's ministry avoided the complete breakdown of the military machine which would have brought the war to an abrupt and unfavourable end. While much of this study will be concerned to examine the political and social costs of waging warfare beyond the financial and administrative resources of the regime, the chapters will also seek to show how it was that this breakdown was avoided in the face of what might seem almost overwhelming administrative inadequacies. It is certainly reasonable to ask whether a ministry which had been committed to a more aggressively reformist policy, pursuing the kind of administrative rationalization so often attributed to Richelieu's ministry, would not have precipitated exactly this type of collapse. A compromising, minimalist, *ad hoc* response to the war-effort might suggest a regime in the grip of an ill-considered conservatism which failed to confront the central problems of maintaining an army in a rational and well-planned manner; yet it may have been this very factor which explains the survival of Richelieu's army and his foreign policy in the face of military setbacks, strong hostility from the French people and a lack of political commitment from much of the political elite.

PART I

The military context

I

The French art of war during Richelieu's ministry

Accounts of French military practice during the seventeenth century have traditionally taken 19 May 1643 as their point of departure, the date of the battle of Rocroi and the defeat of the *tercios* of the Spanish army of Flanders by French forces under the command of the young Louis II de Bourbon, duc d'Enghien and future Grand Condé. Strongly influenced by the cult of the great commander, such studies have focused upon the middle and later seventeenth century, giving detailed attention to the campaigns waged by Turenne and Condé and the sophisticated siege warfare of maréchal Vauban.[1] The relationship of the period from the mid-1640s to the military experience of the earlier part of the century has been largely ignored; little interest is shown in how French armies were deployed for campaigns, battles or sieges during the period of Richelieu's ministry.

The neglect of the way in which French armies fought at the time of Louis XIII and Richelieu reflects another long-held assumption, that French military practice can be subsumed under a wider process of European military evolution; France was simply following those progressive states, the Dutch and the Swedes, whose army reforms were the decisive factor in shaping the military history of the late sixteenth and early seventeenth centuries. The opinion that the tactics, deployment and discipline of European armies were radically reshaped by reforms introduced by the princes of Orange, Stadholders of the Dutch Republic – most notably Maurits of Nassau, but also his younger brother Frederik Hendrik and his nephew Willem Lodewijk – and then adopted and developed by Gustavus Adolphus, king of Sweden (1611–32), has a long ancestry. Indeed, the origins of

---

[1] A. Pascal, *Histoire de l'armée et de tous les régiments* (5 vols; Paris, 1847–50), II. 13–58; E. de La Barre Duparcq, *Histoire de l'art militaire depuis l'usage de la poudre* (Paris, 1864), pp. 95–212; R. Quarré de Verneuil, *L'armée en France depuis Charles VII jusqu'à la Révolution (1439–1789)* (Paris, 1880), pp. 147–75; L. Dussieux, *L'armée en France* (3 vols; Versailles, 1884), II. 17–223; L. Dussieux, *Les grands généraux de Louis XIV. Notices historiques* (Paris, 1888), pp. 1–111; J. Roy, *Turenne, sa vie et les institutions militaires de son temps* (Paris, 1884), pp. 15–78; M. Hardÿ de Périni, *Turenne et Condé, 1626–1675* (Paris, 1906); F. Reboul, 'Histoire militaire de la France', in G. Hanotaux (ed.), *Histoire de la nation française* (15 vols., Paris, 1920–35), VII. 349–418; H. Guerlac, 'Vauban: the impact of science on war', in E.M. Earle (ed.), *Makers of Modern Strategy: Military Thought from Machiavelli to Hitler* (Princeton, 1944), pp. 26–48; R. Foerster, 'Turenne et Montecuccoli. Une comparaison stratégique et tactique', in F. Gambiez and J. Laloy (eds.), *Turenne et l'art militaire. Actes du colloque international* (Paris, 1975), pp. 217–18; M. Blancpain, *Le mardi de Rocroi* (Paris, 1985).

The military context

this argument for military change lie in the conscious dissemination of reform plans by Maurits of Nassau as early as the 1590s.

The key elements in the Orangist military reforms have frequently been identified by historians. Though infantry had dominated the battlefields of Europe since the victories of Swiss pikemen over Burgundian cavalry in the later fifteenth century, this supremacy had rested upon crude mass and impact: foot-soldiers bearing pikes, halbards or swords were pressed into huge blocks as many as sixty men deep and containing 3,000–4,000 soldiers in total, and advanced slowly and remorselessly across a battlefield against enemy formations of cavalry or infantry. When, as with the Swiss or the German *Landsknechte*, these infantry phalanxes possessed strong *esprit de corps* and a cohesion based on accumulated campaigning experience, they appeared invincible. What proved their fatal flaw was the development and increasingly widespread use of firearms. Artillery deployed on the battlefield, and a larger proportion of infantry armed with arquebuses, then from the mid-sixteenth century with the heavier and more effective musket, were gradually changing the face of battle. Attempts to modify infantry tactics to make allowance for the development of firearms were characteristic of sixteenth-century tactical thinking, but they were piecemeal bids to reconcile the traditional packed infantry formation with the new technology. Most notably, the Spanish *tercio*, an infantry formation of 3,000 soldiers, combined the traditional solid square of pikemen with an encircling belt of musketeers, able to return fire while sheltering beneath the protection of the massed pikes, and to disappear amongst them when the square began its lumbering advance across the battlefield. But according to the Orangist interpretation of tactical change, this type of redeployment was little more than tinkering with a traditional conception of battlefield tactics dominated by mass and the 'push of pike'. What was required, and provided by Maurits of Nassau's reforms, was a new conception of battlefield deployment which would take full account of warfare dominated by the killing-power of firearms. The result was a radical rethinking of the organization and deployment of infantry. In place of the massed square, the Orangist reforms substituted shallow formations initially ten rows deep but progressively reduced to eight, then six, rows. The proportion of musketeers rose in these formations to become two-thirds of the total, and instead of being spread in a girdle around four sides of a square so that the great majority were unable to use their firearms unless the formation were completely surrounded by enemy troops, they were placed in increasingly elaborate deployments amongst smaller groups of pikemen, deployments whose primary intention was to ensure that all of them should have the opportunity to fire their muskets. This decision to redeploy the infantry in shallower formations had two consequences. It greatly reduced the size of the basic tactical unit; if the Spanish *tercio* had contained 3,000 men, the reformed Dutch battalion was of 550 men. A Dutch or other 'reformed' general would now find himself in command of an army with a large number of small individual

The French art of war during Richelieu's ministry

units, rather than five or six great blocks of infantry. This itself would encourage more flexible and complex battlefield deployment: a general with two or three dozen individual infantry units would more readily think in terms of drawing up his army in two or three successive lines, providing greater defence in depth and more capacity to adjust to changing battlefield circumstances. The second consequence of this shift to smaller units and more complicated deployment was the need to impose much more rigorous training upon the ordinary soldiers and a far higher level of initiative and flexibility upon NCOs and officers. While a recruit carrying a pike in the fortieth rank of an infantry square barely required any qualities beyond brute strength, musketeers and pikemen deployed in these new and more complex formations were to be subjected to rigorous and uniform drill, enabling units to perform more sophisticated manoeuvres and allowing individual soldiers to handle weapons more effectively – facilitating musket fire through the countermarch system, for example, which would allow successive rows of musketeers to discharge their weapons in sequence. When the loading and firing of a musket was taught, via printed manuals, as a sequence of carefully prescribed actions, a uniform rate of fire could be achieved which would further enhance the battlefield effectiveness of the unit. All of this was supervised and, outside the combat-zone, taught by a much larger group of unit officers and NCOs. These officers were themselves better trained and subordinated to commanders who were aware that maximizing the advantages of this military system required more sophisticated systems of control and communication. A disciplined, professional, cohesive officer-corps would reduce the dangers of misinterpretation or an ill-judged individual initiative which might jeopardize a complex battlefield strategy.[2]

If the essential elements of this change in the 'art of war' were attributed to the reforms of the princes of Orange, and first demonstrated by the Dutch army, no less a debt is attributed to Gustavus Adolphus of Sweden in the process of evolution. Though the Dutch reforms were the self-proclaimed starting point of

---

[2] G. Roloff, 'Moritz von Oranien und die Begründung des modernen Heeres', *Preußische Jahrbücher*, 111 (1903), 255–76; J.W. Wijn, *Het krijgswezen in den tijd van Prins Maurits* (Utrecht, 1934), pp. 433–48, 467–86, 533–41; W. Hahlweg, *Die Heeresreform der Oranier und die Antike* (Berlin, 1941), pp. 136–9, 191–6; H. Delbrück, trans. W. Renfroe, *History of the Art of War within the Framework of Political History* (4 vols.; Westport, Conn., and London, 1975–85), IV. 155–73; J.W. Wijn, *New Cambridge Modern History* (14 vols.; Cambridge, 1958–70) IV. 215–22; M.D. Feld, 'Middle class society and the rise of military professionalism: the Dutch army, 1589–1609', *Armed Forces and Society*, 1 (1975), 419–42; B.H. Nickle, *The Military Reforms of Prince Maurice of Orange* (Michigan, 1984), pp. 145–56; H. Ehlert, 'Ursprünge des modernen Militärwesens. Die nassau-oranischen Heeresreformen', *Militärgeschichtliche Mitteilungen*, 18 (1985), 27–56; G.E. Rothenberg, 'Maurits of Nassau, Gustavus Adolphus, Raimondo Montecuccoli and the "Military Revolution" of the seventeenth century', in P. Paret (ed.), *Makers of Modern Strategy: Military Thought from Machiavelli to the Nuclear Age* (Princeton, 1986), pp. 32–63; M. van der Hoeven (ed.), *Exercise of Arms. Warfare in the Netherlands (1568–1648)* (Brill, 1998), especially essays by J.A. de Moor and J.P. Puype; A. Wiekart and J.P. Puype, *Van Maurits naar Munster: tactiek en triomf van het Staatse leger* (catalogue of exhibition at the Legermuseum (Delft, 1998), pp. 7–15.

the development of tactics and organization, the next generation of commanders, those whose military experience was to be consolidated on the battlefields of the Thirty Years War, recognized the limitations of some of these initial reforms. Above all, the Dutch reforms were the product of a military environment characterized by relatively static warfare dominated by the set-piece siege. The reforms, by maximizing the firepower of infantry and strengthening the effectiveness of the defensive, could create armies that were better adapted through discipline, drill and essentially linear deployments to the conduct of sieges. What the reforms did not resolve was the problem of seizing the initiative when taking the offensive on the battlefield. Shallow, linear formations could throw up a hail of fire which might render an enemy attack unacceptably costly, but did not resolve the problem of how the Dutch army, in turn, could successfully assume the offensive with its lightweight formations, its heavy emphasis on firearms rather than pikes and the weakness of training in the inter-unit cohesion required for successful assault tactics.[3] It was in developing the offensive capacity of his troops that the originality of Gustavus Adolphus was considered to lie. Although the Swedish infantry were deployed in small 'squadrons' of around 500 soldiers, these could be combined in larger 'brigades' of 1,500–2,000 troops, possessing the weight and cohesion to take the offensive. Linear formations and elaborate musket drill indicated that Gustavus was no less preoccupied with maximizing the firepower of his infantry; but pike drill and direct training in assault tactics facilitated hard-hitting offensives supported by a readiness for hand-to-hand combat. Numbers of light, three-pound, artillery pieces were distributed amongst the infantry to provide mobile firepower with far greater range and deadliness than muskets, able to give effective support to infantry assaults. The cavalry, which apparently played the most limited part in the tactical thinking of the princes of Orange, was rehabilitated under Gustavus, who emphasized the shock-value of the mounted charge. While cavalry tactics in the sixteenth century had been preoccupied with the *caracole*, an elaborate and arguably ineffectual manoeuvre to allow riders to fire pistols in sequence at close range into enemy formations, Gustavus stipulated the return to a cavalry whose basic weapon was the sabre, and whose tactic was the charge to contact, seeking to exploit the disarray and weakness that infantry firepower might have sown in enemy formations. The cavalry were to be coordinated with the offensive capacity of the other arms, and their training and tactics were to be developed accordingly.[4]

This location of this 'second stage' of developments in the art of war amongst

[3] M. Roberts, 'Gustav Adolf and the art of war', in M. Roberts, *Essays in Swedish History* (London, 1967), pp. 60–64; M. Roberts, *Gustavus Adolphus. A History of Sweden, 1611–1632* (2 vols; London, 1953–8), II. 182–9.
[4] E. Carrion-Nisas, *Essai sur l'histoire générale de l'art militaire. De son origine, de ses progrès et de ses révolutions* (2 vols.; Paris, 1824), II. 54–9; T.A. Dodge, *Gustavus Adolphus* (Boston, 1895; reissued, London, 1996), pp. 28–62; Delbrück, *History of the Art of War*, IV. 173–83; Roberts, *Gustavus Adolphus*, II. 247–62.

The French art of war during Richelieu's ministry

the practical reforms of Gustavus Adolphus, reforms which are held to have shown their full potential at the great Swedish victory at Breitenfeld in September 1631, is an equally well-established element in traditional military studies of early modern Europe. What gave a new sharpness and wider relevance to such commonplace arguments about early seventeenth-century tactical development, and what makes them particularly familiar to a modern readership, was their incorporation into a much more extensive theory of 'military revolution', articulated so effectively by Professor Michael Roberts.[5] Roberts started from these familiar assumptions about changes in tactics and military deployment, but his distinctive contribution was to argue that they could be shown to have radical political and social consequences for the states fielding the armies. As the introduction to the present book emphasizes, Roberts' assertion that changes in the nature of warfare represented 'a great divide separating medieval society from the modern world' has served to familiarize historians and students who might never have applied such concepts to early modern Europe with a series of arguments about the role of warfare in state formation.[6]

Successive chapters in the book will take issue with many of the assumptions underlying the theory of state development brought about through the demands of warfare. However, the concern of the present chapter is more specifically focused on the extent to which this framework of assumed changes in the nature of tactics, deployment and drill stands up to an investigation of France's 'way of warfare' during Richelieu's ministry. It is typically assumed that France stands in some form of apostolic succession to the reformist initiatives of the Orange princes and to Gustavus Adolphus: while the benefits of tactical and organizational reform only really bear fruit in the period following the battle of Rocroi and the age of the 'great commanders', the period of Richelieu's ministry is one of internal consolidation during which the lessons and prescriptions of the military reformers were being absorbed into the training, experience and assumptions of the French army.[7] The intention of this chapter is to show, from the evidence of training, troop deployment and military practice, how unconvincing such assertions appear when examining the French army of the 1620s to early 1640s. Moreover, by raising doubts about the extent to which these prescriptions were adopted in the French case, it is possible to question the wider European context of military change. While aspects of this process have been subjected to critical

---

[5] Roberts, 'Military revolution'; Roberts, 'Gustav Adolf and the art of war', pp. 56–81; Roberts, *Gustavus Adolphus*, II. 169–271.
[6] Roberts, 'Military revolution', p. 195.
[7] Carrion-Nisas, *Essai*, II. 47–102; E. de La Barre Duparcq, *Eléments d'art et d'histoire militaire* (Paris, 1858), pp. 160–2; Dussieux, *L'armée en France*, II. 26–9; Avenel, *Richelieu*, III. 90–4; Hanotaux, *Histoire de la nation française*, VII. 339–43; J. Revol, *Turenne. Essai de psychologie militaire* (Paris, 1910), pp. 158–68; E. Carrias, *La pensée militaire française* (Paris, 1960), pp. 113–24. John Lynn identifies the fallacy behind this assumption in 'Tactical evolution in the French army, 1560–1660', *French Historical Studies*, 14 (1985), 178–80.

The military context

scrutiny by other historians in the last two decades, the role of France in this reassessment has remained surprisingly restricted.[8]

THE FRENCH 'ART OF WARFARE' IN THEORY

In so far as any attempts have been made to examine French military activity in the period of Richelieu's ministry, historians have relied upon literary sources, and particularly tracts on the art of war.[9] Such military tracts can provide useful insights into contemporary warfare, but it can be misleading to take their elaborate and frequently impractical theoretical prescriptions as an actual account of a cruder and much more diverse military reality.[10]

A rhetoric of military reform

An apparently good reason for taking such writings seriously as an indication of changes in tactical organization, deployment and drill in the late sixteenth and early seventeenth centuries is the extent to which early modern contemporaries

---

[8] G. Parker, 'The "Military revolution, 1560–1660" – a myth?', *Journal of Modern History*, 48 (1976), 195–214, at pp. 89–90 (reprinted in G. Parker, *Spain and the Netherlands, 1559–1659* (London, 1979), pp. 85–103, and in C.J. Rogers (ed.), *The Military Revolution Debate. Readings on the Military Transformation of Early Modern Europe* (Boulder, Colo., 1995), pp. 37–54), raises doubts about the chronological boundaries established by Roberts, and argues that the responsiveness of the Spanish army to developments in the potential of firearms and tactical flexibility has been underestimated. Other historians have echoed Parker's points about overly restrictive chronology and the focus on a narrow group of 'reformist' states: J.R. Hale, *War and Society in Renaissance Europe, 1450–1620* (London, 1985), explicitly places change after 1560 within the context of the developments of the preceding century (pp. 46–74), while a stimulating examination of the evidence for change before 1560 and its wider impact outside of Europe is provided by J.F. Guilmartin Jr, 'The military revolution: origins and first tests abroad', in Rogers (ed.), *The Military Revolution Debate*, pp. 299–333. Similar criticism is launched by D. Eltis, *The Military Revolution in Sixteenth-Century Europe* (London, 1995); F. Tallett, *War and Society in Early Modern Europe, 1495–1715* (London, 1992), pp. 21–68; J. Bérenger (ed.), *La révolution militaire en Europe (XV–XVIIIe siècles)* (Paris, 1998), essays by Bérenger and Chagniot. Other historians have emphasized the geographical limitations of the original thesis, the extent to which it was far too focused on specifically Western European warfare: R. Frost, 'The Polish-Lithuanian commonwealth and the "military revolution"', in J.S. Pula and M.B. Biskupski (eds.), *Poland and Europe: Historical Dimensions. Selected Essays from the 50th Anniversary International Congress of the Polish Arts and Sciences in America* (Boulder, Colo., 1994), pp. 19–47, demonstrates that the Poles had a different set of military traditions, which reflected the geographical circumstances of vast, sparsely populated and open, territories. In encounters with the Swedish army on Polish territory such traditions, which placed a premium on light cavalry, proved more successful than the Swedish preoccupations with maximizing firepower and offensive tactics sustained by the infantry. This argument is elaborated in R. Frost, *The Northern Wars, 1558–1721* (London, 2000), esp. pp. 16–19, 304–27.

[9] Carrion-Nisas, *Essai*, II. 41–102; E. de La Barre Duparcq, *Histoire sommaire d'infanterie* (Paris, 1853), pp. 29–30; Carrias, *Pensée militaire*, pp. 108–32; Lynn, 'Tactical evolution', 176–91.

[10] The problems of relying on military tracts is made clear for the case of the better-studied sixteenth-century French army, where elaborate theoretical prescriptions can be shown to be largely irrelevant to the style of warfare actually practised: see J.B. Wood, *The King's Army. Warfare, Soldiers and Society during the Wars of Religion in France, 1562–1576* (Cambridge, 1996), pp. 78–85.

The French art of war during Richelieu's ministry

themselves appear to have acknowledged extensive debts to a previous literary tradition. From the outset of the period identified with the military changes of the Dutch, what impressed contemporary observers was the extent to which the princes of Orange claimed to be deriving their own reforms from the military prescriptions of classical antiquity. The reformers themselves stated explicitly that the basis of their tactical and organizational changes was a renewed study of the military prescriptions of classical authors – above all, Flavius Vegetius Renatus, Claudius Aelian and the Byzantine Emperor Leo VI[11] – which had provided the decisive impetus behind the development of linear formations, smaller units and a greater emphasis on drill, training and discipline. If later generations of historians have chosen to see the Dutch reforms as an apparently logical response to the growing importance of firearms on the battlefields of Europe, contemporary exponents of the changes were emphatic that they reflected the careful reading and adoption of the prescriptions of classical theorists. The amount of contemporary and subsequent discussion surrounding this classical revival certainly cannot be denied. What can be questioned, however, is whether this well-publicized structure of reforms supposedly based on classical antiquity was more than a rhetorical exercise, deploying language and concepts familiar and convincing to an audience easily susceptible to the authority of classical tradition, and above all, to the martial excellence of the Roman Republic.[12] The works of Vegetius and Aelian had been available in printed translations since the late fifteenth and early sixteenth centuries respectively, and classical military theorists had been studied throughout the middle ages.[13] A century before Maurits of Nassau, Machiavelli's Florentine militia provides a notorious example of an attempt to use classical prescriptions as the basis of modern military discipline and organization. At the most general level this emphasis on ancient military prescriptions should be seen as part of a wider preoccupation with classical, and especially Roman, culture and political organization. The debate about the superiority of Roman institutions, law, art, civic organization and the practicality of their adoption in contemporary

---

[11] Hahlweg, *Heeresreform*, pp. 304–5.

[12] Two of the studies which have contributed most to affirming the link between classical prescriptions and early modern military practice both accept that this adoption was not unconditional: Hahlweg, *Heeresreform*, stresses that the employment of 'classical' models was selective and shaped to the perceived needs of modern warfare (pp. 194–5); Wijn, *Krijgswezen*, pp. 480–2, underscores the point that the direct influence of Roman military organization is at times difficult to demonstrate.

[13] In the case of France, a printed translation of Vegetius, *L'art de [la] chevalerie selon Végèce* – trans. attributed to Jean de Meung 'et surtout à Christine de Pisan' is dated to 1488 (Paris), with a series of subsequent editions in 1494, 1495, 1505. Aelian, *De l'ordre et instruction des batailles* – trans. N. Volkyr de Sérouville – appeared in a volume combined with Vegetius, *Du fait de guerre et fleur de chevalerie*, in 1536 (Paris). Although seventeenth-century strategists also acknowledged a debt to the writings of Leo VI, his *De bellico apperatu liber e graeco in latinum conversus* was not translated into French until 1758. For a degree of scepticism about the Maurician innovations, see C. Schulten, 'Une nouvelle approche de Maurice de Nassau (1567–1625), in P. Chaunu (ed.), *Le soldat, la stratégie, la mort. Mélanges André Corvisier* (Paris, 1989), pp. 42–53.

25

The military context

societies had a long pedigree, and was far more extensive than historians' concentration upon military reforms in isolation would suggest.[14]

In the case of the Dutch Republic, military reform had a specific aim: the repackaging of the Dutch army after decades in which it had been outclassed by the Spanish army of Flanders. The rhetoric surrounding the presentation of this 'new model army', stressing the Roman origins of its new drill and tactics, should be contrasted with the reality of a force overwhelmingly composed of foreign mercenary troops serving under contract. Military success in the decade of the 1590s, when the reputation of the reformed army was established, owed more to the absence or reduced scale of the Spanish army than to any demonstrable superiority of Dutch fighting methods.[15] However, encouraging the notion that the Dutch army had undergone a decisive improvement in organization and fighting techniques was obviously in the interests of the Republic and its princely generals, as a means to convince both wavering citizens and undecided foreign powers that the United Provinces could sustain their independence into the future.[16]

As the Dutch in the early seventeenth century both enhanced their territorial security and consolidated their position as leaders of embattled Calvinism, so their well-publicized military reforms were imitated by lesser protestant states, especially those whose rulers were related to the Orange-Nassau. The creation of a military academy at Siegen, established in 1617 by Johann von Nassau-Dillemberg, nephew of Maurits and Frederik Hendrik, was explicitly dedicated to the propagation of these classically derived theories of drill and deployment, and sought to attract pupils from amongst the German protestant princes, their relatives and their nobilities.[17] Disseminated across Europe during the 1610s

---

[14] Gerhard Oestreich makes a good case for the incorporation of most of these developments into the neo-Stoicism which was central to late sixteenth-century philosphy and political assumptions: Oestreich, *Neostoicism and the Early Modern State* (Cambridge, 1982), pp. 39–117. Schulten, 'Une nouvelle approche', pp. 49–50.

[15] G. Parker, *The Dutch Revolt* (London, 1977), pp. 228–32, who cited the papal legate in Brussels in July 1593: 'We can say that this progress of the Protestants stems more from their diligence and their energy than from military strength; but even more it stems from the absence of any obstacle'; J. Israel, *The Dutch Republic. Its Rise, Greatness and Fall, 1477–1806* (Oxford, 1995), pp. 241–62.

[16] Even Gualdo Priorato, whose military manual is in some respects an anti-Orangist tract, proposes that Maurits of Nassau 'vedendo le forze de gli Spagnuoli poderosissimi, e gli soldati di singolar virtù, usò ogni studio per resister loro . . . pose in osservanza gli ordini Greci, quali riuscendoli mirabilmente' ('seeing the strength of the Spanish armies and the outstanding military virtue of their soldiers, employed military science against them, making particular use of the ordinances of the Greeks, which proved greatly successful'). Galeazzo, count Gualdo Priorato, *Il Maneggio dell'armi moderno* (Bologna, 1643), p. 49.

[17] Hahlweg, *Heeresreform*, pp. 140–8; J.R. Hale, 'The military education of the officer class in early modern Europe', in Hale, *Renaissance War Studies* (London, 1983), pp. 225–46, at pp. 229–30. The military academy at Siegen survived only until 1623, and during this time attracted a total of twenty students: Parker, *The Military Revolution: Military Innovation and the Rise of the West, 1500–1800* (Cambridge, 1988), p. 163 n. 44, quoting from L. Plathner, *Graf Johann von Nassau und die erste Kriegschule* (Berlin, 1913).

The French art of war during Richelieu's ministry

through a flood of publications by Johann Jacobi von Wallhausen, briefly director of the Siegen *Kriegsschule*, the idea of military reform deriving from classical antiquity became common currency amongst reform-minded rulers. Johann von Nassau's initiatives were first copied by his stepson, langraf Moritz von Hessen. As military tensions in the Empire intensified, advisers from Maurits' army were summoned to Brandenburg in 1610, then later to the Palatinate, Baden, Württemberg, Brunswick, Saxony and Holstein.[18]

The primary factor underlying this adoption of a reformist programme was confessional and dynastic solidarity. It was also underpinned by the princely elite's educational and cultural responsiveness to the lessons of ancient history and to classical institutions.[19] But despite the enthusiastic embracing of the military rhetoric, the military prescriptions were not in practice effective. Encountering the realities of warfare after 1619, the protestant armies organized on these principles of small units, complex deployments and prescriptive drill suffered a virtually uninterrupted series of defeats stretching from the White Mountain to Wolgast, leading to the consequent annihilation of protestant military power in Germany by the later 1620s. It was one thing to deploy the Dutch army for war in the Netherlands, where success or failure owed most to a consistent flow of finance, and to skill and endurance in besieging and defending the innumerable fortifications spread across territory; it was quite another to employ Dutch-style tactics in circumstances where wars involved manoeuvring across relatively open country and where pitched battles were less easily avoided. The last great demonstration of the inadequacy of these tactical and organizational reforms in the face of military experience came at the battle of Breitenfeld in September 1631. The Saxon army, drawn up in a 'progressive' formation on the left flank of Gustavus Adolphus' Swedes, was shattered by the assault of Count Tilly's Imperial and Bavarian regiments within the first hour of the battle.[20]

French military theorists were aware of the well-publicized military reforms of the princes of Orange; plenty of evidence can be found that these reforms influenced French military manuals in the first decades of the seventeenth century.[21] However, examination of these writings reveals two obvious points, both of which suggest the rhetorical rather than the practical significance of such

---

[18] Hahlweg, *Heeresreform*, pp. 154–64; Parker, *Military Revolution*, p. 21.

[19] See for example the catalogue of the exhibition surrounding the reign of Moritz, Pfalzgraf von Hessen: H. Borggrefe, V. Lüpkes and H. Ottomeyer (eds.), *Moritz der Gelehrte. Ein Renaissancefürst in Europa* (Eurasburg, 1997).

[20] A detailed account of the battle which differs in certain respects from that of Roberts, *Gustavus Adolphus*, II. 250–61, is provided in T. Barker, *The Military Intellectual and Battle. Raimondo Montecuccoli and the Thirty Years War* (Albany, N.Y., 1975), pp. 174–81. The over-complex and fragile deployment of the Saxon army at Breitenfeld is clearly evident from plans and engravings.

[21] The major works of Johann Jacobi von Wallhausen were translated into French during the 1610s, and were republished during the 1620s and 1630s, though interestingly almost all the editions were printed outside of France: *L'art militaire pour l'infanterie* (trans. J. de Bry, Oppenheim, 1615); *Art militaire à cheval* (trans. J. de Bry, Frankfurt, 1616); *De la milice romaine* – Wallhausen's own

The military context

reform programmes. First, the French writers who make explicit reference to the Orangist reforms were in the great majority of cases themselves Calvinists, writing for a Huguenot audience; some of them were either related to the Orange-Nassau, or had served closely with the princes in the Dutch armies. Secondly, many of these texts show clear incompatibilities between the material explicitly derived from Orangist tactical and organizational prescriptions, and the more traditional – and supposedly obsolescent – ideas for organizing troops and fighting battles derived from traditional French texts on the art of war.

The Huguenot adoption of the Orangist military rhetoric and its alternatives

Given the level of dynastic and confessional solidarity within what might with justice be termed a 'Calvinist International', it comes as no surprise that a significant group of French texts on the art of war published in the early seventeenth century were written by Huguenots, and indeed in some cases by those specifically affiliated with the House of Orange-Nassau. Of the leading writers on military theory in the early seventeenth century, Jean de Billon, author of *Les principes de l'art militaire* (Paris, 1612) and the *Instructions militaires* (Lyon, 1617), began his career in the military service of the Orange-Nassau before moving back to France to join Henri IV, and was closely associated with Jacobi von Wallhausen, who translated Billon's *Instructions militaires* into German in 1617.[22] Louis de Montgommery, sieur de Courbouzon, author of *La milice Françoise réduite a l'ancien ordre et discipline militaire des legions* (Paris, 1610) states that 'je ne puis oublier le brave Prince Maurice de Nassau . . . Estant pres de luy, en l'année 1600 . . . il me faisoit cet honneur de me discourir de plusieurs bons enseignemens pour la guerre.'[23] The sieur du Praissac's *Discours militaires* and *Les questions militaires* (Paris, 1614) makes specific, detailed reference to the military campaigns of Maurits of Nassau, especially the sieges of the 1590s, and addresses one of the annexed letters in the *Discours* to the Calvinist duc de Bouillon.[24] The key work of the quintessential military Calvinist, Henri duc de Rohan – *Le parfaict capitaine, autrement l'abrégé des guerres de Gaule des Commentaires de César* (Paris, 1636) – is influenced by his military experience of the Dutch armies, where he had served a military apprenticeship with prince Maurits in 1606.[25] Lostelneau, *Le maréchal de*

---

translation of Vegetius, followed by his commentary – (Frankfurt, 1616); *Militia Gallica* (Hanau, 1617).

[22] La Barre Duparcq, *Eléments d'art et d'histoire militaire*, p. 159; Hahlweg, *Heeresreform*, pp. 168, and 166 n. 115.

[23] Montgommery, *La milice françoise*, p. 127, taken from section pp. 103–32: 'Les evolutions et les exercises qui se font en la Milice de Hollande.'

[24] Du Praissac, *Discours militaires* (Rouen 1625).

[25] A. Laugel, *Henri de Rohan. Son rôle politique et militaire sous Louis XIII (1579–1638)* (Paris, 1889), pp. 37–8.

bataille, (Paris,1647) makes clear his debt to the reforms of 'le feu prince d'Auranges, Maurits de Nassau'.[26] From the early 1660s, the *maréchal de camp*, the sieur d'Aurignac, wrote his *Livre de guerre* on the basis of his military experiences in the Swedish army of Gustavus Adolphus, and also drew upon the lessons of the Dutch army.[27] Like du Praissac he was a Huguenot, and part of the extended clientele of the Tour d'Auvergne.[28]

There were also clear signs of confessional and family allegiance in the actual military service undertaken by French nobles in the early seventeenth century. Those military officers and memoirists who served with the Dutch – and later the Swedish – armies were, like the theorists who adopted the Nassau reforms in their writings, predominantly protestant. Gaspard de Coligny III, maréchal de Châtillon from 1622, was from a Huguenot family whose links with the Orange-Nassau had been exceptionally close; he had served under Maurits, commanded one of the three French regiments in the Dutch army, and became overall *colonel général* of the French troops in Dutch service in 1614. Frédéric-Maurice de La Tour, duc de Bouillon, travelled to Holland in 1621 to take service with the army of his uncles, Maurits and Frederik Hendrik. He served in the Netherlands until 1635 when he returned to take up the office of *maréchal de camp* with the French armies.[29] His brother Henri de La Tour, vicomte de Turenne, also began his military career serving with the army of Maurits.[30] Of the two other regiments in Dutch service in the 1610s one was commanded by Léonidas de Béthune, seigneur de Congy and kinsman of the duc de Sully, the other by Bertrand de Vignolles, seigneur de Casaubon.[31] At a slightly lower social level, Bénédict-Louis de Pontis, relative of the protestant François de Bonne, duc de Lesdiguières, was a cadet in the *gardes* until his involvement in a duel led to his imprisonment. Escaping in 1602, he entered the service of prince Maurits, where he served until 1604.[32]

It would be mistaken, however, to see service with the Dutch as the only source of military experience. There were catholic alternatives for those in France seeking military experience, and the Dutch army was not seen as the only 'school of war' in the early seventeenth century. François d'Aubusson, seigneur de Beauregard, went to serve with the Spanish army in 1598, taking part in the siege

---

[26] The full identity of a number of these French theorists has proved frustratingly elusive, and would perhaps merit a serious study in its own right.
[27] Aurignac's *Livre de guerre* (1663) was edited from manuscript by P. Azan, *Un tacticien du XVIIe siècle* (Paris, 1904).
[28] Bérenger, *Turenne*, p. 519.
[29] J. de Langlade, baron de Saumières, *Mémoires de la vie de Frédéric-Maurice de La Tour d'Auvergne, duc de Bouillon* (Paris, 1692), pp. 9–33.
[30] Roy, *Turenne*, pp. 7–8; Bérenger, *Turenne*, pp. 33–5, 63–4; R. Mousnier, 'Conditions sociales et politiques de l'action de Turenne', in Gambiez and Laloy, *Turenne et l'art militaire*, p. 107.
[31] Anselme, *Histoire généalogique*, IX. 145: Vignolles ultimately converted from protestantism, but was deeply entrenched amongst Henri IV's Huguenot supporters for most of his career.
[32] B.-L. de Pontis (Pierre-Thomas du Fossé) *Mémoires* (Paris, 1986), pp. 10–11, 44.

The military context

of Ostende.[33] Henri de Campion – adherent of Gaston d'Orléans during his exile in the Spanish Netherlands – served with the Spanish army of Flanders in 1634 during the Spanish siege of Maestricht, when the Dutch garrison was commanded by Frédéric-Maurice, duc de Bouillon.[34]

If service with the Spanish army of Flanders involved the potential problem of fighting against fellow Frenchmen – albeit mostly protestants – in the Dutch armies, a more straightforward catholic alternative was found in service with the Imperial armies in Hungary, fighting against the Ottomans, their Transylvanian allies and Hungarian clients in the protracted war from 1593 to 1606. The scale of this alternative should not be underestimated; at the time when the French had three regiments of volunteers in Dutch service, they also had some 5,000 troops serving in Hungary with the Imperial forces under the overall leadership of Philippe-Emmanuel de Lorraine, duc de Mercoeur, until his death in 1602.[35] Relatives of Mercoeur involved in the Hungarian campaigns included Charles de Lorraine, fourth duc de Guise, Henri de Lorraine, marquis de Mouy and brother of Mercoeur, and Claude de Lorraine, duc de Chevreuse (who assumed overall command of the French forces after 1602).[36] The status of the extended Guise–Lorraine clan as both *princes étrangers* through their family links to the duchy of Lorraine and representatives of an ultra-catholic position in France may have conditioned their involvement in warfare on behalf of the Habsburgs, just as dynastic and confessional affiliations determined those who served with the Dutch. Others acquiring experience in this theatre included another *prince étranger*, Charles de Gonzague-Nevers, François de Bassompierre, who served as a volunteer with the Habsburg armies in Hungary and refused the colonelcy of a Bavarian regiment because he wished to acquire direct military experience, Henri de Schomberg, comte de Nanteuil, and Henri Duval, comte de Dampierre.[37] Just over a decade later, another member of the House of Guise who, exceptionally, was to become one of Richelieu's generals, Henri de Lorraine, comte d'Harcourt, began his career

---

[33] J. de Gangnières, comte de Souvigny, *Vie, mémoires et histoire de messire Jean de Gangnières* ... (2 vols.; Paris, 1906), II. 44: Souvigny specifically emphasizes that Beauregard served with the Spanish forces 'parce qu'il était bon catholique'.

[34] H. de Campion, *Mémoires* (Paris, 1967), pp. 49–51; Saumières, *Duc de Bouillon*, pp. 30–1.

[35] Hanotaux, *Histoire de la nation française*, VII. 340; J.-P. Niederkorn, *Die Europäischen Mächte und der 'Lange Türkenkrieg' Kaiser Rudolfs II* (Archiv für österreichische Geschichte, 135) (Vienna, 1993), pp. 163–4.

[36] For the overall command of Chevreuse, who had assumed the title of prince de Joinville, see François de Bassompierre, *Mémoires*, in Petitot and Monmerqué, XIX. 299.

[37] E. Baudson, *Charles de Gonzague, Duc de Nevers, 1580–1637* (Paris, 1947), pp. 49–52; Bassompierre, *Mémoires*, XIX. 292–333. Bassompierre was also briefly present with Spinola's army at the siege of Ostende; for Schomberg, see F. Redlich, *The German Military Enterpriser and his Work Force, 14th to 18th Centuries* (Vierteljahrschrift für Sozial- und Wirtschaftsgeschichte, Beihefte 47 and 48 (2 vols.; Wiesbaden, 1964), I. 155; O. Chaline, *La bataille de la Montagne Blanche* (Paris, 2000), p. 323, on Dampierre.

The French art of war during Richelieu's ministry

in the service of the catholic armies which fought at the battle of the White Mountain in 1620.[38]

Moreover, while confessional allegiances clearly dictated the character of military service for a large number of French nobles, there was a group who simply served in armies without any strong religious commitment to either camp. Claude de Létouf, baron de Sirot, began service in 1616 as an ordinary soldier acquiring experience in the regiment of *gardes*. He then travelled to the United Provinces to serve with the army of Maurits of Nassau. After the conclusion of the Twelve Years Truce, he passed across to the army of Carlo Emanuele I, duke of Savoy. Thereafter he raised a company of *chevaux légers*, with which he served the Emperor on the Hungarian frontier. Subsequently he served with both the Imperial generalissimo, Albrecht Wallenstein, and was then part of the Imperial army which sacked the city of Mantua in 1630. Apparently incongruously after this period of overtly catholic service, he joined the Swedish army of Gustavus Adolphus. Taken prisoner by Wallenstein, he ransomed himself and returned to France where he served on the north-east frontier after 1635, ultimately becoming a close *fidèle* of the young duc d'Enghien.[39] An only slightly less colourful military career was provided by Antoine III, comte de Gramont, who began his military career accompanying the king in the campaign against the Huguenots in 1621, where he served with distinction, but considered that he had not acquired enough experience. He travelled to the United Provinces in 1623, and served in the besieged Dutch garrison of Breda in 1625. Gramont would seem to offer an example of a catholic *grand* acquiring his military experience from the Dutch 'school of war'. However, following Breda, Gramont transferred to the Catholic League army of Johann Tserclaes, count Tilly, where he participated in Tilly's victory over the army of Christian IV of Denmark. Gramont's memoirs are effusive about the outstanding military capacities, skills and effectiveness of Tilly and Wallenstein as commanders. Only when the prospect of Habsburg war with France in north Italy loomed did Gramont decide to abandon Imperial service, and return to France.[40] Of lower social rank, but a considerably better-known example, René Descartes followed a similar path, beginning service in summer 1618 with the army of Maurits, but changing sides to fight in the Bavarian army after January 1619, where he probably remained until late 1621.[41]

Substantial numbers of French nobles who left France to acquire military experience did not take the 'protestant option' of fighting for the Dutch, and did

---

[38] Pinard, *Chronologie*, I. 455–64.
[39] C. de Létouf, baron de Sirot, *Mémoires* (2 vols.; Paris, 1683), I. 9–17; Henri d'Orléans, duc d'Aumale, *Histoire des princes de Condé pendant les XVIe et XVIIe siècles* (7 vols.; Paris, 1863–96), IV. 12–13.
[40] Antoine III, maréchal de Gramont, *Mémoires*, in Petitot and Monmerqué, LVII. 146–52.
[41] S. Gaukroger, *Descartes: An Intellectual Biography* (Oxford, 1995), pp. 65–6, 132. For a discussion of whether Descartes served under Tilly at the battle of the White Mountain, see Chaline, *Montagne Blanche*, pp. 120–1.

The military context

not therefore consider that the Dutch way of warfare was the only valid military apprenticeship in the first years of the seventeenth century. Indeed, it might be suggested that there was a distinct type of 'catholic' military experience – both in the Hungarian Marches and in the catholic armies during the first decade of the Thirty Years War – which generated a different range of practical military experiences. Against the relatively static warfare of the Dutch–Spanish conflict, this provided experience of greater mobility, involving much more use of light cavalry, and placing much more dependence on the initiative of local commanders both in the conduct of raiding parties and small-scale skirmishes, and in responding to more substantial threats. While fortification was certainly a factor in this style of warfare – on the Hungarian frontiers, for example – it was of a much more rudimentary nature than the massive constructions of the Netherlands.

There was also a third area of experience, the common property of those, frequently the most senior commanders by the 1620s and 1630s, who had never left France, but had passed their early military careers in the Wars of Religion down to 1598. François de Bonne, duc de Lesdiguières and *connétable de France* from 1622, Jean-Louis de Nogaret de La Valette, duc d'Epernon, Jacques-Nompar de Caumont, maréchal de La Force, were all in their seventies and eighties during Richelieu's ministry, and had military experience which went back to the 1580s and even before.[42] A slightly younger generation, for example, Charles de Valois, duc d'Angoulême, Honoré d'Albert, maréchal de Chaulnes, Charles de Blanchefort, maréchal de Créqui, and Louis, maréchal de Marillac, had been born in the 1570s and had served their military apprenticeships in the last decade of the Civil Wars.[43] This was a military experience shared by both protestants and catholics, and in its emphasis on cavalry, its deployment of relatively smaller numbers of infantry and concern with problems of territorial control and denial, it offered lessons that were both different from, and predated, the publicized 'reforms' in the Netherlands.[44] If this type of cumulative experience appears piecemeal and haphazard in comparison with the more systematic lessons proposed by the Dutch reformers, there is certainly evidence in a work like Charles de Gontaut, maréchal de Biron's *Maximes*, that such practical military experience could be used to criticize some of the impractical military theory of the Dutch.[45] Moreover if Henri de Rohan's *Parfaict capitaine* can claim to be the most influential French

---

[42] C. Dufayard, *Le connétable de Lesdiguières* (Paris, 1892), pp. 22–116; L. Mouton, *Un demi-roi: le duc d'Epernon* (Paris, 1922), pp. 44–9; Auguste de Caumont, duc de La Force, *Le maréchal de La Force, 1558–1652* (2 vols.: Paris, 1928), I. 44–120.

[43] J.A. Clarke, *Huguenot Warrior: The Life and Times of Henri de Rohan, 1579–1638* (The Hague, 1966), p. 11; *L'affaire du maréchal de Marillac, 1630–1632* (Paris, 1924); J. Humbert, *Le maréchal de Créquy. Gendre de Lesdiguières, 1573–1638* (Paris, 1962), pp. 23–42.

[44] A point well made by Lynn, 'Tactical evolution', 178–83.

[45] Henri de Gontaut, duc de Biron, *Maximes et advis du maniement de la guerre . . .*, mistakenly attributed to André de Bordeille (elder brother of Brantôme), and published in Brantôme, ed. J. Buchon, *Œuvres* (2 vols.; Paris, 1838), II. 509–24. Biron is particularly interesting on systems of military apprenticeship and the acquired skills of *vieux* soldiers.

The French art of war during Richelieu's ministry

military treatise of the seventeenth century,[46] then its predecessor in the later sixteenth century was probably the *Discours politiques et militaires* (1587) of François de La Noue. La Noue's eclectic approach to tactics, deployment, training and weaponry, supported by a wealth of classical examples, tells against the claims of the Dutch reformers that their deliberate borrowings from the military theory of antiquity contributed something brand new to the contemporary debate.[47]

The significance of tactical theory

It is striking that those French authors who wrote theoretical tracts on the art of war in this period should have been so preponderantly the product of a single area of military experience in which there was already an established rhetorical emphasis on classical models. Links of family and confessional allegiance, which were the determining factor in the adoption and publicizing of the Orange-Nassau military reforms in the Holy Roman Empire, were no less evident amongst the French authors. It is also pertinent to ask why those more numerous groups of French *noblesse* whose service had been in different military contexts were less attracted to the composition of military tracts. There is no reason to consider that the experience of war on the Hungarian frontier or in the Midi during the 1620s was a less valid basis on which to write about the art of war.

That many of the French elites acquired military experience from a variety of other sources may none the less have been an indirect factor contributing to the second problematic element in these written tracts, the often confused and contradictory military prescriptions that they contain. This, however, is not solely an issue with French tactical manuals. The work of Johann Jacobi von Wallhausen, the most celebrated exponent of the Dutch reforms, regularly combines descriptions of 'reformed' small units, deployed in linear formation, with an extraordinary variety of rectangular, circular and geometrically diverse formations of infantry, intended to accommodate between 100 and 6,000 soldiers.[48] Historians have arguably been anachronistic in interpreting early modern military manuals, assuming a degree of consistency and coherence that is incompatible with their rhetorical and even aesthetic character. It is notable that in discussing a series of increasingly elaborate and large-scale infantry formations, Jean de Billon remarked that all systems for the ordering of military units should have two

---

[46] Guerlac, 'Vauban', p. 32.
[47] The alternative candidate would be Blaise de Montluc's *Commentaires* (1571) – reprinted as late as 1661.
[48] Wallhausen, *L'art militaire pour l'infanterie*, pp. 85 *et seq*. Although Wallhausen was appointed as professor at Johann von Nassau's academy in Siegen in 1617, a year earlier he had dedicated his work *De la milice romaine* to Ambrosio Spinola, commander of the Spanish army of Flanders from 1604 to 1629. Even in the case of a writer taken to epitomize the new tactical reforms, the evidence is less than clear-cut and Wallhausen fits uneasily into a straightforward typology of 'radical protestant theorist'.

The military context

qualities, first 'la beauté', and only subsequently 'la promptitude à se faire, ou desfaire, et l'utilité pour toutes actions de guerre'.[49]

The French manuals do not offer a coherent guide to military organization on 'modern principles' that fits the model of progressive military evolution as depicted by subsequent historians. Although parts of these manuals can be read as accounts of Dutch-style reforms in tactics and deployment, most – like Wallhausen – also propose the formation of large infantry squares and other complex and impractical formations. Jean de Billon provides a series of instructions for the formation of an elaborate 'cross-shaped' formation of musketeers and pikemen, and for deploying up to 4,000 infantry into squares and other formations.[50] Louis de Montgommery gives details of a *bataillon* of 2,500 pikes.[51] Du Praissac depicts regiments of 2,760 men in twenty companies and proposes square formations for up to 4,096 infantry, while Lostelneau stipulates that – 'si vous avez 2048 picquiers pour faire cette grande croix . . . il y faut aussi 2,192 mousquetaires', and goes on to describe a series of equally impractical formations for the formation of crosses of Lorraine, hexagons, octagons, etc.[52] Nor was this process, which obviously appealed to the aesthetic sense of the writers, outmoded in ensuing decades. As late as 1675 the sieur de La Fontaine provided an 'ordre pour former toutes sortes de bataillons', a series of prescriptions for the deployment of between 1,000 and 2,600 infantry in various elaborate geometrical formations – octagons, crosses, etc. – whose tactical benefits from an Orangist or any other standpoint are dubious.[53]

The Dutch military experience of many of these authors may have led them to give limited attention to the role and deployment of cavalry, so that prescriptions for its deployment were frequently vague and apparently contradictory. The debate about the relative merits of cavalry equipped with firearms and traditional edged weapons or lances remained unresolved. De La Noue had proposed in the 1580s that a squadron of pistol-firing *reiters* would always defeat a squadron of lancers if the former were prepared to stand their ground and hold fire, while half a century later Rohan argued that the lance had died out as a cavalry weapon because only one rank could be effective, thus forcing the cavalry to attack *en haie* (in an extended line), rendering them extremely vulnerable to an attack by other cavalry deployed in deeper formations.[54] Yet Wallhausen, whose *Art militaire à*

---

[49] J. de Billon, *Suite des principes de l'art militaire* (Rouen, 1641), p. 38.
[50] Billon, *Instructions militaires*, pp. 271–8, includes ever more elaborate ways of deploying eight *bataillons* of 500 men each – grouping together pikemen and musketeers in large blocks. Indeed for Billon the chief advantage of a unit of 4,000 infantry was the variety and complexity of possible formations that could be built from such a force: *Suite des principes*, p. 29.
[51] Wallhausen, *La milice françoise*, pp. 80–91, 95–7.
[52] Du Praissac, *Discours militaires*, pp. 3–6, 223–8, who explicitly takes examples of deployment from both Maurits of Nassau and Spinola; Lostelneau, *Le maréchal de bataille* (Paris, 1647), pp. 244 *et seq.*
[53] La Fontaine, *Les devoirs militaires des officiers de l'infanterie* (Paris, 1675), pp. 245–308.
[54] F. de La Noue, *Discours politiques et militaires* (Basel, 1587), pp. 307–14 (first military paradox); Henri, duc de Rohan, *Le parfaict capitaine, autrement l'abrégé des guerres de Gaule des Commentaires de César* (Paris, 1636), p. 230.

cheval was translated into French in 1616, stresses the preeminence of the lance as the most important cavalry weapon, though he regretfully admits that it was increasingly superseded by cheaper, less well-trained, cavalry armed with pistols. Because of this ambiguity, his manual includes both cavalry deployments *en haie* – suitable for lancers – and in deep columns, characteristic of cavalry practising the *caracole*, the sequential firing of pistols as they approached an enemy formation.[55] Jean de Billon appears to be approaching a compromise with the proposal that cavalry should be grouped in squadrons of 100 horse, five ranks deep, but does nothing to challenge the assumption that the cavalry would regard the pistol as their principal weapon. Aurignac, writing in the 1660s on the basis of his experience of the campaigns of Gustavus Adolphus, still proposed that a possible strategem for a commander with a superiority in cavalry would be to outflank the enemy on both wings and use the *caracole* to disrupt the exposed flanks of infantry formations.[56] Though the theorists were moving towards a consensus that the usual deployment of cavalry was in formations between six and three rows deep, all leave unresolved the problem that in an engagement with other cavalry, a force drawn up in deeper columns would have the mass and cohesion to force its way through an extended, shallow, formation. They are also unconvincing in their arguments that the cavalry should in some vague sense demonstrate their seriousness of intent by 'charging to contact' armed with swords or lances. For this ignores the obvious fact that an experienced formation of infantry, well buttressed with pikemen, is invulnerable to a cavalry charge. Cavalry horses cannot be trained to run into an apparently solid object, and a hedge of pikes presents a formidable obstacle to even the most suicidally reckless sabre-wielding cavalier. Hence the main preoccupation of most of these theorists is not with some simplistic transformation of pistolier tactics into reliance on the *arme blanche*, but with attempts to combine firepower and cavalry action in such a way that initial fire could sufficiently disrupt the cohesion of an infantry formation to allow a cavalry assault with sabres, preferably against a flank, to exploit the confusion. In some accounts a part of this firepower was to be provided by the cavalry itself; so, for example, La Fontaine (1675) describes how a deep formation of cavalry should pass close to the infantry unit, deploying the *caracole* to direct fire against one of the angles of the unit.[57] Another part might be provided by platoons or squadrons of musketeers, deployed in a number of possible ways alongside the cavalry squadrons, purportedly in order to provide sufficient firepower to facilitate a subsequent cavalry charge into a wavering enemy unit.[58] Lacking in all of this is

---

[55] Wallhausen, *Art militaire à cheval*, pp. 3–24, 52–3, 70–1.
[56] Azan, *Un tacticien*, pp. 88–9.
[57] La Fontaine, *Les devoirs militaires*, pp. 17–18.
[58] Du Praissac, *Questions militaires*, pp. 36–7; Lostelneau, *Maréchal de bataille*, pp. 420–9; Azan, *Un tacticien*, pp. 84–7; La Valière, *Pratique et maximes de la guerre* (Paris, 1675), p. 66 (text dates to no later than 1652, when the manuscript, taken from the library of cardinal Mazarin, was illicitly published by Laon d'Aigrémont in his own name). Other theorists examined the possibility of using

The military context

any obvious sense of evolution, a clear consensus about cavalry tactics and weaponry from lessons learned on the battlefield which could serve as a model for military practice; indeed, it is arguable that the problem was intractable given the existing state of military technology.

A potential means of increasing the effectiveness of firepower against infantry formations that were drawn up in close order to resist cavalry would be the better deployment of battlefield artillery. Curiously again, the various French theorists offer little support for a reconsideration of the role of cannon. Most who have a section on artillery confine themselves to detailing the various calibres and weights of the cannon in service, and discuss issues of transport and the supply of adequate munitions.[59] In so far as the deployment of artillery on the battlefield is considered at all, it is in the most conventional manner: La Valière (*c.* 1652), for example, specifies that the artillery must be deployed before a battle in front of the first line of infantry 'sçavoir le plus gros canon au milieu et les moindres pièces vis-à-vis de l'intervale des bataillons qui sont le plus sur les aisles'.[60]

It might be tempting to assume that there was a logical evolution in military manuals through the first half of the seventeenth century, such that the early works of du Praissac and Louis de Montgommery, with their projects for the deployment of troops in large-scale, deep formations, give way to treatises in which the advantages of small units have been learnt. This does not appear to be the case. The influential Jean de Billon, whose prescriptions are taken, after the duc de Rohan, as the most significant theoretical writings of the period, is characteristic of the confusion and contradictions of such works, and was reprinted at least six times into the 1640s. Montgommery and du Praissac were also republished on numerous occasions into the 1630s.[61] The evidence for a shift towards a more recognizably modern and coherent view of tactics and organization is hard to detect. La Fontaine was far from unusual in his continued emphasis on large, over-elaborate formations later in the century, while the works of Lostelneau and La Valière could sustain a model of progressive evolution only by ignoring much which contradicts such a thesis.

Historians who have tended to filter out much of what is contradictory and conventional in these military manuals have also glossed over the large element of the impractical. Most manuals continue to emphasize the importance of the pike

---

dragons or *carabins* to provide the supporting firepower for the *chevaux légers* to exploit: Azan, *Un tacticien*, p. 90.

[59] Du Praissac, *Discours militaires*, pp. 120–39; Rohan, *Parfaict capitaine*, pp. 315–20.

[60] La Valière, *Pratique et maximes*, p. 66; d'Aurignac discusses the important role of Swedish artillery superiority at Breitenfeld and the crossing of the Lech, but does not extend this to any general prescriptions for the tactical deployment of artillery with the French armies: Azan, *Un tacticien*, pp. 93–5.

[61] Lynn, 'Tactical evolution', 181, on Billon; editions of Montgommery, *La milice françoise*, appeared in 1603, 1610, 1615, 1636; du Praissac was republished in 1614, 1617, 1622, 1638, and translated into Dutch in 1623 (E.A. Bardin, *Dictionnaire de l'armée de terre, ou recherches historiques sur l'art et l'usages militaires des anciens et des modernes* (17 vols.; Paris, 1841–51)).

The French art of war during Richelieu's ministry

in infantry formations, and give little weight to the developing importance of infantry firearms – supposedly the *raison d'être* for increasingly linear formations. Indeed, Rohan lamented the relative decline in the proportion of pikemen, arguing that Swiss units with their large numbers of pikemen had a great advantage on the battlefield and that the shift to muskets reflected the contemporary preoccupation with siege warfare.[62] The drill proposed for pikemen in exercise-manuals such as those of Jacob de Gheyn or Wallhausen involve numbers of elaborate manoeuvres of apparently limited relevance to training newly recruited armies or providing tactically relevant basic skills.[63] Such elaborate pike drills could be contrasted with the functional proposals made by a contemporary Italian theorist such as Gualdo Priorato, whose main concern was to ensure that the pikemen were able through simple drills to use their weapons in a number of defensive and offensive postures without obstructing each other.[64] Influenced by Roman practice a number of theorists saw fit to propose the reintroduction of legionary weapons. Both Montgommery and Rohan were enthusiastic proponents of the use of small shields (*rondeliers, targes*) to defend musketeers against pikes, and both attribute this proposal to Maurits of Nassau.[65]

A further aspect of the manuals that sits uneasily with a reformist model is the typical concern to lay out the duties of each rank in the military hierarchy, a process at least as concerned to stipulate what a self-respecting officer should refuse to do as with providing a functional guide to service. There is a contrast between the supposed Orangist ideal of neostoic subordination to authority, and constant reiteration in the French texts that officers must never do anything which reflects badly upon their own social status and particular rank. Billon, for example, in his advice to captains stressed that 'celuy qui commande ne doit laisser rien passer à son desadvantage, soit pour le rang de marcher, de loger ou de combattre, . . . ou d'avoir toutes payes et droicts qui luy appartient'.[66] The impact of this preoccupation may be seen in the over-formulaic prescriptions for the deployment of troops on the battlefield, where, for example, La Valière proposes that though the regiment of *gardes* and the *gendarmes* should always be placed in the second line (the *bataille*), the most honourable place to be accorded to the other senior regiments is the first line (the *avant-garde*), with a descending hierarchy of status allocating positions on the right wing first, then those on the

---

[62] Rohan, *Parfaict capitaine*, p. 233. J. de Billon, *Les principes de l'art militaire*, p. 46, proposed that an ideal company of 200 infantry should contain 120 pikes, one of 100 should contain 60 pikes.
[63] Jacob de Gheyn, *Waffenhandlung von den Röhren, Musqueten und Spiessen* (The Hague, 1608); J.J. von Wallhausen, *Kunstliche Piquenhandlung* (Hanau, 1617).
[64] Gualdo Priorato, *Il Maneggio dell'armi moderno*, pp. 70 *et seq.*
[65] Montgommery, *La milice françoise*, pp. 127–8; Rohan *Parfaict capitaine*, p. 220: Rohan's ideal infantry regiment consisted of 1,440 soldiers, composed of 600 pikemen, 600 musketeers and 240 sword-and-buckler men (p. 233).
[66] Billon, *Principes de l'art militaire*, p. 50; earlier he had stressed that the captain 'doit sçavoir disputer son rang quand on loge, quand on marche . . . et ne laisser rien passer au prejudice de sa charge' (p. 36).

The military context

left, with the centre as 'toujours la moindre place'.[67] If such prescriptions were more than a rhetorical convention, the difficulties faced by a commander in trying to exploit an element of surprise in deploying his army would be insuperable.

THE FRENCH 'ART OF WARFARE' IN PRACTICE

Leaving tracts and manuals on the theory of war, it is enlightening to observe how French troops were trained and deployed in practice – how they actually fought in warfare from the 1620s to the 1640s, especially in the period from the 1630s when the variety of military commitments faced by the French armies greatly increased. It is clear that the military activity of these armies owed little to theoretical prescription but was shaped by the practical imperatives involved in the recruitment and maintenance of troops and the effective use of existing resources. It is true that innovation and reformation are little in evidence. Yet the lack of conspicuous French military success during Richelieu's ministry seems very little to do with the adoption or rejection of the fashionable doctrines of military reform.

Training and drill in the French armies

One of the central assumptions about the modernization of warfare in the early modern period is that armies which had been characterized by extravagant levels of independence on the part of the noble officer or *gendarme*, alongside inflexible passivity on the part of the pikeman or halberdier, now gave way to forces in which individuals were subordinated to a rigid discipline which excluded independent initiative yet sought to achieve far higher levels of collective flexibility and skill. The means to achieve this was through standardized drill, strictly imposed by officers and NCOs on the base of instructions backed by printed texts. It was these latter, the products of Jacob de Gheyn and Wallhausen, which encouraged the widespread view that drill was essentially an invention of the Dutch, and spread across Europe through contact with the Dutch armies.[68]

Both de Gheyn's and Wallhausen's drill manuals for the use of pike and firearms were translated into French, and de Gheyn was competently plagiarized by Lostelneau in the first part of his *Maréchal de bataille*,[69] but these seem to have had no practical impact on the military establishment.[70] A few references to the

---

[67] La Valière, *Maximes et pratiques*, p. 62.

[68] L. Susane, *Histoire de l'ancienne infanterie française* (8 vols.; 1849–53), I. 215; J. Lynn, *Giant of the Grand Siècle* (Cambridge, 1997), pp. 515–18; for an argument which links drill explicitly to a burgeoning 'middle-class' culture, see Feld, 'Middle class society', 419–23.

[69] De Gheyn's *Waffenhandlung* appeared in a French translation, although published in Amsterdam, in 1608: Lynn, 'Tactical evolution', 189; Wallhausen's *L'art militaire pour l'infanterie* was published at Oppenheim in 1615.

[70] Despite frequently reiterated claims that these drill manuals were used to train French recruits,

The French art of war during Richelieu's ministry

régiment des gardes and the régiment de Champagne as 'training schools' for the teaching of military skills certainly give no suggestion that they were intended to act as centres for the dissemination of text-inspired drill.[71] Still greater scepticism is required in dealing with claims that military academies, specifically dedicated to the teaching of drill, were set up under royal or ministerial patronage during this period. Such bogus initiatives include the Académie d'armes at Aix-en-Provence whose foundation was proposed in 1611 for the military instruction of the lesser nobility, Richelieu's own proposal in 1635 for an Académie militaire,[72] and the notion to create an Académie royale des exercices de guerre in 1639 to provide drill for men newly levied by *mestres de camp* and captains.[73] All of these theoretical proposals fit neatly into an impractical reforming rhetoric to which monarchs and their servants none the less felt it desirable to subscribe.[74] The unemployed lesser *noblesse d'épée* who, for want of proper military training, were apparently unable to bring their untutored martial *virtù* to the service of the monarch, were a favourite target for this reformist concern.[75] The proposals are endemic to the period; the vast majority never progressed beyond ideas on paper, or even reached the point of establishing the type of military curriculum that would have been taught.

There were certainly academies in France for the sons of the nobility, but their curricula and aspirations reflected a traditional concern to develop a range of individual practical and theoretical skills appropriate to a young nobleman who might, *inter alia*, serve as an officer in the king's armies: equestrian skills, swordsmanship, an element of rhetoric and mathematics. Antoine de Pluvinal's

---

evidence for such a contention is non-existent. For a typical unsubstantiated statement of the orthodoxy see Carrias, *Pensée militaire*, pp. 116–17.

[71] Carrias, *Pensée militaire*, p. 115, who specifically mentions these units in the context of the 1627–8 siege of La Rochelle, and adds that the *petit-vieux* regiment of Rambures, under the command of Fabert, also served this training function. Bénédict-Louis de Pontis, in his *Mémoires*, claims that the king sent him to investigate the training being carried out by Pierre Arnaud, *mestre de camp* of the regiment of Champagne, during the siege of La Rochelle (pp. 107–10). Yet there is no evidence here or in the *Mémoires* of Robert Arnaud d'Andilly that Pierre Arnauld, his older brother, was using military manuals of the Dutch school; a vague reference to 'la discipline des Romans' would hardly distinguish him from any educated officer of this period: Petitot and Monmerqué, xxxiii. 332–3.

[72] Both of these initiatives are cited in Carrias, *Pensée militaire*, p. 115, but with the admission that neither got beyond the level of intentions.

[73] Cited by Lynn, 'Tactical evolution', 189, quoting Caillet, *De l'administration en France*, pp. 376–7. Also in Dussieux, *L'armée en France*, II. 70–1. Hale, 'Military education', pp. 241–2, dates the foundation of this academy to 1629, and suggests that Richelieu himself provided scholarships for twenty sons of poor gentlemen. No archival evidence is cited in any of these works to confirm that this institution ever came into existence.

[74] R. Briggs, 'Richelieu and reform: rhetoric and political reality', in J. Bergin and L.W.B. Brockliss (eds.), *Richelieu and his Age* (Oxford, 1992), pp. 71–97, especially p. 90 on this question of reforming ideas and the lesser nobility.

[75] A good example of such a paper scheme, drafted by Richelieu himself, is provided in Avenel, v. 721–3, [1636], 'académie pour mil gentilshommes' – 400 for the church, 600 for military service; Richelieu was here repeating a proposal made by the Assembly of Notables in 1626: Hale, 'Military education', p. 246 n. 85.

The military context

Academy, established in Paris in 1594, provides the classic example of such an institution seeking to inculcate into its noble students essentially personal military skills. Some military science – gunnery, fortification and marshalling of troops – was taught, but there is little evidence that the Academy was a means by which Orangist reforms were imported into France.[76] Pluvinal's was one of a number of such academies with similar aims and types of curriculum, aimed as much at educating nobles as creating military professionals, and looking southwards towards a sixteenth-century Italian tradition rather than eastwards towards the United Provinces or Siegen.[77] Another notable example of such a traditional academy, one specifically concentrating on equitation, was founded by the father of the vicomte de Turenne, Henri de La Tour, duc de Bouillon, whose institution at Sedan was considerably more successful than the short-lived Nassau Academy at Siegen in attracting young protestant nobles from across Europe.[78]

Documented evidence for the practical enforcement of Orangist drill in France is extremely thin, whether this was to be achieved through military academies or through attempts to inculcate such skills once the troops were present with the army-corps. This is less surprising when it is recognized that the French traditions of military training at the level of ordinary soldiers were modelled on the practical system of the Spanish, by which experienced troops taught the new recruits basic formations, weapon drill and manoeuvres.[79]

There was no expectation in this period that an entirely inexperienced force would be shaped from scratch through training camps and drill manuals.[80] Instead, new recruits were introduced into existing units and distributed amongst the veterans. The critical building-block of French drill and training was provided by a group of soldiers variously known as the *anspessades*, the *appointés*, or simply the

---

[76] Hale, 'Military education', pp. 236–7, 241: 'the best-known martial finishing school in Europe'.

[77] L.W.B. Brockliss, 'Richelieu, education and the state', in Bergin and Brockliss (eds.), *Richelieu and his Age*, pp. 237–72, at pp. 240–5, which also discusses the foundation of the short-lived college and academy at Richelieu in 1640.

[78] M. Motley, *Becoming a French Aristocrat. The Education of the Court Nobility, 1580–1715* (Princeton, 1990), pp. 123–68, emphasizes that in this period the essential focus of the curricula was the trio of riding, dancing and fencing (p. 139). For Bouillon's Academy at Sedan see Motley, *French Aristocrat*, p. 127 n. 9. Jean III, comte de Montdejeux and future maréchal de Schulemberg, had been a pupil at Sedan: S. Briet, *Le maréchal de Schulemberg, 1598–1671* (Mézières, 1960), pp. 24–5. Turenne himself attended both his father's academy and also spent time from 1626 to 1628 at the Académie chez Benjamin in Paris: Bérenger, *Turenne*, pp. 59–60.

[79] La Noue, *Discours*, p. 268; Parker, 'The "military revolution 1560–1660" – a myth?', p. 90. Parker makes use of Sir Roger Williams, *A Brief Discourse of Warre* (London, 1590), which presents a clear-eyed view of the strengths and weaknesses of the Spanish military system, and describes this means of training the *besoños* (pp. 12–13).

[80] A document, probably of 1635, 'The means to have the best infantry in Christendom' offers eleven proposals, none of which mention drill or formal training, but do emphasize the need to obtain good-quality recruits and to keep them with the companies for the first six months without granting *congé* (arts. 2 and 3), implying that such training was an obvious consequence of serving with more experienced troops within the unit: AAE MD 819, fo. 84 (no date, but included in a volume for 1635).

The French art of war during Richelieu's ministry

vieux soldats – all being ordinary soldiers with some military experience.[81] Receiving higher pay than their less experienced colleagues,[82] they would occupy the three crucial positions in a file of troops, the front rank (*chef de file*), the rear rank (*chef de serre-file*), and, depending on the depth of the file, a position around the fourth or the sixth rank (*chef de demi-file*).[83] It was the *anspessades* and *appointés* who held a formation together, and it was these and any additional *vieux soldats* who executed fire and pike drills with reasonable precision and who took the lead in any military initiative undertaken by the unit. Meanwhile, the recruits would eventually, it was hoped, acquire a reasonable degree of independent skill through emulation.[84] Thus when the *Code Michau* prescribed that 'l'exercice se fera au moins une fois la semaine dans les garnisons, pour instruire et adextrer les soldats', these exercises would be a forum in which the *anspessades* and *appointés* would provide basic instruction by demonstration, taking the initiative in carrying out fire-drill, in redeployment of the unit in a different formation, and other operations.[85]

Such a system necessarily reinforced existing patterns of military behaviour, frequently evolved by the veteran troops themselves as the most convenient, and from their own point of view safest, means of fighting. A characteristic instance of this was the tendency of veterans to discard pieces of armour or weapons which they regarded as encumbrances. Fierce legislation from the *secrétaire*, demanding

---

[81] *Anspessades* were a small group of elite veterans, virtually treated as NCOs, immediately subordinate to the corporals. It was widely assumed in financial documents of the period that there would be no more than two *anspessades* per company. *Appointés* was a generic term for the veteran soldiers who held specific functions, such as the *chef de file*, in the company. Those with the title *appointés* overlapped with the most general group of those with some military experience, the *vieux soldats*. In theory if a company were richly endowed with experienced troops it would be possible for numbers of *vieux soldats* to be in service although they occupied none of the crucial positions in a company formation which would give them the title of *appointés*. See, for example, the idealized structure of a company of 200 troops provided in a memorandum of 1633, which proposes 6 *anspessades*, 45 *appointés*, 100 *vieux soldats* and only 37 *cadets*: AAE MD 819, fo. 102, *Mémoire sur les causes des désordres de l'infanterie*. This might just be a realistic proportion of veteran to newly recruited troops in the *gardes françaises*, but in the majority of regiments, even amongst the *régiments entretenus*, it would be unlikely that the veteran troops would outnumber the inexperienced, especially after 1635.

[82] The *anspessade* received a *montre* – in theory – of 15 *livres*, against the 14 *livres* for *appointés*, 12 *livres* for *vieux soldats* and 10 *livres* for the recruits: AAE MD 819, fo. 59 (1633 or 1635), expenses of a regiment. The *secrétaire* remained concerned throughout the war years to ensure that the principal of *haute paye* to the *anspessades*, *appointés* and *vieux soldats* was maintained: SHAT A^1 63, fo. 191, 22 Jan. 1641, general instruction to the *commissaires généraux* charged with the payment of troops in winter quarters to respect the additional payments to be made to the experienced troops; A^1 64, fo. 28, 18 Mar. 1641, instruction to *intendant* Bellejamme to ensure that the full number of *hautes payes* are provided for the experienced troops in the regiment of Picardie.

[83] Billon, *Principes de l'art militaire*, pp. 166–8; du Praissac, *Discours militaires*, p. 3, proposes a more elaborate system for a file of ten soldiers, in which four are *anspessades* or *appointés*, occupying the first, fourth, fifth and tenth positions. However, the practical evidence of armies on campaign before 1635 and other military manuals suggest that the proportion of three *vieux* per ten soldiers was customary.

[84] AAE CP Savoie 26, fo. 216, 17 May 1638, cardinal de La Valette to Richelieu on the shortage of skilled pikemen in the army of Italy, and the effects on the general quality of the infantry.

[85] *Code Michau*, art. 286.

The military context

that regulation breastplates be worn by cavalry and pikemen, or that swords and other weapons and equipment be carried, probably had little effect in practice when the experienced troops considered that this armour or equipment added to their burdens and reduced their movements without increasing their security.[86] Any attempt to impose an external system upon the veterans would be accepted only in so far as it was regarded as compatible with their own military habits; the military authorities recognized that it would have been counter-productive to force them into unaccustomed drill or manoeuvres prescribed by text-books.

Thus, the role of experienced troops in providing an example for new recruits was the basis of the *ad hoc* system of training and drill within the French army. The main issue to be resolved was how these troops were to be deployed, and the priorities concerning their use. When the army simply consisted of the core of *entretenus* units, the *gardes*, *vieux* and *petits vieux* regiments, and the established companies of *gendarmes* and *cavalerie légère*, there was no necessary clash of interest. The crown wanted elite units containing a high proportion of experienced veterans, but these were the same 'standing' units into which raw recruits would be introduced. However, as the army expanded to meet the military challenges of the 1630s an obvious dilemma emerged. If the fundamental priority was to use the veterans as the means to induct inexperienced troops into the rudiments of weapons-drill, formations and tactical manoeuvres, then the logical step would be to spread them out across all the regiments and cavalry companies of the army, seeking to ensure that every unit had at least some troops who had seen combat, possessed some idea of how to stand fast within a formation and could carry out basic firing drill. But if the minimum theoretical proportion of veterans to relatively or totally inexperienced troops was three to seven, then the numbers of those with previous experience, mostly gained in the *entretenus* units, would be insufficient to supply the needs of all the newly raised units after 1635. Moreover, veterans were not merely expected to provide apprenticeship in military skills for recruits; they were also expected to fight more reliably, more doggedly and with greater commitment. Modern combat theory does not hesitate to ascribe this greater effectiveness of veterans to *esprit de corps* and competitive unit pride, to mutual support and confidence between the officers and soldiers and, above all, to the social and psychological dynamic of soldiers operating together in small groups. The early modern Spanish army had recognized this basic truth. François de La Noue in his *Discours* drew attention to the Spanish system of *camarades*: groups of ten soldiers who were placed together under the

---

[86] SHAT A¹ 28, fo. 269, 14 July 1636, king's ordinance condemning these practices, 'whether because of the officers' laxity, the bravado or the obstinacy of the soldiers'; Aubery, *Richelieu*, II. 291, 9 June 1639, Châtillon, commander of the army on the Flanders' frontier, to de Noyers, *secrétaire de la guerre*, reporting that in his corps only the pikemen in the *régiment des gardes* still appeared at the *revue générale* equipped with the regulation body-armour (*corselets*); AAE MD 832, fo. 112, 2 Sept. 1638, 'ordonnance pour obliger les cavalliers a porter des armes'.

The French art of war during Richelieu's ministry

informal leadership, either of one of their own number whom they had elected or of someone chosen by the captain of the company.[87] The essence of this system was a respect for the stability of these groups; getting the best service out of veterans was therefore totally incompatible with breaking up these bonds and distributing the experienced soldiers across the rest of the army.

The French crown may not have been explicitly aware of the importance of 'small group dynamics' when handling its veteran troops, but it was anxious to ensure that the most prestigious units within the army retained their elite status, and the primary way to strengthen the fighting quality of the *gardes*, the *régiments entretenus* of the *vieux* and the *petits vieux*, or the *gendarmes* and prestige *chevaux légers* companies, was to ensure that they contained a significant proportion of all the experienced veteran troops available in the army. All the expectations of military prestige and status worked *against* the parcelling out of desirable veteran troops to assist in the formation of new regiments. Indeed, the flow ran in the other direction; precisely because the *entretenus* survived the successive disbandments and *réformations* imposed on lesser units – whose existence was regarded for the most part as a war-time expedient – troops with experience who had stayed in the ranks of these units until the moment of disbandment were frequently redeployed into the *entretenus*, thus reinforcing the preponderance of veterans in a small number of elite units.[88]

The same reservations must be laid against the frequently reiterated notion that the *gardes*, the *vieux* and the *petits vieux* regiments provided a training-ground for officers. There are cases of individuals who served as an ensign or a lieutenant in one of the elite units, and who then went on to become a captain or even a *mestre de camp* of a less prestigious unit, but there were powerful reasons for not taking this course, above all, the obvious hazard of moving from an *entretenue* unit which would be kept in being – albeit in a reduced form – regardless of military circumstance to a unit which would be unlikely to be preserved in any form after the end of the war, and might well be disbanded before that time.[89]

---

[87] La Noue, *Discours*, pp. 294–7.

[88] See, for example, SHAT A^1 61, fo. 173, 11 Nov. 1640: order for the disbandment of regts of La Douze, Saint-George, Humières, Tavannes, Roux, Laroche, Polignac and four companies of the regt of Guyenne; the officers were to be sent home, the soldiers incorporated into *régiments entretenus* designated by the comte d'Harcourt, commander of the army in Italy. A^1 31, fos. 73, 76, 12 Dec. 1636, de Noyers to *intendant* Alexandre Sève and colonel Egenfeld, ordering that 200 or so dragoons remaining from Egenfeld's regt should be incorporated into the *gardes françaises*; Avenel, v. 42 (end May 1635), Richelieu to Servien, concerning the distribution of *officiers réformés* from the army of the duc d'Angoulême amongst the separate companies of the *vieux régiments*, maximizing the extent to which they would bring their 'own' soldiers into the companies: 'il n'y a point de capitaine, de lieutenant, d'enseigne ny de sergent qui n'aient quelques soldats attachez d'affection, lesquels ils mèneront avec eux'. Maréchal Bassompierre noted how in June 1620 it was decided to transfer 400 infantry from the *petit vieux* regiment of Vaubecourt to the *vieux* regiment of Picardie: *Mémoires*, xx.170.

[89] The early career of Abraham de Fabert, later *maréchal de France*, reveals the perils of abandoning the relative security of lesser officerships in *régiments entretenus* for promotion into a regiment with

The military context

The crown's inclination was to concentrate its experienced troops and officers into an elite core of the army; this left the problem of the unpreparedness of the newly recruited regiments unresolved. As larger and larger numbers of inexperienced recruits were raised after 1635, the crown and its ministers took one or two reluctant initiatives to try to mitigate the worst effects of lack of training, but they still worked within the same inadequate framework of redeploying veterans rather than rethinking the whole question of training and drill. In 1640, the *secrétaire de la guerre*, Sublet de Noyers, wrote to Charles d'Halluin, maréchal de Schomberg, ordering him to designate one company from each of the experienced regiments in Guyenne and Languedoc, whose troops would serve as a 'stiffening' in newly levied regiments *en route* for Italy.[90] But this is certainly not a typical policy. In the same year Louis XIII wrote to the commander of the army of Italy, Henri de Lorraine, comte d'Harcourt, that 'l'experience ayt faict cognoistre qu'il est presque impossible d'obliger les soldats qui ont esté d'un regiment a servir dans un autre'.[91] Given the notoriously high desertion rates amongst troops despatched across the French frontiers the net result may well have been the loss not merely of most of the new units but also of the veterans, who would have remained in service had they been left in their original regiments. It may also be doubted whether inserting a core of veteran troops and experienced lesser officers and NCOs into newly levied regiments would have produced results without a matching willingness to provide time for these new units to undergo training and exercises before going to join the armies; this the crown considered it impossible to provide after 1635.

The role of veteran and foreign troops in military effectiveness

The conviction that veteran troops were the decisive key to military success was a central preoccupation of the French generals throughout this period.[92] The

---

no long-term stability. Abandoning the post of ensign in a company of the Piémont regiment he assumed a company command in a regiment newly levied by Marie de' Medicis in 1619, only to find himself unemployed when the regiment was disbanded on the orders of the duc de Luynes. Re-established as an ensign in Piémont, he again accepted a captaincy in a regiment of *nouvelle levée* in 1625–6, once more to find himself a victim of the disbandment of the regiment in 1627. Only when he gained the office of sergeant-major in the *petit-vieux* regiment of Rambures through the patronage of the duc d'Epernon did his military career enjoy any stability: J. Bourelly, *Le maréchal de Fabert, 1599–1662* (2 vols.; Paris, 1881), I. 11–26.

[90] SHAT A^1 57, fo. 310, 5 Feb. 1640. Significantly, this was a stiffening under their own terms by inserting cohesive veteran companies within the regiments, rather than parcelling individual veterans out amongst all the other companies. An earlier example from 1636 ordered that soldiers from elite companies of *gendarmes* and *chevaux légers* should be employed amongst the newly levied troops to provide examples of drill and tactical discipline, but the absence of any subsequent orders of this nature suggests that it was either unenforceable, or resulted in the desertion of the elite troops: A^1 29, fo. 15, 16 Aug. 1636, Louis XIII to Louis de Bourbon, comte de Soissons.

[91] AAE CP Savoie 31, fo. 392, 11 Nov. 1640.

[92] And of most other European contemporaries with practical experience of warfare: see, for example,

The French art of war during Richelieu's ministry

correspondence of French commanders with Louis XIII, Richelieu and the *secrétaire de la guerre* provide abundant evidence of the overriding importance contemporaries placed upon obtaining soldiers with practical military experience, regardless of their particular tactical and organizational background or training. The better fighting qualities of veterans were matched by relatively higher resilience and staying power. Harcourt wrote from Italy in late 1640, citing the wastage rates amongst the new levies and emphasizing that the only troops who could be relied upon not to desert were some 3,000 *vieilles trouppes*.[93] In the negotiations for the troops who were to be allocated to the army-corps at the beginning of each campaign, global totals of troops were regarded as relatively unimportant. The critical issue likely to determine the effectiveness of the corps, its survival through the campaign season and its ability to match the military qualities of its enemies, was the proportion of veteran troops present, especially measured in terms of *entretenus* regiments and cavalry companies. The cardinal de La Valette wrote to Richelieu in July 1635 to complain about the respective allocation of troops between his army-corps and that of the maréchal de La Force; overall numbers were of considerably less concern to him than the fact that amongst the twenty-nine regiments on the *état* of La Force were substantial numbers of *vieilles trouppes* 'qui sont touttes . . . les meilleures qu'on ait jamais veues . . . car il est vrai qu'avec que les 12 000 hommes qu'il avoit dans son armee on n'en doibt pas craindre une de 30 000'.[94] Certainly the *état* of La Force's army, revealing the presence of two of the *vieux régiments* (Picardie and Navarre), two of the *petits vieux* (Normandie and Vaubecourt), together with a run of regiments of established reputation (Tonneins, d'Halincourt, Effiat, Navailles, Bussy-Rabutin, La Meilleraye, Nanteuil), offers some credence to La Valette's hyperbole.[95] Thanks to the efforts of Richelieu on behalf of his *fidèle*, La Valette was eventually to be provided with twelve companies of the *gardes françaises* and four of the *gardes suisses*, probably the best troops possessed by the king. This was not achieved without cost to Richelieu's political credit; Louis XIII appears to have regarded the 6,000 elite infantry of the two *gardes* regiments as part of his military entourage, and was not initially willing to allow them to be deployed to strengthen

---

Williams, *Brief Discourse*, p. 4, for an explicit statement of the centrality of veterans to military success, and one which deploys classical examples to buttress the case: 'What caused Caesar to overthrow Pompey, Romane to Romane, with farre lesser number? Because he had olde trained Legions, against more than halfe new levied rawe men.'

[93] AAE CP Savoie 30, fo. 556, 26 Oct. 1640, Harcourt to Richelieu.

[94] AAE CP Lorraine 25, fo. 287, 18 June 1635. In a different context a similar point was made in 1631 by Sébastien Lustrier, Imperial Resident at the French Court, who proposed that 40,000 French troops, mostly of *nouvelle levée*, were not equal to 15,000–20,000 Germans with a higher proportion of veterans in the ranks: Fagniez, *Père Joseph*, appendix v, II. 501.

[95] AAE MD 819, fo. 1 (1635), *Etat des trouppes* – Angoulême and La Force; La Valette's own corps included only one *petit vieux* (Rambures), and the regiments of Turenne and Nettancourt as the other relatively experienced infantry.

the army-corps on the frontiers.[96] Given the dangers of an enemy breakthrough in Picardy, Champagne or Burgundy, the armies on the eastern frontier claimed – and received – the largest share of the veteran units. Elsewhere, commanders hoped for one or two regiments from amongst the *vieux* or *petits vieux* to strengthen the fighting spirit and discipline of their other troops, and were sometimes unable to gain even this allocation.[97] The importance of elite units was emphasized out of all proportion to their numbers; as Châtillon gratefully wrote in May 1641, having just heard that the Picardie regiment was to be sent to join his army-corps: 'j'avais besoin de ce vieux corps pour animer tout le reste de nostre infanterie. Je me suis grandement obligé a son Eminence de me l'avoir accordé'.[98] This preoccupation with gaining as many veteran units as possible before or during a campaign gave rise to the identification of 'bons régiments', those with an *esprit de corps* and reasonable levels of military experience, and the concept achieved wide currency in the correspondence between commanders and with the ministers.[99] In a letter lamenting the quality of the troops sent to him, maréchal Schomberg incidentally underlined the extent to which the ideals of military theorists were out of touch with reality when he suggested dismissively that the regiment of des Touches, recently arrived from the Lyonnais, far from being a *bon régiment*, 'n'est que milice'- troops of the (low) quality of a citizen militia.[100]

The quality of the *vieux régiments* certainly rested on large numbers of experienced soldiers in their ranks, but also the officers were, in general, considered to be far more capable than their counterparts in the ordinary units. There was no assumption that all officers in the army had achieved a basic level of expertise and professionalism. In 1635 cardinal de La Valette contrasted the qualities and hardiness of the *vieux* in comparison with the other units in his

---

[96] AAE MD 814, fo. 210, 30 June 1635; Léon le Bouthillier, comte de Chavigny, the *secrétaire d'Etat* for foreign affairs, reported that the tone of Richelieu's request for the *gardes* to be moved to La Valette's army had made an extremely bad impression on the king: fo. 228, 3 July 1635.

[97] Maréchal Bassompierre claimed that when he was offered command of the troops to be sent to the Valtelline in 1625 he stipulated that he should have one *vieux* regiment, two other *entretenus* and further infantry up to 6,000 which he should be allowed to choose from the army of Champagne: *Mémoires*, xxi. 22–3. A decade later the bargaining power of the commanders in Italy was considerably smaller: AAE CP Savoie 25, fo. 24, 30 Jan. 1637, Michel Particelli, sieur d'Hémery, extraordinary ambassador in Piedmont, writing on behalf of the commander of the army of Italy, Charles de Blanchefort, maréchal de Créqui, stressed that it would be impossible to take the offensive unless the army contained one regiment carrying the *drapeau blanc*; Savoie 26, fo. 699, 11 Dec. 1638, La Valette to Richelieu, emphasizing once again that for the forthcoming campaign it will be essential to have one *vieux* regiment and some foreign units to strengthen the army: 'parce qu'ayant un bon regiment françois a la teste de nos trouppes il nous aiderons a remettre la discipline que j'ay trouvé entierement perdue dans cette armée'.

[98] AAE MD 1680, fo. 58, 6 May 1641, Châtillon to de Noyers.

[99] See, for example, La Valette to de Noyers in early 1639, pessimistic about the likely success of the forthcoming campaign, 'a cause du peu de bons regiments que nous aurons': AAE CP Savoie 28, fo. 25, 12 Jan. 1639.

[100] AAE MD 1631, fo. 265, 26 Dec. 1639, Schomberg to Richelieu.

The French art of war during Richelieu's ministry

corps, pointing out that the latter had almost entirely disbanded 'principallement par la faulte de la pluspart des officiers qui n'ont authorité sur leurs soldats et ne sont pas trop soigneux de leur devoir'.[101] The collapse of these new regiments did not reflect shortage of food supplies, La Valette suggested, but 'le desir qu'aient quelques uns des chefs de retourner à Paris'.[102] The solution to this problem of indiscipline and disbandment proposed by La Valette was in keeping with the conviction that it was better to strengthen the elite units than try to salvage military qualities from the others; his suggestion was 'd'augmenter le nombre des compagnies des régiments qui sont levés depuis trois ans, et les quelles sont recogneus pour les meilleurs'.[103]

In late 1635 a response from Richelieu to La Valette's proposal accepted that the *vieux* regiments should be increased up to twenty-five companies each, while another *état* proposed that the *petits vieux* should be increased from fifteen to twenty companies, evidence that the ministers were prepared to consider embarking on this further policy of concentrating the best troops in a small number of units.[104] In fact neither of these projected augmentations occurred in 1636.[105] The *petits vieux* were increased to twenty companies in 1637,[106] but the augmentation of the *vieux* regiments was not carried out until 1640, when their company strength was increased from twenty companies up to thirty.[107] Although some of this augmentation would be made up from new recruits, the project was in large part a capitulation to the principle that the qualities of the elite units would justify a further input of the veteran troops from the rest of the army.

If one part of the strength of an army-corps was considered to lie with French

---

[101] AAE CP Allemagne 12, fo. 217, 1 Aug. 1635, La Valette to Louis XIII.
[102] AAE CP Allemagne 12, fo. 220, 1 Aug. 1635, La Valette to Richelieu.
[103] AAE CP Allemagne 12, fo. 220, 1 Aug. 1635, La Valette to Richelieu.
[104] AAE CP Allemagne 12, fo. 384 (Nov.) 1635; AAE MD 816, fo. 159, Nov. 1635, *état* drawn up by Abel Servien, *secrétaire de la guerre*, for the augmentation of the seven *petits vieux* (Neerestang, Maugiron, Rambures, Vaubecourt, Sault, Bellnaue and Saint-Luc). The augmentation of the *petits vieux* was part of a wider project to create prestige regiments of twenty companies each, which was also to include Nettancourt, Turenne and Rebé: Avenel, v. 371, 8 Dec. 1635, Richelieu to La Valette. The new companies for this augmentation were to be created explicitly from the best officers and experienced soldiers *réformés* from the *nouveaux régiments* of 1635.
[105] One plausible reason for the rejection of the project is that it would have involved an unavoidable increase in the authority and prerogatives of the *colonel général de l'infanterie*, the duc d'Epernon. This was certainly the reason why a scheme to establish a series of *régiments des provinces* was abandoned in the same year. By 1640 the power of Epernon had been definitively broken, and he would have been unable to exploit the augmentation of the *vieux* regiments which was ordered in this year. This collapse of Epernon's prerogative power after his disgrace in 1639 would not explain the decision to augment the *petits vieux* two years earlier, in 1637, but given the fall in the strength of individual companies in the years after 1635, it may have been decided that the only way to keep these second-rank prestige regiments at an effective overall level was to increase the number of companies regardless of Epernon's prerogatives.
[106] AAE MD 828, fos. 269–82 (1637), *états* of troops for the army-corps of 1637.
[107] AAE MD 837, fo. 276 (1640), *états* of the regiments composing the armies, and fo. 216, a specific *état* of the *régiment de La Marine*, all showing this increase to thirty companies, continued in 1641 and 1642 and extended to a large number of other prestige regiments.

The military context

veterans, the other great desideratum was foreign mercenaries. In part, this was because they were rightly seen in most cases to possess exactly what the majority of French regiments and companies lacked: large numbers of long-serving, quasi-professional veterans who were inured to the hardships of lengthy campaigns and had substantial experience of fighting the Spanish or Imperial armies.[108]

Yet it was not just the veteran component of such forces which persuaded the French crown to give priority to negotiating contracts with foreign entrepreneurs, and made individual foreign units so attractive to French commanders in the field.[109] Given that levels of desertion amongst ordinary French units reached catastrophic proportions when an army-corps moved across the frontiers, the solution was widely held to be reliance upon foreign mercenaries for those armies which, it was hoped, would fight deep in enemy territory.[110] Cardinal de La Valette wrote in early January 1639 to his confidant Léon le Bouthillier, comte de Chavigny and *secrétaire d'Etat* for foreign affairs, that he hoped for two or three foreign regiments in the allocation to his north Italian army-corps 'qui se fussent mieux conservés que les François'.[111]

Thus for the majority of French commanders, military effectiveness was a question of acquiring soldiers with practical experience of campaigning and combat rather than taking raw recruits and hoping to train and drill them before they began campaigning or experienced combat. In so far as the high command considered other factors which might determine the success of their army-corps, these also had little to do with prescriptive tactical theory and a lot to do with the realities of the forces at their disposal.

Optimum unit size and the decline of effective troop numbers

A critical issue in the thinking of theorists and commanders alike was the size and composition of the units in which the infantry – forming the bulk of the army – carried out military operations, and if necessary were brought together to fight battles. Pragmatism and necessity were the shaping factors here, not tactical theory concerned to maximize the deployment of infantry firearms. The regiment certainly had a distinct role in establishing the identity of a group of soldiers, and

---

[108] For a more detailed discussion of the role of foreign mercenaries, see chapter 5, pp. 292–312.

[109] In October 1635 La Valette wrote enthusiastically to Richelieu that if the king had 4,000 cavalry of the quality of the foreign regiments of colonels Hums and Rantzau he would have no difficulty in defeating the enemy: AAE CP Allemagne 12, fo. 332, 8 Oct. 1635.

[110] La Valette wrote to Richelieu in 1635 that 'nos trouppes ont un effroy si grand d'Allemagne qu'il est quasi impossible de le comprendre . . . il est quasi impossible d'en empescher le debandement': AAE CP Allemagne 12, fo. 330, 5 Oct. 1635; Richelieu himself made the comment that news of their imminent despatch into the Empire would reduce a force of recruits by 50 per cent overnight: AAE MD 816, fo. 226 (1635), Richelieu to Servien.

[111] AAE CP Savoie 28, fo. 3, 4 Jan 1639.

The French art of war during Richelieu's ministry

amongst the elite troops it was the basis of a shared *esprit de corps* focused upon the symbol of the regiment's prestige, the *drapeau blanc*. But until 1638 the companies of French cavalry were not grouped into regiments, and even in the infantry there were more differences between individual regiments than obvious similarities. Administratively, the French army, like its Spanish, Imperial and Dutch counterparts, took the company as its basic organizational unit.[112] Troops, whether cavalry or infantry, were recruited and paid by companies, and the captain had direct administrative responsibility for the soldiers in his company. Indeed, although most infantry commissions in the war years were given to those who aspired to command entire regiments, and who would then distribute the individual commissions for the captaincies to their clients or relatives, the convention was retained that the *mestre de camp* was the 'first captain' of the regiment, and would receive a captain's salary in addition to his pay as *mestre de camp*.[113] Additional recruitment took place by companies, and it was with the captains that the *intendants* and the *commissaires* negotiated the *traités* for new levies of troops.[114] The difference, however, at least in comparison with the Imperial and Spanish armies, was that the French companies were smaller. The theoretical strength of a company in the Imperial army, and indeed most German companies in regiments brought into French service, was 200 men.[115] Against this, the notional full-strength company even in a *vieux* regiment numbered only 100 soldiers, and in practice even 'full' strength would mean somewhere between 70 and 90 troops.[116] This would be at the opening of the campaign, or just after the arrival of numbers of recruits. A few months into the campaign, even without

---

[112] G. Parker, *The Army of Flanders and the Spanish Road, 1567–1659* (Cambridge, 1972), p. 274; Wijn, *Krijgswezen*, p. 474; V. Löwe, 'Die Organization und Verwaltung der Wallensteinischen Heere', dissertation, Freiburg im Breisgau, 1895, pp. 18–22.

[113] AAE MD 819, fo. 62 (1635) gives the pay of an infantry captain as 150 *livres* per *montre*, that of the *mestre de camp* as 250 *livres* – including his pay of 150 *livres* as captain of the first company.

[114] See for instance AAE CP Lorraine 31, fo. 49, 24 Apr. 1639, Choisy to de Noyers, giving details of the *traités* that were drawn up and signed by all of the cavalry and infantry captains for the recruitment of their companies up to full strength over the winter quarter.

[115] The theoretical strength of an Imperial infantry company was actually 300 soldiers in 1632–33, but this was rarely maintained: F. Konze, 'Die Stärke, Zusammensetzung und Verteilung der Wallensteinischen Armee während des Jahres 1633', dissertation, Bonn, 1906, p. 15; 300 infantry was also the theoretical company strength in the Bavarian army, with cavalry companies composed of 100 horse: C. Kapser, *Die bayerische Kriegsorganization in der zweiten Hälfte des Dreißigjährigen Krieges, 1635–1648/9* (Münster, 1997), p. 58. SHAT A^1 26, fo. 30, 28 Feb. 1635, capitulation drawn up with Eberhard III, duke of Württemberg for the levy of a regiment of ten companies of infantry of 200 men each; A^1 65, fo. 11, 18 June 1641, order to colonels of three Swiss regiments to see that the company strength of their units is made up to 200 men.

[116] The exceptions to this were the companies of the *gardes françaises and suisses*, theoretically of 150 men each in 1635, though by 1639 the companies of the *gardes françaises* had been increased to 200 men, and in 1642 the companies of the *gardes suisses* were similarly increased: SHAT A^1 51, fo. 60, 6 Mar. 1639, order to complete companies of *gardes* up to 200 men; A^1 68, fo. 121, 18 Jan. 1642, similar order for augmentation of the *gardes suisses*. The most prestigious cavalry companies, the *gendarmes* and the *chevaux légers* of the king, queen and some other members of the royal family, were also theoretically of 200 men each: AAE MD 832, fo. 1 (1638), *état* of the king's army; BN

The military context

an action such as a protracted siege, and the average company strength would have declined precipitately. *Etats* of the regiments in the armies of the maréchaux de La Force and Urbain de Maillé, marquis de Brézé, some way into the 1638 campaign reveal that even the *vieux régiment* of Piémont had fallen to an average company strength of 64, while the *petit vieux* Rambures had an average company strength of 42 soldiers.[117] These were companies in elite regiments, and the *revues* were being conducted before the most serious, late-campaign levels of wastage had occurred. The obvious conclusions can be drawn about the company strengths of ordinary regiments a few weeks after their recruitment or assembly. *Revues* conducted of individual companies in such regiments show these to be more or less consistently below 50 men: a *revue* of a company from the regiment of Saint-Martial conducted on 23 May 1636 gave a total strength of 44 men, whereas a company of the regiment of Florinville, evidently destined for *réformation*, was given as 14 infantry at a *revue* on 13 October 1636.[118] There is no reason to doubt the figures of Bernhard Kroener, who suggests that the average real company strength in infantry regiments for the period 1635–40 was around 42 men.[119]

The essential point about the French infantry company was that it was too small to operate as an autonomous military unit. The simplest tactical formations of the period required substantially more than 30–50 men; the firepower of 20–30 musketeers would be of limited effect, and it was certainly questionable whether 10–20 pikemen could offer the cohesion and strength capable of protecting a body of musketeers, let alone launching an attack in their own right. Even at the level of raiding parties or a localized *guerre de partisans*, a company was too small to defend itself effectively, as numbers of reports of companies being wiped out by local populations attest.[120]

It might be assumed therefore that the regiment would provide a means to bring together the constituent companies into a militarily effective unity. But the fundamental problem with this solution was that 'regiments' in no sense represented uniform tactical building-blocks. At their most extreme, the numerical differences between regiments could vary between 3,000 men for the *gardes françaises* at full strength, down to the point at which ordinary regiments were already marked for disbandment but still in service; evidence suggests that totals of 180, even of 150, infantry per regiment were possible by the last months of a

---

Ms.fr. 25857, pce 1141, 5 Sept. 1641, *revue* of the company of *chevaux légers du roi*, establishing the unit at full strength of 200 *maîtres*.

[117] AAE MD 832, fos. 27, 38 (1638).

[118] BN Ms.fr. 25853, pce 850; 25854, pce 950.

[119] B. Kroener, 'Die Entwicklung der Truppenstärken in den französischen Armeen zwischen 1635 und 1661', in K. Repgen (ed.), *Forschungen und Quellen zur Geschichte des Dreißigjährigen Krieges* (Münster, 1981), pp. 163–220.

[120] For example, Avenel, v. 760, 10 Mar. 1637, Richelieu to Louis XIII, reporting on the massacre of a cavalry company by peasants in the Auvergne.

The French art of war during Richelieu's ministry

campaign.¹²¹ On a more regular basis, generals would command an army-corps in which regiments could vary in size between 1,200 and 300 men. While a *vieux* regiment which had lost half its strength could bring together 600–700 infantry and was still capable of acting as an effective military unit, an ordinary regiment reduced to fewer than 300 effectives had probably reached the point where neither its firepower nor its cohesion in defence or attack would be sufficient in an engagement, even if the infantry in the unit had some military experience.¹²²

These variations between the numerical strength of regiments created considerable practical problems for French commanders attempting to deploy their forces in battle or at a siege. The solution was clearly established, but proved difficult to achieve in practice. The remedy for discrepancies between the size of regiments was to deploy troops in an alternative formation for combat, the *bataillon*.¹²³ This was a unit with neither the administrative existence of the company, nor the clear identity of the named regiment; it was simply a uniform grouping of infantry into a formation of between 500 and 600 men, made up of pikemen and musketeers in what became the increasingly universal proportions of approximately 1:2.¹²⁴ Jean de Billon refers to the *bataillon* as a unit of 500–600 infantry, assuming that the formation is no more than ten men deep, though he adds that 'si on veut plus grand, l'on peut faire les files de vingt hommes au plus'.¹²⁵ At a practical level, maréchal Bassompierre described in his *mémoires* how the French infantry being deployed for the assault on the pass at Susa in March 1629 were organized into *bataillons* of 50 *enfants perdus*, a supporting advance guard of 100, and a main block of 500 soldiers.¹²⁶

---

¹²¹ The *intendant* Jean Choisy, writing about the state of the army of Manassés de Pas, marquis de Feuquières after its defeat at the hands of the Spanish and Imperial troops and the decision to abandon the siege of Thionville, indicated that eleven infantry regiments had been reassembled, and that they now totalled 2,000 men, an average of around 180 per regiment: AAE CP Lorraine 31, fo. 135, 9 June 1639; an *état* of a series of *revues* conducted for the army of the maréchaux de La Force and Angoulême at the end of the 1635 campaign show a group of regiments whose effective strength was between 200 and 160, all of which were marked down for disbandment: AAE MD 823, fo. 270.

¹²² An *état* of a sequence of *revues* of regiments dated 24 Oct. 1637 makes this point clearly: the *vieux* regiments of Picardie, Piémont and La Marine contained 700, 793 and 696 troops respectively; the *vieux* regiment of Champagne was weaker, at 474 effectives, but had been badly hit by the plague; two *petits vieux* and two other prestigious regiments – Bellenaue, Nettancourt, Brézé *père* and *fils* – had managed to retain 350, 444, 522 and 524 effectives. Of the other regiments none exceeded 300 effectives: Du Gué – 290, Montmège – 276, Saint-Luc – 280, Effiat – 220, Bellefonds – 288: AAE MD 828, fo. 92.

¹²³ L. Susane, *Histoire de l'infanterie française* (5 vols.; Paris, 1872–4), I. 188, dates the formation of *bataillons* to 1635, though it was a feature of infantry organization before then; but he correctly emphasizes that the purpose was 'd'avoir une unité de formation régulière, d'une force convenable et déterminée'.

¹²⁴ Lostelneau, *Maréchal de bataille*, pp. 243–4; Lynn, 'Tactical evolution', 179, cites La Barre Duparcq to suggest that the *bataillon* became the standard combat unit under Henri IV, when they numbered around 400 infantry each.

¹²⁵ Billon, *Principes de l'art*, pp. 166–8.

¹²⁶ Bassompierre, *Mémoires*, XXI. 190–1.

The military context

Opinion remained consistent about the optimum size for a *bataillon*, and it is significant that this size corresponds to the Dutch battalion of 550 men, the smallest type of Spanish *escuadrón* of 600, the Swedish squadron of 504 infantry plus officers and NCOs, or the Imperial and Bavarian formations of 600.[127] But the reason that this basic unit size was so universal appears to have nothing to do with any tactical theory of the superiority of small units. As both Billon and later writers imply, the real issue is simply the geometrical relationship between the depth of a formation and the width of its front.[128] Formations of infantry drawn up on the battlefields of seventeenth-century Europe and facing an enemy advancing from a single direction were, in most circumstances, no more than ten files deep, and this depth was progressively declining towards a typical six files by the 1660s. Given this relative shallowness of formations, drawing up a large number of troops into a single block, pikemen flanked by musketeers, would run the risk of creating an over-extended and unwieldy front. A formation of 600 soldiers ten files deep would be numerous enough to be self-supporting on the battlefield, but would involve a front of sixty men. Drawn up in 'close' order – which for the safety of musketeers equipped with matchlock muskets still implied three paces between soldiers – this formation would be only some 180 feet across, a manageable, sufficiently compact size for the transmission of orders by officers and NCOs.[129] This was widely considered to be an optimum balance between firepower, independent cohesion and manageability.[130]

Given the previous discussion surrounding the numerical strength of regiments, it is obvious that the deployment of French infantry in *bataillons* does not, for the most part, fit the thesis that reformed armies were distributing their troops into more numerous, smaller units. In practice, the average size of a standard French infantry regiment, albeit not one of the *entretenue* elite, was smaller than the 500–600 men of a *bataillon*. Far from being a response to the supposed desirability of deploying smaller units, in the 1630s and 1640s the function of the *bataillon* was to amalgamate small regiments of different overall stengths into militarily viable and reasonably uniform tactical units.[131] This was not a case of

---

[127] Wijn, *Krijgswezen*, pp. 474–5; Parker, 'The "military revolution, 1560–1660" – a myth?', p. 89; Roberts, *Gustavus Adolphus*, II. 219–20; A. Åberg, 'The Swedish army from Lützen to Narva', in M. Roberts (ed.), *Sweden's Age of Greatness, 1632–1718* (London, 1972), p. 282; Löwe, 'Wallensteinischen Heere', pp. 19–20; J. Pohl, *Die Profiantirung der keyserlichen Armaden ahnbelangendt. Studien zur Versorgung der kaiserlichen Armee, 1634–1635* (Mitteilungen des Österreichischen Staatsarchives, Sonderband 1; Vienna, 1994), pp. 29–32.

[128] For example, La Fontaine, *Les devoirs militaires*, p. 227.

[129] Billon's calculation of close order allows two feet per soldier: *Principes de l'art militaire*, p. 168, but it was generally considered that the danger of one soldier inadvertently igniting his neighbours' cartridges with the smouldering match that he carried dictated three paces distance. See for example, La Valière, *Pratique et maximes*, pp. 61–4.

[130] And the extent to which this was an innovation in the seventeenth century is raised by the existence of the *bandes* of infantry during the Wars of Religion, also grouped together as 500–600 men: E. de La Barre Duparcq, *L'art militaire pendant les guerres de religion* (Paris, 1864), p. 27.

[131] See, for example, the plan of the French forces drawn up for the battle of Rocroi in Aumale, *Princes*

The French art of war during Richelieu's ministry

scaling down, but of trying to scale up, the size of the fighting unit. Tactical theory and practice during the Thirty Years War cannot be discussed without reference to the military reality on the ground, and a crucial aspect of this reality, particularly in the case of the French army, is the gulf between notional and real troop numbers, and the dramatic decline in unit strength during each campaign.

While the forming of the available infantry into *bataillons* seemingly avoided the dangers of engaging an enemy with an assortment of regiments of varied strength, it was a solution not free of problems. Given the endemic competition between officers over matters of command and precedence, bringing together different units and their officers developed tensions. Maréchal Bassompierre claimed that, as early as October 1621 during the Béarn campaign, he had expressed doubts about the wisdom of amalgamating troops from different units in order to maintain *bataillons* at reasonable strength.[132] The disputes and confusions that would arise over precedence could all too easily neutralize any tactical benefits that might come from the amalgamation. Indeed, one of the main reasons why the relative ranking of regiments, even those beneath *entretenue* status, was such a thorny issue was precisely because such rankings would determine officers' seniority when two regiments were brought together in a *bataillon*.[133] Organization into *bataillons* could create a fluidity in matters of rank that would be exploited by officers seeking precedence; in 1641 it was necessary to stipulate that *aides de camp* should not have the right to exercise the function of major in a *bataillon*, a claim which would never have been at issue within the more clearly defined *état major* of a regiment.[134] So long as the average size of a regiment was smaller than a *bataillon* the potential for conflict was considerable, and it is not surprising that the crown should have devoted effort to creating numbers of regiments with higher company strength from 1637, since the only long-term solution was to ensure that the individual regiments were closer to the ideal of *bataillon* strength. In comparison with these attempts to amalgamate, the attempts to divide *vieux* regiments with perhaps 1,200–1,400 effectives into two or three *bataillons* seem less contentious, though once again, the difficulties of establishing seniority within the separate *bataillons* were significant. There are certainly cases

---

de Condé, IV. facing page 82, which shows regiments doubled – and in one case tripled – into *bataillons*.

[132] Bassompierre, *Mémoires*, xx. 348–9.

[133] BN Châtre de Cangé, 23, fo. 173, 16 Apr. 1636, Richelieu, writing to *mestre de camp* La Touche, might stipulate that *bataillon* commands should go to the most senior captains, but that could hardly plaster over the fertile potential for disputes and competition about what constituted seniority. SHAT A^1 70, fo. 21, 18 July 1642, instructions for the ranking of the regiments of Mercurin and Birasse; A^1 64, fo. 296, 19 April 1641, order regulating precedence between the regiments of Oysonville, Vandy and Rebé, specifically declaring that the *lieutenant colonel* of Oysonville should have precedence over his counterpart in Vandy.

[134] SHAT A^1 64, fo. 293, 19 Apr. 1641; A^1 65, fo. 450bis, 4 Sept. 1641, ordinance to confirm that a regimental *lieutenant colonel* will have precedence over all captains in a *bataillon*, even when these belong to regiments which are more senior than that of the *lieutenant colonel*.

The military context

in which the field commander deploying his troops thought better of trying to divide up a major regiment, and allowed it to fight as a single unit at the centre of the front line.[135]

The deployment of the 500–600 strength *bataillon* did not, moreover, mean that an enthusiasm for larger units had disappeared. While *bataillon*-strength units were favoured in defence, the weight and shock-effect brought by larger infantry units in an assault was still highly regarded. Since 1630 Gustavus Adolphus had brought his Swedish squadrons together in groups of three or four to form brigades of 1,500–2,000 men,[136] while the Imperial and Spanish armies had never abandoned the use of large infantry units when initial shock was sought as a battle-winning weapon.[137] As contemporary military manuals attest, the formation of larger infantry units continued to be seen as a desirable part of the tactical repertoire of the French commander.[138] Moreover, individual *bataillons* of more than 500–600 infantry continued to be formed by commanders who had sufficient troops at their disposal to make larger units practical. César de Choiseul, comte du Plessis-Praslin, noted in his *mémoires* that the weakness of the individual infantry regiments in Italy in 1630 persuaded the commanders to deploy the entire infantry in eighteen *bataillons*, each of between 1,000 and 1,200 men.[139] Three years earlier, at the siege of La Rochelle, the French siege army had been drawn up in fifteen *bataillons* of about 1,200 men each.[140] After 1635 the relatively small total size of most French army-corps made the distribution of infantry into such large individual units impractical, but they continued to be held in high regard by contemporary commentators. Claude de Mesmes, comte d'Avaux, wrote from the Empire in 1638 commenting on the Swedish field army under marshal Johan Banér, emphasizing that its quality lay specifically in the 'douze escuadrons [Avaux clearly means 'brigades'] des gens de pied . . . dont quelques uns se montent à quinze et seize cens hommes'.[141] The largest *bataillons* assembled by the French commanders during the years after 1635 appear to have

---

[135] See, for example, BN Ms.fr. 6385, fo. 132, 3 Aug. 1635, plan of an order of battle in which the Champagne and Normandie regiments are divided into *bataillons*, but the regiments of Navarre and Vaubecourt are left as single units.

[136] Roberts, *Gustavus Adolphus*, II. 250–1; Gustavus' decision to bring together his troops into these brigades from early 1630 is described in R. Monro, *Monro his expedition with the worthy Scots regiment call'd Mackays* (2 parts; London, 1637), II. 2.

[137] Despite the tendency to treat it as an example of the 'military revolution' in practice, the 1631 battle of Breitenfeld was fought between Imperial and Swedish infantry formations that were between 1500 and 2,000 men strong, and both placed the greatest emphasis on cohesion in attack and defence.

[138] In the 1650s La Valière still proposed that the ideal *bataillon* should number up to 1,000 infantry: *Pratique et maximes*, p. 61.

[139] Plessis-Praslin, *Mémoires*, in Michaud and Poujoulat, VII. 357.

[140] Lynn, 'Tactical evolution', 179, citing F. de Vaux de Foletier, *Le siège de La Rochelle* (Paris, 1931), p. 238.

[141] AAE CP Allemagne 15, fo. 123, 25 Sept. 1638, 'Des affaires d'Allemagne'.

numbered 800–900 men, and even units of this strength would represent a heavy investment in a small number of units for an army of 8,000–12,000 infantry.[142]

If enthusiasm for larger units of infantry reflected a persistent conviction that cohesion in both defence and attack was the most desirable of tactical qualities, another major reason for favouring larger units was straightforwardly organizational and financial. Desertion amongst the ordinary soldiers – the largest single cause of unit attrition in the army – was accompanied by an officer-ethos which regarded military service in the ranks, except as a cadet in one of the royal companies, as socially demeaning and unacceptable.[143] As a result, the continuous loss of other ranks from their regiments in the course of a campaign left a pool of company and regimental officers, who continued to exercise their functions, even though this could mean that a serving captain, lieutenant, ensign and a couple of sergeants might command a company of only fifteen to twenty soldiers. Contemporaries would have been amused to note that one of the 'progressive' changes ascribed to the armies of the early seventeenth century was the much higher proportion of officers, supposedly required in order to execute complex drill and manoeuvres with larger numbers of smaller units.[144] In fact, a surplus of expensive officers was one of the besetting problems faced by the French army of the period.[145] As a *mémoire* for the winter quarter arrangements of 1641 emphasized: 'la plus grande despense consiste a l'entretenement d'un nombre infiny de chefz et officiers dont les régiments sont remplis'.[146] The Spanish had managed to circumvent this problem, in that the lesser nobility had long accepted the principle of serving as gentleman rankers, and surplus officers could be kept in the ranks as *particulares* until such time as a military expansion permitted them

---

[142] H. de Besse, *Relation des campagnes de Rocroi et de Fribourg* (Paris, 1673; reprinted 1826), p. 98.

[143] Despite a widely held, but false, assumption amongst earlier historians that all military service was considered honourable: for instance, A. Babeau, *La vie militaire sous l'Ancien Régime* (2 vols.; Paris, 1890), II. 14.

[144] Roberts, 'Military revolution', p. 197; even an exponent of Orangist reforms such as Jacobi of Wallhausen was sceptical about the reduction in the effective size of infantry units, precisely because it would lead to an increase in the number of serving officers, the putative military advantages of which would be outweighed by high costs: *L'art militaire pour l'infanterie*, p. 102.

[145] Attempts could be made to dismiss all the 'superfluous' officers in a regiment whose strength had declined substantially, but this could mean wasting the military talents of a pool of relatively experienced soldiers, and further reinforcing the officers' perception of an essentially exploitative relationship between themselves and the crown: SHAT A^1 5oii, fo. 262, 22 Feb. 1638, order for the dismissal of all the surplus officers from the *régiment réformé* of Suze; A^1 68, fo. 520, 12 Mar. 1642, similar for superfluous officers of regt of Tavannes.

[146] AAE MD 841, fo. 221 (n.d. 1641). The *mémoire* goes on to propose that 50 per cent of the officers should be sent home over the winter quarter to reduce the financial burden on the local populations forced to support the garrisons. The recognition that the officers forced up the costs of the army-corps without increasing military effectiveness was widespread; see, for example, La Valette's comment to Chavigny about the costs of the army of Italy in 1638, greatly augmented by the officers 'qui sont tousjours presents quoy qu'il ny ait que des valets dans leurs compagnies': AAE CP Savoie 26, fo. 607, 9 Nov. 1638.

The military context

to resume officerships.¹⁴⁷ In contrast, the French officers' reluctance to serve in the ranks had been identified as a problem by François de La Noue in his *Discours politiques et militaires* back in the 1580s, and the situation had not changed by the 1630s.¹⁴⁸ A further attraction of foreign mercenary regiments with their substantially larger companies, was that they employed far fewer officers to begin with, and for the most part therefore avoided the situation of large numbers of company officers presiding over declining numbers of soldiers. Cardinal de La Valette wrote to *secrétaire d'Etat* Chavigny in 1639 about the advantages of enlarging the German regiment of colonel Schmidtberg: 'si on peut obliger Schmidtberg a mettre son régiment a 2,000, cela espargne au Roy le payement de beaucoup d'officiers[,] les françois ne peuvent faire deux mille hommes qu'en quatre régiments . . . Je dis la mesme chose des autres régiments estrangers, et c'est la methode dont se servent les ennemis pour espargner le payement.'¹⁴⁹ The year before he had written that the cost of the 6,000 infantry in twenty-two regiments which he had under his command in Italy was as great as 15,000 men in fifteen regiments would have been, since the latter would have involved significantly fewer officers.¹⁵⁰

Yet the financial logic of larger regiments composed of larger individual companies could not change the underlying reality of an army in which the units were becoming smaller, not because of any conscious tactical imperative but because of the high rates of attrition and the difficulty of ensuring that stipulated recruitment actually took place. The average company size, which according to Kroener stood at 42.16 men over the five years from 1635 to 1640 had shrunk to 21.57 men per company between 1641 and 1647;¹⁵¹ despite recognition of the problem, the French army grew increasingly over-officered, and the main result of this was simply to raise overall military costs.

A WAR OF SIEGES

How far were French field commanders influenced by tactical theory or shared European experience in the fighting of battles? The relative silence of archives and memoirs on this subject is remarkable. One or two of the tactical theorists spend time discussing ideal orders of battle. The *maréchal de bataille*, d'Aurignac,

---

[147] Parker, *Army of Flanders*, pp. 40–1. The surrender of the town of Elna in Roussillon to the French in 1641 revealed a Spanish garrison of 1,200 in which 28 captains and 28 ensigns were supplemented by 250 *officiers réformés (particulares)* serving as rankers: AAE MD 1633, fo. 463, 3 July 1641; an account of the Spanish failure to relieve Collioure, described in the royal edict creating Philippe de La Mothe-Houdancourt a *maréchal*, stresses the particular significance of the French triumph in that the Spanish relieving force was an elite corps, composed substantially of *officiers réformés*: MD 842, fo. 131, 2 Apr. 1642.
[148] La Noue, *Discours*, p. 274.
[149] AAE CP Savoie 28, fo. 3, first days of Jan. 1639.
[150] AAE CP Savoie 26, fo. 422, 10 Aug. 1638, La Valette to Chavigny.
[151] Kroener, 'Die Entwicklung der Truppenstärken', pp. 172–8.

The French art of war during Richelieu's ministry

writing his *livre de guerre* in 1663, makes some basic points about a classic order of battle from the period of Richelieu and Mazarin, stressing that the army should be drawn up in two lines and a reserve, the first and second line being 300 paces apart, the second line and the reserve 600 paces. Some reserve units may be placed between the first and second lines to replace units suffering casualities or to shore up weak points. Aurignac stipulates that the reserve must be ready to support the left wing of the front line, which will always be placed under heavy pressure by the enemy's right.[152] All contemporaries take it as axiomatic that the infantry occupy the centre of both first and second lines, while the cavalry hold position on the flanks, though various opinions allow the possibility of deploying platoons of musketeers between the squadrons of cavalry, or deploying small groups of *dragons* or *carabins* betwen the infantry *bataillons* in the centre.[153] Setting aside these rather formulaic examples, neither in tactical theory nor in military reality is a great deal of time spent discussing the deployment of soldiers for battles or strategems in the field. The limited role allocated to the pitched battle in tactical theory was also evident outside of France, but was by no means universal; Raimondo Montecuccoli's treatise *Sulle Battaglie*, probably composed between 1639 and 1642 and written directly out of his experience in the Imperial army during the Thirty Years War, provides a detailed and exhaustive examination of preparing, fighting and exploiting field engagements quite unlike anything produced in France in the same period.[154]

The reason for this was straightforward; the French crown, its ministers and the high command were with few exceptions attuned to thinking in terms of sieges as the normal means of waging warfare. The two extremes envisaged in warfare were the large, set-piece siege, which might admittedly involve some type of pitched battle if besiegers and relieving force clashed, and the *guerre de course*, warfare consisting of limited raids into enemy territory, skirmishes with small enemy forces and attempts to establish a *de facto* domination of local territory. Sieges implied not elaborate plans for orders of battle but familiarity with a complex and extensive range of information about a form of trench warfare: the construction of double sets of circumvallations to face inwards towards the defenders and outwards towards potential relief forces; a mass of techniques for the construction of specific types of earthworks; entrenchment, mining and the

---

[152] Aurignac, ed. Azan, *Livre de guerre*, pp. 48–58. Exactly similar prescriptions for an order of battle are laid out in La Valière's *Pratique et maximes*, pp. 58–65, La Fontaine's 1675 *Devoirs militaires*, pp. 227–44, and in Louis de Gaya, *L'art de la guerre* (Paris, 1689), pp. 99–100.

[153] For the proposal to place groups of musketeers between the cavalry squadrons, see Aurignac, ed. Azan, *Livre de guerre*, p. 84; for the distribution of cavalry squadrons between infantry *bataillons* see the order of battle sketched out in BN Ms.fr. 6385, fo. 132, 3 Aug. 1635; La Fontaine, *Les devoirs militaires*, p. 231, describes how cavalry were inserted between the infantry *bataillons* of the French first line at Rocroi, and that this had a beneficial effect on the infantry. For a series of plans incorporating cavalry squadrons amongst the infantry *bataillons* in orders of battle, see Lostelneau, *Maréchal de bataille*, pp. 422–9.

[154] Barker, *Military Intellectual*, pp. 73–173, provides a translation of *Sulle Battaglie*.

mechanisms of blockade; the organization of raiding and assault parties, supply convoys and the deployment of troops across open country to guard against surprise attempts at relief. The amount of space in most contemporary military manuals devoted to all of these aspects of siege warfare far exceeds the rather perfunctory accounts of deploying an army in a standard order of battle.[155] Rohan, in *Le parfaict capitaine* – the most influential treatise of the period – was categorical that wars were no longer about battles, but about sieges.[156] This was a widely held view, despite the obvious point that a war of sieges required the prior existence of fortifications and these were in fact patchily spread through early seventeenth-century Europe. Those serving in the French high command whose military experience had been of a different type of warfare – whether in the civil wars or in the Marches of Hungary – have left no evidence of a willingness to challenge this dominant view. That war was about the defence and capture of *places* remained the all but unchallenged military orthodoxy in France both in the high command and amongst the ministers. Although a French army-corps defeated the Spanish troops of Tommaso Francesco di Savoia, prince of Carignano, at Avein on 22 May 1635, this was incidental to the army's strategic objective, which was to join forces with the Dutch and to lay siege to Louvain or Brussels; attempts to press the Spanish forces harder in the aftermath of the battle were sacrificed in favour of this bid to launch the siege of a prestigious city. From 1635 until 1642 the French war-effort was conceived in terms of sieges, and this had a profound effect on strategic thinking and military organization.

One consequence was to reinforce a style of 'dynastic warfare', a preoccupation with prestige and reputation, which saw the loss or gain of fortified *places* as an affront or boost to sovereign pride quite disproportionate to their real strategic significance. Debates about the choice of a city for a siege were frequently decided not by considerations of the importance of the *place* in terms of lines of communication or the possibility of facilitating future conquests, or even the relative ease of taking the city. Perceived prestige of the *place* was likely to prove the clinching argument, at least so far as the crown and the ministers were concerned, even when the field commanders may have favoured softer targets more likely to yield success at lower cost.[157] The conduct of major sieges after

---

[155] Du Praissac, *Discours militaires*, for example, devotes 5 pages to deployment for battles and field warfare (pp. 35–9), compared with 100 pages concerned with fortification and the conduct of sieges (pp. 40–139); La Valière's *Pratique et maximes* devotes 15 pages to deployment for battle, and 126 pages to siege warfare (pp. 57–72; pp. 73–116, 128–211).

[156] Rohan, *Parfaict capitaine*, p. 257. Ironically, it was Rohan, as commander of the French forces in the Valtelline in 1635 and 1636 who fought the largest number of battles in the field, defeating Austrian and Spanish troops at Livogno, Mazzo, Val Fraela and Morbegno. Admittedly the forces involved were not large, but the geography of the Grison territories had prevented the establishment of elaborate fortifications in more than a few locations.

[157] These issues are explicit in the debate about the target for a siege in the second half of the 1638 campaign, when the perceived prestige of Arras and Hesdin are weighed against the need to achieve a positive success to restore the king's reputation after the failure at Saint-Omer: Aubery,

The French art of war during Richelieu's ministry

1638 – Hesdin, Arras, Perpignan – became intimately linked with the personal involvement of the king in the war-effort. Resources were poured into the multiple army-corps which conducted these sieges since it became a matter of dynastic pride that a siege once begun under the leadership of the king should not be abandoned without success. There was a stark contrast between the huge military resources committed to the 'royal' siege of Arras in 1640 and the relatively meagre provision of troops and finance granted in the same year to Harcourt, general of the army of Italy. In contrast to the siege of Arras, which would have a limited effect on the ultimate outcome of the war, Harcourt used his restricted resources to organize the relief of the key fortress of Casale in April, and went on to recapture Turin for the French in September, thereby preventing the total collapse of the French position in north Italy.

In this context, it is important not to overestimate the extent to which warfare in this period was conceived in terms of *Realpolitik*. The stakes in the struggle between France and the Habsburg powers may have been high, but this does not mean that the war-effort would necessarily be fought on 'rational' principles. Dynastic assertiveness bulks large in military calculations, even when it was incompatible with the most effective use of military resources, in the same way that assumptions about the priority due to princely families in the allocation of military commands frequently deprived army-corps of the most experienced commanders.

The shortage of cavalry

One consequence of the preoccupation with sieges was a tendency to reinforce an order of priorities for military resources informed by a notion of dynastic warfare; another consequence was far more immediately serious. Siege warfare, it was generally agreed, was infantry warfare. Cavalry were considered of limited use in a siege army; its main purposes were to escort convoys of supplies and munitions, to counter enemy raiding parties and to see off attempts to organize relief by surprise, none of which required an especially numerous force. Speaking of the campaign in Italy in September 1638, Bernard, duke of Saxe-Weimar and military contractor in French service, suggested that Henri II d'Orléans, duc de Longueville, could be relieved of almost all his cavalry as he would be committed to a war of sieges in northern Italy in which they would be of limited use.[158]

Believing that they were committed to a war of sieges, the crown and its

---

Richelieu, II. 212–13 (9 Aug.) 1638, 'mémoire secret envoyé de la part du Roy audit maréchal de Châtillon'.

[158] BN Ms.fr. 3767, fo. 98, 22 Sept. 1638, Saxe-Weimar to Louis XIII: Saxe-Weimar stated that Longueville possesses 5,000 cavalry 'inutilles dans la Savoye', of which Saxe-Weimar could easily be sent 3,000; d'Hémery, present in Italy, had made the same comment to Chavigny two years earlier: 'L'Italie estant d'un autre nature que l'Allemagne [-] extremement estroit et remply de places fortes': AAE CP Savoie 24, fo. 660, 23 July 1636.

The military context

ministers assumed that the main effort in recruitment after 1635 should be infantry. Some sense of the relatively low priority given to the recruitment of cavalry can be seen from the allocations of funding for 1635: against a provision for the payment of *montres* sufficient to recruit a total of 115,000 infantry throughout the campaign, the *bureau des finances* allocated funds for the total recruitment of only 9,500 cavalry. And the relatively small numbers of cavalry raised in the first years of war after 1635 can be seen in practice from the various composite *revues* of the armies: an *état* of the corps serving in Germany under the command of François de l'Hospital, seigneur du Hallier, during 1637 gave its strength at 10,250 infantry and 1,440 cavalry, while maréchal Châtillon's army operating on the eastern frontier was of 11,700 infantry and 1,980 cavalry.[159]

In this priority given to recruitment of infantry, the French crown was out of touch with military developments amongst the other combatants in the Thirty Years War. For a number of reasons the other major belligerents had progressively increased the proportions of cavalry in their armies from the early 1630s. Even in those areas which were heavily encrusted with modern siege works it was not considered that cavalry were useless. On the contrary, in the manoeuvring and movement of troops which might precede the decision to settle down to undertake a siege, cavalry played a vital role, as they did in organizing disruptive raids deep into enemy territory so that a besieging army might weaken itself by sending some of its troops to counter them. As systems of orderly contributions and other mechanisms for the supply of armies came under increasing strain in territories that had been fought over for decades, so cavalry, with its greater capacity for foraging and requisitioning at distances from the army, became an even more attractive option. Finally, if and when troops were drawn into a pitched battle, whether in open territory or in the vicinity of a siege, it became increasingly clear that the battle-winning arm was not the infantry, but the cavalry. Veteran infantry, drawn up in defensive positions in the centre of an army, were virtually invulnerable to direct frontal assault. The typical means to break a deadlock in the centre of the battlefield was the use of cavalry operating on the flanks: having broken through the opposing horse in the enemy army, the cavalry could destabilize the central core of infantry by a rapid and disorienting attack on their flank or the rear.[160] As a result of all these factors, cavalry came to play an increasingly important role in the armies of France's enemies and allies. The army of Fernando, the Cardinal Infante, which invaded Picardy and Champagne in 1636 consisted of 10,000–12,000 infantry and 13,000 horse, and it was squadrons of light cavalry, the 'croats', who sowed panic by raiding as far as the outskirts of

---

[159] AAE MD 828, fos. 279v, 273 (1637).
[160] D. Parrott, 'Strategy and tactics in the Thirty Years War: the "military revolution"', *Militärgeschichtliche Mitteilungen*, 18 (1985), 7–25, at 13–15 (reprinted in Rogers (ed.), *The Military Revolution Debate*, pp. 227–51).

Paris in August.[161] In 1639 the Swedish army of Banér was given at approximately 15,400 infantry and 15,000 cavalry,[162] while if the regiments of the Imperial army were taken at full theoretical strength, in 1635 the total army would consist of 61,000 infantry and 39,500 cavalry.[163]

This structural shift in the main armies of the Thirty Years War had become well established by the time of France's full commitment to war, and the consequence became rapidly apparent from a chorus of dismay amongst the high command of the French army-corps who found themselves critically short of cavalry.[164] The first response was a straightforward decision to allow regiments of cavalry to be raised. Hitherto, and unlike the situation in other European armies, cavalry had only been recruited at the level of individual companies, and this appears to have imposed restraints on the number of commissions issued. The king and his ministers had feared that many of those who would enjoy the prestige and status of being *mestres de camp* of a cavalry regiment would not in fact be able to afford the extremely high costs of maintaining such a unit in the inevitable circumstances of delayed and inadequate support from the centre. They were equally concerned that the strong tradition of autonomous command amongst the cavalry captains could lead to severe problems of discipline and control. As so often, practical necessity overrode organizational scruples, and the first commissions were despatched for the levy of cavalry regiments of 500 horse in June 1635, the accompanying letters stressing that the decision was a direct response to the great need for cavalry in the campaign theatres.[165] In an attempt to ensure that the authority of the *mestres de camp* would be respected, the initial commissions were issued to individuals of high social status – for example, Ambroise-François,

---

[161] AAE MD 821, fo. 106, 25 July 1636; M. Poëte, *Paris devant la menace étrangère en 1636* (Paris, 1916), pp. 309–11. Frenchmen confronted with the invasion were specifically concerned by the very substantial number of cavalry in the Spanish army: Poëte, *Paris*, p. 145. R. Stradling, 'Spain's military failure and the supply of horses, 1600–1660', *History*, 69 (1984), 212–14 (repr. in Stradling, *Spain's Struggle for Europe* (London, 1994)), provides evidence of Spanish discussions about the need to build up the cavalry component of their army before invading France.

[162] AAE CP Lorraine 31, fo. 169, 29 June 1639, *état* of the army of Banér sent to Chavigny by M. de St Aubin.

[163] Pohl, *Profiantierung der keyserlichen Armaden*, pp. 25–7; Pohl points out that these are in no sense 'real' figures, and discusses at length the problems of arriving at any accurate notion of the size of the Imperial army, but for the purposes of establishing the relative importance of the cavalry – some 40 per cent of the army – the figures are useful.

[164] AAE CP Lorraine 15, fo. 82, 8 Feb. 1635, Rohan to Chavigny, emphasizing that the duke of Lorraine's army numbered 7,000–8,000 infantry and 6,000 cavalry, and that the French cavalry was hopelessly outnumbered; AAE CP Lorraine 25, fo. 172, 22 Apr. 1635, La Force to Richelieu.

[165] L. Susane, *Histoire de la cavalerie française* (3 vols.; Paris, 1874), I. 90–7; H. Choppin, *Les origines de la cavalerie française: organization régimentaire de Richelieu, la cavalerie Weimarienne, le régiment de Gassion* (Paris and Nancy, 1905), p. 147, dates the creation to May but lists the first regiments; SHAT A¹ 24, fo. 412, 23 June 1635, Servien to Honoré d'Albert, duc de Chaulnes, emphasizing that the creation of regiments was a response to the high priority being given to the recruitment of cavalry.

The military context

marquis de Bournonville and Timoléon d'Espinay, maréchal de Saint-Luc.[166] But from the outset the cavalry regiments proved particularly ill-disciplined, while financial shortfalls confronted the *mestres de camp* with the prospect of meeting wage and subsistence bills far greater than those involved in supporting an infantry regiment.[167] The experiment limped into 1636; a flurry of new regiments were created at the beginning of the campaign, again placed mostly in the hands of those whose social prestige it was hoped would curb the worst indiscipline.[168] However, in late September the project was finally abandoned; a royal ordinance frankly admitted that the experiment of cavalry regiments under *mestres de camp* had been a failure, and that in future the independent companies would simply be grouped together in tactical *escadres* under the temporary command of the most senior captain.[169]

The concern about inadequate cavalry was even more marked in the 1636 campaign, above all in Picardy and Champagne, where the Spanish invasion force with its massive cavalry contingent encountered almost no effective resistance.[170] Even before the campaign began, reports from the north-eastern frontier had emphasized the damage and demoralization being caused by raiding parties of up to 2,000 Spanish cavalry, forces which could only be opposed by comparable numbers of mounted soldiers.[171] North Italy, because of its fortifications, was judged to be primarily territory for infantry, yet from 1636 the commanders and ministerial agents began to complain of the shortage of cavalry and the problems this posed in any confrontation with the Spanish.[172]

---

[166] SHAT A¹ 24, fos. 410, 411, 23 June 1635, letters to Bournonville and Espinay. In early August, Condé received a commission for a regiment of cavalry, to deliver to 'whoever he judged capable of levying such a unit', and was notified of a further such commission despatched to his son, the duc d'Enghien: A¹ 25, fo. 180, 4 Aug. 1635. J. de Chastenet de Puységur, *Les guerres de Louis XIII et Louis XIV* (2 vols.; Paris, 1883), I. 194, emphasizes that the primary concern in choosing high-ranking nobles for the commissions was to attempt to ensure that they had some authority over the constituent company captains.

[167] SHAT A¹ 25, fo. 249, 25 Aug. 1635, Servien to Louis-Emmanuel de Valois, comte d'Alais, *colonel général de la cavalerie légère*, complaining of the endemic levels of indiscipline in the cavalry, and especially the problems of controlling the assertive behaviour of captains in the new regiments. In late June the *maréchal de camp*, Charles de Sourdis, marquis d'Alluye, had been sent to take command of the cavalry with the army of La Force to try to impose some discipline: A¹ 24, fo. 445, 29 June; Choppin, *Les origines*, p. 149.

[168] SHAT A¹ 32, pce 251, 1636, commission for the post of *mestre de camp lieutenant* and first captain of the regiment of Gaston, duc d'Orléans; A¹ 27, fo. 221, 8 Apr. 1636, regts of cavalry of Charles de Sourdis and Armand de Caumont, marquis de La Force. The hope that commanders of high standing would control insubordinate captains was no more justified in this campaign than the last; the maréchal de Brézé reported that during the Spanish invasion of Picardy the small numbers of French cavalry were further constrained by the disagreements between the *mestres de camp* and the *vieux capitaines*: AAE MD 821, fo. 105, 4 July 1636, Brézé to Richelieu.

[169] SHAT A¹ 29, fo. 270, 21 Sept. 1636.

[170] AAE MD 821, 7 July 1636, Soissons to Chavigny, reporting that Roye fell to a detachment of the Spanish army that included 5,000 cavalry, and that the French had only 150 horse to oppose them.

[171] AAE MD 1678, fo. 29, 9 Mar. 1636, Soissons to Richelieu.

[172] AAE CP Savoie 24, fos. 315, 340v, 342, 28 Apr., 1 May, 2 May 1636, d'Hémery to Richelieu, who

The French art of war during Richelieu's ministry

It was in the context of this shortage in both 1635 and 1636 that the attempts to raise the old feudal *ban* and *arrière-ban* should be understood – as another initiative to remedy the imbalance of cavalry against infantry without contemplating fundamental changes in the allocation of funding. It was assumed that noble fief-holders, not already in arms, who were summoned to serve the king in his armies for the prescribed forty days of service, would consider themselves honour-bound to appear with full military equipment and, as befitted their noble rank, mounted.[173] This would provide a convenient solution to the scarcity of regular cavalry as large numbers of local nobles, trained during adolescence to manage weapons on horseback, would pour into the armies on the frontiers. Richelieu, faced with the inadequate provision of cavalry for the armies on the eastern frontier in 1635, wrote optimistically that 'dans le 20e de ce mois Ms d'Angoulesme et de La Force seront fortiffiez du régiment de cavalerie de Matignon et de plus de 2,500 gentilshommes'.[174]

But it was already clear by the end of the 1635 campaign that the *ban et arrière-ban* was a failure in this primary objective of increasing the quantities of cavalry at the disposal of the commanders. Impoverished lesser nobles were reluctant to equip themselves adequately; *a fortiori*, they were unwilling or unable to provide an expensive horse for service.[175] Many simply ignored the summons, despite the crown's threats to confiscate fiefs and to impose liability for taxes; but even those nobles who did come to the armies did not feel bound to appear adequately equipped; their horses, if these were brought at all, were inadequate even by the flexible standards of the military administration. The attrition-rate of the gentlemen assembled under the *arrière-ban* was so high that the forty days of service, which might otherwise have been a limitation on the activities of commanders, proved irrelevant; almost all of the fief-holders had retired well before the expiry of their term.[176]

---

pointed out that even if the troops were assembled as expected, the army would consist of 15,000–16,000 infantry and only 1,300 cavalry, while the Spanish had been substantially strengthening the cavalry element of their north Italian army.

[173] For the medieval background to the *ban* and *arrière-ban* and its evolution, see P. Contamine, *Guerre, état et société à la fin du moyen âge. Etudes sur les armées des rois de France, 1337–1494* (Paris, 1972), pp. 26–38; G.A. de La Roque, *Traité de la noblesse, de ses différentes espèces . . . et du ban et arrière-ban* (Rouen, 1734); G. Daniel, *Histoire de la milice françoise* (2 vols.; Paris, 1721), II. 489–96; Boutaric, *Les institutions militaires*, pp. 349–54.

[174] BN Ms.fr. 6645, fo. 88, 11 Aug. 1635, Richelieu to cardinal de La Valette. The king's army, notionally to be assembled around Saint-Dizier at this time (though in fact it never came into existence) was projected to have an additional 5,000 *gentilshommes* from the *arrière-ban*: fo. 104, 28 Aug., Servien to La Valette.

[175] AAE MD 254, fo. 178, 18 Oct. 1635, Charles de La Porte de La Meilleraye to Richelieu, complaining about the quality of the *arrière-ban*; SHAT A¹ 26, pce 99, 1 Nov. 1635, order to disband the *noblesse* of the *arrière-ban* of Poitou, heartily condemned for the feebleness of their commitment – only seventy men responded to the convocation, the majority serving as substitutes for fief-holders, and the quality of equipment and horses was totally inadequate.

[176] AAE MD 815, fo. 311, 7 Oct. 1635, Chavigny to Richelieu, reports that the king finds it difficult to believe that the *noblesse* (of the *arrière-ban*) could have behaved with such *lâcheté*, but those

The military context

Despite the discouraging experience of 1635 the experiment was repeated in the following campaign, though with greater hesitancy. There were a number of cancellations of summonses and also various local initiatives to try to commute the *arrière-ban* into a levy to raise ordinary cavalry units.[177] In the event it was clear, once again, that the patchy response, the limited period of service, and the inadequate mounts and equipment of those who did appear with the armies, rendered this a wholly inadequate substitute for additional 'regular' cavalry.[178]

The lack of success, both in raising regiments of cavalry and in using the *ban et arrière-ban* as a source of additional mounted troops, emphasized the gravity of the problem. In late 1637 a *projet de la cavallerie* drawn up for Richelieu emphasized the worsening situation, and pointed out that inadequate funding for the recruitment and maintenance of the cavalry during the campaigns was leading the captains to try to recoup their expenses by laying off all their experienced troops at the end of the campaign, collecting the sums allocated to the company for the winter quarters and re-forming the unit out of totally inexperienced troops in the spring.[179] The most attractive possibility for improving the number and the quality of the cavalry – buying foreign regiments into French service – was too expensive as a general solution.[180] The *arrière-ban* was once again revived in 1638 and in the subsequent campaigns, but it had effectively become a tax, aimed at obtaining a small number of *noblesse* who would actually serve with the armies in regular cavalry units, supported by the great majority of fief-holders who would be assessed in lieu of service.[181] In 1639 the *ordonnance* for the convocation

---

informed that they were to join the army of La Force simply deserted *en masse*. If the *noblesse* had not disbanded, the army would have contained 3,000 cavalry.

[177] SHAT A¹ 27, fo. 403, 17 May 1636, orders for the convocation of the *arrière-ban*; A¹ 27, fo. 443, 29 May, cancellation of the *arrière-ban* in the *sénéchaussées* of Haute and Basse Marche; A¹ 29, fo. 118, 24 July, negotiations of Jacques II de Beauvau, seigneur de Rivau, *lieutenant général* in Haut-Poitou, to raise a company of *chevaux légers* in place of the local *arrière-ban*, choosing the most suitable *noblesse*, and allowing the others to contribute to the costs of the company. A later letter to Rivau from the Council recognized his efforts and deplored the reluctance and ill-will of the 'contribuables aux ban et arrière-ban' towards the scheme: AAE MD 821, fo. 281 (1636).

[178] The only group of *noblesse* who appear to have satisfied the crown were those raised towards the end of the campaign by the duc de Longueville in Normandy, and these had been given the fullest guarantees that they would serve less than forty days and would not be forced across the frontiers; moreover, they were engaged in the attempt to push the Spanish out of Picardy, an objective which, for many Norman landowners, was clearly in their own interests: AAE MD 821, fo. 329, 28 Sept. 1636, Richelieu to Longueville; SHAT A¹ 30, fo. 337, 27 Nov. 1636, Louis XIII to the *noblesse* of Normandy, expressing his satisfaction with their service.

[179] AAE MD 828, fo. 362 (1637).

[180] The notional costs of a foreign cavalry regiment were not necessarily higher than those of a French one, but the possibilities of transferring some of the costs of recruitment and maintenance to the foreign colonel were far more restricted. In 1634, when the size of the army was more manageable, Richelieu had discussed the advantages of recruiting all of the cavalry abroad: Avenel, IV. 312, 21 June 1634.

[181] AAE MD 832, fo. 112 (late 1638), 'pour rendre la cavallerie meilleure'; P. Deyon, 'The French nobility and absolute monarchy in the first half of the seventeenth century', in P.J. Coveney (ed), *France in Crisis, 1620–1675* (London, 1977), pp. 235–6.

The French art of war during Richelieu's ministry

insisted that the service should be provided in the form of infantry, both discouraging fief-holders from serving in person, but also recognizing the limited sums to be obtained from commutation of service compared to the costs of maintaining cavalry.[182]

Whatever the *arrière-ban* was meant to achieve by the later 1630s, generating additional cavalry had ceased to be its goal. In 1638 the crown returned to the creation of cavalry regiments. The obvious disadvantages of larger units of cavalry had not been overcome, but the need for more cavalry remained, and the earlier unsatisfactory experiment had to be resumed.[183] The cavalry regiments remained a great deal smaller than their infantry counterparts, even allowing that the average strength of these latter was declining. The *états* of 1638 show all of the *cavalerie légère* organized into regiments, typically of six companies each, and with an average strength at the pre-campaign musters of 400 *maîtres*.[184] The proportion of cavalry in the French armies gradually increased: the planned strength of the army of the maréchal de Brézé in 1638, for example, was to be 12,250 infantry and 4,050 cavalry, while that of the duc de Longueville was to have 13,800 infantry and 3,560 cavalry. These numbers of cavalry were still well below the proportion of cavalry in the armies of France's allies and enemies, though by 1641 an *état* of the army of Italy gave a total of 10,855 infantry and 7,261 cavalry – when the cavalry units of the duchess of Savoy were included.[185] If this was indicative of a real change of policy on the part of the crown and its ministers, it came just in time: Rocroi was a decisive victory won by the French cavalry led by the duc d'Enghien. Had the French cavalry not been strong and confident enough to break through the Spanish horse of the left flank, the outcome of a battle dependent upon the qualities of the respective infantries was far less likely to have been a French victory.[186]

The French armies and their artillery

Although the French ministers and high command were preoccupied by siege warfare, this did not, paradoxically, lead to a great development in the quality and quantity of artillery in the armies. Letters from 1635 drew attention to the grave shortage of artillery in both the armies of cardinal de La Valette and the maréchal

---

[182] SHAT A¹ 52, fos. 18, 154, 295, 2, 14 and 31 May 1639, letters concerning this convocation and the commutation into infantry service.

[183] Choppin, *Les origines*, pp. 194–208, takes a positive view of this 1638 return to regimental organization, based upon an optimistic reading of the practical effects of legislation; Susane, *Histoire de la cavalerie française*, I. 98–100, notes in contrast that disorders were rife in these new cavalry regiments during 1638.

[184] AAE MD 832, fos. 1 *et seq.*, (1638) *états des trouppes en 1638*.

[185] AAE MD 841, fos. 229, 230 (1641), 'état abregé de la revue qui a esté faite aux regimens d'infanterie et de cavallerie de l'armée d'Italie'.

[186] Aumale, *Princes de Condé*, IV. 105–6; Stradling, 'Spain's military failure and the supply of horses', 213.

de La Force.[187] The situation for the corps campaigning in Lorraine was no better in 1640, when du Hallier complained of the absence of artillery and supporting services.[188] In 1638 the *états* of the army of Italy indicated a strength of 9,000–10,000 infantry, 3,000 cavalry and a total of five artillery pieces.[189] Two years later, in February 1640, Harcourt reported that the total serviceable field artillery for the army of Italy consisted of only four 'moyennes', cannon firing a ten to twelve pound shot.[190] Even the major siege armies were surprisingly short of artillery: the combined forces of La Meilleraye, Châtillon and La Force assembled for the siege of Câtelet at the end of August 1638 possessed fourteen siege cannon and four lighter 'moyennes'.[191] Nor had the situation much changed by the end of the ministry; at the battle of Rocroi the French army of the duc d'Enghien possessed only twelve cannon.[192]

These extremely small numbers of artillery are in striking contrast to the forces of France's allies and enemies. In April 1632, at the crossing of the Lech, when Gustavus Adolphus' army was advancing down into Bavaria, the Swedish assault was supported by a total of ninety cannon, while in 1639 Banér's Swedish army was reported to total 18,000 troops and eighty cannon.[193] The Imperial army under Matthias Gallas which invaded Burgundy in 1636 was said to consist of some 25,000–30,000 troops and forty-two cannon, while the Spanish invasion of Picardy earlier in the year made great use of lighter cannon 'qu'ils mettoit parmi les bataillons' in the fashion of Swedish regimental artillery.[194]

A number of explanations for this relative weakness of the French artillery can be suggested.

One major problem was presented by the limited capacity to found cannon within France. Arms manufacturing was extremely underdeveloped, and an inability to meet more than a small part of the demand for artillery from domestic production was matched by a lack of expertise or willingness to risk innovation in

---

[187] AAE CP Lorraine 25, fos. 250, 252, 16, 18 June 1635, Servien to La Valette, La Force to Richelieu.
[188] AAE CP Lorraine 31, fo. 410, 3 Sept. 1640.
[189] AAE CP Savoie 26, fo. 236, 26 May 1638, d'Hémery to Richelieu.
[190] AAE CP Savoie 30, fo. 111, 28 Feb. 1640, Harcourt to de Noyers.
[191] AAE MD 831, fo. 106, 27 Aug. 1638, de Noyers to Chavigny; the letter does explain that further artillery pieces might be brought up from Péronne, Corbie and St Quentin, but it none the less emphasizes the extremely small number of artillery specifically allocated to joint army-corps which, on paper, totalled over 40,000 troops.
[192] Aumale, *Princes de Condé*, IV. 82–3. La Barre Duparcq, *L'art militaire*, pp. 22–4, proposes that the French army had twenty cannon on the field, but Aumale's well-documented chapter on Rocroi is more reliable.
[193] Roberts, *Gustavus Adolphus*, II. 261; Pappenheim is alleged to have attributed the Swedish victory at Breitenfeld in significant part to the superior firepower of Swedish artillery: B. Stadler, *Pappenheim und die Zeit des Dreißigjährigen Krieges* (Winterthur, 1991), p. 552; this was also the opinion of Monro, *Monro his expedition*, II. 65–7. For the report on Banér's army in 1639 see Griffet, *Louis XIII*, III. 211.
[194] AAE CP Allemagne 14, fo. 198, Nov. 1636, 'relation de ce qui s'est passé despuis l'entrée des ennemis en Bourgogne'; AAE MD 1678, fo. 124, 24 July 1636, marquis de La Force to Chavigny.

the type and design of artillery manufactured.[195] This reluctance to contemplate innovation may be less surprising when the French government was confronted with projects such as that put forward in 1635 by an Italian manufacturer and – presumably – financial adventurer, Piero Leoni, for the construction of 'leather guns' capable of firing a twelve pound shot. Leather guns firing shot of one quarter of this weight had been abandoned by Gustavus Adolphus of Sweden after a brief trial, and even the contemporary French commentator, while impressed by the savings that the innovation appeared to offer, doubted whether such leather guns could really deliver comparable performance.[196] Most of the French artillery was bought from Dutch, English or Scandinavian foundries; this further increased the costs of what was already an exceptionally expensive military commodity.[197]

Even more important, the demand for artillery came from three directions: the armies, fortifications and the navy. The primary consumer of newly founded artillery was Richelieu's expanding Atlantic navy, while the extensive fortifications at Le Havre, Brouage and Brest created a further heavy demand. Richelieu's nomination of his cousin, Charles de La Porte de La Meilleraye, to the office of *grand maître de l'artillerie* in 1634 specifically ensured that the cardinal would take priority in the commissioning and allocation of artillery for naval purposes, and may well have contributed to an inadequate provision for the armies.[198] Moreover, a large part of the artillery which was potentially available to the armies had to be removed from fortifications, which involved further difficulties. Governors of *places* were never happy to hand over the guns to local field commanders. The great developments in fortification, the proliferation of the *trace italienne* in the sixteenth and seventeenth centuries, had generated a theoretical need for defensive artillery far greater than any state could afford to supply. Most governors in possession of sets of reconstructed walls, multiple bastions and citadels found that they had to defend these with a fraction of the artillery which would ideally have been required to provide covering fire against a besieging army.[199] This led to frequent disputes, as for example in 1634 when the governor of Nancy, Jean de Gallard de Béarn, comte de Brassac, simply refused to allow any of his artillery to be removed to meet the needs of La Force's field army. In this case Brassac's

---

[195] See, for example, AAE MD 819, fo. 41 (1635), *advis sur les fontes de l'artillerie*, concerned with the inadequate quality and reliability of French-founded artillery, essentially because of the poor-quality metal being used.

[196] AAE MD 819, fo. 54 (1635), *Mémoire au Roi par Pierre Leoni*. For Gustavus Adolphus' abandonment by 1629 of thin-barrelled guns wrapped in leather, see Roberts, *Gustavus Adolphus*, II. 232.

[197] A report on certain pieces of artillery made in Sweden, presumably as examples to serve as the basis of a larger contract, makes the point that while good, they are 'bien plus cher' than cannon from other sources: AAE MD 819, fo. 53 (1635).

[198] For the consequences of this family *politique* applied to the artillery, see chapter 9, pp. 475–7.

[199] S. Pepper and N. Adams, *Firearms and Fortifications. Military Architecture and Siege Warfare in Sixteenth-Century Siena* (Chicago, 1986), pp. 23–4.

The military context

refusal was upheld by the *grand maître*, and the artillery was obtained instead from the more pliant governors of Châlons and Verdun.[200] In some cases the artillery defending fortifications was so meagre that removing some of the cannon for field service would leave the *places* virtually without firepower. The three *places* which surrendered to the Spanish in 1636, La Capelle, Câtelet and Corbie, possessed totals respectively of six, four and seven cannon of varying weights.[201] When artillery could be requisitioned from fortifications, it was frequently mounted on carriages so dilapidated that they needed to be rebuilt before the cannon could be moved, or the cannon were mounted on purpose-built gun carriages only intended for stationary pieces mounted in bastions.[202]

Within the armies themselves the demand for artillery was divided between the needs of siege warfare, assumed to be the more typical requirement, and for a field artillery to add weight to the firepower of French forces in battle. The French armies were accompanied by relatively heavy guns, firing six to a more frequent twelve, sixteen or twenty-four pound shot. While some of these may have been built as siege guns, cast with thicker barrels and mounted on stronger frames to sustain the heavier charges of powder used to propel shot against fortifications, in practice the artillery seems to have been indiscriminately mixed between these and guns manufactured to a lower specification.[203] Whichever type of artillery, the issue of overall weight may have influenced commanders trying to decide on an optimum number of pieces to take on campaign, assuming that these were available from artillery parks or neighbouring fortifications.[204] All the available types of cannon required teams of draught animals for transport, and a shortage of artillery horses was one of the constant problems of campaigning in this period. The gun team for a heavy cannon needed up to thirty draught horses, and there was little point in making demands for substantial numbers of cannon if the army was allocated a mere 400 horses to transport the guns, the munitions and the gun

---

[200] AAE CP Lorraine 14, fo. 518, 3 June 1634, La Force to Bouthillier. A similar long-running dispute over the provision of artillery for campaigns can be found between the governors of Casale and Pinerolo and the successive commanders of the army of Italy throughout the later 1630s: AAE CP Savoie 26, fo. 143, 24 Apr. 1638.

[201] AAE MD 1676, fo. 479 (end 1635), extrait de l'inventaire de l'artillerie de Picardie.

[202] AAE MD 832, fo. 74 (1638/9) project for the preparations necessary for the artillery in 1639, includes the reconstruction of gun carriages as the highest priority; SHAT A^1 51, fo. 4bis, 2 Mar. 1639, lieutenant of the artillery to travel to *places* in Guyenne and Languedoc and to requisition artillery for the army being assembled, seeing that gun carriages are constructed and repaired where necessary.

[203] AAE MD 819, fo. 50 (1635), *état de l'artillerie*, which makes this intermixing obvious. The crown was obliged to issue an instruction in 1641 that the artillery officers should not overcharge the artillery with gunpowder, suggesting regular confusion between siege and field deployment: SHAT A^1 65, fo. 353, 10 Aug., Louis XIII to La Meilleraye.

[204] AAE MD 806, fo. 249 (1632) gives some weights for cannon, culverines, *bâtardes* and *moyennes*: the lightest, the *moyenne*, still weighed 2,890 pounds with its carriage, while the heavier cannon weighed in at 7,867 pounds.

crews.²⁰⁵ Thus to an even greater extent than shortage of artillery pieces themselves, the principal cause of complaint and appeals to the ministers against the *grand maître* and his agents concerned the inadequacy of the supply of artillery horses, their poor quality and the consequent high rates of wastage.²⁰⁶ Attempts to levy such horses ran into competition from the cavalry, and from the demands of *munitionnaires* requiring transport for grain waggons. A royal edict of 1636 concerned with abuses and corruption amongst the artillery officers was entirely focused upon financial irregularities involved in the procurement and upkeep of artillery horses.²⁰⁷ The problem of providing adequate transportation for the artillery was further compounded by the convention that the entire *equipage* of horses, waggons and teamsters would be dismissed at the end of each campaign season, to be recruited again, it was hoped, in time for the opening of the next campaign.²⁰⁸

Not merely did the French armies suffer from a comparative lack of artillery of all types, surviving evidence (or rather its absence) suggests that they failed to develop the use of light field pieces attached to individual infantry units, although such tactics have frequently been taken as the hallmark of 'military revolution' in the development of artillery.²⁰⁹ That the French developed such light 'regimental' guns has been asserted by historians since the nineteenth century, presumably on the familiar grounds that France, as the 'heir' to the military reforms of the Dutch and the Swedes, must have followed the Swedish lead in matters concerned with the artillery. Curiously, having suggested that a French 'regimental' artillery flourished after 1635, it is then equally rapidly dismissed as 'une affaire de la mode', more or less completely abandoned by 1643.²¹⁰ Quite apart from the

---

²⁰⁵ Rohan, *Parfaict capitaine*, proposes that 100 horses were required to pull a single siege gun, its equipment and enough shot and munitions for 100 rounds: p. 318; BN Ms.fr. 4561, fo. 50 (n.d.) establishes that twenty-five horses are required to pull a single campaign piece, quite apart from the munitions and provisioning of the gun team.

²⁰⁶ See, for example, AAE CP Savoie 26, fo. 169, 5 May 1638, cardinal de La Valette's complaints of totally inadequate provision of artillery horses, and his inability to take any cannon on campaign without a minimum of 400 horses, and preferably double that number to guard against inevitable sickness and loss; BN Ms.fr. 3768, fo. 12v, 2 May 1639, Schomberg to Richelieu, pleading the absence of artillery horses as a principal reason for his inability to begin campaigning.

²⁰⁷ AAE MD 823, fo. 226 (1636).

²⁰⁸ See for example, SHAT A¹ 47, fos. 131, 132 and 160, 22/26 Oct. 1638, orders for the disbandment of the artillery *equipages* of the armies of Languedoc, Champagne and Italy.

²⁰⁹ In preparation for the campaign of 1636, an extensive *état de l'artillerie* lists the cannon available at various *places* for the use of the generals, none of which fired less than a six pound shot and which was very far from being a light, mobile regimental artillery: AAE MD 819, fos. 32–3 (1635). One document of 1635 proposes as a 'secret de guerre' the construction of light cannon, easily carried by four men, but there is no evidence that these were manufactured: AAE MD 819, fo. 95 (1635).

²¹⁰ The historian most recently to emphasize this chimerical development is Lynn, 'Tactical evolution', 185; Lynn cites J. Brunet's *Histoire générale de l'artillerie française* (2 vols.; Paris, 1842), II. 57, who suggested that the 'regimental' artillery enjoyed a rapid flourishing and even more rapid decline by 1643. Brunet may have influenced L. Susane, *Histoire de l'artillerie française* (Paris, 1874), who also argues for the development of light field pieces. Neither historian provides references for these assertions.

unjustified assumptions of flexibility in manufacturing and deployment of different types of cannon which underpin this argument, an overview of the administration of the French army in this period would recognize an obvious problem in distributing artillery pieces to infantry regiments. Historically, the French artillery had grown up as a strongly autonomous institution within the army. Run by the *grand maître de l'artillerie*, it had an entirely separate personnel, independent systems of jurisdiction, and it received and disbursed its own funds. The *grand maître* had direct control over all the artillery and supporting services, just as he was directly charged with the appointment and command of his personnel. When he was not personally present with an army-corps, a *lieutenant* would be appointed to act in his place. Even if regimental field guns were recognized as a decisive factor in success on the battlefield, it would be unlikely that the complex administrative issues of control and authority could be easily resolved or, above all, that the *grand maître* would be prepared to give up his direct authority over a significant part of the artillery. But without this willingness to hand over control, the coordination of infantry and artillery at regimental level would be paralysed in the same way that a plan to place complete companies of infantry on the galleys in 1636 foundered on the conflicts and refusal of the galley and infantry captains to cooperate.[211]

Moreover, lacking supplies of good quality horses, caissons and gun teams, even the supposedly 'light regimental' artillery offered limited flexibility in coping with and exploiting rapidly shifting and developing battlefield situations.[212] Yet even these modest levels of manoeuvrability were not available to the French, and the traditional deployment of an immobile artillery lined up in front of the centre of the army remained unchanged down to Rocroi. At this battle not merely were the French guns initially overrun by the advancing Spanish infantry, but in its last stages when the *tercios viejos* had drawn themselves up in a vast rectangular formation, the French infantry were forced to launch three costly assaults before three or four cannon could be moved up across the battlefield in order to bring their firepower to bear on the Spanish.[213]

Shortage of artillery also ensured that while sieges were the characteristic form of warfare in this period, the role of artillery in these was relatively limited. Few of the French sieges of this period were brought to a conclusion because artillery bombardment had rendered the defences untenable. The great majority of sieges were ended either by the threat of starvation or by the besieged garrison's realization that they would not be relieved and that further resistance would simply harshen the terms of a final surrender. If gunpowder had a role in bringing the siege to an end, it was far more likely to be a result of its use in mining the

---

[211] A. James, 'The administration and development of the French navy and the ministry of cardinal Richelieu', PhD thesis, University of Manchester, 1997, pp. 110–13.
[212] Parrott, 'Strategy and tactics', 15–16.
[213] Aumale, *Princes de Condé*, IV. 103–17.

The French art of war during Richelieu's ministry

walls of the fortress than in an artillery bombardment.[214] The idea that concentrated firepower could shorten a siege – a concept certainly recognized by Gustavus Adolphus and his Swedish army when campaigning in north Germany and the Rhineland – does not seem to have played a part in the calculations of the French commanders during the years of Richelieu's ministry.[215]

Success and failure on the battlefield

It was earlier suggested that tactical and strategic theory, and indeed the working assumptions of the ministers and commanding officers, were shaped by the conviction that sieges were the characteristic form of early seventeenth-century warfare. Yet battles and sieges were not in fact two distinct and exclusive styles of combat; the French high command, by opting for a 'war of sieges', was not necessarily excluding the possibility of engaging in battle with the enemy. The outcomes of numerous sieges were decided by pitched battles fought between the besiegers and a relieving army. Commanders may have regarded sieges as the primary aim of their strategy, but they were forced to accept the possibility of battle as a consequence of these sieges. Battles took place when an enemy force would try to lift the blockade by engaging the French army surrounding a *place*. Or they could occur in order to save a French fortress under siege, as in 1640 when Harcourt recognized that the only way to save Casale from falling to the Spanish was to advance through Monferrato with all the troops and speed that he could muster in order to engage the Spanish in their siege works.

When it came to such battles, however, contemporary sources offer little real sense of how and why they were won or lost. Much is made in memoirs of the *furia francese*, the blind courage in assaulting enemy positions which might carry the day. Numerous cases exist of officers who would defend their independence to the point of mutiny in the army camp or on the march, yet were prepared to lead their men in suicidal attacks on prepared positions on the order of the same commanders whose authority they would have defied in more mundane matters. Henri de Campion, introspective fellow traveller of aristocratic conspirators against Richelieu, spent the 1630s as an ensign, then lieutenant, in the Normandie regiment. In late 1639 after the disastrous collapse of the army with which Henri II, duc de Condé, had been trying to relieve the French garrison at Salces in Roussillon, the decision was taken to launch the *avant-garde* of the remaining troops in an assault against fortified Spanish positions outside the fortress. All

---

[214] In 1639, for example, it was the explosion of two mines under the walls of Hesdin which persuaded the garrison to make terms: Griffet, *Louis XIII*, III. 197–99.
[215] Roberts, *Gustavus Adolphus*, II. 261. When Henri II de Condé's army arrived to conduct the siege of Dôle in the Franche-Comté in 1636, his artillery had only enough gunpowder to last for two weeks: François de Paule de Clermont, marquis de Montglat, *Mémoires*, in Petitot and Monmerqué, XLIX. 115.

those involved recognized that it would be impossible to force the Spanish lines. But Condé, under orders from the Court to relieve Salces and fearing that if he did not attempt something Richelieu would disgrace him, had resolved to throw some of his infantry units into a suicidal attack. Campion and his fellow officers in the Normandie regiment, deprived of any support from cavalry or artillery, 'et jugeâmes alors qu'on ne vouloit hasardier que nous . . . résolûmes de mourir de bonne grâce'. The assault took place, with Campion and the rest of the Normandie regiment deployed in a central *bataillon* of 800 men. At less than thirty yards from the entrenchments the Spanish discharged their artillery loaded with musket-shot together with a salvo from the first rank of their musketeers. The French grimly continued their advance, which swept up to the Spanish lines and was then, as expected, repulsed, but in its course demonstrated an extraordinary level of courage on the part of the subalterns. Of thirty-five officers involved from the Normandie regiment, twenty-nine were killed or severely wounded, while of 800 soldiers, 200 were killed and a similar number wounded. Campion reports laconically that the next day Condé retired to Narbonne and the surviving troops were moved into winter quarters. Yet such an attack, lacking any real chance of success, all too obviously a sop to Condé's frustration at the failure to relieve Salces, could none the less mobilize a level of heroism and sacrifice that would be remarkable in any combat in any period.[216]

Many other examples could be found of such collective courage and self-sacrifice in the face of heavy odds and the certainty of extremely high casualties. The association of the officer-corps with the traditional values of a warrior nobility could still serve as a rallying cry for such heroic commitment. The highest levels of physical courage were simply taken for granted amongst those who sought a career as an officer in one of the prestige regiments, and contemporary memoirs appear to provide no examples of those who betrayed this expectation.[217] Perhaps more impressively, the ordinary soldiers in these prestige regiments provide collective evidence of a similar level of courage and determination in such circumstances.

That said, such commitment, and the phenomena of the *furia francese* itself, need some qualification. For those officers who were appointed to prestigious *régiments entretenus*, whose patronage links to the high command or the Court meant that they were already an object of attention, or who envisaged a military career in which actions would vie with connections in determining promotion, the

---

[216] Campion, *Mémoires*, pp. 113–18; the official account dictated by Condé did emphasize that the infantry were so battered by this first assault 'et tellement imbuë de l'impossibilité du dessein, qu'il luy fut impossible de luy persuader un second effort': Aubery, *Richelieu*, II. 407–8.

[217] And it is these memoirs which influence the picture of combat offered, for example, in the novels of Dumas or in Rostand's *Cyrano de Bergerac*. There is no reason to doubt that, for the most part, this is a realistic presentation of the honour-code and heroism of officers in the prestige regiments; with some rhetorical embellishment it is aptly conveyed in G. d'Avenel, *Richelieu*, III. 74–5, 94, and in Babeau, *Vie militaire*, II, *passim*.

highest levels of bravery and commitment were expected and, for the most part, delivered.[218] The same assumptions probably could not be extended to the officers and men of temporary units, whose ambitions and sense of being under the gaze of the king, the *grands* or other senior officers were much more limited. The comments of cardinal de La Valette, commanding the army of Italy in 1638, that the captains and lieutenants of the newly levied regiments 'fuyent comme les soldats', and that the main concern of the unit commanders was to return to Paris, suggest considerably less fortitude.[219] And even the *officiers d'élite* and their men could find themselves in situations where panic or miscalculation could provoke a disintegration of morale and military effectiveness. The defeat at Thionville (1639) was made all the more shocking by the collapse of the Picardie regiment, which caused the breaking of the French first line and led to a general rout – greatly worsened by the refusal of the French cavalry to enter the combat.[220] The defeat of the French army at La Marfée (1641) was brought about by the reluctance, once again, of much of the French cavalry to provide adequate support for the infantry.[221] The collapse of Condé's army as it advanced into Roussillon to relieve the siege of Salces in late 1639 saw the demoralized flight of prestige regiments as well as local levies.

Moreover, a reckless, heroic and ostentatious style of military behaviour, which was essentially an extension of the values of noble individualism, could easily get out of control and become divorced from any sense of collective responsibility. On numerous occasions, cavalry successes and infantry assaults against the odds were not followed up with the disciplined consolidation which would allow the situation to be exploited to the benefit of the entire French army. Defeats were sustained in circumstances where part of the army had distinguished itself against the enemy force, gaining a local advantage but being insufficiently disciplined to exploit its potential. As such, the *furia francese* could excite criticism as much as admiration, most notoriously on the part of Richelieu, who wrote in his *Testament politique* towards the end of his ministry that: 'Il n'y a point de nation au monde si peu propre à la guerre que la nostre: la légèreté et l'impatience qu'elle a dans les moindres travaux sont deux principes qui ne se vérifient que trop.'[222] The reverse side of the coin of heroic, self-sacrificing and impulsive bravery was, according to Richelieu, a lack of resilience and acceptance of hardship, reluctance to persist after the failure of a first effort and resistance to discipline.

---

[218] J. Smith, *The Culture of Merit. Nobility, Royal Service and the Making of Absolute Monarchy in France, 1600–1789* (Ann Arbor, 1996), pp. 37–9, on the imperative of military heroism as a visible sign of 'generosity' towards the king.

[219] AAE CP Savoie 26, fo. 422, 10 Aug. 1638; CP Allemagne 12, fo. 220, 1 Aug. 1635, La Valette to Richelieu.

[220] Aubery, *Richelieu*, II. 384, 26 Nov. 1639, Louis XIII to Châtillon, detailing the companies and regiments of cavalry to be disbanded with ignominy for their cowardice at Thionville.

[221] Montglat, *Mémoires*, XLIX. 319; Aumale, *Princes de Condé*, IV. 469–70.

[222] Richelieu, *Testament politique*, pp. 296–305, (quotation p. 296).

The military context

Like so much of Richelieu's writing, these assertions need to be treated with caution. The notion that the French soldier was impulsive, heroic, but lacked the stolid endurance and discipline of the Germans or the Swiss, was a received opinion that extended back at least into the sixteenth century, when it had provided an easy justification for hiring foreign mercenaries.[223] In fact, the evidence that the French were particularly ill-suited to sustained, positional warfare – sieges that required endurance and patience – is less obvious than contemporaries, frustrated by the wider French inability to capitalize on material and numerical superiority, believed. With the glaring exception of Fuenterrabía in 1638, when the French army collapsed in the face of an ill-organized Spanish attack on the (half-completed) siege works, once the French armies established themselves and began to conduct a major siege they were, in general, at least as likely to carry it to a successful conclusion as the Dutch or the Spanish. When sieges failed, they did so not because the French troops became demoralized, listless or discontented, but because the supply system broke down (Louvain, 1635; Tarragona, 1641) or because a significantly stronger enemy army moving up to relieve the *place* threatened the besiegers with a battle fought under unfavourable circumstances if they tried to hold the fortifications (Vercelli and Saint-Omer, 1638). The prospect of taking a town and benefiting from the opportunities for plunder or ransoms, or even from the bribes that were habitually paid to the ordinary soldiers in the siege trenches to carry out dangerous actions, made siege warfare potentially more attractive than campaigning in the field. And while aspects of siege warfare could certainly be more dangerous than any battle in the field,[224] large stretches of time were spent in more mundane activity: the construction of entrenchments, expeditions to gather forage or to escort supply convoys, guard duty outside of the range of the guns of the besieged *place* – precisely the activities which in theory the French troops would abandon or neglect.

The outcome of battlefield combats between French forces and their enemies in the 1630s and 1640s cannot be explained by single causes such as the strengths and weaknesses of French 'military spirit'. An overview of the campaigns shows that a number of distinct issues could contribute to success or failure. There are certainly instances in which a decisive factor contributing to defeat appears to have been quarrels between the commanders, especially a refusal of one of the generals to permit his units within the joint army-corps to cooperate in a shared

---

[223] Wood, *The King's Army*, pp. 110–11 cites La Noue, amongst others, who suggested that the 'natural impatience' of the French made them poor soldiers. Wood goes on to argue that this was a myth in the later sixteenth century (as it was in the seventeenth), and that it was in fact the hired foreign infantry who were unsuitable for siege warfare, which was largely sustained by the native infantry (p. 113).

[224] Wood, *The King's Army*, p. 113, quotes Brantôme who suggested that 'in a single hour of a siege, you are in greater danger than in an entire day of battle'.

strategy, whether through rivalry or mutual antagonism. This *may* have been what precipitated the defeat at Fuenterrabía in 1638; it certainly contributed to the defeat at Honnecourt in 1642.[225] In this respect the commanders of the 'lesser' army-corps – Harcourt in Italy, Jean-Baptiste Budes, comte de Guébriant and later Turenne in Germany – may have had an easier time, even though they received a far less substantial portion of the available military resources, in that they did not have to struggle to assert themselves against a rival commander. Other factors influencing defeat and success in battle include the obvious issue of numerical superiority. The French greatly outnumbered the Spanish forces of Tommaso Francesco di Savoia at the victorious battle of Aveins in May 1635, but were in turn heavily outnumbered by the Imperial troops of Ottavio Piccolomini at the defeat of Thionville in 1639.[226] In the first half of 1636, thanks to the systematic reduction of forces based in Picardy and Champagne to maintain the French armies in Alsace, Lorraine and Franche-Comté, the comte de Soissons could not offer effective resistance to the Spanish invasion and fell back behind the Somme: the question of fighting qualities, morale and organization were simply irrelevant. Similarly, the forces of cardinal de La Valette were unable to prevent the fall of Vercelli in 1638.[227] But numerical superiority or inferiority cannot explain the outcomes of all engagements. As noted earlier, it was generally recognized by contemporaries that the more elite, veteran, units serving in a particular army, the more likely it was to win battles and to hold the advantage in a campaign. The Spanish continued to deploy the majority of their elite troops in the Netherlands, and the French armies engaged on the north-eastern frontier were thus set against forces possessing the highest proportion of experienced veterans. The risk that an army composed of newly recruited and inexperienced troops would be defeated on the Flanders frontier, even if it possessed numerical superiority, was much greater than in other theatres. The setback at Saint-Omer

---

[225] The discussions surrounding the failure at Fuenterrabía are confused by the concern of Richelieu to exonerate Henri II de Condé, and the concern of Condé, Henri d'Escoubleau de Sourdis and Bernard de Nogaret, duc de La Valette, to cast the blame on each other. None the less, the evidence in common suggests that, justifiably or not, La Valette did not intervene with his troops at the time of the Spanish attack and allowed the other forces to be caught in their (uncompleted) fortifications: Henri d'Escoubleau de Sourdis, *Correspondance*, ed. E. Sue (3 vols.; Paris, 1839), II. 57–9, 59–67, 9 Sept. 1638, Sourdis to Richelieu and to Charles, marquis de Sourdis. At Honnecourt the rivalry between the maréchal de Gramont and Harcourt, both relatives by marriage to Richelieu, and Gramont's reluctance to ask for support from Harcourt, certainly precipitated the disaster: Montglat, *Mémoires*, XLIX. 353–4; AAE MD 843, fo. 35, June 1642, Séguier to Chavigny.

[226] R. Quazza, *Tommaso di Savoia-Carignano nelle campagne di Fiandre e di Francia, 1635–1638* (Turin, 1941), pp. 48–52; Montglat, *Mémoires*, XLIX. 79–81; Aumale, *Princes de Condé*, IV. 468–9, gives the Imperial army at Thionville as at least 50 per cent stronger than Feuquières' force.

[227] La Valette, who may have been guilty of special pleading, argued that with 5,000 effectives it would have been hopeless to assault the Spanish besieging forces of 12,000–14,000 men, and that the garrison had in any case made terms before La Valette had the opportunity to undertake any manoeuvres to try to break the siege: AAE CP Savoie 26, fo. 347, 8 July 1638, La Valette to Richelieu.

in 1638, if not exactly a defeat, was a clear case in which the superior discipline and hardiness of Spanish and Imperial troops, especially the cavalry under Piccolomini, forced superior French forces into a disorderly abandonment of their positions.[228] In the context of the north-east frontier, the battle of Rocroi was, as Robert Stradling emphasized, 'against the run of play', in that most encounters between Spanish and French troops before that time had seen the advantage fall to the Spanish.[229]

Yet in other campaign theatres where the French confronted Spanish troops the story was rather different; in Italy and on the Pyrenean frontier the quality of Spanish troops was markedly lower, and the balance of victory and defeat much more even. In 1637 Charles de Schomberg, with an army made up of local levies from Languedoc, a few ordinary regiments and no elite units at all, managed to defeat a Spanish invasion force at Leucate.[230] On the other hand, the failure of Condé's forces in late 1639 to prevent the recapture of Salces in Roussillon by a motley collection of Castilian levies and reluctant Catalans, and indeed the complete collapse of the French relieving army, reveals how even in these circumstances superiority was difficult to guarantee. In Italy the arrival of Harcourt, with military resources no greater than those of his predecessors, Créqui and the cardinal de La Valette, began to tip a military balance which had previously favoured the Spanish. In 1635 Rohan had achieved remarkable success in the Valtelline with a small army composed of local Grison troops and a few French regiments, cut off from French supply bases and given a low priority in the government's allocation of funds.[231]

The role played by Harcourt in shoring up the situation in Italy from 1639 and by Rohan in the Valtelline in 1635 raises the issue of generalship as one significant aspect of success and failure on the battlefield. The French suffered during Richelieu's ministry from a shortage of competent commanders. It was a situation which Richelieu himself recognized, complaining to the king of the limited choice of good generals.[232] The advancement of mediocre *créatures* and the destruction of talented senior officers who had incurred ministerial distrust, was a regular theme of writers and memorialists hostile to Richelieu and his regime.[233] And while it is idle to speculate whether Rohan, for example, could have broken through more of

---

[228] Jacques-Nompar de Caumont, maréchal de La Force, *Mémoires* (4 vols.; Paris, 1843), III. 200–7.
[229] R. Stradling, 'Seventeenth-century Spain: decline or survival?'*European Studies Review*, 9 (1979), 154–94; R. Stradling, 'Catastrophe and recovery: the defeat of Spain, 1639–1643', *History*, 64 (1979), 205–19 – both reprinted in Stradling, *Spain's Struggle for Europe*.
[230] C. Vassal-Reig, *La guerre en Roussillon sous Louis XIII (1635–1639)* (Paris, 1934), pp. 56–60.
[231] Laugel, *Rohan*, pp. 323–33.
[232] Hanotaux, *Histoire de la nation française*, IV. 435–75, provides a transcription *in extenso* of a manuscript of 1641 written and corrected in the hand of Richelieu's established secretaries, including Le Masle, offering an overview of the available military commanders: BN Ms.fr. 15644. In many cases tendentious and prejudiced, the document none the less provides a sense of the limited pool of military talent available.
[233] Griffet, *Louis XIII*, III. 184, captures the opinions of many of these memorialists when he asserts

The French art of war during Richelieu's ministry

the limitations and constraints upon the French war-effort had he held senior commands after 1637, it is hard to avoid the suspicion that just as the military expansion outran the administrative and financial resources of the state, so it seems to have drained the shallow pool of competent commanders.

A 'good' general, it should be stressed, does not imply a military genius, someone with the ability to out-think his contemporaries and repeatedly subvert the existing conventions of warfare to the advantage of his army. What was lacking was the more mundane, but vitally important, figure with sufficient charisma – an aura of success and confidence – to persuade his troops to march the extra few miles, to campaign for the extra week, to make one last assault on the fortifications. The armies needed generals who could command sufficient respect, admiration or fear from their troops, and above all from their officers, to ensure that plans would be executed, that orders would be carried out and that criticism would be muted. In this context, the great majority of Richelieu's generals appear lacklustre, unfortunate in combat and largely without ability to inspire their troops to make the kind of sacrifices that might have tipped the balance in marginal situations. It is undeniable that this was partly the responsibility of Richelieu himself. Anxious to avoid having to present defeats to the king, the cardinal was known to react harshly and often punitively to failure by his commanders in the field. Lacking confidence that they could carry through risky or demanding operations, they had a strong incentive to be cautious and unimaginative in the formulation of strategy.[234]

War-winning strategies

Was it possible to win a war through direct military means in the first half of the seventeenth century? The previous discussion about particular sieges and battles in the field could justifiably be regarded as giving a false impression of what led to overall success in warfare.[235] Were states in practice locked into a conflict which was simply about the expenditure of resources until one or the other side broke down under the strain, or, if this did not occur, until a negotiated settlement was finally accepted on the basis of the military *status quo*? An overview of the European war from 1618 to 1659 certainly supports both of these views: the domestic crises which assailed Castile and France in the 1640s significantly reduced the capacity of either state to maintain their European military commitments at the same level; the treaties of Westphalia and the Pyrenees were more

---

simply that Richelieu 'avait coutûme d'employer tout son crédit pour couvrir les fautes de ses proches'.
[234] For a more detailed discussion of Richelieu's effects on the high command, see chapter 9, pp. 485–504.
[235] A point well made by D. Croxton, 'A territorial imperative? The military revolution, strategy and peacemaking in the Thirty Years War', *War in History*, 5 (1998), 253–79, esp. 278–9.

The military context

obviously a compromise reflecting an existing balance of forces than a military *diktat* imposed by victorious powers. These interpretations can induce a scepticism about the importance of military leadership, or indeed any other factor which might be related to military success and failure. A battle won or lost, a *place* captured, do not make much difference to the overall outcome in such a struggle of attrition.

In practice this was true for much of the French period of the European war, though it is not necessarily the case that all conflict in this period was doomed to be an indecisive, attritional struggle. What was essential for a decisive outcome was the achievement of clear military superiority on the ground – such as, for example, the Catholic League and Imperial armies enjoyed over their protestant rivals in the 1620s, or the Swedish army established over the Danes in 1643–4. This was difficult though not impossible to achieve when the military resources of the warring powers were relatively evenly matched. Yet if the French armies *had* been able to establish a clear and lasting control over an area of territory across the frontiers, then the balance of military and political advantage would have been changed, opening the prospect of a favourable peace settlement.

This territorial control would bring two advantages. Evidence suggests that the willingness of garrisons to sustain a protracted resistance to a besieging army was based less on the strength, sophistication or modernity of their fortifications or even the quantities of food and munitions in hand, more on a calculation about the chances that a relieving army would arrive to drive off the besiegers and end the siege. If the besieging army enjoyed military predominance across a large area of surrounding territory, few garrisons or their commanders would be inclined to sustain a lengthy siege. The lengthier the resistance, the harsher the terms for surrender and, in the case of towns, the worse treatment likely to be inflicted by the victorious besieging army on the civil population. If the possibility of relief was eliminated by the clear military superiority of the besieging army, only in the most exceptional circumstances would a town or fortress opt for a heroic and protracted resistance.[236] The usual result, as seen in the Netherlands in the 1580s when Alessandro Farnese's Army of Flanders was dominant in the field, or in the Empire immediately after Gustavus Adolphus' victory at Breitenfeld, or in the Spanish Netherlands in the campaign of 1667 when Louis XIV's forces were overwhelmingly superior to the remnant of the Army of Flanders, was a cascade of surrenders by cities and fortresses, often after minimal resistance.

This collapse of the will to resist amongst the fortified *places* would be

---

[236] The author explores this theme in the context of north Italian fortifications: 'The role of fortifications in the defence of states: the Farnese and the security of Parma and Piacenza', in A. Bilotto, P. Del Negro and C. Mozzarelli (eds.), *I Farnese: Corti, guerra e nobiltà in antico regime* (Rome, 1997), pp. 509–60, at pp. 520–4, and 'The utility of fortifications in early modern Europe: Italian princes and their citadels, 1540–1640', *War in History*, 7 (2000), 127–53.

The French art of war during Richelieu's ministry

accompanied by a second consequence of holding unchallenged military control over a particular territory. Once the army was able to secure this control, the systematic extortion of contributions and other financial and material support could begin. To a significant extent, the costs of warfare could be sustained from the enemy economy; the war was no longer a struggle of attrition between powers, as one of the warring states was now shouldering the costs not only of its own army, but also a significant part of that of the enemy. The state capable of maintaining its army on enemy soil – establishing winter quarters, maintaining garrisons in numerous captured *places*, and imposing regular taxes on the local populations – could force the ruler whose territory was being overrun to take the need for peace much more seriously.

Louis XIII, Richelieu and the king's other ministers certainly recognized this as a winning strategy. Isolated, set-piece sieges still dominated the campaign theatres of the later 1630s and early 1640s, and these sieges were often concerned more with dynastic prestige rather than real military benefit. Nevertheless, these co-existed with, and on occasions played their part in, a wider strategy aimed at controlling large swathes of enemy territory so as to open the possibility of a war fought entirely at the expense of France's opponents. Two territories, Alsace and Lorraine, were from the outset clearly linked with such policies, though the situation was complicated by territorial ambitions, especially in the case of Lorraine. While Louis XIII may initially have wished to spare Lorraine the full burden of war-taxes – contributions – the persistence of localized guerrilla war led to a much tougher, short-term, policy of extracting whatever was possible, as much in reprisal for the population's continued support for duke Charles IV as with the clear aim of making the French troops in Lorraine self-supporting. This latter goal proved elusive throughout Richelieu's ministry; a force small enough to sustain itself from war-taxes levied on the ravaged duchy was unable to control local unrest, and found itself trapped in a number of key fortifications, unable to risk the sweeps through the countryside necessary to collect contributions. When, periodically, the full weight of a French army-corps was turned against the duchy in a short-term attempt to reassert control, the numbers of troops were far in excess of what could be supported locally.

An alternative possibility in the first years of the 1630s was opened up by French 'protection' in Alsace. Less obviously an element in the crown's territorial ambitions, a series of prosperous cities, principalities and ecclesiastical territories offered rich pickings for well-established garrisons. Given that much of Alsace was under the overlordship of the Habsburgs, this occupation presented a means of hitting at the resource-base of France's enemies. However, the hope that Alsace might provide a means to subsidize the French war-effort was shattered by the battle of Nördlingen in 1634. The changed balance of power in the Empire soon revealed that the French would have the greatest difficulty holding these forward positions up to the Rhine, and by mid-1635 Richelieu was considering evacuating

The military context

the last French garrisons.[237] When the Habsburg grip on Alsace was weakened from early 1638 it was largely through the efforts of France's ally-entrepreneur, Bernard of Saxe-Weimar, and given the reluctance of the *surintendant des finances* to provide adequate funding for Saxe-Weimar's forces it was a foregone conclusion that the first call on contributions exacted from Alsace would be for France's *condottiere*-in-chief. As late as the mid 1640s the resurgence of Bavarian power in the Rhineland militated against tight and permanent control of Alsace.

The third, and in many respects most plausible, area contemplated by Louis and Richelieu for the self-financing of the French armies was the Spanish Habsburg's territory of the Franche-Comté. A document of April 1635 identified Lorraine, but especially the Franche-Comté, as obvious *places d'armes*, where the 'gens de guerre de sa majesté pourront estre entretenus sans leur donner beaucoup d'argent, en leur donnent seulement un peu plus de liberté pour vivre . . .'.[238] The document went on to propose contribution-systems which could be imposed on the population of the Franche-Comté. All that was required was clear military dominance over the territory. That proved unattainable in 1635, and when a serious attempt was launched to invade the territory in 1636 it foundered on Condé's failure to take Dôle. The inability to settle with duke Charles of Lorraine and to destroy his army consistently frustrated attempts to bring the Franche-Comté under control in the later 1630s. Reluctant to commit overwhelming military force to the territory, French garrisons found themselves isolated in hostile territory, and small field armies were consistently subject to an order of priorities which committed their troops to other campaign theatres, whether in the Rhineland or north Italy.

The result of this triple failure to gain outright military control of an adjoining territory forced France once more to try to dominate the areas of Spanish territory across the north-eastern frontier; here the chances of gaining outright territorial dominance were slim. Indeed in 1636 France herself was nearly a victim of this means of inflicting the costs of war on the enemy, when the Army of Flanders moved into Picardy and Champagne. The real danger was that the Spanish would establish a powerful military presence in the two French provinces, that this would precipitate a collapse of resistance amongst the remaining French fortified *places* and from this position of military and fiscal strength the Spanish could wait for the French crown to make terms. While Louis and Richelieu were able to mobilize forces to see off this threat in 1636, they never in subsequent years found themselves able to inflict the same treatment on the Spanish Netherlands or Luxembourg. The huge French armies committed to the set-piece sieges of the period from 1638 never managed to hold the surrounding territory in a sufficiently tight grip to bring about the collapse of resistance and to establish

---

[237] Avenel, v. 134 [early Aug.] 1635.
[238] AAE MD 813, fo. 318, 28 Apr. 1635, 'Résultat du conseil tenu à Compiègne chez Monseigneur le Cardinal'.

themselves across the frontiers securely enough for the troops to remain *in situ* over the winter.

Failure to achieve this goal in the north-east was not counterbalanced by anything comparable in the southern theatres, where the political situation was very different. Acting as the ally of the duke of Savoy, the duke of Mantua or the Catalan rebels, France was required to respect the rights and privileges of the populations of these territories, and to pay heavily for the subsistence of her armies in Piedmont, Monferrato or Catalonia. The successful breakthrough into the Milanese or Castile, which would have allowed the troops to impose contributions and to live at the expense of the Spanish king's subjects, never occurred. In fact the French monarchy found itself with the worst of both worlds: unable to shift the financial burden of these troops on to the allied territories, they still found that the casual extortion, pillage and violence of the soldiers alienated the local populations and ensured that the French troops, regardless of their formal financial restraint, were treated as an army of occupation.

It was ultimately to be in the Empire itself, especially from the mid 1640s, that the crown finally managed to foist some of the costs of a particular army-corps on to a territory outside of France. Greatly assisted by the victories of the Swedes, above all at Breitenfeld/Leipzig in 1642 and Jankow in 1645, the army-corps of Guébriant, then Turenne, took on the characteristics of the other self-sustaining armies operating in the Empire. They lived by contributions, employed a high proportion of cavalry for foraging and tax extraction over a broad area, and allowed strategy to be shaped, where necessary, by the demands of logistics. If military pressure brought the Emperor to the negotiating table, then this pressure was imposed through the Franco-Swedish dominance in the Empire, allowing their armies to live from resources which they could now systematically deny to the Imperial and Bavarian soldiers.[239]

The Peace of Westphalia demonstrated that France and Sweden could bring the Emperor to terms on the basis of military pressure, especially when this coincided from the mid-1640s with a powerful group of Imperial privy councillors urging Ferdinand III to cut his losses in the Empire in order to consolidate political and religious control in the Hereditary Lands.[240] It was equally evident, however, that the same policy had not persuaded the Spanish of the need to make peace with France. Another eleven years of warfare between the two great rivals revealed the failure of France to get herself into a comparable military position in which she could dominate the resources of an area under Spanish control; indeed the critical factor moving the Spanish crown to peace negotiations was Anglo-French intervention in the Portuguese revolt, and an increasing conviction that the rebels

---

[239] D. Croxton, *Peacemaking in Early Modern Europe. Cardinal Mazarin and the Congress of Westphalia, 1643–1648* (Selinsgrove, 1999), pp. 56–94.

[240] Croxton, 'A territorial imperative?', pp. 266–72; R. Bireley, 'The Thirty Years War as Germany's Religious War', in Repgen (ed.), *Krieg und Politik*, pp. 85–106, esp. pp. 104–5.

could not be brought back into the Spanish *monarchia* without shedding some of the crown's external commitments.[241]

CONCLUSION

Inevitably perhaps, much consideration of military change in early modern Europe has taken place in the context of historical generalization and abstraction. Understanding the nature of warfare in early seventeenth-century Europe entails making a distinction between what is said in contemporary theoretical tracts and what can be inferred from the evidence of how war was waged in practice. It is also necessary not to be over-influenced by the evidence of those one or two states whose armies were presented in terms of a self-conscious reforming ethos, and to assume that these armies established models that were widely accepted and imitated by contemporaries. Concentration on the French army in this period is instructive, for it has been assumed, on the basis of almost no evidence, that the French stood in succession to the Dutch and Swedes as one of the major 'reformed' armies of the earlier seventeenth century, able in its turn to dominate the battlefields of Europe by virtue of tactical, organizational and disciplinary innovations. There is little evidence that the French 'art of war' was in practice reshaped in this period to conform with the prescriptions of these supposedly progressive reforms. Only in a few areas did a clearly perceived military crisis force changes in the manner that the French organized and deployed their armies; for example, the progressive increase in the cavalry component of French army-corps. In other cases, where change appears to indicate an adoption of innovatory military practices – for example, in reducing the size of individual fighting units – the change can be shown to be due to very different factors and concerns. It can be suggested in other cases that there were good reasons for maintaining a *status quo* which recognized the qualities and military potential of existing French soldiers: concentrating veteran troops in elite units, for example, or accepting a traditional system of military apprenticeship within companies and regiments as the basis of drill and tactical discipline.

The rhetoric of new and 'battle-winning' tactics and organization based upon the precepts of classical military theorists certainly penetrated France in the early seventeenth century. However, this was to a great extent the product of individuals who shared religious or family affiliations with the originators and patrons of the theories, the House of Orange-Nassau. In the wider European context, it is more convincing to place the rhetoric less as a series of universal military prescriptions, more as a 'protestant (and in large part, Calvinist) way of warfare'. What is most remarkable in the French case is the diversity of military experience amongst those who held military command at all levels during Richelieu's ministry. Those

---

[241] R. Stradling, *Philip IV and the Government of Spain, 1621–1665* (Cambridge, 1988), pp. 290–9.

The French art of war during Richelieu's ministry

who had fought in Hungary or for the catholic powers at the outset of the Thirty Years War, those whose experience went back to the religious struggles of the 1580s and 1590s, and those who had fought in the Huguenot wars in the Midi during the 1620s, seemed far more reluctant to deploy their military experience in the writing of theoretical tracts on the art of war. Yet though these contemporaries of the 'protestant' theorists lacked a set of comparable, ready-made literary conventions in which to cast their military theories – above all, the claim that their tracts were reviving the military practices of antiquity – this does not invalidate the relevance of their experiences to the way that the French fought wars after 1630. It is true that some issues and debates appear to have gone by default to the articulate minority whose experience was shaped in the Netherlands – the acceptance that warfare was fundamentally about the conduct of sieges, for example – despite the fact that so many of the French commanders would have experienced types of warfare in which sieges were considerably less central to the art of war. Nevertheless, underpinning the character of warfare was a much richer and more varied range of experience than is suggested by the frequent claim that the Dutch army was the 'school of warfare' in early seventeenth-century France.

This diversity of French military experience tends to underpin another characteristic of actual European warfare in this period; in matters of tactics, dissimilarities between armies were outweighed by broader similarities between their military deployments. By the 1630s, linear formations which allowed the reasonably effective use of firearms were the rule; whether the armies drew their battalions or equivalent formations close together in the line of battle or kept spaces between them was of marginal importance. If some armies made substantially greater use of field artillery or different infantry firing drills, pitched battles continued to see armies drawn up against each other with an infantry centre that was flanked, with small variations, by cavalry wings, and where the course of battle followed a sequence of fairly predictable moves. The eventual outcome continued to depend more upon the quality and number of veteran troops serving within those armies than upon innovative tactics.

And looking beyond the individual engagement, the critical factors in determining success and – more often – failure were far more frequently the inadequacies and breakdown of general administration, finance and supply. As Richelieu himself wrote: 'Il se trouve en l'histoire beaucoup plus d'armées péries faute de pain et de police que par l'effort des armes ennemies, et je suis fidèle tesmoin que toutes les entreprises qui ont esté faites de mon temps n'ont manqué que par ce défaut.'[242] It is with these crucial issues of logistics, control and organization – the raising and maintenance of adequate numbers of troops, their supply, funding and discipline – that the analytical chapters of the present book will be concerned.

---

[242] Richelieu, *Testament politique*, p. 318.

2

France at war, 1624–1642

AIMS AND METHODS, 1624–1634

With the formal declaration of war on Spain in May 1635, France moved from subsidy war (*guerre couverte*) against the Habsburgs to *guerre ouverte*. From the early summer of 1635 France embarked upon a war which was unprecedented. While the civil wars of the later sixteenth century had lasted longer than this Franco-Spanish – and from 1636, Franco-Imperial – war, the scale of the individual conflicts was much smaller. Moreover, both this lengthy period of civil war and indeed the Hundred Years struggle against the English and the House of Burgundy were intermittent conflicts. The war which began in 1635 required a major military commitment every campaign season for twenty-five years. There were no truces, no years in which campaigning was substantially scaled down, no respite for the financial and military administration or for French subjects subjected to the burdens of warfare.

Yet there were considerable continuities with earlier foreign policy aims and aspirations, and with the assumptions and methods of waging war inherited from previous conflicts, particularly from the Habsburg-Valois wars of the first half of the sixteenth century. In 1559 the results of French foreign policy had not been deemed wholly negative. The defeat at Pavia (1525) is often taken as the death-knell of French aspirations in the Italian peninsula, but this ignores the subsequent decades of conflict in which the balance of advantage was more evenly distributed. The legacy of this period was in fact particularly dangerous in its impact on the assumptions of those making policy a century later. The Habsburg-Valois wars demonstrated that military progress could be made by French armies prepared to exploit the weaknesses and the over-extended defences of the *monarchia* of Charles V. It was then easy to allow these assumptions to influence strategic thinking in the very different military context of the first half of the next century.

FRANCE AND THE EUROPEAN CRISIS, 1618–1626

The decision of the Palatine Elector, Frederick V, to give support to the revolt of the Bohemian Estates against Habsburg rule expanded the issues of a localized revolt into the already intensely charged confessional environment of the Holy Roman Empire. The question of France's involvement in this impending conflict was crucial. The success of the Austrian Habsburgs in mustering support from the Spanish branch of the family and from the League of German catholic states, led to demands for an interventionist foreign policy from those in France who argued the need to secure Bohemian independence and the survival of German protestantism.[1] Though the attempt to draw France into solidarity with the Bohemian rebels and the protestant League foundered on Louis XIII's reluctance to sponsor revolt abroad while seeking to suppress Huguenot and aristocratic factionalism at home, the situation was to change as a result of strategic considerations closer to France's traditional sixteenth-century sphere of interest.[2] The control of the Valtelline, the series of passes and valleys which commanded communications between Lombardy and the Tyrol, offering access up into south Germany and an important route down into Venice, had been a highly charged political issue since the early sixteenth century.[3] In 1619, the Spanish took advantage of their military commitment to the Emperor in central Europe to occupy the Valtelline, ostensibly on the grounds that the protestant Grisons were persecuting the local catholic inhabitants. In the face of strong diplomatic protests from France, the Spanish appeared willing to negotiate a compromise.[4] But as the international situation tipped more and more decisively in favour of the Habsburgs, the Spanish proved reluctant to implement the terms of the resulting treaty of Madrid. A series of French diplomatic protests achieved nothing, and only when this was followed by the threat of military intervention did Philip IV and his ministers offer an apparent compromise, proposing to replace Spanish troops with Papal garrisons.[5] However, it soon became clear that the presence of these Papal troops would not be followed by any thorough exclusion of the Habsburgs from the territory.[6] This intransigence within what was claimed as a French sphere of

---

[1] V.-L. Tapié, *La politique étrangère de la France et le début de la Guerre de Trente Ans (1616–1621)* (Paris, 1934), pp. 311–24, 587–94; Hanotaux, *Richelieu*, II. 376–82, on the role of Henri, duc de Bouillon in the cause of international protestantism.

[2] A reluctance compounded by a concern not to destabilize the Austrian Archduke Ferdinand, whose election to the Imperial throne was regarded by French ministers as strongly preferable to the possibility that Philip III of Spain might seek to gain the election for his son: Tapié, *Politique étrangère*, pp. 131–7, 367–72.

[3] L. Bély, Y.-M. Bercé, J. Meyer and R. Quatrefages, *Guerre et paix dans l'Europe du XVIIe siècle* (3 vols; Paris, 1991), II. 112–14.

[4] Tapié, *Politique étrangère*, pp. 595–6, 620–1; R. Quazza, 'Politica europea nelle questione valtellinica (La Lega Franco-Veneta-Savoiarda e la pace di Monçon)', *Nuovo archivio veneto*, 42 (1921), 50–151, at 52–3; Hanotaux, *Richelieu*, II. 395–405, 433–5; P.-M. Bondois, *Le maréchal de Bassompierre* (Paris, 1925), pp. 210–21.

[5] B. Zeller, *Richelieu et les ministres de Louis XIII de 1621 à 1624* (Paris, 1880), pp. 141–58, 183–90; R. Pithon, 'Les débuts difficiles du ministère du cardinal de Richelieu et la crise de Valteline', *Revue d'histoire diplomatique*, 74 (1960), 298–322, at 308; Bergin, *Rise of Richelieu*, pp. 240–1.

[6] E. Rott, *Histoire de la représentation diplomatique de la France auprès des cantons suisses, de leurs alliés et confédérés* (10 vols; Berne, 1900–35), III. 592–609.

The military context

interest shifted Louis XIII back towards a more traditionally anti-Habsburg stance, and placed strong pressure on his ministers to negotiate or force a solution that would uphold the king's honour in the face of this breach of the treaty.[7] A sequence of ministers and ministerial teams grappled unsuccessfully with the problem of a suitable response to the Valtelline impasse until, in August 1624, the dismissal of the *surintendant des finances*, Charles, marquis de La Vieuville, left Armand-Jean du Plessis, cardinal de Richelieu, dominant in the Council. The failure of previous negotiations had already committed the uneasy partnership of Richelieu and La Vieuville to military intervention, which was being planned from May onwards.[8] Richelieu's ascendancy pushed these plans another stage forward, and the *maréchal de camp*, François-Annibal d'Estrées, was despatched with a small army to the Valtelline to encourage resistance by the Grisons to the Habsburg and Papal forces.[9] However, this campaign immediately revealed the logistical difficulties of effective French intervention. Access down into the Valtelline was subject to continual negotiation with the Swiss cantons along the routes from France.[10] A French force large enough to challenge the Habsburg troops who could be passed into the valleys would pose insuperable problems of supply and reinforcement. High levels of desertion in these circumstances would rapidly reduce the army-corps to ineffectiveness.

As the difficulty of conducting an operation aimed only at opening up and controlling the valleys became evident, the ministers looked for a way to wage the war on more favourable terms. One possibility would be to widen the conflict into a European struggle in which France allied herself overtly with the other enemies of the Habsburgs and adopted a much broader strategy, seeking to engage the Spanish and Austrians in multiple theatres. There was, however, considerable doubt about whether such an escalation could be sustained by France. What Richelieu and his ministerial team envisaged instead – characteristic of French policy in the sixteenth century – was the probing of Habsburg territory to select a weak point that would force the Spanish in particular to draw some of their troops away from the Valtelline.[11] The area most likely to lead to a redeployment of Spanish forces in north Italy would be the territories to the west of the Milanese. But this would require either a preliminary French invasion of Savoy-Piedmont to enforce the subsequent passage of troops deeper into the peninsula, or a working alliance with Carlo Emanuele I, duke of Savoy, which would permit French troops passage and *logement* in the duke's territories, as well as providing Savoyard military support for a chosen operation.[12] Louis and Richelieu chose the second

---

[7] Bergin, *Rise of Richelieu*, pp. 250–2.
[8] Zeller, *Richelieu*, pp. 270–91; Hanotaux, *Richelieu*, III. 6.
[9] Bergin, *Rise of Richelieu*, pp. 255–8; Chevallier, *Louis XIII*, pp. 298–9.
[10] Rott, *Représentation diplomatique*, III. 784–89, 856–62
[11] Rott, *Représentation diplomatique*, III. 841–4; Quazza, 'Politica europea', 104–6, who credits Lesdiguières as the main exponent of this second course; Dufayard, *Lesdiguières*, pp. 534–5
[12] Pithon, 'Débuts difficiles', 307; Quazza, 'Politica europea', p. 85.

option. Drawing on the territorial acquisitiveness and the political and military brinkmanship of Carlo Emanuele, they negotiated a secret treaty in early November 1624 which aimed at the joint conquest and partition of Spain's ally, the Republic of Genoa.[13] Yet while the strategic importance of the city and port of Genoa to the Spanish military system ensured that an attack would certainly succeed in drawing off Spanish troops, it presented France with military difficulties that were as considerable as those of the Valtelline theatre. Above all, Spanish naval superiority would make an effective seaward blockade of Genoa impossible, and greatly reduce the likelihood of success if the siege proved to be lengthy. Moreover, an attack on a third party, albeit a firm ally of Spain, was hard to reconcile with the rhetoric of liberating the peninsula from the yoke of Habsburg servitude; other secondary powers such as Mantua, Modena, Parma and especially France's habitual ally, Venice, drew the obvious conclusion and declined to join the Franco-Savoyard initiative.[14]

Despite these dangers, in February 1625 François de Bonne, duc de Lesdiguières and *connétable* of France, moved down through Piedmont to blockade Genoa with an army of 23,000 men, one third of whom were French.[15] At first, Richelieu sought to present the military situation to the king in the most optimistic light, maintaining in May 1625 that: 'toutes choses conspirent maintenant à rabattre l'orgueil de l'Espagne'.[16] Yet even this *mémoire* could not avoid reference to the growing concern that Spain might widen the conflict by an attack from Flanders or up from Spain itself.[17] And even as Richelieu was penning his memoir to the king, the French and Savoyard forces had been driven out of Genoa by a combined Spanish land and sea operation.[18]

Richelieu was saved from the prospect of having to expand the French war-effort under these circumstances by the reemergence of a perennial French problem: an opportunist Huguenot revolt, led by Benjamin de Rohan, duc de Soubise, who seized the isle of Oléron off La Rochelle in June 1625.[19] The Huguenot 'treason' was taken seriously by Richelieu, and there is no reason to doubt his frequently stated contention that the persistence of this organized and

---

[13] Dufayard, *Lesdiguières*, pp. 536–8; R. Quazza, 'La politica di Carlo Emanuele I durante la guerra dei trent' anni', *Carlo Emanuele miscellanea*, 120 (Turin, 1930), pp. 1–45, at 23–4; D. Parrott, 'The Mantuan succession, 1627–1631: a sovereignty dispute in early modern Europe', *English Historical Review*, 112 (1997), 20–65, at 39–41.

[14] Rott, *Représentation diplomatique*, III. 848–53; Pithon, 'Débuts difficiles', 312.

[15] Dufayard, *Lesdiguières*, pp. 538–44; Pithon, 'Débuts difficiles', 312–13.

[16] Grillon, I. 181–6, [beginning of May] 1625, *Mémoire pour le Roi*.

[17] Grillon, I. 184; J.H. Elliott, *The Count-Duke of Olivares: The Statesman in an Age of Decline* (New Haven and London, 1986), p. 229.

[18] Dufayard, *Lesdiguières*, pp. 544–53. Problems of funding and supplying the army in the Valtelline were also taking a heavy toll on its military effectiveness: Rott, *Représentation diplomatique*, III. 898–9.

[19] Hanotaux, *Richelieu*, III. 51–2; M. Schybergson, *Le duc de Rohan et la chute du parti protestant en France* (Paris, 1880), pp. 35–6.

The military context

independent military power within France jeopardized the prospect of waging a successful war abroad. None the less, the revolt allowed Richelieu to back away from an Italian venture that was unlikely to be resolved in French favour by military force and which threatened a major confrontation with Spain for which France was ill-prepared.[20] While Richelieu's propaganda machine stressed the need to make terms with the Huguenot rebels – at least in the short term – in order to continue the war abroad, simultaneous negotiations were begun with Spain.[21] These were to culminate on 5 March 1626 with the treaty of Monzón, a treaty that Richelieu felt it prudent to repudiate publicly, blaming the French ambassador in Madrid, but which he none the less considered that France had no choice but to accept.[22]

LA ROCHELLE AND RENEWED WAR IN NORTH ITALY, 1627–1631

War against the Huguenots

Having extracted France from her commitments in north Italy, Richelieu was able to focus political and military resources on an issue capable of uniting a catholic ruling class which had proved alarmingly divided over the confrontation with the Habsburgs.[23] His standing with the king could be repaired by the reasonable assertion that the elimination of the Huguenot 'fifth column' was the precondition of any successful subsequent foreign policy. In practice, the timing and the nature of what turned from a punitive campaign against Soubise and his elder brother Henri, duc de Rohan, into an increasingly large-scale struggle against Huguenot military power owed little to Richelieu's choice. The English declaration of war against France while King Charles I was already fighting Spain could hardly have been predicted on any rational diplomatic calculation, and war with England was not an obvious route to curbing protestant military power within France. That said, Richelieu seems to have assumed from early in the 1627 campaign that the attempt to force the English off the Île de Ré would lead on to a campaign against

---

[20] Optimistic talk of an army of 7,000 men in Picardy and Champagne would do little to inspire confidence in the event of an invasion by the Spanish Army of Flanders: Grillon, I. 184; Richelieu's concern at the deteriorating military situation and the need for substantial new levies was evident in August: Avenel, II. 102–7, 5 Aug., 'Mémoire sur lequel il plaira au Roi'; R. Quazza, 'Il periodo italiano della guerra dei trent'anni', *Rivista storica italiana*, 50 (1933), 64–89, at 66.

[21] Grillon, I. 218–20, [Sept. 1625], 'Sur la nécessité de la paix du dedans'; I. 226–33, 25 Nov. 1625, 'Discours tendant à voir si, ayant la guerre avec l'Espagne en Italie, il faut la faire aussy au-dedans du royaulme'; Avenel, II. 142–5, 4 Oct. 1625, 'Négotiation avec le Légat', already indicates a considerable softening of the position originally taken in May, that under no circumstances would France pull her troops out of the Valtelline.

[22] Avenel, II. 187–93, 4 Feb. 1625, Louis XIII and Richelieu to Charles d'Angennes, comte du Fargis, French ambassador in Madrid, expressing their discontent at the terms of the treaty which was none the less subsequently ratified; Pithon, 'Débuts difficiles', 314.

[23] G. Pagès, 'Autour du "grand orage": Richelieu et Marillac', *Revue historique*, 179 (1937), 63–97; W. Church, *Richelieu*, pp. 103–72.

France at war, 1624–1642

the Huguenots, and above all, against the great port and fortress of La Rochelle.[24] Even as the French forces were being massed on the coast against Ré, some 15,000 additional troops were being stationed in positions that indicated that La Rochelle was also the objective.[25] Faced with the impending prospect that force would be used against them, the Rochelais decided to throw in their lot with the English expedition and to support the siege of Saint-Martin de Ré, the beleaguered French garrison on the island.[26] As a result the campaign to defeat the English was merged with a siege of La Rochelle.[27] Both involved considerable risks for Richelieu: certainly until Saint-Martin had been relieved and the English driven off the coast, the outcome of the siege of La Rochelle was not assured. The abandonment of the siege of Montauban in 1620 had been a clear warning of the dangers of insufficient preparation and limited resources committed to a major siege.[28]

Richelieu himself had an obvious interest in presenting the siege of La Rochelle as an example of efficient military planning and administration, but other commentators were also prepared to support the view that this was a successfully managed campaign.[29] Investigation of the detail of the siege presents a different picture. Confusion and mistaken priorities were frequent throughout the campaign.[30] The celebrated dyke which finally ensured that the harbour of La Rochelle was cut off from the sea was a subject of contradictory plans and instructions, while to Richelieu's increasing frustration its completion was constantly postponed.[31] Complaints about shortages of funds and supplies were made throughout 1627 and 1628, especially by the governor at Saint Martin de Ré, Jean du Caylar de Saint-Bonnet, marquis de Toiras, anxious to guard himself against later accusations of *légèreté* should he be forced to surrender to the

---

[24] Schybergson, *Rohan*, pp. 46–56; Laugel, *Henry de Rohan*, pp. 212–19.
[25] D. Parker, *La Rochelle and the French Monarchy. Conflict and Order in Seventeenth-Century France* (London, 1980), pp. 15–16.
[26] Vaux de Foletier, *La Rochelle*, pp. 134–44; A.D. Lublinskaya, *French Absolutism: The Crucial Phase, 1620–1629* (Cambridge, 1968), pp. 217–18; Grillon, II. 479–81, 11 Sept. 1627, duc d'Angoulême to Louis XIII and to Richelieu.
[27] Grillon, II. 493–94, 15 Sept. 1627, *mémoire* of Crusy de Marsillac (bishop of Mende in 1628) to Richelieu.
[28] Lublinskaya, *French Absolutism*, pp. 190–3.
[29] Richelieu, *Mémoires*, IV. 37–8, 84–5, who suggested that the three great advantages at the siege were that the troops were regularly paid, that corruption and indiscipline were eliminated and that the king actually knew how many troops he had in his army.
[30] Parker, *La Rochelle*, p. 120, who draws on Bassompierre's *Mémoires*, in Petitot and Monmerqué, XXI. 97–105, for the quarrels over the allocation of commands; Avenel, II. 365, 12 Feb. 1627, Richelieu to Jean de Rechignevoison de Guron, governor of Brouage, urging Guron to do all possible to concentrate troops on Oleron, as the English would be unlikely to attack Ré, with its existing garrison at Saint-Martin; Grillon, II. 664–5, 23 Nov. 1627, Richelieu to Louis XIII, complaining of the general failure to carry out instructions; Avenel, III. 47–8, 28 Feb. 1628, Richelieu to *prévôt général*, Mestivier, concerning the indiscipline amongst the troops.
[31] Vaux de Foletier, *La Rochelle*, pp. 152–4; R. Mousnier, *L'Homme Rouge ou la vie du cardinal de Richelieu (1585–1642)* (Paris, 1992), pp. 346–50.

The military context

English.³² While sympathetic commentators suggested that the army before La Rochelle was outstandingly well controlled and disciplined, reports and letters provide evidence of high levels of desertion and frequent cases of hungry troops engaged in pillage and violence against local communities.³³

Yet there were a number of important factors at work during the siege of La Rochelle which were not reflected in later conflicts. There was a degree of unanimity and consensus amongst the catholic elites both at the centre and in the neighbouring provinces that the policy against the Huguenots was a valid and legitimate deployment of resources.³⁴ At critical points during the siege major *grands* were prepared to use their resources to support the campaigns; François V, duc de La Rochefoucauld, for example, arrived from Poitou with 1,500 soldiers raised entirely through his clients. The additional forces engaged in carrying out local destruction in other areas of Huguenot resistance were largely raised and maintained by catholic *grands*, particularly Henri II de Bourbon, prince de Condé, Jean-Louis de Nogaret de La Valette, duc d'Epernon, and Henri, maréchal de Schomberg.³⁵ The bulk of the revenues, resources and organization of the central government could be focused on the royal siege army. Though the king was to leave the siege for a period during which progress was limited, his presence in the first months and in the latter stages, and the constant presence of Richelieu, could go some way to preventing the worst effects of insubordination and disputes.³⁶ Not only did Richelieu rely upon the organizational and financial support of his *fidèles* to keep the siege army together, he himself claimed to have dispensed over 1 million *livres* on his own credit to meet the immediate costs of the army.³⁷ Given the decision to pursue the siege until the Rochelais were finally brought to surrender, some attempts were made to provide better support facilities for the army.³⁸ Though the army cost around 2 million *livres* per month to sustain,

---

³² Grillon, II. 417–18, 23 Aug. 1627, Argencour to Richelieu, discussing the (claimed) weakness and demoralization of Toiras' garrison; II. 501–2, 18 Sept., Crusy de Marsillac to Richelieu; II. 558–9, 4 Oct., Richelieu to Gaston d'Orléans, doubting the extremity to which Toiras claims the garrison has been reduced. [Where a sequence of correspondence is exchanged within the same year and cited in a single reference, the year itself will be given only in the first citation.]

³³ Aubery, *Histoire du cardinal de Richelieu*, pp. 71–2.

³⁴ Grillon, II. 610–12, [Oct. 1627], *Mémoire de M. le Prince* (de Condé), concerning the need to pursue the siege to final victory, and to resist any negotiated settlement; D. Parker, *The Making of French Absolutism* (London, 1983), pp. 56–7.

³⁵ For the campaign of Condé in Bas-Languedoc, the Cévennes and Foix see Grillon, III. *passim*. Grillon, III. 359, 369, 24 June, 4 July 1628, Epernon and Plessis-Baussonière to Richelieu, discussing Epernon's campaign to *faire le dégât* in the territory around Montauban; Grillon, III. 169–72, 9/10 Apr. 1628, letters discussing Schomberg's campaign in the Vivarais.

³⁶ Mousnier, *L'Homme Rouge*, pp. 347–8; this was certainly Richelieu's own view: Avenel, III. 179–213, p. 203, 13 Jan. 1629, *Advis donné au Roy après la prise de La Rochelle*: 'le seul moyen d'empescher que l'absence du roy ne ruinast son premier dessein estoit que je demeurasse'.

³⁷ Avenel, III. 205, *Advis*.

³⁸ Grillon, III. 66–8, 13 Feb. 1628, d'Effiat to Richelieu, concerning financial provision for the siege army; Avenel, III. 49–54, 6 Mar. 1628, 'Mémoire de ce qui s'est passé au siège de La Rochelle', concerned with provision of clothing and supplies.

enough money was found to prevent any militarily disastrous shortfall on the one hand, or a resort to heavy-handed and counter-productive fiscal expedients on the other.[39]

The campaign was dogged by planning failures, miscalculations, insubordination, the indiscipline and desertion of troops, occasional shortages of funds and supplies. Yet, when it is compared with the subsequent difficulties faced by the French army in action, it has an almost text-book measure of success; some attempt was made to ensure that the army was regularly paid and supplied in proportion to the size of the forces; the troop strengths within the army were monitored, and additional recruitment was carried out to try to keep units at an effective strength. The campaign presented a rare example of a realistic relationship of aims to means. For once, the war being fought – a single major theatre and a group of secondary interrelated theatres in close geographical proximity – corresponded to the accessible resources and the administrative capacities of early seventeenth-century French government. This was a point that was recognized by Richelieu's critics within a couple of years of the expansion of France's military ambitions.

The Mantuan succession

The concentration of military resources on the objective of besieging La Rochelle ensured Richelieu's determination, until the end of 1628, to avoid French implication in the new crisis that was developing in north Italy over the succession to the duchies of Mantua and Monferrato. The death of Vincenzo II Gonzaga in December 1627 marked the extinction of the direct male line of the Gonzaga di Mantova. The closest heir from a collateral branch was Charles de Gonzague, *prince souverain* of Arches, duke of Nevers and Rethel, and governor of Champagne. Despite a strong tradition of partible inheritance within the much-divided Gonzaga territories, Charles de Gonzague-Nevers resolved that he had inherited the duchies of Mantua and Monferrato in their entirety, and from the outset ruled out any compromise with those who held their own claims over parts of the inheritance. This declared intransigence had the obvious effect of driving rival claimants, most notably the duke of Savoy and the Gonzaga duke of Guastalla, to seek support from the major European powers, whether Spain, the Emperor or France. By early March 1628 it was widely suspected that Carlo Emanuele of Savoy and the Spanish governor of Milan had negotiated a partition treaty to occupy and divide Monferrato.[40]

---

[39] R. Bonney, *King's Debts*, pp. 147–8.
[40] For Charles de Gonzague–Nevers and the background to the succession crisis: R. Quazza, *Mantova e Monferrato nella politica europea alla vigilia della guerra per la successione (1624–1627)* (Mantua, 1922); R. Quazza, *La guerra per la successione di Mantova e del Monferrato (1628–1631)* (2 vols;

The military context

Despite the strategic and personal considerations which had deterred Louis XIII and Richelieu from any early intervention in the succession issue,[41] the Spanish–Savoyard partition treaty raised concerns in France. The Spaniards' military aim in cooperating with Savoy was not indiscriminate territorial aggrandizement, but control of the powerful fortress of Casale-Monferrato, dominating one of the key gaps in the Alpine barrier leading down on to the Lombardy plain. As the Spanish siege army slowly tightened its grip on Casale in the second half of 1628, Louis and Richelieu were forced to contemplate the prospect of a considerable strengthening of the Spanish defensive system in north Italy, making any subsequent French intervention in the peninsula correspondingly more difficult. The failure of an expeditionary force raised by Charles de Nevers on his own sovereign authority, recruiting troops from his French duchies with the tacit permission of Louis XIII, considerably worsened the situation.[42] For military action on Nevers' part had weakened the diplomatic position of his partisans at the Imperial Court in Vienna, where the rival claims to the Gonzaga inheritance would ultimately be adjudicated by the Emperor, acting as sovereign overlord of Reichsitalien.[43] Were the Spanish to take Casale, the prospect that any subsequent arbitration brokered by the Emperor would evict them seemed even more remote.

Immediately after the surrender of La Rochelle, Richelieu drafted a document for the king discussing the feasibility of a rapid intervention down through Piedmont to relieve the siege of Casale in early 1629. This rapid strike was to be followed by the transfer of the majority of the troops back into the south of France to take the remaining Huguenot strongholds during the summer.[44] Initial doubts that the plan could achieve both objectives were confounded by the speed and effectiveness of the French bid to relieve Casale in early 1629. Personally directed by Richelieu, his ministerial colleagues and a number of *fidèles*, the preparations for the army that was to force its way through Piedmont and into Monferrato were thorough. Richelieu and his ministers wanted a quick and decisive campaign, and were prepared to ensure that adequate funds were provided. Moreover, the intention that the campaign should be extremely short allowed some of the larger financial issues to be evaded; no attempt would be made to pay the troops in full, but the *prêt*, or subsistence money, would be guaranteed each week, while the remainder of their wages would be paid 'on return to France'.[45] On 6 March, the

---

Mantua, 1926); Baudson, *Charles de Gonzague*; Parrott, 'The Mantuan succession', pp. 38–59; Parrott, 'A *prince souverain* and the French crown: Charles de Nevers, 1580–1637', in Oresko, Gibbs, and Scott (eds.), *Royal and Republican Sovereignty*, pp. 149–87.

[41] Discussed in Parrott, 'The Mantuan succession', 53–5.
[42] Grillon, III. 426, 10 Aug. 1628, Charles Sanguin, sr. de Livry, to Richelieu, reporting the collapse of Nevers' force; Humbert, *Le maréchal de Créqui*, pp. 142–4.
[43] Quazza, *Guerra per la successione*, I. 200–1.
[44] Avenel, III. 150–2, Dec. 1628.
[45] Avenel, III, 284–6, [27] Apr. 1629; Grillon, IV. 103, 15 Feb. 1629, Michel de Marillac to Richelieu: 1.3 million *livres* despatched with d'Effiat for payment of the first sums due. Separate accounts for

advance guard of the French army pushed through the fortifications at Susa, defended by a small force of ill-prepared Savoyard troops, stiffened with a regiment of troops from the Spanish Milanese.[46] The duke of Savoy saw clearly enough the danger of French military occupation and the permanent loss of territory that might follow, and made terms on 11 March, handing over the fortress at Susa as security.[47] The French were saved from the considerably greater complications of a campaign carried further into north Italy by the Spanish commander's decision to abandon the siege of Casale.[48] Considering that the fortress of Casale was too important to be left to the military resources of a minor Italian prince, the French occupied it themselves, placing five regiments of infantry and six cavalry companies under the command of the maréchal de Toiras, hero of the resistance to the English on the Île de Ré.[49]

Richelieu's tough, decisive, action had apparently succeeded in achieving a limited aim, the preservation of Casale and the breaking of the Spanish/Savoyard alliance. Beneath the surface, however, Richelieu was faced with the persistent dilemma about the deployment of French military force. The cardinal's main concern immediately after the French had garrisoned Casale was to ensure a substantial commitment of troops to the unfinished struggle against the Huguenots.[50] In fact the protestants proved reluctant to sustain a drawn-out campaign against an army led by the king in person, and recognized that the fall of La Rochelle in the preceding year had decisively shifted the balance of power.[51] After the sack of Privas and the massacre of its garrison, few fortified towns were prepared to offer more than token resistance.[52] However, in the north Italian theatre the Spanish were not prepared to accept the débâcle of early 1629. The defection of the duke of Savoy, the abandonment of the siege of Casale and the French occupation of the fortress were grave blows to Spanish interests. Supporters of Spain at the Imperial Court argued successfully that the Emperor's authority in Reichsitalien was directly challenged by the possibility of a French-brokered settlement between Nevers and the other claimants to the Gonzaga succession – defying the Emperor's customary rights to arbitrate such disputes.[53]

---

buying supplies, negotiating food and munitions contracts and transport; IV. 118, 25 Feb., Marillac to Richelieu, concerning supply contracts to be negotiated in Paris.

[46] Grillon, IV. 136–7, 8 Mar. 1629, Richelieu to Queen Mother, reporting the French victory.
[47] Grillon, IV. 149–150, 14 Mar., Richelieu to Queen Mother; Quazza, *Guerra per la successione*, I. 322–3.
[48] Grillon, IV. 165, 20 Mar., Richelieu to Queen Mother.
[49] G. di Ricaldone, *Annali di Monferrato (951–1708)* (Turin, 1972), p. 787.
[50] Avenel, III. 312–14, 9 May 1629, Richelieu to Louis XIII.
[51] Laugel, *Rohan*, pp. 252–4, 260–5.
[52] Grillon, IV. 341, 28 May 1629, Richelieu to Queen Mother, concerning sack of Privas; Avenel, III. 351–3, 18(?) June 1629, *Relation des progrès du Roy dans le Vivarez et le Languedoc*.
[53] R. Bireley, *Religion and Politics in the Age of the Counter-reformation. Emperor Ferdinand II, William Lamormaini, S.J., and the Formulation of Imperial Policy* (Chapel Hill, 1981), pp. 94–6; A. Wild (ed.) *Les papiers de Richelieu – Empire Allemand*, vol. I (1616–29) (Paris, 1982), pp. 559–61, 31 Aug.

The military context

As a result, substantial portions of the Imperial army were moved down from the German territories into north Italy after May 1629.[54] This influx of Imperial forces was matched by Philip IV and Olivares' decision to strengthen the Spanish forces in the Milanese and to give control of a second siege of Casale to marquis Ambrosio Spínola.[55] Both Imperial and Spanish forces began operations in autumn 1629, the Imperial army under count Rombaldo Collalto and Johann von Aldringen advancing into the duchy of Mantua, while Spínola prepared the ground for a siege of Casale by occupying a number of lesser *places* in Monferrato.[56]

If the siege of La Rochelle was a good example of military resources and activity deployed towards an attainable objective, the second French intervention in north Italy offered a prefiguration of the situation which was to develop from 1635. The gap between the objectives of the military intervention and the resources and organization committed to them was to become unbridgeably wide: the spectre of a protracted and inconclusive struggle hung over the French war-effort for the first eight months of 1630, and was finally lifted for reasons that had little to do with the effective or successful application of military force.

The report of the *conseil général* of July 1629 indicated that Richelieu had absorbed the implications of the arrival of Imperial troops in north Italy, but stressed that it would be completely impossible for the French to reenter Italy until September: 'il ne faut pas penser d'aller en Italie [avant] que la récolte ne soit faite, et les vendanges bien avancées'.[57] Apart from the troops garrisoning Casale itself, and a small force holding Susa, all other French troops had been pulled back into the Midi, and there was no possibility of a rapid response to these Habsburg moves.[58] Even after the Huguenot struggle had been brought to an end by the Grace of Allais (28 June 1629) Richelieu recognized that the renewal of war in Italy in the face of such a Habsburg military commitment would be a severe test for French military resources.[59]

In discussing the issues, Richelieu asserted that 35,000 infantry and 4,000

1629, Bouthillier to Richelieu, announcing the decision of the Emperor to lend military aid to the Spanish in north Italy.
[54] E. Straub, *Pax et Imperium. Spaniens Kampf um seine Friedensordnung in Europa zwischen 1617 und 1635* (Paderborn, 1980), p. 367; AAE CP Mantoue 2, fo. 646, 18 Sept. 1629, Nevers to Richelieu, reporting that some 30,000 Imperial troops were now assembled in the Milanese.
[55] Elliott, *The Count-Duke of Olivares*, pp. 387–8.
[56] Quazza, *Guerra per la successione*, I. 421–6; Bély, Bercé, Meyer and Quatrefages, *Guerre et paix*, II. 125–6.
[57] Avenel, III. 375–80, p. 377, [14] July 1629.
[58] Initial plans to keep strong forces on the border with Savoy were abandoned in the face of financial and military demands elsewhere: Avenel, III. 286–90, p. 290, 28 Apr. 1629.
[59] Avenel, III. 376–8, [14] July 1629, *Conseil général*. For much of the rest of 1629 Richelieu remained hopeful that it would be possible to obtain a negotiated settlement: Wild (ed.), *Papiers de Richelieu*, pp. 565–70, 8 Oct. 1629, Richelieu to Charles de Blanchefort, maréchal de Créqui, instructing him to offer a number of concessions to gain a peace settlement in Italy. However, by early November this hope had finally evaporated: AAE CP Mantoue 2, fo. 682, 11 Nov., Louis XIII to Créqui, asking

cavalry would be required to save the territories of the duke of Mantua, and added ominously that 'une moindre armée nécessiteuse ne fera autre effet qu'adjouster à la perte de ce prince [Mantua] celle de la réputation du Roy'.[60] For a number of reasons the armies raised for north Italy failed to approach anywhere near the target established by Richelieu for effective military operations. In the first case, the risk of an Imperial or Spanish counter-attack on the eastern frontier of France was sufficiently great to require the presence of a powerful corps under the command of maréchal Louis de Marillac.[61] In the event, this army was both badly funded and consistently under-strength, but its existence had inevitable consequences for the commitment to the Italian theatre.[62] Richelieu's exasperated sense that Marillac was asking for too much support and demanding the impossible in terms of financial and logistical support erupted in the middle of 1630, when he demanded of those who were critical of his management of the war:

s'il y a royaume au monde qui puisse paier régulièrement deux ou trois armées en mesme temps. Je voudrois qu'ils me disent si la raison ne requiert pas qu'on paie plus soigneusement une armée qui agit en pays estranger contre de puissantes forces qu'elle a en teste et où la cherté et les incommodités sont indicibles, qu'une qui demeure dans le royaume pour précaution du mal qui y pourroit arriver.[63]

The conviction that it was neither financially nor logistically practical to support more than a single major campaign army echoes a theme raised at the time of the Valtelline war and the Huguenot revolts. The problem, however, was not just that other forces raised for wider strategic objectives would be subject to financial and supply shortfalls, would be made up of poor quality and under-strength units and would receive little or no positive direction from the centre; maintaining these additional forces acted as a brake on the concentration of logistical and military resources required for the pursuit of an effective strategy in the main campaign theatres. A military system that was geared to the fighting of short campaigns in a single theatre was finally confronted in 1630 with the reality of a very different type of war. After 1635 Richelieu's ministry was constantly faced with the problem illustrated by his rhetorical question in 1630.

The need to divert troops to the army of Champagne was one factor preventing the concentration of resources on behalf of Mantua and Monferrato. An even

---

the latter to devote his efforts henceforth to discovering the attitude of the duke of Savoy to a renewal of war.

[60] Grillon, IV. 681, 21 Nov. 1629.

[61] Grillon, V. 222–3, 18 Apr. 1630, Louis de Marillac reports that Imperial forces were being concentrated, but suggests that this may be against Strasbourg rather than France; v. 267, 18 May, Louis de Marillac to Richelieu; Avenel, III. 859, 12 Aug. 1630, Richelieu to Michel de Marillac, reporting the rumour that Wallenstein was proposing to invade France through Burgundy.

[62] Grillon, V. 265, 18 May, Louis de Marillac's complaints about the delay in sending funds to his army; v. 550, 21 Aug. 1630, Marillac to Richelieu, complaining that revenues assigned to his army have proved entirely worthless.

[63] Grillon, V. 563, 30 Aug. 1630.

The military context

greater constraint was the political and military problem posed by the duke of Savoy and his territories. The commitment of military force to Monferrato or an attack on the Milanese required the voluntary or enforced acquiescence of the duke of Savoy in the passage of troops, matériel and supplies through his territories. The short campaign of 1629 had made gaining this acquiescence quite straightforward: the French army was relatively small, mobile and had a limited, quickly attained, objective. French diplomacy after the forcing of the pass of Susa had been more concerned to provide reasonable satisfaction to the ambitions of Carlo Emanuele than to defend the interests of Charles de Nevers.[64] However, the French decision to retain control of Susa for an unspecified period as a guarantee of good behaviour, and Carlo Emanuele's calculation that the build up of Habsburg forces in north Italy would lead to a decisive shift in the military balance, created growing suspicions of the duke's behaviour.[65] It remains unclear whether military intervention in the duke's states had been anticipated by Richelieu ever since he had voiced these suspicions in the autumn of 1629, whether it reflected the frustrated sense by early March 1630 that the supply and transport of the French troops across these territories was being systematically obstructed,[66] or whether it was finally ordered after the opportunistic seizure of the fortress of Pinerolo in late March.[67] The critical point about the decision was that it involved a military commitment not just to the occupation of a corridor through Piedmont, but to a second operation in the duchy of Savoy itself.[68] The reasoning behind this decision was military: it was not considered possible to sustain a substantial army in north Italy for a full campaign solely along the routes which linked Provence and Dauphiné directly with Piedmont. From the first, Richelieu had assumed that it would be necessary to move large numbers of men and supplies down from Burgundy and the Lyonnais through Savoy and thence into Piedmont, and to maintain a series of supply routes through Savoy for the duration of the war.[69]

---

[64] Carlo Emanuele was rewarded for his cooperation by the treaty of Bossolino of 10 May 1629 which, to the anger of Charles de Nevers, granted Savoy the disputed areas of Monferrato and promised French assistance in ensuring that this partition was guaranteed at any subsequent general peace settlement: AAE CP Savoie 9, fos. 114–19.

[65] Grillon, IV. 680–1, [21 Nov. 1629], 'Considérations pour estre veues par le Roi devant que je parte pour aller en Italie pour la seconde fois'; in mid-August, the ministers were already growing suspicious of the duke's re-fortification of various strategic *places* in Piedmont: Grillon, IV. 552, 19 Aug., Bullion to Richelieu.

[66] Grillon, v. 130–1, 10 Mar. 1630, *mémoire* of Richelieu to Bouthillier.

[67] Grillon, v. 149, 23 Mar. 1630, Richelieu to Queen Mother; v. 159, 30 Mar., Richelieu to Louis XIII; J. Humbert, *Une grande entreprise oubliée. Les Français en Savoie sous Louis XIII* (Paris, 1960), pp. 71–7.

[68] Humbert, *Les Français en Savoie*, pp. 103–4, assumes that the invasion of Savoy itself was a self-evident political necessity and required no explanation. In view of the near-disastrous burden that this extra commitment imposed on the French war-effort, and all of Richelieu's previous comments about the difficulty of sustaining a war in multiple theatres, the issue seems less straightforward.

[69] Grillon, v. 37–8, 20 Jan. 1630, 'Ordres donnés à Lyon par le cardinal de Richelieu pour la marche des troupes et leur concentration à Suse.'

France at war, 1624–1642

Primitive communications stretched over Alpine passes, the need to move soldiers by the shortest possible routes and the devastation that would be created by the constant movement of troops and supplies along a single line of communication meant that access to the campaign theatre needed to be widened as far as possible, with or without the cooperation of the duke of Savoy. Once the French Court had learnt that Carlo Emanuele was negotiating with the Spanish for a military alliance, it became clear that this cooperation would need to be forced; the logic of military occupation appeared irrefutable.

Richelieu expressed the hope that the campaign against the duchy of Savoy itself would require only a couple of months to bring to a conclusion, but he did register concern that this military operation would considerably reduce the strength of the army able to campaign in north Italy.[70] Having originally estimated that 35,000–40,000 troops would be necessary to take the offensive against the Spanish and Imperial forces, Richelieu was now in the process of raising a force of 18,000 troops under the direct command of the king for the conquest of Savoy.[71] What remained of these forces were to move on, after overrunning the duchy, to form the core of the campaigning army to be assembled in Piedmont.[72] Unsurprisingly, however, the campaign in Savoy, far from being the two-month *Blitzkrieg* that Richelieu had anticipated, dragged on through the summer. At the end of 1630 substantial French forces were still committed to the siege of Montmélian, less than ten miles from the capital, Chambéry.[73]

The military commitment to Savoy had a damaging effect upon the waging of the campaign on the Piedmont/Lombardy plain, influencing the timing of the intervention, the number of troops allocated to the theatre and the organization of supplies and reinforcements. Despite low-level Savoyard resistance, Toiras' garrison in Casale was reinforced and supplied as long as it was still possible for French forces to move across Monferrato, but Spínola's encirclement of Casale was finally completed on 24 May.[74] By 8 July, Richelieu had managed to pass 12,000 infantry and 1,400 cavalry down from Savoy into Piedmont, and two days later these troops had forced the duke of Savoy's troops back from Avigliana in a small-scale combat.[75] With the forces that were already in Piedmont, the French

---

[70] Grillon, v. 133–5, 10 Mar. 1630, Richelieu to Bouthillier, v. 164, 31 Mar. 1630, Richelieu's assurance to the king that the campaign in Savoy would require only two months to complete.

[71] Grillon, v. 164, 31 Mar. 1630, *Mémoire pour le roi*.

[72] Grillon, v. 211–12, 13 Apr. 1630, *mémoire* of Richelieu to the king; v. 377, 9 July 1630, letter of Louis XIII to the Queen Mother informing her that some 13,500 troops have passed down to Piedmont; Humbert, *Les Français en Savoie*, pp. 159–61, gives details of the troop movements in late June.

[73] Humbert, *Les Français en Savoie*, pp. 207–10; on 30 July, Bouthillier had reported that the siege of Montmélian was proving less straightforward than originally anticipated: Grillon, v. 454–5.

[74] Quazza, *Guerra per la successione*, II. 78.

[75] Grillon, v. 376, 377, 8/9 July 1630, letters from Richelieu and from the king to the Queen Mother, detailing troop movements; Grillon, v. 387, 12 July 1630, Louis XIII to Queen Mother on the

were able to muster a campaign army of some 20,000 foot and 2,600 horse.[76] But this was considered insufficient to challenge the Spanish and Imperial forces that were entrenched around Casale and held every other *place* in Monferrato.[77] Richelieu wrote that he had ordered the recruitment and despatch to Piedmont of a further 20,000 soldiers by the end of August, and while awaiting these reinforcements, the French troops spent the following month spread out across various fortified positions in Piedmont.[78]

The situation deteriorated further when on 18 July the fall of the city of Mantua itself to the Imperial army effectively ended the struggle in the main duchy.[79] The bulk of the Imperial army, paid and supplied from the booty of the sacked city and with several months of the campaign season remaining, would be free to move across to the western theatre, building up a formidable concentration of troops in Monferrato. In this new situation the arrival of reinforcements would not necessarily tip the military balance in favour of France.[80] Richelieu expected Casale to hold out until September, but this did not leave much time to undertake a relief operation.[81] In the event, the fears proved justified. French reinforcements took much longer to arrive in Italy than had been anticipated: Richelieu wrote to Antoine Coeffier de Ruzé, marquis d'Effiat, at the end of August that the main body of reinforcements could not be expected until the second week of September, 'qui sera bon pour vous renforcer, mais non pas pour le secours de Casal, qui doit estre fait devant'.[82] But without the reinforcements, the commanders were unprepared to act. Far from the 22,000 troops that they were reported to have at their disposal in July – still a considerably smaller force than had originally been considered desirable for the campaign – the force available by mid-September may have been whittled down by sickness and desertion to as few as 7,000 troops.[83] On paper, well over 20,000 additional troops had been raised to maintain the armies in Savoy and Piedmont, yet all of this effort could not sustain even a single army-corps at effective strength.[84] Moreover, initial estimates of the cost of

---

French success at Avigliana; J. Jacquart, 'Le marquis d'Effiat, lieutenant général à l'armée d'Italie (été 1630)', *Dix-Septième Siècle*, 45 (1959), 298–313.

[76] Avenel, III. 789–95, 17 July 1630, *Estat des affaires du Roy en Italie*, p. 792.

[77] Avenel, III. 789–95, 17 July 1630, *Estat des affaires du Roy en Italie*, p. 792.

[78] Avenel, III. 760, 13 July 1630, Richelieu to Toiras. The need to maintain the morale of the garrison at Casale may cast doubt on this statement of French intentions.

[79] Bély, Bercé, Meyer and Quatrefages, *Guerre et paix*, II. 128–30.

[80] Avenel, III. 865, 15 Aug. 1630: Richelieu informed the generals of the despatch of new regiments.

[81] Avenel, III. 780, 22/3 July 1630, Richelieu to the generals of the armies in Savoy and Piedmont; III. 866, 15 Aug. 1630, Richelieu to the generals, ordering them to act immediately to relieve Casale although reinforcements had not yet arrived.

[82] Avenel, III. 890, 28 Aug. 1630.

[83] Avenel, III. 907, 23 Sept. 1630, Richelieu to Schomberg: 'A la vérité il y a bien eu de la malice à ceux qui ont fait paroistre la première armée de Piedmont n'estre que de 7 mil hommes, lorsqu'il estoit question de résoudre le secours, ou consentir à la trefve, puisque depuis elle s'est trouvée de 13 mil.'

[84] Avenel, III. 760, 13 July 1630; III. 829, 6 Aug. 1630. Though both of these letters were written by Richelieu to Toiras, possibly to encourage his resistance at Casale.

France at war, 1624–1642

the *traités* required to supply the troops were set too low for the real price of obtaining and transporting the bread rations. The *munitionnaires* quickly discovered that the costs of transport from Dauphiné, Lyonnais and Provence were much higher than they had originally assumed, so that supply became erratic and delays mounted.[85] The mountain passes and narrow tracks that ran through Savoy and down into Piedmont were impassable for carts and waggons, and grain had to be transported on the backs of mules, forcing up the unit cost of supply, and also requiring the forced purchase of mules from large parts of southern France.[86]

The struggle for Casale was actually decided not on the plains of Piedmont or Lombardy but in north Germany and at the Electoral Diet of Regensburg. On 26 June Gustavus Adolphus landed at Peenemünde with a mere 14,000 troops.[87] Of greater immediate concern to the Habsburgs was the opening of the Diet of Regensburg on 3 July, which brought to the surface a mass of tensions created by the Imperial and catholic triumphs of the preceding half-decade.[88] Even before the concessions made by the Emperor at Regensburg which culminated in the dismissal of the Imperial generalissimo Albrecht Wallenstein, the Imperial forces in Germany were dangerously weakened and dispersed, ill-prepared to meet any threat more formidable than the demoralized and disunited troops of the protestant states.[89] The slow growth of Gustavus Adolphus' army in north Germany presented a potentially destabilizing challenge that the Emperor could not ignore.[90] Ferdinand II was left with little choice but to turn to north Italy, where the core of the Imperial army was still committed to the Habsburg war-effort and, if Olivares had his way, might remain there for years to come. At just the time, following the fall of Mantua, when the military advantage in north Italy seemed to have tipped against the French, the Emperor's willingness to press the

---

[85] The initial contracts assumed a price of 17 *livres* per charge of grain – Grillon, v. 111, 28 Feb. 1630; by early August, 24 *livres* per charge was considered an acceptable price and many new contracts were substantially more expensive than this: Grillon, v. 483, 4 Aug.; v. 491, 5 Aug. For inadequacies and increaing delays in ensuring supply see, for example, Grillon, v. 569, 3 Sept. 1630, Ferté-Imbault to Richelieu, who stresses that he is already able to provide only one and a half rations of bread every two days to his soldiers and that even this situation cannot be sustained in the future.
[86] Grillon, v. 393, 13 July 1630, Michel de Marillac to Richelieu; v. 394, 13 July, Claude Mallier, sieur du Houssay and *intendant des finances*, to Richelieu; v. 453/4, 30 July; v. 481, 3 Aug., Marillac to Richelieu: requisitioning of mules.
[87] Roberts, *Gustavus Adolphus*, II. 417.
[88] Straub, *Pax et Imperium*, pp. 412–13; Bireley, *Religion and Politics*, p. 117; Fagniez, *Père Joseph*, I. 439–59.
[89] Roberts, *Gustavus Adolphus*, II. 439–40, gives around 45,000 Imperial troops, but of low quality, largely unfit for campaigning in the field; B. Rill, *Tilly. Feldherr für Kaiser und Reich* (Munich, 1984), p. 209, gives 39,000 Imperial troops and 30,000 soldiers of the Catholic League. All figures are estimates, and the figures are less important than the general awareness that a large proportion of these troops were not battle-worthy.
[90] The Swedish army had been recruited up to around 26,000 by September: Roberts, *Gustavus Adolphus*, II. 444.

war to its conclusion evaporated, and his ministers prepared to negotiate a compromise settlement with the French representatives at Regensburg.[91]

Olivares was outraged that the Emperor should have made a settlement with the French without consulting Spain, but the treaty served notice that the Spanish could not look to Imperial support for any renewal of the military struggle in Italy.[92] Demoralized by the death of Spínola while the siege of Casale remained unconcluded, and aware that they could no longer afford to risk an all-out war with France, the Spanish commanders in Italy began peace negotiations.[93] French troops finally advanced into Monferrato, confronting the Spanish besieging forces outside the walls of Casale on 26 October. This provided the final impetus to the conclusion of a settlement, allowing the French forces to relieve Casale and opening the way to formal negotiations.[94] As the Habsburgs' difficulties and divisions mounted, Richelieu could simply afford to wait until they were brought to accept the two treaties of Cherasco in April and June 1631.[95]

FRENCH POLICY FROM CHERASCO TO NÖRDLINGEN, 1631–1634

Cherasco was a triumphant vindication for Richelieu and for the aims of his foreign policy. It wiped out the humiliating setbacks of the mid-1620s and forced the Spanish to accept a French settlement, imposed on territories that were considered to be well within their sphere of influence; it provided an immediate and dramatic enhancement of the king's international reputation, while opening up vistas of territorial expansion which had previously seemed elusive or unrealistic. For the next half-decade Richelieu could count upon the virtually unconditional support of the king in any debate about priorities and objectives in the formulation of state policy.[96] If the Day of Dupes (11 November 1630) enhanced the personal authority of the cardinal through the destruction of a major group of political rivals, the treaty of Cherasco represented the positive aspect of Richelieu's ascendancy.

Yet this diplomatic triumph had emerged from a high-risk military policy,

---

[91] H. Ernst, *Madrid und Wien 1632–37: Politik und Finanzen in den Beziehung zwischen Philipp IV und Ferdinand II* (Münster, 1991), pp. 40–1; H.G. Koenigsberger, *The Habsburgs and Europe, 1517–1660* (Ithaca and London, 1971), pp. 243–5.
[92] Elliott, *The Count-Duke of Olivares*, pp. 400–2; Straub, *Pax et Imperium*, pp. 433–6.
[93] Quazza, *Guerra per la successione*, II. 204–5; Elliott, *The Count-Duke of Olivares*, p. 402.
[94] Quazza, *Guerra per la successione*, II. 205–6.
[95] Quazza, *Guerra per la successione*, II. 271–8.
[96] Chevallier, *Louis XIII*, pp. 457–9; Richelieu's opponents regarded 1631 as the beginning of the period during which the cardinal exercised almost complete control over the mechanisms of patronage and favour: see the manifesto of Gaston d'Orléans written to the king, 30 May 1631, printed in G. Mongrédien, *10 Novembre 1630. La journée des dupes* (Paris, 1961), pp. 215–18; the king, in his response, saw fit explicitly to emphasize the central role of Richelieu in ensuring that 'ce Royaume n'a jamais esté si puissant ny si considéré qu'il est à present': Aubery, *Histoire du cardinal de Richelieu*, pp. 178–9.

which had revealed critical weaknesses in the organization and capacity of France's war-effort. In July/August 1630 Richelieu's whole policy in north Italy had seemed set for disaster. The French government was haunted by the fear that the Emperor would extend the war by an invasion across the eastern frontier, and that with the fall of Casale France would be powerless to shape the course of events in Italy. After Cherasco, therefore, Richelieu's policy was founded upon two working principles. The first of these was that France must avoid at all costs a war fought on multiple fronts, and by implication a war fought against both branches of the Habsburg dynasty simultaneously. The dangers of overcommitment and the problems of concentrating and controlling troops in more than one major campaign theatre were obvious after the experience of 1630. The fears were not entirely concerned with the military power of the Habsburgs; they also reflected the awareness of the strains placed upon a state whose administrative structures were still rudimentary, and where political authority was insecure. The challenge to an over-ambitious war-effort was as likely to come from inside France as from the armies of her enemies. Richelieu's policy to return to waging war whose scale and duration were more suited to France's existing capacities appears short-sighted and unrealistic only with the hindsight that assumes that an all-out struggle between Habsburg and Bourbon was inevitable. There is little to suggest that this was more than an outside risk before September 1634. For the second lesson that Richelieu had learned from the Mantuan war, and which was to shape his subsequent policy, was that allies could be used to ensure that Habsburg power was not brought to bear upon France.

As Richelieu and his colleagues recognized, the situation in Italy in 1630 was saved by events in the north of the Empire; these events had confronted the Habsburgs with too many pressing military commitments, so that the Emperor tried to try to gain a settlement in Italy regardless of the relative strengths and weaknesses of the military situation.[97] The expansion of Swedish power in north and central Germany, the leadership and revitalization that this gave to the military forces of the Protestant states, is the most obvious instance of this shift in military power. The tide might still have turned back in favour of the Habsburgs, but the battle of Breitenfeld in September 1631 ensured that the Swedes would remain a military force in the Empire for the forseeable future.[98] Of equal importance was the decision by the United Provinces to assume the offensive in

---

[97] The factor which both allowed the French plenipotentiaries to negotiate the favourable agreement with the Emperor at Regensburg, and allowed Richelieu subsequently to repudiate the treaty: Fagniez, *Père Joseph*, I. 510–12.

[98] Within a month, Tilly had reassembled a campaign army of 25,000 troops: Rill, *Tilly*, pp. 280–1; Roberts, *Gustavus Adolphus*, II. 551, suggests that Tilly had between 40,000 and 45,000 men under his command by mid-October. For the symbolic importance of Breitenfeld for protestant Europe see S. Adams, 'Tactics or politics? The "military revolution" and the Habsburg hegemony, 1525–1648', in J. Lynn (ed.) *Tools of War. Instruments, Ideals and Institutions of Warfare, 1445–1871* (Urbana, Ill., 1990), pp. 28–52, at p. 28.

The military context

the land war for the first time since the expiry of the truce in 1621. In 1629 the Dutch army captured 's-Hertogenbosch, and breached a key element in the defences of the Spanish Netherlands. The Army of Flanders, run down in order to sustain the costs of war in Italy, was underpaid, demoralized and mutinous. The nobility of the Spanish Netherlands appeared on the verge of revolt.[99]

Encouraged by these developments, Richelieu's carefully balanced policy was to try to ensure that France's allies could play a major role in the struggle against the Habsburgs, while not being so successful that they might be in a position to break away altogether in order to make a separate peace treaty. To help the allies maintain military pressure on the Habsburgs, France was prepared to pay increasingly heavier subsidies, to lend diplomatic support in disputes with third parties and in the last resort to provide covert military support. Every inducement was provided to keep France's allies in the war, except an open and full-scale military intervention on their behalf. It was because of this refusal that negotiations with the Dutch and the Swedes progressively soured and at times came close to collapse, while attempts to create a catholic 'third force' in the Empire and a League of Italian states remained matters for discussion rather than action.[100] But this refusal was the key to Richelieu's pre-1635 strategy. It accounted for the considerable successes of French policy in the years from 1631 to 1634.

Sustained by the military effort of France's allies, Richelieu's European policies from 1631 were confrontational and ultimately expansionist in character. Richelieu assumed that Spain, the main target of French assertiveness, could not afford to add another major power to her enemies, and so would not respond to these steps with measures that would push local hostilities towards all-out war.[101] Spanish evidence indicates that Richelieu was correct in this assumption. While acknowledging that France was 'the source of all our troubles', neither Philip IV nor his councillors were prepared to consider an additional burden on Spanish resources so long as her other military commitments remained in place.[102] During

---

[99] J. Israel, 'Olivares and the government of the Spanish Netherlands, 1621–1643', in J. Israel, *Empires and Entrepots. The Dutch, the Spanish Monarchy and the Jews, 1585–1713* (London, 1990), pp. 174–6; Elliott, *The Count-Duke of Olivares*, pp. 388–92.

[100] The creation of a 'third force' in the Empire, founded upon the separation of Bavaria from the Habsburg alliance, was a cherished ambition of Père Joseph: Fagniez, *Père Joseph*, I. 535–544. Avenel, VII. 694–704, [mid-February 1633], *Mémoire pour M. le duc de Créqui*, followed by a discussion of the various projects for a League of Italian states before and after 1633. By July 1634 the representatives of the king of France were prepared to discuss in general terms the allocation of troops to support a movement by the Italian princes against Spain, but the commitments remained vague and dependent upon the princes, led by the duke of Savoy, taking the initiative. The best and most comprehensive account of French policy towards Italy is provided by S. Externbrink, *'Le cœur du monde': Frankreich und die norditalienischen Staaten (Mantua, Parma, Savoyen) im Zeitalter Richelieus, 1624–1635* (Münster, 1999), pp. 202–325.

[101] An assumption made explicit in his *Mémoires*, VIII. 212: 'en assistant nos alliés contre lesquels ils [the Habsburg powers] employoient leurs armes, qu'ils ne pouvoient cependant, comme ils eussent bien désiré, tourner contre nous'.

[102] Elliott, *The Count-Duke of Olivares*, pp. 435–8, 469; Straub, *Pax et Imperium*, p. 452; R. Stradling,

this period, which could be described as the most cost-effective and successful for French foreign policy until the 1660s, Richelieu pursued a number of long-standing dynastic and territorial aims. Assertive policies reflected, as might be expected, a fluid notion of French 'vital interests'; but the areas which she sought to occupy or to deny to the Habsburg armies reduced the threat to France's vulnerable eastern frontier, and gave her the capacity to intervene more quickly and easily in territories which might serve for the assembly of enemy forces.[103] Moreover, advancing beyond the eastern frontier provided the possibility of disrupting the main axis of Habsburg communications, cutting the part of the 'Spanish Road' which ran from the Franche-Comté up along the Rhine.

Richelieu remained cautious during 1631 about exploiting France's position on the edge of the European conflict. He took the opportunity in October unilaterally to modify the terms of the treaty of Cherasco with the duke of Savoy in order to keep the fortress of Pinerolo permanently in French hands.[104] At the same time, Charles de Nevers, newly installed as duke of Mantua, realized that the fortress of Casale was not going to be handed back to his own troops, but was to remain garrisoned by French forces.[105] The future direction of French policy could be seen most clearly in the increasing diplomatic and military pressure that Richelieu placed upon Charles IV and his duchy of Lorraine. The refusal of the successive dukes of Lorraine to accept France's claims to the bishoprics of Metz, Toul and Verdun represented one of the most persistent obstacles to the full incorporation of the *Trois Evêchés* into France.[106] The army of Champagne which had been established in 1629/30 against the threat of an Imperial invasion was retained and expanded through 1631. The military threat to Lorraine was real, although it was not until the end of the year that Richelieu seized the opportunity to overawe the duke and to use the army to assert France's authority over the *Trois Evêchés* by seizing the fortress of Moyenvic.[107] Richelieu was aware that this action would almost certainly lead to armed clashes between French and Imperial troops, but as

---

'Olivares and the origins of the Franco-Spanish War, 1627–1635', *English Historical Review*, 101 (1986), 68–94, at 83–4.

[103] Richelieu, *Mémoires*, VII. 270–324 [Jan. 1633], overview of political and diplomatic aims of Richelieu's interventionist policies.

[104] Grillon, VI. 710 n. 2, secret negotiations for the (ultimately) permanent cession of Pinerolo to France; Avenel, IV. 206/7, 25 Oct. 1631, Richelieu to Toiras; Externbrink, *Cœur du monde*, pp. 190–201.

[105] Avenel, VII. 673–4, 24 Jan. 1632, Louis XIII to Toiras; Hanotaux, *Richelieu*, III 420–1; Straub, *Pax et Imperium*, p. 449.

[106] J.-O., comte d'Haussonville, *Histoire de la réunion de la Lorraine à la France* (4 vols; Paris, 1854–9), I. 29–30, 144–5; G. Zeller, *La réunion de Metz à la France (1552–1648)* (2 vols; Paris, 1926), II. 76–8, 230–6; R. Babel, *Zwischen Habsburg und Bourbon. Aussenpolitik und europäische Stellung Herzog Karls IV. von Lothringen und Bar vom Regierungsantritt bis zum Exil (1624–1634)* (Sigmaringen, 1989), pp. 51–2. An equally contentious issue was the homage that the dukes owed to the kings of France for part of the territory around Bar: Babel, *Karls IV*, pp. 22–3.

[107] Grillon, VI. 695–6, 30 Nov. 1631; VI. 713, 9 Dec. 1631: Louis XIII to maréchal de La Force; Zeller, *Réunion de Metz*, II. 241–2.

The military context

the cardinal wrote to the commander of the army of Champagne, Jacques-Nompar de Caumont, maréchal de La Force: 'Sa Majesté estant résolue d'une façon ou d'[une]autre d'avoir ceste place [Moyenvic], et principalement à ceste heure qu'elle a advis des extraordinaires progrez que faict le roy de Suède . . .'[108] Rather than be crushed between the forces of France and Sweden, Charles accepted the treaty of Vic on 6 January 1632, by which he handed over Marsal to the French for three years as a guarantee of his good behaviour.[109]

Strengthening France's position in Lorraine and up to the frontiers of Alsace was particularly desirable, because the westward advance of the Swedish army had created deep concern amongst the numerous territorial princes in Alsace, Franconia and the middle valley of the Rhine. In December, Louis had issued a declaration offering protection to all sovereign princes within the Empire who requested French support.[110] But while the mantle of 'protector' of the German states allowed France a clear and ultimately profitable role in the Empire, it also implied an obligation to offer military support against the Emperor or, more immediately, the Swedes, when required. In December, Mainz was occupied by the advancing Swedish army, openly defying French declarations of support for the neutrality of the electorate.[111] Bavaria, the key to France's 'catholic' policy in the Empire, was to be invaded in March 1632 despite all French attempts to discourage the Swedes from taking this step.[112]

As the Swedes continued their sweep down the Rhine and into Bavaria, the most important of the Rhineland princes who had so far escaped Swedish occupation, the Trier Elector, archbishop Philipp Christoph von Sötern, decided that open-ended French guarantees were a better safeguard than nothing, and formally requested Louis XIII's military support in April 1632.[113] The Spanish, concerned at the French advance eastward, took the opportunity to occupy Koblenz, the archbishop's key fortress on the west bank of the Rhine and directly opposite Ehrenbreitstein, now garrisoned by French troops. For several weeks French and Spanish troops skirmished over the territory surrounding the two fortresses.[114] The unremarkable discovery that duke Charles of Lorraine was

---

[108] Avenel, IV. 212–13, 9 Dec. 1631, Richelieu to La Force; AAE CP Lorraine 9, fos. 127–8, [Jan. 1632], assessment of the position of Lorraine in the light of Swedish military success.

[109] AAE CP Lorraine 9, fos. 131–8, Jan. 1632, treaty of Vic; C.J. Burckhardt, *Richelieu* (3 vols; London, 1970), III. 24; d'Haussonville, *Lorraine*, I. 228–33; Babel, *Karl IV*, pp. 139–42.

[110] Zeller, *Réunion de Metz*, II. 251–69; H. Weber, *Frankreich, Kurtrier, der Rhein und das Reich, 1623–1635* (Bonn, 1969), pp. 122–42; H. Weber, 'Richelieu et le Rhin', *Revue historique*, 239 (1968), 265–80, at 273–4; W.H. Stein, *Protection Royale. Eine Untersuchung zu den Protektionsverhältnissen im Elsaß zur Zeit Richelieus, 1622–1643* (Münster, 1978), pp. 85–6.

[111] Avenel, IV. 245 [8] Jan. 1632, Richelieu to the Elector of Mainz, reporting French attempts to discourage the Swedes from occupying the Electorate.

[112] G. Pagès, *The Thirty Years War* (Eng. trans., London, 1970), pp. 141–5; D. Albrecht, *Die auswärtige Politik Maximilians von Bayern, 1618–1635* (Göttingen, 1962), pp. 320–1, 343–5.

[113] Weber, *Frankreich, Kurtrier*, pp. 174–96.

[114] Weber, *Frankreich, Kurtrier*, pp. 206–29.

giving tacit support to the Spanish gave Richelieu the excuse to concentrate French forces on the border with Lorraine during April 1632.[115] Faced once again with overwhelming military superiority, Charles had to submit, making peace in late June by the treaty of Liverdun.[116]

Beneath the facade of these successful foreign initiatives were signs of danger. The effort of sustaining armies – in Languedoc to counter the revolt of Henri II, duc de Montmorency, in Trier against the Spanish, in Lorraine and in the north Italian garrisons – revealed weaknesses in the administration and financing of the war-effort which recalled the situation of 1630. Richelieu had been fortunate in that all three field campaigns had been conducted against enemies who had no wish to fight a lengthy war, and in the case of the Spanish and the duke of Lorraine had backed away from an intensification of hostilities. Despite this, the army in Trier ran out of funds, and was close to mutiny by the time that the Spanish decided to evacuate the Electorate.[117] The evidence of 1632 suggested that the problems of sustaining multiple armies in dispersed campaign theatres were as great as ever.

The end of the year brought a piece of unexpected good fortune for Richelieu in the death of Gustavus Adolphus at the battle of Lützen (16 November 1632). Lützen removed a leader whose ambitions and charisma had caused Richelieu considerable concern, while simultaneously vindicating the reputation of the Swedish army as the most formidable military force in the Empire. Richelieu was hopeful that the result of the battle would be an amenable Sweden, a still powerful ally but one more prepared to respect French wishes in return for subsidies and political support.[118] 1633 thus appeared an opportune moment for a further stage in Richelieu's policy – a wider occupation of the territory of the duke of Lorraine.[119] By the end of August French troops under La Force had occupied the Barrois, and then moved on to lay siege to Nancy, which fell on 20 September. Faced with the loss of his capital and the non-appearance of support from Spain or the Imperial army, Charles once again felt obliged to seek terms; by the treaty of Charmes he was forced to accept a French occupation of Nancy for thirty years.[120]

---

[115] Avenel, IV. 275–8, 1 Apr. 1632, 'Instructions à M. de Guron, allant en Lorraine'; IV. 311–12, 21 June, Richelieu to Charles IV: 'je suis extresmement fasché que le roy ayt esté constraint de s'avancer dans vos estats pour tirer raison de ce dont il vous l'a demandée plusieurs fois'.

[116] AAE CP Lorraine 9, fos. 139–43, 25 June, treaty of Liverdun; D'Haussonville, *Lorraine*, I. 267–9; Babel, *Karl IV*, pp. 150–4.

[117] Bonney, *King's Debts*, p. 163, quoting the testimony of de Noyers.

[118] Avenel, IV. 415–16, 15 Dec. 1632, Richelieu to Louis XIII; Fagniez, *Père Joseph*, II. 105–6.

[119] Avenel, IV. 479–80, 18 Aug. 1633, Richelieu to M. de La Grange-aux-Ormes: 'Maintenant que le roy a desjà, dans les Estats dudit duc, une armée de quinze mil hommes de pied et mil chevaux'; Babel, *Karl IV*, pp. 175–8.

[120] Avenel, IV. 483–6, 20 Sept. 1633, Richelieu to Bouthillier and to La Force; Babel, *Karl IV*, pp. 180–1. The importance of the fall of Nancy for subsequent French military action in Alsace is underlined by Stein, *Protection Royale*, pp. 235–7.

The military context

In October 1633 Eberhard III, duke of Württemburg, placed the duchy of Monbéliard in French hands as the price of French protection for his territories.[121] He was followed in December by count Philipp-Wolfgang of Hanau-Lichtenberg, who opened the towns of Bischweiler, Ingwiller and Neuwiller in Lower Alsace to French troops.[122] In January 1634 Hermann Adolf, count of Salm, who had previously made the miscalculation of looking to Charles of Lorraine for protection, now switched across to the French, who gained control of Haguenau, Saverne and Hohbar. Johann Georg von Ostein, bishop of Basle, followed this example a few weeks later.[123] By the limited deployment of military means, Richelieu had dramatically increased French power over Lorraine; through forceful diplomacy based on the fear of Spanish and Swedish intentions, France now held a significant number of the major fortifications on the Rhine from Ehrenbreitstein and Koblenz down to Basle.

Richelieu had every intention of pursuing the same policy through 1634. In April Richelieu accepted terms for a renewal of the alliance with the United Provinces whose military pressure had proved such a valuable support to France's own policies in 1632 and 1633.[124] The Dutch proposal that the alliance be turned into a full offensive treaty and that France should make an open and immediate break with Spain was once again rejected by Richelieu.[125] The dilemma for the Habsburg powers had now became intense; they could ignore the wider issue of French military involvement in support of their enemies, and simply fight French troops in the campaign theatre to which Richelieu and Louis XIII chose to commit them; alternatively, they could take France's action to be tantamount to a declaration of war, and broaden the scale of the conflict – although this would add a formidable, possibly fatal, additional burden to what was already a war-effort stretched to capacity. Contemplating this second possibility on 13 April 1634, the Spanish Council of State resolved that, while open war against France was entirely justified, it would not be desirable to take such a step at this point.[126]

These calculations were to be swept aside in striking manner on 6 September by the battle of Nördlingen, when the main Swedish and German protestant campaign armies were annihilated at the hands of a Spanish and Imperial force which had come together for a limited operation to drive the Swedes out of upper

---

[121] J. Ellerbach, *Der Dreißigjährige Krieg in Elsaß (1618–1648)* (3 vols; Mülhausen, 1912–28), III. 25; Stein, *Protection Royale*, pp. 221–32.
[122] Stein, *Protection Royale*, pp. 240–4.
[123] Stein, *Protection Royale*, pp. 275–89; L. Vautrey, *Histoire des Evêques de Bale* (2 vols.; Einsiedeln, 1884), II. 193–201.
[124] Fagniez, *Père Joseph*, II. 202–6; J. de Pange, *Charnacé et l'alliance franco-hollandaise (1633–1637)* (Paris, 1905), pp. 100–13.
[125] Avenel, VII. 726–7, 23 July 1634 – reiterates the determination to avoid an open break with Spain, and seeks to maintain the agreement of 15 Apr.; Fagniez, *Père Joseph*, II. 206–7; Pange, *Charnacé*, p. 108; Israel, *Dutch Republic*, pp. 303–4.
[126] Stradling, 'Olivares and the origins', 88; G. Parker, *The Thirty Years War* (London, 1984), p. 144; Elliott, *The Count-Duke of Olivares*, pp. 469, 472.

France at war, 1624–1642

Bavaria.[127] Over-confidence in Swedish military capability inherited from Gustavus Adolphus and inadequate local information encouraged the protestant commanders to risk a battle fought from a position of unnecessary weakness, the consequence of which profoundly altered the balance of military power in the Empire. Suddenly, the prospect of an offensive aimed at the elimination of France's military capacity and the removal of cardinal Richelieu became a possibility. Despite a traditional historiography which argues that 'for a long time Richelieu had been prepared for the day when France would have to move from covert to open war', there was no reason for Richelieu to anticipate that an event such as the battle of Nördlingen would occur, or to shape his policies against such a remote eventuality.[128]

Even after the battle, there still seemed little reason to consider that the military situation had changed decisively.[129] The Spanish army was not to be a permanent force in the Empire, but was *en route* for the Netherlands, where the political situation had again worsened since the death of the regent Isabella Clara Eugenia on 1 December 1633.[130] Yet this period of renewed French confidence could not last. A critical factor in the growing realization that France would find it difficult to continue with existing policies was the worsening military situation of the German protestant army of Bernard, duke of Saxe-Weimar, during the last months of 1634, and the weakening of the will to further resistance amongst the protestant states of the Empire.[131] The protestant Assembly of Frankfurt resolved in September that it would not support Saxe-Weimar's army if Johan Banér and the remaining Swedish army refused to be drawn into the western territories of the Empire.[132] Faced with this weakening of the protestant position, Louis proposed to station a substantial French army on the west bank of the Rhine, and to threaten active intervention across the river if any of the territories under French protection were menaced.[133]

Tension was exacerbated as the Imperial forces operating in the western territories of the Empire were regularly reinforced throughout late October and November. The first point of conflict was the Lower Palatinate, and in particular

---

[127] A. van Der Essen, *Le Cardinal-Infant et la politique européenne de l'Espagne (1609–1634)* (Brussels, 1944), pp. 411–23; W. Struck, *Die Schlacht bei Nördlingen* (Stralsund, 1893).

[128] Pagès, *Thirty Years War*, p. 173; Richelieu's own *Mémoires* are perceptive about the battle, and the unnecessary and hazardous decisions which precipitated it: VIII. 176–7; Le Vassor, *Louis XIII*, VIII. 281: 'ces deux habiles Politiques [Richelieu and Père Joseph] se trouvoient autant embarassez qu'Oxenstiern'.

[129] The strengthening of the Habsburg position ensured that a final series of territories in Alsace accepted French protection, thus seemingly reinforcing her position up to the Rhine: Stein, *Protection Royale*, pp. 313–51; Ellerbach, *Elsaß*, III. 80–1, 103–9.

[130] Van Der Essen, *Cardinal-Infant*, pp. 425–50.

[131] E. Charvériat, *Histoire de la Guerre de Trente Ans* (2 vols; Paris, 1878), II. 301; Noailles, *Saxe-Weimar*, pp. 134–6.

[132] Noailles, *Saxe-Weimar*, pp. 131–3.

[133] Fagniez, *Père Joseph*, II. 189–90.

the major fortified cities of Heidelberg and Mannheim, both of which had been taken and garrisoned by the Swedes in 1633, and were seen as the key to control of the territory between the Rhine and the Neckar.[134] The imminent fall of Heidelberg presented Louis XIII and Richelieu with a critical moment of decision on the road to open confrontation. The refusal of Saxe-Weimar to carry out the relief of Heidelberg, using the remnants of his own army, together with French troops acting as an 'independent' force, persuaded the French into direct military action across the Rhine. The arrival of 6,000 French troops forced the Imperial and Bavarian forces to raise the siege and allowed the garrison to be reinforced and supplied.[135] France was now directly and openly involved in the struggle in the Empire, and had supplemented the army of La Force, which carried out the relief of Heidelberg, with a second army commanded by the duc de Rohan intended to secure the French garrisons and positions in Upper Alsace.[136]

At the same time that Louis and Richelieu were initiating policies that would lead inexorably towards war on the Rhine, evidence started to accumulate that the victory at Nördlingen had allowed the Habsburgs to reconsider their overall strategy: a war fought entirely in the Rhineland was one fought to a large extent on terms favourable to France. The lessons of the previous conflicts were quite clear to Spanish and Imperial statesmen; if France was to be defeated it would be through forcing her to dissipate her military resources rather than concentrating them in one chosen theatre. In late 1634 the primary concern had been the possibility that the Spanish would start this process of widening the struggle by launching an amphibious attack on the coast of Provence. A series of letters during October to the governor of Provence, Nicolas de l'Hospital, maréchal de Vitry, and to various governors of key *places*, warned of this possibility, and urged them to press ahead with defensive measures.[137] At the same time, it is clear that Louis and his ministers feared an attack directed against France by parts of the Army of Flanders, especially if the pressure of the Dutch in the north was reduced.

Back on the Rhine, the Imperial response to the relief of Heidelberg came with the surprise capture of Philippsburg one month later, on the night of 23/4 January.[138] The Habsburg powers were now clearly unperturbed by the possibility

---

[134] Charvériat, *Guerre de Trente Ans*, II. 295–8.
[135] Burckhardt, *Richelieu*, III. 54–5; La Force, *Mémoires*, III. 96–9.
[136] Ellerbach, *Elsaß*, III. 114–29.
[137] SHAT A^1 23, fo. 96, 8 Oct. 1634, Abel Servien, *secrétaire d'Etat de la guerre*, to Vitry concerning Spanish plans for a descent on Provence; fo. 99, 8 Oct., Servien to Sr de Sollier, governor of Toulon, concerning defensive preparations, fos. 100, 101, 8 Oct., similar instructions for Marseilles and for the Provençal coast in general. By 18 Oct., the crown was able to inform Vitry that the projected Spanish attack would be of 3,000 Spanish and 4,000 Neapolitan troops: fo. 134.
[138] AAE CP Allemagne 12, fo. 45, 31 Jan. 1635, marquis de Brézé to Grange-aux-Ormes, blaming the commanders of the French army for allowing the capture; Avenel, IV. 660–1, 8 Feb. 1635, Richelieu to La Force; Noailles, *Saxe-Weimar*, pp. 155–6.

of provoking all-out war with France. The treaty of 8 February 1635 with the States General of the United Provinces finally ended the period during which the French king had refused to make an open diplomatic commitment to war against the Habsburgs.[139] The shift in the French negotiating position was even more evident in the case of Oxenstierna and the Swedish Council; if France was committed to open war with the Habsburgs, the support of even the reduced forces at the disposal of the Swedes was considered essential.[140] Furthermore, now that France appeared on course for war, Louis and Richelieu seem to have returned to some of the aims and ambitions of earlier foreign policy. The hope of achieving political and territorial advantage in Italy was once again revived, though the argument for an extension of the conflict was set in terms of the need to secure alliances, and the creation of an anti-Spanish 'Italian League'.[141] A similar willingness to return to 'unfinished business' can be seen in the decision to reopen the struggle for control of the Valtelline.[142]

The last acts in the progress towards open war occurred as these alliances and military arrangements were being finalized. Saxe-Weimar, drawn towards cooperation with the French by the necessity to which his army had been reduced, proposed a surprise attack, launched in collaboration with troops from a French army-corps, to recapture Speyer.[143] The capture was seen very largely in psychological terms; it was a much-needed boost to the reputation of the king after a period during which the military initiative had been held by the Habsburgs.[144] However, the balance of advantage swung dramatically back once again when on 26 March a Spanish force entered the archbishopric of Trier and kidnapped the Elector. Despite the ambiguous attitudes of his subjects, the Elector himself had been one of the earliest and most consistent adherents of French protection. His abduction was an outright challenge to the credibility of French military and political guarantees, and demanded a French response.[145] France finally issued a formal declaration of war, delivered by one of the royal heralds in Brussels on 19 May and – with apparent anachronism – presented as a personal challenge from one king to another.

---

[139] Pange, *Charnacé*, pp. 114–22; Fagniez, *Père Joseph*, II. 202–11; Israel, *Dutch Republic*, pp. 524–8.
[140] Fagniez, *Père Joseph*, II. 199.
[141] Externbrink, *Cœur du monde*, pp. 303–25, 348–60.
[142] Hanotaux, *Richelieu*, V. 95–6; Laugel, *Rohan*, pp. 319–23.
[143] Noailles, *Saxe-Weimar*, pp. 162–4.
[144] La Force, *Mémoires*, III. 111.
[145] AAE CP Allemagne 12, fo. 117, 3 Apr., Brézé to *surintendant* Bouthillier, concerning the humiliation of the loss of Trier; though as Gustave Fagniez correctly insisted, the abduction of the Elector was no more than a 'prétexte bien choisi'. Louis and his ministers had already resolved to go to war: *Père Joseph*, II. 266–7.

The military context

THE FRENCH WAR-EFFORT, 1635–1642

Les plus grands princes de la terre ayant toujours fait difficulté d'entreprendre deux guerres à la fois, la postérité aura de la peine à croire que ce royaume ait esté capable d'entretenir séparément à ses seuls despens sept armées de terre.[146]

The failures and near-disaster of the first years of France's open involvement in the Thirty Years War have always presented an historiographical problem for studies of Richelieu's ministry. The usual explanation assumes that France's armies lacked experience and were unprepared for the war to which they now found themselves committed.[147] Moreover, the organization of a war-effort on this scale proved a formidable challenge to the administrative and organizational capacities of the government, which floundered for the first few years before managing to solve the fundamental problems of control, finance and supply. This interpretation assumes that a *tournant militaire* could occur as soon as these fundamental problems were resolved and that France's superior resources could be deployed to ensure her military advantage over the battered and overstrained Habsburg powers.[148] Yet this interpretation seems incompatible with an earlier stage of the traditional interpretation of Richelieu's ministry, which asserts that France avoided large-scale involvement in the European war before 1635 precisely in order to make those military and administrative preparations that would allow her to deploy her resources more effectively.[149] The thesis that the preceding period was one of preparation for *guerre ouverte*, like so many other myths surrounding Richelieu's ministry, originated in the cardinal's own writings, in this

---

[146] Richelieu, *Testament politique*, p. 83.
[147] The thesis that France was unprepared for large-scale war in 1635 has had a long history: Richelieu, *Mémoires*, VIII. 212–13; Le Vassor, *Louis XIII*, VIII. 394; Fagniez, *Père Joseph*, II. 263–5; Hanotaux, *Richelieu*, IV. 398–432; Pagès, *Thirty Years War*, pp. 176–9; V.-L. Tapié, *France in the Age of Louis XIII and Richelieu* (Eng. trans., London, 1974), pp. 332–5; M. Carmona, *Richelieu. L'ambition et le pouvoir* (Paris, 1983), pp. 568–73; Mousnier, *L'Homme Rouge*, pp. 543–8; the opinion that France's entry into the war in 1635 was dangerous and ill-considered was held by a number of contemporary memoirists: see, for example, François VI de La Rochefoucauld, *Mémoires*, in Petitot and Monmerqué, LI. 350: 'On avoit considéré la déclaration de la guerre . . . comme une entreprise hardie et douteuse'; Montglat, *Mémoires*, XLIX. 76–7; Henri-Auguste de Loménie, comte de Brienne, *Mémoires*, in Petitot and Monmerqué, XXXVI. 54: 'Les plus éclairés furent étonnés de cette résolution, prévoyant bien les malheurs que cause la guerre.'
[148] Tapié, *France in the Age*, pp. 332–76: 'The great ordeal', and pp. 377–427: 'The fight to the death'; Chevalier, *Louis XIII*, pp. 499–546: 'L'année de Corbie', and pp. 560–600: 'Le tournant militaire de 1640–1641'; Carmona, *Richelieu*, pp. 619–44: 'Le grand tournant'; Mousnier, *L'Homme Rouge*, pp. 566–606: 'Les affres d'angoisse (1635–1638)', and pp. 684–706: 'Vers la victoire (1638–1642)'.
[149] The notion that the 1630s were a period of preparation for the 'great ordeal' sometimes, and confusingly, co-exists with the traditional argument that France was unready for the war which broke out in 1635: see, for example, Pagès, *Thirty Years War*, pp. 173–4; Chevalier, *Louis XIII*, pp. 499–504; Burckhardt, *Richelieu*, III. 61–6, who both argues that Richelieu had been rearming France since 1624, and that the French military contingents in 1635 were much too small; H. Weber, 'Vom verdeckten zum offenen Krieg. Richelieu's Kriegsgründe und Kriegsziele', in Repgen (ed.), *Krieg und Politik,*, 203–17, at pp. 211–12.

case the 'succincte narration des grandes actions du Roy', from the *Testament politique*.[150] The notion of a period of relative peace being used to carry out administrative and fiscal reform is hard to reconcile with the general reluctance or inability of early seventeenth-century governments to undertake any such restructuring not imposed upon them by external necessity. France's policies after 1631 cannot, as has been shown, be understood as a period of passivity abroad deliberately decided upon in order to facilitate reform at home.

By April 1635 Louis XIII and Richelieu had underpinned firm diplomatic commitment to France's allies with plans for large-scale military intervention in a number of different campaign theatres. On one level these extensive military plans are entirely comprehensible, as was Richelieu's initial confidence that the allied cause would make rapid progress.[151] Although the Swedish gains of the early 1630s had been overturned, Swedish forces were to remain a source of stubborn resistance in north-east Germany, and by 1638 they were able to retake the offensive in the Empire. The interminable conflict with the Dutch made the full deployment of Spanish forces against France impossible; in fact a predominant element in Spanish strategy continued to be the concentration of the war-effort against the Dutch, in the hope of bringing them to accept a separate peace.[152] The overcommitment of France's enemies was combined with their exhaustion; the commitment of the Austrian and Spanish Habsburgs since 1619 had been massive and virtually unbroken. To these troubles may be added the economic stagnation of Castile, the precipitate collapse of the New World bullion yields from the 1620s and the growing levels of resentment in the other territories of the Spanish Empire at the attempts to extract compensatory financial support.[153] The ravaging of parts of the Hereditary Lands and of the states of Austria's allies in the Empire had a similar effect on their military capacity, as did the endemic peasant revolts in territories such as Upper Austria, subjected to profound religious, economic and military disruption throughout the 1620s and 1630s.[154]

In contrast, France possessed far greater natural resources, especially population, and the French crown could draw upon tax revenues and other sources of

---

[150] Richelieu, *Testament politique*, pp. 74–5: 'c'est un effet d'une prudence singulière d'avoir occupé dix ans durant toutes les forces des ennemis de vostre Estat par celles de vos alliez en mettant la main à la bourse et non aux armes'.

[151] AAE MD 814, fo. 157, 11 June 1635, Richelieu to Bouthillier, expressing his optimistic belief that Olivares would not long be able to delay negotiations for a general peace; the general tone of Richelieu's correspondence in these opening months of the war was positive, almost jaunty: Avenel, IV. 709, 18 Apr. 1635; IV. 712–13, 20 Apr.; IV. 715, 21 Apr., etc.

[152] J. Israel, *The Dutch Republic and the Hispanic World 1606–1661* (Oxford, 1982), pp. 251–2; J. Israel, 'Olivares, the Cardinal-Infante and Spain's strategy in the Low Countries (1635–1643): the road to Rocroi', in R. Kagan and G. Parker (eds.), *Spain, Europe and the Atlantic World. Essays in Honour of John H. Elliott* (Cambridge, 1995), pp. 267–95.

[153] Elliott, *The Count-Duke of Olivares*, pp. 442–95, on the growing crisis of the 1630s.

[154] H. Rebel, *Peasant Classes. The Bureaucratization of Property and Family Relations under Early Habsburg Absolutism, 1511–1636* (Princeton, 1983), pp. 230–84; Bély, Bercé, Meyer and Quatrefages, *Guerre et paix*, I. 245–52.

The military context

income in excess of any other European power. These resources needed only to be deployed in conjunction with the continuing war-effort of the allies to bring the war to a decisive conclusion. The thesis that France was 'unprepared' in 1635 can be refuted: it can be shown that significant numbers of French troops had seen military action on a more or less permanent basis in the preceding decade; it is not clear that the elite troops in the French armies were significantly less experienced than those of her enemies, or that these armies lacked a core of long-serving veterans. And even where French troops were not able to match the military quality of the best Habsburg forces, veteran troops were an international commodity in the Thirty Years War. Numerous army-corps were either overtly or potentially available to the highest bidder; there was no reason why France could not have supplemented her own military efforts by purchasing the military capability of German, Irish, Scottish or Swiss veterans on a large scale.

Yet despite all these apparent conditions for rapid military success, there were critical differences between the way that war had been waged in the past and the style of conflict that emerged after 1635. In employing the precedents of past foreign policy, and making theoretical assessments of the French resources that would be available for war, certain crucial issues were neglected or ignored. French success in the past – whether in the 1530s or 1630s – had depended upon holding the strategic initiative. The French crown and its ministers had consistently sought to select a particular weak point in the Habsburg system, whether north Italy, Artois, Luxembourg or Lorraine – and had concentrated overwhelming forces against that position. The Italian wars of the 1620s had revealed the concern of the French at the prospect of warfare that was not fought on these terms; during both the siege of Genoa in 1625 and the invasions of Piedmont and Savoy in 1629 and 1630, it was feared that the Habsburgs would choose to broaden the conflict into other theatres. Yet before 1635 the dangers of this had been masked. In 1625 or 1630 the Spanish might discuss the possibility of escalating the scale of war with France but had recognized that the consequences would be as damaging for them as for the French. Nördlingen changed this situation dramatically; the Habsburg plans for combined invasions of France were indicative of their realization that the way to place France at a disadvantage was to force her into a large-scale war on multiple fronts. After 1635 France needed to sustain conflict in five or six – sometimes more – separate campaign theatres, and the neglect of any one of these threatened setbacks that would rapidly outweigh any gains made elsewhere. In this situation the inadequacies of administration, command and control, finance and human and material resources became overwhelmingly clear. Only when the Habsburg system itself was temporarily overwhelmed by the twin blows of the Catalan and Portuguese revolts in 1640, with the dynastic priority that this imposed on Philip IV of returning the two kingdoms to obedience, was France able to attempt a partial return to a strategy conducted on her own terms – the overwhelming concentration of force in particular campaign theatres. However, this respite proved temporary and, as the war-effort under Mazarin in the 1640s reveals, France's war aims continued to be dogged by the problems of over-dispersed resources, leading to local collapses and the resounding failure of many of the most promising initiatives.

The campaign of 1635 began – indeed had begun even before the formal declaration of war delivered by Louis XIII's herald – with a Franco-Dutch invasion of the Spanish Netherlands.[155] On 22 May one part of the French army under the command of Urbain de Maillé, maréchal de Brézé, successfully engaged a smaller force of Spanish troops near the village of Avein, in Liège.[156] The news of the victory caused huge enthusiasm in Paris, and generated unrealistic optimism about the likely success of the rest of the campaign.[157] In fact the victory at Avein caused a breach between the victor, Brézé, and his co-commander Gaspard III de Coligny, maréchal de Châtillon, who considered that he and his army-corps had been deliberately sidelined to permit Brézé to gain the glory from the engagement.[158] The resulting dissension between the French high command weakened the capacity to influence Frederik Hendrik, prince of Orange, after the meeting of the French and Dutch armies. The result was acceptance of Frederik Hendrik's decision to lay siege to the small *place* of Tirlemont. The capture of Tirlemont served no strategic purpose, but the sack which followed united the Spanish Netherlands in opposition to the invading forces.[159] After this operation the combined army moved towards Brussels, but was met by predictably strong defences. The local population had stripped the surrounding territory of supplies, and the shortage of forage and inadequacy of food convoys for the soldiers forced the abandonment of any project for a siege of the capital. Instead, the army-corps moved back to besiege Louvain, a target originally rejected as having 'bons fossez et remparts', which would force the army to accept a lengthy siege.[160] However, supply proved just as difficult to maintain here; the population was hostile to all attempts to obtain forage or grain, and the presence of Piccolomini's Imperial cavalry on the borders of the Netherlands succeeded in blocking the passage of

[155] The military agreement was explicitly written into the treaty of 8 Feb. 1635: Pange, *Charnacé*, p. 115.
[156] Griffet, *Louis XIII*, II. 578–9; Montglat, *Mémoires*, XLIX. 79–81, emphasizes the importance of overwhelming numerical superiority; Quazza, *Tommaso de Savoia-Carignano*, pp. 48–52.
[157] Avenel, v. 30–2, 27 May 1635, Richelieu to Bouthillier; Montglat, *Mémoires*, XLIX. 81; Griffet, *Louis XIII*, II. 580–1, suggests that the chief victim of overconfidence after Aveins was Richelieu himself: 'Il s'imagina que les Espagnols ayant perdu toutes leurs forces . . . et que leurs [French and Dutch] progrès seraient encore plus rapides que ceux du grand Gustave en Allemagne.'
[158] Avenel, v. 35–6, 30 May 1635, Richelieu to the ambassador with the States General, Hercule-Girard, baron de Charnacé: 'je crains un peu que cette occasion soit le commencement de quelque division et jalousie . . . je vous prie de faire ce qu'il faut envers Messrs de Chastillon et de Brézé sur ce sujhect'; Griffet, *Louis XIII*, II. 579.
[159] Aubery, *Richelieu*, I. 488, 14 June 1635, Châtillon to Servien; Israel, *Dutch Republic and the Hispanic World*, p. 252.
[160] Aubery, *Richelieu*, I. 489, 14 June 1635.

The military context

supply convoys.[161] Finally on 26 July the Spanish captured the fortress of Schenkenschans, on the border of Cleves and Gelderland. This finally broke the fragile Franco/Dutch coalition as Frederik Hendrik and his Dutch troops left the allied army in a bid to recover the fortress.[162] Though Richelieu finally ordered the removal of Châtillon from the Spanish Netherlands, leaving his own relative, Brézé, in sole command, the forces were by now so depleted that nothing more could be undertaken.[163] By the end of the campaign it was clear that an army originally of 20,000–25,000 men, acting in conjunction with a similar Dutch campaign force, had failed to achieve anything in the Netherlands during 1635. Indeed, by the end of the year serious concern was being expressed by the ministers that the French military presence was so weak that Spanish forces might be able to winter in Picardy.[164]

Campaigning in the Rhineland did not progress any better. By early 1635 Richelieu and Louis XIII had accepted that France would need to support the remnants of Swedish and German protestant forces in the Empire with a more substantial military presence. However, both the army-corps under the maréchal de La Force and that commanded by Richelieu's *fidèle* Louis de Nogaret, cardinal de La Valette, had been weakened by the decision to detach troops for the Flanders army, and in the case of La Valette by sending an additional block of units under the command of the duc de Rohan to conduct a new campaign in the Valtelline.[165] Only gradually, and with protracted and acrimonious complaints from La Valette, were the two army-corps brought up to effective campaigning strength.[166]

The French strategy on the eastern frontier was in theory extremely simple. France faced two armies, that of Charles of Lorraine, far weaker in fact than the French commanders were prepared to admit, and the indisputably powerful forces of the Imperial generalissimo, Matthias Gallas, the body of Wallenstein's army.[167] Richelieu's aim was to keep Gallas in check while French forces defeated the duke, overran those areas of Lorraine that were still resisting French occupation and established military predominance in all of the territory west of the Rhine. As

---

[161] Aubery, *Richelieu*, I. 498, 14 July 1635; Israel, *Dutch Republic and the Hispanic World*, p. 253.
[162] Israel, 'Spain's strategy in the Low Countries', pp. 274–6; Elliott, *The Count-Duke of Olivares*, pp. 492–3.
[163] SHAT A¹ 25, fo. 148, 1 Aug. 1635, Louis XIII to Châtillon; A¹ 25, fos. 354–5, 18 Sept. 1635, Servien to Charnacé.
[164] Avenel, v. 309, 16 Oct. 1635, 'Instruction du Roy pour le mareschal de Brézé.'
[165] Laugel, *Rohan*, pp. 318–19: Rohan was allocated seven regiments of infantry and four companies of cavalry.
[166] For La Valette's complaints about the respective quality of troops allocated to his army-corps and that of La Force, see chapter 1, p. 45.
[167] Avenel, v. 186, 6 Sept. 1635, Richelieu to Claude Bouthillier, *surintendant des finances*, criticizing the *maréchal de camp*, Louis d'Arpajon, comte de Rodez, for having exaggerated the size of the duke of Lorraine's army: 'Je croy . . . que ceux qui auront la commission de chasser les ennemis de Saint-Mihel acquerront de l'honneur à bon marché.' Noailles, *Saxe-Weimar*, p. 183, suggests that the total Imperial forces in this campaign theatre amounted to 20,000 foot and 12,000 horse.

it became clear that neither of the French army-corps considered themselves strong enough to stand alone, even on the defensive, against Gallas, an additional part of this strategy became the creation of a third army-corps on this part of the frontier. The third corps, to be assembled around Langres, had an additional purpose: to provide a suitably prestigious force for the king himself to command.[168] All of Richelieu's arguments in terms of prudence, the insecure succession and the need to maintain overall responsibility for the war-effort, failed to convince Louis XIII that he should relinquish this ambition to command in person. The factor which finally dissuaded the king in the early summer was straightforward organizational failure: it became apparent that if the army-corps of La Valette and La Force were to sustain even modest effective strengths, new recruits and existing 'spare' units would have to be allocated to them; there was simply no scope for the creation of an additional army-corps, certainly not one on a scale prestigious enough for the king to assume personal command.[169]

In the face of Imperial successes in Alsace, the king and Richelieu finally decided that the cardinal de La Valette should amalgamate his army-corps with the remaining protestant troops of Saxe-Weimar, and that both should advance together to relieve the beleaguered Swedish garrison at Mainz.[170] Mainz was reached on 21 August, but the enemy forces which left the city isolated in the midst of hostile territory were not drawn into battle, and no permanent French presence was established.[171] The advancing armies, moving into territory which had been devastated by successive military occupations since late 1631, were dependent upon the magazine set up at Metz for bread supplies. This bread could only be brought as far as Saarbrücken, three or four days distant.[172] Beyond this, and throughout the retreat from Mainz, the Franco-protestant forces depended upon the surrounding countryside, already severely ravaged by the Imperialists during this campaign. The result was a disastrous collapse in the effective strength of La Valette's army-corps through desertion, sickness and starvation.[173]

The results of this French failure shattered any remaining optimism. Even

[168] AAE MD 813, fo. 318, 28 Apr. 1635, result of a council (of war) held at Compiègne, proposing the establishment of a prestige force of 12,000 infantry and 2,000 cavalry.
[169] J. Cornette, *Le roi de guerre. Essai sur la souveraineté dans la France du Grand Siècle* (Paris, 1993), pp. 196–8; Mousnier, *L'Homme Rouge*, pp. 568–71; SHAT A¹ 25, fo. 167, 1 Aug. 1635, Servien to Henri-Robert Gigault, marquis de Bellefonds, governor of Langres, concerning the distribution of troops to La Force and La Valette.
[170] Louis XIII to cardinal de La Valette, 20 July 1635, quoted in A.M.R.A. vicomte de Noailles, *Le cardinal de La Valette, 1635–1639* (Paris, 1906), pp. 140–1; BN Ms.fr. 6645, fos. 69–73, 26/7 July 1635, letters of Servien and Bullion to cardinal de La Valette, both concerned with the logistics and financing of the operation to relieve Mainz.
[171] Noailles, *Cardinal de La Valette*, p. 156–7; Hanotaux, *Richelieu*, v. 119–21.
[172] B. Kroener, *Les routes et les étapes. Die Versorgung der französischen Armeen in Nordostfrankreich (1635–1661)* (Münster, 1980), pp. 85–94; BN Ms.fr. 6645, fo. 93, 14 Aug. 1635.
[173] BL Add. MS. 35,097, fo. 7, [undated – *c.* early Oct. 1635], despatch from Viscount Scudamore, suggested that the army was reduced by two-thirds of its strength; Kroener, *Les Routes*, p. 91; Noailles, *Cardinal de La Valette*, pp. 177–80; Bourelly, *Maréchal de Fabert*, I. 54–67.

The military context

before the destruction of La Valette's army, Richelieu had been debating whether or not to abandon Alsace entirely, given the hazards involved in its defence and the failure of the main campaign armies to make any progress.[174] Matters were scarcely better in Lorraine, where the small forces of duke Charles presented an easy target assuming that one French army-corps could profit from the ability of a second corps to check the movements of the Imperial army. Yet this situation was not achieved, and neither of the corps could be freed for operations in Lorraine. As a measure of the failure to make progress, in September the governor of Nancy, Jean de Gallard de Béarn, comte de Barrault, frankly admitted that the duchy of Lorraine was infested with enemy troops, and that anyone stepping outside the walls of Nancy ran a considerable risk of being captured.[175] At the end of the campaign season a detachment of regular troops, supplemented by *noblesse* raised under the *arrière-ban*, were placed under the direct command of the king, and deployed in a small-scale operation in Lorraine to recapture the fortified town of Saint Mihiel.[176] Though the siege itself was successful, the collapse of the *arrière-ban* and the heavy wastage amongst the regular units made any further actions impossible.[177]

In 1635 French resources were concentrated on the eastern frontier and in Flanders, as Richelieu gambled on decisive and rapid success against the main Habsburg forces. The commitment to reopen campaigning in north Italy was a late decision, and the theatre was relatively neglected by France in the first year of open war, largely in the hope that the Italian princes would support the main burden of the war-effort. The decision to give overall command of the coalition army to the duke of Savoy, Vittorio Amedeo I, accorded with the normal hierarchical conventions of awarding commands, but antagonized Charles de Blanchefort, maréchal de Créqui, commander of the French corps, without – as events proved – winning the full support of the duke.[178] Despite his key role in the anti-Spanish 'League of Rivoli', Vittorio Amedeo apparently sought to avoid any irrevocable breach with the Spanish; his support was consistently half-hearted, if not positively obstructive.[179] The siege of Valenza collapsed amidst

---

[174] Avenel, v. 134, [early August] 1635, Richelieu to Louis XIII, 'Il faut se résoudre à de deux choses l'une: Ou à abandonner Colmar, Schélestat, Haguenau, Montbelliard et Porentru, ou tascher à les conserver.'

[175] AAE CP Lorraine, 26, fos. 81, 176, 16, 22 Sept. 1635, Barrault to Louis XIII; Scudamore also commented on the failure of the French to place military pressure on duke Charles' army: BL Add. MS. 35,097, fo. 8 [early Oct.]; F. des Robert, *Les campagnes de Charles IV, duc de Lorraine et Bar, en Allemagne, en Lorraine et en Franche Comté, 1634–1643* (2 vols; Paris and Nancy, 1883–8), I. 128–9.

[176] AAE CP Lorraine 26, fo. 200, 24 Sept. 1635, La Force to Louis XIII, congratulating him on the decision to take the field in person; des Robert, *Campagnes de Charles IV*, I. 149–53.

[177] Des Robert, *Campagnes de Charles IV*, I. 158–9; Cornette, *Roi de guerre*, pp. 198–9.

[178] AG A¹ 26, piece 65, 15 July 1635, *Pouvoir* of captain-general for the duke of Savoy; G. de Mun, *Richelieu et la Maison de Savoie. L'ambassade de Particelli d'Hémery en Piémont (1635–1639)* (Paris, 1907), pp. 84–5.

[179] The Mantuan representative in Paris, Giustiniano Priandi, had good reason to pay close attention

general recriminations, particularly Créqui's charge that Vittorio Amedeo had connived at the admission of a Spanish relief force into the place.[180] Though the French military commitment to Italy was to increase in subsequent years, suspicions of the motives and commitment of the allies remained, and it was only after the French position in the peninsula was threatened with total collapse in 1638/9 that the theatre started to enjoy a grudgingly accorded higher priority in the war-effort.

The only unqualified French success of 1635 was achieved in the Valtelline, where Rohan managed the twin feat of holding together his own small, badly paid and supplied army, while maintaining cooperation with the forces from the Grisons. Arriving in the Valtelline on 20 April, Rohan conducted one of the outstanding campaigns of the war, successively defeating Imperial troops at Livogno, Mazzo and, most decisively, Val Fraela. A final battle at Morbegno on 10 November 1635 left Rohan in complete control of the Valtelline.[181] But in late 1635, Rohan's progress was the only cause for satisfaction amidst mounting failure. Moreover, this success was counter-balanced by Spain's own diversion, a long-planned amphibious operation off the coast of Provence. Between 13 and 15 September, an amphibious Spanish expedition captured the Isles of Saint Marguerite and Saint Honorat, just off Marseilles, offering a base from which they could launch subsequent raids against the coast.[182]

The lessons of the 1635 campaign were clear. In numerous areas, administrative, supply and command failure had undermined whatever initial advantages had been enjoyed by the French forces. However, it was one thing to recognize that these initial setbacks owed so much to organizational weakness, quite another to provide practical responses.

On 12 May 1636 it was announced that the army of Italy would be ready to begin campaigning within three days.[183] In a pattern that was to become characteristic, despite strenuous efforts to avoid this situation, the army of Italy was not actually

---

to Franco-Savoyard relations, and reported in numerous letters upon the suspicions amongst the ministers about the commitment of Vittorio Amedeo: A.S.Ma AG E. xv. 3, vol. 678, 27 Sept. 1635, Priandi to the duke of Mantua; Mun, *Richelieu et la Maison de Savoie*, pp. 54–5, 82–3.

[180] Aubery, *Histoire du cardinal de Richelieu*, pp. 256–61, reports the mutually critical accounts of Créqui and Vittorio Amedeo; Mun, *Richelieu et la Maison de Savoie*, pp. 89–93, recognizes that blame was spread widely after the débâcle, but that on the basis of the reports Richelieu authorized d'Hémery to offer to replace Créqui if the duke of Savoy made this a condition of future cooperation.

[181] Laugel, *Rohan*, pp. 321–33; Rohan, *Mémoire sur la guerre de la Valtelline*, in Petitot and Monmerqué, xix. 75–123; J.A. Clarke, *Huguenot Warrior. The Life and Times of Henri de Rohan, 1579–1638* (The Hague, 1966), pp. 197–203.

[182] Sourdis, *Correspondance*, I. 7–12, emphasizes the importance of these Isles to the defence of Provence, and the risk that the neighbouring coastal fort of La Croisette would also fall to the Spanish attack.

[183] Avenel, v. 459, [12] May 1636, Richelieu to Louis XIII.

The military context

assembled until the end of June.[184] Though this failure in part reflected decisions to allocate troops to the forces being assembled in Provence to drive the Spanish off the Lérins, it was also symptomatic of much wider organizational problems involved in carrying out recruitment and getting units to the frontiers. As a result, any opportunity to launch a combined attack on the Milanese, acting in concert with the duc de Rohan's army from the Valtelline, was lost.[185] Indeed, the delay in assembling the army for Italy allowed the Spanish to take the initiative, launching an attack on the territory of Odoardo Farnese, duke of Parma, and laying siege to Piacenza.[186] A Spanish invasion of Piedmont threatened Vercelli, and the prospect of Spanish occupation was prevented only by the victory at Tornavento on 22 June, a victory which the allies proved unable to follow up.[187] The position of the duke of Parma, whose territories were subject to Spanish occupation, was now untenable, and in early February 1637 he was to make peace with the Spanish, renouncing any further commitment to the League of Rivoli.[188]

Matters were no better expedited in the other theatres, despite equal awareness of the need to enter the campaign as early as possible.[189] The assembly of the army of the cardinal de La Valette and a second corps being brought together from the remains of La Force's army of the previous campaign were both painfully slow. Koblenz fell to Imperial troops on 3 June, having been under siege since early May.[190] No French force was in a sufficient state of preparedness to attempt its relief without the assistance of the Dutch, and the Dutch forces were fully committed to the attempt to recapture the vital fortress of Schenkenschans, lost in the preceding campaign. It was not until mid-June that the French were in a position to launch a counter-attack on the eastern frontier. Saxe-Weimar, whose army had now been officially brought into the pay of the French crown, together with La Valette's corps, jointly laid siege to Saverne. The two forces were tied to this siege until the second half of July.[191]

The overall French plan for 1636 once the forces had been assembled was once again strongly focused upon the defence or reconquest of the strategic centres in Lorraine, Alsace and on the Rhine. However, a more ambitious project to facilitate

---

[184] Aubery, *Richelieu*, I. 633, 20 June 1636, de Noyers to d'Hémery.
[185] Laugel, *Rohan*, pp. 334–9; Clarke, *Huguenot Warrior*, pp. 204–6; Mun, *Richelieu et la Maison de Savoie*, pp. 106–8.
[186] Mun, *Richelieu et la Maison de Savoie*, pp. 119–22.
[187] AAE CP Savoie 24, fo. 262, 7 Apr. 1636, d'Hémery to Richelieu; Vercelli was relieved at the end of Apr.: fo. 340, 1 May, d'Hémery to Richelieu; Mun, *Richelieu et la Maison de Savoie*, pp. 141–2, on Tornavento.
[188] E. Nasalli Rocca, *I Farnese* (Varese, 1969), pp. 165–6.
[189] Avenel, v. 397–402, 16 Jan. 1636, Richelieu to Servien, stressing the urgency of raising recruits so that the armies would be ready by the end of March.
[190] Avenel, v. 461, 16 May 1636, Richelieu to Charnacé, stressing the king's concern to raise the siege; v. 475, 3 June 1636, Richelieu to Louis XIII, reporting the fall of Koblenz.
[191] SHAT A¹ 28, fo. 304, 23 July 1636, Richelieu to cardinal de La Valette, congratulating him on the capture of Saverne.

this strategy was proposed in the form of an invasion of the Franche-Comté.[192] Overrunning this territory would serve to cut the communication and supply lines of France's enemies, especially Charles of Lorraine. It would also provide France with a *place d'armes* on which her troops could subsist on the basis of contributions exacted from the local population.[193] The conquest was to be undertaken by the prince de Condé and Richelieu's cousin, the *grand maître de l'artillerie*, Charles de La Porte de La Meilleraye, whose joint army-corps moved into the Comté without encountering significant resistance and laid siege to Dôle.[194] The successful outcome of this siege became an absolute priority for the ministry, one to which all other military effort was subordinated.[195] This had particularly serious consequences for the small army-corps commanded by the prince of the blood and governor of Champagne, Louis de Bourbon, comte de Soissons. There was already concern at the build-up of Spanish forces on the Picardy frontier. On 4 July a Spanish force of 10,000–12,000 foot and 13,000 horse under the command of the Cardinal Infante Fernando crossed the frontier and took La Capelle.[196] This was the beginning of a Spanish advance which proceeded almost uninterrupted to the siege of Corbie, which fell on 15 August, crossed the Somme and culminated in the capture of Roye.[197] The comte de Soissons fell back, his troops suffering heavy loss in an attempt to prevent the Spanish crossing of the Somme, and was in turn forced to pass the Oise and to abandon Noyon.[198] Noyon itself was not reached by the Spanish, but was said to have powder and shot for no more than half an hour's defence.[199] While the main concern was that the Spanish would push further into Champagne and towards Paris, it was also feared that they would divert troops to take the remaining fortified *places* in Picardy: Doullens, Peronne, Abbeville and, above all, Amiens.[200]

The Spanish invasion represented a dangerous threat to French territory and a dramatic challenge to the assumption that the war would consist of a series of

---

[192] Aumale, *Princes de Condé*, III. 269–72, who emphasizes the rashness of opening up another campaign theatre in a territory that had hitherto been neutralized by a Franco-Spanish treaty; BL Add. MS. 35,097, fo. 12, 8 Apr. 1636, Viscount Scudamore reported the assembly of the army for the invasion of the Franche-Comté.

[193] AAE MD, 813, fo. 318, 28 Apr. 1635, *Résultat du conseil tenu à Compiègne* – for an early discussion of this project.

[194] For a detailed account of the siege of Dôle: L. de Piépape, *Histoire de la réunion de la Franche-Comté à la France* (2 vols; Paris and Besançon, 1881), I. 402–33, II. 1–34; Aumale, *Princes de Condé*, III. 275–80.

[195] Aubery, *Richelieu*, I. 629, 17 June 1636, de Noyers to Condé, speaking of the siege of Dôle as the primary concern of Louis XIII and Richelieu; this remained the case even after the fall of La Capelle: Aubrey, *Richelieu*, I. 645, 6 July.

[196] AAE MD 821, fo. 106, 25 July 1636, Chavigny to Mazarin.

[197] AAE MD 821, fo. 78, 7 July 1636, Soissons to Chavigny.

[198] AAE MD 1678, fos. 178 *et seq.*, 5 Aug. 1636, Brézé to Louis XIII giving an account of the Spanish forcing of the Somme; fo. 198, 8 Aug., Fontenay to Chavigny, emphasizing the danger to Noyon.

[199] AAE MD 1678, fo. 198, 8 Aug.

[200] Aubery, *Richelieu*, I. 651, 666, 18/28 July 1636, de Noyers to Chaulnes, governor of Picardy, specifically about the risk to Amiens; Avenel, v. 549, 17 Aug. 1636, Richelieu to Chavigny.

The military context

French initiatives against an overstretched Habsburg system. Despite French concerns and the massive levels of panic sown in the capital, it seems clear that Paris was not the object of the Spanish advance; indeed the Cardinal Infante was expressly to rule out an advance against the French capital.[201] The real risk was that the Spanish would succeed in consolidating a strong position in Picardy and Champagne.[202] If Spanish troops could be maintained in a number of important *places* over the winter, supporting themselves by contributions on the French population, then France would be involved in a struggle in which large areas would be continually vulnerable to a *guerre de course* by enemy raiding parties, and where the population would be forced to sustain the burden of enemy as well as French troops, together with most of the destruction and dislocation of the successive campaigns.

Faced with this challenge, Louis and his ministers saw little alternative but to abandon existing plans, and to authorize a wave of panic recruitment. Even when these new units were funded by private or institutional initiatives, the subsequent costs of maintaining the troops was usually the responsibility of the *épargne*.[203] Other troops, whether newly recruited regulars or *noblesse* raised from another convocation of the *arrière-ban*, were a burden laid on the provinces, who responded with varying degrees of enthusiasm.[204] But such rapidly levied troops would be of limited military effectiveness, and everyone knew that rates of desertion and wastage would be high even by the standards of the normal campaign armies. The main strength of the army to move up into Champagne was to be composed of 9,000 troops taken from the army of Condé. Even before the Spanish invasion, the resistance of Dôle and the increasing frequency and confidence of attacks by Charles of Lorraine's army had raised doubts about the outcome of the siege.[205] Judging it essential to obtain a block of experienced troops to form the core of the army of Champagne, the decision was taken to order the abandonment of the siege and to move the bulk of Condé's troops northwards.[206]

---

[201] Burckhardt, *Richelieu*, III. 177; Mousnier, *L'Homme Rouge*, pp. 586–7, suggests that only Jean de Werth favoured a strike against Paris. Nicholas Goulas, *Mémoires* (3 vols; Paris, 1879–82), I. 289: 'Enfin les Espagnols ayant passé la rivière de Somme et remply Paris mesme d'une épouvante si grande que de mémoire d'homme il ne s'étoit vu telle chose'; for an emotive account of the panic in Paris at the approach of Spanish raiding parties, see Poëte, *Paris*, pp. 145–63.

[202] Two years later, in 1638, letters between Olivares and the Cardinal Infante intercepted by the French make this intention quite clear: 'Et ailleurs qu'il faut bien faire en sorte de loger leurs troupes en France que c'est le seul remède et le vray moyen pour avoir la paix': AAE CP Espagne 19, fo. 152, 2 Aug. 1638.

[203] Montglat, *Mémoires*, XLIX. 125–6; La Force, *Mémoires*, III. 175–7; Chevallier, *Louis XIII*, pp. 514–18.

[204] Aubery, *Richelieu*, I. 680–1, 17 Aug. 1636, de Noyers to La Valette.

[205] Aubery, *Richelieu*, I. 670, 31 July, de Noyers to La Meilleraye; I. 674, 4 Aug., Richelieu to Condé.

[206] SHAT A¹ 41, fo. 176, 23 Aug. 1636, Louis XIII and de Noyers to Condé, ordering him to lift the siege and to despatch his troops to Picardy; Avenel, V. 555, 20 Aug. 1636, Richelieu to Chavigny, proposed to draft some of the new levies into these units coming up from Burgundy – an expedient fraught with danger – c.f. chapter 1, pp. 42–4.

France at war, 1624–1642

Partly through concern at the Imperial invasion of Burgundy, partly because of the immense problems of trying to assemble an army towards the end of the campaign season, the new army of Champagne proved slow to assume the offensive against the Spanish, although the latter were clearly losing momentum throughout the later summer. Neither Richelieu nor the king reached the army before the end of September, by which time the opportunity to engage the Spanish forces in the field had been missed.[207] Richelieu was able to assume direct control only after the siege of Corbie. The attempt to recapture this town, begun on 30 September, absorbed the entire army, and by the time the Spanish garrison was finally brought to surrender on 14 November, the opportunity to prevent the orderly withdrawal of the Spanish troops across the Somme and ultimately out of Picardy had been lost.[208]

While the Spanish invasion of the north-east was occupying almost the entire French war-effort, Gallas moved his Imperial army into Burgundy. Richelieu and the king were subsequently haunted by the fear that the Imperialists would gain decisive successes in Burgundy, possibly even the capture of Dijon, while the main French forces were tied down before Corbie.[209] Even after the end of the siege of Corbie, the troops desperately needed by La Valette and Condé if they were to press the retreat of Gallas from Saint-Jean-de-Losne could not be despatched for another ten days, being required as a safeguard while the fortification works were being demolished.[210] Gallas suffered heavy losses on this retreat, but this owed little to French military pressure, much more to successful looting in Burgundy, followed by growing supply difficulties when the troops were held up at the siege of Saint-Jean.[211] Ultimately, the retreat, like that of the Cardinal Infante from Picardy, was more directly motivated by events in the Empire, where the Swedish army had overrun Brandenberg after its victory at Wittstock on 4 October.[212]

---

[207] Avenel, v. 588, 27 Sept. 1636, Richelieu to Chavigny, written from Roye; v. 590, 27/8 Sept., Richelieu to Louis XIII, in anticipation of his imminent arrival with the main army; Richelieu, *Mémoires*, IX. 237–45.

[208] AAE MD 1678, fo. 478, 12 Nov. 1636, anonymous letter to the king, stressing the need to demolish the siege works around Corbie, the extent to which the Spanish had garrisoned other *places* on French territory, and the continued presence of a large Spanish campaign army – all of which would make it dangerous, if not impossible, to push the campaign further in the remaining part of the year.

[209] Avenel, v. 661, 5 Nov. 1636, Richelieu to Chavigny: 's'il faut demeurer devant la place [Corbie] six mois par le blocus, comme apparemment on n'en aura pas meilleur marché, les affaires du roy iroient très-mal. Si Galasse gagnoit un combat qu'on est à la veille de donner, on seroit en mauvais estat si Corbie retenoit les forces du roy'; E. de Vernisy, *Episodes de la Guerre de Trente Ans; l'invasion allemande en Bourgogne en 1636* (Dijon, 1928), pp. 14–18.

[210] AAE MD 1678, fo. 478, 12 Nov. 1636, *mémoire* to Louis XIII.

[211] Vernisy, *L'invasion allemande*, pp. 43–56; the siege began on 25 Oct., and with the failure of the second assault on 2 Nov., Gallas was sufficiently concerned at the precarious supply situation of his army to begin his retreat. Noailles, *Cardinal de La Valette*, pp. 302–8.

[212] Parker, *Thirty Years War* (London, 1984), p. 163; Charvériat, *Guerre de Trente Ans*, II. 353–4; Israel, 'Spain's strategy in the Low Countries', pp. 281–2.

The military context

The opportunism that had marked the first two invasions of France during 1636 was to be equally characteristic of the third, the advance of a small Spanish force along the French Atlantic coast in November. A series of French levies that Richelieu had intended to defer until spring 1637 had to be raised at short notice.[213] This imposed additional strains on the resources of the government and those of the provincial elites, especially the governor of Guienne, the duc d'Epernon, whose loyalty to the ministry had clear limits.[214] The Spanish invasion was limited in scope, but its gains, the towns of Saint-Jean-de-Luz and Socoa, were held for the whole of 1637.[215] This new danger presented by Spanish troops in Guienne was compounded by the successive postponement throughout 1636 of operations to try to retake the isles of Sainte-Marguerite and Saint-Honorat off the coast of Provence.

The first months of 1636 had been characterized by a relative openness about the organizational failures of the preceding campaign. Early 1637 saw the French high command, and Richelieu himself, on the defensive, pessimistic about the probable failure of any grand strategy, and unprepared to take the field before it was made necessary by the enemy.[216] Part of this reflected the upheavals at the Court, and the all-consuming effort to achieve a satisfactory agreement with Orléans and Soissons after their implication in plots against Richelieu at the end of 1636 and hurried departure from France.[217] At least as important was the effect of the unanticipated level of military spending in 1636. The financial shortfalls and the need to meet interest and repayments on ever-growing borrowing took their toll in early 1637, contributing directly to the collapse of the duc de Rohan's underfunded forces operating in the Valtelline – a collapse for which *surintendant* Bullion was publicly blamed by

---

[213] Avenel, v. 684, 19 Nov., Richelieu to Louis XIII, notifying the king of the despatch of the regiments of Roquelaure, Le Vigan, Navailles and Tonneins to Guienne; SHAT A¹ 30, fos. 334, 338, 358, 27/8/9 Nov. 1636, de Noyers to Epernon, informing him of troops being despatched to Guienne, and imposing the burden of subsistence on the province, together with the obligation of trying to build the units up to effective strength; Avenel, v. 698–9, 27 Nov. 1636, Richelieu to duc de La Valette, giving him permission to advance the levy of a number of units in Guienne.

[214] J.N. Fessenden, 'Epernon and Guienne: provincial politics under Louis XIII', PhD thesis, Columbia University, 1972, pp. 146–51; L. Mouton, *Le duc et le roi – le duc d'Epernon, Henri IV et Louis XIII* (Paris, 1924), pp. 264–5. Both Epernon and his third son, the duc de La Valette, were strongly suspected of complicity in the Amiens assassination plot directed against Richelieu earlier in the year: Claude de Bordeille, comte de Montrésor, *Mémoires*, in Michaud and Poujoulat, III. 204–7; Avenel, v. 692–3, 23 Nov. 1636, Richelieu to Epernon and La Valette, warning them against giving support either to Soissons or Gaston.

[215] G. Girard, *Histoire de la vie du duc d'Espernon* (Paris, 1655), pp. 540–6; Fessenden gives the invading army at over 10,000 Spanish troops: 'Epernon', p. 147.

[216] AAE MD 827, fo. 159, 7 Feb. 1637, Bullion to Richelieu, deeply pessimistic about the potential for funding the next campaign; Richelieu, *Mémoires*, IX. 324–5, on the setbacks of 1636; Carmona, *Richelieu*, pp. 598–601.

[217] Goulas, *Mémoires*, I. 302–12; Chevallier, *Louis XIII*, pp. 521–9; J.-M. Constant, *Les conjurateurs: le premier libéralisme politique sous Richelieu* (Paris, 1987), pp. 130–45.

France at war, 1624–1642

Richelieu.[218] Failure in the Valtelline marked the end of any serious attempt to block the main line of communication between the two branches of the Habsburgs, and the tacit abandonment of a foreign policy objective which had explicitly dominated French thinking since the early 1620s.

This setback both to reputation and a coherent European strategy was compounded by the simultaneous maladministration and ceaseless disputes between those charged with the attempt to recapture the Îles des Lérins off Provence. An effective strategy for their recapture would have required the cooperation of the provincial governor, Nicolas de l'Hôpital, maréchal de Vitry, with Henri de Lorraine, comte d'Harcourt, and Henri Escoubleau de Sourdis, archbishop of Bordeaux, the commanders of the land and naval forces respectively, but this had proved unattainable throughout 1636.[219] Under direct threats and pressure from the crown and Richelieu, the joint commanders were forced into action. But even after French forces landed on the Isles, no attempt was made to impose a full blockade of the main fortress on Sainte-Marguerite, and for several weeks after the French landing the Spanish were still able to get supplies to their garrison.[220] Only in late May were the Spanish garrisons finally brought to make terms.[221]

The protracted operation to recover the Isles and the sense that financial limits to the French war-effort had already being reached combined to generate a debate about the extent of a future French commitment to Italy. In a bid to reduce the multi-campaign warfare that was playing havoc with the early years of the French war-effort, it was decided to abandon any plan for an offensive and to rely upon a large number of garrisons to hold down Spanish forces. This, it was calculated, would save France an estimated 2 million *livres* in the theatre.[222] Standing on the defensive in Italy was now seen as a desirable means to relieve pressure on the royal finances with – it was hoped – fewer dangerous consequences than the

---

[218] Avenel, v. 762–3, 28 Mar. 1637, Richelieu to Bullion: 'L'accident qui est arrivé en la Valtelline est si grand que je ne sçay si on y pourra apporter remède . . . Ce mal est arrivé faute d'argent; pour un escu qu'il eust fallu donner à temps il en faudra dix, et encores ne réparera-t-il pas la perte qu'on a faicte.'

[219] Disputes between the high command in Provence and the assertive behaviour of Vitry in particular had been cited by Sourdis in mid-1636 as a major reason for the failure of the attempt to organize the relief of the Isles: Sourdis, *Correspondance*, I. 56–7, 59. In August 1636 Louis XIII had attempted to establish a formal order for the command of the operation, depending on the location of the army: Sourdis, *Correspondance*, I. 74–5, 27 Aug. 1636, Louis XIII to Sourdis. But this had evidently proved of limited effectiveness in avoiding subsequent disputes.

[220] Sourdis, *Correspondance*, I. 341–5, 6 Apr. 1637, Sourdis to Richelieu, discussing the delays in pressing the attack since the landing on Sainte-Marguerite.

[221] Sourdis, *Correspondance*, I. 368–9, 6 May 1637, 'Trève accordée au gouverneur de Sainte-Marguerite'; SHAT A^1 35, fo. 250, 5 Apr. 1637, Louis XIII to Harcourt, congratulating him on the successful landing on Saint-Honorat; Sourdis, *Correspondance*, I. 386, 25 May 1637, Sourdis to Richelieu: 'comme je traitais avec le gouverneur de Saint-Honorat . . . de se rendre avant la descente dans son île, moyennant deux mille pistoles'.

[222] AAE CP Savoie 25, fos. 24–7, 30 Jan. 1637, *mémoire* from d'Hémery (the estimated costs were respectively 5 million *livres* or 3 million *livres* for an offensive or a defensive war).

stepping down of military commitments in other theatres. The result in practice was that the borders of Piedmont and Monferrato were exposed to a major Spanish counter-offensive. By 2 July d'Hémery, acting as special ambassador in Piedmont, was writing to Léon le Bouthillier, comte de Chavigny and secretary of state for foreign affairs, that Vittorio Amedeo had already reconciled himself to the imminent loss of the town of Alba, under siege by the Spanish.[223] Subsequent correspondence from d'Hémery, seconded by Créqui, reflected alarm verging on panic at the possibility of a military catastrophe; the unfortunate duc de Rohan cannot have been far from the minds of other commanders who felt that their own forces did not enjoy a high priority in the ministry's allocation of funds and resources.[224] The immediate cause of the collapse of the French position in north Italy in the following (1638) campaign was the Savoyard succession crisis.[225] But the low priority given to the Italian theatre in the preceding year, and the inertia of French forces throughout the 1637 campaign, made both the rapid development of a Spanish faction in the ducal family more comprehensible and the subsequent Spanish conquest of most of Piedmont far easier to achieve.

The defensive policy pursued in Italy during 1637 did not, in fact, offer many benefits to the war-effort in other campaign theatres. The problem of coordinating several army-corps on the frontier from Picardy to Burgundy, both to counter invasion threats and to try to obtain some military or territorial advantage, proved as intractable as ever. With considerable delays, losses of newly recruited troops and heavy expenses connected with redeployment, three army-corps were fielded on the eastern frontier. The first of these was placed under the command of the cardinal de La Valette and was intended to operate across the frontier from Champagne.[226] Châtillon would once again command a second army, and would begin operations later in the year in support of La Valette.[227] The third army-corps was to be sent into the Franche-Comté, but in 1637 the command was given to Henri II d'Orléans duc de Longueville, brother-in-law of the prince de Condé whose siege of Dôle in the preceding year had proved such an expensive failure.

The preoccupation of the Spanish Army of Flanders with the relief of Breda, besieged by a substantial Dutch army from early June, made the slowness and hesitation of La Valette's, and later Châtillon's, campaigning very obvious.[228] The

---

[223] AAE CP Savoie 25, fos. 191–2, 2 July.
[224] AAE CP Savoie 25, fo. 340, [end July] 1637, d'Hémery to Richelieu, raising the notion of a suspension of arms in Italy; fo. 401, 22 Aug., d'Hémery to Richelieu, concerning inadequacy of financial provision; fo. 420, 9 Sept., d'Hémery on the weakness of Créqui's field army.
[225] R. Oresko, 'The House of Savoy and the Thirty Years War', in K. Bussmann and H. Schilling (eds.), *1648 War and Peace in Europe – Politics, Religion, Law and Society* (Münster, 1998), pp. 142–53, at pp. 147–8; G. Quazza, 'Guerra civile in Piemonte, 1637–1642 (nuove ricerche), *Bollettino storico-bibliografico subalpino*, 42/3 (1959/60), 281–321 (42), 5–63 (43).
[226] AAE MD 828, fo. 269 (1637), material relating to 1637 *revues* of the French armies.
[227] AAE MD 828, fo. 273 (1637).
[228] BN Ms.fr. 6648, fo. 40, 1 June 1637, de Noyers to La Valette; fo. 48, 3 June 1637, Richelieu to La Valette. The Dutch campaign against Breda had itself been considerably delayed by an original

first target selected by La Valette was the small and ill-fortified *place* of Landrecies.[229] Despite its modest garrison and limited supplies, Landrecies held out until the 23 July, and the siege was followed by a lengthy pause during which La Valette's subsequent proposals were discussed.[230] The decision to throw the main weight of the French field armies behind the recapture of La Capelle, lost to the Spanish in 1636, was comprehensible in terms of royal prestige. However, the siege lasted until 23 September, and effectively destroyed any chance of achieving anything further during the campaign.[231]

In contrast, the campaign begun by Longueville in Franche-Comté enjoyed a series of successes; the absence of any relief forces in the area encouraged a significant number of *places* to capitulate after token resistance.[232] On 26 August the army took Bletterans, but this was to be the last French gain and the army subsequently fell into inactivity.[233] Richelieu's first set of instructions to Longueville at the beginning of 1637 had been to cooperate with Saxe-Weimar and La Valette (initially commanding the army in Lorraine before the redeployment of forces on the eastern frontier) to counter any threat from Gallas and Charles of Lorraine.[234] Early in the campaign, Saxe-Weimar, supported by French troops under François de l'Hôpital, seigneur du Hallier, took the bridgehead at Rheinau and defeated the Imperial general Jean de Werth at Kentzingen.[235] But despite this victory, Saxe-Weimar grew more and more discouraged by the extent to which the Imperial troops held the initiative in the Rhineland.[236] In May, he crossed the Rhine and began his own operations in the Franche-Comté, along the Saône valley – operations principally concerned with supplying his army in consequence of what he considered to be the French failure to honour their part of the contract with his force.[237] In the course of this operation he facilitated the campaign of Longueville by defeating Charles of Lorraine's army near Ray-sur-Saône on 2 June.[238] This success could not, however, conceal the fact that Saxe-

plan to launch a land and sea attack on Dunkirk, abandoned after a storm scattered the Dutch fleet: Avenel, v. 771, n. 2.

[229] Noailles, *Cardinal de La Valette*, pp. 330–1, who cites Richelieu's low opinion of the *place* and its likely resistance.
[230] AAE MD 827, fo. 157, 26 June 1637, Richelieu to Charost, reporting that the garrison was of only 500 troops.
[231] Aubery, *Richelieu*, II. 80, 6 Sept. 1637, Chavigny to cardinal de La Valette; La Capelle had been selected because it was agreed to be an easier target than Aveins.
[232] Piépape, *Franche-Comté*, II. 62–84; A.M.R.A. vicomte de Noailles, *Le maréchal de Guébriant, 1602–1643* (Paris, 1912), pp. 64–79.
[233] Avenel, v. 1049, 13 Aug., Richelieu to Longueville.
[234] SHAT A¹ 34, fo. 1, 1 Jan. 1637, de Noyers to Longueville.
[235] Noailles, *Saxe-Weimar*, pp. 232–7; BN Ms.fr. 3767, fo. 23, 11 Sept. 1637, de Noyers to Saxe-Weimar, congratulating him on the passage of the Rhine and the successful engagement with Jean de Werth.
[236] Noailles, *Saxe-Weimar*, pp. 241–2.
[237] Noailles, *Saxe-Weimar*, pp. 237–40; BN Ms.fr. 3767, fo. 14, 4 June 1637, Louis to Saxe-Weimar, reprimanding him for allowing his troops to extort goods from the town of Chaumont.
[238] Noailles, *Saxe-Weimar*, pp. 215–16.

The military context

Weimar was now unwilling to try to secure the remaining *places* held on the middle Rhine with his own troops. In early October he withdrew his army southwards to take up winter quarters around Bâle, leaving the French *maréchal de camp* Achille de Longueval, seigneur de Manicamp, in charge of the remaining Rhine fortifications, especially Rheinau whose garrison costs at 1,000 *riksdaler* per day the duke was no longer prepared to meet.[239] Provided with inadequate funds and no significant reinforcement, Manicamp was unable to hold the conquests; Rheinau fell to a surprise attack by the Imperial general Jean de Werth in early November.[240] Not only was the French position in Alsace now as weak as that in north Italy, confidence in the commitment of France's subsidy-ally, Saxe-Weimar, stood at an all-time low.

The one campaign theatre in which the French gained a decisive and unexpected success during 1637 was Languedoc. A Spanish invasion, attempting once again to probe France's overstretched defences, pushed up along the coast towards Narbonne and was resoundingly defeated at Leucate.[241] This was all the more remarkable given the high proportion of militia in the army commanded by the governor of Languedoc, Charles de Schomberg, duc d'Halluin.[242] The mistake was to expect more. A governor organizing such a campaign would have to bear a heavy financial burden; this would increase out of all proportion if he sought to follow up a defensive strategy with an invasion of enemy territory. Not surprisingly, Halluin decided to consolidate the reconquest rather than push across the frontier into Roussillon.[243]

On the Atlantic coast, in Guienne, no such decisive success was evident, despite the increasingly strident demands from Paris that the duc d'Epernon and his third son Bernard de Nogaret, duc de La Valette, should organize forces to drive the Spanish invading forces out of St Jean de Luz and Socoa.[244] This inactivity was partly the consequence of the ministry's wish to turn the whole operation into a provincial matter, carried out at the expense of the province and its governor with troops raised locally.[245] More immediately, it reflected concern at the peasant

---

[239] Noailles, *Saxe-Weimar*, pp. 248–9.
[240] Richelieu, *Mémoires*, IX. 471; Noailles, *Saxe-Weimar*, p. 248.
[241] Sourdis, *Correspondance*, I. 506–15, 29 Sept. 1637, 'Relation de la levée du siège de Leucate fait par les Espagnols'; Vassal-Reig, *Roussillon*, pp. 33–62.
[242] Sourdis, *Correspondance*, I. 504, 509–10 – 'Relation'; AAE MD 828, fo. 260, 1637: details of the regiments allocated to Languedoc, all severely under strength; Vassal-Reig, *Roussillon*, pp. 36–40; it was hoped that the line regiments could be reinforced with up to 8,000 local militia. Halluin was the son of Henri maréchal de Schomberg, comte de Nanteuil, who had been made governor of Languedoc in 1632, but was succeeded by his son when he died in the same year.
[243] Vassal-Reig, *Roussillon*, pp. 71–3, describes the collapse of the army in the wake of the defeat of the Spanish, and pp. 77–8, presents a series of accusations levelled against Halluin for extortion and illegal activities in the province in the aftermath of the military success.
[244] Avenel, v. 780, 30 May 1637, Richelieu to duc de La Valette, urging him to act rapidly to drive the Spanish out of Guienne, and suggesting that this will be the best means to allay the 'mauvais bruicts' about Epernon's and La Valette's commitment.
[245] Girard, *Espernon*, p. 546: 'Le roi lui promettoit des hommes, des vivres, des munitions de guerre

unrest in Saintonge and Angoumois, requiring the commitment of some of the forces raised in Guienne.[246] Virtual immobility followed and was justified by the need to put the *noblesse* and all available troops into the field to defeat the *croquants*.[247] Finally, on 25 October, the Spanish forces themselves abandoned the year-long occupation and retreated back to Spain.[248] The subsequent desire for an invasion of Atlantic Spain to wipe out the humiliation of 1637, together with the alienation of Epernon and his son, were to fuel the difficulties, and ultimately the disaster, of the campaign in the following year.

Acting with a caution which reflected an awareness of the shortage of funds and of troops, and the severe challenge to French military confidence which had been presented by 1636, the commanders of the various army-corps in 1637 had achieved nothing of strategic significance capable of influencing the outcome of the war. They had also managed to avoid any of the crushing setbacks that were to characterize some of the later campaigns of Richelieu's ministry. The year marked a low point in French military activity. It presented the cardinal with the possibility of a war that would not necessarily lead to outright defeat, but would lose all momentum under the impact of supply and financial failures, the reluctance of the generals to risk their reputations and their fortunes and the practical difficulties involved in any attempt to exploit success in one campaign theatre without excessively weakening all of the others. It was this threat of military stagnation, with its consequences both for strategy and for the loss of royal reputation, that drove the ministers to place greater pressure on the individual commanders to undertake more ambitious strategies in subsequent campaigns. Unfortunately, this increased pressure was not matched by any significant improvement in the administrative structure or the resources available for the war-effort.

The campaign of 1638 therefore saw a return to large-scale offensive strategy, supported from the outset by high levels of recruitment and expanding military commitments. On the Flanders frontier there were the usual delays in getting the main army into the field, a situation not helped by the lacklustre and lethargic generalship of maréchal Châtillon. Fortunately for the French strategy, Frederik Hendrik with a Dutch army of 18,000 infantry and 4,000 cavalry had invaded the Spanish Netherlands in the last week of May.[249] As ever, the Spanish high

... Tout cela néanmoins demeura toujours dans les termes des promesses, sans venir jamais à la moindre partie des effets'; pp. 553–4: first attempts to repel the Spanish with two of the Epernon 'House' regiments (Guyenne and Mun); Fessenden, 'Epernon', pp. 151–2.

[246] Bercé, *Croquants*, I. 443–54; Avenel, v. 780, 30 May 1637, Richelieu to duc de La Valette.
[247] Avenel, v. 788–9, 18 June 1637, Richelieu to Louis XIII, concerning a plan to enlist the defeated *croquants* in the army that would move against the Spanish.
[248] Girard, *Espernon*, pp. 554–5; Fessenden 'Epernon', p. 152; Bercé, *Croquants*, I. 451–2: all emphasize the anger at court that the duc de La Valette had missed the opportunity to draw the Spanish into battle.
[249] Aubery, *Richelieu*, II. 136, 23 May, d'Estampes to Richelieu; Israel, *Dutch Republic and the Hispanic World*, p. 259.

The military context

command in Flanders were not prepared to leave the Spanish Netherlands exposed to a Dutch attack in order to launch an offensive into French territory.[250] Châtillon, although possessing by his own account only 10,000 infantry and 3,000 cavalry out of the forces he considered necessary to sustain a siege, was persuaded to advance into enemy territory, and on 1 June invested Saint-Omer.[251] The ministers swung between exasperation at the unrealistic and immoderate demands of Châtillon, and genuine concern that his fears might be justified and an inadequate army would be overwhelmed in its siege works.[252] When, on the night of 8/9 June the besieging army was surprised by a force of Spanish troops, who established a small fort in the middle of the French lines, and placed an additional 1,500 soldiers in Saint-Omer, the ministers decided not to run the risk of a major setback, and ordered the entire army-corps of maréchal de La Force to move immediately towards Saint-Omer to support Châtillon's siege.[253] The king himself had now moved as far as Amiens, Richelieu up to Abbeville, in order to be closer to what was perceived as the crucial siege of this campaign. But on 12 July a further Spanish force entered Saint-Omer in full view of the French army, and Châtillon and La Force together resolved that it would be impossible to continue the siege.[254]

Following the failure at Saint-Omer, the two commanders followed Louis XIII's instructions to advance against an easier target, the town of Renty, which fell on 9 August.[255] But even this small operation had taken its toll on the effective strength of the troops, and from 11 August it was decided formally to amalgamate the two armies. A substantial detachment of this combined army was sent, under the command of the more vigorous du Hallier, to lay siege to Le Câtelet, another *place* lost by the French in the Spanish invasion of Picardy in 1636.[256] Even the presence of the king and Richelieu does not seem to have eliminated disorders and indiscipline.[257] Only on 14 September was the place finally taken by assault.[258]

---

[250] Quazza, *Tommaso di Savoia-Carignano*, p. 229; Israel, 'Spain's strategy in the Low Countries', pp. 286–7.

[251] Aubery, *Richelieu*, II. 144, 145, 1 June, Richelieu to Châtillon, Châtillon to de Noyers.

[252] Aubery, *Richelieu*, II. 154, 8 June 1638, de Noyers to Châtillon: 'L'on a esté un peu estonné à la Cour, de vous voir desia [déjà] crier au secours, et nous obliger à quitter les desseins, qui avoient esté donnez pour partage l'armée de Monsieur de La Force. Neanmoins, le Roy la vous envoye, comme vous l'avez desirée'; II. 157–8, 10 June, de Noyers à Châtillon.

[253] Avenel, VII. 1033, 13 June 1638, Richelieu to Châtillon, orders him to continue the siege; La Force, *Mémoires*, III. 199.

[254] SHAT A¹ 48, fo. 75, 14 July 1638, notification that Louis XIII consented to the abandonment of the siege of Saint-Omer; Avenel, VI. 65–6, 19 July 1638, Richelieu to cardinal de La Valette, reported the decision to lift the siege of Saint-Omer by Châtillon, and discussed the responsibility for the setback, suggesting that while many blamed the lack of cooperation between Châtillon and La Force, 'la lenteur de M. le mareschal de Chastillon est la première origine de nostre mal'.

[255] Aubery, II. 210–11, 9 Aug. 1638, Châtillon to de Noyers reporting the capture of Renty, accompanied by the articles of the capitulation with the governor.

[256] Initial, optimistic, discussion about the possibility of laying siege to Hesdin was rapidly abandoned: Aubery, II. 213–14, 9 Aug., Châtillon to Richelieu.

[257] Avenel, VI. 130, 31 Aug. 1638, Richelieu to Chavigny.

[258] Avenel, VI. 177 n. 2, 17 Sept. 1638, Richelieu to Louis XIII,: the news reached the king on 15 Sept.

France at war, 1624–1642

While no territory had been lost by the French in the Saint-Omer campaign, there was no denying the impact of a siege which had drawn upon unprecedented numbers of troops, had distorted the war-effort in virtually every other campaign theatre, had used up the best months of the campaign season and thousands of recruits, and had failed in the face of substantially inferior enemy forces. As a result of this setback, Louis XIII and Richelieu decided in future to assume direct control of a specific army-corps, abandoning the principle of command from the centre. The ministry and the *bureau des finances* had always accepted an effective hierarchy of campaign theatres; once the king travelled to be present with a particular army-corps, the order of priorities was immutable.

Despite the angry disputes at the end of 1637 between Saxe-Weimar and the French ministers, the spectacular victory won at Rheinfelden on 2 March, three days after apparent defeat at the hands of the same Imperial troops, transformed his standing with his French paymasters.[259] Heartened by his unexpected success, Saxe-Weimar proposed that in return for adequate military support from France he would be prepared to attempt the siege of Breisach, a fortress which was seen as the key to control of the middle Rhine. The decision to undertake the siege hung in the balance throughout May.[260] Saxe-Weimar's own army appeared too small to attempt such an operation, which would certainly provoke a strong Imperial response, while French promises of support foundered on both the potential availability of troops and the knowledge that units ordered into the Empire would suffer catastrophic and immediate levels of desertion.[261] However, the lure of taking Breisach in the midst of setbacks and failure elsewhere was irresistible; the final decision to order an entire French army-corps to support Saxe-Weimar if and when this should become necessary avoided the dangers of piecemeal allocation and heavy desertion. The duc de Longueville, who had again been given the command of the troops in the Franche-Comté in 1638, was ordered to avoid any engagement or substantial commitment that would prevent him being able to support Saxe-Weimar when the latter's strategy made reinforcement essential.[262]

Despite its sensible rationale, the result of this decision was the worst of both worlds. Longueville was established in the Franche-Comté with an army-corps capable of conducting further military operations against a territory in which

---

[259] BN Ms.fr. 3767, fo. 43, 3 Feb. 1638, Louis XIII (de Noyers) to Saxe-Weimar, offering a rather lukewarm denial that he had spoken critically of Saxe-Weimar's conduct; money will be provided for Saxe-Weimar, despite the king's knowledge of the extremely small number of effectives in his army; fo. 54, 17 Mar., Louis to Saxe-Weimar, congratulating him on the victory at Rheinfelden.

[260] Noailles, *Saxe-Weimar*, pp. 310–27.

[261] Ellerbach, *Elsaß*, III. 322–33; AAE CP Savoie 26, fo. 225v, 21 May 1638, Chavigny to Richelieu. Despite an attempt to bribe them to remain in service, the first contingent of 4,000 troops sent to Saxe-Weimar's army had fallen to 2,500 on arrival: BN Ms.fr. 3767, fo. 52, 14 Mar. 1638, de Noyers to Saxe-Weimar; Noailles, *Saxe-Weimar*, pp. 312–13.

[262] BN Ms.fr. 3767, fo. 60, 22 Apr. 1638, de Noyers to Saxe-Weimar.

The military context

there was initially no major enemy force.[263] At the same time, however, his freedom to campaign was circumscribed by the need to stand on alert to move to relieve Saxe-Weimar, and to avoid any operation that would involve a significant loss of troops or which might tie him to commitments from which he could not extricate himself. The situation was further complicated by the arrival of the duke of Lorraine and his army in the Franche-Comté so that Longueville was no longer operating in a territory which was virtually empty of enemy troops. In consequence of orders from the king and his wariness of the army of the duke of Lorraine, Longueville conducted a low-key campaign which led him to besiege the *château fort* of Rahon in early June, but kept him away from any of the major *places* in the Franche-Comté.[264] But confronted by the forces of Charles of Lorraine, and uncertain how to respond to this threat to French control, Longueville was drawn reluctantly into battle by duke Charles and defeated at Poligny on 19 June.[265] By early July Louis XIII felt obliged to write to Saxe-Weimar to explain why it would not be possible to send Longueville's army to support him. Instead, Henri de La Tour d'Auvergne, vicomte de Turenne, would be sent with 2,000 infantry and 1,500 horse originally intended to conduct operations in Lorraine, and Longueville would be instructed to send an additional 2,000 of his infantry.[266] Predictably, all of these promises proved more or less illusory: Turenne finally arrived on 27 July with 1,800 soldiers, most of whom were unfit for immediate service.[267] Despite further pleas from Saxe-Weimar, additional French forces failed to materialize; as late as 15 September Saxe-Weimar wrote to Louis to complain that the 2,000 troops promised from the army-corps of Longueville still had not arrived.[268]

Astoundingly, given the failure of the French crown to provide the promised military support, Saxe-Weimar was able to sustain the siege and to defeat a series of Imperial counter-attacks. A final Imperial bid to break the siege, launched on 19 November, was beaten off, though Saxe-Weimar lacked the troops for a direct assault and could only hope to starve the garrison of Breisach into submission.[269] The surrender of the garrison on 12 December provided the one positive

---

[263] Piépape, *Franche-Comté*, II. 95, suggests that Longueville had 5,000 infantry and 800 cavalry effectives at his disposal at the opening of the campaign. Campion, *Mémoires*, pp. 88–9, stresses that Longueville's army was intended to be of 10,000 infantry and 3,000 cavalry, and though many of these had not arrived, the duc expected to make progress in a territory which was 'abandoné, comme l'année précédente, à ses seules forces'.
[264] Piépape, *Franche-Comté*, II. 96–7.
[265] Des Robert, *Campagnes de Charles IV*, II. 25–33; Piépape, *Franche-Comté*, II. 102–9; Campion, *Mémoires*, pp. 89–92.
[266] BN Ms.fr. 3767, fo. 64, 3 July 1638, Louis XIII to Saxe-Weimar.
[267] Noailles, *Saxe-Weimar*, pp. 326–7; .
[268] BN Ms.fr. 3767, fos. 80–2, Saxe-Weimar to Louis; Saxe-Weimar had written in similar terms over a month previously concerning reinforcements promised from Longueville and du Hallier: fo. 69, 12 Aug.
[269] Noailles, *Saxe-Weimar*, pp. 365–6.

achievement in a year that had otherwise been filled with setbacks. However, the failure or inability of the French to provide anything approaching the military support that had repeatedly been promised rankled with Saxe-Weimar and certainly contributed to his reluctance to accept the implied agreement that his conquests would be transferred directly to the king of France.

In the Italian theatre, the French extraordinary ambassador, d'Hémery, had no doubt that the Spanish would profit from the dynastic crisis in Savoy-Piedmont to launch a major offensive.[270] The dynastic instability of late 1637 had already encouraged the Spanish to advance into Monferrato, capturing the fort of Pomaro on 16 October.[271] But with the Flanders theatre apparently offering the possibility of greater and more prestigious gains in early 1638, Richelieu was not about to make a substantial military provision to Piedmont. After the French commander Créqui died of wounds suffered while unsuccessfully trying to prevent the fall of Breme, Richelieu decided to replace him with his *fidèle*, the cardinal de La Valette.[272] La Valette inherited a situation in which the existing troops were demoralized, the commanders embroiled in disputes with the Savoyard government over rights of *logement*, and where the new units eagerly anticipated to build up the strength of the army turned out to be delayed and, once arrived, heavily under strength.[273]

On 20 May the Spanish army of the Milanese began a full-scale campaign in Monferrato. Even with the grudging support of Savoyard troops, the French were not able to resist the Spanish offensive, and on 5 July La Valette failed to prevent Vercelli capitulating to the Spanish.[274]

To compound military failure on the frontier with Monferrato, concern was now growing that the whole of Piedmont was on the verge of falling to the pro-Spanish cause of Tommaso Francesco, prince of Carignano and cardinal Maurizio, uncles of the young duke of Savoy. For the death of the young Francesco Giacinto

---

[270] AAE CP Savoie 26, fos. 70, 90, 18/24 Feb. 1638, d'Hémery to Richelieu, complaining that financial incompetence had resulted in the loss of some 50,000 *écus* destined for the army, and stressing the need for the extra three regiments anticipated on the new *état* for the army of Italy.

[271] Mun, *Richelieu et la Maison de Savoie*, p. 227.

[272] AAE CP Savoie 26, fo. 121, 8 Apr. 1638, loss of Breme; fo. 138, 20 Apr., report of death of Créqui; Avenel, VII. 186, 6 Apr. 1638, Richelieu to Chavigny, urging him to do all possible to hasten the departure of the cardinal de La Valette for Italy to shore up the military situation after the fall of Breme.

[273] AAE MD 830, fo. 96, 6 Apr. 1638, Richelieu to Chavigny: 'la prise de Bresme abbatera les coeurs des gens de guerre'; CP Savoie 26, fos. 101, 123, 5 Mar./10 Apr., d'Hémery to Richelieu, reporting that the regiment of Vaillac had arrived with only 230 men, while the comte de Sault had suggested that he should send the units being raised in Dauphiné 'in their present state', implying that they were seriously under strength. D'Hémery in a later letter implied that the deteriorating position of the French in Piedmont was acting as a further disincentive to the troops, who were deliberately finding reasons to delay their departure down to Italy: Savoie 26, fo. 152, 25 Apr. 1638; fo. 214, 17 May 1638, La Valette to Richelieu.

[274] AAE CP Savoie 26, fo. 347, 8 July 1638, La Valette to Richelieu; BN Ms.fr. 6644, fos. 311–13, 8 July, *factum* related to failure to relieve Vercelli.

The military context

on 4 October 1638 had left Marie-Christine with only one surviving infant son, now duke Carlo Emanuele II, and in this even more unstable situation his uncles were prepared to draw upon Spanish support to assert their claims to involvement in the Regency.[275] On 1 December Richelieu wrote to La Valette, urging him to do all possible to ensure that the regent Marie-Christine, Louis XIII's sister, should secure the major cities and fortification in Piedmont.[276] D'Hémery's arguments had been ignored throughout 1638, and the scene was set for the near-total collapse of the French position that would take place in Piedmont during the following year.[277]

Although the decision had been taken to add the Atlantic frontier with Spain to France's existing military commitments in 1638, it was not evident if and where the king and his ministers proposed to scale down the war-effort to compensate for this new burden. It was clear that neither Epernon nor Charles duc d'Halluin (created maréchal Schomberg in late 1637), respectively governors of Guienne and Languedoc, was happy with the decision to give overall authority in this campaign theatre to the prince de Condé.[278] As the only loyalist *prince du sang*, Condé was considered more likely to maintain their obedience than anyone other than the king himself. Sufficient cooperation was achieved to decide that the first target should be Fuenterrabía, just across the Spanish frontier from Guienne.[279] The fall of this city would, it was hoped, open up the possibility of the subsequent capture of San Sebastián, Bilbao or Laredo and permit a French military presence on Castilian territory.[280] But disputes between the various subordinate commanders began almost immediately, focused above all on the feud between Epernon's third son Bernard, duc de La Valette, and Henri Escoubleau de Sourdis, commander of the supporting navy. It was clear that Condé lacked either the diplomatic skill or the personal authority to contain these disputes.[281] But despite concern at these tensions within the high command, and the slowness with which Condé began operations, on 3 July the army managed to cut off the promontary

---

[275] Quazza, *Tommaso di Savoia-Carignano*, pp. 239–49.
[276] Avenel, VI. 250–255, 1 Dec. 1638, Richelieu to cardinal de La Valette and the duchess of Savoy.
[277] Just before the Spanish invasion of Monferrato, d'Hémery had urged Richelieu to decide between a defensive or an offensive strategy, though both would require a more substantial military provision than the ministry had been prepared to offer to date: AAE CP Savoie 26, fos. 202–6, 15 May.
[278] Aumale, *Princes de Condé*, III. 384–5; in fact Richelieu had been contemplating sending the prince down to Guienne as early as October 1637 as a means to push Epernon and his son into a more energetic offensive against the invading Spanish: AAE CP Espagne 18, fo. 572, 6 Oct. 1637.
[279] Bernard du Plessis, sieur de Besançon, *Mémoires* (Paris, 1892), pp. 18–19.
[280] Sourdis, *Correspondance*, II. 9, 12 May 1638, *Instruction pour l'Archevêque de Bordeaux*; Aumale, *Princes de Condé*, III. 390. In the struggle to gain credit and approval with the king, it should not be forgotten that Richelieu was anxious to find opportunities to demonstrate the military contribution that could be made by the French Atlantic fleet, in a real sense his personal creation. This point is effectively made by A. James, 'The administration and development of the French navy and the ministry of cardinal Richelieu', PhD thesis, University of Manchester, 1997.
[281] Sourdis, *Correspondance*, II. 32–3, 22 June, Louis XIII to Condé, concerning the open disputes amongst the senior commanders.

France at war, 1624–1642

on which Fuenterrabía was situated, isolating it from land communications.[282] Once a naval blockade was in place, the conviction grew that a successful siege was a foregone conclusion.[283] Indeed by the end of August Richelieu was presenting the fall of Fuenterrabía as the key to an overall victory over the Habsburgs.[284] By 1 September a breach had been opened in the main defences of the *place*, and Richelieu was confident that the end was in sight.[285] Although a Spanish relief army began to arrive and assemble, the threat posed by this force of 7,000–8,000 troops was underestimated by everyone connected with the siege, from Richelieu downwards.[286] On 7 September the Spanish opened an attack against the main French position commanded by Condé himself. The French troops, even the elite regiments, panicked, although the Spanish attack was relatively small scale and disordered.[287] Part of the problem, as Sourdis pointed out in a private letter to his brother, was that the French circumvallation, both facing inwards towards the city and outwards, were totally inadequate.[288] At the time of the defeat, however, wider questions of responsibility were subordinated to Richelieu's determination to protect his *fidèle*, Sourdis, and his most powerful aristocratic ally, Condé.[289] The scapegoat, much assisted by his own history of non-cooperation and obstruction during the campaign, was the duc de La Valette and, through him, his father Epernon, whose power and hostility Richelieu had regarded as an obstacle to his own and to royal authority in the south-west since the early 1630s.[290]

Though La Valette prudently fled from France, and the power of Epernon as governor of Guienne was broken, this was poor compensation for a campaign which had failed so dismally to achieve the breakthrough in the south that Richelieu had sought.[291] If 1638 could hardly be compared with 1636, *l'année de*

---

[282] Sourdis, *Correspondance*, II. 34–5, 8 July, Condé to Bordeaux.
[283] Avenel, VI. 67, 19 July 1638, Richelieu to Condé, relieved to hear that Condé's siege works were progressing well; VI. 87, 16 Aug. 1638, Richelieu to Condé: 'Je ne doute point que vous n'ayés maintenant pris Fontarabie'; VI. 103, 22 Aug. 1638, 'Projet d'instruction pour M. de Nantes' (Gabriel de Beauvau de Rivarennes, bp of Nantes); Aumale, *Princes de Condé*, III. 396–7, comments on the tensions that developed as soon as Bordeaux joined the siege with his marine units.
[284] Avenel, VI. 128, 31 Aug. 1638, Richelieu to Louis XIII.
[285] Avenel, VI. 139/40, Richelieu to Chavigny, mentioning his hopes with regard to the siege on two separate occasions in the letter.
[286] Sourdis, *Correspondance*, II. 52, 1 Sept. 1638, Richelieu to Sourdis.
[287] Avenel, VI. 195–209 [end Sept.] 1638, 'Factum du prince de Condé sur le lèvement du siège de Fontarabie'; Elliott, *The Count-Duke of Olivares*, pp. 539–540.
[288] Sourdis, *Correspondance*, II. 59–62, 9 Sept. 1638, Bordeaux to Sourdis.
[289] Aumale, *Princes de Condé*, III. 399–400, emphasizes that Condé was far from certain that he would be spared disgrace in the aftermath of the defeat.
[290] Sourdis, *Correspondance*, II. 75–8, 21 Sept. 1638, letters of Richelieu and Louis XIII to Bordeaux, Condé, duc de La Valette and Epernon; Avenel, VI. 191–2, 22 Sept., 'Copie d'un mémoire envoyé a M. de Chavigny sur le sujet de Ms. D'Espernon et de La Valette.' Henri Griffet provides an account of Fuenterrabía that is quite sympathetic to the role and actions of the duc de La Valette, suggesting that contemporaries were surprised that Richelieu should have pursued his relative by marriage with such ferocity, but emphasizes La Valette's role in the conspiracy of 1636: *Louis XIII*, III. 142–3, 181–91.
[291] Girard, *Espernon*, pp. 569–70; Mouton, *Duc et le roi*, pp. 271–85.

The military context

Corbie, in terms of the overt threat posed to French territory and political survival, it was just as comprehensive a failure in terms of French strategic objectives. As with 1636, a massive commitment of men, matériel and finance had left the war-effort in a worse position than before the campaign began.

Despite the failures of 1638, a return to the reactive, defensive, policy of 1637 was no longer a serious option for the next campaign. Successive defeats in 1638 had ensured that the 1639 campaign would be an *affaire d'honneur*: the king's reputation required that France should seize the initiative and recover lost ground with some notable successes. On 27 April Richelieu expressed guarded optimism about the military preparations for the forthcoming campaign. Though the Spanish had made 'progrez inopinez' in Italy, Longueville was being despatched with 10 regiments of infantry and 2,000 cavalry to bolster up resistance. Meanwhile, another massive concentration of troops on the northern and eastern frontiers was to be the centrepiece of French strategy: La Meilleraye, *grand maître de l'artillerie*, was to cross the Flanders frontier in four days' time, and would be seconded by the activities of a further army under Manassés de Pas, marquis de Feuquières. Anticipating the usual massive levels of wastage, Châtillon was to be placed in command of a third army, being levied slightly later in the year, which would march to join La Meilleraye when falling troop numbers started to endanger operations. While it might be doubted whether, in early 1639, Saxe-Weimar was 'plus satisfait de la France que jamais', it was indicative of Richelieu's hopes for the forthcoming campaign that he assumed the duke would prove both tractable and likely to achieve further successes after the capture of Breisach. Richelieu also expressed considerable optimism about the activities of France's main allies, claiming that the Dutch would enter the campaign by 10 May, and that Johan Banér 'fait merveilles en Allemagne'. Having presented this overview of the other theatres, Richelieu stressed that it was for the recipient of the letter, Condé, to do all possible to facilitate the king's service in the south.[292]

For although Condé's military reputation had been preserved by the condemnation of La Valette, the humiliation of Fuenterrabía was not an event Louis XIII or Richelieu proposed to forget. Even before the end of 1638 Richelieu had suggested to Condé that not everyone was convinced that La Valette was solely to blame, and that Condé should attempt 'quelque bon dessein que vous puissiés réussir l'année qui vient' to allay the suspicions that had been generated.[293] Experience during 1638 indicated to Condé that maréchal Schomberg would be unlikely to attempt any effective diversion on his own part if Condé launched the main offensive through Guienne.[294] Moreover, Condé was anxious to deploy the military resources of Languedoc to try to achieve a rapid military success. In

[292] Avenel, VII. 800–2, 27 Apr., Richelieu to Condé.
[293] Avenel, VI. 217–18, 16 Oct. [1638].
[294] Indeed, Schomberg himself said as much, writing to Richelieu that Condé wanted him to launch a

France at war, 1624–1642

consequence, he decided in early June to undertake the invasion of Roussillon, proposing a move against Perpignan or Clairac.[295] Command of the forces operating across the border from Languedoc was given to Schomberg, Condé having received orders from the Court that he should not lead the army in person since the Spanish forces which might be encountered would not be commanded by someone of equivalent rank.[296] Schomberg's troops advanced into Roussillon as far as the fortress of Salces, which it was assumed would capitulate rapidly and leave time to pursue other objectives in the campaign.[297] However, the siege was still in progress on 19 July when a large mine was exploded under the fortifications, and the fortress was finally stormed by the French army.[298] If Louis and his ministers saw this as a prelude to greater achievements during the remainder of the year, Condé now wanted to call the campaign to an end on a note of success, and was already discussing the question of winter quartering for the army.[299] When news was received that Spanish forces were being raised in Catalonia to try to recapture Salces and to push the French out of Roussillon, the commanders did not feel confident that they could confront the advancing Spanish. Condé was back in Narbonne, and Schomberg decided that rather than risk a military disaster by accepting battle with the Spaniards, it would be better to leave a large garrison in Salces and to withdraw from Roussillon.[300] A large force of French troops could then be raised in Languedoc and would move against the Spanish siege army when it had exhausted itself in a protracted siege of Salces.[301] In the last week of October, Condé set out to lift the siege and engage the Spanish forces, by his own admission with an army under his command that numbered 22,000 infantry and 4,000 horse.[302] Admittedly, a proportion of these were irregular troops, yet this could hardly have accounted by itself for the catastrophic collapse of the army after twenty-four hours of exceptionally heavy rain. According to Condé's account the army simply deserted *en masse*, discipline and order collapsed, there was a chaotic general retreat, he and his fellow commanders being left with some 2,000 infantry and 500 cavalry.[303] Fearing disgrace at the hands of

---

poorly supported advance into Roussillon in order to facilitate another assault through Guienne on Fuenterrabía led by Condé: BN Ms.fr. 3768, fos. 15–17, 23 May 1639.

[295] BN Ms.fr. 3768, fos. 22–3, 6 June 1639, Schomberg to Richelieu, who was already complaining that Condé had been responsible for the delay in beginning the campaign into Roussillon.

[296] Vassal-Reig, *Roussillon*, pp. 92–3.

[297] Richelieu was clear that he did not consider Salces an adequate objective for the campaign: Avenel, VII. 213, 1 Apr. 1639, Richelieu to Schomberg.

[298] AAE MD 1631, fo. 20, 31 July 1639, Condé to de Noyers; Campion, *Mémoires*, pp. 103–4.

[299] AAE MD 1631, fo. 29, 22 Aug. 1639, Condé to de Noyers.

[300] Vassal-Reig, *Roussillon*, pp. 111–26.

[301] AAE MD 1631, fo. 156, 30 Sept., Condé to Richelieu, reporting that the Spanish army had suffered 2,500 casualties in the first week of assaults on Salces; Avenel, VI. 572–4, 6 Oct. 1639, Richelieu to Condé, approving this course of action.

[302] AAE MD 1631, fo. 202, 27 Oct. 1639, Condé's account of the failure to relieve Salces; Aumale, *Princes de Condé*, III. 408–10.

[303] AAE MD 1631, fo. 202, 27 Oct.

The military context

an enraged Richelieu, Condé scraped together another, much smaller, force and tried to lift the siege. But the French were outnumbered, the Spanish were now well entrenched around the fortress, and the weather was worsening. After a futile assault on the Spanish positions, Condé withdrew back to Languedoc once again and the garrison surrendered to the Spanish, and marched out of the fortress on 6 January 1640.[304]

At the end of 1639 the balance sheet on the Spanish frontier appeared overwhelmingly negative. It was true that the relief of Salces had placed great strains on the Spanish system, and that the decision to billet some of the Castilian troops in Catalonia over the winter months of 1639–40 was a recipe for potential trouble.[305] The full extent of this trouble could hardly have been predicted, however, and the Catalan revolt did not erupt as a serious and potentially lasting challenge to Castilian authority until July 1640. Even then, the French crown could not immediately assume that it would shift the entire balance of power on the Spanish frontiers, or that the revolt would drag on through the 1640s. If the principle of achieving a breakthrough by concentrating forces against a weak point in the Spanish system was a sound one, it was clear that the Pyrenean frontier had confounded French hopes of easy success in 1638 and 1639.

In the north-east, the opening of a major campaign was once again beset with indecision and conflicting advice. Richelieu had ensured that his relative, Charles de La Porte de La Meilleraye, should have command of the largest army-corps, and that the campaign should be a means to further La Meilleraye's career.[306] Richelieu himself discussed various possible objectives for La Meilleraye's army, particularly Arras, but in the end felt obliged to give him *carte blanche* to use the army as he thought fit.[307] In consequence, La Meilleraye and his *conseil de guerre* decided to move against Hesdin, well fortified but with easier lines of communication back to the French frontier than Arras.[308] As Richelieu's initial plan suggested, command of the second army-corps was entrusted to Châtillon, and it was understood that the purpose of this force was simply to second La Meilleraye.[309] The arrival of Louis XIII to assume overall control of the siege army had the beneficial effect of giving direct royal authority to La Meilleraye and

---

[304] Hanotaux, *Richelieu*, VI. 14.
[305] J.H. Elliott, *The Revolt of the Catalans. A Study in the Decline of Spain (1598–1640)* (Cambridge, 1963), pp. 387–417.
[306] This was widely recognized by contemporaries: Montglat, *Mémoires*, XLIX. 225; Puységur, *Guerres*, I. 217–18.
[307] Avenel, VI. 354–6, 17 May 1639, Richelieu to la Meilleraye: 'car je vous redis encore un fois que le roy vous laisse la carte blanche'. Ironically, La Meilleraye's own letter to Richelieu of three days earlier had already considered a number of possible objectives, regarding Hesdin as the *least* useful gain for the crown: BN Ms.fr. 3769, fos. 1–2, 14 May.
[308] BN Ms.fr. 3769, fo. 4v, 19 May 1639, La Meilleraye to Richelieu.
[309] Avenel, VII. 226, 26 May 1639, Richelieu to La Meilleraye, emphasizing the role of Châtillon in providing a covering force; Griffet, *Louis XIII*, III. 192.

stifling many of the conflicts that might have arisen from more senior officers.[310] But it also had the consequence of ensuring that the king's prestige was tied to the effective outcome of the siege, and that all necessary resources would now be poured into the attempt to capture the chosen *place*.

In some respects this was a return to the strategy of the early sixteenth century – a massive thrust against a single point in the Habsburg system. Yet what made good sense in the 1530s or 1550s when the total size of armed forces was much smaller was a far less sensible deployment of resources in the 1630s when other campaign theatres would be neglected only at considerable peril.

At the same time that La Meilleraye moved against Hesdin, the army of Lorraine, commanded by Manassés de Pas, marquis de Feuquières, had been instructed to do everything possible to attract the attention of the Imperial forces operating between Flanders and Lorraine. In following these instructions, Feuquières laid siege to Thionville.[311] Feuquières counted on taking the *place* quickly, despite its size and fortifications,[312] but on 6 June he learnt that the enemy were advancing towards him, and his outnumbered forces were routed by Ottavio Piccolomini's elite Imperial army-corps.[313] Though Richelieu was concerned to minimize the impact of the defeat at Thionville, the destruction of one of the main French armies left other Imperial and Spanish forces free to deploy themselves against La Meilleraye's siege army.[314] Charles of Lorraine was preparing to use the opportunity presented by Thionville to renew the attempt to drive the French out of his duchy. This rendered the position of du Hallier, commanding a small and underfunded force in Lorraine, untenable. On 25 August he excused himself for the fact that so little progress had been made in holding the duchy, but pointed out that the army was deteriorating by the day, and that even the small number of reinforcements were weak and demoralized.[315]

All effort was being focused on the siege of Hesdin, and the primary concern was to avoid any risk of setbacks or defeats before the place capitulated. The army stayed within the siege works, avoided substantial dispersal and offered no

---

[310] Hanotaux, *Richelieu*, v. 361–2.

[311] Feuquières had argued since the opening of the campaign season that his capacity to launch a diversion towards the Rhine was a good reason for not reducing the numbers of troops at his disposal: AAE CP Lorraine 31, fo. 55, 29 Apr. 1639, Feuquières to de Noyers, arguing against redeploying some of his forces down to Italy.

[312] AAE CP Lorraine 31, fos. 86–7, 29 May.

[313] AAE CP Lorraine 31, fo. 93, 4 June 1639, letter to Feuquières, warning him of the advance of Piccolomini; fos. 97–9, 6 June, Feuquières to de Noyers; Roger de Rabutin, comte de Bussy, *Mémoires* (3 vols; Paris, 1712), I. 66–72, describes the battle from his perspective as a *mestre de camp* present with his regiment, which was largely destroyed.

[314] The initial concern was that the victorious army would attempt a siege of Metz, but by 22 June this had been discounted as a threat: AAE CP Lorraine 31, fo. 159, Choisy to de Noyers; Avenel, VI. 387–8, 16 June 1639, Richelieu to La Meilleraye, reporting that Piccolomini had been moving towards a rendez-vous with the Spanish troops of the Cardinal Infante since 12 June.

[315] AAE CP Lorraine 31, fo. 200, 25 Aug. 1639, du Hallier to de Noyers.

The military context

opportunity to the Spanish–Imperial forces to try to draw parts of the forces into local conflicts. Finally, after the explosion of two mines beneath the walls, the governor made terms for surrender on 29 June.[316] Because the fall of Hesdin had been achieved relatively early in the campaign, it was possible for the bulk of the army to advance into Flanders in order that it could live off enemy territory – arguably the first time that a main French campaign army was in a position to do this since 1635.[317] Châtillon's forces were able to move into Luxembourg, taking the town of Ivoy in early August, though unsurprisingly he proved reluctant to launch his forces into a second siege of Thionville.[318]

Over the winter of 1638–39 and following the capture of Breisach, Saxe-Weimar moved his army back into the Franche-Comté in search of winter quarters.[319] Encountering ill-prepared garrisons and no field-corps, his army had little difficulty in capturing a series of towns and fortresses. A small contingent of French troops, five infantry regiments under the command of Jean-Baptiste Budes, comte de Guébriant, was still serving with Saxe-Weimar, and joined in the occupation and quartering of the Comté.[320] As Saxe-Weimar held Breisach with his troops, having appointed Hans Ludwig von Erlach as governor, it would clearly be necessary for the crown to make some concessions if Louis wished ever to see Breisach under French control.[321] In order to try to draw out Saxe-Weimar about his intentions and to try to hammer out a compromise in an atmosphere of growing suspicion, Guébriant was given an elaborate set of instructions on 30 June and told to meet both the general and Erlach to discuss possible terms.[322] Despite Guébriant's standing with the duke, the situation over Breisach reached an impasse that was broken only by the death of Saxe-Weimar, news of which Richelieu received on 27 July.[323] In order rapidly to exploit this unanticipated turn of events, the duc de Longueville was recalled from Italy and formally established as the commander of the army of Germany.[324] Though the rest of the campaign was spent in renegotiating terms of service between France and the directors of the Weimarian army, it now appeared that France would have more direct control over an army operating in

---

[316] Aubery, II. 320, 30 June 1639, de Noyers to Châtillon, reports the king's entry into Hesdin.
[317] Avenel, VI. 434–6, 16 July 1639, Richelieu to La Meilleraye; Hanotaux, *Richelieu*, V. 371–2.
[318] Avenel, VI. 456, 30 July 1639, Richelieu to Frederik Hendrik, prince of Orange, reporting Châtillon's advance against Ivoy; VI. 465, 9 Aug., Richelieu to La Meilleraye, notifying him of the capture of Ivoy and subsequent plans to move against Thionville.
[319] Piépape, *Franche-Comté*, II. 127–33; des Robert, *Campagnes de Charles IV*, II. 80–1.
[320] Piépape, *Franche-Comté*, II. 133–40.
[321] Noailles, *Saxe-Weimar*, pp. 398–400; Ellerbach, *Elsaß*, III. 341–57.
[322] Avenel, VII. 220, 30 Apr. 1639, instructions for Guébriant; Noailles, *Saxe-Weimar*, pp. 400–1.
[323] Avenel, VI. 450, 27 July 1639, Richelieu to La Meilleraye.
[324] Avenel, VI. 463, 1 Aug. 1639, Richelieu to cardinal de La Valette; AAE CP Allemagne 15, fo. 314, 27 July 1639, *mémoire* for comte d'Avaux, concerning the bribes to be paid to Saxe-Weimar's colonels, and the despatch of Paul Le Prevost, marquis d'Oysonville, to negotiate the transfer of the army; Ellerbach, *Elsaß*, III. 359–62.

France at war, 1624–1642

the Empire with a strong French contingent and overall French command.[325] On 27 December, Guébriant, acting as Longueville's lieutenant, organized the passage of the Rhine, and the bulk of the Weimarian-French army reassembled around Limburg.[326]

In north Italy, French policy was riven by contradictory strategies. One view was that vigorous military action in 1639 would be the only means to recover some of the ground lost in the previous campaign and to preserve the reputation of France amongst the Italian princes.[327] However, an alternative argument put the case, implicitly at least, for continuing a low-level, defensive, strategy, and accepting that in the short term most of Piedmont would be overrun by the Spanish. In the face of this Spanish invasion, the regent Marie-Christine would be forced to ask, as the Rhineland princes had done in the 1630s, for protection from the French. Thus the king would gain control of a number of significant Savoyard and Piedmontese strongpoints, rather than having to negotiate with independent-minded and frequently obstructive rulers, whose previous cooperation in projects such as the 'League of Rivoli' had always been limited and conditional.[328] This ambiguity was to have near-fatal consequences for the French presence in north Italy. For despite protestations to La Valette that the army would receive the highest priority and would be ready to campaign early in the year, the reality was the same slow and incomplete process of moving troops down into Italy, the same half-hearted promises about funding.[329]

By late March the Spanish governor of the Milanese, the marquis of Leganés, had captured Chivasso and was now marching towards Turin accompanied by Tommaso Francesco, prince of Carignano and uncle of the young duke of Savoy.[330] Confronting this substantial Spanish force, La Valette had only 3,500 men available to serve in his field army. Meanwhile, however, d'Hémery was under instructions to increase pressure on Marie-Christine to hand over a list of important fortifications to French garrisons as the price of saving her son's inheritance from his Spanish-backed uncles.[331] In May 1639, the Spanish took

---

[325] AAE CP Allemagne 15, fos. 329–33, 4 Aug. 1639, Richelieu to d'Avaux, concerning Saxe-Weimar's testament; fos. 373–7, 22 Oct., treaty of Breisach.

[326] Noailles, *Guébriant*, pp. 136–9.

[327] AAE CP Savoie 28, fo. 3, 4 Jan. 1639, cardinal de La Valette to Chavigny, expressing the hope that a well-paid and equipped army will be able to press the campaign in Italy 'd'une autre façon quelles ne l'ont usé les années passées'.

[328] Oresko, 'Savoy and the Thirty Years War', p. 149; even Hanotaux, whose uncritical enthusiasm for virtually every decision taken by Richelieu is the hallmark of his biography, recognizes that this policy may have placed Marie-Christine in an invidious situation: v. 381–3. The duchess herself warned Richelieu in mid-January about the dangerous consequences of another purely defensive campaign: BN Ms.fr. 3770, fo. 7v, 14 Jan.

[329] BN Ms.fr. 3770, fos. 23v, 28v, 6 Feb., 15 Apr. 1639, La Valette to Richelieu, concerning the slow arrival of troops and inadequate funding.

[330] AAE CP Savoie 28, fo. 154, 30 Mar. 1639, La Valette to Richelieu on fall of Chivasso.

[331] BN Ms.fr. 3770, fo. 83, 5 Apr. 1639, instructions to d'Hémery: 'si les affaires du Piémont [sont] reduictes au point que la perte du pais fut à craindre, en ce cas led. Sr d'Hémery doibt remonstrer à

Moncalvo, Pondesture and Trino.³³² La Valette was unable to lift any of these sieges, since with his limited forces it would have meant leaving Turin almost undefended; those troops he could spare were placed within Casale-Monferrato, considered an even more vital strongpoint.³³³ Only on 10 June did Marie-Christine finally announce that she would grant Carmagnola, Avigliano, Cherasco and Revello to French garrisons in return for more energetic military support for her son's rights. This itself created a substantial problem for the French war-effort, since the full garrisoning of all the places handed over to France, together with existing commitments, would involve over 10,000 troops, rendering it impossible to support a field army in the Italian theatre.³³⁴ In La Valette's opinion, the last remaining possibility of halting the Spanish offensive depended on the arrival of the duc de Longueville and his complete army-corps which would – at least temporarily – create a force large enough to confront the troops of Tommaso Francesco and Leganés.³³⁵ Longueville's arrival in Italy did permit a brief recovery in French fortunes, and the commanders felt strong enough to attempt the recapture of Chivasso, which was invested on 17 June.³³⁶ However, initial success by Longueville and La Valette, and the diversion of French troops towards Casale, simply permitted Tommaso Francesco to occupy the city of Turin on 27 July, although the citadel itself continued to be held by a French garrison.³³⁷ Immediately after this, Longueville was summoned back to take command of the army of Germany. Paralysed by inadequate funding, and with an army that was still only large enough to hold the existing *places* under French control, La Valette saw no option but to agree to a truce with the Spanish, which lasted from 14 August until 24 October, and allowed the Spanish to consolidate their recent conquests.³³⁸ Richelieu himself was prepared to accept such a truce, above all 'parce qu'il sera plus difficile que jamais de vous envoyer autant d'hommes que vous en aurez besoin'.³³⁹ However, if Richelieu had hoped that the truce would

Madame que le seul expedient . . . [est] de remettre son fils et ses places entièrement entre les mains du Roy'.
³³² Avenel, VI. 338, 3 May 1639, Richelieu to Chavigny.
³³³ AAE CP Savoie 28, fos. 360–7, 18 May 1639, d'Hémery and Chavigny to Richelieu.
³³⁴ Avenel, VI. 349, 13 May 1639, Richelieu to Chavigny: 'la plus grande difficulté que nous aurons est à trouver des gens'. Part of the solution chosen would appear to be self-defeating: the enlistment of substantial numbers of Piedmontese troops to serve in the garrisons.
³³⁵ AAE CP Savoie 28, fo. 457, 1 June 1639, La Valette to Richelieu. Though La Valette's desire was not shared by Longueville himself: Chavigny had reported on 25 May: 'qu'il paroist qu'il n'a pas grande inclination à passer en Italie': Savoie 28, fo. 396v, letter to Richelieu.
³³⁶ AAE CP Savoie 28, fo. 607 [n.d.] *état* of the army of Longueville entering Piedmont Savoie; 28, fo. 585, 30 June 1639, La Valette to de Noyers, reporting capture of Chivasso.
³³⁷ AAE CP Savoie 29, fo. 58, 27 July, La Valette to Chavigny, reporting the loss of Turin; fo. 72, 4 Aug., La Valette to de Noyers, informing him that following heavy fighting, in which a number of senior French officers were killed, the citadel of Turin had remained in the hands of the French garrison.
³³⁸ AAE CP Savoie 29, fo. 97, 13 Aug. 1639, La Valette and Longueville to de Noyers, notifying the court of the decision to accept the truce.
³³⁹ Avenel, VI. 488–93, 25 Aug. 1639, Richelieu to La Valette; this had followed a period of mounting

France at war, 1624–1642

last into the next campaign, the illness and on 28 September the death of La Valette caused immediate concern that Leganés would take this as an excuse to break the treaty and to begin hostilities in Piedmont again.³⁴⁰ La Valette's replacement was Henri de Lorraine, comte d'Harcourt, and his arrival seems to have been linked to greater awareness that, if the French garrisons were not to be picked off one by one, a concerted military commitment would be required in the Italian theatre, both in the last stages of the 1639 campaign and in the year to come.³⁴¹

The campaign of 1639 was characterized by the maintenance of offensive strategies in an attempt to counteract the setbacks of 1638; the following campaign of 1640 saw no less determination to continue the pressure, above all in the northeast, where the capture of Hesdin seemed to vindicate the policy of large-scale siege warfare. It was clear that Italy would require a heavier commitment but owing to disillusionment with the prospect of achieving any breakthrough across the Spanish frontier there was an initial willingness to scale down the commitment there.

Once again, the centrepiece of French strategy was to be a massive concentration of forces on the Flanders frontier. La Meilleraye, made maréchal after his success at Hesdin, was to command the principal – and ultimately 'royal' – army, while Châtillon would stand in reserve. A complicating factor was the initial hope that operations could be combined with the Dutch, dividing the Spanish forces in the Netherlands to the profit of both allies.³⁴² Previous experience would indicate that such attempts at combined operations were more likely to generate frustration than positive results, and indeed La Meilleraye's actions across the frontier in the early part of the campaign did more to weaken the effective strength of his army-corps than bring any positive achievements.³⁴³ By the time that these operations had been abandoned it had already become clear that a major siege on the frontiers would require the amalgamation of the armies of La Meilleraye and Châtillon.³⁴⁴

exasperation by Richelieu at what he considered to be La Valette's lack of initiative – itself indicative of the gap in understanding between Paris and the commanders in Piedmont: Avenel, VI. 470–1, 16 Aug.
³⁴⁰ Avenel, VI. 561–2, 30 Sept. 1639, Richelieu to Leganés.
³⁴¹ AAE CP Savoie 29, fo. 278, 27 Sept., Argenson to Chavigny, reporting the death of La Valette; Noailles, *Cardinal de La Valette*, pp. 539–40; overall command was divided between Turenne and Vignolles in the 'interregnum' before Harcourt's arrival: Savoie 29, fo. 372, 9 Oct.; Avenel, VI. 578–9, 16 Oct. 1639, Richelieu's *mémoire* for the *ambassade* of Claude Mallier, sieur du Houssay, to the Republic of Venice, discussing further troops to be sent to Italy.
³⁴² Bourelly, *Maréchal de Fabert*, I. 158–9.
³⁴³ Griffet, *Louis XIII*, III. 266–8, quoting Richelieu: 'je ne saurois vous exprimer la douleur de M. le maréchal de La Meilleraye, de voir son armée à demi-délabrée dès l'entrée d'une campagne, et sans avoir rien fait'.
³⁴⁴ Choppin, *Maréchal de Gassion*, pp. 64–5: though Gassion was serving with La Meilleraye's army, he enjoyed the confidence of Châtillon, and wrote to Châtillon to explain the necessity of amalgamating the two armies after the wastage suffered by La Meilleraye's corps in supporting the

The military context

The forces thus collected seemed sufficiently large to make an attack on Arras practical, and on 14 June the two armies met together before the city and began to construct siege works.[345] A large siege army, encamped well within enemy territory presented considerable challenges of supply. Initial *ad hoc* organization of supply convoys attracted heavy criticism from Richelieu who did not consider that they had been provided with an adequate escort to cross enemy territory.[346] Because of the need to maintain a large force to man the siege works, and of the consequent demands of organized supply, the siege of Arras rapidly overrode all other strategic considerations.[347] An army-corps under du Hallier had been built up at the beginning of the campaign season in order to conduct a major operation in Lorraine, a bid to reassert direct French control over the territory which had slipped away in preceding years when the theatre had enjoyed the most limited priority in the ministry's strategic planning.[348] Only on 5 July did du Hallier suggest with confidence that he could now open the campaign, but in the interim he had received orders for a complete change of plan. He was now to move his entire army northwards to act as a support for Châtillon and Chaulnes' force at Arras, and in particular to escort the convoys of *vivres* required to support the siege.[349] Once this further concentration of French forces made any further attempt at relief impossible, the governor of Arras decided to negotiate with the besieging army, and on 8 August the city made terms.[350]

In early September du Hallier's forces were still being employed in activities around Arras, and any possibility of resuming the original, planned campaign in Lorraine was now out of the question.[351] It was equally clear that Châtillon, acting as spokesman for the other army-corps, did not consider that the army should

---

Dutch campaign; Avenel, VII. 261, 2 June, Richelieu to Châtillon, instructing him to rendez-vous with La Meilleraye.

[345] Hanotaux, *Richelieu*, VI. 49–50; Bourelly, *Maréchal de Fabert*, I. 159–60; Bussy-Rabutin, *Mémoires*, I. 73–6.

[346] Avenel, VI. 712, 1 July, Richelieu to MM. les généraux: 'je ne sçay quelle raison ils peuvent avoir de hasarder une affaire sy importante avec sy peu de seureté'. This followed the loss of one of the convoys to a Spanish raiding force: Griffet, *Louis XIII*, III. 272.

[347] And generated a level of misappropriation of funds and supplies which would have been inconceivable in other army-corps: after the siege Châtillon saw fit to write a lengthy justification to de Noyers concerning the supply of the army at Arras, noting that Richelieu had written to him on this matter – 'qui tesmoigne nestre pas bien edifiée de la largesse qui s'est faicte du pain': AAE MD 1679, fos. 245–6, 5 Sept.

[348] AAE CP Lorraine, fos. 306–8, 310–11, 21 Mar./1 Apr. 1640, du Hallier to de Noyers, concerning arrangements and requirements for the army to be set *sur pied*.

[349] AAE CP Lorraine 31, fo. 361, 5 July, du Hallier announces that the army is ready to begin campaigning; fo. 363, 6 July, du Hallier confirms that he has received orders for this change of strategy.

[350] AAE MD 1679, fos. 182, 199, 2/9 Aug. 1640, Châtillon's account of defence of the siege works, and text of the capitulation of Arras; Griffet, *Louis XIII*, III. 272–4; Bénédict-Louis de Pontis (Pierre-Thomas du Fossé), *Mémoires* (Paris, 1986), pp. 244–50, provides a convincing account of the defence against Spanish counter-attacks.

[351] AAE CP Lorraine 31, fo. 423, 7 Sept. 1640, du Hallier to de Noyers.

attempt anything further during the present campaign.[352] This reluctance was confirmed by a crisis in the supply of food to the army during the last week of September, when bread ran out altogether for three days, leading to illness and desertion 'par nécessité'.[353] Despite the obvious financial advantages in trying to establish the armies in winter quarters on enemy territory, the risks involved in spreading out forces which had already suffered high rates of campaign attrition persuaded the ministers and the commanders to move most of the troops back on to French soil.

The death of Saxe-Weimar had opened a new chapter in the relations between the French crown and the army operating in the Empire. In practice, initial hopes that the 'directors' – proprietor colonels – of the army would prove tractable tools of French ambition proved misplaced. Despite the social status of the duc de Longueville and the military qualities of Guébriant, there was concern throughout the mid-1640s that the army was dominated by the Weimar colonels, whose loyalty to France was attenuated by a strong sense of their own political and financial interests. Richelieu remained concerned throughout most of 1640 that the directors might decide to repudiate the Breisach agreement and make a deal with a German prince, or, most probably, with the Swedes.[354]

Largely because of this uncertainty about the loyalty of the Weimarian colonels, and because their financial interests dictated that campaigns should be at least as concerned with the exaction of war taxes – contributions – as with the pursuit of political objectives, the army was increasingly allowed to be a quasi-autonomous force, operating with far less direct control from the crown and its ministers. Maintained permanently across the Rhine, for the most part composed of Weimarian units and German regiments in French service, the army conducted campaigns that were increasingly based on overt cooperation with the Swedes, whether in the Rhineland or deeper in the Empire. Longueville, worn down by fever, ceded command of the army in the Empire to Guébriant in September,[355] and under Guébriant, and, later, Turenne, the army became the success story of the French war-effort in the 1640s. It did so in large part because it abandoned the typical character of French campaigning and fought – as all the other successful forces of the late 1630s and 1640s fought – as a decentralized, self-sufficient and to a large extent strategically autonomous corps. The French army of Germany

---

[352] AAE MD 1679, fos. 228–9, 28 Aug., Châtillon to de Noyers; Puységur recounts having been given permission to leave the army by Châtillon immediately after the siege, and being challenged by the king, who had explicitly instructed Châtillon that no *congés* were to be issued: *Guerres*, I. 266.

[353] AAE MD 1679, fos. 289, 291, 1/3 Oct. 1640, Châtillon to de Noyers, Louis XIII; indications that there would be problems in maintaining supply had been evident from early September: Avenel, VI. 722–3, 7 Sept., Richelieu to Louis XIII.

[354] AAE MD 835, fo. 206, 16 June 1640, Richelieu to Hector d'Aubusson, seigneur de Beauregard, French representative with the army of Banér.

[355] Noailles, *Guébriant*, pp. 165–6.

The military context

became very effective at fighting a war in the style of her enemies and her chief ally.

Despite the appointment of Harcourt to the command of the army of Italy, and his initial success in late 1639 in defeating a larger Spanish force near Chieri,[356] the attitude of the crown and ministers to the Italian theatre remained uncertain. Slowness in getting troops and money down into the peninsula at the beginning of the campaign gave Leganés the opportunity to move out of the Milanese and lay siege to Casale-Monferrato, the major French strongpoint in north Italy.[357] Despite inadequate numbers of troops, Harcourt none the less decided to take the field in a bid to relieve the siege, reducing all the other French garrisons to skeleton strength to build up his force, so that there was considerable concern at the possible response of prince Tommaso in the rear of the French army.[358] With some 10,500 French and Savoyard troops, Harcourt engaged the Spanish besiegers and drove them off from Casale with heavy losses.[359] This success did much to boost Harcourt's reputation at court, and gave more weight to his requests for additional troops in order to conduct the siege of Turin, the key to any French attempt to stem the tide of Spanish success in Piedmont.[360]

On 12 May Harcourt began the siege of the Piedmontese capital, though letters make it clear that he and the other commanders were still extremely worried at the inadequacy of financial provision for the army.[361] Given the importance of the objective, Harcourt's frustration at the lack of practical support for the siege of Turin is understandable. Yet increasing Richelieu's or even Louis XIII's awareness was never a guarantee that practical consequences would follow, any more than had been the case for Saxe-Weimar at Breisach.[362] As the siege continued, Harcourt's complaints became more vociferous. Reinforcements for the army came only from Languedoc, where they were collected together so slowly and sustained such heavy losses *en route* that their benefit to the army of Italy was

---

[356] Hanotaux, *Richelieu*, v. 395–6.
[357] AAE CP Savoie 30, fo. 134, 8 Mar. 1640, Harcourt to de Noyers, spoke of a total of 10,000 Spanish reinforcements; fo. 307, 3 Apr., fo. 328, 11 Apr., Harcourt to Chavigny, reported Spanish manoeuvres and the opening of the siege of Casale.
[358] AAE CP Savoie 30, fo. 363, 20 Apr. (intercepted letter to Leganés, informing him of the weakness of the French garrisons); fo. 374, 23 Apr., Harcourt to de Noyers.
[359] AAE CP Savoie 30, fo. 400, 4 May 1640, Harcourt to Louis XIII.
[360] AAE CP Savoie 30, fo. 281, 6 May 1640, Richelieu to Louis XIII; fo. 406, 6 May, Harcourt to de Noyers, using Casale as a means to buttress his requests for a higher priority in the allocation of troops; the king made a series of promises in a *mémoire* discussing the practicalities of the siege: Aubery, II. 819–21, 28 May 1640.
[361] AAE CP Savoie 30, fo. 417, 9 May to de Noyers; fo. 420, 12 May, Plessis-Praslin to de Noyers.
[362] Richelieu seems to have responded positively to some of Harcourt's complaints, writing on 20 June to Condé, urging him to use all care and diligence in ensuring that the troops are levied and despatched in the largest possible numbers to Italy: Avenel, VI. 702. But between good intentions and the arrival of troops a large gap could exist – as Harcourt repeatedly pointed out: c.f. AAE CP Savoie 30, fo. 624, 20 July, replying specifically to Richelieu's assurances about the arrival of reinforcements.

minimal. Harcourt had established from the *états* drawn up in January that the total funding due to the army of Italy and the garrisons for the first six months of 1640 was 4,152,215 *livres*. Of this he had actually received 1,250,000 *livres* from the *bureau des finances*.[363] But despite his constant warnings that he would be forced to abandon the siege, in fact the plight of the besieged townspeople and garrison grew critical before the French besieging army had to retire, and on 19 September the governor made terms.[364]

The combination of a large French garrison in Turin composed of seven full regiments totalling 2,000 infantry without officers, Harcourt's determination to wait for some of the arrears of funding for the army before even contemplating another move, and the imminence of the winter quartering season, all combined to ensure that nothing further would be attempted in the remaining months of 1640.[365] The ministry itself was divided between elation at Harcourt's military success with a belief that the deteriorating situation in Italy might now be reversed, and the conviction that only a diplomatic solution – an agreement with Tommaso Francesco – could offer a cost-efficient means to reestablish a French presence in Piedmont.[366] This lack of clarity about an essentially military or diplomatic policy in Savoy was to afflict strategy throughout the next campaign.

Following the surrender of Salces to the Spanish siege army in early January, Condé retained supreme command in this theatre but spent less time in Languedoc.[367] Though this by no means eliminated disputes amongst the subordinate commanders, these quarrels lacked the paralysing intensity of Condé and Schomberg's hostility.[368] The crown's main concern was that the Spanish might launch a retaliatory campaign into Languedoc in early 1640, and that the demoralization of the French troops after the failure to hold Salces, together with the lack of cooperation amongst the commanders, would turn this into a real threat.[369] In practice, the worsening unrest between Spanish soldiers and Catalan civilians during April and May delayed and ultimately cancelled the anticipated Spanish counter-strike into Languedoc.[370] As the territory slid inexorably into

---

[363] AAE CP Savoie 30, fos. 501–3, 13 June 1640, Harcourt to de Noyers.

[364] AAE CP Savoie 31, fo. 53, 20 Sept. 1640, articles for capitulation of Turin; fo. 100, 23 Sept., Harcourt to de Noyers, describing the final stages of the siege.

[365] Harcourt vetoed the possibility of an attack on Alessandria on grounds of the bad weather, and an attempt to take Asti by surprise failed: AAE CP Savoie 31, fos. 771 (no date – late 1640), 704, 24 Dec., Harcourt to de Noyers.

[366] A series of – ultimately fruitless – diplomatic initiatives to try to win the princes over to the French occupied much of late 1640: e.g., Aubery II. 831, 2 Nov. 1640, *pouvoir* for Harcourt and d'Hémery to treat with the Savoyard princes.

[367] Aumale, *Princes de Condé*, III. 415–16.

[368] For example, AAE MD 1633, fos 15 and 28, 25 Nov./26 Dec. 1640, letters concerning a quarrel between Schomberg and the *maréchal de camp*, d'Espenan.

[369] Moreover, the burdens involved in quartering most of the army in Languedoc over the winter of 1639–40 were heavy, and local disorders and non-cooperation widespread: Beik, *Absolutism and Society*, pp. 173–5.

[370] Elliott, *Revolt of the Catalans*, pp. 418–51.

The military context

open revolt after the murder of the viceroy on 7 June, a different series of possibilities began to present themselves to the French ministers. Once a revolutionary leadership started to emerge in Barcelona, Louis XIII lost little time in opening negotiations; on 9 August a *pouvoir* sent to the *sergent de bataille*, Bernard du Plessis-Besançon, allowing him to treat in the name of the king with the estates and people of Catalonia.[371] At this stage the revolt was seen by Louis and his ministers primarily in terms of alleviating a military burden; there were few illusions about the commitment of the revolutionary *junta* to the French, still less about the enthusiasm of the Catalan population in general for the presence of French troops.[372] Negotiations were threatened by Catalan claims that Roussillon was traditionally part of their principality, effectively blocking any possibility of a French war of conquest in the territory – claims that were flatly rejected by Plessis-Besançon on behalf of Louis XIII, but which left a zone of potential conflict.[373] Quite apart from the attitudes of the Catalans to French protection on French terms, Languedoc had been identified by the ministers as the key area from which recruits for Harcourt's siege of Turin could be drawn, and this had a predictable effect on the strength of forces which might be able to intervene in Catalonia.[374] There was little confidence in France that the revolt would be able sustain itself, and with the invasion of Catalonia by a Castilian army under the marquis de Los Vélez, the worst fears of the French government were confirmed; the Catalans seemed incapable of organized resistance. Despite the successful defence of Illa, saved by the arrival of Espenan and a French relief force, the general military situation started to deteriorate.[375] Faced with the collapse of their new allies, the small number of French troops who had moved across the frontier found themselves pushed back out of Aragon into Languedoc. The *maréchal de camp* Roger de Bussolts, comte d'Espenan, who had been given a handful of French troops to stiffen Catalan resistance, had been pinned down at Tarragona and had made terms with Los Vélez to allow his troops to retire to Languedoc.[376] The obvious question in the French Court in the last months of 1640 was whether further military resources devoted to the Catalan rebels would be support for a lost cause.[377] The rebellion had allowed the crown to cut back on its military

---

[371] Plessis-Besançon, *Mémoires*, pp. 115–18, 29 Aug. 1640, first set of instructions for Plessis-Besançon's mission in Catalonia; *Mémoires.*, pp. 23–7, Besançon's own account; C. Vassal-Reig, *Richelieu et la Catalogne* (Paris, 1935), pp. 102–3.
[372] Elliott, *Revolt of the Catalans*, pp. 471–4 for the attitudes of the Catalan leadership.
[373] Vassal-Reig, *Catalogne*, pp. 115–16.
[374] Avenel, VI. 702–3, 20 June 1640, Richelieu to Condé.
[375] Vassal-Reig, *Catalogne*, pp. 121–3; J. Sanabre, *La Acción de Francia en Cataluña en la pugna por la hegemonía de Europa (1640–1659)* (Barcelona, 1956), pp. 108–110.
[376] Plessis-Besançon, *Mémoires*, pp. 135–7; Hanotaux, *Richelieu*, VI. 70
[377] Vassal-Reig, *Catalogne*, pp. 164–7; Espenan had moved rapidly to secure the garrison of Tarragona with only 1,000 troops; Sanabre, *La Acción de Francia*, pp. 111–17, emphasizes that the defence of Tarragona against los Vélez's army was hopeless.

France at war, 1624–1642

commitments in the south over one campaign, but it was not clear that it would offer any long-term possibilities. However, the news in early December that revolt had also broken out in Portugal served to encourage flagging French enthusiasm, and ensured endorsement for the agreement that Plessis-Besançon finally concluded with the Catalan deputies on 16 December.[378]

The last months of 1640 appeared to offer the possibility that France might be able to reduce her military commitments on the Spanish frontiers; the opening months of 1641 began with the prospect that another campaign theatre might be entirely eliminated, allowing military resources to be concentrated elsewhere. By 1641 the duchy of Lorraine had been exposed to over a decade of war, invasion and occupation. Duke Charles had been fighting with his own army since 1635 as a general contractor in the service of the Emperor and the Spanish. Like every army of the period it suffered high levels of attrition, and Charles was finding it difficult to obtain replacement troops. From the French perspective, the reputation of Lorraine amongst the French recruits was appalling. Troops despatched to the duchy would desert *en masse*, and any attempt to maintain a corps at effective strength required massive levels of additional recruitment. Holding Lorraine required the deployment of an additional campaign army, yet with French troops operating in Alsace and on the Rhine, Lorraine represented a kind of territorial fifth column, draining military resources in an apparently unending struggle.

Hence in early 1641 the French were willing to listen to proposals from Charles IV for a settlement.[379] The comte d'Harcourt, Charles' kinsman, and the only member of the House of Guise in the service of Richelieu, was deputed to meet the duke to discuss the terms for an alliance with France. The treaty was signed at the end of March – at this juncture Charles felt that he had little choice – but in circumstances which made the duke's lasting adherence to the treaty tantamount to a betrayal of his dynastic obligations.[380] Lorraine's army was hastily incorporated into the French campaign plans for 1641, and Charles was offered command of a combined Franco-Lorraine corps.[381] The prospect that the long-running struggle over the status of the duchy could be frozen until after the end of the war with the Habsburgs was extremely attractive to Louis and Richelieu. But by 28 July Lorraine had defected from the new French alliance.[382] Charles argued that Richelieu and Louis XIII had refused to accept his terms for the neutrality of the duchy and for his complete restitution after a general peace, thus breaking the

---

[378] AAE CP Espagne 20, fos. 106–7, 16 Dec. 1640, text of treaty; Sanabre, *La Acción de Francia*, p. 111.
[379] d'Haussonville, *Lorraine*, II. 82–4, 88–9; des Robert, *Campagnes de Charles IV*, II. 204–10.
[380] Aubery, *Richelieu*, II. 655–8, 29 Mar. 1641, full text of treaty; d'Haussonville, *Lorraine*, II. 89–92; des Robert, *Campagnes de Charles IV*, II. 218–21.
[381] D'Haussonville, *Lorraine*, II. 98–9.
[382] AAE CP Lorraine 32, fo. 289, 1 Aug. 1641, *maréchal de camp*, Lambert to Chavigny.

terms of the agreement.[383] In retaliation, on 15 August 1641, France declared war against Charles IV, forcing the crown into yet another time-consuming operation of reconquest and requiring the deployment of a further campaign army of 6,000 troops.[384]

Charles of Lorraine's rejection of the French alliance occurred against a background of aristocratic and princely unrest within France more serious than anything since the early 1630s. From early January 1641 Richelieu and Louis XIII were convinced that the comte de Soissons, in self-imposed exile since 1636, was plotting actively in the frontier principality of Sedan, acting in conjunction with the duc de Bouillon, sovereign of Sedan and brother of the vicomte de Turenne, whose own actions and loyalties came under considerable suspicion in the following months.[385]

By the end of April the court had obtained details of the secret treaty between Soissons, Bouillon, the disaffected archbishop of Reims, Henri de Guise and the Habsburgs. Both Spanish and Imperialists agreed to provide troops to support an invasion of France, and to fund the costs of arming and paying troops raised by the conspirators.

The seriousness of the threat could not be ignored. Although Louis and his ministers had opted for the now characteristic strategy of creating two mutually supporting armies on the Picardy/Champagne frontier, both of which would be deployed to facilitate the siege of a chosen *place*, the conspiracy forced a change of plan. Richelieu ordered Châtillon to advance with the entire army of Champagne towards Sedan in order to block the advance of the Habsburg-backed army of the comte de Soissons.[386] While crown and ministers wanted a quick resolution to the threat posed by Soissons, they were also concerned that laying siege to Sedan would involve a considerable military risk. The main French campaign army in the north-east was already engaged at the siege of Aire, and after the experience of Thionville in 1639 Richelieu was wary of trying to sustain two sieges on this frontier simultaneously.[387] The uncertainty at the centre left Châtillon even more indecisive than usual, losing almost a month before pushing forward towards Sedan, and giving Soissons and Bouillon time to raise soldiers and to incorporate 7,000 Imperial troops into their army.[388] Finally goaded by a letter from de Noyers which considerably underestimated the strength of Soissons' forces, on 6 July Châtillon's army

---

[383] The duke's defection had been suspected by du Hallier since late June: AAE CP Lorraine, 32, fos. 238–9, 28 June 1641; on 8 July du Hallier proposed a contingency plan in the event that the duke should break the treaty: Lorraine 31, fo. 260; des Robert, *Campagnes de Charles IV*, II. 261–3.

[384] Hanotaux, *Richelieu*, VI. 105; AAE CP Lorraine 32, fo. 295, 15 Aug. 1641, du Hallier to Richelieu, concerning plans for occupation of the principal *places* in Lorraine; Montglat, *Mémoires*, XLIX. 329.

[385] Saumières, *Duc de Bouillon*, pp. 54–5.

[386] AAE MD 1680, fo. 53, 3 May 1641, Châtillon to de Noyers.

[387] AAE MD 1680, fo. 172, 8 June 1641, Richelieu (to Louis XIII?).

[388] AAE MD 1680, fo. 219, 14 June 1641, Richelieu to Charles, marquis de Sourdis.

advanced towards Sedan, and was routed at La Marfée.[389] That the defeat did not have catastrophic consequences for the war-effort was due only to good luck: Soissons was killed on the battlefield, and without his leadership the invading army lost momentum and disintegrated over the ensuing weeks.[390]

Less than a week after the battle, Richelieu was already playing down the consequences of the defeat, suggesting that the losses suffered by Châtillon's army had been exaggerated, and that it would soon be possible to reassemble his corps so that it could play a further part in the rest of the campaign.[391] In reality, La Marfée served to vindicate the extravagant military policy over the two previous years, when two or three campaign armies had been simultaneously committed to a single siege on the north-east frontier. While Châtillon's army had been locked into a stand-off, followed by defeat outside Sedan, the other campaign army under the command of La Meilleraye had been blockading Aire since 19 May. François de Paule de Clermont, marquis de Montglat, serving with La Meilleraye's army, stressed that in past campaigns La Meilleraye had always been given overwhelming military support for his campaign objectives, largely thanks to his family link with Richelieu. Now that a substantial reserve army was unavailable to facilitate his siege, and military resources were divided between two separate objectives, the truth of his mediocre generalship rapidly emerged.[392] This verdict, reflecting the widespread animosity felt towards the *créatures* of Richelieu and the extent to which they had been projected into senior military commands, was not entirely just to La Meilleraye, who found himself in a virtually impossible position after La Marfée. Conducting an operation well over the frontier into Spanish Flanders, confronting a Spanish army determined to try to relieve the siege or to gain some compensatory advantage, and without a supporting army-corps to block an enemy initiative, his situation would have challenged a considerably more able general. Aire fell to the French on 26 July, but by that point the Spanish forces had besieged and retaken the town of Lilliers, previously captured by the French during the siege of Aire.[393] In a series of manoeuvres that followed the surrender of Aire, the Spanish army managed to drive La Meilleraye away from

---

[389] Aubery, *Richelieu*, II. 701, 4 July, de Noyers to Châtillon; Abraham de Fabert had been sent to Châtillon's army in early June to encourage him to put more pressure on Soissons, and took part in the battle: *Mémoires*, I. 166–74; Aubery, II. 702–6, *c.* 19 July, Châtillon's account of La Marfée; AAE MD 1680, fos. 267–8, 8 July 1641, *intendant* Grémonville to Richelieu, emphasizing the poor performance of the majority of royal troops in the battle, above all the cavalry.

[390] La Meilleraye, in discussing the death of Soissons, had no doubt that it had saved the ministry from a grave challenge: AAE MD 1680, fo. 291, 20 July 1640, letter to Richelieu; Saumières, *Duc de Bouillon*, pp. 73–86.

[391] Admittedly in a letter addressed to duke Charles of Lorraine which attempted, unsuccessfully, to discourage his repudiation of the French alliance: AAE CP Lorraine 32, fo. 271, 12 July.

[392] Montglat, *Mémoires*, XLIX. 320–2.

[393] Aubery, II. 729, 30 July 1641, Louis XIII to Châtillon, having just heard of the surrender of Aire; Griffet, *Louis XIII*, III. 331.

The military context

Aire, and laid siege to it themselves.[394] Only when the army of Châtillon had been reconstituted by amalgamating the remnants of his forces with a new corps being raised for the maréchal de Brézé was it possible to attempt to draw the Spanish away from Aire while simultaneously preventing them settling down to besiege another target further along the frontier.[395] On 10 September Richelieu wrote that the Spanish siege of Aire was still continuing, but that the French had taken Lens and La Bassée, that Bapaume was besieged and that all the area surrounding Lille was ruined.[396] On 26 September Bapaume surrendered to the French forces of La Meilleraye. These successes, however, resulted from the determination of the Spanish not to be distracted from the siege of Aire; La Meilleraye and Brézé, who were succeeded in late September by another *créature* of Richelieu, Antoine III de Gramont, comte de Guiche, all proved unable to organize an effective relief.[397] At the end of November the French governor ran out of supplies and on 7 December surrendered the *place* to the Spanish.[398]

The final result of this campaign in the north-east had provided France with three captured *places*, albeit none as significant as either Hesdin or Arras. It had also indicated beyond any doubt that a successful campaign on this frontier could be pursued only by a massive deployment of troops. The need to concentrate two, and preferably three, entire army-corps on a particular siege – blockading the *place*, safeguarding supply convoys and countering an enemy relief operation or an attack further along the frontier – seemed more evident than ever. Yet this concentration could only be achieved at the cost of all the other campaign theatres, where the commanders were being deprived of the most basic troop allocations and finance. Given the finite total resources available, the prospect that this could be the pattern of the war-effort for the foreseeable future was daunting.

The costs of this strategy were, once again, to be borne in the Italian theatre. Despite Harcourt's success at Turin, there was little sign that the ministers were anxious to give Italy a higher priority in the following campaign. The costs of supplying the army of Italy were regarded with suspicion at Court, and there was a reluctance to provide the levels of military support that would allow the French forces to resume an offensive in this theatre.[399] Yet the failure to negotiate an agreement with the Savoyard princes in the autumn of 1640 made a resumption of campaigning inevitable. Though Harcourt had not yet returned to assume command, his immediate subordinate, Turenne, led a small field army against the town of Ivrea, garrisoned by troops of Tommaso Francesco, and guarding one of

[394] Montglat, *Mémoires*, XLIX. 323–4.
[395] Aubery, *Richelieu*, II. 716, 14 July 1641, Louis XIII to Châtillon; II. 719, 16 July, Châtillon to de Noyers, welcoming the arrival of Brézé's good-quality troops.
[396] Avenel, VI. 871; AAE MD 1680, fo. 387, 8 Sept. 1641, Brézé and La Meilleraye to de Noyers, explaining that supply problems have forced them to opt for the siege of Bapaume.
[397] AAE MD 1681, fo. 27, 21 Oct. 1641, Guiche to de Noyers.
[398] Griffet, *Louis XIII*, III. 342–3.
[399] For these ministerial suspicions, see chapter 8, pp. 458–9.

the passages between Piedmont and Savoy.[400] In attempting this, he encountered the perennial problem that tying his campaign force down at one siege gave the Spanish army the opportunity to counter-attack elsewhere. Though Turenne began the siege in late March, and was joined by Harcourt a few days later, the projected assault was abandoned in the face of a Spanish attempt at relief and the subsequent, more important, news that Chivasso had in turn been besieged by Tommasso and a Spanish-Savoyard army.[401] Not merely was Harcourt's field army weak even by the standards of the second-rank campaign theatres, but none of the garrisons except Turin, Casale and possibly Pinerolo were strong enough for the French commander to permit them to be besieged with any expectation that they could hold out for months, or even weeks.

Following the abandonment of the attempt to take Ivrea and the relief of Chivasso, Harcourt moved south of Turin, laying siege to Ceva in July.[402] Success was followed by the siege of Cuneo, urged on Harcourt by Richelieu.[403] Meanwhile, as expected, the Spanish moved against Cherasco, which forced Harcourt to send part of his field army to strengthen the garrison, leaving the remainder of his forces too weak to attempt a siege even of another small *place*.

While this fruitless manoeuvring with minimal campaign armies suggested that the ministry placed its real hopes in a diplomatic solution in Italy, neither Tommaso Francesco nor his brother, cardinal Maurizio, showed any more signs during 1641 of being prepared to move towards a French alliance.[404] Moreover, the heavy-handed treatment of the regent Marie-Christine during the 1639/40 campaigns had done nothing to make her more accommodating to French interests.

The Italian theatre was paralysed by inadequate military resources and deep suspicions amongst some of the ministers about the management and deployment of such resources as were despatched down into the peninsula. Above all, there was a lack of clear vision about what would constitute a desirable political outcome now that the prospect of outright Spanish conquest of Monferrato and Piedmont had been checked, but any immediate prospect of a successful offensive against the Milanese by a confederate 'League of Italy' lay in ruins. Down on the

---

[400] N.L. Caron (ed.), *Michel Le Tellier: son administration comme intendant d'armée en Piedmont, 1640–1643* (Paris, 1880), p. 55, 10 Apr. 1641, Le Tellier to de Noyers, announcing that Turenne and Castellan are about to join the troops assembled for the siege, and that he has informed Harcourt, at Lyon, of the project.

[401] J. Humbert, 'Turenne en Italie, 1630–1645', and R. Cruccu, 'Turenne et le siège d'Ivrée en 1641', both in Gambiez and Laloy (eds.), *Turenne et l'art militaire*, pp. 178–80 and 187–200; Bérenger, *Turenne*, pp. 166–8; Caron (ed.), *Le Tellier*, pp. 63–4, 17 May 1641, Le Tellier to de Noyers; p. 69, 5 June, Le Tellier to de Noyers.

[402] Caron (ed.), *Le Tellier*, p. 90, 17 July 1641, Le Tellier to de Noyers, reporting progress of siege.

[403] G.D. de Albertis, *Cristina di Francia. Madama Reale* (Turin, 1943), pp. 236–7; Caron (ed.), *Le Tellier*, p. 109, 16 Sept. 1641, Le Tellier to de Noyers.

[404] Albertis, *Cristina di Francia*, pp. 232–4, 238–9.

The military context

Mediterranean frontier with Spain, the events of early 1641 had ensured that a set of strategic and political aims were more clearly grasped; the essential problem remained the competition for only slightly less limited military resources, which would need to be allocated between two distinct objectives.

The Portuguese revolt against Castile which had broken out in December had encouraged the French ministers to believe that they might be supporting something more than a short-lived spasm of popular unrest in one part of the Spanish *monarchia*.[405] The commitment to provide military support for the Catalan revolt was further strengthened by the unexpected repulse of the Castilian army of reconquest on 26 January 1641 at Montjuic, just outside Barcelona, at the hands of a force made up substantially of Catalan militia.[406] By mid-December 1640 Louis XIII had already agreed a treaty with the Catalans, offering military support in the form of 8,000 troops for Catalan service, though – a fruitful source of later contention – these were to be paid by the Catalans.[407] During January 1641 the military commitment was stepped up further. The *état* of troops to be sent to Catalonia was to include thirteen infantry regiments, five cavalry regiments and six companies of *gendarmes*, and command was to be given to another ministerial *créature*, the *maréchal de camp*, Philippe de La Motte-Houdancourt.[408]

This commitment had its price. Despite subsequent acrimonious disputes about allocation of troops between the various military commanders in Languedoc and Catalonia, the crown was effectively giving priority to the defence of Catalonia, rather than the conquest of Roussillon; at the same time it was expected that the commanders involved in the Roussillon campaign would use their credit and standing in Languedoc to raise troops and to ensure their subsistence.[409] Thus although both Condé and Schomberg were expected to conduct a campaign in Roussillon, with Collioure or even Perpignan as the ultimate objectives, the troops available in Roussillon were progressively reduced throughout the spring and summer to support Motte-Houdancourt in Catalonia.[410] Moreover, the shared interests of Richelieu and Sourdis, the commander of his navy, in waging a combined land and naval operation in Catalonia, led to the high-risk decision to launch an attack against Tarragona, well down the Mediterranean coast beyond

---

[405] Concerning the despondency at the end of 1640 about the prospects that the Catalan revolt could sustain itself, see Vassal-Reig, *Catalogne*, p. 168.
[406] Vassal-Reig, *Catalogne*, pp. 205–19; Sanabre, *La Acción de Francia*, pp. 136–7. A battle described by Robert Stradling as more important than Rocroi in determining the fortunes of the Spanish monarchy in the mid-seventeenth century: 'Catastrophe and recovery', 217.
[407] AAE CP Espagne 20, fo. 106, 16 Dec. 1640, text of the Franco-Catalan alliance; Sourdis, *Correspondance*, II. 549–50, 4 Apr. 1641, Louis XIII to Sourdis.
[408] Plessis-Besançon, *Mémoires*, pp. 138–40.
[409] Sourdis, *Correspondance*, II. 549–50, 4 Apr. 1641, Louis XIII to Sourdis, concerning the two possible projects for an attack on Collioure or on Tarragona.
[410] C. Vassal-Reig, *La prise de Perpignan (1641–1642)* (Paris, 1939), pp. 20–2; by 24 June Condé claimed that he had already raised 150,000 *livres* on his own credit to sustain the campaign: Aubery, *Richelieu*, II. 696.

Barcelona.[411] This campaign to blockade Tarragona, ineffective on both the landward and seaward sides, dragged on from May through into August.[412] Even after Sourdis recognized the likelihood of failure and began to oppose the continuation of the operation, it continued to enjoy the support of Condé, who threw his weight behind successive demands for reinforcements for the Catalan front.[413] Although the first month of the campaign had seen some successes in Roussillon, culminating in the successful siege of Elna in early June,[414] an attempt to lay siege to Collioure was abandoned as the demands for troops to sustain the siege of Tarragona grew.[415] When Sourdis' fleet suffered a reversal at the hands of a superior Spanish force, and was forced back towards the Provençal coast, the game was up for the attempt to capture Tarragona, and the siege was abandoned in early September.[416] By this stage the remaining French forces in Roussillon were struggling to hold their various *places* against Castilian counter-attacks, a struggle which lasted through the winter, and permitted the Castilians to put substantial reinforcements into both Collioure and Perpignan.[417]

While the political imperative of sustaining the Catalans undoubtedly determined the military priorities in 1641, unrealistic expectations about what could be achieved in Roussillon with minimal forces were compounded by a hopelessly ambitious strategy in Catalonia. If the crown wished to give substantial support to the Catalans, and simultaneously exploit their revolt to conquer Roussillon, then French troop concentrations on this frontier would be required at a level not seen since 1639.[418]

Even in the Holy Roman Empire an apparently clear-cut triumph for Franco-

---

[411] Sourdis, *Correspondance*, II. 558–9, 13 Apr., 'mémoire de MM de Lamotte-Houdancourt et d'Argenson'; Richelieu was still determined to press the siege of Tarragona in early August, by which time the difficulties had increased substantially: AAE MD 1633, fo. 301, 3 Aug. 1641, Richelieu to Sourdis.

[412] Both La Mothe-Houdancourt and the *intendant* Argenson were increasingly resentful that they found themselves conducting the siege under Condé's orders, and aware that it was highly unlikely to prove successful: AAE CP Espagne 20, fo. 194 [late June 1641].

[413] Aubery, *Richelieu*, II. 694, 716, 26 June, 14 July 1641, Condé to Richelieu, reporting on Sourdis' pessimism about the outcome of the blockade of Tarragona, but Condé's own continued enthusiasm; AAE MD 1633, fo. 454, 3 July 1641, Condé to Richelieu, reporting the despatch of a further 3,000 infantry and 300 cavalry to support La Mothe-Houdancourt at Tarragona.

[414] AAE MD 1633, fo. 456, 3 July, *Relation de la prise d'Elne*.

[415] Vassal-Reig, *Perpignan*, pp. 38–41; Condé had argued back in late April that it was only practical to besiege Collioure when some of La Mothe-Houdancourt's troops had returned: Sourdis, *Correspondance*, II. 579, 25 Apr. 1641, Condé to Sourdis.

[416] Vassal-Reig, *Perpignan*, pp. 55–67; Aubery, *Richelieu*, II. 732, 17/18 Aug. 1641, account of the engagement at sea resulting from the Spanish attempt to relieve Tarragona; La Mothe had in fact announced that the siege would be called off on 24 Aug., immediately after the defeat of the fleet: AAE CP Espagne 20, fo. 203, La Motte-Houdancourt to Chavigny.

[417] Vassal-Reig, *Perpignan*, pp. 68–88.

[418] AAE MD 1633, fos. 519, 525, 547, 15/23 Dec. 1641, Brézé to Richelieu, emphasizing the French failure to contain the Spanish garrisons in Collioure and Perpignan, and the inability of the French to achieve territorial control in Roussillon without substantially more troops in the forthcoming campaign.

The military context

Swedish military cooperation was followed by inertia and disagreement. Despite all the hopes raised by the agreements extracted by Guébriant, the difficulties involved in controlling the Weimarian directors had not disappeared in the early months of 1641.[419] Yet Guébriant was able to draw upon the self-interest of the colonels in the face of substantial Imperial troops movements to argue that decisive action was necessary if the Franco-Swedish forces were to continue to control Brunswick and to safeguard their position in north-eastern Germany. At the battle of Wolfenbüttel on 29 June the Swedish and French forces inflicted a significant defeat on the Imperial and Bavarian armies.[420] The prospect of exploiting this victory was jeopardized by worsening relations with the Swedish army which, since the death of Banér on 20 May, had been divided between rival claimants to the succession, long-standing grievances which the field marshal's personal authority had held in check, and sharp differences over subsequent Swedish strategy and war-aims. Guébriant's letters make it clear that the Swedish army was collapsing into disorder, and that it would be dangerous to rely on them in any attempt to take the offensive against the Imperialists.[421] Only with the arrival of Lennart Torstensson to assume command of the main Swedish field army in October 1641 was discipline and strategic coherence restored.[422] But Torstensson's immediate decision on assuming command of this army was to propose the formal separation of the Swedish corps from the Franco-Weimarians, arguing that the Swedes were now powerful enough to operate autonomously and that this would place more pressure on the Imperial forces.[423] The next campaign would see Guébriant and his army acting without the support of a Swedish veteran contingent, and against Imperial and Bavarian corps which retained considerable striking power and mobility.

In strategic terms the campaign of 1642 presented an abrupt change in the strategy and assumptions of the previous half-decade. The failure of the 1641 campaigns in Catalonia and Roussillon to achieve anything other than propping up the revolt and gaining a handful of small *places* for the crown had its effect on

---

[419] Noailles, *Guebriant*, pp. 206–7.
[420] Noailles, *Guébriant*, pp. 203–17.
[421] AAE CP Allemagne 16, fo. 299, 25 Aug. 1641, Guébriant to Chavigny: 'l'armee de Suede estant presque ouvertement mutinu (?) et ne se tenant en discipline que pour leur conservation particulière', Allemagne 16, fo. 337/44v, 29 Sept./4 Oct., Guébriant to de Noyers, on Swedish colonels' mutiny for arrears of pay. This state of affairs in the Swedish army was confirmed by d'Avaux: Allemagne 16, fo. 311, 10 Sept., diplomatic despatch to Richelieu.
[422] AAE CP Allemagne 16, fo. 361, 17 Oct. 1641, d'Avaux to Richelieu, reporting the arrival of Torstensson in Mecklenburg with new contingents of Swedish troops.
[423] AAE CP Allemagne 16, fo. 383, 2 Dec. 1641. Torstensson's articles as reported by Guébriant are contradictory, suggesting both that the better financial provision of the French army was causing resentment amongst the Swedish troops, but also that the French army, in the greatest necessity that it has ever experienced, needs to act to support itself financially, and cannot hope to pursue a shared strategy with Sweden.

both Louis XIII and Richelieu. At the end of the 1641 campaign in Roussillon, maréchal Brézé had already made the suggestive comment that 'il est plus aysé de conquerir icy une Province qu'une place en Flandres'.[424] Brézé's motive was clear; appointed viceroy of Catalonia in March 1641, he considered that his political career was now tied to success in this theatre, and had seen the problems created by the limited resources available during the last campaign. The implication was that increased military commitment could achieve exactly this type of conquest. And Brézé's presentation of a theatre in which military pressure was likely to yield results coincided with a willingness of both Louis and Richelieu to reassess their strategic priorities in the face of the massive expense and painfully slow progress which had been the hallmark of the war-effort elsewhere.

An undated 'déclaration' of the king in 1642, justifying the decision to shift the fulcrum of the war-effort from Flanders to Roussillon, provides a clear indication of the thinking that underpinned this shift. Richelieu, who appears to have encouraged Louis to write this formal 'déclaration', had reminded the king that after the successful siege of Bapaume, Louis had remarked on the difficulty of finding another viable target in Flanders for the next campaign season. Problems of supply on this frontier were becoming increasingly intractable, as was the recognition that the quality of enemy troops made any substantial military breakthrough unlikely. All that could be expected: 'estoit de prendre une place en chaque campagne, ce que ne ruineroit pas les affaires du Roy d'Espagne et ne l'obligeroit pas de venir a la paix'.[425] The alternative was to commit a very large campaign army to Roussillon, and for the king to lead the campaign in person, avoiding the formidable problems of command and control that had dogged this theatre. By overrunning Roussillon, the French would be striking a blow not only at the fundamental hereditary possessions of the Spanish monarchy, but would raise the prospect of major French intervention in the Catalan revolt. If they attacked the king of Spain 'dans son propre pays' Philip IV would realize that he had far more to lose by a refusal to accept negotiations for a 'just peace'.[426]

Whether the argument presented by this document was correct, and whether Roussillon now offered the key to overall military success, is questionable. More important are the circumstances in which such a proposal to shift the weight of the French war-effort had been made, and the frank assessment of the problems of trying to force a favourable settlement through focusing military effort on the Flanders frontier. Moreover, events at the end of 1641 had left the French crown

---

[424] AAE CP Espagne 20, fo. 297v, 22 Nov. 1641, Brézé to Chavigny.
[425] AAE MD 843, fo. 186 [1642], *déclaration du Roy sur son voyage de Roussillon*.
[426] The circumstances in which this explanation of policy was committed to paper are unclear. The most likely motive, hinted at in the last paragraph, is that it was a bid to exculpate Richelieu from the charge made by Cinq Mars that the king was persuaded to travel down to Roussillon, despite the considerable risks posed to his health, in order to facilitate the cardinal's own (unspecified) 'mauvais dessein'.

with little choice but to make an increased military commitment to Roussillon if any progress were to be made in this theatre. An extraordinary military effort on the part of the overstretched Spanish monarchy had reinforced the garrisons of Perpignan and Collioure to the extent that the French troops left both in Roussillon and just across the Languedoc frontier were considerably outnumbered.[427] The crown's decision to commit greater military resources to Roussillon, and the king's own decision to accompany the army southwards, were both taken at the very beginning of the year. While awaiting the arrival of the king, who had left Paris in February, the army was to be placed under the command of La Meilleraye, seconded by Schomberg.[428] The decision to give higher priority to the campaign theatre ensured that La Meilleraye had an army of 16,000 troops by the beginning of the campaign and that some of these troops could be used to block enemy movements across Roussillon, while La Motte-Houdancourt laid siege to Collioure, which surrendered on 10 April.[429] The capture of Collioure blocked the obvious land route by which the Spanish might seek to bring a relief force to Perpignan. By the time that the siege of Collioure had ended, the king and Richelieu had arrived at Narbonne, and La Meilleraye had moved south with the bulk of the army to lay siege to Perpignan.[430] Ministerial instructions to La Motte-Houdancourt expressly ruled out any offensive in Catalonia until Perpignan had been taken. Aware that he could expect minimal support from France until then, La Motte-Houdancourt moved what remained of his field army into the kingdom of Aragon in order to sustain its costs through contributions.[431]

The siege of Perpignan was as elaborate and lengthy as any of the sieges on the north-east frontier in previous campaigns. Like those sieges, it devoured reinforcements from across France, and though it could legitimately be regarded as the key to control of Roussillon, it was clear that this siege also imposed strains on the war-effort that were as disruptive as the attempts to take Hesdin or Arras.[432] Despite Richelieu's optimism in early May that the siege would soon be over,[433] the garrison resisted until 9 September, and though some troops were despatched immediately afterwards to reinforce La Motte's army, it was clear that little of

---

[427] Vassal-Reig, *Perpignan*, pp. 88–91; AAE CP Espagne 20, fos. 357–9, 27 Dec. 1641, Brézé to Chavigny: 'les ennemis sont maistres de la campagne', and Brézé is unable to act against the substantial forces operating out of Perpignan and Collioure.
[428] Vassal-Reig, *Perpignan*, pp. 94–5.
[429] Bourelly, *Maréchal de Fabert*, I. 183–5; Vassal-Reig, *Perpignan*, pp. 113–34.
[430] Montglat, *Mémoires*, XLIX. 361–3.
[431] Vassal-Reig, *Perpignan*, p. 180.
[432] In justifying the despatch of reinforcements from Lorraine down to the siege, Chavigny explicitly cited the king's view that the siege of Perpignan was 'la plus importante quelle ayt eu depuis cette guerre': AAE MD 843, fo. 203, 10 Aug. 1632, Chavigny to Richelieu.
[433] Avenel, VI. 911, 8 May 1642, Richelieu to de Noyers; though Montglat, *Mémoires*, XLIX. 365, suggested that it had always been intended to prosecute the siege by blockade, rather than by military action, and that it was inevitably going to take several months to conclude.

significance could be achieved in Catalonia during the remainder of the year.[434] The reinforcements did allow La Motte to relieve Lerida, which the Castilian forces had moved against in early October, but did not allow him to follow up this success.[435]

The heaviest price for the decision to focus French military resources southwards was paid on the Flanders frontier. Although the king himself had moved down to Narbonne, campaign armies had, as usual, been established in Picardy and Champagne with instructions to their commanders, Harcourt and the maréchal de Gramont, to hold the frontier and to take the offensive only if opportunity permitted.[436] But whereas these forces had received the highest priority in preceding campaigns so that the combined armies on the north-eastern frontier had reached total strengths of 30,000–40,000 men, the two corps allocated to Gramont and Harcourt were officially intended to be of only about 10,000 troops each, and in reality were somewhat smaller. The weakness of the forces on this frontier was compounded by the refusal of the mediocre Gramont to cooperate with Harcourt, who he rightly suspected would overshadow him in any combined operation.[437] The new commander of the Spanish Army of Flanders, Francisco de Melo, saw an opportunity to roll back the losses of the previous campaigns. The Dutch were by this stage reluctant to take the offensive against a Spanish army that was seen as less and less of a threat to the United Provinces themselves; Melo was able to throw his sizeable campaign army against the Flanders frontier, taking Lens in late April, and moving on to besiege and recapture La Bassée.[438] Gramont allowed himself to be outmanoeuvred by Melo's army in the aftermath of this siege, failed to draw back towards Harcourt's corps, and was overwhelmingly defeated at Honnecourt on 29 May.[439] The shock waves generated by this defeat were considerable. With the king and the main campaign army in the south, the cities of Picardy and Champagne, possibly even Paris, seemed exposed to a threat as great as anything since *l'année de Corbie*.[440] In the event, Melo decided to pull his army back towards the Rhineland, where Guébriant and his Franco-Weimarian army had established itself in the Electorate

---

[434] Vassal-Reig, *Perpignan*, pp. 264–73.
[435] Montglat, *Mémoires*, XLIX. 368.
[436] Montglat, *Mémoires*, XLIX. 352.
[437] Puységur, *Guerres*, II. 1, lays the blame for the defeat on Gramont's impetuousness and reluctance to wait for the arrival of Harcourt; Gramont's own memoirs seek to blame Harcourt, arguing that he failed to obey Richelieu's injunction that the two armies should remain within marching distance of each other: Antoine III maréchal de Gramont, *Mémoires*, in Petitot and Mommerqué LVII. 338–41.
[438] AAE MD 842, fo. 182, 30 Apr. 1642, de Noyers to Chavigny; Griffet, *Louis XIII*, III. 451–2.
[439] Montglat praised Melo's tactical astuteness in seeing his chance to defeat Guiche's army, but emphasized that the result of Gramont's foolishness in being drawn into battle was a Spanish numerical superiority of 2:1: *Mémoires*, XLIX. 353; Griffet, *Louis XIII*, III. 452–3; Gramont's *Mémoires* further heighten the numerical disparity, suggesting (for obvious reasons) that his 10,000 troops were overwhelmed by 27,000 Spanish: LVII. 341.
[440] Avenel, VI. 925–6, 927, 4/5 June 1642, Richelieu to de Noyers; Richelieu to Louis XIII.

The military context

of Cologne, threatening the southern Netherlands. Moreover, Gramont's defeat gave effective military command on the frontier to Harcourt, who, reinforced with the remnants of the defeated army and potentially able to summon du Hallier's corps from Lorraine, presented a considerably more effective obstacle than Gramont.[441] Contenting himself with a sweep northwards that culminated in the capture of Ardres in the Boulonnais, Melo withdrew from France.[442]

The consequences of this Spanish offensive were felt most heavily in Picardy and Champagne, where the combination of demoralized troops and a project for recruiting the army up to strength which depended on the efforts of Gaston d'Orléans and Condé left even Harcourt reluctant to attempt to retake the initiative. The effects were also felt in Lorraine, where the Spanish victory at Honnecourt, and the prospect that du Hallier's corps might subsequently be ordered into Champagne, encouraged duke Charles, allied again with the Habsburgs, to take the offensive in his duchy.[443] Du Hallier's immediate concern was that Charles might move against either Saverne or Haguenau, and he hoped that by laying siege to the fortress of La Mothe it would be possible to occupy Charles' army in its defence. However, du Hallier's already small campaign army was further reduced by the decision to despatch the *maréchal de camp*, Grancey, and a block of troops down to join the forces at the siege of Perpignan.[444] Commanding an army that had lost over half its effective strength through these demands and through sickness and desertion, du Hallier felt unable to stand up to the army of duke Charles and abandoned the siege of La Motte rather than risk being attacked in the trenches. In the manoeuvring that followed the abandonment of the siege, du Hallier was drawn into a minor engagement and beaten by duke Charles at Liffol-le-Grand.[445]

In contrast to this stalemate in Lorraine, the campaigning in the Empire proved considerably more successful. In January, Guébriant's army – which shared with most of the German forces a preparedness to fight during the winter months if this was required to safeguard communications or maintain control of territory – engaged the Imperial army-corps of Wilhelm von Lamboy at Kempen (17 January) on the frontier between Westphalia and the United Provinces. The victory cemented the growing reputation of the Franco-Weimarian army, and

---

[441] Though this seemed less evident at the time: AAE MD 844, fo. 230, 4 June 1642, Marie duchesse d'Aiguillon to her uncle, Richelieu ('Vous ne trouverez point estrange . . . que je me mesle de ces affaires là, elles sont si importante au Roy'), stressing the need to strengthen Harcourt's army, especially given that the remnants of Gramont's army are 'bien inutiles en ce temps la'.

[442] AAE MD 843, fo. 197, 9 Aug. 1642, Chavigny to Richelieu, reporting Harcourt's concern that the Spanish troops appear to be moving towards the Boulonnais, and might attempt a siege of Hesdin, Ardres or Calais.

[443] Des Robert, *Campagnes de Charles IV*, II. 325.

[444] AAE MD 843, fo. 167, 2 Aug. 1642, Richelieu to de Noyers; fo. 197, 9 Aug. 1642, Chavigny to Richelieu.

[445] D'Haussonville, *Lorraine*, II. 107–8; des Robert, *Campagnes de Charles IV*, II. 326–7.

confirmed the military qualities of Guébriant, who was subsequently promoted to the rank of *maréchal*.[446]

Kempen was to have the most important consequences for the wider fortunes of the French campaign; in the first place, it prevented a possible junction of Spanish and Imperial troops which would have created a force significantly larger than anything that the French or their allies could field on the eastern frontiers or into the Empire.[447] In the second, it allowed Guébriant to move his army into the Electorate of Cologne, where it attracted the attention of both the Spanish Army of Flanders and the Imperial/Bavarian forces, pulling both armies away from the French frontiers, where, after Honnecourt, the defences were in disarray.[448] Acting in coordination with the forces of Frederik-Hendrik, prince of Orange, the two commanders were able to safeguard the Dutch frontiers and ensure that neither was confronted on its own with a powerful Habsburg offensive.[449] Yet this capacity to distract the Habsburg armies, undoubtedly of importance in allowing the French military system to ride out a dangerous setback, also immobilized Guébriant's army in anticipation of attacks by considerably superior forces.

In mid-September Richelieu discussed the need to provide Guébriant with reinforcements if he was to assume the initiative in the present campaign, though stressed that such new recruits would be better raised in the Empire than in France.[450] In response to appeals from Torstensson, Guébriant moved his army further into Westphalia in order to block the advance of other Imperial forces eastwards. Helped by Guébriant's ability to contain Habsburg forces in the West, Torstensson won an impressive victory at Breitenfeld/Leipzig on 2 November, going on to take Leipzig and opening up Saxony to the Swedish army. Though Guébriant was to be the beneficiary of this shift in military power in the east of the Empire, the season was too late to turn it to any advantage in 1642, and he explicitly ruled out a plan to quarter his own army closer to the Swedes, on the borders of Bohemia.[451]

In Italy, 1642 was marked by the final achievement of the long-sought diplomatic solution: agreement was reached between Tommaso Francesco, his brother cardinal Maurizio and the regent Marie-Christine that the two uncles would return to obedience to the young duke, abandon their military alliance with Spain and join the French party. The settlement was finally achieved in July, and cemented by the marriage of Maurizio to his niece, Ludovica Cristina, princess of Savoy.[452] The agreement brought an upturn in fortunes after what

---

[446] Noailles, *Guébriant*, pp. 254–9.
[447] AAE CP Allemagne 16, fo. 456, 8 Mar. 1642, Guébriant to de Noyers.
[448] AAE CP Allemagne 16, fo. 524, 22 July 1642, Guébriant to de Noyers, explaining that he has been forced to hold his present positions in the face of threats from both these armies.
[449] Israel, *Dutch Republic and the Hispanic World*, p. 316.
[450] AAE MD 844, fo. 48, 22 Sept. 1642, *mémoire* of Richelieu.
[451] Noailles, *Guébriant*, pp. 297–9.
[452] Oresko, 'Savoy and the Thirty Years War', pp. 149–50.

The military context

had initially been a monumental miscalculation on the part of Louis and Richelieu. Following his implication in Soissons' conspiracy in the previous year, the duke of Bouillon had made terms for a settlement with the crown which had involved an explicit repudiation of his alliance with the Habsburgs and – as a gesture of good faith – a willingness to serve as Harcourt's immediate subordinate in the army of Italy.[453] When, in 1642, it was decided to place Harcourt in command of the army-corps in Picardy, Bouillon was left in control of the army of Italy.[454] Despite having supplicated for return to royal favour in 1641, Bouillon remained deeply hostile to Richelieu, and in the first months of 1642 he was a principal participant in the Cinq Mars conspiracy to obtain Spanish support for a bid to oust the cardinal and to make peace.[455] In consequence, and until his arrest on 23 June, Bouillon was commanding the army of Italy while actively conspiring with Spain to end the war.[456] Unsurprisingly, and despite vociferous criticism from his immediate subordinates, the *maréchaux de camp* César de Choiseul, comte du Plessis-Praslin and Olivier de Fortia, seigneur de Castelan, the campaign was marked by total inertia in its first months.[457] Only following the arrest of Bouillon and his replacement by the duc de Longueville did the campaign army take the offensive, and after a delay of over six weeks.[458] And the consequence of the treaty between Tommaso Francesco, Maurizio and Marie-Christine was that for the first time the French army started to make progress, rather than simply shoring up a situation that had all but collapsed.[459] Acting now as an ally of France, Tommaso Francesco took Crescentino on 14 August, while ten days later Longueville was able to capture Nizza della Paglia, on the borders of Monferrato.[460] At the end of the campaign season Longueville and Tommaso achieved a far more significant goal,

---

[453] Avenel, VI. 835–8, 15 July 1641, *mémoire* of Richelieu concerning the terms for Bouillon's return to grace.
[454] Saumières, *Duc de Bouillon*, pp. 113–14, suggests that Richelieu deliberately sent Bouillon to Italy to get him away from the court in the midst of the domestic uncertainty surrounding the ill-health of the king and the Cinq Mars conspiracy, placing him: 'dans une Armée où il n'auroit aucune troupes à lui, pas même un seul ami'.
[455] Saumières, *Duc de Bouillon*, pp. 96–104; Bérenger, *Turenne*, pp. 180–2.
[456] Bérenger, *Turenne*, pp. 182–3.
[457] Caron (ed.), *Le Tellier*, p. 193, 21 Apr. 1642, Louis XIII to Le Tellier, concerned that the troops of the army of Italy have now been in winter quarters for seven months; Montglat, *Mémoires*, XLIX. 356; Plessis-Praslin, *Mémoires*, VII. 367.
[458] Caron (ed.), *Le Tellier*, p. 199, 19 July 1642, Le Tellier to Mazarin, notifying him of the arrest of Bouillon at Casale; p. 213, 4 Sept. 1642, Le Tellier to Séguier, reporting on the delay in restarting the campaign; Saumières, *Duc de Bouillon*, pp. 169–72.
[459] Though the state of the army was a source of profound concern to Le Tellier, who wrote to de Noyers on 22 Aug. that he feared the mass-desertion of the troops, who would pass into the enemy garrisons: Caron (ed.), *Le Tellier*, p. 210.
[460] Le Tellier's correspondence with de Noyers suggests that the capture of these two places, with the additional financial burden of restoring the fortifications and the necessary provision of troops for the garrisons, was more than the army of Italy could sustain: Caron (ed.), *Le Tellier*, p. 217, 5 Sept. 1642.

taking Tortona – within the Milanese and standing on the all-important communication route between Milan and Genoa.[461] For the first time since 1635 it appeared that close military cooperation between France and Savoy might open the possibility of incursions into the Milanese.[462] This promising military achievement was to be followed in the course of 1643 by the *coup d'état* which brought cardinal Mazarin to the position of first minister of France and ensured his primacy in the formulation of foreign policy. Under Richelieu, the Italian theatre had never enjoyed outright primacy within French military strategy; under Mazarin, and encouraged by the upturn in 1642, it enjoyed a higher priority, though with results that were, in the event, not significantly more productive.

CONCLUSION

Such an overview of the conduct of the French war-effort between 1635 and 1642 is inevitably partial and limited. Above all, and contrary to Richelieu's own most firmly expressed opinions, it is an account which has largely ignored diplomatic factors and their interaction with the formulation of strategy. The concern to achieve at least the appearance of cooperation with the Dutch and the Swedes; initiatives to accommodate – or intimidate – neutral powers; the creation of 'third forces' of potentially anti-Habsburg secondary powers in the Holy Roman Empire and in Italy: all of these factors have been touched on only in the most cursory way.

However, the purpose of this overview has been different. First it examined the magnitude of the military task that France confronted from 1635, and the extent to which her previous military experience, in the earlier sixteenth century and in the fifteen years from 1620 to 1634, provided models that were often inappropriate to the nature of war after 1635. Second, it raised some preliminary questions about why the considerable optimism that had been shown by Richelieu and his fellow ministers in the opening months of the 1635 campaign should have proved largely misplaced. That the war-effort brought successes and revealed some of Louis XIII's commanders and army-corps to be very effective is not disputed. Rohan's victories in the Valtelline in 1635, Schomberg's defeat of the Spanish invasion at Leucate in 1637, Harcourt's relief of Casale and siege of Turin in 1640, are dramatic and impressive military achievements. It is indisputable, however,

---

[461] Externbrink, *Cœur du monde*, p. 336; Plessis-Praslin, *Mémoires*, VII. 367–8, who stressed that 'la conservation de Tortone seroit de plus grande utilité pour la paix que tout qu'on pouvoit faire aux Pays Bas'.

[462] Caron (ed.), *Le Tellier*, pp. 226–7, 23/4 Oct. 1642, Mazarin and de Noyers to Le Tellier, suggesting that the capture of Tortona offered the possibility of advancing further into the Milanese and billeting French troops there over the winter; Plessis-Praslin, *Mémoires*, VII. 368, regretted that the ministers had not been prepared to provide the fresh troops which would have allowed the success to be followed up with a winter invasion of the Milanese.

The military context

that the war brought spectacular military defeats and setbacks, and that these cannot be seen as 'teething problems' in the first few years of conflict, to be increasingly solved as Richelieu and his ministerial team came to grips with the challenge of an unprecedented war-effort.

Wars in early modern Europe were rarely, in the final outcome, about winning and losing individual battles, nor even about the capture or loss of individual *places*. Much of this was discussed in chapter 1: the state of military technology; the means by which armies were raised and maintained; the near-insuperable problems of logistics and communications; all of these combined to render the 'decisive' (war-winning) battle or siege an all-but unattainable objective. In these circumstances, a successful strategy for an early modern ruler would be one which placed sufficient pressure on an enemy to make peace on terms satisfactory to the ruler, confronting that enemy otherwise with the likelihood of greater territorial, economic or political losses by continuing the war. Individual battles and sieges can be part of that strategy, elements in a wider concern to achieve military dominance, if not outright occupation, of enemy territory. But much of the detailed examination offered above shows that this recipe for success was not followed in the struggle waged by France against the Habsburgs after 1635. Above all, the massive set-piece sieges on the north-eastern frontier which absorbed a huge proportion of the available manpower and resources of the war-effort from 1638 to 1641, proved a clumsy, uneconomic and ill-conceived way of trying to force the Habsburgs to terms, and one which drained away the possibility of achieving more decisive results in other campaign theatres.

By halting the narrative at the end of the 1642 campaign, the battle of Rocroi (19 May 1643) is omitted from this account, and with it the notion that this great French victory vindicated the strategy and organization of Richelieu's war-effort.[463] Yet the notion that Richelieu had laid the foundations for a strategy that was about to yield fruit in the 1640s must be questioned. The traditional argument that Rocroi first broke the myth of the invincibility of the Spanish *tercios* is not supported by a detailed overview of the period after 1635, where numerous examples were seen of Spanish armies going down to defeat at the hands of French opponents. The wider significance of Rocroi is also open to question, especially given the obvious circumstance that the battle occurred as a result of a Spanish invasion of France, not because of a French advance into the Spanish Netherlands. A *Spanish* victory at Rocroi, occurring in the context of a royal minority and uncertainty about the nature of the French governmental regime after the deaths of both Richelieu and Louis XIII, would have been more disastrous for France than the heavy loss of veteran infantry which was the main consequence for Spain of her defeat. Moreover, while Rocroi has often been

---

[463] That Rocroi validated Richelieu's war-effort, and could be regarded as a direct consequence of his organizational and political skills, is a conviction deeply embedded in political and military history of this period: see, as one amongst innumerable examples: Hanotaux, *Richelieu*, IV. 489–502.

projected as the harbinger of a *grande tournant* in French military fortunes, it can be shown that in the campaigns after 1643 such an upturn failed to appear. There was no decisive French breakthrough in Italy or in Catalonia, though both received increased allocations of troops and funding through the mid-1640s. A huge commitment of resources to the Flanders frontier produced a number of *places* captured after protracted sieges – most notably Gravelines in 1644 and Dunkirk in 1646 – but came no nearer to forcing the Spanish to make terms. Even in the Empire, military progress was halted for a campaign after the setback of late 1643, when the army of Germany was surprised during the winter quarters and virtually destroyed at Tuttlingen. Only from 1645 was there evidence of real movement towards military/political objectives in this theatre. And while the 1648 Peace of Westphalia ended France's war with the Emperor and Bavaria on terms which yielded major diplomatic, though modest territorial, advantage, the same year was also marked by the beginning of the *Frondes*. The ensuing collapse of military funding and supply and the complete lack of central direction wiped out many of the gains that the armies of Richelieu and Mazarin had so painfully and expensively accumulated since the late 1630s. In 1652, Barcelona fell to a Castilian army and all but ended the Catalan revolt, Dunkirk was recaptured by the Army of Flanders and the French garrison was finally driven out of Casale where it had been established since 1629.

The question of why France had such difficulty waging a multi-theatre European war after 1635 is given additional force by the contrast with the decades after 1660. Why should an army and a military organization that proved so successful from the first decade of Louis XIV's personal rule have so signally failed in the previous decades to take advantage of a military situation in which its enemies were straining their resources to the utmost and were beset with internal crises? The following chapters provide an answer to some of these questions.

3

The size of the French army

A large increase in the size of forces under arms through the later sixteenth and the seventeenth centuries is believed to be the clearest manifestation of fundamental change in the nature of warfare during the early modern period. In recent writing, doubts have been expressed about the extent, novelty and effectiveness of tactical and organizational change in European armies of this period. Yet an assumption that the average size of armies increased by a factor of at least ten between 1500 and 1700 seems still to be accepted as evidence that warfare underwent a transformation, and that in consequence combatant states and societies had to sustain a massively increased military burden.

In the case of France, the growth in the size of the army over this two hundred year period seems in theory to offer irrefutable justification for this assertion. The theoretical strength of the army with which Charles VIII invaded Italy in 1494 was some 30,500 troops of all types, both native French and foreign mercenaries. Ferdinand Lot, in his classic study of troop numbers during the first half of the sixteenth century, suggests that the true total was somewhere between 16,000 and 20,000 combatants.[1] In dramatic contrast, the theoretical strength of the French army in 1690 during the first phase of the War of the League of Augsburg was about 340,000 troops, including around 74,000 foreign mercenaries, but not including the conscript militia, which was increasingly used as a recruitment pool to supply the manpower needs of the regular army. André Corvisier suggests that, even after the reforms of Louvois, it is still necessary to draw a distinction between the theoretical size of the army and the real, effective, strength, but even allowing for this, 'on peut tout de même retenir comme vraisemblable le chiffre de 300,000 hommes réellement sous les drapeaux'.[2] The view of a progressive increase in the size of the French army, gathering momentum in the seventeenth century, is given additional weight by the typical figures for troop numbers at

---

[1] F. Lot, *Recherches sur les effectifs des armées françaises des guerres d'Italie aux Guerres de Religion, 1494–1562* (Paris, 1962), pp. 16–21.

[2] A. Corvisier, *Louvois* (Paris, 1983), pp. 344–5. An order of magnitude confirmed by J. Lynn, 'Recalculating French army growth during the *grand siècle*, 1610–1715', *French Historical Studies*, 18 (1994), 881–906 (reprinted in Rogers (ed.), *The Military Revolution Debate*, pp. 117–47), and by G. Rowlands in his doctoral research into the army of the 1690s: 'Power, authority and army administration under Louis XIV: the French crown and the military elites in the era of the Nine Years' War', DPhil thesis, University of Oxford, 1997.

certain key points between the late fifteenth and the late seventeenth century. The overall impression is of a slow upward movement in the numbers of troops under arms, boosted by one or two dramatic leaps, for example in 1635, 1667 and 1689.[3] This tends to reinforce the assumption that there is a close link between army size and the development of a more centralized and effective state administration. Whether the demands of foreign policy fuelled the increase in the size of the army, which in turn required a more sophisticated supporting administration, or whether improvements in the structures of state finance and bureaucracy themselves permitted military expansion, the growth of state power seems in some way linked directly to the growth of military force. But this does not mean that military growth can necessarily be linked to the development of the modern centralized state. By assuming that the army increased in size by steps over a long period, it is equally possible to suggest that the existing systems expanded and stretched to absorb a growing burden without at any point being confronted with an increase so great as to overwhelm the existing administration. At least until the 1660s, the slow upward growth in the French army could be accommodated within existing administrative structures.

Yet both these possible interpretations require some qualification. If crude figures and army strengths selected at chosen dates suggest progressive growth, the broader evidence suggests a rather different model of development, in which a maximum size for the total of military forces was achieved by the 1550s and was rarely surpassed again before 1635, certainly not for any length of time. When the troops under arms did rise above that level, the consequent strain on the existing military administration was considerable, and had extensive consequences for the relationships between the army, state and society which will be explored in subsequent chapters.

First, however, we need to raise the most obvious question. What, in fact, *was* the approximate size of the French army in the period after 1635, or indeed in any particular year during the reign of Louis XIII? It is difficult to answer this question, for it poses problems like those that arise when we attempt to make accurate assessments of the French crown's income and expenditure in this period. In both cases a large quantity of documentary evidence is missing or destroyed; in both cases the material that survives can be extremely – sometimes deliberately – misleading. Yet it is important to have even an approximate notion of the strength of the army at points between 1620 and 1642, since this is closely linked to issues surrounding the management and effectiveness of the French

---

[3] A pattern of upward growth primarily defined by sudden increases would give support to Clifford Rogers' interpretation of military change in general as following a 'punctuated equilibrium' paradigm: 'The military revolutions of the Hundred Years' War', in Rogers (ed.), *The Military Revolution Debate*, pp. 55–93, at pp. 76–7. This type of progression for France is well summarized in A. Corvisier (ed.), *Histoire militaire de la France* (4 vols, Paris, 1992–5), I: *Des origines à 1715* (ed. P. Contamine), pp. 241–3, 341–6, 361–3.

The military context

war-effort. If, for example, it is supposed that the number of troops increased from 80,000 men in 1634 to around 200,000 by 1636, then it is extremely doubtful that such an increase – proportionately the greatest single expansion of forces under arms during the *Ancien Régime* – could be accommodated within the existing financial and administrative systems, or that traditional mechanisms for recruitment and maintenance could absorb this additional burden. If the military expansion was smaller than this, and the subsequent burden of the French army during the campaigns down to 1659 was less heavy, it is important to know at least approximately how much larger the army raised for 1635 and subsequent campaigns was than that of the previous decade. A second, related reason for trying to discover the real size of the army is linked to strategy: improbable though it may seem, given the figures of 200,000 soldiers or more that are frequently cited for the army after 1636, shortage of troops appears to be one of the major reasons why the French found it difficult to make military progress in the years after the declaration of war on Spain. Bearing in mind that it was not merely the army which expanded in the years after 1635, but that there was also an expansion in the scale of France's military commitments, a realistic assessment of the numbers of troops under arms leads to the conclusion that there could not have been enough soldiers to provide adequate military support for all of the major campaign theatres. This conclusion is, in fact, supported by considering the difficulties and setbacks encountered by the secondary armies in successive campaigns.

METHODOLOGICAL PROBLEMS IN CALCULATING ARMY SIZE

Reliance upon regimental listings

There are two typical approaches used in attempting to establish the numbers of troops serving in the French army during the seventeenth century. What was considered an orthodox method in the nineteenth century is employed in major works such as Victor Belhomme's *Histoire de l'infanterie en France*, or the multi-volumed studies of General Susane.[4] The working assumption of these calculations is that companies should be taken at full theoretical strength, 200 men in the case of the *gardes* and the *vieux* regiments, 100 men for the others. The size of the army is established by discovering the names of the regiments *sur pied* during a particular campaign, assuming that they possess the stipulated numbers of

---

[4] Lt.-Colonel V. Belhomme, *Histoire de l'infanterie en France* (5 vols; Paris, 1893–1902); Susane, *Histoire de l'ancienne infanterie française*; Susane, *Histoire de l'infanterie française*; Susane, *Histoire de la cavalerie française*; Susane, *Histoire de l'artillerie française*; Pascal, *Histoire de l'armée*, II. 20. A similar approach is taken in Audouin, *Histoire de l'administration*, II. 156–65; J. Servan and le comte P.H. de Grimoard, *Recherches sur la force de l'armée françoise, depuis Henri IV jusqu'en 1806* (Paris, 1806).

companies and taking these companies at full strength.[5] Belhomme's calculations produce an army in 1635 whose infantry effectives alone amount to 149 regiments, calculated to full strength at 210,000 men. By 1638 this had been increased to 220,000 men, and for the rest of Richelieu's ministry stood between 220,000 and 230,000.[6] When Susane's inflated figures for the cavalry are added to these totals, and an allowance is made for the *équipage* of the artillery, the army's total strength after 1635 approaches 300,000 men, not significantly different from the forces officially under arms during the 1690s.[7] But these calculations are no more than a convenient fiction. Louis XIII's government neither expected regiments and companies to be at this theoretical full strength, nor did the crown and its ministers base their own calculations, other than for rhetorical effect, on such simplistic assumptions. Deliberate exaggeration is evident in 1625 when Richelieu claimed, obviously for Spanish consumption and to try to discourage Madrid from opening up further campaign theatres outside Italy, that France had 60,000 troops *sur pied*.[8] A more realistic indication of the state of the French army came from Richelieu's frank admission in the following campaign that the army-corps in Champagne, supposedly of 14,000 troops, was actually less than half that strength.[9]

Indeed the concept of 'full strength' is itself very ambiguous. In practice even *entretenus* regiments such as the *petits vieux* composed of twenty companies were rarely assumed to stand at their notional full strength of 2,000 men, and the far more frequently employed figure was 1,200.[10] Similarly, many of the *états* disposing troops between army-corps at the beginning of the campaign season

---

[5] Though even establishing the global number of regiments serving in a particular campaign, regardless of their actual strength, is contentious. Belhomme, for example, states that there were between 166 and 185 infantry regiments *sur pied* in 1637, while a document in the handwriting of the secretary of state for war, Sublet de Noyers, lists only 134 regiments: AAE MD 828, fo. 287 [1637]; Belhomme, *L'infanterie*, I. 373–5.

[6] Belhomme, *L'infanterie*, I. 365, 379, 382, 387, 392.

[7] André Corvisier illustrates the unrealistic nature of these calculations when he points out that if all of the established regiments were taken at full strength, the army in 1648 would be of 273,000 infantry and 50,000 cavalry: *Histoire militaire*, I. 363.

[8] Parker, *French Absolutism*, p. 61; for a similar calculation motivated by diplomatic expediency, AAE MD 837, fo. 162, [1640], which boasted that the crown was maintaining 205,000 troops *sur pied*. Richelieu was no less concerned to impress the king himself with his mobilization of French resources, and his 'succincte narration des grandes actions du Roy' at the opening of the *Testament politique*, makes the fantastic proposition that in each of the five campaigns since 1635 the crown had fielded 150,000 infantry and 30,000 cavalry at the cost of 60 million *livres* p.a., and without resort to extraordinary financial expedients 'ausquels vos prédécesseurs ont esté souvent contraints de recourir': *Testament politique*, p. 84.

[9] Grillon, I. 179, 11 Apr. 1625, Richelieu to the duc d'Angoulême.

[10] AAE MD 822, fo. 412, Dec. 1636, list of regts – including four *vieux* – to be accorded quarters and subsistence on the basis of 1,200 men each; fo. 416, Dec. 1636, new regts to be levied also at 1,200 men; AAE MD 828, fos. 265–86, 1637, *états* of the theoretical strengths of the army-corps which gives the maximum strength of regiments of twenty companies – even the *vieux* – as 1,200 men; MD 832, fos. 1–15, 1638, *états* for the army-corps for 1638 – twenty companies at a maximum of 1,200 men, and more frequently, 1,000; MD 837, fos. 247–59, similar for 1640.

The military context

proposed that cavalry companies were at full strength with 60 *maîtres*, although once again, 100 was the 'official' complement.[11] This concept of *vingt pour douze* was deeply entrenched in the administration and financing of the army. Indeed, whatever the situation earlier, it is clear that this assumption was fully taken into account in the funding and subsistence of the army after 1635.[12] In practice, neither the figure of 2,000 nor that of 1,200 corresponded to the reality of individual regiments on campaign, but the lower figure was by convention most frequently used to determine allocations of troops between army-corps and the provision of subsistence, while a 'full' company strength of sixty men was frequently used as a target for recruitment.[13]

However, the problem of establishing the size of the army cannot be simply resolved by making a 40 per cent reduction across the board, for this ignores a significant number of other factors serving to reduce the number of troops in an average company. Unfortunately, few of these factors have agreed implications for the overall strength of the army. The crown and its ministers applied a number of formal and informal assumptions about the strength of units, either to avoid overpayment for non-existent troops, or in some cases to encourage the officers to make more effort to recruit troops and to maintain their units at an acceptable strength. To these factors can be added calculations for 'natural' wastage, in the forms of sickness, desertion, absenteeism and deliberate fraud. A *mémoire* of 1637 made the matter-of-fact statement that to have a campaign army in Italy of 15,000 infantry and 2,000 cavalry effectives required that the crown should *fund* 22,000 infantry and 2,500 cavalry. This calculation had nothing to do with the issue of how many additional troops would need to be recruited to achieve and then maintain this target figure of 15,000 infantry and 2,000 cavalry. It was simply a statement of the typical financial wastage, the money that would be 'lost' through payment of valets instead of troops, through other forms of explicit or tacit corruption, the funding of recruitment premiums to officers, and other factors.[14]

All of this presents problems in attempting to find any agreed strength to which it might be suggested the 'average' regiment could be reduced. The difference between discounting the average size of an infantry regiment by 25 per cent or by 50 per cent over and above the 40 per cent reduction for the *vingt pour douze* is the difference in 1635 between an army of 94,500 infantry and one of 63,000

---

[11] AAE MD 828, fos. 265–86, companies of *chevaux légers* consistently given at sixty *maîtres*, prestige companies of *gendarmes* at eighty; MD 837, fos. 247–59, 1640, records all cavalry companies with the exception of a few prestige units of *gendarmes* at sixty *maîtres*.

[12] AAE MD 814, fo. 262, 14 July 1635, Richelieu to Servien specifically stipulating that the French troops in the Valtelline were to be paid as twenty-company regiments assumed to contain 1,200 men in total – 'non pas en payer vingt pour douze'.

[13] Corvisier, *Histoire militaire*, I. 365, cites the system in 1645 when a 300 *livres* bonus was paid to captains raising over sixty men for their companies, while 6 *livres* was deducted from the recruitment pay for each soldier fewer than fifty-six.

[14] AAE CP Savoie 25, fo. 24, 30 Jan. 1637, Michel Particelli d'Hémery to Richelieu.

The size of the French army

infantry.[15] If a further 50 per cent reduction seems fanciful, a letter from Sublet de Noyers to cardinal de La Valette in 1637 contrasts the French army with that of the United Provinces, asking whether the Dutch would have been able to fund an army in which

si les Estats [the States General] payent pour soixante hommes, l'on en deduit trente quatre pour les imaginations des Chefs . . . Le Capitaine de gens de pied en Hollande a cinquante escus pour sa montre; l'on luy passe son fils et son page, et rien plus. Jugez, Monseigneur, si cela reduit une Compagnie de soixante hommes à vingt-six.[16]

It can simply be suggested that the 'real' figure would fall somewhere between the most conservative and the most extreme percentage discounts.[17] However, there are more fundamental objections, which will be examined later, to this attempt to arrive at a 'real' strength by finding an agreed discount figure per unit.

Using global calculations of army size; the contrôles généraux in context

A second method of trying to calculate the size of the army has been widely used by historians in more recent decades, and employs a series of working assumptions made by central government. It takes as its essential source a number of specific *contrôles généraux* emanating from the *bureau des finances*, preserved amongst the papers of the Archives des Affaires Etrangères, and in cases reprinted in Avenel's *Lettres de Richelieu*.[18] This, together with various letters and discussion documents – almost entirely correspondence between Richelieu and the *surintendant des finances*, Claude Bullion – provides an apparently convincing archive-based means to establish the strength of the army from 1634 onwards.

From these *contrôles* emerges the typical assertion that the crown projected the levy of 134,000 infantry and 20,880 cavalry for the campaign of 1635, though this is sometimes moderated with reference to another document, a letter from Bullion to Richelieu, dated 7 November 1634, in which Bullion agreed to prepare funds for 115,000 infantry and 9,500 cavalry.[19] The *contrôle* for 1636 gives the totals of

---

[15] Belhomme's figure of 210,000 for the infantry strength in 1635 × 40 per cent = 126,000; × 75 per cent = 94,500; × 50 per cent = 63,000.

[16] Aubery, *Richelieu*, II. 37, 9 June 1637.

[17] John Lynn, 'Recalculating French army growth', seeks to overcome these divergences by splitting the differences and consolidating the agreements between various historians who have considered the question of army size up to 1659, and arrives in consequence at what might appear to be a fairly unobjectionable conclusion, setting the 'peak size' for the army between 1635 and 1642 at about 125,000 men (901). But given the discretionary working assumptions employed by each of the historians whose figures he has utilized, the end result is necessarily as arbitrary as any of the individual calculations that he brings together and collates in his text.

[18] AAE MD 812, fos. 385–92, assigned to a volume for 1634, but given the campaign theatres cited, these folios clearly refer to preparations for the 1635 campaign; abridged transcription in Avenel, v. 3 [1st fortnight of May 1635]; MD 820, fo. 200, 15 Apr. 1636; Avenel, v. 723 [December (1636)] – Avenel's reasoning in placing this at the end of 1636 rather than December 1635 is obscure.

[19] AAE MD 811, fo. 120.

The military context

172,000 infantry, 21,400 cavalry, together with another 6,000 cavalry which are accounted as part of Saxe-Weimar's army, and a further 6,000 that were to be funded from an obscure 'taxe des financiers qui reviennent à quatre millions'.[20] These figures would appear to confirm the contention that the French army underwent a dramatic increase in size at the beginning of the war with Spain. They also support another widely held view, that the emergency of the *année de Corbie* ratcheted the army upwards by another substantial notch, with the implication that 170,000–200,000 troops then represented the typical army strength in each successive campaign down to 1648.[21] There is no suggestion that the army grew any larger than this during the ministries of Richelieu and Mazarin, and most accounts allow that the forces under arms underwent a numerical decline during the *Frondes* from which they were not subsequently to recover during the 1650s.

The attractiveness of drawing upon evidence from the written word of contemporaries is undeniable, especially when the alternative, as discussed earlier, is to engage in an inconclusive attempt to discount the theoretical full strengths of individual units. Moreover, the figures provided by such letters sound plausible in terms of the supposed war-effort of other European powers; informed that Gustavus Adolphus was able to maintain 170,000 troops under Swedish banners after Breitenfeld, that Wallenstein's army totalled over 100,000 troops in 1632/3, and that, in an often-quoted but misleading citation, the total Spanish forces in 1635 numbered 300,000 men, a French army of 125,000 rising to 175,000 sounds compatible with a particular stage in European military development.[22] However, the use of such *contrôles généraux* is not so straightforward. First, although they give specific totals for troops, and indeed allocate these totals to the various army-corps in the campaign theatres, they are none the less figures drawn up from the centre, a statement of intentions rather than of military reality on the ground. We cannot assume that the provision of funding, contracts for recruitment and orders to local authorities to facilitate the recruitment, passage and assembly of troops, despatched by the ministers in Paris in the interests of raising and maintaining the army, produced a force in the field of the size initially envisaged. Wastage, unanticipated difficulties in recruitment, straightforward corruption, all ensured that the real totals were likely to fall short of the numbers originally projected in

---

[20] AAE MD 820, fo. 200; Avenel, v. 723. The projected *taxe des financiers* of 1636 appears to have been abandoned, quite possibly because of the considerable dangers involved in manipulating the crown's creditors in a period of military emergency. I am grateful to Professor Richard Bonney for confirming that he has no information concerning any attempt to investigate or prosecute a group of financiers in 1636.

[21] Corvisier, *Histoire militaire*, I. 363.

[22] Roberts, *Gustavus Adolphus*, II. 676; Konze, *Die Stärke*. For a sceptical view of the figure of 300,000 Spanish troops under arms, see Elliott, *The Count-Duke of Olivares*, pp. 238, 509. General studies of war and society in this period almost invariably reproduce a table originally drawn up by Geoffrey Parker – *Europe in Crisis, 1598–1648* (London, 1980), p. 70 – which brings together these figures from the principal European powers as a distinct stage in the development of early modern warfare.

The size of the French army

Paris. It might seem that this is no great improvement on the employment of regimental listings to establish the strength of the army. Yet the use of the *contrôles* could still be defended as superior if only on the grounds that it provides a picture of what the crown was *aiming* to achieve in the later 1630s. Even if the actual results were less impressive, the French state was geared to raising an army on this scale, clear evidence that Louis XIII and Richelieu had committed France to an unprecedented war-effort.

A more fundamental objection is raised by the nature of the documents themselves. The *contrôles généraux* emanated from discussions at the opening of the campaign season between the *surintendant des finances*, Richelieu and Louis XIII. The role of the *secrétaire d'Etat* for war is marginal to these discussions, a situation in keeping with his modest, executive, status in the direction of the war-effort.[23] Equally, though, the secretary was absent because these discussions and the resulting *contrôles* are not primarily about troop numbers, but about the allocation of financial resources. The *surintendant* was faced with the problem of planning for military expenses in a situation where the total number of troops that might be deemed necessary for a chosen strategy could become very large. Such troops did not merely represent a burden on the *épargne* when they were initially recruited; indeed, given the possibility of transferring some, or all, of the recruitment costs on to the shoulders of the officers raising the units, this was frequently the least of the burdens. The real financial issue was the subsequent maintenance of the forces *sur pied*, and the burden which this would impose upon the anticipated ordinary and extraordinary sources of revenue over the course of the campaign – and possibly into the winter quarter. The cost of getting the calculations wrong, and allowing too large an army to be raised at the beginning of the campaign, would be a breakdown in the payment of the troops, since too large a proportion of the available funding would be used up in the first months of the campaign. In practice, this was a regular occurrence, at least for some of the army-corps and garrisons deemed of secondary importance to the war-effort. But the situation would be much worse and more dangerous if the attempt to maintain a balance between troop numbers, financial requirements for the entire campaign, and available revenues were to be abandoned altogether.

On the one hand, Louis XIII and Richelieu, acting in consultation with favoured field commanders, and with foreign affairs specialists such as Joseph Le Clerc du Tremblay, Manassés de Pas, marquis de Feuquières, Hercule-Girard, baron de Charnacé, and Michel Particelli, sieur d'Hémery, formulated strategy based upon attempts to anticipate enemy troop movements, the operations of allies and the crown's own territorial and political aspirations. This dictated which campaign theatres would be opened up, and the relative priority that would be

[23] See chapter 7, pp. 367–73.

The military context

given to the allocation of troops in these theatres. Potentially, and even within the context of warfare in the first half of the seventeenth century, the requirements of French strategy after 1635 could easily have suggested that a total military strength of at least 200,000 to 300,000 troops was desirable. On the other side of this debate stood the *surintendants*, Claude de Bullion and Claude Bouthillier, both well aware of the dire fiscal consequences of unlimited military expansion, and concerned to restrain a military system which, via the delegation of recruitment to the individual officers, could well impose a financial burden beyond the available fiscal resources of the state.

The *contrôles généraux* of 1635 and 1636 were an attempt to reconcile these conflicting strategic and fiscal concerns. The critical information to which they allude is not the number of troops that the crown proposes to set *sur pied*, but the estimated military budget that will be available for the entire campaign, and the subdivision of this budget into the number of *montres* considered necessary to pay the army through the campaign season. As a result of a 1634 decision taken in response to the increasing burden of military demands, the ten *montre* payments stipulated in *ordonnances* and apparently distributed, at least in principle, to the prestige regiments, were reduced to eight.[24] In 1635 Bullion had evidently established a total budget of 36 million *livres* for all military expenses, and calculated that this sum, divided between eight *montres*, would sustain 132,000 infantry through the campaign; another letter stipulates an upper limit of 12,400 cavalry as the maximum for 'toute l'année presente'.[25] This was a maximum figure for the total number of troops that could be maintained *throughout the campaign* for the given resources of 36 million *livres*.

However, the army was not composed of 132,000 basic rank-and-file soldiers, and every combatant from the veteran *appointé* or *anspessade* occupying a key position in an infantry or cavalry formation, through the various ranks of NCOs, junior officers, up to the regimental *état major*, were paid in multiples of the ordinary soldiers' wages.[26] The multiple pay of NCOs and officers had a dramatic effect upon any calculation of total troop numbers. A series of *états des fonds* for an army-corps in 1637 explain that though the cavalry should be taken as 2,250 officers, NCOs and men in total, an additional 450 men should be added for the additional 'pays' of the 'chefs, officiers, petits officiers'; equally, pay should be provided for 11,740 infantry in total, but an additional 3,260 men should be added

---

[24] *Code Michaud*, art. 221; AAE MD 808, fo. 77, Oct. 1633; Avenel, IV. 523, Jan. 1634, 'Mémoire concernant la diminution du payement des troupes.'

[25] Avenel, IV. 712, 20 Apr. 1635, Richelieu to Bullion, 'nous avons merveilleusement travaillé pour ne passer . . . le fonds de trente-six millions que vous avez destinez pour toutes les despenses de la guerre'. AAE MD 812, fos. 385–6, repr. Avenel, v. 5, [May 1635], Contrôle Général: 'et qu'ils avoient fait leur projet de 132,000 hommes, comme s'ils les eussent deu payer toute l'année présente'; Avenel, IV. 686, 22 Mar. 1635, Richelieu to Servien.

[26] See a typical breakdown of company and regimental pay provided in SHAT A^1 26, pce 30, 28 Feb. 1635.

The size of the French army

to this to allow for the multiple pays to 'chefs, officiers, sergens'.[27] These multiples of the basic unit of pay would ensure that the global total of troops which could be maintained for the campaign of 1635 was considerably lower than 132,000 infantry and 12,400 cavalry.

Richelieu accepted this element of the calculations, but then introduced a further factor which allowed in its turn for higher levels of recruitment. By arguing that a large proportion of the forces being raised would not be maintained for an entire campaign, and would not expect to receive the stipulated eight *montres*, Richelieu was able to justify the recruitment of significantly more troops than these maximums established by the *surintendants*. Richelieu's justifications in the *contrôle général* itself for higher levels of recruitment provide clear evidence that this was not an explicit statement about the size of a specific army that was to be established for the duration of the campaign; instead, they were running calculations concerning the deployment of available funding, divided for convenience into units of account – the *montre* that was notionally allocated to the individual soldier every forty-five days. A very significant proportion of the troops raised for the opening of the campaign would never draw on more than two or three *montres*: sickness, desertion or the disbandment of the unit would rapidly decimate the ranks of these initial levies. Part of the funds allocated to such units, notionally for the entire year, would be withheld by the *commissaires pour les montres* as *deniers revenans bons* – pay held back now that the regiment or company was significantly reduced from its initial size. This money would be redeployed to pay the costs of units that were newly levied some time into the campaign season, or to pay for new recruits brought to the army-corps to 'refresh' existing units. Depending upon the point in the campaign season at which the commissions were issued and the troops levied, such units would receive some small proportion of the total projected eight *montres*. Indeed, in 1635 Richelieu suggested that a number of Swiss units were being levied so late in the year that they should be left 'hors de compte . . . ne venant qu'à la fin d'année, leur solde et leur levée se trouvera bien dans l'espargne de la montre' – that is, from the savings that would be made because so many units would not, for various reasons, need to receive a full eight *montres*.[28] In essence the ministry was making the working assumption that the *surintendants*' funds would pay 132,000 + 12,400 × 8 *montres*. But as few of the troops maintained by the crown would actually be in service for an entire campaign measured as eight *montres*, then, even when allowance is made for the multiple pays to NCOs and officers and for additional subsistence and munitions costs, the total number of troops actually levied overall – *though not maintained throughout the entire campaign* – could quite possibly *exceed* the notional maxima of 132,000 infantry and 12,400 cavalry stipulated by the *surintendants*. Richelieu

---

[27] BN Ms.fr. 6648, fos. 19–21 [Mar. 1637].
[28] AAE MD 812, fo. 385v; this section of the *contrôle* printed in Avenel, v. 5–6.

The military context

argued in the *contrôle* that 'On lève 21 régimens nouveaux, qui ne seront prestz qu'au commencement de septembre, qu'il ne faut compter tout au plus que pour une montre. . . le pis qui en puisse arriver est une montre, ce qui ne peut estre sy le roi est bien servy aux deniers revenans bons des trouppes qui sont présentement sur pied.' He proposed the same calculation with respect to thirty-nine of the companies of cavalry.[29]

As Richelieu freely admitted, some of these calculations are rough-and-ready: 'encore ne sçait-on pas, avec tout cela, si on les tiendra au nombre auquel on l'a présuposé'.[30] Certainly there was nothing precise about a system that tried to balance the rate of wastage from existing regiments against new recruitment, and which made large numbers of necessarily arbitrary assumptions about the extent to which units could be paid fewer than the full number of *montres*. Evidently, though, the *contrôle* offers no support for the notion that a specific number of troops was raised at the beginning of the 1635 campaign and then maintained to its end. Richelieu's use of the figures generated for him by the *surintendants* shows that what appear to be statements concerning the size of the army are, on the contrary, attempts to allocate funding across the length of the campaign and to justify recruitment levels in terms of the anticipated burden on this funding.

This purpose of the *contrôles généraux* becomes even more explicit in 1636. In the course of the 1635 campaign the *surintendants* had become aware that a system based upon the payment of a theoretical maximum of eight *montres* was unrealistic given the new scale of the war-effort. An attempt was made during the 1635 campaign to reduce the maximum number of *montre* payments to six, but this was resisted both at the time of its implementation and towards the end of the year.[31] The forceful logic of Bullion's position was none the less accepted for the following campaign, and to hammer home the point the *contrôle* for 1636 was drafted explicitly in terms of six *montres*. The figures given by Bullion were for a maximum of 172,000 infantry and 21,400 cavalry, specifically qualified 'sur le pied de six monstres'.[32] The total funding of 29,800,000 *livres* allocated to the costs of infantry and cavalry is specified, while additional sums are stipulated for artillery (3 million *livres*), the navies (2,070,000 *livres*), the additional costs of providing and transporting *vivres* (1,600,000 *livres*) and the ordinary costs of fortification and garrisons (1,200,000 *livres*). As a result of this newly implemented six *montre* system, what looks like a substantial increase in the numbers of troops that were to be raised is nothing of the kind. Only a small proportion of the army would expect

---

[29] AAE MD 812, fo. 385v.
[30] AAE MD 812, fo. 385v.
[31] Aubery, *Richelieu*, I. 444, 5 Apr. 1635, Châtillon to Servien; Avenel, v. 367, 2 Dec. 1635, Richelieu to Louis XIII, attacking Bullion's attempt to restrict the remainder of the French forces now in the United Provinces to only seven *montres* during 1635.
[32] Avenel, v. 723.

The size of the French army

to receive either six – or previously eight – *montres* in the course of the campaign: that minority of units which were already *sur pied* and at full strength at the opening of the campaign, and capable of maintaining a high effective strength through to the following winter. In all other cases the crown and its ministers would be anticipating the maintenance of units for some fraction of the total of six *montres*, and would be engaged in the same calculations as for the 1635 *contrôle* about wastage, *deniers revenans bons*, and additional units recruited in the middle or late in the campaign. Bullion had reduced the number of *montres* to six in order to avoid overpaying a minority of long-serving units, and to avoid disbursing *montres* at the end of the campaign when it was justifiably suspected that a large proportion of the overpayments went into the pockets of the unit officers and/or the *commissaires des guerres* charged with the inspections of the units.

But for the purposes of allocating funds for the maintenance of troops through 1636, there was not a significant difference between the 1635 calculation of 132,000 infantry × 8 *montres*, and the 1636 figures of 172,000 infantry × 6 *montres*.[33] This similarity is also evident in the global totals of anticipated financial allocation for 1635 and 1636: 36 million *livres* for 1635, 37,670,000 *livres* in 1636.[34] Although neither of these anticipated totals bears much relation to financial reality, their similarity is a clear indication of ministerial intentions. There is nothing particularly surprising about this. At the opening of the 1636 campaign there was no reason to foresee the multiple Spanish and Imperial invasions that would bring the threat of military and political collapse and force the crown into a period of unprecedented recruitment through the summer and autumn months.

All of these pre-campaign discussions of budgeting simply reinforce the awareness that the primary concern was the rational allocation of funding to avoid over-heavy recruitment in the first months of the year with its dangerous consequence of severe financial shortfalls as the campaign progressed. As has already been implied by various comments, these attempts to manage the war budget by trying to control the allocations of *montres* to the army throughout the campaign were not particularly effective. What could not have been anticipated after 1635 was the exponential increase in the levels of wastage – sickness and above all, desertion – which accompanied the attempt to create a larger army. The notion of rational planning for recruitment, by which a regular rate of troop loss, and the consequent *réformation* or disbandment of units, could be neatly balanced by the arrival of newly levied units and additional bodies of recruits, came to

---

[33] That is a 'total' of 1,056,000 *montres* to allocate to recruitment and maintenance of infantry in 1635, against 1,032,000 *montres* for 1636. Though as the frequency of *montre* payments was largely determined by a combination of political, military and financial considerations rather than any rigid adherence to a regular 'monthly' schedule, these literal calculations are of limited comparative significance.

[34] An additional 4 million *livres* was added for the army of duke Bernard of Saxe-Weimar, but this was balanced against the specifically earmarked 4 million that the crown expected to obtain from the *taxe des financiers*: Avenel, v. 723–4.

The military context

pieces in the face of a far more disorderly reality. A primary problem was that the units recruited later in the campaign, and, even more, recruits raised outside the regimental structure to be distributed piecemeal among existing under-strength companies, suffered still heavier and more rapid losses from desertion than the units which began the campaigns.[35] Neither the military nor the financial administration had anticipated the huge levels of additional recruitment that would be required to keep even quite modest forces at a reasonable effective strength, and to prevent campaigns being abandoned prematurely. The reluctance of the *surintendants* to face this issue is understandable. From their point of view, excessive additional recruitment at a time when troops raised earlier in the campaign were still on the *montre* rolls was little better than setting the total of initial recruitment too high. Both would threaten to undermine the fragile structure of financial provision that had to be sustained through the campaign season. But in fact, experience revealed that from the point of view of trying to keep armies effective it was literally impossible to raise too many additional recruits. In September 1636, after an unprecedented recruitment effort, some levies were cancelled because it was felt that enough troops had now been raised. Yet within a month it proved impossible to divide the army-corps engaged at the siege of Corbie because of the 'shortage of infantry'.[36] Moreover, while the king and Richelieu subscribed in principle to the notion that recruitment should be limited by the availability of financial resources, a crisis that opened the possibility of military defeat would override such finance-led considerations. This was the case in summer 1636 when the Spanish invasion of Picardy and Champagne brought the abandonment of any attempt to relate recruitment to resources. The immense strain that this placed upon the crown's financial resources and borrowing capacity led the *surintendants* to attempt a drastic retrenchment over the winter quarter, and indeed to try to reduce the projected funding for the army-corps for the 1637 campaign. This bore disastrous fruit in March 1637 when the duc de Rohan's army-corps in the Valtelline collapsed 'faute d'argent', and Richelieu rounded on Bullion to condemn his 'short-sighted' concern to try to curb military expenditure.[37]

When confronted by the king and Richelieu's presentation of the strategic case for increased numbers of troops, and the maintenance of armies at effective strength

---

[35] For example, SHAT A^1 57, fo. 252, 30 Jan. 1640, de Noyers to La Ferté-Imbault, reporting that ten companies raised for the maréchal de Brézé are already so weak that he is to carry out a *réformation* to reduce them to four companies of fifty men each. A^1 61, fo. 116, 26 Oct. 1640, de Noyers to Saligny, *maréchal de camp* in Normandy, ordering him to disband a regiment of *nouvelle levée*.

[36] SHAT A^1 29, fos. 144–5, 5 Sept. 1636, instructions to Jacques d'Estampes sr de Valençay, to defer the levy of additional troops in Languedoc and to ensure that they should be ready for the following year. AAE MD 1678, fo. 302, 1 Sept. 1636 [misdated; actually mid-October], account of the campaign for the defence of Picardy.

[37] Avenel, v. 762–3, 28 Mar. 1637, Richelieu to Bullion: 'pour un escu qu'il eust fallu donner à temps il en faudra dix, et encores ne réparera-t-il pas la perte qu'on a faicte'.

regardless of the burden that this would place on the *épargne*, the *surintendants* found it impossible to sustain their position. This probably lay behind the abandonment of the *contrôles généraux* from 1637. By the end of the 1636 campaign it was clear to the *surintendants* that any agreement made at the beginning of a campaign to try to establish levels of phased recruitment would simply be overridden by Louis and Richelieu in the interests of whatever strategic imperative they considered should have priority. From 1637 formal *états* were produced which gave general totals of troops that could be raised for the army, and which divided these troops between the various army-corps and through the campaign season, but gave no indication of the total available funding, nor did they make any attempt to discuss recruitment in terms of *montres* or financial provision for the campaign.[38] The *surintendants* could not sustain an objection on financial grounds to the scale of the war-effort that crown and first minister argued was necessary. By establishing an agreed limit of 36 or 37 million *livres* at the beginning of the campaign, the *surintendants* were not stating that they would refuse to meet expenditure above this level, for that would be beyond their authority. They were, however, making it impossible to resist or delay demands for expenditure *up* to this level. At the centre of government was a clear conflict between the *surintendants*, who interpreted these figures as the upper limit of the financially possible, and Richelieu, who regarded them as a guarantee of the immediately practical, and who assumed that only sums above this level would require further negotiation. Hence the decision to do away with a system which merely weakened the bargaining position of the *bureau des finances*, in favour of one which left the *surintendants* with more freedom to oppose large-scale recruitment and military planning from the outset, without declaring beforehand the sums that would be available for the campaign.

The 'Estat des trouppes dont seront composées les armees du Roy durant l'année 1637' is still a document emanating from the *bureau des finances*. Once again, the concern is to impose limits upon the forces to be levied, and the document is not intended as a specific statement of the troops that the ministry was intending to set *sur pied* at the beginning of the campaign. Substantial – though still insufficient – allowance is made for a series of additional levies to be despatched to the main army-corps later in the campaign. At least 27,750 additional infantry and 7,060 cavalry are listed, but the total of reinforcements would be greater if a number of unspecific mentions of *renfort* were taken into account. An attempt to anticipate – and thereby to try to control – the need for

---

[38] For the *états* of notional troop allocations for 1637 see AAE MD 828, fos. 311–23, 330–51, [1637]; for 1638 see MD 832, fos. 1–16; for 1640, MD 837, fos. 245–68; *états* for 1639, 1641 and 1642 are missing from the material in the AAE. The *état* for 1639 survives in the BN Ms.fr. 17555, fo. 1, état des troupes ... durant l'année 1639'. Orest Ranum, *Richelieu and the Councillors of Louis XIII* (Oxford, 1963), p. 126, also comments that the attempt to establish and maintain a budget for the war-effort was abandoned after 1636.

The military context

more troops was now established as an integral part of the *surintendants*' planning. The *états* for troop numbers drawn up for 1637 and subsequent campaigns are thus no more of a guide to the real size of the French army than the previous *contrôles généraux*. All are statements of intention, but the intention is not the establishment of the army at a particular stipulated size, rather the attempt, either directly or implicitly, to try to *limit* the size of the army in terms of declared or undeclared financial resources intended to last throughout the entire campaign.

The fundamental problem of calculating army size

A consistent theme has emerged in the discussions of the limitations of both 'regimental' and '*contrôle*'-based attempts to establish the size of the army. This is the problem of ascertaining the size of military forces in which rates of troop loss are so extraordinarily high, and in a situation where any army-corps that was to be kept at modest effective strength for the few months of the campaign season needed both piecemeal reinforcements and the regular injection of substantial numbers of reallocated or newly recruited units at points throughout the period of military activity. The calculations of the size of the army therefore have to be placed in the context of successive levies of troops, paid progressively fewer campaign 'pays', in addition to those units which were operating from the opening of a campaign but whose real strength declined markedly in the ensuing months.

This process defeats any attempt to speak of the 'size of the army' as if there was one figure that had any general relevance to the forces *sur pied* across an entire campaign. Discussions of the size of the French army in this period have been locked into a totally unrealistic steady-state model, more appropriate to nineteenth- or twentieth-century warfare. Armies were institutions whose size and composition fluctuated continually.[39] A crude model of the French army in this period – indeed for all armies except for a few elite corps made up of quasi-professional veterans where the process was slightly more attenuated – is of a bath half full of water, but without a plug, being intermittently refilled from a tap. The moment the tap is turned off – the moment that additional recruitment stops for some reason – the existing water rapidly runs out of the bath. At other times the rate at which additional levies are raised may be slower than the rate at which existing troops desert or become unfit for combat, so that the army-corps falls beneath an effective campaigning strength. On a few occasions a massive recruitment drive in mid-campaign may have the effect of rendering the 'bath' fuller than it was at the beginning of the campaign, though once again, when the recruitment slows down the overall strength of the army will quickly start to decline. In a situation where the crown was committed to keeping only one – or at

---

[39] A point clearly recognized in recent studies of other contemporary armies. See, notably, Pohl, *Profiantirung der keyserlichen Armaden*, pp. 25–7; Kapser, *Die bayerische Kriegsorganization*, pp. 56–8.

The size of the French army

most two – main campaign corps at a high effective strength, the problem was potentially manageable: enough new recruits could be levied and despatched to the campaign theatres, enough effort could be made to slow the rate of desertion and other attritional factors. But after 1635 the French crown was trying to perform this feat for six or seven army-corps simultaneously. In most cases one or two of these were simply ignored, and their effective strength was left to drain away during the campaign season, explaining the regular amalgamations of army-corps seen in almost every campaign after 1635. An alternative to this entailed the impossible task of levying huge numbers of new recruits throughout the campaign season and allocating them to the different forces in sufficient numbers and sufficently quickly to keep the army-corps at effective, campaigning, strength. The other alternative – that the crown's agents and officials should try to do more to control the rates of wastage from the army-corps during the campaigns, proved equally impractical. This view of the fluctuating strength of French army-corps may seem exaggerated, but even a summary overview of the campaigns after 1635 provide numerous examples of rates of attrition which destroyed the capacity of particular army-corps to continue campaigning, often in spite of the arrival of large numbers of additional recruits to try to boost the flagging numbers.

To assume that the army-corps of the 1630s and 1640s were capable of sustaining themselves at the strength which they might temporarily have achieved at the opening of the campaign gives an exaggerated view of the effectiveness of the military administration. If a military establishment of 125,000 men is attained by the French crown through massive recruitment at the beginning of a campaign, but can only be sustained for a few weeks before undergoing dramatic decline, then it is misleading to suggest that this in a real sense represents 'the strength' of the French army, the size of the force that the French crown could maintain *sur pied*.

In any case, even if it could be maintained that the French crown had decided for strategic reasons to set 125,000 men *sur pied* for the beginning of a particular campaign, it cannot be assumed that this number would automatically be ready and assembled for a chosen date. Fixing the opening of the campaign too early in the year would have the consequence that a high proportion of the units would not have completed their recruitment; fixing it too late into the year would mean that those units which had managed to accomplish their recruitment early would already be suffering losses from desertion and sickness before the army-corps was fully assembled and had opened the campaign.

Once set in this context of a continual process of attrition and replacement, attempts to fix upon a figure for the size of the army are to be seen as arbitrary selections of temporary high-points, in many cases quite meaningless in themselves, since the situation would already have changed dramatically within a few weeks of campaigning. When such extensive correspondence is concerned with the ever-changing gap between the paper strength of the units that were destined

The military context

to compose particular army-corps and the far less impressive reality, then all attempts to attach a specific figure to the size of the army relevant even to a particular campaign, let alone to the course of the war, are likely to be wildly astray.

THE DEVELOPMENT OF THE EFFECTIVE
STRENGTH OF THE FRENCH ARMY

Calculating the size of the army from revues *and their* extraits

An alternative to these methods does exist, and is based on further material in the Archives des Affaires Etrangères and in the Bibliothèque Nationale. The Bibliothèque Nationale contains a series of volumes of *revues* of numerous individual companies in the army of Louis XIII, carried out by named *commissaires des guerres*. The material in the Archives des Affaires Etrangères comprises a series of surviving composite reports – *extraits* – from specific *revues* or *montres* of all the companies in a particular army-corps. Setting aside the issue of successful fraud, or the complicity of the *commissaires* in such activities, the figures provided can be taken as a reasonable indication of the strength of constituent companies, and even, from the *extraits*, of entire army-corps at a particular moment in the campaign. There is no reason to assume that these strengths would be the same a week later, but to establish the approximate strength of a particular army-corps, even if only for a particular historical moment, is useful, not least because it can provide some sense of the fluctuations in the numbers of troops under arms.

Both sets of evidence are problematic. The collection of individual *revues* undertaken by the *commissaires* and conserved in the Bibliothèque Nationale gives a clear indication of how far actual company strength could diverge from notional full strength, and allows the historian to chart the inexorable process of declining company strength through successive campaigns.[40]

But the *revues* are an arbitrary collection: only very rarely does the strength of an entire regiment survive through a complete series of company rolls, and even specific individual companies do not appear in the volumes with any regularity. They are a cross section of the companies in the army, spread over a wide chronological span. It is impossible to use them to establish the effective strength of the French army, or even a particular army-corps, at any historical moment.

The survival of the *extraits* from the *revues* provides the historian with exactly this information.[41] They give details about the total strength of an army-corps on a particular date. The problem here is that these *extraits* have survived on a very

---

[40] BN Mss.Fr. 25853–8: company *revues* from 1635 to 1642.
[41] Most of these *extraits* survive in the AAE, but a few are preserved in the BN – for example, Ms.Fr. 3765: a series of revues of army-corps in 1641, or Ms.Fr. 17555: a *revue* of the armies from July 1639.

The size of the French army

patchy basis. Moreover, given the fluctuations in the strength of units during the campaigns it would anyway be difficult to decide how many separate *extraits* would ideally be required to plot the strength of a particular corps over any significant period of warfare. On occasions the surviving *extraits* do offer a glimpse of a particular army-corps at various points in the same campaign, underlining the dramatic changes in troop numbers. But the material is insufficient to provide any comprehensive overview of the fluctuating strength of the entire French army. However, the *extraits* can also be examined in conjunction with documents which have survived in larger numbers in the Archives des Affaires Etrangères and the Bibliothèque Nationale, a series of formal *états* of projected allocations of troops drawn up before each campaign. Such *états* should be taken only on their own terms, as pre-campaign estimates of the maximum numbers of recruits that it was envisaged would be allocated to specific corps, though often with useful indications about additional recruitment in the course of the campaign. But taking both the *extraits* and the *états* together, and adding occasional specific evidence from individual *revues*, it is possible both to give an impression of the crown's general recruitment targets and to give some impression of the extent to which the numbers on the ground corresponded to these targets.

One examination of this material has been undertaken by Bernhard Kroener, whose work represents the most valuable contribution to the debate about real strengths of the French army in the period 1635 to 1661.[42] Kroener considers that these *extraits* are too fragmentary to provide global totals for the strength of the army during this period, and he is fully aware of the insuperable problems presented by fluctuating numbers during the campaigns. Instead, his concern is to give a sense of the discrepancy between assumed and real unit strengths (*Sollstärke* and *Iststärke*) and to show the remorseless decline through the 1640s of what was already a surprisingly low actual company strength. For the first phase of the struggle from 1635 to 1640, Kroener suggests that the average real company strength of infantry units stood at 42.2 men. During the next phase, from 1641 to 1647, the average strength declined to 21.6 men per infantry company, while the period of the Fronde and its aftermath sees a further decline to an average of 16 men. Kroener relies upon complete or partial *extraits* of army-corps to support his contentions about company averages, but the evidence from the individual company *revues* strongly reinforce his contentions about the low – and declining – real strength of the individual companies.

Even before an attempt is made to piece together information about the actual strength of the army in order to provide some rough idea of the scale of the French war-effort, the evidence of Kroener's average company strengths and of the mass of individual company *revues* would call into question even the more modest typical estimates of a military establishment after 1635 of 100,000–

---

[42] Kroener, 'Die Entwicklung der Truppenstärken'.

The military context

120,000 troops. The evidence both of company *revues* and of the larger-scale *extraits* shows that the real totals of troops established at the outset of campaigns, still more the forces that were maintained through the campaigns, were considerably lower than either of the two methods of calculation previously examined would allow.

The approximate size of the French army before 1635

One of the single most significant proportional increases in the number of troops maintained under arms by the French crown occurred in the first half of the sixteenth century. If Charles VIII invaded Italy in 1494 with a relatively small army of 16,000–20,000 combatants, by the time that François I was defeated at Pavia in 1525 the main French campaign army operating in Italy was between 24,000 and 26,000 infantry, and 4,800 to 6,000 cavalry.[43] Even these figures, the lowest cited for the army at Pavia, should certainly be further reduced to allow for the reality of forces on campaign; but the army in Italy was not the only military force maintained by the French crown. When taking into account forces raised to pursue the border conflicts in Picardy and on the Spanish frontier, and those troops required to garrison key *places* on the eastern frontier and the coast, an additional 10,000 troops must be added to the military establishment, creating a war-time strength of somewhere around 40,000 men. As the Habsburg–Valois conflict continued through the 1540s and 1550s, the French military establishment was eased upwards from 40,000 to nearer 50,000 by the wars of the later 1550s.[44]

A military establishment of around 50,000 represented a significant peak in the development of the French army. François I was of the opinion that this was the largest military force that could be sustained by the kingdom, and if the number of effectives did pass much above 50,000 before 1559 it was only for a few weeks of specific campaigns.[45] Moreover, this total of 50,000 troops, of which a high proportion was composed of foreign mercenaries raised on expensive contracts for successive campaigns, was large enough to plunge the French monarchy into a financial crisis, and into a declaration of bankruptcy in 1557.[46]

If troop numbers occasionally increased beyond this level during campaigns in

---

[43] Lot, *Recherches*, pp. 55–6.
[44] During the Anglo-Imperial invasion of 1544, for example, the main campaign army was supposedly of 30,000 infantry and 5,000–6,000 cavalry: Lot, *Recherches*, pp. 102–5. To this should be added other defensive forces, and the considerable garrisons committed to securing Piedmont since its French occupation in 1536. The one apparently reliable *revue* of the 1550s, that held at Pierrepont on 8 Aug. 1558, gives Henri II's main campaigning forces at between 40,150 and 40,550 men, to which, again, could be added a very rough notion of 10,000 additional troops in garrisons and minor standing forces within and outside of French frontiers: Lot, *Recherches*, pp. 179–85.
[45] Corvisier, *Histoire militaire*, I. 305; that troop totals of 60,000–70,000 (if they are accepted at all for this period) were no more than specific, short-term, peaks is a point made by Lynn, 'Recalculating French army growth', 887.
[46] In 1558 at the Pierrepont *revue* some 8,000 cavalry out of a total of 11,000 were mercenary *reiters*,

The size of the French army

the Wars of Religion, this was due in large part to the initiatives of great provincial nobles, raising private forces essentially to wage local wars, but prepared to lend their military support to crown, Huguenots or Catholic League when conflict assumed a national significance.[47] After the Wars of Religion the standing, peacetime, army of Henri IV returned to the diminutive size of the 'ordinary' forces of the earlier sixteenth century, with a typical military establishment between 1601 and 1609 of around 2,650 cavalry and 6,750 infantry.[48] The project for intervention in the Jülich/Kleve dispute seems to have entailed increasing the military establishment up towards the 50,000 barrier again.[49] Between 1610 and the intervention in the Valtelline in 1625 there was a great deal of military activity within France, but no reason to believe that the military establishment approached the maximum levels of the mid-sixteenth century.

Richelieu's original plans for intervention in the Valtelline were to have involved an army of 14,000 infantry and 2,000 cavalry, to be raised in Dauphiné and the surrounding provinces.[50] These were intended to reinforce the levies made by the Grisons themselves, who were the 'official' belligerents seeking to exclude Papal and Habsburg troops from the valleys. However, both the levying of troops in France and the problems of getting them down through the Swiss cantons meant that in mid-November the marquis de Cœuvres had only 7,000 infantry and 400 cavalry, of whom just the cavalry and 1,200 men of the Vaubecourt regiment were French.[51] Though further French forces trickled into Cœuvres' army in early 1625, it was the failure to achieve a sufficient concentration of force in the Valtelline which encouraged the diversionary scheme against Genoa. This invasion of the Republic was to be in alliance with Carlo Emanuele I, duke of Savoy, but it led to an increase in the number of French troops budgeted for 1625. The terms of the treaty with Savoy stipulated that the army which would invade the Republic of Genoa would be 30,000 men, of which France would provide

---

while about 21,000 infantry were Swiss and German out of a total of just over 29,000: Lot, *Recherches*, p. 184.
[47] Wood, *The King's Army*, p. 64, summarizes his findings for the royal army between 1562 and 1575, showing a couple of substantial (60,000–70,000) peaks between 1567 and 1569, but an army that usually fell below the 50,000 mark, and by the mid-1570s was suffering a significant decline in numbers.
[48] Servan and Grimoard, *L'armée française*, pp. 2–4.
[49] Though there is considerable uncertainty about the actual size of the forces set *sur pied*, and by implication the relationship of the Rhineland expeditionary force to the wider military establishment. Audouin, *Histoire de l'administration*, II. 154, indicates a modest but convincing total of 25,000 foot and 4,000 cavalry for the intervention. J.-P. Babelon, *Henri IV* (Paris, 1982), p. 967, proposes that 37,000 troops were raised for the intervention, and both he and Mark Greengrass, *France in the Age of Henri IV* (London, 1984), p. 197, support the notion of a military establishment of around 50,000 men.
[50] Grillon, I. 95, 18 July 1624, Richelieu to cardinal de La Valette.
[51] Rott, *Représentation diplomatique*, III. 799.

15,000.⁵² In the event the duc de Lesdiguières moved down against Genoa with an army of 23,000 men, of whom only 8,000 were French.⁵³ Raising and maintaining even this number of troops proved a severe challenge to the administration. Even more serious for France's overall military commitments than the commitment of forces to the Genoa campaign was the concern that the Habsburgs would broaden the scale of the war by an attack across France's eastern frontier. The forces raised in response to this threat were not large, but the gap was no less significant between an army-corps that was theoretically of 14,000 men yet in practice reported to be less than half that strength.⁵⁴ By the summer of 1625 the ministers were engaged in additional recruitment to maintain the war-effort, with plans to raise another 6,000 troops for Italy and 4,000 for the Champagne frontier.⁵⁵ By the standards of the conflict after 1635 the French war-effort seemed small scale and well within the capabilities of the crown. However, in 1625 it was judged that the simultaneous campaigns in the Valtelline, the Genoese Republic and the forces standing on the defensive in Champagne and the *Trois Evêchés* represented the limits of France's military commitment; to raise a further large-scale army to operate in the Midi against tough and possibly sustained Huguenot resistance was out of the question. It was this military impasse which persuaded Richelieu to accept the terms of the treaty of Monzón (5 March 1626).

The timing of the plan to reduce the protestant 'state within a state' by military force had grown out of the exigency of the 1627 English landing on the Île de Ré. Even as the French forces were being massed on the coast against Ré, some 15,000 additional troops had been stationed in positions that pointed to La Rochelle as their ultimate objective.⁵⁶ However, until the English had been driven off Ré, the ministers and commanders were reluctant to take on the major challenge of a siege of La Rochelle; once again, the total numbers of troops were insufficient to make two simultaneous projects practical. The army which was deployed against the city from the end of 1627 was maintained at an average strength of around 20,000 troops.⁵⁷ Richelieu himself offers a plausible account in his *Mémoires* of how, at the time of the king's departure from La Rochelle (February 1628), the army contained some 18,000 soldiers, many of whom were sick or exhausted, but that by Louis' return in April 1628 the army had been built up to 25,000 men – an

---

⁵² A.S.To LM, vol. 25, Carlo Emanuele I to the Abbé Alessandro Scaglia, pce 39/3, 2 Feb. 1625, specifies total forces of 25,000–30,000 infantry, and 6,000 cavalry; pce 28/2, 30 Nov. 1624, had already confirmed that 15,000 infantry of this total were to be provided by France.
⁵³ Dufayard, *Lesdiguières*, p. 541. Dufayard proposes that the total French forces available for the campaign against Genoa totalled just over 15,000 troops: pp. 539–40.
⁵⁴ Grillon, I. 179, 11 Apr. 1625, Richelieu to Charles de Valois, duc d'Angoulême
⁵⁵ Avenel, II. 102, 5 Aug. 1625, 'Mémoire sur lequel il plaira au Roi'.
⁵⁶ On 1 Aug. 1627 Angoulême already had 7,000 foot and 600 cavalry in the environs of La Rochelle, and was expecting another 4,000 troops by 10 Aug.: Avenel, II. 531, 1 Aug., Richelieu to de La Saludie; Parker, *La Rochelle*, pp. 15–16.
⁵⁷ Kroener, 'Die Entwicklung der Truppenstärken', p. 167.

The size of the French army

early campaign strength that would certainly decline again through the summer months.[58] While this total may seem unimpressive as a one-off figure for a concentration of troops, it was a significant achievement to maintain a siege army at this strength for nearly twelve months, against all the pressures of disease, wounds, fatalities and desertion. The experience of sieges undertaken on the Flanders frontier from 1638 provide examples of joint army-corps with higher original strengths sustaining far more dramatic levels of wastage. The additional troops raised to *faire le dégât* – wage destructive, small-scale, war – against the Huguenots in the Midi were to a large extent recruited through the initiative and patronage of catholic *grands* such as Condé, Epernon and Montmorency.

The reluctance to offer support to the duc de Nevers in north Italy during 1628 is comprehensible in the context of this existing military commitment to La Rochelle. It was clear that the struggle against the Huguenots would continue after the fall of the great protestant stronghold, and in the light of this Richelieu proposed his plan for a rapid intervention in north Italy to lift the siege of Casale-Monferrato and establish a strong French garrison there. The same troops used for this operation early in 1629 would then, Richelieu hoped, be freed to participate in the campaigning against the Huguenot in the Midi. Though the project involved considerable risks, it avoided the burden of trying to sustain two campaign armies simultaneously. On 3 March, Richelieu wrote to Philippe de Béthune, ambassador at Rome, that the king would enter Piedmont with 25,000 infantry and 2,000 cavalry, and that this would be supplemented by another force of 12,000 infantry and 800 cavalry under the command of the maréchal de Créqui.[59] If these numbers sounded like optimistic pre-campaign estimates, Richelieu wrote to Béthune four days later to report that the pass of Susa had been forced by the *gardes*, the *gardes suisses* and the regiments of Sault and Navarrre, a total of 9,400 infantry.[60] The rapid collapse of Savoyard and Spanish resistance allowed Richelieu's plan to work as anticipated. A main army commanded by the king, and reported to be of 10,000 foot and 600 horse, moved against Privas and other Huguenot strongholds, while smaller corps of 3,000–4,000 infantry and a few hundred cavalry continued the localized destruction in the countryside begun in the previous year.[61]

As it grew clear that the Spanish, far from accepting their rebuff over

---

[58] Richelieu, *Mémoires*, IV. 84.
[59] Avenel, III. 238.
[60] Avenel, III. 246, 7 Mar., Richelieu to Béthune.
[61] Grillon, IV. 278, 9 May 1629, Schomberg to Richelieu; Avenel, III. 286–90, 28 Apr. 1629, 'Advis donné au Roi par son commandement'; Grillon, IV. 330, 23 May, Louis XIII to Queen Mother, proposes that Condé will have 8 regts and 900 cavalry to *faire le dégât* around Montauban, d'Estrées will have 7 regts and 800 cavalry to operate around Nîmes, while Henri de Lévis, duc de Ventadour, will command 5 regts and 400 horse around Castres. Given the strengths of the corps cited here, Richelieu's suggestion that the king would have 50,000 troops operating in the Midi (Avenel, III. 287) by the summer seems wildly optimistic.

The military context

Monferrato, were negotiating with the Emperor for greater Habsburg intervention in the territories of the duke of Mantua, it became necessary to build up forces on the frontiers again. By 13 October, Richelieu informed maréchal Toiras, governor of Casale, that the king had assembled 18,000 troops on the frontier with Piedmont, and had given order to levy another 20,000 men to sustain this army.[62] At this point Richelieu continued to hope that French pressure could persuade the Habsburgs to accept a negotiated solution in north Italy. By November 1629 it was clear that such a diplomatic solution was not attainable, and that it would be necessary to intervene for a second time in north Italy, this time against massively strengthened Habsburg forces. For this operation, Richelieu asserted that 35,000 infantry and 4,000 cavalry would be required to save the territories of the duke of Mantua.[63] At the same time French concern was heightened that the Emperor might be persuaded to support Spain by launching a diversionary attack on the *Trois Evêchés*, leading the crown to create an additional force in Champagne, supposedly of 18,000 infantry and 1,450 cavalry.[64] When the decision was taken to launch an attack on the duchy of Savoy, 2,000 infantry and 300 cavalry from these forces on the Champagne frontier were transferred southwards, contributing to a third army which Richelieu hoped to recruit up to 18,000 troops.[65] Anticipating the likely levels of loss and wastage, Richelieu had also made arrangements for a large part of the new levies in France and Switzerland to be allocated to this army-corps rather than being despatched directly to Piedmont.[66]

By 8 July, Richelieu had managed to pass 12,000 infantry and 1,400 cavalry down from Savoy into Piedmont.[67] With the forces that were already in Piedmont, the French were able to muster a campaign army of some 20,000 foot and 2,600 horse.[68] This was judged insufficient to challenge the Spanish and Imperial forces already in Monferrato, and Richelieu wrote that he had ordered the recruitment and despatch to Piedmont of a further 20,000 soldiers by the end of August.[69] The 22,000 troops theoretically available in mid-July for a campaign in Piedmont suffered huge levels of attrition, so that the force available to the commanders by mid-September may have been reduced to 7,000 troops, though Richelieu's relatively more optimistic calculation suggested that the effective strength was nearer to 13,000.[70] The fundamental problem of raising troops to serve across the

---

[62] Avenel, III. 449, 13 Oct. 1629.
[63] Grillon, IV. 681, [21 Nov. 1629].
[64] Grillon, V. 36, 17 Jan. 1630, Louis de Marillac to Richelieu; Grillon, V. 164, 31 Mar. 1630, Richelieu to Louis XIII.
[65] Grillon v. 164, 31 Mar.
[66] Avenel, III. 575–8, 9/10 Mar. 1630, Richelieu to Louis XIII; Grillon, V. 164, [31 Mar. 1630].
[67] Grillon, V. 376, 377, 8/9 July 1630, letters from Richelieu and from the king to the Queen Mother.
[68] Avenel, III. 789–95, 17 July 1630, 'Estat des affaires du Roy en Italie', p. 792.
[69] Avenel, III. 760, 13 July 1630, Richelieu to Toiras.
[70] Avenel, III. 907, 23 Sept. 1630, Richelieu to Schomberg: 'A la vérité il y a bien eu de la malice à ceux qui ont fait paroistre la première armée de Piedmont n'estre que de 7 mil hommes, lorsqu'il estoit question de résoudre le secours, ou consentir à la trefve, puisque depuis elle s'est trouvée de 13 mil.'

frontiers was the speed and scale of desertion, leading to the disintegration of units, often before they had even arrived at the campaign theatre.[71] This spectacular wastage rate was recognized by Richelieu and the king, who proposed in July that regiments – notionally of 1200 soldiers – which were 'réduitz à cent ou six vingts hommes' should be dissolved and the soldiers distributed to other units.[72] On paper, well over 20,000 additional troops were raised to maintain the armies in Savoy and Piedmont, yet all of this effort could not sustain even a single army-corps at effective strength.[73] Finally bringing the campaign in the duchy of Savoy under control,[74] and running down the corps on the Champagne frontier to the point where it would have been unable to provide any effective resistance in the event of an Imperial invasion, Richelieu managed to build up the army in Piedmont to 18,000 infantry and 2,300 cavalry by mid-October, a force large enough to confront the Spanish army in its entrenchments around Casale.[75]

The campaign of 1630 introduced many of the problems of maintaining multiple army-corps that were to reappear after 1635: the attempt to establish a number of forces simultaneously had a predictable impact on the effective strength of each. Despite Richelieu's optimistic hopes of setting 35,000 infantry and 4,000 cavalry *sur pied* to intervene in north Italy, the main campaign army never got much above 20,000–25,000 at its highest point. The other corps operating in Savoy and on the eastern frontier were far smaller. Moreover, the levels of wastage were sufficiently high as to undermine the strength of even the largest of the three armies within a couple of months, so that only sustained and concentrated recruitment could recover its effective strength. At the highest point in 1630 the crown may have managed to raise the total number of troops in the three armies to around 40,000 men, though allowing for corruption, losses of troops, even before units had arrived with the armies, and the failure of anticipated recruits to materialize, the real total could have been nearer to 30,000. To maintain one of these army-corps at an effective strength until the end of the campaign may have required a further 20,000–25,000 recruits.

The war-effort of 1630 was not surpassed in the years down to 1634. A foreign policy which aimed to subsidize allies and to avoid any outright commitment to the European conflict allowed Richelieu to concentrate military resources on particular objectives, so far as possible avoiding the burdens of trying to sustain multiple campaign armies simultaneously. In 1632 the largest element of the

---

[71] Grillon, v. 474, 2 Aug. 1630, Bouthillier to Richelieu on the high levels of desertion even from the elite regiments; v. 516, 15 Aug.: Châtillon to Richelieu, 'Et avec cela, le dégoust général, qui est aujourd'hui parmy la soldatesque, du voyage de Piedmont en feroit beaucoup déserter.'
[72] Avenel, III. 792, 17 July 1630.
[73] Avenel, III. 760, 13 July 1630; iii. 829, 6 Aug 1630. Though both of these letters were written by Richelieu to Toiras, possibly to encourage his resistance at Casale.
[74] Châtillon continued to blockade Montmélian, but in July wrote that he had only 2,200 men to sustain the siege: Grillon, v. 441, 27 July 1630, Bouthillier to Richelieu.
[75] Grillon, v. 597, 15 Oct. 1630, cites Richelieu, *Mémoires*, VI. 324.

The military context

French war-effort was represented by the 23,000 men placed under the command of maréchal d'Effiat, with orders to try to drive the Spanish out of the Electorate of Trier, whose archbishop had claimed French protection.[76] This military effort was matched both in 1632 and 1633 by the military campaigns in the duchy of Lorraine. Having decided on military action to overrun the duchy completely, Richelieu proposed that 20,000 foot and 3,000 cavalry would be required for the campaign, together with another 6,000 infantry and 800 horse in the event that Louis led the campaign in person.[77] In reality the forces were smaller – an undated *mémoire* for the army operating in Lorraine in 1633 listed twelve infantry regiments (though including the *vieux régiments* of Picardie, Champagne and Navarre) and twenty-five companies of cavalry[78] – but the burden of maintaining these at effective strength through a protracted campaign still represented a major military commitment.

The success of foreign policy in these years could be measured by the extent to which France was able to occupy important towns and fortresses in both north Italy and beyond her eastern frontier, but this process itself had a military cost; in 1633 the garrisons in Piedmont and Monferrato and on the frontier of the Empire required 8,500 troops, maintained at an expense of 1.5 million *livres*.[79]

Well before the battle of Nördlingen (6 September) made it more likely that France would be drawn into the European war, military activity reaching and surpassing the levels of 1630 seemed probable in 1634. The attempt to crush resistance in Lorraine had not ended in the previous year, and Louis and Richelieu were resolved to increase France's military commitment for the 1634 campaign in order to occupy the territory and to draw duke Charles' forces into battle. The army was to be placed under the command of maréchal de La Force, and an *état* of the troops assigned to the force listed twenty-one named infantry regiments, including the *vieux* Picardie, whose strength was given at 1,800 soldiers. The other units were calculated at between 900 and 1,200 men, with the exceptions of the Swiss regiment of La Bloquerie, given at 2,400 men, the Scottish regiment of Hebron (Sir James Hepburn) at 1,300, and the prestige Normandie regiment, recruited under Longueville patronage, set at 1,700. Taking the regiments at these target strengths gave 23,400 infantry, and a further thirty-two companies of cavalry, calculated at 3,000 horse.[80] Even if the recruitment of these units fell short of these anticipated totals, it was indicative of ministerial intentions to create a significant force, and one which was also to receive the regular despatch of reinforcements, not least to provide sufficient numbers of troops for the garrisons

---

[76] Pagès, *Thirty Years War*, p. 144; Avenel, IV. 319–20, 14 July 1632.
[77] Babel, *Karls IV*, p. 177.
[78] AAE MD 807, fo. 112 [1633].
[79] AAE MD 808, fo. 304 (1633), *état* for the garrisons.
[80] AAE CP Lorraine 15, fo. 503, [1634], *Armée de Lorraine*; this was confirmed in a letter of the *intendant*, Gobelin, to Bouthillier, who reported that the army was of 22,000 infantry and 3,000 cavalry: AAE CP Lorraine, 14, fo. 72, 15 Jan. 1634.

The size of the French army

that were being created across Lorraine.[81] In mid-August an *état* of La Force's army – both the field force and the garrisons, showed that he had twenty-five infantry regiments and fifty-seven cavalry companies. Even if it is assumed that the average strength of the infantry regiments had fallen to only 400 men by this stage in the campaign, it would still represent a large corps by the standards of these years.[82] In addition to the army of La Force (now jointly commanded by maréchal Brézé), the garrison at Nancy was being maintained on the basis of $4\frac{1}{2}$ regiments with a strength at *revue* of 2,747 troops, 'sur quoy il ne trouve dans le service que 2,183'.[83]

Having taken the remaining *places* still resisting French occupation, and established garrisons across the duchy by mid-August, the bulk of La Force's campaign army, optimistically given at a theoretical strength of 29,000 soldiers, was now pushed forward on to the Rhine, where it was maintained between Koblenz and Breisach, and intended to shore up the weakening position of the German protestant forces.[84]

The duchy was subsequently to provide the assembly point for the creation of a further army, placed under the command of the duc de Rohan and indicating the extent to which the crown and ministers saw the situation in late 1634 as both an opportunity and a threat. A formal *revue* of the regiments in this army in late November 1634 reveals impressive regimental strengths. Rohan had been allocated eight second-rank regiments whose strength varied between 656 and 1,036 men, together with the regiment of la Meilleraye (1,175 men) and the *vieux* regiment of Champagne (1,433 men), a total of 9,536 infantry. To this, the *revues* added 478 *cavalerie légère* and 445 *carabins*.[85] On 6 December, Rohan wrote that the most recent *état* of the army gave 12,200 infantry and 1,550 cavalry, but that taking into account the 10 per cent paid to the captains for maintaining their companies at 70 men or above and the number of officers themselves and their valets, this total was reduced to 10,380 infantry and 1,380 cavalry.[86] Though Rohan was sending this *mémoire* to express concern at the shortfall indicated by these *revues* compared to the size of the army-corps that he had originally been promised, in practice these forces could be seen as evidence of an impressive ability to maintain effective strength during months in which troops were normally assigned to winter quarters. It was an achievement which would be less frequently repeated after 1635.

---

[81] Avenel, IV. 591–3, 18 Aug. 1634.
[82] AAE CP Lorraine 15, fos. 135–6, 17 Aug. 1634, *contrôle* of the *logement* of La Force's troops in Lorraine.
[83] AAE CP Lorraine 15, fo. 405 [1634] *extrait de la revue*.
[84] Fagniez, *Père Joseph*, II. 179; Hanotaux, *Richelieu*, v. 46.
[85] AAE CP Lorraine 15, fos. 332–8, *état* of revues carried out on 24/25 Nov. 1634.
[86] AAE CP Lorraine 15, fo. 369, 6 Dec., Rohan to Louis XIII: Rohan also cited a second *revue* of the army which did not take the officers into account, and gave 9,536 infantry and 923 cavalry – itself indicative of the fluctuations in unit strength even over the short term that were discussed earlier.

The military context

The maintenance of the army-corps of la Force and Rohan, together with substantial garrisons in north Italy and on the Rhine, probably pushed the overall strength of the forces under arms to their highest point since 1624, and to the levels which had been anticipated by Henri IV in 1610. Thus in late 1634, on the eve of the first year of war with the Habsburgs, France may well have recruited – and maintained – as many as 45,000 infantry under arms. Relatively small numbers of French cavalry were to prove a besetting problem in the first years of open war, and given the assumption that they were of limited use in garrisons, the total of horse in the same period would have been considerably lower, perhaps 3,000–4,000 in total.[87]

The French army from 1635 to 1642

French military preparations in March and April 1635 were dominated by the concern to meet the treaty obligation to the Dutch that each power should field an army of 25,000 infantry and 5,000 cavalry for the invasion of the Spanish Netherlands. The French army that was to cooperate with the Dutch was subject to a detailed *revue* in late May, and reported to consist of 22,000 infantry and 4,500 cavalry.[88] The fate of this army-corps provides an instructive example of the problems of recruitment and maintenance besetting the French administration. By the end of June, and after a period during which the army had been operating on enemy territory and with increasing supply problems, the effective strength had fallen to 13,000 foot and 4,000 cavalry, and Richelieu had promised the senior officers that an additional 8,000 infantry and 2,000 cavalry would be sent to Flanders by 10 July.[89] Despite these reinforcements the effective strength of the army continued to fall, and had declined to fewer than 8,000 foot and 2,000 horse by mid-October.[90] A winter spent on Dutch territory with no subsistence provided by the French treasury accomplished a final wasting away of the remaining troops, and those units which were finally shipped back to French ports in May 1636 were subject to large-scale disbandment or *réformation*.[91]

Yet despite the rapid collapse of the effective strength of the Flanders army, the initial creation of a corps on this scale had been achieved at considerable cost to the other French forces. To create such an army of 25,000–26,000 men, Châtillon's troops from Picardy had been amalgamated with a substantial block of

---

[87] For the shortage of cavalry after 1635 and its impact on campaigning, see chapter 1, pp. 59–65.
[88] Aubery, *Richelieu*, I. 481, 1 June 1635. Even at the opening of the campaign season an army of this size had been created only by amalgamating the previously separate corps of the maréchal de Brézé and that of the maréchal de Châtillon: Aubery, *Richelieu*, I. 443, 30 Mar. 1635.
[89] Richelieu, *Mémoires*, VIII. 334; Avenel, V. 74, 28 June 1635, Richelieu to Charnacé.
[90] Avenel, V. 309–11, 16 Oct. 1635, 'Instruction du Roy pour M. le maréchal de Brézé.'
[91] Pange, *Charnacé*, p. 133, indicates that the troops returning to France in February 1636 numbered 7,100 infantry and 2,600 cavalry; SHAT A^1 28, fo. 92, 20 June 1636, instructions to La Meilleraye to receive and 'reform' the returning units.

The size of the French army

troops under the command of maréchal Brézé, which had been detached from the army of maréchal de La Force intended to safeguard France's positions in Lower Alsace.[92] As Brézé's troops abandoned their positions on the Rhine to move northwards, concern was expressed about the size of the army-corps left with La Force, the key to French control of Lorraine and her forward positions in Alsace. In April 1635 La Force's army-corps was reported to contain some 14,300 infantry and 5,000 horse, but the priority of allocating troops to Brézé's corps had meant that wastage through sickness, absenteeism and desertion was not being made good by the arrival of new recruits.[93] The intention from the *états* of mid-April attached to the *contrôle général* of 1635 was that La Force's army should be maintained at 15,000 infantry and 4,000 cavalry, yet reports on the actual numbers varied between La Force's claim to have 12,000 foot, and accounts that the infantry numbered no more than 7,000, and that the cavalry companies were at half strength or less.[94] Despite attempts to push forward recruitment and to despatch new units to La Force, *extraits* from the *revues* of 28 July confirmed the lower figure, giving 7,558 infantry, together with 231 *malades presens* and 149 soldiers with no weapons. Simultaneous *revues* of the cavalry gave 1,576 horse, not including officers, NCOs and a few prestige companies of *gendarmes*.[95] Another *revue* for La Force's army, unfortunately undated, but certainly a little later into the campaign, records modest success in increasing the size of his army, recording 8,076 infantry and 2,652 cavalry.[96]

This relative weakness of La Force's army would have been less important if the army-corps under the duc de Rohan had been left in Lorraine and Upper Alsace, able to move up to the Rhine in a supporting operation if required. But Louis and his ministers had taken the decision to despatch Rohan and a substantial part of this army – albeit shorn of the most prestigious regiments – to the Valtelline. Fearing in consequence that La Force, left with an army of this reduced size, would be in no position to sustain France's position in Alsace, Louis XIII and Richelieu decided that a further army-corps should be created under the command of cardinal de La Valette, although this decision inevitably implied the diversion of troops who might otherwise have strengthened La Force. Although the *états* envisaged an allocation of 15,400 infantry and 4,800 cavalry to La Valette's army, *extraits* from the *revues* carried out at the same time as that of La

---

[92] Aubery, *Richelieu*, I. 443, 30 Mar. 1635; Servien himself admitted by 28 Apr. that the infantry from Picardy, some 13 regts, would only produce around 12,500 troops: AAE CP Espagne 18, fo. 31, instructions to Châtillon and Brézé.
[93] AAE MD 813, fo. 284, [16] Apr. 1635, totals extracted from a letter to Henri II de Bourbon, prince de Condé, instructing him to travel to La Force's army to carry out a *revue* – possibly in response to a suspicion that these figures may already be unreliable.
[94] AAE MD 814, fo. 140, 1 June 1635, *mémoire* from Louis XIII to La Force, concerned at the conflicting accounts of the strength of his army.
[95] AAE MD 819, fos. 64, 68, 28 July 1635 – full texts of *revues* by unit.
[96] AAE MD 819, fo. 69, [1635], *état* of the army of La Force, with accompanying figures for *revue*.

The military context

Force's army, around 28 July, indicated effective strengths of 8,730 infantry and 1,403 cavalry.[97]

The 12,000 troops which had been promised as support for France's allies in the Empire, principally duke Bernard of Saxe-Weimar, and which were to be placed under the command of Manassés de Pas, marquis de Feuquières, fell victim to the recruiting efforts being made elsewhere. Although a financial provision was made for the levy of these troops on the *contrôle général*, almost none seem to have been raised.[98] The entire force was to be made up of mercenaries levied in the Empire, and without funds to establish the contracts, Feuquières could do little.[99]

During 1635 the crown and its ministers attempted a short-lived experiment of creating additional, independent, forces which were intended to provide support and, if necessary, defence in depth. The first attempt to create such a *corps de reserve*, the army assembled around Langres, was initially projected at 20,000 foot and 3,000 horse, totals to be attained by the end of June. This would be reinforced by a further 5,000 infantry and 600 cavalry in August.[100] Given the spectacular rates of loss from the main campaign armies, the fate of the Langres force was a foregone conclusion: it was never assembled, and the units notionally allocated to this force were deployed to meet the more urgent need of keeping the primary armies at a basic effective strength. The second attempt, which entailed creating an army-corps directly under the command of the king to be based in Lorraine, proved slightly more successful. The original *état* proposed that this army should be of 30,000 infantry and 5,000 horse, a project which, if seriously attempted, would have absorbed all of the mid-campaign recruitment effort, leaving no other reserves for the other armies. In practice, the force never approached the size originally intended, but a block of troops under the command of the *maréchal de camp*, Jean de Nettancourt, comte de Vaubecourt, was supplemented by recruits and *noblesse* raised under the *arrière-ban* such that a corps was created sufficient for the king to assume command at the siege of Saint-Mihiel. But despite the presence of the king, this remained an extremely modest force; in mid-September the comte de Chavigny wrote to Richelieu, reporting the king's 'melancholy' that his army contained only 1,200–1,500 cavalry.[101] The third attempt to create a reserve army on the eastern frontier, the troops to be collected in Champagne, was

---

[97] AAE MD 819, fo. 70.
[98] SHAT A¹ 24, fo. 258, 7 May 1635, Servien to Feuquières with a full set of instructions for the levy of troops in the Empire to meet this commitment to France's allies.
[99] SHAT A¹ 25, fo. 35, 8 July 1635, Servien to Feuquières, concerned that the levies of German troops have not been proceeding as anticipated; AAE CP Allemagne 12, fo. 220, 1 Aug. 1635, La Valette to Richelieu, mentions that Feuquières has managed to raise two regiments of infantry.
[100] Avenel, v. 49, 8 June 1635.
[101] AAE MD 815, fo. 157, 2 Sept. 1635, Chavigny to Richelieu, warning the cardinal of Louis' considerable dissatisfaction with the lack of progress of the war-effort. AAE MD 815, fo. 212, 18 Sept. 1635.

assembled so late in the year that the force can be assumed to have been of insignificant size.[102] The additional 8,000 infantry and 2,000 cavalry that were sent to reinforce the Army of Flanders from Picardy were for the most part taken from the army that had been assembled around Langres.[103]

Elsewhere, the duc de Rohan's army, transferred to the Valtelline in early 1635, was given at 13,100 infantry and 540 cavalry on an *état* sent to Richelieu, this not counting 3,000 Swiss and two additional French regiments said to be *en route*. Richelieu expressed some scepticism about these numbers, but none the less stipulated that Rohan should be allocated funds for 12,000 men over three months, and it is difficult to see how Rohan's military performance in 1635 could have been accomplished with fewer than 12,000 troops.[104] In Italy, when a campaign against the Milanese was finally opened, the French contingent of the confederate army was reported by the *intendant des finances*, Camus, to be of 10,000–11,000 infantry and 1,800 cavalry.[105]

It is very uncertain how many troops would have been left in garrisons across France. The provision of 30,000 troops for 'garrisons' in 1635 and 1636 is quite disproportionate to the relatively small size of the campaign armies; it is probable that the term 'garrison' on the *états* was a convenient means to designate levies that had not yet been allocated to a particular army and were envisaged as an allowance for recruitment later in the year. A 'projet des garnisons pour 1636' allocates a total of 360 infantry companies to the various garrisoning commitments in France, Lorraine, Alsace, Trier and Italy.[106] For these to total 30,000 men would mean that the individual companies had an average strength of 83 men; to achieve this level of effectives would be remarkable in a *vieux* regiment and inconceivable in units which stood at the lowest priority in the ministry's allocation of funds.[107] Moreover, the heavy drain on manpower though the armies on the frontiers, and the evident shortage of troops to handle internal unrest such as the rising in Bordeaux in May and June, suggests that additional troops who were not allocated to the main armies were not numerous.

Even from this account, based on a few 'snapshots' of the army-corps during the campaign, it is clear that any attempt to suggest that the French crown had a certain number of troops *sur pied* 'in 1635' is not a meaningful conclusion from the evidence. In the first half of the campaign it is probable that initial recruitment

---

[102] Avenel, v. 302, 15 Oct. 1635, Richelieu to Chavigny.
[103] Avenel, v. 63, 75, 19 June, 28 June 1635, Richelieu to Servien, Richelieu to Charnacé.
[104] AAE MD 814, fo. 262, 14 July 1635, Richelieu to Servien.
[105] Avenel, v. 289, 9 Oct. 1635.
[106] AAE MD 819, fo. 36, [no date].
[107] This was even more improbable, given that the maximum strength for companies in garrison was almost never higher than fifty troops, and was sometimes as low as forty or even thirty: SHAT A¹ 61 fo. 57, 18 Oct. 1640: companies of the garrisons at Calais and Corbie to contain a maximum of fifty men; fo. 95, 22 Oct. 1640, instruction to *commissaire* Dosny that companies in garrison on the frontier of Champagne should not contain more than thirty men.

The military context

and the staggered arrival of additional units with the main armies may have ensured that some 65,000 infantry and 9,000–9,500 cavalry were briefly operational.[108] From June to October the attempt to create three additional armies and to maintain the effectives in the existing forces may have involved the levy of as many troops again; 50,000 infantry and 8,000 cavalry would not be an exaggerated estimate. But in practice these levies were almost completely distributed amongst the existing armies, and their effect was *not* to boost these forces up to the 120,000–130,000 troops so frequently ascribed to Richelieu's war-effort, but to provide partial compensation for the heavy rates of loss that the principal armies underwent throughout the campaign. Even this level of additional allocation did not save the armies from such shortages by the end of the campaign season that in October the armies of La Force and La Valette had to be amalgamated to counter the threat from the Imperial forces on the Rhine.

Above all, the examination of a particular campaign in detail confirms that the global totals of 125,000–150,000 troops for the French war-effort have no basis in reality, even as campaign 'high points'. The army-corps operating in the majority of campaign theatres are, by any standards, relatively small: even leaving aside questions of wastage, replacement and real versus 'paper' figures, it is clear from the evidence of specific *états* that an individual campaign army of 15,000 men represented the upper limits of operational strength. This reinforces the conclusion that the overall number of troops being raised and maintained was considerably smaller than has usually been assumed. It also explains the decision, in 1635 and in every subsequent campaign, to concentrate resources in order to create one army-corps – or sometimes to amalgamate two or three corps – with a much greater operational strength. The inevitable effect of this was both to drain the initial strength from other theatres, and to give priority in the allocation of campaign recruitment to one campaign theatre.

Initially, the crown did not envisage an increase in the number of troops to be set *sur pied* for the 1636 campaign. The one extra element in the scale of the French military establishment would come from the addition of a German mercenary army-corps. The negotiations begun with Saxe-Weimar in 1635 had finally been concluded at Saint-Germain on 27 October 1635, with a formal agreement that the crown would pay the duke 4 million *livres* per year to support an army of 12,000 infantry and 6,000 cavalry in French service.[109] In principle this represented a great increase in the number of troops in French service, but as both parties conspicuously failed to honour the terms of the contract down to Saxe-Weimar's death in 1639, the reality – at least in purely numerical terms – was less impressive.

---

[108] 22,000 infantry in the Army of Flanders, 8,000 in La Force, 8,000 in La Valette's army, 11,000 in Italy, 12,000 in the Valtelline, 5,000–6,000 in Lorraine; cavalry: 4,000 with Army of Flanders, 1500 with La Force, 1,500 with La Valette, 1,800 for Italy, 500 for Rohan, 500 (?) initially in Lorraine.

[109] Noailles, *Saxe-Weimar*, pp. 189–90 – full text printed as appendix 1, pp. 481–6.

The size of the French army

Otherwise, the ministers' plan for 1636 simply involved the redistribution of a military establishment similar to that of the preceding campaign. The strategic logic underlying these changes was not always evident. Although Rohan's campaign in the Valtelline had offered one of the few clear successes of 1635, his army-corps was to be scaled down in the next campaign to send more troops to the army of Italy, despite the fact that Rohan was also intended to launch an invasion of the Spanish Milanese from the north.[110] Thus, an *état* for the campaign of 1636 proposed that the army of Italy should be recruited up to 20,600 infantry and 2,520 cavalry, albeit partly made up of 3,000 infantry and 800 cavalry provided by the duke of Savoy.[111] By 15 May this army was reported to have an actual strength of between 15,000 and 16,000 infantry and 1,300 cavalry.[112] Yet despite this initial achievement, by early July d'Hémery reported to Richelieu that the corps was in need of reinforcements, and that it consisted of only 10,500 infantry, with another 3,000 still promised from the duke of Savoy.[113] However, in consequence of this decision to direct recruits towards the army of Italy, Rohan's corps for the Valtelline was budgeted at only 11,000–12,000 infantry and 500–600 cavalry.[114] In early June Richelieu reported to the king that Rohan was preparing to take the offensive against the Milanese with 8,000 infantry and 'whatever cavalry he possessed'.[115]

On the eastern frontier, the priority in the planning of the campaign was to build up the strength of the corps to be commanded by Henri II de Bourbon, prince de Condé, seconded by Richelieu's cousin, Charles de La Porte de La Meilleraye. This corps was intended to overrun the Franche-Comté in order to create a *place d'armes* for the French, who could then extract contributions from the civil population and use the territory as the base for attacks into the Empire. In theory this force was to be raised up to a total of 20,000 infantry and 8,000 cavalry, an effective strength which could only be achieved at the cost of the other corps on the eastern frontier.[116]

The victims of the priority given to Condé's army were the army-corps under the command of cardinal de La Valette operating in Alsace, supposedly in conjunction with the German forces of Saxe-Weimar, and the corps in Champagne under the overall command of Louis de Bourbon, comte de Soissons.[117] The *état* of 1636 allocated only 7,250 infantry and 2,000 cavalry to La Valette, a

---

[110] Richelieu, *Mémoires*, IX. 123.
[111] AAE CP Savoie 24, fo. 27, 12 Jan. 1636; in May Richelieu wrote to the king that the army of Italy was to be of 20,000 infantry and 3,000 cavalry: Avenel, v. 459, 12 May 1636.
[112] AAE CP Savoie 24, fo. 342, 2 May 1636, d'Hémery reporting to Richelieu and still anticipating a number of levies to bring the corps up to this total.
[113] AAE CP Savoie 24, fos. 626, 640, 3/15 July 1636.
[114] AAE MD 820, fo. 201 – *Armées du Roi*.
[115] Avenel, v. 475, 3 June 1636 ('ce qu'il a de cavalerie').
[116] Aumale, *Princes de Condé*, III. 272; Piépape, *Franche-Comté*, I. 389 n. 3.
[117] BN Ms.fr. 6647, fo. 7, 5 Aug. 1636, de Noyers to La Valette, notifying La Valette that Condé has already received two detachments of reinforcements to replenish his army.

The military context

minimal total for the opening of a campaign and which could be contrasted with the decision to allocate 15,400 infantry and 4,800 cavalry to the same corps in the 1635 campaign.[118] Although it was intended that additional troops would raise the army to 12,100 infantry and 2,900 cavalry by the middle of the campaign season, this calculation depended upon the unrealistic assumption that four twenty-company regiments allocated to La Valette's corps could be recruited up to 1,500 infantry each.[119] The forces under Soissons in Champagne were even weaker. In early June the ministers were concerned that this army-corps, which a *revue* had previously established at around 10,900 infantry and 3,300 cavalry, actually consisted of only 4,500 infantry and 1,500 cavalry.[120] The lower figures seem quite probable: by an order of 19 May, Soissons had been commanded to send seven elite cavalry companies and two infantry regiments to support the army of La Valette, while on 22 June he was instructed to send 1,000 cavalry to the army of Condé.[121]

All of this was changed by the successive invasions of France, beginning in the first days of July with the Spanish advance into Champagne with 10,000–12,000 infantry and 13,000 cavalry.[122] Soissons was ordered to combine his troops with those of the governor of Picardy, Honoré d'Albert, duc de Chaulnes, who brought with him a handful of the soldiers who had been transported back by sea after wintering without pay in the United Provinces. Together the forces amounted to no more than 8,000 infantry and 1,000 cavalry.[123]

Up to this point, the main ministerial effort had been focused upon maintaining Condé's corps at a high effective strength to sustain the siege of Dôle. In late July, Sublet de Noyers gave his opinion that the siege army was still of some 15,000–20,000 troops.[124] But the lack of progress in advancing the siege was matched by the growing threat to Paris posed by the Spanish advance. With the

---

[118] AAE MD 819, fo. 70, [1635], *état* of the army of cardinal de La Valette; a *revue général* of the cavalry with the army carried out on 31 May gave the total strength at 2,122, though this depended upon taking the word of colonel Batilly that his foreign cavalry regiment contained 800 soldiers: AAE CP Allemagne 14, fo. 64.

[119] AAE MD 820, fo. 206: regts of Rambures, Nettancourt, Turenne, Rebé.

[120] SHAT A¹ 28, fo. 7, 2 June 1636, de Noyers to Soissons, informing him of the decision to send the sieur Clanleu, *commissaire des guerres*, to investigate the strength of the forces at Soissons' disposal, largely because of suspicions of financial irregularities rather than concern at the military vulnerability of Champagne. AAE MD 823, fo. 240 [undated], instructions to Clanleu.

[121] SHAT A¹ 27, fo. 420, 19 May 1636, de Noyers to Soissons; Avenel, v. 488, 22 June 1636, Richelieu to Louis XIII; Soissons had been promised two companies of *gendarmes* in exchange for these 1,000 cavalry, but these too were despatched to the army of Condé by an order of 23 June: SHAT A¹ 28, fos. 32, 124, 9/23 June 1636, de Noyers to Soissons, de Noyers to Condé.

[122] AAE MD 821, fo. 106, 25 July 1636, Chavigny to Mazarin, reporting the strength of the Spanish army at time of the capture of La Capelle.

[123] AAE MD 1678, fo. 193, 8 Aug. 1636, Soissons to Louis XIII. This could be contrasted with Chavigny's grossly optimistic assessment that the combined forces could muster 4,000 cavalry: Aubery, *Richelieu*, I. 661, 25 July 1636, Chavigny to cardinal de La Valette.

[124] Aubery, *Richelieu*, I. 670, 31 July 1636, de Noyers to La Meilleraye.

The size of the French army

decision to lift the siege of Dôle on 15 August, some 6,000 infantry and 3,000 cavalry were hastily pulled out from the remnants of Condé's army and despatched northwards.[125] Yet by mid-August the troops under Soissons' command had been battered and sustained losses to the point where these reinforcements from the Franche-Comté would not be enough to create a corps capable of confronting even a depleted Spanish invasion force. Anxious both to halt the Spanish advance, and, equally importantly, to push them back out of Champagne before they could establish their winter quarters there, Louis XIII and his ministers projected the creation of a vast new army to be raised around Paris, with a target strength in late August of 25,000 infantry and 11,000 cavalry, a target which had been raised by mid-September to 35,000 foot and 12,000 horse.[126] A huge proportion of this corps thus had to be raised from new and unanticipated levies, imposed during a campaign where the maintenance of Condé's army at the siege of Dôle, the levies of troops in Provence for the army of Italy and the attempt to maintain the positions on the eastern frontier had already imposed considerable strains on the capacity to recruit additional troops.[127] The need to divert troops to suppress revolt in the south-west had added an additional burden to the military establishment; with the news of the *croquant* risings in Angoumois, Richelieu had given his opinion that 'il est impossible de les réprimer que par la force: il faut, par nécessité, de vieilles troupes', and proposed sending the regiments of La Meilleraye, Montmège and Caloñge together with a substantial force of *chevaux-légers*.[128] Some effort was made to shift the financial burden for the levies in north-east France on to the provinces, while the Paris office-holding and merchant oligarchy had offered in principle to raise and support 20,000 troops, including 4,000–5,000 cavalry, for the duration of the crisis.[129] Obtaining these financial contributions proved more difficult in practice; the Paris levy failed to yield the numbers which had been anticipated, while disputes quickly arose concerning the responsibility for the maintenance of the new units.[130] The maréchal de La Force claimed that he assisted in the levy of 7,000–8,000 infantry and 1,200–1,300 cavalry in Paris, substantially fewer than had originally been anticipated.[131] Even the target strength of the army had been

---

[125] SHAT A¹ 41, fo. 176, 23 Aug. 1636, Louis XIII and de Noyers to Condé.
[126] BN Ms.fr. 6647, fo. 49, 23 Aug. 1636, Richelieu to cardinal de La Valette; Aubery, *Richelieu*, I. 691, 13 Sept. 1636, Bouthillier to La Valette; I. 695, 22 Sept. 1636, Richelieu to La Valette.
[127] SHAT A¹ 28, fos. 164, 179, 27/30 June 1636, *états* of troops sent to the provinces in revolt.
[128] Avenel, v. 485, 21 June 1636,
[129] SHAT A¹ 32, fo. 141, 9 Aug. 1636, de Noyers to Valençay, citing the offer in the context of a commission to Valençay.
[130] SHAT A¹ 32, fos. 149, 150, 14 Aug. 1636; A¹ 30, fo. 35, 7 Oct. 1636, de Noyers to the *prévôt des marchands*, ordering him to make arrangements for the support of regiments at Langres which were the financial responsibility of the citizens of Paris; fo. 183, 24 Oct. 1636, de Noyers to d'Argenson concerning pay of six companies levied by Paris.
[131] La Force, *Mémoires*, III. 176.

The military context

scaled down by late September, when Bouthillier reported that the force was to be of 30,000 infantry and 5,000 cavalry.[132]

At the same time that this additional force was being raised, another army of volunteer cavalry, nobles raised under the *arrière-ban*, and infantry recruited largely through the clientele of Henri II d'Orléans, duc de Longueville, was being assembled in Normandy. The subsequent pay and subsistence of these troops was to be met by the crown, adding another 8,000 foot and 2,000 horse to the overall financial burden.[133] By this stage the invasion of Burgundy by Imperial troops was the main cause for ministerial concern, and the Normandy levies, reported to be of 5,000–6,000 infantry and 1,500 cavalry, were ordered southwards.[134] Given the extremely high rates of desertion and illness in the newly levied units, the ministry continued to issue instructions for the levy of new troops through September and October. In late October, La Force reported that 8,000–9,000 men were still being recruited to maintain the strength of the main army in Champagne.[135] The ministry had hoped to defer some of the levies that it had ordered from other provinces until the spring of 1637, but the Spanish invasion of Guienne in November ensured that these had to proceed as planned.[136] This Spanish invasion and the capture of Saint-Jean de Luz resulted in urgent appeals to the governor of Guienne, Jean-Louis de Nogaret de La Valette, duc d'Epernon, to raise troops on his own authority – and credit – to force the Spanish back across the frontier.

The confusion surrounding the levies, and the very short life of large numbers of the units raised in the recruitment panic of August and September makes any evaluation of the numbers of troops raised and maintained across the whole of 1636 exceptionally difficult. Before giving credence to inflated figures for *l'année de Corbie*, it should be recognized that significant numbers of troops were simply moved between campaign theatres: the core of the French army that advanced into Champagne and Picardy in September was made up of troops from Condé's army of the Franche-Comté; the forces in Burgundy resisting the invasion of Gallas and the Imperial army were hastily strengthened with troops, especially from cardinal de La Valette's corps, which had been planned to support the campaign in the north-east but never despatched. However, the total number of troops initially available to face the Imperial invasion was given at no more than 7,000 infantry and 2,300 cavalry.[137] After the recapture of Corbie on 10 November, the ministers decided to despatch 4,000–5,000 infantry and

---

[132] Aubery, *Richelieu*, I. 696, 22 Sept. 1636, Bouthillier to La Valette.
[133] AAE MD 821, fo. 184, 15 Aug. 1636, Jacques Dyel, sr de Miroménil, *intendant* at Rouen, to Richelieu, concerning the details of this levy.
[134] Aubery, *Richelieu*, I. 700, 5 Oct. 1636, de Noyers to La Valette; I. 702, 10 Oct 1636, Louis XIII to La Valette.
[135] La Force, *Mémoires*, III. 183.
[136] For the orders to cancel these levies, see SHAT A^1 29, fos. 144–5, 5 Sept. 1636; A^1 32, fo. 185, 25 Sept. 1636, fo. 250, [no date]. For the revised instructions, see A^1 31, fos. 279–80, 6 Nov. 1636.
[137] Aubery, II. 25, cardinal de La Valette to Père Joseph.

The size of the French army

3,000–4,000 cavalry from Champagne to supplement the army conducting the defence of Burgundy.[138]

No formal *revue* of the army that was first assembled around Paris seems to have survived; it was unlikely that the total of cavalry ever approached the target strength of 11,000 horse, but at the moment when the decision was taken to despatch 3,000–4,000 cavalry towards Burgundy, a series of *revues* gave the total cavalry strength in Champagne at 4,141 horse of all types.[139] Yet even taking into account these twin caveats about the redeployment of existing forces and the gap between aspiration and reality in subsequent recruitment, it is probable that the levels of additional recruitment from August until the end of the campaign briefly raised the numbers of troops under arms above the numbers that had been set *sur pied* at the outset. For a few weeks the ministry may have been maintaining 70,000–80,000 infantry and 10,000–15,000 cavalry, probably the highest real total achieved during either the ministries of Richelieu or Mazarin.

1637 began under the shadow of a financial crisis, and this, manifested in the collapse of the Valtelline army in March, created greater hesitation about exceeding more modest totals for the levies of troops at the beginning of the campaign. As suggested earlier, the *surintendants* abandoned the *contrôle générale* with its explicit undertaking to provide *montres* against an overall, stipulated, budget. But even on the less specific *états* for 1637, the total recruitment targets are considerably smaller than those for 1635 and 1636: the maximum allocation of infantry to the campaign armies was of some 89,000 men, together with an allowance for 21,220 troops in 'garrisons', and about 24,500 cavalry. Moreover, these totals were based upon the assumption that the constituent regiments were at full strength – that twenty company regiments contained 1,200 infantry and cavalry companies contained 60 horse.[140] This intention to limit the size of the armies conflicted with the aspirations of some of the commanders and officials in the campaign theatres. A 'mémoire pour la guerre d'Italie en l'année 1637', written in early January by maréchal Créquy and d'Hémery, expressed the hope that the campaign army in Italy would be recruited up to 24,000 infantry and 5,000–6,000 cavalry, France providing 20,000 of the infantry and 4,500 cavalry.[141] In contrast, the ministerial estimates for the total projected size of the army of Italy varied between 12,000 infantry and 1,960 horse and 16,800 infantry and 1,820 cavalry – all of these allocations assuming that the regiments would serve at the beginning of the campaign with a full strength of 1,200 soldiers.[142]

The reality during the subsequent campaign was an army of Italy that, starting

---

[138] AAE MD 1678, fo. 466, 10 Nov. 1636, Chavigny to Richelieu.
[139] AAE MD 1678, fos. 472–4, 11 Nov. 1636, *extrait général des revues*.
[140] AAE MD 828, fos. 265–89, 311–23, 330–51, [1637].
[141] AAE CP Savoie 25, fo. 12, 11 Jan. 1637.
[142] AAE MD 828, fos. 282–3v [1637].

The military context

from a relatively low initial strength and without significant reinforcements during the campaign, was simply unable to undertake more than token operations. In early September, d'Hémery wrote that the field army had a theoretical strength of only 8,000 which, removing the sick, the *passe-volans* and the valets, left only around 5,500 effectives.[143] By the end of the campaign a *revue* revealed that the army was reduced to 6,200 infantry and 900–1,000 cavalry *including* the troops provided by the duchy of Savoy.[144]

The largest number of French troops were again to be concentrated on the north-eastern frontier in 1637. Two army-corps were to operate here, one under the command of cardinal de La Valette, and the other under maréchal Châtillon. The theoretical strength of La Valette's corps was to be of 15,000 infantry and 5,720 cavalry, while a second estimate suggests 12,160 infantry and 6,440 cavalry, though both sets of figures are based on the calculations of the armies with the units at 'full' (60 per cent: 1,200 per regiment and 60 per company) strength.[145] The variations between the *états* are probably less significant than the indication that the ministers were gaining some perception of the immensity of the task of keeping the army-corps at a reasonably effective strength for several months of campaigning: the first of these *états* projects the levy or despatch of an additional 10,500 infantry and 1,100 cavalry between June and the end of August.[146] The assembly of troops for Châtillon's corps was to take place a few weeks later than La Valette's – again, in an attempt to compensate for the problems of troop loss – and was allocated a theoretical maximum of 11,700 foot and 4,540 cavalry.[147] From the outset it was clear that the actual number of troops available to them was much smaller than the funding projections made before the campaign opened. Reports from general *revues* for the armies of La Valette and Châtillon early in the campaign reveal that the infantry total for La Valette's army was 7,500 infantry, Châtillon's just over 8,000.[148] On 9 June Richelieu wrote to La Valette expressing concern that, although he was receiving funding for 15,000 infantry and 7,000 cavalry, La Valette admitted to having only 10,000 troops in total.[149] In July La Valette was specifically asked to suppress the details of a *revue* of his army, which showed only 8,000–9,000 infantry, out of concern that this would alarm the Dutch allies.[150]

Even in this, the campaign theatre with the highest priority, the scale of military operations was considerably reduced from the two previous years. If such a

---

[143] AAE CP Savoie 25, fo. 420, 9 Sept. 1637, d'Hémery to Richelieu.
[144] AAE CP Savoie 25, fo. 582, 15 Nov. 1637, d'Hémery to Richelieu.
[145] AAE MD 828, fos. 268–9, fo. 311, [1637].
[146] AAE MD 828, fo. 268v.
[147] AAE MD 828, fo. 273.
[148] AAE MD 828, fos. 269, 273 [1637], these figures, specified as the *état au vrai* of the constituent units, is pencilled into the left-hand margin of the formal *états*.
[149] Aubery, II. 37.
[150] Avenel, v. 1044, 22 July 1637, Richelieu to La Valette.

decision had ensured that the existing armies were better provided with additional recruits in the middle and towards the end of the campaign, the overall effect of a lower level of troop allocation to the various theatres might have been beneficial, at least for the continuity of the war-effort. The practical evidence for such an improvement is unconvincing. Certainly La Valette received 7,000–8,000 reinforcements for his corps at the end of August in order to sustain the siege of La Capelle, lost to the Spanish invasion in 1636.[151] Meanwhile, Châtillon was attempting to take Damvillers with his army-corps, a protracted siege which, after the fall of La Capelle, also drew in the remnants of La Valette's army. After the fall of Damvillers in late October, it was clear that even the combined corps was incapable of achieving anything further.

The ministers had still not abandoned the hope of overrunning the Franche-Comté, and in 1637 this operation was to be conferred upon Condé's brother-in-law, the duc de Longueville. The troops were assembled from a variety of different sources: Longueville himself was allocated only 2,500 infantry and 1,590 cavalry on the most detailed *état*, but this was to be supplemented by an (optimistic) estimate of 4,800 foot and 366 cavalry returning after the collapse of Rohan's army-corps in the Valtelline,[152] and by 5,600 infantry and 640 cavalry initially allocated to Condé in Burgundy but transferred to Longueville when he assumed command of the invasion of the Comté. Once again, there was some attempt to make provision for adequate reinforcements later in the campaign season, a theoretical total of 4,500 infantry and 2,100 cavalry.[153] Some of the French troops from the army of the Valtelline did finally reach the army of Longueville, together with a few of the projected reinforcements, but their numbers had no effect upon Longueville's decision to abandon the offensive in mid-August because he considered that his forces had become too weak.[154]

Saxe-Weimar's army-corps, the key to French strategy in the Empire, was admitted to be only 4,000 infantry and 2,000 cavalry in late January, one third of the theoretical obligation under the funding treaty with France.[155] In consequence, it was assumed that if Saxe-Weimar were to achieve any strategic objective he would need to be supported by a French corps operating in Alsace and across the Rhine. These troops were to be placed under the command of François de l'Hôpital, seigneur du Hallier, and were anticipated on the *états* at between 9,650 and 10,250 infantry and 1,500 and 1,440 cavalry.[156] Saxe-Weimar himself was promised 3,000 French infantry and 500 cavalry to strengthen his

---

[151] Aubery, ii. 79, 31 Aug. 1637.
[152] The ministerial estimates of the troops which could be transferred from the Valtelline were slightly higher; in early May it was suggested that 5,000 infantry and 1,000 cavalry would be available: Aubery, *Richelieu*, II. 797, 5 May 1637, Louis XIII to La Cour.
[153] AAE MD 828, fos. 276–8v [1637].
[154] Piépape, *Franche-Comté*, II. 84.
[155] Avenel, v. 735, 26 Jan. 1636, Richelieu to Charnacé.
[156] AAE MD 828, fos. 279b, 340 [1637].

The military context

army in late September, and these were to be made up from the remnants of Longueville's corps, already worn down by campaigning in Franche-Comté.[157]

The late 1636 Spanish invasion of coastal Guienne still needed to be driven back across the frontiers, and *états* at the beginning of the campaign proposed totals of troops between 10,000 and 11,200 infantry and 580 to 680 cavalry.[158] However, these were mostly to be *nouvelles levées*, to be raised in the province by Epernon and his son Bernard de Nogaret, duc de La Valette. Given Epernon's hostility to Richelieu, and the lack of activity that characterized this theatre after the suppression of the *croquants*, it seems unlikely that the levies took place, or that the existing troops in Guienne, aside from the House units of the Epernon, were maintained at a high effective strength.

In the midst of these setbacks and the obvious inadequacy of resources, the ministry was forced to meet a further military commitment generated by the Spanish invasion of Languedoc in September. The Spanish invading force of 12,000–14,000 Spanish infantry and 1,200 cavalry encountered modest resistance and was able to besiege Leucate.[159] The governor of the province, the duc d'Halluin had little choice but to raise an army-corps through his own initiatives, drawing on those regiments which were still being assembled in Languedoc, and summoning the local militias. The corps finally included the regiments of Languedoc, Vitry, Saint-André and Castelan, all with the exception of Languedoc heavily composed of new recruits.[160] A *revue* of this army just before the engagement with the Spanish gave 10,000 infantry and 900 cavalry.[161] Although the relief of Leucate was a success, the victorious forces rapidly dwindled away, with the complete disintegration of the militia contingents and the regular units falling to 3,500 men by October.[162]

It is probable that some 60,000–70,000 infantry and cavalry were either in existence or levied during the first months of 1637, and that, given the relative speed with which the campaign lost momentum, perhaps as few as 30,000–35,000 additional troops were raised as mid- and late-campaign levies. If the attempt to keep units at high effective strength down to the very end of 1636 had imposed such a heavy strain on the *épargne*, in the following year the collapse in the effective strength of many of the army-corps by August contributed to the exceptionally low military expenditure for 1637.

---

[157] BN Ms.fr. 3767, fo. 26, 26 Sept. 1637, Louis XIII to Saxe-Weimar; fo. 23 indicates that these troops are to be drawn from Longueville's army.
[158] AAE MD 828, fos. 284v, 311, 347.
[159] Sourdis, *Correspondance*, I. 507, 29 Sept. 1637, 'Relation de la levée du siège de Leucate par les Espagnols'; Vassal-Reig, *Roussillon*, pp. 44–51.
[160] Aubery, *Richelieu*, II. 49, 28 June 1637, Richelieu to duc d'Halluin (created maréchal de Schomberg – 27 Oct. 1637); Sourdis, *Correspondance*, I. 504
[161] Vassal-Reig, *Roussillon*, p. 56; Sourdis, *Correspondance*, I. 507–8, gives a total of 11,000 infantry and 800–900 horse, and this is confirmed by an undated *revue*: AAE MD 828, fo. 260 (1637).
[162] Vassal-Reig, *Roussillon*, p. 71.

The size of the French army

The lacklustre military performance of 1637, and the failure to regain the initiative after the setbacks of 1636, may have helped to stave off financial crisis but they threatened Richelieu and the other ministers with the no less dangerous prospect of the collapse of royal support for the war-effort. The *états* for 1638 show a reversion to a large-scale offensive strategy. The maximum levels of recruitment for the 1638 campaign season were renegotiated from the modest 85,000–89,000 infantry in 1637 up to 132,000 for 1638, and from 24,500 to 32,000 cavalry.[163] The allocation of troops between theatres in 1638 establishes a pattern which remains characteristic of the French war-effort until 1642, with a massive concentration of troops in the north-east, ultimately drawing on 50 per cent, even 60 per cent, of the available manpower.

The largest of the army-corps in 1638, which was to invade Flanders in accordance with the military agreement made with the Dutch, was variously projected as having a maximum strength of 19,500 infantry and 6,430 cavalry. Neatly making the point about the manner in which these calculations exaggerated even the theoretical number of troops budgeted, allowing for the 10 per cent recruitment premium, the maintenance of officers' valets at unit expense and – possibly – the multiple wages paid to officers and NCOs, the same *états* reduced these totals to 17,100 infantry and 5,395 cavalry.[164] This force was to be commanded by Châtillon, while a supporting army was to be created under the command of La Force, with the intention that it should recruited up to 16,200 infantry and 8,020 cavalry (14,300 and 6,710).[165] A third army was to operate on the north-eastern frontier, carrying out an invasion of Luxembourg under the command of maréchal Brézé, and was projected at a maximum of 15,500 infantry and 4,920 cavalry (12,250 and 4,050).[166] These three armies, envisaged as sharing a single theatre of operations and potentially a common strategy, dominated the war-effort. Yet the scale of the preparations for 1638 ensured that, at least in theory, some of the other army-corps benefited from a more generous allocation of troops. After the setback of 1637 when Longueville was provided with wholly inadequate forces to invade the Franche-Comté, his army in 1638 was given a target strength of 16,700 infantry and 4,190 cavalry (13,800 and 3,560).[167] The target for the army of Italy was also substantially increased, with plans for 21,200 infantry and 3,910 cavalry. In accordance with Louis XIII and Richelieu's strategy of opening up a campaign theatre against Spain itself, Condé was allocated 14,400

---

[163] AAE MD 832, fos. 1–19 [1638]. Etats of the armies to be set *sur pied* for 1638. For the *états* of both 1637 and 1638 the allowance for 'garrisons' is treated separately from the allocations to the field armies.
[164] AAE MD 832, fos. 3–5 [1638].
[165] AAE MD 832, fos. 6–7.
[166] AAE MD 832, fos. 8–9.
[167] AAE MD 832, fos. 10, 11.

The military context

infantry and 2,190 cavalry to operate from Guienne.[168] The *état* included provision for 5,500 troops under the command of Jean-Baptiste Budes, comte de Guébriant, which were to be sent to support Saxe-Weimar's army.

These were, of course, merely ideal allocations of troops, based on the assumption that the units could be recruited up to full strength. Yet in one or two cases at the beginning of the campaign real numbers proved comparable with the ideal. A full *revue* of La Force's army gave the infantry total as 13,392 infantry and 2,508 cavalry, an impressive achievement of above 90 per cent of the target for infantry, even if the cavalry fell two-thirds short of the projected 6,710.[169] Similarly, a full *revue* of the troops to serve in the Franche-Comté under Longueville gave 11,032 infantry and 3,296 cavalry, in both cases within 95 per cent of the target strengths.[170] In other corps recruitment proceeded less smoothly. A *revue* of Brézé's army at the beginning of the campaign gave only 7,052 infantry and 2,466 cavalry, around 60 per cent of the projected totals.[171] Châtillon's army-corps, intended to be the largest of those raised in 1638, proved exceptionally slow to recruit up to effective strength. Arguing that he could not safely attempt the siege of a major *place* such as Saint-Omer or Arras without a minimum of 15,000 infantry and 5,000 cavalry, Châtillon had still not assembled his army at the end of April.[172] By his own account he possessed only 10,000 infantry and 3,000 cavalry when he was persuaded to move across the frontiers and, on 1 June, to lay siege to Saint-Omer.[173]

Though La Force's army, intended to act as a covering force for Châtillon, was of a high effective strength, the inevitable consequence of a protracted siege was to create a virtually bottomless drain on manpower. Châtillon continued to insist that the army required for the siege of a *place* the size of Saint-Omer needed to be maintained at a minimum of 15,000 troops. His letters to Richelieu and de Noyers assumed an ideal strength for the army under his command, and were full of complaints that recruitment targets and arrangements for the despatch of additional units had not been fulfilled.[174] In fact, *revues* indicate that the army had been raised to some 12,000 infantry and 4,000 cavalry in early June, with the promise of up to another 1,800 cavalry.[175] In these circumstances, the ministers decided not to run the risk of a major setback, and ordered the entire army of La Force to move immediately towards Saint-Omer to support Châtillon's siege. On

---

[168] AAE MD 832, fo. 15.
[169] AAE MD 832 fos. 27 *et seq.*, [early 1638], *extrait* of the *revue* of La Force's army.
[170] AAE MD 832, fos. 47–49.
[171] AAE MD 832, fos. 38–46.
[172] Aubery, *Richelieu*, II. 132, 20 May 1638, Châtillon to de Noyers.
[173] Aubery, *Richelieu*, II. 144, 145, 1 June, Richelieu to Châtillon, Châtillon to de Noyers.
[174] Aubery, *Richelieu*, II. 145, 149–50, 152, 1/4/6 June 1638, Châtillon to de Noyers.
[175] Aubery, II. 146, 2 June 1638, de Noyers to Châtillon; a specific *revue* of the army on 17 and 20 May gave Châtillon's army-corps at 12,103 infantry and 4,169 cavalry, proposing that a further 2,610 infantry and 1,070 cavalry were allocated to the army: AAE MD 832, fos. 125–8.

The size of the French army

the basis of the pre-campaign targets for the strength of both corps, this ought to have created a combined army of 35,000 infantry and 10,000 cavalry.[176] In fact a secret *mémoire* gave the total strength of the two armies at 22,000 men, adding that Brézé's force, which was subsequently brought into the theatre to try to safeguard communications, was 8,000 troops.[177] The subsequent abandonment of the siege of Saint-Omer inflicted a further battering on the overall numbers of these army-corps. In an attempt to maintain the combined force at effective strength for the second half of the campaign, orders were despatched for the levy of a further 10,000 recruits, though these did little to encourage the commanders to attempt anything more ambitious than the recapture of Câtelet, so that by mid-September the campaign in the north-east was over.

Though Saxe-Weimar's victory at Rheinfelden on 3 March 1638 had enhanced his status at the French Court, this enthusiasm was not matched by the commitment of French troops to support his military operations.[178] Despite receiving 2,500 reinforcements under the command of Guébriant in early May, Saxe-Weimar still possessed only 13,000–14,000 men in total, and the strength of Imperial forces in Alsace made his projected siege of Breisach extremely hazardous.[179] By late May Longueville's army-corps in the Franche-Comté had been increased by the arrival of recruits to some 13,000 men, and he had also received instructions to form a special corps of 4,000 infantry and 2,000 cavalry ready for rapid despatch 'wherever necessary'.[180] Yet at precisely the moment when Saxe-Weimar had committed himself to the siege of Breisach, the defeat of Longueville at Poligny rendered the situation in the Franche-Comté sufficiently uncertain that the French ministers were not prepared to risk moving the army-corps into the Empire. Instead, Henri de La Tour d'Auvergne, vicomte de Turenne, would be sent with 2,000 infantry and 1,500 horse, originally intended to conduct operations in Lorraine, and Longueville would be instructed to send an additional 2,000 of his infantry.[181] On 15 September, Saxe-Weimar again wrote to the king to complain that he had not received the promised 2,000 reinforcements from Longueville, and that the success of his siege was now very much in doubt.[182]

---

[176] Quazza, *Tommaso di Savoia-Carignano*, p. 232.
[177] Aubery, *Richelieu*, II. 213, 9 Aug. 1638, *Mémoire secrète*.
[178] Noailles, *Saxe-Weimar*, pp. 268–85.
[179] AAE, CP Savoie 26, fo. 225v, 21 May 1638, Chavigny to Richelieu. The decision to send Guébriant's force had been taken in mid-March. There was considerable concern in Paris that when news reached these troops that they were to be sent into the Empire it would lead to mass desertion, and an attempt was made to bribe them to stay in service: BN Ms.fr. 3767, fo. 52, 14 Mar 1638, de Noyers to Saxe-Weimar. This did not prevent the original 4,000 being reduced to 2,500 on arrival with Saxe-Weimar: Noailles, *Saxe-Weimar*, pp. 312–13.
[180] Piépape, *Franche-Comté*, II. 98; SHAT, A¹ 46, fo. 251, 1 June 1638, de Noyers to duc d'Enghien, informing him of this instruction to Longueville. The evasiveness of the destination was once again to avoid the inevitable losses from desertion that would follow upon the news that these troops were to be sent to the Empire.
[181] SHAT A¹ 46, fo. 251, 1 June.
[182] BN Ms.fr. 3767, fos. 80–2, 15 Sept. 1638, Saxe-Weimar to Louis XIII.

The military context

The campaign in Italy was overshadowed by concern that adequate financial and material provision would not be made in the face of an imminent offensive by the Spanish.[183] In mid-May, the army of Italy was reported to be 11,000–12,000 infantry, which the commander, cardinal de La Valette, suggested amounted to no more than 9,000 effectives. Of these, 3,000 needed to be placed in garrison in Casale and 1,000 in other *places*, leaving only 5,000 to form a field army.[184] Financial neglect continued, despite repeated setbacks that brought the Spanish forces deep into Piedmont. The army received reinforcements during the campaign, but these had been of poor quality, and hit by such high levels of desertion that some units had to be disbanded on arrival with the corps.[185] La Valette wrote with some bitterness in late 1638 that had he received the sums intended for the army of Italy it would have been possible to have maintained 12,000 troops in Piedmont. In reality he had never possessed more than 6,000 troops able to take the field.[186]

The opening of a campaign theatre on the Atlantic frontier with Spain had not been envisaged in 1635 as part of France's grand strategy. If the original projection in the *états* of 1638 for an army-corps in the south had been 14,400 infantry and 2,190 cavalry, a combination of inadequate financial allocation and the ministerial awareness that the army would not face any serious opposition on the Atlantic coast combined to scale down the commitment.[187] After Condé had taken Le Passage and had moved on to lay siege to Fuenterrabía, he wrote to Henri d'Escoubleau de Sourdis that the latter should with some urgency provide 3,000 marines to garrison Passage, since his own army was insufficient for the siege of Fuenterrabía.[188] On 23 August Richelieu notified Condé that Charles de Nanteuil, maréchal de Schomberg, had instructions to raise another 4,000 recruits in Languedoc to reinforce the siege army, but before these had been assembled the army had collapsed in the face of a Spanish relief expedition.[189]

As expected, the centrepiece of French strategy and the main concentration of troops in 1639 remained the northern and eastern frontiers. La Meilleraye, *grand*

---

[183] AAE CP Savoie 26, fos. 70, 90, 18/24 Feb. 1638, d'Hémery to Richelieu, complaining that financial incompetence had resulted in the loss of some 50,000 *écus* destined for the army, and stressing the need for the extra three regiments anticipated on the new *état* for the army of Italy.

[184] AAE, CP Savoie 26, fo. 214, 17 May 1638, La Valette to Richelieu.

[185] AAE CP Savoie 26, fo. 735, [late 1638], *état* showing that nine *régiments d'augmentation* had been sent to the army of Italy during the campaign, together with twenty-eight companies of cavalry; fo. 214, 17 May 1638, La Valette to Richelieu on the need to disband newly arrived units.

[186] AAE CP Savoie 26, fo. 607, 9 Nov. 1638, La Valette to Chavigny ('mais je ne jamais passe 6,000 hommes').

[187] Sourdis, *Correspondance*, II. 12–13, 12 May 1638, Condé to Bordeaux: 'Il n'y a pas un sou à la recette générale de toutes les assignations à moi données.'; Avenel, VI. 55, 20 June, Richelieu to Condé, complaining of the inactivity of the army, although it was not facing any significant enemy forces.

[188] Sourdis, *Correspondance*, II. 34–5, 8 July.

[189] Avenel, VI. 105–6.

The size of the French army

maître de l'artillerie, was in theory to cross the Flanders frontier with 20,000 infantry and 7,500 cavalry. Anticipating the usual levels of wastage, Châtillon was to be placed in command of a second army, being levied slightly later in the year, which would march to join La Meilleraye when falling troop numbers started to endanger the siege of a selected *place*, and would provide cover against an enemy relief operation. The *état* proposed that Châtillon's army should be of 11,200 infantry and 8,000 cavalry.[190] Further support was to be provided by a third army under the command of Feuquières, intended to be of at least 10,000 infantry and 3,000 cavalry, and ordered to advance against another *place* so as to dissipate enemy resources.[191] In the interests of this 'major siege' strategy, the first ministerial priority was to strengthen the twin corps of La Meilleraye and Châtillon. Although Feuquières' corps was seen as an important element of the overall plan, drawing substantial Imperial forces away from the siege of Hesdin by a simultaneous operation, he received a much smaller allocation of troops. In early May his army still consisted of only 6,000–7,000 infantry and 1,500–2,000 cavalry.[192] By the time that he moved against Thionville in early June, Feuquières' army had been recruited up to 10,000 infantry and 4,000 cavalry, but surprised by Piccolomini's veteran army well supported by cavalry, the French corps was routed and its effective strength almost entirely destroyed.[193] In the aftermath of the battle, the *intendant* Choisy described assembling ten regiments with a total strength of 1,700 men, of whom many were badly wounded.[194]

On 12 June, just after Thionville, Châtillon reported that he had 10,000 infantry and 4,000 cavalry in his corps, and he proposed that after La Meilleraye's siege of Hesdin had ended, his own army should be strengthened by a further 2,000 cavalry and 4,000–5,000 infantry.[195] However, with La Meilleraye's army reduced to 10,000 infantry and 4,000 cavalry in the last stages of the siege, there was little possibility that Châtillon could be allocated the troops that would allow him to act independently of La Meilleraye without reducing the latter's army to a level of dangerous weakness.

With the ministry determined to wipe out the humiliation of Fuenterrabiá during the forthcoming campaign on the Pyrenean frontier, the initial *état*

---

[190] *Ibid.* Both forces demonstrate the belated ministerial recognition that a substantial cavalry contingent was essential for combat against the army of Flanders and the Imperial troops operating on the French frontiers – see chapter 1, pp. 59–65.

[191] AAE CP Lorraine 31, fo. 70, 11 May 1639, Feuquières to de Noyers.

[192] AAE CP Lorraine 31, fo. 70, 11 May 1639, Feuquières to de Noyers, explaining the dangers of trying to undertake a diversionary siege with the 6,000–7,000 infantry assembled at present; fo. 75, 17 May, justifying his decision to postpone an operation against Longwy.

[193] Avenel, VI. 380, 10 June 1639, Richelieu to La Meilleraye. AAE CP Lorraine 31, fos. 105–8 [*c*. 7/8 June 1639], account of the battle of Thionville which emphasizes that French and Imperial forces were of comparable size, but the Imperial forces possessed the advantage of surprise. Aubery, *Richelieu*, II. 348, 1 Sept. 1639, Châtillon to La Meilleraye on the quality of Piccolomini's army.

[194] AAE CP Lorraine 31, fo. 161, 25 June 1639, Choisy to de Noyers.

[195] Aubery, *Richelieu*, II. 301, 12 June 1639, Châtillon to Louis XIII.

The military context

allocated 16,600 infantry and 2,200 cavalry to Condé for 1639.[196] Far from Paris, and unconvinced that the ministry would give his army a high priority in the allocation of further recruits or finance, Condé showed little enthusiasm for an early opening of the campaign into Roussillon. Anger from Richelieu at this dilatoriness was heightened by a report – vigorously denied by Condé – that the army was drawing 25,000 bread rations a day, which implied that it contained at least 10,000 infantry.[197] When the army finally moved into Roussillon one serving officer spoke of 14,000 infantry and 2,500 cavalry.[198] But the heat of the summer and inadequate supplies took a heavy toll of the troops, and the militia and the *arrière-ban* who formed part of this army proved a consistent though predictable disappointment, deserting in large numbers throughout the summer months.[199] Though the fortress of Salces was captured, by the time the Spanish counter-attacked with 14,000 infantry and 3,000 cavalry the French forces had fallen to around 8,000 troops in total.[200] The decision was taken to withdraw back into Languedoc to reconstitute the army and to launch a relief operation. In the last week of October, Condé set out to lift the siege and engage the Spanish forces with an army of 22,000 infantry and 4,000 horse, a significant proportion of which were irregular troops – noble volunteers and provincial militias.[201] After the mass desertion that followed the collapse of this army, only 2,000 infantry and 500 cavalry regulars remained, though Condé promised that he would be able to rebuild the force to 15,000 troops before the end of the year in a last-ditch bid to relieve Salces.[202]

By 1639 the political and military situation in Piedmont had become so grave that the commander of the army-corps, cardinal de La Valette, could make an apparently irrefutable case for a more substantial commitment.[203] In consequence, the ministerial *état* did allocate some 13,400 infantry and up to 5,000 cavalry to Italy.[204] Despite this, in late March, La Valette wrote that on the basis of existing units and allocations the total infantry strength of his army would not exceed 8,000 men.[205] In reality the situation in early April when the Spanish forces

---

[196] BN Ms.fr. 17555, fo. 1, [July] 1639.
[197] Avenel, VI. 397, 19 June, Richelieu [to Condé]. Condé defended himself vigorously against this charge of drawing 25,000 rations in a letter of 28 June, arguing that the *états* made it clear that he had only claimed for 12,800 rations, and that the maximum claim for his army at present would be 18,000: AAE MD 1631, fo. 127, Condé to de Noyers.
[198] Campion, *Mémoires*, pp. 99–100. Campion was a lieutenant in the Normandie regiment, which Condé had succeeded in having transferred to Languedoc for the 1639 campaign.
[199] AAE MD 1631, fo. 127, 28 June, Condé to Richelieu, 'nous n'avons pas à l'armée encores trente gentilshommes et pas cinq cent de milice'.
[200] Campion, *Mémoires*, pp. 107–8.
[201] AAE, MD 1631, fo. 202, 27 Oct. 1639, Condé's account of the failure to relieve Salces.
[202] AAE MD 1631, fo. 208, 27 Oct. 1639, La Houdinière to Richelieu: part of this 15,000 was to be made up of 4,000 recruits who had arrived from the Vivarais.
[203] AAE CP Savoie 28, fo. 3, 4 Jan. 1639, cardinal de La Valette to Chavigny.
[204] BN Ms.fr. 17555, fo. 1, [July] 1639.
[205] AAE CP Savoie 28, fo. 157, 31 Mar. 1639, La Valette to Richelieu.

The size of the French army

opened their offensive proved worse than even this pessimistic estimate, and La Valette wrote that he had only 4,400 troops able to take the field.[206] On 20 April Richelieu wrote that an additional army-corps, under Longueville was to be sent down to Italy to buttress the French forces.[207] Longueville's troops finally arrived in Piedmont and joined up with La Valette, providing him with an additional 5,000 infantry and 1,700 cavalry.[208] As a result of this additional force, and allowing for the heavy commitment to garrisoning *places* in Piedmont, a *revue* of La Valette's army reported on 1 June indicated that there were 7,000 infantry in the campaign army, although the cavalry was described as being 'weaker than in 1638'.[209] Despite all these attempts to maintain the strength of the army, by late September, following the death of La Valette and the arrival of the comte d'Harcourt as replacement commander, the forces had been reduced to 5,000 infantry and 1,000 horse, while by late November this had fallen to 3,000 infantry.[210]

On 14 April 1640 Richelieu wrote to comte Godefroy d'Estrades, ambassador with prince Frederik Hendrik of Orange, that he should inform the States General of Holland that the army of La Meilleraye would consist of more than 20,000 infantry and 7,000 cavalry, and that, in addition to this army, Chaulnes (governor of Picardy) and Châtillon were to command another force, of 15,000 foot and 4,500 horse, which would stand against the Flanders frontier to support the actions of La Meilleraye. Furthermore, du Hallier was to have 7,000 foot and 1,500 horse to support operations in Lorraine and towards Luxembourg, while Charles de Neufville, sieur de Villeroy, the same size of force in Burgundy.[211] An element of this report certainly reflected Richelieu's concern to galvanize the Dutch into action by emphasizing France's commitment to the forthcoming campaign; reports to foreign governments are not the most reliable basis on which to establish precise troop strengths. *Etats* of these principal army-corps at the beginning of 1640 qualify some of these figures. La Meilleraye's army was given at 10,600 infantry and 2,200 cavalry, although Châtillon's force was considerably closer to Richelieu's claim, with 15,700 infantry and 4,020 cavalry.[212] In the same

---

[206] AAE CP Savoie 28 fo. 182, 11 Apr. 1639, La Valette to Richelieu.
[207] Avenel, VI. 326–7; the additional corps was to be of ten infantry regiments, and 2,000 cavalry: Avenel, VI. 354, 28 Apr. 1639, Richelieu to Condé.
[208] AAE CP Savoie 28, fo. 607, [no date], *état* of the army of Longueville on entering Piedmont; 2 of the infantry units – the elite foreign regiments of colonels Schmidtberg and Batilly – were not expected in Italy until mid-June.
[209] AAE CP Savoie 28, fo. 457, 1 June 1639, La Valette to Richelieu; a subsequent letter of La Valette indicates the problem of maintaining an effective corps, pointing out that three of his regiments – Roure, Montpezat and Roussillon do not add up to more than 400 men in total: Savoie 28, fo. 471, 2 June.
[210] AAE CP Savoie 29, fo. 536, 29 Nov. 1639, Henri de Lorraine, comte d'Harcourt to Chavigny.
[211] Avenel, VI. 681–2.
[212] AAE MD 837, fos. 247–54.

The military context

series of *états*, du Hallier's army was given at 5,700 infantry and 1,680 cavalry, Villeroy's at 4,500 foot and 1,100 horse.[213]

The corps were smaller to start with, the relative slowness with which the campaign was begun, and the decision that La Meilleraye's corps should launch an early invasion of Flanders specifically to support the activities of the Dutch army, all took their toll. As desertion and sickness depleted La Meilleraye's force, it became clear that a major siege on the frontiers would require the amalgamation of the armies of La Meilleraye and Châtillon. Châtillon's army had received a substantial block of reinforcements – 6,500 infantry and 800 cavalry – and by bringing together the two corps a combined force of some 24,000 infantry and 8,000 cavalry was created.[214] On 1 July the siege works were opened against Arras, and the city cut off. The presence of the king and of Richelieu, the determination to ensure that the siege received the highest priority in provisioning and the available financial resources ensured that the attrition rate for the army, while by no means light, was significantly lower than that prevailing in the other French corps. If the paper strength of the siege army had been around 32,000 troops on 1 July, this – by a rough estimate of Châtillon – had fallen to around 18,000 troops by the end of the month.[215]

Though the army-corps under du Hallier had been significantly enlarged since the opening of the campaign in order to conduct a substantial operation in Lorraine, the almost inevitable instruction arrived to move northwards in order to buttress the forces around Arras.[216] On 2 August, Bouthillier reported to Richelieu with some triumph that du Hallier's army of 19,000 men had arrived in the siege camp with 1,500 carts full of supplies and munitions, having fought off an enemy attempt to block their arrival.[217] Although the arrival of du Hallier assured the outcome of the siege, this commitment had a predictably destructive effect on the strength of his army-corps. As a result it was impossible for him to return to the original plan of an offensive in Lorraine after the conclusion of the siege.[218] Following the capitulation of Arras on 9 August it was equally clear that neither of the commanders of the other two forces proposed to undertake anything further, although six weeks later the two armies would still have contained a respectable number of troops if acting together: on 15 September a *revue* established the army of la Meilleraye at 9,750 infantry and 3,557 cavalry, that of Châtillon at 5,730 infantry and 3,094 cavalry.[219]

---

[213] AAE MD 837, fos. 255–6.
[214] AAE MD 837, fos. 250–4; Aubery, *Richelieu*, II. 524, 31 May 1640, memoir to Châtillon.
[215] AAE MD 1679, fo. 182, 2 Aug., Châtillon: 'Relation de ce qui s'est passé le deux^{me} aoust'.
[216] AAE CP Lorraine 31, fo. 361, 5 July, du Hallier announced that the army was ready to begin campaigning; fo. 363, 6 July, du Hallier confirmed that he has received orders for this change of strategy.
[217] Avenel, VI. 716–17, 2 Aug. 1640.
[218] AAE CP Lorraine 31, fo. 423, 7 Sept. 1640, du Hallier to de Noyers.
[219] AAE MD 1679, fo. 261, 15 Sept. 1640.

The size of the French army

Acting in cooperation with the Swedes, the French army in Germany was to prove the most successful of the forces operating in the last years of Richelieu's ministry, though the strength of the corps remained relatively low. An *état* of early May 1640 shows that the army of Germany, now commanded by Longueville, was roughly 4,000–5,000 cavalry and 3,000–4,000 infantry.[220] When the French contingent was amalgamated with the regiments remaining from the army of Saxe-Weimar, and the two forces cooperated with the Swedish army of Johan Banér, this created an impressive campaign army, said to be of 32,000 men. However, the majority of these were serving under the Swedish commanders, with total forces of 22,000 ascribed to Banér, and the French forces in Germany – increasingly German mercenary regiments – remained small.[221]

In the south, Henri de Lorraine, comte d'Harcourt, was no more sanguine than his predecessors that the Italian theatre would receive a realistic allocation of troops, although once again the theoretical allocation appeared substantial. Richelieu made the revealing comment in a letter to the French representative in the United Provinces that the ministry had made provision for some 30,000 'recrues arrêtées, payées et assurées pour le cours de cette année en Italie'.[222] The *état* for 1640 offered the apparently generous target of 22,900 infantry and 4,580 cavalry, and included a provision for additional recruitment during the campaign of 14,410 infantry and 1,160 cavalry.[223] These were, however, all calculations based upon the assumption that the units would be recruited up to an agreed target, for the most part twenty-company regiments at 800 men each. The assumption that the captains could be held to agreements to recruit their companies up to an average strength of forty soldiers may have been realistic in 1635, but the deluge of complaints from commanding officers, administrators in the field and ministers indicate that this had ceased to be the case by 1640.[224] The defiance of these contracts was so widespread that it proved impossible to threaten punishment of offending officers with any conviction, and by the end of 1640 a company strength of thirty men had been officially accepted in the Italian theatre.[225] When the Spanish army of Lombardy moved against Casale-Monferrato in April, Harcourt had to run the risk of reducing all the other French-held garrisons to skeleton strength in order to put together a modest field army.[226] With some 10,500 French and Savoyard troops, Harcourt engaged the Spanish

---

[220] AAE MD, 835, fo. 102, 9 May, *état* of troops *sur pied*.
[221] Noailles, *Guébriant*, p. 154 – though it is far from clear whether this force is established on the basis of *revues* or simply taking units at 'full' strength. The figures for the Swedish contingents are given in AAE MD 835, fo. 102, 9 May 1640.
[222] Avenel, VI. 681, 14 Apr. 1640, Richelieu to d'Estrades.
[223] AAE MD 837, fos. 265–71.
[224] Caron (ed.), *Le Tellier*, p. 20, 4 Dec. 1640, Le Tellier to de Noyers; AAE CP Savoie 31, fo. 641, 16 Dec., Harcourt to de Noyers.
[225] AAE CP Savoie 31, fo. 392, 11 Nov. 1640, Louis XIII to Harcourt.
[226] AAE CP Savoie 30, fos. 363, 374, 20 Apr. (intercepted letter to Leganès, informing him of the weakness of the French garrisons), 23 Apr., Harcourt to de Noyers.

The military context

besiegers and drove them off from Casale.[227] This success did much to boost Harcourt's reputation, but having placed 880 additional troops in Casale, an *état* of his army left him with only 6,000 infantry and 3,500 cavalry, of which 1,000 cavalry and 1,500 infantry were troops of the duchess of Savoy.[228] The most vital strategic concern was to try to retake Turin, though Harcourt warned that he would need additional troops for a siege of the capital, whose garrison contained 6,000–7,000 troops.[229]

On 12 May Harcourt began the siege of the Piedmontese capital, though letters make it clear that he and the other commanders were still extremely worried at the inadequacy of the army and of financial provision.[230] Most of the reinforcements to be allocated to the army of Italy came from Languedoc, where they were collected together so slowly and sustained such heavy losses *en route* that their benefit to the army of Italy was negligible.[231] In response to the urgent needs of the siege – Harcourt claimed that he had only enough troops to man two-thirds of the circumvallations adequately – a corps of reinforcements was promised, largely to be made up from troops recruited in Burgundy.[232] Promises that this corps would amount to 7,000–8,000 troops were scaled down to 6,000 by mid-July.[233] When the troops finally arrived in late July they consisted of only 4,500 infantry and two cavalry regiments.[234] One of the regimental officers in the lines outside Turin, the comte de Souvigny, suggested that Harcourt had 14,000 infantry and 5,000 cavalry to sustain the siege.[235] This would be supported by a *revue* of all the French troops in Italy during the last phase of the siege of Turin, which gave 12,360 infantry and 4,183 cavalry, though the *revue* also indicated a staggering additional 10,472 infantry who were (or claimed to be) sick, and 5,288 cavalry who were either sick or lacked horses.[236] These figures did not include the companies of *gardes françaises* and *suisses*, a further fourteen companies, given at 2,100 infantry on the original (full strength) *état* for 1640.[237]

The successful conclusion of the siege required Harcourt to commit seven full

---

[227] AAE CP Savoie 30, fo. 400, 4 May 1640, Harcourt to Louis XIII; Campion, who arived in Italy later in the year, gave 5,000 infantry and 3,500 cavalry for Harcourt's relief force: *Mémoires*, p. 123.
[228] AAE CP Savoie 30, fo. 406, 6 May 1640, Harcourt to de Noyers.
[229] AAE CP Savoie 30, fo. 613, 16 July 1640, Harcourt to de Noyers, who also mentioned that the city was defended by a similar number of armed citizens.
[230] AAE CP Savoie, 30, fo. 417, 9 May, Harcourt to de Noyers; fo. 420, 12 May, Plessis-Praslin to de Noyers.
[231] AAE CP Savoie 30, fo. 433, Harcourt to de Noyers, 19 May 1640.
[232] Sourdis, *Correspondance*, II. 177–8, 16 June 1640, Harcourt to Sourdis.
[233] AAE CP Savoie 30, fo. 580, 10 July 1640, La Cour to de Noyers speaking of 7,000–8,000; Campion, whose regiment was part of this reinforcement, writes that 8,000 troops passed down into Italy to join Harcourt: *Mémoires*, p. 125; Savoie 30, fo. 613, 16 July 1640, Harcourt to de Noyers, speaking of 6,000 men.
[234] AAE CP Savoie 30, fo. 657, 27 July 1640, Harcourt to de Noyers.
[235] Souvigny, *Mémoires*, II. 57.
[236] Caron (ed.), *Le Tellier*, p. 4, 11 Sept. 1640, instructions from Bullion to Le Tellier.
[237] AAE MD 837, fo. 264, [1640].

regiments totalling 2,000 infantry without officers to form the French garrison in Turin.[238] Following the siege, the effective strength of the army in Italy collapsed, with Harcourt reporting in early November that his field army was of less than 3,000 men.[239] In a revealing comment, Harcourt wrote that the fundamental problem was now a company strength that averaged under twenty soldiers, which ensured that although the money sent to Italy should have funded 6,000 infantry and 2,000 cavalry, in fact the costs of too many company officers and the *état major* of each regiment brought the real strength of the army down to half of that.[240]

The loss of Salces in Roussillon at the end of 1639 despite a heavy commitment of troops, finance and supplies had profoundly discouraged the crown and ministers, and it was widely considered that military investment on the Pyrenean frontier had produced a singularly poor return. When revolt erupted in Catalonia in June 1640 this position was slightly revised, and a modest military commitment was to be made over and above the troops required to defend Languedoc against possible Spanish incursions. In September 1640, the Catalans proposed that 6,000 French infantry and 2,000 cavalry should be sent into the Principality.[241] However, while Espenan was sent down briefly into Roussillon with 12,000 infantry and 1,000 cavalry to lift the Castilian siege of Illa in late September, it was clear that the numbers of French troops actually based in Catalonia would be much smaller. The first detachments of French troops despatched to the Principality in October totalled 3,000 infantry and cavalry.[242] When Tarragona was threatened by the Castilian army, Espenan moved to reinforce the garrison with 1,000 French troops then based in Barcelona.[243] The surrender of the *place* and the agreement that the French troops in the garrison would withdraw directly to Languedoc, left only 1,500 French infantry and 300 cavalry in Barcelona by the end of 1640.[244]

The pattern for the allocation of troops between army-corps remained much the same in 1641. Two major armies were to be reestablished, one under the command of La Meilleraye, which was to take the offensive against the Spanish Netherlands, targeting another major fortification. This army was to be seconded by a corps under the command of Châtillon, initially independent, but committed to support the siege when falling troops numbers and the threat of an enemy counter-attack overstrained the army of La Meilleraye. Despite efforts to raise both armies to respectable operational strength, the process was slow and patchy

---

[238] AAE CP Savoie 31, fo. 139, 1 Oct. 1640, 'Mémoire de ce qui est à faire en Piémont.'
[239] AAE CP Savoie 31, fo. 357, 6 Nov. 1640, Harcourt to Chavigny.
[240] AAE CP Savoie 31, fo. 795, [late?] 1640: Harcourt described the companies as 'almost entirely composed of officers and valets'.
[241] Vassal-Reig, *Catalogne*, p. 109.
[242] Sanabre, *La Acción de Francia*, p. 103.
[243] Vassal-Reig, *Catalogne*, p. 164.
[244] Vassal-Reig, *Catalogne*, pp. 174–5.

even by the standards of previous years. Both commanders blamed the system of recruitment *traités* with the unit commanders, which entailed an unrealistic combination of high expectations imposed upon the captains, and limited sanctions in the event that they proved unwilling to comply.[245] In mid-May, Châtillon wrote that many of the regiments which had arrived with his army were still expecting significant numbers of reinforcements, and until these arrived the units would remain seriously under strength. He calculated that at present his campaign army consisted of 6,000 infantry and 1,400 cavalry – insufficient to carry out any effective action across the frontier.[246] Not unreasonably, Châtillon suggested that he would need 8,000 infantry and 2,000 cavalry to take the offensive, and that in addition 3,000 infantry and 600 cavalry should be left on the frontier under the command of Charles d'Escoubleau, marquis de Sourdis, to form a 'poste asseuré'.[247] The situation remained unchanged at the end of May, with large numbers of reinforcements expected, but individual company strengths for the regiments present with the army as low as seventeen or eighteen soldiers, figures which frequently included officers' valets, treated as soldiers for the purposes of the *montres*.[248] Châtillon's reluctance to begin operations in these circumstances was understandable, but the delay threatened to have more dangerous consequences as evidence accumulated that the disaffected comte de Soissons, together with Frédéric-Maurice de La Tour d'Auvergne, duc de Bouillon, were preparing to launch an invasion of France.[249] The troops raised through the conspirators' clienteles were supplemented by 7,000 Imperial troops under the command of Wilhelm von Lamboy. As these forces assembled, Châtillon came under overwhelming pressure to move against Bouillon's principal territory of Sedan. The armies met at La Marfée on 6 July, and Soissons' 7,000 infantry and 2,000–2,500 horse triumphed over Châtillon's 9,000 infantry and 3,000 cavalry.[250] Although the death of Soissons undermined the revolt, Châtillon's army had suffered severe losses and was in no state subsequently to carry out its 'real' task of seconding La Meilleraye. The latter had followed the appointed campaign plan and laid siege to Aire with the expectation that his army, of rather less than 15,000 troops, would be supported by Châtillon.[251] After La Marfée, the decision was taken to amalgamate the remains of Châtillon's troops with a third corps that was being levied under the maréchal de Brézé and had been intended to

---

[245] AAE MD 1680, fo. 114v, 29 May 1641, Châtillon to de Noyers: 'c'est une faute quasy generale principalement dans les troupes que vous m'avez commises'; fo. 132, 1 June 1641, La Meilleraye to Richelieu.
[246] AAE MD 1680, fo. 78, 16 May 1641, Châtillon to de Noyers.
[247] Aubery, *Richelieu*, II. 667, 6 May 1641, Châtillon to de Noyers.
[248] AAE MD 1680, fos. 191–213, *revues* of regiments conducted on 9/10 June 1641.
[249] AAE MD 1680, fo. 219, 14 June 1641, Richelieu to the marquis de Sourdis, complaining of Châtillon's failure to open the campaign and the great humiliation which his dilatory behaviour was heaping upon the king.
[250] Avenel, VI. 831–2, 10 July 1641, Richelieu to Bouthillier.
[251] Montglat, *Mémoires*, XLIX. 322.

operate in Luxembourg. As a result it was anticipated that a single supporting army of 10,000–12,000 men could be created, which was moved north to provide support for La Meilleraye.[252] Following the capture of Aire the two army-corps continued to operate together, and given the efforts of the Spanish to recapture the *place*, a concerted effort was made to ensure that both corps were provided with additional recruits through the late summer and autumn.[253] When the two armies were formally amalgamated, *revues* in late October established the combined force at 16,000 infantry and 7,500 cavalry.[254]

The opening of the 1641 had also been marked by the hope that the crown would rid itself of one campaign theatre and gain the support of an additional army-corps following the agreement that duke Charles IV of Lorraine would enter French service. The gradual realization that Charles would evade cooperation with the French forces and that he intended to break the treaty with Louis XIII as soon as opportunity permitted undermined these plans. The ministry had no choice after Charles' official defection in July but to strengthen du Hallier's corps in the duchy, and some 4,000 infantry and 1,000 cavalry were despatched in early August, troops which would otherwise have been used to reinforce the armies of La Meilleraye and Brézé.[255]

Despite Harcourt's success at the siege of Turin, the crown's military commitent to Italy followed the now predictable pattern of generous allocations in theory, but reluctance to give the theatre a high priority in practice. In mid-April, when Turenne had taken the offensive against Ivrea, the campaign army was reported to be of 6,000 infantry, 2,400 cavalry and two cannon.[256] The siege had to be abandoned because there were insufficient troops to force a rapid result, and because the commanders recognized that reinforcements were arriving in Italy so slowly that this situation was unlikely to improve before the Spanish moved against another city. On 28 May the army *intendant* Michel Le Tellier wrote with some concern that there would only be 7,000 infantry for the campaign, given the present rate at which recruits were arriving and the commitments to maintain garrisons in Piedmont.[257] By 20 July this had been raised to 10,000 infantry, and a more accurate, undated, *revue* of the same period gave 10,855 infantry and an impressive 7,261 cavalry, though 1,836 of the latter were Savoyard. To this were added 7,869 anticipated additional infantry recruits, intended to ensure that a reasonable effective strength was maintained through the campaign.[258] It was these forces which allowed Harcourt to take the initiative to the south of Turin

---

[252] Aubery, *Richelieu*, II. 722, 12 July 1641, de Noyers to Châtillon and Brézé.
[253] Aubery, *Richelieu*, II. 727, 22 July, de Noyers to Brézé and Châtillon, notifying them of the despatch of 3,000 reinforcements to strengthen their corps.
[254] AAE MD 1681, fo. 25, 21 Oct. 1641.
[255] AAE CP Lorraine 32, fo. 293, 9 Aug. 1641, Richelieu to du Hallier.
[256] AAE CP Savoie 33, fo. 541, 9 Apr. 1641, Mazarin to Richelieu.
[257] Caron (ed.), *Le Tellier*, p. 65, Le Tellier to de Noyers.
[258] AAE MD 841, fos. 229–33, [1641].

The military context

during the summer months, though once again high levels of wastage and the systematic failure of recruitment contracts rapidly reduced these numbers to a far more modest campaign army; indeed, in early September Le Tellier reported that the officers charged with levies for their units had raised fewer than one third of the stipulated numbers of recruits.[259]

The consolidation of the Catalan revolt and the successful defeat of the Castilian army of reconquest at Montjuic in January 1641 had considerably altered the French crown's perception of the possibilities that this theatre might offer. The problem was the existence of two potentially competing demands: the provision of French troops to honour the king's alliance with the Catalans and to prop up the revolt, and the opportunist awareness that the revolt provided an unparalleled opportunity to conquer Roussillon, locked between Catalonia and Languedoc. The French commitment to Catalonia had been agreed in December 1640 at 8,000 troops.[260] In April it was proposed to establish the army of Philippe de La Motte-Houdancourt in Catalonia with 6,000 infantry and 1,200 cavalry.[261] However, in late June 1641 a *revue* indicated that the French had only 3,409 infantry and 368 cavalry (3,000 and 300 effectives respectively) supporting the Catalans.[262] Initially, the military priority was Roussillon, where the French hoped to establish an army of 10,000 infantry and 2,000 cavalry to undertake the siege of Collioure.[263] However, as the project of a land and sea operation against Tarragona began to gain influential supporters from Richelieu and Condé downwards, the balance of military resources began to shift towards Catalonia.

The operations in Roussillon were not abandoned, but the army which moved out of Languedoc in early June was of only 7,000 infantry and 1,000 cavalry.[264] Plans to take a major *place* such as Collioure or Perpignan were abandoned as it became clear that these forces would be further reduced to strengthen the army engaged at Tarragona. Faced with a Spanish relief force reported to be of 10,000–12,000 infantry and 1,500–2,000 cavalry, the demands for additional troops to sustain the siege of Tarragona became more intense.[265] The failure of the siege in mid-August exposed both an over-ambitious strategy, and the catastrophic levels of troop loss sustained by an army operating deep within Catalonia. On 24 August, La Motte-Houdancourt sought to justify the decision to abandon the siege, arguing that he would have needed 14,000–15,000 infantry and

---

[259] Caron (ed.), *Le Tellier*, p. 83, 1 July 1641, de Noyers to Le Tellier; p. 93, 20 July, Mazarin to Le Tellier; p. 103, 3 Sept., Le Tellier to Mazarin.
[260] Vassal-Reig, *Catalogne*, p. 144.
[261] Sourdis, *Correspondance*, II. 549–50, 4 Apr. 1641.
[262] AAE CP Espagne 20, fos. 192–3, late June, *état* of money and troops sent to La Motte-Houdancourt.
[263] Sanabre, *La Acción de Francia*, pp. 153–5.
[264] Aubery, *Richelieu*, II. 676, 25 May 1641, Condé to Richelieu: 'nostre petite armée entrera en Roussillon samedi prochain, et fera ce qu'elle pourra'.
[265] Aubery, *Richelieu*, II. 682, 8 June 1641, *conseil de guerre* of senior officers in Roussillon and Catalonia.

2,500 cavalry to blockade Tarragona, and that at the time of writing his army consisted of no more than 4,000 infantry and 300 cavalry.[266]

The destructive effects of this setback on the French military presence in both Catalonia and Roussillon during the rest of 1641 were profound. A *mémoire* concerning the military situation in Catalonia written in late October noted that the combined Franco-Catalan army was of 12,000 infantry and 4,000 cavalry, of whom only 2,000 infantry and 1,200 horse were French.[267] The maréchal de Brézé, left in command of the forces in Roussillon in the latter part of 1641, wrote with mounting frustration of missed opportunities and the weakness of the remaining French forces in the face of Castilian strengthening of the principal garrisons at Collioure and Perpignan.[268] In a letter despatched on the last day of 1641 he provided a full account of the troops in Roussillon, based on a series of *revues*: these revealed a total cavalry strength of 207 *chevaux légers* and 152 *gendarmes*, to which could be added 53 new recruits just arrived for the company of Saint-Simon; the infantry amounted to 2,124 soldiers fit to serve, of whom 1,038 were in garrisons, leaving Brézé a campaign force of 1,126 foot.[269]

Brézé's frustration and assurances of what could be achieved in Roussillon and Catalonia with adequate numbers of troops did make their mark on Louis XIII and Richelieu in 1642, however, leading to the first major shift in strategic priorities since 1637. Richelieu took the view that Perpignan, the key to the conquest of Roussillon, was the decisive objective of the 1642 campaign, and by his own presence and that of the king indicated the extent to which resources would be channelled towards this theatre. It was initially proposed to raise an army of 16,000 infantry and 3,000 cavalry for the siege.[270] Once again, the theoretical total for the army was considerably less important than the sustained burden of maintaining the force at an effective strength, a problem which was immensely heightened by the length of the siege. Although Richelieu had optimistically assumed that Perpignan would capitulate by the end of May, providing the opportunity either to press the offensive down through Catalonia or to reduce the commitment to the theatre, the siege continued throughout August, and the governor finally fixed the capitulation for 9 September. In consequence, a steady stream of reinforcements needed to be despatched to Roussillon throughout the campaign season, soaking up the available recruits not merely from Languedoc and Guienne, but from as far afield as Burgundy and Lorraine.[271]

---

[266] AAE CP Espagne 20, fo. 203, 24 Aug., La Motte-Houdancourt to Chavigny.
[267] AAE CP Espagne 20, fo. 283, 24 Oct. 1641.
[268] AAE CP Espagne 20, fo. 304, 28 Nov.; fo. 342, 14 Dec.; fos. 357–9, 27 Dec. 'je suis mort de lassitude et de deplaisir aussi'.
[269] AAE CP Espagne 20, fo. 366, 31 Dec., Brézé to de Noyers.
[270] Vassal-Reig, *Perpignan*, p. 94; Bourelly, *Maréchal de Fabert*, I. 183.
[271] AAE MD 843, fo. 103, 20 July, Richelieu to Chavigny and de Noyers, ordering them to press

The military context

The priority given to the siege of Perpignan as the destination for recruits throughout the summer months all but halted the flow of troops to La Motte-Houdancourt in Catalonia. Although La Motte-Houdancourt and Brézé, now viceroy of Catalonia, had been informed in March of the despatch of 6,000 infantry and 2,000 cavalry to Catalonia, real allocations proved less impressive.[272] On 20 July concern was being expressed that the French troops under La Motte-Houdancourt's command numbered fewer than 3,000 cavalry and 2,000 infantry.[273]

The consequence of this heavy and sustained commitment to a major siege in Roussillon was the relative neglect of the army-corps elsewhere. The impact of this was felt above all in the north-east. Although two army-corps were once again raised in Picardy and Champagne and placed under the command of Harcourt and Antoine III, maréchal de Gramont, their combined allocation of troops was much lower than in previous campaigns. Gramont's *mémoires*, written admittedly with the aim of exonerating his role in the defeat at Honnecourt, proposed that at the beginning of the campaign Harcourt had 14,000 infantry and 6,000 cavalry, while Gramont's own army was half that number.[274] An account by Chancellor Séguier suggests that this may have considerably exaggerated the size of Harcourt's corps, which Séguier establishes at 6,000 infantry and 6,000 cavalry.[275] Even this may have exaggerated the cavalry component of Harcourt's army, for in the aftermath of the battle of Honnecourt the remains of Gramont's corps were incorporated into Harcourt's army to give a reported total of 9,000 infantry and 4,000 cavalry.[276] Though another account gave the strength of the combined army at 15,000 troops, it was considered essential that the corps should be recruited up to 20,000 soldiers to ensure a secure defence against a Spanish army estimated at 25,000. It was also pointed out that Harcourt had only ten pieces of assorted artillery against a Spanish force with over thirty cannon.[277]

Harcourt's forces were not put to the test of a confrontation with the Spanish, but the decision of the governor-general of the Spanish Netherlands, Francisco de Melo, to withdraw his troops out of France had as much to do with the combined Franco-Dutch operations in the Cologne Electorate as with any later reinforce-

---

forward the recruitment and despatch of a further 7,000 infantry and 1200 cavalry in Languedoc and Guienne; Vassal-Reig, *Perpignan*, pp. 183, 260, etc. For the movement of troops from du Hallier's army-corps in Lorraine down to Languedoc, MD 843, fo. 197, 9 Aug., Chavigny to Richelieu; similar instructions for despatch of troops recruited in Lyonnais and Dauphiné, fo. 203, 10 Aug. Chavigny to Richelieu; MD 844, fo. 183bis, 24 Aug., Abbé de Médavy to Richelieu, concerning 2,000 recruits assembled at Saint-Jean-de-Losne about to be despatched to Perpignan.

[272] SHAT, A¹ 68, fo. 463, 3 Mar. 1642, de Noyers to Brézé.
[273] AAE MD 843, fo. 103, 20 July, Richelieu to Chavigny; however, proposals to increase the size of the forces in Catalonia would have to wait upon the conclusion of the siege of Perpignan.
[274] Gramont, *Mémoires*, LVII. 338.
[275] AAE MD 843, fo. 33, [early June] 1642, Séguier to Chavigny.
[276] AAE MD 843, fo. 35, 30 June 1642, Chavigny to Richelieu.
[277] AAE MD 844, fo. 230, 4 June 1642, duchesse d'Aiguillon to Richelieu.

The size of the French army

ment of Harcourt's army. Guébriant's army of Germany consisted of twelve regiments of infantry and twelve of cavalry, but the effective strength of these was low: at the beginning of 1642 the French troops numbered no more than 3,500 cavalry and 2,000 infantry, to which were added the corps of Hessians under the command of Graf von Eberstein, a further 2,000 infantry and 1,500–2,000 cavalry.[278] After the battle of Kempen, these were joined by 3,000 Dutch troops, officially 'disbanded' from the army of the Estates, which together with some Breton and some German recruits created a campaign army in late June of 8,000 cavalry and 7,000 foot.[279]

That the military situation in the Italian theatre improved during 1642 owed considerably more to the diplomatic success of bringing the two princes Tommaso Francesco and Maurizio, uncles of the young duke of Savoy, into a French alliance than to a greater troop allocation. The enlistment of Tommaso Francesco on the French side brought a significant corps of troops into French service, so that, even allowing for the setback of the duc de Bouillon's inaction and subsequent arrest for treason, the French finally possessed a military advantage over the Spanish army of the Milanese. On 30 January, Le Tellier wrote that the French corps in Italy contained fourteen regiments of infantry and eight of cavalry, but given the exceptionally low average strength of companies and the chronic problems of persuading the unit commanders to obtain adequate recruits, there is little reason to think that the army numbered more than 6,000–8,000 troops at most.[280] The arrival of reinforcements during the campaign appears to have maintained an infantry strength of 6,000 men as late as September, though various comments suggested that the cavalry had suffered high rates of wastage.[281] In late December, Le Tellier wrote that eleven regiments had been garrisoned at Tortona both to defend the newly captured *place* and as a base for the winter quarter. Although these regiments amounted in theory to 3,489 soldiers and 480 officers, a *revue* carried out on site had revealed that only 1,246 men, excluding the officers, were fit for service.[282]

CONCLUSION

Most assessments of the strength of the French army during Richelieu's ministry have aimed to calculate a global 'grand total' for each successive year of campaign, either assumed to represent a permanent military establishment, or, in more sophisticated accounts, to be regarded as a 'high-point' of recruitment, inevitably whittled down by death, sickness and desertion. Such grand totals start from

---

[278] Noailles, *Guébriant*, pp. 252–3.
[279] Noailles, *Guébriant*, pp. 276–81.
[280] Caron (ed.), *Le Tellier*, p. 171, 30 Jan., Le Tellier to de Noyers.
[281] Caron (ed.), *Le Tellier*, p. 223, 22 Sept., de Noyers to Le Tellier.
[282] Caron (ed.), *Le Tellier*, p. 244, 23 Dec., 'mémoire sur Tortone, concernant les troupes'.

The military context

assumptions about what the strength of the army ought to be, made on the basis of ministerial calculations, and then engage in various forms of discounting to take into account conventions surrounding 'full-strength' units, officers' and *commissaires*' corruption and other factors. The essential weakness of such methods is that they still accept administrative targets and objectives which were in practice overwhelmed by a vast process of recruitment and wastage characteristic of each of the campaigns after 1635. As a result, the selection of even a discounted 'high-point' for the strength of the army in a particular campaign is usually the arbitrary choice of a figure selected from a constantly fluctuating military establishment, and presents an exaggerated notion of the capacity of the administration to maintain large numbers of troops *sur pied* for any length of time.

If, despite this caveat, some attempt is to be made to calculate the average number of troops under arms in the campaigns from 1635, then it is important to examine the individual army-corps operating within particular theatres. As will have been evident from the present chapter, such examination is a patchy and unsystematic process, and the evidence simply does not survive in sufficient quantity to offer a high level of precision.[283] Nevertheless, the substantiated figures for the strength of individual army-corps, derived where possible from *revues* in the field, combined with knowledge of the number of specific military commitments in different theatres in each year of campaigning, call into doubt the traditional assumptions about the total size of the army set *sur pied* between 1635 and 1642. From this evidence, the maximum strength of one of the larger army-corps which could be sustained over a four to six week siege or field operation was between 12,000 and 18,000 troops, while the smaller corps more usually numbered 6,000–10,000 men. The average number of corps operating in each campaign between 1635 and 1642, albeit sometimes with two or even three corps concentrated within a single theatre, stood at between five and seven. On the basis of these calculations, it is evident that the troops on campaign numbered no more than 70,000–80,000 in total. These, moreover, are liberal estimates of the numbers in specific corps, numbers which could easily be pulled downwards by focusing exclusively on actual *revues* rather than balancing these against some of the ministerial *états* of recruitment targets at the beginning of each campaign. To reach a 'traditional' grand total of 100,000–120,000 or more troops under arms during these years, it would thus be necessary to assume that at least 25,000 troops were maintained in garrisons or established in provinces outside of the main theatres of conflict during the months of campaigning. The evidence for such a huge reserve of garrison troops within France is entirely absent from the archival material, which merely indicates a number of frontier garrisons, for the most part

---

[283] And is the reason for my reluctance to try to commit the information on troop strengths to tabular form, which, while convenient for subsequent syntheses, would risk generating precisely the misleading assumptions about 'average annual troop strength' which I have been concerned to avoid.

The size of the French army

severely undermanned. And where the garrisons were substantially larger – the major fortified *places* in Piedmont, for example, or at Nancy – they were garrisoned from the strength of the troops allocated to those theatres, one of the main reasons for the extreme weakness of their respective campaign armies. It was also notorious that garrisons stood at the lowest point of the ministerial scale of financial priorities; if, improbably, 25,000+ troops had been recruited and placed in garrisons, the wastage rate caused by delayed and inadequate pay would have dwarfed even the rates of loss from the normal campaign armies. In the final analysis, moreover, had such numbers of soldiers been maintained in garrisons within France, this itself would raise questions about the administrative competence and priorities of a ministerial regime which had simultaneously permitted the effective strength of the army of Italy to fall to under 5,000 soldiers in successive campaigns.

The truth was that garrisons outside the period of winter quartering were small, formed of poor-quality soldiers and usually greatly in arrears with pay.[284] Many of the campaign armies were extremely small, not because troops were being kept in France, but because the overall scale of the war-effort did not allow the allocation of any more soldiers to these theatres. The military system was running at full-stretch, but simply could not meet the full range of strategic commitments that had been created from 1635. Above all, it could not meet the twin burdens of rapid recruitment at the beginning of each campaign season, followed by massive levies of replacement troops throughout the campaign. Hence, as has been demonstrated for successive campaigns, the prioritization of resources towards a single theatre, where an objective was usually sustained by the successive commitment of multiple army-corps. But the effect of this was not merely to restrict the initial allocations of troops to the 'subsidiary' theatres, but also to impose considerable limits upon the number of additional recruits which would be made available to them during the months of the campaign. The result created a vicious circle, which further confirms the need to examine the individual army-corps rather than seeking to arrive at some overall figure for the composite strength of the army. Not merely were some of the army-corps the perpetual 'poor relations' in the ministerial scheme of priorities, but because they were allocated more low-quality troops in the first instance, and were subject to more irregular funding, they suffered heavier rates of attrition. These troop losses were, in turn, less rapidly and less comprehensively made good by the despatch of recruits later in the campaign. Thus the overlapping processes of recruitment and troop loss operated at different rates between the various army-corps, so that while the army of Italy, for example, was regularly reduced to as few as 3,000–4,000 troops in total by the end of a campaign, such a collapse in effective strength would never have been permitted in the corps on the Flanders frontier.

---

[284] For a discussion of garrisoning during the winter quarter, see chapter 10, pp. 509–16.

The military context

The French crown lacked the troops to sustain the extensive strategy and military objectives which it was pursuing after 1635. It is not immediately obvious why this should have been so; the total French population in the 1630s was not significantly smaller than that of the 1690s, yet in the latter decade an army of 300,000–350,000 troops could be recruited and maintained. The key issue in explaining this failure to recruit and maintain more substantial armies is that of finance. The crown and its ministers consistently failed to mobilize sufficient funds to cover more than a small fraction of the costs of the army. As such, the crown drew heavily upon the resources of the officer-corps to meet the shortfalls in military funding and this, as will be indicated in chapter 6, imposed considerable limitations upon the number of troops who would be recruited by unit commanders. The latter were well aware that much of the cost of this would be sustained from their own pockets, and used a variety of obstructive and illicit methods to avoid recruitment and to force the crown to accept ever-declining average unit strengths. More immediately, however, it needs to be considered why Richelieu's ministry should have experienced such difficulties in allocating an adequate proportion of tax and *extraordinaire* revenues to meeting the costs of the army.

PART II

The administrative context

4

Paying for war

> Il ne fault plus que les Espagnols se mettent en peine d'assembler des armées pour nous défaire, il fault seulement qu'ils laissent faire M. de Bulion, apres avoir fait perdre Trèves et Philisbourg pour avoir empesché qu'on n'y ait mis des garnisons suffisantes, apres avoir causé la revolte des soldats qui ont livré a l'ennemy noz places frontières fault de payement, apres la dissipation des meilleurs forces du Royaume qui son opiniastreté a faict perir beaucoup plus que les coups ny les malades, apres la defection de la pluspart de nos alliez, ou il les a reduitz fault de leur tenir parolle. . . je ne sçay ce que peult attendre M. le cardinal d'un ministre sy ignorant lequel ayant enfermé l'argent du Royaume dans sa bourse ou dans celle de ses affairistes, ruyne toutes les plus grandes affaires de l'Estat par le manquement d'un peu de secours.[1]

> s'il n'y a du fonds il est impossible de vous rendre l'obeissance que vous est due. Si nous l'estions dans l'abondance com[m]e les Annees passées qu'il y avoit dans vostre épargne plus de quatorze milliers contents [comptant] il nous serait facile de vous obeir en tout.[2]

This chapter is concerned with two related issues: why, despite the large potential revenues that it could obtain both from ordinary taxation and from the exploitation of the *parties casuelles*, was the French monarchy unable to fund more than a small proportion of its military costs during Richelieu's ministry? Secondly, how did the *bureau des finances* manage the distribution of those funds that were available for the war-effort? Related to this second question is the issue of whether the existing system could have been made to operate more effectively within the existing constraints.

CROWN REVENUES AND THE COSTS OF THE WAR-EFFORT

The preceding chapter emphasized the limited value of attempts to arrive at a meaningful figure for the 'total size' of the royal army during Richelieu's ministry, given the continuous fluctuations in effective strength and the multiplicity of factors which separate theoretical from real troop strengths. However, by

---

[1] AAE MD 820, fo. 217, [April]1636, *mémoire*, seemingly written by a *fidèle* of Richelieu judging from its emphasis upon the *prévoyance* of the cardinal in the face of the incompetence and possible corruption of the *surintendant des finances*, Claude Bullion.
[2] AAE MD 820, fo. 258, 9 May 1636, Bullion to Louis XIII.

The administrative context

assembling data for individual army-corps at specific points during particular campaigns it can be shown that the French army in the period after 1635 had a considerably lower effective strength than has traditionally been assumed. But if it has proved difficult to establish the overall size of the army with any accuracy, the same is not true for calculations of the expenses involved in recruiting and maintaining individual units. A number of surviving documents are concerned to establish the costs involved in maintaining infantry regiments or cavalry companies for a complete campaign – defined as requiring the payment of ten, or more usually eight, monthly *montres*. In 1635 a regiment of twenty companies with a notional full strength of 2,000 men was costed, via a breakdown of both company wages and the salaries of the regimental staff and officers, at 33,000 *livres* per *montre*; depending upon whether the regiment received eight or ten *montres* per annum, an annual cost of 264,000 or 330,000 *livres*.[3] These calculations for a 2,000 strong unit were specifically relevant to the prestige *régiments entretenus*: the two units of *gardes* and the four *vieux régiments*. The ordinary line regiments were taken at ten companies totalling a notional 1,000 soldiers, and costed at 17,000 *livres* per *montre* or, in a more specific calculation, at 16,388 *livres*.[4] On campaign, of course, the reality was that units' actual effectives fell below this full strength, so that large sums would be recycled as *deniers revenans bons* to pay for other units.[5] A similar set of calculations established the cost of a company of *gendarmes* of fifty *maîtres* at 2,400 *livres* per *montre*, while some more specific calculations for prestige – *entretenues* – companies of *chevaux légers* drawn up in 1632 gave a cost of 2,767 *livres* per *montre*.[6] To this should be added the cavalry *surtaux*, a considerable payment intended to cover the additional costs of providing forage for cavalry horses and to compensate for cavalry not receiving the ration of *pain de munition* distributed to the infantry. A document of 1632 which set the *montre* of a company of sixty *chevaux légers* at 3,167 *livres* also allocated the company 1,950 *livres* of *surtaux* – a total of 23,400 *livres* of *surtaux* over eight *montres*.[7] On this calculation, the *surtaux* could be added as approximately 60 per cent on top of the wage bill of the cavalry.[8] In the case of the infantry, the crown accepted the costs

---

[3] AAE MD 819, fo. 59, [1635 – or 1633].
[4] AAE MD 819, fo. 63.   [5] See chapter 3, pp. 173–4.
[6] AAE MD 806, fo. 176 [1632] *état* of funds required to support 16,000 infantry and 1,500 cavalry for an entire year (in this case taken as eight *montres*). The lower figure of 2,400 *livres* seems a good working assumption for ordinary companies of *chevaux légers*, which would in fact be cheaper to maintain than companies of *gendarmes*.
[7] AAE MD 806, fos. 175–6.
[8] The scale of which incidentally explained both the considerable ill-feeling that attempts to retrench on the *surtaux* caused amongst the cavalry officers, and the very hostile reaction from the ministers when local commanders succumbed to pressure to distribute *pain de munition* to cavalry who had already received (at least in theory) this financial supplement: AAE CP Allemagne 12, fo. 177, 3 Apr. 1635, Brézé to *surintendant* Bouthillier on the irritation caused by the reduction of the *surtaux*; AAE CP Lorraine 31, fo. 97v, 6 June 1639, Feuquières to de Noyers, defending his decision to provide bread rations to his cavalry.

of providing a daily bread ration (the *pain de munition*) over and above a basic deduction of 1 *sol* per day from the ordinary soldiers' wages.[9] This *pain de munition* was also provided to the NCOs and officers in multiples of the basic ration, and used by these either to support their valets and other servants with the armies, or commuted into a payment which could be used to buy better-quality supplies.[10] The calculation of this element of military expenditure is complicated by the fact that the unit cost of providing a bread ration varied considerably from one campaign theatre to another, and depended upon the ministers' or their agents' capacity to negotiate favourable *traités* with the entrepreneur-suppliers – the *munitionnaires*. In 1632, bread rations supplied to the army on the eastern frontier were priced at 2 *sols*; in Piedmont during 1641, the *intendant d'armée* Le Tellier was proposing to negotiate a contract with the *munitionnaire* at 4 *sols* and 4 *deniers* per ration.[11] A figure between the two extremes would suggest that the crown committed itself (again in theory) to paying 2 *sols* per ration over and above the 1 *sol* automatically deducted from the soldiers' wages.[12] Specific recruitment payments might also be taken into account, though in the majority of cases these would be treated as the first month of the *montre*. Indeed, the official payment for the levy of a new regiment of twenty companies was between 31,000 and 34,000 *livres*; one of twelve companies between 14,000 and 18,000 *livres*. This was more or less exactly a *montre* payment.[13]

To the infantry and cavalry should be added the artillery. The overall costs of the artillery are difficult to establish thanks to the separate administration under the authority of the *grand maître de l'artillerie*. Moreover, much that might be classified as artillery expenses, such as the stockpiling of powder, match and lead, could be considered general military expenses, since these *munitions de guerre* were also distributed to the infantry and cavalry. The *contrôle général* of 1636 allocates a reasonable-sounding total of 3 million *livres* to artillery expenses.[14] The question of winter quartering is problematic chiefly because the crown seems to have made

---

[9] For the 1 *sol* deduction see SHAT A¹ 30, fo. 310, 16 Nov. 1636, instruction to *trésorier de l'extraordinaire des guerres* to deduct the sums from the soldiers' wages and pay these to the *munitionnaires*; A¹ 50ii, fo. 35, 3 Feb. 1639, similar instruction.

[10] AAE MD 1679, fo. 105, 28 June 1640, La Meilleraye to de Noyers; by the later seventeenth century it appears that the officers' rations were provided as small quantities of good bread made from high-quality grain: F. Nodot, *Le munitionnaire des armées de France . . ..* (Paris, 1697), p. 57.

[11] BN Ms.fr. 6385, fo. 28, 30 July 1632, articles for the provision of *pain de munition*; Caron (ed.), *Le Tellier* p. 37, 27 Jan. 1641, Sublet de Noyers to Le Tellier: de Noyers did complain that this price was excessive: the more usual price in this theatre was 45–8 *deniers* per ration: AAE CP Savoie 24, fo. 27v, [early 1636]. The lowest price for a bread ration in the documentation is 1 *sol* 8 *deniers*: Grillon, IV. 85, 7 Feb. 1629.

[12] Nodot, *Le munitionnaire*, p. 5, proposes that 30 *deniers* per ration was a reasonable price for a late seventeenth-century bread contract: against this, the estimate of 3 *sols* (36 *deniers*) used for these calculations is probably an overestimate of the average cost per ration.

[13] AAE MD 816, fo. 159, Nov. 1635, *état des fonds auquel il fault pourveoir pour les nouvelles lévées*.

[14] AAE MD 823, fo. 255, Dec. 1635; the *extraict de l'épargne* for 1641 gives 3,836,287 *livres* for the artillery: MD 844, fo. 128 (late Nov. 1642).

The administrative context

Theoretical army size	Infantry wages	*Pain de munition**	Cavalry pay	*Surtaux*	Artillery	Total costs
35,000 infantry, 5,000 cavalry	4,760,000	1,092,000	1,920,000	1,152,000	3,000,000	10,924,000
50,000 infantry, 10,000 cavalry	6,800,000	1,560,000	3,840,000	2,304,000	3,000,000	17,504,000
65,000 infantry, 15,000 cavalry	8,840,000	2,028,000	5,760,000	3,456,000	3,000,000	23,084,000
75,000 infantry, 20,000 cavalry	10,200,000	2,340,000	7,680,000	4,608,000	3,000,000	27,828,000

Note: all figures in *livres* and rounded; infantry and cavalry wages calculated at eight *montres* per campaign.
* *Pain de munition*: cost to crown calculated at 2 *sols* per soldier per day (+ 30 per cent for NCOs and officers) x campaign of approx. 8 months (240 days).

little realistic provision for the maintenance of the majority of troops over the winter months in the first years of open war, and subsequently attempted to impose the burden upon the localities either through *ad hoc* additional impositions or, from 1637, the *subsistances* tax.

Despite the vagueness surrounding some elements of military expense, it is none the less possible to extrapolate from the figures for individual units some idea of the theoretical cost of maintaining an army at certain sizes (see table above).

None of these figures represents more than the most approximate calculations of the costs of maintaining armies *sur pied*; at least one of these calculations implies an army which was much larger, at 95,000 troops, than evidence suggests was maintained in the campaigns after 1635. However, the conclusion is striking: in theory at least, the royal army of the war years represented an expense that was well within the capacity of the crown to meet from its revenues. From a slightly broader historical perspective this is not surprising; the peace-time army of Louis XIV and Le Tellier, established in the years after 1660, was not significantly smaller in practice than the armies of the cardinal ministers and was supported very largely out of taxes which continued to be extracted at close to war-time levels.[15] It could be argued that war-time expenses were inflated by numbers of significant additional factors: fortification work, the stockpiling of munitions, the (very substantial) additional costs of conducting sieges, the payment of subsidies to allies and to foreign entrepreneurs such as Bernard of Saxe-Weimar. Moreover,

[15] Corvisier, *Louvois*, pp. 77–118.

Paying for war

the navy under Richelieu was in strong financial competition with the land forces; for whatever reason, the estimated naval budget in the 1636 *contrôle général* of 2,070,000 *livres* for both the Atlantic and Mediterranean fleets must be a considerable underestimate of the real naval expenses.[16]

Yet against this could be placed plenty of evidence that the crown and its ministers were seeking to lower the unit costs of the troops after 1635. The decision to reduce the number of *montres* from eight to six per campaign was discussed in chapter 3.[17] Though it was unlikely that eight *montres* had been paid to more than a handful of the most prestigious regiments and companies before 1636, the reduction would contribute to reducing the theoretical wage bill. Moreover, in 1634 the ministers took the decision to stop paying the *surtaux* to cavalry when they were serving outside of France, on the grounds that the cavalry would be able to seize forage and supplies from the localities.[18] As late as 1642 the ministry was still trying to cut its military costs, promulgating an ordinance to reduce the salaries of the regimental officers and staff by 50 per cent.[19]

More important than these attempted economies was a military culture which assumed that a proportion of army expenses would be shouldered by provincial governors and other *grands* whose personal relationship with the king had traditionally been defined through military service. There was no question here of a formal contractual relationship of the sort which developed elsewhere in Europe; it was simply taken for granted that a provincial governor would sustain his military household – frequently a company each of *gendarmes* and *chevaux légers* – at his own or the province's expense.[20] If the province was subjected to a military threat he would use his clients to raise further troops, which again would not enter the accounts of the central *épargne*. Although their military effectiveness was limited, the governors could also call upon the provincial militias to supplement the regular troops in these military operations. This was a regular recourse of Charles de Nanteuil, duc d'Halluin, for example, who called up elements of the Languedoc militia in every campaign after 1637 – again, at the expense of the province.[21] Moreover, aristocratic and princely families regarded the maintenance of one or more regiments as an essential means to provide employment for clients while making a clear statement about the status and military prestige of their house. Although it was not anticipated that such regiments would be entirely self-supporting, it was none the less the case that the ministers could make far greater assumptions about the willingness of the

---

[16] AAE MD 823, fo. 255, Dec. 1635.   [17] See pp. 174–5.
[18] Avenel, IV. 523–4, Jan. 1634, 'mémoire concernant la diminution du payement des troupes': this memoir also proposed the formal reduction of the number of *montres* from 10 to 8 per campaign, emphasizing that in the majority of armies no more than two or three *montres* were paid to their troops during the year.
[19] SHAT A¹ 70, fo. 229, 7 Oct. 1642.
[20] Harding, *Anatomy of a Power Elite* pp. 99–105.
[21] Vassal-Reig, *Roussillon, passim*.

The administrative context

particular *grand* to sustain part of the financial burden of the régiment d'Enghien or the régiment de Turenne than a unit which was less intimately linked to the family's reputation. And although it proved of little greater military effectiveness than the provincial militias, the *ban et arrière-ban* offered an apparent means by which the crown could raise large forces of cavalry at minimal cost by exploiting the traditional obligations of fief-holders. Both in 1635 and 1636 the summons failed to produce the large forces of additional cavalry that had rather naïvely been anticipated; nevertheless a few hundred noble cavalry could be found serving with many of the armies in the campaigns after 1635, and were doing so by virtue of their feudal obligations, not as a burden on the *épargne*.

Such economies are impossible to quantify, and it could be argued that in the larger context of the ceilings to financial resources that could be extracted from French society, money raised and spent by the governors in their provinces was money that did not contribute to meeting the demands of the central government. None the less, the rough calculations offered above of the total costs of supporting an army on the scale of that maintained after 1635 are more likely to overestimate than underestimate the costs to the centre of the war-effort, at least part of which was sustained from provincial sources and the private funds of greater subjects.

In meeting its military costs the crown had access to substantial financial resources.[22] The *taille*, the main direct tax, had originally been levied by Charles VII specifically to support the costs of the royal army. In general, the *taille* was levied only on those areas within the traditional realm of the king of France, though in some other provinces – Normandy, for example – it was imposed with the consent of the provincial Estates. The full *pays d'Etats* had their own elective systems of direct taxation, which protected them from some of the burden of the crown's direct tax system, but could still involve heavy burdens when presented – as in the case of Provence and Dauphiné – as a charge for the maintenance of troops within the provinces. To the major direct tax of the *taille*, whose yield had been rising steadily through the sixteenth century, was added the *taillon*, the specific levy for the costs of the *gendarmes* first imposed by Henri II, and a further tax to cover the costs of the *prévôts des maréchaussées*. Both of these were levied across the whole of France, as was a further *grande crue*, initially raised by Henri IV to assist in the demobilization of the troops which had fought in the civil wars, and subsequently to pay for troops in garrison.[23] The direct tax system was thus heavily tied to the military needs of the crown, and the implication of all of these levies was that they contributed directly to the support of the king's army. Moreover, as James Collins points out in his study of direct taxation, the king did

---

[22] In summarizing the financial resources of the crown, this section draws upon the studies of Mousnier, *Institutions* II. 71–8, 180–92, 413–29; A. Guéry, 'Les finances de la monarchie française'; Bonney, *King's Debts*; R.J. Bonney, 'Louis XIII, Richelieu and the royal finances', in Bergin and Brockliss (eds.), *Richelieu and his Age* pp. 101–20; Collins, *Fiscal Limits*.
[23] Collins, *Fiscal Limits*, pp. 45–8.

Paying for war

not restrict himself to ordinary levies when meeting the ever-increasing expenses of warfare. From the reign of François I, the crown came to depend more and more upon extraordinary impositions specifically intended to meet military costs – levies which, especially in the *pays d'Etats*, could be greater than the total of ordinary direct taxation.[24]

Estimates for the revenue derived from the direct tax system before the reign of Louis XIII are inevitably subject to a large margin of uncertainty and error. Taking the figures recorded by Jean-Roland Mallet, the early eighteenth-century *commis* of the *épargne*, the income obtained by the crown simply from the *taille* and its related *crues* had reached a plateau of around 9.5 million *livres* by the first decade of the seventeenth century.[25] James Collins emphasizes that a significant proportion of 'direct' taxes were not brought to the centre after collection, notably the *taillon* and *crue des prévôts des maréchaussées*, but were distributed to meet regional expenses, a process which was particularly relevant when funding a peace-time army distributed across the provinces.[26] Moreover, a further series of local levies devoted to provincial military needs – the costs of *étapes* to supply troops *en route* across the provinces; the maintenance of garrisons and the lodging of billeted troops through the formal requirements of the *ustensile*; in some cases the cavalry *surtaux* – do not even feature on the original tax assessments; they were effectively 'protection payments' intended to reduce the damage and disruption caused by the presence and movement of soldiers across the province.

Although Mallet's figures suggest that yield from the direct taxes was falling significantly in the 1620s and early 1630s – at a time when military expenditure was certainly increasing – it is again necessary to beware of treating his accounts of tax receipts by the central *épargne* as the total sum of money levied through the direct taxes. In practice the burden of direct taxation rose significantly in the 1620s, but a greatly increased proportion of the receipts remained in the provinces. One driving force behind this process was probably the character of war in the 1620s, the protracted struggles against the Huguenots waged within France, and the maintenance of forces on the eastern frontiers to guard against the threat of Habsburg invasion in 1625/6. The more important factor was the cumulative effect of alienating the direct taxes to *traitants*, a process which expanded greatly in the later 1620s and above all in 1632/3. The great bulk of increases in direct taxation were effectively perpetual *rentes* made in return for immediate cash advances, in theory fixed at ten times the annual value of the alienated tax, but often sold for only five or six times the yield.[27] While this

---

[24] Collins, *Fiscal Limits*, pp. 51–3.
[25] Bonney, *King's Debts*, pp. 310–11; Collins, *Fiscal Limits*, p. 111, suggests that the total direct taxation reaching the centre was around 10 million *livres* from a total collected in the provinces of around 16.5 million.
[26] Collins, *Fiscal Limits*, pp. 112–13: he proposes that these two taxes were levied at a total of 1.8 million *livres* p.a. between 1600 and 1620.
[27] Bonney, *King's Debts*, pp. 164–6; Collins, *Fiscal Limits*, pp. 98–100.

The administrative context

process of alienation was to lead to crisis by 1634, during the preceding period it accounted for substantial increases in revenue received by the crown under the category of *affaires extraordinaires*, which Mallet records as generating 21.7 million *livres* in 1625, 13 million *livres* in 1628 and 19.5 million in 1629 – all years of substantial military activity. Moreover, borrowing money against alienated increases in direct (and indirect) taxation was supplemented after 1620 by a massive expansion in the exploitation of venality of office, the *parties casuelles*. Assisted by the crown's evident willingness to sustain and renew the *droit annuel*, huge numbers of newly invented or duplicated offices were created in the twenties and early thirties and found purchasers. The *droit annuel* was itself a pillar of the subsequent exploitation of these office-holders, supplemented by expedients such as 'salary increases', which required the payment of an immediate additional lump sum to the crown to reflect the increase in the value of the office.[28]

The instability of this revenue system cannot be denied. A very large proportion of the income of the French crown was made up from borrowing against alienated taxes and other resources, and from the sale and exploitation of venal office. The unlimited expansion of the one would lead ultimately to bankruptcy and to all the fiscal disruption inherent in a massive rescheduling of debts; the over-exploitation of the other would ultimately exhaust the market for the purchase of office and alienate existing holders, the value of whose posts would have been systematically depreciated. The accounts of Gabriel Guénégaud, *trésorier de l'épargne* in 1632, reveal total receipts of 57.5 million *livres*, of which some 28 million came from the *parties casuelles* and 11 million from *deniers extraordinaires*. The relative weakness of receipts from direct taxation, and the almost complete failure of the main indirect – sales and customs – taxes to cover more than the costs of the *officiers* in charge of their collection, were matters for serious concern.[29] Yet setting these problems to one side, it could none the less be suggested that the revenues indicate the potential to meet the costs of the war-effort both before and, on all realistic assessments, after 1635. If the costs of open war against the Habsburgs were somewhere between 20 and 30 million *livres* p.a., then a state which would expect to devote at least 80 per cent of its revenues to military expenditure should have been able to meet this demand – even before the notorious increases in taxation and other fiscal expedients after 1635.

THE INADEQUACY OF FINANCIAL RESOURCES

Evidence for the period from 1620 to 1642 makes it clear that the crown could not afford to pay the costs of raising and maintaining its army; there was, moreover, a substantial shortfall between what would have been necessary to provide adequate

---

[28] R. Mousnier, *La vénalité des offices sous Henri IV et Louis XIII* (Paris, 1971), pp. 393–454.
[29] Bonney, *King's Debts*, pp. 164–5.

financial support for the army and what was actually received. As early as 1630, when at the height of the campaign the overall military establishment probably fluctuated between 35,000 and 45,000 troops, Richelieu rounded on the maréchal Louis de Marillac for complaining about the inadequacy of payment and supply to his army-corps on the frontiers of Champagne. Richelieu maintained that it was quite unrealistic to expect that a total military commitment on this scale could be adequately supported from available revenues, and that troops operating within the French frontiers should necessarily expect much more modest financial allocations than those operating in the duchy of Savoy and in Piedmont.[30] After 1635, shortfalls in the funding of the army-corps became endemic; even setting aside the complete collapse of the army of the Valtelline in early 1637 'faute d'argent', the letters of the great majority of the commanders and their administrative agents are full of complaints about delays and shortfalls in the arrival of pay for the *montres* – and no less frequently, their complete non-appearance – the inadequate provision for fortification and other extraordinary expenses, the regular collapse of supply contracts with unpaid *munitionnaires*, the apparent assumption of the central regime that military objectives in the campaign theatres could be achieved with totally inadequate financial support.

Why should there have been such a gap between the apparently substantial financial resources of the crown and the ability to provide adequate funds for the war-effort? As might be expected, there is no single answer; a number of factors are involved, some of which were embedded in the financial and military systems, others of which reflected decisions and misjudgements by the finance ministers. Much of the material related to these issues has been extensively explored through a number of outstanding studies of aspects of the French financial system, and these works will figure throughout this discussion.

The burden of deficit finance

One factor in the gap between theoretical revenues and military needs was the nature of seventeenth-century taxation systems, tied in large part to an agricultural cycle whose rhythms were fundamentally different from those of the campaign season. Although the main direct tax, the *taille*, was notionally collected in quarterly instalments, the capacity of the peasantry to meet their financial obligations, and therefore the overall yield of the instalments, was far greater in the autumn and early winter after the harvest and the sale of grain. Early spring and summer saw the peasantry dependent upon their remaining food supplies, lacking specie and resistant to financial demands. This situation was of course exactly the reverse of the financial cycle of the army, whose heaviest expenditure fell in the first half of the year, when the needs of recruitment, replacement of

[30] Grillon, v. 563, 30 Aug. 1630.

The administrative context

weapons, equipment and horses, stockpiling of food and munitions and the building up of transportation were all at their height.[31] Money collected in the autumn or early winter could, in theory, be held over until the following spring or summer, but in practice there would be substantial 'leakage' to meet other, more pressing, financial engagements. Money was at its most scarce in the *épargne* when military needs were greatest. When Bullion confided to Richelieu in January 1636 that the *épargne* was all but empty, having been ordered to make payments of 2.5 million *livres* in the last eight to ten days, largely for garrisons and recruitment, he was dramatizing this very real problem.[32] And the problem was even more intense if the crown sought to fund its military expenditure through the localized distribution of tax revenues, for the time-lag between local collection and redistribution was significantly shorter, weighting the available revenues still further towards the period in which military demands were at the lowest.

The response to this problem, which was as old as the crown's waging of war, was the anticipation of revenues through short-term borrowing. Though this was certainly not a problem restricted to France, it could be argued that such short-term borrowing to finance the army was part of a wider practice of revenue anticipation which was the largest single reason for the French crown's inability to fund its wars with apparently adequate revenues. The system of short-term advances to cover military expenses had been underpinned by the *trésoriers de l'ordinaire et de l'extraordinaire des guerres* since the sixteenth century. These venal office-holders received a percentage of all military expenditure in return for ensuring the flow of specie to the armies in accordance with instructions from the ministers. The percentage appears to have been reduced from 6 *deniers* per *livre* in 1632 (one fortieth of all payments) to 4 *deniers* by 1640 (one sixtieth).[33] The *trésorier de l'ordinaire* had much the smaller financial charge, being responsible for the troops of the royal household and some of the companies of *gendarmes*.[34] The *extraordinaire* was divided into two, with the *département de Picardie* giving responsibility for all military operations north of the Loire, the *département de Piémont* the south of the realm. As might be expected, given the sums of money involved in military transactions, the offices of *trésoriers de l'extraordinaire des guerres* were much sought after by those involved in the financial affairs of the monarchy. In 1636 François Sabathier and a consortium involved in providing munitions for the armies offered to waive 800,000 *livres* owed them in cash in return for the *trésoriers*' offices, and even to accept a reduction in the total *gages*

---

[31] AAE MD 807, fo. 161, 26 Apr. 1633, Bullion to Richelieu, stating that the bulk of military expenses fall in the first six months of the year when little money is expected to flow into the *épargne*.
[32] AAE MD 820, fo. 93, Jan. 1636.
[33] AAE MD 806, fo. 175, [1632]; SHAT A¹ 58, fo. 257, 24 Mar. 1640, de Noyers to the duc d'Enghien, referring to a *commis* of the *extraordinaire des guerres* still attempting to levy 6 *deniers* per *livre*.
[34] To give a representative sample, the *extrait de l'épargne* for 1634 recorded *ordinaire* expenses of 436,063 *livres* and *extraordinaire* of 19,863, 840 *livres*: AAE MD 812, fo. 401.

Paying for war

paid to the existing office-holders (in addition to the *taxations* from the payments to the army) from 100,000 to 40,000 *livres* p.a.[35] The margins for profit on the *trésoriers*' dealings were huge; there would certainly have been cheaper and more efficient means of obtaining cash to meet military expenses before earmarked taxes had been collected. However, given the crown's general reluctance to assume such functions through a formal administrative structure, delegating this into the hands of the *trésoriers* was a predictable response.

Royal borrowing, however, had never simply been about the short-term anticipation of revenues, a means of meeting immediate demands for expenditure against anticipated revenues. War was the greatest catalyst of longer-term financial transactions: the mortgaging of revenues for years in advance, sometimes permanently, in return for cash advances. The tendency to finance war through *affaires extraordinaires* was in no sense a development of Richelieu's ministry, and it could be maintained that the crown in the 1620s and 1630s was already the victim of over a century of accumulated debt, which considerably narrowed the options of the *bureau des finances* in seeking to finance an expanding war-effort.

Within a structure of bewildering complexity, there were broadly two means by which the crown could obtain advances on its revenues. The first of these, straightforwardly, was the formal contracting of loans (*prêts*), whose interest and ultimate repayment would be met from future income. The second, initially far more important, method was the temporary or permanent alienation of parts of the royal revenue in return for a down-payment corresponding to a multiple of the estimated annual yield of the revenue. Whereas the *prêteur* who simply advanced a sum of money to the crown against an agreed rate of interest had (in theory) no control over the revenues from which his interest was paid, the *traitant* who had negotiated a *rente* with the crown against a specific tax revenue, or a *traité* giving him the right to dispose of certain offices or other crown rights, had direct control over some part of the crown's revenues alienated into his hands in return for the loan.[36]

The attempt to raise *prêts* on the financial market encountered the fundamental problems of the lack of credit-worthiness and the unreliability of the crown. Decades, if not centuries, of willingness to manipulate and withhold interest payments, of diverting money to more urgent needs and of borrowing beyond the crown's real resources had all taken their toll and ensured that the costs of raising money by direct loans was always expensive and could prove crippling. However, the cash loan, raised rapidly and in response to particular, often military, needs of the crown, remained a significant element in the dealings of the *bureau des finances*,

---

[35] AAE MD 822, fo. 189, 10 Nov. 1636, Chavigny to Bullion. The negotiations broke down over the problems of compensating Chamlay, holder of the main office of *trésorier*, and Sabathier was ultimately to buy himself into the administration of the *parties casuelles* in 1638: Bonney, *King's Debts*, p. 187.

[36] Bayard, *Monde des financiers* pp. 163–266.

The administrative context

above all in the years from 1636 to 1648.[37] Rates of interest involved in raising money in this way were so high that the evidence needed to be concealed under the cloak of the king's secret affairs of state.[38] Not surprisingly, this expedient was regarded as an emergency measure, primarily a means of meeting budgetary shortfalls. It was not until alternative means of raising advances had all but dried up in the mid-1640s that direct borrowing became the principal means of meeting the financial needs of the monarchy.[39]

The gradual acceleration of reliance on *prêts* reflected both the exhaustion of other means of anticipating revenues and the impact of these other means in draining away the current income of the crown. For although it might seem that raising money by *prêts* was a more flexible and attractive means of obtaining cash advances to finance warfare or other royal expenses, the legacy of perceived fiscal unreliability of the crown made the direct alienation of revenues or rights into hands of creditors by means of *traités* a more attractive, and relatively cheaper, option.[40]

An initial attraction of alienating revenues from direct taxes in the period 1610–30, as we have seen, was the extent to which the advances could be repaid against increases in the total burden of taxation – *droits* held against these revenues. Though the policy was fiscally short-sighted, it had the immediate advantage that while the receipts from direct taxes were holding steady or declining only slightly, the crown was receiving very substantial cash advances against increases in the overall tax burden granted to the *traitants* and sold by them to interested parties in the provinces, most often the tax officials.[41] Given that the main direct taxes evidently had the potential to be increased gradually from a yield of around 10 million *livres* p.a. up to 16–20 million without provoking unmanageable opposition and resistance, the mortgaging of this increase – frequently for no more than five to six times its annual yield – may have been an obvious response to the immediate costs of warfare, but it also eliminated the possibility that the crown could meet subsequent financial demands through

---

[37] Bayard, *Monde des financiers*, analyses 2,723 contracts for loans negotiated in the decades between 1610 and 1660, emphasizing their concentration in the period after 1636: pp. 234–7. For an example of Bullion's borrowing to meet immediate expenses: AAE MD 820, fo. 184, 31 Mar. 1636, the *surintendant* is about to negotiate *prêts* worth 4 million *livres* required by 15 May.

[38] R. Bonney, 'The secret expenses of Richelieu and Mazarin, 1624–1661', *English Historical Review*, 91 (1976), 825–36.

[39] Bonney, *King's Debts*, pp. 197–8.

[40] A. Chauleur, 'Le rôle des traitants dans l'administration financière de la France de 1643–1653, *Dix-Septième Siècle*, 65 (1964), 16–49. An earlier attempt to reconcile the two systems and to raise loans more cheaply, the creation of *Rentes sur l'hôtel de ville* which theoretically alienated crown revenues to the management of the *échevins*, charging them to raise subsequent loans for the crown, had all but lost its credibility by the end of the sixteenth century after several decades of crown manipulation and interference: J. Dent, *Crisis in Finance. Crown, Financiers and Society in Seventeenth-Century France* (Newton Abbot, 1973), pp. 46–54.

[41] Collins, *Fiscal Limits*, pp. 98–100.

Paying for war

increasing direct tax revenues.[42] The systematic alienation of increases in direct taxes was matched by consistently unfavourable agreements contracting out the management of the revenue farms – the indirect taxes ranging from the *gabelles* (salt tax) and *aides* to the complex mass of internal customs dues headed by the *cinq grosses fermes*.[43]

By the early 1630s the crown finances were already showing clear symptoms of what was to be the fundamental malaise of the war years. Though on paper the French crown had substantial ordinary revenues, and had the capacity to increase these further, the actual cash yield which could be devoted to immediate expenses was pitifully low. Not merely had large proportions of royal taxes been permanently alienated or farmed out for relatively modest annual returns, the consequent shortfalls between actual cash receipts and expenditure had to be made good by further alienations, or short-term loans at high rates of interest, both of which further reduced the income of the crown in subsequent years. Even the exploitation of venality of office – the *parties casuelles* – had its longer-term price in the commitment to pay salaries to the new office-holders in return for the cash received for the initial purchase. Moreover, the majority of offices were sold by *traités* with financiers, who often received batches of offices at well below the market price, whether as repayment for existing debts or in part payment for providing new loans.[44]

Even before France was drawn into open war in 1635, the outlines of a vicious circle were clear. Increased expenditure was met by borrowing, most frequently by means of *traités* and *droits* alienating both existing revenues and absorbing tax increases. The regular income of the crown was falling and expenses could only be met by further financial manipulation and alienations and, in the last resort, by more borrowing. The costs of what was an elaborate system of debt servicing cut further into the remaining revenues and forced the crown into still further expedients to increase its cash in hand to meet expenses. The pattern by the early 1630s is clear, with 17 million *livres* raised through *traités* in 1631, 44 million in 1632 and 69 million in 1633. Against this, Mallet's figures for the payments made to meet *extraordinaire* expenses in the same years are recorded at 15 million *livres*, 30 million and 39 million.[45] None of these figures is reliable; by the 1630s the *bureau des finances* had elevated a combination of erratic accounting and systematic

---

[42] Moreover, increases in taxes that were directly and visibly alienated to *traitants* stimulated widespread hostility and resistance during the 1620s in ways that the direct royal perception of these taxes might have avoided: cf. Bonney, *King's Debts*, p. 166.

[43] R. Bonney, 'The failure of the French revenue farms, 1600–1660', *Economic History Review*, 2nd ser., 32 (1979), 11–32; Bayard, *Monde des financiers*, pp. 116–46. The unfavourable terms were often a reflection of local unrest and resistance to tax collection, which had become a major issue by the later 1620s.

[44] Bayard, *Monde des financiers*, pp. 164–8, analyses a total of 2,272 *traités* drawn up in the first half of the seventeenth century, of which 764 (33.6 per cent) are concerned with the sale or exploitation of offices; see also Mousnier, *Vénalité des offices*, pp. 156–65.

[45] Bonney, *King's Debts*, pp. 315–16, 306–7.

obfuscation into an art form. However, it shows clearly that ever larger sums of money as a proportion of total crown revenues were made up of loan contracts, debt servicing and the contracting of further advances through various means to cover the costs of the existing *affaires extraordinaires*. The crown was already relying as a matter of course on the large-scale mobilization of credit to meet its immediate expenses, and the costs of such a system were rising inexorably. Real revenue was being eaten away to service a debt which then had to be expanded in order to meet the crown's regular expenditure.

This steadily worsening situation raises fundamental questions about the extent to which during the early 1630s the finance ministers could have anticipated the likelihood of all-out war with the Habsburgs. As chapter 2 indicated, France was not at peace in the early 1630s, but exploiting a position on the sidelines of the main European conflict to strengthen her eastern frontier and to pursue a number of long-term political goals which in other circumstances would have provoked a vigorous Imperial or Spanish response. Until 1634 the scale of military activity was both smaller than it had been in 1629–30 and was to become after 1635. But it was still sufficient to ensure that the crown could not break out of its existing reliance upon deficit financing. Despite traditional assertions that the first years of the 1630s were intended to husband French resources for the imminent 'great ordeal', the reality was a financial system driven by the needs of warfare in which the problems of managing the *affaires extraordinaires* continued to grow, restricting any attempt to increase the proportion of revenues in hand. The price of sustaining even the limited war-effort of these years was to confirm the dependence on *traités* and to ensure that far too high a proportion of current income was drawn into debt servicing.

The notorious attempt to break this vicious circle in early 1634 can only reinforce the impression that the *surintendants des finances* did not anticipate that France would be drawn into major European war, at least until the impact of their expedient had been given time to subside. Calculating the budget for 1634, the *surintendants* estimated that out of a total levy of 22.6 million *livres* in direct taxes from the *pays d'élections*, only 14.1 million would represent revenues for the crown. The remaining 8.5 million would reimburse holders of alienated royal taxes. In response, the *bureau des finances* issued *rentes* with a face value of 154 million *livres*, which would receive interest paid at 7.1 per cent based upon the allocation of 8 million *livres* of the income from the *taille* and 3 million from the *gabelles*.[46] While this manoeuvre might appear as simply another alienation of royal revenues, its actual purpose was not to supplement but to supplant existing *droits* on the direct taxes. Holders of these original *droits*, often purchased for only five to six times the annual yield of the tax revenue, were to be subjected to a

---

[46] Bonney, *King's Debts*, pp. 165–7, from whose lucid account of this transaction most of the subsequent discussion of this section is drawn; Collins, *Fiscal Limits*, pp. 100–1.

rescheduling of crown debt: the existing *droits* were to be reclaimed and the holders compensated for their purchase from this 154 million *livres* of new *rentes*, which would receive annual interest at one fourteenth of the face value. While this would not liberate revenues for the crown (the new system would tie up 11 million *livres* of tax revenue), it appeared to ensure that the crown was getting a better return on the alienation of its taxes, and, indeed, if it managed to sell the entire stock of 154 million *livres* of *rentes* – needless to say, through a deal with *traitants* – it would be the beneficiary of cash advances which Bullion calculated to be worth 24 million *livres*.[47]

However, such a manoeuvre presupposed that the existing holders of alienated taxes, for the most part financial office-holders, would be prepared quietly to accept the arbitrary transformation of *droits* which had yielded up to 20 per cent interest on their original capital, into *rentes* paying interest of just over 7 per cent.[48] Like all such debt rescheduling, timing was vitally important. Just as attacks on 'corrupt' financiers by means of *chambres de justice* might be threatened with great regularity, but were usually postponed in practice until the end of a war when the crown's need for new loans was reduced, such a massive rescheduling of debt could only be justified if it was believed that a period of political and military stability was imminent, and that the crown and its ministers could therefore ride out the storm of protest and non-cooperation from those – mostly financial office-holders – compelled to accept the new *rentes*.[49] In fact the *surintendants*' manoeuvre was followed, seven months later, by the battle of Nördlingen and the beginning of the slide into open war.

In this context of an imminent conflict which would prove more expensive than any previous war in France's history, the decision to convert the *droits* was foolhardy. It is impossible to disagree with Richard Bonney's verdict that Bullion and Bouthillier took a bad situation and made it considerably worse.[50] The creation of 154 million *livres* of *rentes* grossly misjudged what the money market would sustain; instead of simply undertaking a smaller-scale operation to redeem the alienated *droits* on the direct taxes, the *surintendants* had tried to engage in a

---

[47] AAE MD 808, fo. 77, [early Oct.] 1633, Bullion to Richelieu. Bullion was being economical with the truth here; Bonney points out that by the time the *traitants* had taken their cut, the net payment to the government would be reduced to 14.8 million *livres*: *King's Debts*, p. 167.

[48] Moreover, Collins, *Fiscal Limits*, p. 100, proposes that the actual sum allocated to the payment of interest on these *rentes* in the late 1630s was 3.5 million *livres*: the effective rate of interest (if it is assumed that all the *rente*-holders received the same level of interest) was less than half the originally envisaged 7.1 per cent.

[49] For discussion of the timing of *chambres de justice* see J. Bosher, '*Chambres de justice* in the French monarchy', in J. Bosher (ed.), *French Government and Society, 1500–1850. Essays in Memory of Alfred Cobban* (London, 1973), pp. 19–40, pp. 24–31; D. Dessert, 'Finances et société au xviie siècle: à propos de la chambre de justice de 1661', *Annales ESC*, 29 (1974), 864–7; Bayard, *Monde des financiers*, pp. 318–30. Bonney, 'Richelieu and the royal finances', pp. 121–4, argues that Richelieu had suspended any thought of fiscal reform until after the end of the war.

[50] Bonney, *King's Debts*, pp. 165–8: the following paragraph draws upon Professor Bonney's meticulous clarification of the consequences of the *surintendants*' decision.

The administrative context

huge cash-raising exercise, and the result was a surge of *rentes*, marketed at an uncompetitive rate of interest, which remained stubbornly unsold into the 1640s.

This would have mattered less had France been at peace or been scaling down her war-effort. A much reduced borrowing requirement would have squeezed the options for investment in the tax system, and the crown could simply have waited for the *rentes* to find a market. In contrast, flooding the market with these *rentes* at precisely the moment when the crown's need for cash advances was about to increase out of all recognition was a recipe for fiscal disaster. Confronted with numerous more attractive options for lending to the crown, the value of the *rentes* plummeted; in 1641 a *rente* generating 1,000 *livres* p.a. which, on paper, ought to have been worth 14,000 *livres* was actually selling for 4,000 *livres*.[51] The situation was compounded by the general inability of the crown to meet even modest rates of interest on its debts in the later 1630s, further strengthening the desire of the luckless owners of many of these *petites rentes* to sell them for whatever small portion of their face value they could obtain. This gap between the paper value of the *rentes* and their massively reduced value on the market fuelled speculation at the crown's expense amongst well-placed financiers. For a major financier, whose subsequent loans were desperately needed by an embattled crown, the opportunity to offload a block of *rentes* previously purchased at a discounted rate in return for reimbursement at face value could be made part of the conditions of a new loan. Any hesitations that financiers might have felt about such transactions were doubtless overcome by the example of Cardinal Richelieu, who between 1635 and 1636 redeemed for cash and at face value some 1.5 million *livres* of *droits* which had been converted into *rentes* in 1634.[52] The conversion of 1634 failed to benefit the crown by providing a substantial source of hard cash to sustain the war-effort, while it made the raising of new loans more difficult and more expensive at precisely the moment when they would be more than ever required.

On the eve of France's entry into the Thirty Years War, a huge miscalculation on the part of the *surintendants* had thrown the crown to an even greater extent into the exploitative hands of its financiers. The incongruous leap in the crown's revenues in 1635 given in Mallet's figures is entirely the product of this paper conversion of *droits* into *rentes*.[53] The reality was that the crown entered the war with few cash resources, having created a situation in which subsequent borrowing would impose an ever-increasing burden of excessively high interest payments on the crown's revenues.

To this grave misjudgement could be added the legacy of the over-exploitation of venal office in the 1620s and early 1630s. The exploitation of the wealth of the

---

[51] Bonney, *King's Debts*, p. 166.
[52] Bergin, *Cardinal Richelieu* pp. 173-5.
[53] The inflated figures are recorded in Bonney, *King's Debts*, pp. 307, 311; Mousnier, *Vénalité des offices*, p. 421, fails to take the fictitious nature of this calculation into account and thus greatly exaggerates the fall in the proportional value of receipts from the *parties casuelles* in 1634/5.

office-holding elites was explicitly considered to be the key resource of the crown, and had been systematically exploited to support the war-effort since 1624. Representing 37 per cent of the crown's income in the half decade 1620–4, the *parties casuelles* declined slightly to 33.5 per cent from 1625 to 1629, then reached a peak of nearly 39 per cent from 1630 to 34. The consequences of this overexploitation of office became apparent as the proportion of revenue fell to 24.5 per cent in the later 1630s, and much more strikingly, to 15 per cent from 1640 to 1644.[54] Inevitably the real – cash – yield from the creation and sale of office fell as venality became drawn into the incessant negotiations between the *bureau des finances* and the financiers concerning the servicing and manipulation of a growing burden of debt.[55] The decision to press the sale of office so hard in the early 1630s, and to antagonize existing office-holders in the process, reinforces the perception that the crown was not consciously planning for a lengthy conflict which would require unprecedented cash resources.

Fiscal policy in the years immediately before the 1635 declaration of war had created a situation in which the crown would need to raise an ever-larger proportion of its ordinary revenues through *affaires extraordinaires*, which in turn would impose an increasingly heavy burden of interest payments and debt redemption on unfavourable terms. This certainly represented the most fundamental reason for the crown's inability to meet the costs of the war-effort. There were, however, other structural reasons contributing to this failure.

SHORTAGE OF SPECIE AND PROBLEMS OF CONVERSION

In very large part, military expenses could be met only with specie. Whereas court pensions, salaries of office-holders, large parts of the debts to *traitants*, could frequently be negotiated payments made on credit, adding further to the burden of crown debt but avoiding immediate expense, soldiers required cash if they were to buy food, pay for lodgings and receive the minimal sums to persuade them to remain in service. This presented problems on a number of levels. In the first instance, coin was relatively scarce in early seventeenth-century France. Decades during which France's neighbours had tended to produce devalued coins with a low silver or gold content had drawn French coins with a higher precious metal content out of the realm.[56] This scarcity was compounded by the relatively small quantity of coinage minted in France during the sixteenth and early seventeenth centuries, itself a reflection of the crown's difficulties in laying hands on gold and silver resources.[57] The results were harmful on a number of levels. A large

---

[54] Bonney, *King's Debts*, p. 313: the real value of the *parties casuelles* is sustained in the later 1630s but falls significantly in the early 1640s: Bonney, *King's Debts*, p. 311.
[55] Bayard, *Monde des financiers*, pp. 182–7.
[56] Dessert, *Argent, pouvoir et société* pp. 28–39.
[57] Bonney, *King's Debts*, p. 170; F. Spooner, *The International Economy and Monetary Movements in France, 1493–1725* (Cambridge, Mass., 1972), pp. 179–87; 291–8.

The administrative context

proportion of the stock of coinage in France was in the hands of a small minority of powerful individuals, above all, financier cartels, who would be reluctant to hand over coinage with a high precious metal content if other means could be found to pay debts or meet expenses. The crown had to offer substantial inducements to prise these reserves out of the hands of its wealthiest subjects, above all repayment and interest payments made in coin – thus reinforcing the crown's own long-term shortage of specie.[58]

This situation was compounded by the consequent shortage of coins in mass circulation. The local peasant economy had little need of coinage other than some low-denomination copper coins, and most peasants had accumulated any surplus acquired in preceding years in goods and stock. Expected to meet increasingly heavy tax demands, ordinary peasants were forced to borrow from the wealthier members of the village to meet tax assessments that by the later 1630s amounted to 5–10 *livres* per household, payable in cash. Indeed, James Collins suggests that peasant resistance to growing tax demands may have reflected the difficulty and cost of meeting payments in specie as much as absolute economic incapacity.[59] The crown could increase its tax demands, but this did not imply any consequent ability to lay hands on a proportionately larger quantity of cash, and it is clear that the yield of direct taxes encountered a ceiling in this period above which increases yielded negligible returns.[60]

To obtain the very large quantities of coin required to pay armies in these circumstances forced the price of borrowing money upwards, and ensured that the crown was constantly negotiating for cash from a position of shortage and urgent need. Comparison with the Spanish monarchy emphasizes the obvious point that the *quinto real* levied on the bullion production from the New World had a value in maintaining the liquidity of government finance out of all proportion to its share of the total tax yield.[61] An annual influx of silver which could be minted and distributed as cash, put the Spanish crown in a position of strength vis-à-vis its creditors. In France, on the other hand, the *bureau des finances* considered that there was an upper limit to the cash that could be extracted from within the economy, that whatever the level of taxation, however vigorous the exploitation of the *parties casuelles* and the *affaires extraordinaires*, the *épargne* would never receive much more than 40 million *livres* in cash. Bullion regularly referred to this figure of 40 million in his correspondence, and most of his anguish about overexpenditure reflected the concern that real financial resources could not be increased

---

[58] Dessert, *Argent, pouvoir et société*, pp. 32–5.
[59] Collins, *Fiscal Limits*, pp. 209–10; Collins also cites M. Foisil, *La révolte des Nu-Pieds* (Paris, 1970), pp. 133–5 to argue for the connection between shortage of coinage and revolt in Normandy.
[60] Collins, *Fiscal Limits*, pp. 218–19, suggests that the upper limit to be extracted from direct taxes was around 30–5 million *livres* – of which, of course, only a proportion would go to the central government.
[61] Elliott, *The Count-Duke of Olivares* pp. 70–1.

above this level.[62] For although the accounts of income provided by Mallet and others might suggest that the crown revenues were increasing substantially in the years after 1633, the bulk of these increases represented the ever-increasing sums involved in paper negotiations with financiers, in which new loans were negotiated to pay off old debts and to meet interest payments. Well over 50 per cent of notional revenue and expenditure was tied up in an increasingly elaborate web of these fiscal negotiations after 1635, such that 'a massive operation on paper was required to produce proportionately quite a small increase in specie available to the government'.[63] The crown's concern to obtain a higher proportion of the available cash within the economy after 1635 enjoyed limited success and drove the *bureau des finances* ever deeper into its expensive dependence on financiers.

The *surintendants* made one effort to come to terms with the dangers posed to the war-effort by a shortage of specie within the French financial system. The devaluation of the *livre tournois* in 1636 was aimed at reversing the imbalance that had developed between French and foreign currencies, and which had led to a flow of currency out of the country.[64] As a result, the *bureau des finances* from the late 1630s, and even more from 1640 to 1644, was able to issue significantly more specie, a large proportion of which was reissued foreign coinage now flowing into France as a result of the devaluation. To facilitate this recoinage, in 1640 the *louis d'or* was introduced and was exactly comparable in weight to the Spanish *pistoles* that were now circulating widely in France and in the French armies. This was followed a year later by the creation of the *écu d'argent*, a copy of another piece of Spanish coinage.[65]

Increasing in this manner the amount of coinage in circulation undoubtedly eased some of the problems of funding the war-effort. Moreover, as Richard Bonney convincingly suggests, the devaluation of the *livre* served to discourage the hoarding of cash, since these hoards would now lose part of their value. Those with spare cash were more likely to try to invest, and in many cases contribute to funding the crown's borrowing requirement.[66] And at one level devaluation may have eased the military expenses of the crown: a soldier receiving a nominal wage of 6 *livres* per *montre* would now receive a smaller sum measured in terms of precious metal, even if the *bureau* hoped that within France the purchasing power of the coins would remain the same.

---

[62] AAE MD 811, fo. 120, 7 Nov. 1634, Bullion to Richelieu; 822, 18 Oct. 1636, Bullion to Chavigny: 'nous ne feront pas loin de quarante un milliers d'argent content [comptant], chose non imaginable'; 833, fo. 98, 11 Apr. 1639, Bullion to Richelieu: 'Je prie Dieu que nous puissions aller jusqu'au 35 millions du content dans cette annee.'
[63] Bonney, *King's Debts*, pp. 174–5.
[64] Bonney, *King's Debts*, pp. 170–1; the *livre* was a unit of account, rather than an actual coin, but the decree that 1 *livre* was now represented by a smaller quantity of silver then affected all of the coins whose values were pegged to the *livre* as new coins with the same face value but a lower silver content started to circulate.
[65] Spooner, *Monetary Movements*, pp. 181–2, 330–2.
[66] Bonney, *King's Debts*, p. 171; Spooner, *Monetary Movements*, p. 298.

The administrative context

There were other problems connected with coinage and the payment of the armies. Coins whose value was a function of their intrinsic silver or gold content created problems of transportation. If the *bureau des finances* decided to collect together a *montre* to pay an army-corps in the form of small-denomination silver coins, the quantities of coin, its weight and bulk, posed considerable problems. Dessert points out that in 1676, 200,000 *écus* would represent 5,438 kilos of silver.[67] A cannon and its equipment of this weight required a team of twenty-five horses, and could move along roads at no more than a few miles a day.[68] Michel Le Tellier, *intendant* with the army of Italy in 1641, explained that the operation of moving money in small silver coins to pay the troops on campaign and in garrison had occupied 800 horses, and at a time when they were needed at least as urgently for the transportation of *vivres*.[69] The costs of transporting these quantities of coinage were significant. The accounts of the *extraordinaire des guerres* for the payment of the garrisons in north Italy in 1632 gives the transportation costs of the coinage at 6 *deniers* per *livre*, or nearly 12,000 *livres* on payments of 500,000 *livres* – 50 per cent more than the *taxations* of the *trésorier de l'extraordinaire*.[70] James Collins provides an example from within France of 86,000 *livres* of tax revenues shipped from Brittany to Paris in 1606, an operation which cost just under 2,000 *livres*, required eighteen pack horses, and took twenty-four days.[71]

A solution could be to transport the money for the soldiers in larger denomination gold coins, something under one tenth of the bulk and weight of their silver equivalent.[72] However, while this would reduce the costs of movement and would speed up the despatch of a *voiture* of money for an army, those charged with distributing the pay faced the concomitant problems of trying to exchange these large-denomination gold coins for the equivalent in smaller silver coins which could be used to pay the troops. There were additional costs involved in carrying out such an exchange, above all if the aim was to convert large denomination French coins into Italian, German or Catalan coins for the armies operating over the frontiers. In the same letter in which he had complained of the logistical problems of moving large quantities of silver to pay the army its last *montre*, Le Tellier explained that he had received the *pistoles* to pay the next *montre* to the troops but was holding the money back for the time being since a local financier (Thibault) was proposing to charge between 1.5 and 3 per cent commission for converting these coins into 'monnaie blanche légère'.[73]

The expense, slowness and security risk of transporting large quantities of cash

---

[67] Dessert, *Argent, pouvoir et société*, p. 36.
[68] BN Ms.fr. 4561, fo. 50 (n.d.).
[69] Caron (ed.), *Le Tellier*, p. 101, 3 Sept. 1641, Le Tellier to Mazarin.
[70] AAE MD 806, fo. 232, *état* of expenses up to 11 Sept. 1632.
[71] Collins, *Fiscal Limits*, p. 130.
[72] Dessert, *Argent, pouvoir et société*, p. 36.
[73] Caron (ed.), *Le Tellier*, p. 101.

Paying for war

to pay the armies were particularly evident when the money had to be moved across the French frontiers. Wherever possible the *bureau des finances* tried to meet the needs of troops operating abroad through *lettres de change* cashed in a financial centre as near as possible to the troops. In 1635 Richelieu wrote to the *surintendants* that they were to send a *voiture* of 300,000 *livres* in cash to the troops operating on the Rhine only if there was absolutely no possibility of paying them via a *lettre de change* cashed at Frankfurt.[74] While raising money abroad to pay these armies made good sense in logistical terms, it represented another burden on the hard-pressed *épargne*. An arrangement for the troops in Alsace to be paid via two merchants in Strasbourg involved a commission of 3 per cent, and the enthusiastic endorsement of this arrangement by the *secrétaire de la guerre*, Servien, suggests that this was considered as good a deal as the crown was likely to get.[75] Moreover, while Bullion's decision to devalue the *livre tournois* made sense in terms of increasing the quantities of specie in circulation within France, it had the immediate effect of increasing the costs of those army-corps operating in allied territory where food, drink, forage and equipment needed to be bought with the local currency. It is not clear to what extent the ministerial concern at what was considered to be the disproportionate expense of the army in Piedmont reflected exchange differentials.[76] Certainly Le Tellier reported that the soldiers in Italy in 1640 were resentful at receiving their pay in French currency, and suggested that it would be possible to make economies by bulk exchange of the French funds for Piedmontese coins.[77] Differential exchange rates are perhaps best seen, less as a fundamental reason for the failure to fund troops operating across the frontiers, more as yet another small but regular drain on the already limited funds available to meet the costs of the armies.

For all these debates about small and large denomination coins, exchange rates and the problems of transporting specie need to be set in the context of an *épargne* which was finding it increasingly difficult to lay hands on any cash at all. On 30 October 1640 Bullion wrote to Richelieu that: 'je puis asseurer V.E. qu'entre tous les trois espargnes il n'y a pas cent mil escus de monnaye blanche de toutes sortes d'espèces'.[78] Agreeing to pay a further million *livres* of expenses in cash in October 1636, Bullion reported that this cleared all of the cash from the *épargne*, down to the last *denier*.[79] In this context finding cash in France which could be used to finance *lettres de change* was a more fundamental problem than the

---

[74] AAE MD 815, fo. 206, 18 Sept.
[75] AAE MD 816, fo. 132, 19 Nov. 1635, Servien to Richelieu.
[76] De Noyers' letters to Le Tellier implied that he considered the expenses of the army of Italy to be primarily the result of fraud by the officers, complicity by the *commissaires* and other agents (including the *intendant*) and the latter's failure to maintain accountability in contracts with the *munitionnaires*: see, for example, Caron (ed.), *Le Tellier*, p. 69, 5 June 1641, p. 175, 19 Feb. 1642.
[77] Caron (ed.), *Le Tellier*, p. 9, 3 Nov. 1640, Le Tellier to de Noyers.
[78] AAE MD 836, fo. 134.
[79] AAE MD 822, fo. 72, 18 Oct.

The administrative context

commission paid on these arrangements.[80] Most commanders would willingly accept a *montre* received in high-denomination *louis d'or* given that the likely alternative was an empty promise of payment, a delayed or partial *montre*, and general uncertainty about when any funding would arrive with the armies.[81] Bullion's main tactic to circumvent the acute shortage of cash – by assigning as yet unpaid revenues to expenses – will be considered in more detail later.

Corruption

While the shortage of specie contributed to the problems of the *bureau des finances* in the earlier 1630s, it was a problem which the *surintendants*, by their devaluation of the *livre tournois* and their massive recoining of foreign currency, managed to do something to ameliorate. The same cannot be said for the steady drain upon the available cash for the armies caused by the multiple layers of corruption within the fiscal and military administrations. The expansion of the war-effort both increased the levels of military expenditure and the opportunities for embezzlement, profiteering and collusive practices, developments which the *bureau des finances* was either unable or unwilling to restrain. Discussions of corruption within an early modern context can become entangled in wider debates about the overlap between private and the public funds in the activities of many office-holders, about different attitudes to personal and family enrichment through state service, and the confusions created by proprietary office-holding within a financial administration.[82] The line between opportunistic reimbursement for expenses previously incurred and the straightforward theft of public funds was rarely drawn clearly. The ministers thought that they could identify corruption amongst the administrators and army officers, but in practice they trod very carefully, and few specific prosecutions were pursued to the extent of a formal trial. Setting to one side contemporary perceptions of the legitimacy or morality of such activities, it is clear that a significant proportion of money destined for the payment of the armies stuck to the hands of those involved in their administration. Moreover, this appropriation came after those involved in the local apportioning, collection and movement of taxes had already taken their substantial cut of the original revenues.

Those involved in corrupt practices with regard to the payment of the armies can be divided into two broad groups: those who held established offices which

---

[80] The extraordinary ambassador in Piedmont, d'Hémery, wrote in 1638 that the army was close to collapse, having received less than 50,000 *livres* through the promised *lettres de change*: AAE MD 831, fo. 109, 29 Aug.

[81] BN Ms.fr. 3770, fo. 23v. 6 Feb. 1639, La Valette to Richelieu, emphasizing that the uncertainty about when funds would arrive makes effective military planning impossible, and constantly threatens the breakdown of supply and recruitment contracts.

[82] See J.-C. Waquet, *De la corruption. Morale et pouvoir à Florence aux XVIIe et XVIIIe siècles* (Paris, 1984), pp. 7–27.

gave them the ability to manipulate the system of troop funding to their own profit, and those – the predators – who were able to take advantage of the short-term financial requirements of the armies to develop monopolistic and exploitative positions in the structure of war-finance.

Corruption within the administration of the armies
Amongst those with an institutional position, the foremost group were the *trésoriers de l'extraordinaire des guerres*, and, to a lesser but still significant extent, their *commis* with the army-corps. As indicated earlier in the chapter, the legitimate profits of the *extraordinaire* – the *taxation* of 4 *deniers* per *livre* on all military expenditure – were already immense: the *extraits de l'épargne* for the years after 1635 give the official expenses of the *extraordinaire des guerres* at 33,167,000 livres (1635), 24,481,000 livres (1636), 21,172,500 livres (1637), 21,442,000 livres (1638) – therefore yielding theoretical *taxations* worth between 553,000 and 357,000 livres p.a.[83] The *taxations* were intended as a rough-and-ready means of compensating the *trésoriers* for the expense of using their own resources to meet immediate military expenses against a more irregular flow of tax revenues. As previously noted, they and their subordinate officials also received salaries, effectively paid against the original purchase price of their offices and funded quite separately from the *taxations*. However, as the scale of the war-effort grew, the role of the *trésoriers* changed from managers of the crown's short-term expenditure to a major element of the elaborate system of deficit financing.[84] Henri II de Bourbon, prince de Condé, arguing in 1639 for the advantages of abandoning tax negotiations in Languedoc and Guienne and simply imposing a levy backed by military force, proposed that one obvious benefit would be to: 'descharger [the population] de plusieurs fraiz inutiles et inevitables dans le maniement ordinaire des deniers du Roy pour les trouppes, comme sont les taxations, et droitz des trésoriers de l'extraordinaire des guerres, les frais des comptes de la Chambre, et autres sans fin.'[85]

Moreover, as the *trésoriers* were called upon to advance money to sustain the war-effort over and above the short-term anticipation of revenues, so the temptation to profit from fiscal confusion grew. *Trésoriers* concerned to recover money found numerous opportunities in a system which was in theory overseen by the *bureau des finances* but in practice was ill-monitored and chaotic.[86] It would seem that a favoured technique of the *trésoriers* was to appropriate sums of money

---

[83] AAE MD 819, fo. 153 [1635]; 823, fo. 116 [1636]; 828, fo. 368 [1637]; 832, fo. 250 [1638]. The *taxations* would represent one sixtieth of the overall expenditure.
[84] SHAT A¹ 28, fo. 317, 26 July 1636, concern at the slowness in collecting the *taillon* in Provence and the consequent delays in the repayment of the *trésoriers de l'ordinaire des guerres*.
[85] AAE MD 1631, fos. 31–2, 22 Aug. 1639, Condé to de Noyers.
[86] AAE MD 806, fos. 181–7, [1632], document concerned with abuses and accounting failures in the finances which singles out the artillery specifically, but is equally relevant to all areas of military finance. Bayard, *Monde des financiers*, pp. 314–15.

The administrative context

– the *deniers revenans bons* – which had been withheld from units whose effective strength had fallen below that given at the previous *montre*.[87] It is not clear whether the *trésoriers* hoped that these *deniers revenans bons* would never be traced or, perhaps more likely, they hoped to profit from lending the sums out at interest until finally forced to return them to the crown.[88] Such activities were well known to the ministers, but so long as the *trésoriers* remained an indispensable element of the financing of the war-effort, any attempt to constrain their activities would need to be handled with care. As de Noyers wrote to an exasperated Cardinal de La Valette: 'si les trésoriers qui ruinent les armées du Roy estoient punis comme ils le meritent, V.E. [La Valette] seroit en peine pour les bleds et pain de munition de son armée'.[89]

Had the appropriation of pay for the armies been confined to the *trésoriers* themselves the losses would have been substantial, but it is clear that the subordinate officers of the *ordinaire* and *extraordinaire*, the *trésoriers provinciaux*, the *commis* and the *payeurs* were also making illicit profits from short-changing the troops under their responsibility.[90] Condé, writing again in 1639 left no doubt that the *trésoriers des guerres* enjoyed the worst reputation for corruption, being 'fort odieuse aux peuples et aux trouppes', and stressing that this was particularly a consequence of the behaviour of their *commis*: 'pour le peu d'obeissance qu'ils leur rendent, et les difficultez incroyables qu'il y a de tirer de l'argent d'eulx . . . et a cause de fripponneries qu'exercent leurs commis, dont il y a plusieurs plainctes en cette armée'.[91]

This might be taken as the typical hostility of the high command to civilian officials operating within the army. However, more specific allegations about particular *commis* recur throughout the period, indicating that this was a much more deeply rooted problem, and one which was draining money away from the troops. Condé's son Louis II de Bourbon, duc d'Enghien, specifically charged the

---

[87] See for example SHAT A¹ 58, fo. 628, 30 Apr. 1640, de Noyers to sr Fondriac, ordering him to return 10,000 *livres* of *deniers revenans bons* retained from the payment of the garrison of Nancy in 1636; A¹ 58, fo. 453, 15 Apr. 1640, similar order to Brossier to return 19,400 *livres* to the *épargne*, constituting the *deniers revenans bons* of the first *montre* of 1639 paid to the army of Italy.

[88] As early as 1635 the *secrétaire de la guerre* was indicating disquiet at the tendency of the *trésoriers* to accumulate *deniers revenans bons* rather than repaying them directly to the *épargne*: SHAT A¹ 24, fo. 421, 26 June; AAE MD 822, fo. 96, 23 Oct. 1636, Louis XIII to Richelieu, commenting on this practice by the *trésoriers*.

[89] BN Ms.fr. 6647, fo. 144, 5 Oct. 1636: de Noyers went on to explain that the *trésoriers* had undertaken to ensure the supply of the army on the basis of a down payment of 20,000 *écus*.

[90] In what was evidently a large-scale abuse discovered in 1636, the *trésoriers généraux* of the *taillon* had refused to hand over sums collected across certain *généralités* throughout 1635: SHAT A¹ 32, pce 167, 31 Aug. 1636, 'contrainte du Roy' to enforce repayment.

[91] AAE MD 1631, fo. 31, 5 Sept. 1639; Condé had shown himself hostile to the actions of the *trésoriers* and their *commis* three years earlier: SHAT A¹ 28, fo. 141, 26 June 1636, Louis XIII to Condé, ordering him to retain the *commis* with his army. Other members of the military and provincial elites took no more favourable an attitude: see for example AAE MD 807, fo. 248, 25 July 1633, Bullion and Bouthillier to Richelieu, reporting the maltreatment of a *commis* accused of refusing to pay sums due to the *cavalerie légère* of the marquis de Saint-Chaumont.

Paying for war

commis of the *extraordinaires des guerres* in Burgundy and Bresse of holding back 6 *deniers* per *livre* of all military payments rather than the prescribed 4 *deniers*.[92]

If the officials of the *ordinaire* and, above all, the *extraordinaire des guerres* stood at the apex of corruption amongst the officials, the dubious activities of the *commissaires* and *contrôleurs des guerres* were also significant, and arguably even more damaging to the effectiveness of the armies. The *commissaires à la conduite* with responsibility for specific regiments received, like the *trésoriers de l'extraordinaire*, a share of the sums paid to their particular unit. In the *anciens régiments* (the *entretenus*) this was fixed as a right to the pay of one soldier per company.[93] Assuming eight *montres* of 12 *livres* paid to the soldiers in a twenty company regiment, this would amount to 1,920 *livres* per annum. The other type of *commissaire*, those with charge of the conduct of the *montres*, received a monthly salary of 300 *livres* – in theory 3,600 *livres* p.a.[94]

In neither case were the *commissaires* likely to receive anything approaching their full salaries, so that they had a permanent interest in the corrupt management of the distribution of funds to the troops. Like the *trésoriers*, the opportunities for profit came from the manipulation of the *deniers revenans bons*, the money held back as desertion, death and illness depleted the effective strength of the units, and which was in theory to be used to cover the cost of troops raised later in the campaigns. Balancing the losses incurred during the campaigns against successive waves of new recruits would have presented problems even to a scrupulously accountable administration. In the context of the 1630s it was an irresistible licence to forms of peculation which were relatively hard to detect and still more difficult to prosecute. On occasions *commissaires* would treat the accumulation of *deniers revenans bons* as an end in itself, and would refuse to pay units for more than the official number of soldiers, even though ministerial policy was to encourage unit commanders to recruit as many troops as possible.[95] Pierre-Conty d'Argencour, *ingénieur du roi*, sent on a mission to the fortifications and towns of Picardy in 1634, wrote in his report to Richelieu that the *commissaires* were simply witholding pay from five to six men in every notionally full-strength

---

[92] SHAT A¹ 58, fo. 257, 24 Mar. 1640, de Noyers to Enghien; A¹ 63, fo. 290, 2 Feb. 1641, order for the arrest of Barbe, *commis de l'extraordinaire des guerres*, accused of substantial misappropriation in the allocation of funds to the troops; BN Ms.fr. 17374, fo. 64, 19 Jan. 1641, *intendant* at Moulins, Humbert Chaponay, to Séguier, complaining of the corruption of the *commis* and his attempts to avoid paying over the *deniers revenans bons*.

[93] SHAT A¹ 57, fo. 526, 28 Feb. 1640, de Noyers to Le Lièvre, *commissaire à la conduite* of the regiment of Vaubecourt.

[94] SHAT A¹ 30, fo. 107, 15 Oct. 1636; A¹ 58, fo. 618, 29 Apr. 1640: the *contrôleurs des guerres* received a salary of 200 *livres* per month. An *ordonnance* of 1641 reduced the salaries of the *commissaires* to 200 *livres*, those of *contrôleurs* to 100 *livres* – though it is unlikely that the officials received even these reduced sums with any regularity: A¹ 62, fo. 171, 20 Jan. 1641. For a fuller discussion of the distinctions between the two types of *commissaires des guerres* and their evolution during this period, see chapter 7, pp. 379–80.

[95] AAE MD 815, fo. 49, July 1635, Richelieu to Bullion.

The administrative context

company on the grounds that the unit officers must be guilty of inflating the muster rolls with *passe-volants* or other corrupt means of borrowing soldiers for the *revues*.[96] In none of these cases was the *commissaires*' motive that of concern for the king's service; Argencour pointed out that companies which were well below full strength were passed at *revues* with no attempt to check on corrupt practices. As with the *trésoriers* and their *commis*, the attraction of the *deniers revenans bons* was the availability of a sum of money which could be appropriated, reinvested or, at the very least, treated as a loan by the administrators.[97]

The refusal to pay over-strength units and the exercise of counter-productive rigour in the interests of withholding pay fell an early victim to the expansion of the war-effort after 1635. As the average size of companies and regiments declined in the years after 1636 it became increasingly rare to find units sufficiently close to notional full strength which could be subjected to this arbitrary system of retrenchment.[98] More characteristic of the corrupt practices in the years of an expanding war-effort was overt collusion with the unit commanders. At the heart of the financial wastage connected with the armies was a huge and deliberate failure of accounting, the responsibility for which lay with the *commissaires* and *contrôleurs*. Both groups were willing to acquiesce in large-scale corruption surrounding the actual levies of troops and their arrival with the existing army-corps, calculations concerning the effective strengths of units and their payment, the provision of bread rations and demands for subsistence.[99] Underpinning all of this was the impossibility of establishing with any accuracy the day-to-day strength of an army-corps, the rate of loss through desertion and sickness and the extent to which these losses were being made good by the arrival of new recruits.

The line between unavoidable confusion and deliberate fraudulence was easily crossed. *Commissaires* were regularly criticized for pre-signing the rolls of the *montres* before the numbers of troops were formally entered, implying minimal concern for the detection of abuses at the *revues*.[100] Even more overt were cases of

---

[96] AAE MD 1676, fo. 42, 8 Aug. 1634.

[97] As the governor of Picardy Honoré d'Albert, duc de Chaulnes, pointed out in an angry report to Richelieu, the excessive stringency of the *commissaires* in refusing to pay even those cavalry who were legitimately absent from the garrisons was more calculated to 'ruiner les trouppes et faire les deniers revenans bons que pour servir le Roi dans leurs charges' – with the clear implication that the withheld sums were pocketed by the *commissaires*: AAE MD 1678, fos. 30–2, 13 Mar. 1636.

[98] Though Jacques de Chastenet de Puységur, captain in the Piedmont regiment, records how in 1638 the *commissaire* attempted to withhold *deniers revenans bons* for 150 men by excluding the wounded and sick: *Guerres*, I. 218.

[99] SHAT A^1 51, fo. 561, 28 Apr. 1639, general instruction to the army commanders enjoining them to do all possible to prevent complicity between the officers and the *commissaires* and *contrôleurs*; AAE MD 819, fos. 101–6 [1635], criticizes the 10 per cent bonus awarded to unit officers who keep their units at regulation full strength since this incited collusion with the *commissaires*.

[100] AAE CP Savoie 24, fo. 611, 30 June 1636, Richelieu to d'Hémery: 'quelques uns ont aussy escrit que les commissaires font signer les rooles en blanc et qu'ils remplissent apres . . . avec lesd. tresoriers et quelques autres officyers des finances'; SHAT A^1 61, fo. 296, 2 Dec. 1640, circular on

paying the troops before – or even without – holding the *revue*, a practice which implied dependence upon the word of the unit officer to establish real unit strengths.[101] It is impossible to establish how far the complicity of the *commissaires* was financially motivated, and how far it was a response to intimidation by the officer-corps and the desire to secure some form of *modus vivendi*.[102] A few prosecutions of *commissaires* for corruption do appear in the archival material, but it seems probable that this was the tip of an iceberg and that the great mass of corruption failed to attract the attention of superior judicial officers or the high command.[103]

Moreover, an administrative culture tacitly tolerant of corruption extended into the levels above the *commissaires*, involving even those who had been placed in positions of administrative responsibility as trusted ministerial clients. Richelieu's *fidèle*, Crusy de Marcillac, bishop of Mende, was prosecuted at the end of 1638 for alleged corruption in the administration of supply contracts.[104] Following his failure to prevent the Spanish relief of Tarragona in 1641, Henri d'Escoubleau de Sourdis, archbishop of Bordeaux, was investigated concerning earlier charges that he had misappropriated funds for naval supplies.[105]

At the very top of the hierarchy it was common knowledge that the *surintendant* Claude Bullion had obtained a substantial personal fortune from the manipulation of the financial system.[106] Suggestions that the *surintendant* should 'devote as much attention to the king's affairs as to his own' were never far from Richelieu's criticism of Bullion's financial dealings,[107] while in 1638 Louis and Richelieu imposed formal restrictions upon Bullion's financial profiteering.[108]

---

this subject to commanders of army-corps; A¹ 62, pce 255, 2 Dec. 1640, *ordonnance* forbidding this practice.

[101] SHAT A¹ 61, fo. 181, 12 Nov. 1640; A¹ 68, 29 Mar. 1642; in another case the corps commander of the forces in Picardy, the maréchal de Gramont, defended the decision of his administrators to carry out a 'revue par estimation' of the army: AAE MD 1680, fo. 431, 26 Sept. 1641.

[102] In at least one case a *commissaire*, Lespine, was maliciously charged with corruption by the officers of Richelieu's régiment de La Marine: SHAT A¹ 63, fos. 260, 527, 30 Jan., 8 Mar. 1641. The senior *commissaire* Jean Bragelongne reported to de Noyers on a case in which (cavalry) colonels were engaged in frauds surrounding the payment of their troops, but despite being ordered to collect further information the case disappears from view: A¹ 61, fo. 228, 22 Nov. 1640.

[103] AAE MD 1678, fo. 8, 10 Jan. 1636, Soissons to Chavigny, reporting that he had arrested the *commissaire* Le Vacher. SHAT A¹ 52, fo. 228, 351, 21 May/4 June 1639, arrest and trial of *commissaire* Barbe. In other cases the accusations were less clear-cut: the *commissaire* Jacques Biou was charged with corruption, but at the instigation of another *commissaire*, André Magnan, who subsequently obtained Biou's office: A¹ 40, fo. 73, 30 Nov. 1637; A¹ 45, fo. 53, 7 Apr. 1638. See also Caron (ed.), *Le Tellier*, p. 22, for a similar case of *commissaires* bringing self-interested accusations against their colleague and against the previous *intendant*, Argenson.

[104] SHAT A¹ 49, pce 212, 23 Dec.

[105] Sourdis, *Correspondance* III. 66–72, Sept. 1641.

[106] J. Labatut, 'Aspects de la fortune de Bullion', *Dix-septième siècle*, 40 (1963), 11–39; Bonney, 'Richelieu and the royal finances', p. 126.

[107] AAE MD 820, fo. 100, 7 Feb. 1636; Avenel, VI. 245–8, 18 Nov. 1638.

[108] Ranum, *Richelieu* pp. 150–3. Overall, the most powerful ministers created fortunes far in excess of even the most successful financiers: Bayard, *Monde des financiers*, pp. 413–16.

The administrative context

Moreover, while it is easy to show that the various army-corps were in most cases deprived of adequate funding during the campaigns after 1635, it is equally the case that, when opportunity permitted, the high command were not slow to extort more funds or supplies than the number of troops in the army merited. Correspondence from the centre expressed surprise shading into incredulity at some of the claims made for numbers of bread rations or for the costs of raising recruits, claims which were evidently made with the full awareness of the commanders and, in many cases, the *intendants d'armée*. The claims by François de l'Hôpital, seigneur du Hallier, governor of Lorraine, that he had received no funds for the subsistence of his troops during most of 1635, provoked indignant denials by both Servien and Bouthillier.[109] In 1640 maréchal Châtillon was explicitly accused of overstating the quantity of *pain de munition* required for the army of Picardy. Despite his insistence that a claim for 32,000 rations per day was reasonable, Châtillon's tortuous rationale foundered on the evidence that the army contained no more than 13,000–14,000 infantry.[110] In February 1642 Richelieu wrote to Le Tellier as *intendant* of the army of Italy, expressing considerable scepticism about the subsistence claims for 1,700 troops being made on the part of the Normandie regiment 'n'y ayant point d'apparence que ledit régiment ait a beaucoup près de ce nombre d'hommes'. Even more insulting to the credulity of the ministers was the demand for substantial additional recruitment funds, supposedly to recruit the Normandie regiment up to 'full strength'.[111]

There are certainly suggestions of the involvement of the high command in corrupt practices, albeit seen in many cases as a way to recover from previous financial shortfalls. It is notable that the maréchal de Marillac was finally convicted of misappropriation of funds and the levy of illegal contributions during his command of the army of Champagne in 1630.[112] He defended himself, as most commanders would, on the grounds that he was merely seeking to recoup advances that he had been forced to make out of his own pocket for the subsistence of the army, and that the contributions were a necessary means to keep the army in being in the face of wholly inadequate financial provision from the crown.[113] It was widely recognized that commanders in the field were forced into financial

---

[109] AAE MD 815, fo. 159, 5 Sept. 1635, Richelieu to Bouthillier, in which Richelieu himself expresses scepticism about du Hallier's motives.
[110] AAE MD 1679, fo. 245, 5 Sept. 1640, Châtillon to de Noyers. The view of the ministers was that the army should not have required more than 22,000 rations: SHAT A¹ 61, fo. 71, 21 Oct. 1640, de Noyers to the *intendant*, Gremonville.
[111] Caron (ed.), *Le Tellier*, pp. 172, 175, 10/19 Feb. 1642.
[112] AAE MD 806, fos. 70–6, [1632], account of the eleven charges levelled against Marillac while commanding the army of Champagne, including withholding funds, extorting illegal contributions and selling local offices created on his own authority.
[113] AAE MD 806, fos. 1–17, [1632], *Remonstrance du maréchal de Marillac*, who suggests that his 'crimes' (apart from opposing Richelieu) come down to the fact 'qu'il me faille rendre compte de tout ce que j'ay fait pour faire subsister l'armée en Champagne'; Vaissière, *Maréchal de Marillac* pp. 178–97.

expedients to make good shortfalls of central funding and that, if the line between public and private finance was blurred, this was in large part because the commanders were expected to utilize their own funds to keep their army operational. As a result, attempts to supervise the allocation of funds more carefully at this level inevitably encountered aggressive and self-justificatory responses from the commanders. Maréchal Brézé epitomized this attitude, when he penned an angry letter to Chavigny after he had received an instruction 'de ne rien ordonner soit pour fortifications, munitions de guerre ou provisions de bouche' without prior authorization and written approval from the *surintendants*. Having pointed out the impracticality of imposing such a system while the army was on campaign, he finally exploded that the financial administrators 'nous traittent comme si nous estions les plus grands voleurs de la terre'.[114] While such an assumption by the *bureau des finances* might well be a good working principle, it was clear that an administration composed of *noblesse de robe* and ministerial appointees would be hard pressed to apply it with any regularity to a well-connected and independent-minded high command.

The predators

If one element of fiscal exploitation involved the corrupt practices of those already established within the military administration and the officer-corps, another was provided by those groups who could manipulate the dependence of the crown and the ministry upon their financial capacities and services: the financier cartels on which the government depended for funding the immediate expenses of the war-effort; the *munitionnaires* who ensured the supply of basic bread to the armies; the munitions contractors who met demand for powder, shot and other military supplies. Here, however, the situation was made considerably more ambiguous by the inadequacy and unpredictability of the crown's financial resources; on occasions, the predators could find themselves the prey of massive shortfalls. But this was not a situation that these groups accepted with equanimity, and the balance of advantage by no means lay with the crown and its *bureau des finances*. While it might be assumed that the crown's ministers had a powerful interest in stimulating competition amongst rival groups of financiers and *munitionnaires* in order to acquire the cheapest contracts, the reality was rarely so simple. The most consistent ministerial concern was reliability, above all trying to ensure that the suppliers would not abandon the armies in the midst of a campaign, even when the crown's funds should prove inadequate or delayed.[115] Trying to force down rates of interest or to reduce the unit cost of bread rations as low as possible was short-sighted if the agents simply halted supply the moment that funds dried up.

---

[114] AAE CP Allemagne 12, fo. 64, 31 Jan. 1635.
[115] AAE CP Lorraine 26, fo. 379, 3 Oct. 1635, Barrault to Chavigny, reporting that the *munitionnaire* Du Poux had announced that he was no longer able to supply the garrison of Nancy with bread, having done so for the last four months without receiving a *sol* from his contract.

The administrative context

The financial deals had to be attractive enough to persuade the financier or *munitionnaire* to continue supply even in the face of temporary financial difficulties. Establishing interest rates or a supply contract that were favourable on paper did not guarantee that the agent would continue to meet the real demands of the army in the face of shortfalls, but it rendered it slightly more likely.

An even more important circumstance in obtaining new loans or maintaining supply in the face of inadequate revenues was personal. Though it might be tempting to try to replace one group of financiers or *munitionnaires* with another in the interests of achieving lower rates of interest or a better deal for the supply of an army-corps, the reality was of close-knit groups linked by family and marriage, whose interests were tied firmly into the ministerial/administrative circles at the centre. This was in part a matter of clienteles, of *fidelité* which bound ministers and financiers together as members of a relatively small elite of Parisian *noblesse de robe*. Both Richelieu and Séguier signed the marriage contract of François Sabathier, while the marriage of the financier Nicolas Jeannin de Castille was attended by most of the Phélypeaux clan, by Léon le Bouthillier, comte de Chavigny, by Louis de Crevant, marquis d'Humières, Jacques du Blé, marquis d'Huxelles, and by Louis de Bade, comte de Palluau.[116] It was also a reflection of the heavy involvement of the governing elite in the activities of financier and *munitionnaire* consortia. This reflected a number of interests: the profits to be made from lending to the crown were far higher than those available in almost any other sphere of financial or commercial activity, and it would have required unusual self-restraint for well-connected ministers and financial officials to renounce the opportunity for involvement in highly profitable speculative ventures; less overtly self-interested was the fact that heavy ministerial involvement in loan contracts could reassure financiers that they had a good chance of seeing the payment of interest and the repayment of principal even when the crown's financial plight seemed beyond repair. The ministers and their central agents were far from alone in their involvement in financier and *munitionnaire* cartels, but their presence was a reassuring indication that, short of complete political or fiscal collapse, the favoured agents would receive priority in repayment.

The negative side of this involvement was that it sacrificed potential for flexibility and competition in the negotiation of contracts, and certainly did not ensure that the crown got the best possible deal from these groups. Such flexibility may in any case have been illusory; the financiers were a tight-knit group whose

---

[116] Bayard, *Monde des financiers*, pp. 439–40. See also the indications of a close relationship between the *intendant des finances* Guillaume de Bordeaux and the financier Thomas Bonneau, the presence of a president of the *Parlement* of Paris, Nicolas Potier, and of Henri de Guénégaud, *secrétaire d'Etat*, at the marriage of Nicolas Doublet's daughter, or the presence of Claude Bouthillier at the marriage of the financier Claude Housset to Marie Aguesseau: Bayard, *Monde des financiers*, pp. 335, 272.

interests were in general better served by collaboration than competition. Only when rival ministerial groupings developed, as in the case of Fouquet and Mazarin/Colbert in the later 1650s, was overt competition likely to flourish amongst financier cartels. At the same time it must be noted that treating the financiers and *munitionnaires* with considerable forbearance during the 1630s and early 1640s did not by any means lead to unconditional loyalty to the regime and its military needs.[117] Aware of their indispensibility so long as the war continued through successive campaigns, both groups sought to minimize their financial exposure and, as far as they were permitted, to avoid over-extending their credit. Both groups sought to squeeze the maximum possible benefit from their willingness to provide hard cash or supplies for the armies. It has already been shown that the 1634 conversion of *droits* into *rentes* considerably weakened the ministry's bargaining power with those whose credit it wished to tap on a regular basis. The capacity of privileged financiers and well-connected creditors to obtain reimbursement at face value on *rentes* which they might themselves have previously bought at a heavy discount, was just one element of the accommodation of the financiers' interests in the years after 1635. Beyond those activities tolerated by the crown's agents, the same financiers were no less prepared to make illicit profits when this seemed possible, and misappropriation, reinterpretation of *traités*, local extortion and non-payment of sums due were all commonplace and mostly undetected (or unprosecuted) by the legal system.[118]

Bullion and Bouthillier were haunted throughout the war years by concern about the impact of political and military setbacks on the willingness of financiers to continue lending. The reduction in the *taille* yield in 1635 brought matters to a head, with real fears that the entire financial edifice would collapse. Bullion reported an apparently massive shortfall in the *taille* receipts in 1635, indicating that an assessment of 58 million *livres* from the direct taxes had actually yielded under 20 million *livres*.[119] The immediate concern in 1635, and again in 1637, was that financiers who found that their interest payments had been assigned to provinces which were now in revolt or refusing to pay more than a fraction of the *taille* would refuse further financial cooperation. Even the suggestion of a reduction in the level of interest payments provoked concern about the reaction of the financier cartels.[120] Bullion's response to these threats was a search for extraordinary revenues that might avoid the prospect of a shortfall in payments to the chosen financiers, shifting their payments to other revenues to compensate for

---

[117] Françoise Bayard comments on the ambiguity of the financiers' attitudes: 'on comprend mal l'attitude de ceux qui, tout en manifestant leur attachement à l'Etat, ne craignent pas de le voler': *Monde des financiers*, pp. 334–5.
[118] Bayard, *Monde des financiers*, pp. 311–17.
[119] AAE MD 819, fo. 97, [1635], *mémoire* of M. de Bullion.
[120] AAE MD 820, fo. 160, 14 Mar. 1636, Bullion to Richelieu, discussing the project to reduce interest payments from 24 to 17 *deniers* (per *livre*), and suggesting that the financier Lumagne would probably suspend arrangements for a new loan in consequence.

the failure of the direct taxes.[121] The concern was not simply that financiers would refuse to advance further loans if existing interest and repayments were not met; the finance ministers were also worried by the knock-on effects of financier bankruptcy. In 1641, for example, Bouthillier voiced his grave concern about the disappearance of the financier Le Roy, and the 'terreur panique' that this had generated amongst those in his cartel and the wider financial market.[122] The result of these concerns was that ministers, having paid heavily over the odds for short-term loan contracts and *traités* with the financiers, payments which implied precisely this element of risk in the collection, then found themselves obliged to bale them out when, despite all the attempts to tip the terms in their favour, the situation still went wrong.[123]

To an even greater extent than the financiers, the *munitionnaires* constituted a tightly knit group, bound even more tightly by the ministers' tendency to draw up contracts with an increasingly narrow group of associates.[124] Despite the problems of high expense and presumed inefficiency, the supply contracts for the troops in Italy were almost exclusively handled after 1627 by the brothers Barthélemy, by Jean-Pierre and Jean-Dominique Falcombel and by Jean-Baptiste Palleologo and Jean-Baptiste Carezzano.[125] Similarly, a *munitionnaire* like Jean Roze, who dominated supply of the armies on the eastern frontier, negotiated at least twelve contracts for *pain de munition* with the ministry between 1630 and 1642, frequently acting in association with Guillaume Mignot.[126] Roze's career illustrates the problems of a ministry which, having allowed itself to become heavily dependent upon the efforts of favoured *munitionnaires*, was consequently extremely restricted in the extent to which corruption and simple failure to honour obligations could be restrained. In 1635 Roze was persuaded to intervene to salvage a series of collapsing supply contracts which threatened to wreck the military campaigns along the eastern frontier.[127] There is little evidence that this transfer of responsibility to a favoured *munitionnaire* brought any significant improvement. Indeed, the disadvantage of relying on one key *munitionnaire* rather than on a

---

[121] AAE MD 819, fo. 97, [1635], *Mémoire* of Bullion; 830, fos. 97, 104, 114, 8/14 Apr., 17 May 1638, Bullion to Richelieu.

[122] AAE MD 839, fo. 182, 27 Aug. 1641, Bouthillier to Richelieu; 820, fo. 131, 22 Feb 1636, Bullion to Richelieu on the danger of financier bankruptcy.

[123] Bayard, *Monde des financiers*, p. 252, on the ministers' intervention to save financiers from their creditors.

[124] A limited attempt to play off the *munitionnaires* Lattignan and Bouault on the north-east frontier in 1636 seems to have established no precedent for such manipulation: BN Ms.fr. 17371, fo. 224, 15 Oct. 1636, Guitonneau to Séguier.

[125] Bayard, *Monde des financiers*, pp. 378, 384: all contracts after 1640 involved the trio of Palleologo, Jean-Dominique Falcombel and Carezzano. The central role of Palleologo in the supply of the troops in Italy is emphasized in AAE MD 835, fo. 236, June 1640.

[126] Bayard, *Monde des financiers*, pp. 381, 386; BN Ms.fr. 6385, fo. 28, 30 July 1632, articles accorded by the king to M. Guillaume Mignot, 'munitionnaire sous le nom de M. Jean Roze', and concerning a supply contract for 8,000 rations per day over two months.

[127] AAE MD 814, fo. 3, 1 May 1635, Richelieu to Louis XIII.

Paying for war

group was the huge administrative burden thrown on to the individual, who would have little choice but to remain in Paris in order to try to coordinate the overall operations of grain purchase, stockpiling, milling and baking. The work of supply with the individual army-corps would be left to his *commis*, and in large part to their independent decisions, calculations and manipulations. In this case, the commanders and administrators in the field had no confidence that Roze represented a fundamentally different and more tractable supplier; Charles de Valois, duc d'Angoulême, writing on 8 August 1635 and providing a hugely detailed account of the supply of grain and baked bread being partially assembled at Nancy, stressed that none of the *munitionnaires* – in which he includes Roze with Bouault and Lattaignan – considered themselves in any sense responsible in their 'propre et privé nom' for the supply of the army. Even when they did receive money as stipulated, they still felt no obligation to honour the terms of the contracts, and they and their *commis* made constant excuses to explain the failure of provision and the need for outside support, whether access to magazines of grain or additional transport facilities.[128] There is no evidence that this situation was improved during subsequent campaigns; in 1639 the same criticisms were still being levelled at Roze.[129]

If the attitude of the *bureau des finances* to the financiers was a mixture of critical rhetoric and practical forbearance, this was even more pronounced in the case of the *munitionnaires*, where concern not to destroy the position of established, but over-exposed, individuals was compounded by an overriding concern to provide the armies with enough bread to keep them on campaign. The result was the use of the resources of the crown and its agents to try to bale out *munitionnaires* who were evidently unable to maintain their contracts, or could only do so at a financial risk which they considered too high. Time after time, the ministers reluctantly accepted that grain which had been stockpiled in provincial or town magazines would need to be provided to *munitionnaires* whose own agents had proved unable to collect the quantities stipulated in their contracts.[130] On occasions, attempts were made to conceal the precautions that were necessarily taken to compensate for the likely failure of *munitionnaires* to meet their stipulated aims. In April 1635, Richelieu wrote to his *fidèle*, Gabriel de Beauvau de Rivarennes, just nominated

---

[128] AAE CP Lorraine 25, fos. 355–8, *mémoire pour la subsistance des armées en Lorraine*; Lorraine 26, fo. 253, 27 Sept. 1635, Lefebvre, a smaller-scale *munitionnaire* operating in Lorraine, reports on attempt of Roze to appropriate 350 carts being used to supply the magazine at Nancy.

[129] AAE CP Lorraine 31, fos. 43, 47, 66, 6 and 19 Apr., 7 May 1639, Jean Choisy to de Noyers, complaining of the inadequacy of the *commis* of Roze in carrying out grain distribution – 'gens peu raisonnables' – and stressing the need to compel Roze to meet his obligations; Lorraine 31, fo. 335, 28 May 1639, du Hallier to de Noyers, reporting that the *commis* of Roze has arrived with only 200 horses for transport, rather than the 400 that were contracted. See also BN Ms.fr. 6647, fos. 104, 106, 25 Sept. 1636, Bullion to cardinal de La Valette on his concern about the imminent breakdown of contracts with Roze.

[130] SHAT A¹ 50, fo. 262, 28 Jan. 1639, instruction to the *échevins* of a number of town to deliver up the grain in their magazines to the *munitionnaire* Jean Flan.

The administrative context

bishop of Nantes, ordering him to amass supplies of biscuit to sustain fifteen days campaigning, but to keep this secret from the *munitionnaires* who must continue to believe that they are solely responsible for supplying the army-corps.[131] But such secret preparations could not mask a prevailing culture in which the *munitionnaires* considered that a contract was more of a statement of good intentions than a legal obligation involving potential risks as well as profits. In this context, Richelieu's insistence at the end of 1635 that henceforth no grain from frontier magazines was to be made over to the *munitionnaires*, who were to be held to the terms of their contracts, was totally unrealistic if the ultimate aim was to keep the armies operational.[132] And if the enforced provision of grain to help the *munitionnaires* meet their contracts was one aspect of this support system, it was no less the case that agents of the central administration were regularly drafted in, not merely to supervise the activities and probity of the *munitionnaires* and their *commis*, but to do the work of the latter who were either absent or incapable. In 1639, the *commissaire des guerres*, Jean de La Court, was instructed to oversee the conduct and storage of grain that had been collected by Jean Roze for the provisioning of the army of Languedoc – a task which the contract would have charged squarely to Roze's *commis* and to his own expense.[133] Transportation facilities were consistently neglected by the *munitionnaires*, again forcing the intervention of the ministers and the deployment of horses and waggons required for other military purposes.[134]

Compounding the inadequacy of the *munitionnaires'* administrative arrangements was a straightforward concern, where possible, to renege on their commitments. Both Germain Rolland and Pierre Gargan were criticized by Richelieu in late 1635 for trying to evade the terms of their supply contracts, while earlier in the year Henri, duc de Rohan reported that the *munitionnaires* appeared simply to have given up on their contract to supply his army.[135] In 1640 it was reported that

---

[131] AAE MD 813, fo. 341; J. Bergin, *The Making of the French Episcopate, 1589–1661* (New Haven and London, 1996), p. 571.
[132] AAE MD 816, fo. 230, 1635, Richelieu to Bullion.
[133] SHAT A^1 51, fo. 578, 29 Apr.; A^1 52, fo. 355, 5 June 1639, Bellefonds, captain of the regiment of Normandie, to assist in the transport of grain on behalf of *munitionnaires*; A^1 59, fos. 504, 676/7, 24 June, 11 July 1640, instructions to abbé de Corneilles to raise additional grain and flour for the army besieging Arras; AAE CP Lorraine 31, fo. 43, 6 Apr. 1639, *intendant* Choisy to de Noyers, concerned at the complete absence of any *commis* of Jean Roze to distribute bread to the army of the marquis de Feuquières. For more detail concerning the central administration's commissioning of agents to intervene in the supply administration, see chapter 8, pp. 413–22.
[134] SHAT A^1 60, fo. 224, 23 Aug. 1640, governors of *places* to provide carts for the use of Jean Flan, *munitionnaire*, charged with the supply of the army at Arras; evidently the local authorities had proved reluctant to comply, and on 6 Oct. an order was despatched for the requisitioning of carts from these *places*: A^1 61, fo. 9, 6 Oct. 1640. AAE MD 814, fo. 40, 13 May 1635, de Noyers as *intendant des finances* reporting on his amassing of carts around Charleville for the transport of grain.
[135] AAE MD 816, fo. 230, [late 1635]; CP Lorrraine 25, fos. 83–5, 8 Feb.; see also complaints against the *munitionnaires* Gagnot and Thibaud: SHAT A^1 41, fos. 43, 44, 23/4 Mar. 1635.

the *munitionnaire* for the army of Languedoc was attempting to increase the price of the rations, disregarding the terms of the contract that he had made with the crown.[136] Almost without exception the *munitionnaires* avoided running into debt on their contracts by ensuring that they would obtain only as much grain as they had received cash in hand from the *bureau des finances*.[137] A system in which the entrepreneurs refused to buy more grain, or bake more bread, than they had already been paid to produce was hopelessly inflexible, but the close personal and financial rapports between the ministers and this small group of *munitionnaires* seems to have produced no more than empty expressions of *fidélité* and goodwill.[138] It is notable that the bankruptcy of François Sabathier occurred after he had diversified his activities from the entrepreneurial control of powder and saltpetre into exceptionally large-scale loan contracts to the crown.[139] Although the ministers had expressed unhappiness with the virtual monopoly possessed by Sabathier and his cartel in the provision of powder and saltpetre to the armies, this was seemingly a position from which he could amass a fortune with little or no risk.[140]

Above all, the strength of these predatory groups derived from the reluctance or inability of the crown and its ministers to devise alternative systems of finance or supply for the armies to lessen their dependence upon entrepreneurship. In the case of a financial system, a move away from dependence upon the vast system of deficit financing was probably impossible so long as the war continued. In the matter of army supply, there is evidence that desperate circumstances occasionally caused the ministers to contemplate some form of direct provisioning. In 1641 a group of *intendants* and *commissaires* received instructions to try to negotiate bread contracts with local bakers for the direct provision of bread 'à meilleur compte que le munitionnaire général (Roze)'.[141] In the winter of 1641–2 it was proposed that the troops in quarters should receive their allowance for the *pain de munition*

---

[136] SHAT A^1 57, fo. 376, 13 Feb. 1640, letter to the *intendant* of Languedoc, Barthélémé Dupré; A^1 39, fo. 253, 23 Oct. 1638, *intendant* Sève to investigate the malversations of the *munitionnaire* Langlois.

[137] SHAT A^1 24, fo. 138, 17 Mar. 1635, Servien to Charles de Lameth, comte de Bussy.

[138] AAE MD 816, fo. 231, [late 1635], Richelieu to Bullion, pointing out that the despatch of money for the *munitionnaires* with the *montre* for the troops rather than three months in advance provides them with the excuse to curtail supply.

[139] Sabathier's bankruptcy in 1641 revealed the concerns of the ministers that an individual financial crisis on this scale represented a grave threat to the entire edifice of crown borrowing, and underlined the need to do all possible to hold off Sabathier's creditors: Bonney, *King's Debts*, pp. 186–8.

[140] As early as January 1634 Richelieu was concerned that Sabathier was neglecting his contracted obligations: AAE MD 810, fo. 13, 11 Jan., Richelieu to Bouthillier. The situation did not change during the war years, and correspondence concerning Sabathier's efforts is invariably critical: see, for example, MD 1678, fo. 294, 31 Aug. 1636, Louis-Emmanuel de Valois, comte d'Alais, to Richelieu; CP Savoie 28, fo. 280, 1 May 1639, de Noyers to Chavigny; SHAT A^1 47i, fo. 379, 20 Nov. 1638, failure of Sabathier to meet his contract. For concern about the implications of Sabathier's virtual monopoly on powder production, see chapter 7, pp. 389–90.

[141] SHAT A^1 64, fo. 124, Mar. 1641.

The administrative context

and should negotiate directly with local bakers for supply.[142] Yet the limited scale of such initiatives suggests that they were considered as *ad hoc* palliatives, in no way intended to replace the basic system which consolidated the bargaining power of the *munitionnaires* so comprehensively.

THE IMPLICATIONS OF FINANCIAL INADEQUACY FOR THE DISTRIBUTION OF FUNDING TO THE ARMIES

The most obvious point to be noted about the crown's use of financiers and contracted supply agents is that the limited amount of cash available to the *épargne* each year was not automatically allocated to the army. It is quite evident that the highest priority of the *surintendant* was the repayment of the financiers and the maintenance of a steady flow of new loans. In 1636 Bullion threatened the consequences of putting heavy pressure on the financiers: 'si en fera mettre prisoniers les traitans [,] tout le conseil des finances . . . protestent de la ruine entière des finances'.[143] Cash employed within the financial system had a much higher value relative to the *surintendants*' commitments than cash spent directly on the armies; when financiers were prepared to accept some form of renegotiation of their previous loans in lieu of cash repayment, the ultimate costs were invariably high. Funds employed to meet debts to the financiers and their cartels would benefit the operations of the *bureau des finances* directly, as cash despatched to the armies would not. Thus, although there was constant speculation that the *surintendants* would default on their obligations to the *traitants* in order to honour immediate military demands, in reality it was usually the needs of the troops which were subordinated to the maintenance of the flow of credit. The first claim on the cash received from tax revenues was to meet the most vital elements of the annual deficit left from *extraordinaire* manipulations.

The *surintendants* made the greatest efforts to justify their position to the king himself, to Chavigny, to de Noyers and, above all, to Richelieu. They had a considerable battle on their hands. Richelieu and his fellow ministers were driven by the fear that military failure would destabilize their political position, and had no wish to see military objectives sacrificed to financial stringencies imposed by the *surintendants*, even when the latter insisted that abandoning fiscal restraint would precipitate a far more comprehensive collapse. While insisting that the detailed management of the finances was outside his sphere of responsibility, Richelieu none the less intervened with great regularity to criticize economies and attempts to ration financial supply to the armies.[144] Such criticisms of financial

---

[142] SHAT A¹ 66, fo. 501, 19 Dec. 1641, de Noyers to the *intendant* and the *commissaire pour les subsistances*, Claude Paris and Etienne Pascal.
[143] AAE MD 820, fo. 131, 22 Feb. 1636.
[144] AAE MD 811, fo. 183, 29 Dec. 1634, Richelieu to Bullion: 'quant à l'affaire de finance dont vous m'escrivez, vous scavez bien que je ne m'en mesle point'.

policy were characterized by an absence of positive suggestions as to how the resources of the crown could be increased sufficiently to allow all army-corps to receive equal priority. Richelieu and many of the other non-financial officials seem to have anticipated the assumptions of the *frondeurs* in 1648 that the administration of the finances was characterized by the immoderate and uncontrollable greed of financiers and *munitionnaires*, who needed only to be reined in to achieve a virtuous circle of reduced taxes and higher military expenditure. That the ministers themselves were implicated in a system which required the inducement of huge interest payments to financiers and financial deals which claimed an ever-higher proportion of the tax revenues was conveniently ignored in the essentially rhetorical condemnations of greed and malpractice.[145] Lack of realism about the practicalities of the system of deficit finance was matched by the ministers' – and, above all, Richelieu's – cronyism in demanding financial support or special treatment from the *bureau des finances* for their *créatures* or those who had specifically requested their support. The cardinal de La Valette, the maréchaux Brézé and La Meilleraye were aware that the best way to try to extort extra resources from the centre was to appeal to Richelieu, asking for his direct intervention with the *surintendants*.[146] When Brézé or La Meilleraye held commands in the army where the king was present, the pressure on the *bureau des finances* to channel resources in this direction was overwhelming, despite scepticism about whether this was the best distribution of the available funds or supplies. La Valette or the duc de Chaulnes were equally ready to make use of Chavigny, whose access to the king as a *secrétaire d'Etat* gave him additional leverage over the finances. These strongly formulated demands for additional support were not based on wider strategic priorities, but a favouritism which all too easily involved robbing one army-corps of its financial support, its reinforcements or its supplies in order to over-compensate another, commanded by a better-connected client.

Not surprisingly, Bullion regarded such demands with considerable hostility. While the *surintendants*' prioritization in part reflected their own favouritism, these personal factors were largely subordinated to calculations about the relative importance of campaign theatres, the ability of troops to sustain themselves from local resources or the likely costs of failing to meet promised obligations to foreign powers. The other ministers made demands on behalf of their clients and relatives which were far more arbitrary and, if obeyed by the *surintendants*, would have ensured an even more chaotic and unmanageable distribution of the available funding. Yet it was difficult for the *surintendants* to reject such demands openly, especially those made by Richelieu himself, or, indeed, on occasions, by the king.

---

[145] Bayard, *Le monde des financiers*, pp. 330–4.
[146] BN Ms.fr. 6647, fo. 250, 12 Dec. 1636, de Noyers to cardinal de La Valette, reporting on the high standing that La Valette enjoys in the eyes of Richelieu and the king, and their determination to ensure that his army receives another *montre*, noting with a flicker of sarcasm: 'n'y ait personne qui puisse doubter que vos trouppes la meritent mieux que celles de touttes les autres armées'.

The administrative context

To do so would risk humiliating ministers in the eyes of their clients, and tempting them into peremptory demands that the *bureau des finances* obey instructions. Thus, even when Bullion had no intention of meeting such special pleading on behalf of ministerial clients or well-placed courtier-commanders, his letters invariably stressed that he had achieved the impossible and had met further demands for expenditure, even though his previous correspondence had emphasized that the *épargne* was empty and that no new revenues could be expected.[147]

The use of assigned revenues

The main means by which the *surintendants* evaded 'unnecessary' payments and operated their order of funding priorities was to rely upon a vast system of assigning anticipated tax revenues to military expenses. In doing this Bullion and Bouthillier were fully aware that while some assignations would prove prompt and reliable sources of funds, other assigned revenues would prove slow and expensive to extract, and a significant number would, by the late 1630s, prove all but worthless.

There was nothing innovatory about the practice of assigning military expenses to specifically earmarked anticipated revenues.[148] Indeed, it was a normal and rational practice; most tax revenues would not be collected and transported to the *bureau des finances* in Paris, in order to be counted, stored and then shipped off again to pay the wages of an army on the frontiers. When seeking to fund the costs of building warships or coastal fortification, it made a lot of sense to pay for this directly out of taxes levied in coastal provinces such as Brittany or Provence.[149] However, such a system of assigning local revenues to local expenses could hardly work in a military situation such as that after 1630 when huge forces were concentrated in a relatively small number of frontier provinces. Funds collected from the non-frontier provinces would be devoted to the same military needs, but, once again, the sums were not collected and transported to Paris in order to be trans-shipped in turn to Champagne or Dauphiné. A ministerial regime which was far from wedded to the expense and trouble of centralization for its own sake was fully prepared to grant provincial revenues to financiers in return for cash payments. The financiers would organize the collection of these revenues, incidentally making a significant profit on the arrangement, and the crown would receive cash advances which could be used to meet immediate military expenses. Where assignment of revenues differed from the earlier development of *droits* was

---

[147] In the case of Bernard of Saxe-Weimar, for example, Bullion was particularly resistant to the demands of both the king and Richelieu that the *condottiere*'s financial obligations should be honoured, while simultaneously providing assurances that he had 'done the impossible' to pay the duke: AAE MD 821, fo. 104, 23 July 1636; 822, fo. 52, 13 Oct. 1636.
[148] Bayard, *Monde des financiers*, pp. 245–51.
[149] Collins, *Fiscal Limits*, pp. 131–2, who distinguishes these as 'regular' assignations.

that they were not conceived as a permanent alienation of the tax revenue, but as an arrangement lasting for a fixed term, frequently no more than the year in question.[150]

Financiers understood clearly that all assigned revenues were not equal, and the deals they struck with the *bureau des finances* reflected this. Borrowing from financier cartels against the assignment of revenues in the Île de France or in the Touraine was likely to be a good deal cheaper than persuading them to accept an assignation on the revenues of a war-torn frontier province or on the *taille* of a province convulsed with tax rebellion. Indeed, in a significant number of such cases, the costs of assigning the revenue would either be so high that the ministers would reject the deal, or the financiers themselves would decide not to procede since the revenues were too unreliable.

In 1637 a *traité* was drawn up with Sabathier for the provision of powder and munitions worth 1,489,000 *livres*. Of this, only 150,000 *livres* was to be received in cash; the rest would be paid from *bonnes assignations* which, the contract specified, would be payable at latest by June 1638.[151] In the case of Jean Hoeufft, a merchant-financier from Gelderland who organized the payment of Saxe-Weimar's troops in Germany through *lettres de change* and was heavily involved in the negotiations for the Dutch subsidy, Bullion assigned revenues worth 1 million *livres* to meet his payments, assuring him that they were all payable during the current year (1637), and allowing Hoeufft to inspect the list. In response to Hoeufft's request, one of these assigned revenues was changed for one which the financier considered more reliable.[152] Overall, Françoise Bayard suggests that around 75 per cent of the value of contracts with *munitionnaires* would be met by assigning revenues.[153]

These cases would represent an increasing proportion of provincial revenues as the effects of the rising tax burden, the impact of fiscal demands made year after year and the disruption of warfare, were all felt. The remaining revenues, unsuitable for negotiating any kind of deal with financiers, were none the less regarded as a means to meet elements of military expenditure that did not figure high in the *surintendants*' order of priorities.[154] It was not therefore the case that all

---

[150] Though by 1639–40 this situation was beginning to change to one in which tax revenues were alienated for significantly longer periods. See the details of the arrangement made with Thomas Bonneau and his cartel for a series of advances against the tax revenues of the *généralité* of Poitiers: Bayard, *Monde des financiers*, pp. 251–2.

[151] AAE MD 828, fo. 361, [1637], 'dernier traitté du Sr Sabathier pour les pouldres et munitions en 1637'. See also Bayard, *Monde des financiers*, p. 380, who suggests that all of Sabathier's expenditure for 1637 was to be met through assignations.

[152] AAE MD 827, fo. 113, 16 Jan. 1637, Bullion to Chavigny; 822, fo. 147, 3 Nov. 1636, copy of letter sent by secretary of Saxe-Weimar to Hoeufft, urging him to make available funds established in Basle and Strasbourg to pay the German troops.

[153] Bayard, *Monde des financiers*, p. 380.

[154] Bayard, *Monde des financiers*, p. 243, dates the first indication of serious problems within this system of assignations to 1630.

The administrative context

revenues assigned directly to expenses were bad; but there was the strongest possibility that any tax capable of yielding a prompt and substantial revenue would be employed to negotiate loans or to meet part of the expenses in whichever army enjoyed the highest priority. For provincial governors charged with sustaining military operations, commanders in theatres which were regarded as secondary, or for governors of fortified *places*, assignations were a byword for inadequate, delayed or non-existent funding. While apparently fulfilling the letter of their commitment to military funding by allocating 'bonnes assignations', the *surintendants* were in fact using their discretion to avoid paying more than a fraction of the costs of these troops. In 1641 Bouthillier made explicit what had always been the practice of the *bureau des finances* when he wrote to Richelieu proposing that some expenses could be managed by giving out poor quality assignations.[155] A progressive deterioration of the quality of military assignations is clearly evident before this date. In 1635 their use does not seem to have provoked many complaints. The strongest criticism came from Provence, where it was claimed that the revenues assigned for the costs of fortification work and the casting of artillery had proved valueless.[156] And indeed when the defence of Provence became a priority after the Spanish capture of the Îles de Lérins, the *intendants des finances*, Guérapin and d'Hémery, were ordered to use their personal credit to raise money to compensate for the poor assignations.[157] By 1636 the role of assignations was becoming less acceptable. At the end of the year Bullion wrote to Chavigny, stating that: 'La despense de l'argent comptant desbourse sur la table monte quarante-un millier [millions] et les assignations monterent au mesme a cette année.'[158] While this could be taken as only an approximate figure for the expenditure for 1636, it gives some sense of the scale of the *bureau des finances*' assignment of revenues to expenses. A large part of the notional total of *c.* 82 million *livres* would consist of funds tied up in the elaborate structures of deficit financing – the payment of interest and the repayment of outstanding loans and short-term borrowing.[159] Some of this would certainly be allocated on the better assignations, but this left a high proportion of poor-quality revenues to be allocated where possible to military expenditure.

The *surintendants*' policy of turning expenses away from the *épargne* emerges in their account of the money sent to Italy and the Valtelline during 1636. On 26 April Bullion reported that 8 million *livres* had been allocated to the two theatres

---

[155] AAE MD 839, fo. 386, 12 Dec. 1641: 'Il fault donner de mauvaises assignations jusqu'a la concurance du retranchement.'
[156] SHAT A¹ 25, fo. 442, 14 Oct. 1635; A¹ 33, fo. 74, 14 Oct. 1635: assignations for the payment of two *montres* have proved 'absolument inutiles'.
[157] SHAT A¹ 25, fo. 442, 14 Oct. 1635.
[158] AAE MD 822, fo. 185, 9 Nov. 1636.
[159] Mallet's figures for expenditure in 1636 give a total of *c.* 108 million *livres*, of which 65 million is made up of payments categorized as *extraordinaire*: cited in Bonney, *King's Debts*, p. 307.

Paying for war

since 15 March, and that 'a large part' of this was in cash.[160] Bullion was already in the process of downgrading funding to the duc de Rohan's army of the Valtelline, and the commander abandoned his invasion of the Milanese for lack of financial support. A high proportion of the 8 million was supposedly sent to the army of Italy, yet on 30 June it became apparent in correspondence between Richelieu and maréchal Créqui that the army of Italy had received only 3.7 million *livres* since the beginning of the year.[161] Significant parts of the allocation of funding to the army of Italy was in the form of assignations which either had not or would not fall due. Similarly in late March, Bullion had written to Richelieu about an extra 5 million *livres* that he was expected to find to sustain recruitment expenses. Suggesting that he was 'hors de moy-mesme quand je voy les despenses en argent content [comptant]', Bullion sought to persuade Richelieu that part of this sum should be converted into assignations – as he had earlier persuaded the Cardinal to accept the conversion of half of an additional 600,000 *livres*.[162]

Even Richelieu's closest *créatures* were not always immune from the allocation of poor assignations. The maréchal de Brézé wrote directly to Richelieu in 1636 attempting to hand back the governorship of Calais. The soldiers were owed fifteen to twenty *montres* each, and all he had received to meet this and other expenses were assignations 'dont bien souvent une partie ne valoit rien', and which were allocated on revenues 'en basse Auvergne, Lionnnais et ainsi en des lieux fort esloignes, et dont les ports et voitures me coutoient quatre ou cinq mille francs par an'.[163] Bullion's reluctance to meet the costs of Brézé's garrison at Calais was not due to personal animosity; later in the same year Chavigny wrote to the *surintendant* on behalf of Chaulnes, the governor of Picardy, complaining that assigned revenues for the pay of all the garrisons in Picardy had failed to yield anything during 1636.[164] In neighbouring Champagne the plight of the governors of *places* was no better. On 21 July 1636 the governor of Corbie, Maximilien de Belleforière, seigneur de Soyecourt, wrote to Chavigny stressing the weakness of the fortifications and the garrison of his *place*. He emphasized the critical need for some cash to pay his troops, stressing that 'je ne recois pas un sous'. His own credit had been exhausted, Soyecourt explained, and he was no longer in a position to make good the inadequacy of the revenues assigned to him: 'bref, il y a forces manquements que jay dit et mandé souvent . . . je ne responds point de la place'.[165] The fall of Corbie and a sequence of other *places* to the Spanish invasion in the weeks after mid-July can be seen in part as a consequence of this

---

[160] AAE MD 820, fo. 228, 26 Apr. 1636.
[161] Avenel, v. 976, 30 June 1636, Richelieu to Créqui.
[162] AAE MD 820, fos. 119, 178, 15 Feb./28 Mar. 1636.
[163] AAE MD 823, fo. 58, 31 Aug. 1636.
[164] AAE MD 822, fo. 189, 10 Nov. 1636.
[165] AAE MD 1678, fo. 118, 21 July 1636.

demoralization, reflecting the progressive failure of financial support based on poor-quality assignations.

Assignation of poor-quality revenues became increasingly synonymous with non-payment, as a strong attack on the system delivered by Richelieu in 1638 makes clear. Richelieu suggested that the army of Italy, Swiss mercenaries in French service, the subsidies to the Dutch and the Swedes, the artillery and fortification work had all suffered greatly in the past from the allocation of poor assignations. The greatest criticism is reserved for the treatment of the galleys – which had received only 200,000 *livres* this year from *all* of their assigned revenues – and the garrisons. Richelieu emphasized the real threat that the majority of garrison troops would simply disband unless they were paid some part of their outstanding wages in cash: 'présentement je viens d'aprendre que une des places du royaume, que les ennemis regardent actuellement, est en fort mauvais estat, parce que la garnison s'est toute desbandée pour n'estre point payée'.[166]

Yet indicative of how deeply entrenched was this system of allocating poor-quality revenues is Richelieu's own response to Charles d'Halluin, maréchal de Schomberg, in the following year: the marshal's complaints about the inadequacy of assigned revenues for the troops intended to move into Roussillon received a curt response and the strident injunction 'au nom de Dieu, Monsieur, ne trouvez difficulté a quoi que ce puisse estre'.[167]

The surintendants' *order of priorities and military contributions*

There is no doubt that Bullion and after 1641 Bouthillier were pursuing an order of priorities in the allocation of funding to military needs, and that a key means by which they could appear to be providing adequate funds while in practice cutting back expenses was to assign poor-quality revenues. In pursuing this prioritization they were not entirely immune from personal favouritism and factional alignments. Bullion strongly disliked Particelli d'Hémery, for example, and regarded the administration of the army of Italy by successive generals and *intendants* as a hotbed of corruption and unnecessary expense.[168] It was equally clear that he

---

[166] Avenel, VI. 245, 18 Nov. 1638; a detailed breakdown of the cost of assignations in 1638/9 is provided in a *mémoire* drawn up by Brézé's successor as governor of Calais, Louis de Béthune, comte de Charost, who showed how as a result of having his garrison and fortification expenses assigned to a number of poor revenues, including two *traités* based on profits from the sale of office and the overstretched *taille* yields from the *généralité* of Soissons, he has been forced to advance 144,000 *livres* on his own credit: AAE MD 1679, fo. 323 [1640].

[167] BN Ms.fr. 3768, fos. 15–20, 23/31 May 1639, letters exchanged between Schomberg and Richelieu.

[168] For the bad relations between Bullion and d'Hémery see AAE CP Savoie 24, fo. 4, 3 Jan. 1636, d'Hémery to Chavigny; for Bullion's suspicions of the financial management of the army of Italy: Savoie 26, fos. 383, 448, 27 July/18 Aug. 1638, La Valette to Chavigny. See also chapter 8, pp. 458–9, for Bullion and de Noyers' criticism of Le Tellier's administration of the army in 1641/2.

regarded the expenses of the Pyrenees theatre with suspicion – as his severe strictures upon the campaigns of 1638 and 1639 indicate.[169]

Yet beyond this issue of personal alliances and links, the *surintendants'* prioritization reflected two central concerns. They were predictably resistant to making payment to what were seen as marginal elements and factors in the French war-effort, and Bullion in particular pursued his own agenda in taking the view that armies operating beyond the French borders could and should live to a large extent by locally exacted military taxes – contributions. Squarely within the first category of low-priority expenses, the *surintendants* placed the foreign subsidies to the Dutch and Swedes. Bullion considered that from the moment France had become involved in open war with the Habsburgs these were no longer necessary or desirable. That there were important diplomatic reasons for continuing them cut no ice with the *surintendant*, who lost no opportunity to criticize their burdensome futility, especially since it was not possible to meet the foreign subsidies by assigning poor-quality revenues to them.[170] On the other hand, assignment of poor revenues was the obvious means by which the *bureau des finances* avoided meeting garrison costs within France, and the *surintendants'* priority was very obviously to ensure that the armies on the frontiers received the bulk of funding and to hope that the garrisons would not be put to the test – as in 1636 – of an enemy invasion.

In their attitude to Saxe-Weimar's army, French troops supporting the duke's forces in Germany, the troops occupying Lorraine and the armies operating in Piedmont, the Valtelline and in Roussillon, the *surintendants* were emphatic that some part of military costs should be met through the systematic extortion of contributions, and took the view that this would reduce the level of support provided by the central financial administration. Bullion considered that Saxe-Weimar should be placed under the most stringent pressure to live by contributions – as indeed his army had done in the years before the 1635 agreement with France.[171] The same reasoning – albeit expressed in a less peremptory fashion – was applied to La Valette's troops when they passed into Germany.[172] Bullion was equally anxious that du Hallier and the governors of *places* in Lorraine should be nudged into supporting a higher proportion of their expenses from contributions,

---

[169] Suspicions that Bullion managed to pass on to Richelieu: Vassal-Reig, *Roussillon* p. 102.

[170] For example, AAE MD 820, fo. 266, 14 May 1636, Bullion to Richelieu, complaining about the 'tyranny' of the States General and their demands; Pange, *Charnacé*, pp. 100–5, 122–34. For a summary of the Swedish subsidies see Bonney, *King's Debts*, pp. 163–4, 172.

[171] AAE CP Allemagne 12, fo. 317, 5 Oct. 1635, Richelieu to La Valette, stressing the concern of the *bureau des finances* that any contract with Saxe-Weimar should be beaten down as low as possible in view of the opportunities for his troops to levy contributions in the German territories; BN Ms.fr. 6647, fo. 231, 28 Nov. 1636, de Noyers to La Valette, emphasizing that Saxe-Weimar's troops should sustain themselves over the winter from contributions levied in Franche-Comté.

[172] BN Ms.fr. 6646, fo. 132, 19 June 1636, emphasizes La Valette's dependence upon contributions levied in Alsace; Ms.fr. 6647, fo. 104, 25 Sept. 1636, Bullion to La Valette;

The administrative context

as should the governors of *places* in Alsace.¹⁷³ The *surintendant* extended this view to Italy, where he expressed the hope that Franco-Savoyard forces would be able to break into the Milanese or other hostile territory, or at the very least that French troops should be supported by contributions levied on the population of Piedmont.¹⁷⁴ Only in the case of the massive, multiple armies, operating on the Flanders' frontier did the *surintendants* appear to renounce the view that contributions should make good central financial shortfalls, and this may have been as much a reluctant admission that it was inappropriate for the army over which the king had personal oversight to be engaged in gathering food and money, as a recognition of the difficulties of extracting contributions to support military forces of this scale on the strongly fortified frontier with the Spanish Netherlands.

In the wider context of European warfare in this period, Bullion's conviction that contributions should be used to narrow the gap between the armies' needs and the central funding available was not unreasonable. The effectiveness of the army operating in Germany after 1641 was due in large part to its capacity to sustain itself from contributions and to maintain operations despite the inadequacy of central funding.¹⁷⁵ However, it was a proposal which did not gain wholehearted support amongst the other ministers. Just as the sanctioning of fully fledged entrepreneurship amongst the French unit commanders was closely linked to concerns about the extent of royal control and raised spectres from the civil wars of a militarized, independent, *noblesse*, so the ministers never willingly accepted the uncontrolled levy of contributions by the commanders and unit officers in the field.¹⁷⁶ On paper at least the French crown was categorical that contributions could not be collected from French populations.¹⁷⁷ In practice, this attitude was modified, but only when resistance to the 'legal' taxes could justify military execution of the levy. In early 1639, for example, the refusal of Lyon to pay the *subsistances* tax led to the imposition of what was in all but name a contribution extracted by the troops forcibly lodged in the city.¹⁷⁸ Even across the

---

[173] SHAT A¹ 50, fo. 238, 26 Jan. 1639, three regiments in Lorraine to be sustained entirely from contributions; AAE CP Lorraine 31, fo. 205, Aug. 1639, anonymous memoir concerning the problems of sustaining the garrison of Metz through contributions.

[174] For the hope that by getting French troops into the Milanese it would be possible to levy contributions systematically, see AAE CP Savoie 31, fo. 795 [1640], Harcourt (or Le Tellier) to de Noyers; CP Savoie 31, 11 Nov. 1640, Louis XIII to Harcourt, ordering him to collect contributions from the Piedmontese population on a regular and orderly basis to support the costs of the army.

[175] Croxton, *Peacemaking* pp. 59–63, 73–8.

[176] For discussion of the French attitude to military entrepreneurship and its implications see chapter 6.

[177] SHAT A¹ 61 fo. 190, 14 Nov. 1640, Louis XIII reiterates his prohibition upon the extraction of contributions within France. A substantial number of orders from the *secrétaire d'Etat* are concerned to prohibit or reprimand individual commanders charged with levying illegal contributions within the frontiers: see for example, A¹ 58, fo. 76, 7 Mar. 1640, de Noyers to Jean, comte de Gassion, forbidding his regiment from extracting contributions from Corbie.

[178] SHAT A¹ 50ii, fo. 107, 10 Feb. 1639; A¹ 66, fos. 319–20, 22 Nov. 1641, preparations to enforce the military exaction of the *subsistances* across the Limousin.

frontiers, the attitude to contributions was not straightforward. The crown was reluctant to have them imposed in territories which had been occupied but which were seen as potential acquisitions in a peace settlement. In 1641 the garrison of Saint Quentin were warned off making levies in the territory around Arras, which had submitted to the authority of the king, while a similar reluctance to heap military taxes on to Alsace was evident from the early 1640s.[179] In the case of allied powers, the crown's attitude varied from reluctant aquiescence – the acceptance that contributions might have to be levied in Piedmont if the army of Italy was to be kept in being – to a total refusal to countenance any military impositions, which was the crown's attitude to Catalonia in the first two years after the revolt.[180] Even in territories where contributions were judged acceptable, the crown and its ministers were emphatic that they could be extracted only with the explicit permission of the central authorities, and under no circumstances on the initiative of local commanders or governors.[181] While it might be assumed that these prohibitions and the concern with prior authorization were merely pious injunctions, the execution of both the maréchal de Marillac and the marquis de Saint-Preuil on charges of levying illegal contributions would certainly give pause for thought to commanders and governors.[182] Perhaps most critically, even if the crown had not shown itself at best ambiguous about permitting the extraction of contributions, this was a method of funding the armies which required the military circumstances of unchallenged territorial occupation. During Richelieu's ministry the failure of French armies to establish this type of territorial dominance remained the single greatest obstacle to the large-scale use of contributions to meet military costs.[183] Frontier regions could be subjected to protection agreements and arbitrary exactions, but this would not provide a sufficient and recurrent support for military operations. Above all French armies with few exceptions were never in a position to winter across the frontiers, the obvious means to relieve the burdens on the *épargne* and the French population. Where contributions were extracted systematically and ruthlessly – in the countryside around Nancy, for example – their limited territorial extent came to exhaust the

---

[179] SHAT A¹ 65, fo. 23, 6 June 1641, de Noyers to governor of Saint Quentin; A¹ 63, fo. 524bis, 7 Mar. 1641, de Noyers to the *intendant*, d'Oysonville, concerning abuses in the levy of contributions on Alsace.
[180] AAE CP Savoie 31, fo. 242, 14 Oct. 1640, Chavigny to Mazarin; 1633, fo. 476, 3 Aug. 1641, Richelieu to Condé, explicitly prohibiting the levy of contributions on Catalonia; SHAT A¹ 63, fo. 503, 5 Mar. 1641, severe limits to the contributions that may be imposed upon the territory of the bishop of Basle.
[181] SHAT A¹ 65, fo. 426, Aug. 1641, *ordonnance*, specifically prohibiting governors of individual *places* from levying contributions on their own initiative – repeated in 1641: A¹ 66, fo. 15, 23 Sept.; A¹ 65, fo. 168, 30 June 1641, specific authorization to Louis de Béthune, comte de Charost, to impose contributions in Alsace to pay for his company of *chevaux légers*.
[182] See chapter 9, pp. 492–4.
[183] See the discussion of this issue in chapter 1, pp. 78–81.

The administrative context

financial and supply potential of the population so that the troops were forced back into dependence upon the crown.[184]

The introduction of new taxes

While the *surintendants* might have hoped that contributions could make good the shortfall between the funds available for the armies and their financial needs, it became clear that this would not be the case. Yet the pressure from the crown, the other ministers and the high command to maintain funding to the armies would not disappear. The last and only remaining recourse was in the circumstances both predictable and of limited impact: the creation and systematization of new taxes to support the specific costs of the war-effort. However, locked into the vicious circle of deficit financing and expensive dependence upon the loans of financiers, the inevitable occurred and these 'earmarked' military taxes were increasingly mortgaged in return for further loan injections to keep in being the whole rickety edifice of the crown's finances. In the process, taxes which originally had a high value in relation to the military needs of the crown were sacrificed to the priorities of the *bureau des finances*, whose primary concern was of course maintaining interest and loan repayment to the financiers.

In two cases, the *étapes* and the *ustensile*, systems of support for troops passing through or lodged in France had evolved over decades as a means to try to regularize and distribute the burden of the army. *Etapes* were the prescribed stopping points for companies and regiments of troops marching across France from their places of assembly to the campaign theatres. Obviously, the routes followed by the troops were determined by the physical environment, above all the presence of roads or water routes. As a result the burden of supporting troops *en route* for the frontiers and sustaining the destruction and disorders which were likely to accompany any large-scale troop movement would fall disproportionately upon that proportion of communities – whether villages or towns – which had the misfortune to be on these main communication routes. If there was no attempt to equalize the burden, the result, as seen in many parts of Germany, would be wholesale depopulation and abandonment of those areas on the main march-routes of the armies.[185] The *étape* system aimed to avoid this situation by imposing a general tax across a far wider territory, frequently an entire province, so that the revenues could be used to buy the supplies to furnish the stopping points for the troops and to compensate the local inhabitants of these *étapes* themselves for the likely damage that would be wrought by the soldiers.[186] The tax to sustain the

---

[184] AAE MD 839, fo. 317, 24 Oct. 1641, Bouthillier to Richelieu; CP Lorraine 31, fo. 205, Aug. 1639, impossibility of supporting the garrison of Metz from contributions levied on the Pays Messin.
[185] Kroener, *Les routes* pp. 94–105.
[186] For a full discussion of the history and organization of the *étape* system, see Kroener, *Les routes*, pp. 57–83.

étapes in the period 1623–35 was administered under the aegis of the provincial governors and through the administration of the *trésoriers* of the *généralités*. While it added to the fiscal burdens on the population, it had a clear purpose in seeking to equalize the burden of supporting the troops.[187] However, in March 1636 the decision was taken simply to incorporate the tax for the *étapes* into the main direct tax burden, adding it as a surcharge to the *taille* assessment.[188] This was accompanied by a growing reliance on *munitionnaires* – specifically described as *étapiers* – who accepted contracts to provision the *étapes* within a particular *généralité* or *élection*.[189] Thanks to the rulings of 1636, these contracts were no longer made against specific earmarked revenues, but were simply another element of the negotiations between the *bureau des finances*, the financiers and the *munitionnaires*. The revenues had been appropriated into the general resources of the *bureau*, so that the *étapes* competed with all the other claims on the crown's revenues.[190]

A similar fate befell the *ustensile*, which had originally been established as an attempt to protect local populations who had troops billeted upon them by specifying precisely what the householder was obliged to provide for each soldier in terms of quantity of candle, firewood, straw for bedding, linen, spoon and bowl, etc.[191] Although throughout the sixteenth and early seventeenth centuries repeated *ordonnances* had stressed that the *ustensile* was to be paid in kind, and under no circumstances to be commuted into a cash payment, the same issue arose of a burden which fell heavily upon those communities on the main lines of communication across France. As a result attempts were made to quantify the value of the goods and facilities stipulated, initially with the idea that householders should be compensated through a tax imposed across the entire province.[192] Once

---

[187] In 1641 the places selected as *étapes* were compensated at the rate of 1 *sol* per infantryman and 2 *sols* per cavalryman for each night the troops stayed: SHAT A¹ 66, fo. 468, 11 Dec.

[188] Kroener, *Les routes*, p. 94 – *ordonnances* of 26 Mar. and 31 Dec. 1636. In 1640, for example, an additional sum of 60,000 *livres* was added to the tax burden of the Lyonnais for the expenses of the *étapes*: SHAT A¹ 57, fo. 221, 24 Jan. instruction to the *intendant*, Champigny. Reimbursement for the *étapes* themselves was simply to be made from the *taille* assessment: AAE MD 844, fo. 36, 18 Sept. 1642, arrangements for reimbursement from the *taille* levied on the Lyonnais. In a few cases and for a specific purpose the previous system would be reinstated: A¹ 51, fo. 454, 14 Apr. 1639, François de Créquy, duc de Lesdiguières and governor of Dauphiné, authorized to levy a tax across Dauphiné for the costs of the *étapes* for troops destined for Piedmont.

[189] SHAT A¹ 66, fo. 467, 11 Dec. 1641, general *ordonnance* concerning the duties of the *entrepreneurs des étapes*.

[190] One consequence of this was that the *généralités* frequently found themselves assessed for a supplementary charge to pay the 'real' costs of the *étapes* over and above than the initial levy, which had simply been lost in the larger financial manipulations of the *bureau des finances*: SHAT A¹ 66, fo. 535, [Dec.] 1641, notification of a supplementary charge for the *étapes* levied on Normandy; A¹ 70, fo. 36, 26 July 1642, *arrêt* for a supplementary tax for the *étapes* for 1642/3.

[191] A. Navereau, *Le logement et les ustensiles des gens de guerre, 1439–1789* (Poitiers, 1924), pp. 164–8.

[192] Navereau, *Logement*, p. 170, refers to the ordinance of 18 Oct. 1641: 'Et afin que la dépense de la dite fourniture de bois et chandelle ne tombe pas sur les particuliers qui le feront, elle sera régalée sur tous les contribuables aux tailles de l'élection entière.' The system of a cash commutation had

The administrative context

the notion of a *ustensile* tax had been established – specifically entitled the *ustensile des gens de guerre* – the direct link between the payment of a specified assessment and its earmarking for the needs of those places subjected to the *logement* of troops – whether *en route* for the campaign theatres or in quarters – quickly started to blur.[193] By 1639, for example, the money supposedly collected to meet the costs of the *ustensile* in the area around Châlons was being diverted to meet the recruitment costs of the French regiments garrisoned there.[194] The number of disputes and the violent clashes between local inhabitants and the soldiers over the terms of *logement* in the years after 1636 indicate clearly that householders were finding themselves assessed for an additional tax burden while receiving no material support in the provision of *logement* to the troops.[195]

The absorption of the taxes for the *étapes* and the *ustensile* into the larger financial activities of the *bureau des finances* was, however, a minor matter compared with the third case of an appropriated military tax. The budgeting for military activity before 1635 had made minimal allowance for the need to keep large numbers of troops under arms during the winter months.

Previous wars had rarely been envisaged in terms of multiple campaigns, so that it had been assumed that the great majority of troops would be disbanded at the end of each campaign. If the war continued into a second consecutive year, mass recruitment in the first months of the new year would seek to bring the army up to effective strength on the basis of new recruits. But France would stand little chance of matching even the modest military effectiveness of her enemies so long as her armies were almost entirely newly recruited for each campaign.[196] This led to a conscious effort, especially from the winter of 1636/7, to keep large parts of the army billeted in towns and fortress garrisons over the winter months. The ministry was thus saddled with the unprecedented administrative challenge of maintaining tens of thousands of soldiers (at least on paper) across anything up to half of the French provinces through four or five months of the winter. These soldiers were almost invariably stationed near or with civilian populations and needed constant disciplinary supervision to prevent local violence and disputes. If excuses for disorders were to be minimized, it was essential that the troops should be regularly fed and adequately housed, that the arrangements for quartering

    been in place since at least 1636: SHAT A¹ 32, pce 103, 28 June 1636, specifying sums to be
    provided to each community subjected to *logement* and the costs of the *ustensile*, raised via a tax –
    'forced loan' – on the rest of the *élection*.
[193] SHAT A¹ 71, pce 158, 8 Nov. 1642, *ordonnance* concerned with the provision of the *ustensile* to troops in garrison.
[194] AAE CP Lorraine 31, fo. 22, 25 Feb., François de l'Hospital, seigneur du Hallier, to de Noyers: the *ustensile* tax was being allocated at the rate of 3–4 *livres* per infantry company per day.
[195] See chapter 10, pp. 510–14.
[196] AAE MD 828, fo. 362, 1637, *Projet de la cavallerie pour S.E.* (probably written by Bullion). The document discusses the problem of cavalry captains who find it cheaper to dismiss their troops at the end of the campaign, using winter quarter funds to recruit new soldiers at the beginning of the next campaign, troops who are even more ill-indisciplined and 'ne valent rien pour le combat'.

Paying for war

should run as smoothly as possible. Hard pressed to meet the regular campaign expenses of the armies, there was certainly no realistic possibility that existing financial resources could meet the costs of a massive programme of winter quartering. Initial responses to the challenge – largely aimed at foisting the burdens of the troops on to the local communities on an *ad hoc* basis – proved totally inadequate, and the disastrous experiences of this expedient during the winter of 1636/7 persuaded the ministers that a more effective provision for the troops in quarters was required. The *subsistances*, a direct tax in lieu of local arbitrary winter quarter contributions, was introduced, adding a further 8.5 million *livres* to the total of direct taxation imposed upon the population subject to the main direct tax, the *taille*.[197] Yet although this seemed a more realistic option than relying on local exactions and requisitioning, it proved simply impossible to load a further 8.5 million *livres* of direct taxation on to the taxable population, stipulating that it should be collected from November and distributed immediately. Not merely were the sums received inadequate for the needs of the troops, but in many cases were so delayed as to be of no practical benefit. An *arrêt* of 22 April 1638 transferred all subsequent receipts from the *subsistances* into the hands of *trésoriers de l'extraordinaire des guerres*, to be used as they saw fit for the war-effort.[198] And this process by which monies raised by the *taxe des subsistances* were allocated to the wider needs of the armies and the *bureau des finances* was to be the hallmark of the operation in all subsequent years.[199] The *arrêt* for the imposition of the *subsistances* for the next winter quarter of 1638/9 expressed dissatisfaction with the disorders committed 'en plusieurs bourgs et villes' by the troops who had not received the payments that ought to have been ensured by the tax. In consequence, the *arrêt* was dated 3 August 1638, and it stressed that the collection of the *subsistances* was to commence immediately and to proceed in parallel with the other direct taxes.[200] If the *subsistances* had been levied too late in 1637/8 to serve its intended purpose, in future it was to be levied far too early. By 1640, 18.5 million *livres* were in theory to be levied across France through the *taxe des subsistances*, and the collection was to start from late June.[201] In these circumstances, an increasingly large proportion of the revenue collected was alienated, or

---

[197] SHAT A¹ 49, pce 104, 22 Apr. 1638: refers to the 8.5 million *livres* that were to have been levied from the subsistances tax in the previous (1637/8) winter.

[198] SHAT A¹ 49, pce 104, 22 Apr. 1638.

[199] See the *Mémoires* of maréchal Bassompierre, who, writing from the Bastille, discussed the introduction of the *subsistances*, and pointed out that the revenues were misappropriated first through large-scale corruption by the *commissaires* charged with their levy and distribution, and secondly by the *surintendants*' wholesale redeployment of the tax to meet other expenses: Petitot and Monmerqué, XXI. 372.

[200] SHAT A¹ 49, fo. 155: 'qu'outre ce qui se doibt lever en deniers'. The *subsistances* was to be collected in six instalments, instead of the five instalments of the *taille*, and collection was to begin immediately and to run through until April of 1639: Bonney, *Political Change*, p. 275.

[201] SHAT A¹ 62, fo. 152, 9 June 1640; Bonney, *Political Change*, p. 274, gives a lower figure of 13.6 million *livres*, drawing upon the *fonds du conseil d'Etat*.

The administrative context

allocated to other expenses, before the winter quarter began. The process was systematized in February 1638 when the general control of the *subsistances* funds and any loans contracted upon them was transferred to a specific *contrôleur de la recette et despense des deniers destinés à la subsistance des troupes*, the sieur Arnoul, who was to receive 8 *deniers* per *livre* of the total sums imposed, allocating the tax to a financier who would offer a substantial payment in advance for the right to handle these funds.[202] Even when money from the *subsistances* was actually allocated to troops in garrison, the funds were increasingly used, not to support the communities against the costs of quartered troops, but to make payments to the unit officers to fund recruitment *traités* – agreements that the company or regimental strength would be raised to a specified level at an agreed date before the campaign opened.[203] While officially the revenues continued to be paid to support the costs of the units in winter quarters, it was increasingly the case that the companies were assessed at well over their real strength, the difference being used to fund the levy of new recruits.[204] There is no means to quantify the proportion of the *taxe des subsistances* that was appropriated to purposes other than sustaining the costs of the troops in winter quarters, but the level of complaint and unrest throughout the provinces and the strong resistance to *subsistances* assessments[205] suggest that the populations did not regard this very substantial increase in the overall direct tax burden as an orderly and responsible method of sharing the burdens of troops in garrison. By 1641 Bouthillier was explicitly lumping all the direct taxes together, writing of 'l'imposition de 60 millions des tailles et subsistances' on which the whole structure of financial *prêts* and *traités* would depend.[206]

The dilemma facing the *surintendants* was straightforward; the appropriation of these taxes – above all the *subsistances* – to feed the great edifice of *traités* and high-interest borrowing was depriving the armies and the civil populations of the financial benefits derived from revenues directly allocated to specified military expenses. Yet it was this capacity to mobilize extra sources of funding that kept the relationship with the financiers and the *munitionnaires* operational in a period

---

[202] SHAT A^1 43, fo. 358, 18 Feb. 1638; AAE MD 841, fo. 242, [1641] – gives details of the *taxation* of 8 *deniers*.

[203] There are numerous examples of these *traités* to fund winter recruitment, first introduced in 1639: SHAT A^1 50, fo. 126, 15 Jan. 1639, de Noyers to Jacques d'Estampes, marquis de La Ferté-Imbault, concerning payment of recruitment *traités* with captains of cavalry; A^1 58, fo. 292, 29 Mar. 1640, order to the *commissaires pour les subsistances* to pay 20,000 *livres* from their revenues to meet the recruitment costs of the regt of Colonel Streiff. Noteworthy as an indication of wider ministerial policy was the instruction to the *trésoriers de France* at Lyon in March 1640 that the funding of recruitment should have priority over the payment of existing troops: A^1 58, fo. 117, 11 Mar.

[204] See, for example, SHAT A^1 43, fo. 128, 17 Jan. 1638: order to *commissaire* Vallier to pay a number of companies on the basis of eighty men each; A^1 48, fo. 312, 23 Aug. 1638, companies garrisoned in Pinerolo to be paid on basis of 100 men each.

[205] See chapter 10, pp. 511–12.

[206] AAE MD 839, fo. 92, Bouthillier to Chavigny, 24 July.

where the *surintendants* constantly feared a breakdown of the loan contracts which were based on the ordinary tax resources of the crown. Given the direction that French financing of the war-effort had taken since the early 1630s, it is indisputable that a breakdown of the system of revenue anticipation would be the most disastrous of all eventualities, and that the *surintendants*' decision to give priority to the maintenance of the flow of loans was the only practical option so long as the war continued.

The costs of this were paid for immediately, by the armies in the field, and in the years after Richelieu's death by financial expedients which became ever-more desperate so that crisis and breakdown were more and more unavoidable. Some sense of the scale of the financial shortfalls faced by a corps commander in the late 1630s can be obtained from the correspondence of Henri de Lorraine, comte d'Harcourt, commander of the army of Italy, in 1640 – the year that Harcourt relieved Casale and recaptured Turin. In January 1640, Harcourt was already complaining that the troops remaining in Italy had been promised 100,000 *livres* per month, in addition to 160,000 *livres* remaining from assignations for costs in 1639, but had so far received only 137,000 *livres* in total.[207] By mid-May, as Harcourt was about to begin the siege of Turin, he was complaining that the *bureau des finances* was trying to meet the expenses of the siege with a one-off payment of 200,000–300,000 *livres*, ignoring the *montre* owed to the army and the fact that the troops had received nothing since leaving winter quarters.[208] As the siege progressed, so did Harcourt's anxiety and anger about the non-receipt of promised funds. On 11 June, Harcourt wrote to the *secrétaire d'Etat*, Sublet de Noyers, in explicit terms: according to the *Etat du Roi* of 14 January, the army had been promised total funds of 3,255,898 *livres* for the first six months of the campaign, while the garrisons of Casale, Rusignan and Susa had been promised 886,317 *livres*, a total allocation of 4,142,215 *livres*; at the time of writing Harcourt had received only 1,250,000 *livres* in total – of which some 260,000 *livres* were provided to pay for recruitment expenses which should anyway have come from a separate budget and were not intended to be part of the allocation in the *Etat du Roi*.[209] An equally angry letter on 11 August about the failure to honour any of the promises for the payment of the garrison of Casale, which had received no funds at all for the last forty days and where the garrison had already mutinied twice, suggests that the initial massive shortfall in funding had not been remedied.[210] Taking this failure of support into account with, as previously noted, the ministerial ambiguity about the extraction of contributions from Piedmont, which might have made good some of the funding gap, the achievement of Harcourt, the other members of the high command and the troops themselves in 1640 is

---

[207] AAE CP Savoie 30, fo. 47, 30 Jan., Harcourt to Chavigny.
[208] AAE CP Savoie 30, fos. 433, 441, 19/22 May 1640, Harcourt to de Noyers; Turenne to Chavigny.
[209] AAE CP Savoie 30, fo. 501, 11 June.
[210] AAE CP Savoie 30, fo. 713, 11 Aug.

The administrative context

remarkable. While Italy did not enjoy the highest status in the funding priorities of the ministers, and while Bullion personally regarded the theatre with some animosity, there is no reason to assume that the majority of other campaign armies enjoyed any better treatment.[211]

The gap between the financial resources potentially available to the crown to fund its war-effort and the kinds of shortfall described by Harcourt provide a graphic illustration of the problems inherent in the fiscal system as it had developed by the 1630s. Rising above all the other factors which diverted funds from the immediate needs of the armies – shortage of specie, exchange and transport costs, even systematic corruption by the administrators – stood the mountainous expenses of the extraordinary fiscal system. The *bureau des finances* presided over a system which had long ceased to have any relation to its original *raison d'être* – the provision of short-term funds to meet financial needs which did not mesh easily with the flow of ordinary tax revenues – and had become a vast, wasteful, parasitic system which, to quote Richard Bonney: 'worked to the advantage of few at the expense of many without any real gain to the crown, a system moreover that became much worse as time went on'.[212] Far from assisting the crown to meet its military expenses, it was the largest single reason why these expenses could not be met, and why the crown's funding fell so far short of what would have been even an adequate level of financial support for the armies.[213] Financial failure and the collapse of the armies in the years after 1648 can therefore be seen as the consequence of a fiscal administration which from the mid-1630s, had been forced into ever more expensive and unreliable expedients to maintain the flow of payments on its borrowing. Similarly the capacity of Louis XIV's regime after 1660 to maintain a permanent army on a scale not greatly below that of Richelieu's military effort during the war years can be seen as a direct consequence of breaking out from the worst abuses of the extraordinary fiscal system. The obvious question to be addressed in subsequent chapters is how, despite this obvious financial inadequacy, the armies continued to campaign each year after 1635 and how military collapse was averted.

---

[211] When the cardinal de La Valette was commander of the army of Italy in 1638, he wrote that of a total theoretical allocation of 3 million *livres* for the campaign army, he had actually received a total of 2.1 million, considerably better than Harcourt in 1640 and an indication of the favour which La Valette could mobilize amongst ministers from Richelieu downwards, but by any standards still an alarming shortfall: AAE CP Savoie 26, fo. 735.

[212] Bonney, *King's Debts*, p. 168.

[213] Bonney, 'Richelieu and the royal finances', pp. 120–1, 126–8.

5

Recruiting and maintaining armies during the Thirty Years War: military enterprise

In the previous chapters two trends were delineated, which together threatened to have disastrous consequences for the French war-effort. First of these was the progressive growth in the size of European armies, which ensured that when the French crown found itself sliding into open and large-scale war with the Habsburgs after 1634, France was also forced into great military expansion. The second threat was posed by the increased pressures upon the financial capacities of the state. The fiscal demands of a greatly enlarged army meant that Richelieu's ministry hit a 'ceiling' for the extraction of direct taxation at about 30–5 million *livres* per annum; at the same time it failed to exploit extraordinary sources of income which might in practice have enlarged the tax base. The result was an ever-increasing demand for troops to maintain six or seven army-corps at effective strength for 4–5 months of the combat season, and a financial provision which was certainly not increasing in line with the new scale of warfare.

All of this raises an obvious question. How were unprecedented armies raised and maintained by the French monarchy throughout twenty-five years of warfare, with only one serious breakdown – the financial and administrative collapse during the *Frondes*? One part of the answer lies in the ruthless prioritization enforced by the ministers in their allocation of troops and funding: the 'royal' siege of Arras in 1640 received something approaching five times the funding and resources allocated to Harcourt for the siege of Turin in the same year. But this simply raises more insistently the question of what kept the finance-starved 'secondary' armies in being? In some cases they were not sustained, and the collapse of Rohan's army in the Valtelline in the winter of 1636–7 or the military inertia of the army of Italy in 1637 and 1638 exemplifies this. Yet these were the exceptions; however inadequate the funding and provisioning, the armies of Guienne, Roussillon, Lorraine, Franche-Comté, even Germany, were somehow kept operational.

The same kinds of question, asked of the French war-effort, are even more relevant to other European powers, both France's allies and her enemies. How was the early modern state to raise and then to maintain the numbers of troops that were required for warfare on an unprecedented and growing scale? The inadequacy of normal sources of revenue, and the extremely limited administrative and organizational capacity of all early modern governments, ruled out one obvious

The administrative context

option for the recruitment and subsequent maintenance of troops – a centrally organized and centrally funded army. The later sixteenth and first half of the seventeenth centuries in Europe were consequently characterized by wholesale military decentralization and organizational delegation. Few states successfully escaped the pressures to hand over the organization of all, or large parts, of their armies to their own subjects or to foreign entrepreneurs. How did decentralization of the war-effort assist governments to sustain unprecedented war with inadequate financial resources? At first sight it might be thought that the possible advantages of greater – self-interested – efficiency in administration further down the hierarchy of command might well be outweighed by even greater financial inflexibility, a system which required regular, contracted, payments to *condottieri* captains and colonels. It is important therefore to examine military entrepreneurship as it had developed by the time of the Thirty Years War in order to appreciate the advantages and disadvantages for the states adopting it.

THE ENTREPRENEURIAL SYSTEM

In attempting to increase the size of forces under arms, the various European states followed largely similar strategies. Faced with the administrative and financial strains of unprecedented recruitment, there was a general willingness to delegate responsibility into the hands of private contractors. Although the Spanish and Swedish crowns appear to have been partial exceptions, in practice they confirm the trend to entrepreneurship. During the early decades of the reign of Philip II the Spanish government was committed to centralization and the direct control of military organization, although the debate concerning the merits of the state's *administración* set against private enterprise, *asiento*, was overt and intense. However, as the burdens of war on the Spanish system grew during the 1580s the policy went into reverse; the economies and efficiencies permitted by contracting outweighed the greater control offered by direct state administration, so that more and more of the military system was turned over to entrepreneurs.[1] Faced with the demands of an expansionist foreign policy, and the severe limitations upon the available population resources, the Swedish monarchy of the early seventeenth century introduced a system of conscription, the *utskrivning*, to maintain the infantry nucleus of a standing army.[2] But after Gustavus Adolphus had abandoned his campaigns to consolidate Swedish power along the Baltic

---

[1] Thompson, *War and Government*, pp. 256–73; L. Ribot Garcia, 'Les types d'armées en Espagne au début des temps modernes', in P. Contamine (ed.), *Guerre et concurrence entre les états européens du xvie et xviiie siècles* (Paris, 1998), pp. 61–5; C.R. Phillips, *Six Galleons for the king of Spain. Imperial Defence in the Early Seventeenth Century* (Baltimore and London, 1986), pp. 78–89, 94; J.F. Guilmartin, 'The logistics of warfare at sea in the sixteenth century: the Spanish perspective', in J. Lynn (ed.), *Feeding Mars. Logistics in Western Warfare from the Middle Ages to the Present* (Boulder, San Francisco and Oxford, 1993), pp. 109–36, esp. pp. 115–18.

[2] Roberts, *Gustavus Adolphus*, II. 202–7; J. Lindegren, 'The Swedish military state, 1560–1720',

Military enterprise during the Thirty Years War

seaboard and had invaded north Germany, it became evident that conscription from a small population was quite inadequate to the Swedish crown's military requirements. The vast bulk of the Swedish army of the 1630s was recruited under contract in the Empire and from traditional sources of mercenaries such as Scotland and Ireland.[3] The largest proportion of the Swedish forces which fought alongside the French army in the 1640s were German mercenaries, while the Swedish high command became so assimilated into the German culture of the Empire by the late 1630s that, for example, the general-in-chief, Johann Banér, even wrote his letters to the Swedish Court in German.[4]

The military enterpriser in the Thirty Years War

The examples of Sweden and Spain serve to confirm a more general picture: across Europe, with the exception of France, governments drawn into the Thirty Years War moved towards a system of raising troops that was almost purely entrepreneurial. The raising of armies on an unprecedented scale was an enforced response to changing political and military aims, not a conscious choice taken by the states concerned. The process of military expansion had occurred quite separately from the general development of state administration, and very much more rapidly. The financial and organizational resources for the direct recruitment of 50,000–75,000 troops simply did not exist in the early seventeenth-century state. Governments had neither sufficient control over the timing and the quantity of their revenue receipts, nor sufficient administrative agents to accomplish a task on this scale within the constraints of relatively short military campaigns.

Not merely was it clear that direct administration was not a practical option, an entrepreneurial system offered clear advantages to the rulers of early modern states. For the officer-entrepreneur both employed his own administrative and organizational resources in order to raise troops for the service of his employer and also extended credit to him to fund the initial costs of the levy.[5] Armies had rarely in the past been raised by the direct involvement of central government agencies; systems of recruitment, even if supervised by the centre, had usually drawn upon the expertise and local connections of the provincial nobility. Numerous rulers had been prepared to go further, delegating the raising of troops to *condottieri* captains, whether these were their own subjects or foreigners.[6] By

---

Scandinavian Journal of History, 10 (1985), 305–27; Åberg, 'The Swedish army'; C. Nordmann, 'L'armée suédoise au XVIIe siècle', *Revue du Nord*, 54 (1972), 265–87.

[3] For the demographic costs of the *utskrivning* see Parker, *Military Revolution*, pp. 52–3; As early as March 1632, only 13,000 of the 140,000 troops theoretically in the service of Gustavus Adolphus were native Swedes: Roberts, *Gustavus Adolphus*, II. 206.

[4] Noailles, *Guébriant*, p. 148.

[5] Redlich, *Military Enterpriser*, I. 211–305, esp. pp. 239–57.

[6] M. Mallett, *Mercenaries and their Masters: Warfare in Renaissance Italy* (London, 1974); Contamine, *Guerre*, pp. 55–64, 140–5. For two case studies of a particular constituency of mercenaries, the Irish

the early seventeenth century, two centuries of experiments with mercenary contracting had developed into a massive and elaborate structure of entrepreneurial captains and colonels, sometimes operating as independent agents in the military marketplace, sometimes fronting the military activities of a much more important figure, sometimes subcontractors in the service of the handful of great 'general contractors' who maintained entire armies for the service of their sovereign war-lords.[7]

Had the entrepreneurs not been able or prepared to use their access to credit to meet the high costs of raising their units, armies of the scale of those seen in the first decades of the seventeenth century could not have come into existence. Everywhere, from Spínola's financial commitments to the Army of Flanders, through the role of Pappenheim in the Bavarian army of the 1620s, the financial commitments of the officers and the high command in Wallenstein's Imperial army, or amongst the German officers in Swedish service, the armies of the period depended upon the credit of their officers, and usually upon their direct role in raising and maintaining the armies.[8]

However, this alone would not have been enough to sustain the great entrepreneurial armies; the possibility of delegating administrative and immediate financial responsibility to native or foreign officers solved the basic problem of how a state with limited administrative capacity and a rudimentary and inefficient system for revenue collection and distribution could raise armies two or three times larger than anything previously attempted.[9] But without a second, simultaneous, development, this would have been at best a short-term expedient. The entrepreneur-officers regarded the raising of units for the service of a military power as an investment; they certainly anticipated a return from any initial credit that they might have deployed in order to raise and equip their units, and they expected reimbursement for the costs that they incurred in feeding and paying their troops on campaign.[10] If governments saw in the entrepreneurial system a

---

in Spanish service, see G. Henry, *The Irish Military Community in Spanish Flanders, 1586–1621* (Dublin, 1992), and R. Stradling, *The Spanish Monarchy and Irish Mercenaries. The Wild Geese in Spain, 1618–1668* (Dublin, 1994).

[7] Redlich, *Military Enterpriser*, calculated that at least 1,500 military enterprisers at various levels offered their services during the Thirty Years War, I. 205–10; M.S. Anderson, *War and Society in Europe of the Old Regime, 1618–1789* (London, 1988), is a general study which gives attention to this phenomenon.

[8] Parker, *Army of Flanders*, quotes a Genoese contemporary that 'Spínola could always raise a personal loan of 2 million *escudos* and could do it for half as much as the king of Spain' (pp. 249–50); Kapser, *Die bayerische Kriegsorganization*, pp. 82–8; Konze, 'Die Stärke', pp. 11–16, emphasizes that under Wallenstein the capital investment in the regiments of the Imperial army was divided between the colonel and supreme commander, reimbursement being arranged accordingly – see also Stadler, *Pappenheim*, pp. 604–6.

[9] The impact of Wallenstein's general contracts on the size of the Imperial forces is notorious: Löwe, 'Wallensteinschen Heere', pp. 6–8.

[10] Pohl, *Profiantirung der keyserlichen Armaden*, pp. 32–7, together with a specimen recruitment contract, pp. 181–8.

means to raise armies on a scale and for lengths of time that were beyond the capacity of their tax revenues to support, then relations with the entrepreneur-officers would reach a crisis as soon as it became obvious that the government could not afford to honour the contracts that it had so willingly negotiated with numbers of them.

The 'contributions-system'

Breakdown of this entrepreneurial system was for the most part averted by the elaboration of a system of war taxation which made it possible to offer a level of financial return to entrepreneurial armies well above the yields of traditional taxes. 'Contributions' were either extracted directly by the armies in a particular territory for their maintenance and the reimbursement of the investment of the entrepreneurs, or through a civil administration acting immediately under military instructions and carrying out assessments and collection in the shadow of a continuous military presence in the locality.[11] Regimental and senior officers, who saw in the effective extraction of contributions the chief means to recoup their investment in the army, were unconcerned by the mass of fiscal privileges and exemptions that permeated the society around them. As a result, the barriers to effective fiscal exploitation were broken down: towns, regions and entire states found themselves assessed for levels of contribution over a few months which amounted to more than whole decades of ordinary tax payments.[12]

An orderly system of contributions entails a number of preconditions; if the armies are simply passing through territory, the temptation will be to resort to unlimited plunder and consequent destruction of economic potential.[13] For a

---

[11] Parker, *Military Revolution*, pp. 65–7; F. Redlich, 'Contributions in the Thirty Years War', *Economic History Review*, 2nd ser., 12 (1959–60), 247–54; M. Ritter, 'Das Kontributionssystem Wallensteins', *Historische Zeitschrift*, 54 (1902–3), 193–249; H. Salm, *Armeefinanzierung im Dreißigjährigen Krieg. Der Niederrheinisch-Westfälische Reichskreis, 1635–1650* (Münster, 1990), pp. 22–6; K. Krüger, 'Kriegsfinanzen und Reichsrecht im 16. und 17. Jahrhundert', and N. Winnige, 'Von der Kontribution zur Akzise: Militärfinanzierung als Movens staatlicher Steuerpolitik', in B. Kroener and R. Pröve (eds.), *Krieg und Frieden. Militär und Gesellschaft in der Frühen Neuzeit* (Paderborn, 1996), pp. 47–83. For a later period in France see J.A. Lynn, 'How war fed war: the tax of violence and contributions during the *Grand Siècle*', *Journal of Modern History*, 65 (1993), 286–310.

[12] Redlich, 'Contributions', gives examples of one-off contributions paid by individual cities and towns that were more substantial than the agreed tax burdens of entire Kreise or, in one case, the contributions of all states of the Catholic League over six months; C. Friedrich, *Urban Society in an Age of War: Nördlingen, 1580–1720* (Princeton, 1979), pp. 148–57; T. Robisheaux, *Rural Society and the Search for Order in Early Modern Germany* (Cambridge, 1989), pp. 202–26; T. McIntosh, *Urban Decline in Early Modern Germany: Schwäbisch Hall and its region, 1650–1750* (Chapel Hill, N.C., 1997), pp. 42–5; M. Gutmann, *War and Rural Life in the Early Modern Low Countries* (Princeton, 1980), pp. 41–6, 62–6.

[13] Such a policy was occasionally pursued during the Thirty Years War, as, for example, in the Franco-Swedish devastation of Bavaria in 1646, aimed at forcing the Bavarian Elector to break with the Habsburg alliance: G. Immler, *Kurfürst Maximilian I. und der Westfälische Friedenskongreß. Die bayerische auswärtige Politik von 1644 bis zum Ulmer Waffenstillstand* (Münster, 1992), pp. 316–23.

The administrative context

contribution-system to be operated requires that some parts of the army should be permanently present in the territory that is to be regularly subjected to these taxes. However, a permanent military presence on enemy, or non-aligned, territory entails a very different conception of strategy: it requires numerous garrisons and/or strike-forces of troops; it assumes a large permanent military establishment ready to act to defend the occupied territories against invading armies or to repress large-scale internal unrest. One consequence of this need to view war largely in terms of territorial occupation is that armies themselves became larger: while there is quite clearly an optimum size for a field army,[14] this is a lot smaller than the forces required for permanent military occupation and garrisoning of territory intended to support the army through contributions.[15] The systematic exaction of contributions is attributed to the Spanish Army of Flanders in the first instance, and it is significant that this was the first of the large, semi-permanent, forces that were to dominate European warfare for the next fifty years.[16] The greatest example of a purely entrepreneurial army, the force raised by Albrecht Wallenstein for Imperial service, came into existence with the explicit intention that it should be supported, and the initial costs repaid, through contributions levied on territory in the Empire.[17] Wallenstein's – possibly apocryphal – statement to the Imperial Privy Council that he could afford to raise and finance an army of 50,000, but not one of 20,000, because the larger force could sustain most of its costs through the extraction of contributions, is a convenient encapsulation of this period of warfare and its driving force.[18]

While the development of contribution-systems was undoubtedly a response to

---

Redlich, 'Contributions', 247, draws a distinction between a regular system of agreed contributions and more casual extortion under the threat of destruction by the military – *Brandschatzung* – though the line would have been blurred in many cases.

[14] Turenne's opinion that armies should be of no more than 20,000–30,000 men, with at least 50 per cent of these being cavalry, has been widely noted: cf Susane, *Histoire de la cavalerie française*, I. 106. Paul Hay du Chastelet, *Politique militaire ou traité de la guerre* (Paris, 1757; 1st pub. 1667), pp. 61–5, suggested that the largest force able to operate in the field was 40,000, and that troops above that number contributed nothing to military effectiveness. He also proposed that the smallest force should be no less than 6,000 men. In a central European context, Raimondo Montecuccoli proposed various ideal sizes for field armies varying between 20,000 and 40,000 men: Barker, *Military Intellectual*, p. 60.

[15] Adams, 'Tactics or politics?', pp. 29–34 – reprinted in Rogers (ed.), *The Military Revolution Debate*, pp. 253–72. That Gustavus Adolphus fought the battle of Lützen with under 20,000 men, when his 'army' – that is to say all the troops notionally in his service – was claimed to total anything up to 175,000, has escaped the attention of many historians of military change in early modern Europe.

[16] Parker, *Army of Flanders*, pp. 142–3; Parker, *Thirty Years War*, p. 197.

[17] Redlich, *Military Enterpriser*, I. 229; Ritter, 'Kontributionssystem Wallensteins', esp. 210–49; A. Ernstberger, *Hans de Witte, Finanzmann Wallensteins* (Vierteljahrschrift für Sozial- und Wirtschaftsgeschichte, Beiheft 38) (Wiesbaden, 1954), pp. 162–225; G. Mann, *Wallenstein. Sein Leben Erzählt* (Frankfurt-am-Main, 1971), pp. 421–32.

[18] Mann, *Wallenstein*, pp. 370–1; for an example of the development of the contributions-system in the second half of the Thirty Years War, see Salm, *Armeefinanzierung*, pp. 116–42, which reveals that around 96.3 per cent of the funds for the Imperial army from the Westphalian Circle between 1635 and 1648 were paid in the form of contributions (p. 117).

military demands, there can be no doubt that their proliferation in the Thirty Years War owed a great deal to the juridical and territorial character of the areas over which the war was fought. The Holy Roman Empire, with its multiplicity of small states and its rulers who did not possess full sovereign authority, provided outstanding opportunities for the manageable imposition of contributions. Not the least of the Emperor's real powers in the seventeenth century was his capacity, by virtue of his status as imperial overlord, to license and authorize the imposition of war-taxes both on those Imperial fiefs which could be considered to be in rebellion against his authority, and also – though with more debatable legality – on all of his other 'subjects', whether or not they were opposed to his authority. As the Swedes, Spanish, French and Dutch found, even where their juridical rights to exact contributions were non-existent, the small scale of most of the states in the Empire, whether in Germany or Italy, made them easy targets for the extortion of funds, while the proximity of states to each other made it easy to move troops from one designated 'support-zone' to another. Even when an elaborate system of territorial occupation had been abandoned, the number of small, poorly defended, states of the Empire offered the possibility that highly mobile campaign armies could operate as self-financing entities, moving from one state to another extracting money by intimidation. On 1 February 1639 field-marshal Banér's campaign army of 18,000 troops and eighty cannon crossed the Elbe:

sans avoir aucune provision pour nourrir ses troupes, ni d'argent pour en acheter. On comptait tout au plus cinq ou six mille écus dans sa caisse militaire ... La terreur de leurs armes leur fit bientôt trouver des vivres en abondance. Bannier les conduisit sur les terres des ducs de Brunswic et de Lunebourg, qui avoient abandonné les Suédois pour accepter la paix de Prague.[19]

The entrepreneurial 'way of warfare'

The contribution-system underpinned military expansion in the first half of the seventeenth century. It provided the prospect of reimbursement to unit commanders who regarded the levying and maintenance of troops as an investment-strategy, and allowed the warring states to inflate their military establishments beyond anything justified by their disposable revenues.

Moreover, if the initial delegation of authority to the entrepreneur was specific and limited, having once raised these troops under contract, the majority of states took the far more significant step of putting the subsequent burden of maintenance and control of the units into the hands of the entrepreneurs. The state which lacked the administrative and financial resources to recruit its army was unlikely to possess the capacity to ensure its effective management and funding once it was established. But in this second step lay the 'prodigal delegation of

[19] Griffet, *Louis XIII*, III. 211.

The administrative context

powers', characteristic of the entrepreneurial military system.[20] For if the entrepreneur was to retain full responsibility for his unit, then it was necessary to grant him permanent powers of appointment and dismissal. As he was responsible for the quality, discipline and military effectiveness of his troops, it was essential that the commander should be able to replace subordinate officers who proved inadequate, and to promote or reward those who gave good service. Even if formal recognition of the changes was reserved by the crown, the entrepreneur, far from being a salaried employee, now held substantial rights of private patronage. The principle that the crown or central government held a monopoly of all military appointments was undermined. Moreover, the entrepreneur-officer would also require substantial autonomous rights of justice over his troops. Finally, the commander of the unit, now made financially and administratively responsible for the day-to-day effectiveness of his unit, needed some formal assurance that his 'investment' would be respected: rights to compensation in the event of dismissal or the unanticipated end of the war; a willingness to pay his ransom in the event of capture, to keep the unit in the hands of his relatives or to compensate them in the event of his death.[21] All of these concessions run contrary to the assumption that governments were seeking to achieve more control over the military resources of the state.

Yet the European sovereigns presiding over the development of this enterprise system conceded their authority more willingly than might have been expected. Delegation of power to the military entrepreneurs worked. The result, in a significant number of cases, was an army created at a supportable financial and administrative cost to the government prepared to accept the system. The nature of the enterprise system for raising and maintaining an army, the stake in the well-being of the army held by the 'investors' – the entrepreneur-officers – ensured that a significant part of the delegated authority was exercised in the interests of military effectiveness.[22] There were, of course, exceptions: some officer-entrepreneurs were badly chosen, lacked personal authority or the will to control their units. It was always possible to envisage situations where immediate gain would

---

[20] C. Jones, 'The military revolution and the professionalization of the French army under the Ancien Régime', *Exeter Studies in History*, 1 (1980), 28–48, at 30.

[21] Many of these were traditional rights extending back to the *condotte* between fifteenth-century Italian states and their mercenary captains: Mallett, *Mercenaries*, pp. 77–88. As usual, however, the archetype of this system was Wallenstein's army raised for the Emperor: see esp. Ritter, 'Kontributionssystem Wallensteins', 207 *et seq.*; Redlich, *Military Enterpriser*, I. 227–30. The interested parties did not necessarily number only the commanding officer; AAE MD 845, fo. 243, [n.d. 1642], accords colonel Rosen 2,000 *livres* compensation on the disbandment of a regiment which he did not command but in which he was 'fort interessé'.

[22] For the careers of two successful military entrepreneurs see Stadler, *Pappenheim*, and T. Barker, 'Ottavio Piccolomini (1599–1659): a fair historical judgement?', in T. Barker, *Army, Aristocracy, Monarchy. Essays on War, Society and Government in Austria, 1618–1780* (New York, 1982), pp. 61–111. For the military effectiveness of the army of Saxe-Weimar see Noailles, *Saxe-Weimar*, *passim*.

Military enterprise during the Thirty Years War

outweigh the longer-term interest involved in ensuring that the army as a whole was capable of preserving itself and acting as a coherent military force. The area in which this temptation became most apparent was in the possibilities for private extortion and plunder from civil populations, and it is necessary to avoid confusing consistent indiscipline and the pursuit of self-interest in this sphere with a lack of coherence and structural weaknesses within the army itself. Wallenstein's army, a mercenary force whose 'rank and file, dredged up from all over Europe, and incapable of solidarity . . . poorly and irregularly paid . . . [resulting] in a rapid turnover', was none the less able to stand up to a numerically superior Swedish army at Lützen, and had already checked Gustavus Adolphus' forces outside Nuremberg a few months earlier.[23] Levels of casualties and the ferocity of the fighting during the Thirty Years War make it quite clear that the enterprise system as it had developed was capable of generating armies that were all too effective.

In examining the phenomenon of the entrepreneurial army, historians have tended to focus on the general contractor – commanders with overall responsibility for the levy and operations of an entire army raised under contract. Yet even these armies actually rested upon substantial individual financial commitments made below that level. Wallenstein, while initially offering to raise 24,000 troops for the Emperor and increasing this offer to 100,000 by 1627, did not intend to use his private resources for this. His army was made up of regiments raised by subcontracting unit officers, who were drawn by Wallenstein's reputation and the hope of subsequent profit from their investment in military service.[24] It was these colonels, sometimes captains, who made the initial advances to raise, equip and provide a first payment for the troops. In fact, if they themselves had a military reputation or a large network of clients, they might be in a position to further subcontract, giving responsibility for the levying of companies to a number of aspiring captains. The essential factor was that the regimental commander and possibly some of his subordinates had made an initial financial commitment in their own right. The possibility of recovering this 'investment' and of continuing in service to make a profit depended upon the army's military success. Gaining a tactical advantage, or a victory in the field, permitted the occupation of enemy or neutral territory, from which contributions could be extracted at well above the

---

[23] V.G. Kiernan, 'Foreign mercenaries and absolute monarchy', *Past and Present*, 11 (1956–7), 66–86, at 78, provides a convenient summary of the typical prejudices and misconceptions about the organization and quality of mercenary armies. The oft-repeated platitude that mercenaries were reluctant to fight battles and to accept heavy casualties, popularized by Machiavelli amongst others, is probably indestructible. W. Block, *Die Condottieri. Studien über die sogenannten 'unblutigen Schlachten'* (Berlin, 1913), subjected the myth to an empirical examination of five major battles involving *condottieri*, but nearly a century later the assumptions remain widespread: 'Vielleicht ist keine Epoche in der Geschichte der Kriegskunst mit so viel Tadel überhäuft worden wie das Kriegswesen der Condottieri' (p. 13).

[24] Mann, *Wallenstein*, pp. 369–72, 406–15; Redlich, *Military Enterpriser*, I. 229–32; Ernstberger, *Hans de Witte*, pp. 229–30.

The administrative context

level required for the immediate subsistence and wages of the troops.[25] This squeezing of the economic resources of territory could be combined with supplementary gains from looting and plunder, allocated according to rank within the army.[26] Defeat on the other hand deprived the army of almost all sources of revenue, threatened its dissolution and the loss of the capital investment of the officers. The commander of a unit was far more than a passive investor; the possibility of realizing his investment depended largely upon his own and his colleagues' efforts to keep the army an effective fighting force and to ensure that it could defeat or fend off enemy forces. The achievement of the entrepreneurial system was thus to ensure that the interests of the commanding officers of the units stood opposed to those of their subordinates and troops – at least in the medium and long term. In this context the officer-proprietors had considerable reason to restrain insubordination, indiscipline and the misappropriation of funds, and to maintain the unit as an effective contribution to the army's military strength.

It may appear mechanistic to attribute the success of an army to the financial commitments made by its unit commanders and by the senior officers. Undoubtedly loyalty, a desire for reputation, the 'military spirit' of some of the veterans in the army, would count for a lot, as would the prevalence and deliberate sustaining of a noble honour code amongst the officers. But, in any case, we are speaking of relative, not absolute, standards of discipline, coherence and military effectiveness. By any exacting standards, the armies of the Thirty Years War were unwieldy and inadequately supported; they faced near insuperable problems of supply and mobility, extraordinary wastage rates amongst the troops, and usually an inability to pursue more than the most rudimentary strategies. Overall control was haphazard, and the forces were held together by no more than a veneer of discipline and subjection to common objectives, under which individual insubordination and corruption were almost universal. Yet for all this, the armies did cohere and could serve as instruments for the pursuit of political and dynastic objectives, however blunt and imprecisely destructive they might prove; and they did so because, not in spite, of their entrepreneurial structure. The ultimate sanction of financial commitments which could either produce substantial returns for the participating entrepreneurs or be completely lost, depending upon the

---

[25] Redlich, *Military Enterpriser*, I. 331–43, 359–60; Adams, 'Tactics or politics?', pp. 43–4; B. Kroener, 'Soldat oder Soldateska? Programmatischer Aufriß einer Socialgeschichte, militärischer Unterschichten in der ersten Hälfte des 17. Jahrhunderts', in M. Messerschmidt (ed.), *Militärgeschichte: Probleme, Thesen, Wege* (Stuttgart, 1982), pp. 100–23.

[26] F. Redlich, *De Praede Militare. Looting and Booty, 1500–1815* (Vierteljahrschrift für Sozial- und Wirtschaftsgeschichte, Beiheft 39) (Wiesbaden, 1956), pp. 41–53. For the wealth – in cash and objects – obtained by the Swedish officer-corps during the war, see H. Trevor-Roper, *The Plunder of the Arts in the Seventeenth Century* (London, 1970), pp. 40–6; Sully, during his service under Henri IV during the French civil wars, estimated that his total profits from war-taxes, plunder and ransoms came to some 330,000 *livres*: I. Aristide, *La fortune de Sully* (Paris, 1990), pp. 29–30.

effectiveness of the army in which they served, should not be underestimated in explaining how the Thirty Years War could be fought on the scale that contemporaries recognized as unprecedented.

The price of this entrepreneurial, decentralized and largely self-financing warfare was paid at the strategic level – the wider military and political aims of the states who unleashed this military system on Europe. Entrepreneurial warfare required that obtaining funds to pay and supply the army and to allow the officers some financial return on their 'investment' should be the first priority of military action. It was not the only priority, but a strategic or political objective could only be pursued if and when this precondition was met. As the war in the Empire continued, it became increasingly difficult for the commanders to escape from an all-consuming preoccupation with territorial occupation and the extraction of financial and material support. It was the extreme, albeit devastating, bluntness of this instrument which was ultimately to drive European rulers to reduce their dependence on entrepreneurial warfare with its inbuilt tendency to ignore or even undermine the war-aims that had set their armies in motion. While contributions continued to occupy a prominent position in the landscape of warfare, states sought to reduce, by more direct administration and a higher proportion of direct funding, the independence of the commanders and their consequent tendency to give priority to the army's subsistence rather than to the war-aims of the state.[27] The entrepreneurial recruitment and maintenance of troops itself was finally phased out, or reduced to a manageable number of foreign mercenary units, in armies that became more effectively subject to direct state control and funding.[28]

FRENCH RESPONSES TO MILITARY ENTERPRISE

Political fears

Entrepreneurial models for military organization were adopted by almost every major state in the first half of the seventeenth century. Even where, as in the case of Spain or Sweden, the state did not move across to a totally entrepreneurial military system, the trend was clearly in the direction of increasing devolution. The notable exception to the trend was France. As with the other European states, the development of mechanisms for the recruitment and maintenance of troops did not reflect any clear-sighted pursuit of an administrative ideal. But whereas elsewhere the pressures which shaped the emergence of the largely entrepre-

---

[27] Lynn, 'How war fed war', 303–6, though Lynn would argue that the collection of contributions remained central to the formulation of strategy.

[28] For the decline of contract armies in the later seventeenth and eighteenth centuries see Redlich, *Military Enterpriser*, II. 103–69; Barker, 'Armed forces and nobility: Austrian particulars', in Barker, *Army, Aristocracy, Monarchy*, pp. 37–40; J. Black, *European Warfare, 1660–1815* (London, 1994), pp. 87–118.

The administrative context

neurial systems were economic, in France the most powerful considerations in raising the army were political.

Just as the experience of the *Frondes* contributed to the shaping of French political life in the second half of the seventeenth century, so decisions concerning administrative practice and the delegation of authority in the 1620s and 1630s were still determined by the civil wars of the later sixteenth century and the rebellions of the Regency of Marie de Médicis. Concern at the potential fragility of monarchical institutions and their vulnerability to the challenge of widespread disorder had been an issue long before the later sixteenth century. Successive kings and their ministers had sought to restrict the means by which revolt and disorder were facilitated. Central to this attempt was the desire to maintain an exclusive right to authorize the levy of troops throughout the realm. Charles VII had first promulgated this claim as a royal ordinance in 1439. The ordinance 'Pour obvier aux pilleries et vexations des Gens de Guerre' stipulated that 'certain nombre de Capitaines des gens d'armes et de traict sera ordonné pour la conduite de la guerre, lesquels Capitaines seront nommez et esleuz par le Roy'.[29] Yet in practice the situation was much more ambiguous; the theoretical rights of the crown were set against a reliance upon the executive authority and influence of the nobles in the provinces, who remained the best and most efficient agents for the recruitment of troops.[30] Not all contemporaries accepted this practical delegation of authority, and the experience of the civil wars of the later sixteenth century created considerable unease in some quarters about the independent military powers possessed by the upper ranks of the traditional *noblesse d'épée*.[31] A limited effort was made to confront this unease during the reign of Henri IV, and to reassert a stronger element of royal control over the recruitment and control of the army.[32] However, Louis XIII's minority was marked by the resumption of

---

[29] Charles VII at Orléans, 2 Nov 1439: *Ordonnances des rois de France de la troisième race*, ed. L.G. de Vilevault, L. Oudart de Brequigny and J.M. Pardessus (21 vols.; Paris, 1773–1849; repr. 1967), XIII. 306–13. The terms of this ordinance were frequently recapitulated in subsequent decrees, particularly at times of particular crown weakness: *Compilation chronologique contenant un recueil en abrégé des ordonnances* . . . (2 vols.; Paris, 1715), I. 1119, 1161, 1177: similar ordinances for 1581, 1583, 1585. Charles VII had also established the principle of a directly levied royal army based upon a small force of *gendarmes* and conscripted *francs archers*: Redlich, *Military Enterpriser*, I. 28; Contamine, *Guerre*, pp. 278–90, 304–7.

[30] This ambiguity is best illustrated in the studies of the relations between the crown and the governors and *lieutenants-généraux* in the provinces: R.G. Tait, 'The king's lieutenants in Guyenne, 1580–1610', DPhil thesis, University of Oxford, 1977; M. Greengrass, 'War, politics and religion during the government of Montmorency-Damville, 1574–1610', DPhil thesis, University of Oxford, 1979; Harding, *Anatomy of a Power Elite*.

[31] C. Loyseau, *Cinq livres du droit des offices* (Châteaudun, 1610), p. 450; J. du Tillet, *Recueil des roys de France leurs couronne et maison* (Paris, 1602), p. 306. At the same time as acknowledging the force of some of these arguments, it is possible to ask how far these tracts by *officiers* are representative of a wider mood of antagonism to the military role of the great nobility in society, and indeed how far even amongst a politically self-conscious group of *officiers* this was seen as more than a rhetorical exercise, devoid of serious political intent.

[32] Audoin, *Histoire de l'administration*, II. 142–90, treats the reign of Henri as a crucial turning point in

Military enterprise during the Thirty Years War

factional and religious conflict. The weakening of central authority, the re-emergence of aggressively autonomous noble power in the provinces, the private levy of troops to wage rebellion or to engage in local conflicts, are all typical of the period after 1614. Letters drawn up during Richelieu's brief tenure of power as *secrétaire d'Etat* in 1616–17 emphasize the resurgence of the problem of the crown's incomplete control of the recruitment and maintenance of its armed forces.[33] While the crown remained in theory preoccupied with the need to prevent the levy of troops without specific royal commissions, and to proceed against those who carried out such levies with severity, in practice the ministers seems to have been prepared to tolerate some levies provided that they were for royal service.[34]

The *coup d'état* of 24 April 1617 did not end the series of challenges to the crown's authority. The practical capacity of provincial nobles to raise troops remained considerable, especially after the resurgence of Huguenot unrest from 1620. The Huguenots resumed the system of eight 'areas', responsible for conscription and for the collection of all royal and ecclesiastical revenues within their jurisdiction.[35] Until the surrender of La Rochelle in 1628 and the final suppression of protestant unrest across the Midi, the crown was engaged in an intermittent struggle, over nearly a decade, with groups who rejected its fiscal and military authority. In order to wage this war, the crown found itself obliged – particularly when engaged in simultaneous foreign ventures – to delegate extensive military authority to catholic *grands* with governorships or political influence in the south: Condé, Montmorency, Epernon.[36] The king's position was not so weak as it had been in the 1580s, in that no single *grand* or family grouping

---

the organization and administration of the army. Other historians have been unconvinced by this interpretation, while none the less according some credit to the initiatives of Henri and Sully: D. Buisseret, *Sully and the Growth of Centralized Government in France, 1598–1610* (London, 1968), pp. 140–69; B. Barbiche and S. de Dainville-Barbiche, *Sully* (Paris, 1997), pp. 203–5, 260–5.

[33] Avenel, I. 375, 378, 10/12 Mar. 1617, concern of the ministers to respect the rights of the *colonel général de l'infanterie*, the duc d'Epernon, over newly levied units.

[34] *Les ordonnances militaires tirées du code du Roi Henri III, auxquels ont esté adjoustez des edicts du roi Henri IV et Louis XIII* (Paris, 1625), p. 257, Paris, July 1575: 'Puis qu'au Roy seul appartient de faire la guerre, ceux qui font levées d'hommes de guerre sans permission commettent crime de leze Majesté.' Illegal levies of troops were certainly a preoccupation of the ministry in these years: Avenel, I. 408, 16 Mar. 1617; I. 418, 19 Mar. 1617; I. 491, 4 Apr. 1617. Yet as the need for troops became greater, this basic principle of control over levies could be abandoned. The sieur de Saragnac was pardoned for his offence of having raised troops without a royal commission, on condition that they should be deployed in the king's service: Avenel, I. 483, 1 Apr. 1617.

[35] Chevallier, *Louis XIII*, p. 226; Lublinskaya, *French Absolutism*, pp. 157–63, 183–5; see also the description of the original Huguenot military organization: J. de Pablo, 'L'armée huguenote entre 1562 et 1573', *Archiv für Reformationsgeschichte*, 48 (1957), 192–216.

[36] Grillon, III. 323, 6 June 1628: Henri II de Bourbon, prince de Condé, was to *faire le dégât* around Nîmes, Castres and Montauban, in cooperation with Jean-Louis Nogaret de La Valette, duc d'Epernon, and Henri II de Montmorency, carrying out similar operations, while the royal army was engaged at La Rochelle. Operations during the following year's campaign in the Midi were divided in a similar manner: Grillon, IV. 319–20, 382–3, 443–4, 21 May, 9 June, 6 July 1629.

looked likely to gain a dominant position in the military structure. Yet the provincial nobility emerged out of this period with their military role substantially intact. Of the Huguenot *grands*, only Henri, duc de Rohan, and Benjamin de Rohan, duc de Soubise, had been prepared to assume the leadership of resistance, while the suppression of Huguenot rebellion had required the crown to draw heavily upon the provincial influence and military resources of other *grands*, both catholic and loyalist Huguenot.

These political developments up to 1630 are of crucial importance in explaining the attitude of the crown and Richelieu's ministry to the recruitment and maintenance of the army. In contrast to every other major European state, France rejected in principle the entrepreneurial system for the raising of troops. This rejection, it can be proposed, had in turn considerable consequences for the relationship between the crown and its military officers. The Spanish Councils of State and Finance could discuss the relative advantages of *administración* and *asiento* on the basis of their respective military and financial merits. For the French, the issue carried inescapable political implications: proprietorship of units, overall control perhaps of a substantial army-corps on the basis of a general contract would imply, as elsewhere, the loss of the ruler's autonomy in the organization of military force. In France the legacy of massive and destructive civil unrest, experienced as recently as the 1620s, made such a transaction unacceptable to the crown. Moreover, any willingness to modify this position in the light of military needs after 1635 would have been checked by the successive noble plots and revolts which continued to challenge the policies and authority of Richelieu's ministry. As late as 1641, Soissons, with a corps of his own troops and supporters, joined up with Imperial troops and routed the royal forces under maréchal Châtillon at La Marfée. The provincial status and patronage of the great nobility continued to provide them with the capacity to raise forces on their own account. And precisely because of this ability, the French government was determined to resist a move towards the formal delegation of military authority implied by the regularization of an entrepreneurial system.

At the same time, however, the crown's regular and urgent military needs created an awareness amongst some of the *grands* that there might be the potential for negotiating some form of entrepreneurial general contract with the French crown. In 1625, as Richelieu was gathering French resources for intervention in the Valtelline and the Franco-Savoyard attack on Genoa, the *connétable* François de Bonne, duc de Lesdiguières, proposed that he should raise and sustain an army of 20,000 infantry, 4,000 cavalry and some field artillery in return for a monthly payment by the crown of 200,000 *livres*.[37] Not surprisingly in view of the crown's attitude to such delegation of military authority, the offer was not accepted,

---

[37] Quazza, 'Politica europea', 57, quoting a letter from the Mantuan representative in Paris to duke Ferdinando, 21 Apr. 1623 – A.S.Ma AG, E. XIV 3, vol. 616.

Military enterprise during the Thirty Years War

despite the obvious convenience of making use of the influence and resources of Lesdiguières in his government of Dauphiné to raise and maintain troops for Italy. The crown's unwillingness to negotiate over this issue seems to have discouraged any similar proposals during the 1630s and 1640s. Even in 1651, in the midst of the *Frondes*, when the maréchal d'Aumont revived the notion that a great military noble should act as a general contractor, the crown remained hostile. D'Aumont proposed that 'Moyennant sept millions par an, il entretiendra vingt mille hommes effectifs toute l'année en bonne conche (équipage) et exacte discipline, sans que le peuple en soit aucunement incommodé.'[38] The offer was rejected, though not without some debate in the Council. There remained an overwhelming reluctance to establish an entrepreneurial army in the hands of a great noble, above all in a situation in which a number of the great *Frondeur grands* had already managed to turn the army-corps which they commanded against the ministerial regime.

The crown was equally sensitive about less extreme forms of delegation. In 1636 Louis XIII wrote to Richelieu concerning a proposal to raise a number of regiments of twenty companies each, holding the status of *régiments entretenus*, bearing the *drapeau blanc*, the sign of elite status conferred upon permanent regiments by the king. Louis considered that: 'Faisons les régiments de province, mon cousin le Duc d'Epernon pourroit avoir les [mesmes] pretensions sur eux, que sur les vieux régiments, ce que je ne puis consentir pour plusieurs raisons.'[39] While the established powers of Epernon over the existing *régiments entretenus* would be tolerated by the crown, Louis XIII had no wish to extend this authority further into the army, to the possible prejudice of the crown's own military authority. He asked Richelieu to negotiate with Epernon's son, Bernard de Nogaret, duc de La Valette, to try to persuade the old duke to abandon his claims: 'Et en cas qu'ils veullent tenir ferme, je me resoudrais plustot a ne point faire lesdits regimens de province.'[40]

Neither Epernon nor his son, who held the *survivance* of the office of *colonel général*, appear to have been prepared to concede their rights in this issue. Most of the regiments had already been established by the time that the king began to have misgivings about the additional influence that this would give to Epernon.[41] Nevertheless, the project was abruptly halted; the duc de La Trémouille was instructed to raise the regiment for which he had received the commissions, but explicitly not to adopt the provincial title that had been proposed, or – by

---

[38] André, *Michel Le Tellier et l'organization*, p. 276.
[39] AAE MD 821, fo. 251, Aug. 1636, Louis XIII to Richelieu; BN Châtre de Cangé, 23, fo. 247 (copy).
[40] AAE MD 821, fo. 251, Aug. 1636.
[41] SHAT A^1 41, fo. 63, 21 Nov. 1635, de Noyers to Charles de Schomberg, duc d'Halluin; BN Châtre de Cangé, 23, fo. 129, 8 Dec. 1635, Richelieu to cardinal de La Valette, giving details of the existing units that are to be promoted to this new provincial status; A^1 27, fo. 8, 11 Jan. 1636: Abel Servien, *secrétaire d'Etat de la guerre*, reports that the majority of these regiments are being levied; A^{1}28, fos. 174, 263, 28 June/12 July 1636: further orders for the levy of regiments of Bourgogne and Perigord.

291

The administrative context

implication – the *entretenu* status.[42] Despite the original intention that all of these units should have the status of permanent regiments, a standard order was drawn up later in the year for the disbandment of the regiment of Anjou.[43] Although the names of provinces attached to a few regiments do occasionally recur in letters from the secretary of state – Lyonnais, Périgord, Saintonge – a coherent group of *régiments provinciaux*, with status as *entretenus* units carrying the royal *drapeau blanc*, did not come into being at this stage.[44]

Despite these instances of a determination to stand on the principle of not delegating more military authority, the unprecedented demands of warfare placed the same financial and organizational pressures upon Richelieu's ministry as upon other governments. France was not immune from these conflicting pressures, but the result in her case was not the adoption of fully fledged entrepreneurship, but an insidious and mutually damaging network of compromises between the government and the unit and staff officers with the army. Yet even here the issue in the French case was less than straightforward; for at the same time that the crown and cardinal Richelieu were concerned with the political principles underlying the means by which native French troops were levied and maintained, they showed no hesitation in adopting an overtly entrepreneurial system with regard to foreign mercenaries brought into French service.

The French monarchy and foreign mercenaries

In theory the political implications which would preoccupy the government when considering possible means of levying native troops were of no relevance when raising foreign units. While granting contracts to French nobles or others who wished to raise native troops might appear a clear infringement of the crown's sovereignty, the use of foreign mercenaries appeared a far more manageable option. The foreign entrepreneur brought his troops directly into the service of the crown, and had no personal or territorial connections with the crown's subjects. Moreover, they were in service for a particular, often stipulated, period, after which the contract could either be renewed or, it was hoped, the troops would be decommissioned and *en route* back to their places of origin outside of France. In practice this neat line between potentially over-powerful subjects and salaried, professional and obedient foreign captains and colonels was less clearly marked, especially when these foreign units found themselves in the service of field commanders who were hostile to the ministerial regime. The government was very sensitive to these threats. When it became known that some 500 soldiers

---

[42] SHAT A¹ 29, fo. 149, 5 Sept. 1636.
[43] SHAT A¹ 31, fo. 89, 29 Dec. 1636. Whether this was the model for a series of orders to disband all the provincial regiments is not evident.
[44] Despite the assertions of numerous earlier historians: for example, Quarré de Verneuil, *L'armée en France*, p. 149.

in the garrison at Nancy were native Lorrainers, who had previously served in the army of the duke, the loyalty of the comte de Brassac, into whose regiment they had been recruited, became a matter of concern for Richelieu. Chamblay, one of the *commissaires* at Nancy, admitted that he had not approached Brassac earlier on this matter because 'je l'ay veu se picquer contre commissaires en de pareilles rencontres', but was prepared to vouch for his absolute loyalty, if not his sobriety.[45] Yet despite these flurries of concern at the potential loyalty of foreign units, Richelieu and his fellow ministers showed themselves prepared to negotiate contracts with foreign entrepreneurs of a size and autonomy that would have been inconceivable in the case of French subjects.[46]

Saxe-Weimar and 'general contractors' in French service
The most extensive single agreement with a foreign entrepreneur was that made at Saint-Germain-en-Laye on 27 October 1635 with Bernard, duke of Saxe-Weimar, stipulating that he should maintain an army of 12,000 infantry and 6,000 cavalry, all German troops with, it was hoped, previous military experience. In return the French crown would pay Saxe-Weimar 4 million *livres* for the costs of the army per annum, and a pension of 150,000 *livres* for his own expenses.[47] This contract with Saxe-Weimar was in some respects an anomaly; the duke and his army formed the rump of the German troops who had served in the Heilbronn League, and who had been deprived of Swedish support after the defeat at Nördlingen. Having found it increasingly difficult to levy contributions or to obtain informal subsistence from territories now dominated by the Imperial armies, Saxe-Weimar considered that the contract with Louis XIII would provide

---

[45] AAE CP Lorraine 25, fo. 152, 3 Apr. 1635; in 1641 Guébriant, commanding the army of Germany, was instructed to assure himself of the loyalty of his foreign units before paying them the *montre*: SHAT A^1 66, fo. 166, 13 Oct. 1641. In this case, however, the concern was not that these troops would defect to the enemy but would accept the inducements to join the 'Swedish' – largely German – army of Johan Banér.

[46] Jean-Baptiste Budes, comte de Guébriant and commander of the Weimarian army after 1641, found a useful riposte to the ministry's neglect of funding for the army of Germany by repeatedly stressing that the majority of the troops in the army, German mercenaries, served through interest rather than affection or loyalty, and could not be expected to continue to serve the crown in the absence of pay: e.g. AAE CP Allemagne 16, fos. 154–5, 7 Apr. 1641. However, it is quite clear that loyalty and commitment to a commander who was prepared to defend their interests played a large part in keeping the officers and soldiers of the army of Germany in French service at precisely those times when support from France was lacking: for example, Noailles, *Guébriant*, pp. 182–221, on the period from the mutinies amongst the Weimarian regiments to the victory at Wolfenbüttel, March–29 June 1641.

[47] Aubery, *Richelieu*, I. 550–3, 27 Oct. 1635; also printed in Noailles, *Saxe-Weimar*, pp. 481–6. Even this original agreement had been hotly debated, and negotiations between the French crown and Saxe-Weimar had stagnated through the summer and autumn of 1635. Richelieu considered that France could not wage war in the Empire without Saxe-Weimar, but initially considered that the cost of the treaty and the absence of guarantees that Saxe-Weimar would subordinate himself to French policy were unacceptable. He was eventually to give way on both grounds: Noailles, *Saxe-Weimar*, pp. 185–90.

The administrative context

him with some prospect of partial financial support to pay the existing troops and to recruit up to an effective, operational, strength. Until Saxe-Weimar's death in 1639 there was no question of the army serving on French territory or in conjunction with French troops as part of a single army-corps. Saxe-Weimar had full autonomy over appointments, recruitment, justice and administration in his army, and had merely agreed to act in pursuit of French military and political aims, sometimes as commander of an independent army-corps, sometimes in conjunction with a French commander such as cardinal de La Valette (1635, 1636), François de l'Hospital, seigneur du Hallier (1637) or Guébriant (1638, 1639). Concern that the French crown might be subsidizing an army that pursued aims in the Empire reflecting the ambitions of the commander rather than the aims of French foreign policy was evident from the outset, though the military quality of Saxe-Weimar's troops and the general difficulties encountered in the first years of the French war-effort ensured that the French ministers had no wish to allow these tensions to develop into serious disputes.[48] The treaty of 27 October 1635 had also made concessions to Saxe-Weimar's own interests, most notoriously in the 'secret articles' where the duke was accorded full titles, seigneurial rights, rents and other financial benefits pertaining to the Landgraviat of Alsace, hereditary territory of the Habsburgs.[49] When Saxe-Weimar started to take fortresses and fortified cities in Alsace, above all, of course, Breisach in 1638, it inevitably generated disputes with the French, who considered that such strongpoints were specifically excluded from the 1635 treaty and belonged to the king. For Saxe-Weimar the ambition to carve out a territory for himself on the Rhine was hardly compatible with the transfer of the key strategic centres in this territory to France.[50] Saxe-Weimar's death on 18 July 1639, with the question of Breisach and the fortified towns of Alsace still unresolved, undoubtedly saved the French ministers from a quarrel which threatened to become extremely damaging. It did not resolve the loyalties of Saxe-Weimar's troops, however, who, though prepared to remain in the service of the king of France after 1639, did not consider that they had entered into any binding contract. Throughout 1640 and 1641 there was considerable concern that the Weimarians might desert *en masse* to the Swedish army. The claim made by the spokesmen of the army during the illness

---

[48] Notwithstanding this dependency, Bullion still wrote to Richelieu on 13 Oct. 1636 that in matters of the financial allocations due to him, Saxe-Weimar was proving 'extrêmement attaché a ses interests et contre raison': AAE MD 822, fo. 52.

[49] BN Ms.fr. 3767, fo. 1, 6 Nov. 1635, Louis XIII to Charles de Monchy, marquis d'Hocquincourt, governor of Schlestadt, instructing him to facilitate Saxe-Weimar's assumption of Habsburg seigneurial rights in Alsace.

[50] AAE CP Allemagne 15, fos. 62–9, 16 July 1639, *mémoire* for Claude de Mesmes, comte d'Avaux, concerning the agreements with and the treatment of Saxe-Weimar. Some concern had been voiced that the dispute over Breisach was so intense that Saxe-Weimar might be prepared to leave French service, though the ministers drawing up the memoir seemed relatively unconcerned by this risk. Noailles, *Saxe-Weimar*, pp. 395–417, provides an account of the dispute as it developed between November 1638 and June 1639.

of the duc de Longueville in March/April 1640 that they were 'pas plus Français que Suédois, mais simplement gens de bien et indépendants' raised worrying questions about their future loyalty and commitment to the French war-aims.[51] Considerable effort was made to ensure that overall command of Saxe-Weimar's units, while they should be kept together as a specific army-corps, should pass to a French commander, and that, on paper at least, a series of undertakings should be extracted from the colonels to ensure their loyalty to the crown. The duc de Longueville had been chosen deliberately as a commander of high social status who would both emphasize the value the king placed upon the Weimarian forces and, as the most senior *prince légitimé*, and thus the highest ranking French *grand* beneath the Princes of the Blood, might be able to overawe those involved in disputes and ensure loyalty.[52]

This attempt to replace Saxe-Weimar with a French commander exposed a series of intractable problems about the control and character of this army. The duke on his deathbed had left the overall control of the army to four 'directors', Hans Ludwig von Erlach, baron of Castelan and Gauwestein in the canton of Berne, Reinhold Rosen, baron von Grossropp, Othon-Guillaume, comte de Nassau, and colonel Öhm.[53] But Saxe-Weimar had not intended that the four directors should take decisions without consulting the other colonels who constituted the majority of proprietors and share-holders in the army. While the French crown wanted an agreement with the Weimarians, it did not want to obtain this through an arrangement that would give *de facto* control to one or more of the directors and might thereby threaten to recreate the independence and capacity to exploit the relationship with France shown by Saxe-Weimar. Negotiations surrounding the reincorporation of the colonels of Saxe-Weimar's army into the king's service began in late July 1639 and lasted until the directors and the other colonels finally signed the treaty of Breisach on 9 October 1639, although even then the oath of allegiance to Louis XIII to be taken by all the troops of the army remained an outstanding issue.[54] While Erlach was treated as the most senior, and also the most reliable, of the directors in these negotiations, there was no attempt to establish him as overall field commander of the army and to negotiate with him to the exclusion of the other directors or colonels. The policy of dealing with the officer-entrepreneurs as a collectivity was understand-

---

[51] Noailles, *Guébriant*, p. 147.
[52] A point made by Guébriant, who was relatively low ranking in both social and military terms, and found himself representing the French crown in command of the army during the illness and subsequent absence of Henri II d'Orléans, duc de Longueville. Faced with hostility and non-cooperation from the colonels, Guébriant wrote back to the French court stressing that a high-ranking commander should be sent to fill Longueville's place as soon as possible if the army was to be kept under control: AAE CP Allemagne 16, fo. 299v, 25 Aug. 1641, Guébriant to Chavigny; fo. 318, 17 Sept.1641, Guébriant to de Noyers.
[53] Noailles, *Saxe-Weimar*, pp. 450–4.
[54] Noailles, *Saxe-Weimar*, pp. 458–69.

The administrative context

able, but in the event it proved no more satisfactory. As a result of these protracted negotiations the formal oath was not taken, and the attempts of the French agents with the army, Guébriant, Paul le Prévost, baron d'Oysonville and the *intendant* and *conseiller d'Etat*, Jean de Choisy, to consolidate the authority of the king encountered all the problems of dealing with an institution in which power was so diffused. In August 1640 matters reached a crisis when procrastination by some of the colonels turned to an outright refusal to take the oath of loyalty, a refusal given underhand encouragement by field-marshal Banér who wanted to draw the Weimarians into his Swedish army.[55] The potential revolt was brought under control by Longueville and Guébriant through a combination of intimidation and bribery, and on 17 August 1640 the army finally assembled to swear the full oath of allegiance to Louis XIII.[56]

Yet the dilemma remained: allegiance to the crown of France could never exert more than a tenuous claim on the loyalty of an army whose outstanding military qualities came from a strong and long-standing corporate identity as an association of independent German-speaking units formed under the charismatic leadership of Saxe-Weimar, and with a very limited sense of responsibility to any higher civil authority. Even at its most successful, the relationship between Saxe-Weimar and the French crown depended more upon a coincidence of interests than upon any institutional subordination of the army to the French crown or its military administration. Simply placing Longueville or Guébriant at the head of such an army would not immediately turn it into an obedient agent of French political and military ambitions. If the army was genuinely to be subordinated to France, then the solution, as Banér perhaps disingenuously proposed in 1640, was to flood the army with French units, up to the point where the Weimarians were outnumbered and would be deterred from taking any step which might be defined by the more powerful half of the army as mutiny. But in the first place this would pose almost insuperable problems of recruitment. Sending French troops into the Empire and keeping them there was almost impossible, and involved rates of wastage through desertion so high as to make any campaign strategy hopeless. Moreover, even if an effective presence of French troops could be maintained within the army of Germany so as to 'dilute' the Weimarians, it is far from clear that this would be militarily desirable. The very effectiveness of Saxe-Weimar's army depended upon its cohesion as a long-standing force containing a high proportion of veterans who considered themselves a military elite with a reputation to defend.

Yet to take the other route, as in fact the French were increasingly to do during the 1640s, and to reduce the proportion of French troops in the army of Germany so that the army consisted of the 'rump' of Weimarians and numbers of

[55] Noailles, *Guébriant*, pp. 159–63. At one point the directors sought to change the terms of the treaty of Breisach, and to substitute the word 'promise' for that of 'oath' to obey the king of France, a proposal that was, of course, strongly resisted by the French agents.
[56] Noailles, *Guébriant*, pp. 161–4.

transferred German regiments already in French service or newly levied east of the Rhine, left the problem of control unresolved. The colonels simply did not recognize that their obligation to the French monarchy outweighed their concern as entrepreneurs to sustain their units and to obtain the best possible terms for themselves and for their troops. At times when the Swedes appeared to be making substantial progress in the Empire and when French strategy seemed to require the colonels to remain bogged down in unprofitable campaigns in the Rhineland, it was inevitable that some of the officers should contemplate a change of allegiance.[57] In February 1641, and before the dispute between the colonels had been resolved, three of the regiments mutinied, ostensibly over quartering arrangements and the inadequacy of pay, but with the tacit support of their colonels who saw this as a means of placing pressure on the relationship with the French crown. On this occasion they declared that they were prepared to pass over to the Bavarian army.[58] Threats of mutiny and insubordination continued throughout the summer of 1641, right up to the victory at Wolfenbüttel on 29 June when the Weimarians once again vindicated their reputation as a *corps d'élite* and brought the disputes in the army to a temporary conclusion.[59] Yet the loyalty and commitment of the army of Germany to French war-aims continued to be an issue throughout the 1640s.

It is probable that the example of Saxe-Weimar served to discourage the French monarchy from the negotiation of further general contracts with entrepreneurs whose personal ambitions were likely to conflict with the crown's own interests. Set against this threat, however, there remained the overwhelming concern to obtain veteran troops under experienced foreign commanders. The attractiveness of a contract which could bring a major, long-serving, army-corps into French service might still outweigh prudential concerns about the loyalty of the corps once in service. The first attempt to enlist the services of Jean de Werth and his Bavarian army-corps was made in 1635, and the experience of fighting against his ferociously effective 'croat' light cavalry in subsequent campaigns encouraged further efforts.[60] Werth's capture after the second battle of Rheinfeld on 3 March 1638 provided an unexpected opportunity to remove him from the war altogether, though soon after his capture the Swedish raised the possibility that he might be exchanged for field-marshal Horn, held by the Bavarians since the battle of Nördlingen in 1634. Negotiations for this exchange dragged on until 1642, with the French interested in the possibility of recruiting Jean de Werth for their own service, but at the same time concerned not to antagonize the Swedes by an

---

[57] Noailles, *Guébriant*, p. 179.
[58] Noailles, *Guébriant*, pp. 182–6.
[59] Noailles, *Guébriant*, p. 207.
[60] AAE CP Allemagne 12, fo. 430, 16 Dec. 1635, 'Mémoire sur les propositions de Jean de Werth . . . de venir a nostre service, et nous amener toutes les troupes qu'il pourra.' For Jean de Werth's military actions against France from 1635 to 1637 see Noailles, *Saxe-Weimar*, pp. 290–1.

The administrative context

apparent refusal to undertake the exchange for Horn. In September 1641 a secret agreement was reached by which Jean de Werth would be exchanged for the Swedish field-marshal, but six weeks after the exchange he would return to France to enter the service of Louis XIII.[61] For reasons that are unclear this arrangement broke down, and though the exchange took place in the following year, Jean de Werth simply returned to Bavarian service, leading his forces against the French army of Germany in the mid-1640s.[62]

In another bid to bring German troops across *en masse* into the French army, the sr de La Boderie, French resident at the court of Hesse-Kassel, was given repeated instructions to try to recruit the army of this state into French service. This in part reflected French knowledge that the widow of landgrave Wilhelm V of Hesse-Kassel, Amelia of Hanau, was negotiating simultaneously with the French, the Swedes and the Habsburgs in order to try to preserve the neutrality of her state and to defend the interests of her son, the future landgrave Wilhelm VI. It also reflected suspicions that the commander of the Hessian army, count Mélander von Holzappel, was sympathetic to an Imperial alliance. Duke Wilhelm V had died in October 1637, and the first proposals that the entire Hessian army – given at about 7,000 troops at the time of the death of the last landgrave[63] – should be recruited into French service were introduced in instructions to La Boderie in August 1638.[64] These French initiatives were successively blocked by Mélander in 1638 and 1639, who was himself seeking to negotiate an arrangement for the transfer of the army into the service of the Emperor.[65] It was only with his departure from the army to take service with the Spanish in 1640 following clashes with the regent over her concern to maintain neutrality that a serious possibility existed of absorbing the landgrave's army. But by this time the French had renegotiated a treaty with Amelia of Hanau on terms that considerably reduced the scope for diplomatic ambiguity in her policies, and the plan to incorporate the army directly into French service was allowed to lapse.[66]

A general contractor can be defined as one who was expected to bring a complete military force from outside into the service of the king of France. The implications of this simple definition were sometimes complicated by political

---

[61] BN Ms.fr. 3833, fo. 244, 18 July 1641, discussion of Jean de Werth's proposals and terms for entry into French service; AAE CP Allemagne 16, fo. 317, 12 Sept. 1641, text of agreement.

[62] Noailles, *Saxe-Weimar*, pp. 297–8.

[63] Noailles, *Saxe-Weimar*, p. 241 n. 1. Landgrave Wilhelm had employed this army in a particularly aggressive local war with his cousin, George II of Hesse-Darmstadt, and the soldiers were of far higher quality than a locally recruited and inexperienced militia: cf. Parker, *Thirty Years War*, pp. 222–3.

[64] AAE CP Allemagne 15, fo. 94, 8 Aug 1638, instructions for sieur de La Boderie. A further set of instructions – fo. 133, 10 Oct. 1638, emphasized the need to deal with the colonels directly.

[65] D'Avaux warned of Mélander's attempts to draw the Hessian troops into Imperial service in early 1639, thus increasing the pressure on the French to try to acquire these units first: AAE CP Allemagne 15, fo. 229, 1 Mar. 1639.

[66] Noailles, *Guébriant*, pp. 150–1.

Military enterprise during the Thirty Years War

relationships. A clear example of this can be seen in the arrangements for the army of Savoy-Piedmont at the time of the regency of Marie-Christine. Confronted by substantial hostility to the French presence in Piedmont, Marie-Christine would obviously have found it politically convenient to allow the French to assume the main financial burden of supporting the Savoyard army – that is, in effect, for her to have acted as a general contractor in French pay. Louis XIII and Richelieu rejected such an arrangement, arguing that the terms of the League of the Italian States had specified a military contribution from each state according to its resources.[67] But political priorities could dictate a different approach, especially when it was a question of incorporating a dangerous enemy into a French alliance. After the settlement which brought prince Tommaso Francesco of Savoy into an active military alliance with France in late 1640, Tommaso's own troops were entered into French service on the basis of a contract which allowed him to retain the role as their corps commander.[68] A similar arrangement was made with the duke of Lorraine in 1641. The accord between Charles IV and Louis XIII agreed on 29 March 1641 stipulated that the army of the duke should be incorporated into French service, and should immediately enter campaign against the Bavarian and Habsburg forces on the Rhine.[69] One of the first signs that Charles IV had no intention of keeping to the wider terms of the treaty was his evasion of this military stipulation.[70] Rejecting French calls that he should take the offensive, he argued that his army was too depleted for any such action and proposed that either the army-corps in Lorraine under François de l'Hospital, seigneur du Hallier, should be amalgamated with the remnant of his own army and subject to his command, or that the French crown should provide funds for him to recruit his army up to its previous effective strength.[71] Not surprisingly, the French crown rejected both proposals.

Foreign mercenaries within the French military establishment
Yet while such general contracts are an indication of the attitudes of the French crown to large-scale foreign recruitment and the delegation of authority, they remain exceptional in the pattern of French recruitment of foreign mercenaries, and as the previous section indicates, the number of successfully negotiated arrangements of this sort was small. Much more frequent in a descending scale of

---

[67] The terms of the League negotiations of 1633–4 had explicitly established the military contributions to be made by the participating states: see S. Externbrink, '*Cœur du Monde*', pp. 351–3; AAE CP Savoie, 26, fo. 101, 5 Mar. 1638, d'Hémery to Richelieu, discussing the duchess of Savoy's intention of raising fewer Savoyard troops than specified in the treaty of the League, intending to treat French subsidies to raise a further 3,000 infantry and 1,200 horse as part of her commitment.
[68] AAE MD 843, fo. 179, 4 Aug. 1642, La Vrillière to Chavigny.
[69] AAE CP Lorraine 32, fos. 54 *et seq.*, 29 Mar. 1641, text of treaty.
[70] AAE CP Lorraine 32, fos. 183–92, late May 1641, letters of Charles IV, duke of Lorraine, to Richelieu and Chavigny.
[71] AAE CP Lorraine 32, fo. 210, 11 June 1641, *mémoire* sent to Richelieu by du Hallier, who, not surprisingly, was unenthusaistic about both proposals.

The administrative context

entrepreneurial contracts was the practice of contracting with a particular foreign colonel to raise more than a single unit for French service. A colonel with a long career of successful military service behind him would find it easier to recruit and retain good-quality veteran troops than an entrepreneur raising a unit for the first time. It made sense to identify a number of reliable, experienced, colonels and to entrust a relatively high proportion of the total levies of foreign troops to them. Of those in the Empire raising troops after 1635, Josias, count of Rantzau (1609–50), was one of the entrepreneurs most frequently employed by the French crown. Descended from an old military noble family from Holstein, Rantzau had served in the Dutch, Swedish and Imperial armies before entering French service in 1635. From the outset Rantzau's reputation was such that he was persuaded to raise two regiments of German troops, one of infantry and one of cavalry.[72] In 1636 he was given the rank of *maréchal de camp* with the army of the prince de Condé serving in Franche-Comté. His standing was already far above that of an ordinary enterpriser colonel bringing a unit into French service. In 1637 Louis XIII recognized the losses of estates and revenues that Rantzau had suffered as a result of entering the service of the French crown by awarding him compensation from French territories, together with a pension of 36,000 *livres*.[73] However, for all Rantzau's reputation as a courageous, experienced and talented commander, the French ministers constantly encountered problems with his reliability and sustained commitment. His reputation was quite sufficient to draw large numbers of high-quality recruits into his service, and the French crown was perfectly correct to see him as an asset in the Empire. But Rantzau's application to such schemes was highly unpredictable: in 1637 he received the charge of *lieutenant général*, together with orders and funds to conduct a large-scale recruitment operation in the Empire.[74] The project broke down amidst recrimination on all sides, and Rantzau left French service to travel to Denmark, where he remained for the next two years. Yet this setback did not discourage the French from approaching him again in 1639 in the hope of enlisting his services and reputation for the recruitment of further troops in the Empire, and of attracting him back into French service. The French representative Claude de Mesmes, comte d'Avaux, was instructed to provide Rantzau with 18,000 *riksdaler* to cover the costs of the transport of his regiment to France, to assure him that the king would

---

[72] C. Malingre, *Eloge historique de la noble et illustre maison de Rantzow* (Paris, 1641); Noailles, *Guébriant*, p. 371 n. 3: the two units were to be unusually large, even by the standards of regiments recruited abroad, consisting of 4,000 infantry and a cavalry 'regiment' of 3,000 light horse and 1,000 dragoons. It is not clear that this was more than a strategy to recruit additional troops and to distribute them amongst the other German regiments in French service; in late 1636 cardinal de La Valette was notified of Rantzau's despatch to join his army with a regiment of infantry and one of cavalry: SHAT A¹ 30, fo. 194, 27 Oct. 1636.

[73] SHAT A¹ 42, pce 70, Mar. 1637.

[74] SHAT A¹ 35, fo. 39, 4 Mar. 1637, de Noyers to Saint-Chaumont, informing him of Rantzau's mission in the Empire.

Military enterprise during the Thirty Years War

be prepared to support the costs of as many troops that he was able to raise over and above the notional full strength of his regiment, and that if he returned to France 'venir continuer ses services à S[a] M[ajesté] il recevra toute sorte de bon traittement de France'.[75] D'Avaux succeeded in negotiating a contract with Rantzau which restored his pension of 36,000 *livres* per annum, and offered him a 60,000 *livres* additional payment towards the costs of raising two regiments of 1,500 infantry each, whose upkeep would subsequently be supported by the crown.[76]

Rantzau provides the best example of the foreign entrepreneur who rose within the French army not as an independent general contractor – a commander of an army-corps in his own right – but as a career-officer who served alongside French senior officers, and achieved successive promotions through his own military skill and leadership. Engaged at the siege of Arras, he was the immediate subordinate of the maréchal de Guiche at the defeat of Honnecourt in 1642, where he was captured. Ransomed through the intervention of the king and in accordance with his capitulation as a foreign colonel in French service, he returned to service to fight both at Rocroi and Tuttlingen in 1643. Yet on two occasions when a more general authority might have been granted to him, the decision was taken to pass over Rantzau in favour of other senior officers. In 1636 Richelieu and de Noyers decided to create an office of *commissaire général* to have a general supervisory role over all German units serving with French forces across the Rhine.[77] The functions of the post were equivalent to the administrative and financial duties of an *intendant d'armée*, but as German colonels serving under capitulations negotiated with the French crown enjoyed considerably more independent authority than their French counterparts, it was considered essential to appoint a military officer rather than a civilian administrator to this post. The problems of enforcing some degree of financial and administrative control over independent-minded proprietor-colonels required a level of authority and capacity to command respect that would not be attained by a French civil administrator; indeed, the *intendant d'armée*, Jean de Choisy, was recalled from the forces serving across the Rhine in order to be replaced by the new *commissaire*. In terms of the respect and authority that Rantzau could command over the German officers, he would have seemed an ideal choice for this new post, but the commission in fact went to Alexandre de Prouville, baron de Tracy, colonel of a cavalry regiment, who had served in the French armies since 1632. In the same year Louis XIII created an office of *colonel général* of the German cavalry, again granted not to Rantzau who would have seemed the obvious candidate, but to Colonel Streff.[78]

---

[75] AAE CP Allemagne 15, fo. 288, 16 July 1639, instructions for comte d'Avaux.
[76] AAE MD 848, fo. 66, 22 Oct. 1639, *extrait* of the accord between Louis XIII and Rantzau, drawn up in Lyon.
[77] SHAT A^1 32, pce 255, [1636], full text of commission for *commissaire général*.
[78] SHAT A^1 32, pce 48, 3 Apr. 1636, commission for *charge* of *colonel général* of the German cavalry.

The administrative context

Rantzau's own concern with titles and status was clear. Insisting that he should be granted a commission as *lieutenant général* as a condition of returning to French service, he explained to d'Avaux at the beginning of negotiations in 1638 that he would prefer to serve in this rank as the subordinate of a French commander than have full command of a lesser corps but with the inferior title of *maréchal de camp*.[79] Unless it is assumed that Tracy and Streff possessed a degree of influence with the king of France or his ministers that Rantzau was unable to assert – and Rantzau's pension of 36,000 *livres* was considerably greater than the annual *appointements* of 6,000 *livres* attached to the *charge* of *colonel général* of the cavalry[80] – it must be assumed that the crown sought to avoid the delegation of too much authority to an already powerful entrepreneur commander, and therefore chose figures of less weight – and potential independence – for these posts.

The death of Guébriant on 24 November 1643 from a wound received at the siege of Rottweil left Rantzau the most senior and experienced officer with the army of Germany.[81] Yet while he appeared the obvious replacement general for the army, once again the French crown chose to look elsewhere for its commander. The overwhelming defeat of the army at Tuttlingen on the same day that Guébriant died, and the capture of Rantzau together with all of the rest of the general staff, imposed a decisive break in the history of the army of Germany. Rantzau was ransomed – for the second time in two years – by the French crown and the army was reconstituted for the campaign of 1644, but overall command was given to the Henri de La Tour d'Auvergne, vicomte de Turenne. The French crown still considered that there was a significant risk involved in setting a German entrepreneur at the head of the army, even though Rantzau had been much more clearly integrated into the French military structure than either Saxe-Weimar or the subsequent directors of his army had been.

Beneath Rantzau were a series of German colonels who had been granted multiple contracts to raise units that were commanded by themselves personally, by their relatives or though subordinates granted lieutenant colonelcies. Colonel Streff, though *colonel général* of the German cavalry, had both a regiment of cavalry and one of infantry under his command.[82] In 1641 Colonel Rosen, one of the directors of the Weimarians, had two cavalry regiments of his own in French

---

[79] AAE CP Allemagne 15, fo. 43, 20 Apr. 1638, considerations concerning Rantzau's return to French service, presented as a memoir for d'Avaux.

[80] SHAT A¹ 32, pce 72, 10 May 1636, *brevet d'assurance* for a salary of 500 *livres* per month for the *colonel général* of the German cavalry.

[81] The *maréchal de camp* Hector de Saint-Maur, marquis de Montausier, was the notional head of the French troops in the army, but as these were a minority compared to the German regiments, and as Montausier's military experience was considerably inferior to Rantzau, there was no serious opposition to his assumption of direction: Noailles, *Guébriant*, pp. 392–3.

[82] SHAT A¹ 58, fos. 290, 292, 29 Mar. 1640, *brevet* for the payment of Streff's infantry regiment; 20,000 *livres* to pay for recruits to his cavalry regiment.

Military enterprise during the Thirty Years War

service, and one regiment of dragoons commanded by his cousin.[83] In the following year Rosen wrote directly to Richelieu to request permission to take over the proprietorship of a further regiment of cavalry, that of the late colonel Müller, in which Rosen had been 'fort interessé' while the colonel was alive.[84] Such multiple contracts were not restricted to German colonels or to troops intended to operate in the Empire. Alfonso Gonzaga di Bozzolo, marquis of Pomaro, was granted contracts for the levy of 4,000 infantry in two regiments intended for the service of the army of Italy.[85] English, Irish and Scottish colonels of established reputation were also approached for the levy of additional units.

The Swiss stood in a rather different relationship to the crown of France by virtue of the treaty and agreement negotiated at Freiburg on 21 November 1516 and consolidated by a further agreement on 7 May 1521. The king paid pensions to all the cantons which had accepted the alliance, guaranteed to uphold their political autonomy, and in return obtained the right to maintain between 6,000 and 16,000 Swiss troops in his service.[86] The long-standing relationship with the French crown had consolidated very considerable juridical autonomy, both within the Swiss units and in relations between the Swiss soldiers and the civilian population.[87] The *régiment entretenu* of *gardes suisses* created in 1616, together with the *cent-suisses* who continued to form part of the king's bodyguard, created a permanent career structure for ambitious Swiss officers that was far more clearly integrated into the French military establishment than was the case for other foreign entrepreneurs. The cantons themselves frequently undertook the levy of the troops for French service, appointing officers rather than allowing these to come forward as potential investors in the unit. It was not the case that the Swiss colonels would be encouraged to raise multiple units in their own name; it was therefore more likely that investment would be made in a company which was within French service. As a number of Swiss regiments were effectively treated as *entretenues*, maintained in both war and peace, and sustained regardless of the death or retirement of the commanding officer, individual Swiss were more likely to invest in a company within such an existing regiment.

In granting the same colonel a number of contracts to raise troops for French service, the crown was concerned to obtain the maximum benefit from the

---

[83] AAE CP Allemagne, 16, fo. 112, 24 Feb. 1641, Choisy to de Noyers.
[84] AAE MD 845, fo. 253, [n.d. – 1642]: Rosen was taking issue with the proposal that the regiment should be transferred to another colonel-proprietor, and that he should be compensated for his stake in the unit by a payment of 2,000 *livres*.
[85] AAE CP Savoie, 25, fo. 28, Jan. 1637. In this particular case a political motive may be suspected, in that the Gonzaga di Bozzolo, a cadet branch of the Gonzaga dukes of Mantua, had previously shown themselves strong supporters of the Habsburgs in Italy, and the opportunity to attract a member of the family into a substantial commitment to France may have seemed a desirable political objective in its own right.
[86] Jérôme Bodin, *Les Suisses au service de la France de Louis XI à la Légion Etrangère* (Paris, 1988), pp. 83–4.
[87] C. Salerian-Saugy, *La justice militaire des troupes suisses en France* (Paris, 1927).

The administrative context

entrepreneurial system on the broad principle that the stronger the reputation of the colonel-proprietor, the better subordinate officers and soldiers he would be able to attract into his service. If objections were raised to a proposal by an individual foreign contractor for raising a number of units, these would be on practical grounds. In 1635 the *secrétaire d'Etat de la guerre*, Abel Servien, wrote to cardinal de La Valette concerning a proposal by Colonel Hums to carry out a multiple levy of a regiment of infantry, two companies of *chevaux légers* and two of dragoons, expressing his doubts about the feasibility of this because 'il y a eu sy peu d'advancement jusques ici en la levée entière de son premier regiment qu'on n'a pas estimé le devoir embarquer a une plus grande levée'. However, Servien did stress that should Hums prove more successful in raising his companies of cavalry and dragoons then the contracts would be maintained.[88]

Even where the individual entrepreneur was only prepared, or only contracted, to raise one unit for French service, it is significant that the individual unit strengths could be considerably higher than was normal amongst the native French troops. Entrepreneurs of proven reliability were encouraged by the crown to raise units whose company strength would be 120, 160 even 200 troops.[89] Initial contracts for recruitment at a company strength that was usually higher than for French units could be followed by revised contracts in which entrepreneur-colonels would be paid to increase the strength of existing units up to 150 or even 200 men per company.[90]

The majority of foreign mercenaries in French service were recruited within the Empire, from the Swiss cantons, the British Isles and Italy. However, efforts were made to widen the net of recruitment and to create new networks of contracts. In 1636 a general authorization was prepared for cardinal de La Valette to raise troops from Poland, and similar efforts were made to obtain light cavalry – 'Croats' – from the Balkans.[91] Corsica provided the recruiting ground for at least one regiment, that of colonel Isola, raised for French service in 1641.[92] The patchy success of these initiatives should not detract from the impression of a

---

[88] BN Ms.fr. 6645, fo. 104, 28 Aug. 1635.
[89] SHAT A¹ 63, fo. 77, 10 Jan. 1641: Swiss colonels of Greder, Watteville and Molondin are to raise regiments based on companies of 120 men; A¹ 65, fo. 74, 13 June 1641, newly levied Swiss companies to be of 160 men; A¹ 65, fo. 186, 4 July 1641, request to the Swiss cantons for the levy of two more regiments of 2,000 men each organized into ten companies. This was no less the case with cavalry companies: A¹ 50 ii, fo. 204, 18 Feb. 1639, de Noyers to d'Erlach, agreeing to support his company on the basis of 200 *maîtres*; AAE CP Lorraine 31, fo. 452, 1 Oct. 1640, du Hallier to de Noyers, reporting on proposals to raise more cavalry companies of 200 *maîtres* for the regiment of Fittinghof.
[90] SHAT A¹ 65, fo. 111, 18 June 1641, Swiss colonels Molondin, Watteville and Greder are to increase the company strength in their units up to 200 by additional recruitment in the cantons; A¹ 68, fo. 101, 17 Jan. 1642, order for companies of the *gardes suisses* to be made up to 200 men.
[91] BN Ms.fr. 6647, fo. 78, 13 Sept. 1636, *pouvoir* of Louis XIII for La Valette; fo. 120, 17 Sept. 1636, de Noyers to La Valette, reporting that he is sending the money for this levy of Croats.
[92] SHAT A¹ 65, fos. 9–10, 2 June 1641, de Noyers to Isola, concerning assembly and transportation of his regiment.

Military enterprise during the Thirty Years War

government which placed great importance on the levy of foreign troops and was prepared to go to considerable lengths to obtain them from any possible source.

Foreign mercenaries: the balance sheet

Indeed, given the concern about the consequences of placing autonomous military force in the hands of the crown's greater subjects, and the respect for the military qualities of troops recruited abroad under contract, it might be thought that the French crown would make the decision, in the manner of the United Provinces, to fight wars on the basis of armies composed preponderantly of foreign mercenaries. The tradition that states should rely upon troops hired outside of their own country to fight for them, thereby avoiding the loss of skilled manpower at home and sustaining military force more cheaply and flexibly than would be possible with a national army, was at least as venerable and influential as the classically derived humanist obsession with militias and citizen armies. The unprecedented armies with which François I and Henri II had waged their wars against Charles V had been sustained by an infantry (and substantial cavalry components) which had been mainly composed of Swiss and German mercenaries.[93] A century later the ministerial consensus was still that foreign mercenaries, often with a high proportion of experienced veterans, were better troops, and provided a vital stiffening for the native forces. Richelieu, reflecting upon the experiences of the first years of war after 1635, wrote that: 'il est presque impossible d'entreprendre avec succes de grandes guerres avec des Français seuls'. He even went so far as to suggest that the Roman deployment of 50 per cent foreign auxiliaries was the ideal proportion of foreign troops.[94] This was the ministerial attitude to the composition of French forces in principle; the same concern can be seen in practice when an army-corps was to be assembled to serve across the frontiers, whether in the Empire or in the Italian states. The commanders themselves, all too aware of the rates of attrition amongst the French troops once they crossed the borders, did all they could to ensure that they were allocated the largest possible number of foreign units. The cardinal de La Valette was clearly capitalizing upon his close understanding with Chavigny in early 1639 when he asked the secretary to try to ensure that he received an allocation of foreign units for the army of Italy when the *états* were drawn up, because these troops 'se feussent mieux conservés que les François'.[95] Similarly, du Hallier, faced at the beginning of 1640 with the prospect of another grim campaign of guerrilla warfare in Lorraine and the high attrition amongst his own troops that this would inevitably entail, made a direct request to

---

[93] Wood, *The King's Army*, pp. 38–41: in 1558 slightly more than 70 per cent of the troops in Henri II's campaign army were foreign mercenaries.

[94] Richelieu, *Testament politique*, pp. 305–6.

[95] AAE CP Savoie 28, fo. 3, [early Jan.] 1639. The ministers needed little convincing in this respect. In 1635 Servien had written to La Valette, urging him to recruit as many foreign troops as possible to strengthen his army in preference to waiting for the arrival of levies raised in France: BN Ms.fr. 6645, fo. 24, 18 May 1635.

The administrative context

de Noyers, stressing that 'il faut des Estrangers pour bien servir du costé que je dois aller'.[96] In the following year du Hallier himself offered to levy a regiment of infantry and one of cavalry within Lorraine to ensure that his army had a higher proportion of foreign troops.[97] The most dramatic example of this dependence on foreign levies was within the Empire, in the army of Germany. Until 1639 there had been no French units permanently allocated to the army of Germany. After Saxe-Weimar's death in 1639, a positive decision was taken to keep control of the army by the appointment of a French commander, but not to build up the number of French units with the army.[98] Instead, a number of German units which had previously served with predominantly French armies were despatched to Germany, such as Rantzau's regiments, Schmidtberg's and Koulas' infantry regiments, and a large number of Liégeois *cavalerie légère*.[99] Further recruitment into the army of Germany would be necessary, but so far as possible the crown sought to raise these troops in the Empire, rather than despatching units from France.[100] The result, of course, was that the army of Germany became one of a series of forces operating in the Empire in the last decade of the Thirty Years War whose troops were made up from a pool of predominantly German 'professionals' and whose essential characteristics and shared strategic and logistical assumptions ensured that there was little to distinguish between notionally Swedish, French, Bavarian or Imperial armies except their intermittent paymasters.[101]

Whether they were intended to serve beyond French frontiers or in the main French field armies, the French crown was prepared to offer considerable concessions to attract foreign troops into service. Referring to the provision of additional subsistence for 3,000 or more German mercenaries, Servien stressed: 'que l'on ne peut prendre trop de soin de contenter les estrangers qui viennent de leur franche vollonté au service du Roy'.[102] Over subsequent campaigns this proved to be more than empty rhetoric. Despite the financial problems that beset the ministry, money could almost always be found to try to *débaucher* troops of other powers into French service, especially if these troops were perceived to be

---

[96] AAE CP Lorraine 31, fo. 304, 31 Mar. 1640.
[97] SHAT A¹ 66, fo. 307, 21 Nov. 1641, de Noyers to du Hallier, approving these proposals and allocating various *rendez-vous* within Lorraine for the assembly of the recruits.
[98] SHAT A¹ 59, fo. 754, 19 July 1640, de Noyers to Longueville, announcing that no further French units would be sent to the army of Germany.
[99] AAE MD 832, fo. 16, [1638], *état* of troops to be allocated to Saxe-Weimar under the command of Guébriant and Turenne; A¹ 64, fo. 362, 30 Apr. 1641, de Noyers to Choisy.
[100] SHAT A¹ 65, fos. 449bis–50, 3 Sept. 1641, de Noyers to d'Avaux, giving orders for a German regiment of 2,000 infantry to be levied for the army of Germany; A¹ 68, fo. 576, 18 Mar. 1642, de Noyers to d'Oysonville, concerned with the levy of units in the Empire explicitly for the army of Guébriant.
[101] For an account of this transformation of the army into a typical entrepreneurial force operating in the Empire, see Guébriant's *mémoire* concerning the state of the army of Germany written on 24 Nov. 1642: AAE CP Allemagne 16, fos. 550–3.
[102] SHAT A¹ 27, fo. 42, 23 Jan. 1636, Servien to Bertrand d'Eschaux, archbishop of Tours, concerning the provision of subsistence in the province for English and German mercenaries.

veterans.¹⁰³ Incidental expenses were also met as part of the crown's concern to facilitate the effective incorporation of these troops into French service; at least one regiment, the Scottish infantry of colonel James Douglas, received an additional financial allowance to pay the salary of an interpreter.¹⁰⁴ Above all, the ministry was concerned to raise foreign cavalry. As late as 1634, Richelieu still hoped to impose a moratorium on any further levies of cavalry within France, obtaining all further levies from Liège and the Empire.¹⁰⁵ In the circumstances of large-scale recruitment in 1635 such a restriction proved impractical, but considerable levies of foreign cavalry took place throughout the war.¹⁰⁶ Although the crown was consistently half-hearted about recruiting native French cavalry in units larger than individual companies (*cornettes*), foreign contracts for the levy of cavalry had consistently sought the levy of entire regiments.¹⁰⁷

The superiority of foreign mercenary troops was acknowledged, not so much for their actual fighting qualities on the battlefield, which were felt to be easily matched by the best French units, but for their endurance and relatively lower rates of attrition. When Richelieu made his proposal to the king in 1634 that cavalry levies should henceforth be drawn from Liège and other states in the Empire, he emphasized that this was not because the foreigners fought better, but because the French horse were 'moins bon pour les fatigues, qui est ce dont on a à faire'. Louis XIII agreed, adding that the advantage of recruiting in Liège and Germany was that these were also the primary recruiting grounds for the Spanish armies.¹⁰⁸ In general this opinion of foreign mercenaries as better able to survive at an effective strength through successive campaigns seems justified by the evidence, and indeed supports the earlier contention about the advantages of an army made up of officer-proprietors who had a personal interest in keeping their units at fighting strength. It was not inevitably the case for all foreign levies: du Hallier, despite his insistence on the quality of foreign units and the desirability of incorporating them into the army, made an exception for his Irish soldiers, writing to de Noyers 'je me trouve embarassé dans l'estat que je vous envoye des hirlandois estant des oyseaux de passage tantost forts et tantost

---

¹⁰³ For example: Avenel, IV. 312, 21 June 1632; AAE MD 815, fo. 17, 21 July 1635: attempt to attract troops of the duke of Lorraine into French service; MD 816, fo. 220, [1635]: project to *débaucher* the troops of Neuburg and Saxony; MD 843, fos. 65–6, 20 July 1642, project to incorporate 800 Liégeois cavalry who have left the service of Spain and the Empire.

¹⁰⁴ SHAT A¹ 52, fo. 135, 11 May 1639, de Noyers' notification of arrangements for payment.

¹⁰⁵ Avenel, IV. 599–600, 12 Sept. 1634, Richelieu to Louis XIII: 'J'ay pensé . . . qu'il valoit mieux lever de la cavalerie estrangère que françoise . . . et cependant on verra si on en peut lever en Liège et en Allemagne, par les gens que pourroit trouver Fequières [*sic*].'

¹⁰⁶ BN Ms.fr. 6645, fo. 24, 18 May 1635, Servien to La Valette, giving details of a further levy of 3,000 German cavalry in addition to four regiments each of 500 horse that have already been raised; SHAT A¹ 67, fo. 174, 8 Aug. 1641, capitulation for levy of six companies of Liégeois cavalry.

¹⁰⁷ SHAT A¹ 32, pces 73, 74, 10 May 1636: two contracts, each for the levy of a regiment of 500 German cavalry. Even larger units could be raised: A¹ 25, fo. 58b, 13 July 1635 – 800 horse; A¹ 40, fo. 33, 24 Nov. 1637 – 1,000 cavalry.

¹⁰⁸ Avenel, IV. 599–600, 12 Sept. 1634, Richelieu to Louis XIII.

The administrative context

foibles'.[109] Complaints of the weakness of Irish units were frequent, but it would seem that the reputation of Irish soldiers as effective, if rather exotic, warriors may have outweighed their tendency to be 'birds of passage'.[110] Certainly these misgivings did not halt regular attempts to recruit additional Irish units throughout the war.

But even if they were in general more reliable and better able to sustain the rigours of campaigning, troops levied abroad were expensive. Although the cost of maintenance might not in theory appear greater than that of their French counterparts, this was deceptive.[111] In the first place, transport and subsistence costs were very much higher.[112] The ministers and the commanders admitted that foreign units found it much more expensive to obtain food and basic subsistence in France and that this had to be taken into acount when negotiating contracts.[113] While it might also prove expensive if French troops were being raised far from their intended campaign theatre, increasingly their subsistence costs *en route* were borne by a network of *étapes* which took on the form of an additional local tax.[114] But if the troops were raised abroad these costs had to be paid in cash and in advance by the central government. Moreover, mercenary forces that were recruited to serve within the French armies held formal contracts – capitulations – which specified the rate and regularity of wages. In the case of the crown's negotiations with the potential commanders of units of French troops, the authorization for the levy, the payment for all or part of the costs of recruitment, and the timetable for the assembly of the new unit and its movement to the campaign theatre was fixed in a *traité* quite separate from any subsequent undertaking to pay and maintain the unit once engaged in campaign, for which no formal undertaking was ever made. With foreign contracts, the costs of recruit-

---

[109] AAE, CP Lorraine 31, fo. 450, 1 Oct. 1640.
[110] For the 'exotic' perception of Irish troops see the illustration in Parker, *Military Revolution*, p. 50; for general perceptions of the qualities of Irish mercenaries, Stradling, *Spanish Monarchy and Irish Mercenaries*, pp. 25–6, 123–37. Complaints about the weakness of Irish units are frequent: SHAT A^1 61, fo. 225, 21 Nov. 1640, circular from de Noyers, criticizing five Irish colonels – du Val, Fitzwilliam, Canlon, Sinot, Belin; A^1 63, fo. 295, 3 Feb. 1641, ordinance concerned with abuses of Irish officers in the presentation of their units for *montres*; A^1 66, fo. 489, 16 Dec. 1641, regiments of Canlon and Sinot are to be amalgamated to create a single regiment at acceptable strength.
[111] SHAT A^1 26, pces 27, 30, 16 Feb./28 Feb. 1635: two contracts for the levy of regiments of German infantry stipulate pay for the ordinary soldiers at 12 *livres* per montre, the captains at 150 or 300 *livres* – the higher figure probably indicating a financial commitment made by the captain. These figures are identical to those established for French soldiers' pay in the *Code Michau*, article 226, and, in practice, to the wages paid, albeit intermittently, to the French companies: AAE MD 819, fos. 59, 62, [1635].
[112] AAE CP Allemagne 15, fo. 288, 16 July 1639: 18,000 *riksdalers* allocated to meet the costs of moving Rantzau's regiment to France.
[113] SHAT A^1 58, fo. 510, 21 Apr. 1640, de Noyers to sr de Caumartin, *commissaire des guerres*, ordering him to treat the foreign troops stationed in the *généralité* of Soissons with particular attention; A^1 65, fo. 307, 2 Aug. 1641, de Noyers to Charost, governor of Calais, ordering him to make full provision of subsistence for an English regiment (curiously, unnamed) about to arrive.
[114] Kroener, *Les routes*, pp. 71–9, 94–6; see also chapter 4, pp. 270–1.

Military enterprise during the Thirty Years War

ment were frequently a small part of the detailed capitulation. The main part consisted of a detailed agreement for the levels of pay to be provided once the unit was *sur pied*, fixed from the colonel down to the most junior common soldier, for the frequency of such pay – usually stipulated as ten *montres* of thirty-six days each per year – and for other financial arrangements concerning transportation, food and munitions, ransoming of prisoners, etc. The relationship between the crown and its foreign units was thus fundamentally different from that with the native regiments; the crown had explicitly contracted to make specified payments at fixed and agreed intervals, and could thus be held to have broken the contract in the event of default or delay in payment. So formalized was the system for the payment of foreign units that in 1640 the crown had to intervene to end a long-running dispute between Scots and Irish regiments, whose officers and soldiers were paid at different rates in accordance with different types of capitulation drawn up for the units from the two states.[115] In practice, of course, the experience of most mercenary colonels serving in other armies across Europe was of regular default by their paymasters, but it was expected that the collection of contributions would make good some of this gap between payment due and money actually paid, preventing regular mutiny or defection by the troops. While this might be acceptable to the French crown when the foreign units were operating beyond France's own borders, Louis XIII and his ministers had no intention of recruiting mercenary units with an ill-defined right to collect contributions on French or neutral territory.[116] But without this, or at least the imminent prospect of plunder or other informal sources of gain, the foreign troops would insist upon the regular payment of wages in accordance with the capitulation and might well threaten to withdraw their services if these obligations were not met.[117] This issue was raised by Richelieu in 1630, when the state was substantially more capable of meeting its financial commitments to foreign mercenaries: 'La difficulté que j'y trouve e[s]t le manque d'argent qu'il faut donner aux estrangers, qui veulent estre payez leurs levées à point nommé.'[118] The problem was confirmed in almost the same words

[115] SHAT A^1 58, fo. 395, 7 Apr. 1640, circular letter to the *lieutenants généraux* and *intendants* with the armies, drawing attention to this anomaly and ordering that henceforth the capitulation negotiated for the regiment of colonel Douglas should be the model for all Scots and Irish regiments.

[116] And even beyond the French borders, the crown had considerable reservations and hesitation about the elaboration of contribution-systems: see chapter 4, pp. 267–70.

[117] This did not, of course, prevent regular conflicts over claims that foreign units were extorting illegal contributions in France to make up for delayed or inadequate pay: SHAT A^1 50, fo. 303, 31 Jan. 1639, circular addressed to srs Caumartin, Fontaines, Bellejamme, *commissaires des guerres* and *intendant* in Picardy, ordering them to do all possible to prevent illegal contributions exacted by foreign units; A^1 58, fo. 76, 7 Mar. 1640, cavalry regiment of Gassion prohibited from exacting contributions from the population of Corbie; A^1 61, fo. 215, 19 Nov. 1640, *intendant* Grémonville to investigate widespread reports of foreign units exacting contributions in Champagne and the Soissonnais.

[118] Grillon, v. 511, [12 Aug. 1630], Richelieu to Louis de Marillac, referring to a proposal of Marillac's to negotiate with an (unnamed) German colonel offering to bring 4,000 troops into French service. See also Aumale, *Princes de Condé*, IV. 39.

The administrative context

by maréchal Châtillon, writing to the *secrétaire* Sublet de Noyers in 1639 concerning the Swiss colonel Greder, who 's'est resolu d'aller trouver le Roy, voyant qu'il n'y avoit point de fonds pour sa Montre: il tesmoigne grande affection luy et ses Officiers. Si on ne les paye à point nommé, il n'y a pas moyen de tirer aucun service d'eux; vous sçavez comme ils sont fort pressans sur ce suject.'[119] The system for the levy of French troops was particularly advantageous for the government in a situation in which funds were not merely inadequate, but where their receipt was irregular and frequently delayed. In the context of entrepreneurial contracts with foreign mercenary commanders, delayed or insufficient payment could be evaded far less easily. Enterprisers were often making a substantial personal investment in setting up their regiments for French service.[120] The costs of getting troops to France and keeping them together *en route* were very high, and there was a significant possibility of serving in a hostile foreign environment far from the German-speaking lands of the Empire. The great majority of those foreign contractors who raised troops for the French government expected an advance payment to cover some of these costs, and regarded this as a precondition of the levy taking place. Without an advance, the foreign levy might well fail to take place; in 1635 the raising of 12,000 German infantry which had been entrusted to Feuquières, yielded only a fraction of the troops anticipated because the necessary funds were not despatched to make good the contracts.[121]

This question of the advance did not merely impose upon the government the frequently embarrassing necessity of producing a substantial payment 'à point nommé', before the levy would proceed or the existing unit would begin to move towards France; it also implied a degree of risk for the government. Servien wrote that foreign levies were: 'Bien souvent de l'argent perdu si on n'y observe des précautions et des prévoyances.'[122] Once the money had been made over to the foreign colonel, the crown relied upon his good faith to raise the troops in the stipulated time, fully equipped and to bring them to France.[123] If the contract were to be broken abroad, the crown possessed few real sanctions that could be

---

[119] Aubery, *Richelieu*, II. 332–3, 18 July.
[120] AAE MD 812, fo. 398, [1634], proposal by Erlach to recruit a regiment of 4,000 infantry in twenty companies for French service, the costs of recruitment being born partly by the French crown which would pay 4 *écus* per recruit, and partly by Erlach himself, who would pay an additional 2 *écus* per man 'pour avancer le service du roi'.
[121] SHAT A^1 24, fo. 258, 7 May 1635, Servien to Feuquières; A^1 25, fo. 35, 8 July 1635, Servien to Feuquières.
[122] AAE MD 816, fo. 118, 15 Nov. 1635, Servien to Richelieu.
[123] See for example the great concern at the sudden death of colonel Erlach, relative of Jean-Louis d'Erlach, in the midst of recruiting a regiment of 4,000 German infantry, and the haste to find another colonel so that the funds for the levy should not be lost: AAE MD 813, fo. 184, 22 Mar. 1635, de Royaumont to Chavigny. SHAT A^1 65, fos. 449bis –50, 3 Sept. 1641, despatch of 32,000 *livres* for d'Avaux to pay to whomever he considered appropriate to raise a German regiment of 2,000 foot. Even when the troops arrived in France, it could transpire that the full terms of the contract had not been met, as the governor of Picardy, the duc de Chaulnes, discovered in 1635

employed against the defaulter.[124] The ministry relied upon a relatively narrow network of trusted entrepreneurs, and depended upon recommendations from ambassadors and military specialists in the selection of suitable new colonels.[125]

All of these considerations imposed limits to the number of troops who could be raised abroad. It is extraordinarily difficult to establish the proportion of foreign troops in French service in this period, not least because the overall number of troops in service fluctuated so considerably. Taking some examples of *contrôles* from particular army-corps, it would seem that the proportion of foreign troops varied between about 10 and 30 per cent of the total forces. The higher figure would be obtained by including the troops on the German frontier, especially the army of Saxe-Weimar, where, after 1636, the *plus part* of the forces were foreign.[126]

Could France have fought a war against the Habsburgs on the basis of armies that, aside from a core of *régiments* and *compagnies entretenues*, were almost entirely composed of foreign mercenaries? From late 1634, it was clear that Philip IV and Olivares, with tacit support from the Emperor, intended to broaden the conflict with France into a full-scale European war. But even if the Habsburgs had not taken this decision, it is unlikely that in 1635, optimistically expecting to make substantial and rapid gains, Louis XIII and Richelieu would have been prepared to restrict themselves to a cautious, defensive, foreign policy. The large-scale conflict envisaged by both belligerents made the option of mercenary warfare financially unviable for the French crown unless it could be ensured from the outset that the vast bulk of the forces would be operating beyond French borders and therefore able to sustain a large part of their costs from contributions. Though Richelieu might have been sanguine about the possibilities of French success at the outset of the war, he was not so confident as to believe that the

---

when he wrote that 1,200 German recruits had just arrived at Calais with no arms or banners, leaving him no choice but to provide these at local expense: AAE MD 1676, fo. 382, 30 Sept. 1635.

[124] SHAT A¹ 47, fo. 215, 2 Nov. 1638: de Noyers to Bellièvre, ambassador in London, to obtain information concerning a captain Lansfort, who embezzled the money intended for the levy of a regiment; A¹ 59, fo. 422, 21 June 1640, de Noyers to Laffemas, lieutenant civil in Paris, ordering him to reclaim 2,000 *livres* from the banker of colonel Leslie, who received this sum in advance payment from the king, and has left France with no intention of returning.

[125] BN Ms.fr. 6645, fo. 104, 28 Aug. 1635, Servien to La Valette; SHAT A¹ 52, fo. 349, 4 June 1639, Bellièvre was to investigate the reputation of an Irish gentleman who had offered to levy a regiment for the king.

[126] SHAT A¹ 32, fo. 255, 1636, *pouvoir* justifying the creation of Baron de Tracy as *commissaire général* of the troops serving the king in the Empire; see also AAE MD 820, fos. 201–16, [1636], MD 837, fos. 245–76, [1640], *états* and *revues* of troops for 1636, 1640. The rather low figure of 6.6 per cent given by Belhomme, *L'infanterie*, I. 360, 362, 368, 373, is a result of calculating all of the French units at full strength. Belhomme and, especially, Susane, *Histoire de l'ancienne infanterie française*, VIII, provide listings of all foreign units in French service. E. Fieffé, *Histoire des troupes étrangères au service de la France* (2 vols.; Paris, 1854), I. 131–65, provides similar listings, though with substantial omissions.

conflict could immediately be carried beyond France's borders and sustained there, thus passing the costs of warfare to enemy or neutral states.[127]

Yet had political circumstances and aspirations been different, then a decision to fight a more limited war based upon subsidies and mercenaries was by no means an unreasonable choice. A mercenary army made up of veteran troops recruited in the Empire and operating on and across the Rhine in French pay, smaller mercenary forces standing on the defensive on the eastern and southern borders of France, neutrality or a defensive policy in Italy, more substantial financial support for, and co-ordination with, the war-effort of the Dutch and Swedes, would probably have served French *defensive* interests as well, and with far lower risk and cost, than the large-scale war embarked upon after 1635. That the whole pattern of warfare in this latter decade of the Thirty Years War was shifting away from large-scale, wasteful and expensive operations mounted at the cost of catastrophic attrition rates amongst excessive numbers of poor-quality newly recruited troops, and was moving towards mobile, self-sustaining, warfare waged by small armies of long-serving veterans, would merely reinforce the military logic of this decision by France.[128]

Beyond the question of the financial burden of armies based on foreign mercenaries, and any concerns about their reliability and loyalty – especially in the case of the large-scale general contractors – stood a more fundamental social issue: the expectation of large elements of the French elites that they should be actively involved as officers in the French army.

---

[127] A point rightly recognized by Downing, *Military Revolution*, pp. 121–3.
[128] Kroener, 'Soldat oder Soldateska', pp. 118–19.

6

The French rejection of entrepreneurship

MILITARY SERVICE AND NOBLE STATUS

The higher costs and financial inflexibility of raising foreign levies were not the only reasons why Louis XIII and his ministers rejected a 'subsidy and mercenary war' against the Habsburgs. In practice, and regardless of the foreign policy pursued, an army largely composed of foreign mercenaries would have proved unacceptable in a society which still regarded service in the armies as a critical source of prestige and social definition.

A number of studies in recent decades have examined the nature, the self-definition and *mentalité* of the noble caste in seventeenth-century France.[1] Some of these have drawn their evidence from printed and published sources concerned to construct moralistic or polemical arguments about the nature of nobility in French society. Such contemporary tracts are of considerable value in reflecting the thought and assumptions of articulate and reflective groups within the caste, and have resonances that may well extend far deeper into the nobility. That said, the writings were produced by those who considered that the nobility itself was either under threat or required redefinition; they reflect conflicts and divisions within the caste over role, function and the allocation of benefits and status.[2] This is a literature of crisis – or at least a literature of malaise – inevitably focusing on disruption and the breakdown of roles within the nobility, rather than on the

---

[1] D. Bitton, *The French Nobility in Crisis, 1560–1640* (Stanford, 1969); A. Devyver, *Le sang épuré. Les préjugés de race chez les gentilshommes français de l'Ancien Régime, 1560–1720* (Brussels, 1973); G. Huppert, *Les Bourgeois Gentilshommes: An Essay on the Definition of Elites in Renaissance France* (Chicago, 1977); A. Jouanna, *L'idée de race en France au XVIe siècle et au début du XVIIe siècle, 1498–1614* (2 vols.; Montpellier, 1981); J.-M. Constant, *La vie quotidienne de la noblesse française aux XVIe et XVIIe siècles* (Paris, 1985); E. Schalk, *From Valor to Pedigree: Ideas of Nobility in France in the Sixteenth and Seventeenth Centuries* (Princeton, 1986); F. Billacois, *Le duel dans la société française des XVIe–XVIIe siècles. Essai de psychosociologie historique* (Paris, 1986), pp. 131–6, 146–61; Jouanna, *Le devoir de révolte*; K. Neuschel, *Word of Honor: Interpreting Noble Culture in Sixteenth-Century France* (Ithaca, 1989); Motley, *French Aristocrat*; J. Meyer, *La noblesse française à l'époque moderne (XVI–XVIII siècles)* (Paris, 1991); J. Dewald, *Aristocratic Experience and the Origins of Modern Culture: France, 1570–1715* (Berkeley, 1993); Smith, *Culture of Merit*.

[2] Bitton, *French Nobility*, pp. 92–117; Devyver, *Sang épuré*, pp. 56–108; Huppert, *Bourgeois Gentilshommes*, pp. 24–33, 162–77; Schalk, *Valor to Pedigree*, pp. 65–144, 202–19; F. Billacois, 'La crise de la noblesse européenne (1550–1650): une mise au point', *Revue d'histoire moderne et contemporaine*, 23 (1976), 258–77.

continuity of assumptions that lay behind the nobility's self-perceptions about its status and role in society. Although these continuities receive less attention in contemporary literature, they are the bedrock on which the nobility continued to build its social, economic and ideological hegemony in European societies down to the end of the eighteenth century. Recent works on the nobility, whether French or European, based on a broader field of archival reference, have been increasingly concerned to emphasize continuity rather than crisis; the supposed 'decline' of the nobility, or the 'crisis' of the aristocracy in the first half of the seventeenth century has been shown to sit uneasily with what then has to be explained as the 'resurgence' of the caste's power and authority for the ensuing 150 years of the *Ancien Régime*.[3]

In understanding the continuities in their power, status and self-perception, a critical factor is the relationship of the nobility to military service. The exponents of a noble 'crisis' in the first half of the seventeenth century argue for a decline in the military role of the nobility on the basis of two general assumptions. The first of these is the contention that the nobility – defined narrowly as the *noblesse d'épée* – were gradually being excluded from military life. Changes in the nature of warfare, in particular the supposed professionalization brought about by the military revolution with its demands for technical skills and its emphasis on subordination to drill and collective discipline, was rendering obsolete a traditional nobility with its individualist behaviour and chivalric honour code.[4] An elaboration of this contention suggests that, as warfare became more expensive, so the lesser *noblesse*, who were assumed to be losing out in the struggle to sustain prosperity and position throughout the sixteenth and seventeenth centuries, were squeezed out of military life. In consequence, military service became increasingly the prerogative simply of the rich whatever their background, rather than of nobles by birth. These latter were rusticated in the French provinces, pleading poverty in the face of the French crown's attempts to extract from them some form of voluntary military service or taxation as noble fief-holders.[5] The other assumption is concerned with the notion of a progressive demilitarization of

[3] J.B. Wood, *The Nobility of the Election of Bayeux, 1463–1666: Continuity through Change* (Princeton, 1980), pp. 5–10; H. Ellis, *Boulainvilliers and the French Monarchy. Aristocratic Politics in Early Eighteenth-Century France* (Ithaca, 1988), pp. 4–11; Scott (ed.), *European Nobilities*, I. 1–52; J. Dewald, *The European Nobility 1400–1800* (Cambridge, 1996); J. Duindam, *Myths of Power. Norbert Elias and the Early Modern European Court* (Amsterdam, 1995), pp. 35–48; A. Corvisier, 'La noblesse militaire. Aspects militaires de la noblesse française du XVe au XVIIIe siècles', *Histoire Sociale/Social History*, 11 (1978), pp. 336–55.

[4] Bitton, *French Nobility*, pp. 27–41; Schalk, *Valor to Pedigree*, pp. 11–20. Such assumptions can generate a facile social determinism which asserts that the 'military revolution' laid the ground for 'middle-class' warfare, an idea which is implicit in Michael Roberts' original thesis, and becomes explicit in some later work – cf. Feld, 'Middle class society'. For a comprehensive challenge to the view that the 'military revolution' marginalized the traditional nobility and its values within European armed forces see C. Storrs and H. Scott, 'The military revolution and the European nobility, c.1600–1800', *War in History*, 3 (1996), 1–41.

[5] Deyon, 'French nobility'; Devyver, *Sang épuré*, pp. 96–100.

The French rejection of entrepreneurship

French society, the decline of a military ethos and of a culture dominated by the ideal of the warrior elite, an element of the wider 'civilizing process' which was supposedly turning noble power-brokers into courtiers.[6]

These assertions have not passed unchallenged. General surveys of seventeenth-century France based on different, frequently less self-conscious, sources have had little difficulty in pointing to the survival and continuity of military values in this society.[7] If alternative models of noble culture and behaviour can be shown to have some currency in seventeenth-century elite society, this does not mean that they are excluding or devaluing the traditional links between warfare, the honour inherent in military service – especially when this is offered to the crown – and the cultural values of nobility.[8] Increased awareness of the civilizations of Greece and Rome and their writings on history and philosophy, literary discussions about the nature and demands of honour, reverence for the pursuit of *gloire*, are all evidence of wide cultural interests, but not of a rejection of the centrality of war and military service as dominant social values.[9]

The study of army officers and their role in raising and maintaining units for the army during this period can make an important contribution to this debate, and can provide cogent evidence for the persistence of military values in French society in the decades after 1620. The scale of the recruitment of new units; the extent to which the crown was able to transfer the costs of such recruitment on to the shoulders of the aspiring officers; the clear evidence that military service as an officer in this period was personally costly and that willingness to undertake it

---

[6] For the first assumption, that the 'civilizing process' was undermining the nobles' military enthusiasm and commitment, see N. Elias, trans. E. Jephcott, *The Civilizing Process*, II: *Power and Civility* (Oxford, 1982), pp. 258–70. The loss of military spirit amongst the seventeenth-century nobility was a staple of nineteenth-century historiography, see, for example, Avenel, *Richelieu*, II. 69–95. The classic study by Emile Léonard, *L'armée et ses problèmes au xviiie siècle* (Paris, 1958), pp. 33–53, discusses the decline of military values amongst the French elites, but dates this decline well into the eighteenth century.

[7] See, for example, Wood, *Nobility of Bayeux*, a study of a small region, but with valuable observations about the persisting military assumptions of the nobles. J.-M. Constant, *Nobles et paysans en Beauce aux XVIe et XVIIe siècles* (Lille, 1981), pp. 158–85; A. Jouanna, *L'idée de race*, I. 323–78; L. Bourquin, *Noblesse seconde et pouvoir en Champagne aux XVIe et XVIIe siècles* (Paris, 1994), pp. 24–33, 135–70; Hickey, *Coming of French Absolutism*, p. 158, affirms the centrality of military service to promotion into the nobility in Dauphiné; D. Bohanon, *Old and New Nobility in Aix-en-Provence, 1600–1695: Portrait of an Urban Elite* (Baton Rouge and London, 1992), points to a high level of participation in military service amongst the urban noble families of Aix: of forty-six noble families in Aix who had sons in the army or the navy, twenty-six were old nobles, twenty from newly enobled families: pp. 114–18.

[8] Cornette, *Roi de Guerre*, pp. 294–8, 308–15; F.E. Sutcliffe, *Guez de Balzac et son temps: littérature et politique* (Paris, 1959), pp. 113–69; A. Corvisier, *Le France de Louis XIV* (2nd edn, Paris, 1979), pp. 59–81; J. Chagniot, 'Guerre et société au XVIIe siècle', *Dix-septième siècle*, 148 (1985), 232–56; Constant, *Les conjurateurs*, esp. pp. 114–22; J. Chagniot, 'Ethique et pratique de la "profession des armes" chez les officiers français au XVIIe siècle', in V. Barrie-Curien (ed.), *Guerre et pouvoir en Europe au XVIIe siècle* (Paris, 1991), pp. 79–93; Dewald, *Aristocratic Experience*, pp. 45–68; Smith, *Culture of Merit*, pp. 44–9, 152–7.

[9] Dewald, *Aristocratic Experience*, pp. 15–44, 81–97; Motley, *French Aristocrat*, pp. 68–122.

The administrative context

could only reflect social, rather than financial, aspirations: all of these factors reinforce arguments for the continuity of military values in this society, and for a clear link between military service and the wish to confirm, consolidate or attain a generally recognized noble status. The capacity of the crown to draw financial and personal sacrifices out of its wealthier subjects pursuing a military career shows that such a career was still valued highly within contemporary society, and that for most of the elite (and perhaps a wider proportion of the population) it was still seen as the acid test of 'real' nobility. At the same time it is clear that levels of military participation varied considerably between regions, depending on diverse factors such as local military traditions, proximity of the provinces to the frontiers, aristocratic clientele-structures, the social hegemony enjoyed by families who could lay claim to present or past military service.[10]

The examination of military service in practice also throws light on the contention that the increasing sophistication, skill and expense of army service tended to exclude the traditional, lesser, *noblesse d'épée* from the profession of arms. The officer-corps, it is argued, was being filled instead with *annoblis* and wealthy bourgeois, who were both better educated in a science of war based upon discipline, drill and the denial of individual assertiveness, and more able to sustain the financial burdens of military service. It is true that a proportion of rural *hobereaux* were economically below the level where military service, unless entirely subsidized by the crown or by a powerful and wealthy patron, was viable. A number of provincial studies reveal a group of local nobles who were indeed too poor to play any part either in the civil administration of the locality or in military service.[11] Yet the expenses of military service, while heavy, were mitigated by the fact that relatively few regarded military service as a lifetime's profession. Large numbers of newly appointed officers raised their own units and met many of their own and their soldiers' campaign expenses, but had no expectation that they would serve for more than a limited period, a few campaigns at most.[12] Most officers presenting themselves for service in the king's army in the first half of the seventeenth century did not do so in the manner of the younger sons of Prussian *Junker*, as a means to build a lengthy professional career away from a family estate. Like so many other aspects of the French military system, assumptions about service in the officer-corps still drew upon the experience of campaigning in the first half of the sixteenth century, where the royal army would rarely be engaged in intensive warfare for more than two or three successive campaigns.

---

[10] R. Chaboche, 'Les soldats français de la Guerre de Trente Ans: une tentative d'approche', *Revue d'histoire moderne et contemporaine*, 20 (1973), 10–24, gives some indication of the regional – and urban – patterns of French military participation; the works of Wood, Hickey and Constant (n 7) show divergent patterns of noble participation in warfare.

[11] Wood, *Nobility of Bayeux*, pp. 88–98; Constant, *Nobles et paysans*, p. 159.

[12] Although this characteristic will emerge from the subsequent detail of this chapter, it was a point previously recognized by Wood in his study of the *Nobility of Bayeux*, pp. 88–9.

The French rejection of entrepreneurship

For the great majority of the French elite who served as officers, military activity was a *rite de passage*, a crucial element in defining their subsequent social status. It was an activity explicitly concerned with building up or reinforcing an appropriate aura of nobility within a society which still regarded service in the army as the defining mark of noble status. In a society in which wealth, influence and political resources, especially in developing urban environments, rarely corresponded to the idealized hierarchy of social status, military service provided a vital buttress for the traditional social order.[13] Membership of the *noblesse d'épée*, those whose titles stretched back generations and had originally rested upon military service, created a theoretical bond between the greatest aristocratic families of the realm and the most impoverished provincial *hobereau* whose family had once served in the royal armies. 'Real' noble status was still linked inextricably to the values of a warrior culture; the titles held by a military nobility were still regarded as intrinsically superior, and the holders set apart from those whose status was achieved through service in government, law or finance. When Montaigne described the nobles' 'exclusive and essential characteristic' as military activity, he was simply echoing the assumptions of contemporaries about the constitution of the 'true' nobility.[14] Moreover, while the *robe* were disinclined to accept a view which denied them noble status altogether, few *robe* theorists dissented in practice from the view of Etienne Pasquier, who: 'en vertu de ce droit du soldat . . . reconnaît aux chevaliers des armes une supériorité sur les chevaliers des lois. La risque mortel qu'encouraient les gentilshommes dans les batailles lui semblait justifier une telle précellence.'[15]

The development of a racial myth amongst the *noblesse d'épée* during the sixteenth and seventeenth centuries gave additional force to this notion of a distinct warrior nobility.[16] Instead of undermining the values of an elite that saw military service in its own right as a badge of social status, this construction of a racial theory of nobility, because it laid great stress on the martial prowess of the

---

[13] The social hierarchy defined by Mousnier, *Les Institutions*, esp. I. 13–46, has been criticized both for its dependence on *a priori* social theory, and for presenting as political reality the self-justifications of an established elite: A. Ariazza, 'Mousnier and Barber: the theoretical underpinning of the "Society of Orders" in early modern Europe', *Past and Present*, 89 (1980), 39–57; Beik, *Absolutism and Society*, pp. 6–9. None the less, it is hard to escape the conclusion that the status accorded to military service enjoyed an objective reality amongst contemporaries of a quite different order from generalized assertions about 'service to the king': R. Mousnier, Y. Durand and J. Labatut, *Problèmes de stratification sociale: deux cahiers de la noblesse pour les Etats généraux de 1649–1651* (Paris, 1965), presents contemporary views about social status and the role of military service in defining that status, cf. pp. 58–65, 128–33, and the texts of the *cahiers* themselves. See also J. Chagniot, 'Mobilité sociale et l'armée', *Dix-septième siècle*, 31 (1979), 37–49.

[14] M. de Montaigne, *Œuvres complètes* (Paris, 1962), book 2, ch. vii: 'Des recompenses d'honneur'.

[15] E. Pasquier, *Les recherches de la France*, cited in Devyver, *Sang épuré*, p. 118; Jouanna, *L'idée de race*, I. 130.

[16] Devyver, *Sang épuré*, pp. 109–14; Jouanna, *L'idée de race*, I. 347–52, though Jouanna argues that this co-existed with a widespread opinion that military service was capable of elevating individuals socially: Blaise de Monluc: 'les armes ont donc en elles-mêmes une vertu propre' (p. 351).

The administrative context

superior, conquering Franks, merely heightened the attractiveness of service. The profession of arms was not merely of high status in itself, but was linked explicitly to a warrior caste that originally combined racial with martial exclusivity.

Much of this concern to establish or 'rediscover' the credentials of traditional military nobility may sound like little more than a petty concern with outward status, pursued by groups whose acquisition of nobility through office-holding or purchase satisfied the legal requirements of the rank without providing access to its cultural and social values. But the military values of French society were more institutionalized than this account would suggest. As late as 1610 the connection between military service and nobility had been made explicit, with an edict which specified that twenty years of service in the rank of captain, lieutenant or ensign would serve as the basis of a claim to the immunities offered by noble status.[17] Such institutionalization of military values was also emphasized in the rigid defence of access to the ranks of the *grands*, the inner elite of the French nobility enjoying a *de facto* close relationship with the king, and encompassing the hierarchy of secular and ecclesiastical aristocrats whose lowest tier was represented by families who held the title of duke. To a very great extent the upper reaches of seventeenth-century French society were closed to all those who were not of military backgrounds. Of the sixty-eight French noblemen created *ducs et pairs* in the period from 1589 to 1723, sixty-two had held military office, and their military services were cited to justify their elevation to the peerage.[18] The award of a *maréchal*'s baton for distinguished military service certainly conveyed social prestige upon the holder; in court ceremony and etiquette the *maréchal* held a rank equivalent to a simple duke. But it was a purely personal recognition of service and status, not transferable to family or successors. For most *maréchaux* the achievement of this status was part of a longer-term strategy to achieve the elevation of their family into the ranks of the *ducs et pairs*. Moreover, the military route made it genuinely possible for a member of the *noblesse de robe* or of the very minor *noblesse d'épée* to rise through successive senior military officerships to achieve the title of *maréchal*, and from this status to take his family across into the ranks of the *grands*. An obvious example of a member of the *robe* who managed this ascent in the first half of the seventeenth century was Abraham Fabert, son of the *maître échevin* of Metz.[19] Of the minor *noblesse d'épée*, good examples of those who achieved promotion to *maréchal* would be Jean du Caylar de Saint-Bonnet,

---

[17] Devyver, *Sang épuré*, p. 68; A. Texier, *Qu'est-ce que la noblesse?* (Paris, 1988), pp. 27–32; L. Tuetey, *Les officiers sous l'Ancien Régime. Nobles et roturiers* (Paris, 1908), pp. 258–9; a specific example of ennoblement through military service is provided by Bénédict-Louis de Pontis.

[18] J. Labatut, *Les ducs et pairs de France au XVIIe siècle* (Paris, 1972), pp. 118–29. Labatut discusses the six examples of those promoted to a *duché-pairie* without holding military office, arguing that all of these were special cases, outside the run of normal social expectations: pp. 129–30; C. Levantal, *Ducs et pairs et duchés-pairies laïques à l'époque moderne (1519–1790)* (Paris, 1996), esp. pp. 180–1.

[19] Bourelly, *Maréchal de Fabert*, I. 8–10.

The French rejection of entrepreneurship

marquis de Toiras, Louis de Marillac and Philippe de Clérambault, comte de Palluau.[20]

And though many more of the minor *noblesse d'épée* played no part in military life, resisting even the attempts to press them into service through the *arrière-ban*, the continued respect accruing to an impoverished class of small-scale *noblesse* was due very much to the social consideration that was still attached to the profession of arms, and could provide them with a veneer of social prestige despite economic and political insignificance.

The holding of a military officership represented a powerful assertion of noble values to the outside world, even for those who had only recently acquired or purchased noble status, or those who still aspired to it. In addition to this association, service as a unit commander or officer also permitted a practical degree of social intermingling between wealthy and traditional nobles, sword and robe, established and aspiring, under the umbrella of a common set of military values. Participation in the military by the *noblesse de robe*, and even by an *arriviste* bourgeoisie, seemed not to devalue the 'nobility' of the profession of arms. It was precisely the association of war and nobility that attracted many wealthy individuals into the officer-corps, and created a strong vested interest in the maintenance of the association between military service and nobility. For a family which had recently acquired a title, with seigneurial rights through landed estates, obtaining a captaincy or even a regimental command for an elder son could be an important step in consolidating status by making contacts within the established hierarchy, arranging a prestigious marriage or gaining other social benefits. For established nobles, even of the highest status, military service was a generational exercise in validating the status of the family through service in the army-corps of a *grand* patron, through direct association with the king and a militarized court, or simply through the assertion of the family's own authority to command.[21]

It is important to stress the attractiveness of military service by virtue of its social cachet to explain the consequent buoyancy of demand for officerships throughout the period of Richelieu's ministry. For the inadequate supply of officerships to meet potential demand, even after the expansion of the army after 1635, was to shape the policy of the crown towards military appointment.[22] Even in civil society the purchase of office in seventeenth-century France is a phenomenon which cannot be explained satisfactorily in financial terms. Only at

---

[20] M. Baudier, *Histoire du maréchal de Toiras* (Paris, 1644), pp. 3–4; Vaissière, *Maréchal de Marillac*, pp. 13–18; for a later period see A. Corvisier, 'Les généraux de Louis XIV et leur origine sociale', *Dix-septième siècle*, 45 (1959), 23–53, reprinted in A. Corvisier, *Les hommes, la guerre et la mort* (Paris, 1985), pp. 145–75, which indicates a small but significant proportion of high-ranking officers drawn from the lesser *noblesse d'épée*.

[21] Dewald, *Aristocratic Experience*, pp. 45–68; Chagniot, 'Mobilité sociale'; A. Corvisier, in A. Corvisier (ed.) *Histoire militaire*, I. 372–6; for the notion that military service to a higher-ranking patron conferred honour see Neuschel, *Word of Honor*, pp. 93–102.

[22] A point made for the mid-seventeenth century by Chagniot, 'Guerre et société', 251–2.

The administrative context

the very highest levels of the fiscal administration could it be suggested that the possibility of large-scale profit motivated the purchasers of office.[23] Elsewhere, the attraction of venality has no such straightforward explanation. Office conferred status, a visible position in the ranks of the governors, not the governed. Many of the senior posts also conferred nobility, albeit in most cases only after three generations of office-holding.[24] And these predominantly social considerations which led the French elites to invest in civil office applied with still greater force to the purchase of military office; for while civil office might prove a poor investment, military office would almost inevitably cause considerable financial loss.

THE MAINTENANCE OF THE CROWN'S RIGHTS
OVER ITS MILITARY OFFICERS

The appointment and replacement of officers

The French crown's hostility to a directly entrepreneurial system for the recruitment and maintenance of its native troops may also have contributed to the popularity of military office. For the attraction of the French system was its ostensibly non-venal nature; the officer-corps was theoretically selected on the basis of merit and of past service to the crown. While beneath this facade it can be shown that the allocation of the available officerships reflected a process of bargaining in which financial commitments were frequently made by the potential officers, this was never allowed to permeate the documentation concerned with the levy of troops. The form of the *Code Michau* was observed, even if the reality was very different.[25] The acquiring of 'non-venal' military office did not became the subject of cynical comment, as did the oaths of judicial officers, obliged to swear that they had not obtained their offices through purchase.[26] In theory the award of an officership reflected the king's awareness of an individual's preeminent personal or family merit, and his social eligibility. While little was actually done to restrict the number of *roturiers* obtaining military office, the principle of military service as the prerogative of the nobility was still affirmed.[27]

This dichotomy between high social prestige and an informal system of venality created a market for military office which was different from that elsewhere in

---

[23] Mousnier, *Vénalité des offices*, pp. 77–83, 455–69, 553–69; W. Doyle, *Venality. The Sale of Offices in Eighteenth-Century France* (Oxford, 1996), pp. 152–95, makes similar points for the attitude to office-holding in the eighteenth century.
[24] Texier, *Qu'est-ce que la noblesse?*, pp. 42–57.
[25] *Code Michau*, art. 190, '[Nous] avons prohibé et defendu . . . toute vénalité d'offices . . . de toutes charges militaires, capitaineries et gouvernements de provinces, places et forteresses.'
[26] Mousnier, *Vénalité des offices*, pp. 35–6.
[27] *Code Michau*, arts. 196, 200; for further general prescriptions favouring the nobility in military service see Richelieu, *Testament politique*, pp. 151–2.

The French rejection of entrepreneurship

Europe. In theory the officers were envisaged as direct employees of the crown, serving in accordance with revocable commissions in return for a salary and payment by the crown of the costs that they might incur in the levy of a unit. Military office held no rights of survivance or inheritance; the officer was treated exactly as if he were a direct employee of the crown, selected for his abilities and replaceable at will.[28]

However, given a military system in which a very large proportion of regiments and companies was raised by the efforts of individuals, using their established connections and influence, and frequently in practice their own funds, to raise and equip the soldiers, NCOs and subordinate officers of their units, it might be assumed that the disposition of the office, still more the choice of subordinate officers in the unit, would be in the hands of the existing commander. In certain units this was certainly the case. Those *grands*, provincial governors or military commanders in their own right, who raised regiments of infantry and cavalry in their own name or in the name of one of their clients or relatives, had a high degree of control over appointments within these. The five infantry regiments raised by Henri II de Bourbon, prince de Condé, and his sons Louis II, duc d'Enghien and Armand, prince de Conti, officered with clients and filled with troops recruited in the Condé governorship of Burgundy, were to all intents and purposes outside of the control of the crown or the war minister.[29] Richelieu might complain vociferously in 1642 that Condé and Enghien had allowed their regiments to fall seriously under strength, but it was never seriously proposed that officers in these units should be replaced through the intervention of the crown, or that they should be subject to outside interference in the form of disbandment of companies, or *réformation* to consolidate the regiments.[30] No other aristocratic house sustained so many military units under their patronage as the Condé; on the other hand, there were few families in an aristocracy whose status reflected present or past military service which did not maintain at least one regiment.[31] Not surprisingly, Richelieu himself was heavily involved in the raising and maintenance of units under his own patronage, and these included the infantry

---

[28] *Code Michau*, art. 191.

[29] Aumale, *Princes de Condé*, III. 594–5; see also Béguin, *Princes de Condé*.

[30] Avenel, VI. 898–9, 20 Feb. 1642, Richelieu complained of the weakness and poor quality of recruitment of Enghien's cavalry regiment, and the generally poor state of the Condé House regiments in the king's service: 'La bonté dont le roy use en vostre endroit . . . mérite bien que vous faciés quelque despense pour son service, proportionnée au rang que vous tenés dans l'estat.' Similar complaints had been made to Condé in 1639 about the weakness of Conti's infantry regiment, serving in the army commanded by Feuquières: SHAT A¹ 51, fo. 396, 9 Apr. 1639.

[31] SHAT A¹ 44, fo. 154, 6 Mar. 1638, de Noyers to Bernard de Nogaret, duc de La Valette, Claude de Rouvroy, duc de Saint-Simon, and Charles de La Porte de La Meilleraye, permitting them, as titular colonels of new regiments of cavalry, to appoint directly to the officerships in these units. J. Labatut, 'La fidélité du duc de Navailles', in Durand (ed.), *Clientèles et fidélités*, 183–97, at pp. 191–2, examines the transfer in 1641 of the *mestre de camp* of the Navailles regiment from uncle to nephew.

The administrative context

Régiment de La Marine, promoted to the most prestigious rank of the *vieux régiments* in 1640.[32] While in most cases such status as one of the limited number of *entretenue* regiments would imply greater subordination to the king's rights of appointment, and indeed to the rights of the *Colonel général de l'infanterie française*, it was clear that Richelieu jealously guarded his rights of patronage and appointment within his first-rank unit.[33] Equally the companies of *gendarmes* and *chevaux légers* which were granted to provincial governors were regarded as subject to their proprietary rights.[34]

At the opposite end of the scale from the regiments and companies raised through the patronage of the most powerful *grands* were numbers of units raised rapidly on the initiative of members of local elites, not expected to serve for a lengthy term, and of minimal interest as sources of patronage to the crown or the secretary for war. A regiment, supposedly of 6,000 men, to be raised in 1639 through the contributions of part of the *noblesse* of Dauphiné, and a second unit to be levied by the Third Estate of the province, were precisely the type of units not anticipated as a permanent element in the crown's forces.[35] Changes amongst the officers of what were seen in practice as temporary regiments were of marginal concern, especially, in this case, when the crown was eager to take advantage of contributions made from the *pays d'Etats*, or more generally when it wished to encourage participation in the war-effort from those who might otherwise escape involvement altogether.[36] The crown and its ministers remained extremely concerned that formal permission should be sought for such levies, but once this was granted, the organization, funding and staffing of the units were left to those who had submitted the proposal.[37]

---

[32] SHAT A¹ 59, fo. 272, 5 June 1640, de Noyers to La Meilleraye, stipulating that the *régiment de La Marine* has fifth rank after the four older *vieux* regiments.

[33] Susane, *Histoire de l'infanterie française*, III. 1–7; M. Deloche, *La maison du cardinal de Richelieu – document inédit* (Paris, 1912), pp. 404–9.

[34] Harding, *Anatomy of a Power Elite*, pp. 21–7, who none the less tends to dismiss the power of the governors to appoint to their units during the seventeenth century: p. 203–4. The treaty of Péronne (8 July 1641) which brought the Grimaldi prince of Monaco into the service of France, and in return for the court status of *prince étranger* reduced him to acting as governor of the principality, also granted him formal permission to raise a company of *gendarmes* to be supported as part of the military establishment garrisoned in Monaco, and to which he would make all appointments: SHAT A¹ 68, fo. 235, 29 Jan. 1642.

[35] SHAT A¹ 50, fo. 18, 2 Jan., fo. 223, 24 Jan. 1639. Another example of this type of recruitment through the efforts of the provincial nobility for units which were envisaged as a temporary stop-gap can be seen in the authorizations given for the organization into regiments of local recruits from Normandy: SHAT A¹ 69, fo. 331, 29 May 1642.

[36] This was especially the case when a major provincial *grand* was asked to nominate a number of reliable figures to raise additional regiments in his province: SHAT A¹ 25, fo. 259, 30 Aug. 1635, approval for the duc d'Halluin's proposal of two *mestres de camp* to recruit and command two regiments to be raised in Languedoc.

[37] For a typical example of an order to recruit a new regiment at all speed and with full discretion in the choice of officers, see SHAT A¹ 65, fo. 221, 11 July 1641, de Noyers to Henri de Saulx-Tavannes, marquis de Mirebeau, an authorization which even allows Tavannes to select the town where the levy will take place.

The French rejection of entrepreneurship

However, between these two categories were a very large number of units, of varying prestige and permanence, over which the crown was concerned to assert an overall right of patronage, giving force to the assertions of the military *ordonnances* and *règlements*. In practice, many of the decisions of the king, expressed through the *secrétaire de la guerre*, confirmed petitions for the transfer of units or the appointment of officers, thus reflecting the wishes of the commander or the overall patron of the unit. The king might choose to hand over an office to a member of the same family or a client of that family, especially if the original holder was killed in action, but he was under no obligation to do so. Any changes that might be made amongst the regimental or company officers required explicit royal permission, and might be challenged if it were felt to be unjustified.[38] When vacancies arose in the 'temporary' units, the selection of replacements would most frequently be granted to the commanding officer, although observing a formal procedure that they were simply 'proposing' suitable persons.[39] In many such cases acceptance of the proposal would be constrained by the practical circumstances in which the regiment or company had been raised and maintained. Louis XIII wrote to Richelieu in 1628, emphasizing that he had confirmed the regiment of Ribeyrac in the hands of the dead commander's son, because: 'si je l'eusse donné a un autre, le reg[imen]t se fut tout debandé, a cause que les cap[itai]nes sont tous de autour de ches luy et estoi[en]t tous parens ou amis du defunt'.[40] Numerous cases of a willingness to acquiesce in structures of clientage and family existed, and it would be surprising if they did not.[41] Petitions for appointment to

---

[38] AAE MD 830, fo. 250, 18 July 1638: letter of François de Bonne et de Créqui, duc de Lesdiguières, to the king on behalf of certain officers in his regiment who wished to *remettre* their charges to persons more capable; SHAT A¹ 44, fo. 145, 5 Mar. 1638, authorization to César de Choiseul, comte du Plessis-Praslin, to change the officers in his company of *chevaux-légers*; Roger de Rabutin, comte de Bussy, required the permission of the king before he could assume the command of his father's regiment: *Mémoires*, I. 18; A¹28, fo. 117, 23 June 1636: the crown rejected a bid by a colonel to buy out one of his captains.

[39] SHAT A¹47ii, fo. 241 bis, 27 Dec 1638: Rostaing-Antoine d'Urre du Puy-Saint-Martin, sieur d'Aiguebonne, was ordered to select officers 'qui me soit agréable', which was the standard formula used by the crown to authorize the unit commander's choice of candidate; A¹ 60, fo. 277, 29 Aug. 1640, *mestres de camp* of the *vieux* regiments to put forward proposals for new officers to staff the *companies d'augmentation* that the crown wishes to be raised, and the king will pay due regard to their proposals.

[40] Grillon, III. 381, 15 July 1628; previously cited in Pagès, *Monarchie*, p. 95.

[41] Documented examples of transfers of units or appointments to officerships which reflect family ties or the interests of patrons are too numerous to cite; however, it should be stressed that the reason the documentation exists is precisely that such transfers could not be taken for granted; each had to be proposed to the crown, with supporting evidence to justify maintaining the family's interest, and each nomination had to be approved. See for example SHAT A¹ 69, fo. 55, 9 Apr. 1642, the baron de Cauvisson has raised a regiment and is given permission to establish his son as the *mestre de camp*; A¹ 60, fo. 186, 12 Aug. 1640, nomination of Charles de Monchy, seigneur de Longueval, to the command of the regiment commanded by his late brother; A¹ 66, fo. 311, 21 Nov. 1641, son of captain Gaya to receive command of cavalry company in response to petition; A¹ 71, fo. 159, 15 Nov. 1642, formal provisions for the transfer of the cavalry company of the late Jean de Nettancourt, comte de Vaubecourt, to his son, Nicolas, following a petition for this replacement by Vaubecourt-

The administrative context

vacancies frequently cite family connections as the basis of the claim to consideration.[42] There was an assumption, obviously reflecting the element of proprietorship which will be discussed in more detail below, that these family interests carried weight in appointments to commands, or in promotions within units.

Yet, given this assumption, a surprisingly large number of appointments were made in defiance of the expectations of family or clientele.[43] Part of this undoubtedly reflected the complex and intersecting mass of patronage networks which ensured that different interests would always be in competition, so that the family ties that dominated many regiments were not the only force which might determine an appointment.[44] The tendency of the king to award a successful petitioner the first office of a specified rank that became vacant in a particular regiment provided a mechanism that was likely to break up *de facto* family proprietorship.[45] The ministers, above all cardinal Richelieu, were also prepared to intervene in appointments to commands, as in late 1639 when Richelieu arranged for the cavalry regiment of the recently deceased cardinal de La Valette to be transferred to the vicomte de Turenne.[46] Even when the crown did not intervene directly in promotions, the attempts of unit commanders to keep their officerships within the family or the clientele could also run foul of the patronage rights of the high command of the army-corps. The commander of a particular

---

fils to Richelieu, written during the father's serious illness of the previous year: AAE MD 840, fo. 49, 20 Apr. 1641.

[42] For example, AAE CP Lorraine 15, fo. 387, 21 Dec. 1634, Henri, duc de Rohan, petitions on behalf of colonel Biez, who wishes one of his companies to be transferred to his son, who can be relied upon to keep it at an effective strength; AAE MD 1679, fo. 176, 30 July 1640, Châtillon to de Noyers, petitioning for the brother of a captain, proposing that he should receive the first available captaincy in the same unit; fo. 230, 28 Aug. 1640, Châtillon to de Noyers, petition for sr de Réaux, based on the service rendered by his father in the regiment of *gardes*. AAE MD 845, fo. 64 [1642], Amador de La Porte, *grand prieur*, to his nephew, Richelieu, supporting a petition that a younger brother should assume the company of a recently deceased captain.

[43] See, for example, SHAT A¹ 69, fo. 311, 25 May 1642, de Noyers to Manicamp, *mestre de camp*, ordering him to establish a specific royal selection of an *enseign* in one of the companies of his regiment.

[44] Many instances exist of competition to fill vacant officerships: AAE CP Savoie 28, fo. 58, 2 Feb. 1639, cardinal de La Valette to Richelieu, writing of the various groups of petitioners trying to place their chosen candidate in a vacant captaincy in the regiment of Rivarre; AAE MD 1680, fo. 439v, 28 Sept. 1641, Antoine III, comte de Gramont, to de Noyers, proposing two candidates for a vacant officership, without prejudice to either. SHAT A¹ 58, fo. 171, 14 Mar. 1640, de Noyers to *mestre de camp* Mercurin, asking him to propose three candidates for any vacant officership. It may be wondered what clashes of patronage underlay an *ordonnance* of 30 Dec. 1642, which reinstated a captain in the regiment of Saint-Estienne, his *charge* having been given *par surprise* to another officer: A¹ 70, fo. 616.

[45] Louis XIII offered Jacques de Chastenet de Puységur such an arrangement in 1622 after the siege of Montpellier for the first post of *enseign* that became vacant in a *gardes* company: Puységur, *Guerres*, I. 42–3.

[46] Henri de La Tour d'Auvergne, vicomte de Turenne, *Lettres* ed. S. d'Huart (Paris, 1972), p. 356, 13 Oct., Turenne to his mother, Isabelle de Nassau, dowager-duchess of Bouillon, in which he gave assurances that he had not asked for the transfer of the regiment to his command, and that 'je n'en négligerai pas pour cela mon régiment d'infanterie'.

The French rejection of entrepreneurship

army-corps possessed considerable influence, sometimes to the extent of specifically delegated authority, to make promotions on the basis of his own judgement.[47] Much of this patronage might be used to support the interests of the subordinate unit commanders and their own choice of appointments and replacements, but on occasions it was quite clear that the interests of unit officers and the overall commander of the corps diverged. The cardinal de La Valette, when commander in Italy, became involved in the replacement of the *mestre de camp* for the regiment of Maugiron. The obvious petitioner, Maugiron's nephew, was regarded with suspicion by La Valette, who wrote that 'je crains qu'il ne le puisse maintenir', and went on to inform de Noyers that he was making enquiries as to whether the sr de La Passage would be prepared to take over the regiment.[48]

The crown's policy of interfering with the 'normal' expectations of the family of previous holders of office in promotion could cause considerable dissatisfaction; confirming a replacement captain in the regiment of Charles de Livron, marquis de Bourbonne, Servien wrote to Bourbonne that he was to placate the lieutenant of the company for being passed over, and to try to prevent him leaving the king's service.[49] Moreover, the simple threat of such interference could itself prove an effective means of achieving some degree of action from unit commanders who were over-inclined to protect the interests of their subordinates when these were their own clients. Louis XIII wrote directly to the *mestres de camp* of the *vieux* regiments in December 1641, complaining of the number of officers absent from their regiments without permission. These officers were to be replaced, and the *mestres de camp* were to send lists of proposals to fill the vacancies. Should they fail to provide these lists of alternative candidates, the crown would intevene to fill the vacancies directly.[50] Even when the end result, as in this case, was that the *mestre de camp* or the captain still nominated replacements within the unit, these may not have been the individuals they had initially appointed or wished to promote.[51]

---

[47] See chapter 9, p. 467.
[48] AAE CP Savoie 28, fo. 44, 17 Jan. 1639. This also serves as a demonstration of the lack of proprietary control that the original *mestre de camp* held over his regiment. For another example of the corps commander operating against the interests of the unit commander or his heirs, AAE MD 1679, fo. 232, 29 Aug. 1640, Châtillon to de Noyers, reported that the sieur de Pierre, captain of *chevaux légers* in the *régiment colonel*, is obliged by illness to retire from service: 'je nay peû dénier au sieur de Fumel son lieutenant la recommandation quil a desire que je vous fisse de ses interests' – followed by a seventeenth-century example of that familiar genre, the letter of reference which damns with faint praise.
[49] SHAT A¹ 24, fo. 161, 22 Mar. 1635.
[50] SHAT A¹ 66, fo. 510, 22 Dec. 1641.
[51] Similar instructions were sent to Bussy-Rabutin and Aiguebonne, ordering them to submit lists of replacements for officers in their regiments who had served inadequately in the previous campaign: SHAT A¹ 57, fo. 331, 8 Feb. 1640, de Noyers to Bussy-Rabutin; A¹ 58, fo. 206, 17 Mar. 1640, de Noyers to Aiguebonne. An instruction was sent in May 1639 to the lieutenant-colonel of Brassac's regiment (the comte de Brassac himself having recently died of wounds suffered while serving with his regiment in the army of Saxe-Weimar), offering him the command of the regiment if he was prepared to accept its *réformation* on the terms imposed on all comparable units. If not, de Noyers'

The administrative context

Proposals for appointments were vetoed by the crown on occasions and the commanders were ordered to present an alternative. This was particularly frequent when a company lieutenant was judged to be unsuitable for promotion to a captaincy, and the crown would order the regimental commander to present someone more suitable for the company command.[52]

We cannot assume that all of these recommendations, criticisms and counter-suggestions were simply motivated by an impartial concern to ensure that the best-qualified officers were appointed to posts in the army. Senior officers may well, on occasions, have genuinely opposed the appointment of those they judged incapable of maintaining units, and may have argued strongly for those, not within their own clienteles, whom they considered to have outstanding potential.[53] More frequently, it may be suspected, the intersection of regimental, corps and ministerial patronage in the allocation of a limited supply of officerships generated a degree of conflict and unpredictability about the allocation of posts in which 'obvious' candidates – the choices of the unit commander – were not always the beneficiaries.

Yet it should be stressed that these conflicting pressures concerning appointments to units applied almost without exception to regiments and companies which were already *sur pied*. It was in this process of selecting officers to augment an existing unit with additional companies, or to replace existing officers for whatever reason, that the crown chose to exercise its theoretically unrestricted power over the officer-corps as its direct employees. At any one time, an extremely large part of the French army was made up of newly recruited regiments and companies, levied by persons of influence who were considered capable of raising a full unit quickly and effectively. To avoid delays in assembling the unit, the crown was prepared to sacrifice its rights to control appointment, and at times even to abandon the formality of scrutinizing the proposals for subordinates made by the *mestre de camp* or the colonel.[54] Such delegation of authority was not always

---

letter warns, the regiment will be transferred to the command of one of Brassac's relatives: A¹ 52, fo. 219, 20 May 1639.

[52] SHAT A¹ 51, fo. 136, 15 Mar. 1639, de Noyers to colonel Lignan, who is to propose a replacement for the captaincy of the company of *chevaux légers* of sr Bouchart as the lieutenant is incapable; AAE CP Lorraine, 31, fo. 423, 7 Sept. 1640, François de l'Hospital, comte du Hallier, to de Noyers, discussing a proposal for the creation of a number of new companies in the regiment of Picardie. Du Hallier wrote that all of the lieutenants of the regiment have put themselves forward as potential captains for the new units, but only a minority of the lieutenants would be capable of raising and maintaining the new companies, and their names, together with others considered capable, are on the enclosed list (which has not survived with the letter).

[53] On at least one occasion, maréchal Châtillon, petitioning for a captaincy in the *gardes suisses* for the brother of an established captain, saw fit to stress that this was a serious recommendation based on his own knowledge of the military qualities of the candidate, not simply a piece of favouritism: AAE MD 1679, fo. 176, 30 July 1640.

[54] SHAT A¹ 57, fo. 474, 22 Feb. 1640, nomination of sr de Murette as *mestre de camp* of a regiment, and arrangements for him to levy troops in Dauphiné; A¹ 59, fo. 419, 16 Feb. 1640, Malissy given full discretion to raise an additional regiment.

The French rejection of entrepreneurship

explicit, and in some cases unit commanders were nervous of exercising the full extent of this right of appointment. When he was raising a regiment for royal service for the first time in 1630, Turenne wished to substitute an alternative candidate for one of the companies of this regiment: 'Je parlay à M. de Marillac de cela. Il me dit qu'il n'y avoit qu'à oster de dessus le parchemin le nom et en remettre un à la place de qui je voudrois . . . Il me dit qu'il n'y avoit nul danger.'[55] The attraction of raising such units for the prospective *mestre de camp* or captain, apart from the status obtained from the possession of military rank, was the opportunity for patronage that it afforded. The future *mestre de camp* was sent a bundle of commissions *en blanc* to establish the number of companies agreed, selecting persons suitable for the subordinate officerships.[56] The privilege of raising a regiment was particularly attractive to provincial governors, allowing them to feed some of the requests for patronage and preferment amongst their provincial clients. Indeed, governors were frequently sent commissions for the levy of several units simultaneously.[57] Other figures with substantial provincial influence could be asked to nominate suitable persons to levy regiments. Those bishops regarded as particular *fidèles* by Richelieu were an obvious group called on to exercise this patronage. Crusy de Marcillac, bishop of Mende, responded to Richelieu's request for a suitable person to raise a regiment in the Cévennes with a substantial discussion of the strengths and weaknesses of candidates before making a nomination, but also stressing that there would be plenty of others who could be recommended if more troops were required from this area: 'certainement estant dommage de laisser tant de braves gens inutiles dans les Cévennes'.[58] Leading figures in the provincial estates, presidents of the *Parlements* and other very senior *robins* were also regarded as good intermediaries in the distribution of commissions.[59]

It is clear that there was tension between the crown's *de facto* willingness to hand out blank commissions and to delegate powers of appointment to the unit commanders in raising and sometimes in making subsequent appointments or changes of officers in their regiments and companies, and a preoccupation in

---

[55] Turenne, *Letters*, p. 132, 18 June 1630.
[56] SHAT A¹28, fo. 161, 27 June 1636: commissions for a regiment of twenty companies despatched to Chastelier-Barlot; A¹ 52, fo. 71, 6 May 1639, commissions *en blanc* and place of assembly to be sent to sieur de Marin, whose offer to raise a regiment has been accepted.
[57] SHAT A¹24, fo. 167, 22 Mar. 1635: commissions for four regiments of infantry and three companies of *chevaux légers* to be sent to Charles de Schomberg, duc d'Halluin and governor of Languedoc, to distribute as he sees fit; A¹24, fos. 410, 424, 23/6 June 1635: Ambroise-François, marquis de Bournonville, and Henri II, prince de Condé, given commissions to levy one regiment of infantry and one of cavalry each; A¹ 43, fo. 339, 13 Feb. 1638, letter to Charles de Valois, duc d'Angoulême, and his son, Louis-Emmanuel, comte d'Alais and governor of Provence, to nominate a series of *mestres de camp* to take command of new cavalry regts.
[58] AAE MD 839, fo. 140, 11 Aug. 1641.
[59] SHAT A¹ 68, fo. 30, 8 Jan. 1642, invitation to the *premier président* of the *Parlement* of Rennes to allocate the levy of 4,000 troops for royal service.

The administrative context

principle with the defence of royal authority in matters relating to the levy and maintenance of troops. A severe response could still be provoked by attempting to recruit soldiers without having received a formal commission.[60] It would be difficult to quantify the relative proportions of appointments of officers made to units which reflected the respective wishes of the unit commanders, the commander of the army, other powerful or influential individuals, or the crown itself and its ministers. Certainly the crown was not prepared to relinquish the rights to make such appointments, but it is equally clear that in practice the king and his ministerial agents had neither the administrative capacity nor the will to exercise detailed and routine control over every appointment in every ordinary unit. At the same time, they considered it vital not to concede full rights of ownership to the commanding officers. By retaining a discretionary power over replacement and appointment in the lesser units and – to a greater though by no means total extent – over the officers in the *régiments entretenus*, the crown went some way to stifling any belief amongst the commanders of units that they held unrestricted rights of proprietorship and patronage over their subordinates.

The réformation *and* licenciement *of units*

On its own, this capacity to intervene in appointments would probably have proved insufficient to maintain an effective claim by the crown to direct proprietorship over its army. The very reliance on the local connections, administrative effort, and personal credit of the unit commanders considerably attenuated the extent to which the crown was prepared to override their judgements concerning suitable subordinates, or to impose its own choice upon them. Only in the *régiments entretenus*, and in subsequent appointments, promotions and transfers of officers in the ordinary regiments and companies, was the crown prepared to assert its right of nomination with any regularity, and even here it is doubtful whether this was seen as more than an arbitrary and sporadic intervention in a system that was basically fuelled by networks of patronage and connection within the army-corps and, most often, within the individual regiment. In practice, the

---

[60] AAE MD 810, fo. 400, 20 Aug. 1634, instructions to the *chevalier du guet* in Paris, Teston, to prosecute those charged with levying soldiers without permission; SHAT A^1 28, fo. 475, 14 Aug. 1636, order to Claude, comte de Maugiron, to dismiss one of the *enseigns* of his regiment for having tried to levy troops without formal permission; A^1 38, fo. 170, 8 Aug. 1637, strong criticism of marquis de Bourbonne for allowing levies to take place across his *charge*. More forceful are the instructions to Armand de Caumont, marquis de La Force, reporting rumours of illegal levies on the frontiers of Lorraine, and ordering him to pursue those involved and to massacre them: AAE CP Lorraine 15, fo. 246, 5 Oct. 1634. The unauthorized levy of troops continued to be a concern right up to the end of Richelieu's ministry: A^1 65, fo. 370, 14 April 1641, A^1 71 fo. 85, 3 April 1642, letter and *ordonnance* concerned to ensure that *commissaires* should not pay officers unable to produce documentary evidence that they had been appointed by the king, and had been granted specific permission to raise troops; SHAT A^1 70, fo. 35, 26 July 1642, order for the arrest of sieur Nourry at Le Mans, charged with having raised troops without commission.

The French rejection of entrepreneurship

primary weapon at the disposal of the crown in asserting itself over the assumptions of the officers was the power to disband or reduce units at will – *licenciement* and *réformation* – carrying out these reductions without acknowledging any rights to compensation that might be claimed by the officers in respect of their own commitments to the units. This authority was crucial. Fritz Redlich suggests that those monarchs and princes who commissioned the entrepreneurial armies operating in the Empire had the right to disband or reduce units, to change the commanders or to transfer the entire unit to the army of another power.[61] However, when this involved financial loss to the entrepreneur, it was expected that compensation be paid. In some cases, the contracting authority might default upon this responsibility, but this would entail a formal breach of contract, and would be imprudent in a situation where the army was heavily composed of similar entrepreneurs.[62] In France, however, whatever sums might be owed to the French unit commander as a result of raising and maintaining his unit, however much administrative effort, expenditure of social and political credit and deployment of patronage had gone into the raising and upkeep of his troops, no formal liability to the commander was acknowledged by the crown.

The principle of disbanding or reducing the units of the army was, in organizational terms, entirely rational. Rates of attrition amongst ordinary soldiers were considerably higher than amongst the officers, and the result was all too frequently that an army organization, in 1635 calculated on a ratio of three officers to each company of eighty to one hundred soldiers and NCOs, would fall to a far less favourable ratio as the army was increasingly composed of companies whose total strength was twenty to thirty officers and men. Under-strength units were expensive and of dubious military benefit. The purpose of amalgamating troops from different units, reducing the number of companies within a regiment, or, in the last resort, simply dissolving whole regiments and reallocating their soldiers, was to try to keep this expense under control by dismissing large numbers of superfluous officers. But the process was more than a simple piece of military rationalization. The threat of *réformation* or *licenciement* was employed throughout the period after 1635 as a calculated pressure to persuade commanders to support the upkeep of their units with their own funds. As the crown had asserted the principle of its full control over the army, and had maintained by implication that the officers were merely its employees, then it was a logical consequence for the crown to assert that the officers had no rights to compensation or to recognition of service should their units be disbanded. The standard terms of an order for the *licenciement* of a unit made no acknowledgement of any financial commitment that might have been made by the commanding officer, or any sense in which his military service implied any reciprocal obligation on the

[61] Redlich, *Military Enterpriser*, I. 171–3.
[62] See the example of a recruitment contract in Pohl, *Profiantirung der keyserlichen Armaden*, pp. 181–8.

The administrative context

part of the crown.[63] In the case of regiments recognized as being of higher quality, the unit would not be fully disbanded, but cut back to a handful of companies. However, as the company was the unit of recruitment, the effects of this *réformation* could be equally destructive of any proprietary interest for most of the captains.[64]

Some generalized concern was expressed that the officers of elite regiments should not be treated with such little regard for their past services. In April 1635 a proposal was drawn up for the payment of a form of gratuity to *officiers réformés* if they were thrown out of their charges by the reduction in the number of companies in the regiment.[65] The relative levels of compensation proposed – a captain would receive 500 *livres*, a lieutenant 450 and an ensign 400 – makes it clear that these sums were not envisaged as reimbursement for any financial commitment that may previously have been made, but more as a financial recognition of good service. And in fact the financial demands of the war-effort ensured that such a scheme, proposed in 1635, stood no chance of implementation. The best that an *officier réformé* could expect was to be allowed to serve with another unit on half pay, and perhaps to be appointed to another full officership again if a vacancy occurred and other claims were not more strongly presented.[66] Moreover, this treatment was exceptional; most officers in this period whose regiments were reduced or disbanded were simply sent home, having gained nothing but a certain degree of military experience, which might be of value in petitioning for another office.[67] At a lesser level they would echo the bitterness of Bénédict-Louis de Pontis, whose lengthy military service was ultimately rewarded with dismissal when he was captured and his unit was disbanded.[68]

This authority to reform or disband units was the ultimate sanction of the crown. It served as a persistent and inescapable reminder of the monarch's claim to hold direct control over the army, and as a check upon the officers' tendency to

---

[63] SHAT A¹ 27, fo. 367, 7 May 1636, standard orders for the *licenciement* of three companies of dragoons and one of *chevaux légers*. Such orders typically assert that the unit is the property of the crown ('la compagnie de chevaux légers de laquelle je vous avois donné le commandement'), and is therefore simply dismissing the captain and other officers from functions delegated to them.

[64] For example: SHAT A¹ 30 fo. 323, 19 Nov. 1636, order to Jean de Lambert, marquis de Saint-Bris and *maréchal de camp*, to *réformer* the regiment of Rostinguet down to four companies; A¹ 70, fo. 438, 23 Nov. 1640, regiment of Courtemar to be reduced to two companies; A¹ 70, fo. 578, 20 Dec. 1640, Noailles' regiment to be reduced to ten companies.

[65] AAE MD 813 fo. 281, 16 Apr. 1635.

[66] André, *Michel Le Tellier et l'organization*, pp. 180–5.

[67] AAE CP Allemagne 12, fo. 443, 11 Dec. 1635, proposal to disband the regiment of Aurélio, but to reemploy some of the more experienced officers immediately; SHAT A¹ 65, fo. 105, 17 Jan. 1641, captain Gaya, whose company has been disbanded, is offered the opportunity to serve as a captain in the regiment of Magalotte; A¹ 66, fo. 323, 22 Nov. 1641, Saligny is ordered to disband five companies that he is maintaining in Normandy, but his son, serving as captain of one of these, is offered employment as captain in another newly levied unit.

[68] Pontis, *Mémoires*, pp. 306–11.

The French rejection of entrepreneurship

regard units which they had raised and often funded through their own efforts as their own property.

VENALITY AND THE EXPLOITATION OF THE OFFICER-CORPS

Both in the appointment of officers to units and in the powers of *réformation* and disbandment the crown showed itself concerned to challenge the proprietary tendencies that were likely to emerge within the officer-corps. For political reasons, overtly entrepreneurial contracts to finance and organize large-scale warfare were unacceptable to the crown and its ministers. Yet the numbers of potential officers petitioning to serve the king, the competition for the finite numbers of new units to be levied and for places in existing regiments and companies created a considerable temptation. Opposed in principle to the delegation of authority to its officers, in practice the crown and its ministers were prepared to take the opportunities offered by competition for places in the military system, exploiting the potential of the officers as royal creditors and using bribes and coercion to persuade them to provide a significant part of the cash required for the raising and maintenance of their units.

Venality within the officer-corps

Briefly setting aside the temptations posed to the crown by the competition for officerships, an existing consequence of this demand for posts had long been the conventional practice of payments made by the aspiring officer to the established holder of a regimental or company position or his heirs. Such 'internal' venality, though officially prohibited, was not seriously challenged by the crown, provided that it was kept tacit.[69] Again, the chief concern was to maintain the principle of the crown's military authority. An edict of 1619, attacking venality in the *garde du corps* was more concerned to prohibit civil judges, particularly members of the sovereign courts, from registering such transactions, than with the practice itself.[70] In fact, venality of this sort flourished largely unchecked; Charles Loyseau criticized the sale of military office in terms that make it clear that it was a widespread and recognized phenomenon: 'on commence desia bien fort, d'en vendre les charges, non pas le Roy, mais les particuliers par sa tolerance, qui est certes un gra[n]d desregleme[n]t à la discipline militaire'.[71]

The military memoirs of this period mention the purchase of military office with far less concern, as an unavoidable aspect of an ambitious military career.

---

[69] *Code Michau*, art. 190, for a formal prohibition of venality within the officer-corps. Occasional edicts condemn the practice, but in a formulaic way which suggests no real commitment to its abolition: BN Ms.fr. 4223, fo. 125 (mid-1650s).
[70] *Les ordonnances militaires tirées du code du roi Henri III*, Dec. 1619, pp. 405–8.
[71] Loyseau, *Cinq livres*, p. 445.

The administrative context

Roger de Rabutin, comte de Bussy, paid 12,000 *écus* to buy the office of lieutenant in the company of *chevaux légers* of Henri II de Condé.[72] Jacques de Chastenet de Puységur positively relished the details of his various purchases and sales of office, and wrote of his disposal of his office of *enseign* in the *Gardes* for 18,000 *livres*, and his purchase of a post of major in the regiment of Piedmont for 15,000, together with a captaincy in the same regiment – to be held conjointly – for which he offered 12,000 *livres*.[73] The latter figure may be exaggerated by Puységur; the 'standard' price for a captaincy in one of the *vieux régiments* was 6,000 *livres*.[74]

In general the conventions were respected; venality was concealed behind private 'certificates of demission', which treated each sale as a unique event, requiring a specific set of negotiations.[75] The reality, that this was one transaction within a network of conventional prices and accepted arrangements for the transfer of office, was kept at arm's length. Yet beneath these conventions venality was tacitly accepted up to the level of Richelieu and the king himself, who would certainly have authorized the edict of April 1639 creating a series of new officers in the royal *gendarmes* companies, which was passed to the *chambre des comptes* for registration in August.[76] When the state negotiated the sale of a senior military office, the distinction between the secret negotiations and the formal commission is striking. In late 1636, Claude de Langlée, seigneur de l'Epichelière, proposed the revival of the office of *maréchal général de logis d'armée*, and, as a letter from de Noyers revealed, had offered 50,000 *livres* for the position.[77] Prepared to create such a post for ready cash, the formal commission for Langlée was drawn up by

---

[72] Bussy-Rabutin, *Mémoires*, I. 147–8.

[73] Puységur, *Guerres*, I. 143–4, [1632]. The comte de Souvigny recorded that he paid 11,600 *livres* in 1628 for the office of major in the regt of Estissac: Souvigny, *Mémoires*, I. 178–9.

[74] This figure emerged in a quarrel over the part-payment of this sum, owed for a captaincy in the Navarre regiment, which forced the intervention of the king: SHAT A^1 26 fo. 58, 2 June 1635. The price of captaincies fluctuated according to levels of demand: AAE MD 830, fo. 51, 21 Feb. 1638, mentions some 9,000–10,000 *livres* paid for the captaincies in Chamblay's regiment, obviously of considerably lower status than a *vieux* unit. The 'standard' price for a captaincy in the *vieux* may have fallen over the following decades. A formal 'certificate of demission' allowing Puységur's son to acquire a company in the regiment of Piedmont in 1656 records that he was to pay 3,000 *livres* 'a telle personne qu'il plaira a S.M. d'ordonner' – i.e. to the present incumbent or his relatives: A^1 147, 8 Nov. 1656.

[75] AAE MD 815, fo. 282, Sept. 1635: lieutenant of Richelieu's *gendarmes* expressed his contentment with a contract on the basis of which he handed back his office in return for 6,000 *livres*; SHAT A^1 28 fo. 273, 15 July 1636, transfer of office of *mestre de camp* to sr Chambret; A^1 42, pce 151, 25 June 1637.

[76] SHAT A^1 65, fo. 376, 16 Aug. 1640, order for the registration of the edict. In September 1642, Jean de Pontevez, comte de Carces and *grand sénéchal* of Provence, wrote to Richelieu concerning the payment that he had made to his sister, Gabrielle, the widow of Guillaume de Simiane, marquis des Gordes, to obtain the captaincy in the *gardes* vacated by her husband's death. Clearly Richelieu himself had some undisclosed proprietary interest in the company, for Carces was at pains to stress of the arrangement that he was 'parfaictement sousmis aux volontés de V.E. [et] j'abandonneray celle cy d'abord que je pourray cognoistre quelle en a en quelque autre ce sera': AAE MD 845, fo. 194, 5 Sept. 1642.

[77] AAE MD 822, fos. 214, 227, 13/17 Nov. 1636.

The French rejection of entrepreneurship

the secretary of state in the king's name; needless to say, no mention of the circumstances of the creation appeared in the document, which simply stressed Langlée's preeminent suitability for the charge.[78] Only if the practice of venality was permitted to become offensively overt would the secretary of state intervene to reassert a notional principle of promotion through merit. The comte de Mercurin, *mestre de camp* of an infantry regiment in which the sale of office by his subordinates was felt to be too blatant, was told to intervene to prevent such sales, and in future to submit a list of three candidates to the crown for each vacant post.[79] In practice it would seem that the only aspect of this system which caused the crown and its ministers serious concern was the possibility of pluralism in the holding of purchased office, a concern evidenced by a series of ordinances and specific instructions to senior officers, though less obviously by any direct action.[80]

This discretion was sufficiently complete that it is effectively impossible to calculate how high a percentage of all office transfers were venal, or how prices fluctuated relative to supply during Richelieu's ministry. However, there seems no reason to underestimate the extent of payment for transfer of office at the level of the *régiments* and *compagnies entretenus*, and good reason to suppose that it frequently took place in other prestigious regiments and companies, even though they did not enjoy formal 'maintained' status. The crown's forbearance about this system of internal venality was possibly motivated by its own willingness to exploit the demand for office in a slightly different manner. The system of venality was not really questioned at an official level until the 1660s, and even then attempts to eliminate it were small scale and largely ineffective: in fact as a higher proportion of the units in the army gained *entretenue* status, the system flourished; more officerships had the potential to become family property, secure from unexpected disbandment or amalgamation into another unit.[81]

---

[78] SHAT A¹ 32, pce 211, 11 Nov. 1636. Similar venal negotiations surround the transfer of the governorship of Péronne in the same period: AAE MD 822, fos. 57, 70, 94, [1636]. The proprietary rights over governorships of *places* both inside and outside of France are a critical issue only hinted at in the documentation, but see for example, AAE CP Savoie 25, fo. 127, 15 May 1637, *demission* made by du Passages of the governorship of Valenza, in Piedmont, in return for payments totalling 40,000 *livres*.

[79] SHAT A¹ 58, fo. 171, 14 Mar. 1640; as payment to the present incumbent or his relatives would *follow* the appointment of the successful candidate to the office, it is difficult to see that referring the candidates to the crown for the final choice would make any difference to the practice of venality.

[80] SHAT A¹ 63, fo. 259, 30 Jan. 1641, *ordonnance* to deprive officers of multiple charges; fo. 434, 26 Feb. 1641, *ordonnance* to dismiss officers because of extreme youth or pluralism; A¹ 64, fo. 2, 16 Mar. 1641, *intendant* Bellejamme to investigate accusations that some officers are holding multiple charges. See, however, A¹ 32, pce 21, 1 Feb. 1636, *lettres patentes*, permitting Descraignolles to hold the charges of lieutenant governor and *sergent-major* at Antibes for a period of three years.

[81] See Corvisier, *Louvois*, pp. 102–4, and C. Rousset, *Histoire de Louvois et de son administration politique et militaire* (4 vols.; Paris, 1879), I. 165–6, 180–3, for discussion of the attempts to restrict venality within the army. Guy Rowlands, 'Power, authority and army administration', makes a convincing case for the persistence of venality throughout the military hierarchy.

The administrative context

The purchase of unit commands

The system of venality described above was concerned with the payments made, notionally outside of the crown's knowledge, by those who sought to replace existing officers in established posts. Such venality was not a system restricted to captains and colonels/*mestres de camp*, indeed the purchase of an ensign or lieutenant's office in one of the *vieux régiments* was a time-honoured way of beginning a prestigious military career.[82] It recognized that officers had made a substantial financial commitment during their period of service and the payment of an agreed sum to the existing holder of the office or, if deceased, to his relatives, as a kind of 'entry fine' on appointment, would serve as some form of reimbursement for previous service.[83] But it is important to note that this system of payments made on the transfer of office was not the same as selling officerships to the highest bidder. A payment of 6,000 *livres* would be made to the present holder of a captaincy in a *vieux régiment*; it was not open to anyone to pay this sum to purchase such an office on the open market. With the exception of particular, individual, offices at the top of the military hierarchy, some governorships and a few apparent anomalies such as the pricing (and *possibly* the open sale) of officerships in the royal *gendarmes*, the crown did not 'sell' military offices in the sense of marketing them openly. Like many other parts of the structure of venal office in its higher or more prestigious reaches, the market for officerships was closed and depended primarily upon the deployment of influence and favour.[84] Most of those who wished to become officers and whose primary qualification was the financial capacity to sustain the expenses of military service would obviously prefer to buy a post in a prestigious *régiment entretenu* rather than establishing their own unit for royal service, but that more attractive option was not open to them. Even allowing for the increase of the *vieux régiments* to five, the elevation of the status of the *petits vieux*, and the systematic increase in the number of companies in prestige regiments from twenty to twenty-five to thirty, the demand far exceeded supply for positions in such units. The allocation of officerships consequently reflected the influence of patrons or relatives, and on occasions the personal wishes of the king, those *grands* holding the great *offices de la couronne* in the army, or the ministers.[85] Such officerships went to those who could mobilize

---

[82] Abraham de Fabert began his long military career in 1613 with a cadetship in the *gardes françaises* at the age of fourteen, followed in 1618 by the office of *enseign* in the Piedmont regiment: Bourelly, *Maréchal de Fabert*, I. 11–13.

[83] The system was alive and well in the eighteenth century, and is described by Léonard, *L'armée et ses problèmes*, pp. 163–9; see also the more impressionistic Tuetey, *Les officiers*, pp. 129–60.

[84] Doyle, *Venality*, pp. 64–5, 134–6, 153, 217.

[85] Abraham de Fabert provides the classic case of an officer whose career was made explicitly through the patronage of Jean-Louis de Nogaret de La Valette, duc d'Epernon, in the latter's role both as *colonel général* and as governor of Metz, where Fabert's father was *maître-échevin*: Bourelly, *Maréchal de Fabert*, I. 11–26. The comte de Souvigny also hoped that his close friendship with Bernard, duc de La Valette, would mobilize Epernon patronage to gain him the post of *aide-major*

The French rejection of entrepreneurship

such connections and prevail over the competition, though even at the highest levels of power it was not a foregone conclusion that patrons would always be able to obtain officerships or promotions for their clients.[86]

Those who were not successful in this competition, but who wanted to enjoy the social prestige of military service, were left with the option of raising their own units or – at the sacrifice of status – serving as subordinate officers in one of these newly recruited companies or regiments. Even in the first case, however, the number of individuals prepared to levy units for the king's service in return for command of the units was considerably greater than the number of units that the crown considered it necessary or desirable to raise. Even after the expansion of military commitments from 1635 and the larger army that these demanded, the crown's policy towards recruitment was shaped by a flow of petitioners for military office which always surpassed the number of units which at any one time the crown considered it desirable to set *sur pied*. In these circumstances it was relatively easy for financial criteria to play a dominant role in the allocation of newly created unit commands. While the policy was never articulated as a general principle, the discussions and negotiations surrounding particular cases give a clear indication of the crown's working practice in granting commissions. In circumstances in which there was competition for officerships, but where the great majority of those petitioning lacked significant military experience or any other factor that would distinguish them from one another, it was a logical step to favour applicants who were prepared to fund all or part of a levy from their own resources.

At the level of the great provincial power-brokers, whether governors, lieutenants or those with an established family affinity in the province, this was a familiar pattern. The use of private or provincial funds to maintain infantry regiments or companies of cavalry – troops whose main purpose might be to defend the province or particular *places* held by the family – was well established.[87] The crown accepted that this gave the provincial aristocracy rights of appointment and probably ensured that the loyalty of the unit would be explicitly to them. Governors and other members of the provincial elite were prepared to meet the costs of maintaining these units either privately or locally because it gave them practical power and prestige and the opportunity to deploy substantial

---

with the regiment of Estissac: *Mémoires*, I. 130–1. Benedict-Louis de Pontis obtained his first military experience in one of the Lesdiguières' family regiments, subsequently benefiting from this family connection to gain an *enseign* in the regiment of Champagne, whose *mestre de camp* in 1612 was Charles de Blanchefort de Créqui, successively married to two of Lesdiguières' daughters: Pontis, *Mémoires*, pp. 39–40, 54.

[86] Béguin, *Princes de Condé*, pp. 98–102, provides a list of petitions made by Henri II de Condé and his son the duc d'Enghien between 1643 and 1648, and (where known) the outcome.

[87] See for example the great concern of the Epernon family to maintain direct control over the garrison at Metz. The governorship was regarded as sufficiently important to the family that the cost of paying most of the troops there was regarded as an acceptable price to ensure their loyalty: Girard, *Espernon*, pp. 215–18, 250–3, 451–3.

The administrative context

patronage amongst their lesser noble supporters. Yet the involvement of unit commanders in funding the recruitment of their soldiers extended well below the level of the greatest provincial nobility.

The provision of credit

While the system was never made explicit, the ministry proposed in effect that potential officers should be willing to assume all or part of the financial burden of raising their unit – taking on what was the true entrepreneurs' second role, the provision of credit. But while this provision of funds was encouraged, it was equally clear that the ministry would not concede to those who advanced their own money the proprietary rights over the unit that would be the consequence of this elsewhere in Europe. Instead the officers' credit was accepted in a number of ways, all of which circumvented the terms of a formal contract. Despite his financial commitment, the officer continued to receive a simple commission, not an entrepreneurial capitulation.

Concern to strengthen a petition for a command could lead a candidate to make a direct offer to raise a unit at his own expense.[88] Such offers were frequently made both to obtain the prestige of a command, but also to emphasize political solidarity with the regime.[89] The aim in all cases was the direct purchase of ministerial goodwill, and sometimes to obtain support for a candidacy which might not otherwise have been accepted. This type of direct offer was also characteristic in cases where the commander had previously possessed a unit which had dispersed or been disbanded in the course of the campaign. Realizing that he stood little chance of having his unit reconstructed at government expense, he would offer to provide the funds to set the unit up for a second time.[90] The ministry was also inclined to use this as a disciplinary penalty if it considered that insufficient care had been taken of the company.[91]

---

[88] AAE MD 816, fo. 198, 31 Dec. 1635: captain of a company of dragoons has already raised this unit with his own funds, and offers to raise another if granted the necessary commission; SHAT A^1 52, fo. 149, 13 May 1639, sr La Douze thanked for his 'bonne volonté' in raising a regiment for the king's service; fo. 168, 15 May, similar to sr Caumarin.

[89] SHAT A^{1}28, fo. 413, 8 Aug 1636: offer by those involved in the *ferme générale* of the *gabelles* to raise and maintain a company of fifty *chevaux légers*; A^1 69, fo. 263, 13 May 1642, *lettres patentes* related to the levy of 4,000 infantry through the efforts of the *Parlement* of Brittany.

[90] AAE MD 816, fo. 22, 23 Oct. 1635: offer to replace a company of *chevaux légers* which had dissipated, the levy to be carried out 'à ses despenses'; SHAT A^1 59, 9 Jan. 1640, Croisille-Melun authorized to reestablish a company of *chevaux légers* at his own expense, and is warned of the king's anger if he does not maintain it in a better state than his previous company.

[91] AAE MD 823, fo. 267, Dec. 1635: four out of six companies of *gendarmes* are to be levied at the captains' expense, in order that they should escape disciplinary proceedings for a previous inadequate levy; SHAT A^1 40, fo. 141, 9 Dec. 1637, captains of the regiment of Nangis have been ordered to recruit their companies up to full strength at their own expense; A^1 58, fo. 72, 7 Mar. 1640, Bussy-Rabutin has been permitted to transfer his regiment to the command of his son, but the unit is in a very poor state, and he is to undertake to recruit it up to full strength in return for the

The French rejection of entrepreneurship

Private credit might also be obtained, again, more as a grant than as a loan, by adopting the convention that the costs of the levy would be recovered from operations in enemy territory. In contrast to the explicit arrangements for the levy of contributions made with entrepreneurs in the service of other European powers, these arrangements were unspecific and cannot realistically have been regarded as a means to recover the initial outlay.[92] In a similar category of units whose recruitment was completely funded by the future commanding officer can be included cases in which the agreement is never stated openly in any form. It was simply understood that the officer would employ his own resources in return for the commission, and without any clear mention of the costs involved.[93] This convention was often adopted in cases where the commander was not merely anxious to raise a unit, but was a prominent supporter of the ministry.[94]

In cases where the ministerial commitment was less overt, another formula was used: a commission was granted, but it was stressed that the urgency of the levy was such that the commander should begin recruitment immediately, using his own funds.[95] Money from the treasury would follow to make good the expenses incurred.[96] Whereas in the previous examples it was evident that the officer had

---

transfer of command; A¹ 63, fo. 175, 21 Jan. 1641, *ordonnance* to oblige *mestres de camp* and captains of units in the army of Italy to raise recruits at their own expense or face disbandment.

[92] SHAT A¹ 24, fo. 355, 24 May 1635: letter to Honoré-Albert, duc de Chaulnes and governor of Picardy, informing him of the king's willingness to concede commissions for cavalry companies to any of the governors of frontier places who request them, provided that the costs of these were entirely supported by exactions from the enemy. AAE MD 814, fo. 78, 24 May 1635, commission for a cavalry company on condition that its costs are met from levies on enemy territory; A¹ 50, fo. 238, 2 Jan. 1639, recruitment of additional troops for regiments of Picardie, Plessis-Praslin and Saint-Luc are all to be met from contributions exacted from Lorraine.

[93] AAE MD 814, fo. 249, 8 July 1635, although Richelieu had expressed his doubts to Servien about granting commissions to raise units of infantry and carabins simultaneously, he was prepared to accept this in the case Jacques Ferron, seigneur de La Ferronnaye, recognizing that 'l'argent faisait tout'; MD 820, fo. 18, 6 Jan. 1636: 'Roche-Giffard est un homme riche et de bonne volonté' (Henri de La Chapelle, marquis de La Rochegiffart); MD 839, fo. 140, 11 Aug. 1641, Crusy de Marcillac, bishop of Mende, to Richelieu, stressing the qualities of the sr de Gabriac, who has agreed to raise a regiment of infantry of twenty companies and a regiment of cavalry of five. His military and organizational qualities are mentioned 'et avec celle il a du credit'.

[94] A very explicit case was the commission for L'Hermitte, director of finances at Casale, who was granted permission to raise a company in his own name for service at Casale, and where it was clearly assumed that he would meet the expenses of this levy, although the unit would subsequently be placed on the garrison roll of the citadel: SHAT A¹ 59, fo. 439, 21 June 1640. A very different set of circumstances was evident in the duchy of Lorraine in 1634, where four French captains who had obviously been serving in the army of Charles IV duke of Lorraine judged it prudent to offer to raise companies at their own expense for the service of the king, simply receiving a first *montre* when their companies had reached the assembly-point: AAE CP Lorraine 14, fo. 170, 7 Feb. 1634, *mémoire* from Jacques-Nompar de Caumont, maréchal de La Force petitioning on their behalf.

[95] SHAT A¹28, fo. 73, 16 June 1636, Léon de Sainte-Maure, comte de Jonzac and *lieutenant* of Saintonge and Angoumois, is to provide the funds for the immediate levy of a company of *carabins* in Saintonge to help to restore order after the peasant unrest.

[96] SHAT A¹25, fo. 471, 27 Oct. 1635: Lasure is to raise a regiment immediately for the garrison at Montbelliard. Money will be sent as soon as possible; A¹ 58, fo. 15, 2 Mar. 1640, Mignoux's nomination of ten additional captains to augment his regiment has been accepted, and they are to

The administrative context

made a long-term loan, and quite possibly a gift, to the crown, here the impression was far less clear. In some of these cases the crown certainly felt it necessary to stress the intention of making repayment.[97] The plight of the *épargne* was such that even loans of the shortest duration were welcome, providing some financial flexibility in meeting the immediate costs of raising troops. However, it would seem that at least a part of these 'advances' were either not repaid or were reimbursed only after a long delay.[98] Moreover, in a situation where so much military expenditure was assigned to unreliable revenues, an agreement to meet expenses incurred was very far from a guarantee of full or prompt reimbursement.[99] Having once advanced the money for the levy of a unit that the crown probably regarded as a temporary creation, the commanding officer was very badly placed to obtain reimbursement through direct pressure on the military administration.

Persuading committed individuals to meet the full costs of levying their units, or presenting such financial commitment as a short-term advance, was one means by which the ministry could support the financial burden of raising additional troops. However, these methods only accounted for a minority of the total number of units raised. The majority of units were levied with some direct government funding. The crucial factor was that these funds were seldom adequate to support the real costs of the levy. Company and regimental commanders were confronted with a situation in which the money provided by the crown would only cover a proportion of the recruitment costs, and where it would be necessary to make up the difference with private funds if the unit were to be raised to an acceptable strength and fully equipped. Once again, the possibility of obtaining any subsequent reimbursement, or even recognition of the expenses incurred, was slight.[100] Sometimes the ministry was prepared to admit beforehand that it would not be able to provide the 'accustomed sum' for the costs of a levy.[101] The crown

---

begin recruiting immediately, without waiting for the formal letters of commission or, by implication, any funds for this levy.

[97] AAE MD 816, fo. 137, 22 Nov. 1635: 'vous ne laisserez pas de presser lesd. cappns. de les envoier faire faire, les asseurant que le Roy les leur payer, et que l'intention de Sa Mte. n'est pas qu'il leur en couste aucune chose'; AAE MD 843, fo. 167, 2 Aug. 1642, Richelieu to de Noyers, reporting that he had persuaded Nicolas de Neufville, duc de Villeroy, the governor of Lyonnais, to raise an additional 500 troops for royal service 'luy promettant que je luy payerez la levée a mon passage a Lyon'.

[98] SHAT A^{1}24, fo. 425, 26 June 1635: in an unpromising reply to a request by Louis de Béthune, comte de Charost, for reimbursement of the costs incurred in the levy of two companies of cavalry, Servien agreed in principle to authorize repayment, 'Bien que [la] grande maison [épargne?] n'a pas d'argent de [que?] vostre . . . j'ai fait mis en despense ce que vous avez faict en cette occasion.' AAE MD 826, fo. 172, 15 Feb. 1637, captain Rénier to Richelieu, petitioning for his support over a ten-month delay in the payment of recruitment expenses.

[99] SHAT A^1 52, fos. 359–60, 6 June 1639, captains who have been offered funds from the new *subsistances* tax to raise their companies, are not to use these new troops to try to extract the tax from the local populations, despite the difficulties of making good the promised revenues.

[100] AAE MD 815, fo. 256, 25 Sept. 1635: de Bergues to Richelieu, 'en ayant bien déjà employé au double de celuy que je receus de Sa Ma^{te}'.

[101] SHAT A^1 24, fo. 410, 23 June 1635: 6,000 *écus* for Ambroise-François, marquis de Bournonville, of

The French rejection of entrepreneurship

also deployed the example of its foreign entrepreneurs, who were occasionally prepared to divide the costs of actual recruitment in the interests of a good capitulation.[102] Inadequate financial provision was frequently the consequence of allocating the recruitment costs to a local revenue judged too unreliable to be assigned to a *traité* or some more important item of government expense. In 1636 Henri de La Trémoïlle, duc de Thouars, was offered a tax on wine levied across two *élections* in return for the levy of two regiments of infantry.[103] This financial agreement ran into almost immediate difficulties: the *cour des aides* refused to recognize the letters patent until late October, and then only under pressure.[104] Faced with delays and obstruction, La Trémoïlle had little choice but to levy the units at his own expense, against the hope that the tax would finally yield a small part of the costs.[105] In some cases, specific revenues were assigned to the recruitment costs; in others it was simply assumed that the governors would find local or private means to fund units, which allowed them to reward their clients and supporters.[106] The combination of the personal relationship with the king enjoyed by the great aristocracy, and the intermingling of private and public roles that characterized their position in the provinces, allowed the crown to transfer much of the expenditure of raising troops to these individuals with little risk that this would be challenged or rejected.[107]

Across the entire range of French military expenditure in the 1630s and 1640s this attempt to evade full payment of the costs of recruitment may seem petty or insignificant, especially as many of the units raised did receive all – or part – of these costs. But it should be emphasized that the sums involved in levying troops were not small. A company of *gendarmes* cost 6,000 *livres* to raise, mount on decent horses and provide with necessary equipment.[108] A similar allowance was made

---

the 10,000 *écus* that the king customarily provided for a regiment of 500 cavalry; A^{1}35, fo. 276, 7 Apr. 1637, Jacques de Rouxel, comte de Grancey, is informed that the crown cannot provide him with the accustomed sum for the levy of a company of *chevaux légers*; Avenel, VI. 898, 20 Feb. 1642, additional costs of recruitment to be met by Condé.

[102] AAE MD 812, fo. 398, 1634: Colonel Erlach offers to provide an extra 2 *écus* per recruit above the agreed advance of 4 *écus* per man from the crown.

[103] SHAT A^1 29, fos. 219–21, 13 Sept. 1636; letters setting out and discussing the agreement.

[104] SHAT A^1 30, fos. 180, 220, 24/8 October 1636.

[105] See also SHAT A^1 41, fo. 78, 3 Feb. 1636: governors of Languedoc, Bourbonnais and Burgundy were informed that numerous companies of the army of Italy were to be raised in their provinces. The king stressed that money for the recruitment cannot be provided from the central treasury, and that the governors should fund the levy. If justified, the money may be deducted from the *dernier quartier* of the *taille* for 1636.

[106] SHAT A^1 65, fo. 210, 8 July 1641, Claude de Rouvroy de Saint-Simon thanked for his offer to levy troops, and asked to set *sur pied* four companies of *chevaux légers*; fo. 221, 11 July, Henri de Saulx-Tavannes to raise a regiment of infantry with all speed to join the army on the Flanders frontier; A^1 51, fo. 354, 4 Apr. 1639, recruitment of the regiment of Rambures assigned on revenues from a tax to be levied on the *généralité* of Orléans.

[107] Turenne, *Lettres*, p. 293, 20 Mar. 1636: Turenne agrees to pay for the levy of a unit for one of his provincial clients.

[108] AAE MD 823, fo. 267, Dec. 1636.

The administrative context

for the levy of a company of *chevaux légers*.[109] The captain of a company of infantry would require as much as 3,000 *livres* to set his company *sur pied*, though this was the highest figure, and the sums officially provided could be as low as 600 *livres* per company.[110] For purposes of comparison, and confirming that the basic recruitment cost of raising foreign mercenaries was not greater, Josias, count Rantzau, was provided in 1635 with 102,000 *livres* for the levy of 500 cavalry and 3,000 infantry in the Empire.[111]

Needless to say, this sum represented the absolute minimum required for an effective levy, and hence the overwhelming number of complaints that officers had been forced to subsidize their recruitment operations in order to get acceptable troops.[112] That the crown and its ministers were well aware of this emerges in a document drawn up by *surintendant* Claude de Bullion in 1637, a 'projet de la cavallerie'. The crisis in the numbers and effectiveness of the French cavalry which had characterized the previous two campaigns, led Bullion to assert that 'Je scay par experience que pour vingt pistolles [*c.* 120 *livres*] on n'a que de tres mediocres cavaliers. Ainsy pour une Recreue de vingt maistres ... on ne peut donner moings de 4,000 *livres*.'[113] A company of 80 horse would cost, on this realistic basis, some 16,000 *livres* to raise, while one of 100 horse would cost over 20,000. In effect the real cost of raising an acceptable company of *chevaux légers* was between two and a half and three and a half times the sum allowed by the crown, even where that sum was paid at all.

---

[109] SHAT A¹ 24, fos. 410, 424, 23/6 June 1635, where the sum stipulated is 10,000 *écus* to raise a regiment of five companies of *chevaux légers*; AAE MD 820, fo. 11, 4 Jan. 1636, proposed to offer 8,000 *écus* for the levy of 500 *chevaux légers*, but the discussion made it clear that this was below the 'standard' rate. The figure of 6,000 *livres* for a company of *chevaux légers* was still current in 1640: A¹ 57, fo. 475, 22 Feb. 1640, instruction to François de Villemontée, *intendant* of Poitou, to allocate this sum for the levy of a company from the taxes levied on the *généralité* of Poitiers. The identical allowance for the raising of *gendarme* and *chevau léger* companies suggests that the captains of *gendarme* companies were expected to pay for the more lavish equipment and better horses out of their own pocket, or persuade their recruits to do so. Service as an ordinary *gendarme* was the only rank-and-file position – outside of the royal *garde du corps* – which a French noble would regard as compatible with his status.

[110] SHAT A¹ 28, fo. 86, 19 June 1636; A¹ 30, fo. 13, 5 Oct. 1636, stipulation of 3,570 *livres* per company, but this was to include the first *montre*; the figure of 600 *livres* per company is cited with reference to one of Epernon's regiments, and may reflect the fact that the captains are regarded as his clients (even though the duke and his son were in semi-disgrace at this time), and could therefore look to make up additional costs from the titular head of the regiment: AAE MD 837, fo. 60, [1640], rough notes under heading 'despense pour l'infanterie'. One agreement of early 1641 specifies a recruitment payment of 9,600 *livres* for a levy of 800 soldiers for François de Bonne et de Créqui, duc de Lesdiguières' regiment, which would give 1,200 *livres* per company: A¹ 63, fo. 98, 12 Jan 1641.

[111] AAE MD 814, fo. 92, 25 May 1635.

[112] For example AAE MD 809, fo. 120, 12 July 1633, Servien reports the complaints of Melchior Mitte de Miolans, marquis de Saint-Chaumont, that he cannot be expected to raise troops on the crown's allowance of 1 *écu*, 6 *sols* per recruit; SHAT A¹ 70, fo. 501, 10 Dec. 1642, circular letter to *intendants*, concerning the complaints of captains about the inadequacy of recruitment allowances and the impossibility of raising troops for the sums provided.

[113] AAE MD 828, fo. 362, [1637].

The French rejection of entrepreneurship

Some potential officers, especially those who possessed powerful or well-placed patrons, were certainly prepared to plead mitigating circumstances to try to evade the burden of these recruitment costs.[114] However, in attempting this they ran up against the realities of the crown's own financial position, which made it impossible to provide adequate levels of support for these recruitment operations. The ordinary petitioner for a command was faced by the choice of paying for his unit – whether in the form of a loan, or partial/full payment for his troops written off to the crown – or of not becoming an officer. To wait for the provision of adequate funds from the *épargne*, or more usually from some unreliable provincial tax source, would be to wait for ever. Certainly in the context of rushed levies to meet military needs over relatively short campaigns, a reluctance to act directly to carry out recruitment might mean that the officer missed the chance to serve, and this would greatly weaken any subsequent petition for a command. Moreover, a series of sixteenth-century ordinances, once again concerned with possible abuses in the delegation of authority to levy troops, specified that commissions were only valid for two months after the date of issue.[115] This would rarely have been long enough to raise a unit if the commander had insisted on receiving funds before he began recruitment.

It was not the case that the crown had acted deliberately to create this mechanism for the funding of recruitment, or that it was exploiting the credit of its military office-holders in accordance with a clearly defined and articulated policy. This aspect of the military system emerged through pressure of circumstance, above all, the crown's antipathy to an entrepreneurial, proprietary, mechanism for raising its armies, combined with the scale of military requirements after 1635, and the widespread desire of the elites to hold military commands as a mark or a confirmation of social status. For the crown and its ministers not to exploit this evident willingness of wealthy subjects to pay for the officerships they wished to hold would have been a self-defeating assertion of principle over pragmatism. Above all, the mass recruitment of 1635 and 1636 saw these expedients transformed into practices so commonplace as to become almost integral to the military system. The raising of an unprecedented army in these years was not underpinned by a vast expansion of the monarchy's bureaucratic and financial resources, but by a systematic exploitation of the crown's officers to raise their own units – entrepreneurship in all but title and proprietorial rights.

---

[114] AAE MD 1676, fo. 297, 20 Aug. 1635, Artus de Moreüil, seigneur de Caumesnil, claimed that he was unable to sustain the costs of raising two companies of cavalry for which he had received the commissions because of his lost *rentes* from the Spanish Netherlands; AAE MD 839, fo. 75, 25 Mar. 1639, maréchal de Brézé to Richelieu, presenting excuses for not lending money to set his regiment *sur pied*.

[115] *Les ordonnances militaires tirées du code du roi Henri III*, pp. 256–61: 'lesquelles commissions ne peuvent avoir lieu, si elles ne sont executées dedans deux mois apres l'expédition et datte d'icelles'.

The administrative context

Maintaining the army sur pied

Had the crown and its ministers been prepared to restrict themselves to the exaction of this specific financial contribution from its officers, above all from those who lacked powerful patrons or an established family tradition of military service which gave a presumptive right to serve the crown in a military command, the consequences might have remained largely insignificant. Entry into the officer-corps had always been determined by elaborate networks of patronage and influence; payment for all or part of the levy of the new unit might well be regarded as an acceptable 'entry charge' made in return for the status granted by the title and rank of army officer. Moreover, by definition, those who had to pay to set their units *sur pied* would not be liable to the system of 'internal' venality which applied when the petitioner was granted an existing, vacant, officership in an *entretenue* regiment or company.

Yet just as the resources of the judicial and financial *officiers* were exploited beyond the initial purchase of their office in the forms of 'salary increases', forced loans and negotiations surrounding the renewal of the *droit annuel*, so their military counterparts did not escape with a simple contribution to the initial costs of the levy.[116] The subsequent exploitation of *mestres de camp* and captains to meet the shortfalls in the running costs of their units was altogether more dangerous for the interests of the crown and the ministry. In the first place, it was all pervasive. Some officers had obtained adequate funds from the crown to raise their troops, or at least to meet a significant part of the costs of setting their unit *sur pied*; others had raised units as the clients of the *grands*, whether commanders of the army-corps or provincial govenors, and had received subventions from their patron to meet the expenses of the levy. Very few unit commanders could escape from the subsequent pressures to employ their own funds to maintain the unit once it was in being. In the second place, these demands for a financial commitment to the subsequent maintenance of the unit were an open-ended commitment. However expensive the costs of the levy might have been, it was at least a one-off payment. As some officers had borrowed all or part of this initial sum, the imposition of further and recurrent charges could prove an overwhelming burden.[117]

The mechanism by which the troops were paid once *sur pied* would appear to have been devised with the express purpose of spreading the financial burden across from the crown to its officers. The *montre* remained the basic theoretical unit of payment for the troops. The *Code Michau* stipulated that the ordinary soldier was to receive a 'monthly' *montre* of 12 *livres*, and these *montres* were to be paid ten times per year, every thirty-six days.[118] However, in practice the soldiers

---

[116] Mousnier, *Vénalité des offices*, pp. 393–414, 645–63.

[117] Puységur provides at least one case of an aspiring officer who borrowed part of the sum required to obtain an officership, a loan of 9,000 *livres* from 'un de mes amis': *Guerres*, I. 144.

[118] *Code Michau*, pp. 284–5, arts. 221, 226. This was later reduced to eight *montres* and, in 1636, to six.

The French rejection of entrepreneurship

were to be paid in much smaller instalments, by *prêts* made each nine days.[119] The *prêt* was a basic subsistence allowance, permitting the soldier to buy the wine, meat and other provisions required to supplement the crown's issue of *pain de munition*. In theory the 4 *prêts* made in the course of the thirty-six days between *montres* would amount to between 5 *livres* 2 *sols*, and 7 *livres* 2 *sols* in total.[120] This is anticipated in the *Code Michau*, which stipulates:

> Que de trois mois en trois mois de monstre toutes lesdites compagnies feront monstre [used here synonymously with *revue*] en laquelle ce qui doit revenir bon à chacun soldat à cause de sa solde par dessus les prests qui lui auront esté faits, et le pain de munition qui lui auront esté délivré, lui sera donné par ledit payeur pour son décomte.[121]

The term 'prêt' carries the implication of an advance, a loan made against the full settlement of the soldiers' monthly wages. In theory, the advances were to be made by the *payeur* attached to each regiment, 'pour les payer des prests et monstres sans discontinuation, et secourir les soldats en leur nécessitez'.[122] The officers were also to receive their salaries from the *payeurs*, but not in the form of *prêts*: 'Les capitaines, lieutenans, enseignes et officiers des régimens ne seroient pas payez par prests comme les soldats, mais que seulement aux monstres leur gages leur seront délivrez.'[123]

The *Code Michau* indicates a system in which officers and soldiers/NCOs are paid on different systems; archival evidence indicates that this was also the case in practice.[124] Such a system might reflect a prudent concern to ensure that the ordinary soldiers did not receive too much money at once; but in practice it allowed the crown and the ministers to operate a system of financial priorities not merely between, but also within, the army-corps. The main concern was to placate the ordinary soldiers by providing a minimum bread ration and a subsistence payment which would allow for the purchase of some additional food and drink. During the Italian campaign of 1629, Richelieu spoke of the capacity of

---

[119] *Code Michau*, pp. 285, 287, arts. 223, 239.

[120] *Code Michau*, p. 287, art. 239, which specified that the *prêt* was to be of 3–4 *sols* per day; SHAT A¹ 32, pce 271 [1636], specifies a *prêt* of 4 *sols* per day; A¹ 59, fo. 392, 19 June 1640, provision of a *prêt* of 4 *sols* for troops in garrison at Doullens.

[121] *Code Michau*, p. 287, art. 240. The *pain de munition* was deducted at the rate of 1 *sol* per day: SHAT A¹ 30, fo. 310, 16 Nov. 1630; A¹ 50ii, fos. 9 and 11, 2 Feb. 1639.

[122] *Code Michau*, p. 286, arts. 232, 233: the *secours* was to be a further loan, whether for replacement clothing, arms or other needs, to be deducted from the three-month accumulation of the pay remaining after the payment of the *prêts* to the soldiers.

[123] *Code Michau*, p. 288, art. 250.

[124] For e.g. Avenel, IV. 268, 31 Mar. 1632, specifies that 45,000 *livres* were allocated for the expenses of the *prêts*, 11,000 *livres* for the *montres* of the officers; Grillon, IV. 498, 31 July 1629, Bassompierre to Richelieu, using the distinction between 'l'argent de la montre et les prêts pour les soldats'; SHAT A¹ 28, fo. 19, 4 June 1636, de Noyers to Soissons, concerning money to pay the *montres* to the officers of his corps; A¹ 66, fo. 270, 13 Nov. 1641, order to pay *prêts* to troops at ten- (rather than nine-) day intervals; additional funds for the officers to be despatched separately; A¹ 63, fo. 540, 11 Mar. 1641, *intendant* Grémonville to make provision to pay one month of *montre* to the officers and one month of *prêts* to the soldiers of the regiment of Castelnau.

The administrative context

the Spanish army in Monferrato to sustain itself for eight months solely on the issue of bread rations, but in terms which imply that this would not be possible in the French army.[125] If the basic needs of the soldiers were attended to, then the officers could be left to fend for themselves with fewer ill-effects. The ministers would simply decide to prioritize the payment of the soldiers, ordering the commanding officers to pay out the *prêts* as regularly and fully as possible, but to ignore the *montres*. In north Italy during 1630, a campaign theatre enjoying the highest priority in the allocation of funding and resources, Montmorency wrote that he had not been provided with enough money both to pay the *monstre des officiers* and to continue the fortification-work at Pinerolo. Richelieu's emphatic response was that the money should be spent on the fortifications. The officers would be paid from the next *voiture*, which would probably arrive a month or six weeks later.[126] Obviously such delays in meeting the officers' salaries, even if this was in order to concentrate the available resources on the ordinary soldiers, were likely to generate ill-feeling. The frequency of petitions and letters concerning arrears of pay indicate that this was a major problem for the officers. An order of July 1640 to Le Clerc, *Trésorier général de l'extraordinaire des guerres*, to pay officers' salaries which were outstanding from 1638, followed by a similar letter concerning monies owing from 1637, provides evidence of the widespread accumulation of arrears.[127] In 1640 the maréchaux Chaulnes and Châtillon despatched a graphic plea from the camp before Arras, stressing that the failure to honour the financial obligations of the winter quarter payments, and the arrears in the payment of *montres*, had led to the point where 'nous vous pouvons asseurer qu'il y a nombre d'officiers d'infanterie qui sont contrainct de vivre du pain de munition comme de simples soldats'.[128] Concern that officers had not been paid their salaries and the impact of mounting arrears, was widespead.[129] Cases of officers being forced to borrow money from each other were reported, and at least

---

[125] Avenel, III. 465, 15 Nov. 1629. In fact it seems likely, given the complaints about their depredations by Charles de Gonzague, duc de Nevers and chief claimant to Mantua and Monferrato, that the Spanish troops occupying Monferrato were supplementing this bread ration with other, locally requisitioned, supplies: AAE, CP Mantoue 3, fo. 428, 2 Oct 1630, Nevers to Père Joseph.

[126] Avenel, III. 699, 15 June 1630; SHAT A¹ 27, fos. 442, 452, 30 May 1636, Nicolas de l'Hospital, maréchal de Vitry and governor of Provence, seized the wages of the officers with his army-corps in order to pay for clothing for the troops; A¹ 60, fo. 125, 5 Aug. 1640, money provided to pay only the *prêts* of the regiment of Guébriant, stationed at Ardres; A¹ 68, fo. 39, 9 Jan 1642, de Noyers to Henri de Saulx-Tavannes, informing him that insufficient money has been sent to pay the officers of the regiment of Motte-Houdancourt.

[127] SHAT A¹ 59, fos. 607, 608, 4 July 1640. The situation for officers in garrisons was even worse, cf. A¹ 65, fo. 27, 7 June 1641, order to *intendant* Bellejamme to pay arrears of salary to lieutenant at the garrison of Abbeville accumulated since 1636; A¹ 60, fo. 405, 13 Sept. 1640: order to the inhabitants of Queyras requiring them to pay arrears owed to the governor since 1630!

[128] AAE MD 1679, fo. 118, 4 July 1640.

[129] BN Ms.fr. 6647, fo. 231, 28 Nov. 1636, de Noyers to La Valette; AAE MD 845, fo. 183bis, 24 Aug. 1642, abbé de Médavy to Richelieu, concerning the likely disintegration of six regiments bound for Roussillon unless the captains receive money owed them from the winter quarter; SHAT A¹ 50ii, fo. 286, 25 Feb. 1639, order to pay 7,000 *livres* specifically to meet the arrears of salaries of the

The French rejection of entrepreneurship

one certified case of a captain being reduced to bankruptcy was cited by the maréchal de Châtillon in 1642.[130] For the high command, of course, the concern was particularly immediate, as it was they who most frequently provided the additional credit to keep their subordinate officers in service despite the arrears of salaries.[131] Prudently or not, the crown regarded the payment of its officers, the vast majority of whom positively wished to serve with the armies, as a line of limited resistance that could be exploited with far fewer ill consequences than the non-payment of the troops. In 1642 the crown carried this view to a logical extension by cutting the pay of the officers attached to the *état major* of the regiments by 50 per cent, though this was probably of notional importance when the salaries of all officers was so frequently delayed or paid only in part.[132]

The willingness to overlook, delay or make inadequate provision for the officers' salaries might have been less resented, as one or two of the earlier cited examples suggest, if it had been a direct consequence of the crown's concern to honour its commitment to meet the soldiers' *prêts*. But here again the system operated against the interests of the officers. In theory the *prêts* were paid to the troops by the regimental *payeur*, who would have the necessary money in hand to pay these 'sans discontinuation'. In practice, the distribution of the *prêts* was the responsibility of the individual unit commander. The *commissaire* would carry out a *revue* of the unit, certify the number of effectives and draw up his *roolle* as the basis of subsequent payment. After the arrival of the *voiture* from the *épargne*, a lump sum would be given to the commanding officer both to pay his subordinate officers their *montres* and the troops their *prêts*.[133] If the *voiture* arrived on time

---

officers of the regiment of Aiguebonne, so that they will no longer have a pretext for failing to carry out their duties.

[130] Châtillon to de Noyers, concerning captain Buson of Plessis-Praslin's cavalry regiment; the concern about Buson was less his bankruptcy, rather that he had tried to salvage his situation by absconding with money provided for additional recruitment to bring his company up to strength: AAE MD 1680, fo. 53, 3 May 1641. For an example of captains lending each other money to compensate for the inadequacy of the crown's provision, and the subsequent problems that this has caused, AAE MD 1680, fo. 193, 9 June 1641, report on the state of the regiment of Castelnau. Avenel, *Richelieu*, III. 70–4, has some perceptive comments about officer indebtedness and the threat of bankruptcy.

[131] This issue of the financial contributions of the *grands* to the war-effort is discussed in more detail in chapter 9, pp. 499–500; however, the extent of the commitment of funds and credit can be gauged from sums ranging from 100,000 *livres* raised on Condé's credit in Oct 1641 to support the operation in Catalonia – a sum which Condé was at pains to point out represented a small fraction of his financial commitment to the costs of the army – AAE MD 1633, fo. 504, 31 Oct. 1641 – to 10,000 *livres* of credit provided by Turenne as a junior *maréchal de camp* with the army of Italy in 1640: SHAT A^1 58, 30 Apr. 1640.

[132] SHAT A^1 70, fos. 229, 245, 7 Oct., 12 Oct. 1642, *ordonnance* ordering this cut, and arrangements for its implementation.

[133] There were occasional exceptions to this practice; at the siege of La Rochelle it was reported that troops were paid directly by the administration: Chevallier, *Louis XIII*, p. 332. In 1636, Richelieu considered the possibility of paying the *prêts* directly to the troops: Avenel, v. 547, 16 Aug. 1636; however, the practical advantages of holding the officers responsible for the payment of their troops inevitably prevailed.

The administrative context

and with sufficient funds to pay the troops in advance, the *mestres de camp* and captains would have found the system acceptable. Certainly they would not have permitted themselves to suffer financial loss merely to ensure that their troops received full pay.[134] But in fact the *voitures* were almost always substantially in arrears, and usually contained less than was required to make anything approaching a full payment to the army.

As early as 1627 Richelieu had made explicit the principle that even when the money was available the soldiers' pay should not be met in full, as this encouraged desertion and disorder.[135] The government and its administrators wished to steer a course between provision that was so inadequate as to generate mass desertion and the collapse of armies, and the concern that soldiers who were paid all that they were owed would feel no constraint to remain in service. There was of course little risk that this latter situation would arise: the practice of assigning army expenses on taxes whose yield would prove inadequate or impossible to collect ensured that even notional 'full payment' would result in the delayed arrival of a percentage of the allocations.[136] Moreover, there was never any serious suggestion that a full number of *montres* would be paid to an army in the course of a year. When it became increasingly obvious that some provision had to be made either to maintain units over the winter months or to allow the unit commanders to recruit up to effective strength in the spring, this was funded via the different and more flexible system of *traités* for the *quartier d'hiver*. The first *montre* of the campaign could be paid relatively late, and the crown took the view that the payment of full *montres* in the latter part of the campaign was simply a licence for fraud; it was also unnecessary, given the tendency of the army-corps to lose energy and momentum by the late summer, especially if an initial objective had already been gained.[137]

---

[134] Cases certainly exist where relatively regular payments allowed the unit commanders to withhold money from their troops to cover their own 'expenses': Caron (ed.), *Le Tellier*, p. 159, 11 Jan. 1642, Le Tellier reported to Mazarin and de Noyers that the officers of the army of Italy were withholding pay from their men; SHAT A^1 61, fo. 228, 22 Nov. 1640, de Noyers acknowledged the report of *intendant* Bragelongne concerning the frauds perpetrated by the *mestres de camp* in making payment to their troops.

[135] Grillon, II. 154, 23 Apr. 1627.

[136] See, for example, the complaints of Michel Particelli, sieur d'Hémery, concerning the proposal to make up part of the total payment to the army of Italy in 1636 from an assignation of 480,000 *livres*, which will certainly arrive later than the projected date, and will inevitably yield less than the stipulated sum for an army which has increased in size since the financial projection: AAE CP Savoie, 24, fos. 370, 385, 6 May 1636.

[137] Taking an example of an army which enjoyed a high priority in the crown's funding – the corps of Châtillon and Chaulnes engaged at the siege of Arras in 1640 – the first *montre* was not paid until the end of June, and in circumstances where complaints were still rife amongst the officers about the non-payment of monies outstanding from the last instalment of the winter quarter/recruitment allowance: AAE MD 1679, fo. 114, 30 June 1640, Châtillon to de Noyers. The second *montre* of the campaign was being prepared in mid-September for despatch to the army: 1679, fo. 263, 17 Sept., Châtillon to de Noyers. A discussion surrounding the disbandment of the regiment of Noailles in early November suggests that a third *montre* may have been paid to the army, though this could

The French rejection of entrepreneurship

While the crown and its ministers could take a minimalist view of the number of *montres* required to keep a campaign army in being, the officers in the field had less flexibility. The highest priority was ensuring that the bread ration was distributed without interruption – the failure of this basic supply would have the most direct effect upon the effective strength of the army. In theory the costs of the *pain de munition* were met directly by the crown through large-scale contracts with the suppliers, the *munitionnaires*. Far more correspondence between the field commanders and the ministers was concerned with the threat or reality of the breakdown of *munitionnaires'* contracts and the supply of bread than with the inadequacy or delay of financial provision. However, the soldiers could not be expected to subsist indefinitely on a poor-quality ration of bread, and if the army was to be maintained, the *prêts* would have to be provided. Thus the officers found themselves caught between a crown policy towards *montres* which saw these as flexible and almost discretionary, and their soldiers, whose demand for basic, regular, payment to allow them to feed themselves, was far less flexible. Innumerable letters make it clear that the consequence of these delays, inadequacies and the crown's attitude to the distribution of pay was to force the unit officers into the role of creditors to their own soldiers, providing them with the basic *prêts* when the *montres* failed to appear, or were inadequate for the full needs of the army.[138] The alternative, equally common, was for the officers to purchase the provisions needed by the soldiers on their own credit, and to distribute these in kind.[139]

Placed in this situation, the unit commanders had an unenviable choice. If they did not advance the money to pay for the immediate subsistence of the troops, large-scale desertion would follow. The commander would gain a bad reputation for failing to control and retain his troops, although this would be largely irrelevant, since his unit would almost certainly have fallen to a strength where it was no longer deemed capable of effective service. The alternative would be to pay the *prêts* to his troops – and quite possibly part of the *montres* to his subordinate officers – until financial provision from the crown finally arrived. The danger of

---

equally refer to the delayed payment of the second *montre*: 1679, fo. 307, 9 Nov. 1640, Châtillon to de Noyers.

[138] See, for example, SHAT A¹ 31, fo. 187, 29 Dec. 1636, officers of the regiment of Maugiron have been forced to provide 15,000 *livres* for the *prêts* of their soldiers (and fo. 106, 19 Dec., similar for officers of the regiment of Saint-André); A¹ 30, fo. 1, 1 Oct. 1636, officers of regiments of La Tour and Vaillac have been paying cash advances to their soldiers throughout the present year; AAE CP Lorraine 31, fo. 304, du Hallier to de Noyers, informing him that the regiment of Saint-Estienne is the one unit in 'bon estat' in the garrison at Nancy, but only because the captains advance the *prêts* to the soldiers each week; A¹ 64, fo. 48, 21 Mar. 1641, order to pay the accumulated debts of the captains and *mestre de camp* of the regiment of Lorraine.

[139] SHAT A¹ 36 fo. 229, 18 May 1637, captains of regiment of Brézé have been purchasing subsistence for their companies; A¹ 51, fo. 462, 15 Apr. 1639, officers of regiments in Alsace, who have advanced money to provide their soldiers with *pain de munition*; A¹ 69, fo. 11, 3 Apr. 1642, compensation to be paid to a captain of the regiment of Saulx for expenses incurred in supplying his company while in garrison.

The administrative context

this was that the captain or the *mestre de camp* would fall into debt himself, with no guarantee the reimbursement would be timely or complete. In this respect another article of the *Code Michau* was of significance, stipulating 'Que l'argent presté par les capitaines, officiers ou autres aux soldats, ne pourra estre par eux repris ni répeté dans les prests, ainsi seulement dans les monstres [i.e. the notional residue of the soldiers pay after the *prêts* had been allowed], à cause que cela les empêcheroit de vivre jusques a l'autre prest.'[140] If this were to be rigorously enforced, then the chances that the officers would recover their loans from the small residue not required for future *prêts* would be small. The supervisorial duty of the *intendants* and the *commissaires pour les montres* suggest that this stipulation may well have been applied in practice.[141]

The problem of the deployment of the officers' credit lies at the heart of the military system of the *Ancien Régime*. The purchase and subsequent exercise of a military command under such circumstances could prove literally ruinous. An order in January 1640 to François Bochart, sieur de Champigny, *intendant* of Provence, to repay 24,000 *livres* owed to the sieur d'Evennes, captain of the *gardes françaises*, from provincial revenues provides an indication of the potential scale of indebtedness amongst relatively junior officers.[142] And while these specific, large, sums advanced by individuals have generated correspondence in the archives and implied an acceptance by the crown that the debts existed even if the mechanisms for their repayment seem haphazard, many other groups of unit officers found themselves drawn into less well-defined relationships as creditors to the king. A group of artillery officers in Lorraine during the winter quarter of 1634–5 presented a petition through the duc de Rohan, explaining that they had been forced to pay far greater sums to ensure the subsistence of the artillery train than had been provided for them from the funds that arrived in November, 'ce que les met en desespoir[,] je masseure que Sa Mate y aura esgard'.[143]

---

[140] *Code Michau*, p. 287, art. 244.

[141] The *intendant* René Voyer d'Argenson wrote to Chancellor Séguier in August 1636, concerning the officers' expectations that they will be repaid the money for *prêts* which they have advanced to their men, and the measures to evade these demands on the *montre* that is about to arrive: BN Ms.fr. 17372, fo. 186, 25 Aug.; Caron (ed.), *Le Tellier*, p. 4, 11 Sept. 1640, instructions from *surintendant* Bullion to Le Tellier which clearly imply that he is to oversee the distribution of the *montres* and to ensure that priority is given to the provision of the *prêts*.

[142] SHAT A¹ 57, fo. 74, 10 Jan. 1640; see also A¹ 60, fo. 221, 22 Aug. 1640, Guillaume Frémin, *intendant* of the Limousin to find means to repay 10,000 *livres* owed to Léon d'Aubusson, comte de La Feuillade for the upkeep of his regiment; A¹ 69, fo. 542, 28 June 1642, Louis-Emmanuel de Valois, comte d'Alais and governor of Provence was to provide means for the reimbursement of the captains of the regiment of Mazarin, who had to meet the full subsistence expenses of the march across Provence.

[143] AAE CP Lorraine 15, fo. 371, 6 Dec. 1640, Rohan to *surintendant* Claude Bouthillier; SHAT A¹ 58, fo. 4, 1 Mar. 1640, de Noyers to Rigault, naval captain (presumably a *fidèle* of Richelieu's on commission): order to investigate the requests for reimbursement of 'large sums' of money which the officers of the garrison of Metz claimed to have advanced for the upkeep of their troops. The obvious means of seeking reimbursement – through the Epernon family as governors of Metz – having presumably been disrupted by the death, exile or disgrace of the members of the family;

The French rejection of entrepreneurship

The crown's sanctions against its officers

In every period of large-scale military effort by the French crown during the seventeenth century, expenses ran far beyond the crown's revenues and extraordinary resources. Beyond the 'supportable' levels of inadequate pay and supply inflicted upon the soldiers, who, even in periods of peace and retrenchment, were extremely unlikely to receive their statutory wages, this shortfall was borne by the unit commanders.[144] The extent to which the unit officers suffered in consequence of advancing their own funds depended upon the location of their units. The worst victims were inevitably those unfortunate enough to find themselves in a permanent garrison within the frontiers of France, at the lowest point on the crown's scale of financial priorities. The letter sent by the governor of Calais, Louis de Béthune, comte de Charost, to de Noyers in 1640, which carefully itemized the 144,000 *livres* that he had advanced on his own credit to the upkeep of the garrison from 1637 up to the end of 1639, provides a graphic case of such indebtedness.[145] However, a petition from La Rivière for reimbursement of 50,000 *livres* advanced as lieutenant of Calais and governor of Fort Nieulay, or the request for repayment of 30,000 *livres* owed to La Chapelle for expenses incurred as governor of Charleville, indicate that heavy debts were easily built up in this role.[146] Yet even in the field armies it was possible in almost all cases for the ministry to assume that pressure could be placed on the officers to provide support for the expenses of their units.

It was apparently simple to apply this pressure; if the unit commander was not prepared to act personally to maintain his unit in circumstances where central funding was delayed or inadequate, he would rapidly find that he had lost his military command. In some cases, particularly if supply difficulties were compounded by a military defeat or a severe setback, the unit might disperse completely. More frequently, the unit suffered the type of heavy loss, especially through desertion, which reduced a company to a few dozen soldiers. At this point the administration would usually intervene; the very weak companies would appear on the muster rolls, probably still padded above their actual strength, and the decision would be taken to disband the unit altogether or, more frequently, to conduct a *réformation* which would incorporate the soldiers into other companies while dismissing the officers. Had the *mestres de camp* and the captains actually

---

AAE CP Savoie 30, fo. 533, 19 June 1640, *mestre de camp*, François de Havart-Senantes, marquis de Ruffiers, to Chavigny, recording advances of 1,000 *écus* to meet the cost of maintaining his regiment which he was concerned would not be repaid.

[144] Indeed in the 1660s when a peacetime 'standing' army was created on the basis of much more reliable financial provision, the wages of ordinary soldiers were subject to a general reduction, from 6 to 5 *sols* per day: Corvisier, *Louvois*, pp. 108–9.

[145] AAE MD 1679, fo. 323, [1640].

[146] AAE MD 815, fo. 281, 30 Sept. 1635, Bouthillier to Richelieu, discussing La Rivière's petition, and suggesting that the outstanding sum is nearer to 40,000 *livres*; SHAT A¹ 65, fo. 343, 9 Aug. 1641.

The administrative context

been crown employees, then the disintegration of their units might have been accepted more lightly. The crown, having once recognized their 'preeminent suitability' for military service, would be prepared to do so again, overlooking a setback which had left them with a ruined unit, since this was the fault of central provisioning not of their failings as officers. The reality, as has already been made plain, was very different. There was a strong possibility that the commander had paid all, or part, of the initial costs of recruiting his unit, and he may have found himself obliged to invest in its subsequent maintenance before it had finally dropped below acceptable effective strength. All of this would be irrelevant if the company was disbanded. In such circumstances the unit commander could look to no compensation from the crown for past service, still less for any recognition of financial commitments that he might have made to the setting up or maintenance of his company or regiment. In some cases companies and regiments were explicitly disbanded as a disciplinary penalty, and both the ceremony and the formal instruction for the *licenciement* made the crown's dissatisfaction entirely plain.[147] In most cases the order for disbandment was accompanied by a formulaic satisfaction with the service rendered, yet left the inevitable impression that disbandment was, in an unspecific sense, a disgrace, and certainly marked the end of a military career. Bussy-Rabutin's status and influence did not prevent his regiment of cavalry being reformed down to four companies in 1640. He left this rump under the command of his son, retired from military service for three years, and took up arms again only in 1643 when he bought the office of lieutenant in the company of *chevaux-légers* of Condé for 12,000 *écus*.[148] Most officers, faced with the disbandment of their unit, and the polite but uncompromising order to return to their homes, would not make a subsequent venture into military command. If the captain did wish to re-enter service it was most unlikely that the crown would be prepared to meet any of the costs involved in carrying out a subsequent recruitment.[149]

The crown and its ministers were well aware that in the threat of disbandment and dismissal they had a considerable weapon which could be used to force the

---

[147] SHAT A¹ 31, fos. 79, 13 Dec.1636, company of captain Culley to be disbanded with ignominy for illegal requisitioning of horses; A¹ 46, fo. 216, 29 May 1638, order for the public disbandment of the regt of Chanceaux; Aubery, *Richelieu*, II. 383, 23 Nov. 1639, order for the exemplary disbandment of three companies of *chevaux légers* for their cowardice at Thionville; A¹ 68, fo. 668, 31 Mar. 1642, public disbandment of the company of *carabins* of La Noue for having committed substantial disorders.

[148] Bussy-Rabutin, *Mémoires*, I. 111; see also SHAT A¹ 58, fo. 72, 7 Mar. 1640, *réformation* of the regiment of Léonor de Rabutin, sieur de Bussy, and transfer of remaining troops to his son, Roger.

[149] There are certainly cases where the commander was permitted to reconstitute his company or regiment after it has been reformed, but few of these make any mention of funding to cover the costs of this levy of new troops: SHAT A¹ 59, fo. 341, 12 June 1640, permission for the reestablishment of the regiment of Chalançay; A¹ 63, fo. 334, 8 Feb. 1641, company of *chevaux légers* of Castelet is to be reestablished, and is to be incorporated into the regiment of Louis de Baschi, marquis d'Aubais.

The French rejection of entrepreneurship

captains and *mestres de camp* to make a greater commitment to the maintenance of their units. Even as Bullion and Richelieu were discussing the plans for the great expansion of the army for the campaign of 1635, the *surintendant* emphasized the salutary effect on the captains of threatening them with dismissal if they failed to keep their companies at full strength.[150] There is no doubt that the crown was prepared to use the threat of disbandment to persuade its officers both to pay advances to keep their troops in service and to recruit more soldiers to replace losses which threatened to render the units too weak for service.[151] The threat of *réformation* was negotiable, moreover; orders for the disbandment of particular units might be rescinded, either through the deployment of powerful influence or through undertaking to carry out the recruitment or reorganization deemed necessary to ensure that the unit could serve.[152] In late 1634 the duc de Rohan, commanding an army being assembled in Lorraine, was playing a *double jeu* with his unit commanders. In a *mémoire* to the king he passed on the complaints of his captains about the threat to disband all companies whose effective strength fell below fifty-five men: 'pource que par ceste voye leurs honneurs et leurs fortunes sont entre les mains de 35 ou 40 soldats impatiens qui peuvent s'en aller a la vieille d'une monstre'. At the same time Rohan stressed how salutary this threat was proving: 'la crainte qu'ils ont de perdre leurs compagnies les reveillent et travaillent a faire des recreues'.[153] The shadow of disbandment could be anticipated in letters from captains and *mestres de camp* well aware of the weakness of their units and their potential vulnerability, but concerned to excuse this on grounds of protracted service, limited opportunities to maintain unit strength or promises to act rapidly and decisively to render the unit effective in the near future.[154]

---

[150] AAE MD 811, fo. 120, 7 Nov. 1634, Bullion to Richelieu.
[151] SHAT A¹ 39, fo. 166, 5 Oct. 1637, du Hallier to disband all companies whose captains have failed to keep them at effective strength; A¹ 51, fo. 379, 7 Apr. 1639, *licenciement* of regiment of Manicamp, which has been inadequately maintained and is no longer in a state to serve; A¹ 57, fo. 398, 15 Feb. 1639, Charles de Châtillon, marquis d'Andelot, to dismiss four captains of his regiment and to disband their companies for having failed to bring these units up to 'bon estat'; A¹ 58, fo. 72, 7 Mar. 1640, Léonor de Rabutin to intervene to bring his son's regiment of cavalry up to an acceptable state, or it will be disbanded; A¹ 68, fo. 590, 20 Mar. 1642, *ordonnance*, threatening the disbandment of all units under an – unspecified – acceptable strength; A¹ 70, fo. 479, 7 Dec. 1642, captains of the regiment of Navarre must accept the agreement to strengthen their companies or face disbandment.
[152] SHAT A¹ 57, fo. 60, 6 Jan. 1640, a regiment is to be reprieved from disbandment if the *mestre de camp* acts with all speed to reestablish it at twenty companies; A¹ 57, fo. 188, 22 Jan. 1640, revocation of an order for disbandment of a company of *chevaux légers*; A¹ 61, fo. 370, 12 Dec. 1641, retracts order for disbandment of *gendarme* company; A¹ 68, fo. 642, 26 Mar. 1642, cavalry regiment of Jacques Ferron, seigneur de La Ferronnaye, to be recruited back to full strength instead of being disbanded as originally stipulated.
[153] AAE CP Lorraine 15, fo. 369, 6 Dec. 1634, Rohan to Louis XIII.
[154] See, for example, the letter from the *mestre de camp*, La Clavière, written to Richelieu, and giving detailed reasons for a company strength of around fifty men in terms of the length of the previous campaign, the inadequacy of financial provision during the *quartier d'hiver* and the commitment of

The administrative context

Behind all of these negotiations surrounding the survival or disbandment of particular units was the crown and its ministers' calculation that there were always aspiring officers prepared to contribute to the costs of raising entirely new companies able to replace those subject to *réformation*. In consequence, apart from the *régiments* and *compagnies entretenues*, units in the army were not envisaged as more than temporary creations. The crown accepted a high turnover of units because it appeared cheaper and more efficient to encourage new petitioners to come forward prepared to organize and – quite possibly – fund the levy of their troops, rather than trying to salvage the existing units.[155]

Consequences for the crown's war-effort

This tendency to favour the creation of new units rather than the preservation of old imposed a heavy price on the effectiveness of French armies. In circumstances where military success depended so much upon the numbers of experienced veteran troops in an army, the crown appeared to be limiting its experienced soldiers to a small core of *entretenus* units and accepting that a very high percentage of a given army-corps would be made up of newly enlisted troops, commanded by inexperienced officers. The massive wastage rates and military ineffectiveness of the campaigns of 1635 and 1636 led to the realization that this was unsatisfactory from a military point of view, even if it minimized the administrative and financial burden on the crown. However flawed in practice, the introduction of the *subsistances* tax from 1637 can be seen as marking the crown's decision that more adequate provision had to be made for the maintenance of the army over the winter quarter. This was followed by a discernable shift in policy towards sustaining existing units, above all through the increasingly elaborate attempts to negotiate recruitment *traités* aimed at bringing units back up to acceptable strength before the beginning of the next campaign.

Yet this change of approach appears to have had a limited impact on a system which, in practice, continued to operate on the assumption that there would be a very high level of wastage amongst ordinary units.[156] Large numbers of units

---

the captains' own credit to keeping their troops fed and equipped: AAE MD 1680, fo. 201, 9 June 1641. A similar, lengthy, letter from a *mestre de camp* in the army of Italy, the sr de Senantes, stresses the exemplary military service of his unit and his own wounding in royal service at the relief of Casale – which prevented him writing earlier to de Noyers – to challenge the imputation that his regiment has fallen below effective strength through his own negligence: AAE CP Savoie 30, fo. 428, 16 May 1640.

[155] On occasions this is made quite explicit: SHAT A^1 57, fo. 177, 22 Jan. 1640, letter to *mestre de camp* Mignoux, ordering him to enforce the disbandment of the company of captain Marché in his regiment; the company will be replaced by one of *nouvelle levée*, commanded by sieur Guy; A^1 57, fo. 270, 27 Mar. 1640, Grémonville is to investigate complaints that captains of *nouvelle levée*, arriving with established regiments, are being held responsible for the debts and the exactions of their predecessors and their companies, now disbanded.

[156] Regardless of accuracy in specific cases, the mass of *licenciements* and new creations described in

The French rejection of entrepreneurship

continued to be disbanded at the end of each campaign, while the threat of *réformation* still served as a means to try to compel officers to use their own resources to maintain their units and replace troops up to an effective strength.[157] Indeed, in 1642 this threat was supplemented by a new and impractical proposal that captains whose companies were below strength should be subjected to a 50 per cent reduction in salary.[158] In theory, this ought to have mitigated one of the besetting problems of under-strength units, the disproportionate costs of a far too numerous officer-corps. In practice, the officers' salaries were not paid with sufficient regularity for this to have an obviously punitive effect, and, more importantly, given the extent to which the captains deployed their own resources to maintain their units, a further reduction in their income could only worsen the problem of sustaining their soldiers in periods of inadequate central provision.

One part of the price paid by the crown for a system which assumed and exploited a high level of wastage amongst its regiments and companies was the perpetuation of army-corps in which a substantial proportion of the serving soldiers – and officers – were wholly inexperienced at the beginning of a campaign. This placed French armies at a considerable disadvantage when faced by those Habsburg and Bavarian forces which comprised a high proportion of long-serving veterans.[159] A less tangible price was paid by the crown in terms of the attitudes within the officer-corps that this system generated. In the immediate interest of funding armies which were of a size beyond the direct financial resources of the crown, the administration was placing excessive demands upon the officers and granting them nothing in return. The captain would be reluctant to see a large part of the unit which he had recruited desert or disband for lack of

---

V. Belhomme, *L'histoire de l'infanterie en France* (5 vols.; Paris, 1893–1902), I. 360–93, or in Susane, *Histoire de l'ancienne infanterie française*, VIII. 73–166, give an impression of the scale on which the French army was regenerated through newly raised units at the beginning of each campaign. This could be compared with the situation in the Empire, where Fritz Redlich suggests that most regiments lasted from two to five years during the Thirty Years War, and very few less than two years: *Military Enterpriser*, I. 226; see also Kroener, 'Soldat oder Soldateska?', on the growing number of long-serving veteran-based regiments operating in the Empire.

[157] For examples of large-scale disbandment at the end of Richelieu's ministry, see, for example, SHAT A¹ 66, fo. 103, 4 Oct. 1641, Philippe de La Motte-Houdancourt to supervise the disbandment of five regiments, including Polignac and Lecques; A¹ 70, fo. 313, 1 Nov. 1642, disbandment of regiment of Bellefonds; fo. 316, 1 Nov., lengthy *état* of individual companies from numerous regiments to be disbanded; fo. 443, 24 Nov, fo. 461, 28 Nov. 1641, orders relating to disbandment of companies of *chevaux légers*. For the threat of *réformation*, see A¹ 68, fo. 590, 20 Mar. 1642, *ordonnance* threatening disbandment for all units below effective strength; A¹ 69, fo. 647, 12 July 1642, *ordonnance* for the disbandment of companies of less than thirty soldiers in the army of Italy; A¹ 70, fo. 317, 1 Nov. 1642, instruction to Henri de Lorraine, comte d'Harcourt, Gramont and du Hallier, concerning the *réformation* of companies that are too weak, and the incorporation of troops into other regiments.

[158] SHAT A¹ 70, fo. 144, 27 Aug. 1642; this would bring delinquent captains into line with the officers of the *état major*, who were in theory to be subjected to a 50 per cent cut in salaries across the board.

[159] Kroener, 'Soldat oder Soldateska?', p. 118: by 1643 over 50 per cent of the troops in the Bavarian army had military experience extending over more than one campaign and by 1648 this was the case with over two-thirds of the troops.

The administrative context

pay and food, and would probably feel constrained to make the advances to his soldiers, if only to safeguard his initial 'investment' in raising the unit. This subsequent financial commitment by the officers to their units was not in general motivated by any immediate concern with the military effectiveness of the company or regiment, but rather with the crown's typical response to units which fell below acceptable strength. The additional funds were not a recognizable 'investment'; they could not enhance the value of the company, for this had no accepted market value – above all because the survival of an ordinary unit was so uncertain.[160] Such officers were not elements in an entrepreneurial army. They were under no illusion that their financial efforts would confer any recognized status as proprietors of their units, or that they could do anything to turn these offices into a long-term property in the way that their civil counterparts had accomplished in the judicial and financial administration.

In consequence, while the officers sought to ensure that their units appeared on the muster rolls at an acceptable strength which avoided the possibility of *réformation*, they had no financial interest in doing more than the absolute minimum to meet this requirement. Certainly they had no incentive, as did their genuinely entrepreneurial counterparts, to invest in the military effectiveness of their units. Unlike the colonel-enterpriser of the armies operating in the Empire, the French officer had no financial stake in the military success of the army measured in terms of controlling territory, excluding enemy forces and exacting contributions. What the French *mestre de camp* or captain who invested in building up the military effectiveness and quality of their units faced instead was the prospect of substantial personal loss without compensation if, during or at the end of the campaign, the crown's administrators or the high command became concerned at excessive numbers of under-strength units and too many expensive officers. Disbandment made it clear how uncertain the prospect of a lengthy military career would prove, and how little material benefit could be salvaged from a period of service. If the requirement of maintaining the unit at an acceptable strength could be met by collusion with the *commissaire* carrying out the *revues*, by overt fraudulence in borrowing troops or peasant 'passe-volants' to pad out the muster of the unit, or by recruiting additional soldiers at the last possible moment and as cheaply as possible to make good the losses from the ranks, then the unit commander would probably not hesitate to pursue such methods. It is impossible to arrive at an accurate figure for this endemic fraud, but André Corvisier's

---

[160] Cf. Turenne's reluctance to raise two additional *compagnies d'augmentation* for his regiment, on the grounds that this would prove expensive, and apart from providing him with the opportunity to favour some of his clients, would offer no enhancement of the value of the regiment: Turenne, *Lettres*, p. 386, 29 Dec. 1643. A reluctance to raise these *compagnies d'augmentation* was widespread amongst *mestres de camp* who suspected that the costs of this could not be passed on to the aspiring captains.

The French rejection of entrepreneurship

proposal that 20 per cent of the official troops strength should be discounted is certainly a conservative estimate.[161]

Muster fraud gave the officers the potential means to avoid paying from their own resources to maintain the numbers or the quality of their units, or at least to reduce this amount to the bare minimum. If the *commissaire* was prepared to collude in the presentation of a company as being in *bon état* when 50 per cent of its soldiers were under fifteen, or where a sudden influx of new recruits from the local peasantry could swell the ranks up to 'effective' strength for the period of the *montre*, then the captain would look upon this as a satisfactory means to avoid the risk of losing his unit, without having to pay heavily for its maintenance. Muster-fraud could also be used as a means to embezzle money paid by the government for non-existent 'paper' soldiers and officers. The problem, of course, was that the money reaching the armies was rarely frequent or generous enough to make systematic embezzlement from this source an effective means to recover the resources that the captains or *mestres de camp* had been obliged to commit to their units. The shortfalls and delays in payments also handicapped the few royal initiatives to raise the number of soldiers in individual units by offering a financial bonus to officers who could maintain their companies at near to full strength. The offer, current in the early 1630s, of a 10 per cent bonus to captains who maintained their units at over 90 per cent strength, was quite unrealistic from the captains' viewpoint.[162] Enormous expense would be involved in keeping the unit at nearly full strength, as opposed to allowing it to fall to a (barely) acceptable forty to fifty soldiers. Personal funds would have to be committed to the careful nurturing of the existing soldiers, and then to regular recruitment of replacements to fill gaps in the ranks. Even if the 10 per cent bonus had been paid regularly and in full, it is unlikely that this would do much to reduce the heavy personal outlay involved in trying to sustain units at near full strength. As the bonus would be subject to the same delays, shortfalls and economies as the ordinary pay of the officers, it would have been extremely imprudent to have taken steps to render a company or regiment complete on anything other than grounds of loyalty to the crown or its ministers.[163]

If the ordinary payments to the army offered limited opportunities to officers anxious to claw back some of their own financial commitments, a far more promising possibility was presented by the money that the crown was prepared to pay to permit unit commanders to engage in additional recruitment. It is no small irony that the funds for additional levies stood at the centre of the corrupt

---

[161] Corvisier, *Louvois*, pp. 344–5.

[162] AAE MD 808, fo. 89, 12 Oct. 1633; in late 1634 this had been formalized as maintaining an infantry company with over seventy effectives: AAE CP Lorraine 15, fo. 369, 6 Dec. 1634, Rohan to Louis XIII.

[163] Such proposals for bonus payments largely disappear in later correspondence, either because it was quite evident that the crown's resources were not adequate to their payment, or because they had no impact on the officers in persuading them to raise the number of soldiers in their units.

The administrative context

practices of the army officers. It has been proposed that in the years immediately after 1635 the crown had developed and exploited a system which drew upon the officers' own resources precisely through the working assumption that the great majority of units were temporary creations and were not expected to last more than one or two campaigns. However, as the military consequences of this system became disastrously clear, so the crown and its ministers attempted expedients aimed at keeping a reasonable proportion of the units *sur pied* from one campaign to the next. It was recognized that companies and regiments, even if run down to a skeleton strength during the winter quarter, would still provide a better base for new recruitment at the beginning of the spring than would the establishment of completely new units. In the majority of cases these units would still not be expected to survive a large number of campaigns, but a regiment composed of companies whose officers, NCOs and *haute-payes* had seen service even in one previous campaign was widely regarded as greatly superior to one which had been newly recruited.

Yet moving towards such a system, whatever its military advantages, had its price. While commanding officers may have been prepared to contribute to setting their unit *sur pied* in the first instance, they would be far less anxious to fund a second, or third, recruitment operation intended to restore the unit to full strength. If the crown wished to ensure that a significant part of the army was reconstructed from existing units at the beginning of each campaign, or equally that large-scale losses during the campaign were made good by new recruitment, it would have to pay for a large part of this operation itself. As the administrative mechanisms for raising recruits by *commissaires*, *intendants* or other specific royal or ministerial agents were rudimentary and inadequate to the scale of the task, this recruitment was in the main carried out by the officers of the units, despatched to selected recruitment grounds with sums of money given them by the *payeurs* of the army-corps.

For many of the officers this represented a unique opportunity in their relationship with the royal administration: a single, large, sum of money – in the case of a *mestre de camp* of a regiment this could amount to 10,000 or 20,000 *livres* – was placed in their hands with instructions to spend the money on recruits.[164] The temptation to appropriate all, or a significant part, of this money in order to replace previous sums committed to the cost of the regiment or the company was overwhelming. The crown had no choice but to offer these sums if this additional recruitment were to take place, yet the provision of these funds greatly enhanced the possibilities for large-scale corruption by the officers.

---

[164] SHAT A^1 52, fo. 116, 10 May 1639, 12,000 *livres* for recruits for regt of Montauzier; A^1 57, fo. 204, 23 Jan. 1640: *mestre de camp* of regt of Tavannes to receive 34,000 *livres* partly as reimbursement for subsistence provided over the winter quarter, mostly to fund the levy of new recruits; A^1 63, fo. 98, 12 Jan. 1641, payment of 12 *livres* per soldier for the replacement levy of 800 men for regt of Lesdiguières.

The French rejection of entrepreneurship

Initially, the arrangements for additional recruitment had been made on an *ad hoc* basis; the money was frequently drawn from the *deniers revenans bons* held back from units whose strength had already fallen substantially since the beginning of the campaign, and then allocated at the discretion of the high command and the administrators with the army.[165] Alternatively, specific arrangements could be made for particular units; it would, for example, be agreed with the *commissaires* or *payeurs* with the army that a particular unit should be paid at full strength although it was far weaker than this, the additional sum being intended to fund recruitment.[166] The characteristic of most of these arrangements for additional recruitment was the vagueness of the stipulations and, frequently, of the mechanisms for recruitment. If, for whatever reason, the captain proved unable to raise his additional soldiers – and the precise numbers of these were rarely specified in these informal arrangements – then it was not clear whether he would be liable to disciplinary penalties, the enforced refund of the sums advanced, or simply ordered to continue with the recruitment operation until he had satisfied the administration.[167]

Faced with the obvious weakness of the system for raising additional troops, the crown recognized that it was necessary to impose some form of legal obligation upon the officers, and from 1639 the use of recruitment *traités* became commonplace. These were documents which stipulated the number of troops to be raised, the sum paid to the *mestre de camp* or more frequently to the captains for the recruitment, and the time and place allocated to the levy. They were clearly intended as legally binding contracts, a means to replace vague and informal agreements which had been regularly broken in the past.[168] It was through this system of *traités* that the large-scale levy of troops for existing regiments was carried out. Such *traités* were unpopular with the officers forced to sign them.[169]

---

[165] SHAT A¹ 51, fo. 428, 11 Apr. 1639: 12,000 *livres* of the *deniers revenans bons* is to be used to allow the officers of the regt of La Tour to recruit this unit back up to 2,000 men.

[166] Avenel, v. 60, 18 June 1635, grant of 10 per cent made to incomplete companies to facilitate recruitment; SHAT A¹ 30, fo. 13, payment of a large first *montre* to the Touraine regt of Dumont, intended to cover the costs of recruiting up to full strength.

[167] SHAT A¹ 39, fo. 166, 5 Oct. 1637, order to du Hallier to proceed against the officers of his army who refuse to raise their units to effective strength; A¹ 31, fo. 214, 31 Dec. 1636, Bussy Rabutin's failure to raise more than 300 of a total of 1,000 additional recruits for his regiment is noted, but the letter stipulates only that he should continue the operation until the total is achieved.

[168] It seems that these *traités* were initiated not by the central administration, but by a number of agents operating with particular army-corps: SHAT A¹ 50i, fo. 126, 15 Jan. 1639, approval given to treaties drawn up by the *maréchal de camp*, Jacques d'Estampes, marquis de La Ferté-Imbault, with captains of cavalry; A¹ 50i, fo. 201, 22 Jan. 1639, *intendant* Pierre Imbert is to base the *traités* for the *mestres de camp* of the army of Italy on those drawn up by de Castelan for the officers in Languedoc; A¹ 50ii, fo. 84, 7 Feb. 1639, Imbert to 'reach an agreement' with Jacques de Cominges, seigneur de Montpezat, to set his regiment *en bon estat*, fixing a realistic sum for the additional recruits and a place for the levy.

[169] SHAT A¹ 51, fo. 83, 11 Mar. 1639, *ordonnance* to force the captains of the regt of Castelnau to accept the *traité* made by the *mestre de camp* (fo. 91bis, 11 Mar., similar for captains of regt of Cabrières); A¹ 58, fo. 54, 5 Mar. 1640, king's dissatisfaction that the *mestres de camp* Bussy-Lamet,

The administrative context

The agreements were far more inflexible, and it was considered that they made unreasonable demands in terms of the quantities of available recruits, the money required to obtain those who were available for service and the time taken to carry out the operation.[170] In numerous cases officers had to be forced to accept *traités* against the threat of dismissal.[171] The crown was certainly prepared to make occasional examples and to dismiss or imprison those officers considered to have broken their agreements.[172] In cases judged less culpable, the captain concerned could still be forced to carry out the levy again, at his own expense.[173] Yet even this combination of a more clearly defined contractual system accompanied by penalties for default seems to have had little practical impact. Without the imposition of *traités* the situation might well have been worse, but there is little evidence that the *traités* acted as a serious deterrent to the officers.[174] In early 1639 the crown was already confronted by *mestres de camp* and their captains who had broken the first of these signed and contractual agreements. De Noyers, writing in the king's name, despatched an abrasive letter to the comte de La Suze on 27 February 1639, reminding him of the 'advantageous terms' which the crown had offered him for the recruitment of his regiment up to effective strength, criticizing his failure to honour the terms of the *traité*, and emphasizing the lack of concern that he had thereby shown for the king's service.[175] But the problem was not one

---

Effiat and Saint-Aubin have refused to sign the recruitment *traités*; A^1 70, fo. 501, 10 Dec. 1642, difficulties being made about the *traités* by some captains.

[170] AAE MD 1679, fo. 269, 18 Sept. 1640, Châtillon to de Noyers, concerning the discontent of the *mestres de camp* and captains who have been expected to accept *traités*, but given no indication of the support and contacts that they are to draw upon in the designated places of recruitment; AAE CP Savoie 28, fo. 93, 1 Mar. 1639, cardinal de La Valette to Richelieu, that although the *traités* have been agreed with the officers designated to carry out additional recruitment, the money for these levies has not yet been received. Without it, La Valette is concerned that the army will not be in a state to begin the campaign by 20 April.

[171] SHAT A^1 57, fo. 17, 2 Jan. 1640, Henri de Saulx-Tavannes to compel the captains of his regt to meet the terms of their *traités* or to dismiss them; A^1 58, fo. 578, 27 Apr. 1640, officers of regt of Nettancourt threatened with dismissal for refusing to carry out levies; A^1 70, fo. 479, 7 Dec. 1642, captains of the regt of Navarre must accept the *traité* for the strengthening of their companies or face dismissal.

[172] SHAT A^1 52, fo. 56, 5 May 1639, François de Bonne et de Créqui, duc de Lesdiguières, to dismiss captains of his regiment who, despite signing a *traité*, have failed to recruit the stipulated numbers of troops; A^1 57, fo. 398, 15 Feb. 1640, François de Coligny, marquis d'Andelot, to dismiss four of the captains of his regt for having failed to honour their *traités*; A^1 66, fo. 138, 140, 10 Oct. 1641, orders to Harcourt and Le Tellier to arrest those officers of the army of Italy who have broken their *traités*, and to place them on trial for misappropriation of funds.

[173] SHAT A^1 51, fo. 220, 24 Mar. 1639, *mestre de camp*, de Genlis, criticized for the inadequacy of the recent recruitment for his regiment, and he and his captains are to carry out further recruitment; A^1 68, fo. 577, 18 Mar. 1642, captain Commarin ordered to repeat the levy of his company which he failed to carry out in accordance with the *traité*.

[174] And in 1640 the maréchaux de La Meilleraye and Châtillon argued that the imposition of the *traités* had positively hindered the assembly of their army-corps at the opening of the campaign: AAE MD 1679, fo. 48, 25 May 1640, Châtillon/Chaulnes to de Noyers.

[175] SHAT A^1 50ii, fo. 320, 27 Feb. 1639; for a similar example from a few days earlier: A^1 50ii, fo. 240, 19 Feb. 1639, La Ferté-Imbault to investigate those captains who have not fulfilled the terms of

The French rejection of entrepreneurship

of isolated, individual, captains trying to evade the terms of the contracts. As Châtillon wrote in 1641, the failure to honour the terms of the recruitment contracts was all but universal. Although the king had met his side of the agreement in full, and the captains had all received their money, designated places for recruitment and local assistance, the officers had not reciprocated: 'c'est une faute quasy generale [mais] principalement dans les troupes que vous mavez commises, dont les plus fortes [compagnies] sont bien esloignees du nombre quelles devroyent avoir'.[176]

The correspondence of Michel Le Tellier while *intendant* of the army of Italy reinforces this impression. Writing to Mazarin in September 1641, Le Tellier suggested that less than one third of the recruits stipulated in the *traités* had actually been raised during the campaign, and that the levels of fraud were so great that he and the comte d'Harcourt were inhibited from administering rigorous punishments that would fall on the great majority of officers.[177] Le Tellier's letters provide a catalogue of means by which the unit officers defrauded the crown, and makes it clear that the impunity of those who had previously broken their *traités* acted as a standing encouragement to those who might otherwise have been more scrupulous.[178] In one particularly irritable outburst Le Tellier complained that not only were the officers of the army of Italy embezzling the recruitment money, they were openly boasting of their intention of doing so.[179]

Le Tellier's last comment is significant, for it emphasizes the extent to which the fraudulence of the officers was not seen by them as a criminal activity but as a legitimate means to recover costs incurred. In the same correspondence which complains of the corruption of the officers, another letter, from Louis XIII to Le Tellier, emphasizes the deeper character of the problem, familiar from the discussion earlier in the chapter. The letter concerns a general proposal to convert all the companies of *mousquetaires à cheval* into *carabins*, equipped with lighter, more robust, firearms. The companies were to be increased to a minimum strength of fifty men, and the officers were to equip the soldiers – at their own expense – with the new firearms, recouping the cost of this from the soldiers'

---

their *traités*, to dismiss the officers *sur le champ*, and to reallocate the soldiers amongst the other companies.

[176] AAE MD 1680, fo. 114v, 29 May 1641, Châtillon to de Noyers. Later in the year Richelieu wrote to the maréchal de Gramont concerning the same army, ordering him to arrest 'une vingtaine de petits officiers fort gallants hommes qui ont pris la peyne de prendre l'argent de leurs recreues et leurs quartiers d'hiver . . . pour venir a l'armée accompagnez seulement de trois ou quatre valetz': AAE MD 1681, fo. 15, 17 Oct. 1641.

[177] Caron (ed.), *Le Tellier*, pp. 101–2, 3 Sept. 1641.

[178] Caron (ed.), *Le Tellier*, p. 65, 28 May 1641, Le Tellier to Mazarin on the slowness of recruitment; p. 80, 27 June 1641, Le Tellier to de Noyers on the recycling of troops in order to counterfeit recruitment; p. 199, 19 July 1642, Le Tellier to Mazarin on the officers' enlistment of troops simply to serve long enough to appear at the first *revue*.

[179] Caron (ed.), *Le Tellier*, p. 57, 18 Apr. 1641, Le Tellier to de Noyers.

wages in the future.[180] In its automatic assumption that the captains will meet this considerable expense as the price of retaining their companies, and its stipulation of an uncertain and impractical method of obtaining reimbursement, it would seem to justify the views of the officers that their own appropriation of money was legitimate in view of past – or quite possibly future – financial demands that they would be required to meet.

Obviously not all officers would seek to evade the financial demands of the crown, nor would all take the opportunities presented by the arrival of *montres* and payment for recruits to engage in fraudulence. For some officers, especially those with a heavy commitment of personal *fidélité* to Richelieu or the other ministers, renouncing corrupt opportunities for reimbursement was an acceptable price to pay, a gauge of loyalty to the regime, which would, it was hoped, be recognized and rewarded.[181] For the *grands*, once again, conspicuous personal extravagance in the upkeep of their regiments and cavalry companies was seen both as a mark of their closeness to the king, and of their responsibilities to maintain the status and prestige of their entourage and clientele.[182] Certainly the aristocratic ethos of conspicuous consumption in military life was sufficiently entrenched that in 1641 it was considered necessary to promulgate the first of many ordinances attempting to restrict extravagant dining amongst the senior army officers, ordering that no more than two *services* should be offered at dinner.[183] A minority of officers, whether for family or personal reasons, who envisaged a permanent military career would probably also prove less willing to exploit opportunities for corruption, and would show greater readiness to commit their own credit to their units. For many such individuals, building a career depended upon the capacity to bring themselves to the attention of the king or to one of the aristocratic commanders as someone prepared to make both personal and financial sacrifices for the king's service.[184] By doing so, the officer might gain a sufficient reputation to be considered for another, perhaps more prestigious, charge, whether an officership in a *régiment entretenu* or the possibility of financial assistance from the crown or a *grand* in the purchase of a more senior post.

But these groups were exceptional; the majority of unit officers wished to exercise their command long enough to accrue social prestige from the *métier*

---

[180] Caron (ed.), *Le Tellier*, p. 200, 22 July 1642, Louis XIII to Le Tellier.

[181] The decision of the *conseillers d'Etat* to raise a regiment and to support its costs for three months in summer 1636 was an initiative which few individual *conseillers* felt they could safely ignore: BN Ms.fr. 6647, fo. 7, 5 Aug. 1636, de Noyers to cardinal de La Valette.

[182] SHAT A^1 29, fo. 297, 25 Sept. 1636, Henri de La Trémoïlle congratulated on the extravagant fitting out of his company of *gendarmes* and his establishment of two regiments of infantry; A^1 50i, fo. 219, 23 Jan. 1639, gratitude to duc de Lesdiguières for the speed and personal commitment to the levy of his regiment.

[183] SHAT A^1 67, pces 134–5, 23 Apr. 1641.

[184] The memoirs produced by 'career' officers – de Pontis, Puységur, Montglat – demonstrate their concern to display a combination of individual heroism and responsible concern for their units, preferably in the presence of the king himself.

The French rejection of entrepreneurship

d'armes, but did not envisage a lifetime's career in military service. Thus the threat of disbandment, which was very real when the unit had just been recruited, became increasingly less important once the officer felt that he had acquired this personal military association, and at the point where he may even have sought the excuse to retire from the army. While newly commissioned officers may have done all possible to maintain the effective strength of their units, both through the deployment of personal credit and through defrauding the *commissaires* at the *montres*, those officers with two or three campaigns' experience were less concerned about running the risk that their units would suffer disbandment for being under-strength and were more prepared to engage in apparently self-defeating manipulation of the system intended to fund additional recruitment.

Enough of the officers clearly operated on such assumptions to have a serious effect upon the crown's administration of the army. By acting *en masse* the unit officers effectively forced the crown to accept military service on their terms. The period was marked by an ever-diminishing average company strength, as the officers, despite receiving recruitment bonuses to raise their units up to a notional full strength, persistently recruited far fewer troops than stipulated. This was despite concessions such as that of August 1635, which permitted each captain the right to present two valets at the *revue*, these being taken as members of the company by the *commissaires*.[185] And if bribery failed to persuade the officers to make the necessary effort, penalties proved equally ineffective. Above all, the ever-falling company strength brought about by the refusal of the officers to carry out recruitment eroded the possibility of using disbandment with any systematic rigour as a disciplinary penalty. Individual officers whose failure to maintain their units was felt to be especially culpable might well see their units disbanded or reformed; but the great mass of officers existed in a nebulous world in which they were well aware that allowing their units to suffer heavy wastage for lack of pay and supplies *might* lead to direct intervention by the crown, especially as the campaign drew to a close, but where the crown's policy would depend to a large extent on the state of the other units in the army. As early as September 1636 maréchal Créqui was ordered to carry out the disbandment of all infantry companies in the army of Italy containing fewer than thirty men, dismissing the officers and incorporating the troops into other units.[186] Yet an almost immediate reconsideration followed; if all companies of thirty men or less were to be reformed, the army would be left with so few regiments that the corps would be unable to operate as a campaign force and an alarming signal would be given to France's allies in Italy. Instead, Créqui was to use his discretion, and reform only those companies from regiments that he considered to be especially weak or badly

---

[185] SHAT A¹ 26, pce 78, 23 Aug. 1635, 'ordonnance du Roi portant punition de mort contre les passe-volants'. Such concessions were inevitably abused: in 1641 the regiment of maréchal Brézé contained 189 valets amongst a total of 943 infantry – AAE MD 1680, fo. 191 (late May).
[186] SHAT A¹ 29, fo. 311, 27 Sept. 1636.

The administrative context

run.[187] While excessively weak companies were still regularly disbanded, the notion of a statutory minimum number of soldiers per company, below which the company would automatically be disbanded, was almost entirely abandoned.[188] Orders for *réformation* were more typically concerned with making a proportion of the companies up to an effective strength, rather than giving inflexible instructions concerning the disbandment of those beneath this number. In September 1640 Poupart, *commissaire des guerres*, was ordered to carry out the *réformation* of the three regiments in garrison at Doullens. Instead of specifying the criteria for the disbandment of some of the companies, the instruction merely stressed that the *commissaire* was to ensure that all the remaining companies of the regiment had been established at a minimum strength of fifty men.[189] A similar instruction was given to Harcourt with reference to three regiments of the army of Italy in 1641, in which he was ordered to ensure that they should be reformed in order to ensure a minimum of forty men per company.[190] These arrangements for *réformation* obviously left a great deal more discretion in the hands of the high command with a particular army-corps and even, in cases, with the *commissaires des guerres* charged with the disbandment. While the threat posed by disbandment to captains and to *mestres de camp* was a real one, the possibility that influence or reputation could prove sufficient to mitigate its impact was equally evident. While no evidence of such favouritism and special arrangements would be likely to survive in the archival records, it seems probable that the disbandment of units fits into a broader pattern of clientage and reciprocal arrangements operating within the army-corps, and militating against any effective administrative control.

The problem of officer absenteeism

The crown was forced to accept an ever-declining average company strength because the failure to carry out adequate recruitment and to maintain the unit while in service were so universal that both disciplinary penalties and even the practical threat of disbandment proved largely unworkable. This situation, which suited the immediate interests of the officers, can be seen as one of a number of ways in which the officers, acting as a self-interested corporation, were able to impose terms of service upon the crown that were most harmful to the war-effort and the effectiveness of royal authority over the army. Another significant part of

---

[187] SHAT A^1 29, fo. 336ii, 29 Sept. 1636.
[188] Cf. SHAT A^1 35, fo. 88, 13 Mar. 1637, order for the *réformation* of all companies under fifty strong in Picardy; A^1 65, fo. 507, 14 Sept. 1641, Philippe de La Motte-Houdancourt to carry out the *réformation* of all companies in his army under fifty strong.
[189] SHAT A^1 60, fo. 446, 19 Sept. 1640 (similar instructions for other regiments fos. 448, 450, 19 Sept.); A^1 61, fo. 197, 17 Nov. 1640, instructions to four governors in Picardy to keep their companies of *chevaux légers sur pied*, but to distribute the soldiers to ensure that they have a minimum of thirty horse in each.
[190] SHAT A^1 66, fo. 134, 9 Oct. 1641.

The French rejection of entrepreneurship

these 'terms of service' concerned attitudes to the indiscipline of their soldiers, and the willingness to pursue a range of activities varying from exactions of dubious legality to downright extortion and robbery at the expense of the local populations where the units were billeted, recruited or *en passage*. These will be considered in chapter 10 as part of the general problem of relations between the army and wider French society. Another distinctive aspect of the French officers' implicit 'terms of service' was their own right to be absent from service as frequently and for as long as they wished. Officer absenteeism, as opposed to the universal problem of desertion amongst the ordinary soldiers, seems to have been a peculiarly French problem in its scale and intractability.[191] During the first months of the 1635 campaign an *ordonnance* was promulgated with respect to the army-corps of maréchal de La Force, whose effectives at a contemporary *revue* numbered 7,938 infantry and 1,576 cavalry, condemning 140 officers absent without official *congé*, and actually naming 111 of these in the document.[192] Nor was this in any sense an initial problem as the administration struggled to create a more experienced and committed officer-corps. In 1642 the correspondence of the *bureau de la guerre* was particularly concerned with officer absenteeism from the army of Catalonia – despite the presence of the king and of Richelieu. On 5 March the officers of the army of Catalonia were ordered to rejoin their regiments within eight days, or face penalties for absenteeism.[193] On 12 March Condé was ordered to have published in Paris a list of all the officers of the army of Catalonia absent from their posts, while on 17 March de Noyers wrote to Brézé, La Meilleraye and La Motte-Houdancourt, concerned at the extremely high levels of absenteeism, far greater than could be justified by the normal arrangements for one third of the officers to be absent during the winter quarter.[194] This was accompanied by a warning that *congés* were being granted too freely by the generals with the armies, and by a major *ordonnance* condemning all absenteeism by officers.[195] Judged by the frequency with which such general and specific *règlements* were promulgated throughout the period of Richelieu's ministry, the problem of absenteeism continued largely unchecked from one campaign to the next.[196]

---

[191] Parker, *Army of Flanders*, gives no indication that this was a comparable problem for the Spanish army. Equally, with a few notable exceptions at the very highest ranks, it does not appear to have been an issue in a fully entrepreneurial army such as Wallenstein's: cf. Redlich, *Military Enterpriser*, I. 443–6.

[192] SHAT A¹ 26, fos. 74–5, 10 Aug. 1635; the *revue* of La Force's army from AAE MD 819, fos. 64, 68, 28 July 1635. A similar list of absentees can be found for Rohan's army in 1637: A¹ 35, fo. 225, 1 Apr. 1637. More general condemnations of officers for absenteeism were generated in every year of campaigning. Eleven such documents survive in the archival material for 1636 alone.

[193] SHAT A¹ 68, fo. 478.

[194] SHAT A¹ 68, fo. 515, 12 Mar.; fo. 558, 17 Mar.

[195] SHAT A¹ 68, fo. 598, 21 Mar.; A¹ 71, fo. 184, [1642].

[196] The issue of officer absenteeism is given detailed attention in the excellent *Mémoire de maîtrise* of Captain Bernard Masson, 'La lutte contre l'absence et la désertion dans les armées de Louis XIII,

The administrative context

The motives for large-scale absenteeism amongst the officers are difficult to establish with any certainty. Bernard Masson points with good reason to the disillusionment of many officers when the expectations of a short and glorious war in 1635 encountered the setbacks of 1636.[197] The mass recruitment of the summer of 1636 generated a significant number of newly created officers with little enthusiasm or aptitude for service, who decided to absent themselves from the armies. Even after the mid-1630s, it is reasonable to suggest that for some young, previously inexperienced, nobles or bourgeois, the brutal realities of fighting as it was practised by the armies of the later stages of the Thirty Years War may have been too much for them. It was certainly the case that officer absenteeism, like the desertion of the soldiers, was especially high in the campaign theatres beyond the French frontiers – Italy, Catalonia, the Empire – or in territories such as the duchy of Lorraine where the fighting was especially vicious.[198] Yet the fact that so many of the absentee officers did not return quietly to their estates, but travelled to Paris and other major cities, suggests that the problem ran deeper than simple discouragement, cowardice or revulsion. Obtaining and holding an officership was a statement about social prestige in a society which was particularly sensitive to visual symbols of hierarchy and power. In the long term a period of military service could be seen as a way to enhance the status of the family, and to build up prestige in a provincial or a local context. In the short term, however, the flaunting of high status as an army officer, whether at the level of a company captain, or even as an ensign or lieutenant, could be far more gratifying in a major population centre, whose elites were attuned to nuances of hierarchy, and prepared to offer deference and respect to officers in the midst of a major war. The confluence of officers in Paris and the provincial capitals reinforces the notion that for many, social prestige, far more than any possibility of building a career through gallant and dutiful military service, was their real motivation. Many of these officers had never separated themselves from the preoccupations of a civil society into which they soon expected to return, and the preoccupations of that society had determined their military ambitions. Absenteeism, both during the winter quarter and during the campaign itself, was a temptation for those whose primary concern

---

1635–1643', *Bibliothèque de la Guerre*, Vincennes (1981), 17–50. Masson suggests that there was a peak of officer absenteeism in 1636, an amelioration in 1637 and a slow drift upwards during the later 1630s, which falls again in 1641 and 1642. Whether this represents, as he suggests, an 'évolution dans la mentalité de l'officier' (p. 44), or whether it reflects the ministry's own realism in accommodating with the officers over questions such as absence during the period of winter quarters, thus reducing 'unofficial' absenteeism, seems open to question. Masson certainly does not suggest that this was a struggle won by the crown, and points to the pervasiveness of the problem into the eighteenth century (p. 50).

[197] Masson, 'La lutte contre l'absence', 20.
[198] Some sense of the unpleasantness of this unchivalric style of warfare for an educated and reflective serving officer can be found in Henri de Campion's accounts of the campaigns in Catalonia and Italy: *Mémoires*, pp. 103–32. The subject is well treated, *inter alia*, in Dewald, *Aristocratic Experience*, pp. 45–68.

The French rejection of entrepreneurship

was with social prestige in a wider society. So pervasive was this attitude that in 1641 Sébastien le Hardy, marquis de La Trousse, *mestre de camp* of Richelieu's own *régiment de La Marine*, was instructed to send an *état* of absentee officers from the regiment so that the ministerial agents could attempt to apprehend and punish them.[199]

The absenteeism of the officers was undoubtedly one of the prime causes of the disorders and desertion of the troops. It was also part of the fundamental problem that concerns the remaining chapters of the book: the extent to which the government could control an army which it had set up on principles of a rejection of entrepreneurship and the exploitation of the officers' own resources.

---

[199] SHAT A¹ 66, fo. 374, 29 Nov. 1641.

7

The civil administration of the army: the structures

> Le roy sçait bien que je me suis tousjours plaint des retardemens des trésoriers et munitionnaires, et que j'ay dict plusieurs fois publiquement . . . que ce n'estoit rien de mettre des armées sur pied, sy on ne donnoit ordre de les faire payer à temps, et sy on ne pourvoyoit soigneusement aux vivres.[1]

However deeply entrenched its compromises with the officer-corps over the financing and maintenance of the army, the French crown had remained reluctant to adopt a system of direct military entrepreneurship which would have delegated overall responsibility for military administration into the hands of the unit and corps commanders. Even in the first half of the sixteenth century, when a majority of French soldiers were foreign mercenaries, a civil administration still undertook those financing, disciplinary and organizational functions which did not intrude upon the specific rights and autonomy of the Swiss and German *condottiere*.[2] Though battered by the usurpation of independent military authority by both *grands* and lesser provincial nobles during the Wars of Religion, the civil administration survived, and in certain respects expanded, during the second half of the sixteenth century.[3] When Louis XIII and Richelieu committed France to war with the Habsburg powers in 1635, the army administration was a reasonably developed, comprehensive, structure. Admittedly it was almost entirely based upon purchased office, but on paper at least it was capable of encompassing most of the issues concerned with raising, controlling, feeding, disciplining and paying armies, with coordinating the provision of supplies and munitions, with the organization and financing of siege and fortification work and with the maintenance of multiple channels of information from the armies in the field to the central government. The principal weakness lay not in its size: the number of administrators was probably adequate for the scale and typical duration of warfare, at least as it had been envisaged in the decades up to 1635. The real problems within the system were those of overlapping and contested jurisdictions, ill-defined spheres of authority and responsibility, multiple hierarchies of

---

[1] Avenel, v. 231, 16 Sept. 1635, Richelieu to Louis XIII.
[2] G. Zeller, *Les institutions de la France au XVIe siècle* (Paris, 1948), pp. 323–7; D. Potter, *War and Government in the French Provinces: Picardy, 1470–1560* (Cambridge, 1993), pp. 179–99.
[3] La Barre Duparcq, *L'art militaire*, pp. 108–13;. Wood, *The King's Army*, pp. 86–106, 226–74.

The civil administration of the army: the structures

command and control and a fundamental reluctance at both local and central level to challenge the vested interests of the military elites. Confronted with the expansion in the scale of military operations after 1635 and the general inadequacy of resources to match this expansion, these weaknesses in the military administration became disastrous liabilities. Despite a number of legislative initiatives, *ad hoc* expedients and direct interventions in the system, the capacity of the ministers to develop the administration to meet the challenges of European-scale warfare in the years down to 1643 was to remain limited.

THE CENTRAL STRUCTURE OF THE WAR ADMINISTRATION

In 1661 Michel le Tellier, *secrétaire d'Etat ayant le département de la guerre*, was formally recognized as a *ministre d'Etat*, giving him the right to participate in the restricted and powerful *Conseil d'en haut*.[4] This promotion should be seen primarily as the personal achievement of Le Tellier: recognition of his astute political manoeuvring during and after the *Frondes*, his seniority within the Mazarinist team and the young Louis XIV's concern to achieve a balance of power amongst his ministerial servants and to ensure that no one of them could again achieve the status of *premier ministre*. The personal element in the rise of Le Tellier should be stressed to counter the frequent suggestion that the authority and responsibilities of the office of *secrétaire de la guerre* increased progressively through the secretaryships of Charles de Beauclerc (1624–31), Abel Servien (1631–6) and François Sublet, sieur de Noyers (1636–43).[5] While the quantity of business handled by the secretary increased considerably in the period down to Richelieu's death, the character and functions of the office underwent more modest change. The secretary may have become in certain respects more influential as a result of the greatly increased work load evident from the 1630s, but the outlines of an essentially secondary, executive and reactive role did not change in this period.

THE DEVELOPMENT OF THE *SECRETAIRES D'ETAT*

In a *règlement* of 1588, Henri III defined a specific group of four royal secretaries, already possessing the title *secrétaire d'Etat*, who were to receive commissions granting them the authority to conduct most of the king's epistolary business – writing his letters, keeping copies and reading him

---

[4] L. André, *Michel Le Tellier et Louvois* (Paris, 1942), pp. 77–9; Corvisier, *Louvois*, p. 119.
[5] Avenel, *Richelieu*, III. 55–6; André, *Le Tellier et Louvois*, p. 308–9; Ranum, *Richelieu*, pp. 100–19 (whose work still provides the most perceptive account of the personalities and power structures amongst Richelieu's ministerial team); Corvisier, *Louvois*, pp. 67, 77.

The administrative context

incoming correspondence.[6] The value of this newly defined office of *secrétaire d'Etat* certainly did not lie in its direct political influence. There was no expectation that the *secrétaire* would do more than record the decisions of the king and his ministers, whether in the king's private apartments or in the formal atmosphere of *séances* of the *conseil d'Etat*. The attraction of the office, the reason that its price had reached 180,000 *livres* by 1608[7] and that the posts had become virtually monopolized by a number of major families – the l'Aubespine, Bochetel and Neuville, in particular[8] – was the potential for informal influence with the king that the role of intimate private secretary could afford.

The early seventeenth century saw the development of a foreign affairs specialization by one of the *secrétaires*. Nicholas de Neuville, marquis de Villeroy, by virtue of his standing with Henri IV, was able to unite all of the foreign correspondence in his own hands and to establish the principle that one *secrétaire*, while not relinquishing the *département* of French provinces for whose general correspondence he had responsibility, should have overall control of the receipt and despatch of diplomatic despatches.[9] While the secretaryship with charge of foreign affairs thus acquired a more defined administrative role, there was no comparable pattern for military affairs. Although a *règlement* of 29 April 1619 identified one of the *secrétaires* as having charge of matters related to war, it also specified that this *secrétaire* had responsibility only for the 'première et principale armée', the one commanded by the king or his chosen *lieutenant général*. Other armies, defensive forces and garrisons were to remain the responsibility of the *secrétaire* in whose geographical department they lay. If one of these lesser forces crossed a frontier into a province which belonged to another *secrétaire*, the conflict of jurisdiction would have to be resolved between the two *secrétaires*, who would decide which of them should now handle the correspondence with that force.[10]

Like so many aspects of the military administration, the compromise laid down in 1619 for the jurisdiction of the *secrétaire d'Etat de la guerre* looked back to an early sixteenth-century model for warfare in which it was assumed that one major royal army would be engaged in campaigning while other 'provincial' forces simply held defensive positions or undertook very limited activities elsewhere. As

---

[6] R. Doucet, *Les institutions de la France au XVIe siècle* (2 vols; Paris, 1948), I. 159; Zeller, *Les institutions*, pp. 117–19; N. Sutherland, *The French Secretaries of State in the Age of Catherine de Medici* (London, 1962), provides an account of the *secrétaires* before 1588; Mousnier, *Les institutions*, II. 145.

[7] The price paid by Pontchartrain for the office: Mousnier, *Vénalité des offices*, p. 343. Other figures for the sale of the secretaryship vary between 150,000 *livres* in 1624, 300,000 negotiated with Abel Servien for the sale of the secretaryship to Sublet de Noyers in 1636, and 700,000 *livres* in 1645: Mousnier, *Vénalité des Offices*, pp. 341–3.

[8] Doucet, *Les institutions*, I. 160; Mousnier, *Les institutions*, II. 145; Ranum, *Richelieu*, p. 51.

[9] Doucet, *Les institutions*, I. 163–4; Ranum, *Richelieu*, p. 51; E.H. Dickerman, *Bellièvre and Villeroy. Power in France under Henry III and Henry IV* (Providence, 1971), p. 6; D. Buisseret, *Henry IV, King of France* (London, 1984), pp. 97, 99–101.

[10] Ranum, *Richelieu*, p. 53; the *règlement* is printed on pp. 189–91.

The civil administration of the army: the structures

secondary armies became more important, so the potential for disputes between the *secrétaires* and confusion in the despatch of instructions to the armies grew. In 1626 a new *règlement* attempted a further clarification, strengthening the hold of the *secrétaire de la guerre* over correspondence connected with all operational armies.[11] Yet this enhancement of the authority of the *secrétaire de la guerre* sprang not from a reconsideration of his own office and responsibilities, but as compensation for the decision to confirm that all foreign affairs would henceforth be consolidated in the hands of one of the other secretaries, in this case Raymond Phélypeaux d'Herbault. The superiority of the *secrétaire d'Etat* for foreign affairs was made clear in a final *règlement* of 1633.[12] The military operations in Italy, the *Trois Evêchés* and Lorraine had generated a conflict between the secretary for foreign affairs, who claimed jurisdiction over correspondence emanating from outside of France whether it was diplomatic or military, and the secretary for war, who claimed that correspondence with armies operating across the frontiers fell within his authority. The 1633 *règlement* compromised, establishing a complex arrangement for control of garrisons in foreign and conquered territory. So long as these garrisons were composed of troops from a field army under the direct command of an officer of that army, the responsibility for them rested with the *secrétaire* with charge of war, 'mais dès l'heure qu'il y aura un Gouverneur etably avec une garnison reglée non tirée du corps dont l'armée sera composée ou d'autres sous la charge et autorité des colonels . . . le pouvoir [and subsequent correspondence] dudit Gouverneur sera expedié par ledit Secretaire d'Etat qui aura les étrangers'.[13] The potential for ambiguity and uncertainty generated by such a compromise was considerable: many governors were officers drawn from the armies, not clearly separated from wider military operations, but certainly in command of a 'garnison réglée'; it did little to facilitate the overall coordination of the war-effort if established garrisons at *places* such as Casale, Pinerolo or Nancy communicated with the secretary for foreign affairs while the military activities in the surrounding territories were the responsibility of the secretary for war.

The main factor in averting such disputes between the secretaries would appear to be Richelieu's appointment in 1632 of his *créature*, the young Léon le Bouthillier, comte de Chavigny, as *secrétaire* with charge of foreign affairs. Chavigny had considerable abilities, but these were primarily personal and social, not administrative. For Richelieu, Chavigny's value lay in the close relationships that he managed to establish with both the king and – curiously – with Louis' brother, Gaston d'Orléans.[14] He had not been made *secrétaire* in order to play a

---

[11] Ranum, *Richelieu*, p. 55, text given p. 191.
[12] Ranum, *Richelieu*, pp. 192–4, for full text.
[13] Ranum, *Richelieu*, p. 193.
[14] Ranum, *Richelieu*, pp. 77–99; P. Grillon, 'Lettre du Secrétaire d'Etat Claude Bouthillier au Cardinal de Richelieu', in Durand, *Clientèles et fidélité*, 71–90 at pp. 72–5, 84–90; for the relationship between Chavigny and Gaston see Goulas, *Mémoires*, I. 272, 303–10, 349.

The administrative context

part in the formulation of foreign policy, which was very largely handled by Richelieu himself. In consequence, Chavigny does not seem to have been inclined to provoke quarrels over disputed jurisdiction nor to see his power and influence in terms of the institutional extent of his office. At a personal level it seems clear that Chavigny did not like Richelieu's last and longest-serving *secrétaire* for war, Sublet de Noyers, and played a critical role in ensuring his disgrace after the cardinal's death.[15] Yet the quarrels between them, including the major dispute in 1639 over de Noyers' provision of funds for Chavigny's diplomatic mission to Savoy-Piedmont, were personal, not institutional.[16] Despite the potential for quarrels and rivalries over the control of the war-effort, and the vulnerability of the *secrétaire de la guerre* to the encroachments of the *secrétaire des affaires étrangères*, this does not appear to have been a great problem during the ministry after 1633. But there is little evidence that the absence of serious conflict was due to any marked increase in the power and effectiveness of the *secrétaire de la guerre* during this subsequent period.

THE *SECRETAIRE DE LA GUERRE*: FUNCTIONS AND AUTHORITY

When Abel Servien assumed the office of *secrétaire de la guerre* in 1631, he took over a post which had never been held by a powerful individual comparable with Villeroy or even Villeroy's successor, Raymond Phélypeaux d'Herbault, and had consequently not undergone a broadening of function and authority comparable with the secretaryship for foreign affairs. However, as with the *secrétaire* for foreign affairs, the *secrétaire de la guerre* combined responsibility for military affairs with a provincial *département*. The *secrétaire* was responsible for the promulgation of administrative decisions in, and receipt of correspondence from, the provinces of Poitou, La Marche, Limousin, Angoumois, Saintonge, Lyonnais, Dauphiné and Provence.[17] In the direct administration of war, which came to occupy a larger and larger amount of the secretary's business, the concerns were essentially subsidiary and connected with execution, rather than the formulation, of policy. It is easy to point to the presence of Servien and de Noyers at formal and informal meetings of the king and his ministers, to show the rapidly growing volume of correspondence despatched and received by the *secrétaires* during the 1630s, and to adduce the remarks of other ministers which show that the *secrétaire*

---

[15] For Chavigny's role in the fall of de Noyers, see the comte de La Châtre, *Mémoires*, in Michaud and Poujoulat, III. 273–4; André, *Michel le Tellier et l'organization*, pp. 52–5; L.-N. Tellier, *Face aux Colbert. Les Le Tellier, Vauban, Turgot et l'avènement du libéralisme* (Québec, 1987), pp. 61–3.

[16] Ranum, *Richelieu*, pp. 88–9, citing the exchange of correspondence in AAE CP Savoie 28, fos. 230, 232, 21 Apr. 1639, letters between de Noyers and Chavigny.

[17] Ranum, *Richelieu*, p. 191, text of *réglement* of 11 Mar. 1626: the *secretaire* with responsibility for war also had charge of the *marine du Levant*, the galley-fleet which operated out of Provençal ports. The *réglement* stipulates that 'pour le regard des fortifications chacun en fera les Estats en ce qui sera son departement'.

de la guerre was treated as a colleague rather than a subordinate administrative agent. All of this is certainly the case, but cannot sustain an argument that the *secrétaire de la guerre*, whether Servien or de Noyers, carried weight and influence in the formulation of military policy. Considerable administrative responsibility was placed upon the shoulders of the *secrétaire* and his staff in the *bureau de la guerre* for the execution of decisions related to the war-effort, but there is little evidence that the *secrétaire* played a significant role in the making of major military decisions over, for example, funding and army size, the formulation of strategic priorities or appointment to the high command.

The chief obstacle faced by the three *secrétaires de la guerre* between 1624 and 1642 in any attempt to increase the power and the status of the *office* was the existence of the cardinal de Richelieu. Losing no time in assuming the military commands for which his initial education had prepared him,[18] Richelieu considered that the overall administration of the war-effort was too important to be left to anyone except himself. The two secretaries charged with war and foreign affairs were entirely subordinated to Richelieu's overall authority.[19] While in matters of foreign policy Richelieu was prepared to delegate some authority to ambassadors and specialist advisers such as Joseph Le Clerc du Tremblay, Claude de Mesmes, comte d'Avaux, Michel Particelli sieur d'Hémery or Giulio Mazzarini, there was no such willingness in the administration of the war-effort. Not only was the *secrétaire* subordinated to Richelieu as *premier ministre*, he was also part of a hierarchy in which much greater weight was carried by the *surintendants des finances* in the planning and formulation of strategy and in discussions of general military policy. The centrality of the chief finance minister to the waging of warfare was recognized on a number of occasions in the most direct way, through the appointment of senior military commanders as *surintendant* while they were still exercising their military commands. This was the case with Henri de Schomberg, comte de Nanteuil, created *surintendant* in 1619, and Antoine Coeffier de Ruzé, marquis d'Effiat, elevated to the post in 1626.[20] The appointment of the *robins* Claude Bullion and Claude Bouthillier in 1632 brought the practice of combining military and financial high office to an end until the appointment to the surintendancy of Charles de La Porte, maréchal de La Meilleraye in June 1648.[21] But this did not curtail the direct involvement in military decision-making by the *surintendants* and little ground was conceded to the *secrétaire de la guerre* during Louis XIII's reign.[22] While the secretary's correspondence in the Archives de la

---

[18] Bergin, *Rise of Richelieu*, pp. 55–8; Richelieu assumed direct command of armies in 1627 and 1628 at Ré and La Rochelle, and in 1629 at Susa and in the Midi.
[19] Ranum, *Richelieu*, accepts this for Chavigny – pp. 93–7 – but is less willing to affirm the equally evident subordination of Sublet de Noyers.
[20] Bonney, *King's Debts*, pp. 102, 121; Dent, *Crisis in Finance*, pp. 197–8.
[21] Bonney, *King's Debts*, p. 206.
[22] See the perceptive remarks of Avenel, *Richelieu*, I. 70–1, on the over-powerful position of the *surintendant*.

The administrative context

Guerre remains primarily concerned with the executive business of the army,[23] the regular letters from Bullion to Richelieu are concerned with the central issues of overall policy and its funding, the assessment of military priorities and the deployment of forces. It was Bullion who ensured the disgrace of the second *secrétaire de la guerre*, Servien, by drawing him into a quarrel over financial estimates in which it was clear that Richelieu's support would go to the *surintendant*.[24] The incoming *secrétaire*, Sublet de Noyers, proved himself as amenable to Bullion's wishes as he was to those of his official superior, Richelieu. This was hardly surprising; de Noyers had previously held the office of one of the four *intendants des finances* in the central *bureau des finances*, working directly under Bullion and his co-*surintendant*, Claude Bouthillier.[25] Under de Noyers, Bullion was able to extend his authority in military affairs. In 1638 he obtained control of the *taillon*, the direct tax which had supplemented the levy of the *taille* since 1549.[26] Hitherto, this had been the rather anomalous preserve of the *bureau de la guerre*, and by acquiescing in this transfer, de Noyers abandoned the small element of financial flexibility remaining to the *secrétaire*, and became dependent upon the *surintendant* in every aspect of war finance. When the new *subsistances* tax was first levied in 1637, notionally for the support of the troops in winter quarters, it was a foregone conclusion that the allocation and control of the funds would be in the hands of the *surintendant*, even though the tax was in the first instance collected by a group of *commissaires des guerres*.

Nor was it the case that the secretary had outright executive control over all matters related to the administration of the war-effort. A number of *officiers de la couronne* held traditional prerogatives in matters related to adminstration and justice within the armies, often through the right to appoint to offices within the administrative hierarchy. These prerogatives were held by the *colonel général de l'infanterie française*, by the *connétable* down to the abolition of this *office* in 1627, and by the individual *maréchaux*. While their appointees were supposedly subject to the overall authority of the *secrétaire d'Etat*, ties of *fidélité* made such agents only conditional supporters of ministerial policies.[27] Richelieu himself

---

[23] And even in this executive business, the secretary could be subordinated to the chancellor, for e.g. BN Ms.fr.17372, fo. 230, de Noyers to Séguier, 7 Sept. 1636, defers to Séguier in matters of food supply for the army in Champagne.

[24] Servien himself accused Bullion of engineering his disgrace in a letter to his *fidèle*, Montigny d'Oisement, in 1636: SHAT A¹ 41, fo. 117, 27 Feb. 1637. This was confirmed by François de Paule de Clermont, marquis de Montglat in his *Mémoires*, Petitot and Monmerqué, XLIX. 110–11.

[25] Bonney, *King's Debts*, pp. 160, 289. For an aspect of de Noyers' career as an *intendant des finances*: C. Schmidt, 'Le rôle et les attributions d'un "intendant des finances" aux armées: Sublet de Noyers de 1632 à 1636', *Revue d'histoire moderne et contemporaine*, 2 (1900–1), 156–75.

[26] Ranum, *Richelieu*, p. 108; Doucet, *Les institutions*, II. 575.

[27] Although Bassompierre had been imprisoned in the Bastille since 1631, he retained his right, as a *maréchal*, to nominate a *prévôt* to the armies. When his original appointee died in 1636, his nomination for a replacement – Cognesceau, sieur de Bevandière – was accepted by the king: SHAT A¹ 32, fo. 121, 17 July 1636; A¹ 71, fo. 99, 23 Apr. 1642, royal ordinance registers the nomination of

The civil administration of the army: the structures

contributed to this dilution of the authority of the *secrétaire d'Etat* both by the accumulation of posts for himself and his relatives, and by his active intervention in the military administration. The office of *grand maître de l'artillerie*, which in 1634 was placed in the hands of Richelieu's compliant cousin, La Meilleraye, largely to guarantee that Richelieu's navy would receive priority for the distribution of scarce and expensive artillery resources, remained outside the wider structure of the military administration. Similarly, a number of Richelieu's initiatives in the provision of food supply for the armies had the effect of removing parts of the logistical system from the control of the *secrétaire de la guerre*.

It would appear, moreover, that neither Servien nor de Noyers sought to compensate for their rather limited role in strategic decision-making by trying to impose more elaborate, detailed regulation on the day-to-day administrative practice of the army. The 1630s and early 1640s show no evidence of a concern for systematic legislation in military affairs, and the instructions deriving from the *secrétaire de la guerre* are far more concerned with the solution of immediate problems than with extensive regulation.[28] For both men the administration of the war-effort was essentially a responsive, reactive task. The quantity of correspondence handled by the *bureau de la guerre* increased dramatically in the period 1634–43, while the structures and the personnel of the *bureau* remained small scale and informal. Beneath this level of the *secrétaire* and his modest team of clerks were the administrators who operated in the provinces, the campaign theatres or with the armies.

THE ADMINISTRATORS WITH THE FRENCH ARMY BEFORE 1635

The most important functions of army administrators can be placed within three broad categories: financial administration, justice and *police*, and supply. While special commissions might occasionally delegate an authority which encompassed two of these areas, the system was originally developed as tripartite, each section being handled by different administrators, owing responsibility to different authorities.

---

the Sr Bidal as the *commissaire des guerres* of the maréchal de Gramont, and reaffirms the right of each newly appointed *maréchal* to make such a nomination.

[28] This is based upon an examination of the ten volumes of *expeditions* compiled for the period of Richelieu's ministry. (SHAT, A^1 14, 21, 24, 32, 42, 49, 56, 62, 67, 71). While these volumes represent only a selection of the legislative material originally generated by the administration, it seems probable that it would have been precisely this type of 'major' legislation that would have been preserved had it existed in the earlier period.

The administrative context

THE FINANCIAL OFFICIALS

The intendants des finances

The *surintendant des finances* wished to appoint a trusted and senior agent to each of the army-corps to coordinate the receipt and distribution of funds, to report irregularities and quite possibly to defend ministerial fiscal policy to the high command. Depending upon the size of a particular army-corps and the consequent problems of financial administration, the *surintendant* could either appoint one of the four *intendants des finances*, his immediate subordinates in the *bureau des finances*,[29] or could select a lesser agent. These latter would also, confusingly, bear the title of *intendant des finances*, but described as 'acting with' the army of Champagne, Picardy or whichever other specific force to which they were allocated.[30] The *intendants des finances* who were not themselves holders of one of the intendancies in the *bureaux des finances* tended to be drawn from a financial background. Gaspard du Gué, sieur de Bagnols, for example, was also a *trésorier de France* at the *bureaux des finances* in Lyon, while Guillaume Bordeaux, sieur de Génitoy, was secretary to the *conseil d'Etat et direction des finances*.[31] Though the *intendant des finances* who replaced him in the army of Germany, Robert Arnaud d'Andilly, held no specific financial office, he had worked in the *bureaux des finances* under his uncle, one of the central *intendants des finances* during the *surintendance* of maréchal Schomberg.[32] Nicolas Le Camus, *intendant des finances* with the army of Italy in 1635/6, was also *procureur général* of the *cour des aides*.[33]

The trésoriers des guerres *and their subordinates*

If the *surintendant* regarded an *intendant des finances* of whichever type as his primary representative with a particular army-corps, his control over much of the rest of the financial administration with the armies was more limited. The French financial administration was characterized by systematic exploitation of the sale of office in all its spheres, and the fiscal administration of the war-effort was no exception. The actual payment of funds to the armies was not carried out directly from central or provincial treasuries, but through the hands of the *trésoriers de*

---

[29] For de Noyers as an *intendant des finances* in 1634–5 see Schmidt, 'Le rôle et les attributions'; Michel Particelli d'Hémery acted with the army in Provence: SHAT A¹ 24, fo. 23, 16 Jan. 1635.
[30] Before becoming one of the central *intendants des finances*, d'Hémery held at least one specific commission of *intendant* of finance acting with an army: Grillon, IV. 81, 4 Feb. 1629; SHAT A¹ 21, fo. 86, [1634]: Guillaume Bordeaux; A¹ 25, fo. 190, 11 Aug. 1635: Nicolas Le Camus.
[31] SHAT A¹12, fo. 131 [1630]; Baxter, *Servants of the Sword*, p. 15.
[32] Arnaud d'Andilly, *Mémoires*, in Petitot and Monmerqué, XXXIII. 392–3.
[33] SHAT A¹ 25, fo. 190, 11 Aug. 1635, Servien to maréchal Créqui, mentioning the commission of intendancy for Le Camus, granted in response to the petitioning of Particelli d'Hémery, then extraordinary ambassador in Savoy; R. Mousnier (ed.), *Lettres et mémoires adressés au Chancelier Séguier, 1633–1649* (2 vols; Paris, 1964), II. 1208.

The civil administration of the army: the structures

l'ordinaire and *de l'extraordinaire des guerres*. Proprietorship of these offices was a direct form of financial speculation, and in the case of the *trésoriers de l'extraordinaire* brought a percentage payment of all the funds allocated to the infantry and most of the cavalry in return for a willingness to make advances to the armies against incoming tax revenues.[34]

The distribution of funds to the armies was thus handled by the *trésoriers*, or rather by their subordinates, the *commis* and *payeurs*, whose offices were also venal and distributed through the patronage of the *trésoriers des guerres* themselves. The possibility of expanding the system of venal office to the immediate profit of the crown and the increasing power and influence of the *trésoriers* led to two edicts in 1627, which multiplied these subordinate offices of the *trésoriers des guerres*, and introduced the triennial system. The expansion of an official structure which was not directly accountable to the crown or its finance minister continued at the same pace into the 1630s.[35] Characteristic of much of the *Ancien Régime* financial administration, the *trésoriers* and their subordinates were both financial officials and self-interested financial speculators, whose private aims were likely to include withholding or appropriating funds due to the troops.

The contrôleurs des guerres

The concern of the financial administration to regulate the payment of the troops might appear to be demonstrated by the introduction of the *contrôleurs des guerres* in the later sixteenth century, whose tasks were to supervise the execution of *revues* and *montres* and to keep records of these. In fact, though, while the *contrôleurs des guerres* were formally part of the financial hierarchy, their creation was not a serious attempt to come to terms with the supervision of the payment of the troops, but was simply another financial expedient. In 1582, eleven *conseillers contrôleurs provinciaux ordinaires des guerres* were created, followed in 1592 by twenty-four *contrôleurs provinciaux extraordinaires*.[36] It has been maintained that in contrast to the *commissaires des guerres* – the other officials responsible for assessing the numbers of troops and authorizing payment – the *contrôleurs'* charges were non-venal and they were commissioned to undertake specific assignments.[37] This is not the case: *contrôleurs* purchased a departmental (provincial) office, on the basis of which they would be assigned to the *revues* and *montres* that were to take place within their area.[38] The administration showed itself intent upon the

---

[34] For further discussion of the role of the *trésoriers de l'ordinaire et l'extraordinaire des guerres* see chapter 4, pp. 234–5, 247–9.
[35] Belhomme, *l'infanterie*, I. 337–9; BN Châtre de Cangé, 23, 16 May 1635; P. Frémont, *Les payeurs des armées* (Paris, 1906), pp. 41–9.
[36] J. Milot, 'L'évolution des corps des intendants militaires', *Revue du Nord*, 50 (1968), 386.
[37] André, *Michel Le Tellier et l'organisation*, p. 611.
[38] SHAT A¹ 26, pce 21, Jan. 1635: copy of *lettres patents* concerning the *démission* of an office of *contrôleur provincial des guerres*, implying that the office was the property of the original holder.

maintenance of property rights possessed by the *contrôleurs* as office-holders, and was rigorous in the definition of the provincial areas of responsibility. An order from the *secrétaire d'Etat* of November 1636, for example, forbade the *contrôleurs* to take cognizance of *revues* outside of their own province, and ordered the *trésorier de l'extraordinaire* to ignore *rôles* drawn up by an inappropriate *contrôleur*.[39]

As administrators, the *contrôleurs des guerres* owed their authority to a *contrôleur général des guerres*, and were responsible to the *bureau des finances*.[40] While the *contrôleurs* were in theory established as supervisory agents, it is unclear how this controlling function could be exercised – whether, in practice, they had any effect upon the operations of the financial administration. The *contrôleurs* are treated as if their functions were effectively those of the *commissaires des guerres*, whose higher salary would suggest that they had precedence in the conduct of the *revues*.[41] This is even echoed in the *Code Michau*, where the two titles are treated as synonymous, and in large numbers of instructions for the conduct of *montres*, which simply refer to *commissaires et contrôleurs*.[42] It seems probable that the existence of the two officers owed most to their different sources of authority: the *commissaires* as the appointees of the *secrétaire de la guerre*; the *contrôleurs* working within and responsible to the financial administration.

THE JUDICIAL OFFICIALS

The prévôts

Traditionally, the exercise of justice and the maintenance of discipline in the armies had rested in the hands of the *prévôts*, assisted by their lieutenants and *archers*. One group of those *prévôts*, the older and more prestigious, with disciplinary responsibilities that extended into the civil sphere, were responsible to the court of the *connétablie et maréchaussée*. At least some of the *prévôts* were still directly nominated by the *maréchaux* on the latters' appointment to office.[43] Their authority was enshrined in an *ordonnance fondamentale* of twelve articles,

---

[39] SHAT A¹ 30, fo. 296, 12 Nov. 1636.
[40] *Les ordonnances militaires tirées du code du roi Henri III . . .*, pp. 243–8, *ordonnance* of 1567 related to the office of *contrôleur général des guerres*, which should not be confused with the *contrôleur général des finances*, the immediate subordinate of the *surintendant* in the central financial administration. The *contrôleur général des guerres* during the 1630s was Jacques Bigot: Baxter, *Servants of the Sword*, p. 47. Baxter suggests that Bigot was made *intendant* of the army of Champagne in 1636, citing a commission in SHAT A¹ 88, fo. 8, but there is no documentary evidence that he held this post in practice or served as an *intendant d'armée* before 1642.
[41] The *contrôleurs* received 200 *livres* per month in comparison with the *commissaires*' salary of 300 *livres*: SHAT A¹ 30, fo. 107, 15 Oct. 1636; A¹ 31, fo. 215, Dec. 1636; A¹ 58, fo. 618, 29 Apr. 1640.
[42] *Code Michau*, art. 247; SHAT A¹ 32, pce 260, 1636, order for a *commissaire* and a *contrôleur des guerres* to carry out a *revue* of the cavalry regiment of the comte de Guiche, with no indication that the two officials had different tasks or responsibilities.
[43] SHAT A¹ 32, pce 121, 17 July 1636, *prévôt* nominated by Bassompierre (though in the Bastille at the time) to replace his original appointee, recently deceased.

The civil administration of the army: the structures

which claimed the most extensive rights over all aspects of military jurisdiction.[44] As late as the 1660s, this and subsequent ordinances were still being cited as the basis of a claim to a virtual monopoly of military justice.[45] However, in the later sixteenth century an alternative and specifically military system of *prévôts* emerged, the *prévôts des bandes*, owing their authority to the *colonel général de l'infanterie française*.[46]

The areas of competence held by these two groups of *prévôts* were not defined, and were the subject of numerous assertions and counter-assertions by the *colonel général* and the *maréchaussée*.[47] The jurisdiction of the *prévôts des bandes* extended in theory only over crimes committed by the infantry. The other great *office de la couronne*, the *grand maître de l'artillerie*, presided from the Arsenal in Paris over a further independent judicial system. This in turn was fiercely guarded against the incursions of the *colonel général* and the *maréchaussée*.[48]

This still left the cavalry, and here the situation was even more complex. In theory, the *colonel général de la cavalerie légère* had the equivalent jurisdiction of the *colonel général* of the infantry.[49] In practice, as much the more junior *colonel général*, the *colonel général de la cavalerie légère* possessed a judicial authority that was subject to appeal both to the *maréchaussée* and the *colonel général de l'infanterie*.[50] Although the *colonel général* lacked undisputed authority even over the *cavalerie légère*, his nominal charge also extended to the increasing numbers of *carabin* companies serving with the armies, although such authority appears never to have been officially granted.[51] It emphatically did not extend over the companies of *gendarmes*. These units, frequently raised from the clients of the great nobility, particularly when these were serving as provincial governors, and responsible only to their commanding officer, had a reputation for indiscipline quite disproportionate to their small number and elite status.[52]

---

[44] J. Pinson de La Martinière, *La juridiction de la connestablie et mareschaussée de France* (Paris, 1661), pp. 1–4; J.H. Mitchell, *The Court of the Connétablie* (New Haven, 1947), pp. 39–62.

[45] Pinson de La Martinière, *La juridiction*, introductory section (unpaginated).

[46] *Les ordinances militaires tirées du roi Henri III*, pp. 248–50: ordinance of Dec. 1584, 'Du Colonel Général', art. II: the *colonel général*, acting through his *prévôts*, may take cognizance of all 'cas, crimes et délits' committed by captains, soldiers and valets of the infantry.

[47] C. Salerian-Saugy, *La juridiction du colonel général de l'infanterie de France* (Bourges, 1927), pp. 24–9.

[48] Daniel, *Histoire*, I. 193–4, II. 544–5; Boutaric, *Institutions militaires*, p. 365; Susanne, *Histoire de l'artillerie française*, pp. 125–6.

[49] SHAT A^1 29, fo. 204ii, 12 Sept. 1636: ordonnance creating François de Bourbon-Vendôme, duc de Beaufort, acting *colonel général de la cavalerie légère* with the army of Picardy in the absence of the comte d'Alais, and providing an account of the disciplinary functions of the office.

[50] Montgommery, *La milice françoise*, p. 30: 'il [the *colonel général de la cavalerie légère*] fait justice ayant son prévost particulier... Toutefois les lieutenants et enseignes peuvent aller de lui au général et aux maréchaux de France, et au colonel général de l'infanterie françoise.'

[51] SHAT A^1 32, pce 122, 18 July 1636: typical commission for the levy of a *carabin* company, which stresses the oath of allegiance and disciplinary accountability to the comte d'Alais, the *colonel général de la cavalerie légère*.

[52] Harding, *Anatomy of a Power Elite*, pp. 75–6. See the comments of cardinal de La Valette regarding

The administrative context

Also beyond the reach of the *prévôts* were the various groups of foreign mercenaries. The most elaborate and well-established set of judicial privileges were possessed by the Swiss,[53] but the growing number of German cavalry in French service led, in 1636, to the creation of a *colonel général de la cavalerie allemande* in an attempt to ensure the effective operation of the independent judicial machinery possessed by the officer-proprietors of these units.[54]

It is misleading therefore to speak of the *prévôts* as a single mechanism for the enforcement of military justice; a number of officers held compartmentalized authority over specific elements of the army, and owed their authority to a range of different sources. Moreover, unless they had actually caught a soldier or an officer in the act of committing an offence, many of the *prévôts (des bandes* and of the *cavalerie légère*) were forced to carry out prosecutions for suspected crimes through the *conseils ordinaires des guerres*, composed of a minimum of six military officers who passed judgement without consultation with, or reference to, the *prévôt*.[55] For the trial to take place at all, it required the authorization of the general or other commanding officer, who was quite capable of suppressing accusations brought by the *prévôts* in contentious cases.[56] In contrast, the oldest group of *prévôts*, those owing their authority to the *connétablie et maréchaussée*, would attempt to have the soldier or officer brought before their own tribunal, the *table de marbre* at the Châtelet.[57] The troops, and especially the officers, had the strongest interest in obtaining trial by *conseil de guerre*, and in encouraging the disputes between the different groups of *prévôts*.[58] As none of the *prévôts* were directly under the control of the government ministers, they found it difficult to ensure that the armies were even sufficiently provided with disciplinary officers; still less were they able to preside over these conflicts concerning jurisdiction.[59]

---

the poor service and the bad example of the units of *gendarmes* present with his forces in the Empire: AAE MD 816, fo. 22, 23 Oct. 1635; AAE CP Allemagne 12, fo. 324, 12/16 Oct. 1635.

[53] Salerian Saugy, *La justice militaire*, pp. 30 *et seq.* as early as 1620 the Swiss officers had succeeded in having all French judicial officials removed from Swiss judicial tribunals.

[54] Daniel, *Histoire*, II. 448–9; ordinance for the creation of the office of *colonel général*: SHAT A¹ 32, pce 48, 3 Apr. 1636, office accorded to Colonel Streff.

[55] BN Châtre de Cangé, 22, fo. 37; L. de Ville, *La justice militaire de l'infanterie* (Paris, 1633), pp. 26–44, emphasizes that the *prévôt* must simply await the verdict of the *conseil*.

[56] C. Salerian Saugy, *Les conseils de guerre judiciaires en France sous l'Ancien Régime* (Bourges, 1925), pp. 29–30.

[57] Pinson de la Martinière, *La Juridiction*, pp. 1–4.

[58] Pinson de la Martinière, *La Juridiction*, p. 100: 'lettres de confirmation de la jurisdiction de la connestablie et mareschaussée de France', 24 Apr. 1621; Pinson de la Martinière, *Juridiction*, p. 819: 'Règlement fait par Messieurs les Mareschaux de France', 18 Jan. 1630. For an example of the manner in which the authority of the *prévôts* could be challenged by the officer-corps, see, for example, SHAT A¹ 29, fos. 136–7, 3 Sept. 1636: an order for two *chevaux légers* arrested in Paris by the *prévôt* of the Île de France to be returned (supposedly for trial) to their captain.

[59] SHAT A¹ 25, fos. 97–8, 23 July 1635, Servien to Arnaud d'Andilly, *intendant* with the army of La Valette, responding to complaints about the inadequate numbers of *prévôts*; Grillon, v. 270, 18 May 1630: complaints of Louis de Marillac to Richelieu about the inadequacy of *prévôts* with his army.

The civil administration of the army: the structures

The commissaires des guerres

The jurisdiction of the *prévôts* had been shared, or, perhaps more realistically, contested, from a much earlier period by another group of administrators with supervisorial and judicial functions, the *commissaires des guerres*. The origins of the *commissaires* can be traced back to the fourteenth century.[60] Once again, the appointment and subsequent employment of *commissaires* had originally rested with the authority of military officers; they had been appointed directly on the authority of the *connétable* and the *maréchaux* commanding the armies.[61] The same right was given to the *maître des arbalétriers*, later to become the *grand maître de l'artillerie*; this was the origin of the independent and influential corps of the *commisssaires de l'artillerie*, which remained under the direct control of the *grand maître* into the seventeenth century.[62] Ordinances and decrees stressed that the *commisssaires* of the *maréchaux* were purely disciplinary agents, distinct from the *clercs de montres* who were charged with the specific task of carrying out the *revues* of the troops and verifying their effective strength. By 1483, the judicial *commissaire*s had come to be designated *conducteurs des gens de guerre*, distinguished from a group who had become known as *commissaires pour les montres*, who became known increasingly as *commissaires des guerres*.[63] Influenced by the continued division between the two groups of *commissaires*, and by simple financial calculation, the crown began to sell the two types of *commissaires'* posts systematically.[64] Only the office of *commissaire des guerres* was to confer the right to conduct *montres* and *revues*, while the offices of *commissaire à la conduite* were to be valued according to the status of the *régiment entretenu* or *compagnie d'ordonnance* to which they were attached.

The division between the two spheres of responsibility was artificial; the motive for the continued separation of the two groups continued to be the financial benefits of the sale of office. The result, inevitably, was disputes over jurisdiction and the tendency of the *commissaires* to obstruct each other's authority. The *commissaires à la conduite*, charged with the *bon ordre et police* either of individual units or of all the troops within a particular area, were also duplicating the functions of the *prévôts*, whether of the *maréchaussée* or of the *bandes*. The *commissaires* did not possess a judicial tribunal of their own. Admittedly, a large part of military justice was executed *sur le champ*, against soldiers or others caught in the act of committing one of a large number of statutory offences. Numerous edicts against desertion, pillage and violence against the civil population specify punishment 'sans autre forme de procès'. Yet in other cases which required a

---

[60] Contamine, *Guerre*, pp. 86–8.
[61] The clearest account of this development is given in Milot, 'L' évolution'.
[62] *Les ordonnances militaires tirées du roi Henri III*, 'Du Grand Maistre', pp. 310–28, art. v.
[63] Milot, 'L'évolution', 384.
[64] Milot, 'L'évolution', 385–7; Boutaric, *Institutions militaires*, pp. 378–9.

The administrative context

formal investigation and trial, the *commissaires* would be forced to present their cases before the military *conseils de guerre*, like the *prévôts des bandes* with limited powers to influence the course or result of the procedure.

The intendants de la justice *serving with the armies*

One method of attempting to compensate for the obvious inadequacies of these mechanisms was for the chancellor to appoint an *intendant de la justice* to the army. The *intendant* would be an agent of the central authority, acting on the basis of temporary, delegated, power, holding a commission to supervise the operation of the judicial administration and to enforce justice within a particular army.[65] Before 1635 the *intendants'* significance lay in the possession of an independent legal authority; unlike the *commissaires* and the majority of *prévôts*, they were fully empowered to investigate and judge cases in their own right. This did not in any sense imply that they would wish to set up their authority against that of the senior officers serving with the armies; their role was perceived very clearly as one of support to the commander of the army, and as a legal agent able to circumvent some of the disputes over authority and competence that might arise between the groups of *prévôts* and *commissaires*.[66] Trials would still be carried out before a *conseil de guerre*, but with the *intendant* acting as president and selecting the other judges from among officers whom he considered suitable.[67]

Significantly, however, the *intendants de la justice* were not directly linked with the *secrétaire de la guerre*. They were the chancellor's appointees, and looked to him for support and authorization. Much of their correspondence concerning military affairs was addressed to the chancellor, and this served further to reduce the sense that the *secrétaire de la guerre* possessed a defined and separate sphere of authority.[68] One consequence of this was that the distinction between provincial

---

[65] G. Hanotaux, *Les origines de l'institution des intendants des provinces d'après les documents inédits* (Paris, 1884), pp. 117–21; Bonney, *Political Change*, p. 265; Baxter, *Servants of the Sword*, pp. 3–19.

[66] See particularly M. Antoine, 'Genèse de l'institution des intendants', *Journal des savants* (1982), 287–317, and M. Antoine, 'Institutions françaises en Italie sous le règne de Henri II: gouverneurs et intendants', *Mélanges de l'école française de Rome*, 94 (1982), 759–818; Bonney, *Political Change*, pp. 30–3; D. Moulias, 'Les origines du corps de l'intendance', *Revue historique de l'armée*, 23 (1967), 83–8.

[67] Baxter, *Servants of the Sword*, pp. 67–9. Baxter makes the confusing suggestion, via a *mémoire* of Bassompierre, that the *intendant* might call upon *prévôts* with the armies to act as co-judges, but this ignores the fundamental issue of the different bases of authority on which the various judicial agents acted, the besetting problem of the entire system: Baxter, *Servants of the Sword*, p. 67. I have found no evidence of this practice.

[68] Mousnier, *Lettres à Séguier*, together with the series of volumes in the Bibliothèque Nationale from which the collection is derived: Ms.fr. 17367–74 (Séguier correpondence from 1633 to 1643). A.D. Lublinskaya (ed.), *The Internal Policy of French Absolutism, 1633–1649* (2 vols; Moscow and St Petersburg, 1966). These collections of correspondence reveal the extent to which *intendants* serving with the army-corps regarded the chancellor as the obvious recipient of information and the channel of communication to the centre, as, conversely, does the relatively small quantity of correspondence relating to the *intendants* in the Archives de la Guerre.

The civil administration of the army: the structures

and army *intendants* remained vague; powers of justice accorded both within a province and over the troops within the borders or passing through, were common. There was no clear sense that the intendants who held judicial responsibilities with the armies were a group set apart from those with such responsibilities in the provinces.[69]

THE SUPPLY ADMINISTRATION

The central organization of supply and the commissaires généraux des vivres

An ordinance of 1557 established the rudiments of a supply administration, decreeing that an 'ancien conseiller du roi' should assume overall control of the provision of *vivres* to the army. This informal appointment was to be supported by two *commissaires généraux des vivres*.[70] All three figures' primary responsibility was to coordinate the supply of *vivres* collected and assembled by the local and regional authorities. In practice it would seem that the *ancien conseiller* was rarely nominated: Sully assumed the function in 1610, when preparing the French forces for intervention in the Kleve-Jülich succession, and Richelieu's appointment of himself as *surintendant des vivres* in July 1635 may be seen as an institutionalized version of this post.[71] Overall central responsibility for the direction of *vivres* was in the hands of the *sécretaires d'Etat*, and the edict of 1619 explicitly divided up responsibility for the supply of the armies on a regional basis reflecting the *départements* of the secretaries.[72] In 1627 an edict doubled the number of *commissaires généraux des vivres* from two to four, partly to raise revenues for the *parties casuelles* but also to allocate one *commissaire* to each of the four *secrétaires*.[73] In 1631 a further office was created, that of the *grand maître et contrôleur général des vivres*, responsible to the *trésoriers généraux de l'extraordinaire*

---

[69] SHAT A¹ 14, fo. 44, 6 Feb. 1633, commission of intendant 'tant en nos dictes armées qu'ès villes de ladite province de Champagne, Metz, Toul et Verdun' for Isaac de Laffemas; Hanotaux, *Origines des intendants*, p. 295, 1630, Potherie and Aubray to act as joint *intendants* in Provence and in the army sent to put down the rebellion in Aix; A¹ 26, fo. 49, 28 Apr. 1635, commission for the *intendant* of the army of Champagne and for the troops passing through the province for Jean de Choisy, in which it emerges that Choisy is already *intendant de province* for Champagne. This issue of the confused jurisdiction between the *intendants des provinces* and the *intendants d'armée*, and the wider issues of the effective powers of the intendants will be considered in more detail in chapter 8, pp. 448–59.

[70] Kroener, *Les routes*, pp. 7–8; J.E. Iung, 'Service de vivres et munitionnaires sous l'ancien régime: la fourniture du pain de munition aux troupes de Flandre et d'Allemagne de 1701–1710', Thèse pour le diplôme d'archiviste, Ecole Nationale des Chartes, Paris, 1983, pp. 4–5.

[71] For Sully's control of *vivres*, see Buisseret, *Sully*, pp. 160–1, who accepts Sully's claim that he had refused the *surintendance des vivres* for the campaign of 1610. However, this was probably a matter of terminology rather than function, since Sully was certainly acting as the *ancien conseiller* with charge of supply in 1610: Kroener, *Les routes*, p. 8; for Richelieu's assumption of the *surintendance générale des vivres*, Aubery, *Richelieu*, I. 501, 26 July 1635, Bullion to La Valette.

[72] Ranum, *Richelieu*, pp. 189–90; Kroener, *Les routes*, p. 9.

[73] Kroener, *Les routes*, pp. 9–10.

The administrative context

des guerres, obviously intended to have a specific supervisorial function over the costings and payments for supply of *vivres* to the armies.[74]

The provincial administration of vivres

In practice the central coordination of supplies remained skeletal; the main burden of supplying the armies, coordinating and stockpiling *vivres*, rested with provincial officials. The assumption of the crown, whether made in the 1550s or the 1630s, was that local authorities would cooperate in matters of supply, and that it was in their interests to ensure timely and sufficient distribution of *vivres* to soldiers whose behaviour and potential disorders would otherwise prove more difficult to control.[75] While this was probably true, it did nothing to resolve the perennial problem of allocating and maintaining specific responsibility for aspects of particular supply operations, a situation which had deteriorated to crisis point by 1635. Provincial supply was divided between existing civilian administrators in the provinces and a number of specifically appointed *commissaires*. The supply requirements of the armies were tripartite. Provision needed to be made for armies in the field, which either involved collecting grain in the French frontier provinces and transporting it to the armies on campaign, or contributing to the stockpiling of supplies in specified magazines near to or across the frontiers.[76] Troops *en route* for the campaign theatres needed to be supplied by means of *étapes* or stopping points, stocked from the localities in preparation for the arrival of troop detachments. Finally, the heaviest burden was imposed for the subsistence of the troops in winter quarters, the period from November to April during which large parts of the armies were billeted upon the French provinces.

The actual purchase and collection of grain, the grinding of flour and baking of the *pain de munition*, and finally the distribution of the bread to the soldiers were delegated under contract to entrepreneurial *munitionnaires*.[77] But this system needed supervision: the *munitionnaires* frequently required assistance in finding and purchasing grain locally. Transport provided by the *munitionnaires* and their agents was rarely adequate to meet the burden of collecting and distributing supplies, and the *munitionnaires* and their *commis* inevitably saw corruption as the

---

[74] BN Ms.fr. 4811, fos. 1–72 [n.d.]: 'instructions pour la charge de grand maistre, surintendant général des vivres, munitions, magazines estappes et avitaillement de France, et de l'ordre qui doibt estre observer pour la conduite et administration des vivres des gens de guerre.' (copy of edict of creation, fos. 55–6).

[75] An assumption made explicit in letters to consuls and magistrats of Frankfurt, Strasbourg and Basle, who were instructed to give all practical assistance to the French *munitionnaire*, Lattignan, in the collection of *vivres* for the French forces on the Rhine, by this means 'preventing the disorders that necessity otherwise render inevitable': SHAT A¹ 24, fo. 114, 26 Feb. 1635. These self-interested requests for assistance had first been made a couple of months earlier: A¹ 23, fo. 361, Dec. 1634.

[76] SHAT A¹ 23, fo. 62, 30 Sept. 1634, Servien to the *trésoriers* at Châlons, ordering them to establish magazines for forage on the frontier of Champagne.

[77] BN Ms.fr. 4811, fos. 26v–32, various forms of contracts and instructions for *munitionnaires*.

means to maximize their profits from the contracts. In the front line of the provincial administrators stood the *trésoriers de France* in the *généralités* and – where they had been appointed – the provincial *intendants*. Rivalries between the two groups were endemic, and it was not until the mid-1640s that the crown's consistent favouring of the provincial *intendants* in the supply administration began to resolve the tensions in their favour.[78] The provisioning of the *étapes* was entrusted to the *trésoriers* during this period, though they shared responsibility for their supply with the provincial governors.[79] These latter, the key figures for the military administration in the provinces, obviously enjoyed complete social and political superiority over the *trésoriers*, but at the same time would not have wished to be involved in the fine detail of a supply operation.[80] Also involved in military supply were the governors of fortified *places* and the governors and urban authorities of major towns, who were instructed to ensure adequate provision both for *étapes* fixed within their jurisdiction and for the subsistence of the troops during the winter quarter period.[81] Their priority was to ensure that adequate quantities of supplies were kept within the locality to meet these immediate demands, and not drained away to meet the needs of the campaigning armies; they necessarily opposed the attempts of *munitionnaires* and provincial officials to use towns and *places fortes* equipped with magazines as sources of food supplies for troops stationed elsewhere.[82]

All of the previously mentioned figures were involved in the supply of *vivres* as a subsidiary task to their main functions. From the later sixteenth century there had also grown up an administrative structure that was concerned primarily with the provision of *vivres*. A group of lesser, venal, office-holders, entitled specifically *commissaires des vivres*, or *commissaires particuliers des vivres*, was brought into being when, in 1597, a *commissaire particulier* was appointed to each *élection*.[83] The attraction of the office – whose numbers were doubled in 1622 and tripled in 1631

---

[78] A shift in the balance of provincial power temporarily overturned by the effects of the *Frondes* after 1648: Kroener, *Les routes*, pp. 12–21; for the role of the *trésoriers* in the provisioning of the *étapes* and the recovery of this authority during the *Frondes* see also J.P. Charmeil, *Les trésoriers de France à l'époque de la Fronde* (Paris, 1964), pp. 168–70, 388–96.

[79] SHAT A¹ 22, fo. 215, 9 June 1634, circular to six provincial governors, drawing attention to changes in the collection and allocation of supplies through the *étape* system.

[80] The governors were permitted to fix the itineraries of troops passing through their provinces, for example, and would work with the lesser officials in their provinces to ensure that the chosen *étapes* were adequately prepared and that the troops kept to their itinerary: SHAT A¹ 22, fo. 356, 13 Aug. 1634, Servien to Charles de Neufville-Villeroy, marquis d'Alincourt, governor of Lyonnais, Forez and Beaujolais, confirming the governor's right to establish itineraries through his provinces for the conduct and ordering of the troops.

[81] For example, SHAT A¹ 19, fos. 238, 240, 21 Sept. 1633, letters from Servien to Claude Frère, sr de Crolles, *premier président* of the *Parlement* of Grenoble, instructing him to ensure the collection and distribution of provisions through the *étapes* for troops about to pass through Dauphiné.

[82] BN Ms.fr. 4811, fo. 7v: 'lettres pattentes et autres expeditions necessaires pour faire lesdites levées des magazines de bled '.

[83] BN Ms.fr. 4811, fo. 63v.

The administrative context

– was entirely financial: the *commissaires* received a payment of 2 *sols* per *livre* on all transactions connected with the payment and reimbursement of sums for the provisioning of troops in the *élection*.[84] By the 1620s the military activities in the frontier provinces threatened to overwhelm a supply system based upon *commissaires* working at the level of individual *élections*, especially when these *officiers* were constantly being challenged in their jurisdiction by other local office-holders.

A further group of *officiers* involved in matters of supply held posts specifically connected with the upkeep, replacement and distribution of grain held in particular towns or *places fortes*. These, entitled either *gardes magasins* or *commissaires gardes particuliers*, were holders of a venal office specifically attached to their particular *magasin*.[85] Their independence and insistence that they were accountable only to the crown and its ministers led to direct conflict with the governors of the *places*, especially when the latter considered that the distribution of grain to the garrison was necessary to make good shortfalls elsewhere in the supply system.[86] Attempts were made to mitigate the confusion of the system by appointing *commissaires des vivres* with responsibility for supply across an entire province.[87] Such figures were subdelegated officials, nominated by the *commissaires généraux des vivres* to provide assistance with the supervision and control of *vivres*.[88]

The control of vivres *within the armies*

The *intendants d'armée* had existed before 1635, but their commissions were rarely drawn up in the standardized form of the intendancies of *justice, police et finances* which later became typical. As a result, many of the earlier intendancies specifically included the function of overseeing the *vivres* of the army. In 1629 Gaspard Du Gué was *intendant des finances, vivres et magasins* with the army of La Force established in Burgundy and Bresse, and the following year held the same appointment with the army of Italy, specifically concerned with the problems of supplying the forces in Piedmont.[89] Similarly in 1634, Claude Gobelin, sieur d'Aunoy, was given charge of the *finances et vivres* with La Force's army in Germany.[90] Intendancies created with specific responsibility for a particular *place*

---

[84] Iung, 'Service des vivres', p. 17.
[85] Some of these posts, in strategically important centres, could be extremely responsible, see, for example, the commision appointing the sr Duman to the *garde générale* of *vivres et munitions* at Pinerolo: SHAT A¹ 21, fo. 58, 10 July 1634.
[86] Kroener, *Les routes*, pp. 48–50.
[87] SHAT, A¹ 24, fo. 109, 25 Feb. 1635: sr Videl created *commissaire des vivres* for Dauphiné.
[88] Kroener, *Les routes*, pp. 52–3.
[89] SHAT A¹ 13, fo. 149, 1629; A¹ 12, fo. 131, May 1630; Grillon, v. 85–6, 16 Feb. 1630, Du Gué to Richelieu. In the same period the *intendant de justice* with the army of Italy was Abel Servien.
[90] Avenel, IV. 618, 1 Oct. 1634, Richelieu to Servien: 'mémoire de diverses dépesches pour l'Allemagne'; SHAT A¹ 26, pce 64, 11 July 1635: Guillaume Bordeaux appointed *intendant des finances, vivres et magasins* in Champagne and the surrounding provinces. Although the subsequently

The civil administration of the army: the structures

forte, or newly conquered city, invariably had as the major priority the duty to maintain supplies of food for the garrison. Balme, made *intendant de la justice et finance* at Pinerolo in 1635 having previously been *contrôleur des fortifications*, was immediately informed that the provisioning of Pinerolo was his most important function.[91]

The duties of *intendants d'armée* to supervise the provision of *vivres* to the troops in the field or in garrisons were supplemented by a further group of *commissaires des vivres*, given charge of supply in specific armies.[92] The duplication of authority between *intendants* and *commissaires des vivres* once again reflected their appointment by different authorities, the *commissaires des vivres*, like their counterparts in the provinces, being the subdelegates of the *commissaires généraux des vivres*.

The regulation of supply was not entirely left to civilian office-holders. Taking into account the greater complexity of the needs of the cavalry, the formal duties of the *maréchaux des logis* for the cavalry included responsibility for the supply of the troops, and above all the supply of forage for the horses.[93]

Munitionnaires *and* vivandiers

Throughout Richelieu's ministry an increasingly heavy responsibility for supply was placed in the hands of a decreasing number of substantial entrepreneurial *munitionnaires*. The advantage of this lay in the extremely close relations that could be established between the ministers and one or two *munitionnaires* such as the srs Rose or Lattignan, both of whom dominated the supply of the armies in the campaigns of 1635 and 1636. The provision of supplies other than the statutory *pain de munition* to the infantry depended upon the local initiatives of *vivandiers*, individual vendors or food-producers who were prepared to take advantage of the presence of troops to expand their market opportunities. The numbers of *vivandiers* and the variety of goods that they would offer could vary widely depending on the location of the army, the regularity with which troops formed a part of the local economy and were perceived to have money to buy food and drink other than their basic *pain de munition*, and upon the state of local agriculture and animal-rearing. But in all cases for the system to operate

---

appended description of the commission entitles it an *intendance de justice, police et finances*, the text makes no reference to justice and police, and emphasizes the role as coordinator of the supplies to the army: A¹ 41, fos. 56–7, 13 July 1635, accompanying instructions to Bordeaux.

[91] SHAT A¹ 25, fo. 8, 2 July 1635, notification of appointment; fo. 71, 16 July, extensive instructions for the collection and accumulation of grain supplies at Pinerolo.

[92] SHAT A¹ 14, fo. 37, 30 Dec. 1632, commission for an intendancy of *vivres* and *munitions* in the army of Germany for Coquer, *commissaire des guerres*; A¹ 14, fo. 54, 28 Mar. 1633, commission granted to Le Caumar to exercise the *charge* of *garde général des vivres et munitions*, apparently over all of the armies of the king.

[93] Kroener, *Les routes*, p. 51. Despite their title, it should be stressed that the *maréchaux des logis* were simply high-ranking NCOs, company quartermasters, in effect.

The administrative context

demanded effective organization and policing – supervision of markets, establishment of mutually acceptable prices, rudimentary guarantees of order and security for the tradesmen and women.[94]

By 1634 the ministry was well aware of the need for more direct administrative intervention in supply through the already existing supervisory officials.[95] A lengthy document arising out of the experience of campaigning in Lorraine emphasized both the need to stockpile grain in substantial magazines at key points on the frontiers, quite independently of the supply efforts of the *munitionnaires* and whatever could be purchased locally for the needs of the troops. The use of such magazines implied more effective transport from the magazines to the army camps, and the author of the *mémoire* proposed giving priority to obtaining horses and waggons of the highest quality for the transport of *vivres* rather than for the artillery. The teams of horses for the artillery operated intermittently; the horses were rested and grazed when the artillery was in camp or assembled for a siege, whereas the supply of *vivres* was a constant necessity, requiring the troops of horses to be continually active. Moreover it was futile to think that the *munitionnaires* would lessen their profits by obtaining horses of adequate quality for these duties. Only the direct assumption of a large part of the transport responsibilities by the army administration could make this part of the system work.[96] The *mémoire* was taken seriously, at least at the level of planning: in the details of the *contrôle général* establishing the available funding for 1635, Bullion made an explicit allocation for the transport of *vivres*, stipulating that each army-corps of 15,000 troops should be accompanied by 500 waggons for the transport of *vivres*, which was to be in addition to a further 50 waggons stipulated as the responsibility of the *munitionnaires* for the day-to-day supply of the army.[97] The waggons were to be provided by the *élections* in return for a rebate on the *taille*. Whether the responsibility for this levy was to be in the hands of the *commissaires particuliers* or the *élus* is not clear; in practice neither group did much to requisition waggons and horses, and nothing was to be done during the 1635 campaign to maintain these prescribed levels of transport for supplies.[98]

If the transport of *vivres* was identified as one area in which the government

---

[94] SHAT, A¹ 14, fo. 46, 14 Feb. 1633: characteristic *ordonnance* to regulate the prices of foodstuffs brought to the army camps by *vivandiers*.
[95] As early as January 1634 Louis d'Arpajon, vicomte de Montal, and *maréchal de camp* with the army on the Rhine, had written to La Force of the failure of the *munitionnaires* to ensure adequate supply of the troops, of his short-term advances to keep the army supplied with the basic *pain de munition*, and of the vital need for direct intervention to stockpile *vivres*: AAE CP Lorraine 14, fo. 10, 1 Jan. 1634.
[96] AAE MD 811, fos. 194–5 [1634], *mémoire* concerning the subsistence of the army; BN Ms.fr. 4811, fos. 34, 39, two *ordonnances* concerning supplementary provision of transport for supplies.
[97] AAE MD 812, fo. 385, [late] 1634, *abrégé du contrôle général*.
[98] For example, AAE MD 815, fos. 34, 90, 6 Aug. 1635, Servien to Richelieu; fos. 228, 325, 20 Sept./10 Oct. 1635, Bouthillier to Richelieu – all concerned with the chronic shortage of waggons to transport *vivres* to the armies.

The civil administration of the army: the structures

would need to intervene with its own agents, the stockpiling of grain in magazines was also given priority, though whether this was to safeguard the garrisons in *places fortes*, or to provide an emergency supply for the armies on campaign is not clear. In September 1634 de Noyers, acting as one of the *intendants des finances* directly under the authority of the *surintendants*, was commissioned to establish supplies of hay and oats for the cavalry in a number of designated frontier *places*.[99] The maréchal de La Force was equally concerned that his troops operating in Lorraine and on the Rhine should be able to draw upon magazines containing three months' supply of grain and requested money and administrative assistance to accomplish this, rather than relying on the efforts of the existing *munitionnaires*.[100]

Provision of munitions de guerre – shot, powder and match

The appointment of Charles de La Porte de La Meilleraye in 1634 was further to reduce the control of the *grand maître de l'artillerie* over the founding and distribution of artillery, to the benefit of Richelieu and his preoccupation with the navy and coastal defence.[101] However, the *grand maître* retained full control of the purchase, storage and distribution of gunpowder, shot and the slow-burning match which was the means by which virtually all muskets and arquesbuses were fired.[102] Although the quantity of artillery with the French armies, even when engaged at a major siege, remained comparatively small, the provision of powder, shot and match for the infantry and cavalry was of a different order of magnitude.[103] It was common for batches of gunpowder or match of 100 or 200 *milliers* (a *millier* being around 1,000 lb.) weight or more to require storage or transport.[104] However, in comparison with the supply of *vivres* the longer shelf-

---

[99] AAE MD 1676, fo. 80, 14 Sept. 1634; 811, fo. 38, 25 Sept. 1634, Sublet de Noyers to Richelieu, who also points out the difficulties of creating these magazines without a direct order from the king to the municipalities that they should cooperate in the provision of the fodder; this supply operation was also a concern of Pierre Conty d'Argencour, *ingénieur du roi*, acting under commission to survey the state of fortifications and garrisons on the north-east frontier: MD 1676, fo. 78, 12 Sept. 1634.

[100] AAE CP Lorraine 14, fo. 170, 7 Feb. 1634, *mémoire* from La Force; the message was repeated later in the month by the despatch of the *munitionnaire* with the army, the sr Toison, to the court: fo. 196, 18 Feb. 1634; AAE CP Lorraine 15, fo. 379, 11 Dec. 1634, *intendant* Gobelin to Richelieu.

[101] For the reduction in the control of the *grand maître* over the artillery see chapter 9, pp. 475–7.

[102] Daniel, *Histoire*, II. 372–6; Brunet, *Histoire générale de l'artillerie française*; Boutaric, *Institutions militaires*, pp. 362–5; Susane, *Histoire de l'artillerie française*, pp. 109–26; Buisseret, *Sully*, pp. 140–61.

[103] Boutaric, *Institutions militaires*, p. 362, suggested that there was an average of four artillery pieces for each 1,000 men in a French field army, but for Richelieu's ministry this is certainly an overestimate; Avenel, *Richelieu*, III. 124–5, comments on the shortage of artillery with the French field armies; see also chapter 1, pp. 65–71.

[104] SHAT A¹29, fo. 283, 23 Sept. 1636, d'Halincourt to de Noyers, discussing the transportation of 200 *milliers* of powder to Lyon; AAE CP Lorraine 31, fo. 325, Du Hallier to de Noyers, reporting arrival of 100,000 lb of gunpowder at Nancy; CP Savoie 28, fo. 326, 13 May 1639, Richelieu's

The administrative context

life of munitions ensured at least that stockpiling and storage was a less complex operation. Munitions were stored in bulk in a series of key magazines in Paris, Metz, Châlons, Amiens, Lyon, Calais, Narbonne and in a large number of other major garrisoned *places* near the frontiers. There, supplies could be doubled either for defence in the event of a siege, or to allow quantities of munitions to be despatched to the field armies.[105] The greatest challenge facing the munitions administrators was not the collection of adequate supplies, but their distribution; finding sufficient horses and waggons and adequate escorts to transport powder or shot to the campaign theatres was by far the main preoccupation of the artillery administration.

The structure of the artillery and munitions administration had been established in the sixteenth century. Immediately below the *grand maître* were one or more immediate subordinates, the *lieutenants généraux de l'artillerie*, who held authority over the artillery itself, munitions, and control and discipline of the artillery officers in the absence of the *grand maître*.[106] Though in theory all such appointments were in the gift of the *grand maître*, it is clear that in an increasing number of cases such nominations were made by the crown, or delegated to the commander in the field. During the grand mastership of Sully's son, Maximilien-François de Béthune, marquis de Rosny (1618–33), a series of *lieutenants généraux* were granted control of the artillery in particular campaign theatres by the direct intervention of the king, notably Henri d'Orléans, marquis de Rothelin, who was made *lieutenant général* of the artillery at the siege of La Rochelle, and subsequently the marquis d'Effiat (1630) and La Meilleraye himself in 1632.[107]

Beneath the *lieutenants généraux* was a hierarchy of venal office, headed by three *contrôleurs généraux* who held office on a triennial basis, for four months of the year each. The distribution of funds to the various artillery *départements* was handled by two *trésoriers généraux*, exercising the office on a six-monthly *alternatif*. Beneath these were the *commissaires ordinaires* and *extraordinaires*. The latter were appointed only in wartime, but with a possibility, through extended service or patronage, of being appointed into the ranks of the permanent *commissaires ordinaires*.[108] The main task of these agents was the supervision of the lower ranks of the artillery staff – the *canonniers*, unskilled *pionniers*, founders, carpenters and

---

response to d'Hémery's request for 500 *milliers* of powder, match and lead for the army of Italy; A¹ 52, fo. 208, 20 May 1639, arrival of 1,200 *milliers* of powder ordered from the United Provinces.
[105] Daniel, *Histoire*, II. 389; AAE MD 828, fo. 263, [1637], *état* of powder stored during 1636 and 1637 in seventeen locations, together with a further 200 *milliers* to arrive from the United Provinces; MD 832, fo. 74v, [1638], similar for 1638 – ten locations.
[106] Daniel, *Histoire*, II. 376.
[107] Grillon, III. 396, 25 July 1628, Louis XIII to Richelieu.
[108] Susane, *Histoire de l'artillerie française*, pp. 130–4; SHAT A¹ 62, fos. 107, 108, 10 Apr. 1640, commission establishing sr de Beaupré as *commissaire ordinaire de l'artillerie* with the army of Germany, accompanied by a series of detailed instructions from La Meilleraye. The salaries of the *commissaires* were bewilderingly varied, presumably reflecting either the jurisdiction or the internal seniority of the posts: BN Ms.fr. 4561, fo. 69, *état* for payment of the artillery officers in 1622.

The civil administration of the army: the structures

others, who transported, maintained and fired the cannon – and control of the disbursement of munitions with the armies. The direct control of the munitions stored in magazines was the responsibility of a different hierarchy, composed of *gardes provinciaux*, appointed by the king in order to assume charge of the main arsenals, and *gardes particuliers*, appointed by the *grand maître*, and placed in charge of temporary or less substantial stockpiles of munitions.[109] The distribution of munitions from the magazines to the armies was, at least in theory, contracted out to twenty 'capitaines de chevaux', allocated on a provincial basis, each with the obligation to provide 200 horses, 50 waggoners and 25 waggons for the transport of munitions whenever required.[110] Such a system may have been adequate to the transportation needs of the army in 1552, when the *ordonnance* was promulgated; it was wholly inadequate for warfare after 1635, and the movement of substantial quantities of munitions was delegated on a largely *ad hoc* basis to governors of *places*, local officiers and others.[111] It was equally the case that the crown's willingness to obtain supplies via the activities of large-scale entrepreneurs, who offered the short-term advantage of providing goods on credit, could backfire in the same way as the use of *munitionnaires* for the supply of *vivres*. Richelieu's ministry saw an ever-growing dependence on a single entrepreneur, François Sabathier, for the provision of saltpetre, the vital component in manufacturing gunpowder.[112] Although the situation was mitigated by the huge quantities of powder bought abroad, above all from the United Provinces and Denmark, the dependence on Sabathier and his *commis* for the provision of domestic saltpetre had clear disadvantages. In 1636 it was necessary to warn Sabathier against seeking to establish a *de facto* monopoly on the gathering of saltpetre within France.[113] Subsequent correspondence from commanders and other administrators suggested some dissatisfaction with the efforts of Sabathier and his *commis*, especially when his role was extended to the production of powder as well as the collection of saltpetre. In turn, Sabathier was clearly encountering difficulties in extracting contracted payments from the crown, and discovering that he had been assigned revenues which proved inadequate to cover his outlay.[114] When he diversified his

---

[109] Daniel, *Histoire*, II. 389.
[110] Susane, *Histoire de l'artillerie française*, p. 124; the *ordonnance* also specified the daily sums (50 *sols* per day for each team of four horses) they would be paid for the maintenance of the horses and waggons.
[111] SHAT A¹ 30, fo. 167, 22 Oct. 1636, de Noyers to the *lieutenant général* of the *siège présidial* of Rouen, ordering him to make arrangements to transport 140 *milliers* of gunpowder to Abbeville – this to be in conjunction with the efforts of the *commissaire* of the artillery, de Saincton, who also received orders to raise horses and waggons: fo. 168, 23 Oct.
[112] Bonney, *King's Debts*, pp. 186–8; Sabathier had received a nine-year lease to provide the armies with saltpetre from 1 July 1634 (Bonney, *King's Debts*, p. 187); J.U. Nef, *Industry and Government in France and England, 1540–1640* (Ithaca, N.Y., 1957), pp. 59–68.
[113] SHAT A¹ 29, fo. 21, 16 Aug. 1636, *ordre du roi*.
[114] SHAT A¹ 59, fo. 291, 7 June 1640, instruction to *intendant des finances*, Jacques Tubeuf, concerning payment of arrears claimed by Sabathier.

The administrative context

activities into direct involvement in the crown's finances, purchasing the office of *trésorier des parties casuelles* in 1638 and engaging simultaneously in large-scale loan contracts, his situation became more precarious still. Contracting with the crown for the huge sum of 9 million *livres* in February 1640, Sabathier became heavily overextended, and by summer 1641 was only staving off bankruptcy by a series of orders from the Council of Finance suspending the legal claims of his creditors.[115] The bankruptcy of Sabathier carried a real threat for the provision of gunpowder to the armies; after eight years in which he dominated the supply of saltpetre, there was no obvious alternative able to step in to replace his network of *commis* and agents. How far this explains the considerable efforts to keep him financially afloat and to hold off his creditors is unclear, but the danger to the war-effort of such concentration in the hands of one entrepreneur was obvious.[116]

CONFLICTS OF JURISDICTION

The principal characteristic of the military administration was the confused tangle of senior authorities presiding over the activities of the agents in the provinces and with the armies. The military administration was not a pyramid, focusing authority upwards towards the *secrétaire de la guerre*, or any of the senior government ministers. It was a series of different administrative hierarchies, each looking to a different central authority: the *surintendant des finances*, the *secrétaire de la guerre*, the chancellor, or the traditional great military *offices de la couronne* – the *grand maître de l'artillerie*, the *colonels généraux*, the *maréchaux*, the tribunal of the *connétablie et maréchaussée*. There was no single, coordinating authority standing over all of these to resolve disputes over jusrisdiction, let alone rationalize the functions of the officials. As suggested earlier, it would be quite false to speak of the *secrétaire de la guerre* as 'controlling' the war-effort. He neither did so at the level of policy-making, nor did he control more than a portion of the administration charged with the supervision and coordination of the armies. Such divided and incomplete authority, not subject to any shared hierarchical superior, greatly increased the opportunities for evasion, for the overturning of administrators' decisions and for appeals against successful attempts to enforce or maintain regulations.

With the exception of a few harmonious working relationships, especially those between *intendants* and commanders such as that between the *intendant* Jean Choisy and the commander of the army in Germany, Jean-Baptiste Budes, comte de Guébriant,[117] the high command rarely had a good word for *prévôts*,

---

[115] Bonney, *King's Debts*, pp. 187–8.
[116] See the discussion about the impending bankruptcy of Sabathier in AAE MD 845, fo. 175, [1642], *mémoire* of Etienne III d'Aligre, *conseiller d'Etat*.
[117] For example, AAE CP Allemagne 16, fos. 318, 322v, 17 Sept. 1641, letters of Guébriant and Choisy to de Noyers, giving strong support to mutual decisions about pay and discipline.

The civil administration of the army: the structures

commissaires or the agents of the *munitionnaires* and *trésoriers*. A *commissaire des guerres*, Boyer, who had the temerity to criticize Henri de Rohan for allegedly holding the *montre* on a day other than that anticipated by the *commissaires*, was denounced by the duke to Servien as 'un petit fou presomptueux ignorant en sa charge et incapable de faire aucune chose de bien'.[118] The maréchal de Gramont was doubtless echoing a typical prejudice when he wrote to de Noyers that: 'ce que je trouve de joly est que les commissaires ne paraissent jamais que pour recevoir leurs taxations'.[119]

In such circumstances, a clear and unambiguous hierarchy would be essential if relatively minor agents of the central government were to have any chance of standing up against the interests and assertions of the officers.[120] In practice, the lack of this clear hierarchy, the confusions of jurisdiction, the potential to play off one group of administrators against another, contributed to making impossible what would in any case have been a difficult task.

Not only did this structure of multiple authorities create ambiguity about the location of authority, it also conditioned the willingness of senior officials to defend the interests of administrators in the field. It was clear that in any clash between an official and the high command, the extent to which a minister or a senior military office-holder would stand up for the interests of the official would depend on whether he was perceived as a client. The *secrétaire de la guerre* would certainly act to defend the interests of his *commissaires des guerres* in the event that they were involved in a quarrel with a military officer, but would be far less likely to stand up for a *contrôleur*, a *prévôt* or even an *intendant*. In cases where *commissaires* were attacked or abused by troops or officers, the *secrétaire* would take considerable pains to investigate the cases and to do all possible to have those guilty punished. A flurry of correspondence and decisive action by the *secrétaire* followed the information in June 1637 that the *commissaire* Jean-Baptiste de Bretagne had been assaulted by the marquis of Courcy, captain of a cavalry company.[121] In March 1639 Sublet de Noyers sent a peremptory order for the dismissal of the

---

[118] AAE CP Lorraine 25, fo. 84v, 8 Feb. 1635, Rohan to Servien; Nicolas de l'Hospital, maréchal de Vitry went further than Rohan in demanding – and obtaining – the recall of *commissaire* Savyer, whom he charged with obstruction and lack of respect: SHAT A^1 25, fos. 599, 630, 6, 19 Dec. 1635, Servien to Vitry and Savyer; A^1 41, fo. 68, 15 Jan. 1636, Servien to Vitry, notifying him of the decision to replace Savyer with La Berche.

[119] AAE MD 1680, fo. 439v, 28 Sept. 1641.

[120] Indicative of the failure of confidence in this respect was the practice of getting senior military officers to accompany and support the civil administrators in their functions: AAE MD 1679, fo. 35, 7 May 1640, instructions to the sr de La Ferté, maréchal de camp, to attend the *revue* of the troops assembling on the Flanders frontier.

[121] SHAT A^1 37, fos. 142, 143, 147, 150, 153, 17/18 June 1637, letters to Coucy, Bretagne, maréchal Châtillon, and orders for the arrest of Coucy and the disbandment of his company. See also A^1 47i, fo. 232, 3 Nov. 1638, order for the dismissal of captain Beaulieu 'qui a levé le baton sur le commissaire Chantelou'.

The administrative context

aide-major of the regiment of Bretagne, charged with assault upon the *commissaire* Pierre Guignard.[122] De Noyers showed similar resolution in response to the maltreatment of *commissaire* Anthoine Desmaretz in 1640, and in 1641 when the *commissaire* Jacques Magnan was threatened by captain du Hamel.[123] Though the *secrétaire* was obliged to transfer *commissaire* Henri d'Aubray from Arras to Landrecies in response to the complaints of the newly installed governor of Arras, François de Jussac d'Ambleville, seigneur de Saint-Preuil, it is evident that this humiliation of one of de Noyers' clients was a factor in the antagonism that the *secrétaire* subsequently maintained towards Saint-Preuil.[124]

Yet this willingness to defend those whom the *secrétaire* recognized as his clients stands in sharp contrast to the indifference or positive lack of support for administrators whose authority was not clearly linked to his own. In a quarrel between the *grand prévôt* and Charles d'Aumont, sieur de Villequier in 1635, Servien made it clear that his support would go to Villequier.[125] The intendant Pierre Imbert was reprimanded by de Noyers for making 'difficulties' in the negotiation of a recruitment *traité* with François de Blanchefort de Créqui, duc de Lesdiguières, although the previous correspondence, mostly to *commissaires*, had been specifically concerned with fraud and corruption in recruitment.[126] In similar fashion, a peremptory letter from de Noyers to Le Tellier, then *intendant* with the army of Italy, simply ordered him to reinstate a captain whom he had dismissed for fraud and absenteeism.[127]

---

[122] SHAT A^1 51, fo. 171, 18 Mar. 1639, de Noyers to Henri II de Saint-Nectaire, marquis de La Ferté, governor of Lorraine; A^1 51, fo. 342, 3 Apr., order for investigation and punishment of officers who insulted *commissaire* Charrault.

[123] SHAT A^1 58, fo. 601, 29 Apr. 1640, de Noyers to Charles de La Porte, maréchal de La Meilleraye. This rigorous defence of Desmaretz was despite the *commissaire* having received a reprimand from de Noyers in the preceding month for absenteeism from his charge as *commissaire à la conduite* with the regiment of Picardie: A^1 58, fo. 194, 15 Mar. 1640, de Noyers to Desmaretz; A^1 63, fos. 108, 129, 13, 16 Jan. 1641, de Noyers to *intendant* Bellejamme and to the *maréchal de camp*, Jean Gassion.

[124] SHAT A^1 61, fo. 21, 9 Oct. 1640, de Noyers to Saint-Preuil. A hostility that was to lead to Saint-Preuil's trial and execution in 1641, allegedly for massacring the Spanish garrison of Bapaume after they had received a safe conduct. Saint-Preuil himself wrote to Richelieu after the massacre to defend himself and to assert that *commissaire* Aubray was behind the wider accusations of misconduct: AAE MD 1680, fo. 370, 1 Sept. 1641.

[125] SHAT A^1 25, fo. 28, 7 July 1635, Servien to Charles, comte de Lannoy, *conseiller d'Etat*. In the same year Servien refused support to Balme, *intendant de justice* and president of the *conseil souverain* at Pinerolo, affirming that he was to yield precedence in his dispute with the military governor of Pinerolo, Henri, marquis de Malissy [Maleissy], over the discipline and control of the garrison: A^1 25, fo. 548, 24 Nov. 1635, Servien to Malissy.

[126] SHAT A^1 63, fo. 544, 12 Mar. 1641, de Noyers to Imbert (François de Blanchefort de Créquy was created third duke of Lesdiguières in March 1638).

[127] SHAT A^1 68, fo. 612, 22 Mar. 1642, de Noyers to Le Tellier.

The civil administration of the army: the structures

Clashes between the military administrators

Perhaps the most obvious consequence of the diffuse structure of authority was that different groups of officials spent their time fighting over demarcation disputes and locked in quarrels over jurisdiction. Sublet de Noyers himself had direct experience of such conflicts, when as *intendant des finances* commissioned to investigate the state of fortifications on the Picardy/Champagne frontier in 1634 he clashed with the *intendant* of Champagne, Isaac de Laffemas. De Noyers' letter of complaint was addressed to Richelieu, and given the status of Laffemas as a *fidèle* of the cardinal, this may well have reduced the efficacy of the appeal.[128] It would be unlikely, however, that Sublet would not have complained in similar terms to his direct patron, *surintendant* Bullion, and it is probably significant that this feud was contemporaneous with the decision to transfer Laffemas from his intendancy over Champagne and over the troops concentrated around Metz, Toul and Verdun, to the intendancy of Limousin, while Sublet de Noyers continued to pursue his commission in Picardy and Champagne into early 1635.[129]

Any dispute between different groups of administrators ran the risk of involving rival patrons higher up the military or governmental hierarchies. A dispute between the *intendant d'armée*, Jean Choisy, and the *commissaires des guerres* over the effective strength of units serving in Feuquières' army inevitably raised tensions and led to appeals to senior authorities. Choisy's high standing with Feuquières, and the latter's careful handling of the issue, protected him from Sublet de Noyers' involvement, which would probably have been to the benefit of the *commissaires*.[130] In a subsequent conflict between some of the *commissaires* and the successive *intendants* with the army of Italy, Sublet was certainly inclined towards those he considered to be his clients. Le Tellier was appointed to the intendancy of the army of Italy in September 1640 after his predecessor, René Voyer, sieur d'Argenson, had been captured by a Spanish raiding party in Piedmont.[131] At the time of his capture, Argenson had been embroiled in a dispute with the *commissaires* of the army, Louis Bourguignon and Bernard Dreux.[132] The *commissaires* alleged that Argenson was administratively incompetent and had acquiesced in corrupt deals with the army officers, a claim given weight by the exceptionally high level of expenses for the army of

---

[128] AAE MD 1676, fo. 51, 19 Aug. 1634.

[129] G. Mongrédien, *Le bourreau du cardinal de Richelieu. Isaac de Laffemas (1584–1657)* (Paris, 1929), p. 98 n. 2: 'Aucun historien n'a signalé le passage de Laffemas à l'Intendance du Limousin'. Bonney, *Political Change*, p. 138, cites the commission's concern with potential unrest by supporters of Gaston and the Queen Mother in Limousin, but the decision to replace Laffemas in Champagne and with the army in the Trois Evêchés in the middle of the campaign season remains mysterious.

[130] AAE CP Lorraine 31, fo. 41, 6 Apr. 1639, Feuquières to de Noyers.

[131] AAE CP Savoie 30, fo. 742, 22 Aug. 1640, Harcourt to de Noyers, reporting Argenson's capture.

[132] AAE CP Savoie 31, fo. 664v, 17 Dec. 1640, de Noyers to Mazarin; Caron (ed.), *Le Tellier*, p. 22, 15 Dec. 1640, de Noyers to Le Tellier.

The administrative context

Italy.[133] In retaliation, Argenson and his supporters, above all, Jules Mazarin, alleged that the *commissaires* were spreading malicious rumours because Argenson had sought to reduce their *taxations*, the percentage of the pay of the troops taken by the *commissaires* as part of their salary.[134] De Noyers, while not convinced of Argenson's guilt, saw the dispute as a challenge to his own authority and considered that the appointment of Le Tellier under the patronage of chancellor Séguier and Bullion, and before the dispute had been resolved, was likely to weaken his control over the army of Italy.[135] Correspondence between de Noyers and Le Tellier in the first few months of the appointment was characterized by *froideur* and overt criticism on de Noyers' part.[136] The combined support of Bullion and Mazarin stabilized Le Tellier's position and ensured that the *commissaires* were disciplined for having brought malicious charges against Argenson.[137] At the same time, de Noyers was persuaded to make his peace with Le Tellier, but relations between the two, undoubtedly aggravated by the high expense and, after 1640, the limited achievement of the army of Italy, continued to be characterized by the *secrétaire*'s outbursts of irritation and his suspicions of mismanagement and local complicity.[138]

Elsewhere, in cases where de Noyers sought to reinforce the authority of the *commissaires*, his instructions anticipated clashes with different groups of administrators. The *intendant* Jean Martin, sieur de Laubardement, was explicitly warned in 1638 to do nothing to obstruct or interfere with the activities of *commissaire des guerres*, Gilles Renard, and a similar instruction was sent by de Noyers to Geoffroy Luillier, sieur d'Orgeval, *intendant* at Soissons, who was ordered to alter nothing in the arrangements for the *logement* of the troops in Champagne made by Charles Besançon de Bazoches, *commissaire pour les subsistances* in 1637/8.[139]

---

[133] Suspicions of financial irregularities in Argenson's management of the army were not allayed by the discovery that no *revues* of the army had been carried out during the siege of Turin: Caron (ed.), *Le Tellier*, p. 10, 3 Nov. 1640, Le Tellier to Bullion.

[134] AAE CP Savoie 31, fo. 664, 17 Dec. 1640, de Noyers to Mazarin. Another of the *commissaires des guerres* in north Italy, Jean de La Cour, charged with *montres*, discipline and fortifications at Casale, was writing to de Noyers in the same period, complaining that Bullion himself was acting to block payment of his salary and to undermine his position in Italy: CP Savoie 30, fo. 410, 8 May 1640; fo. 580, 10 July 1640.

[135] AAE CP Savoie 31, fo. 664, 17 Dec. 1640, de Noyers to Mazarin.

[136] Caron (ed.), *Le Tellier*, p. 17, 26 Nov. 1640, de Noyers to Le Tellier.

[137] Caron (ed.), *Le Tellier*, p. 28, 4 Jan. 1641, Louis XIII to Le Tellier.

[138] Caron (ed.), *Le Tellier*, p. 29, 4 Jan. 1641, de Noyers to Le Tellier. For characteristic outbursts against Le Tellier see Caron (ed.), *Le Tellier*, p. 70, 5 June 1641; p. 175, 19 Feb. 1642. Nor was it the case that the *surintendant*'s support in disputes would always go to the *intendant*. The memoirs of Robert Arnaud d'Andilly accuse Bullion of trying to destroy his professional reputation during his 1634 intendancy with the army of the maréchaux Brézé and de La Force operating on the Rhine. Only the combined support of Richelieu and Servien, and, Andilly suggested, his own impeccable book-keeping, saved him from Bullion's malice, and even then Bullion was able to insist that Andilly repaid a disputed sum of 23,000 *livres* out of his own pocket: *Mémoires*, XXXIV. 56–7.

[139] SHAT A^1 44 fo. 6, 21 Feb. 1638, de Noyers to Laubardement; A^1 45, fo. 202, 18 Apr. 1638, de Noyers to Orgeval.

The civil administration of the army: the structures

CONCLUSION

The army administration, even as it had developed before the expansion of the war-effort from 1635, owed little to rational planning or the concern to establish clearly defined spheres of authority. There is no evidence that it had grown up in response to a well-structured plan based upon an overview of military requirements. Much of the system had come into existence, either as the legacy of a 'feudal' concept of the army, in which the *grands* played a predominant part in the recruitment and command of troops, and expected to exercise some degree of patronage over the appointment of military officials, or through financially motivated venality of office. The factor which had mitigated the worst effects of this unstructured and largely unaccountable administration, and had concealed some of the fundamental problems, was the character of warfare before France's full involvement in the Thirty Years War from 1634 to 1635. The type of warfare envisaged – and very largely practised – before 1635 involved a concentration upon one main army, which would absorb the bulk of the royal troops and undertake the major campaigning, and a number of subsidiary defensive forces. All of the problems connected with the army administration were apparent in the main army, but with the difference that such a force was either commanded by the king himself, or was campaigning in the presence of a significant number of ministers and officers of state. Many of the inefficiencies and jurisdictional conflicts arising from officials whose authority was owed to different figures in the central and military hierarchies could be resolved or avoided if central officials were present with the army, able to coordinate their own agents and to use their authority to harmonize to some extent the operations of the administration. After 1635, this was no longer practical. Although the crown was increasingly to resort to personal control over the 'principale armée' in a particular campaign, the other forces could not be dismissed as small-scale corps, based on locally raised troops and engaged in defensive sideshows. The presence of the king with the army at Arras in the campaign of 1640, for example, or Perpignan in 1642, rendered effective administration within the other armies even more essential, since the central authorities were even less capable of rapid and effective responses to crises than they would have been when based in Paris.

Documentation surrounding the 'crisis-years' of 1635–6 leaves no doubt that the chief ministers considered that the failures of the French army were, to a significant extent, the failures of its administration. The inability to provide food supplies for the armies sufficient for even a modest campaign; the epidemic levels of desertion amongst the troops and the casual attitudes to discipline and absenteeism of the officers; the extent of fraud and corruption at the *revues* and *montres* of the troops; the mounting levels of resentment and resistance in the country to the disorders and exactions of the soldiers: all of these were recognized to be playing a major part in reducing the effectiveness of the war-effort. If the military performance of the army were to be improved, it would be as a result of better management and control of supply, the better distribution of financial resources, the control of absenteeism and desertion, the regulation of troops' movements and quartering to preserve the strength of the individual units and to avoid the destruction of local resources that were needed to generate tax revenues for the crown.

PART III

Responses and reactions

8

The management of the war-effort from 1635 to 1642: *commissaires des guerres* and *intendants*

The expanding scale of France's military commitments after 1635 posed a challenge to the fragile institutions of the early seventeenth-century French state. Richelieu and his fellow ministers could recognize the inadequacy of existing mechanisms for control and the allocation of resources, but this would not necessarily lead them towards radical reforms and innovations. They were well aware of the dangers of provoking resistance and non-cooperation from established interests within the armies: officers, venal administrators, private contractors, all of whose support was becoming more important as the scale of military activity expanded after 1635. Administrative changes were piecemeal, often incomplete or open-ended, frequently modified or abandoned, and, above all, not part of any coherent and integrated strategy for better and more responsive control over troops and resources.

This view contradicts the typical interpretation of the period, which presents the evolution under the pressure of warfare of a 'fully fledged' military bureaucracy proceeding from the 1630s and culminating in the achievements of the war ministers, Michel Le Tellier and his son, the marquis de Louvois, during the 1660s.[1] By the end of the first decade of Louis XIV's personal rule a wide-ranging structure of military administration had come into existence, capable of sustaining the burdens of an expanding war-effort through the subsequent decades of the reign.[2]

It is tempting to look for continuity with Richelieu's ministry, to argue that Le Tellier and his son were building on earlier initiatives of Richelieu and his

---

[1] Audoin, *Histoire de l'administration*, II. 156–90; F. Sicard, *Histoire des institutions militaires des Français* (4 vols.; Paris, 1834), I. 416–74; Dareste de La Chavanne, *Histoire de l'administration en France* II. 310–18; Chéruel, *Histoire de l'administration monarchique* I. 298–301, 301–31; Caillet, *De l'administration en France*, pp. 25–54, 360–79; Boutaric, *Institutions militaires*, pp. 374–95; Pagès, *Monarchie*, pp. 93–5; G. Pagès, *Les institutions monarchiques sous Louis XIII et Louis XIV* (Paris, 1937); Baxter, *Servants of the Sword*, pp. 201–8; Corvisier (ed.), *Histoire militaire*, I, pp. 359–61, 389–93; Lynn, *Giant of the Grand Siècle*, pp. 79–97.

[2] Rousset, *Histoire* I. 164–255; André, *Le Tellier et Louvois*, pp. 315–427; Corvisier, *Louvois*, pp. 77–118. Though it remains outside the scope of this work, doubt may be cast on the completeness and the practical achievements of the reforms of the 1660s in the light of the problems confronting the French army from the later 1680s. See, above all, Rowlands, 'Power, authority and army administration', which presents a wide-ranging critique of the traditional argument that the military hierarchy was fully subordinated to the authority of the war minister and his officials.

fellow ministers. This is especially the case with what has traditionally assumed to have been the principal 'centralizing' achievement of the years of war after 1635, the development of the authority and the role of the *intendants d'armée*, and the enhancement of the military functions of the provincial *intendants*. This assumption imposes a simple cause and effect pattern on developments that were a great deal more arbitrary and less coherent. In the context of Richelieu's ministry, the first significant response to the challenge posed by the new scale of warfare was the extension of the authority and functions of the *commissaires des guerres*. This extension needs to be seen in the light of the second response, the very marked increase in the use of commissions to delegate administrative authority. While some of these commissions were intended to institutionalize responsibility in the hands of selected groups of officials, this process was by no means synonymous with the rise of the *intendants d'armée*. Indeed, at various points after 1635 it appeared that the process of delegating authority under commission might sideline the *intendants d'armée* rather than facilitate their rise to preeminence.

THE DEVELOPMENT OF THE OFFICE OF *COMMISSAIRE DES GUERRES*

The most striking conclusion to be drawn from the evidence of administrative development during Richelieu's ministry is that the 'natural' agents in the attempt to develop the military administration were the *commissaires des guerres*. The first years of open war saw a significant increase and diversification of the functions of this group as the ministry attempted to tackle the problems posed by the war-effort.

The *commissaires* were already entrenched within the administrative structure and between the two groups of *commissaires des guerres pour les montres* and *commissaires à la conduite* were a relatively numerous group of agents with the armies. It was likely that an essentially cautious, conservative administration would consolidate the position of an existing group, rather than seek to impose a new set of agents. It is also significant that before Michel Le Tellier achieved more considerable powers and influence as *secrétaire de la guerre*, the *commissaires* were the one group of administrators fully within the clientele and under the authority of the *secrétaire*.

The expansion of the administrative competence of the commissaires

In general, the practice of venality led to the sale of office within the military administration with a permanent, but non-specific, financial or disciplinary function. Specific tasks were allocated to authorized agents through particular, limited, commissions. For the *commissaires des guerres* or the *commissaires à la conduite*, this could include commissions ordering them to carry out what were already ostensibly their prescribed functions, whether the administration of a *montre* or *revue* of particular troops at a particular place and time, or the conducting of a unit from one location to another.[3] In both cases the specific commission heightened the authority of the official, and simultaneously emphasized for that *commissaire* the weight that the minister placed on the effective accomplishment of the particular task. It also created the possibility, attractive to the *secrétaire de la guerre* in a situation where a large part of the administration of the army lay outside his direct authority, of commissioning 'his' officials – the *commissaires* – to carry out a range of other functions within the army.

Well before the introduction of the new *taxe des subsistances* in 1637, the *commissaires* were being given a growing role in the ordering and management of the troops in winter quarters, additional to their traditional responsibilities, mainly the conduct of *revues* and *montres* while the troops were on campaign.[4] Individual *commissaires* were also called upon to carry out the disbandment or *réformation* of selected units, albeit under the authority of a senior officer or governor.[5] In some cases this authority could extend further, to permit certain *commissaires* discretionary power to disband those units that they felt to be seriously under-strength or unfit for service.[6]

Although individual units of infantry and cavalry were very rarely recruited in the first instance on the basis of the *commissaire* system, this was not the case with

---

[3] For typical examples, SHAT A¹ 25, fo. 195, 11 Aug. 1635, sr Savier to carry out *montres* and *revues* of troops in Provence; A¹ 50, 13 Jan. 1639, Christophe Royer to carry out *revues* of companies at Langres; A¹ 59, fo. 641, 8 July 1640, Jacques Le Vacher to conduct regt of La Feuillade to siege of Arras. For an example of a more general commission – A¹ 32, pce 233, 16 Dec. 1636, authorization for Jean-Baptiste de Bretagne, *commissaire ordinaire des guerres*, to carry out the *montres* and *revues* of the troops in Lorraine and Barrois, specifically permitting him to choose times of day or night for the *revues* as he sees fit. This tradition of authorizing the conduct of *montres* by commission was a legacy of the period before the *commissaires des guerres* were venal office-holders, when specific *commissaires pour les montres* were appointed on an *ad hoc* basis to carry out the *revues* of the troops. From 1633 the *maréchaux* in command of armies were permitted to order *revues* on their own authority, and to pass this instruction, as a commission, to the *commissaires ordinaires* with their forces: AAE MD 819, fo. 56, 1633, 'ordre necessaire pour la montre et revue des gens de pied ou cavalerie, soit en l'armée, soit en garnisons'. As an example of this authority A¹ 28, fo. 336, 28 July 1636, notification to *intendant* Jean Choisy of the despatch of *commissaire* d'Aubray to carry out *revues* of the troops in the army of Picardy as and when ordered by the commander, the comte de Soissons.

[4] SHAT A¹ 31, fo. 165, 27 Dec. 1636, circular letter to *commissaires des guerres* Bragelongne, Desmarests, La Birche and Dancy, ordering them to travel to the *places* of Picardy to carry out *revues* of the troops quartered in these *places* every ten days – general draft ('projet') of this commission given in A¹ 32, pce 271, 1636. A¹ 34, fo. 322, 22 Feb. 1637: order for *commissaire* Bretagne to carry out *revues* of the troops in the two garrisons in Alsace (Saverne and Hautbar) every ten days.

[5] SHAT A¹ 32, fo. 98, 22 Sept. 1636: Sétoubre to carry out the *réformation* of certain regiments under the supervision of the maréchal de Chaulnes; AAE MD 820, fo. 4ii, Jan. 1636, Bullion to Richelieu, suggesting that *commissaire* Gilles Renard carry out the disbanding of units under the supervision of the cardinal de La Valette; A¹ 57, fo. 184, 22 Jan. 1640, de Noyers to *commissaire* Pierre de Naberat, instructing him to disband the two Irish regiments of Tirrell and Langford.

[6] SHAT A¹ 68, fo. 590, 20 Mar. 1642, ordinance giving powers to commanding officers and *commissaires* to disband units which fall below a minimum strength, yet to be specified.

Responses and reactions

the augmentation of units already in existence.[7] These extra levies of recruits encouraged levels of fraudulence remarkable even by the normal lax standards of the time, and the ministers' response was on occasions to entrust such recruitment to the *commissaires*.[8] Even further removed from the official functions of the office of *commissaires des guerres* was their employment in overseeing the construction or maintenance of fortification work.[9] While it would appear more logical to entrust such functions to the *commissaires* of the artillery, fortifications had been outside the jurisdiction of the *grand maître de l'artillerie* since the assumption of the office by La Meilleraye in 1634.[10] Numbers of *commissaires* were also granted commissions to investigate cases of desertion and to try to apprehend deserters.[11] In 1638 a project was considered which would have allocated specified *commissaires* to groups of provinces, granting them authority to control and punish desertion. This scheme would have transferred the major element of responsibility for the control of desertion from the *prévôts* to the *commissaires des guerres*, and those named as its agents – Gilles Renard, Jacques Magnan, Charles Desgranges, Pierre Clozier, François Prouville, Charles de Bragelongne and the sieurs Montmaur, Croisilles and Destouches – constitute a roll-call of the most experienced and reliable *commissaires des guerres* of the late 1630s.[12] The *secrétaire* also showed

---

[7] For an apparent exception see Richelieu, *Mémoires*, v. 461. The few examples of *commissaires* apparently raising troops for newly created units are ambiguous: SHAT A¹ 48, fo. 127, 4 Aug. 1638, instruction to *commissaires dans les provinces*, concerning the raising of troops – probably, given the month, additional troops to augment existing units; A¹ 50ii, fo. 64, 6 Feb. 1639, circular to those *commissaires* concerned with recruitment of what are simply described as 'nouvelles levées'.

[8] SHAT A¹ 28, fo. 477, 14 Aug. 1636, Besançon de Bazoches to carry out recruitment to raise the effective strength of the regt of Roncières to 1,200 men; A¹ 45 fo. 481bis, 9 May 1638; Châtillon informed of despatch of a *commissaire* to carry out additional recruitment for units in his army; A¹ 48, fo. 426, 1 Nov. 1638, instructions for *commissaire* Imbert to carry out recruitment in Languedoc and Dauphiné for the army of Italy; A¹ 60 fo. 369, 9 Sept. 1640, *commissaires* charged with levy of troops for armies of Châtillon and du Hallier.

[9] SHAT A¹ 26, fo. 44, 14 Apr. 1635: commission for Saurès, *commissaire des guerres*, to have charge of the *montres* of the garrison and the fortifications of Pinerolo; A¹ 36, fo. 298, 26 May 1637, *commissaire* Destouches to travel to Soissons to examine the state of the fortifications; A¹ 65, fo. 246, 15 July 1641, notification to *maires*, *échevins* of Saint Dizier and Vitry, informing them of the despatch of Vallier with order to repair the fortifications of their *places*. (The commission was subsequently transferred to Besançon de Bazoches: A¹ 65, fo. 255, 17 July.)

[10] Even before this, it was simply the case that Sully, and subsequently his son and heir to the posts by *survivance*, Maximilien-François de Béthune, marquis de Rosny, had held the office of *grand maître* and *surintendant des fortifications* conjointly: Buisseret, *Sully*, p. 120.

[11] SHAT A¹ 46, fo. 494, 28 June 1638, *commissaire* Lespine to travel to the Nivernais to try to prevent desertion; A¹ 57, fo. 206, 23 Jan. 1640, *commissaire* Pierre Gaucher to supervise return of deserters to their original regiment; A¹ 60, fo. 339, 5 Sept. 1640, *commissaire* Roche to arrest nineteen named deserters from the company of *gendarmes* of Richelieu, and to enjoin the *maréchaux* and other judges to proceed against them in accordance with the ordinances against desertion; A¹ 70, fo. 51, 4 Aug. 1642, *commissaires* Pingault and Budée to guard passages of the Aisne and Oise to prevent desertion, and fo. 91, 21 Aug., *ordonnance* giving Pingault the authority to levy fines on inhabitants of *places* who refuse to hand over deserters.

[12] AAE MD 832, fo. 110, 1638: 'order to be established to prevent the disbandment of the soldiers'; there seems no practical evidence for the wholesale transfer of responsibility envisaged in the document.

himself prepared to draw up specific disciplinary commissions for *commissaires des guerres*, assigning them the duty of maintaining order in a particular army or province.[13] Charles Besançon, sieur de Bazoches, was given a specific commission to enforce justice in Champagne during the winter of 1636. As he possessed no authority to carry out trials, it was stipulated that he should hand over those suspected or accused of disorders to Choisy, the *intendant de la justice* in the province.[14] *Commissaires* were frequently despatched to particular *places* where there had been disorders or violence between soldiers and civilians, to carry out enquiries and, where appropriate, to order that compensation be paid from the soldiers' wages to the inhabitants.[15]

The use of commissions and the local availability of *commissaires des guerres* could lead to more anomalous assignments from the *secrétaire*. The *commissaire* Jean Martin was ordered to assemble all the inhabitants of Noisy capable of bearing arms,[16] and, in an extremely rare example of military conscription, *commissaire* Nicolas Boullet (Boullé) was ordered to enlist all the men capable of bearing arms in the *élection* of Laon.[17] Henri d'Aubray was given the task of provisioning frontier magazines,[18] while Destouches was charged with the levying and conduct of waggons for the army of cardinal de La Valette.[19] When the task of collecting additional *vivres* for the army across all of Languedoc and Guyenne in early 1639 was considered too great to be carried out by Richelieu's *fidèle*, Gilles Boutault, bishop of Aire-sur-l'Adour, the burden was divided, with responsibility for Languedoc going to *commissaire* Destouches.[20] The *commissaires* were ordered to intervene in order to ensure the adequate supply of the *étapes* when the ministers suspected that the local authorities or the contractors would prove inadequate.[21] In

---

[13] SHAT A^1 27, fo. 233, 11 Apr. 1636: Destouches sent to Susa to act as a general disciplinary officer for the army of Italy; A^1 41, fo. 84, 4 Feb. 1636: Breteche acting in a similar capacity in Brittany.

[14] SHAT A^1 32, fo. 242, 30 Dec. 1636.

[15] SHAT A^1 69, fo. 179, 12 Nov. 1640, order for the investigation of corruption amongst the governors of *places* in Italy: commission to be held jointly by *commissaire des guerres*, Talon, and the *intendant d'armée*, Michel Le Tellier; A^1 32, fo. 233, 16 Dec. 1636: Bretagne ordered to reside in Lorraine and Barrois to ensure the good order of the troops, acting 'as appropriate to the office of *commissaire des guerres*'; A^1 59, fo. 340, 12 June 1640: Besançon was ordered to gather information about a riot against soldiers billeted in the city of Tours.

[16] SHAT A^1 28, fo. 446, 12 Aug. 1636 – though this was in the midst of the crisis of the Spanish invasion, when administration was particularly chaotic.

[17] SHAT A^1 65, fo. 225, 12 July 1641.

[18] SHAT A^1 36, fo. 326, 30 May 1637: he was emphatically not a *commissaire des vivres*; A^1 63, fo. 283, 1 Feb. 1641, *commissaires* Arnoul and La Court charged with purchase of grain for troops in quarters; A^1 66, fo. 227, 27 Oct. 1641, *commissaire* Talon ordered to find ways of providing the *pain de munition* for the army of Italy more cheaply.

[19] SHAT A^1 37, fo. 200, 22 June 1637.

[20] SHAT A^1 51, fo. 238, 26 Mar. 1639.

[21] For example, SHAT A^1 58, fo. 391, 7 Apr. 1640, general order to *commissaires* who had been charged with subsistence of troops in winter quarters to take cognizance of supplies in the *étapes* on the routes to the campaign theatres. A^1 66, fos. 257, 259, 10 Nov. 1641, *commissaires* Langlée and Pingault to ensure that *étapes* are adequately supplied for the passage of troops.

Responses and reactions

dealing with the aftermath of campaigns, *commissaire* Pierre Gigon, sieur de Lespine, was assigned the demolition of the siege works around La Capelle,[22] while in 1642 Pingault was instructed to escort Spanish prisoners of war into captivity.[23] During the siege of Perpignan, the *commissaire*, Claude de Langlée, received a commission to enforce the ordinance forbidding French subjects to trade with the inhabitants of the city.[24] One example from this period survives of a commission granted to a *commissaire des guerres* to oversee medical provision and to provide supplies and food for wounded troops.[25] Many such specific commissions imply the control and management of substantial sums of cash which the ministers were evidently willing to entrust to the *commissaires*.[26] An extension of this responsibility was to charge *commissaires* with the often difficult and dangerous assignment of transporting sums of money for the payment of the armies when it proved impossible to arrange letters of credit to obtain the cash locally.[27]

The redefinition of the office of commissaire

The *secrétaire* was thus projecting the *commissaires des guerres* into a range of functions which went far beyond their original responsibilities for the administration of *montres* and *revues* or the conduct and discipline of specific units of troops. To a great extent, as many of the examples cited above attest, this was an exercise in clientelism. Judging by the frequency with which certain *commissaires* received regular assignments over and above the basic duties of carrying out *montres* and *revues*, the *secrétaire* was looking less for an institutional structure to meet the needs of the expanding war-effort, more for a pool of individuals of proven reliability to carry out specific tasks. One reason for this *ad hoc*, personalized, role for the *commissaires* has already been suggested: in crucial respects their powers were limited and subdivided. They lacked the judicial authority to preside as judges in trials of military offenders, and the more important group, the *commissaires des guerres*, were still primarily concerned not with discipline or the control of troops (still the responsibility of the *commissaires à la conduite*) but with

---

[22] SHAT A¹ 39, fo. 221, 17 Oct. 1637.
[23] SHAT A¹ 69, fo. 166, 22 Apr. 1642; similar instructions for the escort of Spanish prisoners of war to the citadel at Montpellier were given to *commissaire* Langlée: A¹ 69, fo. 465, 15 June 1642.
[24] SHAT A¹ 69, fo. 40, 8 Apr. 1642.
[25] SHAT A¹ 65, fo. 491, 12 Sept. 1641, instructions to *commissaire* Chaufourneau.
[26] And in at least one case a *commissaire* found himself in the position, regularly encountered by the servants of the French crown, of making cash advances to cover the immediate costs of his assignment in the absence of funds received from the centre: SHAT A¹ 57, fo. 510, 27 Feb. 1640, order to the *trésorier de l'épargne* to reimburse *commissaire* Jacques Charles 6,022 *livres* provided for the costs of establishing garrisons in Picardy.
[27] SHAT A¹ 41, fo. 151, 8 Aug. 1636: Jean-Baptiste Colbert, *commissaire des guerres*, to transport 350,000 *livres* to the Valtelline for the payment and subsistence of the army of the duc de Rohan. This was the second cousin of the future *contrôleur général des finances*.

The management of the war-effort from 1635 to 1642

the very specific task of carrying out the *montres* and *revues*. Thus, in theory at least, any task beyond this basic function would require special authorization – a formal commission – if the *commissaire* was to carry any weight in conflicts with other officials or the military officers.

The first stage in the institutional redefinition of the *commissaires* after 1635 was, predictably, a renewed attempt to come to terms with the inefficient division that existed between the financial and judicial groups of *commissaires*. A royal edict of May 1635 sought to link administrative rationality with immediate financial advantage by establishing 69 new offices of *commissaires provinciaux* combining the authority of the two groups of *commissaires*.[28] The principal effect of the sale of these sixty-nine offices was the segregation of the *commissaires*, not according to function, but by their area of operations.[29] It has been claimed that very few of these new officials were actually appointed.[30] In fact the list of *commissaires provinciaux* is substantial; the *secrétaire* obviously regarded them as a major instrument in the maintenance of the expanded war-effort.[31] Nevertheless, it was probably inevitable that the crown's financial plight would ensure that this rationalization was not left undisturbed; in 1637 two ordinances restored the *commissaires à la conduite* of the *vieux* and *petit-vieux* regiments[32] – abolished by the edict of May 1635 – and created an additional eleven resident *conducteurs* of troops.[33] The process of creating further resident or regimental *commissaires* continued. In late 1638, the crown found it necessary to order that the number of *commissaires* employed for the discipline and police of the troops should be reduced to four per *généralité*.[34] This overloading of the *généralités* with *commissaires* stood in sharp contrast to the continued complaints about the inadequate

[28] BN Châtre de Cangé, 23, fo. 124, 11 Oct. 1635.
[29] There had been a previous experiment in 1595 with the creation of a group of twenty-four *commissaires à la conduite* who held regional authority rather than being attached to a particular regiment or cavalry company, but the edict of creation was explicit that these offices conveyed no authority to conduct *montres* and *revues*, and it is not clear whether they had any significant or long-term existence: Milot, 'L'évolution', 385–6.
[30] André, *Michel Le Tellier et l'organization*, p. 613, suggests that they were appointed only in Picardy and Champagne; Milot, 'L'évolution', p. 387, is of the same opinion.
[31] SHAT A^1 28, fo. 263, 12 July 1636: L'Hermitte – Champagne; A^1 28, fo. 281, 18 July 1636: D'Osny – Picardy (replaced by Charost: fo. 332, 28 July 1636); A^1 30, fo. 246, 30 Oct. 1636: Clozier – Normandy; A^1 32, fo. 243, 30 Dec.1636: Le Comte and Bretagne – Hte Alsace, Lorraine; A^1 39, fo. 218, 16 Oct. 1637: Montmaur – Burgundy; A^1 40, fo. 268, 27 Dec. 1637: Bouteret – Normandy; A^1 41, fo. 84, 4 Feb. 1636: Bréteche – Picardy; A^1 44, fo. 242, 14 Mar. 1638: Cornuel – Touraine; A^1 44, fo. 343, 22 Mar. 1638: Magnan – Saintonge/Angoumois; A^1 45, fo. 111, 13 Apr. 1638: (*en blanc*) – Maine; A^1 46, fo. 496, 28 June 1638: Lespine – Nivernois; A^1 47, fo. 25, 27 Nov. 1638: (*en blanc*) – Rouen; AAE MD, 830, fo. 41, 8 Feb. 1638: Gaillard – Marseilles. These examples do not constitute a definitive list. Many *commissaires* whose functions were not clearly emphasized on the relevant documents have been omitted. It would seem probable that all, or most, of the sixty-nine *commissaires* were created.
[32] SHAT A^1 42, pce 44, 30 Jan. 1637: together with the regiments of Chamblay and La Valette, which had received *drapeau blanc* status in 1635: Susanne, *Histoire de l'infanterie française* I. 186.
[33] SHAT A^1 42, pce 177, July 1637: these were the original *commissaires à la conduite provinciaux*.
[34] SHAT A^1 47ii, fo. 219, 21 Dec. 1638.

Responses and reactions

numbers of *commissaires* present with the armies to carry out adequate *revues*.[35] In response to this overpopulation in the *généralités*, a further ordinance of late 1638 sought to establish a *commissaire des recrues* in each *généralité* with specific powers to supervise the orderly recruitment and mustering of soldiers, but unlike the *commissaires provinciaux* there is little evidence that such a group came into being.[36]

The establishment of commissaires with overall supervisory authority

The attempt to amalgamate the responsibilities of the *commissaires* to create a group with much wider competence was unlikely to succeed so long as the crown's primary need, exacerbated by the costs of the war-effort, remained the sale of office. It was not, however, the only means by which the *secrétaire de la guerre* sought to improve the effectiveness of some of these agents. An attempt was made to create a working hierarchy amongst the *commissaires* by formalizing the charge of *commissaire général des guerres*, granted extensive powers of supervision over his colleagues. Although examples of this practice can be found in 1625 and 1635,[37] it was in 1636 with the establishment of three such commissions that the policy becomes clear.[38] To these might be added the commission creating an office of *commissaire général* with the army of Germany for Alexander de Prouville, baron de Tracy, explicitly established in lieu of an intendancy.[39] The same rationale – the establishment of a single administrative figure of undisputed authority – may be seen in a parallel series of commissions establishing *prévôts généraux* with some of the armies.[40]

---

[35] AAE CP Lorraine, 31, fo. 401, 13 Aug. 1640, Du Hallier to de Noyers on the shortage of *commissaires* with the army in Lorraine; a similar shortage with the army of Italy was also cited as a reason for the difficulty of conducting adequate *montres*: CP Savoie 24, fo. 299, 23 Apr. 1636, Créquy to Richelieu.

[36] SHAT A^1 47ii, fo. 269, 28 Dec. 1638.

[37] Charles Besançon de Bazoches was *commissaire général* with the army in Italy in 1625: Grillon, v. 178; SHAT A^1 25, fo. 630, 19 Dec. 1635: Savyer specified as *commissaire général* with the army of Provence.

[38] SHAT A^1 30, fo. 164, 22 Oct. 1636, commission for sieur de La Four to assume the office of *commissaire général* with the army of Picardy; A^1 32, fo. 53, 8 Apr., commission for sieur de Cosade with the army of Provence; A^1 32, fo. 263, [late 1636], Christophe Royer to act as *commissaire général* with the army in Flanders.

[39] SHAT A^1 32, pce 255, 1636: there is a clear implication that the French official, the *intendant* Choisy, had authority only over the French troops with the army, and that the German colonels, by virtue of their capitulations with the French crown, enjoyed a *de facto* juridical independence that only a high-ranking military officer would be likely to overcome. Tracy still held this position of *commissaire général* in 1642: BL Egerton 1689, fo. 49, 6 Feb., and the commission had been formally renewed in 1641: A^1 67, pce 201, 14 Sept. Biographical note on Tracy in Noailles, *Guébriant*, p. 246 n. 1.

[40] SHAT A^{1}32, pce 29, 24 Feb. 1636, commission for sieur le Grain, *lieutenant criminel de Paris*, to assume office of *prévôt général* for the army of Italy; pce 86, 31 May 1636, commission for Gilles Renard, *prévôt de la maréchaussée* at Rethel, to assume the office of *prévôt général* of the army of Champagne (by 1637 Renard had purchased the office of *commissaire des guerres* and rapidly became one of the *secrétaire's* most trusted agents); pce 95, 16 June 1636, commission for sieur de Verchamp to serve as *prévôt général* in the army of the Valtelline.

The management of the war-effort from 1635 to 1642

The practical success of this expedient is difficult to assess. The title of *commissaire général des guerres*, or indeed *prévôt général*, ceased to be granted under commission after 1636, and the policy of granting overall authority to a specific *commissaire* allocated to a particular army was abandoned.[41] However, there is evidence that by the end of the 1630s a less formal hierarchy was emerging amongst the *commissaires*, and that those who had been allocated the largest share of special assignments and commissions were also being given powers to treat the others as subordinates, even to the point of investigating allegations of misconduct.[42] In a few other cases the senior *commissaires* were employing *subdélégués* to carry out part of their tasks, implying an increasing weight of responsibility, especially as the ministry seems to have accepted at least some financial responsibility for these *subdélégués*.[43] The commissions for *commissaires (généraux) pour les subsistances* were further to strengthen the distinction between an elite of *commissaires* and their subordinates.

Moreover, although the practice of issuing commissions establishing *commissaires généraux* with particular armies was abandoned after 1636, a small number of individuals continued to be qualified as *commissaire* or *prévôt général*, but as a personal office rather than as a specific delegation of authority. Montifault bore the title of *prévôt général* into the 1640s,[44] while the most significant example, the *commissaire général*, Charles Besançon, sieur de Bazoches, was still holding the post when it was converted into an *office de la couronne* in 1654. Bussy-Rabutin claimed in his *Mémoires* that the office of *commissaire général des armées* was abolished after Besançon's death 'puisqu'elle avoit trop d'autorité'.[45] Yet there is

---

[41] One or two later documents refer to *commissaires généraux*, but for the most part this is simply used as an alternative or supplementary title for the *commissaires pour les subsistances* to be discussed below: for example, SHAT A¹ 58, fo. 286, 26 Mar. 1640; A¹ 63, fo. 279, 1 Feb. 1641: both are circulars addressed to the 'commissaires généraux' – in fact to the *commissaires pour les subsistances*, as the contexts make plain.

[42] For example, SHAT A¹ 40, fo. 210, 18 Dec. 1638, Renard instructed to provide funds for *commissaire* Berger to distribute for the subsistence expenses of the regt of Brézé; A¹ 43, fo. 54, 8 Jan. 1638, Besançon de Bazoches to investigate conduct of *commissaire* Guillaume Belot, sieur Du Clos; A¹ 44, fo. 186, 10 Mar. 1638, Vallier instructed to delegate other *commissaires* to oversee the discipline of particular regts lodged in Normandy.

[43] SHAT A¹ 50ii, fo. 38, 3 Feb. 1639, order to the *trésoriers de l'extraordinaire des guerres* to pay the salaries of the *subdélégués* of Christophe Royer; A¹ 50ii, fo. 123, 11 Feb. 1639, de Noyers to *intendant* Choisy, ordering him to recognize the *subdélégué* of commissaire Clozier; later in the month de Noyers found it necessary to stress that the *subdélégués* were only to assist the *commissaires* in the conduct of *montres*, and were not to carry them out in their own right: A¹ 50ii, fo. 267, 24 Feb. 1638.

[44] SHAT A¹ 58, fo. 289, 28 Mar. 1640, order for Montifault to proceed to the army of La Meilleraye to exercise his office; A¹ 64, fo. 216, 10 Apr. 1641, Montifault to proceed (again) to take up duties with the army of La Meilleraye. There exists a commission *en blanc* to establish a *prévôt général* with the army of Catalonia in 1641, commanded by the maréchal de Brézé, but whether this was an alternative destination for Montifault or whether the ministry was contemplating the revival of the office of *prévôt général* is unclear: A¹ 67, fo. 145, 14 May 1641.

[45] Bussy-Rabutin, *Mémoires* I. 19; this opinion has been echoed by subsequent historians, for example Corvisier, *Louvois*, p. 94: 'les commissaires des guerres . . . avaient eu une sorte de supérieur, le commissaire général'.

Responses and reactions

no evidence that Besançon de Bazoches controlled all the other *commissaires*, and it is certainly not the case, as has sometimes been suggested, that he bridged the worlds of administration and the officer-corps.[46] Neither the commission renewing his appointment as *commissaire général des guerres* in 1643 nor the edict of 1654 erecting the commission into a permanent *office de la couronne*, suggests that Besançon had any overall authority over the *commissaire* hierarchy; all that is accorded is responsibility to report upon any frauds committed by *commissaires* that he might discover.[47]

THE WIDER USE OF COMMISSIONS AFTER 1635

Much of the expansion of the role of the *commissaires des guerres* in the years of war after 1635 was based upon special commissions. But while the *commissaires* formed a significant group of recipients of such specialized commissions, they were by no means unique.

Specific commissions

The use of the specific commission was characteristic of *Ancien Régime* government; its great advantage lay in the fact that it was a response to particular circumstances which would not, in theory, entail a challenge to the vested interests of existing office-holders, nor a radical reshaping of established institutional structures. On the one hand, the commission could be depicted as no more than crisis-management, a response to the need for decisive action in a specific sphere, which ought not generate too much obstruction and resistance. On the other hand, the commission-holder was granted superior authority within his particular area of responsibility through the legal tradition that the holder of a specific commission enjoyed precedence over all those agents who were simply exercising their normal functions.[48]

---

[46] The main reason for the exaggeration of the extent of Charles Besançon de Bazoche's authority and the suggestion that he also held direct military command has been historians' tendency to confuse him with his brother, the *aide de camp*, later *maréchal de bataille*, Bernard de Besançon, sieur du Plessis. This confusion was identified by comte Horric de Beaucaire in the introduction to his edition of the *Mémoires* of Plessis-Besançon, pp. iii, xiii–xxvii. Plessis-Besançon did, while holding positions as an officer in the high command of armies in Provence and Languedoc, undertake certain specific ministerial commissions concerning fortifications and the conduct of regiments, while in the same period Besançon de Bazoches was engaged in substantial operations concerning the subsistence and discipline of troops in Picardy and Champagne.

[47] BN Ms.fr. 4224, fos. 58v–61: this edict renewed the commission held since 1625; BN Ms.fr. 4189, fos. 310–14, Dec. 1654.

[48] R. Mousnier, 'Le Conseil du Roi', in Mousnier, *La Plume*, p. 178, where it is used in the context of the developing powers of the *maîtres de requêtes*; Mousnier, *Les institutions* II. 466–500, 561–606; Bonney, *Political Change*, pp. 135–7, draws attention to the distinction between specific and general commissions, emphasizing that 'hundreds, possibly thousands of *commissions particulières* were issued each year'. Commissions to carry out military functions in the sixteenth century are discussed

The management of the war-effort from 1635 to 1642

Individuals were regularly commissioned to supplement the efforts of *commissaires* and *prévôts* to maintain discipline over troops *en route* for the armies, in garrisons, or lodged in winter quarters. In some cases those commissioned were military officers, the rationale presumably being that they were more capable of intimidating or controlling the unit officers than a civil agent would be. Thus, for example, the sieur de Cornillon, *aide de camp*, received a commission in the winter of 1638/9 to travel around the *places* of Picardy to ensure that the troops were living with discipline in their quarters.[49] Numerous civil officials, including the *commissaires pour les subsistances*, would be charged with the same duties, but given the inadequacy of attempts to restrain disorders, extortion and violence during the winter months, it was clearly considered that additional agents, operating within a different hierarchical structure, might be able to achieve some results. It was not merely relatively high-ranking military officers who received such commissions; members of the royal household, *fidèles* of the ministers or provincial officials could also find themselves authorized to investigate disorders or to oversee the *police* of troops in garrison. Potrincourt, *écuyer ordinaire du Roi*, was commissioned to inspect the troops lodged in Normandy,[50] while Mayolas, captain of the *gardes* of Richelieu, was given the commission to travel to Nancy to carry out a *revue* of the garrison and to maintain order and discipline amongst the troops.[51] The abbé de Médavy, a *fidèle* of Richelieu, was charged with the *police* of six regiments being assembled at Saint-Jean-de-Losne in Burgundy prior to being marched down to Roussillon, while the judges of the courts of the *sénéchaussées* of Lyonnais, Forez and Beaujolais were commissioned to investigate disorders and unrest in recruitment in these provinces.[52]

A similar concern was evident in a number of cases in which newly created, temporary, regiments – who did not therefore have their own *commissaire à la*

in H. Michaud, 'Les institutions militaires des guerres d'Italie aux guerres de religion', *Revue historique*, 257 (1977), 29–43. The theoretical arguments for the superiority of commission-holders are discussed in R. Bonney, 'Bodin and the development of the French monarchy', *Transactions of the Royal Historical Society*, 5th Ser., 40 (1990), 43–61.

[49] SHAT A¹ 50i, fo. 26, 3 Jan. 1639. For a further example from the same period, A¹ 50i, fo. 247, 27 Jan. 1639, de Noyers to the comte de Saligny, *maréchal de camp*, congratulating him on the successful conclusion of his commission to investigate disorders amongst the troops 'dans plusieurs généralités'.

[50] SHAT A¹ 58, fo. 104, 10 Mar. 1639; similar instructions to oversee the *police* of the regt of Guébriant were given to de Lisle, *gentilhomme de la chambre du Roi*: SHAT A¹ 60, fo. 125, 5 Aug. 1640.

[51] AAE MD 816, fo. 136, 22 Nov. 1635, Richelieu to Servien, informing the *secrétaire* that Mayolas has been given authority to carry out *revues* in Nancy; Avenel v. 356, 23 Nov. 1635, Richelieu to Louis XIII, notifying him of Mayolas' instructions to maintain discipline in the garrison. For a general account of Richelieu's use of members of his *maison militaire* to execute special commissions see Deloche, *Maison de Richelieu*, pp. 392–8.

[52] AAE MD 845, fo. 183bis, 24 Aug. 1642, abbé de Médavy to Richelieu; SHAT A¹ 27, fo. 194, 4 Apr. 1636, de Noyers to the *lieutenants-généraux* of the *sénéchaussées*; A¹ 58, fo. 370, 5 Apr. 1640, de Noyers to Belot, *trésorier de France* at Tours, granting a commission to investigate the disorders of the regt of Périgord.

conduite – were either based in, or passing through, areas that were not under the jurisdiction of the *commissaires provinciaux*. In such cases the *secrétaire* would draw up a specific commission for the conduct of the particular unit, entrusting the responsibility either to a *commissaire des guerres* or to any other person whom he considered capable or available. This might be an official or an *officier exempté* from the king's or Richelieu's households,[53] an officer from another unit or from the general staff.[54] The besetting problem of desertion generated numbers of special commissions, not merely granted to *commissaires des guerres*, but to numerous civil officials and, again in the hope that they might prove more effective, to military officers.[55] Civilian officials across France had, since 1635, received a blanket authorization to seize and investigate deserters, even permitting them to impose capital sentences where appropriate, but as usual the ministry found it prudent to combine general authorizations with specific commissions and continued to issue more specific instructions to individuals or groups.[56]

Commissaires des guerres were involved in the recruitment of additional troops for existing units, but so were a variety of *fidèles*, especially those whose own networks of patronage and influence in the provinces were likely to facilitate the levy of troops of acceptable quality and to minimize the local disruption of the recruitment process. In particular this led, through Richelieu's own patronage, to a reliance on bishops: in 1640 Anthime-Denis Cohon, bishop of Nîmes, Nicolas Grillié, bishop of Uzès, and Louis-François La Baume de la Suze, bishop of Viviers, were commissioned to levy troops in their dioceses for the army of Italy, while in 1641 Claude de Rebé, archbishop of Narbonne, the bishops of Uzès, Nîmes, and Crusy de Marsillac, bishop of Mende, received instructions to levy troops to reinforce the army of maréchal de Brézé.[57] The levying of troops was one of the functions of provincial governors, but even here the crown saw fit on

---

[53] SHAT A¹ 26, fo. 61, June 1635, Lespine, *huissier* of the king's cabinet, commissioned to conduct Richelieu's regiment of dragoons; A¹ 27, fo. 233, 11 Apr. 1636, notification of the despatch of the sieur Destouches, *ordinaire de la Maison du Roi*, to conduct a number of newly recruited regiments down to Italy.

[54] SHAT A¹ 30, fo. 351, 28 Nov. 1636: Saint-Tour, *aide de camp*, to conduct three regiments to Guienne, where he is then to take up service in his military capacity; A¹ 29, fos. 125, 1 Sept. 1636, Oysonville, *aide de camp*, to take charge of a regiment of foreign cavalry – name left *en blanc* – and to conduct it to the army of Picardy.

[55] SHAT A¹ 25, fo. 330, 331, 15 Sept. 1635, commissions to the *lieutenant-général* and the *vice-sénéchal* of Poitiers, to investigate and punish those gentlemen from Poitou who have deserted from the *arrière-ban*; A¹ 32, fo. 28, 20 Feb. 1636, commission for the sieur de Saint-Julien, *sergent-major* of the regt of Chalabre, to investigate and prosecute deserters from the regt; A¹ 63, fo. 313, commission to Jacques de Chastenet de Puységur, captain of the Piémont regt, to carry out an investigation in the environs of Soissons for deserters from his regt.

[56] SHAT A¹ 24, fo. 456, 30 June 1635, circular addressed to mayors, councillors, consuls and other officers of justice in the realm.

[57] SHAT A¹ 60, fo. 393, 12 Sept. 1640; A¹ 66, fo. 505, 21 Dec. 1641. Although Crusy de Marsillac had been prosecuted for claimed misappropriation of funds in military supply operations on the eastern frontier in 1638, it is interesting to see that he was still expected to exercise a commission on behalf of the ministry in 1641.

occasions to draw up specific commissions for governors to carry out levies, such as that despatched in 1642 to Charles de Valois, duc d'Angoulême, governor of Provence.[58] Powerful provincial nobles were frequently commissioned to levy troops that neither they nor their relatives would necessarily command. Claude de Rouvroy, duc de Saint-Simon, had fallen from his position as royal favourite in 1636, and this may have made him anxious to demonstrate his subsequent loyalty to the regime. In July 1641 he was instructed to raise four companies of *chevaux légers* and to despatch these for service with the corps of the maréchal de Schomberg.[59] Commissions for recruitment were also entrusted to the familiar group of household officers, *officiers exemptés, gardes*, and others amongst the clienteles of king and ministers. Varennes, *maître de l'hôtel du Roi*, was commissioned in 1642 to carry out the levy of 1,000 infantry in Touraine, Anjou and Maine, while in the preceding year a number of *gentilshommes ordinaires du Roi* had been commissioned to travel to the *élections* around Paris to provide additional soldiers not generated by the most recent recruiting operations.[60]

It was the inadequacy of the existing institutions for the supply of the armies that threatened the most immediate and disastrous consequences for the war-effort, and which ensured a heavy reliance upon specialized commissions as a direct form of crisis-management. Much of the effort of the ministers was focused upon dealing with the immediate circumstances of the *munitionnaires'* failure or inability to meet their contracts with the armies. In trying to make good these failures, there was a marked tension in ministerial policy between reliance on short-term, limited, commissions to resolve immediate problems, and a concern to deploy varieties of the second type of 'comprehensive' commissions for a more fundamental restructuring of the supply system. In the former category, the ministers drew on the now familiar groups in addition to the *commissaires des guerres*. Churchmen figure prominently amongst the recipients of commissions, whether in the form of a circular letter to all of the bishops calling upon them to do whatever possible to facilitate the collection of *vivres* and other measures for the subsistence of the armies,[61] or in the form of more specific commissions for individuals. The abbés of Coursan, Mouzon, Corneille and Cinq Mars were all

---

[58] In 1634 the crown had despatched a whole series of commissions to the provincial governors for the levy of specified units in conjunction with a reminder that all governors should reside within their provinces or face penalities of *lèse-majesté*: AAE MD 813, fo. 274, Apr. 1634; MD 844, fo. 226, 4 June 1642, Angoulême to Chavigny; SHAT A¹ 68, fo. 115, 18 Jan. 1642, de Noyers to La Meilleraye, governor of Brittany.

[59] SHAT A¹ 65, fo. 210, 8 July; de Noyers to Saint-Simon; A¹ 65, fo. 221, 11 July 1641, Louis XIII to Henri de Saulx-Tavannes, marquis de Mirebeau.

[60] SHAT A¹ 69, fo. 6, 3 Apr. 1642; A¹ 65, fo. 241, 14 July 1641. AAE MD 839, fo. 62, 14 July 1641, Léonard Goulas, sieur de Frémoy, *trésorier* and *secrétaire des commandements* of Gaston d'Orléans, to Chavigny, concerning a special commission for the levy of three new regiments.

[61] SHAT A¹ 69, fo. 91, 14 Apr. 1642; A¹ 68, fo. 538, 14 Mar. 1642, de Noyers to the archbishops and bishops of Languedoc, asking them to select suitable locations for the establishment of *étapes*.

Responses and reactions

requested to carry out specific supply operations,[62] and as *fidèles* of Richelieu presumably wished to emulate the career of the abbé Gabriel de Beauvau, *maître de chambre* of Richelieu, who was nominated to the bishopric of Nantes in March 1635, certainly in part as a reward for carrying out a succession of commissions to ensure the supply of royal armies since the siege of La Rochelle.[63] Once again, it was not simply ecclesiastical *fidèles* who received these commissions; the practice also extended to various household officials and *exemptés*, such as des Touches, *gentilhomme ordinaire de la maison du Roi*, and La Prugne, *maréchal de logis des gardes* of Richelieu, who jointly received a commission for the transport of munitions from Compiègne to the army of the cardinal de La Valette at Guise.[64] Not surprisingly, in view of their position and contacts in an urban, and market, context, and also their possible access to greater transport facilities, supply commissions were frequently made over to established civil office-holders. In June 1640 the *trésoriers de France* at Tours, Orléans and Paris received a typical commission to coordinate the provision of *vivres* for four regiments *en route* for the siege of Arras, while the *élus* of the *élections* of Amiens, Péronne, Montdidier and Roye received a commission to raise peasants and labourers to construct the siege-works at Arras.[65] As royal appointees, the *premier présidents* of the *cours souveraines* were another obvious group to find themselves involved in specific supply operations. In 1641 the *premier président* of the *Parlement* of Rouen received

---

[62] SHAT A¹ 25, fos. 58, 70, 13/16 July 1635, abbé Mouzon – based at Liège – to coordinate the collection of grain to supply the army in Flanders; A¹ 27, fo. 376, 9 May 1636, de Noyers to Mouzon, ordering him to sell the grain that he had previously gathered in magazines at Liège. A¹ 59, fo. 504, 24 June 1640, notification to the inhabitants of Beauvais that the abbé de Corneille has been charged with the production of the largest possible quantities of *pain de munition* for the army besieging Arras; A¹ 59, fo. 677, 11 July 1640, specific commission to the abbé de Corneille. A¹ 44, fo. 351, 22 Mar. 1638, commission to the abbé de Cinq Mars to provide *pain de munition* to two regiments; A¹ 46, fo. 103, 18 May 1638, Cinq Mars to assist with the supply of the army of maréchal Châtillon. (Pierre de Broc, abbé de Cinq Mars, took his title from his family *seigneurie*, although this was sold in 1620 by Pierre's father, Jacques de Broc, to Antoine Coeffier de Ruzé, marquis d'Effiat, whose son Henri subsequently carried the title marquis de Cinq Mars: Deloche, *Maison de Richelieu*, pp. 80–2.)

[63] The abbé's long record of service to Richelieu in military assignments is summarized in Deloche, *Maison de Richelieu*, pp. 77–80. Having rewarded him with the bishopric, Richelieu expected Beauvau to demonstrate his *fidélité* through the execution of further commissions. For Beauvau's assignment to bake biscuit to support a 15-day campaign, see AAE MD 813, fo. 341, April 1635. Notification of Beauvau's elevation to the bishopric of Nantes appears in a letter announcing that he is *en route* to oversee supply of the army being assembled in Provence: SHAT A¹ 25, fo. 596, 7 Dec. 1635, Servien to maréchal Vitry. The abbé de Cinq Mars was to be rewarded for his efforts with consecration as bishop of Auxerre in March 1640: Deloche, *Maison de Richelieu*, p. 83. His obligations to the supply of the armies continued with a commission in 1640 to assist in the supply of the army of the maréchal de La Meilleraye: A¹ 59, fo. 89, 14 May 1640.

[64] SHAT A¹ 41, fo. 265, 22 June 1637.

[65] SHAT A¹ 59, fo. 426, 20 June; A¹ 59, fo. 368, 16 June. *Elus* were also instructed to provide grain for the armies – for example A¹ 37, fo. 315, 8 July 1637, *élus* of Meaux to provide *vivres* for the company of Roches Saint-Quentin.

412

The management of the war-effort from 1635 to 1642

one such commission, asking him to supply grain from Normandy for the needs of the army commanded by the king.[66]

Such specific commissions had the obvious disadvantage of being hand-to-mouth expedients. In cases like the massive military effort for the 1640 siege of Arras, they proved quite inadequate. Moreover, despite the legal theory that a commissioned agent should enjoy precedence over established office-holders and institutions in the execution of his task, there were frequent clashes and disputes which threatened to undermine whatever benefit might be gained from cutting through the existing systems. Another of Richelieu's ecclesiastical *fidèles*, the abbé de Coursan, had received a commission in 1635 to amass grain in Burgundy to supply the needs of the armies concentrated in Alsace and Lorraine.[67] However, Coursan found himself in a confrontation with the governor of the province, the prince de Condé, and Condé's *fidèle* the *intendant* Charles Machault. The apologetic and conciliatory letter written by Servien to Condé makes clear how keenly the danger of antagonizing a major provincial figure was felt.[68] In another case, Gilles Boutault, bishop of Aire-sur-l'Adour, commissioned to assist with the provision of *vivres* for the troops in Guyenne, had to be extracted by the intervention of the king from a disabling quarrel over jurisdiction with Prouville, the official directly charged with the supply of the army of Condé in Guyenne and Languedoc.[69]

The granting of 'comprehensive' commissions – supplying the armies

It was the issue of food supply which revealed most directly the weakness of the administration and showed up the inadequacy of reliance upon personalized special commissions. Whereas discipline, control of desertion, recruitment and adequate financial control over the army-corps could be allowed to fester – however disastrously in the medium and long term – failure to provision the armies had brought the war-effort to the point of collapse by mid-1635. As early as January 1635, the maréchal de Brézé was complaining that his army had received no money for the past seven weeks, and that this had halted the supply operations since the *munitionnaire* lacked both finance and access to credit.[70] The *munitionnaires* did not trust the crown to honour successive financial instalments

---

[66] SHAT A¹ 65, fo. 56, 11 June: he was to coordinate his activities with the *lieutenant général* of Normandy. A¹ 25, fo. 103, 30 Apr. 1635: the king's satisfaction with the contributions made by the *Parlement* and the *cour des comptes* of Provence to the struggle to recapture the Îles de Lérins.
[67] Avenel, v. 219, 14 Sept. 1635, notification of commission.
[68] SHAT A¹ 25, fo. 528, 17 Nov. 1635; there is no indication of whether Coursan was withdrawn from Burgundy and his commission cancelled, but it is notable that he does not appear to have received any further assignments, although earlier in 1635 he had received a sensitive commission from Richelieu to try to discover the campaign plans and assess the motivation of the maréchal de La Force: Avenel, v. 43, 2 June 1635, Richelieu to Coursan.
[69] SHAT A¹ 59, fo. 176, 22 May 1640, de Noyers to bishop of Aire; Bergin, *French Episcopate* p. 583.
[70] AAE MD 813, fo. 6, [late] Jan. 1635, *mémoire* of the maréchal de Brézé.

of their contracts, so deliberately avoided the stockpiling of grain which would involve the payment of sizeable advances and leave them vulnerable to any later failure to provide reimbursement. Instead, they purchased just enough grain to match the cash which they had in hand from the crown, which meant therefore that there would only be enough for a few days' supply and that any delay or shortfall in the arrival of the next payment would be followed by the almost immediate cessation of the bread rations.[71]

In a *mémoire* written by, or sent in the name of, the co-commander of the army of La Force in 1635, Charles de Valois, duc d'Angoulême, this problem was explicitly discussed. The *munitionnaires* needed more effective regulation, since none of them, even the senior figures of Roze, Bouault and Lattignan, considered themselves in any respect liable in their *propre et privé nom* for the supply of the army and the transport of *vivres*.[72] The *ad hoc* approach to the inevitable shortfalls in stockpiling grain, problems of distribution and even the complete breakdown of supply emphasized the obvious weakness of the entire supply administration, the lack of overall responsibility for the maintenance of *vivres*, either at a central level or, more realistically, at the level of the individual army-corps. By May/June 1635 this weakness was recognized as critical by the ministers, and although numbers of specific functions concerning the collection, transport and distribution of *vivres* were assigned to specially commissioned individuals, more drastic action was considered necessary.

In July 1635 Richelieu announced his intention of assuming the *surintendance générale des vivres*.[73] By placing himself at the head of the administration of *vivres*, Richelieu was emphasizing the importance of this aspect of the war-effort in ministerial budgeting and planning. In the context of ministerial politics, the supply of the armies – largely associated with the *secrétaire de la guerre* – would always stand in danger of being marginalized by the *bureau des finances*. Bullion's critics certainly suspected that the supply failures which beset the armies had more to do with the *surintendant*'s misplaced financial priorities than with wider administrative inadequacy.[74] Yet this assumption of overall authority for supply

---

[71] SHAT A¹ 24, fo. 138, 17 Mar. 1635, Servien to the *maréchal de camp*, Charles de Lameth, comte de Bussy.

[72] AAE CP Lorraine 25, fos. 355–8, fo. 356, 8 Aug. 1635, 'mémoire pour la subsistance des armées en Lorraine'.

[73] Aubery, *Richelieu*, I. 501, 26 July 1635, Bullion to cardinal de La Valette; 27 July, Servien to La Valette, both announcing Richelieu's assumption of the office: 'Il semble que vous ne pouvez recevoir une meilleure assurance d'avoir désormais abondance de toutes choses, puis que l'on n'a jamais encore veu manquer tout ce qui a dépendu de ses soins particuliers.'

[74] See for example Avenel, v. 366, 2 Dec. 1635, Richelieu to the king, complaining of Bullion's obstructive reluctance to provide an eighth *montre* for the French troops stranded in the United Provinces; AAE CP Savoie 24, fo. 4, 3 Jan. 1636, d'Hémery to Chavigny, complaining about Bullion's un-cooperativeness in meeting the costs of supplying the army of Italy; Avenel, v. 444, 18 Apr. 1636, Richelieu to Chavigny, complaining of Bullion's unwillingness to pay a subsistence allowance to the foreign troops in royal service.

The management of the war-effort from 1635 to 1642

was primarily psychological rather than practical, since in trying to tackle problems of supply failure with specific army-corps the effectiveness of a single, central, office was likely to be limited. Ultimately, as the ministers recognized, success and failure would reflect the efforts of administrators either within specific army-corps, or in the surrounding territories.

The response to this was a series of expedients in 1635 and 1636, all of which utilized commissions giving overall local authority in matters of supply to chosen agents and officials. These commissions were not temporary in the sense that those allocating specific assignments to trusted *officiers* or other individuals were temporary, for the latter type would expire with the completion of a particular assignment. However, they were revocable; in contrast to the policy of exploitative venality that characterized most administrative appointments, the crown resisted the temptation to establish further tiers in the existing structure of office-holders. Revocability, and indeed the delegation of authority under commission, should not be overestimated as a means of ministerial control. But to use agents given substantial authority on the basis of commissions was a more focused and direct response to administrative inadequacy; in the last resort it was more difficult for a commission-holder to do nothing towards the fulfilment of his assignments, particularly when the selected commission-holder was a client of the ministerial regime and would be expected to show responsibility and commitment.

However, these extensive supply commissions were granted with a total lack of consistency. One of the reasons why this attempt to delegate authority in army supply has attracted little attention from administrative historians is the bewildering mass of commissions issued under different titles, and of different types of office established for different categories of holder operating with the various army-corps and in the frontier provinces. The ministry had no overall strategy in commissioning agents with general responsibility for supply. The inadequacy of relying on small-scale, specific – and therefore, in general, reactive – commissions was recognized, but there was no plan to create a group of uniformly titled and authorized major commission-holders; there was nothing comparable with the establishment of the formulaic commissions of the *intendants d'armée*, or the 1638 creation of *commissaires pour les subsistances*.

The result, though it gave some authority to a number of individuals who subsequently showed ability in accumulating and distributing *vivres* for the armies, added to the levels of administrative confusion and incoherence. At least three types of general commission concerned with *vivres* appear to have been distributed in 1635 and 1636. The least consequential were those commissions which granted a more general authority to specific *munitionnaires*. The *munitionnaire* Gargan was made *commissaire des vivres* with the army of Condé in 1636. The commission initially reiterated his established functions as a *munitionnaire aux armées*, stipulating responsibility for the collection of grain, the baking of bread and the choice of 'lieux avantageux' for the establishment of magazines.

Responses and reactions

Perhaps the most important aspect of the commission, given the general willingness of military and civil elites to disregard *munitionnaires* as profiteering social inferiors, are the explicit instructions ordering the local and urban elites to recognize the authority of Gargan, and to give him all necessary support. Even the high command were reminded of Gargan's appointment, and the implied royal authority behind his selection for the commission.[75] Gargan's commission only lasted for the 1636 campaign, and by 1637 he appears to have resumed his status as a simple *munitionnaire*, collecting grain in Champagne for the army of Châtillon.[76] In May 1636, a similar post of *commissaire des vivres* was created for the army of cardinal de La Valette, and given to La Point.[77] At least one other example of a similar commission to establish a *commissaire général des vivres* survives, to create the post with the army of the comte de Soissons in Champagne for 1636, but left *en blanc* to be filled at the discretion of the *intendant d'armée*, Jean Choisy.[78]

How far these commissions to establish *commissaires des vivres* were intended to be substantively different from those of the same period establishing *munitionnaires généraux* is not clear. Both Lattignan and Jean Roze received this second title,[79] and once again the status involved the typical responsibilities of the *munitionnaire*, combined with a few concessions in matters of finance, the establishment of supply magazines and the appointment of subordinates. The post of *munitionnaire général* continued to be held by Roze as late as 1640, though his reputation was badly damaged in that year by accusations that his inadequate provision of *vivres* had come close to jeopardizing the siege of Arras.[80] However, while the other title of *commissaire (général) des vivres* continued in use with the armies, it ceased to be a post granted to *munitionnaires*, instead becoming one of a number of titles that could be given to individuals with overall responsibility for

---

[75] SHAT A¹ 32, pce 67, 30 Apr. 1636, commission for sr Gargan to execute the charge of *commissaire des vivres*.

[76] SHAT A¹ 35, fo. 327, 14 Apr. 1637, de Noyers to Châtillon, requesting him to provide escorts for the convoys of grain that the *munitionnaire* Gargan is assembling.

[77] SHAT A¹ 32, pce 88, May 1636. Curiously, a letter to the bishop of Mende a month earlier specified the appointment of Mende's choice of Lorman as *commissaire général des vivres* with this army: A¹ 27, fo. 267, 21 Apr. 1636, de Noyers to Mende.

[78] SHAT A¹ 26, fo. 101, 18 Nov. 1635. An accompanying letter to du Houssay, himself commissioned to stock the grain magazines in Champagne during the campaign of 1635, stressed that he was originally given the right to nominate the holder of this commission, but because he was unable to persuade the *trésoriers de France* of the province to agree upon a candidate, the nomination has been passed to Choisy.

[79] Lattignan held this title in 1635: SHAT A¹ 24, fo. 114, 26 Feb. 1635, while Roze held it in 1636, according to Richelieu's *Mémoires*, cited in E. Legrand-Girarde, *L'arrière aux armées sous Louis XIII. Crusy de Marcillac, évêque de Mende, 1635–1638* (Paris, 1927), p. 21. He is referred to as *munitionnaire général* in the context of the commission to supply La Valette's army in Burgundy in November 1636: A¹ 32, pce 221.

[80] SHAT A¹ 59, fo. 57, 11 May 1640, order to the *commis* of the *munitionnaire général* Roze, serving with the army of La Meilleraye. For the near-disgrace of Roze in 1640, AAE MD 1679, fos. 135, 236, 12 July, 2 Sept 1640, Châtillon to de Noyers.

The management of the war-effort from 1635 to 1642

the supply of an army-corps. In most cases the recipients of these commissions were *commissaires des guerres*. The sieurs d'Osny, de Maistre, Destouches, Boissière, Arnoul and Guillory are all examples of *commissaires des guerres* who were holding wide-ranging commissions as *commissaires des vivres* with specific armies in the last years of Richelieu's ministry.[81] But by the time that these commissions *des* (or *aux*) *vivres* were being distributed regularly, large numbers of other commissioners with responsibility for supply of the army had been created, ensuring that the question of overall authority remained as confused as ever.

In the first years of the war after 1635, the ministry's local response to the threat of complete supply failure on the eastern frontier was to experiment with a number of more extensive commissions, providing authority for individuals to take over or supplement large parts of the existing supply system and assume direct responsibility for the maintenance of supply to the armies. In July 1635 Claude Mallier, sieur du Houssay, one of the four central *intendants des finances*, was despatched to Champagne to establish magazines of grain which would supplement the efforts of the *munitionnaires* and allow the armies to campaign into enemy territory without the risk of outrunning the contracted supplies of *pain de munition*.[82] At first sight this seems a typical case of a *fidèle* being granted a specific commission, but the scale of the assignment was unprecedented: du Houssay was to collect sufficient grain across Champagne and the Barrois to supply an army of 30,000 for a campaign of three months, establishing principal grain magazines in Metz and Nancy and in other *places* as he saw fit.[83] Moreover, the operation involved numbers of additional supervisory responsibilities, including the management of the *munitionnaires* so that they would not consider themselves discharged from their own individual responsibilities, but would have to cooperate with du Houssay. His instructions gave him powers to requisition

---

[81] SHAT A¹ 64, fo. 435, 12 May 1641, appointment of d'Osny as *commissaire des vivres* with the army of Châtillon; A¹ 50ii, fo. 212, 18 Feb. 1639, de Maistre operating as *commissaire des vivres* in Lorraine; A¹ 51, fo. 259, 27 Mar. 1639, Destouches sent to serve as *commissaire des vivres* with the army of Languedoc; A¹ 59, fo. 280, 5 June 1640, Boissière to oversee provision of *vivres* to army-corps in Picardy and Champagne; A¹ 64, fo. 477, 15 May 1641, Arnoul, *commissaire des vivres*, with the army of Picardy; A¹ 64, fo. 367, 30 Apr. 1641, Guillory *commissaire des vivres* with army of Champagne.

[82] Avenel, v. 124–5, 28 July 1635, 'instructions données à M. Du Houssay, s'en allant en Champagne'. For reports from Du Houssay towards the end of the year concerning his assignment see AAE CP Lorraine 27, fos. 239, 267, 311, 10/13/20 Dec. 1635: Du Houssay to Richelieu.

[83] In the past a supply operation of comparable size would have been handled by one of the inner circle of ministers: principal responsibility for the operation to supply the royal army operating in the Midi in 1629 was given to the *garde des sceaux*, Michel de Marillac: cf. Grillon IV. 196–7, 205–6, 214–16, 222–3, 230–1, 5–26 Apr. 1629. In the following year the supply of the army-corps operating in Savoy and Piedmont in 1630 was coordinated by Richelieu himself, present with the army in Piedmont: Grillon v. 56–9, 29 Jan. 1630, *règlement des étapes pour l'armée d'Italie*; v. 129–35, 10 Mar. 1630, Richelieu to Bouthillier, concerning the logistical issues involved in an occupation of the duchy of Savoy.

grain and transport, and involved him in direct consultation with the local elites.[84] Du Houssay had been given an assignment of wide geographical and administrative scope, one which established his responsibility for a large part of the operation to supply the campaign armies on the eastern frontier. But his responsibility for this operation was not based on undivided authority. In the first place he found himself obliged to cooperate on equal terms with the two established *intendants des provinces*, Anne de Mangot, sieur de Villarceaux, in Lorraine, and Jean Choisy in Champagne. He was also flanked by a number of other commissioners carrying out similar, in some cases overlapping, supply operations. In July 1635 Guillaume Bordeaux, sieur de Génitoy, was granted a commission appointing him *intendant des finances, vivres et magasins* for the province of Champagne. Bordeaux was not being commissioned as a provincial or an army *intendant*; these functions were exercised by Choisy, *intendant de justice, police et finance* of Champagne, and *intendant de justice et police* over all troops within or passing through the province.[85] In the same period another recipient of an extensive supply commission, Gagnot, was made *intendant des vivres* with the army of La Force.[86] In this atmosphere of ambiguity about overall responsibility for supply, it seems that the ministers also experimented with the formal addition of the word *vivres* to the commissions of intendancy. One commission of May 1635 – which was drafted twice – for René Voyer, sieur d'Argenson, to exercise an intendancy with the army of the king (which was not in the event assembled), specifies *justice, police, finance et vivres* in both drafts, although the text of the commission suggests no greater powers over the organization and control of *vivres* than was usually granted.[87]

Just as du Houssay found himself in conflict with other officials holding responsibility for supply, so it was impossible for commissioned *intendants des vivres* such as Bordeaux or Gagnot to enjoy clearly defined authority. The results were predictable. Bordeaux's relations with Servien deteriorated through 1635; he claimed that Servien ignored his advice and had over-high expectations of what could be achieved in the field, gaining a rebuke from the *secrétaire*, and also being reprimanded by Richelieu for lack of diligence in organizing the collection and

---

[84] Du Houssay was sufficiently successful in carrying out this assignment to receive another major task in January 1636, when Richelieu issued him with a commission to make good the collapse of the contract previously negotiated with the *munitionnaire* Rolland for the supply of *vivres* to the garrison of Nancy: Avenel, v. 964, 31 Jan. 1636.
[85] SHAT A¹ 26, fo. 49, 28 Apr. 1635.
[86] SHAT A¹ 24, fo. 374, 15 June 1635, letter of de Noyers to La Force and Condé, notifying them of the appointment of Gagnot as *intendant des vivres*. The letter begins with an explicit admission of the logistical problems that have beset the armies, accepting that the majority of the supply failures that the armies have suffered reflect the failure of both the *officiers des vivres* and the *munitionnaires*, and that Gagnot has been despatched, on the part of the king, to do all possible to remedy the failure amongst both groups.
[87] SHAT A¹ 26, pce 52bis, 10 May 1635.

The management of the war-effort from 1635 to 1642

transportation of grain to the armies.[88] Although Bordeaux's responsibilities had been extended to the supply of the garrisons in occupied Lorraine,[89] in August 1635 he was replaced in this capacity by Sylvestre de Crusy de Marsillac, bishop of Mende, and by du Houssay.[90] Gagnot's commission appears to have been more successful, though he became involved in violent quarrels with his subordinates, including the nephew of du Houssay.[91] Gagnot was aware of the limitations of his commission, and had evidently proposed to Servien that he be granted a higher status by receiving a *charge* of *surintendant des vivres*. Although complimenting Gagnot on his efforts for the king's service, Servien stressed in unambiguous terms that 'on n'a pas l'intention d'ériger en charge les fonctions dont il s'agit'.[92] The advantages which might be brought by enhancing the authority of one individual would certainly be lost if too many of the existing administrators were antagonized by this sudden and unwelcome promotion. Even geographically limited commissions, such as that granted to another of the four central *intendants des finances*, Michel Particelli, sieur d'Hémery, to inspect the *places maritimes* of Provence, to give orders for repairs to fortifications, the founding or repair of artillery and to ensure that adequate garrisons were being maintained, ran the risk of antagonizing local elites from the provincial governor downwards.[93] Fortunately for d'Hémery this commission was of limited duration. Entrusting responsibility for the necessary work to a group of subordinates, including the *aide de camp*, Bernard du Plessis, sieur de Besançon, the *intendant des finances* had moved across the Alps by mid-August to take up his military and diplomatic charge in Piedmont.[94]

The problem remained. The provision of an adequate *service des vivres* appeared beyond the resources of any individual, yet the proliferation of duplicated and conflicting authorities with the armies and in the provinces had not improved the situation. It was in the context of this debate that Richelieu decided, after the

---

[88] SHAT A¹ 25, fo. 183, 7 Aug. 1635, Servien to Bordeaux; Legrande-Girarde, *Crusy de Marcillac*, pp. 25–6, copy of a letter of July 1635 from Richelieu to Bordeaux.

[89] AAE CP Lorraine 25, fo. 329, 27 July 1635, Servien to cardinal de La Valette, announcing that the task of revictualling the garrisons of Lorraine and building up magazines at Metz and Nancy was to be shared between du Houssay (charged specifically with the amassing of grain in the major magazines), and Bordeaux.

[90] Legrande-Girarde, *Crusy de Marcillac*, pp. 57–8; shortly after this, Bordeaux was granted a *congé* to retire from his commission: SHAT A¹ 25, fo. 290, 6 Sept. 1635, Servien to Bordeaux, who assures the latter, probably insincerely, of Richelieu's continued favour.

[91] SHAT A¹ 25, fo. 291, 6 Sept. 1635.

[92] SHAT A¹ 25, fo. 322, 13 Sept. 1635.

[93] SHAT A¹ 26, pce 42, 12 Apr. 1635, Commission for sieur d'Hémery. D'Hémery encountered problems not only with the provincial elites but, as soon as he started to give orders for the refounding and redistribution of cannon, with the agents of the *grand maître de l'artillerie*: A¹ 24, fo. 255, 4 May 1635, Servien to d'Hémery, discussing the obstruction and negligence of the *commissaires* of the *grand maître*.

[94] SHAT A¹ 25, fo. 191, 11 Aug. 1635, Servien to du Fauré, *intendant de justice et police* with the army of Italy, notifying him of d'Hémery's imminent arrival; Plessis-Besançon, *Mémoires*, pp. 12–17.

Responses and reactions

winter post-mortem on the 1635 campaign, to take the risk of establishing a single, overall commission for *vivres* on the eastern frontier during the campaign of 1636, awarding it to his *fidèle*, the bishop of Mende.

Crusy de Marsillac, bishop of Mende, had already gained some experience of supply administration in the previous campaign, and his experience of commissions carried out on behalf of Richelieu extended back to the siege of La Rochelle. When Guillaume Bordeaux proved unable to undertake both the supply of the troops in Champagne and the revictualling of the garrisons in Lorraine, the latter responsibility was passed to Mende. In 1636 the bishop was given the formal 'direction générale des vivres, munitions et magasins des armées de Champagne, Barrois, Lorraine et Allemagne', with extensive powers to purchase or requisition grain and transport, and to organize the production of bread, together with additional rights to attend the *conseils de guerre* held by the high command in order to discuss strategy in the light of supply capabilities.[95] Mende had gained an authority in matters of supply which appeared to be the equivalent of the commissions of du Houssay, Bordeaux, Gagnot and a number of lesser commission-holders rolled into one. Yet even in this case, Mende had to work with Mangot, sieur de Villarceaux, *intendant* in Lorraine, and Claude Gobelin, *intendant* with the army of Germany, neither of whom were initially well-disposed towards this great extension of Mende's authority and sphere of operations.[96] While there was no overt rupture or breakdown during 1636, Mende never enjoyed the unimpeded authority of a 'général des vivres' which might have permitted him to achieve significant improvements in the provisioning of the armies. His biographer describes the mission as disappointing, although by no means an outright failure, and attributes the primary responsibility for its partial success to the practical limitations upon Mende's power.[97] In the last resort the ministers were never prepared to delegate sufficient authority and then to stand behind the recipient in a way that would cut through the web of local interests and compromises.

In December 1636 the territorial and functional scope of Mende's task was redefined, and he received a more limited commission as *intendant des vivres* in

---

[95] SHAT A¹ 32, fo. 46, 29 Mar. 1636; the text is printed in Legrande-Girarde, *Crusy de Marcillac*, pp. 279–81, and discussed in detail, pp. 100–5: Legrande-Girarde notes perceptively that the authority of Mende, and a substantial range of his specific tasks, appear to have emanated from Richelieu's instructions and to have had little to do with the *secrétaire de la guerre*: 'celui-ci, que ce fût Servien ou Sublet des Noyers, était laissé en dehors de ces questions traitées au cabinet même de Richelieu' (p. 102).

[96] Legrande-Girarde, *Crusy de Marcillac*, pp. 92–3, 96–7. Servien wrote to Villarceaux, informing the *intendant* of Mende's mission and stressing that he should facilitate the operations: A¹ 27, fo. 291, 25 Apr. 1636.

[97] Legrande-Girarde, *Crusy de Marcillac*, pp. 151–7. Such success achieved is based upon a *mémoire* of the grain collected at the principal magazines by the end of December 1636: AAE CP Lorraine 29, fo. 628, 26 Dec. 1636, transcribed in Legrande-Girarde, *Crusy de Marcillac*, p. 163.

The management of the war-effort from 1635 to 1642

Alsace and Lorraine.[98] The experiment of creating a single figure with wide-ranging territorial and military authority was abandoned in favour of a number of individual commissions which continued to give substantial control of *vivres*, but were limited to a specific army-corps, or a relatively restricted geographical area. These commission-holders continued to hold a variety of titles, none of which had a clear place in an established hierarchy. *Intendants des vivres* were still being created in 1641, when a commission was drawn up for d'Osny to exercise the commission with the army of Champagne.[99] But the approach still remained unsystematic: in the same year the *prévôt général*, Mestivier, was granted the commission of *prévôt général des vivres* with the army of Picardy, a post which involved responsibility for guarding the *vivres* stored for the army and regulating their distribution. He was to work with Arnoul, *commissaire des vivres* with the army, though it remained unclear which of them was the superior agent.[100] Further commissions were granted to establish *directeurs généraux des vivres* with the armies, and, in 1640, a *contrôleur général des vivres* was created with the army of La Meilleraye for Périer.[101] In at least one instance a commission was drawn up to revive the post of *commissaire général des vivres*, not, however, for a *munitionnaire*, but for Gagnot, previously *intendant des vivres*.[102] Some of the *intendants d'armée* continued to receive a specific additional clause in their commissions granting them overall control of *vivres*, as in the case of Dreux d'Aubray, sieur d'Offement and Geoffroy Luillier, sieur d'Orgeval, nominated jointly to an intendancy of *justice, police et vivres* with the army of Gaston d'Orléans in 1636.[103] Although such commissions specifically including responsibility for *vivres* grew less common, the *intendants* continued to receive specific commissions in matters of supply which would cut across the authority of any other *officiers* and commission-holders who had been charged with supply within their armies or provinces. Typical of this was the circular sent in March 1641 to the *intendants* Bellejamme, Villemontée, Villarceaux, d'Orgères, Grémonville, Champigny and

---

[98] A¹ 32, fo. 245, Dec. 1636, transcribed in Legrande-Girarde, *Crusy de Marcillac*, p. 165. Mende's career continued its downward trajectory when he became involved in an extended quarrel with the governor of Lorraine, George de Mouchy d'Hocquincourt, culminating in his being prosecuted at the end of 1638 for alleged malversations in the administration of *vivres*: SHAT A¹ 49, pce 212, 23 Dec. The worsening relations with Hocquincourt are detailed in Legrande-Girarde, *Crusy de Marcillac*, pp. 212–59.

[99] SHAT A¹ 67, pce 144, 12 May 1641, text of commission. Jean Choisy, previously *intendant* in Champagne, was made *intendant des vivres* with the army of Feuquières and in Champagne in 1639, and was *intendant général des vivres* in 1642: A¹ 51, fos. 129, 555, 15 Mar./27 Apr. 1639, A¹ 68, fo. 650, 27 Mar. 1642. De Prouville had received a similar commission of *intendant des vivres* with the army of Guyenne in 1640: A¹ 59, fo. 176, 22 May.

[100] SHAT A¹ 67, pces 141–2, 4 May 1641; for Arnoul as *commissaire des vivres* see A¹ 64, fo. 477, 15 May 1641.

[101] SHAT A¹ 58, fo. 608, 29 Apr. 1640, commission for appointment of Périer; A¹ 62, fo. 308, 1640, commission *en blanc* for *directeur général des vivres* with an army.

[102] SHAT A¹ 62, pce 309, 1640.

[103] SHAT A¹ 27, fo. 224, 13 Sept. 1636, notification to Gaston d'Orléans of the appointment.

Responses and reactions

Chaulnes, ordering them to act independently to make contracts with bakers who would provide bread for the armies more cheaply than the bakers who had been employed by the *munitionnaires*.[104]

The commissaires pour les subsistances

So far, the history of the ministry's initiatives to organize the supply of armies through substantial commissions appears haphazard and arbitrary, possessing no discernable rationale and characterized by a reluctance to sustain any individuals or group of officials with overall authority in matters of provisioning. In many cases the driving force behind appointments was the selection of trusted *fidèles* or clients, for whose activities on behalf of the ministers a commission of some description was the most convenient means of empowerment. A rather different picture emerges in the ministry's approach to a related area of army organization, the provision of *logement* and *vivres* for the troops maintained under arms through the winter months, the *quartier d'hiver*. Once again this was an issue which presented unprecedented challenges to the existing military administration. Previous wars had rarely been envisaged in terms of multiple campaigns, and it had been assumed that the great majority of troops would be disbanded at the end of each campaign. If the war continued into a second consecutive year, mass recruitment in the first months of the new year would seek to bring the army up to effective strength on the basis of new recruits. But France would stand little chance of matching even the modest military effectiveness of her enemies so long as her armies were almost entirely newly recruited for each campaign.[105] This led to a conscious effort, especially from the winter of 1636/7, to keep large parts of the army billeted in towns and fortress garrisons over the winter months. The ministry was thus saddled with the new administrative challenge of maintaining tens of thousands of soldiers (at least on paper) across anything up to half of the French provinces through four or five months of the winter. These soldiers were almost invariably stationed near or with civilian populations, and needed constant disciplinary supervision to prevent local violence and disputes. If excuses for disorders were to be minimized, it was equally essential that the troops should be regularly fed and adequately housed, that the arrangements for quartering should run as smoothly as possible.

The ministers' first response to this challenge was, as usual, *ad hoc* and piecemeal. Mass disbandment of the serving units at the end of the two campaigns of 1634 and 1635 may have protected the civilian populations of the frontier

---

[104] SHAT A¹ 64, fo. 124, Mar. 1641.
[105] AAE MD 828, fo. 362, 1637, *Projet de la cavallerie pour S.E.* (probably written by Bullion). The document discusses the problem of cavalry captains who find it cheaper to dismiss their troops at the end of the campaign, using winter quarter funds to recruit new soldiers at the beginning of the next campaign, troops who are even more ill-indisciplined and 'ne valent rien pour le combat'.

The management of the war-effort from 1635 to 1642

provinces from some of the consequences of ill-disciplined and badly provisioned soldiers.[106] However, even if the ministers had not, on military grounds, sought to move towards a policy of maintaining a higher proportion of the army under arms, the scale of recruitment in the later months of 1636 and the military commitments which persisted into the early months of 1637 led to a great increase in demand for winter quartering.[107] The administrative burdens that this generated were largely tackled by *commissaires des guerres* and other figures holding special commissions, who were employed across the frontier provinces, carrying out regular *revues* of the garrisons and trying to ensure that the local populations should be protected at least in part from the extortionate demands for pay and supplies likely to be made by the troops. Despite the large numbers of such commissions granted, the burdens of quartering the troops, coming after a campaign which had involved expenditure well above that originally budgeted by the *surintendant*, overwhelmed the system. Disorder was almost universal, troops were inadequately supplied with their statutory *vivres*, and lived by pillage and extortion. The *logement* of troops was badly distributed and inequitable.[108] The quartering placed an intolerable burden upon the frontier provinces in general, and upon those places charged with garrisons in particular.[109]

The experience of this disastrous winter persuaded the government that it should act to ensure a more effective provision for the troops in quarters. Instead of hoping that they could be billeted in existing *places*, and that local contributions could be arranged to support the communities actually subject to billeting, a new system was devised. The *subsistances*, a direct tax in lieu of local, arbitrary, winter quarter contributions, was introduced, adding a further 8.5 million *livres* to the total of direct taxation imposed upon the population subject to the main direct tax, the *taille*.[110] This was to be levied from early November throughout the

---

[106] Albeit at the cost of imposing a different and more arbitrary burden upon them – that of large numbers of vagrant, disbanded, soldiers supposedly *en route* for their homes but prone to disorders, theft and violence against the local populations. See chapter 10, pp 539–43.

[107] BN Ms.fr. 3759, fo. 6, 31 Dec. 1636, 'arrêt du conseil d'état pour la subsistance des trouppes'. A document drawn up by Bullion, dated 1635, discusses the problem of quartering the troops over the winter: AAE MD 819, fos. 97–9, [1635]. Bullion speaks of the levy of the general *subsistances* tax to support the costs of the troops who will be billeted largely in the towns of the *généralités*. However, the reference to the *subsistances* as if it already existed, and the sum proposed – 18 million *livres* – leads me to suspect that the document should be dated to 1638/9, or, more probably, to 1639/40.

[108] See, for example, a detailed and explicit letter from Charmouluc, a judicial official at Roye, to chancellor Séguier, complaining of the devastating effects of billeting Irish troops on the town with inadequate regulation and control, and the extent to which the troops were systematically exploiting this situation: BN Ms.fr. 17373, fo. 3, 20 Jan. 1637.

[109] BN Ms.fr. 3759, fo. 16, 17 Jan. 1637, fo. 22, 28 Jan. 1637, fo. 52, 8 Mar. 1637: Maréchal Châtillon to de Noyers, describing the confusion, disorders and inadequacy of the winter quartering arrangements in Picardy; Ms.fr. 6648, fo. 11, 9 Jan. 1637, cardinal de La Valette to Père Joseph, discussing the inadequacy of the winter quarter arrangements for the troops in Burgundy and Lorraine.

[110] SHAT A¹ 49, pce 104, 22 Apr. 1638: refers to the 8.5 million *livres* that were to have been levied from the *subsistances* tax in the previous (1637/8) winter.

Responses and reactions

period of the winter quarter; the sums raised were to be paid to the soldiers as a subsistence allowance every fifteen days.[111] The persons charged with this operation were not the provincial intendants, but a group of *commissaires des guerres*: 'deputtez par Sa Majesté en vertu de ses patentes'.[112] The authority implied by this assignment was immense; a group of half a dozen *commissaire*s had control of the system for the collection and distribution of the *taxe des subsistances*, together with responsibility across large areas of France for all problems of *logement* and discipline that might arise during the quarter. Charles Besançon de Bazoches, the nominal head of the operation, was responsible for the troops and subsistances across Picardy, Champagne, Brie and Île de France.[113] Gilles Renard held similar responsibilities for the *généralité* of Orléans and Tours,[114] while Jacques Biou was charged with Poitou and the Limousin.[115] Jean Vallier was despatched to Normandy – regarded as a sufficient assignment in itself.[116] Charles des Granges was allocated Lyonnais, Forez and Beaujolais,[117] and Montmaur received authority in Burgundy, Bresse and Berry.[118] The great majority of the *généralités* placed under the authority of these *commissaires provinciaux pour les subsistances* possessed an *intendant* in 1637 and 1638.[119] The ministry explicitly demanded that the authority of the *intendants* be subordinated to the *commissaires* in all matters touching the quartering of the troops and the allocation of *subsistances* funds.[120]

In addition to the collection of the *subsistances* tax and the maintenance of good order amongst the troops, the functions of the *commissaires pour les subsistances* extended to the disbanding and *réformation* of the units under their charge,[121] and the adjudication of disputes concerning the payment of subsistence by the communities.[122] If necessary, the *commissaire*s were empowered to oversee the collection of funds by military force.[123]

---

[111] SHAT A¹ 42, pce 214, 20 Nov. 1637, *arrêt* for the imposition of the *subsistances* on the *généralités*.
[112] SHAT A¹ 42, pce 206, 8/12 Nov. 1637, arrangements for the levy and distribution of the *subsistances* by the appointed *commissaires*.
[113] SHAT A¹ 40, fos. 13/14, 20 Nov. 1637.
[114] SHAT A¹ 40, fo. 41, 26 Nov. 1637.   [115] SHAT A¹ 40, fo. 73, 30 Nov. 1637.
[116] SHAT A¹ 40, fo. 47, 28 Nov. 1637.   [117] SHAT A¹ 40, fo. 104, 5 Dec. 1637.
[118] SHAT A¹ 41, fo. 307, [late 1637]. Montmaur's commission may also have extended to the Bourbonnais.
[119] Bonney, *Political Change*, p. 31.
[120] SHAT A¹ 44, fo. 6, 21 Feb. 1638: Laubardement ordered to do nothing to obstruct Renard; A¹ 45, fo. 202, 18 Apr. 1638: Orgeval is not to interfere in the decisions of Besançon.
[121] SHAT A¹ 40, fo. 188, 15 Dec. 1637: Besançon ordered to disband all companies of *chevaux légers* in the armies operating on the Flanders frontier with fewer than thirty effectives. However, this was qualified, two months later, by an order to all six *commissaires* not to carry out the disbandment of under-strength companies: A¹ 44, fo. 7, 21 Feb. 1638.
[122] SHAT A¹ 40, fo. 168, 14 Dec. 1637: Biou to carry out the levy of the *subsistances* on the *généralités* of Poitou and Limousin, starting with the *villes franches*; A¹ 43, fo. 62, 8 Jan. 1638: Besançon is to ensure that *pain de munition* is provided for the billeted troops, not a financial equivalent.
[123] SHAT A¹ 43, fo. 291, 9 Feb. 1638: announcement of despatch of cavalry for Renard and Biou to enforce payment of the *subsistances*; A¹ 32, pce 267, n.d. [1638]; A¹ 45, fo. 139, 14 Apr. 1638.

The management of the war-effort from 1635 to 1642

Above all, the other *commissaires des guerres* present in these *généralités* were fully subject to the authority of the six *commissaires pour les subsistances*. Not merely did the latter receive orders to facilitate the individual *montres* and *revues* carried out by the lesser *commissaires*,[124] but were also charged with the payment of their salaries.[125] In the rare cases of fraud or misappropriation being detected or reported, it was the senior *commissaires* who were ordered to take action against their subordinates.[126]

The *commissaires pour les subsistances* provide an apparently ideal example of government by 'comprehensive' commission. In their jurisdictions they enjoyed explicit precedence over all other administrators for the duration of the winter quarter. Correspondence from the *secrétaire de la guerre* for the winter months of 1637/8 is dominated by letters to these six *commissaires*,[127] and they are certainly regarded as the key agents for discipline, supply and the general oversight of the troops.

Yet despite the apparent coherence of the *commissaire* system, matters had gone badly wrong. It was simply not possible to foist a further 8.5 million *livres* of direct taxation on to the taxable population, stipulating that it should be collected from November and distributed immediately. The ministry resorted to force, and, more characteristically, to concessions.[128] Both methods were implemented by the *commissaires*, but to little practical effect. Not merely were the sums received inadequate for the needs of the troops, but in many cases were so delayed as to be of no practical benefit. An *arrêt* of 22 April 1638 transferred all subsequent receipts from the *subsistances* into the hands of *trésoriers de l'extraordinaire des guerres*, to be used as they saw fit for the war-effort.[129] It was apparent that the levy of the *subsistances* would have to begin well before late November if it were to fund the winter quarter.

Moreover, even the proportion of this tax that was collected by the *commissaires* was not allocated to the subsistence of the troops. The memoirs of maréchal

---

[124] SHAT A¹ 40, fo. 125ii, 8 Dec. 1637: Renard to assist La Court in his *revue* of the regiment of Brézé; A¹ 40, fo. 268, 27 Dec. 1637: *commissaire* Bouteret is to give account to Vallier of the companies which he was ordered to provide with subsistence over the winter.

[125] SHAT A¹ 40, fo. 119, 7 Dec. 1637: Besançon to pay one of 'his' *commissaires* from the *subsistances*; A¹ 45, fo. 214, 18 Apr. 1638: Vallier to pay the salary of the *commissaire* La Retaye.

[126] SHAT A¹ 43, fo. 54, 8 Jan. 1638: Besançon to investigate the affairs of the *commissaire* Thomas Belot; A¹ 45, fo. 224, 19 Apr. 1638: order to Montmaur to arrest his *subdélégué*, Biou, brother of the *commissaire* of Poitou – the *commissaire* is also to be arrested.

[127] For example, SHAT A¹ 43 – minutes for Jan. and first twenty days of Feb. 1638 contains 416 documents, of which 127 are letters to the *commissaires* (including 40 letters to Besançon and 33 to Vallier), and only 7 letters to *intendants*, 6 of which were addressed to a single *intendant*, Villemontée.

[128] SHAT A¹ 44, fo. 331, 21 Mar. 1638, de Noyers to des Granges: the *commissaire* is to administer a *remise* of 2 *sols* 6 *deniers* on each *livre* of the *subsistances* paid immediately for the support of the army of Italy in quarters; A¹ 43, fo. 405, 20 Feb. 1638, Renard is to accept the proposition of the city of Orléans to pay a flat sum of 60,000 *livres* for the upkeep of the troops.

[129] SHAT A¹ 42, fo. 104, 22 Apr. 1638.

Responses and reactions

Bassompierre, written from the Bastille, relate what was presumably widely credited at court. The original plan to introduce the *subsistances* has been greeted with considerable enthusiasm by local communities, and especially by the *places* subjected to garrisons. Bassompierre suggested that overall responsibility for the system rested with Besançon, who acted fraudulently to make a substantial personal profit from the advances of this tax.[130] But even fraudulence by the *commissaires* on the largest scale would not account for the complete failure of the project. More damagingly, money taken in advance to meet the costs of the troops was appropriated by the *surintendant*. This was used to meet a number of immediate military expenses as the 1637 campaign drew to its close, especially for the army of Saxe-Weimar, with no possibility that it could be reimbursed later in the winter. The communities were faced with the choice of paying a double tax – a further payment for the *subsistances* – or submitting to the pillage and disorders of unpaid soldiers. Although the commissions to the *commissaires* gave them the power to collect the revenues from the *subsistances*, they found themselves under pressure from Bullion to reallocate their funds. The short-term aim of meeting the costs of keeping the remaining operational forces funded seemed more important to the *bureau des finances* than the provisioning of the troops over the winter.

Bassompierre's *Mémoires* are corroborated by the *arrêt* for the imposition of the *subsistances* for the next winter quarter of 1638/9, which expressed strong dissatisfaction with the disorders committed 'en plusieurs bourgs et villes' by the troops who had not received the payments that ought to have been ensured by the tax. In consequence, the *arrêt* was dated 3 August 1638, and it stressed that the collection of the *subsistances* was to commence immediately and to proceed in parallel with the other direct taxes.[131] In 1637/8, the *subsistances* had been levied too late to serve its intended purpose. In future it was to be levied far too early; by 1640, 18.5 million *livres* were in theory to be levied across France through the *subsistances*, and the collection was to start from late June.[132] In these circumstances, much of the revenue collected would have been alienated, or allocated to other expenses, before the winter quarter began.

But the failure of the *subsistances* experiment of 1637/8 did not lessen the need to find some means adequately to support a significant portion of the army under arms during the winter months. Nor did it make it any easier to ignore the

---

[130] Bassompierre, *Mémoires*, XXI. 371–2. The fact that Besançon had been arrested on a previous occasion, in 1629, for misappropriation of funds belonging to the army of Italy might seem convincing evidence of his later guilt, except that Bassompierre, together with maréchal Schomberg, had been his judges on that occasion: Plessis-Besançon, *Mémoires*, pp. xiv–xv.

[131] SHAT A¹ 49, fo. 155: 'qu'outre ce qui se doibt lever en deniers'. The *subsistances* was to be collected in six instalments, instead of the five instalments of the *taille*, and collection was to begin immediately and to run through until April of 1639: see chapter 4, pp. 273–4.

[132] SHAT A¹ 62, fo. 152, 9 June 1640; Bonney, *Political Change*, p. 274, gives a lower figure of 13.6 million *livres*.

The management of the war-effort from 1635 to 1642

violence, disorder and economic damage perpetrated by soldiers billeted on French provinces with inadequate mechanisms to ensure that they were fed and received some basic subsistence pay. As the ministers recognized, the failure had been essentially financial rather than organizational, and, whatever doubts may have been raised about the corruption of the *commissaires*, flawed supervision of winter quartering was better than no supervision at all.

However, pushing back the date for the beginning of the collection of the *subsistances* tax created a simple practical problem: the *commissaires* were not available for the levy of a tax in the provinces during the campaign season. The commissions for the *subsistances* expired at the end of the winter quarter in March/April 1638, and the senior *commissaires* were subsequently allocated a number of important functions concerned with the *montres* and administration of the armies in the field.[133] After they had abandoned their *généralités* at the beginning of the campaign, all claim by the late *commissaires pour les subsistances* to formal precedence over the other *commissaires* lapsed.

The *commissaires*' resumption of functions with the armies and on the frontiers thus left the collection of the *subsistances* to the *intendants*, considered to be the most reliable of the provincial administrators when it came to the collection of an unpopular and innovatory tax. As this situation accorded with the wish of the *surintendants* to incorporate the new tax into the existing structures of revenue anticipation and the dealings between the *bureaux des finances* and its financiers, it was unlikely that there would be influential support for a proposal to create a new group of agents to collect the tax in the absence of the *commissaires*. The ruling of 24 July 1638 ordered the collection of the *subsistances* by *intendants* in nineteen *généralités*.[134] Yet while the collection of the tax may have been transferred to the established 'civilian' provincial administrators, the operation and supervision of the winter quarter system from November to March was once again placed in the hands of specific commission-holders. Despite the general accusations, only one of the *commissaires* of 1637/8, Jacques Biou, was prosecuted for misappropriation of funds,[135] but it seems that the ministers decided to make a clean sweep of the entire group, who continued to hold substantial military assignments, but did not receive commissions *pour les subsistances* during the subsequent winter quarters.[136]

---

[133] SHAT A¹ 38, fo. 233, 19 Aug. 1637, de Noyers to Besançon; A¹ 39, fo. 218, 16 Oct. 1637, de Noyers to Montmaur; A¹ 45, fo. 316, 26 Apr. 1638, de Noyers to Vallier; A¹ 48, fo. 127, 4 Aug. 1638, general instruction to *commissaires dans les provinces* concerning levy of additional troops.

[134] Bonney, *Political Change*, pp. 274–5; R.J. Bonney, 'The intendants of Richelieu and Mazarin, 1624–1661', DPhil thesis, University of Oxford, 1973, p. 297, table 15.

[135] SHAT A¹ 40, fo. 73, 30 Nov. 1637: account of claimed corruption of Biou; A¹ 45, fo. 53, 7 Apr. 1638, replacement of Biou by *commissaire* André Magnan, who had himself brought some of the charges against Biou – fo. 50, 7 Apr. The main charge was that Biou was extorting illegal advances from the captains of units for the subsistence of their troops, breaking with the usual tendency for *commissaires* and officers to work together to exploit the civilian populations.

[136] This is one obvious interpretation, based on the allegations of corruption. It was equally possible that the ministers simply decided to allocate other duties to this group of *commissaires des guerres*, or

Responses and reactions

The alternative, established during the winters of 1638/9, 1639/40 and thereafter, was an *ad hoc* mixture of commission-holders, based upon a core of provincial *intendants* but supplemented by a group of other agents, some of whom were *commissaires des guerres*, some *trésoriers de France* and other provincial *officiers*. Of twenty-eight named agents in 1638/9, fifteen were *intendants des provinces*, thirteen were other officials.[137] In the following winter some of the individuals were changed, but the mixture of *intendants* and other *officiers* remained the same. A list of twenty *commissaires chargés de la subsistance des trouppes dans les généralités*, gives twelve *intendants* and eight others.[138] In the latter document the *généralités* to which the *commissaires* were allocated are indicated, revealing no pattern to the appointments. An obvious configuration might have been the appointment of an *intendant* together with another *officier* to each *généralité*, and this is the case with Rouen, for example, where the *intendant* Claude Paris shared these functions with the *trésorier de France*, Etienne Pascal.[139] However, in other cases two *intendants* exercised the commission jointly, as at Limoges, for example, where the winter quarter was administered by Guillaume Fremin, sieur de Couronnes, and Bernard Fortia, sieur du Plessis Clereau. Meanwhile at Soissons neither Caumartin nor Berault were *intendants*. Whether these appointments reflected lobbying on the part of patrons or a willingness to draw on existing administrative expertise in the *généralités* is unclear. No sharp distinction is drawn between a group of officials who already held commissions, the *intendants*, and others, whether *commissaires des guerres* or *trésoriers*, who were venal office-holders; both received identical 'comprehensive' commissions, which would enhance their existing authority and delineate their responsibilities. This practice of creating a mixed team of *intendants* and *officiers* under commission to handle the various tasks and problems

---

that the change in officials reflected a reluctance of the chancellor or the *surintendants* to see a tax-collecting operation in the hands of agents of the *secrétaire de la guerre*. Vallier and Montmaur were to be reemployed as *commissaires pour les subsistances* in the winter of 1641/2: SHAT A¹ 68, fos. 446, 563, 28 Feb./18 Mar. 1642.

[137] SHAT A¹ 50ii, fo. 190, 16 Feb. 1639, A¹ 51, fo. 91, 11 Mar. 1639: the *intendants* were d'Aubray, du Gué, Lauzon, Talon, Le Bret, Choisy, Bellejamme, Heere, Chaponay, Paris, Aligre, Thiersault, Villemontée, Fremin and Fortia; the others were Ribeyre, Loubet, Montraville, Channes, Caumartin, Longay, La Ferté, Villetrin, Duret, Puchot, Croismar, Perreau and Chambonneau. Of these latter, Loubet, Longay (Longuet) and Ribeyre were certainly *commissaires des guerres*. The list of *commissaires pour les subsistances* for this and subsequent years has no pretensions to being comprehensive given the haphazard survival of documentation in the Archives de la Guerre, and the tendency of the material to emphasize the provinces within the *département* of the *secrétaire de la guerre*. Bonney, *Political Change*, p. 274, proposes that these *commissaires* were to be established in nineteen *généralités*, implying the appointment of thirty-eight agents overall.

[138] SHAT A¹ 58, fo. 79, 7 Mar. 1640: the *intendants* were Bellejamme, Heere, Grémonville, Fremin, Fortia, Paris, Thiersault, Potherie, Miron, Dupré, Orgères and Villemontée; the others were Caumartin, Berault, Fontaines, Baye, Pascal, Leconte, Chambonneau and Croismar.

[139] Bonney, *Political Change*, p. 274, suggests that the legislative intention was to establish pairs of *commissaires*, one provincial intendant and one *trésorier* or other provincial office-holder in each *généralité*. As so often, intentions seem to have given way to a more *ad hoc* reality.

The management of the war-effort from 1635 to 1642

connected with the winter quarter continued through the winters of 1640/1 and 1641/2.[140] Indeed, the system began to acquire a stability and familiarity which appears to have reduced the quantity of routine correspondence, especially the generalized circulars, between the *secrétaire* and the *commissaires pour les subsistances*.

The primary responsibility implied by the commissions, and frequently reiterated in the specific instructions to individual *commissaires*, was the distribution of *subsistances* funds to the troops billeted within the area of their jurisdiction.[141] Anxious to spread hard-pressed funds as far as possible, the *commissaires* frequently needed prompting to accept financial responsibility for additional units which they considered fell outside their jurisdiction.[142] Moreover, the question of payment of the winter quarter was considerably complicated by the ministry's aim, from the winter of 1638/9, to use part of the funds from the *subsistances* to meet some of the costs of additional recruitment needed to bring the quartered units up to campaign strength. In theory the *subsistances* had been introduced as a means to reduce and distribute the burden of lodging and supplying the troops through the winter months; above all, given sound practical reasons for billeting the troops in the towns, it was intended to spread a share of these costs across to the countryside.[143] In the interests of ensuring that the burden on the local populations should be no heavier than necessary, it was vital that the *commissaires pour les subsistances* themselves, and their *commissaire* subordinates, should conduct *revues* with the greatest care to ensure that the number of troops in winter quarters was established as accurately as possible.[144] Yet this concern, often expressed in rather generalized terms, was paralleled by

---

[140] Confusingly, in 1640/1 the title of the *commissaires pour les subsistances* was changed to *commissaires généraux*, but these are the same agents, and the original title was resumed in 1641/2. For winter quarters in 1640/1, SHAT A¹ 61, fo. 375, 12 Dec. 1640, lists some of the *commissaires généraux*: Bellejamme, Grémonville, d'Osny, Paris, Pascal, Lecomte, Blanchon, Champigny, Orgères, Villarceaux, Legendre, Villemontée, Fremin and Montmaur. For 1641/2, A¹ 68, fos. 12, 52, 69, 214, 3–27 Jan. 1642: a composite list indicates *commissaires* Vallier, Hardicourt, Montmaur, Aubray, Grémonville, Potherie, Paris, Pascal, Champigny, Briconnet, Villemontée, d'Oisonville, Fontaines. For 1642/3 a similar pattern emerges: A¹ 70, fo. 364, 10 Nov. 1642: Montmaur, Villarceaux, Bellejamme, Choisy, Paris, Pascal, Potherie, Thiersault, Vallier, Orgères, Fontaines.

[141] SHAT A¹ 50, fo. 30, 4 Jan. 1639, Aligre and Croismar informed that the king has accorded 6,000 livres for the upkeep of each company of *chevaux légers*, 6,000 for each company of *mousquetaires à cheval*, and 22,000 livres for each regiment of twenty companies of foot; A¹ 61, fo. 333, 9 Dec. 1640; A¹ 63, fo. 211, 26 Jan. 1640, 26 Jan. 1641: general instructions concerning the basis on which the units were to be paid their *montres* for the winter quarter.

[142] For example, SHAT A¹ 50, fo. 281, 28 Jan. 1639, de Noyers to Mesgrigny, ordering him to pay the regiment of Biscarat from the *subsistances* funds of Champagne; A¹ 63, fo. 319, 6 Feb. 1641, Champigny to pay the subsistence of the company of *chevaux légers* of Bussy de Vere.

[143] The point made explicitly in Bullion's *mémoire* on the subsistence of the troops in winter quarters: AAE MD 819, fos. 97–9, [dated 1635, more probably between 1638 and 1640].

[144] For example, SHAT A¹ 61, fo. 358, 10 Dec.1640, circular to the '*commissaires généraux*' concerned with the accurate conduct of *revues* of the troops in garrison; A¹ 70, fo. 558, 17 Dec. 1642, similar to the *commissaires*, enjoining the greatest care and accuracy in the conduct of *revues*.

Responses and reactions

the apparently contradictory practice of ordering the *commissaires* specifically to overstate the numbers of troops in particular units in order to generate funds for recruitment. Instructions that the *commissaires pour les subsistances* were 'to treat with all possible favour' certain regiments in order to generate recruitment funds were common,[145] while in other cases the *commissaires* were simply ordered to allocate the *subsistances* to the costs of recruitment.[146] By 1640 the ministers were even negotiating specific *traités* for recruitment on the basis of the *taxe des subsistances*: in return for accepting the obligation to raise their units to full strength and then maintain them throughout the winter, the unit commanders from Châtillon's army were to receive funds from the *subsistances* at the rate of 17,000 *livres* per company of *chevaux légers*, substantially more than the standard payment of 6,000 *livres* per company.[147]

Whether through awareness that the *subsistances* was being deployed for purposes other than the 'soulagement des communautés', or whether it was inevitably the result of trying to impose a further substantial tax burden upon the already intolerably burdened peasantry, the attempt to extract the new tax encountered strong resistance.[148] This resistance was evident both during the summer and autumn months, when the first instalments were to be collected by the provincial *intendants*, and during the winters when the responsibility for collecting the further installments and for trying to extract the sums still outstanding from the earlier period, fell to the *commissaires pour les subsistances*. Collection of the *subsistances* in the face of delays, partial payment and outright opposition came to absorb a large part of the time and energies of the *commissaires*. The ministers were concerned that failure to provide the pay and food for the troops in garrisons would result not merely in disorders but in the likely disbandment or disintegration of the units, and possessing a large reserve of coercive force immediately to hand, they were more prepared to force the issue

---

[145] SHAT A¹ 50, fo. 238, 26 Jan. 1639, instructions to Mesgrigny, Lefebvre, Talon and Lebret to use *subsistances* payments to favour the regts of Picardie, Plessis-Praslin and Saint-Luc in their winter quarters; A¹ 64, fo. 176, 6 Apr. 1641, instruction to Orgères that he is to pay subsistence to the regt d'Huxelles throughout the quarter at the strength of 410 soldiers – i.e. regardless of the (doubtless lower) actual strength.

[146] SHAT A¹ 51, fo. 70, 7 Mar. 1639, de Noyers to Fremin and Fortia, ordering them to pay over 32,000 *livres* of the *subsistances* to meet the recruitment costs of the regt de La Suze; A¹ 52, fo. 136, 11 May 1639, although the winter quarter is now over, Talon is to continue to pay money collected from the *subsistances* to meet recruitment costs.

[147] SHAT A¹ 57, fo. 94, 13 Jan. 1640, de Noyers to Lepage, informing him of the new proposals for the *traités* with Châtillon's officers; fo. 132, 17 Jan., specifies the sum of 17,000 *livres* (for the winter quarter subsistence allowance of 6,000 *livres* per company see A¹ 50, fo. 30, 4 Jan. 1639).

[148] SHAT A¹ 50ii, fo. 50, 4 Feb. 1639, general instruction to the *commissaires* concerning the extreme difficulties in levying the *subsistances*; A¹ 50ii, fo. 276, 25 Feb.1639, dissatisfaction of the king with the very poor contribution made by Provence to the payment of the *subsistances*; A¹ 63, fo. 571, 15 Mar. 1641, Bellejamme to address the issue of the numerous towns in the *généralité* (Amiens) which have not paid their *subsistances* allocation for the present winter.

The management of the war-effort from 1635 to 1642

with local communities than in other circumstances. Refusal to pay the *subsistances*, or some acceptable contribution towards the original assessment,[149] could result in the order to billet troops on the recalcitrant area, or – in the event that the majority of the offenders were in the countryside – to use troops to extract the *subsistances* by force.[150]

Aside from the collection of the outstanding *subsistances* and its distribution to the troops, the additional duties of the *commissaires pour les subsistances* became clearly defined and accepted by other authorities: the allocation of troops to particular towns and other *places*; the duty of travelling between the various places of *logement* to maintain discipline and resolve disputes; carrying out necessary disbandment and *réformation* of the units; ensuring that the troops were made ready for campaigning during March and April.[151] The commissions continued to expire at the end of the winter quarter, and the various *intendants* and other officials were granted new commissions or assigned to other duties. In May 1640 Fontaines, *commissaire pour les subsistances* at Châlons, was informed that his *commissaire*-colleague, Nicolas Bretel, sieur de Grémonville, had been commissioned as *intendant* with the army of Picardy. Fontaines was ordered in the meantime to continue his duties as *commissaire pour les subsistances* for the troops still based in the *généralité* of Châlons.[152] Yet winter quarter by winter quarter some continuity of personnel began to emerge, as is evident from the names which recur in many of the instances of their activities. The tendency to use officials drawn from a number of different administrative structures persisted, as did the convention by which the commission of the *intendant* appears to have been

---

[149] An example of this willingness to compromise is provided for the *généralité* of Bourges in 1639, where the *commissaires* Heere and Bigot were simply instructed to try to extract as much as possible from the territory for the *subsistances*, and in any case 'at least 50,000 *livres*': SHAT A^1 51, fo. 389, 8 Apr.

[150] SHAT A^1 50ii, fo. 77, 6 Feb. 1639, general instruction to *commissaires* to use the troops lodged in their *généralités* to extract the *subsistances* from the local populations; A^1 58, fo. 48, 5 Mar. 1640, Ferté and Villetrin, *commissaires pour les subsistances* for the *généralité* of Tours, were to regulate the exaction of the *subsistances* from Tours, and to make use of the company of *chevaux légers* of Annevoux to enforce collection and maintain order; A^1 58, fo. 394, 7 Apr. 1640, Fremin and Fortia to use troops to compel payment of the *subsistances* in the *généralité* of Limoges.

[151] SHAT A^1 58, fo. 11, 1 Mar. 1640, Villemontée and Chambonneau to investigate disorders and violence between troops and civilians in Poitou; A^1 61, fo. 304, 2 Dec. 1640, Paris, Pascal – *commissaires pour les subsistances* at Rouen – notification of despatch of military officers to the troops billeted in the *généralité*, and orders for cooperation; A^1 68, fo. 11, 3 Jan. 1642, *commissaires pour les subsistances* in the *généralité* of Soissons to intervene directly in the distribution of food to the troops in quarters; A^1 57, fo. 473, 22 Feb. 1640, Miron and Dupré to disband three regts in Languedoc; A^1 51, fo. 91, 11 Mar. 1639, general despatch to the *commissaires* to do all possible to ensure that the troops should be ready to campaign by 15 Apr.

[152] SHAT A^1 59, fo. 157, 20 May 1640; see also A^1 51, fo. 259, 27 Mar. 1639, de Noyers to sr Destouches notifying him of the expiry of his commission as *commissaire pour les subsistances* and his reappointment as *commissaire général des vivres* with the army of Languedoc for the forthcoming campaign; A^1 64, fo. 313, 23 Apr. 1641, nomination of Pierre de Naberat, *commissaire pour les subsistances*, as *commissaire* with the army of Italy.

Responses and reactions

overridden by the commission for the *subsistances* for the duration of the winter quarter. As the commissions for the administration of the winter quarter emanated from the *secrétaire d'Etat*, whereas, of course, the commissions of intendancy emanated from the chancellor, this may be one case in which Sublet de Noyers demonstrated an ability to expand the patronage of the secretaryship against the senior ministers. Equally, though, it may simply have been permitted on the rational grounds that the winter quartering of troops was best administered through the secretary for war.

How should the experiment with the comprehensive commissions 'pour les subsistances' be regarded? As a means of controlling the soldiers in winter quarters, reducing the damage and violence inflicted on the local communities and ensuring that relatively full-strength units were ready to take the field at the beginning of the campaign season, its success was limited. Chapter 10 will emphasize that there was no evidence for an improvement in the relations between soldiers and the local populations during Richelieu's ministry. On the other hand, the *commissaires pour les subsistances* can bear only a limited responsibility for a situation which was in largest part the result of inadequate financial and supply provision for the winter quarter, considered to be a low priority by the *bureau des finances*. Yet though provision for the troops in quarters was undoubtedly inadequate, the use and development of the *commissaires pour les subsistances* did offer some benefits. By giving them direct control not only of the organization and discipline of the troops in their quarters, but also over the extraction of that part of the *taxe des subsistances* that was still outstanding by the end of the year, the ministry was tacitly accepting a form of financial decentralization. At least one part of the *subsistances* was being collected locally in order to meet the immediate need of paying some of the costs of the troops billeted in the area. The collection was being undertaken directly by those who had responsibility for distribution, and as such at least a proportion of the monies extracted were going to the relatively 'low priority' – in the eyes of the *bureau des finances* – objective of paying the troops in their quarters. Moreover, unlike the patchwork of commissions granted in an attempt to try to improve the supply of the armies on campaign, which were frequently vague or ambiguous about the relationship between the commission-holder and the existing administrators, and which could impose an outsider such as the bishop of Mende with massive responsibilities and theoretical powers but limited means to secure cooperation, the *commissaires pour les subsistances* were far more effectively integrated into the existing structures for the supply and garrisoning of the troops, with clearly defined powers and responsibilities.

Moreover, the role of an elite of *commissaires des guerres* in the *subsistances* experiment is important in evaluating the status and importance of these officials. It casts doubts upon the assumption that the *commissaires* were minor functionaries of insignificant origins, never seriously contemplated as an administrative alternative to the *maîtres des requêtes* who were to dominate the commissions of intendancy. Charles Besançon de Bazoches was of the Parisian administrative elite, his father being auditor of the *chambre des comptes* and *gentilhomme de la chambre* of Catherine de Bourbon, sister of Henri IV.[153] Charles raised a company of cavalry, and may have levied regiments of foot and horse in 1652.[154] Gilles Renard raised a company of *chevaux légers*, and held in addition to his office of *commissaire des guerres* that of *commissaire à la conduite des gendarmes de la garde du Roi*.[155] Jean Vallier, seigneur de La Martinière, was to become *maître de l'hôtel du Roi*, his son became a president of the *Parlement* of Metz, and the family went on to assume high status in the Paris *Parlement* in the eighteenth century.[156] Another *commissaire* who rose to preeminence in 1638, Jean de Bragelongne,[157] was a member of a family which not only constituted a dynasty of *commissaires des guerres*[158], but which held an office of *trésorier de l'ordinaire des guerres* throughout the first half of the seventeenth century.[159] The Bragelongne went on to hold important positions as *Parlementaires*[160] and at least two prestigious military *charges* in the later seventeenth century.[161]

The high social status of the upper ranks of the *commissaires des guerres* is less surprising in the context of seventeenth-century France. As Daniel Dessert rightly maintains, there were no 'self-made men' in this society; social and vocational advancement was owed to family connections and to existing resources.[162] With hindsight the purchase of an office of *maître des requêtes* leading to an army intendancy would have been the more astute investment for a wealthy member of the *noblesse de robe* with political ambitions. However, in 1637/8, and indeed into the 1640s, it was less obvious that a senior *commissaire* would not prove equally able to progress upwards into the central government. In a situation in which the allocation of intendancies owed a great deal to family proximity to certain members of the ministerial circle, others within the administrative elite

---

[153] Plessis-Besançon *Mémoires*, pp. vi–xxix: Beaucaire also points out that the Besançon were related to Claude Bullion, Charles being Bullion's cousin.
[154] For the company of *chevaux légers*, SHAT A¹ 48, fo. 9bis, 9 Feb. 1638. In the case of the infantry regiments, it seems likely that confusion with the *maréchal de camp*, Charles' brother, Bernard du Plessis-Besançon, is at issue.
[155] André, *Michel Le Tellier et l'organisation*, p. 616.
[156] F. Bluche, *L'origine des magistrats du Parlement de Paris au XVIIIe siècle* (Paris, 1956), pp. 406–7. BN Ms.fr. PO 64924, pces 51, 52.
[157] SHAT A¹ 48, fo. 151, 4 Aug. 1638: placed with Vallier, Renard and des Granges.
[158] BN Ms.fr. PO 26974, pces 13, 20, pce 361.
[159] BN Ms.fr. PO 26974, pces 137, 234. Facilitated by the status of the Bragelongne as relatives-by-marriage to Claude Bouthillier.
[160] Bluche, *L'origine des magistrats*, pp. 107–8.
[161] BN Ms.fr. PO 26974, pce 240: colonel of infantry regiment; 248: captain of the *gardes du corps du roi*, 1667.
[162] Dessert, 'Le "laquais financier" au Grand Siècle'.

Responses and reactions

would be tempted to search for alternative routes to power, above all routes where access might be controlled by different patrons and patronage networks.

THE ROLE OF THE *INTENDANTS D'ARMÉE*, 1635–1642

In their accounts of the developing role of the *intendants*, many historians have been influenced by the interpretation first propounded by Gabriel Hanotaux in his *Origines de l'institution des intendants des provinces*. Hanotaux argued that while *intendants* had received commissions since the sixteenth century in order to carry out specific administrative functions, such intendancies were granted more frequently during the 1620s and 1630s, above all, in response to the multiple military and civil pressures of warfare.[163] Royal agents explicitly commissioned as *intendants de la justice, police et finance* were used to override the authority of the mass of ordinary office-holders, to take responsibility for numerous assignments connected with the general administration of the provinces or the armies, and to act as directly accountable ministerial agents and informers in the field.

Taking a broad chronology, this view that the *intendants*, both in the provinces and in the armies, were the foundation of a more extensive, 'bureaucratic' and centralized administration is irrefutable.[164] In the specifically military sphere, the smaller-scale, adequately funded royal army of the 1660s provided some of the preconditions for the operations of a more effective, centralized, military administration, and the *intendants d'armée* were the key element in this structure. Their position and status was clearly defined, linked upwards to their direct administrative superior and patron, the *secrétaire de la guerre* (now enjoying ministerial status), and downwards to the *commissaires des guerres*, the subordinates of the *intendants*, but the pool from which the *intendants d'armée* were largely selected.[165]

It is reasonable to assume that some elements of this development in the authority and status of the *intendants d'armée* would have been evident before the

---

[163] Hanotaux, *Origines des intendants*, pp. 107–60; Avenel, *Richelieu* IV. 193–215; C. Godard, *Les pouvoirs des intendants sous Louis XIV. Particulièrement dans les pays d'élections de 1661–1715* (Paris, 1901; repr. Geneva, 1974), pp. 1–13; G. Pagès, 'Essai sur l'évolution des institutions administratives en France du commencement du xvie siècle à la fin du xviie siècle', *Revue d'histoire moderne*, 7 (1932), 8–57, 113–37; Mousnier, *Les institutions*, II. 484–500; A. Petracchi, *Intendenti e prefetti. L'intendente provinciale nella Francia d'antico regime* (2 vols; Milan, 1971), I, *1551–1648*, pp. 42–6, 54–61; A. Smedley-Weill, *Les intendants de Louis XIV* (Paris, 1995), pp. 23–36.

[164] The most convincing and scholarly presentation of the critical role of the *intendants* in the emergence of a centralized regime remains Bonney, *Political Change*. This study of the emergence of the role of the *intendants* could be set with the example of their role at the end of the century provided by the volumes reprinting the reports of the provincial intendants *pour l'instruction du duc de Bourgogne*, revealing all of the preoccupations with detailed provincial information and regulation characteristic of the 'well-ordered police state': see the *introduction générale* by L. Trenard, *Les mémoires des intendants pour l'instruction du duc de Bourgogne, 1698* (Paris, 1975).

[165] Baxter, *Servants of the Sword*, is lucid and well-supported on the period after 1660. Dated, but still useful, is the relevant chapter in Godard, *Pouvoirs des intendants*, pp. 379–415.

The management of the war-effort from 1635 to 1642

great changes in military organization during the 1660s. But it is equally important to guard against a view which separates *intendants* from other administrative agents working within the armies, and which assumes that Richelieu, Mazarin and their subordinate ministers had consistently and purposefully recognized the importance of the *intendants d'armée* by heaping an increasingly large share of military authority and responsibility on to their shoulders.[166] The *intendants* were but one part of a larger ministerial initiative: the deployment and increasing formalization of authority under commission to try to mitigate the inadequacies of existing military administrators and institutions.[167] Moreover, the role and development of the *intendants d'armée* should be understood as much in terms of patronage structures as of an element in the progressive march of institutional history.

Simply by being commissioned officials, the *intendants d'armée* had no claim to being unusual or significant, and to an observer in the late 1630s it could not have been at all clear that the *intendants* would necessarily emerge as the primary recipients of such commissions in the administration of the armies. Moreover, the various overlapping, ill-conceived and impractical commissions granted to many of the agents discussed above cast doubt on the view that government by commission represented a progressive and rationalizing approach to the problems of administering an expanding war-effort. Yet, despite this, most accounts assume that a major place should be given to the *intendants d'armée* in any discussion of the administration of the armies after 1635, and in many cases give them considerable importance even before that date.[168] There are, indeed, some positive grounds for that assumption. Unless one of the ministers was present with an army-corps,[169] the *intendant d'armée* was the most senior official present with the troops, and as the number of campaign theatres expanded after 1635 so the position of the *intendant* as the senior military administrator during the campaigns

---

[166] A notable exception to this, a military-administrative study which takes the *intendants* as one group within a much larger administrative whole, is provided by Kroener, *Les routes*.

[167] This has been long understood but insufficiently emphasized. Esmonin, *Etudes sur la France*, pp. 13–17, stressed that the *intendants* were only one example of the increasing tendency to govern through the delegation of authority under commission; D. Buisseret, 'A stage in the development of the French *Intendants*: the reign of Henri IV', *Historical Journal*, 9 (1966), 27–38, also argues that the *intendants* were one group within a wider pool of royal *commissaires*. Mousnier, *Les institutions*, II. 466–8, 500–6, 575–86.

[168] Sicard, *Histoire des institutions militaires*; Baron C.V.E. Boyer de Saint-Suzanne, *L'administration sous l'Ancien Régime. Les intendants de la généralité d'Amiens (Picardie et Artois)* (Paris, 1865), pp. 9–43; J. Milot, 'Du commissaire des guerres à l'intendance militaire', *Revue historique de l'armée*, special number (1968), 39–48; Milot, 'L'évolution'; Baxter, *Servants of the Sword*, pp. 3–19, 60–85; Bonney, *Political Change*, pp. 259–83.

[169] It was rare, but not unknown, for a minister to be present with an army-corps after 1635: Chavigny was present with the army commanded by Gaston d'Orléans and Soissons in the autumn of 1636, and after the king began to assume control of particular army-corps from 1638 one or more of the ministers would be present with him.

Responses and reactions

was consolidated through increasingly regular appointments. Putting aside the division of functions between different *intendants* serving with the same army-corps, in principle the *intendant de justice, police et finances* possessed a direct juridical authority enjoyed by no other military administrator. Only the *intendants*, by virtue both of their commissions, and through being for the most part *maîtres des requêtes* – magistrates of the *Parlement* of Paris – had the power to dispense justice directly and under their own authority. The *intendants d'armée* might choose to exercise this authority through councils of war which drew upon the services of military officers, but this was essentially a question of prudence rather than legal necessity, and as they presided at these councils they had a great deal more control over the outcome of trials than other officials.[170] In the third case, the relationship between the high command of an army-corps and the *intendant d'armée* was much closer than for any other official. Special commissioners, charged, for example, with the supply of the armies, might have specific authority to sit in on the meetings of the high command,[171] but only the *intendants* received this right of presence at the policy meetings as a matter of course.[172] Part of this special relationship reflected the numbers of *intendants* who were specifically chosen by the commanders of army-corps when they assumed their commands; nevertheless, it gave them a standing with the armies that was incontrovertibly higher than that of other officials.

So although it is unconvincing to maintain that the *intendants* were a 'different type' of official simply by virtue of holding authority under commission, as the issuing of commissions was a general means by which the ministers sought to manage the problems of the armies, there is evidence for the superiority of the *intendant* within the hierarchy of military officials. Less defensible is the assumption that this hierarchical superiority was matched by effectiveness. The discussions in this chapter, as will those in chapter 9 below, emphasize the constraints weighing upon all elements of the military administration. It is important that the *intendants d'armée* are not treated in isolation from these constraints, and are not presented as the key element in an idealized picture of expanding administrative competence and effectiveness.[173]

---

[170] In other cases, especially those where the crown wanted a swift and exemplary sentence, the *intendants* were simply instructed to summon judges from other lesser courts in the vicinity and to direct proceedings, giving final and definitive judgement themselves: Baxter, *Servants of the Sword*, p. 67. A practical example is provided by Le Maistre de Bellejamme, writing to Séguier from the town of Guise, that he had summoned civil judges from Laon to conduct the trial of a captain accused of large-scale violence and extortion: BN Ms.fr. 13373, fo. 35, 16 May 1637.

[171] This was the case with the bishop of Mende's commission in 1636: Legrand-Girarde, *Crusy de Marcillac*, pp. 279–80.

[172] Baxter, *Servants of the Sword*, pp. 65–6; Bonney, *Political Change*, p. 266.

[173] Historians have recently raised doubts about the efficacy of the provincial *intendants*, at least in the sense of contrasting the limitations of their authority in practice with the apparently vast scope of their powers in theory, too often assumed in the past to have corresponded to administrative reality. Though Richard Bonney made extensive claims for the significance of the *intendants* to the war-

The management of the war-effort from 1635 to 1642

A number of areas should be examined in assessing the role of the *intendants d'armée* in the years after 1635. The first area is the extent of the autonomy that the *intendants* possessed in relation to the high command of the army-corps in which they served. This involves on the one hand the issue of direct patronage: from whom did the nominations to serve as an *intendant d'armée* come? On the other, the status of the *intendant* in any dispute with army officers: what level of support was he likely to gain from the ministers at the centre? The second area concerns the extent to which the *intendants* could actually achieve a clear field of authority. How far were the *intendants d'armée* able to define a sphere of operations and competence from which other officials – whether different groups of commissioned agents of the crown or indeed other *intendants* – were excluded? The third area requiring consideration is the practical effectiveness of the *intendants*. Beneath the formal level of their commissions, apparently granting and specifying an omnicompetent administrative authority, what functions did the *intendants d'armée* actually perform, and how effectively?

The examination of these three areas raises questions about the authority and capabilities of the *intendants* and places them clearly within the context of the constrained and limited administrative initiatives that have been described earlier in this chapter.

The intendants *and the high command*

The traditional interpretation of the *intendants* placed strong emphasis upon the extent to which they were chosen as commission-holders and allocated to provinces or to armies by the central government – in most cases by the chancellor, acting with the advice of the other ministers. Of all of those who purchased an office of *maître des requêtes* in the period between 1605 and 1643, fewer than 50 per cent were to be granted intendancies during Richelieu's ministry, although a further proportion would receive special, but by definition

---

effort from 1635 to 1659, much of the detailed evidence of his magisterial *Political Change* argues for a more limited and integrated role for these administrators, working within rather than replacing or challenging the existing structures: see for example pp. 46–8 on the problems posed by the territorial extent of some of the *généralités* and the difficulties caused by the potential solution of appointing joint *intendants*; or pp. 300–1 on the links between some of the *grands* and the *intendants* serving in their provinces. More recently F.-X. Emmanuelli has launched a direct assault on what he presents as the exaggerated claims for the *intendants* in the creation of monarchical absolutism: *Un mythe de l'absolutisme bourbonien. L'intendance du milieu du XVIIe siècle à la fin du XVIIIe siècle (France, Espagne, Amérique)* (Aix-en-Provence, 1981), pp. 10–37, 83–6; see also F.-X. Emmanuelli, *Etat et pouvoirs dans la France des XVIe–XVIIIe siècles. La métamorphose inachevée* (Paris, 1992), pp. 61–85. See also F. Hildesheimer, 'Centralisation, pouvoir local et diplomatique: les ordonnances des intendants', *Bibliothèque de l'école des chartes*, 136 (1978), 67: 'l'intendant occupait une situation bien plus ambiguë qui explique dans une large mesure l'évolution de l'institution'. Scepticism about the effectiveness of the provincial *intendants* is also expressed by Beik, *Absolutism and Society*, pp. 98–109, and Roger Mettam, *Power and Faction in Louis XIV's France* (Oxford, 1988), *passim*.

Responses and reactions

specific and temporary, commissions.[174] Those who obtained intendancies gained them through connections and through the patronage of the ministers. The *intendant* in Languedoc, Jean-Baptiste Baltazar, sieur de Malherbe, made his debt to Chavigny explicit in a letter of *fidélité* in April 1642.[175] De Noyers wrote to Séguier in March 1643 informing him that the *députés* of Pinerolo had requested that the king should send an *intendant* to exercise authority within the town and the garrison. The king chose to grant the commission to M. de Champigny, and de Noyers suggested that this should please Séguier as the candidate was the grandson of the Président de Champigny, one of Séguier's oldest family links.[176] It is perhaps no coincidence that one of the few *commissaires des guerres* who received a commission as an *intendant* during the period of Sublet de Noyers' secretaryship, Jean Bragelongne, was related to the *surintendant* Claude Bouthillier, who had married his aunt, Marie de Bragelongne.[177] The *intendants* were part of the structures of clientage and patronage which permeated the whole of society and government. This is, however, assumed to be a form of patronage based upon the power and influence of the ministers, and therefore compatible with the centralizing and modernizing aspirations of a state driven by the needs of warfare.[178]

It is clear, however, that the appointment of the *intendants des provinces*

---

[174] For the number of *intendants* appointed or in service from 1624 to 1642 see Bonney, *Political Change*, p. 117, who calculates that seventy-nine *intendants* received commissions in this period. (Given the problems of distinguishing between provincial and army *intendants* – an *intendant d'armée* who served as a provincial *intendant* at any point will be on Bonney's list – it is reasonable to assume that the total should be increased at most by 10–15 per cent to allow for other *intendants d'armée*.) For a complete list of the *maîtres des requêtes* who purchased this office in the same period, see BN Ms.fr.14018, which gives 190 names of creations made between 1605 and 1643. While this suggests that the *maîtres des requêtes* had a less than even chance of gaining an intendancy, it gives no idea of the number who received other types of limited commission. For a particular case of a *maître des requêtes* who received a commission that was clearly not an intendancy, see BN Ms.fr. 6645, fo. 3, 17 Apr. 1635, Chavigny to La Valette, announcing the despatch of Jacques Dyel, sieur de Miroménil, to carry out a particular investigation and trial. (Miroménil was appointed to the intendancy of Rouen in the following year.) See also Bonney, *Political Change*, p. 136, for further examples.

[175] AAE, MD 842, fo. 152, 18 Apr. 1642: Baltazar emphasized 'que j'ay employé la meilleure partie de mon bien et ma vie' to the service of Chavigny. Chavigny was demonstrably also the court patron of François Bochart de Champigny, and worked with the comte d'Alais to gain Champigny's reappointment to the intendancy of Provence in 1643: Harding, *Anatomy of a Power Elite*, p. 286 n. 97, refers to a letter cited in A. Crémieux, *Marseille et la royauté pendant la minorité de Louis XIV* (Paris, 1917), p. 173.

[176] BN Ms.fr. 17374, fo. 154, 4 Mar. 1643.

[177] Bragelongne was *intendant* at Tours from 1641 to 1648. For the marriage of Marie to Claude Bouthillier and the proximity that this brought the Bragelongne to Richelieu, see P. Grillon, 'Lettre du secrétaire d'Etat Claude Bouthillier au Cardinal de Richelieu', in Durand (ed.), *Clientèles et fidélités*, pp. 71–90, at pp. 72–5.

[178] This is a key contention advanced in Kettering, *Patrons*, pp. 233–5, and in her article 'The decline of great noble patronage during the reign of Louis XIV', *Canadian Journal of History*, 24 (1989), 157–77; Kettering's general overview of the debates about the character and forms of patronage is also important: 'Patronage in early modern France'.

The management of the war-effort from 1635 to 1642

sometimes reflected different patronage structures, both at the level of the original grant of a commission and, to an even greater extent, in the decisions about where to place particular *intendants*. Moreover, in the case of the *intendants d'armée* the entire administrative initiative rested on different foundations, which significantly shaped the operations of patronage and influence in appointments. The origins of the *intendants d'armée* lay with the high command. Just as the appointments of some of the *prévôts* and some of the *commissaires des guerres* lay within the patronage of the *maréchaux*, so the *intendants d'armée* developed as specialized, legally or financially trained assistants of the commanding officers, appointed by all these commanders as a means to deal with administrative problems as they arose.[179] Just as the great aristocrat would not usually manage his own estates or administer seigneurial justice in his own person, the technical elements of running an army were considered beneath the dignity of the commander and were to be delegated to an official who was, in effect, a member of his household. These origins contrast with the notion that *intendants d'armée* were appointed from the centre, and that their primary purpose was to oversee and report upon the loyalty of the commanders, seventeenth-century equivalents of the bolshevik commissars with the Red Army.[180] There is plenty of evidence that the *intendants*' origins as the assistants of the general would render them unsuitable agents for this task, and even in the period of multiple army-corps in the period after 1635, examples of *intendants* reporting on the activities of the generals in such terms are rare.[181]

By the 1630s it was no longer the case that the *intendants d'armée* were

[179] Antoine, 'Genèse'; Antoine, 'Institutions françaises', and private communication with Professor Antoine.

[180] There was a tradition, cited by Baxter, that when the king was present with an army the great government officers performed the most senior administrative and judicial functions with the force: *Servants of the Sword*, pp. 12–13. But this does not appear to have prevented the *grands* acting as commanders from making their own appointments of administrators.

[181] Baxter's example of this, the appointment of René Voyer d'Argenson to accompany the forces placed under Condé in the Limousin, Marche and Auvergne in 1632, simply asserts that the standard formula of the commission, requiring him to do all possible to assist Condé, was implicitly an order to spy on Condé because 'Condé was in royal disfavour': *Servants of the Sword*, p. 66. Setting aside the issue of Condé's fall from favour – he was to be the chief beneficiary from the confiscation of the property of his brother-in-law, Montmorency, and Richelieu was shortly to approach Condé to propose the marriage betwen his son and Richelieu's niece – any standard commission of intendancy could be read in the same way. There is nothing in the copy of the commission (SHAT A¹ 14, pce 32) to suggest a particular concern with surveillance; Bonney, *Political Change*, p. 247 n. 7, gives a more specific example of Cazet de Vautorte writing in code on 16 Aug. 1645 concerning the unsatisfactory conduct of the *maréchal de camp*, d'Espenan, in the levy of contributions. I have found no evidence of uncomplimentary reports by *intendants* concerning their commanders for the period 1630–42, and it would seem overwhelmingly the case that it was not seriously expected that the *intendants* would act in this role. If the ministers were worried about the loyalty or commitment of a commander in the field, they were more likely to appoint another *grand* of known fidelity to serve beside him either in a joint command, or to report on his behaviour: for example BN Ms.fr. 6645, fo. 11, 29 Apr. 1635, Richelieu to the cardinal de La Valette, asking him to execute 'un tour en l'armée de Mons. le Mar. de La Force, où sans doute elle [*sic*] ne sera pas peu utile'.

Responses and reactions

appointed from the household of the aristocratic commander. Indeed the *Code Michau* stipulated that *intendants* were not to be appointed from those who were 'domestique, conseiller ou employé aux affaires ou proche parent des généraux desdites armées'.[182] Instead, as was indicated in chapter 7, the *intendants* were appointed from two sources. Those with fiscal jurisdiction were either one of the four *intendants des finances* from the central *bureau des finances* acting 'on circuit', or were other financial officials commissioned by the *bureau* to hold this post. The *intendants de justice* were either existing provincial *intendants* or *maîtres des requêtes* whose commissions were drawn up by the *secrétaire de la guerre*, but whose ministerial patron was more obviously the chancellor. Yet the role of the commanders in the selection of the *intendants* remained important. Even though it was increasingly unusual for these appointments to intendancies to be made from amongst their own retainers,[183] they continued to ask the ministers for *intendants* to serve with their army-corps.[184] This in itself casts doubt on the view that the *intendants* should be seen as a check upon the authority and independence of the commander. Certainly, the latter did not see the *intendants* in such terms, and requests that they be appointed to serve with the army-corps even when they were not already known and reliable clients suggest that their role was envisaged in neutral or in positive terms by the commanders in the field, and certainly not as spies or investigators. Even if the commander had to tolerate the irritation of regular, detailed, reports made by the *intendants* to the ministers, this was outweighed by the support that the *intendant* might offer in the endless struggle to obtain resources and financial support from the crown. Indeed, though the commanders may have disliked the notion that the ministers should know as much about the state of the army as the reports of the *intendants* would make possible, this could be useful in justifying claims for additional funds and troops, or in explaining decisions to ministers with little understanding of local

---

[182] *Code Michau*, art. 81, quoted in Bonney, *Political Change*, p. 300.

[183] Bonney cites the example of Baltazar, appointed to serve under the maréchal de Schomberg in Languedoc in 1643, who had been in the service of the Schomberg family since at least 1632: *Political Change*, p. 300. Similarly, Jean de Choisy had built up his career in the household of Gaston d'Orléans, and was eventually to become his chancellor, as, in turn, was Choisy's eldest son: Mousnier (ed), *Lettres*, II. 1194.

[184] For example, AAE CP Lorraine 31, fo. 358v, 3 July 1640, letter from François de L'Hôpital, seigneur du Hallier to de Noyers, complaining that he was having difficulty dealing with the supply of the army in Lorraine and that: 'un intendant de justice me soulageroit de ce soin, vous scavez, Monsieur, que les commis des vivres ne font rien s'ils ne sont pressés par quelqu'un'. AAE MD 254, fo. 198, Oct. 1635, request by Charles d'Aumont, sr de Villequier, for an *intendant* to serve with the army before Montreuil, in Lorraine. For a case of a provincial *grand* making a slightly more specific request for an *intendant*, BN Ms.fr. 17373, fo. 164, 8 July 1637, de Noyers to Séguier, the former reporting that the duc de Ventadour, the *lieutenant-général* of Limousin, had managed to restore order in his *gouvernment* and now wished to have an *intendant de la justice* serving beside him 'qui soit homme doux et polytique'. De Noyers expressed confidence that Séguier would be able to select such a candidate.

circumstances who constantly sought rapid and decisive results.[185] Even an *intendant* with no previous connections to the commanding officer could prove a useful tool in negotiations with the centre.

However, in many cases the commanders were not simply calling for the appointment of any *intendant*, but were requesting particular individuals who, even when they were not part of their household, were none the less in some respect part of their extended clientele. The number of established relationships between *intendants* and particular commanders is high, considering the relatively few *intendants d'armée* who were regularly commissioned to army-corps and their links to a small group of commanders who repeatedly held commands. Whichever other commanders he served, the links of Jean Choisy, sieur de Beaumont, with Gaston d'Orléans gave him a prior claim to the intendancy whenever Gaston assumed command of an army, as he was to do in 1636. François de Verthamont, marquis de Manoeuvre, *fidèle* of the duc d'Epernon and the duke's choice for the intendancy of armies that he commanded, was only prevented from assuming this office more frequently by the reluctance of Richelieu to place troops operating in south-west France under the command of Epernon, and by the disgrace of the duke in late 1638.[186]

These close links between commanders and 'their' *intendants* appear on the whole to have been tolerated by the crown and its ministers.[187] When on occasions it appears to have become a matter of concern, the evidence suggests limited resolve to force through change in the face of opposition. The ties between Henri II, prince de Condé, and Charles Machault, *intendant* in Burgundy and for the troops in the province, offers one such example of these tight links. In late 1635, an attempt was made to transfer Machault to the intendancy of Provence.[188] Despite assurances that this was not a disgrace, the proposal aroused the opposition of Machault and of Condé.[189] Encouraged by Condé, Machault

---

[185] AAE MD 1679, fo. 118, 4 July 1640, Chaulnes and Châtillon to de Noyers, registering concern at the underpayment of the *montre*, and emphasizing that 'M de Grémonville vous en rendre compte': a letter from the *intendant* giving a detailed account of the consequences of the financial shortfall was considered the best way of bringing pressure to bear on the ministers. AAE CP Savoie 30, fos. 492, 494, 10 June 1640, letters from Harcourt and Argenson to de Noyers expressing concern at the failure to provide additional troops and financial support for Harcourt's siege of Turin. Argenson's letter was clearly written in conjunction with Harcourt's to reinforce and support the commander's complaints and to provide further details of the consequences of inadequate support.

[186] Verthamont was commissioned as *intendant* with the army that Epernon was to raise to drive the Spanish out of Saint-Jean de Luz: SHAT A¹ 40, fo. 222, 21 Dec. 1637, de Noyers to Verthamont as *intendant d'armée*. For the rest of the period 1630–8, Verthamont served as provincial *intendant* under Epernon's patronage at Bordeaux. For Epernon's disgrace and the replacement of Verthamont with Etienne Foullé, see Bercé. *Histoire des croquants*, I. 453–4.

[187] AAE CP Lorraine 31, fo. 37, 2 Apr. 1639, Choisy to de Noyers, emphasizing his great respect for, and close working relationship with, Manassés de Pas, marquis de Feuquières: 'il y a desia cinq ou six ans que vous me tenez dans l'employ . . . et sans faire tort a pas un, je n'en ay point encore approché qui doibve estre plus a [mon] goût'.

[188] SHAT A¹ 25, fo. 479, 28 Oct. 1635.

[189] SHAT A¹ 25, fos. 503, 529, 619/20, 7/17 Nov., 11 Dec. 1635.

Responses and reactions

formally refused the intendancy of Provence in March 1636.[190] If the *intendants* are assumed to be an elite of career-motivated government servants, this refusal ought to have destroyed Machault's career. Yet on the basis of a letter from Condé, stipulating that he wished the *intendant* to continue to serve in his province and with the army preparing to invade Franche-Comté, the ministry simply abandoned its opposition and confirmed the appointment.[191] Richelieu's opinion of Condé's loyalty to the ministry ensured that the *intendant* would not be placed under pressure from two incompatible duties. But what undoubtedly influenced the ministry's surrender on this point of principle were negative considerations about the likely consequences of installing another *intendant* expressly against Condé's wishes. Despite – indeed perhaps because of – his loyalty, Condé would possess an unlimited capacity to frustrate and disrupt the work of an unwanted royal agent.[192]

Moreover, in those cases where the *intendants* had not already acknowledged some degree of dependence upon the commanders, pressure could be brought to bear to ensure his cooperation. Accusations of incompetence, provocative behaviour or misrepresentation of the military situation could all be used by commanders to attack the reputation of an unwanted or obstructive *intendant* and to demand his replacement.[193] Once again, the ministers, fully aware of how little could be achieved by an *intendant* in the face of opposition from the high command, were extremely reluctant to press the issue and demand that he remain *in situ*. The *intendants* were also well aware of their vulnerability in this respect. It would be difficult to find a closer liaison between *grand* and *intendant* than that between François Bochart, sieur de Champigny, *intendant* of Provence, and the governor of the province, Louis-Emmanuel de Valois, comte d'Alais. Alais had been instrumental in achieving Champigny's appointment to the intendancy in 1637, and an enemy commented that Champigny was 'more like an *intendant* of [Alais'] household than an *homme du roi*'.[194] Yet despite this link of explicit *fidelité*, in early 1640 a quarrel developed between the *intendant* and the governor over the

---

[190] SHAT A¹ 27, fo. 180, Mar. 1636.
[191] SHAT A¹ 27, fo. 373, 8 May 1636; A¹ 32, fo. 83, 29 May 1636.
[192] An opaque comment in a letter from the cardinal de La Valette to Richelieu suggests similar difficulties in placing an *intendant d'armée* with the army of Italy: 'M de Thou ne veult pas estre intendant apres M d'Argenson vous en choisires un autre tel qu'il vous plaira': AAE CP Savoie 28, fo. 157, 31 Mar. 1639.
[193] AAE MD 1678, fo. 32, 13 Mar. 1636, duc de Chaulnes to de Noyers, using the excuse that Laffemas has been the object of local printed libels and attacks to propose that he be removed from the intendancy of the army of Picardy: 'Il seroit necessaire qu'un nouveau comm.ᵣₑ ou intendant feust promptement député pour remedier a ceste affaire.' Such willingness to complain of *intendants* was not necessarily confined to the highest levels of the command structure; in 1642 the *mestre de camp* du Chamblay wrote to Richelieu, complaining of the *intendant* Claude Vignier, marquis de Mirebeau, for his treatment of the garrison at Nancy, and claiming that these complaints were supported by the governor of Lorraine (du Hallier) and three-quarters of the garrison: AAE MD 845, fo. 141, [n.d. 1642].
[194] Quoted in Harding, *Anatomy of a Power Elite*, p. 207.

The management of the war-effort from 1635 to 1642

levy of 300,000 *livres* outstanding on the *subsistances*.[195] Despite the attempted mediation of Alphonse de Richelieu, archbishop of Lyon, and despite Champigny's protestations of loyalty to Alais, the quarrel reached an impasse, and was resolved by the ministers' decision in early June to remove Champigny from Provence and to replace him with François Cazet, sieur de Vautorte.[196] Champigny, evidently also linked to the archbishop, who had intervened on his behalf, was granted a new commission to serve as the *intendant* of the Lyonnais.[197] Alais appears to have regretted this decision, found Vautorte less compliant than Champigny, and in 1643 successfully engineered the return of Champigny to the intendancy of Provence. Yet the obvious conclusion to be drawn by the *intendants* was that they were vulnerable to the whims of the governors or military commanders, even after accumulating several years of obliging service to the same *grand*. Perhaps not surprisingly, the combination of ministerial concern to avoid establishing an *intendant* likely to antagonize the commander, and the deference and willingness of the *intendant* to be accommodating, ensured that there are few surviving examples of demands for the removal of these agents.

It would be simplistic to assume that such divisions of loyalty implied that the ministry would be badly served by its agents. Most recent studies of clientage have emphasized that even the most formal bonds linking together client and patron were rarely an exclusive undertaking on the part of the client. There was no incompatibility between bonds of service, reward and employment contracted with a number of different patrons. When some of the bonds were less formal the potential for multiple links was even greater.[198] In some circumstances a client might have to choose between these loyalties, but in the main he would seek to maintain his relationships with different patrons without having to make a definite choice between allegiances. This was as true of the *intendants* as any other client.

Thus, for example, when it was explicitly claimed that the *intendant* was acting against the interests of the ministry, the accusations seem more often to have been motivated by personal rivalry than by substantial evidence. The *intendant* François Bosquet asserted that his colleague in the joint intendancy of Languedoc, Jean-Baptiste Baltazar, sieur de Malherbe, was giving unconditional allegiance to the

---

[195] SHAT A¹ 57, fo. 438, 17 Feb. 1640, instructions to Champigny concerning the levy of the *subsistances*; A¹ 58, fo. 294, 29 Mar. 1640, letter to archbishop of Lyon, asking him to try to intervene in the quarrel.
[196] SHAT A¹ 59, fo. 262, 4 June 1640, notification of the appointment of Vautorte to Provence.
[197] SHAT A¹ 59, fo. 517, 25 June, letter to the archbishop to inform him of the change of *intendants*.
[198] See, for example, the discussions in Kettering, *Patrons*, pp. 85–97; for a study which makes heavy use of literary sources and speculates a great deal about linguistic expressions of *fidélité*, but none the less proposes a fluid and multifocused interpretation of clientage see Neuschel, *Word of Honor*. The now rather dated discussion initiated by Yves Durand concerning the distinction between relations based on *fidélité*, implying a stronger, more exclusive, link, and *clientélisme*, more shaped by material self-interest and opportunism, is perhaps over-rigid in its categorization, but does emphasize that relations between patron and client could vary considerably: Durand, 'Clientèles et fidélités dans le temps et dans l'espace', in Durand (ed.), *Clientèles et fidélités*, pp. 3–24.

governor, Charles d'Halluin, maréchal Schomberg. However, the rivalry between the two *intendants* was intense, and the substance of the accusation was that Baltazar was using his alliance with Schomberg to frustrate Bosquet's own authority in Languedoc.[199] The accusations reflect the insuperable problems of trying to persuade two *intendants* to cooperate within the same territorial jurisdiction. In general most *intendants* would try to avoid any situation in which they had to choose between their loyalty to the crown and its ministers, and their loyalty to the commander in whose army they were serving.

This also implied, however, that they would not wish to do anything to antagonize their commander, and while there is, unsurprisingly, little evidence of the *intendants d'armée* acting explicitly against the interests of the crown and its ministers, there is certainly evidence of complicity between *intendants* and commanders in the presentation of information to the centre, and in a willingness to tolerate financial practices which served the interests of the officers.[200] Obviously the *intendants* would not publicize the details of financial compromises made with their commanders, yet it would be naïve, for example, to accept at face value Arnaud d'Andilly's justification for paying weakened units with the army of maréchal Brézé at full strength.[201] Arnaud wrote that although this ran against all the prescriptions for the conduct of the *montres*, it could be justified as the extra money was to be used by the officers to obtain recruits of the 'highest quality'.[202] That Arnaud felt the need to produce such a justification at all for the type of financial compromise that was commonplace with the armies probably reflects the close and suspicious interest that the *surintendant* Bullion was showing in Arnaud's financial dealings with the army.[203] Financial compromises certainly formed one part of the working relationship between the *intendants* and the high command, and we can speculate how far the *intendant d'armée* would turn a blind eye to the deals and arrangements between the *commissaires* and the unit commanders in the drawing up of accurate muster-rolls, a practice so frequently condemned by royal ordinances. For the *intendant* to make an issue of such activities would mean a needless complication of an ever-delicate situation in which the support of the commanding officers was all important if they were to sustain any effective authority.[204] It was accepted by all involved in the administration of the armies

---

[199] Lublinskaja (ed.), *Internal Policy*, I. 129–31, 31 Mar. 1645.
[200] AAE MD 1680, fo. 86, 20 May 1641, Châtillon to de Noyers, asking for funds to be placed in the hands of the *intendants* Grémonville and d'Osny to cover future expenses for the army. Châtillon assured de Noyers that these funds would not be spent unnecessarily, but that it was important to have the money available to face unexpected contingencies.
[201] See Baxter, *Servants of the Sword*, p. 83.
[202] Arnaud d'Andilly, *Mémoires*, XXXIV. 55–6. See also the example of the *intendant* with the army of Italy, Argenson, who decided to pay the infantry captains of the army of Italy an advance of 50 *écus* each to quell an incipient mutiny over an attempt by the ministry to cut back on the rate of the *prêt* granted to troops in garrison in Italy: AAE CP Savoie 25, fo. 238, 14 July 1637.
[203] Arnaud d'Andilly, *Mémoires*, XXXIV. 56–7.
[204] For example, AAE, MD 1680, fo. 151, 4 June 1641, Grémonville to de Noyers, admitting that the

that an *intendant* without the support, or indeed without the presence, of a senior officer could carry little or no weight in his dealings with the officers and troops. Choisy made this explicit in 1641 when he wrote, in conjunction with the acting commander and *maréchal de camp* Guébriant, that the crown should send a general of high social rank to assume command of the army of Germany: 'Je n'estime pas que vous envoyez plus icy d'argent sans un general, sans lequel un Intendant est icy entierement inutil'.[205] This was not a point that needed emphasizing to either the provincial governors or the senior army commanders, with their extended patronage networks and preeminent social status. As maréchal Schomberg wrote to Richelieu in 1639 concerning the collection of extraordinary financial levies for the troops in Languedoc:

si l'on peut attribuer ceste diligence à autre qu'à moy, que V. Eminence se donne s'il luy plaist ce divertissement d'ordonner à Messieurs les Intendans et au Sr. Imbert de faire une seulle imposition de six mil livres sur toute la province, sans que je m'en mesle, et je m'oblige à les payer en cas qu'ils les facent lever en six mois, quelques [*sic*] expeditions qu'on leur a envoyé du conseil.[206]

Given this sense of superiority of the commanders, we can well believe that *intendants*, summoned to attend the main *conseils de guerre* at which the overall strategic planning for an army-corps took place, were drawn into complicity with the aims and military perceptions of the senior officers. Flattered by a role within this inner elite of the army, and aware of the difficulties and problems faced by commanders who did not want to sanction military action that might go badly wrong or might involve them in heavy personal expense, there was a strong temptation to write to the centre in terms which reiterated and justified the decisions of the high command. When Richelieu grew impatient with the marquis de Feuquières' slowness in launching a campaign to take the pressure off La Meilleraye who was conducting the siege of Hesdin, the *intendant* Choisy immediately wrote to de Noyers to defend Feuquières' conduct. Choisy maintained that Feuquières was intent on launching the campaign, but was handicapped by shortages of troops, slowness of recruitment and the impracticality of some of the objectives which the ministers had proposed.[207] In one of the few apparent exceptions to this seconding of decisions of the high command, Arnaud

---

majority of the captains in the army of Châtillon have failed to fulfil their recruitment *traités*, but that none the less 'je croy qu'il est necessaire de mettre quelque distinction entre ceux qui ont fait une partie de leur devoir et ceux qui l'ont entierement negligé'.

[205] AAE, CP Allemagne 16, fo. 322v, 17 Sept. 1641, Choisy to de Noyers.
[206] BN Ms.fr. 3768, fos. 14v–15, 10 May 1639.
[207] AAE CP Lorraine 31, fo. 82, 22 May 1639, Feuquières to de Noyers, responding to Richelieu's criticisms; for Choisy's deliberate and explicit support for Feuquières' position, fo. 84, 22 May 1639. A willingness to defend the less than enterprising strategy of the duc de La Valette can be seen in a letter from Verthamont to Séguier: Mousnier (ed.), *Lettres*, 1. 365–6, 11 May 1637. Argenson's letters do not waver for a sentence from Harcourt's line that without reinforcements and more financial support the siege of Turin would have to be abandoned: AAE CP Savoie 30, fo. 494, 10 June 1640, Argenson to de Noyers.

Responses and reactions

d'Andilly claimed that he spoke out strongly against the proposal made in the *conseil de guerre* by colonel Schmidtberg, who suggested that supplies could be infiltrated into beleaguered Mannheim by giving some 5,000 cavalry a sack of grain each so that they could be transported down to the Rhine and placed on river boats that would run through the enemy siege works.[208] Whether or not Arnaud was the first to oppose it, the idea was abandoned by the overall decision of the *conseil de guerre*. Yet it could be argued that this was an example not of an *intendant* standing up to assert himself against the opinion of the senior commanders (all of whom would seem to have changed their minds when confronted with Arnaud's counter-arguments) but of a decision, unpalatable to a central government which wanted military action and could not understand the hesitancy and dilatoriness of its commanders, being presented as a *fait accompli* by the *intendant* and the high command speaking with one voice.

The *intendants*' reluctance to challenge the authority of the senior officers in the army-corps reflected a number of factors. A significant issue was the willingness of the *robe* official to acknowledge the social superiority of a high command that was mainly composed of court aristocracy. The situation described by Roland Mousnier in his study of the relationship between provincial governors and the *intendants des provinces* holds good for the relations between the generals with the armies – the king's lieutenants – and the *intendants d'armée*.[209] Cooperation was achieved through the unambiguous subordination of the *intendant*.

It has already been emphasized that the senior officers had considerable scope to criticize or attack an *intendant*, and it was broadly understood that the ministry would not be prepared to give support to the *intendant* in such a clash.[210] It was considered to be the fault of the commission-holder for having exceeded his instructions and for intruding upon the authority of the commander. The instructions from Bullion to Michel Le Tellier on his assumption of the intendancy with the army of Italy make this quite evident; Le Tellier was warned to avoid any conflict with the senior officers, and to make sure that he discussed every matter with the commander, the comte d'Harcourt, before proposing it to the wider group of senior officers.[211]

The intendants d'armée *and their sphere of authority*

To the constraints caused by client relationships of *intendants* to their commanders should be added a number of other institutional limitations. As previously

---

[208] Baxter, *Servants of the Sword*, p. 65.
[209] Mousnier, 'Les rapports entre gouverneurs et *intendants*', in Mousnier, *La plume*, pp. 201–13.
[210] Pierre Imbert was firmly reprimanded by de Noyers for 'making difficulties' about the negotiation of a recruitment *traité* with François de Bonne et de Créqui, duc de Lesdiguières, to set his regiment *en état*: SHAT A¹ 63, fo. 544, 12 Mar. 1641.
[211] Caron (ed.), *Le Tellier*, p. 4, 11 Sept. 1640: 'on le prie, au nom de Dieu, en mesnageant doucement les gens de guerre' (in this context clearly the senior officers).

The management of the war-effort from 1635 to 1642

emphasized, the army *intendants* were not initially a single group of officials, but divided into two groups holding financial or judicial functions, and owing their allegiance to different parts of the central administration. It may be argued that this division of responsibilities could have been a deliberate policy to prevent an excessive number of functions being heaped upon the individual administrator. Yet the ministers must have been aware of the problems which would inevitably stem from dividing the authority and functions of the *intendants* – in particular the clashes over jurisdiction and the lack of overall responsibility in the hands of a single administrator. It was these issues which influenced the direction of subsequent ministerial policy. For in the years immediately after 1635 the ministry moved towards the creation of composite *intendants d'armée*, commissioned with standardized joint powers of justice/police and finance.[212] The 1635 intendancy of Jacques Dyel, sieur de Miroménil, with the army of Brézé and Châtillon in Flanders is the first clear occasion on which a commission as an *intendant d'armée* with powers of justice, police and finance is accorded to one person.[213] This was the only example of a composite military intendancy granted in 1635. However, there are signs of a tendency towards such a consolidation of functions. The intendancy of justice and *police* with the army of Italy during the 1635 campaign was held by du Fauré.[214] The intendancy of finance was vacant at the opening of the campaign, and was claimed by Servien's relative, Balme, who held the very junior intendancy of justice at Pinerolo.[215] Servien wrote to his relative to apologize for not being able to obtain the intendancy of finance for him; this would infringe the *surintendants*' wish to give overall financial responsibility in Italy to Particelli d'Hémery.[216] In reality, this appears to have been a convenient excuse to avoid appointing Balme to a post claimed by the *bureau des finances*, and which may also have been considered beyond his capacities.[217] Yet while Balme was clearly considered unsuitable, d'Hémery was too involved with diplomatic duties at the Savoyard Court to carry out the financial administration of the army of Italy.[218] It was necessary to make a formal appointment of an *intendant des*

---

[212] The one possible exception might be that of Claude Gobelin, sieur d'Aunoy, *intendant* with the army commanded by the duc de Rohan in the Empire in 1634. G. Livet implies that although he was styled *intendant de justice*, Gobelin was charged with the full burden of *justice, finance et police* over the troops: *L'intendance d'Alsace sous Louis XIV, 1648–1715* (Strasbourg, 1956), p. 41. Unfortunately, his commission does not appear to have survived, and no other corroboration that Gobelin held these multiple functions is extant.

[213] SHAT A^1 26, fo. 42, 14 Apr. 1635; similar powers apparently accorded to Argenson in the same year turn out, on examination of the text, to be simply an intendancy of justice/*police*: A^1 26, fo. 52bis, 10 May 1635.

[214] SHAT A^1 24, fo. 409, 23 June 1635; A^1 25, fo. 9, 3 July 1635.

[215] SHAT A^1 24, fo. 136, 12 Mar. 1635.

[216] SHAT A^1 24, fo. 345, 27 May 1635.

[217] SHAT A^1 25, fo. 548, 24 Nov. 1635: he was given permanent leave of absence from Pinerolo in March 1636, and replaced by La Cour, who, significantly, was given powers of justice *and* finance over the fortress: A^1 27, fos. 129, 186, 15 Mar. 1636.

[218] G. de Mun, *Richelieu et la Maison de Savoie.*, pp. 53–102.

finances, but no qualified candidate was immediately available. As an interim measure it was decided that the *intendant de la justice*, du Fauré, should hold the financial intendancy conjointly.[219] In this particular case, the ministry quickly reverted to the customary practice, and granted the financial intendancy to Le Camus a few weeks later.[220] However, the idea of establishing composite army intendancies had been given further support. In the same period, it was proposed that the *intendant de la justice* in Lorraine, Anne Mangot, sieur de Villarceaux, would benefit from an extension of his authority to include financial administration.[221] Servien assured him that he would speak to the *surintendants* about this. The immediate outcome is uncertain; Mangot's correspondence with Servien during the rest of 1635 was concerned only with disciplinary and fortification matters.[222] In 1636, Lefèbvre was mentioned as *intendant* of finance in Lorraine.[223] But with the administrative reorganization of Alsace/Lorraine in 1637, and the creation of the joint intendancy for the Mangot brothers, Villarceaux and Jacques, sieur d'Orgères, the new policy was clearly being pursued. Both received full powers of justice and finance to exercise across the area of their joint charge, without any functional division between the two.[224]

By 1637, the ministry had effectively abandoned the system of delimiting intendancies to justice or finance in favour of these more extensive, generalized, powers and responsibilities.[225] This would appear then to be an example of a rational response to the likely confusions and conflicts between different types of *intendant* as the number of armies proliferated. Weighing up the benefits of overall administrative autonomy against the cost in heaping excessive functions on to the solitary *intendant*, the ministers made their decision. Yet at the same time that the potential clash of jurisdiction between the two types of *intendant d'armée* was resolved by amalgamation, the equally vital issue of how the geographical extent and authority of the army *intendants* should be defined remained dangerously confused. Army corps operating in the frontier provinces frequently revealed a confused and overlapping group of *intendants'* commissions. To speak of a clash between provincial and army *intendants* is to oversimplify the situation, in that the military role of the provincial *intendants* when troops were within their provinces was, by the terms of their commissions, so extensive that it could not be be said that they were encroaching on the 'rightful' jurisdiction of the *intendants d'armée*.

---

[219] SHAT A¹ 24, fo. 409, 23 June 1635.
[220] SHAT A¹ 25, fo. 190, 11 Aug. 1635.
[221] SHAT A¹ 24, fo. 419, 26 June 1635.
[222] SHAT A¹ 25, fos. 10, 166, 184, 3 July, 1 Aug., 8 Aug. 1635.
[223] SHAT A¹ 29, fo. 197, 11 Sept. 1636.
[224] Livet, *L'intendance d'Alsace*, pp. 49–57.
[225] SHAT A¹ 32, pces 83, 142, 178, 228, 229, 1636, commissions of joint intendancies for Machault, Gobelin, Argenson, Le Fèvre d'Ormesson and Champigny; A¹ 35, fos. 203, 205, 31 Mar. 1637: intendancy of the army of Italy assumed as a joint charge by Argenson after the expiry of the commissions of Du Fauré and Le Camus.

The management of the war-effort from 1635 to 1642

The division of military responsibilities between the two types of *intendant* had been based on the assumption that during the campaign season the armies would be operating across the frontiers, outside of the jurisdiction of the provincial *intendants*. Over the period of winter quartering and early spring recruitment it was anticipated that the provincial *intendants* would hold military authority, and hence the commissions of the *intendants d'armée* were drawn up in March/April and intended to run only for the months of campaigning.

From 1635 this proved not to be the case; armies which should have crossed the frontiers were delayed by slowness in recruiting and assembling troops, and by concern at the potential strength and disposition of enemy forces were they finally to take the offensive. The great sieges of Spanish or Imperial frontier *places* were usually organized from within France, supplies were convoyed from French towns and magazines, large numbers of replacement recruits were levied in the provinces. All of this confused the issue of authority, since these military activities fell precisely into the remit of the *intendants des provinces*, although the execution of such operations had a direct bearing on the successful conduct of the campaign and therefore might have been regarded as the concern of the *intendant d'armée*. The ministry had apparently turned its back on division of functions between separate *intendants* within the armies, but it may well have considered a division of responsibilities between the *intendants d'armée* specifically charged with fiscal and judicial concerns within the army and the provincial *intendants* charged with the more general supporting operations as a sensible division of labour. This would make a virtue of necessity – especially given the unprecedented size of some of the military operations, above all on the north-east frontier. In 1636, for example, Choisy was *intendant* of Champagne and possessed, in addition, extensive powers of justice and police over the armies and troops present in the province.[226] His equivalent in Picardy was Le Maistre de Bellejamme, who also held considerable authority over the troops in his territory.[227] In June the *intendant* Jacques Dyel de Miroménil had received instructions to travel to Calais to receive the remnants of the army returning from Holland, and to distribute them in garrisons across Picardy and Normandy.[228] This duty was evidently considered to be an excessive burden upon Bellejamme, although obviously the *logement* of troops across Picardy would concern him directly. After the Spanish invasion of Picardy in early July the situation became considerably more complicated. The *intendant* of Île de France, Isaac de Laffemas, was ordered to carry out the levy of pioneers, bringing them to Picardy and keeping them supplied.[229] Laffemas' functions were subsequently extended to the billeting of troops once he had arrived in the province; the governor of Picardy, the duc de Chaulnes, was to demand his recall later in the

---

[226] SHAT A¹ 26, pce 49, 28 Apr. 1635: the commission was operative throughout 1636 and renewed in December: A¹ 31, fo. 89, 15 Dec. 1636.
[227] Mousnier (ed.), *Lettres*, I. 152–5.
[228] SHAT A¹ 28, fo. 13, 3 June 1636.   [229] SHAT A¹ 28, fo. 403, 8 Aug. 1636.

year over this issue.[230] As further forces were assembled around Paris, a joint intendancy was created for the army of Gaston d'Orléans, and assigned to Geoffroy Luillier, sieur d'Orgeval, and Dreux d'Aubray, sieur d'Offement.[231] The original plan had been to establish Argenson with the army of La Force,[232] and to grant the intendancy of Orléans' army to Gobelin.[233] However, the dramatic fall in the strength of the new levies of troops, and the irresolution of the commanders prevented the original strategy of splitting the army from being pursued. Argenson and Gobelin were already occupied as simple *maîtres des requêtes*, carrying out supply operations for various places in Picardy in conjunction with Laffemas, who actually held a commission of intendancy at this time.[234] As the formal military intendancy had been granted to Orgeval and Aubray, these latter continued with their existing functions during the campaign.[235] With the subsequent amalgamation of the forces of Orléans with those of the comte de Soissons, the military operation involved the efforts of two *intendants d'armée*, two provincial *intendants* with attached military responsibilities and three *maîtres des requêtes*, one of whom (Laffemas) held an *intendant*'s commission. A particular concern with the defence of Abbeville, felt to be the most likely Spanish target once the momentum of the advance towards Paris had slowed, led the ministry to appoint Alexandre Sève, sieur de Chatignonville, to a specific intendancy of this place, again with full authority over all the troops in and around the town.[236]

This series of appointments, in so far as it reflected conscious policy rather than *ad hoc* and disconnected initiatives, was intended to match the scale of the military operations which the Spanish invasion and the campaign in Picardy and Champagne had forced upon the crown. The obvious cost was a high level of confrontation and dispute between the various *intendants* which did nothing to aid the war-effort.[237] The *intendants des provinces* proved strongly hostile to any move which threatened to challenge the principle of one *intendant* per *généralité*, however rational the decision in terms of the administrative burden.

The situation was still sensitive in the following campaign. The *intendants* of the *généralités* of Soissons and Amiens, Luillier d'Orgeval and Le Maistre de Bellejamme, encountered each other at Laon in June 1637, both under the

---

[230] Bonney, *Political Change*, p. 304.
[231] SHAT A¹ 29 fo. 224, 13 Sept. 1636.
[232] SHAT A¹ 32, pce 178, 12 Aug. 1636.
[233] SHAT A¹ 32, pce 142, 10 Aug. 1632; this episode is misinterpreted by Baxter, *Servants of the Sword*, p. 70.
[234] SHAT A¹ 29, fos. 67, 68, 25 Aug. 1636; Mongrédien, *Le bourreau*, pp. 109–14.
[235] AAE MD 1678, fo. 331, 23 Sept. 1636; Mousnier (ed.), *Lettres*, I. 307–8, 19 Sept. 1636 (d'Orgeval); I. 309–10, 21 Sept. (d'Aubray); I. 322–3, 1 Nov. (Argenson).
[236] SHAT A¹ 30, fo. 271, 3 Nov. 1636.
[237] SHAT A¹ 28, fo. 268, 14 July 1636, de Noyers to Bellejamme, urging Bellejamme to collaborate with the *intendant* Choisy in their joint control over the army in Picardy. BN Ms.fr. 17372, fo. 150, 5 Aug. 1636, Bellejamme to Séguier, complaining that Laffemas was issuing 'ordonnances soubs le nom d'intendant de la justice en Picardie'.

impression that the town lay within their jurisdiction. Orgeval's letter to Séguier presents his own actions in the most cooperative light, but does nothing to play down the difficulties of such divided authority

> si tost que je fus arrivé j'allé voir Mr. de Beliambe que je n'estimois pas trouver icy croiant qu'il fust à expedier la generalité d'Amiens pour advancer cette affaire . . . je venois l'asseurer que je desirois vivre avec luy non seulement comme confrere mais comme pere[,] il me dit qu'il estoit difficile apres avoir souffert un demembrement de la Picardie en la personne de M. de Seve [granted the intendancy of Abbeville] que je vinsse encore à Guise et la generalité de Soixon et qu'une espée divisée en tant de morceaus ne pouvait pas faire un si bon effet.[238]

A similar jurisdictional quarrel between *intendants* arose in 1640 between the provincial *intendant* of Dauphiné, Jean Lauzon, sieur de Liré, and Henri La Guette, sieur de Chazé and Alexandre Sève, both of whom were claiming military authority within Dauphiné which Lauzon considered trespassed upon his own provincial powers.[239] These clashes over jurisdiction certainly influenced the ministers. Yet the problem remained; the combination of provincial and military responsibility was increasingly beyond that which could be sustained effectively by an individual administrator. In general the ministers preferred to accept the inefficiencies of relying on an undivided jurisdiction, yet the sheer scale of some of the military operations would occasionally persuade them to grasp the nettle and try to allocate responsibilities. Anticipating trouble, Sublet de Noyers wrote to the established *intendant* of Picardy, Bellejamme, in December 1640, explaining that the extremely large numbers of troops quartered in Picardy obliged him to divide responsibility for the province. Jacques Chaulnes, sieur d'Epinay, was to be sent to Picardy to take charge of the troops at Ponthieu, the Boulonnais, Hesdin and the *pays conquis*, and Bellejamme was to grant him full authority within this jurisdiction. A further set of letters were sent to governors of *places*, urban authorities and troop commanders, informing them of the new division of reponsibilities, and thereby, it was hoped, reducing the possibility that they would seek to play off the *intendants* against each other.[240] An alternative, and possibly less controversial, means of dividing the jurisdiction of an existing intendancy was

---

[238] Mousnier (ed.), *Lettres*, I. 384, 10 June 1637. Curiously, Mousnier himself seems to have drawn the opposite conclusion about working relationships between *intendants*, citing a 'collaboration constante d'hommes qui concourent à une même fin, dans un esprit de confiance et d'estime réciproque, sans ombre de rivalité', and chooses to characterize this by the relationship between Jean-Baptiste Baltazar, sieur de Malherbe, and François Bosquet, joint *intendants* of Languedoc from 1643 to 1646: 'Les rapports entre gouverneurs et intendants', in Mousnier, *La plume*, p. 203. Yet it was clear that the relations between Balthazar and Bosquet were uniformly, and at times comically, bad: cf. Bonney, *Political Change*, pp. 126–9, and W. Beik, 'Two intendants face a popular revolt: social unrest and the structures of absolutism in 1645', *Canadian Journal of History*, 9 (1974), 243–62.

[239] SHAT A¹ 61, fo. 319, 4 Dec. 1640, de Noyers to Lauzon.

[240] SHAT A¹ 61, fo. 390, 15 Dec. 1640, de Noyers to Bellejamme; fos. 391, 392, 15 Dec., general notification.

to commission an *intendant* with authority over a specific, major *place*, above all, one which had been newly conquered. An intendancy at Arras was created from 1640, and one at Perpignan from 1642.[241] These newly conquered *places* contained large garrisons, presented major problems of security, discipline and supply, and involved the handling of large sums of money for the payment of garrisons, munitions and fortification work. It was certainly rational to separate this responsibility from the provincial intendancies, but it did not significantly reduce the burden of responsibility and duties which still rested upon the *intendant* with a major provincial and military assignment.

Another strategy was to despatch additional *maîtres des requêtes* to theatres where troops were concentrated, but without giving them formal commissions of intendancy. Sublet de Noyers wrote to chancellor Séguier in 1636, proposing the commissioning of some of these *officiers* to levy supplementary funds required for the army: 's'il vous plairons y employer M. les Maistres des Requestes leur temps y serons tres bien occupé'.[242] A number of such lesser commissions were despatched for the levy of horses,[243] and for the investigation of desertion after the collapse of the late 1636 recruitment *en masse*.[244]

During Richelieu's ministry it was not, in fact, clear that the *intendants d'armée* would emerge as the principal *intendants* with military responsibility. There was a strong presumption that the *intendant* with provincial jurisdiction should control all aspects of the administration within his province, in the same way that only the most socially exalted commander of a field army could expect to overrule the military authority of the provincial governor in whose province the army was based.[245] Richard Bonney points to the declining numbers of *intendants d'armée* in the 1650s and the increasing tendency to use provincial intendants for military duties.[246] This can be supported by the experience of the later 1630s and 1640s, where the functions of the provincial *intendants* were considerably broadened to allow them to absorb a significant part of the administrative burden of the armies. This was not simply a phenomenon restricted to the period of winter quartering when the troops were explicitly garrisoned in the French provinces. Because so much of the preparation of the armies, recruitment, supply bases and magazines,

---

[241] SHAT A¹ 63, fo. 549, 12 Mar. 1641, notification from de Noyers to Chaulnes, governor of Picardy, of the appointment of the sieur de La Bastide as *intendant de justice, police et finances* at Arras. A¹ 70, fo. 259, 15 Oct. 1642, nomination of sr des Yvetaux as *intendant-général* in Perpignan. Clashes between the authorities in Picardy and the intendancy of Arras do not seem to have been avoided, judging from the extremely rapid turn-over of *intendants* in the latter *place*.
[242] BN Ms.fr. 17372, fo. 230, 7 Sept. 1636.
[243] AAE MD 822, fo. 169, 6 Nov. 1636.
[244] SHAT A¹ 30, fo. 188, 24 Oct. 1636.
[245] This was notoriously the case in Languedoc and Guienne in 1637–9, when the reluctance of either Schomberg or Epernon to tolerate the intrusion of another military commander in their provinces led the ministry to impose Henri II de Bourbon, prince de Condé, as the only figure of sufficiently high status to overrule their resistance and reluctance to cooperate.
[246] Bonney, *Political Change*, pp. 264–5.

The management of the war-effort from 1635 to 1642

even their camps and assembly points, all fell within the borders of France, the organizational burden inevitably fell within the jurisdiction of the provincial *intendants*. It was certainly the case that numbers of the *intendants d'armée* were commissioned from the ranks of the provincial *intendants*, implying that experience in the provincial sphere was regarded as a suitable background for service as a military administrator.[247] If the ministry seemed uncertain about the status of the *intendants d'armée* for much of this period, it was no less clear, as discussed earlier in the matter of large-scale commissions granted to *commissaires des guerres* and others, that neither group of *intendants* enjoyed a monopoly of major disciplinary or supply assignments with the armies.

The practical effectiveness of the intendants d'armée

Assuming, however, that the *intendant d'armée* accepted the ambiguities of his position and authority, made the necessary compromises to ensure a working relationship with the commander, and built up his credit as a useful, loyal and articulate support of the high command, how substantial then was the role of the *intendant* within the army? What was he capable of achieving, and how important, in the context of the war-effort down to 1643, was he for the running of the army-corps to which he was appointed?

The *intendants* received specific commissions authorizing them to undertake a full range of administrative and judicial functions, and giving the support of the royal council to the decrees that they might issue in the course of exercising these functions. The most striking first impression of the role of the *intendant d'armée*, based upon a reading of the commissions empowering them to serve with a particular army for a particular campaign, was the extraordinary plethora of duties cited in the document.[248] The general commission included the responsibility to attend the *conseils de guerre* and to provide the commanding officers with the fullest information about logistical and financial issues connected with the campaign. The *intendant* was charged with the implementation of all of the edicts related to justice and order in the army, and to hear and judge all appeals that might be made against the verdicts of subordinate judicial officers. He was to investigate all cases of corruption, violence and other abuses that might be committed within the army or between soldiers and civilians, and to hand down judgement that would carry the force of a ruling from the sovereign courts, assembling groups of judges or military officers to preside over the courts as he saw fit. The *intendant* was to oversee expenditure and the management of all funds

---

[247] Though Bonney, *Political Change*, p. 264, does make the point that the majority of army *intendants* taken down to 1661 had not served as *intendants des provinces*.
[248] See, for example, a printed copy of the general commission for Claude Gobelin as *intendant d'armée* in Mousnier (ed.), *Lettres*, II. 1047–9, 10 Aug. 1636. That for Michel Le Tellier in Sept. 1640 is printed in Caron (ed.), *Le Tellier*, pp. 1–3.

Responses and reactions

with the armies, related to every aspect of the forces present, and to check and verify all of the *états* drawn up by the *trésoriers*, their *commis* and any other financial agents with the armies. He was to examine all of the *états* of the *commissaires* and the *contrôleurs*, countersigning the *extraits* of the *revues* and *montres*. He was to assume general responsibility for the purchase of *vivres* and munitions, to supervise the activities of the agents of the *munitionnaires* and to oversee any siege work and any expenditure related to the artillery or the purchase of munitions.[249] To these duties specified in the formalized commissions, the historian of the *intendants d'armée*, Douglas Baxter, would add a certain number of 'implied functions': hospitals, fortifications, the supervision of the *commissaires* and the duty of acting as general informant for the ministry.[250]

However, when we move from the theoretical range of responsibilities to administrative practice, the only practical example drawn upon for an *intendant* 'in action' is Robert Arnaud d'Andilly, whose memoirs provide an accessible, though hardly reliable, account of his intendancy with the army operating in the Empire in 1634/5.[251] Arnaud is not inclined to play down the significance of his own role; he suggests that he had a determining voice in decisions concerning strategy taken in the *conseil de guerre*, that he was to all intents and purposes the paymaster of the army, and was at the centre of all discussion and action concerned with logistical support.[252] Above all, moreover, this is an account of an intendancy that was only of finance/*vivres*.[253] It does not give an idea of the pressure placed upon an *intendant* expected to perform judicial as well as financial functions. And even in his more limited role, Arnaud d'Andilly was conspicuously unsuccessful in all his major assignments; the army in Germany was mutinous for lack of pay and supplies, while the *places* in Alsace were inadequately provisioned. Even the commander, the maréchal de Brézé, who was generally sympathetic to the problems of the administration of the armies, expressed dissatisfaction with his *intendant*.[254] More typical perhaps of the burdens placed upon the *intendants* is a letter of Servien to Charles de Machault in 1635, admitting that he was not surprised that Machault encountered difficulties in his work with Condé's army, since the effective execution of his duties would require: 'Un intendant des finances et deux intendants de la justice tous à la fois.'[255]

---

[249] Duties assembled from Mousnier (ed.), *Lettres*, and SHAT A¹ 32, pce 83, 29 May 1636, commission for Machault as *intendant* with army of Condé.
[250] Baxter, *Servants of the Sword*, pp. 76–80.
[251] Arnaud d'Andilly, *Mémoires*, XXXIV. 40–59, detailed in Baxter, *Servants of the Sword*, pp. 80–5.
[252] Arnaud d'Andilly, *Mémoires*, XXXIV. 40–53.
[253] Livet, *L'intendance d'Alsace*, pp. 41–3, suggests that it also involved powers of justice and *police*, but all the circumstantial evidence, above all, Arnaud's own memoir, argues against this.
[254] AAE CP Allemagne 12, fo. 64, 31 Jan. 1635, Brézé to Chavigny; MD 813, fo. 63 (Jan. 1635), *mémoire* of Brézé to the *surintendants*, expressing his irritation that Arnaud has allowed funds for the *montre* to be diverted, and ending that he has written to Arnaud on this matter 'une fois pour toutes'.
[255] SHAT A¹ 24, fo. 349, 30 May 1635.

The management of the war-effort from 1635 to 1642

Examination of correspondence between the *intendants* and the ministers suggests that the typical, extensive view of the military *intendants*' functions ought to be adjusted. The commission has been regarded as a prescription for the duties of an *intendant* serving with the armies. Yet if these duties were to be carried out automatically, it seems strange that the correspondence of the *secrétaire* with the *intendants* should consist almost entirely of particular instructions to undertake tasks that were already specified in the commission. It is clear that the *intendant* was being authorized by the commission to intervene in all those specified areas of military organization should it prove necessary, and, most importantly, was being given the overriding legal authority of the king's council to do so. On occasions, moreover, an *intendant* might still apply for specific authorization, as Laubardement did in a letter to Séguier discussing his assistance in the levy of some additional recruits in Poitou.[256]

In general, the reality of the *intendants*' work was a blend of those tasks that he considered practical, and which probably reflected his own judicial or financial specialization, together with the execution of specific orders from the *secrétaire*, *surintendant des finances* or chancellor. Thus, although the total correspondence in the Archives de la Guerre makes at least one mention of each of the duties specified in the *intendants*' commissions, this is far from proposing that all of these functions were carried out systematically by all the *intendants* of justice, *police* and finance. Aware of the burden implied by the commissions, the ministry treated the *intendants* as its representatives with the armies. As such, they were to carry out specific instructions from the centre, and to act in response to specific crises or problems rather than as a constant administrative presence performing an extensive series of formally prescribed functions. An example of this is provided by the detailed letters written in summer 1639 by the *intendant* with the army of Lorraine, Jean Choisy, which reveal a hard-pressed and competent administrator dealing with, and reporting upon, a series of local issues and crises which he was clearly handling according to a rigorous order of priority. In the aftermath of the defeat of Feuquières' army outside Thionville, Choisy's first concern was the reassembly and reconstruction of defeated regiments. This involved making emergency arrangements for lodging the remnants of the units, overseeing the payment of a discretionary subsistence to allow the soldiers to replace weapons and to feed themselves in their lodgings. Choisy evidently needed to seek de Noyers' instructions about the methods by which additional troops should be raised, the *intendant* proposing that the money be given directly to the officers 'pour peu que les officiers s'en veulent aquiter jusques à present'. Meanwhile, Choisy was confronted with a dispute with the officers about the level of subsistence that they themselves should receive during this reconstruction of the units; this issue he referred to de Noyers for advice, together with the matter of

[256] BN Ms.fr. 17371, fo. 40, 16 Sept. 1636.

Responses and reactions

paying local workmen who repaired the bridge near Thionville, burnt by the French troops during their retreat.[257] Letters in the subsequent week are concerned with the levels of payment to be accorded to those units to be despatched to serve in the army of maréchal Châtillon, and the disorders of soldiers who, with the active complicity of their *mestre de camp*, the baron de Navailles, had forcibly billeted themselves upon a village belonging to the *président à mortier* of the *Parlement* of Paris, Henri de Mesmes. Choisy also added that he was working on the summons of the *arrière-ban*, but has little confidence that he will have much success in raising the local *noblesse*, and he asked de Noyers to intervene with the *surintendants* to allow him to recover money that he has advanced from his own pocket against the tax receipts at Châlons.[258] The next letter reports the departure of the selected regiments to the army of Châtillon, and the decision of the officers to send the marquis de Canisy as their representative to de Noyers to explain their reluctance to carry out any recruiting until they receive some money. Choisy emphasizes that Canisy served well in the campaign and that his complaints deserve some attention at court.[259]

Admittedly, the content of Choisy's letters show the preoccupations of an *intendant d'armée* in the aftermath of a major defeat, but a lot of the work of the *intendants* in successive campaigns may be assumed to have been crisis-management of a similar, if less extreme, sort.[260] Much of their activity involved focusing on immediate priorities, seeking to resolve problems of direct importance to the war-effort at that moment. The obvious consequence is that a large number of duties ascribed to the *intendants d'armée* by their commissions were rarely, if ever, executed. Detailed examination of the extracts of the *revues* and *montres* is a good example of this type of impractical task. In reality, the *commissaires* and *contrôleurs* were left to carry out these tasks with minimal supervision.[261] Only in the event of large-scale corruption or mismanagement of funds coming to light,[262] or of the

---

[257] AAE CP Lorraine 31, fos. 161–2, 25 June 1639.
[258] AAE CP Lorraine 31, fos. 177–8, 7 July 1639.
[259] AAE CP Lorraine 31, fos. 179, 183, 11/15 July 1639.
[260] A similar impression of prioritization and focus on specific problems can be gained from Le Tellier's correspondence to Séguier and de Noyers from the army of Italy in 1641 and 1642: Caron (ed.), *Le Tellier, passim*. For the *intendant* in Italy the two dominant and insuperable problems were the negotiation of contracts with *munitionnaires* to supply bread at an acceptable unit cost and the establishment and enforcement of recruitment *traités* with the regimental officers.
[261] AAE CP Lorraine 26, fo. 317, 30 Sept. 1635: extensive report from *commissaire* Jean-Baptiste de Bretagne concerning the strength of the garrison at Nancy and the arrangements for hospital provision. Neither Arnaud d'Andilly nor Mangot de Villarceaux were involved in the *revues* of the garrison; MD 1679, fo. 62, 8 June 1640, report by maréchaux Châtillon and Chaulnes of a 'revue secrette' of their army, conducted by the *commissaires* with the help of the *aides de camp*, but with no reference to the role of the *intendant d'armée* or any suggestion that he had countersigned the *états*.
[262] SHAT A^1 25, fo. 191, 11 Aug. 1635, *intendant* du Fauré to investigate instances of corruption in payment of *montres* to regiment of Maugiron; A^1 38, fo. 200, 10 Aug. 1637, Dreux d'Aubray to carry out the *revues* of the companies of *gendarmes* with the army of La Meilleraye.

The management of the war-effort from 1635 to 1642

commissaires' accounts being doubted,[263] would the *intendants* be called upon to exercise this duty.[264] Similarly, the *intendants* were probably not involved regularly in the granting of *congés* to permit officers or soldiers to leave the armies. Correspondence between Le Tellier and Sublet de Noyers reveals that it was 'not the practice' in the army of Italy for the *intendant* to countersign these *congés*.[265] Certainly the reports that Châtillon was permitting large numbers of troops to leave his army after the siege of Arras in 1640, some with *congés* and some without, implies that the *intendants* (Grémonville and Gobelin) had not been using their theoretical authority to prevent this process.[266]

Similar conclusions may be drawn about the enforcement of justice: 'contre les coupables de quelque qualité et condition'. The majority of petty offences such as small-scale desertion or local violence would be left to the jurisdiction of the *prévôts* and *commissaires*. Only when a major case or series of prosecutions arose, would the *intendant* (often with a colleague's support) receive a specific order to take over the proceedings or intervene on his own initiative. In December 1635 cardinal de La Valette wrote to Richelieu that he had charged the *intendant* with his army, Argenson, to carry out trials of those troops who had served badly during the campaign, considering Argenson far more effective than the *prévôt*, who was altogether lacking in the necessary severity.[267] The *intendant* was more likely to deploy his judicial role when it became necessary to prosecute unit officers, rather than soldiers or NCOs. In such cases it was essential for the *intendant* to use his authority to select members of a military court – or *conseil de guerre* – who would be prepared to convict an officer found guilty of extortion, violence or disobedience.[268] Even when the *intendant* intervened, the outcome was far from assured, and the time and effort involved in a successful prosecution was

---

[263] AAE, MD 826, fo. 213, 15 Mar. 1637, de Noyers to Chavigny, concerning *commissaires*' *revues* of companies in garrison at Abbeville, and his decision to refer the *revues* back to Sève, *intendant* at Abbeville. It was not always the case that the *intendant* would automatically be seen as the more reliable source in assessing the veracity of *revues*: in 1639 Feuquières wrote to de Noyers that the *commissaire* whom Feuquières had sent to conduct a *revue* of the regiment of Colonel Streff had given a far less advantageous report of its strength than had the *intendant* Choisy: AAE CP Lorraine 31, fo. 41, 6 Apr.

[264] There are very few specific cases of the *intendants* being ordered to play a direct role in the supervision of the *revues* and *montres*. The *intendant* of Poitou, Villemontée, was ordered to carry out a *revue* of the newly levied regiment of the marquis de Jonzac: SHAT A¹ 65, fo. 93, 15 June 1641. Grémonville reported to de Noyers in Oct. 1641 that he had intervened to prevent the conduct of the *revue* by the *commissaire* at Bapaume because he was anxious to save the available funds – it being dangerous for discipline to conduct a *revue* without providing some subsequent payment to the troops: AAE MD, 1680, fo. 455, 4 Oct.

[265] Caron (ed.), *Le Tellier*, p. 182, 12 Mar. 1642.

[266] Aubery, II. 591, 25 Aug. 1640, Louis XIII to Châtillon and Chaulnes.

[267] AAE CP Allemagne, 12, fo. 445, 11 Dec. 1635.

[268] SHAT A¹ 52, fo. 66, 6 May 1639, order to Machault, Argenson, Miroménil, Choisy and Grémonville to proceed to prosecute and seize the goods of unit commanders who have not produced the recruits specified in their *traités*; A¹ 64, fo. 229, 12 Apr. 1641, Charles le Roy, sr de La Potherie, to prosecute a captain of the regiment of Bretagne, accused of theft from the *montre*.

considerable. Le Maistre de Bellejamme reported to Séguier that in the case of his prosecution of a captain accused of violence and extortion at Guise he had assembled thirty witnesses, and had managed to ensure that the accused was tried before civil judges brought from Laon, as a result of which he had managed to have the captain executed.[269] Yet the frequency of disorder and violence perpetrated by unit officers, and, above all, the failure to restrain the abuses surrounding each successive series of recruitment *traités*, suggest that the success of the intendants in controlling or intimidating the officers was limited.

It may also be suggested that even in their administrative sphere within the armies, the ministers did not regard the *intendants* as entirely reliable. It is evident that *intendants* could fail in their assignments or perform them badly; their capacity to come to terms with the central weaknesses of the war administration was inevitably limited. Even allowing for de Noyers' initial suspicions of Le Tellier and the circumstances of his appointment as *intendant* with the army of Italy, a striking number of the *secrétaire*'s letters criticize the *intendant*'s failure to control expenses, to negotiate satisfactory contracts with *munitionnaires* and to provide adequate control over desertion and absenteeism. In early 1641, de Noyers expressed scepticism at the high unit cost of the *munitionnaires*' contracts for the provision of bread, stipulating that he would only meet these if Le Tellier could assure him that it was not possible to negotiate the price down.[270] Six weeks later de Noyers wrote that Maria Cristina, regent of Savoy, had claimed that the French troops had extorted some 6 million *livres* from her subjects for subsistance over the winter months. De Noyers argued that this was effectively the exaction of illegal contributions, and could only be the result of inadequate supervision of the troops garrisoned in Piedmont.[271] In early June, de Noyers complained to Le Tellier about the cost of food in the army, focusing not on the price of the rations, but on the inadequate control of distribution, 'cette immense profusion de pain', which contrasted with the *intendant*'s protestations that the army was gravely weakened and scarcely able to sustain field operations.[272] Such complaints and ministerial criticism rumbled on through the autumn, to be supplemented in the winter of 1641/2 by increasingly strident complaints about the level of expense for the troops in winter quarters, again seen in terms of poor control and supervision on the part of the *intendant*. De Noyers – supported by Richelieu – cited the example of the Normandie regiment, which was claiming funds for 1,800 soldiers during the winter quarter, yet was also the beneficiary of substantial *traité*-payments for recruitment. With some irritation, de Noyers requested Le Tellier to send him an *état au vrai* of the troops in Italy so that realistic recruitment and subsistence claims could be established and imposed from the

---

[269] Mousnier (ed.), *Lettres*, I. 364–5, 369, 9/16 May 1637.
[270] Caron (ed.), *Le Tellier*, pp. 37–8, 27 Jan 1641.
[271] Caron (ed.), *Le Tellier*, p. 50, 12 Mar 1641.
[272] Caron (ed.), *Le Tellier*, p. 69, 5 June 1641.

centre.²⁷³ The inability to hold the officers to their recruitment *traités* runs through the correspondence of Le Tellier, as do the problems of maintaining adequate discipline over the troops in quarters or on campaign.²⁷⁴ None of this is to argue that Le Tellier was a less able administrator than his colleagues holding other intendancies. Indeed, it could be argued that the problems of administering the army in Italy were particularly intractable.²⁷⁵ Other *intendants* were criticized in similar terms for their failures and misjudgments. D'Orgères was reprimanded for his failure to provision *places* in Alsace,²⁷⁶ while Mangot de Villarceaux was censured for using grain from the magazine at Nancy to supply the troops.²⁷⁷ Criticism for failing to ensure adequate supply was frequent, as for failing to disburse money owed to troops with sufficient promptness.²⁷⁸ The absenteeism of the *intendant* at Bordeaux, Etienne Foullé, was a more unusual case amongst officials whose standard of professional commitment was generally high.²⁷⁹

The *intendants d'armée*, and indeed those *intendants des provinces* with military responsibilities, had a limited capacity to resolve the fundamental problems of army administration and to restrain the self-serving practices of the officer-corps, and government ministers were well aware of this. While more wide-rangingly competent and better able to use their initiative than other groups of officials with the armies, the *intendants* lacked the resources, support-structures and coercive power to reshape the administration of the armies single-handedly.

These failures do not, for the most part, imply that the *intendants* were guilty of corruption or embezzlement, although the suggestion of complicity with the high command carries more weight.²⁸⁰ With the possible exception of Le Camus, the *intendants d'armée* were not implicated in any of the cases of administrators' corruption reported to the secretary.²⁸¹

---

²⁷³ Caron (ed.), *Le Tellier*, p. 175, 19 Feb. 1642; p.172, 10 Feb., Richelieu to Le Tellier, same subject.
²⁷⁴ Caron (ed.), *Le Tellier*, p. 125, 2 Nov. 1641: de Noyers is strongly critical of the tolerance of disorders amongst the troops, disorders which Le Tellier seeks to minimize in his reply: p. 131, 12 Nov.
²⁷⁵ There is a clear implication that Antoine Le Camus, a previous *intendant des finances* with the army of Italy, had gravely mismanaged the financing of the army in 1636, and that this was one of the reasons for the limited success of the campaign: AAE CP Savoie 24, fo. 640, 15 July 1636, d'Hémery to Richelieu, concerning 'l'affaire de M Camus', and 'ses mauvaises offices'.
²⁷⁶ SHAT A¹ 39, fo. 165, 5 Oct. 1635.
²⁷⁷ SHAT A¹ 39, fo. 280, 30 Oct. 1637; Villarceaux was criticized again in 1639 for his failure to ensure the adequate subsistence of the troops in Lorraine: A¹ 50i, fo. 50, 1 Jan.
²⁷⁸ SHAT A¹ 37, fos. 221, 286, 25 June/3 July 1637; d'Aubray is reprimanded for making difficulties about payment of companies; Miroménil is reluctant to pay the units returning from the Valtelline.
²⁷⁹ SHAT A¹ 60, fos. 476, 477, 23 Sept. 1640.
²⁸⁰ The virtual absence of corruption amongst the *intendants* is emphasized by Bonney, 'The intendants', p. 216.
²⁸¹ For Le Camus, see above, n. 275. It was the case that a group of ordinary *maîtres des requêtes*, commissioned to carry out levies of horses in the provinces, were accused of substantial malversations: AAE MD 822, fo. 169, 6 Nov. 1636, Séguier to Chavigny. The assumption of probity linked to the *intendants* would not apply to all administrators with direct ties of *fidélité* to the ministry; Richelieu's chosen agent, the bishop of Mende, was investigated on suspicion of appropriating funds intended for the supply of the armies: SHAT A¹ 49, fo. 217, 29 Dec. 1638.

Responses and reactions

However, the close identification with the ministers and their patronage may have contributed in one respect to the individual *intendant*'s failure in the face of particular administrative assignments. The ministers assumed that the *intendant* would be prepared to use his own credit to make good shortfalls or delays from the *épargne*.[282] They might find themselves assisted by the military officers, who had an equal interest in not seeing the army collapse through financial shortages or delays, but it was the ministry's assumption that it was the responsibility of the *intendant d'armée* to mobilize his own credit in the first instance in these situations. Moreover, the ministry took what might have been a reasonable expectation applied with moderation and pushed it to extremes. The danger for the *intendants* was that an advance could easily turn into a gift to the crown, which had no means of making repayment.[283] And once the *intendant* had begun to provide money to meet a particular emergency, it was far from certain that he could halt the process. In 1636 Miroménil wrote to express his anxiety at his mounting financial commitments to the troops, and his concern at the exhaustion of his credit.[284] Yet this burdening of the *intendants* continued to be one of the props of the war-effort. Bosquet wrote to Séguier in April 1643 that he had been forced to borrow the money for the cost of embarking troops for Catalonia, some 80,000–100,000 *livres*. A proposal to levy this sum from the local dioceses had been rejected by the ministers, who had promised to repay Bosquet with funds from the *épargne*. Bosquet had received none of this reimbursement. It would have been disastrous to have delayed or postponed embarkation after the troops had been assembled, an error for which the *intendant* would have been held responsible.[285] Yet an advance made upon this scale and not recovered would not merely damage the *intendant*'s personal fortune, it would severely limit his ability to undertake any further assignments which might depend upon making good shortfalls or anticipating funds. The *intendants*' failure to carry out substantial provisioning operations becomes comprehensible, not merely in terms of the administrative burden, but also a possible reluctance to commit personal credit on the scale that a major intendancy would entail.[286] If the *intendant* had been prepared to offer support on

---

[282] SHAT A^1 25, fo. 443, 14 Oct. 1635: Le Camus' personal advances for the army of Italy are acknowledged; A^1 30 fo. 29, 6 Oct. 1636: reimbursement of Miroménil; AAE MD 1680, fo. 455, 4 Oct. 1641, Grémonville to de Noyers concerning 15,000 *livres* that he has advanced; A^1 70, fo. 134, 25 Aug. 1642, reimbursement of La Potherie for his advances to fund the *étapes* in the *généralité* of Caen.

[283] Argenson was owed 30,000 *livres* by 1642, and was clearly having difficulty getting repayment: SHAT A^1 69, fo. 147, 21 Apr.; order for payment to the *trésorier de l'épargne* repeated: fos. 396, 420, 6/8 June.

[284] AAE MD 1678, fo. 47, 23 May 1636.

[285] Lublinskaya (ed.), *Internal Policy*, I. 32–3, 24 Apr. 1643.

[286] BN Ms.fr. 17372, fo. 244, 8 Sept. 1636: Choisy to Séguier. In 1639 Choisy was still advancing funds to meet military expenses, but evidently needed to stress to de Noyers that 'je voudrais bien que ma bourse fust assez bien fournye pour aller audevant de tout, je le ferais avec plaisir, mais vous excuserez s'il vous plaist un pauvre Intendant': AAE CP Lorraine 31, fo. 84, 22 May. By 1641 Choisy was appealing to de Noyers to pay some of the monies owing to him in order to stave off the threat of bankruptcy: CP Allemagne 16, fos. 221–2, 18 June.

The management of the war-effort from 1635 to 1642

this level on one occasion, the predicament of the *bureau des finances* made it unlikely that he would be able to do so again.

In the course of the seventeenth century the *intendants d'armée* were to acquire a secure position at the top of the hierarchy of military administrators. The critical stage in the rise of the *intendants d'armée* was the post-1643 consolidation of Michel Le Tellier's authority as *secrétaire d'Etat de la guerre*. Enjoying a status and independence vis-à-vis Mazarin far greater than that of Sublet de Noyers with Richelieu, Le Tellier was able to break the hold of the *bureau des finances* and the chancellor over appointments to military intendancies, and to ensure that the *intendants d'armée* were increasingly his own clients, drawn in the main from the *commissaires des guerres*.[287] With the passing of the *intendants d'armée* into the clientele of the secretary – later minister – for war, a fundamental obstacle to the enhancement of their authority was removed. There was no longer an element of competition between the *secrétaire*, who sought to make the best use of his limited powers by extending and developing his own agents with the armies, and the other ministers of the crown, for whom *intendants*, *contrôleurs*, *prévôts* and *commis* represented a means of access to the army for their own administrator-clients. As the *intendants* were increasingly promoted from the ranks of the *commissaires des guerres*, the notion of the *de facto* subordination of the latter group became generally accepted within the military administration. The role and attributions of the intendancy itself became more formalized; the individual *intendants* themselves were more experienced, and, after 1660, more confident of the support of the *bureau de la guerre* in the event of disputes with the officer-corps.[288]

Yet all of this emerged slowly, and arguably in reaction to, rather than in anticipation of, the disasters of military administration during the Franco-Spanish war. An examination of the role of the *intendants* in the context of the war-effort in the years after 1635 does not support an assumption that they were targeted for development as part of a planned policy to reform military administration. In fact, the one administrative step taken in the mid-1630s, the amalgamation of the *intendants*' functions of justice/police with those of finance, almost certainly led to a reduction of the competence of these agents, by imposing an impracticably heavy burden of duties upon them. At the same time, the ministry conducted a wide-ranging, though ultimately abortive, experiment to develop the functions and authority of the *commissaires des guerres*. Probably the most significant casualty of the overburdening of the *intendants d'armée* was any capacity to play a formal

---

[287] A. Corvisier, 'Clientèles et fidélités dans l'armée française aux XVIIe et XVIIIe siècles', in A. Corvisier, *Les hommes, la guerre et la mort* (Paris, 1985), pp. 191–214, (first pub. in Durand (ed.), *Clientèles et fidélités*). Corvisier, making use of material from Baxter, *Servants of the Sword*, shows the extent to which post-1644 a significant proportion of *intendants d'armée* were not simply clients of the Le Tellier family, but were members of the extended clan itself (pp. 192–5).

[288] Baxter, *Servants of the Sword*, pp. 139–3, 201–8; Corvisier (ed.), *Histoire militaire*, I. 389–93.

and regular role as supervisor and coordinator of the rest of the military administration. Whether in practice, and with their existing authority, the *intendants d'armée* would have been capable of controlling and disciplining the various groups of *commissaires*, *contrôleurs*, *prévôts* and *commis* of the *trésoriers* is questionable. Yet so long as the central issue of a fragmented and partitioned administrative authority remained unresolved, all other attempts at rationalization or reform could do little to change the fundamental weaknesses and inadequacy of the ministry's attempt to control its armies.

Above all, it is important to place the administrators within a wider military context, a context in which the ministry depended upon both the officer-corps in general and the senior officers of the various army-corps in particular. It remained unrealistic to assume that any group of administrators with the armies could carry out the wishes and instructions of the ministry in the face of opposition or non-cooperation from the military elite. The methods by which the ministry had expanded the size of the army after 1635 had reinforced a high level of dependence upon the financial goodwill of the unit officers, and placed limitations upon the extent to which they could be subject to effective discipline or control. The one means by which that control might be facilitated was through the efforts and leadership of the high command, who were both the superiors in rank and, very frequently, the social superiors of the unit officers. The relationship between the ministry and these commanding officers was ultimately the most significant factor in ensuring some degree of control over the war-effort. It was to the attempts to sustain this relationship that initiatives to develop the military administration were sacrificed in the years after 1635.

9

The ministry and the high command

> La plus belle et la plus honorable des occasions est passée pour cette année. L'incommodité des fourrages et des maladies nous vont presser bientost. Je cours le risque de vos reproches de n'avoir jamais assez fait . . . je me prepare desia a tout cela[,] ma patience et souffrance a esté mise souvent a l'espreuve.[1]

In these terms of affected weariness and insolent superiority, Gaspard III de Coligny, maréchal de Châtillon, dismissed the attempt by the secretary for war, Sublet de Noyers, to induce him to continue the campaign in Flanders after Arras had fallen to the French. Châtillon's epistolary style neatly demonstrates the high command's perception of the modest social and political status of the *secrétaire d'Etat de la guerre* before 1661. While Châtillon would never have addressed Richelieu in such terms – deploying in the cardinal's case the relatively more subtle insult of consistently addressing him as Monsieur rather than Monseigneur – the tone and content of this letter point to a bigger and more persistent problem in the management of the war-effort. Châtillon, a mediocre but absolutely loyal commander, was one of the more reliable pillars of the military hierarchy. Yet his ability and willingness to defy the ministry on this and numerous other occasions, making his own judgements about what the army under his command would or would not do, was characteristic of the wider attitude of the high command.

The reasons for this are not difficult to find. Above the level of *maréchal de camp*, senior office was still perceived as the preserve of the great noble houses, the *grands* – the sixty or seventy families ranked hierarchically from the collateral branches of the Bourbon down through the holders of *duchés-pairies* to the handful of *ducs sans pairies*.[2] Central to the political history of this period was the *grands*' sense that they possessed a distinctive, personal relationship with the king, which established them in an intermediate position between the sovereign and his subjects. At the highest levels of the aristocratic hierarchy, amongst the *princes du sang*, the *princes légitimés* and the *princes étrangers*, the situation was compounded by claims to a share in sovereignty, whether that of the kings of France or of

---

[1] AAE MD 1679, fo. 228, 28 Aug 1640, Châtillon to de Noyers.
[2] Corvisier, 'Les généraux de Louis XIV', 41–3. The exceptions to this were a relatively small number of *noblesse d'épée*, and a handful of second-generation *noblesse de robe*. For discussion of this hierarchy within the *grands* see Labatut, *Ducs et pairs*, pp. 41–88, 337–79; Levantal, *Ducs et pairs*, pp. 163–242; Mettam, 'The French nobility'; Parrott, 'Richelieu, the *grands* and the French army', pp. 136–9.

Responses and reactions

foreign ruling houses.[3] In these cases the relationship with the crown was not just that of a superior subject possessing a close personal relationship with the king, but of a sovereign or semi-sovereign individual in his own right, whose 'service' to the French crown was conditional upon reciprocal respect for his rights and status.

The most conspicuous arena for the expression of the close relations between the crown and its *grands* had traditionally been military service. Appearing in the royal army with a host of retainers and clients, living, eating and passing time in close proximity to the sovereign on campaign, fighting with or in his presence; all of these activities crystallized the special relationship, granting the militarized *grands* the informal access to the king which most easily facilitated requests for favour and patronage, and flattered their self-esteem. And just as the *grands* derived status and validation from this close association with the king on campaign or on the field of battle, so the monarch reinforced his own *gloire* and prestige through personal military command in the company of a large proportion of his greatest subjects. The king as military leader remained one of the most potent symbols of royal sovereignty and legitimate authority in the seventeenth century.[4] When this was accompanied by an extravagant and elaborate entourage of *grands*, offering an overt demonstration of their willingness to fight and die for the king, the statement carried even greater rhetorical and visual force – as Louis XIV well understood. A direct consequence of this was to give military command a symbolic weight greater than any other exercise of authority. If the king in command of his army stood at the summit of his sovereign power, then it followed that when armies were not commanded by the king in person, whoever was acting as commander had a status akin to that of viceroy: he was the direct representative of the king, over whose royal army he was exercising authority.[5] The invariable formula that the commander of an army where the king was not present was the *lieutenant général* of that force bears witness to this convention, as does the style of all commissions, which were always written as if by the king in the first person, and refer without exception to 'mon armée d'Italie', 'mes trouppes', 'mes officiers'. Slightly more ambiguous were the great military *offices de la couronne* – the *connétable*, the *grand maître de l'artillerie*, the various *colonels généraux* of the infantry, Swiss, *cavalerie légère*. These *offices* would seem to imply a permanent

---

[3] For the practical impact of *prince étranger* status on relations with the crown, see E. Baluze, *Histoire généalogique de la Maison d'Auvergne* (2 vols.; Paris, 1708), II. 813–20; Bérenger, *Turenne*, pp. 40–52, 303–6; Parrott, 'A *prince souverain*'; A. Cremer, *Der Adel in der Verfassung des Ancien Régime. Die Châtellenie d'Epernay und die Souveraineté de Charleville im 17 Jahrhundert* (Bonn, 1981), pp. 131–4, 169–87.

[4] Cornette, *Roi de guerre*, pp. 120–3, 151–207. The count-duke of Olivares encountered huge problems in trying to discourage Philip IV from assuming this personal military leadership, above all after Louis XIII had taken this role at La Rochelle and at the pass of Susa (1629): Elliott, *The Count-Duke of Olivares*, pp. 375–82, 500–2.

[5] Pernot, 'Le rôle de la guerre', 52.

The ministry and the high command

delegation of military authority rather than a decision to place an individual for a limited period as the representative of the king in command of his army. Yet the texts for the edicts of creation and renewal of these *offices* make it clear that the authority was no less explicitly exercised in the name of the king and as his agent.

However, if on one level this could be seen as a forthright affirmation of royal rights over the army, which created a considerable barrier – as was seen in chapter 6 – to the full development of military entrepreneurship, it had an additional set of implications with regard to the *grands*. If military command was one of the highest manifestations of royal sovereignty, then it followed that only the most prestigious and highest-ranking of the king's subjects should assume this 'viceregal' role. Just as the provincial governors were selected from the *grands*, or on a few occasions the very topmost ranks of the provincial nobility, so military command should be exercised only by those whose social prestige was immediately below that of the king. There was apparent justification for this; effective military authority in this period required constant engagement with those who sought to carve out their own spheres of authority, whether *maréchaux de camp* with aspirations to command smaller, independent, army-corps, provincial power-brokers who would assert their authority over troops within their territorial jurisdiction, or young, socially high-ranking, unit commanders resistant to any form of discipline. In a society profoundly sensitive to nuances of status and hierarchy, a relatively low-ranking commander would encounter obstruction and insubordination from his notional inferiors. It was a point that Jean-Baptiste Budes, comte de Guébriant, made of himself with regard to the army of Germany, when he was the acting commander in 1640/1. Though of a prestigious family of *noblesse d'épée* with a long ancestry, Guébriant none the less argued that a general from amongst the *grands* should be sent to take overall command. Although Guébriant had held the commission of lieutenant commander of the army since 1639 under the command of Henri d'Orléans, duc de Longueville, the latter's retirement on grounds of ill-health led Guébriant to write to the court emphasizing that a commander of high social status would be more likely to keep both the French *mestres de camp* and the German colonels in order.[6]

Yet this argument, while having wide currency in court and military circles, is not entirely convincing. It cannot explain the numbers of senior commands which did ultimately go to those who were not themselves from families situated within the *grands*. Guébriant himself, despite his earlier protestations in favour of Longueville, gained outright command of the army of Germany in 1642 when he was made a *maréchal*.[7] Previous examples of commanders promoted from the ranks of the *épée* included Louis de Marillac, Jean du Caylar de Saint-Bonnet, marquis de Toiras, Antoine Coeffier de Ruzé, marquis d'Effiat, and Manassés de

[6] AAE CP Allemagne 16, fo. 318, 17 Sept. 1641, Guébriant to de Noyers; Noailles, *Guébriant*, pp. 486–7, for formal text of commission to Guébriant.
[7] Noailles, *Guébriant*, pp. 245–75.

Responses and reactions

Pas, marquis de Feuquières.[8] Later in the ministry Guébriant could be placed with Philippe de Clérambault, marquis de Palluau, Abraham Fabert, Jean de Gassion and Philippe de La Motte-Houdancourt.[9] Moreover, if social prejudice were assumed to be invincible, the ascent of foreign colonels such as Josias, Count von Rantzau, or Hans Ludwig von Erlach would have been equally improbable.[10] In many of these cases the dignity of *maréchal* was of crucial importance at least as much for social validation as for a recognition of outstanding military service. Whereas the prince de Condé, the duc de Longueville or Henri de Lorraine, comte d'Harcourt, could assume command of armies without specific title, for lower-ranking commanders the baton of *maréchal* was an essential reinforcement of authority. At this level, its prestige derived precisely from its role as a signifier of likely social ascent. The office of *maréchal* itself was held for life, with no possibility that it could be passed through the family, though it gave the holder lifetime status equivalent to a *duc sans pairie* in the court hierarchy. In most cases, however, the promotion of a family into the ranks of the *grands* came through the king's decision to erect a family title into a *duché-pairie*, with the expectation that the Paris *Parlement* would then register the *pairie*, thus fixing the date from which its seniority would be based. The overwhelming majority of *duchés-pairies* were erected for families of the *noblesse d'épée* on the basis of distinguished and high-ranking military service.[11] Thus, though the award of a baton of *maréchal* was by no means a guarantee of a subsequent and permanent social promotion of the family, it was a good indication that a family might be poised on the brink of the highest social status. The combination of traditional, time-honoured, prestige accruing to the office of *maréchal* with this awareness that the holder might well gain access to the ranks of the *grands*, could do much to overcome social prejudice and enhance the authority of a member of the *noblesse d'épée* who had achieved senior military command.

These promotions to overall command of armies from amongst the second tier of the *noblesse d'épée*, and even in a handful of cases the *noblesse de robe*, cast doubt on the belief that only senior officers from the most socially exalted background possessed enough prestige successfully to command an army-corps. Yet though the social rationale for granting such commands only to the highest-ranking *grands* might be ignored in specific cases, the 'viceregal' theory of military

---

[8] Vaissière, *Maréchal de Marillac*, pp. 13–18; Baudier, *Maréchal de Toiras*, pp. 3–4; Jacquart, 'Le marquis d'Effiat', 300; Manassés de Pas, marquis de Feuquières, *Lettres inédites*, ed. E. Gallois (5 vols.; Paris, 1845–6) I. viii–xix.

[9] Noailles, *Guébriant*, pp. 1–24; Pinard, *Chronologie*, II. 597 (Palluau); H. Choppin, *Le maréchal de Gassion, 1609–1647* (Paris and Nancy, 1907), pp. 1–13; Bourelly, *Maréchal de Fabert*, I. 3–23; L. André, 'Le maréchal de La Motte-Houdancourt, son procès, sa rébellion, sa fin', *Revue d'histoire moderne et contemporaine*, 12 (1937), 5–35, 95–125.

[10] Malingre, *Eloge historique*; Noailles, *Guébriant*, pp. 372–4; A. von Gonzenbach, *Der General Hans Ludwig von Erlach von Castelan* (3 vols.; Bern, 1880–2).

[11] Labatut, *Ducs et pairs*, pp. 118–33.

command continued to exercise a powerful hold on the thinking behind the wider distribution of the charge of *lieutenant général*. A high proportion of all commands were made on grounds of social prestige rather than military competence or experience. In this the crown and the grands were bound together by the network of assumptions about the status of the king's representative with the army-corps, assumptions which subordinated military effectiveness to the selection of a recipient who would appropriately embody the king's sovereign dignity. In principle, it was assumed that military commands would be allocated hierarchically within the caste: the immediate royal family and the princes of the blood should receive commands in preference to any other *grand*, followed by the families of the *princes légitimés* such as the Longueville, the Vendôme or the Angoulême, who were ranked together with the sovereign princes of foreign states such as the dukes of Lorraine and Savoy when these were allied with France, and on down through the ranks.

In reinforcing these assumptions, the *grands* were not overlooking their personal interests; overall military command in a particular campaign theatre or one of the major military *offices de la couronne* was an extremely desirable objective. Representing an unambiguous sign of royal favour, such grants were a clear validation of their status within the caste. Traditional aristocratic education was still primarily aimed at developing a warrior ethos and the capacity for military command. It was therefore expected that the *grands* would assume the role of warrior on at least one or two occasions during their lives.[12] Though a command could involve heavy personal expense, it also offered considerable opportunities for the distribution of patronage and favours, maintaining or winning clients who might be retained long after the particular campaign had ended.[13] This was especially the case after any military advantage achieved against the enemy, when the commander would deluge the crown and its ministers with requests for promotions to fill places vacated by death or wounding, or to reward meritorious service. In 1640, for example, the comte d'Harcourt, then commander of the army of Italy, wrote to the court to announce the capture of Turin. In keeping with such an auspicious event, he accompanied the announcement with a long list of requests for promotions and favours for his officers.[14]

Crown and *grands* thus had a number of interests in maintaining the latter's grip on military commands; the assumption that the great nobility possessed a special status in this as in other areas was not challenged. This had its price in the control of the war-effort. Commands were put in the hands of individuals who,

---

[12] Motley, *French Aristocrat*, pp. 123–68.

[13] The 'personalized' nature of this service to the crown could also mean that expenditure could be recompensed with arbitrary, one-off, gifts from the crown, such as the 50,000 *livres* paid to maréchal Châtillon in recognition of expenses incurred in military service: SHAT A^1 31, fo. 193, 30 Dec. 1636, Louis XIII to the *cour des comptes*.

[14] AAE CP Savoie 31, fo. 100, 23 Sept. 1640.

while they acknowledged the superior status of the crown (and in some cases only on the basis of a reciprocal regard for sovereign rights), believed without question in their social superiority over the rest of the king's subjects, whether these were royal administrative agents or ministers of state. Having granted these powers to its *lieutenants généraux*, the crown found that it possessed no effective means of enforcing their cooperation via its own agents. In 1650, Le Tellier commented that 'L'armée estoit une véritable république et . . . les lieutenants généraux consideroient leurs brigades comme autant de cantons.'[15] This remark was admittedly made at the height of the *Frondes*, but the situation had not been significantly different in the preceding decades. What Eugène Carrias termed 'l'esprit d'insubordination', which he regarded as the principal weakness of the command structure, was an essential element of the ethos of the commanders.[16]

Had the king been directing a foreign and military policy unambiguously presented in terms of his own wishes, then the loyalty and cooperation of the *grands* would have been less problematic. Louis XIV's conspicuous assumption of personal control over the conduct of his wars from 1667 drew a high level of cooperation from the *grands*. But when the foreign policy appeared not necessarily to represent the wholehearted will of the king, when the policies themselves created deep political and religious divisions within the French elites, and when the organization and waging of war and the conduct of foreign policy appeared to be in the hands of a minister-favourite and his *créatures* rather than of the crown, then consensus and cooperation amongst the *grands* at the summit of the army-corps was difficult to achieve. It was not possible to rely on the high command's commitment to policies which were seen by many of the *grands* as ministerial rather than royal and which – as the rhetoric of conspiracies after 1626 demonstrates – many of them regarded with open hostility. This unreliability was exacerbated in practice by the *grands'* social prestige, which encouraged them to defy the authority and instructions of socially inferior ministers and created a culture of self-confident insubordination.

To what extent could Richelieu's ministry confront this problem? Given that the selection of high-ranking *grands* for military commands was deeply tied to the perception of sovereign authority, it would be unrealistic to suppose that a practical alternative was available to the crown for the command of its armies. But even if the *grands'* quasi-monopoly of high office remained unchallenged, it was essential to restrict their potential for autonomy, and to persuade them to accept central direction from and accountability to the ministry. It has been believed that recognition of this need formed the basis of the policies pursued by Richelieu's ministry; the cardinal used his authority to try to break the dangerous concentration of military command and administrative control resting with the senior

---

[15] Cited in Bonney, *Political Change*, p. 262.
[16] Carrias, *Pensée militaire*, p. 142.

officers. The reality is considerably more complex and, like so much else in the conduct of the war-effort, reveals a number of *ad hoc* and sometimes contradictory initiatives.

THE TRADITIONAL PICTURE: RICHELIEU AS THE OPPONENT OF ARISTOCRATIC POWER IN THE ARMY

The belief that the ministry was actively opposed to the excessive power of the great aristocratic commanders has a long ancestry. Richelieu himself, in his *Testament politique* and his *Mémoires*, suggests that some steps were taken to curb their authority. This evidence has been given prominence by historians, although the target for the cardinal's supposed initiative was the military *offices de la couronne* rather than the more fundamental problem of those commanders having authority over the individual army-corps. Above all, the celebrated abolition of the *office* of *connétable* in 1627 is taken as evidence of a new policy towards the high command.[17] Richelieu speaks of the *connétable* as a charge that was earlier of the greatest benefit to France, but which had lately become very harmful 'by the absolute authority that it gave to the holder'.[18] Yet the *connétable*'s most significant power, it is proposed, was that once appointed, the holder could be removed only for some crime or by his death, a characteristic of all *offices* held as private property under the *Ancien Régime*. The cardinal pointed in addition to the *connétable*'s financial authority, the control of the revenues held by the *ordinaire des guerres*. It was emphasized that this separate accounting caused 'uncontrollable confusion' in the king's finances, so that the *surintendant* was unable to make any *règlement* concerning overall military expenditure. Yet the *ordinaire* consistently represented less than 0.5 per cent of official expenditure during the war years.[19] There were better reasons for the confusion in the crown's finances.

The real motive for the 1627 abolition seems more straightforward. In 1626 Richelieu had used the Assembly of Notables to force Henri II, duc de Montmorency, the son of the late *connétable*, Henri I de Montmorency-Damville, to surrender the office of *amiral de France, de Bretagne et de Guyenne* for a cash payment.[20] Although the price of the *amirauté* (1.2 million *livres*) was paid to Montmorency by the *épargne*, the beneficiary was Richelieu, holder of the newly

---

[17] Daniel, *Histoire*, I. 170–88; Audouin, *Histoire de l'administration*, II. 187–8; Hanotaux, *Richelieu*, IV. 382–3; Caillet, *De l'administration en France*, p. 363; E. Boutaric, *Institutions militaires*, p. 377: 'Richelieu eut pour système de supprimer toutes ces grandes charges qui conféraient à de grands seigneurs des droits dont la couronne n'aurait jamais dû se dessaisir'; Quarré de Verneuil, *L'armée en France*, p. 157; Tapié, *France in the Age*, pp. 166–7.
[18] Richelieu, *Mémoires*, III. 212.
[19] AAE MD 819, fo. 153, 1635; MD 823, fo.116, 1636.
[20] L.-A. Boiteux, *Richelieu: grand maître de la navigation et du commerce de France* (Paris, 1955), pp. 81–110; Richelieu argued that the abolition of the *amiral* would save the crown some 400,000 *livres* p.a.: James, 'Administration and development', p. 23.

Responses and reactions

created rival office of *grand maître et surintendant général de la navigation*. However, the despoiling of the Montmorency family raised the stakes when the *office* of *connétable* fell vacant with the death of maréchal Lesdiguières in September 1626. Both by military reputation and by family, Henri II de Montmorency was the obvious candidate for the office of *connétable*, and his claim could only be strengthened by his recent loss of high office. Had Richelieu been confident that he could fill the *connétablie* with one of his allies amongst the *grands*, then the issue of the abolition would probably not have arisen. But the prospect of a prestigious office being held by a great noble who, if not overtly disloyal, was clearly outside the circle of the cardinal's allies, was not acceptable.[21] Precisely because the office of *connétable* implied no specific military function, had been in obvious decline ever since its expedient revival in 1594, and Lesdiguières had made no arrangements for the *survivance* of the office within his own family, it was feasible to carry through its abolition.[22] And despite the rhetoric about the significance of the abolition, the reality seems a great deal more arbitrary. It was certainly alleged that Richelieu was prepared to revive the office as part of the dowry attached to his niece, Marie de Combalet, when he was attempting to lure Louis de Bourbon, comte de Soissons, into the match.[23] It is clear that the abolition was not regarded as definite: in April 1643 another formal edict reiterated the abolition of the *office* of *connétable* conjointly with that of the *colonel général de l'infanterie*, and this was registered just before the *colonel général* was revived for the second duc d'Epernon.[24] There remained considerable speculation that the *connétable* would be revived in favour of Turenne after 1658.[25] Thus the most frequently cited of the ministry's initiatives to restrain the military power of the great aristocracy amounts to little more than the contingent abolition of an office whose powers had become vague and narrowly defined by the early seventeenth century, and for reasons which have more to do with family politics than with any wider strategy for the reduction of aristocratic power over the army.

Scepticism about the intentions of the ministry proves even more justified in the case of *colonel général de l'infanterie française*. In 1638, the disgrace of Jean-Louis de Nogaret de La Valette, duc d'Epernon, and his second son Bernard, duc de La Valette, after the débâcle of Fuenterrabía allowed Richelieu to strip Epernon of his office of *colonel général*, the powers of which Richelieu himself described as insupportable.[26] It is assumed that the relative weakness of the

---

[21] V. Siri, *Anecdotes du ministère du cardinal de Richelieu et du règne de Louis XIII* (Amsterdam, 1717), p. 274, regards this grievance as the fundamental motive for Montmorency's 1632 revolt.

[22] Richelieu, *Mémoires*, VIII. 212. Avenel, *Richelieu*, I. 191, III. 58, suggests that the importance of the office in the decades before 1626 had been much exaggerated.

[23] Siri, *Anecdotes*, p. 320. Although Siri is not an authoritative source, the opinion is compatible with other contemporaries' sense that the abolition was provisional.

[24] BN Châtre de Cangé, 25 fo. 239.

[25] C. Picavet, *Les dernières années de Turenne* (Paris, 1914), pp. 59–62; Bérenger, *Turenne*, pp. 337–8.

[26] Avenel, *Richelieu*, III. 61–2; Fessenden, 'Epernon', pp. 157–70.

The ministry and the high command

Regency government after Louis XIII's death – the need to appease the *grands* who had been excluded from power under Richelieu – led to the reinstatement of Bernard de La Valette, now second duc d'Epernon, with all the rights and prerogatives of the office restored. Only with the rigorously absolutist policies of the early 1660s was the office of *colonel général de l'infanterie* finally abolished, confirming the successful 'shift of power from the independent Grands to the royal bureaucracy'.[27]

This belief about the wider importance of the abolition has been due to a misconception about the powers of the *colonel général*, particularly the idea that the holder had an unlimited right of appointment to all offices in the infantry.[28] Compared with such an extraordinary authority, the colonel's other prerogatives – the control of the one company, *la colonelle*, in each *régiment entretenu*, the right to publish the disciplinary *bans* within the armies and the possession of a disciplinary executive in the *prévôts des bandes* – would have been considered minor. Yet it is clear that this vaunted power of appointment never existed in the form that has been assumed; it was an incidental and personal prerogative of Epernon's, enjoyed in practice only for the few years between 1584 and 1588. The *colonel général* did not possess a right of direct appointment, but one of nomination or *présentement*.[29] This lesser right had been possessed since the creation of the *charge* of *colonel général* (held by commission) in 1542.[30] While potential officers were to be put forward for consideration through the mediation of the *colonel général*, who benefited from patronage opportunities and payments for his services, he was not empowered actually to appoint the officers to the units. Admittedly, he did possess this power for the *compagnie colonelle* in every *régiment entretenu*, but these company appointments of captain, lieutenant, etc., were at a relatively insignificant level. In all other cases, his nominations were subject to the king's approval, who was at liberty to overrule them and select other candidates himself. The practical extent of the *colonel*'s power thus depended upon his relationship with the crown; in exceptional circumstances of great royal favour, a *droit de nomination* could become a full right of appointment.

In 1584, Henri III, pressed by competing court factions and wishing to turn Epernon, a member of the provincial *noblesse d'épée*, into an effective supporter of

---

[27] Fessenden, 'Epernon', p. 200.
[28] Daniel, *Histoire*, I. 270, 281–3; André, *Michel Le Tellier et l'organization*, pp. 160–4; Mouton, *Un demi-roi*, p. 142; P. Viollet, 'Le colonel général de l'infanterie française', *Journal des savants*, 7 (1909), 485–94; Rousset, *Histoire*, I. 175; Tapié, *France in the Age*, p. 463 n. 4. Three studies: Avenel, *Richelieu*, III. 61–2; Corvisier, *Louvois*, pp. 98–100; Fessenden, 'Epernon', pp. 199–200, express some doubt about the practical extent of the colonel's powers of appointment, but all maintain the orthodoxy about the *de jure* extent of these powers.
[29] Girard, *Espernon*, pp. 34–5: 'de nommer generalement a toutes les charges vacantes dans les Bandes Francaises, sans excepter même de cette nomination celle de Mestre de Camp du Regiment des Gardes'.
[30] Charles de Cossé-Brissac was named *Capitaine et colonel général des gens de pied* in that year: Salerian-Saugy, *La juridiction*, p. 5.

Responses and reactions

an independent royal position, elevated the charge of *colonel général* into an *office de la couronne*.[31] The significance of the royal *ordonnance* was merely that it emphasized the immense enhancement of Epernon's standing with the king. Until his disgrace in 1588, the duke could make nominations to infantry officerships in the full knowledge that they would be accepted unconditionally by Henri. Predictably, this alarming and concrete manifestation of the king's particular favour antagonized the other *grands* at Court.[32] A coalition led by Henri de Lorraine, duc de Guise, deploying the power of the *Sainte Ligue* against the crown, finally achieved Epernon's disgrace in 1588 and his suspension from office.[33] With Henri III's assassination a year later, Epernon's capacity to regain his position of previous influence – although he had sided with Henri IV – was permanently lost.

The situation that had existed prior to 1584, for Epernon as for his predecessors, was restored; the king was not inclined to accept the *colonel général*'s nominations as binding in the nomination of officers. In 1602, Henri decided to replace Louis de Berton, sieur de Crillon, as *mestre de camp* of the *gardes françaises* with his own choice of Lesdiguières' son-in-law, Charles de Blanchefort de Créqui. Seemingly out of touch with the extent to which the political climate had changed, Epernon opposed this appointment vociferously, and retired to his governorship of Angoulême. Henri, acting within his established rights and concerned at possible complicity in the Biron revolt, responded assertively, forcing the abandonment of the existing understanding and the adoption of a formal *traité*.[34] In return for an explicit right to make nomination to certain offices – every other captain in the *gardes* and the captains of the *vieux* and *nouveaux* (presumably the *petits-vieux*) regiments – Epernon was forced to sacrifice any general right to make nominations to other regiments, and lost all authority to propose *mestres de camp* and the lesser company officers.[35] A limited compensation of the treaty was that it affirmed Epernon's right to make all appointments to the *compagnies colonelles*, and to appoint a group of officers attached to the regimental *état major* – sergeant majors and their *aydes*, surgeons and chaplains.[36] None the less, the effect was to restrict very severely the scope of the colonelcy, already reduced to a fraction of the authority possessed in the essentially anomalous period of 1584–8.

---

[31] For details of the negotiations surrounding this creation, see Girard, *Espernon*, pp. 34–6. For Henri III's overall political intentions see J. Salmon, *Society in Crisis: France in the Sixteenth Century* (London, 1975), pp. 205–6; P. Chevallier, *Henri III* (Paris, 1985), pp. 426–31; Tait, 'The king's lieutenants', pp. 40–2.

[32] Mouton, *Un Demi-Roi*, p. 142: 'avec une telle augmentation dans ses prerogatives, honneurs et emoluments que cette charge [*sic*] devenait l'une des premières du royaume'.

[33] Chevallier, *Henri III*, pp. 645–6; Guise had tried unsuccessfully to have Epernon disgraced in 1585: Girard, *Espernon*, pp. 35–8.

[34] Girard, *Espernon*, pp. 211–15.

[35] Daniel, *Histoire*, II. 263–4.

[36] La Fontaine, *Les devoirs militaires*, p. 377.

The ministry and the high command

Even this limited *droit de nomination* had disappeared before Richelieu's ministry. Epernon's involvement in revolt on behalf of Marie de Médicis in 1619, and his use of the office of *colonel général* to draw numbers of officers from the *vieux* regiments into revolt, led to his being stripped entirely of this authority as the price of his reconciliation with the crown.[37] There is no evidence that this power was recovered by Epernon.

By the 1630s all that remained to Epernon was the specific control of the *compagnies colonelles* within the *régiments entretenus*,[38] the placing of some of the officers in the *états majors* and an apparently less significant right to receive the oath of allegiance from all newly appointed infantry officers.[39] To this were added certain judicial functions: authority over the *prévôts des bandes* and the *maréchaux de bataille*,[40] and an unspecific disciplinary authority over the troops, particularly the infantry.[41]

The final abolition of the colonelcy in 1638 was one of a series of penalties inflicted on Epernon and Bernard de La Valette for their presumed role in the defeat at Fuenterrabía. This cannot be interpreted as Richelieu's seizing the chance at last to remove an 'intolerable' challenge to royal authority. In so far as Richelieu's ministry showed itself at all concerned with the powers of the *colonel général*, rather than with the specific activities of the duc d'Epernon, it may well have been with the intention of increasing the effectiveness of the *colonel*'s judicial authority. A *mémoire* of 1635 stated that the authority claimed by the *colonel* to publish disciplinary *bans* binding upon all the troops serving with the armies was in fact valid only for the *gens de pied* and not for the cavalry.[42] The issue at stake

---

[37] Belhomme, *L'infanterie*, I. 327. While Belhomme is not in general a reliable source for this period, his assertion is borne out by the archive material. Letters in Avenel's collection from Richelieu's 1616/17 secretariat do make references to Epernon's right of nomination: I. 375, 378, 10/12 Mar. 1617. Subsequently – after 1619 – there are no such letters referring to nomination or seeking Epernon's recommendation. One apparent exception, a letter from 1636, almost certainly refers to an appointment to a *compagnie colonelle*: SHAT A¹ 28 fo. 104, 21 June. Even in this case, the king stresses that Epernon must select a captain 'qui me soit agréable'.

[38] AAE MD 816, fo. 132, 19 Nov. 1635: Servien informs Richelieu that he is sending only nineteen company commissions to be handed over to the *mestre de camp* by Richelieu. The *lettre de cachet* that is being sent to Epernon will serve for the 20th: 'comme il s'est autrefois pratiqué, si S.E. ne desire qu'on en face une commission particulière'. Greatly reduced though this prerogative was, it was still the case that the crown had no wish to expand it, and the decision not to formalize the creation of *régiments provinciaux* in 1635 seems to have reflected this preoccupation: see chapter 5, pp. 291–2.

[39] This right was written into the commissions for the levy of infantry units: e.g. SHAT A¹ 26, fo. 114, 1635: the captain is to hold his company 'sous mon [i.e. the king's] autorité et celle de nostre tres cher . . . cousin le duc d'Espernon, colonel général de l'infanterie françoise'.

[40] SHAT A¹ 26, fo. 113, n.d. [1635].

[41] These disciplinary powers were not threatened by the crown in this period, but they did come under frequent attack from the *maréchaussée*, which asserted that the *colonel général* possessed a purely executive judicial authority, with no power to legislate or to carry out trials: Salerian Saugy, *La juridiction*, pp. 24–9.

[42] AAE MD 819, fo. 107, n.d. [1635]: 'Les gendarmes ont pour chef le général de l'armée, les chevaux légers ont un chef particulier [the *colonel général de la cavalerie légère*] . . . qui a autant d'auctorité sur eux que le colonel de l'infanterie sur les gens de pied.' Apparently contradicting this view, Louis

473

Responses and reactions

appears trivial; the king enacted the military legislation, and this dispute was merely about whether its publication should in all cases be in Epernon's name as well as the king's. While two separate *mémoires* signed by Epernon suggest that he saw this as an attack on the status of the *colonel général*, the most likely explanation was simply that is was an attempt to make the *bans* more effective by focusing them upon the limited area of the infantry.[43] A related document of the same period, a very lengthy 'mémoire sur les causes des désordres de l'Infanterie', indicates that indiscipline amongst the *gens de pied* was already a matter of concern to the ministry.[44] Far from regarding the colonelcy as incompatible with the crown's military authority, it would appear that the ministers were prepared to grasp at any institution which might offer some possibility of maintaining discipline amongst the troops. This motive certainly lay behind the decision to create a new *colonel général* in 1636, holding an overall control of the German cavalry levied for French service.[45] It may also be seen in the willingness to create subsidiary *colonels généraux de la cavalerie légère*, acting as delegates of the office-holder, Louis-Emmanuel de Valois, comte d'Alais, in particular campaign theatres.[46] The concern underlying these creations was exclusively disciplinary; it was intended to establish figures of independent authority and high social status, able to intervene in disputes over precedence and function amongst the cavalry officers. The same rationale justified the maintenance of the *mestre de camp général de la cavalerie légère*, the immediate subordinate of the *colonel général de la cavalerie*, throughout the seventeenth century[47] and the creation of the *commissaire général de la cavalerie* in 1654.[48] In 1643, the office of *colonel général de la cavalerie légère* had been given to Henri de La Tour d'Auvergne, vicomte de Turenne, a

---

de Montgommery, sieur de Courbouzon, argued that cavalry officers had the opportunity to appeal to the *colonel général de l'infanterie*, implying that the latter held at least a right of adjudication in disciplinary cases concerning the cavalry: *La milice françoise*, p. 30.

[43] AAE MD 819, fos. 123, 124, n.d. [1635].

[44] AAE MD 819, fos. 101–6, n.d. [1635]

[45] SHAT A¹ 32, fo. 48, 3 Apr.: creation of office for colonel Streff. The office was passed to colonel Egenfeld in 1638: A¹ 49 fo. 106, 5 Apr.

[46] SHAT A¹ 26, fo. 87, 10 Sept. 1635: acting *colonel général de la cavalerie légère* with the army of Flanders for Frédéric-Maurice de La Tour d'Auvergne, duc de Bouillon; A¹ 28 fo. 465, 13 Aug. 1636; *colonel général de la cavalerie* with army of Soissons for François de Bourbon, duc de Beaufort. This was not paralleled by acting appointments for the infantry. The *survivance* granted to Bernard, duc de La Valette, in 1610 gave him an *a priori* claim to any immediately subordinate infantry colonelcy. As Bussy-Rabutin pointed out, the extremely lengthy tenure of Alais as *colonel général de la cavalerie* (fifty-six years) provided considerable administrative continuity in the exercise of this office: *Mémoires*, II. 151.

[47] Daniel, *Histoire*, II. 457–9; the *mestre de camp général* was held by Roger de Rabutin, comte de Bussy, in succession to Philippe de Clérambault, comte de Palluau, from whom he bought the office in 1653 for 90,000 *écus*: Bussy-Rabutin, *Mémoires*, II. 139–54.

[48] Daniel, *Histoire*, II. 459–61; Bussy-Rabutin, *Mémoires*, II. 171–3, who narrates how he sought to oppose this new creation, fearing that it would diminish the status of his own office of *mestre de camp général*.

The ministry and the high command

certain means of ensuring that its status and new authority would be asserted.[49] As late as 1669, an entirely new *colonel général des dragons* was created to have specific control over this growing element in the armies.[50] It is a misconception to assume that the structure of colonelcies was being eroded. Envisaged as offices or commissions with disciplinary functions of a considerable but non-specific nature, the colonel generalcies contined to play an important role in the military organization. The fact that they were held by *grands* possessing considerable independent power and high social status was certainly not of itself taken as grounds to seek to reduce their significance within the military hierarchy.[51]

The final major *office de la couronne* attached to the armies was the *grand maître de l'artillerie*. In the management of this office after 1634 a different and rather more characteristic *politique* is evident, but once again one which does not indicate the planned increase of centralized crown authority. The incapacity of the duc de Sully's son and *grand maître* by *survivance* from 1610, Maximilien-François de Béthune, marquis de Rosny, was evident by the mid-1620s.[52] In consequence, during the siege of La Rochelle, Henri d'Orléans, marquis de Rothelin, was appointed acting Grand Master, the first of a series of replacements acting in Rosny's name.[53] A copy of Charles de La Porte de La Meilleraye's *pouvoir* of 1634, creating him *grand maître* in succession to Rosny, emphasized his suitability for the office 'particulierement depuis qu'il a eu l'administration de laditte Charge de Grand Mestre . . . laquelle, ayant executé par commission depuis plus de six années'.[54]

The overall authority of the office was certainly dissipated by these commissions. This rendered it more vulnerable to the main attack, made by Richelieu himself. But the appointment of Richelieu's first cousin, La Meilleraye, to the office of *grand maître* concerned more than the marginalization, then replacement, of a none too competent incumbent. Richelieu's assumption in 1626 of the office of *grand maître, chef et surintendant général de la navigation et du commerce de France*, combined with his control of the mechanisms of government and his standing with the king, permitted him to undertake a large-scale expansion of the navy. It is suggested that from thirty-one vessels of all types in 1629, Richelieu had built up an Atlantic fleet of sixty-six vessels by 1635, of which forty-one were custom-built, properly gunned, warships.[55] The significance of this for the *grand*

---

[49] André's suggestion that this was compatible with increasing royal authority over such 'anachronisms' because of Turenne's 'proven and assured loyalty' is unconvincing: *Michel Le Tellier et l'organisation*, pp. 149–50.
[50] Daniel, *Histoire*, II. 505–6
[51] Rowlands, 'Power, authority and army administration', pp. 22–46.
[52] Grillon, III. 453, 564, 22 Aug./12 Nov. 1628; Barbiche and Dainville-Barbiche, *Sully*, pp. 369–71.
[53] Grillon, III. 396, 25 July. Whether he actually held the title is unclear, but maréchal Schomberg was evidently carrying out the functions of the *grand maître* during the campaign of 1627: Avenel, II. 685, 29 Oct.
[54] SHAT A^1 26, fo. 83, 21 Sept. 1635 (copy).
[55] R. La Bruyère suggests that the Atlantic fleet consisted of fifty-one fighting ships in 1637: *Sourdis*,

maître de l'artillerie was obvious. The requirements of the navy, coordinated by Richelieu, quickly came to dominate the founding and distribution of artillery throughout France.[56] Given the limited production of the various foundries, and the immense cost of constructing cannon,[57] a large part of the naval requirement had to be met by transferring cannons from garrisons, or in direct competition with the needs of the armies. This provoked hostility and obstruction from the governors and army commanders, and drew Richelieu into an ever-more central role in determining the distribution of the cannon available, and ensuring that the requirements of the navy were met so far as possible.[58]

In consequence of this, first under the ineffectual Rosny and his commissioned aides, and above all from 1634 under his cousin, La Meilleraye, Richelieu used his maritime office to assume the more significant functions of the *grand maître*. The *grand maître* became less concerned with artillery, and more with supervising munitions in general. La Meilleraye's main task lay in the purchase and distribution of powder, shot and match, and a general responsibility for the provision of military transport. In drawing up an *état* for 1636, the *grand maître* listed supplies of lead, saltpetre, powder, the available horses and waggons, but explained that he was unable to give details of the cannons with the armies and in the *places*.[59] Because the *grand maître* had a large number of horses and waggons at his disposal, his duties were increasingly extended to the transport of *vivres*, as well as munitions, to supply both *places* and the armies.[60]

The change in emphasis did not result in a reduction of the number of the Grand Master's functions, but certain of his prerogatives did atrophy during the ministry. Instructions from the king to Condé drawn up in March 1639 grant him a formal provision to select artillery officers as he considered fit, and to order *revues* of the artillery *matériel*.[61] It may be assumed that this permission granted to

---

archevêque et amiral: la marine de Richelieu (Paris, 1948), p. 52; James, 'Administration and development', chapter 8.

[56] And the artillery purchased abroad: cf. letters concerning the purchase of 60–100 cannon in Holland for use on French naval vessels: Avenel, III. 4, 11, 6/22 Jan. 1628.

[57] Avenel, *Richelieu*, III. 123, suggests a rough guide of 1 *livre* per pound of metal, an eighteen pound cannon costing 8,000 *livres* to produce.

[58] SHAT A¹ 28, fo. 9, 3 June 1636: failure of governor to despatch cannons required for the navy; A¹ 35 fo. 80, 11 Mar. 1637: direct order from the king and Richelieu to hand over artillery required for the army in Provence; AAE MD 816, fo. 217 [mid-]1635: Richelieu corresponds directly with the *lieutenant général* of the artillery, Ferrier, to allocate cannons to the army being assembled at Langres.

[59] AAE MD 819, fo. 32, [late] 1635. Numerous letters testify to the central concern of the *grand maître* with munitions and transport: SHAT A¹ 30, fo. 160, 22 Oct. 1636: instruction to ensure that adequate powder is despatched to Dauphiné; A¹ 35, fo. 260, 6 Apr. 1637: transport of munitions to Neuchâtel. Even in these matters, Richelieu's intervention might still be apparent: e.g. Avenel, VII. 15, 7 July 1642.

[60] SHAT A¹ 27, fo. 390, 14 May 1636: La Meilleraye to provide transport to move 1,000 *rezeaux* of grain to Haguenau; Legrande-Girarde, *Crusy de Marsillac*, pp. 148–9.

[61] Avenel, VI. 299–303; both these powers were clearly the prerogative of the *grand maître*: Daniel, *Histoire* II. 526–7.

The ministry and the high command

Condé was typical of the authority granted to commanders distant from the *grand maître*. It is clear that Richelieu had gained overall control of the artillery budget early in the ministry. Indeed, the comment attributed to the *surintendant* Bullion: 'fermez-moi deux bouches: La Maison de S. Eminence et l'Artillerie', suggests that the two were recognized to be closely related, and that Richelieu may well have profited from their shared independence of the *surintendant*.[62] But this was not to the benefit of any alternative institution, least of all an effective, accountable, state administration. After Richelieu's death, the grand mastership of the artillery continued in the hands of the La Meilleraye family, whose authority revived and expanded to fill the vacuum. The demission of Armand-Charles, second duc de La Meilleraye, in 1669 did not lead to the suppression of the office, but to its transfer to Henri de Daillan, comte de Lude.[63] Despite the obvious inconveniences of an artillery administration which maintained rigorous independence and limited accountability in relation to any other element of the military administration, the situation persisted down to the end of the *Ancien Régime*.

THE REAL POLICY TOWARDS MILITARY APPOINTMENT: INFILTRATION AND COMPROMISE

The appointment of La Meilleraye as *grand maître de l'artillerie*, not as a means to bring the artillery more effectively under the control of the crown and its administrators, but to ensure that Richelieu's preoccupation with the needs of the navy received priority, is characteristic of the ministerial initiatives adopted in response to the independence of the high command. While La Meilleraye's appointment may have had a pernicious effect upon the availability of artillery within the armies, it did ensure that a key military *office de la couronne* remained in the hands of a ministerial supporter.

It was this concern to place allies and to identify and create links with potential allies that was characteristic of Richelieu's approach to the high command. One aspect of this was concerned overtly with Richelieu's own family ambitions. Unlike the great majority of government ministers in seventeenth-century France, who were drawn from backgrounds within the *noblesse de robe*, Richelieu came from a traditional *épée* family with a lengthy background of military service. He could use this background, together with his status as minister-favourite, to lay claim to all the prerogatives of rank amongst the *grands*: the elevation of his territories to the rank of a *duché-pairie* (the family ultimately held three *duché-pairies*: Richelieu, Aiguillon and Fronsac); full membership of the most prestigious Order of the Saint Esprit, rather than the secondary rank of an officer within it normally given to *robe* ministers; the nomination to army command in his own

---

[62] Tallement de Réaux, *Historiettes*, ed. A. Adam (2 vols.; Paris, 1960), II. 19.
[63] Daniel, *Histoire*, II. 553–4.

Responses and reactions

right as the king's *lieutenant général* – a post which Richelieu held at La Rochelle in 1627–8, and in north Italy in the following year. In the military sphere, however, Richelieu's concern was less to press his own claims to command, but rather those of his close relatives. Urbain de Maillé, marquis de Brézé, Richelieu's brother-in-law, was made a *maréchal* in 1632, and given command of the forces operating in the Empire, the first of a sequence of commands that he was to receive throughout the 1630s.[64] Brézé's son, Armand de Maillé, first served in the armies at the level of *maréchal de camp*, but was later transferred to the navy, commanding the Atlantic fleet after the disgrace of Henri d'Escoubleau de Sourdis, archbishop of Bordeaux, in 1641.[65] Richelieu's eldest sister's second husband, René de Vignerot, would almost certainly have been pushed into military commands, but had died in 1625. The only son from this marriage, François de Pont-Courlay, born in 1609, was made *général des galères* in 1635 as soon as his age made this remotely feasible, and proved an extravagant and incompetent embarrassment until his eventual removal in May 1639 and replacement by Armand, marquis de Maillé-Brézé.[66] Of Richelieu's uncles on the maternal side, Amador de La Porte was made *grand prieur* of the Order of Malta, and served as Richelieu's immediate subordinate in naval affairs, holding the office of *intendant général de la navigation*. The marriage of his other maternal uncle, Charles de La Porte, had produced an only son, born in 1602, who was to become the *grand maître de l'artillerie* in 1634.

Though Richelieu might have wished to fill more military commands with his immediate relatives, he was constrained by a network of marriages in his own and the previous generation which had not been notable for their fecundity, and by the need to spread this limited pool of eligible males thinly over the three distinct areas of the church, the navy and the army. Moreover, even had Richelieu possessed an extensive family, it is not clear how far it would have been acceptable to have made large numbers of appointments into the high command. Although the navy might increasingly resemble a family fiefdom, command in the army was far more extensively sought by the *grands*. The advancement of Brézé or La Meilleraye was resented by contemporaries, but such promotions were not individually out of order; like Richelieu himself, they were from traditional *épée* backgrounds, and there was always some scope to promote a few individuals who were not at the summit of the social hierarchy. However, a policy which sought more systematically to colonize the upper reaches of the officer-corps with the extended family of a minister-favourite would be a different matter, likely to raise intense resistance from a great aristocracy who expected a large proportion of these commands to be distributed in their favour.

In consequence, Richelieu's policy towards army command from the mid-1620s

---

[64] SHAT A¹ 21, fo. 74, 12 Nov. 1632, *pouvoir* of *lieutenant général* for Brézé.
[65] R. La Bruyère, *Maillé-Brézé: général des galères, grand amiral (1619–1646)* (Paris, 1945), pp. 1–36.
[66] La Bruyère, *Maillé-Brézé*, pp. 43–9.

was based upon a shrewd and self-interested exploitation of existing alignments amongst the *grands*. Traditional historiography tends to treat the *grands* as an undifferentiated, homogeneous and static group, characterized by common hostility to the reforming, centralizing aspirations of a forward-looking crown and its ministers. In reality they constituted an elite whose status at each tier of the hierarchy was relatively fluid and susceptible to rival claims for precedence and rank. The *grands* were intensely competitive and constantly locked in rivalry for status and ranking, while relations within the caste were marked by long-running factional alliances and feuds.

By involving himself in these factional conflicts, drawing upon the power and patronage of the crown to favour or marginalize different families, Richelieu was able to operate within the structure of the *grands* to establish allies whose military careers would be promoted at the expense of others whose exclusion was the price of keeping the allies on side. There was no suggestion that the 'allies' felt any ideological identification with the aims and objectives which were the public justification for Richelieu's foreign policy. Richelieu certainly could not assume that his policies would of themselves be sufficient to command loyalty and commitment. If he managed to gain the support of a group of *grands* it was because they perceived personal and factional advantage in collaborating with the ministry.

At the very highest level of the Princes of the Blood it was fortunate for Richelieu during the first decade of his ministry that those who were hostile to him, and who could lay claim to military appointments by undisputable right of birth, were for one reason or another out of the way. Gaston d'Orléans, above all, managed to rule himself out of claims to command for almost this entire period. The family crisis of the Chalais conspiracy was followed by a short *rapprochement* with Louis at the time of the brief Montpensier marriage. In late 1628 Gaston was being considered for command of the army that was to be sent down to Italy to relieve Casale and to support the duc de Nevers' claims to the duchy of Mantua.[67] However, Gaston's proposal to marry Marie de Gonzague, the daughter of Charles de Gonzague-Nevers, which would have tied Louis XIII more closely than he wished to the political fortunes of Mantua and would have upset marriage plans that Louis found more congenial, ensured that Gaston was kept away from a military role in which he would have had considerable access to his prospective father-in-law.[68] Louis finally decided to command the army in person, with Richelieu serving as his *lieutenant général*. Until 1634 when he was finally

---

[67] Quazza, *Guerra per la successione*, I. 299; G. Dethan, *La vie de Gaston d'Orléans* (Paris, 1992), pp. 69–70.

[68] M.C. Quazza, *Marie de Gonzague et Gaston d'Orléans: un épisode de politique secrète au temps de Louis XIII* (Mantua, 1925), pp. 6–10, 30–8. Given that Louis XIII had still not produced an heir, it is hard to avoid the conclusion that the most congenial solution for both the king and Richelieu was to prevent Gaston remarrying at all.

persuaded to return to France, Gaston was either at the centre of conspiracies, under suspicion in their immediate aftermath, or in voluntary exile.[69] Richelieu did not have to compete against the individual who had the strongest claim to military command under the king, and who would certainly have used this position in a manner harmful to the cardinal and his clientele.

Instead, the path was eased towards a working relationship with Henri II de Bourbon, prince de Condé, who was to become a central figure amongst the commanders of the later 1630s. Next in line to the throne after Gaston, whose first marriage had produced only one daughter, Condé could see considerable advantage in weakening Gaston's position within France.[70] On the other hand, Condé felt himself threatened by the next princely line to the throne, represented by his cousin Louis de Bourbon, comte de Soissons, who profited from persistent rumours of Condé's illegitimacy to strengthen his own claim to a succession which, even after 1638, appeared anything but assured in the king's line.[71]

The result of these calculations was that Condé proved an early and committed ally of Richelieu, who reciprocated this support.[72] Richelieu needed a collaborator in the royal family, especially after the definitive break with the Queen Mother in 1630. It was also important for Richelieu not to be seen to be denying the claims of all of the *princes du sang* to military commands. The working relationship which was to culminate in the marriage of Condé's son to Richelieu's niece, Claire-Clémence de Maillé-Brézé, began with the appointment of Condé to the main army operating against the Huguenot strongholds in the Midi during 1628.

The absence of Gaston spared Richelieu from one dangerous source of demands for military command in the period down to 1635. The alliance of the duke of Savoy with Spain during the second, 1630, campaign of the Mantuan war, and the French invasions of the territory of the duke of Lorraine after late 1631, saved him from another hazard – the convention that the princes of foreign allies should receive the command of any forces within or close to their territory not directly commanded by the French king. The subsequent duke of Savoy, Vittorio Amedeo I, was married to Louis XIII's sister, and when he was attracted into an alliance with France, Richelieu had no choice but to accept his appointment as *capitaine général* of the Franco-Savoyard army raised for the 1635 campaign in north Italy.[73] From the outset suspicions were voiced about his commitment to the alliance and about his break with Spain. His reluctant subordinate Charles de Blanchefort, maréchal de Créqui, accused him of sabotaging the siege of Valenza by permitting a Spanish relief force to enter the town.[74]

---

[69] Dethan, *Gaston d'Orléans*, pp. 73–106.
[70] Siri, *Anecdotes*, pp. 111–12.
[71] Aumale, *Princes de Condé*, II. 245–8.
[72] Aumale, *Princes de Condé*, III. 180–91; Jouanna, *Le devoir de révolte*, pp. 215–17.
[73] SHAT A¹ 26, pce 65, 15 July 1635, text of commission.
[74] See chapter 2, pp. 116–17.

The ministry and the high command

Richelieu had little scope to deny military commands to *grands* at this social level, and was simply fortunate that Gaston, Soissons or Charles IV of Lorraine could be excluded through political *force majeure*. Below this level, however, there was considerable potential to exploit rivalries amongst families of similar rank, and here Richelieu was able to pursue a more proactive policy, deliberately excluding certain families of *les grands* from military power. Of these, the most obvious victim was the extended Guise/Lorraine clan. Hostility between Richelieu's family and the various branches of this *prince étranger* dynasty may have extended back as far as the reign of Henri III, when Richelieu's father had been subordinated to the duc de Guise at Court, and had taken a strongly monarchist line at the time when the Guise were the directors of the *Sainte Ligue*.[75] From the outset of the ministry, Richelieu's aim was to weaken and undermine the various branches of the Guise-Lorraine family and to deprive them of opportunities for military command. The hostility was unambiguous, and reached its ultimate extent in the invasion and occupation of the duchy of Lorraine, on whose sovereignty the status of the Guise and their cousins rested.

Just as Richelieu's elevation to the charge of *grand maître et surintendant de la navigation* had allowed him to exclude the duc de Montmorency from the admiralty of the Atlantic, so it also allowed him to plan the elimination of the Mediterranean *amirauté du Levant*, held by Charles de Lorraine, fourth duc de Guise, seeking to have him bought out in 1629.[76] This initial attempt to deprive Guise became bogged down by Richelieu's refusal to pay the price for the *amirauté* demanded by the duke. However, when Guise supported Marie de Médicis in 1630 it provided an opportunity not just to suppress the *amirauté*, but to remove Guise from the governorship of Provence, breaking the power of the family in the south of France.[77] Guise died in exile in 1640; his brother, Claude de Lorraine, duc de Chevreuse, never received a military command, despite distancing himself from the conspiratorial activities of his duchess, Marie de Rohan-Montbazon.[78]

The Elbeuf branch of the Guise family was also excluded from commands: Charles de Lorraine, duc d'Elbeuf, resentful of Richelieu's policies towards his

---

[75] François de Richelieu held the office of *grand prévôt* which subordinated him to Henri de Lorraine, third duc de Guise, who was *grand maître de France*. Joseph Bergin warns against any assumption that this automatically created hostility between the two families: *Rise of Richelieu*, pp. 20, 27–8. However, as the hostility between the *Ligue* and Henri III mounted in the later 1580s, it is difficult to see how relations with the loyalist François de Richelieu could have been maintained. Richelieu was involved in action taken against the *Ligue* after the murder of Henri, duc de Guise and the cardinal of Lorraine, and was one of the first courtiers to declare for Henri of Navarre after the assassination of Henri III: M. Deloche, *Le père du cardinal* (Paris, 1923), pp. 261–77.

[76] Avenel, III. 173–4 n. 4 [1628]; Grillon, IV. 689–90, 1 Dec. 1629, Charles Sanguin to Richelieu, refers to Guise's possible acquiescence in the loss of the *amirauté*, but the negotiations continued into 1630; Boiteux, *Richelieu*, pp. 137–43.

[77] Bergin, *Cardinal Richelieu*, pp. 112–13; Constant, *Les conjurateurs*, pp. 79–80; James, 'Administration and development', pp. 99–104.

[78] L. Battifol, *La duchesse de Chevreuse* (Paris, 1924), pp. 181–95; Constant, *Les conjurateurs*, pp. 95–6.

family, was exiled in 1631 when he gave support to Gaston's unapproved marriage with Elbeuf's kinswoman, Marguerite of Lorraine, sister of duke Charles IV.[79] Only one member of the Guise family was involved in the military activities of this period. In a strategy that is a distinctive aspect of aristocratic family policy – an opportunistic 'hedging of bets' – the younger brother of Elbeuf, Henri de Lorraine, comte d'Harcourt, served in the royal armies throughout the later 1620s and early 1630s, though he did not receive a senior command at this time.[80]

This offensive against the Guise strengthened Richelieu's relations with some of the families who had previously shown their hostility towards the Guise/Lorraine clan. In particular, it encouraged the allegiance of a group of traditional, loyalist Huguenot *grands*, notably Jacques-Nompar de Caumont, duc de La Force, the maréchal de Châtillon and the maréchal de Créqui. Both La Force and Châtillon were prepared to support policies opposed to the interests of the Guise and were heavily involved in the campaigns to overrun the duchy of Lorraine.[81] When a commander was needed for the army to be sent against the comte de Soissons' invasion in 1641, it was Châtillon who was chosen, his loyalty outweighing his mediocre military record.[82]

Even more intriguing than gaining the loyalty of these Huguenot *grands*, Richelieu's obvious hostility to the Guise clan permitted him to achieve a tenuous working relationship with the duc d'Epernon and his sons. Epernon's own hostility to the Guise can be traced back to the 1580s, when Henri de Lorraine, third duc de Guise, was the main protagonist in the conspiracy which disgraced Epernon at Court. Epernon's possession of the governorship of Metz, always vulnerable to the ambitions and the juridical claims of the dukes of Lorraine, led him to look favourably on the cardinal's military activities which were consolidating French control in this area.[83] In contrast to this well-founded hostility to the Guise clan, Epernon and Richelieu had found themselves working together after 1617 to reestablish their political fortunes through a *rapprochement* between Marie de Médicis and Louis XIII.[84] In 1626 the duke notified Richelieu of Gaston

---

[79] Avenel, IV. 109–10, [end Mar. 1631], Louis XIII to Catherine-Henriette de Bourbon, duchesse d'Elbeuf.

[80] AAE MD 815, fo. 101, Aug. 1635, Harcourt to Richelieu, affirming his *fidélité* and requesting Richelieu to intercede with the king to provide him with a *charge*.

[81] La Force commanded the army of Lorraine from 1633: AAE MD France 808, fo. 119, 27 Oct. 1633, Chavigny to Claude Bouthillier; Châtillon was nominated to command the army of Lorraine in 1635, but the decision was subsequently changed and he was granted joint command with maréchal Brézé of the army that was to invade Flanders: SHAT A¹ 26, pce 32, Feb. 1635, *projet de pouvoir*; Aubery, I. 443, 30 Mar. 1635. Châtillon campaigned in Lorraine in 1639 and 1640, where he quarrelled vociferously and consistently with the governor, François de l'Hôpital, sieur du Hallier: AAE CP Lorraine 31, fos. 419, 433, 7 and 13 Sept. 1640.

[82] Hanotaux, *Richelieu*, IV. 437.

[83] Girard, *Espernon*, pp. 437, 448–53.

[84] Bergin, *Rise of Richelieu*, pp. 188–97; it may also have been significant that the powerful ministerial ally of Richelieu, chancellor Séguier, had begun his career as a client of Epernon, and used his influence with Richelieu to support the interests of his first patron: Mousnier (ed.), *Lettres*, I. 32.

d'Orléans' request that Metz be used as a base for the Chalais conspirators.[85] In 1632 he refused to move out of Guienne to give military support to the rebellion of his relative, the duc de Montmorency.[86]

Both as a military power-broker in south-west France, a key area for recruitment,[87] and as *colonel général de l'infanterie*, Epernon was important to the management of the war-effort. Moreover, as early as 1612 the *survivance* of the *colonel général* had been fixed upon Epernon's second son, Bernard de La Valette.[88] Recognizing that even the reduced powers of the *colonel général* ensured that the holder held significant patronage and influence in the armies, Richelieu managed to achieve an alliance with the future holder: in 1634 the duc de La Valette was married to Richelieu's first cousin, Marie de Pontchâteau.[89]

The dramatic quarrel between Epernon and Richelieu's *fidèle*, Henri de Sourdis, archbishop of Bordeaux, certainly damaged Epernon's relations with Richelieu after 1633.[90] But this was counterbalanced by the duc de La Valette's marriage into the Richelieu family, and the establishment of the cardinal de La Valette, his younger brother, as one of Richelieu's most trusted military commanders.[91] As with the comte d'Harcourt, it is not clear whether the *fidélité* of cardinal de La Valette should be seen simply as the personal ambition of a younger son, or part of a sophisticated family *politique* aimed at sustaining as many divergent political interests as possible. What is clear is that the cardinal enjoyed Richelieu's trust, even after his father and brother had been disgraced in the wake of the Fuenterrabía episode, and, until his premature death in 1639, cardinal de La Valette received increasingly important military commands.[92]

The exclusion of the Guise clan brought Richelieu the support of other families; his attack on the Vendôme family proved equally fruitful. The opportunity to remove the family permanently from the political and military stage came in 1626, when the two Vendôme sons of Henri IV by Gabrielle d'Estrées were disgraced in the aftermath of the Chalais conspiracy: Alexandre de Bourbon, the *grand prieur* died in prison at Vincennes in 1629, his brother, César de Bourbon, finally escaped to England, where he remained until Louis XIII's death.[93] Their close links with the Lorraine – César had married Françoise de

---

[85] Girard, *Espernon*, pp. 417–18; Fessenden, 'Epernon', p. 55; Mouton, *Duc et le roi*, p. 177.
[86] Girard, *Espernon*, pp. 466–70.
[87] Chaboche, 'Soldats français', 15: only the provinces on the eastern frontier and Normandy provided a higher proportion of the troops recruited for French service.
[88] Girard, *Espernon*, pp. 261–2; it had simultaneously been arranged that Epernon's eldest son, Henri de Nogaret, duc de Candale, would receive a baton of *maréchal* as soon as he was sufficiently experienced.
[89] Girard, *Espernon*, pp. 501–4.
[90] Fessenden, 'Epernon', pp. 87–120.
[91] Noailles, *Cardinal de la Valette*, pp. 94–115.
[92] Noailles, *Cardinal de La Valette*, pp. 464–537.
[93] Constant, *Les conjurateurs*, pp. 84–5; J.-P. Desprat, *Les bâtards d'Henri IV. L'épopée des Vendômes, 1594–1727* (Paris,1994), pp. 212–38.

Responses and reactions

Lorraine-Mercoeur – had won them enemies amongst the other families. Moreover, their position as the most recently legitimized family of royal bastards ensured the lasting animosity of the two other lines of *princes légitimés*, the Longueville and the Angoulême. Richelieu's exclusion of the Vendôme was the basis of an alliance with these two rival families. Charles de Valois, duc d'Angoulême, was given a series of commands into the first years of open war and his son, Louis-Emmanuel, comte d'Alais, held the *colonel général de la cavalerie légère*, while Henri II d'Orléans, duc de Longueville, was consistently favoured in the distribution of military commands until his appointment as one of the plenipotentiaries at the Westphalia negotiations in 1644.[94] Longueville's regular appointments reflected another aspect of the power of the *grands*; his possession of the governorship of Normandy enabled him to levy troops on his own account. In late 1636, for example, he was to raise some 8,000 infantry and 2,000 cavalry in his province to reinforce the French army in Burgundy.[95] The concern of these two families to strengthen their own position against *arrivistes* was further rewarded by Richelieu when François-Annibal, maréchal d'Estrées, maternal uncle of the Vendôme, was disgraced while commanding the army moving towards Trier in 1633. Richelieu suspected him of complicity in Châteauneuf's conspiracy, and although the charges against him were dismissed, the cardinal took the opportunity to bring his military career to an end.[96]

The final factor in shaping and defining this group of commanders was the prolonged fall-out from the Day of Dupes, and the elimination of the Queen Mother's supporters from military commands during the early 1630s. Throughout 1630 Richelieu's correspondence indicates growing uneasiness with those commanders whose posts were owed to the patronage of Marie de Médicis. Louis de Marillac's letters from the army in Champagne are a litany of complaints about the progress of the war, the inadequacy of his allocation of troops and resources and his fears of a possible Imperial invasion.[97] François de Betstein, maréchal de Bassompierre, who had enjoyed command of a separate force at La Rochelle in 1628, had been appointed ambassador to the Swiss cantons in 1630, a step taken, he believed, to remove him from the Italian theatre.[98] Bassompierre subsequently joined in the campaign in Savoy, but Richelieu had already marked him down as talented, but unreliable. His close links with the Guise family, which had culminated in a secret marriage to Louise de Lorraine, princesse de Conti, undoubtedly increased Richelieu's suspicions and hostility. The opportunity was

---

[94] Hanotaux, *Richelieu*, IV. 439.
[95] SHAT A¹ 30, fo. 31, 7 Oct. 1636, de Noyers to Longueville.
[96] François-Annibal, maréchal d'Estrées, *Mémoires sur la régence de Marie de Médicis et sur celle d'Anne d'Autriche*, ed. P. Bonnefon (Paris, 1910), pp. x–xi; Hanotaux, *Richelieu*, IV. 453.
[97] See chapter 2, p. 95.
[98] Bassompierre, *Mémoires*, XXI. 236–7. Bassompierre initially blamed the maréchal de Schomberg for this manoeuvre, but claimed that Richelieu aligned himself with Schomberg and against Bassompierre's counsel by supporting the 1630 invasion of Savoy: XXI. 239–42.

The ministry and the high command

provided to remove both Marillac and Bassompierre in November 1630. Richelieu's most illustrious victim was Henri II, duc de Montmorency. It has already been suggested that Richelieu's pressure on Montmorency to sell the office of the *amirauté du Ponant*, and the subsequent manoeuvre to suppress the office of *connétable* to keep it out of the duke's hands had soured relations between the two men. Despite this, Montmorency received one of the military commands in the army of Italy in 1630, and indeed Louis XIII created him a *maréchal* in that year. He was too important and influential for Richelieu to deprive him of high military status until he had actually taken the step into active revolt, a move which played directly into Richelieu's hands. It is significant that the Montmorency inheritance, rather than falling to the king as was customary in cases of high treason, was parcelled out to Condé on the basis of his marriage to Montmorency's sister, Charlotte.[99] Once again, Richelieu was working to bind himself to a particular group of the *grands* through the ruin or exclusion of others.

A victim of Richelieu's suspicions who did not need to cross the line into open treason was Jean du Caylar de Saint-Bonnet, maréchal de Toiras, disgraced in 1633 despite an outstanding military career which had included the heroic defence of the Fort Saint-Martin on the Île de Ré against the English in 1627, and lengthy defence of Casale in 1629–30.[100] But Richelieu stood high in the king's favour in 1633; he had crushed most of his accessible enemies, and Toiras, who was neither a *créature* nor clearly aligned with Richelieu's group of *grands*, could be removed without questions being asked about the wisdom of destroying the career of an outstanding field commander.[101]

By 1634 Richelieu had taken advantage of a favourable military and political climate to reshape the high command of the army into a group which reflected his own dynastic, familial ambitions and his aristocratic alliances. This system worked well, provided that the scale of the French war-effort remained limited and Richelieu's policies appeared successful to the king. In this situation a relatively small number of armies would almost without fail be commanded by one of Richelieu's family or a loyalist *grand*, a situation which Louis XIII would be prepared to accept, maintaining considerable power in the cardinal's hands to nominate or veto commanders.

After 1635, however, the situation changed dramatically. Following the battle of Nördlingen and the collapse of the military effectiveness of Sweden and the German protestant forces, France was pushed inexorably towards open war with the Habsburg powers, a war fought on a scale greater than any previous conflict and where military and political success proved altogether more elusive. The

---

[99] Aumale, *Princes de Condé*, III. 250–2.
[100] Baudier, *Maréchal de Toiras*, pp. 234–47; Toiras was permitted to enter the service of the duke of Savoy, in whose army he was killed in 1636.
[101] Hanotaux, *Richelieu*, IV. 455–6.

growth in the scale of warfare – the transition to a conflict fought with six, sometimes seven, army-corps simultaneously – required a larger pool of commanding officers, and forced Richelieu to reverse his policy of restricting such appointments to a core of family and allies amongst the *grands*. The sudden change after 1635 from French success achieved at low cost to a much more doubtful and dangerous military situation reduced Louis XIII's willingness to accept Richelieu's nominations to military command. Doubts about the wisdom or justification for the war, which had been muted during the successful years of small-scale and opportunist policies, became more overt now that Richelieu seemed to have committed France to a struggle that might test her resources up to, and possibly beyond, breaking point. As the war seemed to tip towards imminent disaster in 1636, so Richelieu's control of the high command was further undermined. Partly as a result of the decision to give priority to Condé's and La Meilleraye's lengthy and unsuccessful siege of Dôle in Franche-Comté, which had gravely weakened French forces on the north-east frontier, a formidable Spanish army was able to push down from Flanders into Champagne, capturing Corbie in August. The organization of the army which would attempt to push back the Spanish seems to have depended more upon the king than Richelieu.[102] In a gesture which indicated Louis' declining confidence in Richelieu's management, the army was placed under the command of Gaston and the comte de Soissons.[103] Châtillon and La Force were attached to the army, but played a largely passive role in all the decisions of the *conseil de guerre*, presumably because they wished to distance themselves from Richelieu's declining fortunes. Only La Meilleraye was present to try to sustain the ministerial interest, but with little success. Gaston deployed the entire army around Corbie and ostentatiously disregarded Richelieu's instructions to engage the retreating Spanish forces.[104] Only when the king arrived in person could the army be pushed, belatedly, into a wider offensive. Richelieu's own presence with the forces at a time of military frustration and political uncertainty allowed the Amiens plot to be hatched against him, with the support of both Gaston and Soissons.[105]

The campaign of 1636 represented the low-point of Richelieu's control of the armies; in subsequent years he was able to recover some of his influence with the king and some of his capacity to control the allocation of commands to the army-corps. But the continuing scale of the war-effort forced Richelieu to look further afield for potential commanders; by the end of the ministry this had amounted to the virtual abandonment of his earlier policy. In the first case, the increase in the

---

[102] Hanotaux, *Richelieu*, v. 162–8.
[103] SHAT A¹ 32, fo. 113, 7 July 1636 (Soissons); fos. 165–6, 31 Aug. (Gaston d'Orléans).
[104] AAE MD 1678, fos. 302–4, [misdated 1 Sept. – actually considerably later in the autumn] 1636, anonymous report [La Meilleraye or Chavigny] concerning the failure of the army to obey Richelieu's instructions or to seize the initiative in engaging the retreating Spanish.
[105] Montrésor, *Mémoires*, III. 204–5; Constant, *Les conjurateurs*, pp. 122–5.

number of campaign theatres, bringing in Picardy, Provence and, by 1636 and 1637, Guienne and Languedoc, forced Richelieu to accept an *ad hoc* system of giving military commands to the provincial governors who were in place. French resources were committed to the main theatres of Champagne, Lorraine, Burgundy, the Rhineland and Italy; faced with the need to counter Habsburg incursions elsewhere, Richelieu relied upon provincial governors to raise troops at their own expense in order to supplement what were usually extremely small – or non-existent – royal forces, and to lead these against the invaders. The results were unsatisfactory from all points of view.

A number of governors – Honoré d'Albert, duc de Chaulnes, in Picardy, Nicolas de l'Hospital, maréchal de Vitry, in Provence, Charles de Schomberg, duc d'Halluin, in Languedoc and Epernon in Guienne – were confirmed in their opinion that they had the automatic right to command all the forces that might be placed within their provinces, and to obstruct or resist anyone appointed over their heads. At the same time, with the notable exception of Schomberg, who won his baton of *maréchal* leading a largely local force of troops to defeat the Spanish invasion of Languedoc at Leucate in 1637, they were reluctant to commit their own financial resources or those of the provinces to an energetic pursuit of military objectives. Chaulnes was heavily criticized for his failure to prevent Spanish incursions into Picardy in 1635, just as Soissons, acting in his capacity as governor of Champagne, was to be criticized in the following year.[106] In both cases the governors had far too few troops to resist enemy incursions, and had seen numerous regular troops in their provinces reallocated to other theatres. Both governors felt with some justification that they were being placed in overall command by a ministry whose principal aim was to force them to raise new troops on their own credit in a dangerous and unstable military situation. One of the accusations levelled at Soissons in late 1636 was that he had written to the duc de Longueville expressing disgust with the 'grands employs' that he had received from the king, calling them 'commissions ruineuses' and complaining of the heavy costs involved in maintaining his army.[107] Military command in these cases was not being used as a sign of confidence and the basis of a working relationship with *grand* families, but as a desperate measure, thrust on to governors whose provinces were under threat and who suffered all the financial and personal risks of command with none of the advantages.

This type of command could weaken and undermine those ties which had hitherto been cultivated by Richelieu. The demands placed upon Epernon and Bernard de La Valette from 1636 became increasingly heavy. Expected to raise the

---

[106] Avenel, v. 242, 18 Sept. 1635; AAE MD 821, fo. 106, 25 July 1636, Chavigny to Mazarin; MD 1678, fos. 519–24, [Nov. 1636], account of the recapture of Corbie.

[107] AAE MD 1678, fo. 519, [Nov. 1636]; MD 822, fo. 189, 10 Nov. 1636, Chavigny to Bullion, giving details of the extent to which the duc de Chaulnes had committed his own funds to the defence of Picardy during 1635 and 1636.

Responses and reactions

troops to expel the Spanish from Saint-Jean-de-Luz entirely at their own expense, and that of the province, they were subsequently criticized by Richelieu for a failure to act sufficiently quickly or decisively against the invading forces.[108] As the war on the Spanish frontier grew more important, the clashes between Epernon and the central government grew more intense. Having been expected to organize the defence of Guienne in 1636, Epernon considered it an affront that any other *grand* should be given command of a force within the province, and an indication that Richelieu was no longer prepared to abide by the working relationship between the two families.

The arrival of Condé as commander-in-chief in Guienne and Languedoc, with orders to organize an expedition into Atlantic Spain in the next (1638) campaign, brought these tensions to a head. They had been sharpened by the tactless way in which Condé's appointment had been presented, making it appear as a punishment for Epernon's dilatoriness during the 1637 campaign.[109] The subsequent defeat during 1638 at Fuenterrabía may have been precipitated by Bernard, duc de La Valette, who was accused of failing to cooperate with Condé's main siege force.[110] However, the reporting and interpretation of the events and actions surrounding the defeat was extremely confused.[111] The main consideration was not to establish responsibility, but the fact that Condé was vital to Richelieu's political and dynastic strategies, particularly as the projected marriage of Condé's son to Richelieu's niece had yet to be finalized. Having previously tried to buy the support of the Epernon family, Richelieu now decided to destroy the duc de La Valette and his father, and to abandon the attempt to work through the traditional source of power in Guienne.

The decisiveness of this break is underlined by the decision to appoint the comte d'Harcourt as governor of Guienne after the death of Epernon in 1642.[112] Richelieu's apparent volte-face, placing a member of the house of Lorraine in the governorship of one of their most inveterate opponents, can also be explained by the ever-increasing demands of the war-effort and the shortage of capable commanders. Harcourt's military ability and willingness to profess personal *fidélité* to Richelieu, despite his family affiliations, could attract the cardinal's attention both for the command of army-corps and, in this case, for a provincial governorship with an important military dimension. In 1639 Harcourt had been married to Marguerite de Cambout, Richelieu's first cousin, signalling that an arrangement

---

[108] BN Ms.fr. 6644, fo. 275, 28 Oct. 1637, Girard to cardinal de La Valette; Avenel, v. 871, 10 Oct. 1637, letter from the king expressing displeasure at failure of Epernon to engage the Spanish; Girard, *Espernon*, p. 546, emphasizes that the crown failed to keep its promises to provide financial assistance.
[109] Avenel, v. 871, 10 Oct. 1637.
[110] See chapter 2, pp. 132–3.
[111] See Griffet, *Louis XIII*, III. 141–4, for a view that is far more sympathetic to La Valette.
[112] Between Epernon's disgrace in early 1639 and his death in 1642 the governorship had been exercised by Condé.

The ministry and the high command

had been reached to overlook traditional dynastic antagonisms.[113] Richelieu saw this as an important alliance: he needed the military skills of Harcourt to prop up the war-effort; Harcourt did more than anyone else to retrieve the French position in north Italy that had deteriorated since the unexpected death of Vittorio Amedeo I of Savoy in 1637.[114] Yet it also implied the abandonment of a dynastic policy that had previously brought a number of other *grand* families into an alliance with the cardinal. Harcourt's marriage allowed him to found a new branch of the Lorraine, distinct from the Guise and the Elbeuf branches of the family, and to contribute decisively to the family's dramatic recovery in the later seventeenth century.[115]

Richelieu's venture into a marriage alliance with the House of Lorraine at least brought the military capacities of Harcourt into the high command. That which linked Antoine III de Gramont, comte de Guiche and sovereign prince of Bidache, to Richelieu's family through his marriage to Françoise-Marguerite de Chivré, another of Richelieu's cousins on the du Plessis side, was less fortunate.[116] Raised to the status of *maréchal* through Richelieu's intervention, Gramont was placed in command of one of the two armies on the Flanders' frontier in 1642, failed to cooperate with the other commander, Harcourt, and was heavily defeated by a Spanish invading army at Honnecourt.[117] Contemporaries drew the same conclusion that they had previously drawn about Brézé and La Meilleraye, that these military appointments reflected patronage based upon Richelieu family interests rather than military competence or general suitability for command.[118]

Appointment to other commands reflected the real practical difficulties faced by Richelieu in finding suitable *grands* who had not been previously disgraced or removed. The Huguenot Henri, duc de Rohan, whose considerable military ability had been deployed in resisting the crown during the 1620s, had been partially restored to favour in the early 1630s, and had served in a number of supporting roles.[119] In 1635 Richelieu transferred him from the duchy of Lorraine to assume command of the army operating in the Valtelline, where Rohan's leadership brought considerable military success, rare enough in the first years of

---

[113] Ironically, Marguerite de Cambout was the sister of Marie de Pontchâteau, who had been married by Richelieu to Bernard de La Valette in 1634.
[114] See chapter 2, pp. 139–41, 144–5.
[115] Anselme, *Histoire généalogique*, III. 499–501.
[116] Gramont, *Mémoires*, LVI. 308.
[117] SHAT A¹ 71, pce 45, 26 Jan. 1642, *pouvoir* for Gramont; concerning responsibility for the defeat at Honnecourt, see chapter 2, pp. 157–8.
[118] For Brézé, see Bassompierre, *Mémoires*, xxi. 389–90; for La Meilleraye, see Puységur, *Guerres*, II. 1–3, Tallement de Réaux, *Historiettes*, I. 326, and Bussy-Rabutin, *Mémoires*, I. 28–29; For Gramont, see Tallement de Réaux, *Historiettes*, I. 529–30. The Mantuan representative in Paris, Giustiniano Priandi, reported that there was much criticism of the appointment of cardinal de La Valette to command the army of Italy in 1638, an appointment which reflected Richelieu's favour for his *créature*: ASMa AG E. xv. 3, vol. 679, 30 Mar. 1638.
[119] Laugel, *Rohan*, pp. 273–318.

Responses and reactions

war.[120] It is unclear whether Richelieu continued to distrust Rohan, or whether it was assumed mistakenly that the Huguenot duke would seek to purge his previous history by committing unlimited private funds to ensuring that the army of the Valtelline would continue to operate. What is clear was that the army was starved of official financial support and collapsed in early 1637. Richelieu by this time felt his position even more threatened by military failure, and he made no attempt to hide his anger with Rohan; the duke considered it prudent not to return to France, and ended his career as a gentleman-ranker in the army of Saxe-Weimar.[121]

The rise of Turenne towards senior military command was to have important consequences for the French war-effort after Richelieu's death. During the ministry, however, the willingness to promote the military careers of the La Tour d'Auvergne, protestants or recent converts, who possessed the sovereign territory of Sedan, should be seen as a further sign of Richelieu's shortage of able generals, and of his acceptance of conventional assumptions about the right of the highest aristocratic families to hold commands. Frédéric-Maurice de La Tour d'Auvergne, duc de Bouillon, and head of the House, made little attempt to hide his hostility to Richelieu, and had been frequently involved in conspiracies, sometimes based in Bouillon's territories outside France. Nevertheless, after his reconciliation with the king in 1641, there was simply no reason, given the numbers of army-corps in operation, to prevent him assuming a command for which his rank made him eligible.[122] In 1642, at the same time that he became involved in the Cinq Mars conspiracy, he received command of the army of Italy.[123] His younger brother, Turenne, possibly playing a part in a wider family *politique*, had avoided complicity in conspiracies against the cardinal; nevertheless he remained under suspicion throughout Richelieu's ministry as a consequence of his brother's activities.[124] As a result, Turenne had to wait until Mazarin's ministry to receive a full command and to be made a *maréchal*.[125]

The duc de Bouillon had benefited from the same conventions governing the military hierarchy within the *grands* as might other, even more unreliable, sovereign princes. Richelieu was even prepared to grant a military command to Duke Charles IV of Lorraine as one of the concessions of the 1641 Peace of Saint-Germain. The prospect was averted by the duke's decision to reenter Spanish

---

[120] Rohan, *Mémoire*, XIX. 75–123; Laugel, *Rohan*, pp. 319–33.
[121] Avenel, v. 762, 28 Mar. 1637: blame was shared with the *surintendant des finances*, but Rohan was still unprepared to return to France: Laugel, *Rohan*, pp. 348–57.
[122] Saumières, *Duc de Bouillon*, pp. 113–14, suggests that the choice of the army of Italy also reflected Richelieu's concern to distance Bouillon from the court.
[123] SHAT A¹ 71, fo. 44, 24 Jan. 1642, *pouvoir* for Bouillon.
[124] Avenel, VI. 946, 27 June 1642, Richelieu to de Noyers, concerning suspicions of Turenne; Bérenger, *Turenne*, pp. 177–85.
[125] Turenne received the baton of *maréchal* on 16 Nov. 1643, and was made *lieutenant général* of the army of Germany on 3 Dec: Baluze, *Maison d'Auvergne*, I. 459–60.

The ministry and the high command

service after only a few months of reluctant alliance with France, rather than by any reconsideration on Louis XIII and Richelieu's part about the wisdom of such an appointment.[126]

MANAGEMENT BY INTIMIDATION: THE ATTEMPT TO CONTROL THE
HIGH COMMAND AFTER 1635

There was thus no serious attempt to enforce a permanent reduction of the power held by the key aristocratic *officiers* within the military structure; there remained also a general preparedness to accept the principle of a high command dominated by the *grands*. The most serious challenge created by this situation was the possibility that the individual army-corps might be turned into instruments of aristocratic separatism or revolt. With the lower ranks of the officer-corps dominated by the clienteles of the high command, and with the latter sustaining part of the costs of military operations and making most decisions in the field, this was certainly perceived as a threat, although in the event down to 1643 no commander led his army-corps against the ministerial regime. Short of active revolt, however, there was a more characteristic level of insubordination and evasion of instructions from the centre, a marked reluctance of commanders to play their appointed role in the conduct of ministerial strategy. This was compounded by failure to take the initiative in campaigning, and by a reluctance to push beyond a single, clearly defined objective.

The typical explanation for this puts the blame on the personal qualities of the commanders; Richelieu, it is argued, had been saddled at the outset of his ministry with a collection of inferior generals, most of whom lacked the military skills, charisma and daring required for success in the field.[127] The cardinal was developing a new generation of commanders who would remedy these defects, but the benefits of this policy were not fully evident until the mid 1640s.[128] It was an opinion that Richelieu himself did much to propagate, presenting a picture of *grands* like La Force, Angoulême and Châtillon as possessing only limited capacities and lacking commitment to the aggressive prosecution of a campaign.[129] In similar vein, Richelieu suggested that Henri II de Condé, Charles de

---

[126] Aubery, II. 655–8, 29 Mar. 1641, terms of treaty of Saint-Germain; Avenel, VI. 769, 771, 6 and 15 Apr. 1641, Richelieu to Chavigny.
[127] This was certainly the interpretation which Richelieu himself offered to the king: Avenel, VI. 129, 31 Aug. 1638.
[128] A detailed account of this argument is provided in Hanotaux, *Richelieu*, IV. 475–98.
[129] Hanotaux, *Richelieu*, IV. 438, 435–7, Richelieu's comments extracted from a report on all those who had held senior commands since the siege of La Rochelle: BN Ms.fr. 15644. Richelieu's opinions were clearly held by many at court and were picked up, for example, by Viscount Scudamore, English ambassador in Paris, who in 1635 wrote of La Force's 'frigidy, whereunto his age disposes him', and that Châtillon was using the excuse of waiting for his baggage to return from Holland to avoid recommencing the campaign in Picardy: BL Add. MS 35097, fo. 7, early Oct. 1635; fo. 5, 18 Sept.

Responses and reactions

Schomberg, the ducs de Longueville and de Chaulnes, lacked resilience or organizational ability, and were unable to seize military opportunities. Those Richelieu positively distrusted – Marillac, Montmorency, Toiras, Rohan – were branded not just as military incompetents but as real or potential traitors.[130] The view of a high command ill-suited to the tasks that confronted it fits neatly into the scheme laid out in the *Testament politique*, where Richelieu warms to his theme that 'Il n'y a point de nation au monde si peu propre à la guerre que la nostre.'[131]

The notion that Richelieu had the misfortune to depend upon men so much inferior to himself for the execution of his designs provides support for a traditional image of the cardinal as the visionary statesman raised above his mundane contemporaries by his abilities and his 'grand sens de l'Etat'. This view requires some qualification. It is certainly true that many of Richelieu's commanders appear lacklustre and second-rate in comparison with a generation which included the Grand Condé, Turenne, Jean de Gassion and Fabert. But few generations produce more than a handful of commanders with outstanding military qualities. If the 1640s appears fortunate in this respect, it could be contrasted with successive decades of Louis XIV's reign, or much of the eighteenth century, when the number of talented commanders at any one time was certainly no greater than that available to Richelieu. The real problem was not that Richelieu had an unusually small number of able generals at his disposal, but a much more general issue – that an increasing number of army-corps demanded a pool of military talent greater than the available commanders were able to supply.

If it is allowed that Richelieu threw away the considerable military talents of the duc de Rohan and the maréchal de Toiras, then the outstanding commanders of the later 1630s and 1640s were most probably Harcourt and Guébriant. Surrounding them were a large number of other commanders who were not disastrously poor or incompetent, but who would be effective in some circumstances and not in others. The fundamental criticism that can be levelled against the ministerial regime is that it created a political atmosphere in which these second-rank commanders were pushed towards unenterprising and limited activity rather than being encouraged to take initiatives and to run risks in the hope of achieving military advantage. Much of what has been treated as inherent in the personalities of the commanders was in fact generated by ministerial pressures. The vulnerability of Richelieu and his fellow ministers, and the awareness that their policies enjoyed no clear consensus, would always ensure that the first priority in managing the high command was not military ability but loyalty. Those whose loyalty could not be assured by close family connections or

---

[130] Hanotaux, IV. 442–63.
[131] Richelieu, *Testament politique*, p. 296. The extent to which Richelieu is deploying a traditional rhetoric in this argument is discussed in chapter 1, pp. 73–4.

The ministry and the high command

overt *fidélité* which implicated them in the fate of the ministerial regime needed to be coerced or intimidated into adherence. In the interests of trying to compel this obedience, and in reaction to military failure that might have dangerous repercussions for the stability of the ministerial regime, Richelieu pursued a series of expedients which reduced the effectiveness of the second-rank generals who inevitably formed the majority of field commanders.

The ministry's bid for obedience was based on fear. To those members of the high command whose loyalty was suspect or who were felt to be jeopardizing the war-effort by lack of commitment to ministerial policies, Richelieu offered threats, rigged trials and imprisonment, exile or execution. Arranged trials were followed by execution in the cases of the maréchal de Marillac, François de Jussac d'Ambleville, marquis de Saint-Preuil, the duc de La Valette (whose prudent flight to England meant that the execution was carried out in effigy) and a surprisingly large number of governors of individual *places*. The *maréchaux* Bassompierre and Vitry were placed in the Bastille for the duration of the ministry. Epernon, Henri d'Escoubleau de Sourdis, Toiras and Rohan were deprived of their commands and publicly disgraced with the loss of all public office.[132] That this was a deliberate policy is suggested in the *Testament politique*, where Richelieu proposed that 'Les châtiments de Marillac et du duc de Montmorency ont en un instant mis en leur devoir les grands de ce royaume, et j'ose asseurer que celuy de dix officiers et de cinquante soldats maintiendra les armées en discipline et en estat de faire tout ce que l'on voudra.'[133] Yet this was demonstrably not the case, above all because the motives for the application of such draconian tactics were ambiguous: were Richelieu's salutary examples punished for indiscipline and disobedience, for practical failure, or simply for opposition to the regime?

When Marillac was finally sentenced by a majority of the judges on the special tribunal, it was not for treachery or disobedience, but for the misappropriation of funds and the levy of illegal contributions.[134] These charges represented the prosecution's efforts to find a serious crime for which the judges were prepared to accept Marillac's guilt. The frequency of such offences committed by all commanders, and the inconsistency in imposing capital sentences, all provide evidence for the dubious nature of this trial.[135] It was recognized at the time that Richelieu wished to destroy the powerful nexus of *dévot* opponents who had sought to challenge his power on the 10/11 November 1630. To claim, as he did subsequently, that Marillac had shown himself 'déloyal et infidèle', and that this

---

[132] Though Toiras and Rohan, like Charles de Lorraine, fourth duc de Guise before them, wisely decided not to return to France when deprived of military command: Hanotaux, *Richelieu*, IV. 455–6.
[133] Richelieu, *Testament politique*, p. 301.
[134] AAE MD 806, fos. 1–17, 18–34, n.d. [1632]; Vaissière, *Maréchal de Marillac*, pp. 178–97.
[135] Despite ferocious pressure by Richelieu and a hand-picked tribunal, the capital sentence was still opposed by ten out of the twenty-three judges: Vaissière, *Maréchal de Marillac*, pp. 211–14.

had emerged at his trial, did little to justify his severity.[136] The other celebrated case, that of the *maréchal de camp* and governor of Arras, Saint-Preuil, raises similar doubts about the government's real motive for carrying out his trial and execution in 1641. Both Puységur and Bussy-Rabutin emphasize in their memoirs that Saint-Preuil was not eliminated for his supposed offence – massacring Spanish prisoners leaving Bapaume under a safe conduct – nor even the crime which formed the basis of his prosecution: 'quelques prétendues concussions'. Both memorialists suggest that the real motive was the hatred felt by Sublet de Noyers and, above all, the maréchal de La Meilleraye, who exploited their official positions and their standing with Richelieu to obtain the sentence.[137] Nor was the stance of the two authors a simple example of solidarity shown by other members of the *noblesse d'épée*. Puységur reports with approval the king's intervention in 1635 to ensure a capital sentence upon des Chapelles, who surrendered the *château* of Cirk, although this intervention overruled the decision of the formal *conseil de guerre* which had previously tried the governor.[138] Less well known, but perhaps more typical, was the execution of Heucourt, governor of Doullens, accused of treating with the Spanish for the surrender of the *place*. After the execution, Richelieu ordered the investigation to continue, in view of Heucourt's repeated denials of his treachery.[139] Similar uncertainty surrounds the attempted prosecution in 1639 of the governor of Leucate, Henri de Saint-Aunais, who Condé suggested was negotiating with the Spaniards. The charges seem highly improbable given the level of loyalty shown by the family, hereditary governors of Leucate for over a century, but on 4 November Condé had the governor arrested on vague and unsubstantiated charges of treason. When in due course Saint-Aunais was replaced by the dispossessed governor of Salces, Roger de Bussolts, comte d'Espenan, the suspicion grew that Richelieu and Condé were conspiring to place a favoured client in Leucate, a *place* within the jurisdiction of the governor of Languedoc, Schomberg.[140]

Some of this severity reflected the ministry's unease at the prospect of potential opponents who possessed access to military force. But as well as salutary examples made for political purposes, harsh sentences were imposed for simple military failure, sentences showing a complete disregard for any mitigating circumstances. The treatment of the three governors who surrendered their *places* in Champagne in the summer of 1636 was probably to be predicted, even though weak garrisons of the poorest-quality troops and inadequate supplies and artillery made pro-

---

[136] BN Ms.fr. 15644, fos. 852–7.
[137] Puységur, *Guerres*, II. 2–3; Bussy-Rabutin, *Mémoires*, I. 133–9. Bussy-Rabutin also suggests that his own 1641 imprisonment for five months in the Bastille reflected not the failure to maintain discipline over his regiment, but the hatred of de Noyers for his father: Bussy-Rabutin, *Mémoires*, I. 114–28.
[138] Puységur, *Guerres*, I. 165.
[139] Avenel, VI. 165, 13 Sept. 1638.
[140] Aumale, *Princes de Condé*, III. 410–13.

The ministry and the high command

tracted resistance to the Spanish army futile and probably suicidal.[141] Other cases seem less easily justified. Achille de Longueval, seigneur de Manicamp, whose military service in Germany and governorship of Colmar had been highly regarded, was none the less prosecuted for surrendering Rheinau.[142] The *place* had been abandoned by Saxe-Weimar who doubted that it was defensible, and Manicamp had received no financial support or reinforcements from the government.[143] A similarly vindictive response was evident in the prosecution of the comte de Pédamont for the surrender of Lunéville, and of Pierre-Pol de Percin, baron de Montgaillard, for the surrender of Breme in 1638.[144] In the latter case, Montgaillard had been singled out in the previous year by the *intendant* with the army of Italy for his willingness to absorb the costs of fortification related to his governorship while refusing anything more than the 1,000 *livres* of his salary.[145]

The execution of governors for surrendering their *places* created a climate of uncertainty about ministerial reactions which permeated the higher reaches of the command structure. Maréchal Vitry was thrown into the Bastille for allegedly offering limited cooperation to Harcourt and Sourdis in the recapture of the Îles de Lérins, regarded as a badly conducted and humiliating fiasco by Louis XIII and Richelieu. While it is clear that Bernard de La Valette did nothing to avert the defeat at Fuenterrabía, it is equally evident that he was not solely responsible for the débâcle, still less, that he had conspired to facilitate the Spanish victory.[146] These doubts were supported by the attitude of the picked tribunal, whose president, Nicolas de Bellièvre, threw out the prosecution's case, and had to be bullied by Richelieu into bringing a guilty verdict.[147] Epernon and La Valette, by their conspicuous lack of commitment to the war-effort, had cast themselves in the role of scapegoats for the third major defeat of the campaign. The second setback, the French failure to relieve Vercelli in Piedmont, had resulted in scarcely veiled threats made even to as well-established a *fidèle* as cardinal de La Valette.[148] Though he had received a series of naval commands as a favoured *créature* of Richelieu, Sourdis did not survive the cardinal's wrath at his failure to beat off the

---

[141] AAE MD 1676, fos. 474–81 [1635]: Corbie's garrison was recorded at seventy-three men at a *revue*, La Capelle's at eighty, Câtelet at eighty-two.

[142] SHAT A^1 47, fo. 21, 4 Oct. 1638: Avenel, VI. 108, 23 Aug. 1638.

[143] See chapter 2, pp. 129–31.

[144] SHAT A^1 49, fo. 184, 30 Oct. 1638; des Robert, *Campagnes de Charles IV*, II. 50–1; Noailles, *Cardinal de La Valette*, pp. 379–82.

[145] AAE CP Savoie 25, fo. 238, 14 July 1637, Argenson to de Noyers. Montgaillard was a client of the late duc de Créqui, but had no similar relationship with La Valette: Noailles, *Cardinal de La Valette*, p. 379.

[146] Both of these asserted in the *Factum du prince de Condé*, liberally rewritten by Richelieu: Avenel, VI. 195, [1638]. Contrast this with the earlier, undoctored, account by Sourdis: *Correspondance*, II. 56–67, 9 Sept. 1638.

[147] Hanotaux, *Richelieu*, V. 338 n. 4; Griffet, *Louis XIII*, III. 184–5, is more cynical, suggesting that 'après un dîner superbe que le roi leur fit donner', the picked tribunal had little difficulty in finding La Valette guilty on all counts.

[148] AAE CP Savoie 26, fo. 373, 19 July 1638, Richelieu to La Valette.

Responses and reactions

Spanish fleet attempting to relieve Tarragona, which forced the abandonment of the siege in August 1641. He was disgraced and subject to an investigation for his supposed misappropriation of funds, while his brother Charles, marquis de Sourdis, previously a well-regarded *maréchal de camp*, was also removed from military command.[149] On numerous other occasions no specific action was taken in response to military failures, but in the context of these notorious arbitrary punishments, threatening or abusive letters from Richelieu or the king following the abandonment of a siege or a defeat in the field would not be lightly dismissed.

All of this reveals a short-sightedness which can probably be explained by mounting exasperation at the failure of the war-effort to make significant progress. But the effect was predictable; threats and punishment for failure, not for overt disobedience, led commanders to adopt defensive strategies and passivity in the face of opportunities that might well have allowed them to seize military advantages. An example of the pernicious effects of Richelieu's reliance on fear is provided by Henri II de Condé, in Languedoc during 1639. Though Condé had escaped any judicial proceedings for his role in the 1638 defeat at Fuenterrabía, Richelieu had no intention of freeing him from all fear that there might be a subsequent investigation. Fuenterrabía was used by Richelieu to goad Condé into making greater efforts to achieve a significant military objective during the 1639 campaign.[150] By this time Condé had no confidence that he would be able to survive another setback. A marriage into the cardinal's family had after all not saved the duc de La Valette from disgrace, and Condé knew that the political importance of an alliance with a *prince du sang* would be no necessary guarantee of Richelieu's support. Condé began the campaign of 1639 outstandingly late, despite vociferous complaints from the centre, and pursued a policy aimed at minimizing risks throughout the campaign.[151] When the army at last advanced into Roussillon under the command of Condé's immediate subordinate, the maréchal de Schomberg, the objective selected was the relatively insignificant fortress of Salces, even though the absence of any significant Spanish resistance would have made a rapid strike towards Perpignan or Collioure feasible.[152] Condé assured the Court that Salces was just a prelude to more important gains but, in the face of reports of the gradual assembly of a Spanish relief force, the French troops simply held their positions. When the Spanish advanced to relieve Salces, the French high command decided to withdraw the bulk of their forces into Languedoc, simply leaving a garrison to hold Salces, when a direct attack on the Spanish forces while they were disorganized and over-extended might well have

---

[149] Sourdis, *Correspondance*, III. 66–72, Sept. 1641, series of letters concerning Sourdis' disgrace.
[150] See chapter 2, pp. 134–5; Aumale, *Princes de Condé*, III. 399–400, is explicit that Condé feared disgrace in late 1638.
[151] Avenel, VI. 345, 9 May 1639; the army did not move into Roussillon until mid-June.
[152] Avenel, VII. 213, 1 Apr. 1639, Richelieu to Schomberg: Salces 'ne méritait pas un siège . . . étant un château assez inutile, sis sur un roc qui n'ouvre point l'entrée du pays'; VI. 398, 19 June 1638: Richelieu had wished Condé to split his forces rather than concentrating upon Salces.

The ministry and the high command

driven them back into Catalonia. Two months passed before Condé considered himself ready to risk a relief operation against the Spanish besieging forces. Determined to obtain numerical superiority over the Spanish, Condé waited while groups of local militia were assembled even though the military effectiveness of such forces was dubious. By the time that the army was set to move back into Roussillon in the last week of October the weather had become uncertain, and Condé's army collapsed into complete disarray after twenty-four hours of torrential rain before it had reached Salces. Desperate to retrieve a situation that had been largely due to his fearful reluctance to seize earlier opportunities, Condé assembled another force with which he marched to the siege works at Salces. Anxious to be seen to have done something, he ordered some of his best infantry into a futile and costly assault against the Spanish positions before bowing to the inevitable and retiring into Languedoc.[153] Deprived of any prospect of relief, the garrison surrendered on 6 January 1640.

Not only had the campaign been wrecked by hesitancy and over-caution which clearly reflected Condé's experience of the previous year, but, as with the setback at Fuenterrabía, the fall-out included a damaging series of quarrels within the high command as worried senior officers attempted to throw the blame for failure on each other's shoulders. Condé's relations with his immediate subordinate, the maréchal de Schomberg, had been consistently poor, not least because Schomberg had never fully accepted subordination to another commander within his own province. As the campaign began to disintegrate, Condé considered it a useful insurance policy to emphasize the intransigence and insubordination of Schomberg. By September, when the prospect of organizing an effective relief force for Salces was already dwindling, Condé was doing his best to lay the blame for the failure to assemble the relief army on Schomberg's failure to cooperate.[154] The fall of Salces was followed by an even stronger attack on Schomberg, casting him in the semi-treasonable role played by the duc de La Valette the year before, and stressing his failure to make adequate provision for the garrison.[155] Schomberg, far less vulnerable than La Valette, had not hesitated to retaliate, writing to Richelieu to blame Condé for the loss of the relief force, and emphasizing the extent to which the prince was disregarding ministerial instructions.[156]

The result of this conflict was a total impasse at the opening of the following campaign. Schomberg now strongly distrusted Condé and was prepared to use all of his provincial influence to obstruct his senior's plans. He made it clear that he would not cooperate in a military operation in which he would be expected to bear responsibility for the errors and poor organization of his superior; still less would

---

[153] See chapter 1, pp. 71–2, and chapter 2, pp. 135–6, for the background to this campaign and the attempt to force the Spanish lines in November 1639.
[154] AAE MD 1631, fo. 150, 26 Sept. 1639: 'mais il faut que je vous dire que je suis tres mal secondé'.
[155] AAE MD 1631, fo. 420, n.d. [Dec. 1639].
[156] AAE MD 1631, fo. 229, 7 Nov., fo. 268, 27 Dec., Schomberg to Richelieu.

he undertake a small-scale, inadequately supported, operation from Languedoc, drawing Spanish forces down on to himself in order to provide Condé with the opportunity to launch a more important operation across the frontier from Guienne into Atlantic Spain. Despite Richelieu's commitment to a family alliance with Condé, he judged it prudent to edge him out of the south-west; though the prince remained notional *lieutenant général* in this theatre, and titular governor of Guienne, he was encouraged to return to Court. Schomberg, freed from the concern that his superior would try to blame him for military failure, resumed limited cooperation with ministerial instructions.

In the case of these two *grands*, it was at least clear that precedence was accorded to Condé, even if ministerial policy generated intense tensions between them. Ministerial policy did not always encourage a clear-cut chain of command. Doubts about the commitment of the older generation of commanders to the war-effort after 1635 led to a series of experiments in which previously loyalist *grands* were paired with a commander drawn from amongst the *créatures* of the ministers. Châtillon, de La Force, Angoulême, Chaulnes, even Longueville, found themselves sharing commands with Brézé, La Meilleraye, cardinal de La Valette; later in the ministry they were paired with Philippe de La Motte-Houdancourt and Guébriant, commanders whose position and prospects were owed directly to ministerial support.[157] This expedient provided the ministers with a greater sense that they could control or monitor operations in the field, but the benefit was certainly outweighed by the disadvantages of these joint commands. As no commander would accept subordination to anyone other than a clear social superior within the hierarchy of *grands*, the usual arrangement for the exercise of authority within the army was a damaging *alternatif* arrangement, by which each commander was in charge on successive days. If relations between the commanders were already tense, the arrangement was a sure recipe for contradictory instructions, confused channels of communication and ultimate inactivity. Had the commanders shared roughly similar backgrounds and outlooks, the system might have been less problematic. But the *créatures* were, as a rule, a generation younger than the *grands* with whom they shared commands and this made cooperation much more unlikely.

Moreover, the motive for this policy of pairing commanders – suspicion of the military commitment of the *grands* who were not explicitly tied into the ministerial regime – was made more open than was tactful or useful. Well aware that they had been paired up with the older commanders to galvanize them into an aggressive pursuit of the war-effort, the younger *créatures* made little attempt to spare their feelings. The apparent lethargy, reluctance and incompetence of the older generation were derided in letters between *créatures* such as Brézé and cardinal de

---

[157] La Motte-Houdancourt was used as the ministerial *fidèle* in Roussillon during 1641, when his relations were difficult with both Condé, who had now returned to the front, and Schomberg.

The ministry and the high command

La Valette and their ministerial allies such as Chavigny and Giulio Mazzarini.[158] As much as in Richelieu's own writing, these letters and comments have shaped the picture of a mediocre and unenterprising high command, who stifled warwinning strategies until they could be replaced by a younger generation.

Yet as has already been suggested, from the commanders' point of view there were good and prudent reasons for exercising restraint in the pursuit of campaign objectives which they would certainly be blamed for failing to achieve. In practice, La Meilleraye, the cardinal de La Valette or Brézé were little more enterprising than the older generation whom they derided. The main difference, as contemporaries sourly noted, was that they sheltered behind their familial relations or their overt *fidélité* to the ministers to avert the criticism or worse consequences that would fall on others who were less well connected. Brézé's exploitation of his family connection with Richelieu was considered particularly outrageous; actions such as his unilateral abandonment of his governorship at Calais in 1636 because his *appointements* had fallen into arrears, or his abrupt departure from the army on campaign in 1638 after a quarrel with Châtillon, strained even Richelieu's willingness to support his family.[159] Had it been possible to shift outright control of all the army-corps to the ministerial *créatures* then this confrontational atmosphere and the rebarbative relations they generated might have been less important. It should be stressed, however, that these *créatures* were not in most cases the better or more successful generals of the younger generation. But it was in any case not a practical proposition to eliminate the *grands* from the high command, or even reduce them to a token presence. Antagonized and, as they saw it, exploited, the *grands* continued to command army-corps and continued to frustrate unreasonable ministerial expectations by scaling down military activity to a level which they considered to be realistic.

The ministerial distrust of the loyalty and commitment of many of the commanders and the anxieties that this aroused in the high command did not prevent the ministry from exploiting the financial resources of the commanders. They were pressed to mobilize their own resources to make good the shortfalls of the *épargne*, and such pressures increased dramatically after 1635. Condé, again, provides the classic example: as early as 1629, Richelieu spoke of the prince as a suitable commander, since he 'Méprisera toutes les nécessitez que l'armée qui sera

---

[158] AAE MD 831, fo. 225, 12 Sept. 1638, Chavigny to Richelieu on the incapacity and incompetence of La Force; MD 831, fo. 138, 31 Aug. 1638, de Noyers to Chavigny, commenting on the 'ancienne léthargie' of 'celles de nos armées'.

[159] For Calais see AAE MD 823, fo. 58, 31 Aug. 1636, Brézé to Richelieu; fo. 61, 2 Sept., Richelieu to Brézé, stressing that he will only be discharged from the governorship when a new appointment has been made. For Brézé's behaviour in 1638: Griffet, *Louis XIII*, III. 129–30; François de Paule de Clermont, marquis de Montglat, *Mémoires*, XLIX. 203; Richelieu's letter to Brézé following his departure from the army provides an example of the cardinal's most acerbic epistolary style: Avenel VI. 83–5, 11 Aug. 1638.

employée à cet effet pourra avoir, ce que ne feroit pas un autre.'[160] A decade later this justification for selecting Condé as a commander was still being cited.[161]

But the financial burdens that Condé appeared to accept – after all, he received a pension of 150,000 *livres* p.a. from the crown[162] – lesser *grands*, even acknowledged *fidèles*, would be loth to undertake. Knowing that they would be expected to intervene to prevent serious breakdowns in payment of wages or supply, they were reluctant to carry out extended operations which would make such breakdowns more likely. During the 1635 campaign both cardinal de La Valette and maréchal Brézé were forced to sell off all their possessions with the armies to maintain food supplies to their troops.[163] La Valette was reduced to this during the retreat from Mainz in September, Brézé after his army had been stranded in Holland following the earlier inconclusive campaign in the Spanish Netherlands.[164] To less committed *grands*, this was a clear warning; it at least partially explains why Longueville, La Force, Châtillon and others sought to undertake short campaigns, aimed at limited objectives. Harcourt, pressing the siege of Turin through the summer of 1640, inevitably found himself raising money on his own credit to keep the army in basic supplies and to prevent the collapse of the operation; his chief concern was not obtaining reimbursement for money already advanced, but that his own credit could only keep the army going temporarily.[165] Without compulsion from the centre, but anxious to avoid any strategy that involved open-ended expense, the majority of commanders would never have progressed beyond small-scale sieges of frontier *places*, or short *courses* – raiding missions – through territory largely empty of enemy troops. Even then, some financial commitment was unavoidable, if only to ensure that obvious setbacks could be avoided.[166]

As in the case of the unit commanders, the effect of this was to legitimize, in the officers' eyes, any opportunity presented for the misappropriation of central funds. The case of Louis de Marillac was typical; he did not deny that he had levied, strictly speaking, illegal contributions, but claimed in mitigation that the fortifications of Metz and his army-corps had been largely paid out of his own

---

[160] Avenel, III. 290, 28 Apr. 1629. The year before Condé had informed Richelieu that he had provided 45,000 *écus* for the costs of his army: Grillon, III. 340, 16 June 1628.
[161] AAE MD 1631, fo. 150, 26 Sept. 1639: 'Sans mon argent le pain est cessé il y a plus de quinze jours'; MD 1633, fo. 478, 16 Aug. 1641, Condé to Richelieu.
[162] AAE MD 806, fo. 202: pension list for 1632.
[163] The value of the commander's baggage train could be very considerable, cf. Kroener, *Les routes*, pp. 87–8, and Appendix VI.
[164] AAE CP Allemagne 12, fo. 355, 23 Oct. 1635; Avenel, v. 366, 2 Dec. 1635.
[165] AAE CP Savoie 30, fo. 551, 27 June 1640, Harcourt to de Noyers.
[166] Du Hallier, commanding his small army in Lorraine in 1640, still found himself forced to advance his own funds to pay for the demolition of the fortifications of Lunéville, fearing the consequences for his own position if the *place* were to fall back into the hands of Charles of Lorraine: AAE CP Lorraine 31, fo. 335, 28 May 1640, du Hallier stressed that the razing of the fortifications will cost him 8,000 *livres*, and that this will be in addition to 8,000 that he has already advanced for other expenses.

The ministry and the high command

pocket.[167] Once again, the ministry's willingness to confuse public and private finance in its own interest had unwelcome reciprocal consequences. In 1628 even Condé had been accused of expropriating funds intended for his army.[168] While he denied this vociferously, the level of his personal financial commitment makes the charge entirely credible. Whether, on balance, the crown gained more from exploiting the credit of the *grands* than it lost through corruption is impossible to assess. It is improbable, moreover, that all opportunities for illicit profit would have been renounced by the *grands* had their own financial resources not been tapped in this manner. Yet these exactions, combined with the threat of disgrace, could only serve further to destabilize the ministry's relations with the high command.

Nor was it the case that ministers were prepared to permit commanders a degree of independent action in return for such personal financial commitments. Even after the experiment with joint military commands had been almost entirely abandoned, the ministers did not give up their concern to control military activities in the campaign theatres. Suspicion of the commitment and loyalty of many of the commanders remained, and with it a strong impulse to direct the war from the centre, usually in accordance with a strategy which had been formulated at the beginning of the particular campaign. The impact of this preoccupation was, again, largely counter-productive. If a military setback was encountered it was far safer to have been acting according to ministerial instructions than to have seized an initiative which might bring greater success but left the commander dangerously exposed in the event of failure. It was a lesson which Henri II de Condé had certainly grasped, and his slow and unenterprising approach to campaigning reflected a concern to shelter behind ministerial instructions, while simultaneously interpreting such instructions in the narrowest and most limited way.

The ministers themselves recognized that the concern to control the war-effort from the centre could have damaging consequences, but they revealed a characteristic ambiguity in their attitudes to the conduct of field commanders. Time and again, Richelieu wrote to the generals, stressing that they possessed full autonomy and were to act upon their own initiative as circumstances permitted. Such an approach represented an apparently sensible recognition that it was impossible to conduct frontier campaigns from Paris, dependent upon out-of-date information, and with no capacity to adjust to rapidly changing military circumstances. If the war was to be prosecuted effectively, operational freedom had to be granted to the commanders in the field. Yet while this could be accepted intellectually, suspicion of the commitment of the commanders and a compulsion to influence plans that were originally established at Court led in practice to floods of instructions and suggestions based upon the king and his ministers' reading of the military

[167] AAE MD 806, fos. 1–17 [1632]: *Remonstrance*. Also, letters of 1629/30 which emphasize that he was being forced to sustain these expenses from his own pocket: Grillon, v. 36, 485, 17 Jan./4 Aug. 1630.
[168] Grillon, III. 340, 16 June 1628.

Responses and reactions

situation in the particular theatre.[169] The temptation to intervene was constant and rarely resisted. The commander was placed in an unenviable position; central instructions were invariably over-optimistic, based upon outdated assessments of the troop strengths of both French and enemy armies, and on relative positions that had probably changed. Execution of these suggestions would either prove impractical or dangerous. Yet if they were ignored, and the army was defeated or exposed to a major setback while acting upon the commander's own initiative, the response from the Court would be harsh.

Yet the tendency to over-regulate the detailed operations in campaign theatres was not the whole story. It was also true that some of the commanders could regard themselves as victims of the same kind of 'information overload' suffered by the ministry. The coordination of strategy in five or six different campaign theatres; the administration of an unprecedented war-effort; the need to respond to rapidly changing military circumstances: all these factors would have imposed considerable burdens on a government considerably more sophisticated than that of early seventeenth-century France. When these were compounded by the slowness and inadequacy of communications, the difficulties became insuperable. The ministers were unprepared to delegate full responsibility for the operations of the army-corps to the commanders in the field, and were certainly not prepared to allow strategic decisions to be made locally. Nor was this wished for by the commanders themselves, who continued to receive a large part of their financial and material resources from the royal government, and who needed the crown and its ministers to allocate recruits, to ensure the levy and despatch of reinforcements, and at least to note the extent to which the senior and unit officers were sustaining the immediate costs of campaigning.

What was deeply resented was the combination of occasional bouts of intensive interference with long periods of almost total neglect, sometimes even compounded by expressed ministerial irritation that local commanders should be importuning for resources, strategic guidance or repayment of debts incurred. After 1638 these impossible situations became unavoidable. The amount of administrative and organizational effort required for the conduct of the type of siege that became the centrepiece of French strategy in the later years of the ministry effectively crowded out consideration of the 'lesser' campaign theatres. The *bureau de la guerre* was a small, informal and rudimentary structure, and the extent to which its head, the *secrétaire d'Etat*, could make autonomous decisions about military matters of central importance was limited. All the senior ministers were heavily involved in military decision-making and resource-allocation, but

---

[169] See for example two letters to Châtillon, concerning his authority and the strategy to be pursued by his corps in 1637: Avenel, v. 831, 833, 8/16 Aug. 1637; BN Ms.fr. 6645, fo. 93, 14 Aug. 1635, *mémoire* of the king to cardinal de La Valette; AAE CP Allemagne 12, fo. 379, 13 Nov. 1635, Richelieu to cardinal de La Valette and La Meilleraye; Avenel, VI. 354, 17 May 1639: Richelieu to La Meilleraye.

The ministry and the high command

had to place these activities in the context of numerous other demands upon their time and administrative energies; the result was severe rationing not just of resources, but also of attention.

For example, while Châtillon, commanding one of the three army-corps involved in the siege of Arras in 1640, considered that his patience was being tried by extensive ministerial importunities to press the campaign into the autumn, Harcourt's complaints were exactly the reverse. As commander of the army of Italy, locked into the siege of Turin, his letters reveal increasing exasperation at what he felt to be almost total ministerial neglect. Despite despatching detailed accounts of his campaigning and its strategic significance and making elaborate and well-considered requests for troops and resources, replies from the centre were sketchy, failed to answer his questions and, above all, failed to respond to his requests for support. At the height of his exasperation, Harcourt attacked the bland ministerial assumption that the fall of Turin was a foregone conclusion. His letters show how aware he was that the Italian theatre had been relegated not just in terms of resources but even as a focus of ministerial attention. A very similar exasperation can be found in the letters of Saxe-Weimar, and after his death in 1639, of Guébriant. Both found it necessary to emphasize the dangers to French security of a collapse of the Weimarian army, simply to try to elevate the force in the ministry's priorities.

The implications of a low priority were made explicit by maréchal Brézé, writing from Roussillon in November 1641; he comments that in the course of the previous month he had received one letter, of six lines, from the ministers and the Court, which had said nothing of any practical use.[170]

The exasperation of the commanders, who felt that their letters were going unread – or at least unanswered – was matched by occasional ministerial frustration at being forced to pay attention to a theatre which they regarded as of secondary importance. Michel Particelli d'Hémery was a stubborn and tireless partisan of the needs of the army of Italy throughout the later 1630s when he was acting as extraordinary ambassador in Savoy. The result of his importuning the ministers with lengthy and insistent letters was replies that were frequently opaque and failed to answer more than a fraction of his requests for information, but which also revealed considerable irritation on the part of ministers – including Richelieu himself – who wished to concentrate on other elements of the war-effort.[171] Despite strong partisanship from Chavigny, secretary for foreign affairs, d'Hémery acquired the reputation of someone whose judgement was unreliable, who was prone to exaggerate both the poor state of the army of Italy and the threat posed by the Spanish and who encroached excessively on the limited

---

[170] AAE CP Espagne 20, fo. 319v, 30 Nov. 1641, Brézé to Chavigny.
[171] Avenel, v. 845, 27 Aug. 1637, Richelieu to d'Hémery: 'considérés à l'avenir ce qui se peut, et ne vous imaginés pas que les hommes, l'argent, les vivres et les munitions de guerre croissent en France sans nombre'.

amount of attention that the ministers intended to devote to the problems of the army of Italy.

The problems with the high command discussed in this chapter raise the question of whether they were a consequence of this particular ministerial government, or of a deliberate increase in royal authoritarianism. The burden of the argument throughout has been that it was the king's ministers and their ambitions, rather than Louis XIII's desire to increase his own control of the state, which produced both the problems and the failure to solve them. It is suggested, for example, that some of the high command's problems might have been overcome if the various *grands* had participated in the formulation and coordination of overall strategy. An extraordinary *conseil de guerre*, meeting at Court during the winter months, could have provided a forum for such involvement. A similar body had after all been assembled in 1616, and included the 'principaux hommes de guerre, un secrétaire d'Etat et le chef de Finances', although it met for only one sitting.[172] In 1625, a 'Règlement pour toutes les affaires du royaume' had proposed that this type of body be recreated, but no action was taken during Richelieu's ministry.[173] Only in 1643 did Gaston d'Orléans use his authority to create such a *conseil* and to ensure its permanence.[174] The deduction is obvious; for all its practical advantages, the perceived dangers of bringing together the most powerful of the military *grands* were greater than the ministry was prepared to accept.

This example aptly illustrates the central dichotomy in the management of the high command. The interests of the crown clearly lay in the successful prosecution of the war. Yet while the ministry sought victory to justify its foreign policy, its actions were hampered by an even more compelling need to retain its own grip on the state and the mechanisms of government. Overt criticism, unrest and revolt are practical evidence of the ministry's vulnerability; yet it has tacitly been assumed that after 1630 Richelieu's position was unassailable, provided that he could master Louis XIII's temporary moods of self-assertiveness. The truth seems to be that he controlled a far less secure edifice which required constant attention: all of his policies had to be compatible with effective control of potential sources of opposition. Richelieu and his ministers were deeply anxious about the recurring patterns of military failure, but they could not undertake policies which might improve the effectiveness of the army at the price of delegating power. Reappointment of autonomous commanders and the involvement of the *grands* in the formulation of overall strategy made military sense but were considered politically too dangerous. There were political anxieties concerned with the stability of the ministry which were even greater than the military anxieties.

---

[172] R. Mousnier, 'Le conseil du roi de la mort de Henri IV au gouvernement personnel de Louis XIV', in Mousnier, *La plume*, p. 162.
[173] Grillon, I. 249, n.d. [1625].
[174] Mousnier, 'Le conseil du roi', p. 162.

10

The army and the civilian population

> La plus grande surcharge des peuples provenant de la license avec laquelle les dits gens de guerre vivent sur eux à discrétion, ce qui arrive faute du payement, lequel manque tousjours, ou parce qu'il n'y a point de fonds, ou parce que celuy qui est destiné a cest usage est diverty.[1]

As the size of the French army and the scale of its military activities grew in the years after 1635, so inevitably did the problems of the relations between troops and the civilian population. Soldiers across Europe during the first half of the seventeenth century were only to an extremely limited extent segregated from civilians. Armies set apart from non-military life, with troops lodged in barracks and spending most of their time when not on active service being drilled in special encampments, were mostly a phenomenon of the second half of the century.[2] There were a few cases in which French garrisons were lodged in barracks in the 1630s and 1640s, but this was almost invariably when the troops were being maintained in cities beyond the French frontiers, and where concern at disorders and tensions between French soldiers and the populations of (sometimes reluctant) allied states was paramount. This was typically the case in north Italy, where the use of barracks predated the arrival of French troops. After Henri de Lorraine, comte d'Harcourt, had recaptured Turin in 1640, the French garrison of 2,000 soldiers were placed in the existing barracks, though even in this case the officers were lodged with the civilian population.[3] Yet it was quickly recognized that attempts to lodge French soldiers apart in this way exposed them to inadequate food which cost more to provide, and involved them in greater risk of infectious disease. By the end of 1640 the ministers had ordered Harcourt to remove his troops from barracks in Carmagnola, Casale and other *places fortes* and to billet them upon the civilian population.[4] These exceptions aside, the great majority of garrison troops, above all within France, were lodged upon the local populations.

---

[1] Richelieu, 'Propositions qui doibvent estre faictes de la part du Roy à l'assemblée des notables' [late] 1626: Avenel, II. 317–18.
[2] Babeau, *Vie militaire*, I. 79–85; André, *Michel Le Tellier et l'organization*, pp. 361–4; Jones, 'The welfare of the French foot-soldier from Richelieu to Napoleon', *History*, 214 (1980), 193–213, at 200–1; Tallett, *War and Society* (London, 1992), pp. 121–2.
[3] AAE CP Savoie 31, fo. 139, 1 Oct. 1640, *mémoire* from the comte d'Harcourt.
[4] SHAT A^1 61, fos. 35, 42, 15 Oct. 1640, instructions to Harcourt and Plessis-Praslin.

Responses and reactions

Billeting of permanent garrisons had always been the lot of designated fortified towns in the frontier provinces; moreover, some troops from the elite *régiments* and *compagnies entretenues* had always been added to these garrisons during the winter quarter, the period roughly from October through to the end of March during which almost all serious campaigning ceased. However, the shift in emphasis after 1635, which involved maintaining far larger numbers of troops in quarters over the winter months, had a huge impact on the entire system of garrisoning.[5] Winter quartering was no longer a small-scale imposition inflicted on selected frontier *places*, but a major operation encompassing a large number of the French provinces adjoining or near to the frontiers.[6] Within a couple of years – systematic winter quartering had been effectively introduced by the winter of 1636/7 – whole areas of France and their populations which previously had minimal contact with the army now had direct experience of the presence of large numbers of poorly paid and fed, violent and ill-disciplined soldiers for, at worst, nearly half the year. All of the eastern frontier provinces, together with Normandy, the Île de France, Touraine, Provence and Languedoc, were subjected to the *logement* of troops more or less every year after 1636.[7] Although there was some debate about the possible merits of spreading the troops across villages in the countryside, in the event the ministers remained firmly committed to concentrating troops in the towns.[8]

This did not mean that smaller communities escaped the presence of troops. The process of recruitment, assembly and movement of troops from the inner provinces of France to the campaign theatres brought with it recruiting officers and NCOs, who appeared in villages and small *bourgs* far away from the frontiers, and could result in such places being selected as points of assembly. Constant complaints were made to the ministers that recruitment officers were battening on to an appointed area and spending far too long in the process of recruitment and assembly of the troops – during which time the subsistence expenses were largely borne by the local communities.[9] Above all communities could find themselves

---

[5] See chapter 4, pp. 272–3

[6] Corvisier (ed.), *Histoire militaire*, I. 367–8, which includes a project for winter quartering for 1639. Even provinces such as Picardy and Champagne, previously accustomed to lodging troops over the winter, were subjected to unprecedented burdens: see the breakdown of *logement* for 30,000 troops across Picardy for the winter quarter of 1641, involving the billeting of 2,000–3,000 troops on each of the larger cities and towns – Calais, Abbeville, Amiens, Doullens, etc: AAE MD 841, fo. 222, [1641], Projet de logement.

[7] BN Ms.fr. 3759, fo. 6, 31 Dec. 1636, 'Arrêt du conseil d'état pour la subsistance des trouppes', discusses the burdens placed upon the main frontier provinces and the need to devise a system to distribute the financial burden of *logement* during the winter quarter.

[8] Navereau, *Logement*, pp. 52–4, 169, describes a plan in 1641 to lodge the troops in disused and deserted *couverts communs* rather than imposing them on the towns – see also SHAT A^1 66, fo. 468, 11 Dec. 1641 – but the logistical and organizational problems proved so grave that the plan was abandoned in the following year. As early as 1635 Bullion had laid out the arguments for concentrating the billeting of troops for the winter quarter in the towns: AAE MD 819, fo. 97, [end 1635].

[9] SHAT A^1 28, fo. 297, 20 July 1636, *vice-sénéchal* of Limousin to investigate the disorders of sieur de

The army and the civilian population

selected as *étapes*, or stopping points for the troops marching from places of assembly towards the frontiers. The choice of places was determined by the main communication network and by rough calculations of a reasonable distance to expect a column of troops to march in a day. The assumption of the system was that the local community would be supported by a financial levy imposed across the rest of the *élection*. In consequence, ensuring that the chosen *étape* point was large enough to sustain – and control – the burden of companies, even regiments, *en route* for the frontiers was not a high priority.[10]

THE PROVISIONING AND *LOGEMENT* OF TROOPS ACROSS FRANCE – ASPIRATIONS AND INADEQUACY

Systems already existed in 1635 for the provisioning of *étapes* along the routes that led towards the campaign theatres and to allocate responsibility for the feeding and *logement* of troops in garrison. In both cases attempts were made to spread the financial responsibility for such arrangements beyond the particular community which had the misfortune to be selected as an *étape* point, or which had been chosen to play host to a garrison, whether over the winter quarter or because the *place* was considered to be of strategic significance.

The obvious problem confronted by the *étapes* after 1635 was that the volume and frequency of troops moving to the frontiers considerably exceeded the capacity of the chosen *places* to buy in and stockpile foodstuffs.[11] A brief experiment begun in 1633, by which the troops passing through the *étapes* were paid in cash so that they could purchase their own food, proved hopelessly unsuited to the scale of operations from 1635 and an incitement to the most overt corruption and extortion.[12] In practice, the distribution of cash had been largely abandoned during 1635, but in 1636 the crown officially returned to the system of

---

Chamberet in the levy of recruits for the regt of his son, which have ruined numerous of the king's subjects; A¹ 37, fo. 74, 12 June 1637, de Noyers to Charles de Schomberg, governor of Languedoc, with a characteristic discussion about the extreme slowness with which the recruits are being assembled in the province before being marched down to Italy, and the great burdens that this is imposing on the places of assembly. But, equally characteristic: A¹ 41, fo. 78, 3 Feb. 1636, de Noyers to a number of provincial governors, announcing that officers have been sent to locations in their provinces to carry out recruiting, and that they and the recruits will need to live at the expense of the local communities.

[10] Kroener, *Les routes*, pp. 72–83. Indicative of the general thinking about *étape* locations was a specific 1634 instruction that the *étapes* specified for the prestige cavalry companies of the king and Richelieu should be larger – wealthier – than the average: SHAT A¹ 21, fo. 77 [1634].

[11] SHAT A¹ 25, fo. 27, 7 July 1635, Servien to François de Créqui, comte de Sault, concerning his quarrel with the *trésoriers de France* in Dauphiné about responsibility for the provisioning of the *étapes* in the province; fo. 523, 13 Nov. 1635, Sault to do all possible to ensure that the communities of Dauphiné meet their responsibilities for supplying troops *en route* through the province; A¹ 32, pce 93, 12 June 1636, concerning the failure of the Lyonnais to meet the obligations of the *étapes* in the course of 1635.

[12] SHAT A¹ 19, fo. 240, 21 Sept. 1633, Servien to Claude Frère, sieur de Crolles, *premier président* of the *Parlement* of Dauphiné, concerning the implications of the new *règlement* for the *étapes*.

Responses and reactions

providing the troops with specified rations of food at the *étapes* ('l'ancien ordre').[13] This in turn made it even more vital to ensure that adequate supplies could be collected at the chosen places in preparation for successive waves of troops moving through the provinces.[14] Lack of confidence in this provisioning resulted in regular requests both from provincial governors and from corps commanders to make changes in the routes in order to avoid locations where supplies were known to be depleted.[15] However, the ministers were well aware that, whatever the immediate problems with ensuring adequate supplies at the designated locations, allowing discretion to alter march routes through the provinces would be far more destructive for both the supply of the soldiers and the civil population in the long term. Not surprisingly, therefore, such requests were almost invariably refused:[16] the principle of fixed *étapes* and severe punishments for officers and soldiers who diverged from their prescribed routes was asserted throughout the war years, albeit with limited success.[17] The challenge grew worse as from 1635 it became increasingly difficult for an overburdened *secrétaire d'Etat* and his staff to maintain the traditional system of sending each commanding officer and *commissaire à la conduite* a personalized itinerary for the movement of his unit to the campaign theatre.[18] Without this specific instruction it was easy for the officers to interpret routes with a degree of laxness; despite threats and penalties the ministers fought an inconclusive struggle through the 1630s and 1640s to curb the tendency of the officers and their troops to ignore the prescribed *étapes*.[19]

Though a working system of fixed *étapes* was certainly the best means of minimizing damage caused by the troops across the provinces, the failure to ensure that the *étapes* were adequately supplied would threaten not merely the desertion or collapse of individual units marching through the province, but disorder, violence and pillage as the troops attempted to extort their subsistence from an unprepared population. One response of the ministry to this challenge was to specify the precise quantities of food and forage that could be claimed by

---

[13] SHAT A¹ 27, fo. 162, 27 Mar. 1636, circular letter from de Noyers to the provincial governors.

[14] In at least one case, foot-dragging and complaints about the difficulties of gathering the provisions in Provence led the *secrétaire* to insist that the *procureurs* return to the recent system of providing a cash payment to the soldiers passing through the province: SHAT A¹ 27, fo. 132, 17 Mar. 1636.

[15] SHAT A¹ 27, fo. 261, 19 Apr. 1636, failure of the established *étapes* has led to demands to move the troops through Dauphiné via alternative routes.

[16] There are a few cases of *commissaires* and others being specifically authorized to change the route of a particular unit – usually to speed its march down to the campaign theatre: see, for example, SHAT A¹29, fo. 227, 14 Sept. 1636, *commissaire* d'Aubray given permission to select a route to conduct the regiment of Annevaux to the army of Picardy: A¹ 48, fo. 206, 11 Aug. 1638, licence to the *commissaires* to change routes for recruits in the interests of getting them to the campaign theatres.

[17] SHAT A¹ 60, fo. 295, 31 Aug. 1640, de Noyers to Brézé, reporting king's refusal to change the *étapes* in Anjou; A¹ 66, fos. 382, 383, 386, 29/30 Nov. 1641, instructions to *officiers* concerning the adherence of troops to the established *étapes*.

[18] Typical examples in SHAT A¹ 19, fos. 322, 324, 365, 366, 27/8 Oct./9 Nov. 1633.

[19] Kroener, *Les routes*, pp. 114–15.

The army and the civilian population

the troops in the hope that this would reduce the burdens on the *étapes* by preventing units from 'misunderstanding' what was due to them and leaving nothing for units following them along the same route.[20] A further step was to try to regularize the system by which the chosen *étapes* raised money from the surrounding *élection* to meet the costs of supplying and lodging the troops so that shortfalls would be minimized and the *officiers* or the *étape-munitionnaires* would have adequate money in hand to purchase supplies.[21] The questionable effectiveness of these 1636 initiatives is shown by the frequency of subsequent legislation concerning the *étapes* down to and beyond 1642, and the regularity with which different groups of *officiers* were charged with responsibility for the system.[22] The evidence of this legislation was that it was easier to prescribe the use of *étapes* than to devise a mechanism that would ensure that provincial taxes could be turned into rations and that these would be made available for the soldiery in sufficient quantity and at the point required.[23]

A similar set of problems was created by the need to provide lodging and subsistence for the larger numbers of troops now placed in winter quarters. Here again, previous *ad hoc* expedients were no longer viable, while dispersing the troops in small groups across broad areas of the provinces had been rejected on the grounds that it presented insuperable problems of control.[24] Yet the development of a system which concentrated the soldiers in chosen towns and cities and aimed to distribute the burden of support more widely placed no less an obligation on the administrators to ensure that basic provision was maintained, and that these concentrations of troops had no excuse for extortion, pillage and violence against the town population. The great innovation in the provision of the winter quarter was the introduction of the *subsistances* tax in the winter of 1637–8, and the establishment of a specific group of *commissaires pour les subsistances* with general authority to allocate troops to the prescribed towns, to collect the *taxe des subsistances*, to order its distribution to the troops and to deal with all disputes and

---

[20] SHAT A¹ 32, pce 44, 26 Mar. 1636, *règlement* concerning the provision of foodstuffs for the *étapes*, which also took the opportunity to reiterate the precise obligations of the *ustensile* – the bed, table linen, candle, etc., that the host was obliged to provide for troops billeted on his household.

[21] SHAT A¹ 32, pce 103, 28 June 1636, *règlement* to attribute responsibility for the provisioning of the *étapes* to the *officiers* of the *élections*; A¹ 27, fo. 424, 22 May 1636, instructions to Charles de Neufville-Villeroy, marquis d'Halincourt and governor of Lyonnais, and to the *trésoriers* of Lyon concerning the negotiation of contracts with entrepreneurs for the supply of the *étapes* and the system by which money will be raised in the province to fund this; A¹ 57, fo. 221, 24 Jan. 1640, levy of 60,000 *livres* by the *intendant* of Lyonnais for the costs of the *étapes*.

[22] Kroener, *Les routes*, pp. 94–103.

[23] SHAT A¹ 27, fos. 190, 191, 3 Apr. 1636, de Noyers to maréchal Vitry and to d'Hémery concerning the failure of the *étapes* in Provence and the consequent loss of troops, the local disorders and violence; AAE MD 844, fo. 36, 18 Sept. 1642, appeal concerning the non-payment of *étape* expenses.

[24] See, for example, criticism of the *mestre de camp* Valmont that his regiment has been dispersed into the countryside where it is living with great disorder, and must return immediately to its appointed winter quarters at Noyon: SHAT A¹ 58, fo. 196, 15 Mar. 1640.

Responses and reactions

disorders which arose from the winter quarter.²⁵ But neither the institution of the *subsistances* tax nor the establishment of specific administrators to take responsibility for the winter quarter arrangements did anything to eradicate the constant disputes over provisioning, the discipline of troops in garrison, the balance of cash and food to be provided for the soldiers and – still more contentiously – for the officers, and the array of claimed exemptions, rights to compensation and simple refusals to pay the *subsistances*.

The *étape* and the winter quarter systems were developed with the dual aim of ensuring adequate support for the troops, thereby seeking to reduce the levels of desertion while simultaneously providing some safeguards for the civilian population against extortion and violence by an unpaid and unfed soldiery. Neither system was capable of adjusting to circumstances after 1635. For as with so many other areas in the military administration, the increase in the scale of the war-effort was not so great that it completely overwhelmed the existing structures, but it was large enough to ensure that piecemeal expedients and lack of integrated planning could never adequately cope with the problems involved. There were, in addition, other more specific obstacles standing in the way of making these systems work.

The first of these was the ambiguous attitude of the *bureau des finances*. Was the purpose of new regulations for the financing of the *étapes* and the winter quarters actually the protection of the civil population from the violence and extortion of the soldiery? Comments made by the *surintendant* Bullion in his correspondence with the other ministers certainly suggest that the *bureau des finances* was anxious to protect the population from the worst effects of arbitrary military demands. Ministers accepted that the undisciplined passage of troops was the primary cause of the immiseration of the population. As Mazarin wrote in 1643: 'un logement de trois jours avec la licence accoustumée des gens de guerre [n']incommode plus un homme que la taille et la subsistance d'une année'.²⁶ Chancellor Séguier had taken a similarly bleak view when he wrote to Richelieu that 'dans l'Est le logement des gens de guerre a réduict 50 familles sur 80 à l'aumône; on a été obligé de les nourrir à leur tour'.²⁷ Bullion himself wrote that in many areas 'il n'est plus possible de subsister car la pluspart des peuples se voyent tyranniquement traitez par les gens de guerre'.²⁸ Obviously there was an element of interest in the *surintendants*' condemnation of the troops' maltreatment of the civilian population,

---

[25] For the changing identities and roles of the *commissaires pour les subsistances* during the late 1630s see chapter 8, pp. 423–32.

[26] Quoted in P. Landier, 'Guerre, violences et société en France, 1635–1659', thèse de troisième cycle, Université de Paris IV, 1981, p. 36. A similar comment was made – probably by Claude Bouthillier – in a *mémoire* concerning winter quarters for 1641/2, when he suggests that the troops moving down to Italy through Dauphiné 'coustant beaucoup plus aux sujets de Sa Mate qu'une année entière des subsistances': AAE MD 841, fo. 221, [late 1641].

[27] Navereau, *Logement*, p. 55.

[28] AAE MD 835, fo. 257, 6 July 1640, Bullion to Richelieu.

The army and the civilian population

since this diminished the latter's capacity to pay the regular taxes on which the whole structure of war-finance depended.[29] Bullion put it bluntly in a *mémoire* at the end of 1635, when he reminded his colleagues that without the imposition of better discipline over the soldiers there would soon be no *taille* to levy.[30]

Yet this attitude of the finance ministers that the people should so far as possible be spared the depredations of the soldiers was tempered by concern to pursue the highest priority of the *bureau des finances*: the desperate need for new sources of revenue capable of sustaining a further tranche of borrowing from *traitants* and other groups of financiers, on whose loans the financial system in time of war had become entirely dependent. As was suggested in chapter 4, both the *taxe des étapes* and the *taxe des subsistances* were to fall foul of the process by which the *bureau des finances* appropriated new taxes which had ostensibly been intended to meet specific needs, in order to fuel the general borrowing requirement of the *épargne*.[31] The *subsistances* was a large additional burden on an already heavily taxed population.[32] Yet had it fulfilled its stated purpose of providing for the troops in winter quarters, thereby reducing the levels of disorder and destruction inflicted on the civilian populations, there is some evidence that it would have been regarded as acceptable.[33] However, the appropriation of the *subsistances* funds to pay the campaign expenses of the troops and to meet payments due on the ministry's loan contracts turned potential acquiescence into ferocious resistance.[34] The attitude is unsurprising given that the populations were fully aware that a demand for the *subsistances* – a hefty increase in the direct tax burden – would be followed by the passage or billeting of soldiers who would not have received more than a fraction of this money, and would simply set about demanding the payments for a second time.[35] Resistance to the *taille* and the other

---

[29] AAE MD 835, fo. 230, 25 June 1640, Bullion to Richelieu, stating that the disorders of the troops made it all but impossible to levy the *taille* and the *subsistances*.

[30] AAE MD 819, fo. 97.

[31] See chapter 4, pp. 270–5.

[32] The *subsistances* assessment for the city of Rouen in 1638 was 150,000 *livres*; that of Caen was 45,000: SHAT A^1 44, fos. 28, 79, 23/8 February 1638.

[33] Bassompierre, in his *Mémoires*, commented that the initial proposal to introduce the *taxe des subsistances* in 1637 was regarded with considerable support and enthusiasm – if only as an orderly system of protection-payments (XXI. 371–2); Kroener, *Les routes*, p. 130, emphasizes the willingness of populations to pay for the provisioning of *étapes* if they were spared subsequent exactions by the soldiers.

[34] Correspondence in the years after 1635 is full of reports concerning resistance to demands for subsistence for the troops, and outright attempts to refuse lodging or supply to units billeting upon towns. Indicative of the general attitude was a directive sent in 1638 to the authorities in the *généralités* of Riom, Lyon and Grenoble offering a remission of 2 *sols* and 6 *deniers* per *livre* to any community prepared to pay their *subsistances* on time: SHAT A^1 44, fo. 331, 21 Mar. A more general instruction in 1639 to the *commissaires pour les subsistances* and for the *étapes* ordered them to treat with favour any areas which had shown some degree of goodwill and cooperation in the payment of the *subsistances*: A^1 50ii, fo. 10, 2 Feb.

[35] Typical proposals that areas which had both paid the *subsistances* and been subjected to the *logement* of troops should be compensated through a reduction in the *taille* in the following year were unlikely

Responses and reactions

'traditional' direct taxes was strong and growing during the 1630s; yet demand for these taxes at least did not imply a cynical calculation that they would need to be paid twice – once to the crown and its creditors, and once to the soldiers who would turn up in the localities.[36] Not surprisingly, the peasants and townspeople regarded the soldiers as the greater menace and went to all lengths to evade paying the first, official, *subsistances*.[37]

However, there was a major difference between the *taille* and the *subsistances* or *étape* taxes, in that the latter were collected, at least notionally, in direct anticipation of the arrival of troops. By 1638, the *bureau des finances* had reached the conclusion that it could afford to fund the war-effort only if the winter quarter and *étape* costs were itemized and paid separately from the rest of the military budget.[38] Faced with obstruction and refusal to pay these levies, the *bureau* was prepared to abandon its solicitude for the civil populations and to sanction the extraction of the *subsistances* by military force. Both at the level of individual towns and across entire provinces, during the winter quarter and throughout the campaign season, the presence of troops offered the opportunity of imposing the *subsistances* by force. It was an opportunity which the *bureau* was prepared to seize with growing regularity. On 13 January 1639 the *intendant* and *commissaire pour les subsistances* in the *généralité* of Poitou were ordered to use troops to compel payment of *subsistances* which the population had refused to contribute voluntarily.[39] A few weeks later Charles de Villeroy, marquis d'Halincourt and governor of the Lyonnais, received orders to enter Lyon with two regiments of infantry and some cavalry companies to compel payment of the *subsistances*, hitherto resisted by the city.[40] The pattern of such military coercion had been well established during the winter quarter of 1637/8, and had become institutionalized during the 1638 campaign season in *arrêts du conseil* such as that of April 1638, authorizing the maréchal de Schomberg to execute the military levy of the *subsistances* across Languedoc.[41]

---

to gain much support from local communities, who were aware that the *taille* assessment was already higher than they would probably be able to meet: see, for example, SHAT A¹ 43, fo. 197, 28 Jan. 1638, de Noyers to *commissaire* Desgranges, concerning this procedure.

[36] And, moreover, that a significant proportion would be syphoned into the pockets of the *commissaires pour les subsistances*: see, for example, the letter of the *commissaires* of the *généralité* of Moulins, 6 Dec. 1640, printed in Mousnier (ed.), *Lettres*, I. 468–9.

[37] This was openly admitted by the ministers: AAE MD 839, fo. 49, 12 June 1641, Bouthillier to Richelieu. They were also well aware that this opposition received tacit support from local *officiers* and other authorities: for example SHAT A¹ 45, fo. 139, 14 Apr. 1638, *commissaire* Desgranges to send troops to the offices of the *trésoriers de France* at Riom to compel them to impose the *subsistances*; A¹ 43, fo. 251, 4 Feb. 1638, concern at obstruction by sovereign courts in Normandy.

[38] AAE MD 830, fo. 114, 17 May 1638, Bullion to Richelieu, discussing the fall in the tax receipts and stressing that the winter quarter levies are 'le seul moyen d'accommoder les affaires'.

[39] SHAT A¹ 50i, de Noyers to Villemontée and Chambronneau.

[40] SHAT A¹ 50ii, fo. 107, 10 Feb. 1639. See also a general instruction to the *commissaires pour les subsistances* of 6 Feb., authorizing them to make use of the troops in their *généralités* who 'peuvent satisfaire à la levée des subsistances ce qui le faut tirer l'oreille pour payer leur taxe': A¹ 50ii, fo. 77.

[41] SHAT A¹ 45, fo. 363. For examples of the military exaction of the *subsistances* during the winter of 1637/8, see A¹ 39, fo. 147bis, 3 Oct. 1637, de Noyers to Louis-Armand, vicomte de Polignac,

The army and the civilian population

Although there were no 'legal' contributions exacted in France,[42] the forcible extraction of the *subsistances* provides obvious parallels with such a system.[43] The major difference was that contributions exacted by armies campaigning elsewhere in Europe were used by the military commanders directly to meet the costs of paying and supplying their troops and – in many cases – reimbursing their subordinate, subcontracting, unit officers.[44] Within France, these taxes were levied by the military, but the proceeds were destined, at least in theory, for the *épargne*. This is not to deny that, in practice, French military commanders and their officers did not seek to benefit directly from the *subsistances*. In 1640 a comprehensive condemnation was drawn up of the 'arrangement' that existed between the governor of Languedoc, maréchal Schomberg, his company of *gendarmes* and the 'House' regiment of Languedoc. In the course of forty articles the document accused these two units of having extorted some 450,000 *livres* from the province since 1637 on the understanding that they would then pay all of their subsistence/lodging costs. In practice this agreement had been systematically broken and both the cash and all additional support for the units had been extorted from the province.[45] As the document makes clear, such direct exploitation of the *subsistances* by the troops and their commanders was entirely illegal, and not the way the taxes should have operated. Ironically, the 'legitimate' system may have ensured even more unpopularity; the extraction of the *subsistances* was certainly carried out under military duress – action which undoubtedly increased civil–military tensions in the later 1630s – but, since the receipts were held and distributed by the financial administration, they were as likely to be used to fund new *traités* with financiers or to pay for recruitment as to meet the immediate needs of supporting the troops in garrison or *en route* for the campaign theatres. Hated by the population, the extraction of these 'military' taxes none the less placed

---

lieutenant of the Auvergne, concerning military response to non-payment of the *subsistances*; A¹ 40, fo. 49, 28 Nov. 1637, order to march troops into the *généralités* of Tours and Blois to oblige inhabitants to pay the *subsistances*.

[42] Regiments and their officers were regularly disciplined for seeking to exact unauthorized contributions (i.e. sums of money for their own use/reimbursement) from French communities: see, for example, SHAT A¹ 61, fos. 190, 215, 14/19 Nov. 1640, reinforces prohibition upon any exaction of contributions within France; orders *intendant* Grémonville to investigate cases of illegal exaction in Picardy and Champagne.

[43] In 1639, Henri II de Bourbon, prince de Condé, proposed cutting through the negotiations with the *Etats* of Languedoc and the consuls of the *villes et communautez* of Guienne by deploying the threat of military force to collect the *subsistances*: AAE MD 1631, fos. 31–2, 22 Aug. 1639. Beik, *Absolutism and Society*, pp. 174–6, discusses the forcible imposition of the *subsistances* on Languedoc.

[44] See chapter 5, pp. 281–3.

[45] AAE MD 1631, fo. 432 [1640], 'les desordres, exactions et malversations de la compagnie des gendarmes de M. le duc d'Halluin et de son regiment de Languedoc' Some details of the document may require a sceptical eye in so far as it was produced in the period of acrimonious dispute between Schomberg and Condé and their partisans over the management of the war-effort on the Pyrenean frontier.

Responses and reactions

coercive potential in the hands of central government greater than any of the normal sanctions for non-payment of taxes. While companies of *fusiliers* under the authority of the *intendants* might be used to collect the *taille* and the other direct taxes from the later 1630s, this was a response that frequently cost more than the projected tax yields from the localities and could do little to counter determined guerrilla tactics by the peasants.[46] In contrast, the use of troops billeted in an area to collect what was assessed for their maintenance was cost-efficient, while resistance to large bodies of troops carried huge risks of violence and devastation.[47]

The taxes for the troops greatly increased the burden placed by the army upon the civil population, a burden made worse by the *bureau des finances*' appropriation of much of the revenue to meet other financial priorities. But this was not the only obstacle to the attempts to fund more effective means of sustaining the troops within France. Ruthless imposition of taxes which were too often diverted from the immediate needs of communities subjected to the troops was matched by a growing use of patronage and influence within government to obtain exemptions from *logement* and from the burden of the *subsistances* and *étape* impositions. Both were already assessed on the basis of the main direct taxes, giving exemption to the usual groups of nobles, ecclesiastics, office-holders, privileged towns and *bourgs*, and ensuring sharp differentials in the levels of assessment between provinces. However, these exemptions of the most prosperous groups in society were accompanied by even more damaging interventions to ensure that entire communities under the jurisdiction of those with influence and connections should be removed from the tax assessment and spared from the *logement* of troops. From the property and tenants of members of the king's household and the villages on the estates of Richelieu downwards, political influence was deployed to ensure exemption.[48] A test of the influence of major provincial power-brokers was their ability to win exemptions from military impositions for their clients.[49] The situation was made considerably worse after 1636, when Richelieu began systematically to sell exemptions from *logement* and from

---

[46] Bonney, *Political Change*, pp. 214–19, on the difficulties of using troops to coerce payment of the traditional direct taxes; Collins, *Fiscal Limits*, p. 203.

[47] SHAT A^1 47ii, fo. 282, 29 Dec. 1638, de Noyers to Charles, marquis de Sourdis: numerous *élections* in the *généralité* of Orléans have refused to pay the *subsistances*, and troops are therefore to be lodged across all these territories; A^1 61, fo. 187, 13 Nov. 1640, general *ordonnance* warning all towns which refuse to pay the *subsistance* that thay will be constrained to meet their obligations by the billeting of troops. Kroener's argument – *Les routes*, pp. 118–20 – that military force was only used to impose the *subsistances* or to lodge troops in the face of armed resistance by the civil population is not supported by the evidence.

[48] SHAT A^1 40, fo. 269, 27 Dec. 1637, instruction to *commissaires pour les subsistances* to exempt estates and lands belonging to the king's officers and household; A^1 36, fo. 87, 28 Apr. 1637, full exemption for all villages on Richelieu's estates.

[49] SHAT A^1 25, fos. 274–6, 1 Sept. 1635, requests for exemptions by maréchal Vitry on behalf of some of his clients. For a regional example of the competition to gain exemptions through patrons, see Bercé, *Histoire des croquants*, I. 57–9.

contributions to the *étapes*.⁵⁰ In 1638 the ministers had tried to reverse this trend, insisting that exemptions applied only to *logement* itself and not the accompanying taxes, but by 1641 this had been abandoned and general exemptions were once again being confirmed.⁵¹ While recognizing that exemptions were far too widely granted, nothing serious was done to reverse the trend, partly, of course, because the ministers themselves and their clients were prime beneficiaries.⁵² The ultimate result, as described in a *mémoire* sent to Gaston d'Orléans in 1645, was that in each *élection* there would typically be only three to four places without some form of exemption and in which troops could be lodged.⁵³

If the overt use of public office to obtain private benefits was an inevitable characteristic of this society, no less damaging was a high level of corruption in the allocation of *étapes* and *logement* even amongst places notionally subject to the burdens of the troops and their taxes. Towns or local dignitaries might be prepared to offer bribes to unit officers, *commissaires* or others involved in the allocation of troops in return for a change of route or the reduction of the number of troops in the garrison allocation. A characteristic example came to light in March 1640, when it emerged that the cavalry company of Paul Le Prévost, marquis d'Oysonville, had accepted a bribe of 200 *livres* per day not to lodge in the town of Bellême, but to billet themselves in a nearby village (Saint-Martin).⁵⁴ Such local corruption did not benefit the *épargne* and threw the burden of supporting the troops still more heavily upon the remaining communities. These, which were less and less able to sustain repeated burdens, provided a standing incitement to violence by the frustrated soldiery.

A final obstacle to the effectiveness of these systems for the quartering and subsistence of the troops was the corruption and, above all, the administrative incoherence of the agents variously established to try to manage the soldiers within France. This network of expedients, especially the ever-changing identities and authority of the *commissaires pour les subsistances*, was considered in chapters 7 and 8, and does not require detailed reexamination here. Yet the lack of any logical

---

⁵⁰ Kroener, *Les routes*, pp. 115–18; SHAT A¹ 65, fo. 279, 26 July 1641, purchase of exemption from *logement* and *subsistances* by town of Péronne.

⁵¹ SHAT A¹ 50ii, fo. 325, 28 Feb. 1638, *ordonnance* to constrain the *officiers* who consider themselves exempt from *logement* to pay the *subsistances*; A¹ 44, fo. 218, 12 Mar. 1638, order that no exemptions from the *subsistances* are to be granted to the inhabitants of Commercy; A¹ 67, pce 190, 29 Aug. 1641, *ordonnance* concerning exemptions from the *subsistances*; this reversal of policy is discussed in Navereau, *Logement*, pp. 40–1.

⁵² SHAT A¹ 52, fo. 365, 6 June 1638, de Noyers to maréchal Schomberg, emphasizing the problems for the troops' subsistence caused by excessive numbers of exemptions across Languedoc. In granting exemptions, the *bureau des finances* led from the front: A¹ 44, fo. 468, 31 Mar. 1637, disorders caused by troops illegally lodged on exempted property of *surintendant* Bullion; A¹ 60, fo. 242, 25 Aug. 1640, order to exact 3,000 *livres* from regt of Martin Ruzé, marquis d'Effiat, to compensate for damage caused to Bullion's estates.

⁵³ Kroener, *Les routes*, p. 116.

⁵⁴ SHAT A¹ 58, fo. 77, 7 Mar. 1640, de Noyers to Pierre Thiersault, *intendant* at Alençon; for an identical case involving the inhabitants of Montmirail, see A¹ 70, fo. 260, 15 Oct. 1642.

Responses and reactions

structure in the allocation of responsibilities amongst different groups of agents charged with the control of the *subsistances*, the *étapes* or the wider questions of maintaining discipline and rigorous timetabling in the movement and allocation of troops to areas of France is obvious from any chronological survey of the years after 1635. Faced with financial and supply shortfalls, resistance to payment of the *subsistance* from the population and extortion and violence by the troops, the various groups of *trésoriers, commissaires, intendants* and other specially commissioned agents, all proved inadequate as agents of royal control.[55] Following his substantial survey of the structures for the support of the troops in France, Bernhard Kroener concluded that

> Die detaillierten Verwaltungsvorschriften haben in der Vergangenheit häufig zu dem Schluß verleitet, daß die französischen Armeen besser versorgt gewesen wären als die ihrer Gegner und Verbundeten. Bisweilen führte die Suche nach den Ursachen zu den widersprüchlichsten Schlußfolgerungen . . . Unsere Untersuchung hat gezeigt, daß weder Richelieu noch Mazarin, ein klar umrissenes Konzept von militärischer Verwaltung besaßen.[56]

Such a verdict, as Kroener recognized, provided not merely a partial explanation for the relative ineffectiveness of the war-effort of this period, but was the administrative background to a human tragedy unfolding at the level of innumerable individual towns and villages across France after 1635.

INDISCIPLINE AND VIOLENCE: SOLDIERS AND CIVILIANS

The direct consequence of this failure to establish a system capable of sustaining the burden of the army within the frontiers of France was massive levels of indiscipline, disorder and conflict between the civil populations and the military.

On the military side, there was undoubtedly frustration at the civilian failure to meet 'reasonable' financial, supply and logistical demands, a frustration felt at all levels from the high command down to the ordinary soldiers. The corps and unit officers soon recognized that financial resources from the *bureau des finances* would consistently fall short of the needs of the armies, and that the food, money and lodging demanded from local communities *en route* for the campaign theatres and during the winter quarter constituted an important element in a package by which

---

[55] Kroener, *Les routes*, p. 171: 'So blieben die auf allen Ebenen der Heeresversorgung eingesetzten Amtsträger nahezu völlig unabhängig von den Anweisungen der Krone, die ihrerseits außerstande war, eine wirksame Kontrolle auszuüben.' (On all levels the administrators serving with the armies remained almost entirely independent of the directions of the crown, which was itself not in a position to exercise an effective system of control.)

[56] Kroener, *Les routes*, pp. 170–1: ['Examination of] detailed administrative legislation has in the past led frequently to the assumption that the French armies were better supported than those of their enemies and allies. However, the examination of the actual system leads to the opposite conclusion . . . Our investigation has shown that neither Richelieu nor Mazarin possessed a clearly defined concept of military administration.'

they and their soldiers would be remunerated.[57] While the soldiers themselves had little expectation that they would receive either regular or full payment of their wages, they did expect the provision of basic rations; at the very least this would mean the issue of *pain de munition* and some drink, or a sufficient *prêt* in lieu to buy basic foodstuffs from the *vivandiers* present with the armies. When the responsibility for these basic provisions and for the lodging of the troops had been laid upon the local populations by winter quartering or *étape* ordinances and were not forthcoming, the reaction was predictable: what was not given freely would be taken, and the population punished with violence and intimidation for their resistance.

An obvious question when examining the mass of letters and detailed accounts concerning acts of violence by the soldiery against French populations is why soldiers, whose *raison d'être* might appear to be the protection of French civilians against enemy armies, should have been so ready to behave with savagery and lack of any constraint towards their countrymen. A traditional response would stress the supposedly marginal social background of the soldiery. Assuming that the typical soldiers of the Thirty Years War were little more than vagrants, scraped up through gaol-clearings and conscripted from amongst the indigent and idle poor of the localities, it was not at all surprising that they saw the established peasantry and artisans of the civil population as a 'respectable' source of pillage and extortion.[58] But more recent research, both on France and other European states, has challenged this view that typical soldiers were of a social background markedly inferior to the surrounding peasant and artisanal society. R. Chaboche, in his pioneering study of the first soldiers admitted to the Hôtel des Invalides after 1670–1, shows not merely that there was a proportionally larger number of recruits drawn from urban rather than from rural areas in the armies down to 1648, but points to the artisan backgrounds of a large proportion of these – admittedly long-serving – troops.[59] The relatively respectable social background of many of the recruits fits the picture drawn by André Corvisier for the end of the century.[60] The number of *goujats* – menial servants – maintained by the ordinary troops, the notorious reluctance of the French soldiers to carry their own baggage or to undertake heavy manual work such as the building or demolition of fortifications, tell against the view that soldiers were drawn from the dregs of the

---

[57] And many of the officers would have made advances on their own credit both to raise and maintain their units during the campaigns, rendering them even more reluctant to shoulder the burdens of supporting their soldiers over the winter months: see chapter 6, pp. 336–48.

[58] A typical view is that of Babeau, *Vie militaire*, I. 156: 'l'infanterie qui est composée de deux tiers vagabonds, déserteurs et coquins, doit nécessairement être conduite comme des forçats'.

[59] Chaboche, 'Soldats français'; also R. Chaboche, 'Le recrutement des sergents et des caporaux de l'armée française au XVIIe siècle', in *Recrutement, mentalités, sociétés. Actes du colloque international d'histoire militaire* (Montpellier, 1974), pp. 25–43; Chagniot, 'Mobilité sociale'.

[60] Corvisier, *L'armée française de la fin du XVIIe siècle au ministère de Choiseul. Le soldat* (2 vols; Paris, 1964), p. 449–542.

population and were simply vagrants with weapons.[61] Recognition that those who enlisted may have had personal or immediate economic reasons for accepting military service, but that their backgrounds were more usually those of the established lower classes than the entirely marginal, has extended beyond studies of France.[62]

It was not that the soldiers were socially inferior to the mass of the ordinary population, but that they saw themselves, and to an extent were encouraged to see themselves, as a separate group of men, set apart by their profession. Even new recruits, the vast majority of whom would be unlikely to serve more than a single campaign, seem to have absorbed some of this sense of being a distinct caste, governed by its own identity and rules which would pit the soldiers against all outsiders. This perception could vary considerably in intensity. German, Scottish, Irish or Italian mercenaries, serving within France under their own officers, and excluded by language and culture from the populations on which they were billeted, would provide the most extreme example of alienation from surrounding society.[63] Equally, the implacable reluctance of French troops to serve across the frontiers in the Empire or in Italy reflected their sense of isolation and estrangement in the midst of an environment which could prove murderously hostile.[64] In both these cases the surrounding population was seen as little different from the enemy, as the litany of complaint about the behaviour of foreign regiments garrisoned in France, and the violence and extortion of French units campaigning in allied Piedmont bear witness.[65] Yet the attitudes of French units serving within

---

[61] Avenel, *Richelieu*, III. 23. This tolerance of the soldiers' self-perception is substantiated in numerous contemporary documents: Avenel, III. 640, 23 Apr. 1630, Richelieu writes of the need to pay the soldiers to construct basic fortifications near to Susa, pioneers not being available for the task.

[62] Kroener, 'Soldat oder Soldateska?'; Kroener, 'Conditions de vie et origine sociale du personnel militaire subalterne au cours de la Guerre de Trente Ans', *Francia*, 15 (1987), 321–50, at 340–50; B. Bei der Wieden, 'Niederdeutsche Söldner vor dem Dreißigjährigen Krieg: Geistige und mentale Grenzen eines sozialen Raums', and by Rogg, "Zerhauen und zerschnitten, nach adelichen Sitten': Herkunft, Entwicklung und Funktion soldatischer Tracht . . .', both in Kroener and Pröve (eds.), *Krieg und Frieden*, 85–135; Kapser, *Die bayerische Kriegsorganization*, pp. 70–4, 270–3; Burschel, *Söldner im Nordwestdeutschland des 16. Jahrhunderts und 17. Jahrhunderts* (Göttingen, 1994), pp. 54–96. This shift in historiographical perception is ably summarized by Geoffrey Parker, 'The soldiers of the Thirty Years War', in Repgen (ed.), *Krieg und Politik*, pp. 303–15, esp. pp. 305–7.

[63] A situation recognized, at least in theory, by the crown, which ordered the *commissaires pour les subsistances* to treat foreign regiments with favour as they would find it more difficult to subsist within France: SHAT A¹ 58, fo. 510, 21 Apr. 1640, de Noyers to *commissaire* Caumartin, in the *généralité* of Soissons.

[64] Though given the epidemic level of desertion amongst French troops at the moment that they heard a rumour that they were to move eastwards across the frontiers, a more basic factor was undoubtedly the lack of confidence that they would receive adequate subsistence, and the greater difficulties of desertion should their situation become intolerable.

[65] Irish infantry and German cavalry regiments figure most frequently amongst all the complaints levelled against foreign troops within France, with Fitzwilliam's and Streff's units most regularly mentioned in correspondence. For disorders and exactions of French troops in Piedmont, see, for example, AAE CP Savoie 24, fo. 541, 17 June 1636, d'Hémery to Richelieu: 'de continuer la guerre comme on faict c'est un abus[;] cette armee sera un Brigandage [*sic*]'; Savoie 31, fo. 242, 14 Oct.

The army and the civilian population

the French frontiers were not markedly different. A society in which the concept of the *pays* most often identified a group of villages – perhaps linked together with the local town; where even a provincial identity had only the most embryonic existence amongst the ordinary population; where local customs and dialect varied sharply, provided an environment which troops recruited from the other side of France would find scarcely less foreign than service abroad. In so far as the ministry had a policy with regard to the location of regiments and cavalry companies, it was to avoid maintaining them within their provinces or regions of origin. Distancing the units from their area of recruitment made desertion more difficult and dangerous, and prevented the development of a mentality typical of provincial militia and the *arrière-ban*, which either flatly refused to serve outside of its own province or sought to impose stringent limits upon the duration of such service.[66] These were obvious dangers, but it was no less the case that troops from Guienne or Poitou who found themselves garrisoned in towns in Picardy felt little or no common identity with the northern French population surrounding them. They would feel correspondingly little restraint in extorting goods or money, or responding with extreme violence to any attack by civilians on any members of the unit.[67]

Perhaps indicative of this pervasive ethos of apartness, and of a shared identity defined against the civilian population, is the evidence that the more prestigious regiments and companies seem to have behaved with even less restraint in robbing and brutalizing the population than the newly recruited and short-lived units.[68] Possessing a higher proportion of long-serving, veteran, troops for whom military service was likely to be a long-term career, these regiments and elite cavalry companies had developed an *esprit de corps* at least as strong as some of the foreign mercenary units.[69] Taking only one example, the *secrétaire d'Etat* wrote concerning the disorders and outrages committed against French civilian populations

---

1640, Chavigny to Mazarin; SHAT A¹ 68, fo. 74, 12 Jan. 1642; A¹ 70, 27 Oct. 1642 – both concerned with unacceptable level of troops disorders.

[66] SHAT A¹ 59, fo. 362, 15 June 1640, militias of Calais, Ardres and Boulogne to be mobilized to guard the frontiers now that the regular troops had moved into enemy territory; Avenel, *Richelieu*, III. 11–12, suggests in addition that it was felt that troops garrisoned within their own province would find it too easy to settle into a comfortable and undemanding routine.

[67] Conversely, troops from the regt of Normandie billeted in Languedoc felt no compunction about extorting additional money and goods from the inhabitants of Castelnaudery: SHAT A¹ 57, fo. 375, 13 Feb. 1640, instructions to the *intendant* Barthélémé Dupré to investigate the charges.

[68] Such a proposition is inevitably difficult to quantify in any exact way, and is open to the obvious criticism that the war minister might react more vigorously to complaints against the elite units, or even that these units are more likely to be mentioned in the correspondence of the minister than the lawlessness of short-service units which were raised at the expense of the proprietor and where disbandment was the obvious and typical sanction for disorder – often carried out on the initiative of the local commander and his administrators.

[69] It might also be speculated that the attempt to discourage marriage amongst such veteran troops may have contributed to the process of desocialization: Babeau, *Vie militaire*, I. 203–4; This was a policy maintained into the late seventeenth century: Corvisier, *L'armée française*, pp. 757–72; Lynn, *Giant of the Grand Siècle*, pp. 339–40.

Responses and reactions

by the *vieux régiment* of Picardie on at least five occasions between 1636 and 1642.[70] A similar pattern of extortion and violence is evident for most of the elite regiments, whether the other *vieux*,[71] the *petits vieux* or the quasi-permanent 'household' regiments of the *grands* and the major provincial nobles.

Even more significant is the evidence of the involvement of the unit officers in disorders and violence. One of the most surprising aspects of the correspondence related to disorders is not just that officers were engaged in their own private extortion and violence at the expense of the citizenry, but that on numerous occasions, they were prepared to throw in their lot with the soldiers in pillaging goods and money or in 'punishing' local resistance.[72] In July 1639 the *intendant* Jean Choisy wrote to de Noyers of an incident near Châlons in which a village – which happened to belong to one of the *présidents* of the *Parlement* of Paris, Henri de Mesmes – was attacked by the regiment of Navailles, led by the *mestre de camp*, the baron de Navailles in person. Intending to billet some of the troops upon the village in obvious defiance of its exemption, the regiment encountered vigorous resistance from the inhabitants during which Navailles was wounded by a musket shot. He himself then gave the order for the total sack of the village. After looting and destroying what they could, the officers and soldiers forced their way into the church where the majority of villagers had taken refuge, killing one and attempting to hang the peasant suspected of having fired the shot that wounded Navailles. Some thirty to forty of the villagers were dragged off by the regiment to Verdun, where they were to be ransomed at 12–15 *pistolles* per prisoner. Whether the prisoners were released before being forced to pay the ransoms is not revealed

---

[70] SHAT A¹ 31, fo. 37, 7 Dec. 1636, complaints of inhabitants of Epernay; A¹ 51, fo. 201, 23 Mar. 1639, 'continual disorders of regt of Picardie'; A¹ 63, fo. 129, 16 Jan. 1640, violence surrounding regimental recruitment; A¹ 68, fo. 153bis, 22 Jan. 1642, violence of Picardie regt at Beauvais; A¹ 70, fo. 532, 15 Dec. 1642, disorders of regt at Sens. Given the selective nature of the material in the Archives de la Guerre, and the strong possibility that some of the grievances against the regiment would be taken to authorities other than the *secrétaire d'Etat*, these five cases must be assumed as the absolute minimum of incidents involving the Picardie regiment.

[71] Richelieu's own, newly promoted, *vieux régiment* – La Marine – was certainly not immune from such disorders: SHAT A¹ 64, fos. 237, 257–8, 12/16 Apr. 1641; A¹ 68, fo. 433, 26 Feb. 1642. Nor was the *régiment des gardes françaises*: A¹ 51, fo. 14, 3 Mar. 1639, disbandment of a company of *gardes* for disorders.

[72] From 1640: SHAT A¹ 57, fo. 332, 8 Feb., *Parlement* of Metz to investigate charges of violence and pillage against governors of *places* in Lorraine and Barrois; A¹ 57, fo. 462, 20 Feb., corruption, theft and disorders perpetrated by the lt. col. of Crosby's regt; A¹ 58, fos. 381, 382, 6 Apr., *intendant* Bellejambe to arrest major and sergeant-major of Irish regiment of Coulon (Cullen?), charged with local disorders; A¹ 59, fo. 46, 10 May, conflict of jurisdiction in case of a captain who murdered the sieur de Saint-Estienne; A¹ 59, fo. 653, 9 July, arrest of capt. La Borde from regt of Francois d'Aubusson, comte de La Feuillade, accused of violent disorders; A¹ 59, fo. 682bis, 12 July, de Noyers to Châtillon and La Meilleraye, concerning the rape of an eighteen-year-old girl by officers of regt of the marquis d'Aubais; A¹ 60, fo. 59, 27 July, *prévôt* of Langres to arrest captain Yves, charged with theft and extortion; A¹ 61, fo. 176, 11 Nov., *prévôt de l'Hôtel* to travel to Noyon to arrest certain officers guilty of extensive disorders and to conduct them to the Bastille; A¹ 61, fo. 179, 12 Nov., Michel Le Tellier and *commissaire* Talon to investigate the wholesale corruption of governors of *places* in Piedmont.

The army and the civilian population

in the account; the *intendant* simply ended with the comment: 'Vous jugerez M[onseigneur] sy telz crimes sont pardonnables, et sy les armes du Roy peuvent prosperer commandez par telz officiers.'[73] Choisy did act to dissolve the regiment, dismissing the officers and, with a certain irony, transferring the soldiers into the regiment of Picardie.[74] Yet despite this resolute action by an experienced *intendant d'armée*, the attitude of the government to the involvement or complicity of officers in the behaviour of their troops remained ambiguous. A series of *ordonnances* emphasized that officers would be considered financially liable for pillage and destruction caused by their soldiers which they failed to restrain.[75] Roger de Rabutin, comte de Bussy, was arrested and imprisoned in the Bastille for three months for failing to prevent the disorders of his regiment while they were quartered in Moulins during the winter of 1640–1, months during which he was almost entirely absent from his troops and, according to his *Mémoires*, preoccupied by his affair with the comtesse Hélène de Busset.[76] Although he ascribed this imprisonment to the malice of Sublet de Noyers and his release to the intervention of Richelieu's relative-by-marriage, the comte de Guiche, disorders committed by the regiment at Nogent-le-Roi earlier in the year and a flow of letters concerning the unrest at Moulins suggest that the *secrétaire*'s patience was becoming exhausted.[77] Equally, though, the 'continual disorders' of the foreign cavalry regiment of colonel Gassion, which included similar actions in besieging and sacking *places fortes* within France, and involved the complicity of the officers, did not prevent Gassion's appointment as a *maréchal de camp*, and his steady promotion up to the rank of *maréchal*.[78] There was in practice a grudging willingness to accept that the problems of controlling groups of unruly and

---

[73] AAE CP Lorraine 31, fos. 177v–8, 7 July.
[74] AAE CP Lorraine 31, fos. 177v–8, 7 July.
[75] SHAT A¹ 59, fo. 1, 1 May 1640; A¹ 71, pce 183, 1642. There are plenty of warnings in practice to unit commanders that they should act to control the disorders of their soldiers and subordinate officers: typically, A¹ 58, fo. 276, 27 Mar. 1640, *mestre de camp* Bertrand d'Ostove, seigneur de Clanleu, charged with responsibility for ensuring that the damage and looting caused by his officers and soldiers is reimbursed; A¹ 61, fo. 241, 23 Nov. 1640, criticism of *mestre de camp* Martin de Ruzé, marquis d'Effiat, for failure to restrain disorders.
[76] Bussy-Rabutin, *Mémoires*, I. 77–123; J. Duchêne, *Bussy-Rabutin* (Paris, 1992), pp. 31–5.
[77] SHAT A¹ 57 fo. 319, 6 Feb. 1640; A¹ 58, fo. 157, 14 Mar.; A¹ 61, fo. 365, 11 Dec. 1640, *commissaire* Legendre to investigate complaints of inhabitants of Moulins; A¹ 61, fos. 412, 419, 19 Dec., to establish procedures for investigating disorders of regts of Bussy-Rabutin and Effiat in Moulins. Whatever the influence of Guiche, his release from the Bastille was certainly conditional upon signing an agreement that he would reimburse from the funds paid to his regiment the costs of damage in Moulins and the losses caused by the illicit trade in salt practised by the troops: SHAT A¹ 65, fo. 21, 6 June 1641, de Noyers to Charles Le Clerc du Tremblay, governor of the Bastille.
[78] SHAT A¹ 46, fos. 63, 72, 15 May 1638, instructions to *commissaire* Vallier and to *maréchal* Châtillon to withhold 10,000 *livres* from the regt of Jean de Gassion to compensate for pillage and destruction; A¹ 57, fo. 44, 5 Jan. 1640; A¹ 65, fo. 50, 10 June 1641; Choppin, *Maréchal de Gassion*, pp. 40–128. It could be added that the disorders of Bussy-Rabutin's regiment did not prevent its colonel being appointed to the office of *maître de camp général de la cavalerie* in 1653, a *charge* which had also been held by Gassion.

Responses and reactions

unpaid soldiers would strain the officers' relations with their men and could not be pressed too hard.[79] The *Mémoires* of Bénédict-Louis de Pontis recount his promotion to a lieutenancy in the *gardes françaises*: 'Les soldats étaient alors fort libertins et il se gardait très peu de discipline parmi eux . . . Comme je n'étais point d'humeur à souffrir un tel désordre, je me chagrinai si fort, voyant que je m'allais attirer la haine de tous les soldats.'[80] In 1639, when Pontis had been promoted to a captaincy in the *gardes*, he deliberately turned a blind eye to his soldiers' trafficking in contraband salt while garrisoned in Abbeville: 'Nos soldats qui n'étaient pas trop bien payés faisaient un petit trafic fort commode pour les bourgeois et pour eux-mêmes' – in open defiance of the *officiers* of the *gabelle* who were not strong enough to prevent it.[81]

All of this might suggest that the civilian populations were so many defenceless sheep, to be preyed on by a rapacious soldiery more or less at will, with either the active complicity or the tacit support of their officers. That fails to recognize both the levels of preexistent violence within this society, and the extent to which the behaviour of the soldiers drove the population to extremes in their resistance to what they saw as an alien and hostile presence in their midst.[82] The ministerial regime was not guiltless in this upward spiral of violence; as previously suggested, the willingness to use the presence of troops to extort the *taxe des subsistances* and financial support and provisions for the *étapes*, and to treat the forcible *logement* of military units as the immediate penalty for non-compliance with these demands,

---

[79] Bussy-Rabutin describes what may have been a formative incident in his military career when, in 1638 and shortly after having assumed the command of the regiment after the demission of his father, he insisted on executing a soldier who had been convicted of pillaging a church in the vicinity. Bussy-Rabutin describes the pressure from both officers and soldiers to pardon the offence and the considerable unrest when he insisted that the sentence be carried out: *Mémoires*, I. 41–3.

[80] Pontis, *Mémoires*, p. 105. Pontis' *mémoires* include an even more dramatic case than that given by Bussy-Rabutin of Pontis' determination to execute a soldier who had killed a young woman in Troyes, and the subsequent need to quell a riot amongst other soldiers in the regt who wanted to prevent the punishment being carried out (pp. 277–81). Pontis rehearses all the arguments for severity, though ends up by commuting the capital sentence to a year's service in the regt without any leave.

[81] Pontis, *Mémoires*, pp. 237–8: the reported response of Louis XIII about these troops when the matter was brought to his attention – that 'je ne les empêcherai pas d'être faux sauniers; mais s'ils sont pris par la justice, je ne les empêcherai pas aussi d'être pendus' – is no less indicative of the ambiguities about the troops' disorders – albeit in this case a disorder which harmed only the king's own tax revenues.

[82] That the *Code Michau*, article 203, should recapitulate previous ordinances forbidding commoners to own or to carry firearms is a clear indication of a situation in which peasants and artisans possessed and could use the weapons of the troops – indeed many had acquired these weapons through temporary military service. The capacity of local groups in the Auvergne to defend themselves against soldiers is examined in M. Greenshields, *An Economy of Violence in Early Modern France. Crime and Justice in the Haute Auvergne, 1587–1664* (Pennsylvania, 1994), pp. 158–60. For a European perspective and a typology of civil responses to military pressures, see R. Pillorget, 'Populations civiles et troupes dans le Saint-Empire au cours de la Guerre de Trente Ans', in V. Barrie-Curien, *Guerre et pouvoir en Europe au XVIIe siècle* (Paris, 1991), pp. 151–74.

The army and the civilian population

created an atmosphere in which armed resistance, however desperate, might seem the only recourse. Needless to say, the use of troops to compel obedience to tax and quartering demands created considerable ambiguity about legitimate and illegitimate use of force in the minds of the troops and their officers.[83]

As might be expected, the commonest form of resistance to the soldiers was localized attacks by peasants on isolated companies or smaller detachments of troops. Richelieu himself provides a typical example in a 1637 letter to the king, when he cited the massacre of the company of *chevaux légers* of Bussy de Vere in the Auvergne. Originally allocated to a garrison by the *secrétaire*, de Noyers, this placement was overruled by the *bureau des finances* – presumably the (unspecified) town enjoyed an exemption from *logement* – who ordered the company to march to another *place* in the *élection*. The inhabitants of the second town denied that they had received any order for the billeting of the company and took the opportunity to refuse entrance to a company of only thirty to forty soldiers. As Richelieu described: 'ainsy ils ont esté contraints de battre la campagne, ce qui a excité ce désordre'.[84] The administrative confusion, the provocation offered by a small number of soldiers who responded to their exclusion from an official garrison by trying to live off the countryside and the violent response of the peasantry were all characteristic of such incidents.[85] Attacks on small groups of soldiers in the countryside were opportunistic, and were akin to assaults on tax collectors and other outsiders whose presence and demands were considered illegitimate by the peasants. In some cases, it would appear that such attacks had the sanction of, or were even led by, members of the local elite; in 1640 chancellor Séguier was asked to investigate the case of the assassination of captain du Soudé and numerous *maîtres* of his company of *chevaux légers* by the sieur de Récy and his villagers.[86]

Different in some respects was the situation in the towns, where violence between soldiers and the civil populations, less likely to focus on specific outrages, would more usually be a reflection of the steady accumulation of incidents and frustrations over the months during which troops were in garrison. Moreover, the presence of town authorities whose primary concern was to maintain order, and

---

[83] Lynn, *Giant of the Grand Siècle*, pp. 188–91, recognizes this ambiguity in the government's attitude to violence against civilian populations.

[84] Avenel, v. 760, 10 Mar. 1637, Richelieu to Louis XIII

[85] See, for example, SHAT A¹ 28, fo. 280, 17 July 1636, violence committed by local populations in Périgord against the infantry company of captain des Bordeilles; A¹ 34, fo. 219, 3 Feb. 1639, disorders committed by villagers against company of comte de Lignon; A¹ 59, fo. 115, 16 May 1640, attack of villagers on comp. of regt of Castelmoron; A¹ 60, fo. 266, 28 Aug. 1640, *intendant* of Limousin, Bernard Fortia, to investigate murderous attack by peasants on recruits of the regiment of Boissier; A¹ 60, fo. 305, 1 Sept. 1640, *sénéchal* of Angoumois to investigate inhabitants of two villages who attacked a company from the regiment of Noailles.

[86] A¹ 60, fo. 65, 27 July; a month later the *prévôt* of Senlis was ordered to investigate an attack against a company of the regt of Castelan carried out by the *noblesse* of Senlis: A¹ 60, fo. 244, 25 Aug; see also Greenshields, *An Economy of Violence*, pp. 168–70.

Responses and reactions

the obvious danger of allowing a dispute between civilians and soldiers to get out of hand when the latter could be present in regimental strength, usually ensured that the violence was less extreme than the attacks on isolated companies in the countryside. Civil violence might be restricted to particular individuals, usually officers, who had proved particularly corrupt or brutal in their treatment of the townspeople. The latter had no confidence that the military authorities would impose adequate punishment upon these individuals, and so acted in place of a judiciary which they considered unable or unlikely to serve the interest of local justice.[87] Equally characteristic were acts of 'theft' by townspeople; in most cases it can be assumed they were either reclaiming property stolen from them or attempting to lay hands on goods which could compensate for previous losses.[88] More ingenious was an attempt in 1636 by the town government of Guise to impose a 'tax' on the soldiers' booty obtained from enemy and – presumably – French territory, an attempt which was forcefully rebuffed by the king and de Noyers.[89]

On occasions these limited actions against the soldiers turned into something more serious. Townspeople were certainly prepared to attack small groups of soldiers when they had been provoked by excessive or unjustified demands, and when they thought that they could get away with it.[90] In 1637 the inhabitants of Bayeux assaulted, perhaps unwisely, the company of *chevaux légers* of Richelieu, and four of the townsmen were subsequently summoned before the king to explain their behaviour.[91] But the same tensions that could lead to an attack on a company of soldiers might provoke town populations into an attack on larger bodies of troops. An ordinary line regiment in the middle of the winter quarter might number fewer than 200 soldiers; a population who knew that they were subjected to a *subsistances* tax assessed at well above this troop strength to facilitate the recruitment *traités*, and were then victims of disorders and pillage by the

---

[87] SHAT A¹ 39 fo. 112, 24 Sept. 1637, assassination of a captain by townspeople of Laval; A¹ 39, fos. 179bis, 204, 205, 8/13 Oct. 1637, orders for investigation of violence committed by inhabitants of Grandpré against capt. des Barres; A¹ 50, fo. 35, 4 Jan. 1639, maltreatment of a sergeant of regt of Brazeaux by inhabitants of Saint-Quentin; A¹ 58, fo. 377, 6 Apr. 1640, *intendant* Bellejamme to investigate those accused of attempted assassination of a lieutenant of the regt of Gassion; A¹ 63, fo. 363, 15 Feb. 1641, *prévôt de l'Hôtel* to travel to Reims to investigate the assassination of an *enseign* of regt of Turenne by townspeople.

[88] SHAT A¹ 37, fo. 114, 15 June 1637, order to the inhabitants of Reims to return the horses, arms and equipment which they took from the company of captain Vassay; A¹ 45, fo. 396, 3 May 1638, to investigate thefts from a company of *chevaux légers*, carried out by inhabitants of Saint-Estienne, near Vitry.

[89] SHAT A¹ 30, fo. 169, 23 Oct.

[90] The *intendant* Humbert Chaponay, based in Moulins, made this explicit when he stressed that certain of the inhabitants of the town were no less guilty of crimes than the soldiers, and cited assaults on soldiers by their hosts: BN Ms.fr. 17374, fo. 64, 19 Jan. 1641.

[91] SHAT A¹ 35, fo. 109, 15 Mar.; the episode is mentioned in M. Foisil, *La révolte des Nu-Pieds et les révoltes normandes de 1639* (Paris, 1970), p. 113. A¹ 35, fo. 296, 10 Apr. 1637, investigations of violence of inhabitants of Saint-Pierre-sur-Dives against the comp. of sieur Vetanel; A¹ 37, fo. 159, 18 June 1637, attack by inhabitants of Chaumont on the comp. of Damvilliers.

The army and the civilian population

troops actually present, could easily allow their frustration to turn to violence. In 1640 the populations of La Ferté-Bernard and the nearby hamlet of Saint-Germain rioted against the exactions of the regiment of Bellefonds, wounding numbers of soldiers and seizing horses and baggage.[92] But what might start as an explosion of frustration by the townspeople could turn into a protracted struggle when the troops seized the opportunity to retaliate. In the case of a pitched battle which broke out between the inhabitants of Saint-Mathurin and the regiment of baron du Tot the intervention of chancellor Séguier was required to restore order.[93] The *intendant* in Provence, Charles de La Potherie, was despatched to Toulon in 1636 to try to adjudicate a lengthy and serious dispute between the inhabitants of Toulon and the regiment of Vaillac.[94] Frustration in Toulon had been evident in the previous year when the consuls reported that a captain who had been billeted on the same citizen for over twelve months had refused to change his lodgings and had called upon his soldiers to resist any attempt to move him. The consuls, fearing a popular riot in the town because of this and 'numerous other provocations', had tried to calm matters, but were now appealing to the king aganst the excessive demands of the garrison.[95]

In cases where civil/military disorder had got dangerously out of control, the sympathies of the ministers were not always with the civilians. While there was a reasonable presumption that many disorders would originate with the soldiery, the ministers were also concerned and frustrated at the levels of non-payment of the *subsistances*, resistance to which was seen as tantamount to provoking the troops' disorders. Evidence that some of the inhabitants of Troyes had connived in the setting-up of placards denouncing the *subsistances* tax produced a harsh response from the ministers, largely because practical resistance to the military taxes was already perceived as such a problem.[96] In May 1640, de Noyers was categorical that the attack by the inhabitants of Dreux on the regiment of Saint-Aubin should be treated as rebellion, punishable as *lèse-majesté* in the same way as rebellion against the payment of the *taille*.[97] As with much of the purely civil unrest of the period, the ministers were more worried about the implications of disorder *per se* than with trying to sort out the rights and wrongs of the opposing sides. The primary concern was to achieve a pacification as quickly as possible, if necessary by appearing willing to assert the authority of the crown and its agents. An urban

---

[92] SHAT A¹ 59, fo. 533, 27 June; for a similar case in 1638, see A¹ 47, fo. 408, 21 Nov., order for the investigation of the uprising of the townspeople of Verneuil against the troops in garrison.
[93] SHAT A 1 65, fo. 17, 6 June 1641 – Séguier ordered fines upon the regiment *and* the demolition of the walls of the town; see also A¹ 37, fo. 15, 2 June 1637, maréchal Créqui to investigate violent dispute between town of Romans and a billeted regiment.
[94] SHAT A¹ 32, fos. 248, 249 [1636].
[95] SHAT A¹ 33 (lettres reçues), fo. 59, early Oct. 1635.
[96] SHAT A¹ 63, fo. 206, 25 Jan. 1641, orders to inhabitants of Troyes.
[97] SHAT A¹ 59, fo. 183, 23 May: the execution of the judgement was charged to Bussy-Rabutin and his regiment.

Responses and reactions

elite who had allowed disorder to get out of hand within their town would be treated as having failed in their responsibility, regardless of whether they considered that the grievances which had led to the unrest were within their power to control.

THE LAW, LEGAL *OFFICIERS* AND TROOP DISORDERS

Formal legal codifications of the regulations for controlling troops *en route* and in garrison seem to indicate the determination of the crown and its agents to maintain discipline and punish disorders. Officers who permitted their troops to leave their assigned routes and to billet themselves on other villages were, according to the *Code Michau*, to be punished in peacetime by confiscation of office, and by death in time of war.[98] Any soldiers found in villages – even those specified for the *étapes* – without official *départements* 'signez de nous ou de nos gouverneurs des provinces ou de quelqu'un de nos maréchaux de camp', were to be treated as vagabonds or robbers and executed on capture by the *prévôts* or by civilian judges.[99] A soldier marching through a province with his unit who lagged behind or loses sight of the regimental colour would be punished with the *estrapade*.[100] When billeted in a town, the soldiers were constrained 'sur peine de la vie' to occupy only the prescribed billet, and not to try to change their *logement*.[101] Once lodged, any soldier who had 'rompu malicieusement les meubles de son hoste, et pris de ses hardes [clothing] ou argent, sera pendu sur le champ'.[102] All such sentences imposed when the troops were in quarters were to be executed at the head of the regiment 'pour mieux servir d'exemple'.[103] A 1623 *règlement* 'sur le rétablissement de la discipline, forme et ordre de payement', prescribes the death penalty for *commissaires* and officers engaged in corrupt practices surrounding the presentation of the rolls of the *montre* and the payment of the troops.[104]

Thus in all that touched military/civil relations, the formal regulations concerning the behaviour of the troops prescribed the harshest penalties even for first offences, and in many cases dispensed with any judicial procedure, stipulating

---

[98] *Code Michau*, art. 252; the officers were also to be financially liable for destruction and pillage carried out by such troops under their charge.
[99] *Code Michau*, arts. 252, 253.
[100] *Code Michau*, art. 260.
[101] *Code Michau*, art. 264.
[102] *Code Michau*, art 266; art. 267 prescribes punishment varying from the *estrapade* to death for any soldier who tried to claim food from his host or who behaved with violence in the host's house; art. 272 prescribes the death penalty for any soldier attempting to demand more than the prescribed *ustensile* from his host.
[103] *Code Michau*, art. 271.
[104] *Les ordonnances militaires tirées du code du roi Henri III*, *règlement* of 14 Aug. 1623, art. XVI; arts. XXII–XXXIV prefigure the disciplinary sanctions specified in the *Code Michau* for breaking regulations concerning the *étapes* and *logement*.

The army and the civilian population

that those caught would be executed 'sur le champ'. The impression that was deliberately created was of a legal code of unrelenting severity; in this the crown and its ministers were accommodating themselves to the common rhetoric of a population whose sense of vulnerability in the face of military force was acute, and who were convinced that soldiers, precisely because they stood outside the normal structures of society, could be controlled only through the harshest discipline. These formal codifications of French military law have a striking artistic parallel in Jacques Callot's well-known series of engravings 'Les grandes misères de la guerre'. Generations have assumed these engravings to be either a forceful condemnation of the French crown's military occupation of the sovereign duchy of Lorraine or a generalized, heartfelt, response to the miseries of war as inflicted on civilian populations. Recent work has laid far more emphasis upon the final engraving of the series, 'La distribution des récompenses'. Upon a close examination of the accompanying texts in this and the earlier engravings, it seems evident that Callot's series is a precise and rhetorical affirmation of the role of reward and, above all, punishment in military life. If it is a response to war, it is one that is concerned to emphasize the savage punishment inflicted on soldiers who pillage, ransack and extort from the peasantry, commit sacrilege, betray trust or defy military discipline to live as marauders. 'Normality' in war and military life, as Callot presents it to his receptive audience, is of a harsh penal code, inflexibly applied by honest and strong-willed captains, acting under the authority of a warrior leader who knew both how to inspire and reward virtue and to punish vice.[105]

The difficulty with this rhetoric of unrelenting punishment for military indiscipline is that, even at the legislative level, it was realized that a code which prescribed capital punishment as the most common penalty for any disobedience was unlikely to be effective. Richelieu's proposals to the 1626 Assembly of the Notables were torn between a concern to be seen as an advocate of harshness – a response to the proposals of the Notables themselves – and a recognition that 'd'autant que les capitalles sont d'autant moings exécutées que plus elles sont rigoureuses, plus l'on demande s'il ne seroit poinct à propos d'en imposer de moindres . . . avec deffenses très expresses aux particuliers de rechercher la relaxation des dites peines en faveur des déliquans, et obligation au prince de ne s'en dispenser jamais'.[106]

Contemporary tracts specifically concerned with military justice, such as Laurens de Ville's *Justice militaire de l'infanterie*, also show flexibility in their

---

[105] This interpretation of Callot's *Grandes Misères* is explored in P. Choné 'Les misères de la guerre ou "la vie du soldat": la force et le droit', in P. Choné and D. Ternois (eds.), *Jacques Callot, 1592–1635* (Catalogue of exhibition – Nancy, June–Sept. 1992; Paris, 1992), pp. 396–409; M. Richard, 'Les Misères et les Malheurs de la guerre (1633): a work and its context', in K. Bussmann and H. Schilling (eds.), *1648. War and Peace in Europe* (3 vols; Münster and Osnabrück, 1998), II. 517–23.
[106] Avenel, II. 321.

prescriptions for the punishment of offences. De Ville goes to considerable lengths to show how the workings of the judicial *conseils de guerre* should allow maximum discretion amongst the judges in the imposition of appropriate penalties, to be established not by rigid prescriptions but by majority verdict.[107] On grounds which admittedly may have been as much utilitarian as based upon the calculation that mandatory capital punishment would render judges overwilling to dismiss cases, the crown increasingly urged that crimes carrying a death sentence should be punished by the galleys. This became the most common penalty for those convicted of desertion,[108] and by 1642 the *secrétaire* had issued a general order that all military and military/civil crimes should be punished with the galleys.[109]

Scepticism about whether the mandatory imposition of the harshest penalty was the best response to crimes committed by the troops reflected awareness of the practical failure of the various judicial institutions and *officiers* to curb indiscipline and disorders. The fundamental problem in dealing with *délits mixtes* – crimes involving the military and civilians – was the failure to establish any clear set of rules to establish who had the authority to investigate and try such cases. Both military and civil *officiers* claimed cognizance, so that the resulting clashes of jurisdiction did much to disable any effective response to such crimes.

If the crimes were to be judged solely by the military administration, it was strongly suspected that flexibility in the imposition of penalties would verge on laxity or complicity with the soldiers. Senior officers who sat on the *conseils de guerre*, it was assumed, would always tend to share some degree of sympathy with the plight of an unpaid and poorly fed soldiery whose service under arms required that they should get sustenance from somewhere. Yet in practice this may have been less of a factor than was frequently assumed.[110] Once the case had reached the point of being formally tried before a *conseil de guerre*, often with the participation of the legally qualified *intendant d'armée* or the presence of a *commissaire des guerres*, the officers were unlikely to dismiss the offence or to prescribe a mild punishment.[111] The more typical problem, as Bussy-Rabutin intimated in his *mémoires*, was the pressure on commanders to grant reprieves once sentence had been passed. Not merely did the soldiers' sympathies lie with their convicted colleague, but commanding officers were obviously reluctant to execute experienced soldiers for crimes against civilians. In 1640 maréchal Châtillon wrote to de Noyers on behalf of three *chevaux légers* of the regiment of

---

[107] Ville, *La justice militaire*, pp. 26–105.
[108] For example SHAT A^1 59, fo. 327, 10 June 1640; A^1 69 fo. 221, 5 May 1642.
[109] SHAT A^1 70, fo. 368, 11 Nov.
[110] Though Humbert Chaponay wrote to Séguier of the resistance being put up by the officers on a *conseil de guerre* at Moulins to delivering a guilty verdict against an *enseign* of Bussy-Rabutin's regiment charged with rape; the officers argued that it was improbable that the young man would rape a woman of forty, serving in a cabaret: BN Ms.fr. 17374, fo. 64, 19 Jan. 1641.
[111] Salerian-Saugy, *Les conseils de guerre*, pp. 64–82.

The army and the civilian population

Bouillon, who had been found guilty of robbing a merchant of Saint Quentin: one had been sentenced to death, the other two to the galleys. Châtillon wrote that both the colonel and company captain: 'tesmoignent avoir grand regret sil fault qu'ils perdent ces trois hommes qui sont avec eux il y a longtemps, ont fait preuve de leur courage en beaucoup d'occasions', and asked for the sentences to be commuted to a period of unpaid service with the regiment.[112] This kind of lenity was even more evident when the accused was one of the regimental officers, some of whom seem to have remained at large, or even in service, after sentence was passed on them.[113] With unit officers, the ministry was sometimes also torn between the desire to see justice executed and the temptation to accept a financial composition by which the culprit would agree to raise more troops. In February 1642, de Noyers ordered the release of a captain Sanson, whose troops had dispersed in the course of disorders committed during the winter quarter, but who had offered to reestablish the company at his own expense.[114]

More problematic than the presumed bias of the officers assembled in a *conseil de guerre* were the almost insuperable problems of divided and conflicting authority within the military judiciary. The weaknesses and duplication of the various groups of *officiers* with judicial authority were discussed in chapter 7; they were no more effective in handling cases which involved soldiers and civilians than in taking cognizance of exclusively military crimes such as desertion or violence between soldiers. Different groups of *prévôts* and *commissaires* appeared more jealous of their own jurisdiction than prepared to cooperate in a common bid to maintain discipline. Too many of the judicial *officiers* had no formal legal qualification, and could only carry out sentences on soldiers they apprehended in the act of committing a crime.[115] Rivalries between the various groups of military officials were only subsumed by a more general dislike of the involvement by any part of the civil judiciary – even in cases which involved both soldiers and civilians. The crown's official policy in determining whether a case should be subject to civil or military jurisdiction depended on whether the crime was committed in a province where a full army-corps was stationed, or whether the

---

[112] AAE MD 1679, fo. 43, 18 May. Similarly, SHAT A¹ 31, fo. 45, 7 Dec. 1636, king's displeasure with captains Viteaux and Chémerault, who have refused to hand over to the *prévôt* for punishment 'with full rigour' troopers from their companies of *chevaux légers*.

[113] SHAT A¹ 30, fo. 282, 7 Oct. 1636, order to *prévôts* and other judicial *officiers* to arrest Le Clerc, first captain of regt of Vernancourt, who is still at large; A¹ 66, fo. 483, 13 Dec. 1641, order to officers of justice in Paris to arrest captain Lespine of d'Huxelles' regiment, who had been sentenced to death for pillage and extortion; AAE CP Lorraine 27, fo. 228, 9 Dec. 1635, *prévôt* from army of La Valette excuses himself for the failure to carry out a sentence against a *cornette* from the cavalry company of Bouquainville, but was forced to release the man on the express orders of Louis-Emmanuel de Valois, comte d'Alais, *colonel général de la cavalerie légère*. The *cornette* has been restored to his company and is serving in a garrison outside the reach of the *prévôt*.

[114] SHAT A¹ 68, fo. 336, 10 Feb. For other examples of these recruitment 'deals' see chapter 6, pp. 336–9.

[115] See chapter 7, pp. 376–81.

soldiers were simply *en route* or serving as detached garrisons.[116] This would apparently leave a considerable field of jurisdiction to the civil authorities, especially when the troops were established in winter quarters. However, by claiming that a particular crime was a matter of exclusively military concern, it was possible to have cases withdrawn from civil judges and returned to military administrators, both when the troops were not serving with an army-corps and when the crime concerned one non-military party.[117] Evocation of such cases could occur even when the civil court claiming jurisdiction was the *Parlement* of Paris, as was the case in 1640 when the king ordered that the investigation of a captain charged with the murder of a gentleman should be returned to the *intendant* of the army of La Meilleraye, Claude Gobelin.[118] A smaller but no less contentious issue was the claims of foreign colonels in French service that all crimes committed by their soldiers, in any context, could be judged only by a tribunal of their serving countrymen. Against this, French judges asserted that any crime which involved a French civilian would remove the case from the exclusive jurisdiction of the foreign troops.[119] Yet the issue remained ambiguous. In 1640 the colonels of the Irish regiments in French service were permitted to set up a *conseil de guerre* of seven senior Irish officers to try lieutenant-colonel Butler of Crosby's regiment, charged with having authorized extortion and violence committed by the men under his command.[120] Later in the year, however, the crown appeared to side firmly with the 'French' interpretation, asserting that the claims of foreign colonels to comprehensive jurisdiction had been the cause of innumerable abuses of justice and unpunished crimes, and insisting that henceforth all crimes involving persons outside of the foreign regiment were to be judged by the army or the civil judiciary.[121] Needless to say, such orders served more as a clarification of intentions than a solution to disorders; extortion and violence committed by foreign regiments continued, and foreign colonels still

---

[116] The distinction is made expressly in a letter to the *Parlement* of Provence, emphasizing that they did not have jurisdiction over a captain of the regiment of Cornusson, serving with the army commanded by Vitry: SHAT A¹ 25, fo. 391, 30 Sept. 1635.

[117] See, for example, the complaints of the officers of the regiments of Picardie and Rambures that the *présidial* of Troyes was claiming jurisdiction over the crimes committed by soldiers in their regiments, and the response of the *secrétaire d'Etat* that the *présidial* should return all such cases to the jurisdiction of the regiments: S.H.A.T. A¹ 51, fo. 271, 28 Mar. 1639. The officers of Rambures were involved in a similar jurisdictional dispute, this time with the *intendant* at Arras, three years later over the trial and punishment of soldiers from their regt: A¹ 68, fo. 525, 13 Mar. 1642.

[118] SHAT A¹ 59, fo. 46, 10 May; A¹ 29, fos. 136–7, 3 Sept. 1636, arrest of two *chevaux légers* in the vicinity of the Louvre by the *prévôt* of the Île de France – to be handed back to their captain for investigation and trial.

[119] This could also be asserted in practice: A¹ 44, fo. 132, 4 Mar. 1638, *intendant* Claude Gobelin to suppress the disorders committed by the Scottish regiment of Lord James Douglas.

[120] SHAT A¹ 58, fo. 373, 5 Apr.; A¹ 45, fo. 340, 27 Apr. 1638, order to release Irish soldiers who have been imprisoned at Châlons in defiance of their privileges as foreign soldiers.

[121] SHAT A¹ 59, fos. 162, 168, 20/1 May 1640.

needed regularly to be reminded that their soldiers were not exclusively under their own jurisdiction.[122]

Both in the interests of maintaining the status of their own courts and because they believed that the military jurisdiction was likely to prove too lenient, civil judges did not simply accept such evocation of *délits mixtes*. Civil judges won some of their claims to try cases involving soldiers, and there seems evidence that by the last years of Richelieu's ministry the crown and its agents were coming to the conclusion that the civil judiciary was more likely to restrain disorders than the military.[123] Certainly, individual commissions to investigate crimes involving soldiers were very likely to be given to civilians.[124] By late 1641 the crown had accorded authority to mayors and councillors in the towns to arrest officers whose soldiers had committed disorders or violence against the citizens.[125]

Yet there were disadvantages to reliance on the civil judges. Even the most powerful provincial courts were not always able to resist the power of patronage; the deployment of ministerial and court connections was the most typical reason why officers brought before a civilian tribunal had cases against them summarily quashed on higher authority. In 1633 the *secrétaire*, Abel Servien, wrote to the *premier président* of the *Parlement* of Aix, informing him that he was to suppress a case being brought by the *Parlement* against the brother of the first captain of the regiment of Sault.[126] Despite considerable concern at the disorders of the Picardie regiment in Beauvais in early 1642, de Noyers still wrote peremptorily to order the release of a captain of the regiment, imprisoned on the authority of the local justices.[127] There is understandably no explicit evidence that aristocratic army commanders, standing behind the *prévôts* or the *conseils de guerre*, would be more willing to resist undue influence in the matter of officers' criminal offences, at least if the officers accused were not part of their own clientele. Yet the criticism by some of the commanders about the weakness of their *prévôts* and frustration with the ineffectiveness of the legal procedures in their army-corps suggests a greater readiness to assert their authority even in the face of well-connected

---

[122] SHAT A^1 65, fo. 50, 10 June 1642, order to Gassion to hand over two *reiters* of his regt, charged with local disorders and violence.

[123] SHAT A^1 61, fo. 412, 19 Dec. 1641, rights of jurisdiction confirmed in hands of *présidial* of Moulins; A^1 66, fo. 85, 3 Oct. 1641, rights of jurisdiction granted to *présidial* of Amiens.

[124] SHAT A^1 32, pce 247, [1636], commission for the *maître des requêtes*, Henri Gamin, to travel to the *généralité* of Amiens to adjudicate in disputes between the military and the civil population; A 1 37, fo. 295, 4 July 1637: *vice-sénéchal* of Agen to try captain of regt of Calonges; A^1 58, fo. 370, 5 Apr. 1640, *trésorier de France* from Tours to investigate the disorders of the regiment of Périgord, and to receive full support from the *mestre de camp*.

[125] SHAT A^1 66, fo. 524, 26 Dec.

[126] SHAT A^1 41, fo. 11, 13 Aug. 1633.

[127] SHAT A^1 68, fo. 153bis, 22 Jan., concern at disorders; fo. 337, 12 Feb., order for release. A similar order was despatched for the release of a captain of the regiment of Jonzac: A^1 68, fo. 210, 27 Jan. 1642; A^1 71, pce 100, Apr. 1642, *lettres d'abolition* in favour of capt. La Motte and soldiers of his company.

subordinate officers.[128] Henri II de Bourbon, prince de Condé, and a *conseil de guerre* of his senior officers were at least prepared to pass a capital sentence against the baron de Gensac and eighteen of his officers: 'pour les exactions estranges commises par eulx sur le peuple en la levée dud. régiment', whether or not the sentence was carried out.[129]

Moreover, although it may be assumed *a priori* that civil judges would prove more severe in punishing crimes involving soldiers, there are cases of an apparent reluctance to behave with exemplary rigour. No explanation is given of why judicial officials in Cognac were acquitting deserters from Jonzac's regiment in 1642, so that the provincial *intendant* was instructed to investigate the case.[130]

However, the besetting weakness of the civil judges was, perhaps understandably, a narrow preoccupation with jurisdiction; rather than seeing military judges as allies, requiring assistance and support in pursuit of a common goal of curbing disorders which, for the most part, originated with abuses committed by the soldiers, many of the civil administrators saw the military judges as rivals.[131] Cases were to be prised out of the hands of the military tribunals, whatever the effect on the maintenance of local order. The *prévôt général* Montifault described a particular case in Toul, where he was attempting to put on trial and punish the sergeant-major of the garrison, accused of numerous acts of violence and extortion against the bourgeois of the city. Montifault duly arrested the sergeant-major, La Vallée, but was immediately challenged by the lieutenant of justice in Toul and the local *procureur du roi*, who did all possible to block the proceedings. In response, Montifault charged the lieutenant with obstruction, but the latter appealed to the *Parlement* of Metz, which bogged down the case in a lengthy appeal. Montifault now appealed to the king to prohibit the *Parlement* from interference in this case, and to allow him to get on with the business of prosecuting an officer who had been oppressing the citizens of Toul.[132] The crown's response was to tread carefully. The *maître des requêtes*, Claude Gobelin, was sent to investigate the conflict, and produced a lengthy, judicious, report, as concerned to avoid antagonizing the *Parlement* as to ensure that justice was done in the matter of the

---

[128] See, for example, the criticism of both the duc de Rohan and cardinal de La Valette of the *prévôts* serving with their armies: AAE CP Lorraine 15, fo. 387, 21 Dec. 1634, Rohan to Chavigny: 'Je fais aujourdhuy passer deux soldats par les armes, et si jestois tant peu assisté par les prevosts . . . je croirois maintenir l'armée que Sa Mate m'a commise . . .'; CP Allemagne 12, fo. 445, 11 Dec. 1635, La Valette to Richelieu, dismissing the capacities of all of the *prévôts* with his army save Orgelin: 'il a fait luy seul plus d'executions en un jour que les autres en tout le temps qu'ils ont esté à l'armée'.
[129] AAE MD 1631, fo. 31, 5 Sept. 1639.
[130] SHAT A¹ 69, fo. 194, 27 Apr. 1642, order to François Villemontée.
[131] SHAT A¹ 44, fo. 70, 26 Feb. 1638, a strong rebuke to the *présidial* of Auxerre for failing to provide support to the *prévôt* of the regiment of Bourgogne in his attempt to punish disorders committed by soldiers of the regiment.
[132] AAE CP Lorraine 14, fo. 458, 5 May 1634.

The army and the civilian population

criminal offences of the sergeant-major.[133] A still more egregious example of obstruction in the context of local unrest survives in a 1637 letter from the lieutenant-governor of Meaux. In the case of a soldier accused of murdering a butcher in the town, the lieutenant reported the formal proceedings of the *conseil de guerre*, composed of the captains of the regiment of La Meilleraye who investigated the case and sentenced the soldier to execution at the head of the regiment. However, he went on to describe how the process was halted by the intervention of the *lieutenant criminel* of the town, who insisted that the case should be tried before the judges of the *présidial* of Meaux. The report on this incident, addressed to Séguier, made no bones in claiming that 'le lieutenant criminel qui est homme fort prompt et violent n'avoit forme ce debat que pour exciter de la division entre les capitans de la garnison et les habitants'. Whatever the motive, this civil *officier*'s attempt to seize control of a legal procedure, although it was already working to the benefit of the townspeople, angered the soldiers of the garrison, who now intervened to prevent an execution that was to be carried out by the civil authorities. In turn the *lieutenant criminel* stirred up the inhabitants of the town, especially the butchers, and encouraged them to riot against the garrison.[134] Such cases, if widely replicated, must have added to the already huge problems of controlling the troops present in France.

DISBANDED SOLDIERS, DESERTERS AND MARAUDERS

The disorders caused by soldiers in active service were one major issue confronted by the various military and civil authorities. Equally important was the whole question of disbanded troops – released through the end of campaign service, or through wounding or sickness, or the specific *licenciement* of particular companies and regiments. This problem was greatly exacerbated by the numbers of deserters – masses of soldiers who had abandoned their units and were either living in areas where the army-corps had been posted, or were trying to make their way back to their home provinces.

Battle wounds and sickness on campaign were naturally regarded as occupational hazards for which the army commander or the civil government had only a minimal responsibility. In the case of infectious diseases such as bubonic plague, typhus and dysentery, rates of mortality amongst overcrowded, undernourished and badly housed soldiers were devastatingly high. No account of warfare in this period can ignore the impact of infectious illness on the conduct of campaigns and the formulation of strategy.[135] In facing this threat, administrators and officers

---

[133] AAE CP Lorraine 14, fo. 464, 10 May 1634, Gobelin to Chavigny; fos. 466–9, *mémoire* of Gobelin concerning the case.
[134] BN Ms.fr. 17373, fo. 11, 12 Jan. 1637.
[135] A detailed account of disease and its impact on troops is provided in Burschel, *Söldner im Nordwestdeutschland*, pp. 258–72. For a notable addition to the discussion of disease on the conduct

were virtually helpless. Basic sanitary precautions concerning drinking water, for example, were unknown or ignored: military imperatives dictated the location of troops, and their concentration, in siege-works for example, where there was an inadequate and polluted water supply, would guarantee high rates of mortality from any infectious disease. The only precaution generally practised was the avoidance of places of assembly or *étape* points where epidemics were already raging. The plague which had spread through north Italy in late 1629 was particularly intense in the fortified place of Susa, captured by the French in March 1630. In April Richelieu wrote to order that all other units of the army were to be kept apart, on pain of death, from the regiments of Aiguebonne and Saint-Paul, lodged in Susa, while the soldiers of those two regiments were under no circumstances to leave the town.[136]

Higher rates of survival could have been ensured by an adequate provision of military hospitals, if only because these would have served to some extent to isolate the sick from the remaining healthy troops. Moreover, some rest, care and a more suitable diet would have contributed to getting some of the sick back to health and into service with their units. The same arguments could be applied to those recovering from wounds suffered in combat; although rudimentary surgery, post-operational infection and lack of elementary hygiene would ensure that survival rates from even minor wounds were low, these rates could have been improved by modest levels of hospital care.

The principle of establishing hospitals with the armies was certainly accepted by the crown and its ministers.[137] In a much-quoted phrase, Richelieu expressed the opinion that '2,000 soldiers leaving hospital cured and in some respects broken into military service were far superior to 6,000 new recruits.'[138] Projects for hospitals with the armies were regularly established, and were seen as a critical element in the planning for military campaigns.[139] Planning on paper for military hospitals was extensive and comprehensive. In 1629 a proposal was made to set up a hospital for each regiment in service.[140] An *état* for the establishment of a real hospital in March 1636 at Toul itemizes all of the employees down to laundresses

---

of a particular campaign, that in Bohemia in 1619, see Chaline, *Montagne Blanche*, pp. 59–60; Henri de Campion, lieutenant in the Normandie regiment, describes how 'plus de la moitié des soldats et quantité des officiers' died from plague in the army campaigning in the Franche-Comté in the summer of 1637: *Mémoires*, pp. 87–8.

[136] Avenel, III. 640, 23 Apr. 1630, Richelieu to Charles d'Angennes, comte du Fargis.

[137] And was enshrined in legal compilations such as the *Code Michau* – art. 232 – which also accepted the theoretical obligation to provide lifelong care for all soldiers who had been incapacitated by service – art. 231.

[138] Avenel, IV. 717, 22 Apr. 1635, Richelieu to Servien.

[139] Jones, 'Welfare of the French foot soldier', 194–6; J. Guillermand (ed.), *Histoire de la médecine aux armées*, I: *De l'antiquité à la révolution* (Paris, 1982), pp. 348–65; R. Chaboche, 'Le sort des militaires invalides avant 1674', in R. Baillargeat (ed.), *Les Invalides. Trois siècles d'histoire* (Paris, 1975), pp. 131–6.

[140] This is cited by Babeau, *Vie militaire*, I. 212–13, though he admits that the reality fell short of this aspiration.

The army and the civilian population

and gravediggers, and specifies every item of kitchen, ward and surgical equipment, giving a total of 9,497 *livres* 19 *sols* for the equipment and two months of wages for the staff.[141] Overall supervision of medical provision was a task typically granted under commission either to Richelieu's ecclesiastical *fidèles* or to others who would have direct, personal, responsibility for organization and expenditure.[142] Richelieu had expressed the view that 'un ecclésiastique bien entendu, actif et zélé' was far better than appointing, as in the past, 'des maistres des requestes qui scavent mieux plaindre la misère des soldats blessez qu'y apporter remède et les faire secourir'.[143]

As a proportion of a total military budget the costs of the hospital would seem extremely modest: in the Italian theatre a total of 3 million *livres* was budgeted for the six-month campaign during 1636, of which 48,000 *livres* was set aside for hospital expenses.[144] Moreover, in theory the expenses of the hospitals were not an additional charge on the *épargne* but were to be met by a deduction from the soldiers' wages – in a document of 1635 the rate of deduction was specified as 6 *deniers* per *livre* of the soldiers' *montre*.[145]

The problem with turning these proposals into an actual system of provisioning for the sick and wounded was predictable: although the sums involved were small, the general problems of funding military operations were large. Hospitals simply did not occupy a high priority amongst the demands on the *épargne*, or even as a call on the expenditure of the commanders in the field.[146] When, typically, no money was allocated within the *montre* for 1639 to the costs of setting up a hospital for the troops operating in Lorraine, the commander, François de l'Hospital, seigneur du Hallier, reluctantly advanced 1,500 *livres* on his own credit to provide some rudimentary hospital support.[147] The provision that hospitals were to be

---

[141] A¹ 27, fo. 156, 26 Mar.; similarly: AAE CP Lorraine 27, fo. 175, Nov. 1635, *Dépense pour l'hôpital de Nancy*; AAE MD 832, fo. 110v, [1638], 'ordre nouveau pour garantir les soldats de maladie'.

[142] Avenel, III. 734, 5 July 1630, Richelieu to Henri d'Escoubleau de Sourdis, archbishop of Bordeaux, ordering him to establish a hospital in Pinerolo; SHAT A¹ 32, pce 194, 6 Oct. 1636, Léonor d'Etampes de Valençay, bishop of Chartres, to act to create a hospital to serve the army of Picardy; A¹ 62, pce 338, [1640], commission of *intendant des hôpitaux* in Barrois, Lorraine, Alsace and Germany for Crusy de Marsillac, bishop of Mende. For other agents: Avenel, II. 457, 17 May 1627, Richelieu to Jean de Rechignevoisin, seigneur de Guron, *gentilhomme ordinaire de la Chambre*, to set up a hospital; A¹ 32, pce 60, 20 Apr. 1636, commission for sieur Rapine to establish a hospital with the army of Henri II de Condé.

[143] Avenel, V. 726, Dec. 1636, 'observations' to the *contrôle général pour 1636*.

[144] AAE CP Savoie 24, fo. 27, Jan. 1636; 3,000 *livres* was allocated for the upkeep of the hospital at Narbonne during the 1642 campaign: SHAT A¹ 69, fo. 138, 20 Apr., and A¹ 71, pce 98, 21 Apr.

[145] AAE MD 819, fo. 101, [dated 1633, but more probably 1635]. The system of deductions is confirmed in André, *Michel Le Tellier et l'organization*, pp. 478–9. André also provides the best general account of the development of military hospitals into the 1660s: pp. 469–87.

[146] A letter from de Noyers to the *trésorier de l'extraordinaire des guerres* in November 1641 that he should accept and pay the accounts of sr Berthereau, surgeon with the army of Lorraine, relative to expenditure on medicaments and equipment incurred in 1636, gives some sense of ministerial priorities: SHAT A¹ 66, fo. 399.

[147] AAE CP Lorraine 31, fo. 196, 18 Aug. 1639, du Hallier to de Noyers complaining of the absence of

funded from a levy on the soldiers' wages remained a dead letter when wages were paid so irregularly and almost never above the level of the basic *prêt*, which was merely intended to provide for the soldiers' bare subsistence-needs.

One response to the shortage of funds was to attempt to pass the expenses of hospitals on to the religious Orders. Even if the equipment and supplies would have to be funded from the military budget, the religious involved in the care of the soldiers would not require wages.[148] Moreover, the presence of regular clergy in the hospitals would provide an opportunity to offer religious instruction to the soldiery, judged an even more suitable target for missionary endeavour than the most isolated of Breton peasant communities.[149] Thus in 1636 and in 1639 the Superior of the Order of La Charité was encouraged to send some of his religious to run hospitals for the armies in Italy and on the Flanders frontier.[150] Running military hospitals was a role which the Jesuits had assumed with great success amongst other European armies, and in 1638 an *Ordre nouveau pour garantir les soldats de maladie* proposed turning the whole French system of military hospitals and care of the sick over to the Jesuits. Jesuit fathers with the armies would prepare and distribute bouillon to those invalids who could be treated in their units and did not need hospitalization. In the largest of the armies it was proposed that a hospital should be established, staffed by four Jesuit fathers and two lay brothers; teams half this size would be allocated to each of the lesser armies.[151] In practice however, the role of the Jesuits seems to have been more limited. Six Jesuit priests were sent to the army of La Meilleraye in 1639, but explicitly to care for the spiritual well-being of the soldiers.[152] In 1640 a group of Jesuits with the army in Picardy did seem to have some responsibility for the sick and wounded,

---

any funds for the hospital; SHAT A¹ 60, fo. 236, 24 Aug. 1640, refers to the 1,500 *livres* still being claimed by du Hallier twelve months later. The army of Italy seems to have fared slightly better in its hospital provision, at least during the early 1640s. Le Tellier wrote in June 1641 that 20,000 *livres* had been spent on the hospital during the present campaign, and that 400 wounded soldiers were being cared for: Caron, *Le Tellier*, pp. 73–4.

[148] Though as Louis André points out it was necessary to get formal permission from Rome for clergy to serve with the armies, *Michel Le Tellier et l'organisation*, p. 482.

[149] Spiritual care at the Invalides from 1674 was to be provided by the Order of the *prêtres de la Mission*: H. de Buttet, 'La vie aux Invalides sous le règne de Louis XIV', in Baillargeat (ed.), *Les Invalides*, pp. 210–11.

[150] SHAT A¹ 27, fos. 259, 260, 18 Apr. 1636 (Italy); A¹ 30, fo. 318, 18 Nov. 1636 (Corbie); A¹ 51, fo. 547, 26 Apr. 1639 (Flanders frontier).

[151] AAE MD 832, fo. 110v, [1638].

[152] SHAT A¹ 52, fo. 32, 3 May 1639; in contrast to the Spanish Army of Flanders, chaplains were relatively sparse: Parker, *Army of Flanders*, p. 274, indicates that the staff of a Spanish *tercio* consisted theoretically of a chaplain major and two assistants, while each of the constituent companies would contain its own chaplain. The pay structure for a French regiment in 1635 made provision for one chaplain per regiment – apparently regardless of whether the regiment was of ten or twenty companies: AAE MD 819, fo. 59, [1635]. Even this may have overstated the number of chaplains with a French army-corps; a letter to Henri II de Condé in 1636 notifies him of the despatch of three experienced priests being sent to serve as chaplains with the army of Burgundy: SHAT A¹ 28, fo. 173, 28 June 1636.

but La Meilleraye was informed that their duties had finished with the end of the siege of Arras.[153] Though some Jesuits appear to have been reestablished with the garrison at Arras in 1641, it seems evident that the potential of the Order to combine care for the sick with missionary activity was never fully exploited during Richelieu's ministry.[154]

Above all, the ministry's response to the provision of military hospitals was to seek to impose the burden upon the localities. Either the local authorities were to be persuaded or coerced into assuming the costs and the administration of a formally established military hospital, or the sick and wounded soldiers were imposed upon the local communities as an additional burden. In March 1640, for example, the *échevins* of Abbeville were ordered to assume administrative (and it may be supposed, financial) responsibility for the running of the hospital that was to support the army of La Meilleraye.[155] More typical are instructions such as those to the inhabitants of Crécy to look after the sick and wounded soldiers from the regiment of Valmont, with notification that a *commissaire* was being despatched to the town to ensure that suitable provision was made.[156] An initiative was taken in 1636 to establish a permanent military hospital at Nancy paid for out of local taxes, and a similar example exists of an order to the consuls of Montpellier in 1642 to set up a hospital for wounded soldiers to supplement the provision of military hospitals.[157] As with the *étapes* and the *subsistances*, the population would be promised remission from the *taille* in return for meeting these additional costs, but as in those cases, since the *taille* demands were now made well above the level that the communities would in most cases be able to pay, this ensured that remission was of minimal benefit.

The pressure to absorb sick or wounded soldiers into local communites or into civil hospitals can be seen as part of a larger policy, aiming to shift on to the local communities the burden of caring for soldiers too badly wounded to continue to serve, or having suffered debilitating sickness which would effectively exclude them from active service. The crown's obligation to support such *soldats estropiés* was, after 1635, little more than an expression of good intentions. Equally,

---

[153] SHAT A¹ 59, fo. 197, 27 May 1640; A¹ 60, fo. 245, 25 Aug; four Jesuit priests had been sent to provide care for the sick and wounded with the army of Soissons in Champagne in 1636: A¹ 28, fo. 466, 13 Aug.

[154] SHAT A¹ 65, fo. 107, 17 June 1641, arrangements for paying the Jesuits at Arras.

[155] SHAT A¹ 58, fo. 301, 29 Mar.; similar orders in the following year placed responsibility for the military hospitals at Soissons and Reims in the hands of the mayor and *échevins* of Soissons and the Chapter of the Cathedral at Reims: A¹ 64, fos. 527, 532, 23 May 1641; this was a well-established policy: Grillon, IV. 290, 12 May 1629, Richelieu to Consuls of Gap, ordering them to establish a hospital for soldiers who have fallen ill.

[156] SHAT A¹ 65, fos. 490, 491, 12 Sept. 1641.

[157] SHAT A¹ 31, fos. 107–8, 19 Dec. 1636, de Noyers to the *conseil souverain* at Nancy; A¹ 69, fo. 323, 27 May 1642; the consuls subsequently received the less than lavish sum of 2,257 *livres* to contribute to the costs of this undertaking: A¹ 69, fo. 471, 18 June. André, *Michel Le Tellier et l'organisation*, p. 483, suggests that in 1639 Richelieu specifically ordered that a certain number of major 'civil' hospitals should provide beds and care for soldiers on a permanent basis.

however, there was considerable reluctance to set at large numbers of soldiers who, disbanded because of wounding or sickness and mostly incapable of earning their living in civil society, would turn to begging or vagrancy. The traditional solution to the problem of the war-crippled had been to place them as lay assistants in those monasteries whose royal foundation made it more difficult to refuse the request.[158] The project was revisited in correspondence between Michel de Marillac and Richelieu in early 1630, though even at this stage Marillac pointed to problems with funding and a potential clash of jurisdiction between the *colonel général de l'infanterie* and the *maréchaux* over the right to establish which crippled soldiers would receive support.[159] Moreover, this whole expedient was, as Louis André points out, a cause of endless contention; the notion that ex-soldiers could adjust easily to becoming members of a monastic community was to say the least naïve, even when due allowance is made for reformist aspirations to instil catholic piety into a group whose lives had been little touched by religion. In addition, the stipulation reflected a period of irregular and smaller-scale warfare: if requested, each royal foundation was to take at least one crippled soldier. While under pressure abbeys might be prepared to accept this demand, they showed no willingness to respond to the far larger requirements of the years from 1630.[160]

The alternative was to try to place such soldiers into fortified towns to supplement the existing active garrison – as so-called *mortes payes*. As part of the garrison they would be incorporated into units, placed under military discipline and accorded rations and reduced pay. In theory they would be removed from the civil community, where their capacity to band together with other vagrants and to fill the streets of major cities with begging and petty crime was perceived as an increasingly grave threat. The problems were two-fold. The crown lacked the funds even to pay the regular garrison troops, who already occupied the lowest point in the order of military priorities of the *bureau des finances*. As the arrears owed to garrisons mounted inexorably, so governors and others trying to sustain their troops with basic rations and enough petty cash to stave off mutiny or mass desertion certainly did not intend to divert some of their credit to sustaining the *mortes payes*, whose support was seen as little more than charity. Unpaid and lacking basic food, the crippled soldiers would drift out into the urban community, seeking to sustain themselves through begging and all too likely to play a part in the disorders of the regular garrison as it sought to sustain itself by living *à discrétion* on the townspeople and the surrounding area.[161] As French garrison troops were not placed in barracks but billeted on the unprivileged population,

---

[158] Avenel, II. 212–13, provides a reemphasis of this obligation in the March 1624 *Déclaration pour les places de soldats estropiés dans les abbayes*.
[159] Grillon, v. 19, 35, 41–2, 4/16/22 Jan. 1630, letters from Marillac to Richelieu. Marillac's original *mémoire*, and Richelieu's response to the proposals have not survived.
[160] André, *Michel Le Tellier et l'organisation*, pp. 489–90.
[161] BN Ms.fr. 17373, fo. 3, 20 Jan. 1637, Charmolue to Séguier, concerning the garrison of Roye, living *à discrétion* on the inhabitants.

who would be in the front line when pay and food supplies to the troops ran into arrears, the permanently crippled or convalescent soldiers would simply be added to this burden. The obvious conclusion was that this system's main result was to remove a small proportion of the disbanded and crippled soldiers from the most prosperous towns and cities and impose them upon the populations of the already battered and hard-pressed frontier *places*. Elaborate and extravagant schemes, such as that of Richelieu in 1633 to set up a community, the *commanderie de Saint-Louis*, at the Bicêtre in Paris, whose mission would be the feeding and care of crippled soldiers, fell victim to financial exigencies even before it had begun to assume the role of a place of confinement for the ex-soldiers who thronged into Paris.[162]

Crippled soldiers, unable to support themselves through a return into civilian employment, were perceived as a problem for the towns and, to a lesser extent, the rural communities, rather than for the military administration. They became part of the ever-growing proportion of the population dependent upon charitable support, and presented urban and local elites with the familiar dilemma of either trying to ignore a problem which would not go away and would certainly threaten the fragile social balance on which their position depended, or committing hard-pressed funds to a system of relief which might serve simply to attract more ex-soldiers into the town.[163]

Had the problem simply been that of genuinely wounded or convalescent soldiers, unable to serve in their units and obviously dependent upon alms or other charitable support, the challenge might just have been contained. But the *soldats estropiés* represented a small fraction of the much vaster problem of fit, active, but demobilized soldiers. The handling of soldiers after demobilization had always been a sensitive issue. Indeed one of the oft-claimed advantages of reliance on foreign mercenaries had been that once their contract expired they could be driven across the frontiers where they would remain until a large-scale military force was required again. While wars were short, the scale of mobilization and consequent disbandments of French troops were disruptive, but not devastatingly so. From the 1630s the situation lurched into crisis. Although from 1636 the crown aimed to keep a high proportion of the army in being over the winter quarter and lodged in *places fortes* in the frontier provinces, this did not exclude substantial waves of disbandments of units both during and at the end of each campaign. And while many regiments were kept in being over the winter months, they were maintained at a reduced strength with numbers of their soldiers being laid off to reduce the companies to a level that was sustainable by the local

---

[162] Avenel, *Richelieu*, III. 150–1; Chaboche, 'Sort des invalides', pp. 134–5. The proposal to place the Order under the control of Richelieu's brother and to fund it through a tax on all ecclesiastical benefices yielding more than 2,000 *livres* p.a., ensured considerable opposition from the outset.

[163] André, *Michel Le Tellier et l'organisation*, pp. 490–1, emphasizes the problems caused by crippled soldiers in Paris.

Responses and reactions

communities.[164] In both cases there was a lack of any adequate organization for this demobilization. If the systems for supplying and disciplining troops *en route* for the campaign armies were bad, the provision for moving them back from the frontiers to the French heartlands were virtually non-existent. The only important issue was the possession of a formal *congé* signed by the commander and the *intendant* – without which soldiers ran the risk of being arrested as deserters and punished *sur le champ* by the *prévôts* or civilian officials charged with the repression of desertion. Yet *congés* could be given out by commanders with scant regard for the logistical impact of allowing large numbers of troops to disperse from the armies, making their way back towards their home provinces with little or no food and money to sustain themselves.[165] The readiness to disband units without a final pay imposed hardship even upon the officers; Châtillon appealed to de Noyers to pay a *montre* to the officers of the disbanded regiment of Noailles: 'qu'il ny en a pas deux qui ayant dequoy de reconduire, et la pluspart sont d'Auvergne et Languedoc'.[166] A formal notification of disbandment, assuming the ordinary soldiers were not to be incorporated into other units, would specify that they should be sent home in two's or three's 'to prevent disorders'.[167] What usually happened, of course, was that groups of soldiers found it both safer and more effective to band together in larger groups, dependent in the first instance upon begging to sustain their return journey, but slipping easily into poaching, petty theft and extortion as opportunity arose. The status of disbanded soldiers was by no means always clear; communities who might have felt under pressure to contribute food or money to groups of disbanded troops in the hope of encouraging them to pass on more quickly needed to be reminded on occasions that the ordinary soldiers were not, in fact, formally disbanded, but had been instructed to transfer to another unit in order to increase the latter's effective strength.[168] In such cases soldiers begging food for their 'passage home' were to be treated as deserters.

And it was desertion which transformed the scale of this problem. The

---

[164] BN Ms.fr. 6646, fo. 4, 1 Jan. 1636, Richelieu to cardinal de La Valette, concerning the reduction of seven regiments to 'deux ou trois compagnies chacune ... pour les mettre dans les places et chasteaux de la Lorraine'.

[165] The *maréchaux* Châtillon and Chaulnes were heavily criticized after the siege of Arras in 1640 for handing out *congés* too freely: Aubery, *Richelieu*, II. 591, 25 Aug. 1640, Louis XIII to Châtillon and Chaulnes; general orders in 1639 and 1641 addressed to commanders and *intendants* with the armies, condemned abuses in the system of *congés* and called for much greater restraint in their allocation: SHAT A^1 52, fo. 184, 16 May 1639; A^1 65, fo. 24, 6 June 1641.

[166] AAE MD 1679, fo. 307, 9 Nov. 1640; similar letters have survived from the end of the 1641 campaign on behalf of officers from the disbanded regiments of Beausse and Lusignan: AAE MD 1680, fos. 511, 518, 13/14 Oct.

[167] SHAT A^1 31, fos. 74, 120, 12/20 Dec. 1636, formal orders for disbandment of companies of cavalry.

[168] See, for example, SHAT A^1 34, fo. 24, 4 Jan. 1637, letter to the inhabitants of Beauvais, informing them that the soldiers of the disbanded regt of Bachevilliers are under explicit instructions not to disperse, but to transfer to service in the regt of Nanteuil.

The army and the civilian population

principal difference between legitimately disbanded soldiers making their way back across the provinces and deserters was merely that the former held – or ought to have held – explicit, written, *congés* signed by the *intendant* and/or one of the commanding officers of the army. This was not always the case; soldiers arrested from Bussy-Lamet's and Effiat's regiments in September 1640 produced *congés*, but these had been illicitly issued within the regiments: 'les officiers qui ont donné lesd. congés se trouvent plus coupables que les soldats'. So far as the army and civil authorities were concerned these were worthless scraps of paper, and the soldiers were deserters.[169] However, the vast majority of troops disbanding from the armies throughout the campaign season and into the winter quarter had no *congé* of any sort – licit or illicit – and were without question deserters. The scale of this problem in the French armies has already been touched upon in other contexts. Ministerial approaches to desertion, experimenting with a whole range of responses between extreme, mandatory, harshness and the granting of amnesties for those who admitted their crime and agreed to rejoin their units, were consistent only in their failure to do more than scratch the surface of the issue.[170] When de Noyers could write to Châtillon in 1640 that there had been such massive desertion from his army that in a single morning those who were arrested completely filled all the prison cells in Amiens, this was a situation which went far beyond that typically described in historians' graphs estimating comparative monthly rates of loss from field armies.[171] Desertion, whether in the form of spontaneous mass disbandment like that following the capture of Arras, or the constant trickle of troops making their escape from hardship, inadequate food and pay and erratic military discipline, was not simply a challenge to the maintenance of military effectiveness. It also threatened to overwhelm the fragile mechanisms of local order, control and resource distribution.

The crown and its ministers had clear, self-interested, motives in trying to make systems of *étapes* or winter quartering work. For all their inefficiencies, inflexibility and the additional burdens that they placed upon local populations, they were an attempt to keep troops fed and disciplined, to reduce levels of desertion and to control the impact of soldiers on civilians. The ministers had no such agenda for troops who had been disbanded and were making their way back to their home provinces legitimately. As with the crippled or war-wounded soldiers, the implicit aim was to pass the burden across to the local communities, calculating that it was more in their interests to provide minimum subsistence as a means to move them on than to run the risk of having to deal with hungry and

[169] AAE CP Lorraine 31, fo. 421, 7 Sept., du Hallier to de Noyers.
[170] The unpublished *maîtrise* of Masson, 'La lutte contre l'absence', 100–30, offers the best general survey of the problem.
[171] Aubery, *Richelieu*, II. 599, 3 Sept. 1640, de Noyers to Châtillon; on the same day Louis XIII wrote to Châtillon: 'Voyant que le débandement est presque general de toutes les troupes de Cavalerie et Infanterie de mes armées que vous commandez, et que toute la garde que l'on fait aux passages, n'est pas capable d'arrester leur license et laschété': Aubery, *Richelieu*, II. 598.

disorderly disbanded soldiers. The crown and its ministers' aim was different once again in their attitude to deserters: to capture, hold and, in due course, despatch the fleeing troops back to the armies.[172] Infliction of penalties in an attempt to deter others might play a part in this process, but the primary aim was to reintegrate as many soldiers as possible into the armies.[173]

To the local authorities, however, the difference between masses of legitimately disbanded troops flowing through their areas, and even larger masses of deserters, may have been less evident. Both types of disbanded soldier would tend to come together in groups that were larger than most local *officiers* and their systems of law enforcement could handle; both were imposing a problem of disorder, violence and material demands upon communities whose ordinary members were already under great strain in meeting the demands of taxation and the formal burdens of the soldiery.

Furthermore, the crown's policy of seeking to investigate and round up deserters may have had the additional effect of discouraging deserters from returning home, where they could be more easily identified, above all if a unit had been recruited by a local figure of influence on the basis of his tenants or the local population.[174] The absence of uniforms and the failure to carry out in practice any of the proposals for a real system of *contrôles* to give some means of identifying enlisted recruits meant that any system of detection was cumbersome and inefficient.[175] Yet in a society in which geographical mobility was exceptional, and where the scale of desertion from the armies was so massive, civilian justices, *prévôts* and other *officiers* would place the burden of proving innocence on to the apprehended individuals. In certain provinces or on certain routes the balance of suspicion would be tipped heavily against any young man, or group of men, without papers and not grouped under the command of an NCO, officer or *commissaire*.

In these circumstances, the emergence of 'marauders', bands of soldiers living

---

[172] One instruction of 1642 even ordered the setting up of *étapes* to facilitate the return of deserters collected in Toulouse and Narbonne to the army in Catalonia: SHAT A¹ 68, fo. 609, 22 Mar. 1642.

[173] A point well made by Landier, 'Guerre, violences et société', part II.

[174] SHAT A¹ 61, fo. 19, 9 Oct. 1640, Châtillon and du Hallier are to draw up full *états* of deserters from their armies, which will be used as the basis of investigations around the soldiers' places of origin; in some cases the localities proved reluctant to hand over deserters who had managed to get home: A¹ 70, fo. 90, 21 Aug. 1642, *ordonnance* granting *commissaire* Pingault the power to levy fines on communities refusing to hand over deserters.

[175] Masson, 'La lutte contre l'absence', 73–7, considers that some of these *rôles de signal* may have been produced but have not survived in the archives, yet the frequency with which the instruction to draw up these more detailed enlistment documents was repeated suggests that it was an instruction in almost all cases ignored; Wood, *The King's Army*, pp. 86–97, bases an illuminating discussion on the discovery of a couple of such *rôles de signal*, but none survive in the later volumes of the same BN manuscript series; André, *Michel le Tellier et l'organisation*, pp. 212–15, proposes that two *ordonnances* of June 1645 and February 1647 finally established a system of detailed lists/descriptions of all newly enrolled soldiers, but it may be wondered whether this system was any more effectively enforced in the later 1640s than its predecessors.

The army and the civilian population

outside the law and away from established towns or other centres, terrorizing small communities, engaged in robbery and violence on the highways, can be seen as an almost inevitable development.[176] For many deserters who had no wish to return to the armies, who were anxious to avoid the 'sweeps' through the major cities and who might be vulnerable to arrest near to their places of origin having no papers or identification that would protect them from arrest by any civil or military official, this outlaw life might seem the only option.[177] Such groups of deserters or disbanded soldiers probably represented the most insistent challenge to the maintenance of order, and were treated with a severity which certainly indicated the practical difficulties of coming to grips with the problem. The *intendant* at Nancy, Anne Mangot, sr de Villarceaux, wrote of having tried and executed five deserted soldiers '[qui] s'estoient mis parmy les voleurs', and a few months later of seeking to ensure that capital sentences were brought against another ten, two of whom had killed a royal courier.[178] These he suggested were part of a 'grosse troupe' of 300–400 'thieves and bandits', who had taken refuge in the forests of the Barrois, and were preying on merchants and the local populations.[179] It would not be until the return to peace in the 1660s that the violent disorders of such militarized bands of vagrants could be brought under control in the French provinces.[180]

CONCLUSION

Studies of popular revolt in the 1630s and 1640s identify both the direct financial burdens of warfare and the immense, arbitrary costs of the *logement*, passage and disruption of French troops as a primary factor in the incidence of provincial unrest and uprisings.[181] If the fiscal burden of sustaining the troops – which took the form of additional charges for the *subsistances*, the *étapes*, the costs in lieu of

---

[176] B. Kroener, '"Kriegsgurgeln, Freireuter und Merodebrüder". Der Soldat des Dreißigjährigen Krieges. Täter und Opfer', in W. Wette (ed.), *Der Krieg des kleinen Mannes. Eine Militärgeschichte von unten* (Munich, 1992), pp. 51–67; B. Kroener, '"Der Krieg hat ein Loch . . ." Überlegungen zum Schicksal demobilisierter Söldner nach dem Dreißigjährigen Krieg', in H. Duchhardt (ed.), *Der Westfälische Friede. Diplomatie, politische Zäsur, kulturelles Umfeld, Rezeptionsgeschichte* (Munich, 1998), pp. 599–630.

[177] The crown ordered regular searches for deserters (and indeed absentee officers) in Paris: see for example, AAE MD 822, fos. 45, 52, 12/13 Oct. 1636, Bullion to Richelieu on a planned search for deserters; SHAT A¹ 52, fo. 366bis, 6 June 1639, order to *lieutenants civils et criminels* to investigate deserters in Paris.

[178] Mousnier, *Lettres*, I. 295, 24 Aug. 1636; I. 320–1, 25 Oct. 1636.

[179] Mousnier, *Lettres*. I. 321.

[180] And even after 1660 considerable ambiguity existed in the attitudes of the authorities to different types of dependent groups: J. Depauw, 'Pauvres, pauvres mendiants, mendiants valides ou vagabonds? Les hésitations de la législation royale', *Revue d'histoire moderne et contemporaine*, 21 (1974), 401–418.

[181] Bercé, *Histoire des croquants*, I. 44–118; Foisil, *La révolte des Nu-Pieds*, pp. 62–114; Kettering, *Judicial Politics*, pp. 51–80.

billeting – was resented as an intolerable increase in the pressures imposed by an already over-heavy weight of direct taxation, the failure of these additional levies and impositions to restrain the disorders, extortion and disruption of the troops made matters incomparably worse. Far from resolving the problems of civil–military violence and disorders caused by the army, it was clear that the expansion of the war-effort after 1635 was carrying the situation out of the control of the ministers and their agents in the localities. Occasional demonstrative punishments of individual soldiers, and sometimes even officers, could not constrain a military for whom preying on the local populations was a means of survival, and who developed an ethos of separateness from day-to-day civilian activity which made violence and extortion an easy and acceptable response to shortfalls of pay or supplies from the centre, or to local resistance to demands for food and lodging. There is no evidence that these patterns of behaviour were being brought under control in the later years of the war. On the contrary, it could be argued that the legacy of the problems generated by the scale and duration of the war-effort was leading to a crisis of authority in French society. The normal mechanisms of law enforcement and administration simply could not cope with the burdens imposed by the army; and this reduced the perceived legitimacy of these mechanisms in the eyes of subjects at all social levels. As in other areas where the established authorities were considered to have failed in their obligation to maintain order and justice, local communities sought to assume the role of the authorities and responded violently to excessive demands or violence by the soldiers. Rioting and acts of counter-aggression against soldiers proliferated, inevitably provoking reprisals and a rising spiral of tension and disruption. As William Beik argues in his study of Languedoc, 'innumerable petty disputes and conflicts, each of them distinct and local, but coordinated by a common political climate, common superior officials, and mutual exchange of information', were undermining the credibility of authority and contributing to a climate in which popular disturbances and factional confrontations were the norm.[182] Although much of the resistance to the troops was weakened by divisions and hostilities between localities, and the communities' concern was to get the soldiers off their own backs even if this heaped up the burdens on nearby territories or towns, the impact of the war-effort as a solvent of central authority in the provinces should not be underestimated. If the crown and its agents sought to justify their authority by claiming a 'monopoly of violence' within society, it was at the level of the pervasive disorders and violence of the troops that the failure to make good the claim was most evident. It is ironic that a regime intent on retaining some outward semblance of control over its army officers and restricting the proliferation of entrepreneurship in the military should thereby have been forced to assume

---

[182] Beik, *Absolutism and Society*, pp. 196–7: Beik is discussing the conjunction of heightened fiscal burdens, economic problems and the impact of the troops on provincial authority.

The army and the civilian population

greater responsibility for the failures of discipline, control and maintenance amongst the 'royal' troops present in the provinces.

It was during the years of the *Frondes* after 1648 that the progressive legacy of this collapse of control over the soldiery can be seen and its impact on the credibility of central authority becomes most evident. The vacuum which appeared at the centre of government and the overt struggle for power amongst rival political factions undoubtedly exacerbated the scale and intensity of military disorders. Yet the breakdown into what especially in the area around the Paris basin and the north-eastern provinces can be regarded as a state of near-anarchy precipitated by the troops is only explicable in terms of the weaknesses and failings of the military administration in the less grave circumstances of the period 1635–47. The account of Oudart Coquault between 1649 and 1652 describes successive waves of royalist and Condéen soldiery passing through the Champenois and billeting themselves on Couquart's city of Reims, living entirely by extortion and pillage, and behaving with no more restraint than outlaw bands: 'ce que les voleurs pillent en une province, les vivandiers d'armée les vont vendre en une aultre'.[183] Couquault's account, with its detail of a soldiery who, led by their officers, were intent on treating the province as a conquered territory and were using the systematic destruction of villages as a conscious means of intimidation, could be matched by many other contemporary accounts. It is an interpretation confirmed by economic and social historians of the regions; Pierre Goubert's account of the Beauvaisis emphasizes the decisive effect of the *Frondes* on the region: demographically, socially and politically.[184] Jean Jacquart's study of the Île de France treats 'la crise de la Fronde, 1640–1662' as a central event in the history of the province – a combination of a cyclical economic downturn, exacerbated by the unprecedented disorders and burdens of the soldiery. Jacquart stresses that 1648 was by no means the beginning of the troubles caused by the destruction and chaos of the war-effort and the soldiers; he quotes the *avocat général* of the *Parlement* of Paris, Omer Talon, who stated in 1648 that: 'il y a dix ans que la campagne est ruinée'.[185] The capacity of the soldiers to inflict such levels of damage and disruption upon the French provinces in the years between 1649 and 1653 should not be seen as the consequence of a sudden breakdown of previously effective systems of control and discipline, but as the high-water mark in a process of deteriorating authority and central control. Historians have given attention to what is assumed to have been the positive impact of armies and military change on state-building. It is also worth giving attention to the extent to which an over-ambitious war-effort, sustained with inadequate resources and placing pressures on existing administrators which they were unable to meet, could have the

---

[183] Oudart Coquault, *Mémoires, 1649–1668*, ed. Ch. Loriquet (2 vols; Reims, 1875), p. 72.
[184] P. Goubert, *Beauvais et le Beauvaisis de 1600–1730* (2 vols; Paris, 1960), I. 623–4.
[185] J. Jacquart, *La crise rurale en Île-de-France (1550–1670)* (Paris, 1974), pp. 643–748, Talon quotation on p. 645.

opposite effect. The perceived inability of the crown to control its own soldiers, while simultaneously making ever-larger demands for their support, undermined the credibility of the regime in the eyes of its subjects, and incited levels of active and covert resistance which reflected a belief that the central government could no longer provide the protection on which one of its chief claims to obedience was founded.

Conclusion

Much of the argument of the book has challenged the traditional assumption that the pressures of warfare during Richelieu's ministry, and especially in the years after 1635, stimulated the evolution of a more centralized, bureaucratic and effective military administration, itself a counterpart to changes occurring more widely in French government. Although the war fought from 1635 was unprecedented, it was sustained on a much more *ad hoc*, decentralized and traditional basis than has typically been suggested. There was no coordinated ministerial strategy aimed at exercising more effective control over recruitment, supply, payment or discipline; there were simply a series of – frequently contradictory – expedients undertaken in the face of crises precipitated by the size of the army and the scale of the war-effort. The ministers, bombarded with correspondence from the commanders and administrators with the individual army-corps and attempting to control a war-effort extending over most of the French frontier provinces, were simply overloaded with information. The lack of orderly and established systems for the handling of this information led to arbitrary or factional decisions about the allocation of resources, failures of budgeting, regular lapses of communications and an inability to act beyond the most immediate requirements of the war-effort.

In this context it is relevant to return to the broad thesis of early modern European military change, the 'military revolution'. As first articulated in the work of Michael Roberts, the thesis sought to link the tactical and organizational changes in 'progressive' European armies – those developments described at the opening of chapter 1 – with much more widely significant political and social developments.[1] Rather than presenting the reforms of the princes of Orange and Gustavus Adolphus within their own tactical terms, simply as a means to gain the advantage on the battlefield, Roberts incorporated them into a larger framework of state formation and the reshaping of European societies. The result of tactical changes, improvement in drill and more efficient deployment of firepower – especially in their 'offensive' Swedish form – was to allow commanders to break out of a tactical stalemate and revive the decisive battle as a factor in

---

[1] Roberts, 'Military revolution'.

Conclusion

warfare.[2] And this, Roberts argues, led in turn to the emergence of 'grand strategies', a new confidence about the political objectives which could be achieved through military means. The pursuit of such wide-ranging strategies required far larger concentrations of military force, and thus began the progressive increase in the size of armies which is taken to be characteristic of the early modern and modern worlds. But armies could not be expanded in this way without an adequate financial and administrative base to sustain them. Providing this base led directly to the creation of an increasingly centralized, powerful style of government: more effective systems of tax extraction and financial management were implemented; professional, bureaucratic administrators were established; models of ruthless, coercive government developed in the military sphere were imposed upon civil society, and used to deal with revolt and resistance to the demands of the ruler. Finally, massive military expansion and the rising proportion of the state's wealth and political energies expended upon warfare led to social and psychological changes, the widest circle of effects generated by Roberts' thesis. Societies were increasingly imbued with military values, which in turn developed and shaped authoritarian tendencies amongst the political elites, generating a heightened concern with social order to be maintained through regulation and coercion. The experience of military discipline and the habits of military service were increasingly diffused into civil society. The military were no longer synonymous with independent-minded officers, imbued with a 'noble' ethos hostile to any overall command structure. Instead, the army became the microcosm of an orderly and hierarchical society, imbued with a sense of collective discipline. A modern world of centrally imposed uniformity replaced the looser ties of patriarchal, local and family bonds.[3]

The present study is by no means the first work to draw attention to the problems with such an all-embracing thesis of military change and modernization. If historians have proved willing to criticize the exclusivity and chronological narrowness of the initial case for tactical and organizational change in early modern armies, they have been no less ready to attack the subsequent stages in the 'military revolution' thesis. Geoffrey Parker proposed that the critical factor in the growth of early modern armies was not more expansive and ambitious strategies, but the developing science of fortification and its impact on sieges. The scale of the new style of bastioned, low-walled, fortifications and their outworks, and the numbers of troops who might be garrisoned within a major fortress or a

---

[2] Roberts, 'Gustav Adolf and the art of war'; Roberts, *Gustavus Adolphus*, II.173–82 – citing Sir Charles Oman on the indecisive warfare of the sixteenth century. However, as Geoffrey Parker pointed out, it is not evident that sixteenth-century battles and campaigns were especially indecisive: Parker, 'The "military revolution, 1560–1660" – a myth?'. Roberts' claim that the 'decisive battle' was rediscovered in the early seventeenth century is taken as the starting point of R. Weigley's substantial survey, *The Age of Battles. The Quest for Decisive Warfare from Breitenfeld to Waterloo* (Bloomington and Indianapolis, 1991), pp. 3–23.

[3] Roberts, 'Military revolution', pp. 205–17.

Conclusion

strategically important city, forced up the overall size of armies which would be called upon to besiege such state-of-art fortifications.[4] The need to maintain substantial numbers of garrisons to hold occupied territory and to provide frontier defences also absorbed a large proportion of army strength, and ensured that total numbers of troops needed to increase to accommodate this demand.[5] Recent works have raised another fundamental issue shaping the concerns of commanders in the field: the role of logistics in determining the character of warfare, and, above all, the limitations imposed by the economy and communication system of early modern Europe on the capacity to supply and move armies. Wider strategy was consistently subordinated or abandoned in the face of the simple need to ensure that an army could find local food supplies, given the practical problems of supplying armies from magazines on the frontiers via rudimentary and inadequate transport facilities.[6]

The link between war and governmental change, fundamental to Roberts' argument for the wider significance of the 'revolution', has also come under scrutiny.[7] In particular, attention has been given to the means by which the expansion in army size was achieved. The role of the mercenary commander, the 'military enterpriser', in the recruitment, organization and financing of early modern armies has been well documented.[8] What has been insufficiently noted, however, is the implications for the military revolution thesis of military organizations which were very largely dominated by officers who held their units – or army-corps – as mercenary contractors, and whose willingness to utilize their private credit, local connections and administrative skills made the raising and maintenance of unprecedented armies possible. The growth in the size of armies was not necessarily either a product or a cause of administrative and financial developments in the state. Armies raised through the enterprise system could expand beyond the resources available to the governments which were nominally fielding them, and without bringing about any fundamental development in the

---

[4] Parker, *Military Revolution*, pp. 24–33; Eltis, *Military Revolution*, pp. 76–98. The detail of Parker's argument has recently been challenged by John Lynn, who argued that more extensive fortifications did not imply proportionately larger armies to besiege or defend them: 'The *trace italienne* and the growth of armies: the French case', *Journal of Military History*, 60 (1991), 297–330, reprinted in Rogers (ed.) *The Military Revolution Debate*, pp. 169–99. The argument received a robust reply from Geoffrey Parker in Rogers (ed.), *The Military Revolution Debate*, pp. 351–2.

[5] Adams, 'Tactics or politics?', pp. 43–5 (reprinted in Rogers (ed.), *The Military Revolution Debate*, pp. 253–72).

[6] Parker, *Military Revolution*, pp. 45–81; M. Van Creveld, *Supplying War: Logistics from Wallenstein to Patton* (Cambridge, 1977), pp. 5–39; Parrott, 'Strategy and tactics'; J. Lynn (ed.), *Feeding Mars. Logistics in Western Warfare from the Middle Ages to the Present* (Boulder-San Francisco-Oxford, 1993), pp. 9–13, 15–21, 103–7, 137–59; Pohl, *Die Profiantirung der keyserlichen Armaden*, pp. 11–17, 46–61.

[7] Notably, and from a welcome northern and eastern European perspective, in R. Frost, *The Northern Wars, 1558–1721* (London, 2000), esp. pp. 307–27.

[8] See, above all, Redlich, *Military Enterpriser*; M. Howard, *War in European History* (London, 1976), pp. 20–37; Anderson, *War and Society*, pp. 33–76; Parker, *Military Revolution*, pp. 48–52.

Conclusion

state's own administrative structures. Contributions-systems, which effectively delegated the extraction of financial resources into the hands of the military commanders as a means by which they could recover their 'investment', proliferated and by-passed the normal systems of revenue collection.[9]

These points are confirmed and reinforced by the experience of French warfare and army organization during Richelieu's ministry. The conduct of sieges was not the key factor determining the overall size of the French military establishment, but it undoubtedly had a decisive impact on the shaping of strategy and the allocation of resources, as the accounts of the major, set-piece, sieges on the north-eastern frontier detailed in chapter 2 make apparent. Multiple army-corps, frequently amounting to over 50 per cent of the total campaign strength of the French army, were committed to individual sieges which swallowed up a high proportion of the money and supplies of the entire war-effort, leaving the commanders in the secondary theatres to make do with minimal resources.

That a war dominated by the manpower demands of large-scale sieges did not force up the overall size of Richelieu's army more dramatically underlines the failure to develop financial and administrative resources capable of sustaining such an expansion. The recruitment of the French forces has much in common with the entrepreneurial systems of other European powers: an expanding army did not reflect an expanding royal administration so much as increased dependence upon the credit, local connections and organization of the officer-corps. However, the reluctance to sanction a formalized system of military enterprise, and the failure of the great majority of French forces down to 1642 to establish themselves across the frontiers so that they could finance and supply themselves through contributions, imposed limits upon the readiness of the unit officers or the high command to commit personal resources to the war-effort. The officers' reluctance to make open-ended financial commitments, together with their successful manipulation of the internal checks on troop numbers and pay, ensured that the average size of French units was low, and declined steadily through the later 1630s and 1640s.

In France, as elsewhere in Europe during the Thirty Years War, the expanding scale of the war-effort was not matched by any systematic reconstruction of the civil administration, whether the agents directly connected with the control of the army, or the more extensive structures concerned with the control of troops

---

[9] Jeremy Black has argued forcefully that far from being a consequence of the expansion of armies, more effective systems of civil government were its essential precondition. It was not until the later seventeenth century, and a period of increasing administrative effectiveness and control based on better working relations between central and provincial elites, that European states could undertake significant military expansion without relying upon entrepreneurship: J. Black, *A Military Revolution? Military Change and European Society, 1550–1800* (London, 1991), pp. 67–82; Black, *European Warfare, 1660–1815*, pp. 6–15, 87–92.

Conclusion

en route and quartered in France, or with general civil–military relations. Still less could it be argued that a process of military change served to constrain the independence of the nobility, forcing them into the role of disciplined, professional, officers who had abandoned the ethos of insubordinate individualism. As the crown remained heavily dependent on the financial and organizational role of the officer-corps, and less able to depend upon an administration whose primary motive for expansion was the multiplication of venal office, so the autonomy and privileged status of the *noblesse* within the army survived and flourished. It is not surprising that Condé, Turenne, Longueville, Harcourt and other *grands* were able to deploy their army-corps to sustain independent political positions during the *Frondes*; it is equally unsurprising that the honour code of the unit officers made them unconcerned to conceal financial malpractice and an extensive range of other abuses in the maintenance of their units. It is an established element in the hagiography of Cardinal Richelieu that his severity in ensuring the execution of the illustrious duellists François de Montmorency-Bouteville and François de Rosmadec, comte des Chapelles, curbed the practice of duelling amongst the French nobility and submitted them more effectively to the authority of the king. Not merely did duels between serving officers continue throughout these years of war, but the crown intervened regularly to pardon those who had fought each other over points of honour.[10]

What can certainly be said about the war-effort under Richelieu and then his successor, Mazarin, is that the burden of sustaining the army greatly worsened existing weaknesses of control and authority in French society. The recovery of order and the reassertion of the rule of law by the royal judiciary in the French provinces, despite the pacification of Henri IV's reign, had remained incomplete and partial. The pressures of recruiting, supplying, quartering and controlling the troops across France after 1630 tipped a fragile system of local authority, already under challenge from large-scale popular revolt, into breakdown. There is scant evidence that the civilian populations could be protected from the exactions and violence of 'official' troop movements and billeting, still less from the rapacity of bands of deserters and marauders. Not surprisingly, local communities were prepared to risk taking defence into their own hands; confidence in the capacity of the formal administration to defend them was minimal. Army officers and administrators, far from being seen as guarantors of the discipline and order of their troops, were too often seen either as indifferent to, or as the promoters of, their soldiers' exactions and destruction. The notion that a more disciplined and ordered society was emerging through the demands of military expansion would

---

[10] To take simply a handful of examples from 1639: SHAT A^1 51, fo. 274, 28 Mar., pardon for d'Imorville, capt. of regt of Lorraine; fo. 302, 31 Mar., Fiesque and Marsy pardoned; fo. 386, 8 Mar., pardons for Leseure, Roquebouillac, Lagnac. Similar scepticism is expressed by Billacois, *Le duel dans la société française*, pp. 273–5.

Conclusion

have seemed a mockery to contemporary Frenchmen, even at the level of the ministers themselves.

Yet, as in the civil sphere of Richelieu's ministerial regime, it is necessary to return to the critical point about the war-effort after 1635. Though immense strains were certainly generated, there was no complete breakdown. A number of factors could have forced France into a humiliating peace settlement in the face of military collapse: a funding crisis which would bring the armies to a grinding halt in mid-campaign – a prospect which haunted the finance ministers from 1635; the mass disbandment of armies in the face of supply failure or the non-arrival of pay; a refusal of nobles and aspiring nobles to shoulder the financial burdens of serving as unit officers; a high command who simply declined to accept the risks and assume the burdens of taking the offensive with inadequate numbers of troops and inadequate assurances of material support. That something like this *could* happen was evident during the *Frondes* when, in 1652, the various French army-corps almost disintegrated and the war-effort suffered a sequence of reverses in Flanders, Catalonia and north Italy.

That this did not happen under Richelieu owed almost nothing to administrative reform and greater central efficiency. The most important factor in sustaining the conflict through financial inadequacy, supply failure, lack of control over the army-corps, inexperienced troops and absentee officers was the elaborate structures of clientage which underpinned the officer-corps and the military administration. An important element of the clientelism in the armies was maintained by the ministers themselves, above all Richelieu, the finance minister, Claude de Bullion, the secretary for war, Sublet de Noyers, and, increasingly, the secretary for foreign affairs, Léon le Bouthillier, comte de Chavigny. The extent to which they placed their *fidèles* in military offices – from the high command down to company posts in the *régiments entretenus* – and then acted as powerful backers for these *fidèles* in the competition for resources, commands, promotion and favour was crucial. In return, they could expect a greater level of military commitment and responsiveness to ministerial instructions, and more willingness to commit private resources to sustaining the army-corps through periods of crisis. At the highest level, the ministers could also expect the commanding officers to try to keep their own clienteles of subordinate officers and corps administrators committed to ministerial service. Unit officers who looked to the corps commander as their specific patron were more susceptible to honouring recruitment contracts, to accepting financial allocations that might cover the pay of the ordinary soldiers but not the officers, to meeting the additional costs of recruiting better-quality troops, providing better cavalry horses, and the innumerable other areas where success or failure might depend on mobilizing these extra resources. The officer-corps should be seen as a network of clienteles linking company and regimental officers up to the high command through structures that

Conclusion

frequently reflected provincial hierarchies transposed into the armies. Setting aside his ambitions for his own family within the high aristocracy, Richelieu's concern to ensure close alliances with some of the great aristocratic houses is fully explicable in terms of maintaining the informal, underlying, forces of patronage and clientage which kept the armies operating through successive campaigns.

An occasional ambivalence was still apparent towards permitting the development of an officer-corps dominated by clientage relationships (an ambivalence already noticeable in the Wars of Religion during the later sixteenth century), especially where the clienteles were not controlled by ministers or their aristocratic allies. Yet the situation in the 1630s offered no real alternatives. Fewer ambiguities existed in respect to the administrators with the armies, where the various groups of agents were permeated by ministerial patronage which acted as a catalyst within a system staffed by venal office-holders whose commitment in the face of tough, independent-minded, military corporatism had always been questionable. Specific commissions placed in the hands of administrators in this period should be seen primarily as a manifestation of this kind of clientage, whether these were granted to *maîtres des requêtes* serving as *intendants d'armée* or to ambitious *abbés* aspiring to ecclesiastical promotion through the management of a supply or recruitment operation. Such an interpretation is more plausible than the notion that commissions were used as a planned bureaucratic expedient – a means to circumvent the inefficiencies of venal office-holders by deploying agents with a different institutional power-base and administrative priorities shaped by authoritarian and centralizing ambitions.

Yet if patronage lay at the heart of the military system and explained its ability to overcome some of the obvious weaknesses generated by military expansion, there was another aspect to this which serves to explain the extreme unpopularity of a ministerial regime which was not deliberately overriding traditional privileges or seeking to reshape the army in accordance with a modernizing blueprint. Richelieu's ministry combined general dependence upon the goodwill and resources of the officer-corps to keep the forces operational with individual acts of heavy-handed intervention or intimidation. These arbitrary acts could involve the manipulation of patronage and appointment in favour of ministerial *créatures* (a process noted and resented at every level of the military hierarchy), or the imposition of harsh punishments for military 'failure', often visited upon those individuals known to be hostile to the ministerial regime. It was widely felt in both cases that Richelieu, his fellow ministers and aristocratic allies were playing fast and loose with a system which required goodwill and circumspection on the part of a governmental regime – a system which needed to operate by cooperation rather than compulsion. An officer-corps and a military administration which were enmeshed in multiple, overlapping patronage relationships, in which the ministers and their allies played a leading role, was one thing; the belief that the ministers were seeking to dominate the entire system of appointments, rewards

Conclusion

and advantages within the military was far less acceptable. Attempts to link the ministerial regime and its policies with the interests of the crown and the crown's claims to unconditional loyalty were persistently weakened by what was widely recognized as the pursuit of factional advantage. Richelieu's ministry generated resentment and hostility amongst many elements of French society; the main cause of rancour appears to have been that blend of dependence on established interests and arbitrary manipulation from the centre which is illustrated in the present account of the administration of the war-effort. It matches the perceptions of a number of recent provincial studies that what was most hated and rejected in the regime was not some anachronistic notion of a 'drive towards absolutism', but the influence, favour and patronage that were being wielded by a narrow ministerial circle, their allies and clients. Although Louis XIII maintained a strong interest in the practical detail of military organization, in appointments and rewards or promotion for meritorious service, the perception of contemporary memoirs, and on occasions of the ministers and the commanders themselves, was that the king's wishes were not paramount. The notion of 'service to the king' was easily lost in a belief that affiliation to the ministers was the key to military appointment and promotion. Anyone occupying an officership but standing outside of this network was vulnerable both to the burdens of military service and to heavy-handed treatment in the event of a failure to meet the demands of an embattled regime, easily alarmed by the domestic consequences of military failure. While this was not invariably the case, it was seen to be so by contemporaries. It certainly reinforced criticism of Louis XIII, carried into the next reign, as being excessively beholden to his first minister and to the priorities of Richelieu's regime.

Clientage is a key factor in explaining how the army held together and made gradual military progress under Richelieu and under cardinal Mazarin, albeit a progress which continued to be dogged by defeats, reverses and the recognition that gains in one theatre were inevitably bought at the cost of stagnation or setbacks in others. If the military capacities of the Grand Condé or Turenne could win victories at Rocroi, Nördlingen or Lens in the mid-1640s, the grinding, attritional warfare on the Flanders frontier down to 1659 does nothing to modify the general perception of the war-effort. The contrast with the French army after 1660 could hardly be more apparent. In 1667–8 Louis XIV's armies swept all before them and captured more fortified *places* in the Spanish Netherlands in a single campaign than in twenty-five years of war under the cardinal-ministers, while the planning and execution of the first months of the 1672 campaign against the Dutch offered further evidence of extraordinary organizational progress.

The contrast of this effectiveness and success of the French army in the years after 1660 calls for attention. There are certainly organizational and administrative explanations, and these have been discussed in detail by other historians. The

Conclusion

treaty of the Pyrenees inaugurated a period of peace of a length not seen since before 1610, and opened the possibility of reconstructing both the army itself and the financial and administrative structures which supported it. At the centre of the reforms lay a reduction in the military establishment to create a core of 55,000–60,000 permanent troops. This permanent army was to be funded through the maintenance of war-time levels of taxation during a period of peace. As peace allowed more efficient and less wasteful systems of tax collection to be implemented, for the first time a large – but not unmanageable – army could be supported from crown revenues. Most of the costs of the recruitment and wages of the troops were met from central funds, and more effective systems of frontier supply, *étapes* and quartering could be established to provide better support and to remove a perennial excuse for indiscipline and local violence between troops and civil populations. The exploitation of the officers' own financial resources was much reduced, and the units maintained in the army enjoyed a degree of stability and permanence unknown for all but a handful of *entretenus* in the period before 1659. As a result the *bureau de la guerre*, run by the *secrétaire* who in 1661 acquired full ministerial status, could demand higher standards of military commitment from the officers, and could expect their cooperation with the military administrators in the maintenance of discipline over the soldiers. Long-serving troops were now commanded by officers who regarded military service as a career rather than a short-term means to acquire or confirm social status.[11]

Yet at the same time, the officer-corps and the administration continued to be shaped by deeply entrenched structures of patronage which the *bureau de la guerre* scarcely eroded, and had no desire to eliminate. Indeed in the post-1660 army the patronage of the war minister in the appointment of both military administrators and army officers became considerably more significant, expanded at the expense of other ministers of state. The difference in these decades was that the control of appointments to office and promotion was considerably less unaccountable. The much-resented capacity of Richelieu and his allies to manipulate appointments, to deal out favour and resources to their *créatures* and supporters 'as if the king counted for nothing', was far less evident. Patronage and favour may have continued to lie at the heart of the military system, but the network of access through favour was considerably more open to competing influence. Even the marquis de Louvois saw fit to distribute his patronage with more circumspection than Richelieu had done, and to pay attention both to the quality of the appointees he did support and to Louis XIV's clearly expressed desire to be seen to be in ultimate control of all appointments to *his* army. Once again, the army provides a case-study of larger changes in the character of government and society in the period of Louis XIV's personal rule: the reassertion of royal arbitration and

---

[11] Rousset, *Histoire*, I. 163–255; André, *Le Tellier et Louvois*, pp. 307–427; Baxter, *Servants of the Sword*, pp. 139–208; Corvisier, *Louvois*, pp. 77–118.

Conclusion

systematic supervision of the distribution of patronage; the concern to keep open a large number of channels of influence through which benefits could be distributed; the more consistent respect for those – especially the *grands* – who possessed established authority in the military hierarchy. Patronage links may have played no less important a role in determining the composition of the officer-corps and in identifying the real channels of authority in the army, but these operated with fewer of the tensions and hostilities which had been generated by the narrow distribution of favour and benefits evident in Richelieu's ministry. Although the cardinal's system had served to keep the army functioning in the decades after 1630, and had managed to draw upon the resources of the officers with remarkable success, these achievements had been bought at a high cost in military effectiveness, commitment and cooperation from the officer-corps, and in civil/military relations. The years after 1660, which saw the integration of broader networks of clientage into a military organization that was better financed, maintained and controlled, permitted the crown to realize the huge military potential of its French subjects. Here, as in many other respects, the personal rule of Louis XIV may better be seen as a reaction against, rather than a building upon, the regime of the cardinal ministers.

Bibliography

MANUSCRIPT SOURCES

SERVICE HISTORIQUE DE L'ARMÉE DE TERRE – ARCHIVES DE LA GUERRE, VINCENNES

Series A^1: 1630–42

Expéditions (drafts/copies of legislation despatched to commanders, administrators and others in the campaign theatres and provinces): A^1 12, 13, 14, 21, 26, 32, 42, 49, 56, 62, 67, 71.

Minutes (drafts of letters and instructions despatched to officers and administrators): A^1 11, 15, 16, 17, 18, 19, 22, 23, 24, 25, 27, 28, 29, 30, 31, 34, 35, 36, 37, 38, 39, 40, 41, 43, 44, 45, 46, 47, 48, 50i, 50ii, 51, 52, 53, 54, 55, 57, 58, 59, 60, 61, 63, 64, 65, 66, 68, 69, 70.

Lettres recues: A^1 33.

ARCHIVES DES AFFAIRES ETRANGÈRES, PARIS

Series Mémoires et Documents

AAE MD 806, 807, 808, 809, 810, 811, 812, 813, 814, 815, 816, 819, 820, 821, 822, 823, 826, 827, 828, 830, 831, 832, 835, 836, 837, 838, 839, 840, 841, 842, 843, 844, 845.
MD 254, 1631, 1633, 1676, 1678, 1679, 1680, 1681.
MD Italie, 21, 22 (Mantoue).

Series Correspondance Politique

AAE CP Allemagne, 12, 13, 14, 15, 16 (1635–42).
AAE CP Espagne, 18, 19, 20 (1635–41).
AAE CP Lorraine, 14, 15, 25, 26, 27, 29, 30, 31, 32 (1634–42).
AAE CP Mantoue, 1, 2, 3, 4, 5 (1600–39).
AAE CP Savoie (Sardaigne), 7, 8, 9 (1626–30); 24, 25, 26, 28, 29, 30, 31, 32 (1636–41).

BIBLIOTHÈQUE NATIONALE, PARIS

Manuscrits français

3703 (Feuquières); 3759/60/1 (Châtillon, 1637–8); 3767 (Saxe-Weimar); 3768 (Schomberg); 3769 (La Meilleraye); 3833 (*lettres diverses*); 3770 (Italy); 4189 (Besançon);

Bibliography

4223/4 (army material, 1643–60); 4561 (artillery); 4531 (finances for 1637); 4811 (*vivres*); 5223 (*grand maître de l'artillerie*); 6385 (marquis de Sourdis); 6386 (finance); 6644 (Epernon); 6645 (cardinal de La Valette – 1635); 6646/7 (La Valette – 1636); 6648 (La Valette – 1637); 14018 (*maîtres des requêtes*); 17369 to 17374 (Séguier); 20564 (Epernon); 22365 (duc de La Valette); 25853–8 (*montres de gens de guerre*, 1635–42).

Collection Châtre de Cangé

22, 23, 24, 25, 26 (*réglements et ordonnances militaires*, 1635–46).

Pièces Originales

26,974 (Bragelongne); 26,803 (Besançon); 32,356 (Familles de Paris) 41,449 (Magnan); 64,924 (Vallier).

BRITISH LIBRARY, LONDON

Egerton 1689, 1690 (Sublet de Noyers/Richelieu to Brézé, 1630–42).
Additional MS 35097 (Viscount Scudamore).

ARCHIVIO DI STATO DI MANTOVA, ARCHIVIO GONZAGA

AG E xv. 3, vols. 675, 677, 678, 679 (Giustiniano Priandi, Mantuan representative in France, to Charles de Gonzague-Nevers then the regent Maria, 1626–45).

ARCHIVIO DI STATO DI TORINO, LETTERE MINISTRI

Francia, vols. 25, 26, 28, 29, 30 (letters of Pietro Biandrà, Savoyard representative in France, to dukes Carlo Emanuele I and Vittorio Amedeo I, 1624–31).

PRINTED SOURCES AND WORKS PUBLISHED BEFORE 1800

Anselme de Sainte-Marie, Père, *Histoire généalogique et chronologique de la maison royale de France, des pairs, grands officiers de la couronne, de la maison du roi et des anciens barons du royaume* (3rd edn), 9 vols.; Paris, 1726–33.
Arnaud d'Andilly, R., *Mémoires*, in Petitot and Monmerqué, xxxiii–xxxiv.
Aubery, A., *Histoire du cardinal duc de Richelieu*, Paris, 1660.
  Mémoires pour servir à l'histoire du cardinal duc de Richelieu, 2 vols.; Paris, 1660.
Avenel, D.L.M. (ed.), *Lettres, instructions diplomatiques et papiers d'état du cardinal de Richelieu (Collection de documents inédits sur l'histoire de France)*, 8 vols.; Paris, 1853–76.
Azan, P., *Un tacticien du XVIIe siècle* (edition of Aurignac, *Livre de guerre*, 1663), Paris, 1904.
Baluze, E., *Histoire généalogique de la Maison d'Auvergne*, 2 vols.; Paris, 1708.
Bassompierre, F. de, *Mémoires*, in Petitot and Monmerqué, xix–xxi.
Baudier, M., *Histoire du maréchal de Toiras*, Paris, 1644.

Bibliography

Besançon, B. du Plessis, sieur de, *Mémoires*, ed. H. de Beaucaire, Paris, 1892.
Besse, H. de, *Relation des campagnes de Rocroi et de Fribourg*, Paris, 1673 (reprinted 1826).
Billon, J. de, *Instructions militaires*, Lyon, 1617.
   Les principes de l'art militaire, Paris, 1622.
   Suite des principes de l'art militaire, Rouen, 1641.
Biron, Henri de Gontaut, duc de, *Maximes et advis du maniement de la guerre* . . ., mistakenly attributed to André de Bordeille (elder brother of Brantôme) and published in Brantôme, ed. J. Buchon, *Œuvres*, 2 vols.; Paris, 1838.
Brienne, H.-A. de Loménie, comte de, *Mémoires*, in Petitot and Monmerqué, XXXV-XXXVI.
Bussy, Roger de Rabutin, comte de, *Mémoires*, 3 vols.; Paris, 1712.
Campion, H. de, *Mémoires*, Paris, 1967.
Caron, N.L. (ed.), *Michel le Tellier: son administration comme intendant d'armée en Piémont, 1640–1643*, Paris, 1880.
Coquault, Oudart, *Mémoires, 1649–1668*, ed. Ch. Loriquet, 2 vols.; Reims, 1875.
Daniel, Père G., *Histoire de la milice françoise*, 2 vols.; Paris, 1721.
Dugrès, G., *Life of Richelieu*, London, 1643.
du Praissac, *Discours militaires*, Rouen, 1625.
du Tillet, J., *Recueil des roys de France leurs couronne et maison*, Paris, 1602.
Estrées, François-Annibal, maréchal d', *Mémoires sur la régence de Marie de Médicis et sur celle d'Anne d'Autriche*, ed. P. Bonnefon, Paris, 1910.
Feuquières, Manassés de Pas, marquis de, *Lettres inédites*, ed. E. Gallois, 5 vols.; Paris, 1845–6.
Gaya, L. de, *L'art de la guerre*, Paris, 1689.
Gheyn, Jan de, *Waffenhandlung von den Rören, Musqueten und Spiessen*, The Hague, 1608.
Girard, G., *Histoire de la vie du duc d'Espernon*, Paris, 1655.
Goulas, Nicholas, *Mémoires*, ed. C. Constant, 3 vols.; Paris, 1879–82.
Gramont, Antoine III, maréchal de, *Mémoires*, in Petitot and Monmerqué, LVI-LVII.
Griffet, Père H., *Histoire du règne de Louis XIII*, 3 vols.; Paris, 1758.
Grillon, P. (ed.), *Les papiers de Richelieu. Section politique intérieure: correspondance et papiers d'état*, 6 vols. to date; Paris, 1975– .
Gualdo Priorato, G., *Il Maneggio dell'armi moderno*, Bologna, 1643.
Hay du Chastelet, P., *Politique militaire ou traité de la guerre*, Paris, 1757 (1st pub. 1667).
La Châtre, comte Edmé de, *Mémoires*, in Michaud and Poujoulat, III.
La Chesnaye-Desbois, F.A. de, *Dictionnaire de la noblesse* (3rd edn), 19 vols.; Paris, 1866–76.
La Fontaine, de, *Les devoirs militaires des officiers de l'infanterie*, Paris, 1675.
La Force, Jacques-Nompar de Caumont, maréchal de, *Mémoires*, 4 vols.; Paris, 1843.
La Noue, F. de, *Discours politiques et militaires*, Basel, 1587.
La Rochefoucauld, François VI de, *Mémoires*, in Petitot and Monmerqué, LI-LII.
La Roque, G.A. de, *Histoire généalogique de la Maison de Harcourt*, 4 vols.; Paris, 1662.
   Traité de la noblesse, de ses différentes espèces . . . et du ban et arrière-ban, Rouen, 1734.
La Valière, *Pratique et maximes de la guerre*, Paris, 1675.
Le Vassor, M., *Histoire du règne de Louis XIII*, 10 vols.; Amsterdam, 1701–11.
Lostelneau, le sieur de, *Le maréchal de bataille*, Paris, 1647.
Loyseau, C., *Cinq livres du droit des offices*, Châteaudun, 1610.
Lublinskaya, A.D. (ed.), *The Internal Policy of French Absolutism, 1633–1649*, 2 vols.; Moscow and St Petersburg, 1966.

Bibliography

Malingre, C., *Eloge historique de la noble et illustre maison de Rantzow* (Paris, 1641).
Michaud, J., and J. Poujoulat (eds.), *Mémoires pour servir à l'histoire de la France depuis le XIIIe siècle jusqu'à la fin du XVIIIe – 3e série*, 10 vols.; Paris, 1838.
Monro, R., *Monro his expedition with the worthy Scots regiment call'd Mackays*, 2 parts, London, 1637.
Montaigne, M. de, *Œuvres complètes*, Paris, 1962.
Montglat, F. de Paule de Clermont, marquis de, *Mémoires*, in Petitot and Monmerqué, XLIX–LI.
Montgommery, L. de, sieur de Courbouzon, *La milice françoise réduite à l'ancien ordre et discipline militaire des legions*, Paris, 1610.
Montrésor, Claude de Bordeille, comte de, *Mémoires*, Michaud and Poujoulat, III.
Mousnier, R. (ed.), *Lettres et mémoires adressés au Chancelier Séguier, 1633–1649*, 2 vols.; Paris, 1964.
Mousnier, R., J.-P. Labatut and Y. Durand (eds.), *Problèmes de stratification sociale. Deux cahiers de la noblesse pour les Etats Généraux de 1649–1651*, Paris, 1964.
Nodot, F., *Le munitionnaire des armées de France, qui enseigne à fournir les vivres aux troupes avec toute l'oeconomie possible*, Paris, 1697.
Petitot, C., and L. de Monmerqué (eds.), *Collection des mémoires relatifs à l'histoire de France – 2e serie*, 52 vols.; Paris, 1824–9.
Pinard, M., *Chronologie historique militaire*, 7 vols.; Paris, 1760–4.
Pinson de La Martinière, J., *La juridiction de la connestablie et mareschaussée de France*, Paris, 1661.
Plessis-Praslin, César de Choiseul, comte du, *Mémoires*, in Michaud and Poujoulat, VII.
Pontis, Bénédict-Louis de (Pierre-Thomas du Fossé), *Mémoires*, Paris, 1986.
Pure, M. de, *Histoire du maréchal de Gassion*, 4 vols.; Amsterdam, 1696.
Puységur, J. de Chastenet de, *Les guerres de Louis XIII et Louis XIV* (memoirs), 2 vols.; Paris, 1883.
Richelieu, Armand-Jean du Plessis, cardinal de, *Mémoires*, in Petitot and Monmerqué, XXII–XXX (numbered I–IX in text).
  Testament politique, ed. F. Hildesheimer, Paris, 1995.
Rohan, Henri de, *Le parfaict capitaine, autrement l'abrégé des guerres de Gaule des Commentaires de César*, Paris, 1636.
  Mémoires, including *Mémoire sur la guerre de la Valtelline*, in Petitot and Monmerqué, XVIII–XIX.
Saumières, J. de Langlade, baron de, *Mémoires de la vie de Frédéric-Maurice de La Tour d'Auvergne, duc de Bouillon*, Paris, 1692.
Siri, V., *Anecdotes du ministère du cardinal de Richelieu et du règne de Louis XIII*, Amsterdam, 1717.
Sirot, C. de Létouf, baron de, *Mémoires*, 2 vols.; Paris, 1683.
Sourdis, H. d'Escoubleau de, archevêque de Bordeaux, *Correspondance*, ed. E. Sue, 3 vols.; Paris, 1839.
Souvigny, Jean de Gangnières, comte de, *Vie, mémoires et histoire de messire Jean de Gangnières...*, 2 vols.; Paris, 1906.
Tallement de Réaux, *Historiettes*, ed. A. Adam, 2 vols.; Paris, 1960.
Turenne, Henri de La Tour d'Auvergne, vicomte de, *Lettres*, ed. S. d'Huart, Paris, 1972.

Bibliography

Vialart, C., *Histoire du ministère d'Armand-Jean du Plessis, cardinal duc de Richelieu*, 4 vols.; Amsterdam, 1649.
Ville, L. de, *La justice militaire de l'infanterie*, Paris, 1633.
Wallhausen, J. J. von, *L'art militaire pour l'infanterie*, trans. J. de Bry, Oppenheim, 1615.
Art militaire à cheval, trans. J. de Bry, Frankfurt, 1616.
De la milice romaine (trans. of Vegetius), Frankfurt, 1616.
Militia Gallica, Hanau, 1617.
Kunstliche Piquenhandlung, Hanau, 1617.
Wild, A. (ed.), *Les papiers de Richelieu – Empire Allemand*, I (1616–29), Paris, 1982.
Williams, Sir Roger, *A Brief Discourse of Warre*, London, 1590.

COLLECTIONS OF ORDINANCES, EDICTS

Compilation chronologique contenant un receuil en agrégé des ordonnances, édits, déclarations et lettres patentes des rois de France, qui concernent la justice, la police et les finances, 2 vols.; Paris, 1715.
Jourdan, A.L., J. Decrusy and F.A. Isambert (eds.), *Recueil général des anciennes lois françaises depuis l'an 420 jusqu'à la Révolution de 1789*, 28 vols.; Paris, 1821–33.
Les ordonnances militaires tirées du code du roi Henri III, auxquels ont esté adjoustez des edicts du roi Henri IV et Louis XIII, Paris, 1625.
Ordonnances des rois de France de la troisième race, ed. Vilevault, L.G. de, L. Oudart de Brequigny and J.M. Pardessus, 21 vols.; Paris, 1773–1849 (reprinted 1967).

SECONDARY WORKS

Åberg, A., 'The Swedish army from Lützen to Narva', in M. Roberts (ed.), *Sweden's Age of Greatness, 1632–1718*, London, 1972, pp. 265–87.
Adams, S., 'Tactics or politics? The "military revolution" and the Habsburg hegemony, 1525–1648', in J. Lynn (ed.), *Tools of War. Instruments, Ideals and Institutions of Warfare, 1445–1871*, Urbana, Ill., 1990, pp. 28–52.
Albertis, G.D. de, *Cristina di Francia. Madama Reale*, Turin, 1943.
Albrecht, D., *Die auswärtige Politik Maximilians von Bayern, 1618–1635*, Göttingen, 1962.
Anderson, M.S., *War and Society in Europe of the Old Regime, 1618–1789*, London, 1988.
André, L., *Michel Le Tellier et l'organization de l'armée monarchique*, Paris, 1906.
'Le maréchal de La Mothe-Houdancourt, son procès, sa rébellion, sa fin', *Revue d'histoire moderne et contemporaine*, 12 (1937), 5–35, 95–125.
Michel Le Tellier et Louvois, Paris, 1942.
Antoine, M., 'Genèse de l'institution des intendants', *Journal des savants*, (1982), 287–317.
'Institutions françaises en Italie sous le règne de Henri II: gouverneurs et intendants', *Mélanges de l'école française de Rome*, 94 (1982), 759–818.
Ariazza, A., 'Mousnier and Barber: the theoretical underpinning of the 'Society of Orders' in early modern Europe', *Past and Present*, 89 (1980), 39–57.
Aristide, I., *La fortune de Sully*, Paris, 1990.
Audouin, X., *Histoire de l'administration de la guerre*, 4 vols.; Paris, 1811.

Bibliography

Aumale, H. d'Orléans, duc d', *Histoire des princes de Condé pendant les XVIe et XVIIe siècles*, 7 vols.; Paris, 1893-6.
Avenel, vicomte G. d', *Richelieu et la monarchie absolue*, 4 vols.; Paris, 1884-90.
Babeau, A., *La vie militaire sous l'Ancien Régime*, 2 vols.; Paris, 1890.
Babel, R., *Zwischen Habsburg und Bourbon. Aussenpolitik und europäische Stellung Herzog Karls IV. von Lothringen und Bar vom Regierungsantritt bis zum Exil (1624-1634)*, Sigmaringen, 1989.
Babelon, J.-P., *Henri IV*, Paris, 1982.
Baillargeat, R. (ed.), *Les Invalides. Trois siècles d'histoire*, Paris, 1975.
Barbiche, B., and S. de Dainville-Barbiche, *Sully*, Paris, 1997.
Bardin, E.A., *Dictionnaire de l'armée de terre, ou recherches historiques sur l'art et l'usages militaires des anciens et des modernes*, 17 vols.; Paris, 1841-51.
Barker, T., *The Military Intellectual and Battle. Raimondo Montecuccoli and the Thirty Years' War*, Albany, N.Y., 1975.
   Army, Aristocracy, Monarchy. Essays on War, Society and Government in Austria 1618-1780, New York, 1982.
Battifol, L., *La duchesse de Chevreuse*, Paris, 1924.
Baudson, E., *Charles de Gonzague, duc de Nevers, de Rethel et de Mantoue, 1580-1637*, Paris, 1947.
Baxter, D.C., *Servants of the Sword. French Intendants of the Army, 1630-1670*, Urbana, Ill., 1976.
Bayard, F., *Le monde des financiers au XVIIe siècle*, Paris, 1988.
Bean, R., 'War and the birth of the nation state', *Journal of Economic History*, 33 (1973), 203-21.
Béguin, K., *Les princes de Condé. Rebelles, courtisans et mécènes dans la France du Grand Siècle*, Paris, 1999.
Beik, W., 'Two intendants face a popular revolt: social unrest and the structures of absolutism in 1645', *Canadian Journal of History*, 9 (1974), 243-62.
   Absolutism and Society in Seventeenth-Century France. State Power and Provincial Aristocracy in Languedoc, Cambridge, 1985.
Belhomme, lt.-col. V., *Histoire de l'infanterie en France*, 5 vols.; Paris, 1893-1902.
Bély, L., Y.-M. Bercé, J. Meyer and R. Quatrefages, *Guerre et paix dans l'Europe du XVIIe siècle*, 3 vols.; Paris, 1991.
Bercé, Y.-M., *Histoire des croquants. Etude des soulèvements populaires au XVIIe siècle dans le sud-ouest de la France*, 2 vols.; Geneva, 1974.
   'Guerre et etat', *Dix-septième siècle*, 38 (1985), 257-66.
Bérenger, J., *Turenne*, Paris, 1987.
Bérenger, J. (ed.), *La révolution militaire en Europe (XV-XVIIIe siècles)*, Paris, 1998.
Bergin, J., *Cardinal Richelieu. Power and the Pursuit of Wealth*, New Haven and London, 1985.
   The Rise of Richelieu, New Haven and London, 1991.
   'Richelieu and his bishops? Ministerial power and episcopal patronage under Louis XIII', in J. Bergin and L. Brockliss (eds.), *Richelieu and his Age*, Oxford, 1992, pp. 175-202.
   The Making of the French Episcopate, 1589-1661, New Haven and London, 1996.
Bergin, J., and L.W.B. Brockliss (eds.), *Richelieu and his Age*, Oxford, 1992.

Bibliography

Billacois, F., 'La crise de la noblesse européenne (1550–1650): une mise au point', *Revue d'histoire moderne et contemporaine*, 23 (1976), 258–77.

Le duel dans la société française des XVIe–XVIIe siècles. Essai de psychosociologie historique, Paris, 1986.

Bilotto, A., P. Del Negro and C. Mozzarelli (eds.), *I Farnese: Corti, guerra e nobiltà in antico regime*, Rome, 1997.

Bireley, R., *Religion and politics in the age of the Counter-Reformation. Emperor Ferdinand II, William Lamormaini, S.J., and the formulation of Imperial policy*, Chapel Hill, 1981.

'The Thirty Years' War as Germany's religious war', in K. Repgen (ed.), *Krieg und Politik, 1618–1648*, Munich, 1988, pp. 85–106.

Bitton, D., *The French Nobility in Crisis, 1560–1640*, Stanford, 1969.

Black, J., *A Military Revolution? Military Change and European Society, 1550–1800*, London, 1991.

European Warfare, 1660–1815, London, 1994.

Blancpain, M., *Le mardi de Rocroi*, Paris, 1985.

Block, W., *Die Condottieri. Studien über di sogennanten 'unblutigen Schlachten'*, Berlin, 1913.

Bodin, Jérôme, *Les Suisses au service de la France de Louis XI à la Légion Etrangère*, Paris, 1988.

Bluche, F., *L'origine des magistrats du Parlement de Paris au XVIIIe siècle*, Paris, 1956.

Bohanon, D., *Old and New Nobility in Aix-en-Provence, 1600–1695: Portrait of an Urban Elite*, Baton Rouge and London, 1992.

Boiteux, L.-A., *Richelieu: grand maître de la navigation et du commerce de France*, Paris, 1955.

Bondois, P.-M., *Le maréchal de Bassompierre*, Paris, 1925.

Bonney, R.J., 'The intendants of Richelieu and Mazarin, 1624–1661', DPhil thesis, University of Oxford, 1973.

'The secret expenses of Richelieu and Mazarin, 1624–1661', *English Historical Review*, 91 (1976), 825–36.

Political Change in France under Richelieu and Mazarin, 1624–1661, Oxford, 1978.

'The failure of the French revenue farms, 1600–1660', *Economic History Review*, 2nd Ser., 32 (1979), 11–32.

The King's Debts. Finance and Politics in France, 1589–1661, Oxford, 1981.

'Absolutism: what's in a name?', *French History*, 1 (1987), 93–117.

'Bodin and the development of the French monarchy', *Transactions of the Royal Historical Society*, 5th Ser., 40 (1990), 43–61.

'Louis XIII, Richelieu and the royal finances', in J. Bergin and L. Brockliss (eds.), *Richelieu and his Age*, Oxford, 1992, pp. 99–133.

Bosher, J., '*Chambres de justice* in the French monarchy', in J. Bosher (ed.), *French Government and Society, 1500–1850. Essays in Memory of Alfred Cobban*, London, 1973, pp. 19–40.

Bourelly, J., *Le maréchal de Fabert, 1599–1662*, 2 vols.; Paris, 1881.

Bourquin, L., *Noblesse seconde et pouvoir en Champagne aux XVIe et XVIIe siècles*, Paris, 1994.

Boutaric, E., *Les institutions militaires de la France avant les armées permanentes*, Paris, 1863.

Boyer de Saint-Suzanne, Baron C.V.E., *L'administration sous l'Ancien Régime. Les intendants de la généralité d'Amiens (Picardie et Artois)*, Paris, 1865.

Bibliography

Briet, S., *Le maréchal de Schulemberg, 1598–1671*, Mézières, 1960.
Briggs, R., 'Richelieu and reform: rhetoric and political reality', in J. Bergin and L.W.B. Brockliss (eds.), *Richelieu and his Age*, Oxford, 1992, pp. 71–97.
Brockliss, L.W.B., 'Richelieu, education and the state', in J. Bergin and L.W.B. Brockliss (eds.), *Richelieu and his Age*, Oxford, 1992, pp. 237–72.
Brunet, J., *Histoire généralede l'artillerie française*, 2 vols.; Paris, 1842.
Buisseret, D., 'A stage in the development of the French *intendants*: the reign of Henri IV', *Historical Journal*, 9 (1966), 27–38.
Sully and the Growth of Centralized Government in France, 1598–1610, London, 1968.
Henry IV, King of France, London, 1984.
Burckhardt, C.J., *Richelieu and his Age*, 3 vols.; London, 1970.
Burschel, P., *Söldner im Nordwestdeutschland des 16. Jahrhunderts und 17. Jahrhunderts*, Göttingen, 1994.
Caillet, J., *De l'administration en France sous le ministère du cardinal de Richelieu*, Paris, 1857.
Carmona, M., *Richelieu. L'ambition et le pouvoir*, Paris, 1983.
Carrias, E., *La pensée militaire française*, Paris, 1960.
Carrion-Nisas, E., *Essai sur l'histoire générale de l'art militaire. De son origine, de ses progrès et de ses révolutions*, 2 vols.; Paris, 1824.
Chaboche, R., 'Les soldats français de la Guerre de Trente Ans: une tentative d'approche', *Revue d'histoire moderne et contemporaine*, 20 (1973), 10–24.
'Le recrutement des sergents et des caporaux de l'armée française au XVIIe siècle', in *Recrutement, mentalités, sociétés. Actes du colloque international d'histoire militaire*, Montpellier, 1974, pp. 25–44.
Chagniot, J., 'Mobilité sociale et armée', *Dix-septième siècle*, 31 (1979), 37–49.
'Guerre et société au XVIIe siècle', *Dix-septième siècle*, 148 (1985), 232–56.
'Ethique et pratique de la "profession des armes" chez les officiers français au XVIIe siècle', in V. Barrie-Curien (ed.), *Guerre et pouvoir en Europe au XVIIe siècle*, Paris, 1991, pp. 79–93.
Chaline, O., *La bataille de la Montagne Blanche: un mystique chez les guerriers*, Paris, 2000.
Charmeil, J.-P., *Les trésoriers de France à l'époque de la Fronde*, Paris, 1964.
Charvériat, E., *Histoire de la Guerre de Trente Ans*, 2 vols.; Paris, 1878.
Chauleur, A., 'Le rôle des traitants dans l'administration financière de la France de 1643–1653', *Dix-septième siècle*, 65 (1964), 16–49.
Chaunu, P. (ed.), *Le soldat, la stratégie, la mort. Mélanges André Corvisier*, Paris, 1989.
Chéruel, A., *Histoire de l'administration monarchique en France depuis l'avènement de Philippe-Auguste jusqu'à la mort de Louis XIV*, 2 vols.; Paris, 1855.
Chevallier, P., *Louis XIII, roi cornélien*, Paris, 1979.
Henri III, Paris, 1985.
Choné, P., 'Les misères de la guerre ou "la vie du soldat": la force et le droit', in P. Choné and D. Ternois (eds.), *Jacques Callot, 1592–1635* (Catalogue of exhibition – Nancy, June–Sept. 1992), Paris, 1992.
Choppin, H., *Les origines de la cavalerie française: organisation régimentaire de Richelieu, la cavalerie Weimarienne, le régiment de Gassion*, Paris and Nancy, 1905.
Le maréchal de Gassion, 1609–1647, Paris and Nancy, 1907.
Church, W., *Richelieu and Reason of State*, Princeton, 1972.

Bibliography

Clarke, J.A., *Huguenot Warrior: The Life and Times of Henri de Rohan, 1579–1638*, The Hague, 1966.
Collins, J.B., *The Fiscal Limits of Absolutism. Direct Taxation in Early Seventeenth-Century France*, Berkeley, 1988.
Classes, Estates and Order in Early Modern Brittany, Cambridge, 1994.
Constant, J.-M., *Nobles et paysans en Beauce aux XVIe et XVIIe siècles*, Lille, 1981.
La vie quotidienne de la noblesse française aux XVIe et XVIIe siècles, Paris, 1985.
Les conjurateurs: le premier libéralisme politique sous Richelieu, Paris, 1987.
Contamine, P., *Guerre, état et société à la fin du moyen âge. Etudes sur les armées des rois de France, 1337–1494*, Paris, 1972.
Cornette, J., *Le roi de guerre. Essai sur la souveraineté dans la France du Grand Siècle*, Paris, 1993.
'La révolution militaire et l'état moderne', *Revue d'histoire moderne et contemporaine*, 41 (1994), 698–709.
Corvisier, A., 'Les généraux de Louis XIV et leur origine sociale', *Dix-septième siècle*, 45 (1959), 23–53, reprinted in A. Corvisier, *Les hommes, la guerre et la mort*, Paris, 1985, pp. 145–75.
L'armée française de la fin du XVIIe siècle au ministère de Choiseul. Le soldat, 2 vols.; Paris, 1964.
Le France de Louis XIV, 2nd edn, Paris, 1979.
'La noblesse militaire. Aspects militaires de la noblesse française du XVe au XVIIIe siècles', *Histoire Sociale/Social History*, 11 (1978), 336–55.
Louvois, Paris, 1983.
'Clientèles et fidélités dans l'armée française aux XVIIe et XVIIIe siècles', in A. Corvisier, *Les hommes, la guerre et la mort*, Paris, 1985, pp. 191–214 (1st pub. in Y. Durand (ed.), *Clientèles et fidélités en Europe à l'époque moderne: hommage à Roland Mousnier*, Paris, 1981).
'Guerre et mentalités au XVIIe siècle', *Dix-septième siècle*, 38 (1985), 219–32.
Corvisier, A. (ed.), *Histoire militaire de la France*, 4 vols.; Paris, 1992–5.
Cremer, A., *Der Adel in der Verfassung des Ancien Régime. Die Châtellenie d'Epernay und die Souveraineté de Charleville im 17 Jahrhundert*, Bonn, 1981.
Croxton, D., 'A territorial imperative? The military revolution, strategy and peacemaking in the Thirty Years' War', *War in History*, 5 (1998), 253–79.
Peacemaking in Early Modern Europe. Cardinal Mazarin and the Congress of Westphalia, 1643–1648, Selinsgrove, 1999.
Dareste de La Chavanne, A., *Histoire de l'administration en France*, 4 vols.; Paris, 1848.
Delbrück, H., trans. W. Renfroe, *History of the Art of War within the Framework of Political History*, 4 vols.; Westport, Conn., and London, 1975–85.
Deloche, M., *La maison du cardinal de Richelieu – document inédit*, Paris, 1912.
Le père du cardinal, Paris, 1923.
Dent, J., *Crisis in Finance. Crown, Financiers and Society in Seventeenth-Century France*, Newton Abbot, 1973.
Depauw, J., 'Pauvres, pauvres mendiants, mendiants valides ou vagabonds? Les hésitations de la législation royale', *Revue d'histoire moderne et contemporaine*, 21 (1974), 401–18.
Desprat, J.-P., *Les bâtards d'Henri IV. L'épopée des Vendômes, 1594–1727*, Paris, 1994.

Bibliography

des Robert, F., *Les campagnes de Charles IV, duc de Lorraine et Bar, en Allemagne en Lorraine et en Franche Comté, 1634–1643*, 2 vols.; Paris and Nancy, 1883–8.

Dessert, D., 'Finances et société au xviie siècle: à propos de la chambre de justice de 1661', *Annales ESC*, 29 (1974), 847–81.

'Le "laquais financier" au Grand Siècle: mythe ou réalité?', *Dix-septième siècle*, 122 (1979), 21–36.

Argent, pouvoir et société au Grand Siècle, Paris, 1984.

Dethan, G., *La vie de Gaston d'Orléans*, Paris, 1992.

Devyver, A., *Le sang épuré. Les préjugés de race chez les gentilshommes français de l'Ancien Régime, 1560–1720*, Brussels, 1973.

Dewald, J., *Aristocratic Experience and the Origins of Modern Culture: France, 1570–1715*, Berkeley, 1993.

The European Nobility 1400–1800, Cambridge, 1996.

Deyon, P., 'The French nobility and absolute monarchy in the first half of the seventeenth century', in P.J. Coveney (ed.), *France in Crisis, 1620–1675*, London, 1977, pp. 231–26.

Dickerman, E.H., *Bellièvre and Villeroy. Power in France under Henry III and Henry IV*, Providence, 1971.

Dodge, T.A., *Gustavus Adolphus*, Boston, 1895 (reissued London, 1996).

Doucet, R., *Les institutions de la France au XVIe siècle*, 2 vols.; Paris, 1948.

Downing, B., *The Military Revolution and Political Change. Origins of Democracy and Autocracy in Early Modern Europe*, Princeton, 1992.

Doyle, W., *Venality. The Sale of Offices in Eighteenth-Century France*, Oxford, 1996.

Duchêne, J., *Bussy-Rabutin*, Paris, 1992.

Dufayard, C., *Le connétable de Lesdiguières*, Paris, 1892.

Duindam, J., *Myths of Power. Norbert Elias and the Early Modern European Court*, Amsterdam, 1995.

Dunkley, K., 'Patronage and power in seventeenth-century France. Richelieu's clients and the Estates of Brittany', *Parliaments, Estates and Representation*, 1 (1981), 1–12.

Durand, Y., (ed.), *Clientèles et fidélités en Europe à l'époque moderne: hommage à Roland Mousnier*, Paris, 1981, pp. 3–24.

Dussieux, L., *L'armée en France*, 3 vols.; Versailles, 1884.

Les grands généraux de Louis XIV. Notices historiques, Paris, 1888.

Ehlert, H., 'Ursprünge des modernen Militärwesens. Die nassau-oranischen Heeresreformen', *Militärgeschichtliche Mitteilungen*, 18 (1985), 27–56.

Elias, N., trans. E. Jephcott, *The Civilizing Process*, II: *Power and Civility*, Oxford, 1982.

Ellerbach, J., *Der Dreißigjährige Krieg in Elsaß (1618–1648)*, 3 vols.; Mülhausen, 1912–28.

Elliott, J.H., *The Revolt of the Catalans. A Study in the Decline of Spain (1598–1640)*, Cambridge, 1963.

Richelieu and Olivares, Cambridge, 1984.

The Count-Duke of Olivares: The Statesman in an Age of Decline, New Haven and London, 1986.

Elliott, J.H., and L. Brockliss (eds.), *The World of the Favourite*, New Haven and London, 1999.

Ellis, J., *Boulainvilliers and the French Monarchy. Aristocratic Politics in Early Eighteenth-Century France*, Ithaca, 1988.

Bibliography

Eltis, D., *The Military Revolution in Sixteenth-Century Europe*, London, 1995.
Emmanuelli, F.-X., *Un mythe de l'absolutisme bourbonien. L'intendance du milieu du XVIIe siècle à la fin du XVIIIe siècle (France, Espagne, Amérique)*, Aix-en-Provence, 1981.
Etat et pouvoirs dans la France des XVIe–XVIIIe siècles. La métamorphose inachevée, Paris, 1992.
Ernst, H., *Madrid und Wien 1632–37: Politik und Finanzen in den Beziehung zwischen Philipp IV und Ferdinand II*, Münster, 1991.
Ernstberger, A., *Hans de Witte, Finanzmann Wallensteins* (Vierteljahrschrift für Sozial und Wirtschaftsgeschichte, Beiheft 38), Wiesbaden, 1954.
Ertman, T., *The Birth of Leviathan. Building States and Regimes in Medieval and Early Modern Europe*, Cambridge, 1977.
Esmonin, E., *Etudes sur la France du XVIIe et XVIIIe siècles*, Paris, 1964.
Evans, P., D. Rueschemeyer and T. Skocpol (eds.), *Bringing the State Back In*, Cambridge, 1985.
Externbrink, S., *'Le coeur du monde': Frankreich und die norditalienischen Staaten (Mantua, Parma, Savoyen) im Zeitalter Richelieus, 1624–1635*, Münster, 1999.
Fagniez, G., *Le Père Joseph et Richelieu, 1577–1638*, 2 vols.; Paris, 1894.
Feld, M.D., 'Middle class society and the rise of military professionalism: the Dutch army, 1589–1609', *Armed Forces and Society*, 1 (1975), 419–42.
Fessenden, J.N., 'Epernon and Guienne: provincial politics under Louis XIII', PhD thesis, Columbia University, 1972.
Fieffé, E., *Histoire des troupes étrangères au service de la France*, 2 vols.; Paris, 1854.
Finer, S., 'State and nation-building in Europe: the role of the military', in C. Tilly (ed.), *The Formation of National States in Western Europe*, Princeton, 1975, pp. 84–163.
Foerster, R., 'Turenne et Montecuccoli. Une comparaison stratégique et tactique', in F. Gambiez and J. Laloy (eds.), *Turenne et l'art militaire. Actes du Colloque International*, Paris, 1975, pp. 211–19.
Foisil, M., *La révolte des Nu-Pieds et les révoltes normandes de 1639*, Paris, 1970.
Frémont, P., *Les payeurs des armées*, Paris, 1906.
Friedrich, C., *Urban Society in an Age of War: Nördlingen, 1580–1720*, Princeton, 1979.
Frost, R., 'The Polish-Lithuanian commonwealth and the "military revolution"', in J.S. Pula and M.B. Biskupski (eds.), *Poland and Europe: Historical Dimensions. Selected Essays from the 50th Anniversary International Congress of the Polish Arts and Sciences in America*, Boulder, Colo., 1994, pp. 19–47.
The Northern Wars, 1558–1721, London, 2000.
Gambiez, F., and J. Laloy (eds.), *Turenne et l'art militaire. Actes du colloque international*, Paris, 1975.
Gaukroger, S., *Descartes: An Intellectual Biography*, Oxford, 1995.
Giesey, R., 'State-building in early modern France. The role of royal officialdom', *Journal of Modern History*, 55 (1983), 191–207.
Giry-Deloison, C., and Mettam, R. (eds.), *Patronages et clientélismes 1550–1750 (France, Angleterre, Espagne, Italie)*, Lille, 1995.
Godard, C., *Les pouvoirs des intendants sous Louis XIV. Particulièrement dans les pays d'élections de 1661–1715*, Paris, 1901 (repr. Geneva, 1974).
Gonzenbach, A. von, *Der General Hans Ludwig von Erlach von Castelan*, 3 vols.; Bern, 1880–2.

Bibliography

Goubert, P., *Beauvais et le Beauvaisis de 1600–1730*, 2 vols.; Paris, 1960.
L'Ancien Régime, 2 vols.; Paris, 1973.
Greengrass, M., 'War, politics and religion during the government of Montmorency-Damville, 1574–1610', DPhil thesis, University of Oxford, 1979.
France in the Age of Henri IV, London, 1984.
Greenshields, M., *An Economy of Violence in Early Modern France. Crime and Justice in the Haute Auvergne, 1587–1664*, Pennsylvania, 1994.
Guerlac, H., 'Vauban: the impact of science on war', in E.M. Earle (ed.), *Makers of Modern Strategy: Military Thought from Machiavelli to Hitler*, Princeton, 1944, pp. 26–48.
Guéry, A., 'Les finances de la monarchie française sous l'Ancien Régime', *Annales ESC*, 33 (1978), 216–39.
Guillermand, J. (ed.), *Histoire de la médecine aux armées*, I: *De l'antiquité à la Révolution*, Paris, 1982.
Guilmartin, J.F., 'The logistics of warfare at sea in the sixteenth century: the Spanish perspective', in J. Lynn (ed.), *Feeding Mars. Logistics in Western Warfare from the Middle Ages to the Present*, Boulder, Colo., 1993, pp. 109–36.
Gutmann, M., *War and Rural Life in the Early Modern Low Countries*, Princeton, 1980.
Hahlweg, W., *Die Heeresreform der Oranier und die Antike*, Berlin, 1941.
Hale, J.R., *Renaissance War Studies*, London, 1983.
War and Society in Renaissance Europe, 1450–1620, London, 1985.
Hamscher, A., *The Parlement of Paris after the Fronde, 1653–1673*, Pittsburgh, 1976.
Hanley, S., *The "Lit de Justice" of the kings of France: Constitutional Ideology in Legend, Ritual and Discourse*, Princeton, 1983.
Hanotaux, G., *Les origines de l'institution des intendants des provinces d'après les documents inédits*, Paris, 1884.
Hanotaux, G., and duc de La Force, *L'histoire du cardinal de Richelieu*, 6 vols.; Paris, 1893–1947.
Harding, R., *Anatomy of a Power Elite. The Provincial Governors of Early Modern France*, New Haven and London, 1978.
Hardÿ de Périni, M., *Turenne et Condé, 1626–1675*, Paris, 1906.
Haussonville, J.-O., comte d', *Histoire de la réunion de la Lorraine à la France*, 4 vols.; Paris, 1854–9.
Henry, G., *The Irish Military Community in Spanish Flanders, 1586–1621*, Dublin, 1992.
Hickey, D., *The Coming of French Absolutism: The Struggle for Tax Reform in the Province of Dauphiné, 1540–1640*, Toronto, 1986.
Hildesheimer, F., 'Centralisation, pouvoir local et diplomatique: les ordonnances des intendants', *Bibliothèque de l'école des chartes*, 136 (1978), 37–68.
Richelieu; une certain idée de l'état, Paris, 1985.
Hintze, O., 'Military organization and the organization of the state', intr. and trans. by F. Gilbert, *The Historical Essays of Otto Hintze*, New York, 1975, pp. 178–215.
Hodson, S., 'Sovereigns and subjects: the princes of Sedan and the dukes of Bouillon in early modern France, c. 1450–1652', DPhil thesis, University of Oxford, 2000.
Howard, M., *War in European History*, London, 1976.
Humbert, J., *Une grande entreprise oubliée. Les Français en Savoie sous Louis XIII*, Paris, 1960.
Le maréchal de Créquy, Gendre de Lesdiguières, 1573–1638, Paris, 1962.

Bibliography

Huppert, G., *Les Bourgeois Gentilshommes: An Essay on the Definition of Elites in Renaissance France*, Chicago, 1977.
Immler, G., *Kurfürst Maximilian I. und der Westfälische Friedenskongreß. Die bayerische auswärtige Politik von 1644 bis zum Ulmer Waffenstillstand*, Münster, 1992.
Inglis-Jones, J., 'The Grand Condé in exile: power politics in France, Spain and the Spanish Netherlands', DPhil thesis, University of Oxford, 1994.
Israel, J., *The Dutch Republic and the Hispanic World 1606–1661*, Oxford, 1982.
    'Olivares and the government of the Spanish Netherlands, 1621–1643', in J. Israel, *Empires and Entrepots. The Dutch, the Spanish Monarchy and the Jews, 1585–1713*, London, 1990, pp. 163–88.
    The Dutch Republic. Its Rise, Greatness and Fall, 1477–1806, Oxford, 1995.
    'Olivares, the cardinal-infante and Spain's strategy in the Low Countries (1635–1643): the road to Rocroi', in R. Kagan and G. Parker (eds.), *Spain, Europe and the Atlantic World. Essays in Honour of John H. Elliott*, Cambridge, 1995, pp. 267–95.
Iung, J.E., 'Service de vivres d'Allemagne de 1701–1710', Thèse pour le diplôme d'archiviste, Ecole Nationale des Chartes, Paris, 1983.
Jacquart, J., 'Le marquis d'Effiat, lieutenant-général à l'armée d'Italie (été 1630)', *Dix-septième siècle*, 45 (1959), 298–313.
    La crise rurale en Île-de-France (1550–1670), Paris, 1974.
James, A., 'The administration and development of the French navy and the ministry of cardinal Richelieu', PhD thesis, University of Manchester, 1997.
Jones, C., 'The military revolution and the professionalization of the French army under the Ancien Régime', *Exeter Studies in History*, 1 (1980), 28–48.
    'The welfare of the French foot-soldier from Richelieu to Napoleon', *History*, 214 (1980), 193–213.
Jouanna, A., *L'idée de race en France au XVIe siècle et au début du XVIIe siècle, 1498–1614*, 2 vols.; Montpellier, 1981.
    Le devoir de révolte: la noblesse française et la gestation de l'état moderne, 1559–1661, Paris, 1989.
Kaiser, D., *Politics and War. European Conflict from Philip II to Hitler*, London, 1990.
Kapser, C., *Die bayerische Kriegsorganisation in der zweiten Hälfte des Dreißigjährigen Krieges, 1635–1648/9*, Münster, 1997.
Kennedy, P., *The Rise and Fall of Great Powers. Economic Change and Military Conflict from 1500–2000*, London, 1988.
Kettering, S., *Judicial Politics and Urban Revolt in Seventeenth-Century France: The Parlement of Aix, 1629–1659*, Princeton, 1978.
    Patrons, Brokers and Clients in Seventeenth-Century France, Oxford, 1986.
    'The decline of great noble patronage during the reign of Louis XIV', *Canadian Journal of History*, 24 (1989), 157–77.
    'Patronage and kinship in early modern France', *French Historical Studies*, 16 (1989), 408–35.
    'Patronage in early modern France', *French Historical Studies*, 17 (1992), 839–62.
Kiernan, V.G., 'Foreign mercenaries and absolute monarchy', *Past and Present*, 11 (1956–7), 66–86.
Kitchens, J.H., 'Judicial commissions and the Parlement of Paris', *French Historical Studies*, 12 (1982), 323–50.

Bibliography

Knecht, R.J., *Richelieu*, London, 1991.

Koenigsberger, H.G., *The Habsburgs and Europe, 1517–1660*, Ithaca and London, 1971.

Konze, F., 'Die Stärke, Zusammensetzung und Verteilung der Wallensteinischen Armee während des Jahres 1633', dissertation, Bonn, 1906.

Kroener, B., *Les routes et les étapes. Die Versorgung die französischen Armeen in Nordostfrankreich (1635–1661). Ein Beitrag zur Verwaltungsgeschichte des Ancien Régime*, Münster, 1980.

'Die Entwicklung der Truppenstärken in den französischen Armeen zwischen 1635 und 1661', in K. Repgen (ed.), *Forschungen und Quellen zur Geschichte des Dreißigjährigen Krieges*, Münster, 1981, pp. 163–220.

'Soldat oder Soldateska? Programmatischer Aufriß einer Socialgeschichte, militärischer Unterschichten in der ersten Hälfte des 17. Jahrhunderts', in M. Messerschmidt (ed.), *Militärgeschichte: Probleme, Thesen, Wege* (Stuttgart, 1982), pp. 100–23.

'Conditions de vie et origine sociale du personnel militaire subalterne au cours de la Guerre de Trente Ans', *Francia*, 15 (1987), 321–50.

'"Kriegsgurgeln, Freireuter und Merodebrüder". Der Soldat des Dreißigjährigen Krieges. Täter und Opfer', in W. Wette (ed.), *Der Krieg des kleinen Mannes. Eine Militärgeschichte von unten*, Munich, 1992, pp. 51–67.

'"Der Krieg hat ein Loch . . ." Überlegungen zum Schicksal demobilisierter Söldner nach dem Dreißigjährigen Krieg', in H. Duchhardt (ed.), *Der Westfälische Friede. Diplomatie, politische Zäsur, kulturelles Umfeld, Rezeptionsgeschichte*, Munich, 1998, pp. 599–630.

Kroener, B., and R. Pröve (eds.), *Krieg und Frieden. Militär und Gesellschaft in der Frühen Neuzeit*, Paderborn, 1996.

La Barre Duparcq, E. de, *Histoire sommaire d'infanterie*, Paris, 1853.

Eléments d'art et d'histoire militaire, Paris, 1858.

L'art militaire pendant les guerres de religion, Paris, 1864.

Histoire de l'art militaire depuis l'usage de la poudre, Paris, 1864.

Labatut, J., 'Aspects de la fortune de Bullion', *Dix-septième siècle*, 40 (1963), 11–39 (reprinted in J. Labatut, *Noblesse, pouvoir et société en France au XVIIe siècle*, Paris, 1987, pp. 43–72).

Les ducs et pairs de France au XVIIe siècle, Paris, 1972.

'La fidélité du duc de Navailles', in Y. Durand (ed.), *Clientèles et fidélités en Europe à l'époque moderne*, Paris, 1981, pp. 183–97.

La Bruyère, R., *Sourdis, archevêque et amiral: la marine de Richelieu*, Paris, 1948.

Maillé-Brézé: général des galères, grand amiral (1619–1646), Paris, 1945.

La Force, Auguste de Caumont, duc de, *Le maréchal de La Force, 1558–1652*, 2 vols.: Paris, 1928.

Landier, P., 'Guerre, violences et société en France, 1635–1659', thèse de troisième cycle, Université de Paris IV, 1981.

Laugel, A., *Henri de Rohan. Son rôle politique et militaire sous Louis XIII (1579–1638)*, Paris, 1889.

Legrand-Girarde, E., *L'arrière aux armées sous Louis XIII. Crusy de Marcillac, évêque de Mende, 1635–1638*, Paris, 1927.

Léonard, E., *L'armée et ses problèmes au xviiie siècle*, Paris, 1958.

Bibliography

Levantal, C., *Ducs et pairs et duchés-pairies laïques à l'époque moderne (1519–1790)*, Paris, 1996.
Lindegren, J., 'The Swedish military state, 1560–1720', *Scandinavian Journal of History*, 10 (1985), 305–27.
Livet, G., *L'intendance d'Alsace sous Louis XIV, 1648–1715*, Strasbourg, 1956.
Lloyd-Moote, A., *The Revolt of the Judges*, Princeton, 1971.
Louis XIII. The Just, Berkeley, Calif., 1989.
Lot, F., *Recherches sur les effectifs des armées françaises des guerres d'Italie aux Guerres de Religion, 1494–1562*, Paris, 1962.
Löwe, V., 'Die Organisation und Verwaltung der Wallensteinischen Heere', dissertation, Freiburg im Breisgau, 1895.
Lublinskaya, A.D. (ed.), *The Internal Policy of French Absolutism, 1633–1649*, 2 vols.; Moscow and St Petersburg, 1966.
Lublinskaya, A.D., *French Absolutism: The Crucial Phase, 1620–1629*, Cambridge, 1968.
Lynn, J., 'Tactical evolution in the French army, 1560–1660', *French Historical Studies*, 14 (1985), 176–91.
'How war fed war: the tax of violence and contributions during the Grand Siècle', *Journal of Modern History*, 65 (1993), 286–310.
'Recalculating French army growth during the Grand Siècle, 1610–1715', *French Historical Studies*, 18 (1994), 881–906, reprinted in C.J. Rogers (ed.), *The Military Revolution Debate. Readings on the Military Transformation of Early Modern Europe*, Boulder, Colo., 1995, pp. 117–47.
Giant of the Grand Siècle. The French Army, 1610–1715, Cambridge, 1997.
Lynn J. (ed.), *Feeding Mars. Logistics in Western Warfare from the Middle Ages to the Present*, Boulder, San Francisco and Oxford, 1993.
McNeill, W.H., *The Pursuit of Power. Technology, Armed Force and Society since A.D. 1000*, Oxford, 1982.
Major, J.R., *Representative Government in Early Modern France*, New Haven and London, 1980.
Mallett, M., *Mercenaries and their Masters: Warfare in Renaissance Italy*, London, 1974.
Mann, G., *Wallenstein. Sein Leben Erzählt*, Frankfurt-am-Main, 1971.
Mann, M., *The Sources of Social Power*, vol. I, *A History of Power from the Beginning to A.D. 1760*, Cambridge, 1986.
Masson, B., 'La lutte contre l'absence et la désertion dans les armées de Louis XIII, 1635–1643', Mémoire de maîtrise, *Bibliothèque de la Guerre*, Vincennes, 1981.
McIntosh, T., *Urban Decline in Early Modern Germany: Schwäbisch Hall and its Region, 1650–1750*, Chapel Hill, N.C., 1997.
Mettam, R., *Power and Faction in Louis XIV's France*, Oxford, 1988.
'The French nobility, 1610–1715', in H. Scott (ed.), *The European Nobilities in the Seventeenth and Eighteenth Centuries*, 2 vols.; London, 1995, I. 114–41.
Meyer, J., *La noblesse française à l'époque moderne (XVI–XVIII siècles)*, Paris, 1991.
Michaud, H., 'Les institutions militaires des guerres d'Italie aux guerres de religion', *Revue historique*, 257 (1977), 29–43.
Milot, J., 'Du commissaire des guerres à l'intendance militaire', *Revue historique de l'armée*, special number (1968), 39–48.

Bibliography

'L'évolution des corps des intendants militaires', *Revue du Nord*, 50 (1968), 381–410.
Mitchell, J.H., *The Court of the Connétablie*, New Haven, 1947.
Mongrédien, G., *Le bourreau du cardinal de Richelieu. Isaac de Laffemas (1584–1657)*, Paris, 1929.
10 Novembre 1630. La journée des dupes, Paris, 1961.
Motley, M., *Becoming a French Aristocrat. The Education of the Court Nobility, 1580–1715*, Princeton, 1990.
Moulias, C., 'Les origines du corps de l'intendance', *Revue historique de l'armée*, 23 (1967), 83–8.
Mousnier, R., *La plume, la faucille et le marteau. Institutions et société en France du Moyen Age à la Révolution* (collected essays), Paris, 1970.
La vénalité des offices sous Henri IV et Louis XIII, Paris, 1971.
Les Institutions de la France sous la monarchie absolue, 1598–1715, 2 vols.; Paris, 1974–80.
L'Homme Rouge ou la vie du cardinal de Richelieu (1585–1642), Paris, 1992.
Mousnier, R., Y. Durand and J. Labatut, *Problèmes de stratification sociale: deux cahiers de la noblesse pour les Etats généraux de 1649–1651*, Paris, 1965.
Mouton, L., *Un demi-roi: le duc d'Epernon*, Paris, 1922.
Le duc et le roi: le duc d'Epernon, Henri IV et Louis XIII, Paris, 1924.
Mun, G. de, *Richelieu et la Maison de Savoie. L'ambassade de Particelli d'Hémery en Piémont (1635–1639)*, Paris, 1907.
Nasalli Rocca, E., *I Farnese*, Varese, 1969.
Navereau, A., *Le logement et les ustensiles des gens de guerre, 1439–1789*, Poitiers, 1924.
Nef, J.U., *Industry and Government in France and England, 1540–1640*, Ithaca, N.Y., 1957.
Neuschel, K., *Word of Honor: Interpreting Noble Culture in Sixteenth-Century France*, Ithaca, N.Y., 1989.
Nickle, B.H., *The Military Reforms of Prince Maurice of Orange*, Michigan, 1984.
Niederkorn, J.-P., *Die Europäischen Mächte und der 'Lange Türkenkrieg' Kaiser Rudolfs II* (Archiv für österreichische Geschichte, 135), Vienna, 1993.
Noailles, A.M.R.A. vicomte de, *Le cardinal de La Valette, 1635–1639*, Paris, 1906.
Bernhard de Saxe-Weimar, 1604–1639, Paris, 1908.
Le maréchal de Guébriant, 1602–1643, Paris, 1913.
Nordmann, C., 'L'armée suédoise au XVIIe siècle', *Revue du Nord*, 54 (1972), 265–87.
Oestreich, G., *Neostoicism and the Early Modern State*, Cambridge, 1982.
Oresko, R., 'The marriages of the nieces of Cardinal Mazarin. Public policy and private stategy in seventeenth-century Europe', in R. Babel (ed.), *Frankreich im europäischen Staatensystem der Frühen Neuzeit* (Beihefte der Francia, 35), Sigmaringen, 1995, pp. 109–51.
'The House of Savoy and the Thirty Years' War', in K. Bussmann and H. Schilling (eds.), *1648 War and Peace in Europe – Politics, Religion, Law and Society*, Münster, 1998, pp. 142–53.
Oresko, R., G. Gibbs and H. Scott (eds.), *Royal and Republican Sovereignty in Early Modern Europe. Essays in Honour of Professor Ragnhild Hatton*, Cambridge, 1997.
Pablo, J. de, 'L'armée huguenote entre 1562 et 1573', *Archiv für Reformationsgeschichte*, 48 (1957), 192–216.
Pagès, G., 'Essai sur l'évolution des institutions administratives en France du commence-

ment du XVIe siècle à la fin du XVIIe siècle', *Revue d'histoire moderne*, 7 (1932), 8–57, 113–37.
'Autour du "grand orage"': Richelieu et Marillac', *Revue historique*, 179 (1937), 63–97.
Les institutions monarchiques sous Louis XIII et Louis XIV, Paris, 1937.
La monarchie de l'Ancien Régime en France de Henri IV à Louis XIV, 3rd edn, Paris, 1941.
The Thirty Years' War, English trans., London, 1970.
Pange, J. de, *Charnacé et l'alliance franco-hollandaise (1633–1637)*, Paris, 1905.
Parker, D., *La Rochelle and the French Monarchy. Conflict and Order in Seventeenth-Century France*, London, 1980.
The Making of French Absolutism, London, 1983.
Class and State in Ancien Régime France. The Road to Modernity?, London, 1996.
Parker, G., *The Army of Flanders and the Spanish Road, 1567–1659*, Cambridge, 1972.
'The "military revolution, 1560–1660" – a myth?', *Journal of Modern History*, 48 (1976), 195–214 (reprinted in G. Parker, *Spain and the Netherlands, 1559–1659*, London, 1979, pp. 85–103, and in C.J. Rogers (ed.), *The Military Revolution Debate. Readings on the Military Transformation of Early Modern Europe*, Boulder, Colo., 1995, pp. 37–54).
The Dutch Revolt, London, 1977.
Europe in Crisis, 1598–1648, London, 1980.
The Thirty Years' War, London, 1984.
The Military Revolution. Military Innovation and the Rise of the West, 1500–1800 Cambridge, 1988; 2nd edn, 1996.
'The soldiers of the Thirty Years' War', in K. Repgen (ed.), *Krieg und Politik, 1618–1648*, Munich, 1988.
Parrott, D., 'The administration of the French army during the ministry of cardinal Richelieu', DPhil thesis, University of Oxford, 1985.
'Strategy and tactics in the Thirty Years' War: the 'military revolution', *Militärgeschichtliche Mitteilungen*, 18 (1985), 7–25.
'Richelieu, the *grands* and the French army', in J. Bergin and L.W.B. Brockliss (eds.), *Richelieu and his Age*, Oxford, 1992, pp. 135–73.
'Power and patronage in the French army, 1620–1659', in C. Giry-Deloison and R. Mettam (eds.), *Patronages et clientélismes 150–1750 (France, Angleterre, Espagne, Italie)*, Lille, 1995, pp. 229–41.
'The Mantuan succession, 1627–1631: a sovereignty dispute in early modern Europe', *English Historical Review*, 112 (1997), 20–65.
'A *prince souverain* and the French crown: Charles de Nevers, 1580–1637', in R. Oresko, G. Gibbs and H. Scott (eds.), *Royal and Republican Sovereignty in Early Modern Europe: Essays in Honour of Professor Ragnhild Hatton*, Cambridge, 1997, pp. 149–87.
'The role of fortifications in the defence of states: the Farnese and the security of Parma and Piacenza', in A. Bilotto, P. Del Negro and C. Mozzarelli (eds.), *I Farnese: Corti, guerra e nobiltà in antico regime* (Rome, 1997), pp. 509–60.
'The utility of fortifications in early modern Europe: Italian princes and their citadels, 1540–1640', *War in History*, 7 (2000), 127–53.
Pascal, A., *Histoire de l'armée et de tous les régiments*, 5 vols.; Paris, 1847–50.
Pepper, S., and N. Adams, *Firearms and Fortifications. Military Architecture and Siege Warfare in Sixteenth-Century Siena*, Chicago, 1986.

Bibliography

Pernot, J., 'Le rôle de la guerre dans le développement de la théorie de la monarchie moderne', *Revue historique des armées*, 6 (1979), 41–70.

Petracchi, A., *Intendenti e prefetti. L'intendente provinciale nella Francia d'antico regime*, 2 vols.; Milan, 1971.

Phillips, C., *Six Galleons for the king of Spain. Imperial Defence in the Early Seventeenth Century*, Baltimore and London, 1986.

Picavet, C., *Les dernières années de Turenne*, Paris, 1914.

Piépape, L. de, *Histoire de la réunion de la Franche-Comté à la France*, 2 vols.; Paris and Besançon, 1881.

Pillorget, R., 'Populations civiles et troupes dans le Saint-Empire au cours de la Guerre de Trente Ans', in V. Barrie-Curien (ed.), *Guerre et pouvoir en Europe au XVIIe siècle*, Paris, 1991, pp. 151–74.

Pithon, R., 'Les débuts difficiles du ministère du cardinal de Richelieu et la crise de Valteline', *Revue d'histoire diplomatique*, 74 (1960), 298–322.

Poëte, M., *Paris devant la menace étrangère en 1636*, Paris, 1916.

Pohl, J., *Die Profiantirung der keyserlichen Armaden ahnbelangendt. Studien zur Versorgung der kaiserlichen Armee, 1634–1635* (Mitteilungen des Österreichischen Staatsarchives, Sonderband 1), Vienna, 1994.

Potter, D., *War and Government in the French Provinces: Picardy, 1470–1560*, Cambridge, 1993.

Quarré de Verneuil, R., *L'armée en France depuis Charles VII jusqu'à la Révolution (1439–1789)*, Paris, 1880.

Quazza, G., 'Guerra civile in Piemonte, 1637–1642 (nuove ricerche), *Bollettino storico-bibliografico subalpino*, 42/3 (1959/60), 281–321 (42), 5–63 (43).

Quazza, M.C., *Marie de Gonzague et Gaston d'Orléans: un épisode de politique secrète au temps de Louis XIII*, Mantua, 1925.

Quazza, R., 'Politica europea nella questione valtellinica (La Lega Franco-Veneto-Savoiardo e la pace di Monçon)', *Nuovo archivio veneto*, 42 (1921), 50–151.

Mantova e Monferrato nella politica europea alla vigilia della guerra per la successione (1624–1627), Mantua, 1922.

La guerra per la successione di Mantova e del Monferrato (1628–1631), 2 vols.; Mantua, 1926.

'La politica di Carlo Emanuele I durante la guerra dei trent' anni', *Carlo Emanuele miscellanea*, 120, Turin, 1930, pp. 1–45.

'Il periodo italiano della guerra di trent'anni', *Rivista storica italiana*, 50 (1933), 64–89.

Tommaso di Savoia-Carignano nelle campagne di Fiandre e di Francia, 1635–1638, Turin, 1941.

Ranum, O., *Richelieu and the Councillors of Louis XIII*, Oxford, 1963.

Rasler, K., and W. Thompson, *War and State Making. The Shaping of the Global Powers*, Boston, 1989.

Rebel, H., *Peasant Classes. The Bureaucratization of Property and Family Relations under Early Habsburg Absolutism, 1511–1636*, Princeton, 1983.

Reboul, F., 'Histoire militaire de la France', in G. Hanotaux (ed.), *Histoire de la nation française*, 15 vols., Paris, 1920–35, VII. 349–418.

Redlich, F., 'Contributions in the Thirty Years' War', *Economic History Review*, 2nd Ser., 12 (1959–60), 247–54.

Bibliography

De Praede Militare. Looting and Booty, 1500–1815 (Vierteljahrschrift für Sozial- und Wirtschaftsgeschichte, Beiheft 39), Wiesbaden, 1956.

The German Military Enterpriser and his Work Force, 14th to 18th Centuries (Vierteljahrschrift für Sozial- und Wirtschaftsgeschichte, Beihefte 47 and 48), 2 vols.: Wiesbaden, 1964.

Reinhard, W. (ed.), *Power Elites and State Building*, Oxford, 1996.

Repgen, K. (ed.), *Krieg und Politik, 1618–1648*, Munich, 1988.

Revol, J., *Turenne. Essai de psychologie militaire*, Paris, 1910.

Ribot Garcia, L., 'Les types d'armées en Espagne au début des temps modernes', in P. Contamine (ed.), *Guerre et concurrence entre les états européens du xvie et xviiie siècles*, Paris, 1998, pp. 61–5.

Ricaldone, G. di, *Annali di Monferrato (951–1708)*, Turin, 1972.

Richard, M., 'Les Misères et les Malheurs de la Guerre (1633): a work and its context', in K. Bussmann and H. Schilling (eds.), *1648. War and Peace in Europe*, 3 vols.; Münster and Osnabrück, 1998, II. 517–23.

Rill, B., *Tilly. Feldherr für Kaiser und Reich*, Munich, 1984.

Ritter, M., 'Das Kontributionssystem Wallensteins', *Historische Zeitschrift*, 54 (1902–3), 193–249.

Roberts, M., 'The military revolution, 1560–1660', Belfast, 1955 (reprinted in M. Roberts, *Essays in Swedish History*, London, 1967, pp. 195–225, and in C.J. Rogers (ed.), *The Military Revolution Debate. Readings on the Military Transformation of Early Modern Europe*, Boulder, Colo., 1995, pp. 13–35).

Gustavus Adolphus. A History of Sweden, 1611–1632, 2 vols.; London, 1953–8.

'Gustav Adolf and the art of war', in M. Roberts, *Essays in Swedish History*, London, 1967, pp. 56–81.

Robisheaux, T., *Rural Society and the Search for Order in Early Modern Germany*, Cambridge, 1989.

Rogers, C.J. (ed.), *The Military Revolution Debate. Readings on the Military Transformation of Early Modern Europe*, Boulder, Colo., 1995.

Roloff, G., 'Moritz von Oranien und die Begründung des modernen Heeres', *Preußische Jahrbücher*, 111 (1903), 255–76.

Rothenberg, G.E., 'Maurits of Nassau, Gustavus Adolphus, Raimondo Montecuccoli and the "military revolution" of the seventeenth century', in P. Paret (ed.), *Makers of Modern Strategy: Military Thought from Machiavelli to the Nuclear Age*, Princeton, 1986, pp. 32–63.

Rott, E., *Histoire de la représentation diplomatique de la France auprès des cantons suisses, de leurs alliés et de leurs confédérés*, 10 vols.; Berne, 1900–35.

Rousset, C., *Histoire de Louvois et de son administration politique et militaire*, 4 vols.; Paris, 1879.

Rowlands, G., 'Power, authority and army administration under Louis XIV: the French crown and the military elites in the era of the Nine Years' War', DPhil thesis, University of Oxford, 1997.

Roy, J., *Turenne, sa vie et les institutions militaires de son temps*, Paris, 1884.

Salerian-Saugy, C., *Les conseils de guerre judiciaires en France sous l'Ancien Régime*, Bourges, 1925.

La juridiction du colonel général de l'infanterie de France, Bourges, 1927.

Bibliography

La justice militaire des troupes suisses en France, Paris, 1927.
Salm, H., *Armeefinanzierung im Dreißigjährigen Krieg. Der Niederrheinisch-Westfälische Reichskreis, 1635–1650*, Münster, 1990.
Salmon, J.H., *Society in Crisis: France in the Sixteenth Century*, London, 1975.
Sanabre, J., *La Acción de Francia en Cataluña en la pugna por la hegemonía de Europa (1640–1659)*, Barcelona, 1956.
Schalk, E., *From Valor to Pedigree: Ideas of Nobility in France in the Sixteenth and Seventeenth Centuries*, Princeton, 1986.
Schmidt, C., 'Le rôle et les attributions d'un "intendant des finances" aux armées: Sublet de Noyers de 1632 à 1636', *Revue d'histoire moderne et contemporaine*, 2 (1900–1), 156–75.
Schulten, C., 'Une nouvelle approche de Maurice de Nassau (1567–1625)', in P. Chaunu (ed.), *Le soldat, la stratégie, la mort. Mélanges André Corvisier* (Paris, 1989), pp. 42–53.
Scott, H. (ed.), *The European Nobilities in the Seventeenth and Eighteenth Centuries* (2 vols.; London, 1995).
Schybergson, M., *Le duc de Rohan et la chute du parti protestant en France*, Paris, 1880.
Servan, J., and le comte P.H. de Grimoard, *Recherches sur la force de l'armée françoise, depuis Henri IV jusqu'en 1806*, Paris, 1806.
Sicard, F., *Histoire des institutions militaires des Français*, 4 vols.; Paris, 1834.
Skalweit, S., 'Richelieus Staatsidee', *Geschichte in Wissenschaft und Unterricht*, 2 (1962).
Smedley-Weill, A., *Les intendants de Louis XIV*, Paris, 1995.
Smith, J., *The Culture of Merit. Nobility, Royal Service and the Making of Absolute Monarchy in France, 1600–1789*, Ann Arbor, 1996.
Spooner, F., *The International Economy and Monetary Movements in France, 1493–1725*, Cambridge, Mass., 1972.
Stadler, B., *Pappenheim und die Zeit des Dreißigjährigen Krieges*, Winterthur, 1991.
Stein, W., *Protection Royale. Eine Untersuchung zu den Protektions-verhältnissen im Elsaß zur Zeit Richelieus, 1622–1643*, Münster, 1978.
Storrs, C., and H. Scott, 'The military revolution and the European nobility, c. 1600–1800', *War in History*, 3 (1996), 1–41.
Stradling, R., 'Catastrophe and recovery: the defeat of Spain, 1639–1643', *History*, 64 (1979), 205–19.
'Seventeenth-century Spain: decline or survival?', *European Studies Review*, 9 (1979), 154–94.
'Spain's military failure and the supply of horses, 1600–1660', *History*, 69 (1984), 208–21.
'Olivares and the origins of the Franco-Spanish War, 1627–1635', *English Historical Review*, 101 (1986), 68–94.
Philip IV and the Government of Spain, 1621–1665, Cambridge, 1988.
Spain's Struggle for Europe, London, 1994.
The Spanish Monarchy and Irish Mercenaries. The Wild Geese in Spain, 1618–1668, Dublin, 1994.
Straub, E., *Pax et Imperium. Spaniens Kampf um seine Friedensordnung in Europa zwischen 1617 und 1635*, Paderborn, 1980.
Struck, W., *Die Schlacht bei Nördlingen*, Stralsund, 1893.

Bibliography

Susane, L., *Histoire de l'ancienne infanterie française*, 8 vols.; Paris, 1849–53.
    Histoire de l'infanterie française, 5 vols.; Paris, 1872–4.
    Histoire de la cavalerie française, 3 vols.; Paris, 1874.
    Histoire de l'artillerie française, Paris, 1874.
Sutcliffe, F., *Guez de Balzac et son temps: littérature et politique*, Paris, 1959.
Sutherland, N., *The French Secretaries of State in the Age of Catherine de Medici*, London, 1962.
Tait, R.G., 'The king's lieutenants in Guyenne, 1580–1610', DPhil thesis, University of Oxford, 1977.
Tallett, F., *War and Society in Early Modern Europe, 1495–1715*, London, 1992.
Tapié, V.-L., *La politique étrangère de la France et le début de la Guerre de Trente Ans (1616–1621)*, Paris, 1934.
    France in the Age of Louis XIII and Richelieu, Eng. trans.; London, 1974.
Tellier, L.-N., *Face aux Colbert. Les Le Tellier, Vauban, Turgot et l'avènement du libéralisme*, Québec, 1987.
Texier, A., *Qu'est-ce que la noblesse?*, Paris, 1988.
Thompson, I.A.A., *War and Government in Habsburg Spain, 1560–1620*, London, 1976.
Thuau, E., *Raison d'état et pensée politique à l'époque de Richelieu*, Paris, 1966.
Tilly, C., *Coercion, Capital and European States, A.D. 990–1992*, Oxford, 1990.
Tilly, C. (ed.), *The Formation of National States in Western Europe*, Princeton, 1975.
Trenard, L., *Les mémoires des intendants pour l'instruction du duc de Bourgogne, 1698*, Paris, 1975.
Trevor-Roper, H., *The Plunder of the Arts in the Seventeenth Century*, London, 1970.
Tuetey, L., *Les officiers sous l'Ancien Régime. Nobles et roturiers*, Paris, 1908.
Vaissière, P. de, *L'affaire du maréchal de Marillac, 1630–1632*, Paris, 1924.
Van Creveld, M., *Supplying War: Logistics from Wallenstein to Patton*, Cambridge, 1977.
van Der Essen, A., *Le cardinal-infant et la politique européenne de l'Espagne (1609–1634)*, Brussels, 1944.
van der Hoeven (ed.), M., *Exercise of Arms. Warfare in the Netherlands (1568–1648)*, Brill, 1998.
Vassal-Reig, C., *La guerre en Roussillon sous Louis XIII (1635–1639)*, Paris, 1934.
    Richelieu et la Catalogne, Paris, 1935.
    La prise de Perpignan (1641–1642), Paris, 1939.
Vaux de Foletier, F. de, *Le siège de La Rochelle*, Paris, 1931.
Vernisy, E. de, *Episodes de la Guerre de Trente Ans; l'invasion allemande en Bourgogne en 1636*, Dijon, 1928.
Viollet, P., 'Le colonel général de l'infanterie française', *Journal des savants*, 7 (1909), 485–94.
Waquet, J.-C., *De la corruption. Morale et pouvoir à Florence aux XVIIe et XVIIIe siècles*, Paris, 1984.
Weber, H., 'Richelieu et le Rhin', *Revue Historique*, 239 (1968), 265–80.
    Frankreich, Kurtrier, der Rhein und das Reich, 1623–1635, Bonn, 1969.
    'Dieu, le roi et la chrétienté: aspects de la politique du cardinal de Richelieu', *Francia*, 13 (1985), 233–45.
    'Vom verdeckten zum offenen Krieg. Richelieu's Kriegsgründe und Kriegsziele', in K. Repgen (ed.), *Krieg und Politik, 1618–1648*, Munich, 1988, pp. 203–17.

Bibliography

Weigley, R., *The Age of Battles. The Quest for Decisive Warfare from Breitenfeld to Waterloo*, Bloomington and Indianapolis, 1991.

Wiekart, A., and J.P. Puype, *Van Maurits naar Munster: tactiek en triomf van het Staatse leger* (catalogue of exhibition at the Legermuseum), Delft, 1998.

Wijn, J.W., *Het krijgswezen in den tijd van Prins Maurits*, Utrecht, 1934.

Wood, J.B., *The Nobility of the Election of Bayeux, 1463–1666: Continuity through Change*, Princeton, 1980.

The King's Army. Warfare, Soldiers and Society during the Wars of Religion in France, 1562–1576, Cambridge, 1996.

Zeller, B., *Richelieu et les ministres de Louis XIII de 1621 à 1624*, Paris, 1880.

Zeller, G., *La réunion de Metz à la France (1552–1648)*, 2 vols.; Paris, 1926.

Les institutions de la France au XVIe siècle, Paris, 1948.

Index

Total consistency in creating an index which incorporates large numbers of the French *noblesse* would be both difficult to achieve, and in many cases counter-intuitive. For the lower ranks of the nobility, and especially the *noblesse de robe*, I have usually indexed the individuals under family names rather than seigneurial titles – hence Jean *Choisy*, sr de Beaumont, or Jean-Baptiste *Bretagne*, marquis de Courcy. However, there are some cases where such persons were clearly identified by their seigneurial title in contemporary correspondence and by subsequent historians, such that it would be perverse not to use this title: René Voyer, sr d'*Argenson*, Léon le Bouthillier, comte de *Chavigny* (yet, at a similar social level, Claude *Bullion*, not marquis de Gallardon). On a few occasions where confusion may be generated by this I have cross-referenced family name and siegneurial titles. At the level of the *grands*, indexing by (most prestigious) title tends to be the lesser of two evils, precluding some of the confusion over different generations of the family with similar names – maréchal *Créqui* was recognized by contemporaries and subsequent historians in a way that 'Charles de *Blanchefort*' is not. In the case of sovereign families, I have adopted the convention of indexing under first names: Charles VIII, king of France, Carlo Emmanuele I, duke of Savoy.

Abbeville, 119, 128, 344n127, 450, 457n263, 506n6, 522, 537
absenteeism of officers, 14, 47, 325, 362–5, 395, 521, 543n177
academies, French military, 39–40
Aelian, Claudius, 25
affaires extraordinaires, 232, 235, 238, 241, 242, 260
Agen, 531n124
Aigrémont, Laon d', 35n58
Aiguebonne, Rostang-Antoine d'Urre du Puy-Saint-Martin, sr d', 323n39, 325n51
Aiguillon, *see* Combalet
Aire, 148–50, 214–5
Aix-en-Provence, 39
Alais, Louis-Emmanuel de Valois, comte d', *colonel général de la cavalerie légère*, 62, 348n142, 377, 442–3, 474, 484, 529n113
Alba, 124

Aldringen, Johann von, Imperial general, 94
Alençon, 515n54
Alincourt, Charles de Neufville-Villeroy, marquis d', 209–10, 338n97, 383n80, 509n21, 512
Allais, Grace of, 94
Alluye, Charles de Sourdis, marquis d', 62
Alsace, 75, 79, 80, 104, 106, 115, 116, 118, 126, 147, 191, 193, 195, 201, 205, 268, 269, 294, 413, 421, 448, 454, 459, 535n142
Amelia of Hanau, widow of landgrave Wilhelm V of Hesse-Kassel, 298
Amiens, 119, 128, 388, 412, 451, 486, 531n123, 541
amirauté du Levant, 481
amirauté du Ponant, 469–70, 481, 485
Andelot, Charles de Châtillon, marquis d', 351n151

Index

André, Louis, 538
Angoulême, Charles de Valois, maréchal d', 32, 63, 257, 411, 414, 467, 484, 491, 498
Angoumois, 127, 197, 370, 472, 523
Anjou, 411
Anne of Austria, Regency of (1643–51), 162–3, 470–1
Ardres, 158, 519n66
Argencour, Pierre-Conty d', *ingénieur du roi*, 249–50, 387n99
Argenson, René Voyer, sr d', *intendant*, 348n141, 393–4, 418, 439n181, 441n185, 444n202, 445n207, 448n225, 450, 457, 460n283, 495
Arnaud d'Andilly, Robert, *intendant*, 39, 374, 378n59, 394n138, 444, 445–6, 454, 456n261
Arnauld, Pierre, *mestre de camp*, 39n71
Arnoul, sr, *commissaire des guerres* and *contrôleur des deniers destinés à la subsistance des troupes*, 274, 403n18, 417, 421
Arpajon, Louis d', vicomte de Montal, *maréchal de camp*, 114n167, 386n95
Arras, 58, 59, 136, 142, 150, 156, 204, 210, 269, 301, 344, 346n137, 392, 395, 412–13, 416, 452, 457, 463, 494, 503, 530n117, 537, 540n165, 541
arrière-ban, see ban et arrière-ban
artillery, 65–71, 218, 227, 247n86, 388–90, 475–6
  see also grand maître
Artois, 112
Aubray, Dreux d', sr d' Offemont, *intendant*, 381n69, 421, 428n137, 429n140, 450, 456n262, 459n278
Aubray, Henri d', *commissaire des guerres*, 392, 401n3, 403, 508n16
Aubusson, François d', sr de Beauregard, 29
Augsburg, War of League of, 164
Aumont, Antoine de Rochebaron, maréchal d', 291
Aurignac, sr d', *maréchal de camp* (?) and military theorist, 29, 35, 56–7
Austria (Habsburg Hereditary Lands), 1, 86, 111
Auvergne, 265, 439n181, 513n41, 522n82, 523, 540

Auxerre, 532n131
Avaux, Claude de Mesmes, comte d', 54, 294n50, 300–1, 371
Avein, battle of, 22 May 1635, 58, 75, 113
Avenel, vicomte Georges d', 2
Avigliano, 97, 140

Baden, 27
Balme, sr, *intendant*, 385, 392n125, 447
Baltazar, Jean-Baptiste, sr de Malherbe, *intendant*, 438, 440n183, 443–4, 451n238
ban et arrière-ban, 63–5, 116, 120, 192, 198, 208, 230, 314, 319, 410n55, 456, 519
Banér, Johan, Swedish general, 54, 61, 66, 107, 134, 154, 211, 279, 283, 296
Bapaume, 150, 155, 457n264, 494
Barcelona, 146, 153, 163, 213
Barrault, Jean de Gaillard de Béarn, comte de, 116
Barthélemy brothers, *munitionnaires*, 256
Basle, 106, 126, 382n75
Bassompierre, François de Betstein, maréchal, 30, 46n97, 51, 53, 372n27, 426, 484–5, 493
Batilly, colonel, 196n118
Battalion (*bataillon*), 20, 51–54, 57
Bavaria, duchy, then (1625) electorate of, 80, 104, 107, 163
  army, 52, 108, 154, 280, 297, 353
Baxter, Douglas, 454
Bayard, Françoise, 263
Bayeux, 524
Béarn, 53
Beauclerc, Charles de, baron d'Archères et de Rougement, *secrétaire d'Etat de la guerre* 1624–31, 367
Beaufort, François de Bourbon-Vendôme, duc de, 377n49, 474n46
Beaupré, sr de, *commissaire de l'artillerie*, 388n108
Beauvais, 412n62, 520n70, 531, 540n168
Beauvau de Rivarennes, Gabriel de, bishop of Nantes, 257–8, 412
Beik, William, 544
Belhomme, Victor, 166–7
Bellejamme, Louis Le Maistre, sr de, *intendant*, 41n82, 344n127, 421, 428n137,

580

Index

429n140, 430n148, 449, 450–1, 458, 524n87
Bellême, 515
Bellièvre, Nicolas de, sr de Grignon, *président* of *Parlement* of Paris, 495
Bellièvre, Pierre de, sr de Grignan, ambassador to England, 311nn 124 and 125
Belot, Guillaume, sr du Clos, *commissaire des guerres*, 407n42, 409n52, 425n126
Berault, *commissaire pour les subsistances*, 428
Berger, *commissaire des guerres*, 407n42
Bertheneau, sr, surgeon with army of Lorraine, 535n146
Besançon, Bernard du Plessis, sr de, *sergent de bataille*, 146–7, 408n46, 419, 433n154
Besançon, Charles de Bazoches, sr de, *commissaire des guerres*, 394, 402n8, 403, 406n37, 407–8, 424–6, 427n133, 433
Béthune, Léonidas de, seigneur de Congy, *mestre de camp*, 29
Béthune, Philippe de, 185
Bevandière, Cognesceau, sr de, *prévôt*, 372n27
Bidal, *commissaire des guerres*, 373n27
Biez, *colonel*, 324n42
Bigot, Jacques, *contrôleur général des guerres*, 376n40, 431n149
Billon, Jean de, military theorist, 28, 33–4, 35, 36, 37, 41, 51, 52
Biou, Jacques, *commissaire*, 251n103, 424–5, 427
Biron, Charles de Gontaut, maréchal de, 32, 472
Bletterans, 125
Blois, 513n41
Bohemia, kingdom of, 159
  revolt of, 84–5, 534n135
Boissière, sr, *commissaire des guerres*, 417
Bonney, Richard, 8, 239, 243, 276, 452
Bordeaux, 193, 441n186, 459
Bordeaux, Guillaume, sr de Génitoy, *intendant*, 374, 384n90, 418–20
Bosquet, François, *intendant*, 443–4, 451n238, 460
Bossolino, treaty of, 96n64
Bouault, *munitionnaire*, 256–7, 414
Bouillon, Frédéric-Maurice de La Tour d'Auvergne, duke of, 29, 30, 148, 160, 214, 219, 474n46, 490
Bouillon, Henri de La Tour d'Auvergne, duke of, 28, 40
Boullet (Boullé), Nicolas, *commissaire des guerres*, 403
Boulogne, Boulonnais, 451, 519n66
Bourbon, House of, *see* French kings by name, and Condé, Conti, Soissons
Bourges, 431n149
Bourguignon, Louis, *commissaire des guerres*, 393–4
Bournonville, Ambroise-François, marquis de, 62, 338n101
Boutault, Gilles, bishop of Aire-sur-l'Adour, 403, 413
Bouteret, sr, *commissaire des guerres*, 405n31, 425n124
Bouthillier, Claude (le), *surintendant des finances* 1632–43, 172, 198, 210, 238–40, 243, 252, 253, 255–6, 261–2, 264, 266, 270, 274–5, 371–2, 417n83, 433n159, 510n26, 512n37
Boyer, *commissaire des guerres*, 391
Bragelongne, Jean de, *commissaire des guerres*, subsequently *intendant*, 251n102, 346n134, 401n4, 433, 438
Bragelongne, Marie de (wife of Claude Bouthillier), 438
Brandenburg, Electorate of, 27, 121
Brassac, Jean de Gallard de Béarn, comte de, governor of Nancy, 67, 293, 325n51
Breda, 31, 124
Breisach, 129–31, 134, 138, 143, 189, 205, 294, 295
Breitenfeld, battle of, 17 Sept. 1631, 23, 27, 36, 66, 78, 101, 170
Breitenfeld/Leipzig, battle of, 2 Nov. 1642, 81, 159
Breme, 131, 495
Bresse, 384, 424
Brest, 67
Bretagne, Jean-Baptiste, marquis de Courcy, *commissaire des guerres*, 391, 401n3, 403n15, 405n31, 456n261
Breteche, sr, *commissaire des guerres*, 403n13, 405n31
Brézé, Armand de Maillé, marquis de, 478

Index

Brézé, Urbain de Maillé, maréchal de, 50, 62, 65, 113–14, 150, 155, 189, 191, 203–5, 215, 217, 253, 261, 265, 341n114, 363, 410, 413, 444, 447, 454, 478, 482, 489, 498–9, 500, 503, 508n17
Brittany, 244, 262, 403n13
Brouage, 67
Brunswick, duchy of, 27, 154
Brussels, 58, 109, 113
Budée, sr, *commissaire des guerres*, 402n11
Budes, Jean-Baptiste, *see* Guébriant
Bullion, Claude, marquis de Gallardon, sr de Bonnelles, *surintendant des finances* 1632–40, 122–3, 169, 172, 174, 176, 225, 234, 238–40, 242–3, 245–6, 251, 253, 255, 260, 261–2, 263, 264–5, 266, 267, 270, 276, 340, 351, 371–2, 386, 393, 394, 401n5, 414, 422n105, 423n107, 433n153, 444, 446, 477, 487n107, 506n8, 510–11, 512n38, 515n52, 552
bureau de la guerre, 9, 363, 371–3, 461, 502, 555
bureau des finances, 12, 60, 129, 145, 177, 225, 235–9, 241, 243, 244, 245, 246, 253, 257, 259, 260, 261–2, 267, 270–6, 374, 414, 432, 440, 461, 510–12, 514, 516, 523, 538
Burgundy, 46, 66, 96, 121, 124, 198–9, 201, 209, 212, 217, 321, 384, 413, 424, 441, 484, 487, 536n152
Buson, captain, 345n130
Busset, Hélène de, 521
Bussy, Charles de Lameth, comte de, 357n169, 414n71
Bussy, Léonor de Rabutin, sr de, 336n91, 350n148, 351n151
Bussy, Roger de Rabutin, sr de, 323n38, 325n51, 332, 350, 357n167, 407, 474nn46, 47 and 48, 494, 521, 522, 525n97, 528
Butler, lieutenant-colonel, 530

Caen, 460n282, 511n32
Calais, 265, 349, 388, 449, 499, 506n6, 519n66
Callot, Jacques, 527
Calvinism, 25, 28, 82
  see also Huguenots
Cambout de Pontchâteau, Marguerite de, 488
Cambout de Pontchâteau, Marie de, 483

Campion, Henri de, 30, 71–2, 364n198, 534n135
Canisy, marquis de, *mestre de camp*, 456
Carces, Jean de Pontevez, comte de, 332n76
Carezzano, Jean-Baptiste, *munitionnaire*, 256
Carlo Emanuele I, duke of Savoy (1585–1630), 31, 86–7, 91–2, 96, 97, 183, 480
Carlo Emanuele II, duke of Savoy (1638–75), 132, 139, 219
Carmagnola, 140, 505
Carrias, Eugène, 468
Casale, 59, 68n200, 71, 92–3, 94, 97–100, 103, 140, 151, 161, 163, 185–7, 188, 206, 211–12, 275, 369, 479, 485, 505
Castelan, Olivier de Fortia, sr de, *maréchal de camp*, 160, 357n168
Castelnaudery, 519n67
Castile, kingdom of, 81, 111, 132
Catalonia, kingdom of, 81, 135–6, 153, 154–7, 163, 216–17, 269, 363, 364, 460, 497, 552
  revolt of, 81, 112, 136, 145–6, 152–3, 155, 213, 216
Câtelet, 66, 68, 128, 205, 495n141
Caumarin, sr de, *mestre de camp*, 336n88
Caumartin, sr de, *commissaire pour les subsistances*, 428, 518n63
Caumesnil, Artus de Moreüil, sr de, 341n114
Cauvisson, baron de, 323n41
cavalry, 59–65, 149n389, 190, 282n14, 307, 340, 422n105, 473–5
  see also colonel général *and* surtaux
central control of French war-effort, 90, 169–78, 258, 366–7, 381–2, 414–15, 468, 501–4, 539, 547, 552
centralization/decentralization of political authority, 5–13, 165, 262, 277–8, 349–50, 390–2, 395, 432, 434–6, 475, 479, 513–14, 544–6, 547–52
Ceva, 151
Cévennes, 327
Chaboche, Robert, 517
Chalais, Henri de Talleyrand, comte de (and 1626 conspiracy), 479, 483
Châlons, 68, 272, 382n76, 388, 431, 456, 520, 530n120
Chambéry, 97

582

Index

Chamblay, *commissaire des guerres*, 293
Chamblay, sr du, *mestre de camp*, 442n193
chambres de justice, 239
Chamb(r)onneau, *commissaire pour les subsistances*, 431n151, 512n39
Champagne, 46, 60, 62, 75, 80, 95, 103–4, 119–21, 124, 148, 157–8, 167, 176, 184, 186–7, 192, 195–9, 218, 252, 262, 265, 393, 394, 403, 416, 417, 418, 420–1, 424, 449–50, 484, 486, 487, 494–5, 506n6, 513n42, 537n153, 545
Champigny, François Bochart, sr de, *intendant*, 348, 421, 429n140, 438, 442–3, 448n225
Chantelou, *commissaire des guerres*, 391n121
Chapelles, François de Rosmadec, comte des, 551
Chapelles, sr des, governor of Cirk, 494
Chaponay, Humbert, sr de Lisle, *intendant*, 428n137, 524n90, 528n110
Charles I, king of England, Ireland and Scotland, 1625–49, 88
Charles IV, duke of Lorraine and Bar 1625–75, 79, 80, 103–5, 106, 114, 116, 119, 120, 125, 130, 137, 147–8, 158, 188, 215, 299, 480–1, 482, 490–1
Charles V, Holy Roman Emperor 1519–58, 84, 305
Charles VII, king of France 1422–61, 230, 288
Charles VIII, king of France 1483–98, 164, 182
Charles of Gonzaga-Nevers, duke of Mantua 1627–37, 30, 91–3, 96, 103, 185–6, 344n125, 479
Charles de Lorraine, duc d'Elbeuf, 481–2
Charles de Lorraine, fourth duc de Guise, 30, 481, 493n132
Charles, Jacques, *commissaire des guerres*, 404n26
Charleville, 349
Charmes, 105
Charmouluc, sr, 423n108, 538n161
Charnacé, Hercule-Girard, baron de, ambassador to the States General, 171
Charost, Louis de Béthune, comte de, 269n181, 338n98, 349
Charost, *commissaire des guerres*, 405n31

Châteauneuf, Charles de l'Aubespine, marquis de, *garde des sceaux*, 484
Châtillon, Gaspard de Coligny III, maréchal de, 46, 60, 66, 113–14, 124, 127, 128, 134, 136, 138, 141–2, 148–9, 190, 200–1, 203–4, 207, 209–10, 213–14, 252, 290, 310, 344, 358n170, 359, 416, 423n109, 430, 441n185, 444n200, 447, 456–7, 463, 467n13, 482, 486, 491, 498, 499, 500, 502n169, 503, 521n78, 528–9, 540, 541
Chaufourneau, *commissaire des guerres*, 404n25
Chaulnes, Honoré d'Albert, maréchal de, 32, 61, 142, 196, 209, 250n97, 261, 265, 336n92, 344, 441n185, 442n193, 449, 452n241, 456n261, 487, 498, 540n165
Chaulnes, Jacques, sr d'Epinay, *intendant*, 422, 451,
Chaumont, 524n91
Chavigny, Léon le Bouthillier, comte de, *secrétaire d'Etat*, 46n96, 48, 124, 192, 253, 254, 260, 261, 264, 265, 305, 369–70, 435n169, 438, 457n263, 459n281, 487n107, 499, 503, 552
Cherasco, 100, 101, 103, 140, 151
Chivasso, 139–40, 151
Chivré, Françoise-Marguerite de, 489
Choisy, Jean, sr de Beaumont, *intendant*, 49, 51, 207, 258n133, 296, 301, 381n69, 390, 393, 401n3, 403, 406n39, 407n43, 416, 418, 421n99, 428n137, 440n183, 441, 445, 449, 450n237, 455–6, 457n263, 460n286, 520–1
Christian IV, king of Denmark 1588–1648, 31
Cinq-Mars, Henri Coeffier de Ruzé, marquis de, 160, 490
Cinq-Mars, Pierre de Broc, abbé de, 411–12, 412n62
Clairac, 135
Clanleu, Bertrand d'Ostove, sr de, 521n75
Clanleu, *commissaire des guerres*, 196
Claude de Lorraine, duc de Chevreuse, 30, 481
Cleves, 114, 183
clientelism/clientage, 11, 14, 29, 90, 133, 149, 188, 254, 261–2, 321, 324, 326–7, 341, 342, 360, 372, 393–4, 400, 410, 438–9,

Index

clientelism/clientage (cont.)
    441–4, 461, 467, 488, 491, 498, 514, 531, 552–6
Clozier, Pierre, *commissaire des guerres*, 402, 405n31, 407n43
Code Michau (1629), 41, 320, 331n69, 342–3, 348, 376, 440, 522n82, 526, 534n137
Cognac, 532
Cohon, Anthime-Denis, bishop of Nîmes, 410
Colbert, Jean-Baptiste, *controleur-général des finances*, 255
Colbert de Saint-Pouange, Jean-Baptiste, *commissaire des guerres*, 404n27
Collalto, Rombaldo, Imperial general, 94
Collins, James, 230–1, 241, 244
Collioure, 152–3, 156, 216–17, 496
Colmar, 495
Cologne, Electorate of, 158–9, 218
colonel général de l'infanterie, 9, 47, 291, 322, 372, 377, 390, 464, 470–4, 483, 538
colonel de la cavalerie légère, 377n49, 464, 473n42, 474
colonel de la cavalerie allemande, 301–2, 378, 474
colonel des dragons, 475
colonel des Suisses et Grisons, 464
Combalet, Marie-Madelaine Vignerot de, duchesse d'Aiguillon (1638), 158n441, 470
commanderie de Saint Louis, Bicêtre, Paris, 539
Commercy, 515n51
commissaire général de la cavalerie, 474
commissaires des guerres (à la conduite, des montres) 180, 249, 250, 259, 348, 354–5, 356–7, 361–2, 371, 376, 379–80, 391–2, 393, 400–8, 410, 423–4, 433–4, 438, 439, 461–2, 508, 515, 526, 528, 529
commissaires des vivres, 382–5, 416–17, 421
commissaires pour les subsistances, 415, 422–32, 509, 512, 515–16, 518n63
company, as an organizational unit, 48–50, 181, 304, 329–30, 339–40
Compiègne, 412
Condé, Henri II de Bourbon, prince de, 62, 71, 73, 75n225, 76, 80, 90, 119, 120, 121, 124, 132–3, 134, 145, 152–3, 158, 185, 195–8, 201, 203, 206, 208, 216, 247–8, 289, 300, 321, 332, 339n101, 345n131,
350, 363, 413, 415, 439n181, 441–2, 452n245, 454, 466, 476–7, 480, 485, 486, 488, 491, 494, 496–8, 499–501, 513n43, 532, 535n142, 536n152
Condé, Louis II de, *see* Enghien
connétable, 9, 372, 464, 469–70, 485
connétablie et maréchaussée, 376–9, 390, 473n41
conseils de guerre, 136, 378, 380, 420, 445, 453, 486, 494, 504, 528–33
Conti, Armand de Bourbon, prince de, 321
'contributions', 60, 79–81, 119, 120, 143, 156, 195, 252, 267–9, 270n184, 275, 281–3, 285–6, 287, 309n117, 337n92, 439n181, 458, 493, 500, 513, 550
contrôleurs des guerres, 249, 250, 375–6, 461–2
Coquault, Oudart, 545
Corbie, 66, 68, 119, 121, 134, 157, 170, 176, 198, 265–6, 486, 495n141
Córdoba, Gonzalo Fernández de, governor of Milanese, 91
Corneille, abbé de, 411, 412n60
Cornillon, sr de, *aide de camp*, 409
Cornuel, *commissaire des guerres*, 405n31
Corsica, 304
Corvisier, André, 164, 517
Cosade, *commissaire des guerres*, 406n38
Cossé-Brissac, Charles de, *colonel général des gens de pied*, 471n30
Courcy, marquis de, 391
Coursan, abbé de, 411, 413
Crécy, 537
Créqui, Charles de Blanchefort, maréchal de, 32, 46n97, 76, 94n59, 116–17, 124, 131, 185, 199, 265, 335n85, 361, 472, 480, 482, 495n145, 525n93
Crescentino, 160
Crillon, Louis de Berton, sr de, *mestre de camp*, 472
Croats, 60–1, 304
Croisilles, *commissaire des guerres*, 402
croquant rebellions (1635–37), 127, 197, 202
Cuneo, 151

Dampierre, Henri Duval, comte de, 30
Damvillers, 201
Dancy, sr, *commissaire des guerres*, 401n4
Daniel, Père Gabriel, SJ, 3

Index

Dauphiné, 96, 99, 183, 230, 262, 271n188, 291, 322, 370, 451, 507n11, 508n15, 510n26
'Day of Dupes', 10/11 Nov. 1630, 100, 484–5, 493
deniers revenans bons, 173, 175, 226, 248–50, 357
Denmark, army of, 78, 300
Descartes, René, 31
desertion of soldiers, 14, 44–5, 48, 55, 64n176, 86, 90, 91, 98,115, 120, 129, 143, 158, 175–6, 179, 186–7, 205n179, 296, 346, 347, 379, 395, 402, 410, 452, 457, 518n64, 519, 533, 538, 540–42
Desgranges (des Granges), Charles, *commissaire des guerres*, 402, 424–5, 433n157, 512n35
Desmaretz (Demarests), Anthoine, *commissaire des guerres*, 392, 401n4
Dessert, Daniel, 244, 433
Destouches, *commissaire des guerres*, 402, 403, 417, 431n151
Dijon, 121
disbandment/*licenciement* of troops, 43, 50, 51n121, 175, 190, 272, 284n21, 328–31, 349–52, 401, 422–3, 431, 533, 539–40
Dôle, 71, 80, 119, 120, 124, 196–7, 486
Douglas, James, colonel, 307, 309n115, 530n119
Doullens, 119, 362, 494, 506n6
Dreux, 525
Dreux, Bernard, *commissaire des guerres*, 393–4
duelling, 551
Dunkirk, 163
Dupré, Barthélémé, sr de Chatulé, *intendant*, 259n136, 428n138, 431n151, 519n67
Dutch Republic, 101–2, 106, 158, 161, 190, 196, 200, 203, 263, 266–7, 305, 312, 449, 476n56, 500
armies, 27, 28, 49, 52, 102, 113–14, 118, 124, 127, 134, 141, 157, 169, 190, 218–19
military reforms, 19, 20, 21, 22, 25–6, 32, 33, 34, 40, 69, 82, 83, 547
States General of, 109, 209
Dyel, Jacques, sr de Miroménil, *intendant*, 438n174, 447, 449, 457n268, 459n278, 460

Eberhard III, duke of Wurtttemburg, 49, 106
Eberstein, Graf von, colonel, 219
ecclesiastics, involvement in military administration, 251, 257–8, 327, 410–12, 535–7, 553
Effiat, Antoine Coeffier de Ruzé, marquis d', *maréchal* and *surintendant des finances*, 98, 188, 371, 388, 465
Effiat, Martin de Ruzé, marquis de, *mestre de camp*, 521n75
Egenfeld, colonel, 43n88, 474n45
Ehrenbreitstein, 104, 106
Elna, 56, 153
Enghien, Louis II de Bourbon, duc d' (prince de Condé from 1646), 19, 31, 62, 65, 66, 248–9, 321, 480, 492, 551, 554
England, 81, 88, 303, 483, 485
enterprise/entrepreneurship, military, 48, 228, 259, 268, 278–81, 283–7, 290–2, 329, 336–41, 347–8, 350, 353–4, 366, 465, 549–50
Epernay, 520n70
Epernon, Jean-Louis de Nogaret de La Valette, duc d', 32, 47, 90, 122, 126–7, 132–3, 185, 198, 202, 289, 291, 334n85, 441, 452n245, 470–4, 482–3, 487–8, 493, 495
Erlach, Hans Ludwig, baron of Castelan and Gauwestein, 138, 295, 310n120, 466
Espenan comte d', Roger de Bussolts, *maréchal de camp*, 146, 213, 439n181, 494
esprit de corps, 20, 46, 49, 519
Estrades, Godefroy d', 209, 211
Estrées, François-Annibal d', marquis de Cœuvres, 86, 183, 185n61, 484
étapes, 270–1, 272, 308, 383, 403, 411n61, 460n282, 507–9, 510, 511–12, 514–16, 517, 522, 534, 537, 541, 542n172, 543, 555
Evennes, sr d', captain, 348

Fabert, Abraham, *maréchal*, 39, 43n89, 318, 334nn 82 and 85, 466, 492
Falcombel, Jean-Dominique, *munitionnaire*, 256
Fargis, Charles d'Angennes, comte du, 88n22, 534n136
Farnese, Alessandro, duke of Parma, 78

585

Index

Fauré, sr du, *intendant*, 419n94, 447–8, 456n262
Ferdinand II, Holy Roman Emperor (1619–37), 31, 85, 99–100, 186, 285, 311
Ferdinand III, Holy Roman Emperor (1637–57), 81, 147, 163, 298
Fernando, Cardinal-Infante, governor-general of the Spanish Netherlands 1634–41, 60, 119–20, 121
Feuquières, Manassés de Pas, marquis de, 51n121, 134, 137, 171, 192, 207, 310, 393, 421n99, 441n187, 445, 455, 457n263, 465–6
Flan, Jean, *munitionnaire*, 258
Flanders, *see* Netherlands, Spanish
Flanders, Army of, *see* Spain, armies
Fontaines, sr des, *commissaire pour les subsistances*, 428n138, 429n140, 431
foreign mercenaries, French employment of, 293–312
Fortia, Bernard, sr du Plessis-Claireau, *intendant*, 428, 430n146, 431n150, 523n85
Foullé, Etienne, sr de Prunevaux, *intendant*, 441n186, 459
Fouquet, Nicolas, *surintendant des finances*, 255
Francesco Giacinto, duke of Savoy, 1637–8, 131–2
Franche-Comté, 75, 80, 103, 119, 124, 125, 129–30, 138, 195, 197, 201, 203–5, 277, 300, 486, 534n135
François I, king of France 1515–47, 182, 231, 305
Françoise de Lorraine-Mercoeur, 483–4
Franconia, 104
Frankfurt, 382n75
fraud, at musters and reviews, 168–9, 170, 180, 200, 214, 220, 245n76, 250–1, 307–8, 354–5, 392, 395, 401–2, 408, 444, 526
Frederick V, Palatine Elector, 84
Frederik Hendrik, prince of Orange-Nassau, 19, 26, 113–14, 127, 159, 209
Freiburg, 303
Fremin, Guillame, sr de Couronnes, *intendant*, 348n142, 428, 429n140, 430n146, 431n150

Frère, Claude, sr de Crolles, *premier président* of Parlement of Dauphiné, 383n81, 507n12
Frondes, 163, 170, 261, 277, 288, 291, 367, 383n78, 468, 545, 551–2
Fuenterrabía, 74, 75, 132–3, 134, 206, 207, 470, 473, 483, 488, 495, 496–7
furia francese, 71–3

Gagnot, *intendant des vivres*, 418–21
Gaillard, *commissaire des guerres*, 405n31
Gallas, Matthias, Imperial general, 66, 114, 115, 121, 125, 198
Gamin, Henri, *maître des requêtes*, 531n124
Gap, consuls of, 537n155
gardes françaises, 39, 41, 42, 43, 45–6, 49, 50, 185, 226, 332, 348, 472, 520n71, 522
gardes suisses, 45–6, 49, 185, 226, 303, 326n53
Gargan, Pierre, *munitionnaire*, 258, 415–16
garrisons, 230–1, 265–7, 344n127, 368–9, 387, 423, 452, 505–6, 518–19, 526, 530, 538–9
Gassion, Jean, comte de, 309n117, 466, 492, 521, 531n122
Gaucher, Pierre, *commissaire des guerres*, 402n11
Gaya, Louis de, military theorist, 57
gendarmes, 37, 38, 49n116, 168n11, 226, 229, 230, 322, 332, 334, 339
Genlis, sr de, *mestre de camp*, 358n173
Genoa, Republic of, 87, 112, 161, 183–4, 290
Gensac, baron de, 532
Gheyn, Jacob de, military theorist, 37, 38
Gobelin, Claude, sr d'Aunoy, *intendant*, 384, 420, 447n212, 448n225, 450, 453n248, 457, 530, 532, 533n133
Goubert, Pierre, 545
Goulas, Léonard, sr de Frémoy, 411n60
Gramont, Antoine III de, comte de Guiche, 31, 150, 157–8, 218, 301, 324n44, 353n157, 359, 373n27, 391, 489, 520
Grancey, Jacques de Rouxel, comte de, *maréchal de camp*, 158, 339n101
grand maître de l'artillerie, 67–70, 227, 373, 377, 379, 387–90, 402, 464, 475–7
grand maître et surintendant général de la navigation (Richelieu), 470, 475, 481

Index

grands, les (princely and ducal houses), 73, 90, 289, 291, 318, 321, 322, 334, 342, 360, 395, 439, 463–9, 478–9, 484–6, 489–91, 498–9, 501, 504, 520, 551, 553, 556

Granges, Charles des, *commissaire des guerres*, 402, 424, 425n128, 433n157, 512nn35 and 37

Gravelines, 163

Greder, colonel, 304n89, 310

Grémonville, Nicolas Bretel, sr de, *intendant*, 309n117, 352n155, 421, 428n138, 429n140, 431, 441n185, 444n200, 457, 460n282, 513n42

Grillié, Nicolas, bishop of Uzès, 410

Grisons, 85, 86, 117, 183

Gualdo Priorato, count Galeazzo, 26n16, 37

Guastalla, Ferrante Gonzaga, duke of, 91

Gué, Gaspard du, sr de Bagnols, *intendant des finances* and *trésorier at Lyons*, 374, 384, 428n137

Guébriant, Jean-Baptiste Budes, comte de, 75, 81, 138–9, 143, 154, 157–9, 204, 205, 219, 293nn45 and 46, 294, 295, 302, 390, 445, 465, 492, 498, 503

Guénégaud, Gabriel, *trésorier de l'épargne*, 232

Guérapin, *intendant des finances*, 264

Guiche, see Gramont

Guienne, 122, 126–7, 132, 134, 198, 202, 204, 217, 247, 277, 403, 413, 483, 487–8, 498, 513n43, 519

Guignard, Pierre, *commissaire des guerres*, 392

Guillory, *commissaire des guerres*, 417

Guise, town of, 451, 458, 524

Guron, Jean de Rechignevoison de, governor of Brouage, 89, 535n142

Gustavus II Adolphus, king of Sweden 1611–32, 19, 21–3, 29, 31, 35, 54, 66, 67, 71, 99, 105, 107, 170, 278, 282n15, 285, 547

Habsburg, House of, 84, 85, 101, 111, 366, 485

Haguenau, 158

Hallier, François de l'Hôpital, seigneur du, 60, 66, 125, 128, 137, 142, 158, 201, 215, 252, 267, 272n194, 294, 299, 305–6, 307–8, 326n52, 347n138, 353n157, 406n35, 440n184, 442n193, 482n81, 535, 541n168, 542n174

Halluin, Charles de Nanteuil-Schomberg, duc d' (maréchal de Schomberg from 1637), 44, 69, 76, 126, 132, 134, 145, 152, 156, 161, 202, 206, 209–10, 229, 266, 327n57, 411, 440n183, 444, 445, 452n245, 487, 491–2, 494, 496–8, 507n9, 512, 513, 515n52

Hanotaux, Gabriel, 434

Harcourt, Henri de Guise-Lorraine, comte d', 30–1, 43, 44, 45, 59, 66, 71, 75, 76, 123, 141, 144–5, 146, 147, 150–1, 157–8, 160, 161, 209, 211–12, 215, 218–19, 275, 277, 353n157, 358n172, 359, 362, 441n185, 445n207, 466, 467, 482, 488–9, 492, 495, 500, 503, 505, 551

Hay du Chastelet, Paul, military theorist, 282n14

Hebron [Hepburn], Sir John (colonel), 188

Heere, Denis, sr de Vaudois, *intendant*, 428n137, 431n149

Heidelberg, 108

Heilbronn League, 293

Hémery, Michel Particelli, sr d', extraordinary ambassador in Savoy, 46, 59, 124, 131, 132, 171, 195, 199–200, 264, 266, 346n136, 371, 374, 414n74, 419, 447, 459n275, 503, 509n23, 518n65

Henri II, king of France 1547–59, 182n44, 305

Henri III, king of France 1574–89, 367, 471–2, 481

Henri IV, king of France 1589–1610, 183, 190, 230, 288, 368, 433, 481n75, 551

Henri de Guise-Lorraine, archbishop of Reims, 148

Henri de Lorraine, 3rd duc de Guise, 472, 481, 482

Hermann Adolf, count of Salm, 106

Hesdin, 58, 59, 71n214, 136–8, 141, 150, 156, 207, 445, 451

Hesse, Moritz, prince of, 27

Hesse, troops of, 219

Heucourt, sr d', governor of Doullens, 494

Hocquincourt, Charles de Mouchy, marquis d', 294n49

Hocquincourt, George de Mouchy d', governor of Lorraine, 421n98

Hoeufft, Jean, financier, 263

587

Index

Holy Roman Empire, German territories of, 6, 33, 81, 85, 101, 104, 107, 114, 121, 139, 143, 153–4, 158–9, 161, 163, 192, 195, 201, 205, 267–8, 277, 279, 282, 283, 287, 294, 300, 305, 306–7, 310–12, 329, 354, 420, 447n212, 454, 465, 495, 518
Honnecourt, battle of, 29 May 1642, 75, 157–8, 159, 218, 301, 489
Honoré II Grimaldi, prince of Monaco, 322n34
Horn, Gustav, Swedish general, 297
hospitals, and medical provision, 404, 456n261, 534–7
Houssay, Claude Mallier, sr du, *intendant des finances*, 416n78, 417–18, 419–20
Huguenots, 2, 28, 29, 31, 83, 85, 87–8, 92, 93, 95, 184–5, 231, 289–90, 480, 482
Humières, Louis de Crevant, marquis d', 254
Hums, colonel, 48, 304
Hungary, 30, 31, 32, 33, 58, 83
Huxelles, Jacques du Blé, marquis d', 254

Illa, 146, 213
Ile de France, 263, 424, 506
Imbert, Pierre, *intendant*, 357n168, 392, 402n8, 445, 446n210
Imperial armies, 27, 30, 31, 48, 49, 52, 54, 61, 66, 76, 78, 94, 98, 99–100, 105, 106, 108, 112, 113, 116, 121, 125, 129, 137, 148, 154, 159, 194, 198, 205, 280, 290, 353
Imperial (Habsburg) foreign policy, 108, 184, 238
intendant général de la navigation, 478
intendants, 8, 10, 49, 259, 356, 434–62, 512
intendants d'armée, 9, 252, 266, 301, 348, 374, 380–1, 384–5, 400, 415, 434–62, 528, 540, 553
intendants des provinces, 9, 383, 400, 427–8, 449–53, 514
Ireland, and Irish troops in French service, 112, 279, 303–4, 307–8, 309, 423n108, 518, 530
Isabella Clara Eugenia, regent of Spanish Netherlands, 107
Isola, colonel, 304
Italy, French forces in, 54, 56, 59, 65, 66, 73, 95, 116, 117, 134, 140, 150–1, 160, 182, 187, 190, 195, 197, 199, 203, 206, 208–9, 211–12, 215–16, 219, 244, 265, 266, 275, 277, 361, 384, 394, 414n74, 419n94, 431n151, 444n202, 446, 447, 456n260, 457, 485, 490, 495, 536
Italy, campaigns in north, 62, 76, 86, 92–100, 101, 112, 116, 123–4, 131–2, 139–41, 145, 159–61, 163, 187, 193, 211, 219, 264–5, 276, 305, 343–4, 364, 369, 478, 480, 484, 487, 503, 505, 518, 535, 552
Italy, Leagues of, 102n100, 109, 116, 118, 139, 151, 161, 299
Ivoy, 138
Ivrea, 150, 215

Jacquart, Jean, 545
Jankow, battle of, 5 Mar. 1645, 81
Jeannin de Castille, Nicolas, 254
Jesuits, Order of, 536–7

Kempen, battle of, 17 Jan. 1642, 158, 219
Kentzingen, battle of, Aug. 1637, 125
Kleve–Jülich, succession dispute, 183, 381
Koblenz, 104, 106, 118, 189
Koulas, colonel, 306
Kroener, Bernhard, 50, 56, 181, 516

La Baume de La Suze, Louis-François, bishop of Viviers, 410
La Bassée, 150, 157
La Bastide, sr de, *intendant*, 452n241
La Boderie, sr de, French resident in Hesse-Kassel, 298
La Capelle, 68, 119, 125, 201, 404, 495n141
La Chapelle, 349
La Charité, Order of, 536
La Clavière, sr de, 351n154
La Cour(t), Jean de, *commissaire des guerres*, 258, 394n134, 425n124
La Douze, sr de, *mestre de camp*, 336n88
La Ferronaye, Jacques Ferron, sr de, 337n93, 351n152
La Ferté, Henri II de Saint-Nectaire, marquis de, 392
La Ferté, sr de, *commissaire pour les subsistances*, 428n137, 431n150
La Ferté-Bernard, 525
La Ferté-Imbault, Jacques d'Estampes,

Index

marquis de, *maréchal de camp*, 274n203, 357n168, 358n175, 391n120
La Feulliade, Léon d'Aubusson, comte de, 348n142
La Fontaine, de, military theorist, 34, 35, 36, 52, 57
La Force, Armand de Caumont, marquis de, *maréchal de camp*, 62, 328n60
La Force, Jacques-Nompar de Caumont, maréchal de, 32, 50, 63, 65, 66, 67, 104, 105, 115, 118, 128, 188–9, 191–2, 194, 197–8, 203–4, 363, 384, 387, 413n68, 414, 418, 439n181, 450, 482, 486, 491, 498, 500
La Four, sr de, *commissaire des guerres*, 406n37
La Guette, Henri, sr de Chazé, *intendant*, 451
La Marche, 370, 439n181
La Marfée, battle of, 6 July 1641, 73, 149, 214, 290
La Meilleraye, Armand-Charles de La Porte, 2nd duc de La Meilleraye, 477
La Meilleraye, Charles de La Porte de, 63, 66, 67, 119, 134, 136–7, 141, 149, 150, 156, 189–90, 195, 206–7, 209–10, 213–15, 261, 321n31, 363, 373, 387–8, 402, 407n44, 416n80, 421, 445, 456, 475–8, 486, 489, 494, 498, 499, 530, 533, 536–7
La Mothe, 158
La Motte-Houdancourt, Philippe de, *maréchal*, 56, 152, 156–7, 216, 353n157, 362n188, 363, 466, 498
La Noue, François de, military writer and theorist, 33, 34, 40, 42, 56, 74
La Passage, sr de, 325
La Point, sr de, *commissaire des vivres*, 416
La Porte, Amador de, *grand prieur*, 324n42, 478
La Potherie, Charles Le Roy, sr de, *intendant*, 381n69, 428n138, 457n268, 460n282, 525
La Prugne, *maréchal de logis des gardes du cardinal*, 412
La Retaye, sr de, *commissaire des guerres*, 425n125
La Rivière, lieutenant of Calais, 349
La Rochefoucauld, François V, duc de, 90
La Rochegiffart, Henri de La Chapelle, marquis de, 337n93

La Rochelle, 54, 87–91, 92, 93, 94, 184–5, 289, 345n133, 388, 412, 475, 478, 484
La Suze, sr de, *mestre de camp*, 358
La Touche, sr de, *mestre de camp*, 53
La Tour d'Auvergne, House of, 29
La Trémoïlle, Henri de, duc de Thouars, 291, 339, 360n182
La Trousse, Sébastien le Hardy, marquis de, *mestre de camp*, 365
La Valette, Bernard de Nogaret, duc de (2nd duc d'Epernon), 75n225, 126–7, 132–3, 134, 202, 291, 321n31, 334n85, 445n207, 470–1, 483, 487–8, 493, 495, 496–7
La Valette, Louis de Nogaret, cardinal de, 41, 45, 46–7, 48, 55, 56, 65, 69, 73, 75, 76, 114–6, 118, 121, 124, 125, 131–2, 139–41, 169, 191, 194, 195–6, 198, 200–1, 206, 208–9, 246n81, 261, 267, 294, 304, 305, 324, 325, 358n170, 403, 412, 416, 423n109, 439n181, 442n192, 457, 483, 495, 498–9, 500, 532n128, 540n164
La Valière, military theorist, 35, 36, 37, 52n129, 54, 57, 58
La Vallée, sr de, sergeant-major, 532
La Vieuville, Charles, marquis de, 86
Laffemas, Isaac de, sr de Beausemblant, *intendant*, 381n69, 393, 442n193, 449–50
Lamboy, Wilhelm von, Imperial general, 158, 214
Landrecies, 125, 392
Langlée, Claude de, sr de l'Epichelière, 332–3
Langlée, Claude de (may be the same individual as above), *commissaire des guerres*, 403n21, 404,
Langres, 115, 192, 193, 520n72
Languedoc, 105, 126, 132, 134–6, 145, 146, 152, 156, 202, 208, 213, 216–17, 247, 258–9, 403, 413, 431n151, 440n183, 443–4, 487, 488, 494, 496–8, 506, 512, 513, 515n52, 519n67, 540, 544
Laon, 403, 450, 458
Lasure, *mestre de camp*, 337n96
Lattignan, *munitionnaire*, 256–7, 382n75, 385, 414, 416
Laubardement, Jean Martin, sr de, *intendant*, 394, 424n120, 455

589

Index

Lauzon, Jean, sr de Liré, *intendant*, 428n137, 451
Le Bret, Cardin, sr de Flacourt, *intendant*, 428n137, 430n145
Le Camus, Nicolas, *intendant des finances*, 193, 374, 448, 459, 460n282
Le Clerc, *trésorier de l'extraordinaire des guerres*, 344
Le Comte, sr de, *commissaire des guerres*, 405n31, 429n140
Le Gendre, *commissaire des guerres*, 521n77
Le Grain, sr de, *prévôt*, 406n40
Le Havre, 67
Le Roy, financier, 256
Le Tellier, Michel IV, *intendant*, subsequently *secrétaire d'Etat de la guerre*, 215–16, 219, 227, 228, 244–5, 252, 346n134, 358n172, 359, 367, 392, 393–4, 399, 400, 403n15, 446, 453n248, 456n260, 457, 458–9, 461, 468, 520n72, 536n147
Le Vacher, Jacques, *commissaire des guerres*, 251n103, 401n3
Lefèvre d'Ormesson, André, *intendant*, 448n225
Leganés, Diego Mexía, marquis of, governor of Milanese, 139–41
Lens, 150, 157
  battle of, 20 Aug. 1648, 554
Leo VI, Byzantine Emperor and military theorist, 25
Leoni, Piero, engineer, 67
Lepage, *commissaire pour les subsistances*, 430n147
Lerida, 157
'Les grands misères de la guerre' (Jacques Callot), 527
Lesdiguières, François de Bonne, duc de, *connétable*, 29, 32, 87, 184, 290–1, 470
Lesdiguières, François de Bonne (et) de Créquy, 3rd duc de, 271n188, 323n38, 358n172, 392, 446n210, 507n11
Lespine, Pierre Gigon, sr de, *commissaire des guerres*, 251n102, 402n11, 404, 405n31
Létouf, Claude de, baron de Sirot, 31
Leucate, battle of, 28 Sept. 1637, 76, 126, 161, 202, 487, 494
L'Hermitte, sr de, *commissaire des guerres*, 337n94, 405n31

Liège, 113, 306–7
Liffol-le-Grand, 158
Lignan, colonel, 326n52
Lille, 150
Lilliers, 149
Limousin, 268n178, 370, 393, 424, 431n150, 439n181, 506n9
Lisle, sr de, *gentilhomme de la chambre du roi*, 409n50
Liverdun, 105
Livron, Charles de Bourbonne, marquis de, 325
Livogno, battle of, 27 June 1635, 58, 117
logement of troops, 270–2, 514–15, 522–5, 526
  in barracks, 505
  in towns, 268, 506, 525, 538–9
  winter quarters, 55n146, 64, 79, 143, 160n457, 171, 176, 189, 197, 219, 221, 227–8, 272–4, 364n196, 372, 382, 401, 403n21, 409, 422–4, 425–7, 429, 432, 458, 506
Lombardy, 85, 99
Longay (Longuet), *commissaire des guerres*, 428n137
Longueval, Charles de Monchy, sr de, 323n41
Longueville, Henri II d'Orleans, duc de, 59, 64, 65, 124, 125, 129–30, 134, 138–40, 143, 160, 188, 198, 201–2, 203–5, 209, 211, 295, 296, 465, 466, 467, 484, 487, 492, 498, 500, 551
Lorraine, duchy of, 66, 75, 79, 80, 103–5, 112, 114, 116, 118, 125, 137, 142, 147–8, 158, 188–9, 191–2, 193, 205, 209–10, 217, 252, 267, 277, 299, 305–6, 337n92, 348, 351, 364, 369, 386, 387, 401n3, 406n35, 413, 418–21, 440n184, 448, 455, 481, 482, 487, 489, 520n72, 527, 535, 540n164, 543
Lorraine, House of, 467, 481–2, 483–5, 488–9
Los Vélez, Pedro Zúñiga y Requesens, marquis of, 146
Lostelneau, sr de, military theorist, 28–29, 34, 35, 36, 38, 51, 57
Lot, Ferdinand, 164
Loubet, *commissaire des guerres*, 428n137

Index

Louis XIII, king of France 1610–43:
concern to maintain control of policy, 10, 155, 291, 359, 486, 504, 554
and foreign policy, 85, 86
concern to command in person, 115, 136, 192, 435n169, 464n4, 479
control of appointments, 261, 307, 323, 486
Louis XIV, king of France 1643–1715, 367, 464, 468, 492, 555–6
army of, 78, 163, 228, 276, 333, 349, 399, 461, 554–6
Louise de Lorraine, princesse de Conti, 484
Louvain, 58, 74, 113
Louvois, François-Michel Le Tellier, marquis de, 164, 399, 555
Loyseau, Charles, 331
Lude, Henri de Daillan, comte de, *grand maître de l'artillerie*, 477
Lunéville, 495
Lützen, battle of, 16 Nov. 1632, 105, 282n15, 285
Luxembourg, 80, 112, 138, 203, 209
Lyon, 388, 511n34
Lyonnais, 96, 99, 265, 268, 370, 409, 424, 443, 507n11, 509n21, 512

Machault, Charles, sr d'Arnouville, *intendant*, 413, 441–2, 448n225, 454, 457n268
Machiavelli, Niccolo, 25
Madrid, Treaty of, 85
Maestricht, 30
Magnan, André, *commissaire des guerres*, 251n103, 392, 402, 405n31, 427n135
Maillé-Brézé, Claire-Clémence de, 480
Maine, 411
Mainz, 104, 115, 500
Maistre, de, *commissaire des guerres*, 417
maîtres des requêtes, 433, 436, 437–8, 440, 452, 459n281, 535, 553
Malissy, Henri, marquis de, 392n125
Mallet, Jean-Roland, 231–2, 240, 243
Manassés de Pas, *see* Feuquières
Mangot, Anne de, sr de Villarceaux, *intendant*, 418, 420, 421, 429n140, 448, 456n261, 459, 543
Mangot, Jacques, sr d'Orgères, *intendant*, 421, 428n138, 429n140, 430n145, 448, 459

Manicamp, Achille de Longueval, sr de, 126, 324n43, 495
Mannheim, 108, 446
Mantua, duchy of, 31, 479
dukes of, 81
war of succession (1628–31), 91–100, 101, 480
Marcillac, Crusy de, bishop of Mende, 251, 327, 337n93, 410, 416n77, 419–21, 432, 436n171, 459n281, 535n142
Marguerite of Lorraine, 482
Marie-Christine, regent of Savoy, 65, 132, 139–40, 151, 159–60, 212, 299, 458
Marie of Gonzaga-Nevers, 479
Marie de Médicis, regent of France and Queen Mother 1610–42, 288–9, 473, 480, 481, 482, 484
Marillac, Louis de, comte de Beaumont, *maréchal*, 32, 95, 233, 252, 269, 309n118, 319, 378n59, 465, 484–5, 492, 493–4, 500–1
Marillac, Michel de, *garde des sceaux*, 327, 417n83, 538
Marsal, 104
Marseilles, 117
Martin, Jean, *commissaire des guerres*, 403
Masson, Bernard, 364
Maugiron, Claude, comte de, 328n60
Maurits, prince of Orange-Nassau, 19, 25, 26, 28–9, 31, 37
Maurizio of Savoy, cardinal, 131, 151, 159–60, 219
Mayolas, captain of *gardes* of Richelieu, 409
Mazarin, Cardinal Jules (Giulio Mazzarini), 35n58, 113, 161, 255, 359, 367, 371, 394, 435, 461, 490, 499, 510, 551
Mazzo, battle of, 3 July 1635, 58, 117
Meaux, 533
Médavy, abbé François Rouxel de, 218n271, 344n129, 409
Mélander, Graf von Holzappel, 298
Melo, Francisco de, governor of Spanish Netherlands, 157–8, 218
Mercoeur, Philippe-Emmanuel de Lorraine, duc de, 30
Mercurin, comte de, 333
Mesgrigny, *commissaire pour les subsistances*, 429n142, 430n145

Index

Mesmes, Henri de, *président* of *Parlement* of Paris, 456, 520
Mestivier, *prévôt général*, 421
mestre de camp général de la cavalerie, 474, 521n78
Metz, 103, 115, 334n85, 348n143, 388, 417, 482–3, 500, 520n72
Mignot, Guillaume, *munitionnaire*, 256
Mignoux, sr de, *mestre de camp*, 352n155
Milanese, 81, 86, 93, 94, 96, 118, 131, 161, 193, 195, 268
'military revolution', 7, 20, 21, 547–52
militias, 25, 46, 126, 152, 164, 202, 208, 230, 305, 298n63, 395, 497, 519
Miron, Robert, sr de Tremblay, *intendant*, 428n138, 431n151
Moncalvo, 140
Monferrato, 81, 91–2, 95, 97–8, 100, 124, 131, 151, 160, 186, 344
Monro, Robert, 54
Montaigne, Michel de, 317
Montauban, 89
Montbéliard, duchy of, 106
Montdidier, 412
Montecuccoli, Raimondo, Imperial general, 57, 282n14
Montgaillard, Pierre-Pol de Percin, baron de, 495
Montglat, François de Paule de Clermont, marquis de, 149
Montgommery, Louis de, sr de Courbouzon, military theorist, 28, 34, 37, 377n50, 474n42
Montifault, *prévôt général*, 407n44, 532
Montjuic, battle of, 26 Jan. 1641, 152, 216
Montluc, Blaise de, 33n47
Montmaur, *commissaire des guerres*, 402, 405n31, 424–5, 427n133, 429n140
Montmélian, 97
Montmirail, 515n54
Montmorency, Charlotte de, 485
Montmorency, Henri II, duc de, *amiral de France*, 105, 185, 289, 344, 439n181, 469–70, 481, 483, 485, 492, 493
Montmorency-Bouteville, François de, 551
Montmorency-Damville, Henri I, *connétable*, 469
Montpellier, 537

Montpezat, Jacques de Cominges, sr de, 357n168
Monzón, treaty of, 88, 184
Morbegno, battle of, 10 Nov. 1635, 58, 117
Moulins, 512n36, 521, 524n90, 528n110, 531n123
Mousnier, Roland, 8, 446
Mouy, Henri de Lorraine, marquis de, 30
Mouzon, abbé de, 411, 412n62
Moyenvic, 103–4
Müller, colonel, 303
Murette, sr de, *mestre de camp*, 326n54

Naberat, Pierre de, *commissaire des guerres*, 401n5, 431n151
Nancy, 67, 105, 189, 221, 257, 269, 293, 369, 409, 417, 442n193, 456n260, 459, 537, 543
Narbonne, 72, 126, 135, 156, 157, 388, 535n144
Nassau, Otto-Wilhelm, comte de, colonel, 295
Nassau-Dillemberg, Johann von, prince of Siegen, 26
Navailles, François de Montluc, baron de, 321n31, 456, 520
navy (*du Levant* – Mediterranean galleys), 70, 229, 266, 370n17, 478, 528
navy (*du Ponant*), 67, 132–3, 152–3, 229, 262, 475–6, 478
Netherlands, Spanish (and frontiers of), 80, 107, 113, 116, 127–8, 131, 134, 137–8, 141–3, 149–50, 155, 157, 158, 163, 185, 190, 203, 207, 209, 213–15, 218, 221, 268, 447, 463, 500, 536, 552, 554
Nevers, Charles de, *see* Gonzaga-Nevers
Nieulay (fort near Calais), 349
Nizza della Paglia, 160
noblesse, 14, 63–4, 116, 120, 127, 192, 208, 268, 313–20, 322, 465–6, 477–8, 494, 523n86
Nogent-le-Roi, 521
Noisy, 403
Nördlingen, battle of, 6 Sept. 1634, 79, 106–7, 112, 188, 293, 297, 485
Nördlingen (Allerheim), battle of, 3 Aug. 1645, 554
Normandy, 64, 198, 230, 409, 424, 449, 484, 506, 512n37

592

Index

Noyers, François Sublet, sr de, *secrétaire d'Etat de la guerre* 1636–43, 169, 196, 245n76, 260, 275, 301, 307, 310, 325, 349, 358, 363, 367, 368n7, 370–3, 374n29, 387, 391–4, 432, 438, 440n184, 445, 451, 452, 455–8, 460n286, 461, 463, 494, 520, 521, 523, 524, 525, 528–9, 531, 540, 541, 552
Noyon, 119, 509n24, 520n72
Nuremberg, 285

Odoardo Farnese, duke of Parma, 118
Öhm, colonel, 295
Oisement, Montigny d', 372n24
Oléron, isle of, 87
Olivares, Gaspar de Guzmán, count-duke of, 94, 99–100, 311
Orange-Nassau, House of, 25, 27, 28–29, 33, 82, 547
Orders, religious, 536–7
Orgelin, *prévôt*, 532n128
Orgeval, Geoffroy Luillier, sr d', *intendant*, 394, 421, 424n120, 450–1
Orléans, 412, 424, 425n128, 514n47
Orléans, Gaston d', 62, 100n96, 122, 158, 369, 411n60, 421, 435n169, 440n183, 441, 449, 479–81, 482–3, 486, 503, 515
Osny, d', *commissaire des guerres*, 193n107, 405n31, 417, 421, 429n140, 444n200
Ostein, Johann-Heinrich of, bishop of Basle, 106, 269n180
Ostende, 30
Ottoman Empire, 30
Oxenstierna, Axel, Swedish chancellor, 109
Oysonville, Paul Le Prévost d', *aide de camp*, 296, 410n54, 515

Palatinate, Electorate of the, 107
Palleologo, Jean-Baptiste, *munitionnaire*, 256
Palluau, Philippe de Clérambault, comte de, 319, 466, 474n47
Pappenheim, Gottfried Heinrich, count, Imperial general, 66, 280
Paris, 47, 61, 73, 119–20, 157, 196–7, 199, 244, 364, 388, 412, 539n163, 543n177
Paris, Claude, *intendant*, 428, 429n140, 431n151
Parker, Geoffrey, 548–9

Parlement of Aix, 413n66, 530n116, 531
Parlement of Grenoble, 383n81, 507n12, 511n34
Parlement of Metz, 433, 532
Parlement of Paris, 433, 436, 456, 466, 530
Parlement of Rennes, 327n59, 336n89
Parlement of Rouen, 412–13
Parma, duchy of, 118
parties casuelles, 232, 237, 240–41, 242, 390
Pascal, Etienne, *trésorier de France*, 428, 429n140, 431n151
Pasquier, Etienne, 317
Passages, sr du, governor of Valenza, 333n78
patronage, *see* clientelism/clientage
Pavia, battle of, 24 Feb. 1525, 84, 182
Pédamont, comte de, *mestre de camp* and governor of Lunéville, 495
Peenemünde, 99
Périer, sr, *contrôleur général des vivres*, 421
Péronne, 66, 119, 322n34, 333n78, 412, 515n50
Perpignan, 59, 135, 152, 156–7, 158, 216–8, 395, 404, 452, 496
petits vieux régiments, 46, 47, 167, 405, 472, 520:
  Bellenaue, 51
  Maugiron, 325, 347n138, 456n262
  Neerestang, 47n104
  Rambures, 44, 45, 50, 196, 339n106, 530n117
  Saint-Luc, 51, 337n92, 430n145
  Sault, 185, 347n139, 531
  Vaubecourt, 43, 183
Phélypeaux d'Herbault, Raymond, *secrétaire d'Etat*, 369, 370
Philip II, king of Spain 1556–98, 278
Philip III, king of Spain 1598–1621, 85
Philip IV, king of Spain 1621–65, 85, 94, 102, 112, 155, 311
Philipp-Wolfgang of Hanau-Lichtenberg, 106
Philippsburg, 108, 225
Piacenza, 118
Picardy, 46, 60, 62, 66, 68, 75, 80, 114, 119–21, 124, 128, 148, 157–8, 176, 182, 193, 196, 198, 218, 249, 252, 265, 362, 393, 401n4, 409, 421, 424, 431, 442n193, 449–51, 487, 506n6, 508n16, 513n42, 519, 535n142, 536

Index

Piccolomini, Ottavio, Imperial general, 75, 76, 113–14, 137
Piedmont, 81, 92, 96, 97, 99, 112, 118, 124, 131–2, 139–41, 145, 151, 185–6, 188, 206, 208–9, 215, 221, 227, 233, 245, 267–8, 269, 275, 299, 370, 384, 393, 417n83, 419, 458, 495, 518, 520n72
Pinerolo, 68n200, 96, 103, 151, 344, 369, 385, 392n125, 438, 447, 535
Pingault, *commissaire des guerres*, 402n11, 403n21, 404, 542n174
Plessis-Besançon, *see* Besançon
Plessis-Praslin, César de Choiseul, comte du, 54, 160, 323n38
Pluvinal, Antoine de, 39–40
Poitou, 90, 370, 410n55, 424, 431n151, 455, 457n264, 519
Polignac, Louis-Armand, vicomte de, 512n41
Poligny, battle of, 19 June 1638, 130, 205
Pomaro, Alfonso Gonzaga di Bozzolo, marquis of, 131, 303
Pondesture, 140
Pont-Courlay, François de Vignerot, marquis de, *général des galères*, 478
Pontis, Bénédict-Louis de (*mémoires* written by Pierre-Thomas du Fossé), 29, 39, 318n17, 330, 335n85, 522
Portugal, revolt of, 81, 112, 147, 152
Potrincourt, sr de, *écuyer ordinaire du roi*, 409
Poupart, *commissaire des guerres*, 362
Poux, du, *munitionnaire*, 253n115
Praissac, du, military theorist, 28, 29, 34, 35, 36, 58
prévôts, 372n27, 376–8, 390–1, 392, 406–7, 409, 439, 457, 461–2, 471, 523n86, 529, 530n118, 531, 540, 542n174
Privas, 93, 185
Prouville, François de, *commissaire des guerres*, 402, 413, 421n99
Provence, 96, 99, 108, 117, 118, 122, 197, 230, 262, 264, 370, 419, 430n148, 441–3, 476n58, 481, 487, 506, 508n14, 509n23, 525
Puységur, Jacques de Chastenet de, 62, 324n45, 332, 342n117, 410n55, 494
Pyrenean frontier, 76, 136, 267, 513n45
Pyrenees, Peace of (1659), 77, 555

Rahon, 130
raison d'état, 4, 10
Rantzau, Josias, count von, 48, 300–2, 340, 466
Rapine, sr, 535n142
Ray-sur-Saone, battle of, 2 June 1637, 125
Ré, isle of, 88–9, 93,184, 485
Rebé, Claude de, archbishop of Narbonne, 410
Récy, sr de, 523
Redlich, Fritz, 329
Regensburg, 99
regiments
  Aiguebonne, 345n129, 534
  Alincourt, 45
  Anjou, 292, 508n17
  Annevaux, 508n16
  Aubais, 350n149, 520n72
  Bachevilliers, 540n168
  Batilly, 209
  Beausse, 540n166
  Bellefonds, 51, 353n157, 525
  Birasse, 53
  Biscarat, 429n142
  Boissier, 523n85
  Bouillon, 528–9
  Bourgogne, 532n131
  Brazeaux, 524n87
  Bretagne, 392, 457n268
  Brézé, 51, 347n139, 361n185, 407n42
  Bussy-Lamet, 541
  Bussy-Rabutin, 45, 521, 522n79, 528n110
  Calonge(s), 197, 531n124
  Castelan, 202, 523n86
  Castelmoron, 523n85
  Castelnau, 343n124, 345n130, 357n169
  Chalabre, 410n55
  Chalançay, 350n149
  Chamberet, 507n9
  Chamblay, 332n74, 405n32
  Chanceaux, 350n147
  Cornusson, 530n116
  Coulon (Cullen?), 520n72
  Crosby, 520n72, 530
  Dumont, 357n166
  Effiat, 45, 51, 515n52, 541
  Egenfeld, 43
  Enghien, 230

Index

Erlach, 304n89
Estissac, 335n85
Fittinghof, 304n89
Fitzwilliam, 518n65
Florinville, 50
Gassion, 521n78, 524n87
Greder, 304nn89 and 90, 310
Guienne, 43
Hebron (Hepburn), 188
Humières, 43
Huxelles, 430n145, 529n113
Jonzac, 457n264, 531n127, 532
Koulas, 306
La Bloquerie, 188
La Douze, 43
La Feuillade, 401n3, 520n72
La Meilleraye, 45, 197
La Suze, 430n146
La Tour, 347n138, 357n165
La Valette, 405n32
Langford, 401n5
Languedoc, 202, 513
Lecques, 353n157
Lesdiguières, 335n85, 356n164
Lorraine, 347n138, 551n10
Lusignan, 540n166
Lyonnais, 292
Magalotte, 330n67
Manicamp, 351n151
Mazarin, 348n142
Mercurin, 53, 324n44
Mignoux, 337n96
Molondin, 304nn89 and 90
Montauzier, 356n164
Montmège, 51, 197
Montpezat, 209
Motte-Houdancourt, 344n126
Nanteuil, 45, 540n168
Navailles, 45, 321n31, 456, 520
Nettancourt, 45, 51, 196, 358n171
Noailles, 523n85, 540
Oysonville, 53
Périgord, 292, 409n52, 523, 531n124
Plessis-Praslin, 337n92, 345n130, 430n145
Polignac, 43, 353n157
Rantzau, 306
Rebé, 53, 196
Ribeyrac, 323
Rivarre, 324n44
Roncières, 402n8
Rostinguet, 330n64
Roussillon, 209
Saint-André, 202, 347n138
Saint-Aubin, 525
Saint-Estienne, 324n44, 347n138
Saint-George, 43
Saint-Martial, 50
Saint-Paul, 534
Saintonge, 292
Schmidtberg, 56, 209, 306
Streff, 457n263, 518n65
Suze, 55
Tavannes, 43, 55, 356n164
Tirrell, 401n5
Tot, du, 525
Turenne, 45, 196, 230, 524n87
Vaillac, 347n138, 525
Valmont, 509n24, 537
Vandy, 53
Vernancourt, 529n113
Vitry, 202
Watteville, 304nn89 and 90
see also gardes françaises, gardes suisses, petits vieux régiments, vieux régiments
régiments entretenus, 42–3, 45, 52, 72, 167, 226, 291, 303, 311, 328, 333, 334, 342, 352, 360, 471, 506, 519, 552, 555
Reims, 524nn87 and 88, 537n155, 545
Renard, Gilles, *commissaire des guerres*, 394, 401n5, 402, 406n40, 407n42, 424–5, 433
Renty, 128
Revello, 140
Rheinau, 125–6, 495
Rheinfelden, battle of, 2 Mar. 1638, 129, 205, 297
Rhineland, 104, 108, 114, 118, 125–6, 129, 139, 157, 189–90, 191, 194, 201, 294, 387, 446, 487
Ribeyre, *commissaire des guerres*, 428n137
Richelieu, Alphonse de, archbishop of Lyon, 443
Richelieu, Armand-Jean du Plessis, cardinal-duc de
  and historians, 2–3, 110–11, 468–9, 491–2, 551
  Mémoires, 184, 469

Index

Richelieu, Armand-Jean du Plessis (*cont.*)
social/family/career background, 289, 477–8, 481–3, 485, 527
Testament politique, 2, 73–4, 83, 110–11, 167n8, 305, 469, 492, 493
Richelieu, François de, *grand prévôt* at court of Henri III, 481
Riom, 511n34, 512n37
Rivau, Jacques II de Beauvau, sr de, 64
Roberts, Michael, 7, 23, 547–8, 549
Roche, *commissaire des guerres*, 402n11
Rocroi, battle of, 19 May 1643, 19, 23, 52–3, 65, 66, 70, 76, 162, 301, 554
Rohan, Henri, duc de, commander and military theorist, 28, 32, 34, 36, 37, 58, 61, 69, 76, 114, 117, 118, 122, 124, 161, 176, 189–90, 191, 193, 195, 201, 258, 265, 277, 290, 324n42, 348, 351, 363n192, 391, 404n27, 447n212, 489–90, 492, 493, 532n128
Rohan-Montbazon, Marie de, duchesse de Chevreuse, 481
Rolland, Germain, *munitionnaire*, 258, 418n84
Rosen, Reinhold, baron von Grossropp, colonel, 295, 302–3
Rosny, Maximilien-François de Béthune, marquis de, *grand maître de l'artillerie*, 388, 402n10, 475–6
Rothelin, Henri d'Orléans, marquis de, 388, 475
Rottweil, 302
Rouen, 428, 431n151, 511n32
Roussillon, 135, 146, 152–3, 154–6, 208, 213, 216–17, 266, 267, 277, 409, 496–7, 503
Roye, 119, 423, 538n161
Royer, Christophe, *commissaire des guerres*, 401n3, 406n38, 407n43
Roze (Rose), Jean, *munitionnaire*, 256–7, 258, 259, 385, 414, 416
Ruffiers, François de Hervart-Senantes, marquis de, 349n143
Rusignan, 275

Saarbrücken, 115
Sabathier, François, supplier of munitions and financier, 234–5, 254, 259, 263, 389–90
Saint-Aubin, sr de, *mestre de camp*, 358n169

Saint-Aunais, Henri de, governor of Leucate, 494
Saint-Bris, Jean de Lambert, marquis de, *maréchal de camp*, 330n64
Saint-Chaumont, Melchior Mitte de Miolans, marquis de, 248n91, 340n112
Saint-Germain, 194, 293, 490
Saint-Honorat, isle of (Lérins), 117, 118, 122, 123, 264, 495
Saint-Jean-de-Losne, 121, 409
Saint-Jean-de-Luz, 122, 126, 198, 441n186, 488
Saint-Julien, sr de, *sergent-major*, 410n55
Saint-Luc, Timoléon d'Espinay, maréchal de, 62
Sainte-Marguerite, isle of (Lérins), 117, 118, 122, 123, 264, 495
Saint-Martin-de-Ré, 89, 485
Saint-Mathurin, 525
Saint-Mihiel, 116, 192
Saint-Omer, 58, 74, 75–6, 128–9, 204–5
Saint-Preuil, François de Jussac d'Ambleville, marquis de, 269, 392, 493–4
Saint-Quentin, 66, 269, 524n87, 529
Saint-Simon, Claude de Rouvroy, duc de, 321n31, 339n106, 411
Saintonge, 127, 370
Salces, 71–2, 73, 76, 135–6, 145, 208, 213, 494, 496–7
Saligny, Gaspard de Coligny II, comte de, *maréchal de camp*, 330n67, 409n49
San Sebastián, 132
Sanson, captain, 529
Sault-Tavannes, Henri de, marquis de Mirebeau, 322n37, 344n126, 358n171, 411n59
Saurès, *commissaire des guerres*, 402n9
Saverne, 118, 158
Savoy, duchy of, 86, 97, 112, 151, 186–7, 233, 417n83, 484
Savyer, *commissaire des guerres*, 391n118, 401n3, 406n37
Savoy, dukes of, 467
Saxe-Weimar, duke Bernard of, 59, 80, 107, 108, 109, 115, 118, 125–6, 129–31, 134, 138, 143, 170, 192, 194, 195, 201–2, 204, 205, 211, 228, 267, 293–5, 296, 302, 306, 311, 426, 495, 503

596

Index

Saxony, Electorate of, 27, 159
Schenkenschans, 114, 118
Schmidtberg, colonel, 446
Schomberg, Henri de, comte de Nanteuil
  (first maréchal de Schomberg), 30, 90,
  371, 374, 426n130, 475n53
Schomberg, maréchal from 1637, *see* Halluin
Schulemberg, Jean III, comte de Montdejeux,
  maréchal de, 40n78
Scotland, and Scottish troops in French
  service, 112, 279, 303–4, 309, 518
secrétaire de la guerre (office of), 9, 171, 322,
  323, 333, 367–73, 400–1, 404–5, 410,
  414, 420n95, 432, 434, 440, 461, 463,
  502, 555
Sedan, 40, 148, 149, 214, 490
Séguier, Pierre, chancellor of France, 218,
  254, 348n141, 394, 438, 440n184,
  450n237, 452, 455, 456n260, 458,
  459n281, 460, 461, 482n84, 510, 523,
  525, 528n110, 533
Senantes, sr de, 352n154
Senlis, 523n86
Sens, 520n70
Servien, Abel, *secrétaire d'Etat de la guerre*
  1631–6, 245, 252, 291n41, 304, 306, 310,
  325, 367, 368n7, 370–3, 382n76, 391,
  394n138, 413, 418–19, 447, 454, 473n38,
  531
Sétoubre, sr, *commissaire des guerres*, 401n5
Sève, Alexandre, sr de Chatignonville,
  intendant, 43, 450, 451, 457n263
's Hertogenbosch, 102
Siegen, 26–27, 33n48, 40
Socoa, 122, 126
Soissons, 431n151, 451, 518n63, 537n155
Soissons, Louis de Bourbon, comte de, 44, 62,
  75, 119, 122, 148–9, 160, 195–7, 214,
  290, 401n3, 416, 435n169, 450, 470,
  474n46, 480–1, 482, 486, 487, 537n153
Sötern, Philipp Christoph von, archbishop
  and Trier Elector, 104, 109, 188
Soubise, Benjamin de Rohan, duc de, 87, 290
Soudé, du, captain, 523
Sourdis, Charles d'Escoubleau, marquis de,
  214, 496, 514n47
Sourdis, Henri d'Escoubleau de, archbishop
  of Bordeaux, 75n225, 123, 132–3,

152–3, 206, 251, 478, 483, 493, 495–6,
  535n142
Souvigny, Jean de Gangnières, comte de, 212,
  334n85
Soyecourt, Maximilien de Belleforière, sr de,
  governor of Corbie, 265
Spain, Habsburg kingdoms of, 1, 81, 86, 203,
  242, 279, 287
  armies, 19, 20, 26, 29–30, 40, 42–3, 48, 49,
    54, 55–6, 62, 66, 70, 75–6, 80, 98, 102,
    106, 109, 112, 119, 124, 128, 131, 136,
    146, 148, 157, 159, 162, 170, 202, 211,
    219, 280, 282, 344, 496–7, 536n152
  military and political system, 87, 92, 93,
    103, 106, 108, 137, 170
  navy, 87, 108, 117, 496
Speyer, 109
Spínola, Ambrosio, marquis of Los Balbases,
  33, 34, 94, 97, 100, 280
Strasbourg, 382n75
Streff, colonel, 274n203, 301–2, 378n54
subsistances, taxe des, 268n178, 273–4, 372,
  401, 423–32, 509–14, 516, 522, 524,
  525, 537, 543–4
Sully, Maximilien de Béthune, duc de, 381,
  402n10, 475
surintendant (général) des vivres (Richelieu),
  381, 382n74, 414–15, 419
surtaux (additional pay for cavalry), 226, 228,
  229, 231
Susa, 51, 93, 94, 96, 275, 403n13, 518n61, 534
Susanne, Louis, 166–7
Sweden, government and foreign policy, 81,
  101, 102, 143, 153, 161, 266–7, 278, 287,
  297, 312, 485
  army, 52, 66, 71, 78, 106, 107, 109, 111,
    114, 121, 170, 211, 279–80, 285, 293,
    294–6
  military reforms, 19, 21–3, 54, 69, 82, 547–8
Swiss Cantons, 86, 183, 304, 484
Swiss in French service, 49, 173, 186, 266,
  303–4, 305, 366, 378
  see also gardes suisses
Swiss soldiers, 20, 37, 74, 112

taille, 230–1, 233, 238, 255, 263, 266n166,
  271, 273, 274, 339n105, 423, 511–12,
  514, 525, 537

Index

Talon, Claude, *commissaire des guerres*, 403n15, 520n72
Talon, Jacques, *intendant*, 428n137, 430n145
Talon, Omer, *avocat général* of the *Parlement* of Paris, 545
Tarragona, 74, 146, 152–3, 213, 216–17, 251, 496
Thibault, Italian financer, 244
Thiersault, Pierre, sr de Conches, *intendant*, 428n137, 515n54
Thionville, battle of, 7 June 1639, 51, 73, 75, 137–8, 148, 207, 455–6
Thirty Years War, 1, 22, 31, 53, 57, 61, 83, 110, 112, 240, 278, 279, 283, 286–7, 306, 312, 364, 395, 550
Thou, sr de, *commissaire des guerres*, 442n192
Tilly, Johann Tserclaes, count, Bavarian general, 27, 31, 101n98
Tirlemont, 113
Toiras, Jean du Caylar de Saint-Bonnet, marquis de, 89, 93, 186, 318–19, 465, 485, 492, 493
Toison, sr, *munitionnaire*, 387n100
Tommaso Francesco of Savoy, prince of Carignano, 58, 75, 131, 139–40, 145, 150, 159–61, 219, 299
Tornavento, battle of, 22 June 1636, 118
Torstensson, Lennart, Swedish general, 154, 159
Tortona, 161, 219
Touches, sr des, *gentilhomme ordinaire de la maison du roi*, 412
Toul, 103, 532, 534
Toulon, 525
Touraine, 263, 411, 506, 513n41
Tours, 403n15, 424, 431n150, 531n124
Tracy, Alexandre de Prouville, baron de, 301–2, 406
traités, for recruitment of additional troops, 114, 211, 214, 274, 355–60, 392, 401–2, 430, 445n204, 456n260, 458–9, 513, 524–5
Tremblay, Joseph Le Clerc du (Père Joseph), 171, 371
trésoriers de France, 271, 274n203, 374, 382n76, 383, 412, 416n78, 428, 509n21, 512n37, 516, 531n124
trésoriers de l'ordinaire et de l'extraordinaire des guerres, 234–5, 247–9, 273, 374–5, 381–2, 425, 462, 469, 535n146
Trier, 105, 109, 188, 225, 484
Trino, 140
Trois Evêchés, 103, 369, 393
Troyes, 522n80, 525, 530n117
Tubeuf, Jacques, *intendant des finances*, 389n114
Turenne, Henri de La Tour d'Auvergne, vicomte de, 19, 29, 75, 81, 130, 143, 148, 150–1, 205, 215, 282n14, 302, 324, 327, 339n107, 345n131, 354n160, 470, 474–5, 490, 492, 551, 554
Turin, 59, 139–40, 145, 146, 150, 151, 161, 212–13, 275, 277, 441n185, 467, 500, 503, 505
Tuttlingen, battle of, 23 Nov. 1643, 163, 300, 302
Tyrol, 85

United Provinces, *see* Dutch Republic
ustensile, 231, 270, 271–2, 509n20

Valençay, Léonor d'Etampes de, bishop of Chartres, 535n142
Valenza, 116–17, 333n78, 480
Val Fraela, battle of, 31 Oct. 1635, 58, 117
Vallier, Jean, sr de La Martinière, *commissaire des guerres*, 274n204, 402n9, 407n42, 424–5, 427n133, 429n140, 433, 521n78
Valtelline, 58, 76, 85–7, 95, 114, 117, 118, 122–3, 161, 176, 183–4, 191, 193, 195, 199, 201, 233, 264–5, 267, 277, 404n27, 406n40, 489–90
Varennes, sr de, *maître de l'hôtel du Roi*, 411
Vauban, Sébastien Le Prestre de, *maréchal*, 19
Vaubecourt, Jean de Nettancourt, comte de, *maréchal de camp*, 192, 323n41
Vautorte, François Cazet, sr de, *intendant*, 439n181, 443
Vegetius Renatus, Flavius, military theorist, 25
venality of office, 9, 232, 234, 237, 240–1, 319–21, 331–48, 368, 374–6, 379, 383–4, 388–9, 395, 399, 400, 401n3, 406, 415, 428, 494–5
Vendôme, Alexandre de Bourbon, *grand prieur de France*, 467, 483

Index

Vendôme, César de Bourbon, duc de, 467, 483
Venice, Republic of, 85, 87
Ventadour, Henri de Lévis, duc de, 185n61, 440n184
Vercelli, 74, 75, 118, 131, 495
Verchamp, sr de, *prévôt*, 406n40
Verdun, 68, 103, 520
Vere, Bussy de, captain, 429n142, 523
Verneuil, 525n92
Verthamont, François de, marquis de Manoeuvre, *intendant*, 441, 445n207
Vic, 104
Videl, *commissaire des vivres*, 384
Vienna, 92
vieux régiments, 42, 43, 46, 47, 51, 193, 226, 322, 325, 332, 334, 405, 472, 520
  Champagne, 39, 188, 189, 233, 335n85
  La Marine, 51, 251n102, 322, 365, 520n71
  Navarre, 45, 185, 188, 351n151, 358n171
  Normandie, 45, 71–2, 188, 252, 458, 519n67, 534n135
  Picardie, 41, 43, 45, 46, 51, 73, 188, 326n52, 337n92, 430n145, 520, 521, 530n117, 531
  Piémont, 44, 50, 51, 332, 410n55
Vignerot, René de, 478
Vignier, Claude, marquis de Mirebeau, *intendant*, 442n193
Vignolles, Bertrand de, seigneur de Casaubon, *mestre de camp*, 29
Ville, Laurens de, legal theorist, 527–8
Villemontée, François de, marquis de Montauiguillon, *intendant*, 340n109, 421, 425n127, 428n137, 429n140, 431n151, 457n264, 512n39, 532n130

Villequier, Charles d'Aumont, sr de, 392, 440n184
Villeroy, Nicolas de Neufville, marquis de, *secrétaire d'Etat*, 368, 370
Vincenzo II Gonzaga, duke of Mantua (1626–7), 91
Vitry, Nicolas de l'Hôpital, maréchal de, 108, 123, 344n126, 391n118, 487, 493, 509n23, 514n49, 530
Vittorio Amedeo I, duke of Savoy, 1630–7, 116–17, 124, 195, 480, 485n100, 495

Wallenstein, Albrecht von, duke of Friedland, 31, 95, 99, 114, 170, 280, 282, 285
Wallhausen, Jacobi von, military theorist, 27, 28, 33, 37, 38, 55
Wars of Religion, 32, 83, 84, 182–3, 366, 553
Weber, Max, 5, 6
Werth, Jean de, Bavarian cavalry commander, 120n201, 125, 126, 297–8
Westphalia, 158–9
  Peace of, 77, 81, 163, 484
White Mountain, battle of, 3 Nov. 1620, 27, 31, 534n135
Wilhelm V, duke of Hesse-Kassel, 298
Willem Lodewijk, prince of Orange-Nassau, 19
Williams, Sir Roger, 40n79
Wittstock, battle of, 4 Oct. 1636, 121
Wolfenbüttel, battle of, 29 June 1641, 154, 297
Wolgast, battle of, 22 Aug. 1628, 27
wounded and invalids, provision for, 404, 533–4, 537–9
Württemburg, duchy of, 27

Yvetaux, Hercule Vauquelin, sr des, 452n241

CAMBRIDGE STUDIES IN EARLY MODERN HISTORY

*The Old World and the New**
J. H. ELLIOTT
*The Army of Flanders and the Spanish Road, 1567–1659: The Logistics of Spanish Victory and Defeat in the Low Countries Wars**
GEOFFREY PARKER
*Richelieu and Olivares**
J. H. ELLIOTT
*Absolutism and Society in Seventeenth-Century France: State Power and Provincial Aristocracy in Languedoc**
WILLIAM BEIK
*The Princes of Orange: The Stadholders in the Dutch Republic**
HERBERT H. ROWEN
Lille and the Dutch Revolt: Urban Stability in an Era of Revolution
ROBERT S. DUPLESSIS
The Continuity of Feudal Power: The Caracciolo di Brienza in Spanish Naples
TOMMASO ASTARITA
The Nobility of Holland: From Knights to Regents, 1500–1650
H. F. K. VAN NIEROP
Early Modern Democracy in the Grisons: Social Order and Political Language in a Swiss Mountain Canton, 1470–1620
RANDOLPH C. HEAD
*War, State and Society in Württemberg, 1677–1793**
PETER H. WILSON
From Madrid to Purgatory: The Art and Craft of Dying in Sixteenth-Century Spain
CARLOS M. N. EIRE
The Reformation and Rural Society: The Parishes of Brandenburg-Ansbach-Kulmbach, 1528–1603
C. SCOTT DIXON
Labour, Science and Technology in France, 1500–1620
HENRY HELLER
The King's Army: Warfare, Soldiers, and Society during the Wars of Religion in France, 1562–1576
JAMES B. WOOD
Spanish Naval Power, 1589–1665: Reconstruction and Defeat
DAVID GOODMAN
State and Nobility in Early Modern Germany: The Knightly Feud in Franconia 1440–1567
HILLAY ZMORA
The Quest for Compromise: Peace-Makers in Counter-Reformation Vienna
HOWARD LOUTHAN
Charles XI and Swedish Absolutism, 1660–1697
A. F. UPTON

Noble Power during the French Wars of Religion: The Guise Affinity and the Catholic Cause in Normandy
   STUART CARROLL
The Reformation of Community: Social Welfare and Calvinist Charity in Holland, 1572–1620
   CHARLES H. PARKER
Henry IV and the Towns: The Pursuit of Legitimacy in French Urban Society, 1589–1620
   S. ANNETTE FINLEY-CROSWHITE
The Limits of Royal Authority: Resistance and Obedience in Seventeenth-Century Castile
   RUTH MACKAY
Defiled Trades and Social Outcasts: Honor and Ritual Pollution in Early Modern Germany
   KATHY STUART
Kingship and Favoritism in the Spain of Philip III, 1598–1621
   ANTONIO FEROS
Richelieu's Army: War, Government and Society in France, 1624–1642
   DAVID PARROTT
The Emergence of the Eastern Powers, 1756–1775
   H. M. SCOTT
Monarchies, States Generals and Parliaments: The Netherlands in the Fifteenth and Sixteenth Centuries
   H. G. KOENIGSBERGER

Titles available in paperback marked with as asterisk*

The following titles are now out of print:

French Finances, 1770–1795: From Business to Bureaucracy
   J. F. BOSHER
Chronicle into History: An Essay in the Interpretation of History in Florentine Fourteenth-Century Chronicles
   LOUIS GREEN
France and the Estates General of 1614
   J. MICHAEL HAYDEN
Reform and Revolution in Mainz, 1743–1803
   T. C. W. BLANNING
Altopascio: A Study in Tuscan Society 1587–1784
   FRANK MCARDLE
Gunpowder and Galleys: Changing Technology and Mediterranean Warfare at Sea in the Sixteenth Century
   JOHN FRANCIS GUILMARTIN JR
The State, War and Peace: Spanish Political Thought in the Renaissance 1516–1559
   J. A. FERNÁNDEZ-SANTAMARIA
Calvinist Preaching and Iconoclasm in the Netherlands, 1544–1569
   PHYLLIS MACK CREW
The Kingdom of Valencia in the Seventeenth Century
   JAMES CASEY

Filippo Strozzi and the Medici: Favor and Finance in Sixteenth-Century Florence and Rome
  MELISSA MERIAM BULLARD
Rouen during the Wars of Religion
  PHILIP BENEDICT
The Emperor and His Chancellor: A Study of the Imperial Chancellery under Gattinara
  JOHN M. HEADLEY
The Military Organisation of a Renaissance State: Venice c. 1400–1617
  M. E. MALLETT AND J. R. HALE
Neostoicism and the Early Modern State
  GERHARD OESTREICH
Prussian Society and the German Order: An Aristocratic Corporation in Crisis, c. 1410–1466
  MICHAEL BURLEIGH
The Changing Face of Empire: Charles V, Philip II and Habsburg Authority, 1552–1559
  M. J. RODRÍGUEZ-SALGADO
Turning Swiss: Cities and Empire 1450–1550
  THOMAS A. BRADY JR
Neighbourhood and Community in Paris
  DAVID GARRIOCH
The Duke of Anjou and the Politique Struggle during the Wars of Religion
  MACK P. HOLT
Society and Religious Toleration in Hamburg 1529–1819
  JOACHIM WHALEY
Frontiers of Heresy: The Spanish Inquisition from the Basque Lands to Sicily
  WILLIAM MONTER
Rome in the Age of Enlightenment: The Post-Tridentine Syndrome and the Ancien Régime
  HANS GROSS
Renaissance and Revolt: Essays in the Intellectual and Social History of Modern France
  J. H. M. SALMON
Louis XIV and the Origins of the Dutch War
  PAUL SONNINO
The Cost of Empire: The Finances of Kingdom of Naples during the Period of Spanish Rule
  ANTONIO CALABRIA
The Armada of Flanders: Spanish Maritime Policy and European War, 1568–1668
  R. A. STRADLING
After the Deluge: Poland and the Second Northern War 1655–1660
  ROBERT FROST
Classes, Estates and Order in Early Modern Brittany
  JAMES B. COLLINS